Cambridge Handbook of Culture, Organizations, and Work

It is now widely recognised that countries around the world are becoming increasingly interconnected, and that both public and private organizations are of necessity becoming increasingly global. As political, legal, and economic barriers recede in this new environment, cultural barriers emerge as a principal challenge to organizational survival and success. It is not yet clear whether these new global realities will cause cultures to converge, harmonize, and seek common ground or to retrench, resist, and accentuate their differences. In either case, it is of paramount importance for both managers and organizational scholars to understand the cultural crosscurrents underlying these changes. With contributions from an international team of scholars, the *Cambridge Handbook of Culture, Organizations, and Work* reviews, analyzes, and integrates available theory and research to give the best information possible concerning the role of culture and cultural differences in organizational dynamics.

RABI S. BHAGAT is Professor of Organizational Behavior and International Management at the Fogelman College of Business at the University of Memphis. He is a fellow of SIOP, APA, APS, and the International Academy for Intercultural Research. He has edited handbooks in the area of cross-cultural training and has published widely in the area of cross-cultural organizational behavior and international management.

RICHARD M. STEERS is Professor Emeritus of Organization and Management in the Lundquist College of Business, University of Oregon. He is a past president and fellow of the Academy of Management, as well as a fellow of the American Psychological Society and the Society of Industrial and Organizational Psychology. Professor Steers has published widely in the areas of work motivation and cross-cultural influences on management.

Cambridge Handbook of Culture, Organizations, and Work

Edited by

RABI S. BHAGAT
University of Memphis

RICHARD M. STEERS
University of Oregon

CAMBRIDGE
UNIVERSITY PRESS

University Printing House, Cambridge CB2 8BS, United Kingdom

One Liberty Plaza, 20th Floor, New York, NY 10006, USA

477 Williamstown Road, Port Melbourne, VIC 3207, Australia

314-321, 3rd Floor, Plot 3, Splendor Forum, Jasola District Centre, New Delhi - 110025, India

103 Penang Road, #05-06/07, Visioncrest Commercial, Singapore 238467

Cambridge University Press is part of the University of Cambridge.

It furthers the University's mission by disseminating knowledge in the pursuit of
education, learning and research at the highest international levels of excellence.

www.cambridge.org
Information on this title: www.cambridge.org/9780521877428

First published 2009

A catalogue record for this publication is available from the British Library

Library of Congress Cataloging in Publication data
Cambridge Handbook of culture, organizations, and work / [edited by] Rabi S. Bhagat,
Richard M. Steers.
   p. cm.
Includes index.
ISBN 978-0-521-87742-8 (hardback) 1. Corporate culture–Cross-cultural studies. 2. Social
values–Cross-cultural studies. 3. National characteristics. 4. Globalization. I. Bhagat, Rabi S.,
1950– II. Steers, Richard M. III. Title.
HD58.7.H354 2009
302.3′5–dc22   2009012899

ISBN 978-0-521-87742-8 Hardback

This book is dedicated
with sincere appreciation to
HARRY C. TRIANDIS
and
LYMAN W. PORTER,
true scholars and pioneers
in the study of work and
organizations across cultures

Contents

PART IV. FUTURE DIRECTIONS IN THEORY AND RESEARCH

Figures

Tables

Contributors

Soon Ang, National Technical University, Singapore

Rabi S. Bhagat, University of Memphis, USA

Dharm P. S. Bhawuk, University of Hawaii at Manoa, USA

Nancy R. Buchan, University of South Carolina, USA

Ronald J. Burke, York University, Canada

Nathalie Castaño, Wayne State University, USA

Deanne N. Den Hartog, University of Amsterdam, The Netherlands

Marcus W. Dickson, Wayne State University, USA

Gili S. Drori, Stanford University, USA

Miriam Erez, Technion, Israel

Ronald Fischer, Victoria University Wellington, New Zealand

Michele J. Gelfand, University of Maryland, USA

Cristina B. Gibson, University of California at Irvine, USA

Lynn Imai, University of Maryland, USA

Mansour Javidan, Thunderbird School of Global Management, USA

John R. Kimberly, University of Pennsylvania, USA

Bradley L. Kirkman, Texas A&M University, USA

Ben C. H. Kuo, University of Windsor, Canada

Sang Myung Lee, Hanyang University, South Korea

Kwok Leung, City University of Hong Kong, China

Martha L. Maznevski, IMD, Switzerland

Annette S. McDevitt, University of Memphis, USA

Ian McDevitt, University of Memphis, USA

Mark E. Mendenhall, University of Tennessee at Chattanooga, USA

Luciara Nardon, Carleton University, Canada

Joyce S. Osland, San Jose State University, USA

Colleen Beecken Rye, University of Pennsylvania, USA

Carlos Sanchez-Runde, IESE Business School, Spain

Günter K. Stahl, INSEAD, France and Singapore

Taryn L. Stanko, University of Oregon, USA

Richard M. Steers, University of Oregon, USA

Pamela K. Steverson, University of Memphis, USA

Sully Taylor, Portland State University, USA

Fons J. R. van de Vijver, University of Tilburg, The Netherlands, and North-West University, South Africa

Preface

As noted organizational scholar Robert J. House recently observed:

> ample evidence shows that the cultures of the world are getting more and more interconnected and that the business world is becoming increasingly global. As economic borders come down, cultural barriers will most likely go up and present new challenges and opportunities for business. When cultures come in contact, they may converge in some aspects, but their idiosyncrasies will likely amplify.[1]

In this new and more turbulent global environment, a critical question is whether these new global realities will cause various dissimilar cultures of the world to converge, harmonize, and seek common ground or to retrench, resist, and accentuate their differences. In either case, it is important for organizational scholars and managers of multinational and global organizations to understand the intricacies of the cultural undercurrents that are responsible for these changes. To accomplish this, we are in need of the best information possible concerning the role of culture and cultural variations in various macro and micro processes in organizational contexts.

The principal objective of this handbook is to aid in this endeavor by reviewing, analyzing, and integrating available theory and research in the field of organizational studies as they are influenced by cultural differences. More specifically, this handbook focuses on explicating the interactive relationships between culture, work, and organizations, as well as the implications of these findings for future research and theory development.

Organizational studies as the systematic investigation of the ways by which people organize themselves to achieve common objectives is a relatively young endeavor. As such, available information

and tenable theories have evolved only during the past several decades. Still, as the accumulation of intellectual wealth began to mushroom in the 1960s and beyond, serious efforts were required to summarize what had been learned and identify new areas in need of further exploration. One way this academic record has been documented is through the publication of integrated handbooks.

In 1965, James G. March published his now classic *Handbook of Organizations* (Rand McNally, 1965). This handbook aimed to bring together in one volume cutting-edge research and emerging theories focusing on organizations and organizational behavior. A little over a decade later, this was followed by the *Handbook of Industrial and Organizational Psychology*, edited by Marvin Dunnette (Rand McNally, 1976). This volume was – and remains today – a definitive contribution to the field of industrial-organizational psychology. It is rich in theory and research, comprehensive in scope, rigorous in method, well organized, and clearly written. It continues to be widely read, widely cited, and a "must read" for scholars in the field.

These two works were then joined by other equally important handbooks, all aimed at the summary and integration of existing theory and research on the topic. Robert Dubin's *Handbook of Work, Organization, and Society* (Rand McNally, 1976) focused on theory and research on work, occupations, and organizations from a largely sociological perspective, and reflected the national differences in organizations around the world. Shortly thereafter, William Starbuck and Paul Nystron published their

---

[1] R. J. House. 2004. "Introduction", in R. House, P. Hanges, M. Javidan, P. Dorfman, and V. Gupta, *Culture, Leadership, and Organizations: The GLOBE Study of 62 Societies.* Thousand Oaks, CA: Sage, p. 1.

two-volume *Handbook of Organization Design* (Oxford University Press, 1981), focusing largely on the theory and research in the development of organization (or macro organizational) theory.

In 1994, Marvin Dunnette teamed up with Leaetta M. Hough to edit a major revision of his earlier handbook. The new multi-volume *Handbook of Industrial and Organizational Psychology* (Consulting Psychologists Press, 1994) emerged once again as a leader in theory and research and, indeed, Volume 4, edited in collaboration with Harry Triandis, marked the first significant volume devoted exclusively to theory and research on cross-cultural psychology. More recently, in 2002, Martin J. Gannon and Karen L. Newman added to this reservoir of ideas and information with their *Handbook of Cross-Cultural Management*, focusing on the role of culture in management and organized behavior.

Finally, Peter Smith, Mark Peterson, and David Thomas updated the field still further with the publication of their *Handbook of Cross-Cultural Management Research* (Sage, 2008). This handbook provides a systematic examination of management research from thirteen countries on the relationships between employees and employers, organization structure and process, and the management of multinational firms, using a standardized model based on cultural values, cognitions, and social structures that was developed by the editors.

Taken together, the tradition of editing periodic handbooks that summarize, integrate, and hopefully synthesize available theory and research has proven to be a valuable tool for pushing the frontiers of our knowledge. It is our belief that such attention should now be focused on the complex and rather intractable topic of cross-cultural organizational studies. This field has often been characterized by a lack of rigor both in theory development and in empirical research. It has also been characterized by extensive fragmentation and a lack of cohesiveness of results. In our view, there have been too many armchair opinions and too little solid research. Much of this is understandable due to both the difficulty and the distances involved in cross-cultural research. However, it is also our view that sufficient high-quality research

on the impact of national cultural differences on organizations and organized behavior now exists that the time has come to attempt an updated integration and synthesis of the field.

In editing this volume, our principal objective has been to bring together in one place both the knowledge base that currently exists as well as some thoughtful ideas concerning the next steps that could be taken in order to continue the development of this field. Our goal in this new handbook is certainly not to replace earlier handbooks; that would be an impossible task. Rather, our intention is to update and expand on what has been learned previously, specifically as it relates to cross-cultural and cross-national influences on organization and management. In doing so, our aim has also been apply this same level of rigor and inquisitiveness and the same level of theory development to the study of how cultural differences affect – and are affected by – organizations and work behavior. This volume also aims to integrate various bodies of literature in a fashion that makes important ideas readily accessible to scholars.

An important goal of this handbook is to publish major contributions on the various topical domains of research dealing with cultural variations in both the macro and micro areas of organizational behavior and theory. At the macro level of analysis, we know that organizations around the world are influenced by the dominant cultural values that are salient in their societal contexts. Topics that relate to the role of cultural variations to various organizational processes include cultural variations in organizational structure and design in various countries of the world as well as in cross-border mergers and acquisitions. Other topics included here focus on cultural influences on organizational processes, cultural variations in the creation, diffusion, absorption and transfer of knowledge, and cultural variations in organizational innovation. Likewise, on a more micro level, while there have been considerable single-country or two-country studies of such topics as leadership, work motivation, work teams, negotiation, conflict resolution, and stress, it is difficult to find efforts to collectively view these individual empirical results in ways that have meaning for both researchers and managers. Finally, issues relating to the improvement of cross-cultural research methods and future directions for future research and theory development represent an integral part of any discussion of culture, work, and organizations.

Taken together, this handbook aims to collect, organize, and integrate knowledge in the area of cultural variations in macro and micro aspects of organizational behavior, as well as provide important insights into the nature of work in various societies around the world. To accomplish this goal, we invited noted scholars from twelve different countries to contribute chapters based on their particular areas of research expertise. We believe we have brought together people doing cutting-edge research and theory development for this endeavor. Individually and collectively, they have made a signal contribution to this project. Even so, no single volume and no set of authors can incorporate everything relating to the topic under study. In our efforts to organize this handbook, and in view of space limitations, we had to make some strategic choices concerning what could be included and what could not. In this effort, the editors accept full responsibility for the results.

This handbook is divided into four parts, each representing a significant element in understanding how – and why – national cultures and cultural differences influence individual and organizational action. Part I: Cultural Foundations is designed to provide theoretical foundations for conceptualizing the role of cultural variations in work organizations. Three chapters are included. The first, by Luciara Nardon and Richard M. Steers, examines various models of national cultures. On both conceptual and empirical levels, serious research on cultural differences in organizations has been simultaneously facilitated and inhibited by the existence of multiple and often conflicting models of national culture. This lack of convergence across these models has created a culture theory jungle – a situation in which researchers must choose between competing, if sometimes overlapping, models to further their research goals and then defend such choices against a growing body of critics. Based on a review of the more commonly used models of national culture, Nardon and Steers's chapter suggests that a clear need exists to seek convergence across the various models where it exists in order

to facilitate meaningful cross-cultural research. The authors seek this by identifying five relative common themes, or core cultural dimensions, that pervade the various extant models. Based on these core cimensions, culture ratings for country clusters are offered based on multiple evaluative strategies. Finally, new directions for future research are discussed.

Chapter 2, by Kwok Leung and Soon Ang, focuses on the evolution of the field of international business as it is influenced by cultural differences. The role of national culture in international business has received considerable attention partly because of the seminal work of Hofstede on cultural dimensions. In this research tradition, national culture is typically defined by subjective constructs, such as values and beliefs. However, the cultural perspective also encompasses the ecology of a culture and other objective elements, such as physical infrastructure and formal institutions. In a different line of research guided by institutional theory, cultural differences in the choices and behaviors of firms are explained by differences in institutional variables across societies. Leung and Ang provide a review of the constructs of national culture and institution and argue that the cultural perspective can broaden the scope of the institutional approach and highlight the importance of ecology in global management research. Likewise, the institutional perspective is able to spell out the specific nature of the influence of social institutions, which has rarely been studied under the cultural perspective. The authors' integrative review suggests that cultural change is best understood by a joint consideration of subjective culture and social institutions. A synthesis of the cultural and institutional perspectives can also shed new light on firm and individual behaviors in emerging economies.

Chapter 3, by Cristina B. Gibson, Martha Maznevski, and Bradley Kirkman, asks a simple but important question: When does culture matter? Can we simply assume, for example, that whenever members of different national cultures interact, the national cultural differences will drive behavior? Gibson *et al.* question this assumption and attempt to place more precise boundaries around the influence of national culture. They first identify mechanisms through which national culture affects four types of individual-level work outcomes. They then propose moderators of these effects at three levels of analysis, which serve to codify the extent of cultural variations, as well highlight circumstances in which cultural variation is most salient. This framework is illustrated with sample propositions. Implications for theory, research, and practice are discussed.

In Part II: Culture and Organization Theory, attention shifts to an examination of several of the major macro variables that differentiate organizations in one culture from another. In Chapter 4, Richard M. Steers, Luciara Nardon, and Carlos Sanchez-Runde examine the relationship between strategic choice, organization structure, and organizational decision-making as these processes are influenced or constrained by cultural differences. Despite the existence of extensive research on the impact of national culture on managerial behavior, surprisingly little attention has been given to the way in which national culture shapes the structures of organizations. Even though few organizational scholars today disagree that culture directly and independently influences individual behavior, values, norms, and attitudes, we know little about how such forces influence organizing efforts that include hierarchical structure, organizational boundaries, and division of labor.

In Chapter 5, Günter K. Stahl and Mansour Javidan observe that cross-border mergers and acquisitions (M&As) continue to be a popular strategy for achieving growth and diversification. In their chapter, they provide an overview of extant theories and research findings on the role of culture in cross-border M&As. The authors examine several possible explanations for the inconsistent findings that have emerged from previous research on the performance impact of cultural differences in M&As and discuss some of the conceptual and methodological ambiguities inherent in the cultural distance paradigm, which continues to dominate this field. They then introduce an alternative cultural framework, based on the conceptual foundations and empirical findings of the GLOBE research program, and provide an in-depth look at how cultural differences at the national level can affect the integration process and, ultimately,

the post-merger financial performance. Stahl and Javidan conclude with a discussion of remaining questions and future research directions.

Chapter 6, by Miriam Erez and Gili Drori, offers an integrative (micro and macro) perspective to understanding the nature of the work environment in multinational organizations. Linking between institutional theory and behavioral theory, the authors explore the impact of world culture on the structures and operations of multinational organizations and on the identity of their employees. They link between the characteristics of world culture (macro), the nature of the transnational work environment, and the behavior of employees (micro) to develop a theoretical model that captures the nested nature of the cultures of globalization. They further examine the interplay between the macro and micro levels of analyses on the study of global work and global culture by considering both top-own and bottom-up processes.

In Chapter 7, Rabi Bhagat, Annette McDevitt and Ian McDevitt examine the cultural variations in the cross-border transfer of organizational knowledge. Research on organizational knowledge is highly inter-disciplinary in character. Important contributions have been made by economists, political theorists, and information scientists. However, there is a critical need to understand the role of culture-specific influences in the way knowledge gets created, diffused, absorbed and transferred. They provide a list of important facilitators and constraints in the creation, diffusion, absorption, and transfer of organizational knowledge. This chapter should stimulate future theory and research in this growing area of inquiry.

This is followed in Chapter 8 with a discussion of a new way of thinking about the relationship between culture and innovation. This chapter, by John R. Kimberly and Colleen Beecken Rye, uses data on the adoption and implementation of Patient Classification Systems (PCSs), an innovation in hospital management information systems in the United States, France, Italy, Germany, and Japan to show that when innovations are diffused and implemented across regional and national borders, the components of PCSs can change in response to the interests and agendas of key stakeholders in relevant health systems. The authors refer to this phenomenon as the morphology of innovation, and discuss both the theoretical and empirical implications of moving away from focusing principally on organizations as the context for innovation and images of innovations as discrete, fixed, and culture-free.

In Part III: Culture and Organizational Behavior, attention is directed towards developing a better understanding of individual and group behavior in work organizations across cultures. This section begins in Chapter 9, by Marcus W. Dickson, Deanne N. Den Hartog, and Nathalie Castaño, who examine reasons why cross-cultural research is difficult to do well, and why this is particularly the case with leadership research. The authors define terms and then focus on the tension researchers face between seeking leadership universals and leadership cultural contingencies. This includes a discussion of the major cultural dimensions (as well as research on dimension-based culture clusters) as they relate to leadership, while raising questions about the adequacy of the dimension approach for understanding leadership across national boundaries. They conclude with a section on implications for leaders, including topics such as reward systems and expatriate selection/preparation.

In Chapter 10, Joyce Osland, Sully Taylor, and Mark Mendenhall focus on global leadership and its development. Despite some commonalities with traditional leadership, they articulate how global leadership differs in degree and kind due to its global context. Cultural variations, complexity (multiplicity, interdependence, ambiguity), and flux are contextual determinants of global leadership. The chapter's major contribution resides in going beyond the common "competency delineation" approach that is so prevalent in the literature, to present an integrated framework illustrating how the contextual variables of global complexity lead to global leadership. Global leadership is then portrayed as different forms of sense-making, which in turn requires the enacting of particular competencies; the final component of the framework is the ideal sequence of development training to learn these competencies. The authors then

review the limited empirical research in relation to this framework and identify progress, challenges, and needs for future research. Two other frameworks are also discussed: the Pyramid Model that organizes global leadership competencies and a model that integrates the focus, training methods, and HR support related to global leadership development.

Chapter 11, by Taryn L. Stanko and Cristina B. Gibson, reviews articles published between 2000 and 2006 focusing on virtual, distributed, or dispersed work. Their review focuses on four key areas of virtual work: (1) conceptualizations and operationalizations of virtuality, in particular, exploring culture as a defining characteristic; (2) research designs utilized (i.e., experimental, field surveys, case studies); (3) the role of virtuality in the models investigated (i.e., whether it is considered an independent variable, moderator or dependent variable); and (4) outcomes of virtuality (dependent variables investigated). In each of these areas, the authors first summarize the state of the art and the limitations of the current research, and then develop recommendations for future research, essentially laying out a plan for where we can go from here. In this regard, they emphasize the most promising directions for future research concerning cultural variations in virtual work.

Following this, in Chapter 12, Carlos Sanchez-Runde, Sang Myung Lee, and Richard M. Steers examine work motivation theory and practice as it relates – and, in some cases, does not relate – to cultural differences. Despite a long tradition of theory building and empirical research focusing on work motivation and job performance, few rigorous studies have been conducted over the years that look beyond the borders of a small number of highly industrialized nations. It has often been assumed – incorrectly, the authors assert – that western theories of work motivation most likely apply with equal vigor to highly divergent cultures around the world. With this in mind, this chapter reviews what is known – and what remains to be learned – about personal work values, motivation, job attitudes, and performance in divergent global settings. The concept of cultural drivers is used as a framework for understanding how cultural differences can influence action. Implications for research and management are then discussed.

Following this, Lynn Imai and Michele Gelfand focus in Chapter 13 on interdisciplinary perspectives on culture, conflict, and negotiation. In doing so, they draw from a variety of disciplines, each with their unique approach to culture and conflict, including legal anthropology, comparative law, communication, experimental economics, cognitive anthropology, language and disputing, international relations, and primatology. For each field, they identify the major research questions asked, the unit of analysis, the way in which culture is conceptualized, the dominant methodology used, as well as the comparative versus intercultural nature of research. They then review key representative work from each discipline, and discuss the implications of each field for the study of culture and conflict in organizational behavior. By looking outward to representative works on culture and conflict from a variety of disciplines, Imai and Gelfand aim to better understand our own implicit assumptions in organizational behavior as well as to invite new perspectives and interdisciplinary collaborations.

In Chapter 14, Nancy R. Buchan argues that significant potential lies in clarifying the complex influence of culture in the trust process. By drawing on literature from multiple academic fields, a dynamic model is presented that meticulously breaks down the trust development process and demonstrates that trust development is dynamic and fluid, changing in nature from context to context, and is influenced by a multiplicity of economic, sociological, psychological, legal, political, business-related factors in the cultural environment of the trust relationship. The model demonstrates that the bulk of current trust research suggests a trajectory for trust development particular to western-based cultures. Based on research from less-developed and/or non-western environments, this chapter reveals that culture is intrinsically intertwined in trust relationships, that the nature of trust manifested is likely culturally determined, and that different trajectories for trust development exist depending on the cultural environment studied.

In Chapter 15, Rabi Bhagat, Pamela Steverson, and Ben Kuo examine the role of cultural differences in work stress and coping in the era of globalization. They provide a model that explicitly incorporates the role of cultural differences in work stress and coping. Coping with work stress is often infuenced by culture-specific influences and their chapter should facilitate further inquiry into the role of cultural differences on various types of work stress including stresses associated with acculturation.

Next, in Chapter 16, Ronald J. Burke reviews the literature addressing cultural values and women's education, work, and career experiences. Women in management research specifically, while still relatively limited, is increasingly being carried out in a greater number of countries and across countries. The proportion of women in the labor force continues to increase, but these participation rates are uneven. Few women, however, achieve senior executive leadership positions in any country. "Think manager – think male" appears to be widespread. Culture is a major factor, those societies valuing traditional roles for women have fewer women in professional and managerial jobs. National policies and legislation as well as cultural and religous values are important here as well. Two large-scale research projects, Hofstede's and GLOBE, indicate the effects of cultural values in explaining women's work experiences. Hofstede has shown that cultures high on masculinity had a lower percentage of women in managerial and professional jobs, greater gender segregation in higher education, and greater work centrality at the expense of family. The GLOBE study reported more women in higher education and in the workforce, higher levels of male-female equality, women's economic activity and a higher GNP in societies scoring higher on gender egalitarianism. Promising future research directions are then offered.

Rounding out this section of the handbook is Chapter 17, by Dharm P.S. Bhawuk, focusing on intercultural training. A review of the literature on intercultural training shows that this field of research has been theory driven from its early days owing to its founders like Edward Hall, Harry Triandis, Richard Brislin, Dan Landis, and Bill Gudykunst, who were motivated to pursue theory driven research. Three major reviews of the field of intercultural training in the past seven years have helped present a historical overview of the field and also present a synthesis of its theories and methods. This paper builds on these earlier reviews by synthesizing various theoretical ideas to propose an approach to intercultural training that is grounded in theory and can be utilized by business and government or non-government organizations. It also presents a synthesis of learning models that have hitherto been scattered across the literature, which will help young scholars better to focus their research agenda. It is hoped that the chapter will also guide practitioners to systematic develop intercultural training programs that are informed by theory.

This volume concludes with Part IV: Future Directions in Theory and Research, which includes two summary chapters on future research directions, theory development, and research methodology. Chapter 18, by Fons J.R. van Vijver and Ronald Fischer, examines ways of improving methodological robustness in cross-cultural organizational research. More specifically, this chapter deals with two kinds of methodological issues. The first involves bias and equivalence. Tools are described to address the question of whether an instrument measures the same construct in different cultures. Examples are exploratory and confirmatory factor analyses and the numerous techniques that can be employed to identify differential item functioning. The second issue involves the multilevel design of cross-cultural organizational studies. Multilevel analyses address important questions in cross-cultural organizational research, such as determining the most appropriate level of analysis (e.g., individual, group, organization, industry, national culture, etc.), similarity or dissimilarity of meaning at all levels, and the linkage of constructs across levels. The authors argue that a further integration of theory and methods and a more refined use of methodological tools in cross-cultural research will help to increase the replicability of cross-cultural research findings, bolster conclusions against alternative interpretations, and increase validity of organizational theory in a cross-cultural framework.

Finally, Chapter 19, co-editor Rabi Bhagat examines the accomplishments and challenges in cross-cultural organizational research. In his analysis, he discusses various reasons why cross-cultural researchers should take pride in the work that has been accomplished in recent years. Important avenues of research are discussed as the global economies expand and move into different parts of the world. It is argued, based on this review, that little doubt exists that research on the interaction among culture, work, and organizations will continue and grow in importance in the twenty-first century.

In closing, we recognize a significant debt of gratitude to the many people who supported this venture from the beginning. No project of this magnitude could be accomplished without a true partnership between editors, contributing authors, publisher, colleagues, and family members. In this regard, we were very fortunate to have had such a partnership.

First and foremost, we wish to thank our contributing authors for the dedication and commitment with which they approached their research and writing. In our view, these individuals represent the best in academe; they delivered carefully crafted scholarly pieces under relatively tight time constraints, and for this we are grateful.

We owe a particular debt of gratitude to Harry Triandis, University of Illinois, and Lyman W. Porter, University of California at Irvine, for their inspiration and dedication as scholars, mentors, and friends. Mentors serve a very useful purpose in the academic development of both the field in general and individual scholars in particular, and these two mentors are as good as it gets.

We want to recognize Annette and Ian McDevitt for their continued support and encouragement throughout the various phases of preparing this handbook. And thanks are due to our respective schools – the University of Memphis and the University of Oregon – and to our colleagues both at home and abroad for their long-term support and encouragement of academic excellence in teaching and research.

We also wish to thank our editors at Cambridge University Press – Paula Parish and Philip Good – for their enduring patience, untiring support, and dedication to excellence. Publishers and their editors represent the true unsung heroes in scholarly advancement, and the people at Cambridge are clearly in the lead in this regard. We thank them for their interest in pushing the frontiers of research and theory development, for their commitment to quality, and for their sincerity and high standards that guided all of us throughout this project.

Finally, we thank our wives and families – Ebha, Monika, and Priyanka for Rabi and Sheila, Pat, Kathleen, and Allison for Richard – for their warm support and patience throughout this project. Without their support, this project could never have come to fruition.

Rabi S. Bhagat
Richard M. Steers

PART I

Cultural Foundations

The culture theory jungle: divergence and convergence in models of national culture

LUCIARA NARDON and RICHARD M. STEERS

On both a conceptual and empirical level, serious research on cultural differences in organization and management has been simultaneously facilitated and inhibited by the existence of multiple and often conflicting models of national culture. These models offer useful templates for comparing management processes, HRM policies, and business strategies across national borders. Some models have gone a step further and offered measures or numerical indicators for various countries that have been used widely in cross-cultural research. However, a problem that continues to plague organizational researchers in this area is a lack of convergence across these models. This divergence represents what we refer to as the *culture theory jungle* – a situation in which researchers must choose between competing, if sometimes overlapping, models to further their research goals and then defend such choices against a growing body of critics. This reality fails to facilitate either parsimony or rigor in organizational research, let alone useful comparisons across studies and samples.

As such, after a brief review of the divergence that currently exists in the most commonly used models of culture, we argue in this paper that a clear need exists to seek convergence across the various models where it exists in ways that facilitate both research and meaningful cross-cultural comparisons. We then seek such convergence by identifying five relative common themes, or *core cultural dimensions*, that pervade the various extant models. Based on these themes, culture ratings for country clusters are presented based on data secured through the use of multiple measures and multiple methods.

Divergence in models of national culture

At present, there are at least six models of national cultures that continue to be widely cited and utilized in the organizational research literature. These include models proposed by Kluckhohn and Strodtbeck, Hofstede, Hall, Trompenaars, Schwartz, and House and his GLOBE associates. Each model highlights different aspects of societal beliefs, norms, and/or values and, as such, convergence across the models has been seen as being very limited. Below we summarize each of the six models very briefly as a prelude to a comparative analysis and attempted integration later in the paper. (Readers are referred to the original sources for a more in-depth discussion of each model.)

Kluckhohn and Strodtbeck

Based on the initial research by Clyde Kluckhohn (1951), cultural anthropologists Florence Kluckhohn and Fred Strodtbeck (1961) suggested one of the earliest models of culture that has served as a principal foundation for several later models. They proposed a theory of culture based on value orientations, arguing that there are a limited number of problems that are common to all human groups and for which there are a limited number of solutions. They further suggested that values in any given society are distributed in a way that creates a dominant value system. They used anthropological theories to identify five value orientations, four of which were later tested in five subcultures of the American Southwest: two Native American

3

Table 1.1 Kluckhohn and Strodtbeck's cultural dimensions

Cultural Dimensions	Scale Anchors		
Relationship with Nature: Beliefs about the need or responsibility to control nature.	Mastery: Belief that people have need or responsibility to control nature.	Harmony: Belief that people should work with nature to maintain harmony or balance.	Subjugation: Belief that individuals must submit to nature.
Relationship with People: Beliefs about social structure.	Individualistic: Belief that social structure should be arranged based on individuals.	Collateral: Belief that social structure should be based on groups of individuals with relatively equal status.	Lineal: Belief that social structure should be based on groups with clear and rigid hierarchical relationships.
Human Activities: Beliefs about appropriate goals.	Being: Belief that people should concentrate on living for the moment.	Becoming: belief that individuals should strive to develop themselves into an integrated whole.	Doing: belief on striving for goals and accomplishments.
Relationship with Time: Extent to which past, present, and future influence decisions.	Past: In making decisions, people are principally influenced by past events or traditions.	Present: In making decisions, people are principally influenced by present circumstances.	Future: In making decisions, people are principally influenced by future prospects.
Human Nature: Beliefs about good, neutral or evil human nature.	Good: Belief that people are inherently good.	Neutral: Belief that people are inherently neutral.	Evil: Belief that people are inherently evil

tribes, a Hispanic village, a Mormon village, and a farming village of Anglo-American homesteaders. The five dimensions are identified in table 1.1. Each dimension is represented on a three-point continuum.

Initially, Hofstede asserted that cultures could be distinguished along four dimensions, but later added a fifth dimension based on his research with Michael Bond (1991). The final five dimensions are illustrated in table 1.2.

Hofstede

Dutch management researcher Geert Hofstede (1980, 2001) advanced the most widely used model of cultural differences in the organizations literature. His model was derived from a study of employees from various countries working for major multinational corporation and was based on the assumption that different cultures can be distinguished based on differences in what they value. That is, some cultures place a high value on equality among individuals, while others place a high value on hierarchies or power distances between people. Likewise, some cultures value certainty in everyday life and have difficulty coping with unanticipated events, while others have a greater tolerance for ambiguity and seem to relish change. Taken together, Hofstede argues that it is possible to gain considerable insight into organized behavior across cultures based on these value dimensions.

Hall

Edward T. Hall (1981, 1990), a noted American cultural anthropologist, has proposed a model of culture based on his ethnographic research in several societies, notably Germany, France, the US, and Japan. His research focuses primarily on how cultures vary in interpersonal communication, but also includes work on personal space and time. These three cultural dimensions are summarized in table 1.3. Many of the terms used today in the field of cross-cultural management (e.g., monochronic-polychronic) are derived from this work.

Trompenaars

Building on the work of Hofstede, Dutch management researcher Fons Trompenaars (Tromepaars, 1993; Trompenaars and Hampden-Turner, 1998)

Table 1.2 Hofstede's cultural dimensions

Cultural Dimensions	Scale Anchors	
Power Distance: Beliefs about the appropriate distribution of power in society.	Low power distance: Belief that effective leaders do not need to have substantial amounts of power compared to their subordinates. Examples: Austria, Israel, Denmark, Ireland, Norway, Sweden.	High power distance: Belief that people in positions of authority should have considerable power compared to their subordinates. Examples: Malaysia, Mexico, Saudi Arabia.
Uncertainty Avoidance: Degree of uncertainty that can be tolerated and its impact on rule making.	Low uncertainty avoidance: Tolerance for ambiguity; little need for rules to constrain uncertainty. Examples: Singapore, Jamaica, Denmark, Sweden, UK.	High uncertainty avoidance: Intolerance for ambiguity; need for many rules to constrain uncertainty. Examples: Greece, Portugal, Uruguay, Japan, France, Spain.
Individualism-Collectivism: Relative importance of individual vs. group interests.	Collectivism: Group interests generally take precedence over individual interests. Examples: Japan, Korea, Indonesia, Pakistan, Latin America.	Individualism: Individual interests generally take precedence over group interests. Examples: US, Australia, UK, Netherlands, Italy, Scandinavia.
Masculinity-Femininity: Assertiveness vs. passivity; material possessions vs. quality of life.	Masculinity: Values material possessions, money, and the pursuit of personal goals. Examples: Japan, Austria, Italy, Switzerland, Mexico.	Femininity: Values strong social relevance, quality of life, and the welfare of others. Examples: Sweden, Norway, Netherlands, Costa Rica.
Long-term vs. Short-term Orientation: Outlook on work, life, and relationships.	Short-term orientation: Past and present orientation. Values traditions and social obligations. Examples: Pakistan, Nigeria, Philippines, Russia.	Long-term orientation: Future orientation. Values dedication, hard work, and thrift. Examples: China, Korea, Japan, Brazil.

Table 1.3 Hall's cultural dimensions

Cultural Dimensions	Scale Anchors	
Context: Extent to which the context of a message is as important as the message itself.	Low context: Direct and frank communication; message itself conveys its meaning. Examples: Germany, US, Scandinavia.	High context: Much of the meaning in communication is conveyed indirectly through the context surrounding a message. Examples: Japan, China.
Space: Extent to which people are comfortable sharing physical space with others.	Center of power: Territorial; need for clearly delineated personal space between themselves and others. Examples: US, Japan.	Center of community: Communal; comfortable sharing personal space with others. Examples: Latin America, Arab States.
Time: Extent to which people approach one task at a time or multiple tasks simultaneously.	Monochronic: Sequential attention to individual goals; separation of work and personal life; precise concept of time. Examples: Germany, US, Scandinavia.	Polychronic: Simultaneous attention to multiple goals; integration of work and personal life; relative concept of time. Examples: France, Spain, Mexico, Brazil, Arab States.

presented a somewhat different model of culture based on his study of Shell and other managers over a ten-year period. His model is based on the early work of Harvard sociologists Parsons and Shils (1951) and focuses on variations in both values and personal relationships across cultures. It consists of seven dimensions, as shown on table 1.4. The first five dimensions focus on relationships among people, while the last two focus on time management and society's relationship with nature.

Schwartz

Taking a decidedly more psychological view, Shalom Schwartz (1992, 1994) and his associates asserted that the essential distinction between societal values is the motivational goals they express. He identified ten universal human values that reflect needs, social motives, and social institutional demands (Kagitçibasi, 1997). These values are purportedly found in all cultures and

Table 1.4 Trompenaars' cultural dimensions

Cultural Dimensions	Scale Anchors	
Universalism-Particularism: Relative importance of applying standardized rules and policies across societal members; role of exceptions in rule enforcement.	Universalism: Reliance on formal rules and policies that are applied equally to everyone. Examples: Austria, Germany, Switzerland, US.	Particularism: Rules must be tempered by the nature of the situation and the people involved. Examples: China, Venezuela, Indonesia, Korea.
Individualism-Collectivism: Extent to which people derive their identity from within themselves or their group.	Individualism: Focus on individual achievement and independence. Examples: US, Nigeria, Mexico, Argentina.	Collectivism: Focus on group achievement and welfare. Examples: Singapore, Thailand, Japan.
Specific-Diffuse: Extent to which people's various roles are compartmentalized or integrated.	Specific: Clear separation of a person's various roles. Examples: Sweden, Germany, Canada, UK, US.	Diffuse: Clear integration of a person's various roles. Examples: China, Venezuela, Mexico, Japan, Spain.
Neutral-Affective: Extent to which people are free to express their emotions in public.	Neutral: Refrain from showing emotions; hide feelings. Examples: Japan, Singapore, UK.	Affective: Emotional expressions acceptable or encouraged. Examples: Mexico, Brazil, Italy.
Achievement-Ascription: Manner in which respect and social status are accorded to people.	Achievement: Respect for earned accomplishments. Examples: Austria, US, Switzerland.	Ascription: Respect for ascribed or inherited status. Examples: Egypt, Indonesia, Korea, Hungary.
Time Perspective: Relative focus on the past or the future in daily activities.	Past/present oriented: Emphasis on past events and glory. Examples: France, Spain, Portugal, Arab countries.	Future oriented: Emphasis on planning and future possibilities. Examples: China, Japan, Korea, Sweden, US.
Relationship with Environment: Extent to which people believe they control the environment or it controls them.	Inner-directed: Focus on controlling the environment. Examples: Australia, US, UK.	Outer-directed: Focus on living in harmony with nature. Examples: China, India; Sweden, Egypt, Korea.

represent universal needs of human existence. The human values identified are: power, achievement, hedonism, stimulation, self-direction, universalism, benevolence, tradition, conformity, and security.

Schwartz (1994) argued that individual and cultural levels of analysis are conceptually independent. Individual-level dimensions reflect the psychological dynamics that individuals experience when acting on their values in the everyday life, while cultural-level dimensions reflect the solutions that societies find to regulate human actions. At the cultural level of analysis, Schwartz identified three dimensions: conservatism and autonomy, hierarchy versus egalitarianism, and mastery versus harmony, summarized in table 1.5 below. Based on this model, he studied school teachers and college students in fifty-four countries. His model has been applied to basic areas of social behavior, but its application to organizational studies has been limited (Bond, 2001).

GLOBE

Finally, in one of the most ambitious efforts to study cultural dimensions, Robert House led an international team of researchers that focused primarily on understanding the influence of cultural differences on leadership processes (House, Hanges, Javidan, Dorfman, and Gupta, 2004). Their investigation was called the "GLOBE study" for Global Leadership and Organizational Behavior Effectiveness. In their research, the GLOBE researchers identified nine cultural dimensions, as summarized in table 1.6. While several of these dimensions have been identified previously (e.g., individualism-collectivism, power distance, and uncertainty avoidance), others are unique (e.g., gender egalitarianism and performance orientation).

Based on this assessment, the GLOBE researchers collected data in sixty-two countries and compared the results. Systematic differences were found in leader behavior across the cultures.

Table 1.5 Schwartz's cultural dimensions

Cultural Dimensions	Scale Anchors	
Conservatism-Autonomy: Extent to which individuals are integrated in groups.	Conservatism: individuals are embedded in a collectivity, finding meaning through participation and identification with a group that shares their way of life.	Autonomy: individuals are autonomous from groups, finding meaning on their own uniqueness. Two types of autonomy: Intellectual autonomy: (independent pursuit of ideas and rights) and Affective autonomy (independent pursuit of affectively positive experience).
Hierarchy-Egalitarianism: Extent to which equality is valued and expected.	Hierarchy: cultures are organized hierarchically. Individuals are socialized to comply with theirs roles and are sanctioned if they do not.	Egalitarianism: Individuals are seen as moral equals who share basic interests as human beings.
Mastery-Harmony: Extent to which people seek to change the natural and social world to advance personal or group interests.	Mastery: individuals value getting ahead through self-assertion and seek to change the natural and social world to advance personal or group interests.	Harmony: individuals accept the world as it is and try to preserve it rather than exploit it.

For example, participatory leadership styles that are often accepted in the individualistic west are of questionable effectiveness in the more collectivistic east. Asian managers place a heavy emphasis on paternalistic leadership and group maintenance activities. Charismatic leaders can be found in most cultures, although they may be highly assertive in some cultures and passive in others. A leader who listens carefully to his or her subordinates is more valued in the US than in China. Malaysian leaders are expected to behave in a manner that is humble, dignified, and modest, while American leaders seldom behave in this manner. Indians prefer leaders who are assertive, morally principled, ideological, bold, and proactive. Family and tribal norms support highly autocratic leaders in many Arab countries (House *et al.*, 2004). Clearly, one of the principal contributions of the GLOBE project has been systematically to study not just cultural dimensions but how variations in such dimensions affect leadership behavior and effectiveness.

Seeking convergence in models of national culture

Taken together, these six culture models attempt to accomplish two things: First, each model offers a well-reasoned set of dimensions along which various cultures can be compared. In this regard, they

offer a form of intellectual shorthand for cultural analysis, allowing researchers to break down assessments of various cultures into power distance, uncertainty avoidance, and so forth, and thus organize their thoughts and focus attention on what otherwise would be a monumental task. Second, four of the models offer numeric scores for rating various cultures. For example, we can use Hofstede to say that Germany is a 35 while France is a 68 on power distance, suggesting that Germany is more egalitarian than France. Regardless of whether these ratings are highly precise or only generally indicative of these countries, they nonetheless provide one indication of how these countries might vary culturally.

As is evident from this review, there are many different ways to represent cultural differences. Unfortunately, the six cultural models available frequently focus on different aspects of societal beliefs, norms, or values and, as such, convergence across the models seems at first glance to be limited. This lack of convergence presents important challenges both for researchers attempting to study cultural influences on management and for managers trying to understand new cultural settings.

Instead of advocating one model over another, we suggest that all of the models have important factors to contribute to our understanding of culture as it relates to management practices. In order to navigate this culture theory jungle, we argue

Table 1.6 GLOBE's cultural dimensions

Cultural Dimensions	Scale Anchors	
Power Distance: Degree to which people expect power to be distributed equally.	High: Society divided into classes; power bases are stable and scarce; power is seen as providing social order; limited upward mobility.	Low: Society has large middle class; power bases are transient and sharable; power often seen as a source of corruption, coercion, and dominance; high upward mobility.
Uncertainty Avoidance: Extent to which people rely on norms, rules, and procedures to reduce the unpredictability of future events.	High: Tendency to formalize social interactions; document agreements in legal contracts; be orderly and maintain meticulous records; rely on rules and formal policies.	Low: Tendency to be more informal in social interactions; reliance on word of people they trust; less concerned with orderliness and record-keeping; rely on informal norms of behavior.
Humane Orientation: Extent to which people reward fairness, altruism, and generosity.	High: Interests of others important; values altruism, benevolence, kindness, and generosity; high need for belonging and affiliation; fewer psychological and pathological problems.	Low: Self-interest important; values pleasure, comfort, and self-enjoyment; high need for power and possessions; more psychological and pathological problems.
Institutional Collectivism: Extent to which society encourages collective distribution of resources and collective action.	High: Individuals integrated into strong cohesive groups; self viewed as interdependent with groups; societal goals often take precedence over individual goals.	Low: Individuals largely responsible for themselves; self viewed as autonomous; individual goals often take precedence over societal or group goals.
In-Group Collectivism: Extent to which individuals express pride, loyalty, and cohesiveness in their organizations and families.	High: Members assume they are interdependent and seek to make important personal contributions to group or organization; long-term employer-employee relationships; organizations assume major responsibility of employee welfare; important decisions made by groups.	Low: Members assume they are independent of the organization and seek to stand out by making individual contributions; short-term employer-employee relationships; organizations primarily interested in the work performed by employees over their personal welfare.
Assertiveness: Degree to which people are assertive, confrontational, and aggressive in relationships with others.	High: Value assertiveness, dominance, and tough behavior for all members of society; sympathy for the strong; value competition; belief in success through hard work; values direct and unambiguous communication.	Low: Prefers modesty and tenderness to assertiveness; sympathy for the weak; values cooperation; often associates competition with defeat and punishment; values face-saving in communication and action.
Gender Egalitarianism: Degree to which gender differences are minimized.	High: High participation of women in the workforce; more women in positions of authority; women accorded equal status in society.	Low: Low participation of women in the workforce; fewer women in positions of authority; women not accorded equal status in society.
Future Orientation: Extent to which people engage in future-oriented behaviors such as planning, investing, and delayed gratification.	High: Greater emphasis on economic success; propensity to save for the future; values intrinsic motivation; organizations tend to be flexible and adaptive.	Low: Less emphasis on economic success; propensity for instant gratification; values extrinsic motivation; organizations tend to be bureaucratic and inflexible.
Performance Orientation: Degree to which high performance is encouraged and rewarded.	High: Belief that individuals are in control of their destiny; values assertiveness, competitiveness, and materialism; emphasizes performance over people.	Low: Values harmony with environment over control; emphasizes seniority, loyalty, social relationships, and belongingness; values who people are more than what they do.

that the most productive approach is to integrate and adapt the various models based on their utility for better understanding business and management in cross-cultural settings. In doing so, we seek common themes that collectively represent the principal differences between cultures. While no single model can cover all aspects of a culture, we believe it is possible to tease out the principal cultural characteristics through such a comparative analysis.

Table 1.7 Common themes across models of national culture

Common Themes	Culture Models					
	Kluckhohn/ Strodtbeck	Hofstede	Hall	Trompenaars	Schwartz	GLOBE
Distribution of power and authority		1	1	1	1	2
Emphasis on groups or individuals	1	1		1	1	2
Relationship with environment	2	1		1	1	3
Use of time	1	1	1	1		1
Personal and social control	1	1		1		1
Other themes (see text)			1	2		

Note: Numbers indicate the number of cultural dimensions from the various models that fit within each theme.

In our view, five relatively distinct common themes emerge from this comparison (see table 1.7):

1. *Distribution of power and authority in society.* How are power and authority distributed in a society? Is this distribution based on concepts of hierarchy or egalitarianism? What are societal beliefs concerning equality or privilege?
2. *Centrality of individuals or groups as the basis of social relationships.* What is the fundamental building block of a society: individuals or groups? How does a society organize for collective action?
3. *People's relationship with their environment.* On a societal level, how do people view the world around them and their relationship with the natural and social environment? Is their goal to control the environment and events around them or to live in harmony with these external realities?
4. *Use of time.* How do people in a society organize and manage their time to carry out their work and non-work activities? Do people approach work in a linear or a nonlinear fashion?
5. *Mechanisms of personal and social control.* How do societies try to insure predictability in the behavior of their members? Do they work to control people through uniformly applied rules, policies, laws, and social norms or rely more on personal ties or unique circumstances?

To achieve this clustering, we must recognize that in a few cases multiple dimensions in the original models can be merged into a single more general or unifying cultural dimension (e.g., institutional and in-group collectivism in the GLOBE model), as discussed below. In addition, we need to look beyond the simple adjectives often used by the various researchers and seek deeper meaning in the various concepts themselves, also as discussed below.

At first glance, these five themes seem to replicate Hofstede's five dimensions, but closer analysis suggests that the other models serve to amplify, clarify, and, in some cases, reposition dimensions so they are more relevant for the contemporary workplace. Indeed, we believe that the commonality across these models reinforces their utility (and possible validity) as critical evaluative components in better understanding global management and the world of international business. As such, each model thus adds something of value to this endeavor.

Core cultural dimensions: an integrative summary

Based on this assessment, we suggest that the advancement of cross-cultural organizational research lies not in developing new models of national culture or debating the validity of the various extant models, but rather in seeking commonalities or convergence among existing ones. To accomplish this, we examine each of the five principal themes of cultural differences that emerged

Table 1.8 Core cultural dimensions: an integrative summary

Core Cultural Dimensions	Focus of Dimensions
Hierarchy-Equality	*Power distribution in organizations and society:* Extent to which power and authority in a society are distributed hierarchically or in a more egalitarian and participative fashion.
Individualism-Collectivism	*Role of individuals and groups in social relationships:* Extent to which social relationships emphasize individual rights and responsibilities or group goals and collective action; centrality of individuals or groups in society.
Mastery-Harmony	*Relationship with the natural and social environment:* Beliefs concerning how the world works; extent to which people seek to change and control or live in harmony with their natural and social surroundings.
Monochronism-Polychronism	*Organization and utilization of time:* Extent to which people organize their time based on sequential attention to single tasks or simultaneous attention to multiple tasks; time as fixed vs. time as flexible.
Universalism-Particularism	*Relative importance of rules vs. relationships in behavioral control:* Extent to which rules, laws, and formal procedures are uniformly applied across societal members or tempered by personal relationships, in-group values, or unique circumstances.

from our comparison, identifying similarities and differences where they exist and teasing out the details. We refer to these themes as *core cultural dimensions* (CCDs) to reflect both their centrality and commonality in cross-cultural organizational research (see table 1.8). However, it should be emphasized that credit for the identification of these dimensions goes to previous researchers; our focus here is simply to identify a means of integrating, interpreting, and building upon their signal contributions.

Hierarchy-equality

The first common theme running through the various models relates to how individuals within a society structure their power relationships. That is, is power in a society distributed based primarily on vertical or horizontal relationships? Is power allocated *hierarchically* or in a more *egalitarian* fashion?

Hofstede's (1980) refers to this as power distance and defines it as the beliefs people have about the appropriateness of either large or small differences in power and authority between the members of a group or society. Some cultures, particularly those in several Asian, Arab, and Latin American countries, stress "high power distance," believing that it is natural or beneficial for some members of a group or society to

exert considerable control over their subordinates. Subordinates are expected to do what they are told with few questions. However, this control does not necessarily have to be abusive; rather, it could be benevolent where a strong master exerts control to look after the welfare of the entire group. Other cultures, particularly those in Scandinavia, stress a "low power distance," believing in a more egalitarian or participative approach to social or organizational structure. They expect subordinates to be consulted on key issues that affect them and will accept strong leaders to the extent that they support democratic principles.

Schwartz (1994) recognizes a similar cultural dimension, which he calls hierarchy and egalitarianism, the terms we have adopted here. In "hierarchical" societies, the unequal distribution of power, roles, and resources is legitimate. Individuals are socialized to comply with obligations and roles according to their hierarchical position in society and are sanctioned if they do not. In "egalitarian" cultures, individuals are seen as moral equals and are socialized to internalize a commitment to voluntary cooperation with others and to be concerned with others' welfare. According to Schwartz' research, China, Thailand, and Turkey are hierarchical cultures, while Denmark, Sweden, and Norway are egalitarian cultures.

The GLOBE study (House *et al.*, 2004) also includes a cultural dimension referring to the power distribution in society. However, it also adds a more specific cultural dimension, referring to the issue of gender egalitarianism. For the GLOBE researchers, the "power distance" dimension focuses on the degree to which people expect power to be distributed equally, while the "gender egalitarianism" dimension focuses on the degree to which gender differences are minimized.

Trompenaars (1993) takes a somewhat different approach here. Rather than focusing on the distribution of power, he focuses on how status and rewards are allocated in a culture. In "achievement" cultures, status and rewards are based on an individual or group's accomplishments, while in "ascription" cultures, such recognition is based largely on such things as seniority, inheritance, class, or gender. Achievement cultures use titles only when they are relevant and their leaders typically earn respect through superior performance. By contrast, people in ascription cultures use titles routinely as a means of reinforcing a hierarchy and typically select their leaders based on age or background.

As noted in table 1.9, several key questions pertaining to power orientation include the following: Should authority ultimately reside in institutions such as dictatorships or absolute monarchies or in the people themselves? Should organizations be structured vertically (e.g., tall organization structures) or horizontally (e.g., flat organization structures or even networked structures)? Is decision-making largely autocratic or participatory? Are leaders chosen because they are the most qualified for a job or because they already have standing in the community? Are leaders elected or appointed? Are people willing or reluctant to question authority?

Individualism vs. collectivism

The cultural dimension that has by far received the most attention in the research literature is individualism–collectivism. All six models recognize that cultures vary in the fundamental structures of social organization. A common theme that permeates the models is recognition that some cultures are organized based on groups, while others are organized based on individuals. The most common

Table 1.9 Hierarchy-equality dimension

Hierarchical	Egalitarian
Belief that power should be distributed hierarchically.	Belief that power should be distributed relatively equally.
Belief in ascribed or inherited power with ultimate authority residing in institutions.	Belief in shared or elected power with ultimate authority residing in the people.
Emphasis on organizing vertically.	Emphasis on organizing horizontally.
Preference for autocratic or centralized decision-making.	Preference for participatory or decentralized decision-making.
Emphasis on who is in charge.	Emphasis on who is best qualified.
Acceptance of authority; reluctance to question authority.	Rejection or skepticism of authority; willingness to question authority.

terms used to describe this are *individualistic* and *collectivistic*. The fundamental difference across the models refers to the extent to which this dimension is related to or separated from the power orientation dimension (see below). Some researchers suggest that a single dimension dealing with relationships among people (including both group orientation and power) is more appropriate to distinguish between cultures, while others retain these as separate dimensions. For our purposes, we will discuss these two dimensions separately, although we recognize that their relationship to each other is important.

Kluckhohn and Strodtbeck (1961) suggested that there are important variations in how individuals relate to each other across cultures. They classified cultures in three types: individualistic, collateral, and lineal. In "individualistic" cultures, individual goals are considered more important and are encouraged to pursue their own personal interests at the expense of others. In "collateral" cultures, individuals see themselves as part of a social group, formed by laterally extended relationships. In "lineal" cultures, the group is equally important but the nature of the group changes. One of the most important goals of lineal societies is the continuity of the group through time, resulting in a strong emphasis in ordered positional succession.

Hofstede (1980) is generally given credit for introducing the terms individualistic or collectivistic. According to his definition, "individualistic" cultures teach their people to be responsible for themselves and that, in a sense, the world revolves around them. Their job is to become independent and to reap the rewards of their individual endeavors. Individual achievement is admired and people should not be emotionally dependent on organizations or groups. By contrast, "collectivistic" cultures stress group interests over those of the individual. They stress personal relationships, achieving harmony as an overriding societal objective, and the central role of the family in both personal and business affairs. One's identity is difficult to separate from that of one's group. Group decision-making is preferred and groups protect their members in exchange for unquestioned loyalty. This is not to say that individuals are unimportant; they are. Rather, collectivistic cultures tend to believe that people can only attain their full potential as a member of a strong group. The US and western European cultures tend to be individualistic, while Asian cultures tend to be mostly collectivistic.

Trompenaars' (1993) dimension mirrors Hofstede's earlier work. He differentiates between individualism, where people think of themselves first and foremost as individuals, and collectivism, where people think of themselves first and foremost as members of a group. The only difference between these two sets of dimensions can be found in their application. For example, while Hofstede lists Mexico and Argentina as relatively collectivist, Trompenaars lists them as individualistic. Whether this resulted from different measurement techniques or from changes in the cultures in the ten-year interlude between the two studies has not been explained.

Schwartz's (1994) dimension is also closely related to individualism and collectivism. He classified cultures along an autonomy–conservatism dimension, focusing on how individuals see themselves with respect to others. In "autonomous" cultures, individuals see themselves as autonomous entities with independent rights and needs. Individuals in autonomous cultures relate to one another based on self-interest and negotiated agreements. Schwartz distinguishes between two types

of autonomy: intellectual and affective. Intellectual autonomy refers to an emphasis on self-direction and independence of thought, while affective autonomy refers to an emphasis on the pursuit of one's interests and desires. By contrast, "conservatism" cultures stress preserving the status quo, propriety, and the traditional order. Cultures towards the conservatism pole stress closely knit harmonious relationships. Individual and group interests are aligned and one finds meaning in life by taking part in a group. According to Schwartz (1994), Israel, Malaysia, and Bulgaria are conservative cultures, while France, Switzerland, and Germany are autonomous cultures.

The GLOBE project (House et al., 2004) subdivided this dimension into institutional and in-group individualism-collectivism, the distinction being one of level of analysis. "Institutional collectivism" refers to the extent to which society encourages collective distribution of resources and collective action, while "in-group collectivism" refers to the extent to which individuals express pride, loyalty, and cohesiveness in their particular organizations and families. Other researchers have also made a distinction between individual and cultural level of analysis (Triandis, 1986). For our purposes here, however, we will only focus on cultural level of analysis, i.e. national or regional, under the assumption that cultural level influences are more relevant to the study of management practice.

Finally, although Hall (1959, 1981) does not directly refer to individualism and collectivism, his notion of interpersonal communication, specifically how much context surrounds people's messages, is closely related to the way societies are organized. Hall distinguishes between low and high context cultures. In "low context" cultures, such as Germany, Scandinavian countries, and the US, the context surrounding the message is far less important than the message itself. The context provides the speaker and listener with very little information relating to the intended message. As a result, people need to rely more on providing greater message clarity, as well as other guarantees like written contracts or information-rich advertising. Language precision is critical, while verbal agreements, assumed understandings, innuendos, and body language count for little. By contrast, in "high context" cultures, such as Japan and China, the context in which the message is conveyed (that is, the social environment in which the message is communicated) is often as important as the message itself. Indeed, the way something is said is at times even more important in communicating a message than the actual words that are used. Here, communication is based on long-term interpersonal relationships, mutual trust, and personal reputations. People know the people they are talking with, and reading someone's face becomes an important – and necessary – art. As a result, less needs to be said or written down. High context cultures tend to be relatively collectivistic, while low context cultures tend to be more individualistic.

In summary, the individualism-collectivism dimension has been widely identified in previous models of culture as representing a key variable in understanding what differentiates one society from another. In general, this dimension focuses on the fundamental issue of whether society and interpersonal relationships are organized based on individuals or groups as their principal building blocks (see table 1.10). Basic questions here include the following: Do people achieve self-identity through their own efforts or through group membership? Are individual goals or group goals more important? Do group sanctions reinforce personal responsibility or conformity to group norms? Is individual or group decision-making preferred? Is business done primarily based on written contracts or on personal relationships? Is communication characterized primarily by low context (where the message contains all or most all of the intended message) or by high context (where the context surrounding the message also carries significant information)?

Mastery vs. harmony

Five of the six models reviewed here agree that there are important variations across cultures with regard to the degree to which people try to control their environment or adapt to their surroundings. Some models focus on the degree to which individuals believe they can and should control nature, while others focus on the degree to which

Table 1.10. Individualism-collectivism dimension

Individualistic	Collectivistic
Person-centered approach valued; primary loyalty to oneself.	Group-centered approach valued; primary loyalty to the group.
Preference for preserving individual rights over social harmony.	Preference for preserving social harmony over individual rights.
Belief that people achieve self-identity through individual accomplishment.	Belief that people achieve self-identity through group membership.
Focus on accomplishing individual goals.	Focus on accomplishing group goals.
Sanctions reinforce independence and personal responsibility.	Sanctions reinforce conformity to group norms.
Contract-based agreements.	Relationship-based agreements.
Tendency toward low-context (direct, frank) communication.	Tendency toward high-context (subtle, indirect) communication.
Tendency toward individual decision-making.	Tendency toward group or participative decision-making.

individuals value achievement or accommodation with nature. Kluckhohn and Strodtbeck (1961) propose two separate cultural dimensions that relate to this dimension. The first dimension focuses on how humans relate to nature. They identified three main cultural types. In "mastery" cultures, individuals have a need or responsibility to control nature; in "subjugation" cultures, individuals submit to nature; and in "harmony" cultures, individuals work with nature to keep harmony or balance. The second dimension focuses on the degree to which striving for goals is important. "Being" cultures stress spontaneous expression of the human personality; "becoming" cultures stress developing oneself as an integrated whole; and "doing" cultures stress acting on the environment to produce accomplishments.

Hofstede's (1980) dimension, "masculinity" and "femininity," focuses on the extent to which cultures stress achievement or quality of life and personal relationships. Masculine cultures value assertiveness, success, progress, achievement, and control over the environment. Feminine cultures, on the other hand, value modesty, relationships, harmony with the environment, and quality of life. Hofstede argues that a preference for achievement or harmony is related to the role often dictated of men and women in societies. Masculine (achievement oriented) societies also show higher emotional and role differentiation between men and women than feminine societies.

Building on Rotter's (1966) model of locus of control, Trompenaars (1993) distinguishes between inner-directed and outer-directed goal behavior. In inner-directed cultures, individuals believe they can and should control nature, imposing their will on it. In outer-directed cultures, by contrast, individuals believe that societies exist as a part of nature and should largely adapt to it.

Schwartz (1994) suggests that cultures vary in the degree to which individuals seek to master and at times change the natural and social world. Schwartz identified two types of culture: mastery and harmony. In "mastery" cultures, individuals value getting ahead through self-assertion and seek to change the natural and social world to advance personal or group interests. In "harmony" cultures, individuals accept the world as it is and try to preserve it rather than exploit it. Harmony cultures value adapting to the environment.

Finally, GLOBE (House *et al.*, 2004) suggests three interrelated dimensions that may be subsumed under goal orientation: assertiveness, performance orientation, and humane orientation. "Assertiveness" refers to the degree to which individuals in organizations or societies are assertive, tough, dominant, and aggressive in social relationships. "Performance orientation" reflects the extent to which a community encourages and rewards innovation, high standards, and performance improvement. Finally, "humane orientation" reflects the degree to which society encourages individuals for being fair, altruistic, friendly, generous, caring, and kind to others.

A comparison of these models suggests more agreement than disagreement. In general, it is well established that cultures vary in how individuals relate to nature and to one another. The disagreement lies in whether these dimensions are independent or not. While Kluckhohn and Strodtbeck (1961) and GLOBE suggest that there are a group of independent dimensions to account for these

Table 1.11 Mastery-harmony dimension

Mastery	Harmony
Focus on changing or controlling one's natural and social environment.	Focus on living in harmony with nature and adjusting to the natural and social environment.
Achievement valued over relationships.	Relationships valued over achievement.
Emphasis on competition in the pursuit of personal or group goals.	Emphasis on social progress, quality of life, and the welfare of others.
Embraces change and unquestioned innovation.	Defends traditions; skepticism towards change.
Emphasis on material possessions as symbols of achievement.	Emphasis on economy, harmony, and modesty.
Emphasis on assertive, proactive, "masculine" approach.	Emphasis on passive, reactive, "feminine" approach.
Preference for performance-based extrinsic rewards.	Preference for seniority-based intrinsic rewards.

behaviors, Hofstede (1980), Trompenaars (1993), and Schwartz (1994) integrate these behaviors into one cultural dimension. We argue that, for purposes of better understanding organization and management across cultures, it is logical to focus on a small number of critical dimensions that account for most of managerial behavior instead of cutting the cultural pie into several smaller slices.

For this reason, we follow Schwartz's (1994) approach and use *mastery* and *harmony* as representative of cultures that vary in the extent to which they seek achievement and control over the natural and social world or accommodation with it. Table 1.11 compares mastery and harmony cultures, integrating the findings from the researchers reviewed above.

Monochronism vs. polychronism

Five of the six models reviewed regard a society's time orientation as an important cultural variable. While there is widespread agreement that societies vary considerably in how they view or use time, there is less convergence concerning which perception of time is most salient. That is, some culture models focus on the degree to which cultures plan for and focus on the future (House *et al.*, 2004; Hofstede, 2001; Kluckhohn and Strodtbeck, 1961), while others focus on how individuals perceive the flow of time (Hall, 1959; Trompenaars and Hampden-Turner, 1998). Moreover, even when there is a convergence of opinions about which aspect of time is most important to study, there is little agreement concerning how the dimension should be measured.

Kluckhohn and Strodtbeck (1961) suggest that cultures focus on the past, present, or future. "Past oriented" cultures value preserving or restoring traditions of the past. "Present oriented" cultures pay little attention to what happened in the past and think the future is vague and unpredictable. "Future oriented" cultures focus on a better future, stressing change and avoiding traditional ways. In planning, past oriented societies use the past to anticipate the future; present oriented societies resolve current problems without regard for the future; and future oriented societies focus on the long-term implications of past and present actions.

Hofstede, in his work with Michael Bond (1991), classifies cultures in short- or long-term oriented, focusing on the extent to which cultures stress working for today or working for tomorrow. "Long-term oriented" cultures value hard work, personal sacrifice for future benefits, dedication to a cause, and personal thrift. The emphasis is on sacrifice so that future generations can prosper. By contrast, "short-term oriented" cultures focus more on the past or present, stressing respect for traditions and fulfillment of one's social obligations over achievement or investments.

The GLOBE project (House *et al.*, 2004) focuses on the degree to which a society encourages and rewards "future-oriented behaviors" such as planning and delaying gratification. However, in contrast to Hofstede and Bond's (1991) and Kluckhohn and Strodtbeck's (1961) conceptualizations, their alternative to future orientation is not an emphasis on tradition or learning from the past, but rather low economic success, maladaptive managers and organizations, and psychologically unhealthy individuals. Hall (1959) took a very different approach to characterize time. He discusses time as it relates to organizing work activities, noting that some cultures tend to approach work activities

Table 1.12 Monochronism-polychronism dimension

Monochronic	Polychronic
Sequential attention to individual tasks.	Simultaneous attention to multiple tasks.
Linear, single-minded approach to work, planning, and implementation.	Nonlinear, interactive approach to work, planning, and implementation.
Precise concept of time; punctual.	Relative concept of time; often late.
Approach is job-centered; commitment to the job and often to the organization.	Approach is people-centered; commitment to people and human relationships.
Separation of work and personal life.	Integration of work and personal life.
Approach to work is focused and impatient.	Approach to work is unfocused and patient.

in a linear or single-minded fashion, referred to as "monochronic," while others approach multiple tasks simultaneously, referred to as "polychronic." Finally, Trompenaars' approach is a blend of the earlier models, suggesting that one's time orientation (past, present, or future) influences the degree to which people approach tasks sequentially or simultaneously.

While all of these approaches add value to the study of cultural differences, we believe that, from a managerial standpoint, Hall's approach of distinguishing between *monochronic* and *polychronic* cultures seems most useful. In a sense, concerns with the future are closely related to needs for achievement and assumptions of control. Cultures that believe the future is their own doing are more likely to stress planning and future orientation than cultures that believe they cannot affect the turn of events. These cultures are more likely to focus on living the present. In our view, the central point in understanding time orientation is whether people approach their work one task at a time in a somewhat linear fashion or attempt to perform multiple tasks simultaneously (see table 1.12). Do people have a precise concept of time and tend to be very punctual or do they have a relative concept and tend to be late? Do they need a steady flow of information to do their job? Are people more committed to their jobs or to family and friends? Do they separate work and family life or see them as an integrated whole? Do they take a linear or nonlinear approach to planning? And, finally, are they focused and impatient or unfocused and patient?

Universalism–particularism

Finally, one of the more intractable dimensions found in current culture models involves the issue of rules as a means of reducing uncertainty in society. Here there is less agreement across the models. For example, both Hofstede (1980) and GLOBE (House *et al.*, 2004) call this dimension "uncertainty avoidance." However, Hofstede focuses principally on the degree to which societies can tolerate uncertainty and use rules to control personal behavior, while GLOBE focuses on the degree to which societies attempt to reduce uncertainty through rules and regulations. Meanwhile, Trompenaars (1993) follows Parsons and Shills' (1951) classic work and focuses on the relative importance of rules vs. relationships. They all tend to agree, however, that the various social, ideological, and behavioral mechanisms by which social control manifests itself in a society represents an important aspect of culture.

In this regard, we suggest that rather than comparing cultures on the extent to which they attempt to ignore or tolerate uncertainty, it is better to compare cultures based on how they try and deal with it. How cultures deal with uncertainty is largely influenced by other cultural dimensions, including the mechanisms of social control. We believe society's views on rules and rules enforcement is a critical culture dimensions because it influences how cultures cope with uncertainty as well as other critical managerial action.

In *universalistic*, or rule-based, cultures, there is a tendency to promulgate a multitude of laws, rules, regulations, bureaucratic procedures, and strict social norms in an attempt to control as many unanticipated events or behaviors as possible. People tend to conform to officially sanctioned constraints because of a moral belief in the virtue of the rule of law, and will often obey directives even if they know violations will not be detected. Waiting for a red light in the absence of any traffic is a good example here. Rules and laws are universally applied (at least in theory), with few exceptions for extenuating circumstances or personal connections. There is a strong belief in the use of formal contracts and rigorous record keeping in business dealings. Things are done "by the book" and infractions often bring immediate sanctions or consequences. Finally, decisions tend to be made based on objective criteria to the extent possible. All of this is aimed at creating a society with no surprises. Germany, the Netherlands, the Scandinavian countries, the US, and Canada are often identified as rule-based cultures.

By contrast, *particularistic*, or relationship-based, cultures tend to use influential people more than abstract or objective rules and regulations as a means of social control. This social control can come from parents, peers, superiors, supervisors, government officials, and so forth – anyone with influence over the individual. In this sense, relationship-based cultures tend to be particularistic and individual circumstances often influence the manner in which formal rules are applied. In addition, greater emphasis is placed on developing mutually beneficial interpersonal relationships and trust as a substitute for strict rules and procedures. There is generally less record keeping and things tend to be done on an informal basis. There is also greater tolerance for non-compliance with bureaucratic rules in the belief that formal rules cannot cover all contingencies and that some flexibility is often required. Finally, decisions tend to be made based on a combination of objective and subjective criteria and with less formality. Russia, Greece, Venezuela, Italy, Portugal, and Spain are often cited as examples.

This is not to say that particularistic cultures do not value laws and official procedures; they do. Rather, laws and procedures are often followed only to the extent that one's social network embraces them and sees either the virtue or necessity of following them, not because of some innate belief in their moral correctness, as is the case with rule-based cultures. Where predictability of behavior is important, it is motivated largely through

Table 1.13 Universalism-particularism dimension

Universalistic	Particularistic
Individual behavior largely regulated by rules, laws, formal policies, standard operating procedures, and social norms that are widely supported by societal members and applied uniformly to everyone.	While rules and laws are important, they often require modifications in their application or enforcement by influential people (e.g., parents, peers, superiors, government officials) or unique circumstances.
Rule-based.	Relationship-based.
Emphasis on legal contracts and meticulous record keeping.	Emphasis on interpersonal relationships and trust; less emphasis on record keeping.
Rules and procedures spelled out clearly and published widely.	Rules and procedures often ambiguous or not believed or accepted.
Rules are internalized and followed without question.	Rules are sometimes ignored or followed only when strictly enforced.
Do things formally by the book.	Do things through informal networks.
Low tolerance for rule breaking.	Tolerance for rule breaking.
Decisions based largely on objective criteria (e.g., rules, policies).	Decisions often based on subjective criteria (e.g., hunches, personal connections).

contacts, not contracts, and interpersonal trust and mutual support between partners is critical. These differences are summarized in table 1.13.

Country clusters and core cultural dimensions

A major challenge in working with cultural differences is determining how best to assess or measure such differences for purposes of research and theory development. Some culture models, like Hofstede and Trompenaars, offer country-specific numeric scores for each of their cultural dimensions. However, converting cultural differences into numeric scores is an imprecise science at best. Cultures by definition are qualitative, not quantitative, and attempts to attach numbers to various cultures only invite errors and misunderstandings. Moreover, cultures are not monolithic; each culture consists of people who are different in many ways even if central tendencies can be differentiated between various nationalities. For example, while we may describe people from the United States as relatively individualistic and people from Japan as relatively collectivistic, many Americans in fact are highly collectivistic and many Japanese are highly individualistic. It is only a matter of degree

and central tendencies that differentiate between the two cultures.

Despite this limitation, several researchers have made serious attempts to attach numbers to various cultures in order to facilitate country comparisons. Without such numbers, it is argued, comparisons by both researchers and managers become problematic. However, these ratings are based on research methods that have been widely criticized, and the accuracy of the results has frequently been questioned (Trompenaars and Hampden-Turner, 1998; House *et al.*, 2004). Indeed, many of the estimates for specific countries do not agree with each another. For example, while Hofstede assigns Italy a score of 76 on individualism-collectivism (highly collectivistic), Trompenaars assigns it a 20 (moderately collectivistic). While Hofstede (2001) assigns Germany a score of 35 (egalitarian) on power distance, House and his associates (2004) assign it a 5.25 (hierarchical). Moreover, some country estimates by the same researchers change over time. For example, Trompenaars (1993; Trompenaars and Hampden-Turner, 1998) rated Thailand as individualistic in his first assessment, but collectivistic in his second. Such errors call into question the validity of the entire rating system.

An alternative to quantitative measures is qualitative, or ethnographic, measures. But problems exist here too, largely due to potential rater bias in developing both the models and measures. While cultural anthropologists have made earnest attempts to differentiate across cultures using ethnographic or qualitative methods, room for errors persists due to possible cultural biases of the evaluators. For instance, a US born, US educated anthropologist will likely view the world (and hence different cultures) through American eyes, and may possibly overlook important cultural traits because he or she is not looking for them. Indeed, this occurred when Michael Bond and Peter Smith (1996) first noted that looking at cultures through an east Asian perspective led to the identification of different cultural dimensions for purposes of assessment. This human bias in assessment and analysis is itself a natural outcome of cultural differences. As a result, as with quantitative assessments, ethnographic or qualitative measures of cultural differences do not always agree with one another.

In order to operationalize the core cultural dimensions presented here, it is necessary to have a means of classifying cultures so country – or at least regional – comparisons can be made. Mindful of the limitations discussed above, we chose to estimate cultural differences within country clusters (as opposed to individual countries) by adapting a model originally proposed by Ronan and Shenkar (1985). This model focused on identifying regions where ample anthropological data were available, and our use of these clusters reflects this imbalance. Some regions (e.g., Central Asia, Polynesia) are not included, while others (e.g., Europe) are covered in considerable detail. (Our hope is that future research will address this imbalance.) In addition, according to Ronan and Shenkar, several countries (e.g., Brazil, India, and Israel) do not easily fit into such a framework, so again some caution is in order. With these cautions in mind, we used the Ronan and Shenkar model to identify nine country clusters for which sufficient data were available to estimate central tendencies in cultural characteristics: Anglo cluster (e.g., Australia, Canada, UK, USA); Arab cluster (Dubai, Egypt, Saudi Arabia); eastern European cluster (e.g., Czech Republic, Hungary, Poland); east/southeast Asian cluster (e.g., China, Japan, Korea, Singapore, Thailand); Germanic cluster (e.g., Austria, Germany); Latin

American cluster (e.g., Argentina, Costa Rica, Mexico); Latin European cluster (e.g., France, Italy, Spain); Nordic cluster (e.g., Denmark, Norway, Sweden); and Sub-Sahara African cluster (e.g., Ghana, Kenya, Nigeria).

Based on these country clusters, and using multiple measures and multiple methods to the extent possible, we then assessed and integrated a combination of quantitative and qualitative measures from available research in order to categorize cultures along the five dimensions. First, existing quantitative measures from such researchers as Hofstede, Trompenaars, and House and associates were examined and compared. Next, ethnographic data compiled largely from cultural anthropology focusing on specific cultures or geographic regions were incorporated into the analysis and compared against the quantitative findings. Finally, remaining points of disagreement were discussed between the co-authors and other researchers in an effort to reach a consensus on the final ratings. While it is not claimed that this procedure eliminated all errors, it is felt that it represents a superior method to the previous reliance on single-source data. Still, room for error persists, in particular due to the potential rater bias of the authors, and readers are cautioned to use their own judgment in interpreting results.

In making our assessments, we chose to develop a more conservative ordinal rating scale, clustering cultures into four categories (e.g., strongly individualistic, moderately individualistic, moderately collectivistic, and strongly collectivistic) based on the relative strength of the various dimensions compared to other cultures, instead of attempting to calculate specific numeric ratings that may appear to be more precise than they actually are. The results are shown in table 1.14. Note that these are only rough estimates based on available research. While the results shown in the table may appear to be less precise than assigning specific numeric ratings, we believe they are possibly both more accurate and useful because they assume a more conservative stance in data analysis and are based on multiple data points. Finally, in making use of the information presented here, it is important to recognize that no point on any assessment scale is preferred over any other; they are simply different.

Table 1.14 Central tendencies on core cultural dimensions for country clusters

Country Clusters	Hierarchy-Equality	Individualism-Collectivism	Mastery-Harmony	Monochronism-Polychronism	Universalism-Particularism
Anglo	Moderately egalitarian	Strongly individualistic	Strongly mastery-oriented	Strongly monochronic	Moderately universalistic
Arab	Strongly hierarchical	Strongly collectivistic	Moderately harmony-oriented	Strongly polychronic	Strongly particularistic
East European	Moderately hierarchical	Moderately collectivistic	Moderately mastery-oriented	Moderately monochronic	Moderately particularistic
East/Southeast Asian	Strongly hierarchical	Strongly collectivistic	Strongly-harmony-oriented	Moderately monochronic	Strongly particularistic
Germanic	Moderately egalitarian	Moderately individualistic	Moderately mastery-oriented	Moderately monochronic	Strongly universalistic
Latin American	Moderately hierarchical	Moderately collectivistic	Moderately harmony-oriented	Strongly polychronic	Strongly particularistic
Latin European	Moderately hierarchical	Moderately collectivistic	Moderately harmony-oriented	Moderately polychronic	Moderately particularistic
Nordic	Strongly egalitarian	Moderately collectivistic	Moderately harmony-oriented	Moderately monochronic	Strongly universalistic
Sub-Sahara African	Strongly hierarchical	Strongly collectivistic	Moderately harmony-oriented	Moderately polychronic	Strongly particularistic

Note: The country cluster categories used here were adapted from Ronan and Shenkar (1985). The core cultural dimension (CCD) ratings represent central tendencies for selected country clusters (see text for details). Variations, sometimes substantial, around these central tendencies can be found in all clusters and countries. Also note that some regions of the globe (e.g., Central Asia) are not included here due to an absence of substantive data, while others (e.g., Europe) are represented in some detail due to the availability of sufficient data.

In interpreting the results shown in table 1.14, it must also be remembered that significant within-cluster variance can often be found. For example, as noted earlier, all Anglos are not individualistic, while all east or southeast Asians are not collectivistic. While it is sometimes necessary to focus on central tendencies between cultures for purposes of general comparisons, the role of individual and regional differences in determining attitudes and behaviors should not be overlooked. Still, it should not be surprising that cultural ratings for countries in the same cluster of the world (e.g., Denmark, Norway, and Sweden) tend to be closer than ratings for countries located in a different cluster of the world (e.g., Italy, Spain, France). This is a natural consequence of contiguous countries in various regions living side-by-side with their neighbors over centuries and sometimes millennia. Still, important cultural differences can be found across peoples inhabiting a particular region. Finally, it is important to remember that, while these cultural dimensions may be a useful shortcut for gaining conceptual entry into general cultural trends across countries and regions, they are in no way a substitute for more systematic in-depth analyses as they relate to the study of culture, work, and organizations.

Directions for future research

In this paper, we propose a vehicle for understanding cultural differences based on the previous work of Kluckhohn and Strodtbeck, Hofstede, Hall, Trompenaars, Schwartz, and the GLOBE researchers. We further suggest that in order to facilitate future research and cross-cultural comparisons it is useful to integrate and consolidate existing – if sometimes divergent – models of national cultures. While previous researchers have introduced various cultural dimensions, we conclude from our comparative analysis that five specific dimensions – referred to here as core cultural dimensions – are particularly salient for understanding management practices in different cultures. In our view, these five dimensions account for most of the conceptual variance across cultures and help researchers escape from the culture theory jungle – a proliferation of theories that needlessly forces researchers to choose whose side they are on prior to initiating a research project. The five dimensions presented here were derived from a comparative analysis and integration of six competing theories and represent what to us is a useful strategy for reducing the confusion caused by both the overlap and differences across models.

However, any attempted integration such as ours obviously requires further study and validation. Cultural dimensions by their very nature are interrelated and, while they may make sense as a collective whole, each dimension may lose its relevance or even meaning when studied individually or out of context. As such, more research of a comprehensive or integrative nature is called for. Moreover, as is evident from our review, there is widespread agreement among existing models about the themes of the various dimensions, but less agreement about the details of what some of these dimensions actually mean. Below we propose some specific areas for future research within each of the core cultural dimensions discussed above:

1. *Hierarchy–equality*. Variations in power orientation have received considerable attention is recent research. Moreover, a review of this research suggests that this dimension enjoys the most agreement across the various models. The question that remains unanswered, however, is the extent to which power orientation and group orientation are independent dimensions or are closely related and, if so, how? Again, Triandis (1986) laid the foundation for this issue, but more work is needed. In particular, future research may focus on investigating the relationship between power orientation and rule orientation. These dimensions appear to be correlated and further investigation teasing out the role of rules, relationships, and social structure into power distribution are likely to shed light into the relationship of the several culture dimensions and their influence on behavior.

2. *Individualism–collectivism*. There has already been considerable research on individualism–

collectivism. Of particular note here is the work of Triandis (1994), who refined this construct and then tested his approach in fifteen countries. He found seven factors that relate to this dimension: self-reliance and independence, competition, hedonism, interdependence, family integrity, closeness to in-groups, and sociability. The first three were related to individualism and the last four to collectivism. He suggested that collectivism and individualism were polythetic constructs, meaning that there were various kinds of individualism and collectivism. He suggested further that four dimensions were universal attributes of the constructs of individualism and collectivism: (1) definition of the self: independent versus interdependent; (2) structure of goals: compatible with in-group goals, independent of in-group goals; (3) emphasis on norms versus attitudes: social behavior is determined by norms, duties and obligations (collectivism) or attitudes, personal needs, perceived rights and contracts (individualism); and (4) emphasis on relatedness versus rationality: collectivists emphasize relatedness, giving priority to relationships and taking into consideration the needs of others even when the relationships are not advantageous. Individualists emphasize rationality, and calculate the cost benefits associated with relationships. Based on this research, Triandis argued that societies vary in the extent in which the differences among people are minimized or emphasized. In homogeneous cultures people do not want to stand out, while in heterogeneous societies being different is emphasized. Future research may wish to focus on a more explicit examination of how this critical dimension relates to other cultural dimensions, again looking to how the various dimensions that collectively comprise culture work together to influence attitudes and behaviors.

3. *Mastery–harmony*. As noted above, this cultural dimension refers to people's beliefs concerning the degree of their control over the natural and the social world. However, clarifying exactly what this dimension means is not easy. For example, earlier models diverge in the extent to which people's

need for achievement should be included in this dimension or whether this represents a separate cultural dimension. Future research needs to tease out this dimension and explore the degree to which beliefs about control and need for achievement are actually correlated. At the same time, future research should examine the relationship between gender differences across cultures and perceptions of control. While previous research has suggested that there are important cultural variations regarding gender differences, it is not clear if they relate to assumptions of control, need for achievement, power distribution, or even possibly a separate cultural dimension. We believe this is a fruitful area for future research.

4. *Monochronism–polychronism.* Future research should investigate the relationship between perceptions of the flow of time and how tasks are organized (i.e. the monochronic and polychronic distinction) and perceptions of past, present, and future, short and long term. Are these views of time independent or interconnected? It seems that while most researchers agree there is an important cultural component in how individuals perceive time, there are disagreements concerning which aspects of time are more important. Future research should focus on refining the time dimension studying the relationships among several aspects of time.

5. *Universalism–particularism.* Significant research is needed to validate this dimension. We have argued that rather than comparing cultures on how they perceive uncertainty, it is more salient to compare them on how they deal with rules which, in turn, influence how they deal with uncertainty. Two important culture models, those proposed by Hofstede (1980) and the GLOBE project (2004), suggest that cultures vary in the degree to which they avoid uncertainty. While we think uncertainty is not a culture dimension as it is an experience better explained by other more consequential culture variables, we recognize that there are significant variations in how individuals perceive and cope with uncertainty across cultures. We suggest that each of the five main cultural themes proposed here influences perceptions of

uncertainty. For instance, mastery cultures are more likely to try to change the environment to reduce uncertainty than harmony cultures. Moreover, the degree to which individuals see themselves as autonomous or embedded in groups may influence how collectives organize to cope with common uncertainties. The way in which power, status, and authority in a society are distributed is likely to influence the degree to which individuals take responsibility for uncertain events or rely on the guidance, opinion, or protection of superiors. Additionally, time perceptions may influence the timing in which uncertainty is perceived and action is taken. In summary, we suggest that instead of classifying cultures according to their tolerance or ways of dealing with uncertainty, it makes more sense to focus on social control. Social control, as well as other cultural dimensions, influences how cultures cope with uncertainty. Future research should explore how each cultural dimension influences perceptions and ways of dealing with uncertainty.

As indicated in this paper, much remains to be done to understand in a more comprehensive way the etiology of cultural differences as they relate to management practice. In this pursuit, researchers must of necessity come to terms with the fundamentally flawed and imprecise nature of both their theories and their data. In the near term – if not also the long term – accurate data in support of research will frequently be difficult to collect and analyze and, since theory-building and empirical research go hand-in-hand, theoretical development itself will often be constrained. In the meantime, in our view, researchers must rely on personal insight and intuition, reflection, and collaboration, not just in what they believe to be "hard" data, if they are to make genuine progress on this important topic. We believe that the existing models in the field, individually and collectively, represent useful and constructive efforts towards this end. Our hope is that future researchers will attempt to build on these signal contributions instead of merely criticizing them. In our view, cross-cultural organizational research is and must remain a synergistic and collaborative endeavor.

References

Bond, M. H. 2001. "Surveying the foundations: approaches to measuring group, organizational, and national variation", in M. Erez and U. Kleinbeck (eds.), *Work Motivation in the Context of a Globalizing Economy*. Mahwah, NJ: Lawrence Erlbaum, pp. 395–412.

and Smith, P. 1996. "Cross-cultural social and organizational psychology", *Annual Review of Psychology* 47: 205–35.

Hall, E. T. 1959, 1981. *The Silent Language*. New York: Doubleday.

and Hall, M.R. 1990. *Understanding Cultural Differences*. Yarmouth, Maine: Intercultural Press.

Hofstede, G. 1980, 2001. *Culture's Consequences: Comparing Values, Behaviors, Institutions, and Organizations Across Nations*. Thousand Oaks, CA: Sage Publications.

and Bond, M. H. 1991. "The Confucius connection: From cultural roots to economic growth", *Organizational Dynamics* 16(4): 4–21.

Hooker, J. 2003. *Working Across Cultures*. Stanford, CA: Stanford University Press.

House, R. J., Hanges, P. J., Javidan, M., Dorfman, P. W., and Gupta, V. 2004. *Culture, Leadership and Organizations: The GLOBE Study of 62 Societies*. Thousand Oaks, CA: Sage Publications.

Kagitçibasi, C. 1997. "Individualism and collectivism", in J. B. Segal and C. Kagitçibasi (eds.), *Handbook of Cross Cultural Psychology*. Boston: Allyn & Bacon, Vol. 3, pp. 1–49.

Kluckhohn, C. 1951. "Values and value orientations in the theory of action", in T. Parsons and E. A. Shils (eds.), *Towards a General Theory of Action*. Cambridge, MA: Harvard University Press.

Kluckhohn, F. and Strodtbeck, F. 1961. *Variations in Value Orientations*. Evanston, IL: Row, Peterson.

Nardon, L. and Steers, R. M. 2007. "Learning cultures on the fly", in Mansour Javidan, Richard M. Steers, and Michael Hitt (eds.), *Advances in International Management: The Global Mindset*. Amsterdam: Elsevier.

Parsons, T. and Shills, E. A. 1951. *Toward a General Theory of Action*. Cambridge, MA: Harvard University Press.

Ronan, S. and Shenkar, O. 1985. "Clustering clusters on attitudinal dimensions: A review and synthesis", *Academy of Management Review*, 10(3): 435–54.

Rotter, J. 1966. "Generalized expectations for internal versus external control of reinforcement", *Psychological Monographs* 609.

Schwartz, S. H. 1992. "Universals in the content and structure of values: Theoretical advances and empirical tests in 20 countries", in M. Zanna (ed.), *Advances in Experimental Social Psychology* 25, Orlando, FL: Academic, pp. 1–65.

1994. "Beyond individualism/collectivism: New cultural dimensions of values", in U. Kim, H. C. Triandis, C. Kagitçibasi, S. C. Choi, and G. Yoon (eds.), *Individualism and Collectivism: Theory, Methods and Applications*, Thousand Oaks, CA: Sage, pp. 85–122.

Steers, R. M. and Nardon, L. 2006. *Managing in the Global Economy*. Armonk, NY: M. E. Sharpe.

Triandis, H. C. 1994. *Culture and Social Behavior*. New York: McGraw-Hill.

Trompenaars, F. 1993. *Riding the Waves of Culture: Understanding Cultural Diversity in Business*. London: Economists Books.

and Hampden-Turner, C. 1998. *Riding the Waves of Culture: Understanding Diversity in Global Business*. New York: McGraw Hill.

Culture, organizations, and institutions: an integrative review[1]

KWOK LEUNG and SOON ANG

The focus on national culture as a major variable in global management research has been primarily guided and inspired by the now classic work of Hofstede (1980), although there is already a vibrant literature on culture and organizational behavior prior to the popularity of cultural dimensions (for a review, see Bhagat and McQuaid, 1982). Hofstede identified four major dimensions of culture in his framework: individualism-collectivism; power distance; uncertainty avoidance; and masculinity-femininity. Numerous studies have employed his framework to examine diverse organizational issues (for a review, see Kirkman, Lowe, and Gibson, 2006), ranging from the choice of entry mode (e.g., Kogut and Singh, 1988), cultural differences in the popularity of internet shopping (Lim, Leung, Sia, and Lee, 2004), the popularity of employee assistance programs (Bhagat, Steverson, and Segovis, 2007), intercultural negotiation (Brett and Okumura, 1998) to foreign-local employee relationships (Ang, Van Dyne, and Begley, 2003).

While Hofstede's framework is obviously important and influential, there are constant pleas for the development of novel constructs to advance our understanding of culture and international business (e.g., Leung, Bhagat, Buchan, Erez, and Gibson, 2005). The objective of our chapter is to review the development of cultural frameworks in the arena of global management since Hofstede's (1980) monumental work, explore how the cultural perspective can augment the institutional perspective, a popular approach for understanding firm differences across cultures, and identify fruitful directions for future research on culture and global management.

Research on cultural dimensions

Major dimensions of culture

Perhaps because Hofstede's (1980) work is based on work values, the bulk of research on culture in the last two decades is concerned with shared values of members of different societies. The Chinese Culture Connection (1987) raised the issue that the cultural dimensions of Hofstede (1980) may have been biased because of the western origin of the value items. To correct for this bias, the Chinese Culture Connection developed a set of values based on Chinese traditional values, and surveyed college students from over twenty societies. This triangulation effort resulted in the validation of three Hofstede dimensions: *individualism-collectivism, power distance*, and *masculinity-femininity*, as well as the identification of a new dimension: *Confucian Work Dynamism*, which was subsequent relabeled as "*short-term vs. long-term orientation*" by Hofstede (1991).

Schwartz (1992) offered a conceptually different approach to mapping dimensions of culture. Although based also on values, Schwartz (1992) was more interested in general values than in work-related values, and has identified ten value types at the individual or psychological level. At the level of culture, Schwartz (1994) has identified seven value types, which may be regarded as cultural dimensions: (1) *conservatism*; (2) *intellectual autonomy*; (3) *affective autonomy*; (4) *hierarchy*; (5) *egalitarian commitment*; (6) *mastery*; and (7) *harmony*. In comparing his value types with Hofstede's dimensions, Schwartz (1994)

[1] This paper was partially supported by a grant (CityU 1274/03H) provided by Research Grants Committee of Hong Kong.

concluded that individualism is positively related to intellectual and affective autonomy as well as egalitarian commitment, but negatively related to conservatism and hierarchy. Power distance shows a pattern of correlations that is generally opposite to that of Individualism. Masculinity is positively related to mastery, and uncertainty avoidance is related to harmony.

The value frameworks of Schwartz have been adopted in some global management research. For instance, his individual value types have been used in understanding cultural differences in conflict resolution (Morris *et al.*, 1998), and in analyzing cultural differences in corporate debt ratios (Chui, Lloyd, and Kwok, 2002).

In an analysis of work values in a sample of over 8,000 employees from forty-three societies, Smith, Dugan, and Trompenaars (1996) have identified two culture-level dimensions: *egalitarian commitment* vs. *conservatism*, and *utilitarian involvement* vs. *loyal involvement*. The egalitarian commitment vs. conservatism dimension corresponds to power distance, whereas the utilitarian involvement vs. loyal involvement dimension corresponds to the individualism-collectivism dimension. In summary, Smith and Bond (1998, ch. 3) concluded that the three different value surveys subsequent to the work of Hofstede (1980) have produced convergent results, lending support to the validity of his original cultural dimensions.

The latest attempt to develop a cultural framework based on values has been made by House and his associates in their global study with the acronym GLOBE. A major focus of this project is to understand leadership and organizational behavior around the world, and in doing so, nine dimensions of culture based on values and practices salient in an organizational context have been identified: (1) *performance orientation*; (2) *assertiveness orientation*; (3) *future orientation*; (4) *humane orientation*; (5) *institutional collectivism*; (6) *family collectivism*; (7) *gender egalitarianism*; (8) *power distance*; and (9) *uncertainty avoidance* (House, Hanges, Javidan, *et al.*, 2004). Despite the use of measures related to leadership and organizational behavior, most of the cultural dimensions identified are related conceptually and correlated empirically with the dimensions of Hofstede's

(1991). Institutional collectivism and family collectivism are related to individualism-collectivism; assertiveness orientation and gender egalitarianism are related to masculinity-femininity; power distance and uncertainty avoidance are related to two Hofstede dimensions of the same labels; while future orientation is related to long-term orientation.

Two dimensions, performance orientation and humane orientation, seem unrelated to the Hofstede dimensions. However, performance orientation is conceptually related to McClelland's (1961) concept of need for achievement, while humane orientation appears related to the good vs. bad human nature dimension of Kluckhohn and Strodtbeck (1961). In sum, the overlap between the GLOBE dimensions and the Hofstede dimensions are quite substantial, although there is no agreement with regard to the extent of the overlap (Javidan, House, Dorfman *et al.*, 2006; Hofstede, 2006).

Novel cultural dimensions

Broadly speaking, the several global research projects reviewed above are based on values emphasized in society, and many of the items defining the cultural dimensions are concerned with what people regard as important, necessary, and proper in their cultural context. It is obvious that other constructs are needed to broaden the conceptual tools for analyzing culture (e.g., Gelfand, Erez, and Aycan, 2007). Two recent, major developments are reviewed here, one based on beliefs, and the other one on social norms.

To develop a cultural map of the world that is not based on values, Leung and Bond (2004) have turned to social axioms, or general beliefs that are context-free. Social axioms are general beliefs that may be conceptualized as "generalized expectancies," a concept introduced by Rotter (1966) to characterize locus of control. Based on items culled from the psychological literature as well as from qualitative research conducted in Hong Kong and Venezuela, Leung *et al.* (2002) identified five axiom dimensions in each of five cultures: Hong Kong, Venezuela, the US, Japan, and Germany. These five dimensions were subsequently confirmed in a round-the-world study (Leung and Bond, 2004):

(1) *social cynicism* refers to a negative view of human nature, a bias against some social groups, and a mistrust of social institutions; (2) *social complexity* suggests a belief that there are multiple ways to solve a problem, and that people's behavior may vary across situations; (3) *reward for application* suggests that the investment of effort, knowledge, careful planning and other resources will lead to positive outcomes; (4) *religiosity* asserts the existence of a supernatural being and the beneficial social functions of religious institutions and practices; and finally, (5) *fate control* suggests that life events are pre-determined by external forces, but that there are ways for people to influence the negative impact of these forces.

A culture-level factor analysis with cultural means of the items, however, has yielded only two factors (Bond, *et al.*, 2004): (1) *dynamic externality* refers to beliefs in fate, the existence of a supreme being, and positive functions of religious practices as well as beliefs in effort and knowledge and in the low complexity of the social world; while (2) *societal cynicism* is based entirely on items from social cynicism. Dynamic externality is generally related to collectivism and high power distance, but societal cynicism is relatively distinct from cultural dimensions identified previously.

We note that the individual-level axiom dimensions have been adopted in global management research, such as in a cross-cultural study of influence tactics (Fu *et al.*, 2004). However, the culture-level axiom dimensions have not been studied in a global management context.

The second development centers on the notion of tightness-looseness as a major cultural characteristic, which has been around for decades (e.g., Pelto, 1968), and is concerned with the strength of social norms for regulating social behaviors. Compared to tight cultures, social norms in loose cultures allow more latitude for individual behavior, and norm violations are subjected to less social sanctioning. Gelfand, Nishii, and Raver (2006) argued that because of the dominance of value frameworks in global management research, this important cultural dimension has been ignored. To address this gap, Gelfand *et al.* have proposed a multi-level model of looseness-tightness, which distinguishes between societal tightness-looseness as well as

organizational and psychological adaptation to tightness-looseness. Societal tightness-looseness, together with features of the organizational context and psychological adaptations to tightness-looseness at the individual level, are supposed to influence organizational adaptations to tightness-looseness, which in turn influence significant organizational outcomes, such as stability vs. innovation and change. Furthermore, societal tightness-looseness, together with individual characteristics and experiences, are supposed to influence psychological adaptations to tightness and looseness, which in turn influence individual behaviors, such as risk avoidance vs. risk-taking and innovation.

Empirical work on tightness-looseness as a major dimension of culture is just beginning, and given the depth of theorizing that has been proposed regarding this construct, we expect it to emerge as a novel and important non-value-based framework and provide the impetus for some new directions in global management research.

Current development of the dimensional approach to culture

In a review of the literature, Leung *et al.* (2005) noted three major trends in the current work on cultural dimensions in the global management areas. First, it is now recognized that the influence of culture is important, but not omnipresent. Situational variables may override or even reverse the effects of culture (Earley and Gibson, 2002; Leung, Su, and Morris, 2001). For instance, in a study of five multinational firms, Zellmer-Bruhn, Gibson, and Earley (2002) found that information exchange among group members was more affected by cultural heterogeneity only when the groups were newly formed. In other words, cultural backgrounds of group members had a smaller influence on information exchange for well-established groups.

There is a different stream of research showing that cultural influence is stronger in situations where one's actions are identifiable. In a comparison between Chinese and Canadians, Kachelmeier and Shehata (1997) reported cultural differences in the willingness to reveal valuable information in an auditing context in an identifiable condition. When people's preferences were anonymous, however, cultural differences vanished and the pursuit of self-interest was evident for all cultural groups. In general, this line of research attempts to investigate when culture does matter, and what major variables make culture matters more or less.

The second development is concerned with cultural change. In a globalization era, cultures may converge in some areas and diverge in others (Bhagat, Baliga, Moustafa, and Krishnan, 2003). Recently, Erez and Gati (2004) proposed a multi-level model of culture, starting with the macro level of a global culture, to national, organizational, and team cultures. A top-down, bottom-up process is proposed for understanding cultural changes, which may start from some individuals, and eventually shape the global culture. Culture change may also start from the global culture, which will eventually modify the behaviors and thoughts of individuals in a given society. Although their model has not been rigorously tested, there is ample evidence to suggest that culture is not static. For instance, Heuer, Cummings, and Hutabarat (1999) found that Indonesian managers were closer in individualism and power distance to their American counterparts than the gaps previously reported by Hofstede (1980). Ralston, Egri, Stewart, et al. (1999) found that in China, younger managers (under 41 years old) were more individualistic and more likely to act independently, and showed lower endorsement of Confucian values. Finally, Hung, Gu, and Yim (2007) reported that younger consumers in China were more likely to endorse novelty seeking, perceive shopping as a leisure activity, and use foreign goods.

The third development is concerned with the argument that the cultural orientation of individuals is not rigid, but shows some latitude as a function of what is salient on their mind. For instance, based on cognitive psychology, Tinsley and Brodt (2004) proposed a number of knowledge structures for understanding cross-cultural differences in conflict behavior. These knowledge structures are dynamic in the sense that their content and salience are sensitive to situational influences, which may lead to different reactions to the same conflict situation. There is convincing empirical evidence to suggest that people's dominant cultural orientation can be shifted by making salient different markers of cultural orientations (Hong, Morris, Chiu, & Benet-Martinez, 2000; Trafimow, Triandis, and Goto, 1991). In line with a dynamic view of culture, for instance, Molinsky (2007) has provided an analysis of the variables that may influence cross-cultural code-switching, i.e., the act of modifying one's behavior in a foreign cultural setting.

Other theoretical frameworks in the cultural approach

Area-specific cross-cultural theoretical frameworks

In a commentary on the debate between Hofstede and the GLOBE team about the overlap of cultural dimensions, Earley (2006) argued for moving away from conducting value surveys around the world to "developing theories and frameworks for understanding the linkage among culture, perceptions, actions, organizations, structures, etc." (p. 928). Unfortunately, this type of theoretical framework is not common in the field of global management. We review two areas of research that are relatively well developed.

The first area is concerned with the adjustment and performance of expatriates, as well as various issues related to their selection and training, which has a very long history in global management (e.g., Tung, 1998). Considerable research has examined the antecedents of the adjustment of expatriates (e.g., Black, Mendenhall, and Oddou, 1991), and a variety of factors, including personal, job and organizational, and non-work factors, are predictive of expatriate adjustment (Bhaskar-Shrinivas, Harrison, Luk, and Shaffer, 2005). Likewise, many factors have been found to predict the job performance and effectiveness of expatriates (e.g., Mol, Born, Willemsen, & Van Der Molen, 2005). The focus of the research in this area is on the processes underlying the adjustment, performance, and effectiveness of expatriates, although cultural dimensions are sometimes invoked in the explanatory mechanisms (e.g., Stahl and Caligiuri, 2005). Quite a number of mid-range theoretical frameworks have been proposed, which have received considerable empirical support, such as the model of Black, Mendenhall and Oddou, (1991) on the adjustment of expatriates.

The second area of research is nascent, but also touches on intercultural contact. In the latest review on the research in cross-cultural organizational behavior, Gelfand, Erez, and Aycan (2007) lamented that cross-cultural organizational behavior research has focused on comparative research – comparing attitudes and behaviors across cultural groups – but has ignored the dynamics of culture in intercultural encounters. For example, while there is a large literature on cultural differences in motives, justice, negotiation, or leadership across cultures, little is known about what contributes to positive intercultural dynamics (Leung, Bhagat, Buchan et al., 2005). Yet we know that these dynamics can adversely affect effectiveness and performance in culturally diverse settings (Tsui and Gutek, 1999; Williams and O'Reilly, 1998) or in multicultural teams (Earley and Gibson, 2002; Kirkman, Gibson, and Shapiro, 2001)

Gelfand, Erez and Aycan (2007) identified cultural intelligence (Earley and Ang, 2003) as a promising new approach and novel construct for thinking about and researching on effectiveness of intercultural encounters. Cultural Intelligence or CQ (Earley and Ang, 2003), defined as the capability to function effectively in culturally diverse settings, is based on contemporary conceptualizations of intelligence as inclusive of the capability to adapt to others and to situations (Sternberg, 1986). Operationally, cultural intelligence is defined as a multidimensional construct comprising four factors. These four factors mirror contemporary views of intelligence as a complex, multi-factor set of capabilities that is composed of metacognitive, cognitive, motivational, and behavioral factors (see Sternberg, 1986). Metacognitive CQ reflects the mental capability to acquire and understand cultural knowledge. Cognitive CQ reflects general knowledge and knowledge structures about culture. Motivational CQ reflects the individual capability to direct energy toward learning about and functioning in intercultural situations, while behavioral CQ reflects the individual capability to exhibit appropriate verbal and non-verbal actions in culturally diverse settings (Ang, Van Dyne, Koh, 2007; Ang and Van Dyne, 2008). Again, the focus

of this stream of research is on adapting and adjusting to a foreign cultural milieu, and cultural dimensions fade into the background of the theorizing in this area. Ongoing research in this area is examining how cultural intelligence in its comprehensive multifaceted form could facilitate the adaptation of individuals and organizations across cultural boundaries.

In summary, while most studies in global management in the last two decades have been inspired by cultural dimensions, we note that in some topical areas, well-defined theoretical frameworks for explicating the specific processes involved have been developed. We are with Earley (2006) that it is important to connect these area-specific theoretical frameworks to general cultural dimensions, which constitutes a very fruitful topic for global management research.

Indigenous theoretical constructs

Cultural dimensions and area-specific theoretical frameworks are universal in nature and are assumed to be applicable in diverse cultural contexts. However, it is also widely acknowledged that some constructs are only salient and important in some cultural contexts, which means that they may not be intelligible and sensible to outsiders. In global management research, a wide variety of indigenous constructs have been identified and studied, some of which are argued to be loosely related to some cultural dimensions. For instance, guanxi, loosely translated as interpersonal connections, is very important in the organizational context in China (e.g., Luo, 2000) and can be traced to the collectivistic nature of Chinese societies (e.g., Dunning and Kim, 2007). At the firm level, business groups are more common in Japan and Korea than in the West and while the business groups in these two countries have some unique, country-specific characteristics, they can again be loosely connected to the collectivistic orientation of these two countries (White, 2002).

In contrast, some indigenous constructs show no obvious connection to major cultural dimensions. For instance, some Australians and New Zealanders exhibit what is known as a "tall poppy syndrome", i.e., the envy and hostility directed at

Table 2.1 Major research areas under the cultural perspective

Nature of Cultural Effects	Major Research Areas		
Static	Cultural dimensions		
	1980s	1990s	2000s
	Hofstede	Schwartz	GLOBE
		Smith *et al.*	Bond *et al.*
			Gelfand *et al.*
Contingent	Contextual effects of culture	Culture change	Dynamic effects of culture
Multicultural	Adjustment and behavior of expatriates and migrant workers		Intercultural contact
Mono-cultural	Indigenous concepts tied to broad cultural dimensions		Indigenous concepts unique to a culture

successful people, which may deter the drive for improving individual and firm performance (e.g., Mouly and Sankaran, 2002). Siesta, or afternoon nap, is common in some European countries along the Mediterranean Sea, such as Spain, which has significant impact on job design and work hours (Baxter and Kroll-Smith, 2005).

We agree with Gelfand, Erez and Aycan, (2007) that research on indigenous constructs is under-represented in global management research. Hopefully, more researchers will work on such constructs to enrich our conceptual tools and facilitate the development of truly universal management theories. For a summary of the broad research areas under the cultural perspective, see table 2.1.

Institutional perspective on global management research

Institutional perspective and national differences

While the dimensional approach to culture is dominant in global management, there is an independent stream of research that examines national differences in management-related phenomena based on the institutional perspective. With roots in sociology, the institutional perspective in essence takes the view that the economic, legal, political, and technological environment of a society impacts and constrains the strategic choices of organizations (DiMaggio and Powell, 1983; North, 1990;

Oliver, 1991; Scott, 1995). National differences in strategies, organizational structure, management practices and other related constructs can be explained by the corresponding national differences in some institutional variables. For instance, large national differences in investment behaviors were found among Japanese, American, and German firms, which can be traced to some differences in their institutional environments, such as the institutional bargaining power between owners and labor in decision-making and non-financial corporate ownership of other firms (Thomas and Waring, 1999). Luo (2007) found that cultural differences in attitudes toward the continuous learning model of employee training corresponded to cultural differences in institutional logics. Countries that emphasized the statist logic (i.e., collective authority is located in the state) and the corporatist logic (i.e., individuals are members in collectives) were less likely to prefer the continuous learning model of training.

The institutional perspective is frequently used to account for the drastic changes in the strategies and structures of firms observed in transition economies, which are conceptualized as reactions to the corresponding changes in the institutional environment, such as in the case of China (Boisot and Child, 1999; Walder, 1995). In fact, Peng, Wang, and Jiang (2008) argued that the institutional perspective provides a major mechanism for understanding business strategies in transition economies, primarily because the institutional contexts of these economies are very different form those in developed economies.

Institutional perspective and cultural dimensions

Research guided by the institutional perspective or cultural dimensions is voluminous, but there is a surprising dearth of work that explores the interplay between these two paradigms. One major reason may be that cultural dimensions are popular in micro-level studies, whereas the institutional perspective is typically used to account for macro, firm-level phenomena.

Perhaps the most extreme view in the literature on the interplay between institutional variables and cultural dimensions is given by Singh (2007), who argued that "culture provides very limited explanation for variance in firm behavior or performance," and that institutional explanations can provide more comprehensive explanations for firm characteristics and performance across national and cultural contexts. Singh (2007) reviewed a number of studies that demonstrate the importance of institutional variables in explaining national differences in firm strategies and performance, but there is no empirical evidence that unequivocally supports his claim. For instance, in an analysis of foreign subsidiaries of Japanese firms in forty-eight countries, Gaur, Delios, and Singh (2007) contrasted the effects of institutional distance between Japan and the host countries, which captures national differences in institutional environment, and cultural distance, which is based on the original four Hofstede dimensions (Kogut and Singh, 1988), on the use of expatriates in managing the subsidiaries and their labor productivity. In general, the effects of institutional distance were consistent and as predicted. In contrast, although they detected some effects of cultural distance, these effects were less consistent. We note, however, that meaningful effects of cultural distance did emerge independent of the effects of institutional distance in the study of Gaur, Delios, Singh (2007), and that their findings certainly do not suggest that cultural distance should be ignored in their research context. We also note that Gong (2003) reported more consistent effects of cultural distance on the use

of expatriates in managing foreign subsidiaries of multinationals.

Other conceptual analyses of how institutional and cultural variables can be used to explain national differences are less extreme and typically view both types of variables as useful. Kostova (1999) proposed the use of institutional distance to explain the transfer of strategic organizational practices a transnational an alternative to cultural dimensions, but she makes no claim that institutional variables can completely replace cultural variables. In fact, in developing a framework to explain the foreign direct investment of multinational enterprises based on the notion of institutional distance, Xu and Shenkar (2002) explicitly stated that "institutional distance complements, rather than replaces, the cultural distance construct" (p. 615). Aycan (2005) is more explicit about the joint effects of institutional and cultural variables in her conceptual analysis of the influence of cultural dimensions and institutional factors on cross-cultural variations in human resource management practices. For instance, she argues that both universalism and labor laws can promote the use of job-related criteria in the selection of job applicants.

In terms of empirical evidence, there are very few studies that contrasted the effects of institutional and cultural variables in explaining cross-national differences. Typically, these studies show that both institutional and cultural variables have independent effects, and there is no convincing evidence that culture can be ignored in accounting for national differences. For instance, Parboteeah and Cullen (2003) contrasted the effects of culture as represented by Hofstede's dimensions and social institutions on work centrality across twenty-six countries. Three Hofstede dimensions and five social institutional variables were significantly related to work centrality, supporting the importance of both types of variables.

In another study, Lau and Ngo (2001) studied the institutional and cultural perspectives on the receptivity to organization development interventions in domestic and foreign firms in Hong Kong. They concluded that western firms were more receptive of organization development interventions than Hong Kong firms, thus supporting the cultural perspective. However, the effect of organization development practices on employee satisfaction showed little variation across firms of different origins, thus supporting the institutional perspective.

Integrating the institutional and culture perspectives

Overlap between the institutional and cultural perspectives

The debate regarding the relative influence of institutions and culture is actually less controversial than it seems if we scrutinize the scopes of these two perspectives. The institutional perspective is very broad, including regulatory, normative, and cognitive dimensions (e.g., Scott, 1995). These dimensions, representing authority systems and roles and the associated beliefs; norms that guide behaviors and choices; and socially constructed and shared knowledge, actually overlap with the construct of national culture (e.g., Scott, 1995). In fact, deviating from the typical focus on objective institutional variables, some current work under the institutional rubric has forayed into subjective measures based on aggregating individual responses. For instance, Busenitz, Gomez, and Spencer (2000) created survey items to measure the institutional dimensions for entrepreneurship, and a country's score on a dimension was based on aggregating the relevant items in the survey across individuals from the country. Their items involve individual perceptions and are concerned with current practices and perceived preferences in society (e.g., "Individuals know how to legally protect a new business", and "Entrepreneurs are admired in this country"). It is interesting to note that a high rank-order correlation (.64) was found between their normative dimension and Hotstede's individualism-collectivism dimension.

National culture as a ubiquitous, multilayered and multifaceted construct is even broader. It includes not only cultural values and beliefs, but also social institutions. Both Triandis (1972) and Stewart and Bennett (1991) proposed that culture can best be modeled as having objective and subjective components. Objective culture describes what we can see – the observable and visible artifacts of cultures,

which include human-made part of the environment, the economic, political, and legal institutions as well as social customs, arts, language, marriage and kinship systems. Furthermore, the ecocultural model of Berry (1976; 1979) proposes that culture represents an adaptation to its ecological context, and both the ecological context and the sociopolitical context should be viewed as antecedents of culture. In contrast, subjective culture refers to the hidden, psychological features of cultures that reside in individuals. These could include values, beliefs, norms, and assumptions that exist within a society, which is typically mapped by dimensions of culture, such as those of Hofstede (1980).

A cultural model with both objective and subjective components is consistent with Schein's (2004) metaphor that an organizational culture could best be depicted by the metaphor of an iceberg. In the iceberg model, cultural actions and artifacts represent the objective – the part of the iceberg that is visible on the surface. Unspoken rules, values and deep-seated beliefs represent the subjective – the part of the iceberg that is hidden beneath the surface. Trompenaars (1993) offered a different metaphor to describe culture, an onion. The outer layer of the onion represents the objective culture – the visible artifacts we encounter when we first contact a foreign culture. The inner layers then represent its unwritten and subjective norms and values. For the overlap of the scope of the cultural and institutional perspectives, see table 2.2.

We believe that the institutional and the culture perspectives complement rather than compete with each other, and that the two perspectives overlap more than many researchers recognize. Nonetheless, there are indeed major and significant differences between the studies conducted under these two perspectives. Studies guided by the institutional perspectives tend to focus on objective variables associated with characteristics of social institutions, mostly in the economic, legal, and political domains, although, as mentioned before, there is some recent foray into the subjective domain. In contrast, mostly due to the influence of Hofstede (1980), global management studies under the rubric of the cultural perspective typically focus on the subjective culture (Kostova, 2004; Gelfand, Erez, and Aycan, 2007).

Table 2.2 Overlap of the scope of the cultural and institutional perspectives

Cultural Perspective	Institutional Perspective
Ecology	
– climate	
– terrain	
– environmental resources	
– disaster-proneness	
Objective culture	Regulatory dimension
– human-made physical environment	
– other overt, objective elements	
– formal rules	
Subjective culture	
– norms and values	Normative dimension
– beliefs and knowledge	Cognitive dimension

A cultural analysis of institutions

Perhaps because culture has long been studied from the subjective angle, it is easy for researchers to lose sight of the fact that institutions are themselves cultural in nature. As a matter of fact, a number of cultural theorists have provided detailed analyses of social institutions from a cultural perspective, notably in the field of cultural anthropology. Although cultural anthropology has directed its efforts towards discovering cultural differences across a diverse range of human societies, it has also acknowledged that, at a higher level of abstraction, each society has evolved a similar set of cultural systems, known as cultural universals, to cope with various aspects of human functioning and adaptability to its environment. Murdock (1945) offered one of the most comprehensive attempts in creating a taxonomy of cultural universals. More recently, Brown (1991) updated Murdock's work on cultural universals and proposed that these cultural universals should include and are not restricted to: (a) *economic system* – a system of producing, allocating and distributing resources within a society; (b) *legal system* – a system of law in the sense of rights and obligations; (c) *government* – a political system of order where collective decisions and regulations of public order are made; (d) *technology* – a system of producing and using tools; (e) *kinship* – a system of reproduction and social relationships amongst kin groups and outsiders; (f) *religious and supernatural system* – a system of religious or supernatural beliefs for things beyond the visible and palpable; (g) *educational system* – a system of learning and socialization where senior members of a society are expected to transmit norms and patterns of thoughts, beliefs, and behaviors to their offspring; (h) *linguistic system* – a system of communication, both verbal and non-verbal, within members of a society and across members from different societies; (i) *arts and crafts* – a system of aesthetic standards manifested in decorative art and its artifacts, including music and dance.

Conceptually, these cultural systems can be seen as relatively independent of each other, but, in reality, they are tightly interwoven within the objective cultural environment and integral to the subjective cultural environment of values and beliefs. Malinowski's (1944) organic analogy of culture suggests that the complexities of systems associated with a culture is analogous to the complexities of systems associated with a physical human body. Ferraro puts it concisely (2006, p. 42):

> The physical body comprises a number of systems, all functioning to maintain the overall health of the organism: these include the respiratory, digestive, skeletal, excretory, reproductive, muscular, circulatory, endocrine, and lymphatic systems. Any anatomist or surgeon worth her or his salt knows where these systems are located in the body, what function each plays, and how parts of the body are interconnected. Surely no sane person would choose a surgeon to remove a malignant lung unless that surgeon knows how that organ was related to the rest of the body ... In the same way that human organisms comprise various parts that are both functional and interrelated, so too do cultures.

Hence, culture must be examined in its integral whole with its various subjective and objective parts. The institutional perspective in theory can include a wide range of institutions, but in practice most studies are confined to the first four types of cultural universals proposed by Murdoch, namely, economic, legal, political, and technological (e.g.,

North, 1990; Womack, Jones, and Roos, 1990). The cultural perspective on institution can definitely enrich the institutional variables that should be explored in global management research. In the following, we propose four ways for a productive synergy of the institutional and cultural perspectives for future research.

Broadening the scope of social institutions

We argue that to understand global management phenomena fully, we need to include institutional variables that have been ignored. Of all the cultural universals, the kinship system is widely regarded as the single most important aspect of social structure for all societies (Parkin, 1997), but its importance has only been recently recognized by global management researchers. Kinships refer to relationships among members of a society, and serve the critical function of organizing members of a society into social groups and categories and creating a group identity for these members. Kinships therefore serve to form ingroups and create solidarity among ingroup members within a much larger society (Bock, 1979). With an identity to a certain kin group, members then take on pre-specified roles, obligations and responsibilities to the kin. Generally, there are three kinds of kinship systems: (1) consanguineal kinship, where members are related by blood; (2) affinal kinship, where members are related by marriage; and (3) fictive kinship, where members are related neither by blood nor by marriage.

Consanguineal and affinal kinships are also known as kinship organizations where lineages of descent could be traced through genealogical links. By contrast, fictive kinships such as clans claim a stipulated descent, but the tracing of all the genealogical links is not possible. Because of the lack of genealogical links, fictive kinships could be very diverse. For example, namesake kin groups identify members of a society as kin so long as they have the same family name. Other fictive kinships are formed based on close friendships; college fraternities or sororities; affiliations with religious institutions where members are referred to as brothers and sisters; or locale, where members living together in close proximity are regarded as kin.

While many cultures place higher priority on genetically based kinships in terms of members' roles and obligations to such kin groups, other cultures, especially in collectivistic societies, regard fictive kinships as equally important in the daily lives of their members for accessing critical social resources (Lin, 2001). In addition, kinship calculation is the key feature of kinship systems, and can account for the differences in the dominant forms of kinship systems across societies (Kottak, 2006). Kinship calculation refers to a system by which members in a specific society identify, designate, and recognize another member as belonging to a particular kin group (Stone, 2001). One widespread kin calculation is the nuclear family, comprising a married couple and their children. It is the most pervasive kinship organization in western societies and especially in the middle classes. In other societies, however, other kinship calculation may overshadow the nucleus family. Some societies acknowledge extended families where the expanded household includes three or more generations, or fictive kin groups such as clans in terms of legitimate kinship obligations.

Given their fundamental function of organizing members in a society into legitimate social groups, kinship systems have ramifications for the other parts of the objective cultural environments. For example, instead of distributing goods based on the capitalistic principle of one's capacity to pay, societies that place higher emphasis on kinship may distribute resources based on kinship calculation. Goods are distributed based on whether members of a society are classified as an ingroup kin member or outgroup. In some societies, especially tribal societies, law and social controls are also upheld by kinship calculation. A recent *Wall Street Journal* newspaper article (Jaffe, 2007) reported that the US Marines managed to quell violence in Iraq's unruly Anbar province by paying a powerful local Sheik over US $97,000 in cash to pay for food for the Sheik's tribe and for two school renovation projects for which the Sheik is the lead contractor.

The recognition of kinship systems by global management researchers is partly prompted by the emergence of very large, successful family-run overseas Chinese firms (Hamilton, 1996; Redding, 1995). This type of firms is managed by the owner with unquestioned authority, aided by a small group of family members and close subordinates. When the owner retires, the firm is typically passed to the second generation. Although these family-run firms now have a tendency to engage professionals who are outsiders to help them face their competitors (Tsui-Auch, 2004), the owners rarely relinquish control of the firms.

Kinship systems are also crucial for understanding relationships among people who are related by kinship in collectivistic societies. Research in this area is probably more developed in China, and the notion of *guanxi* is used to describe kin-like, personal and business relationships created by gifts and reciprocal favors (Yang, 1994). Some researchers argue that it is on the decline as a result of China's economic transition to a market economy (e.g., Guthrie, 1999), but others have argued that *guanxi* remains resilient given the strong kinship system inherent of the Chinese society (Kipnis, 1997; Tong and Yong, 1998). Yang (2002, pp. 463–4) concluded:

> While impersonal money has begun to replace some of the affectively charged relationships created by gifts and reciprocal favors, guanxixue has also found new territory to colonize … It is in the world of business where entrepreneurs and managers still need to engage in guanxi with what remains of the state economy, with official controls over state contracts, access to imports, bank loans, favourable tax incentives, access to valuable market information and influential persons, and exemptions from troublesome laws and regulation.

Yang (2002, p. 465) further remarked:

> It can be said that, among enterprise managers in contemporary China, whether they are in state enterprises or in village and township enterprises, there is not one person who is not aware of the importance of informal social relationships in business and industrial relations.

Since the bulk of China's industrial and commercial order comprises small and medium enterprises, and without a mature and formalized set of institutional power, overseas investors must also rely on *guanxi* to access state and central governments. With *guanxi* overlaying on a market economy, a new version of economic system – the Chinese *guanxi* capitalism has emerged. This form of capitalism relies on small, flexible firms using fictive or lineal kinships to access new markets and supplies. As a new mode of capitalist production, the flexible, *guanxi*-based capitalism detests huge investments, inventories, and overheads of large vertically integrated bureaucratic firms and favors subcontracting relations and small companies, which can change products and distribution outlets more flexibly (Hamilton, 1990; Redding, 1995). Hence, kinship personal networks rather than objective legal and institutional structure are seen to be functional in this new kind of Chinese *guanxi* capitalism. In a nutshell, flexible capitalism favors business relationships of kinship and *guanxi* networks and personal trust (Ong, 1999).

Given that *guanxi* based on kinship notions and particularistic relationships has acquired new forms and meanings and remained indispensable for business transactions in China, global management research can draw on concepts and principles of kinship such as kinship calculation to predict and understand how *guanxi* grows, develops, and evolves in Chinese capitalism. Kinship concepts could also be used to understand how *guanxi* offers Chinese capitalism with an informal, adaptive mechanism that distinguishes itself from western capitalism, which is more formal, legal, rational, and bureaucratic in nature, as well as its hidden cost on business.

Cultural consequences of neglected social institutions

In a state of equilibrium where there is no drastic cultural change, objective and subjective cultural elements are typically consistent with each other and mutually reinforcing each other's influence. For instance, in the previous example of kinship systems, the salience and importance of kinship in an organizational context is associated with the cultural orientation of collectivism. However, despite decades of research on culture and social institutions, some important social institutions have been neglected in global management research, and we do not know much about the subjective cultural elements associated with these institutions.

The case of religious systems provides a good illustration of these gaps. Understanding the impact of religious systems is important for global management research because religions and other supernatural beliefs can shape work-related attitudes, beliefs, and practices. Weber's (1958) analysis of the relationship between Protestantism and capitalism pioneered this line of thinking. Capitalism was viewed as driven partly by the Protestant work ethic, which is prevalent in western Protestant societies and emphasizes diligence, hard work, and frugality with the aim of accumulating capital. Unfortunately, since Weber's seminal ideas, religion has more or less lapsed into oblivion in global management research.

The tragic events of September 11 have propelled religious cultural systems to prominence. To account for scientifically inexplicable and supernatural events, all societies have developed organized forms of religion, astrology, magic, witchcraft, or sorcery (Kottak, 2006), of which religion is typically the more important and influential form of social institution. Although the current interest in Islamism is more politically than business driven, the impact of Islam on business practices is slowly being recognized. For instance, the Islamic religion places strong emphasis on charity to the poor, and on making profits without exploitative gains. Hence, in Islamic banking, interests on loans are prohibited because gains from loans are seen as a form of exploitative gains from the poor who require loans. As a result, international businesses have evolved innovative practices, such as charging upfront fees for a loan, as a way of circumventing interest payments (Lippman, 1995). For non-Islamic firms to do business with Islamic countries, they must have a full understanding of these practices.

In addition to religious beliefs, research in global management needs to examine the extent supernatural customs and beliefs could affect business operations globally. For example, burial grounds are typically regarded as sanctified grounds in many societies. Ong's (1987) study of a Japanese MNC relocating labor-intensive operations in rural Malaysia showed that constructing a factory on the aboriginal burial grounds precipitated mass hysteria and spirit possession affecting more than 120 factory workers of Malay origin. Another example concerns the Festival for the Dead as a major event in the Chinese calendar (Lip, 1988). Opening new business establishments are to be avoided during the Festival of the Dead. Supernatural customs and beliefs usually play a small role in the work context, but, under some circumstances, their influence can be pivotal and exact a major toll on productivity and staff morale.

The implications of religious and supernatural systems for global management research are wide-ranging. The few examples above show how deeply held religious values and supernatural beliefs could affect the financial, management and marketing decisions associated with conducting businesses across borders. As mentioned before, we do not know much about how religious and supernatural systems are linked to the subjective cultural elements that have important management implications. Nor do we know much about the values and beliefs engendered by different religious and supernatural systems, and how these values and beliefs affect management processes and outcomes across societies. Research that seeks answers to these questions will be very different from the current studies guided by the institutional perspective and cultural dimensions. It is hoped that future research will give rise to elements of subjective culture that are drastically different from constructs based on the cultural dimensions that currently dominate the field.

Beyond institutions: the influence of ecology

The cultural perspective is broader than the scope of institutions because it also encompasses the influence of ecology, i.e., the natural environment, on human behaviors. The eco-cultural model of Berry (1976; 1979), which is based on the works of such anthropologists as Kardiner, Linton, Du Bois, and West (1945) and Whiting (1974), is perhaps the most well-known model that takes into account the influence of the physical environment on social institutions and human behavior. In Berry's model, the ecological context influences both the biological and cultural adaptation of its inhabitants, and the central feature of the ecological context is economic activity, which represents an interaction between the physical environment and human activities. Specifically, means of subsistence of a society is affected by its physical environment, and considerable research has examined the relationships between economic activities and cognitive style.

Two types of economic activities have often been compared: agricultural and hunting. The general finding is that, in agricultural societies, the cognitive style of field dependence is more prevalent, which involves the use of external frames of reference for orienting oneself. One important consequence of field dependence is that one's perception and judgment of an object is more influenced by its background (Berry, 1979). It is also interesting to note that field dependence is correlated with conformity behavior.

The relevance of cognitive styles to management is perhaps not direct but, recently, Van de Vliert and his associates have conducted an impressive research program on the effects of temperature, an important feature of the ecological context, on social and work behaviors. For instance, Van de Vliert and Van Yperen (1996) found that ambient temperature was correlated with role overload across twenty-one societies. Van de Vliert (2003) investigated the relationship between thermoclimate, culture, poverty, and wages in fifty-eight nations. Van de Vliert makes a distinction between three major types of climate with reference to the human body temperature: temperate, hot, and cold. Temperate climate is comfortable, and hot and cold climates are demanding. As predicted, the effect of temperate climate on overpayment (wages received controlled for a country's national wealth) is partially mediated by a mastery orientation. The results further showed that the tendency for overpayment was found in countries that were both poor and had a mastery-oriented culture (and hence a temperate climate).

More recently, Van de Vliert (2007) argued that the influence of climate on culture has been contemplated before, but these previous attempts have failed because they conceptualized temperature in absolute terms, but not with the human body temperature as the reference point, and they did not take into the account the effects of wealth. Van de Vliert (2007) has proposed a theoretical model,

in which climate and wealth exert some intricate, but predictable effects on human behavior. His basic argument is that psychological functioning in terms of individual values, motives, attitudes, and practices is impoverished in poor countries with demanding climates, but flourishes in wealthy countries with demanding climates, because of the success in overcoming the threats associated with demanding climates. Psychological functioning is moderate in countries with a temperate climate, regardless of their wealth.

Consistent with his argument, in a study of thirty-eight countries (Van de Vliert, Van Yperen, and Thierry, 2008), extrinsic work motivation was strongest in poor countries with demanding climates, whereas intrinsic work motivation was strongest in wealthier countries with demanding climate. Moderate levels of intrinsic and extrinsic motivation were found in countries with undemanding climates, regardless of their wealth. In a study of eighty-four nations, Van de Vliert and Smith (2004) found that leaders in wealthier nations, especially those with more demanding climates, relied more on subordinates as a source of information. Based on these results, Van de Vliert (2006; 2008) hypothesized and confirmed that autocratic leadership was viewed as more effective in poorer countries with demanding climates, whereas democratic leadership was viewed as more effective in wealthy countries with demanding climates. In countries with temperate climates, both leadership styles were accepted regardless of the wealth of a country.

The research program of Van de Vliert and his associates on thermoclimate illustrates that the ecology of a society does exert important influence on some management processes and work behavior. The research findings of this program of research have at least two important implications for global management research. First, it is clear that thermoclimate has impact on some work behaviors, and it is entirely possible that thermoclimate may also have impact on the form and dynamics of some social institutions across a wide range of countries. In fact, in Berry's (1976; 1979) ecocultural model, the ecological context and social institutions are hypothesized to have mutual effects on each other. Generally speaking, the examination of the interaction of the ecological context and social institutions in the global management context is an exciting area of research.

Second, thermoclimate is just one type of ecological variable, and other ecological variables may also have important effects on work behaviors and social institutions. For instance, the likelihood of natural disasters, such as volcano eruptions, earthquakes, tsunamis, and hurricanes obviously have significant impact on people's life, including work life. People who live and work in areas threatened by such disasters are likely to be different in some important aspects from their counterparts in safer environments. Likewise, institutions in disaster-prone and non-disaster-prone areas may differ in some significant aspects. Interestingly, natural disasters have been considered by global management scholars under the rubric of risk management (Miller, 1992, 1993), but the focus is on how international firms can prepare for such disasters. There is little research on how the threats of natural disasters shape work behaviors and social institutions across nations, and global management research will be enriched by considering such possibilities.

Lewis and Harvey (2001) recently argued that firms have not taken into account the natural environment into their strategic thinking. Based on the work of Miller (1992; 1993), they have developed a scale to measure perceived environmental uncertainties and, in doing so, they have identified a number of ecological variables relevant for the operations and performance of firms. These variables are primarily concerned with environmental resources, which can be classified with two dimensions: renewable vs. non-renewable and sources (resources) vs. sinks (for disposal of wastes). Generally speaking, sources are economically valuable, whereas sinks have little economic value. Based on this scheme, four types of environmental resources can be exploited by firms: renewable and economically valuable (e.g., hydroenergy); renewable and economically not valuable (e.g., forests as carbon sinks); non-renewable and economically valuable (e.g., hydrocarbons); and non-renewable and economically not valuable (e.g., land fills). Firms can take advantage of these different types of environmental resources by implementing various strategies and actions in

improving their performance. In addition, firms may also be affected by a variety of environmental issues, such as climate change and pollution, and their responses to these threats can have a significance influence on firm performance as well.

To facilitate the understanding of the impact of the ecology on global management practices, a taxonomy of the relevant ecological variables is needed. Four broad types of ecological variables can be identified based on our cursory review of this literature. The ambient environment involves two types of ecological variables: Climatic (e.g., temperature and rainfall) and geological (e.g., terrain). Environmental resources described above constitute the third type of ecological variables. The final category is concerned with the occurrence of natural disasters, such as floods and hurricanes. This typology is obviously crude and future research needs to refine it and identify subdimensions. We are just beginning to understand the interaction between the ecology and human activities in the global management context, and this is definitely a very fruitful avenue for future research.

Cultural jolts: conflict between culture and institution

While some cultures are relatively stable, many societies experience cultural jolts in the form of innovation and diffusion (Rogers, 2003). Innovation refers to cultural jolts generated internally by members of a society. It is typically associated with a change in the objective culture – a new religious practice, a new social practice or policy, a new technological tool, new scientific breakthroughs such as harnessing new sources of energy, stem-cell research, nanotechnology, and others. Diffusion, on the other hand, refers to cultural jolts that come from outside the society, involving the spreading of a cultural element from one society to another (Rogers, 2003). Diffusion therefore occurs when one society adopts an innovation or an existing cultural feature that originated from another society. The adoption of a cultural feature could be a physical technology, such as a tool; or a social technology, such as a human resource practice or a government policy. Linton (1936) estimated that innovation comprised approximately 10 per cent of all cultural jolts while diffusion made up the remaining 90 per cent. Obviously, we do not know whether this proportion has changed since Linton's study in the early 1930s.

In theory, any cultural feature associated with a cultural jolt could be diffused from one culture to another. However, societies that remain relatively insulated from the global economy experience relatively few cultural jolts. By contrast, societies which are highly interdependent with other societies in the global economy experience more cultural jolts.

According to Rogers (2003), whether a cultural feature 'sticks' in a society depends largely on whether the subjective cultural values inherent in the cultural feature are compatible with the sociocultural values and beliefs of the recipient society. This argument suggests that social institutions and organizational practices may also spread from country to country, but adaptation may occur such that the form of an imported institution or practice may remain the same, but its functions and mode of operation may change. For example, Singapore recently implemented a social "workfare" instead of a welfare scheme for addressing low-wage and creeping structural unemployment plaguing the nation. The workfare program is a modification of Wisconsin Works in the US. While the original Wisconsin Works had focused on aid to the unemployed to help them seek gainful employment (e.g., paying for retraining), Singapore's workfare further supports the unemployed by paying for the employed children's education. The extension of aid to supporting the next generation's education embraces Singapore's national value and belief system that education is the primary if not the sole means whereby subsequent generation of the nation could escape the poverty trap of its current generation (Neo and Chen, 2007).

Cultural jolts are sometimes introduced into a system in an attempt to change the fundamental values of a society or an organization, but the intended change may not occur if the imported institution or practice conflicts with local values and beliefs. An example is the adoption of quality control circle (QCC) practices across the world. QCC as a social technology evolved in Japan because Japan's group-centered norms and values naturally promote circle formation and maintenance of circle activities. When QCC was introduced into individualistic (e.g., US: Griffin, 1988) or vertically oriented cultures (e.g., Singapore: Wee, 1995), circle activities fostered consensual group values by promoting team work and collective decision-making. However, although initial attitudes toward teamwork and consensual decision-making were improved in the recipient societies, longitudinal assessments showed that these initial positive reactions were at best ephemeral (Griffin, 1988; Wee 1995). Rarely are subjective cultural values shifted because of cultural jolts. Change in subjective cultural values evolves more slowly because values and beliefs are simply very deep-seated (Inglehart, 2006).

In general, innovation created in one society is rarely universal, and a case in point is information technologies (e.g., SAP from Germany; or Microsoft from the US). Despite efforts by western global technology companies to supply "universal" or "global" technological solutions to the world, such presumably "universal software" is based inherently on western metaphors, representations, color associations, and navigational logic. Yet design features such as metaphors, representations, and color schemes vary widely from culture to culture. According to Callahan (2005), the aesthetics and visual appeal of technological tools are perceived differently across cultures. For example, southern provinces of China prefer bright colors while those in the north prefer more subdued colors (Marcus, 2003).

The use of icons and aesthetic representation across cultures also creates much confusion. Shen, Woolley, and Prior (2006) found that "My computer" in the MS Windows has created much angst. The phrase "My computer" suggests private ownership, which is uncommon in cultures without private property and ownership protection. An interesting dilemma is provided by Callahan (2005, p. 284), who shares the challenge facing universal software designers by using flags to depict the different languages in the world:

> the best visual symbol for language is a flag, but is language an indication of ethnicity and is the flag a symbol of nationality? Which flag would be the best for indicating English on the Web:

British, American, or Australian? What about other countries where English is spoken (India, several African countries)? ... The idea of using a flag to represent a language seems untenable and potentially politically explosive. And we are still left with the problem of the existence of thousands of languages that cannot be represented by a flag.

In summary, symbols that originate from one society are not recognized automatically by other societies, and their recognition requires learning (Marcus, 2003). Cultural misfits or misalignments are especially extensive when ubiquitous information technologies solutions that originate from US/western European spread to Asia, eastern Europe and beyond (Martinsons, 2004). For example, Sia and Soh (2007) documented more than 400 cultural misfits just from customizing a "generic" enterprise resource package that was developed in Germany and transplanted to Singapore for use in its hospitals. The cultural misfits arose from incompatibility of patient care systems, financial accounting practices, and other regulatory requirements between the two nations.

The diffusion of organizational practices is often viewed from an institutional perspective, which examines institutional variables that promote or suppress diffusion (e.g., Guler, Guillén, and Macpherson, 2002; Kostova, 1999). However, some research shows that diffusion is also affected by culture. For instance, Erumban and de Jong (2006) found that across a wide range of countries, the diffusion of information and communication technologies is related to Hofstede's (1980) cultural dimensions. Bhagat, Kedia, Harveston, and Triandis (2002) have recently proposed a framework for examining the cross-border transfer of organizational knowledge. In their model, knowledge is classified in terms of two dimensions: explicit vs. tacit and complex vs. simple. The effectiveness of the cross-border transfer of different types of knowledge is influenced by the cultural patterns of the countries and the cognitive styles of the individuals involved.

The above review provides a compelling case for considering the joint effects of culture and the institutional context in the diffusion of organizational practices and institutions, which has not received much attention in the literature. Nonetheless, the scanty research in this area shows that both culture and institution matter. For instance, Matten and Geppert (2004) reported that the adoption of work systems in engineering in subsidiaries of multinationals was affected by both national culture and the institutional context. No clear convergence in work systems across the subsidiaries of multinationals was found, because it is unlikely that two subsidiaries had an identical cultural and institutional context. The interplay between culture and institution in shaping the diffusion of social institutions and organizational practices across nations is a largely uncharted territory in global management research and much exciting research awaits to be contemplated.

Management in transition economies

Under most circumstances, economically developed societies, such as western European countries, Japan, and the US, tend to be relatively stable in their national culture and institutions. In contrast, the pace of change in transition economies that enjoy rapid growth tends to be much faster, and major institutional reforms and value change are typical. A case in point is China, which has sustained hyper growth since its switch from central planning to a market-oriented economy. These drastic changes make transition economies an excellent context for studying cultural jolts and the interplay between institution and national culture.

In the literature, the majority of studies have examined management processes in transition economies with the institutional perspective, and the typical focus is on relating observed management processes and strategies to the institutional context (e.g., Peng, Wang, Jiang, 2008). In this type of study, institutional features are viewed as independent variables, which exert influence on the strategies and operations of firms. For instance, because of the lack of formal institutions, informal relationships and connections become important in business transactions in many transition economies (e.g., Redding, 1995; Newman, 2000).

We argue that while it is important to examine the effects of institutions, the effects of culture cannot be ignored. Large-scale economic and organizational reforms in transition economies have typically resulted in the introduction of new institutions and organizational practices, as well as the reengineering of existing institutions and practices. While it takes relatively a short time to reform institutions and practices, cultural values are more enduring and take much longer to change. Thus, some newly introduced institutions and practices may contradict dominant cultural values and beliefs and create tension between management and employees.

A good example of this conflict can be found in China, in which state-owned enterprises used to be the dominant form of organizations. Many state-owned enterprises have not performed well, partly because of the lack of incentives for good performance (Warner, 1996). It is interesting that Chinese culture emphasizes interpersonal harmony and hence an equal distribution of resources and rewards among team members (Leung, 1997). The equal treatment of employees in state-owned enterprises despite their different contributions is actually consistent with the cultural norms and values in China (Chow, 2000; Liu, 2003). The economic reform in China has introduced merit-based compensations to motivate employees to perform at a high level. When asked to distribute rewards, Chinese now favor a merit-based rule in a work context, even more so than Americans (Chen, 1995), and a likely explanation is that China now emphasizes a market economy and the competitiveness of firms (He, Chen, and Zhang, 2004). Nonetheless, the introduction of merit-based compensation schemes to state-owned enterprises is slow and difficult, and staff resistance is widespread (Chow, 2004; Ding, Akhtar, and Ge, 2006). People who get less may be jealous about those who get more (termed the red eye disease in Chinese), thus limiting the motivational effects of these incentive schemes (e.g., Warner, 1996).

In summary, the conflict between subjective culture and newly introduced institutions and organizational practices may be especially acute in transition economies, which provides a fertile ground for some innovative global management research. Unfortunately, these issues have not been pursued extensively and we believe that very exciting research on the interplay of institution and national culture can emerge from this context.

Conclusion

The aim of this chapter is to show that global management research needs to go beyond the narrow focus on either subjective culture or social institutions by embracing broader conceptualizations of culture from cultural anthropology and cross-cultural psychology. On the one hand, culture viewed as a deep-level construct of societal values and beliefs is enduring and can survive centuries of societal evolution and revolution. On the other hand, culture viewed as a surface-level construct of institutions and practices, which is ubiquitous and manifests itself in such domains as government, economic institutions, kinship, religion, and family, are less stable and can change significantly in a matter of decades because of economic reforms and intercultural contact. In stable economies or societies, subjective culture and objective cultural elements usually align with each other, and different cultural domains are synergistic and coherent. In the event of rapid social changes, however, different cultural components are likely to be in conflict with each other. In transition economies, for example, institutional changes often clash with deep-seated cultural values and beliefs. The management of firms is likely to be more challenging in transition than in stable economies.

We argue that the current cultural perspective in global management research must acknowledge that culture includes not only its subjective components, but also the objective components, such as constructs emphasized in the institutional perspective and beyond. Furthermore, we argue that the unique and defining characteristic of global management research vis-à-vis domestic management research is the recognition of the complexity of the business context, thus calling for a fully fledged perspective on the institutional context. We believe that a comprehensive view of the business context needs to go beyond economic, political, and legal systems and include such systems as kinship, religion, aesthetics, linguistics, and technologies. An expanded view of the business context provides a richer set of explanatory variables and offers a more comprehensive framework to explain the cultural differences in global management phenomena than either cultural values and beliefs or the narrowly defined social institutions in the current institutional perspective. For instance, we note that by including ecological variables in our frameworks, global management researchers can more fully conceptualize the effects of the environmental context and the subjective cultural elements and their interplay.

Finally, an important corollary of our analysis is that viewing the institutional perspective and the cultural perspective as independent is not likely to be productive. Both perspectives capture essential components that define a culture, and they should be viewed as complementary to each other. We hope that our chapter provides the impetus for a paradigm shift in global management research, where culture is approached and conceptualized as an integrated whole comprising both subjective and objective elements.

References

Ang, S., Van Dyne, L. and Begley, T. M. (2003). "The employment relationships of foreign workers versus local employees: a field study of organizational justice, job satisfaction, performance, and OCB", *Journal of Organizational Behavior*, 24(5): 561–58.

2008. "Conceptualization of cultural intelligence: definition, distinctiveness, and nomological network", in Ang, S. and Van Dyne, L. (eds.), *Handbook on Cultural Intelligence*. New York: M. E. Sharpe, pp. 3–15.

Van Dyne, L., Koh, C., Ng, K. Y., Templer, K. J., Tay, C., and Chandrasekar, N. A. (2007). "Cultural intelligence: its measurement and effects on cultural judgment and decision making, cultural adaptation, and task performance", *Management and Organization Review*, 3: 335–371.

Aycan, Z. 2005. "The interplay between cultural and institutional/structural contingencies in human resource management practices", *International Journal of Human Resource Management*, 16: 1083–119.

Baxter, V., and Kroll-Smith, S. 2005. "Normalizing the workplace nap: blurring the boundaries between public and private space and time", *Current Sociology*, 53: 3–55.

Berry, J. W. 1976. *Human Ecology and Cognitive Style: Comparative Studies in Cultural and Psychological Adaptation*. New York: Sage/ Halsted.

1979. "A cultural ecology of social behavior", in L. Berkowitz (ed.), *Advances in Experimental Social Psychology* Vol. 12. New York: Academic Press, pp. 177–207.

Bhagat, R. S., Baliga, B. R., Moustafa, K. S., and Krishnan, B. 2003. "Knowledge in cross-cultural management in the era of globalization: where do we go from here?", in D. Tjosvold and K. Leung (eds.), *Cross-cultural Management: Foundations and future*. Hampshire, UK: Ashgate, pp. 155–176.

Kedia, B. L., Harveston, P., and Triandis, H. C. 2002. "Cultural variations in the cross-border transfer of organizational knowledge: an integrative framework", *Academy of Management Review*, 27: 204–21.

and McQuaid, S. J. 1982. "Role of subjective culture in organizations: a review and directions for future research", *Journal of Applied Psychology*, 67: 653–685.

Steverson, P. K., and Segovis, J. C. 2007. "International and cultural variations in employee assistance programmes: implications for managerial health and effectiveness", *Journal of Management Studies*, 44: 222–42.

Bhaskar-Shrinivas, P., Harrison, D. A., Shaffer, M. A., and Luk, D. M. 2005. "Input-based and time-based models of international adjustment: meta-analytic evidence and theoretical extensions", *Academy of Management Journal*, 48: 257–81.

Black, J. S., Mendenhall, M., and Oddou, G. 1991. "Toward a comprehensive model of international adjustment: an integration of multiple theoretical perspectives", *Academy of Management Review*, 16: 291–317.

Bock, P. K. 1979. *Modern cultural anthropology*. New York: Alfred A. Knorf, Inc.

Boisot, M., and Child, J. 1999. "Organizations as adaptive systems in complex environments: the case of China", *Organization Science*, 10: 237–52.

Bond, M. H, Leung, K, Tong, K. K., de Carrasquel, S. R., Murakami, F. *et al.* 2004. "Culture-level dimensions of social axioms and their correlates across 41 countries", *Journal of Cross-Cultural Psychology*, 35: 548–70.

Brett, J. M. and Okumura, T. 1998. "Inter- and intracultural negotiation: US and Japanese negotiators", *Academy of Management Journal*, 41: 495–510.

Brown, D. E. 1991. *Cultural Universals*. New York: McGraw Hill.

Busenitz, L. W., Gomez, C., and Spencer, J. W. 2000. "Country institutional profiles: unlocking Entrepreneurial Phenomena", *Academy of Management Journal*, 43: 994–1003.

Callahan, E. 2005. "Interface design and culture", in B. Cronin (ed.), *Annual Review of Information Science and Technology* Vol. 39 Medford, NJ: Information Today, pp. 257–310.

Chen, C. 1995. "New trends in reward allocation preferences: a Sino–US comparison", *Academy of Management Journal*, 38: 408–428.

Chinese Culture Connection. 1987. "Chinese values and the search for culture-free dimensions of culture", *Journal of Cross-cultural Psychology*, 18, 143–64.

Chow, G. C. 2000. "Managerial values and practices sharing common cultural heritage: a comparison of cultural values in Hong Kong, Taiwan, and the People's Republic of China", *Journal of Asia Pacific Business*, 2: 21–38.

Chow, I. H. 2004. "Human resource management in China's township and village enterprises: Change and development during the economic reform era", *Asia Pacific Journal of Human Resources*, 42, 318–35.

Chui, A. C. W, Lloyd, A. E., and Kwok, C. C. Y. 2002. "The determination of capital structure: Is national culture a missing piece to the puzzle", *Journal of International Business Studies*, 33: 99–127.

DiMaggio P. J. and Powell, W. W. 1983. "The iron cage revisited: institutional isomorphism and collective rationality in organisational fields", *American Sociological Review*, 48: 147–60.

Ding, D. Z., Akhtar, S and Ge, G. L. 2006. "Organizational differences in managerial compensation and benefits in Chinese firms", *International Journal of Human Resource Management*, 17: 693–715.

Dunning, J. H. and Kim, C. 2007. "The cultural roots of guanxi: an exploratory study", *The World Economy*, 30: 329–41.

Earley, P. C. 2006. "Leading cultural research in the future: a matter of paradigms and taste". *Journal of International Business Studies*, 37: 922–31.

and Ang, S. 2003. *Cultural Intelligence: Individual Interactions Across Cultures*. Palo Alto, CA: Stanford University Press.

and Gibson, C. B. 2002. *Multinational Work Teams: A New Perspective*. Hillsdale, NJ: Lawrence Erlbaum.

Erez, M. and Gati, E. 2004. "A dynamic, multi-level model of culture: from the micro level of the individual to the macro level of a global culture", *Applied Psychology: An International Review*, 53: 583–598.

Erumban, A. A., and de Jong, S. B. 2006. "Cross-country differences in ICT adoption: a consequence of culture?", *Journal of World Business*, 41, 302–31.

Ferraro, G. 2006. *Cultural Anthropology: An Applied Perspective* (6th edn). Belmont, CA: Thomson Learning, Inc.

Fu, P. P., Kennedy, J., Tata, J., Yukl, G., Bond, M. H., Peng, T. K., Srinivas, E. S., Howell, J. P., Prieto, L., Koopman, P., Boonstra, J. J., Pasa, S., Lacassagne, M. F., Higashide, H., and Cheosakul, A. 2004 "The impact of societal cultural values and individual social beliefs on the perceived effectiveness of managerial influence strategies: a meso approach", *Journal of International Business Studies*, 35: 284–305.

Gaur, A. S., Delios, A., and Singh, K. 2007. "Institutional environments, staffing strategies, and subsidiary performance", *Journal of Management*, 33: 611–63.

Gelfand, M. J., Erez, M. E., and Aycan, Z. 2007. "Cross-cultural organizational behavior", *Annual Review of Psychology*, 58: 479–514.

Nishii, L. H., and Raver, J. L. 2006. "On the nature and importance of cultural tightness-looseness", *Journal of Applied Psychology*, 91: 1225–44.

Gong, Y. 2003. "Towards a dynamic process model of staffing composition and subsidiary outcomes in multinational enterprises", *Journal of Management*, 29: 259–80.

Griffin, R. W. 1988. "Consequences of quality circles in an industrial setting: a longitudinal assessment", *Academy of Management Journal*, 31: 338–58.

Guler, I., Guillén, M. F., and Macpherson, J. M. 2002. "Global competition, institutions, and the diffusion of organizational practices: the international spread of ISO 9000 quality certificates", *Administrative Science Quarterly*, 47, 207–32.

Guthrie, D. 1999. *Dragon in a Three-piece Suit: The Emergence of Capitalism in China*. Princeton, NJ: Princeton University Press.

Hamilton, G. 1990. "The network structures of East Asian economies". In S. R. Clegg and S. G. Redding (eds.), *Capitalism in Contrasting Cultures*. Berlin: Walter de Gruyter, pp. 105–29.
  1996. *Asian Business Networks*. New York: walter de Gruyter.
He, Q. 1998. *The Trap of Modernization: Economic and Social Problems in Contemporary China*. Beijing: Jinri Zhongguo Chubanshe.
He, W., Chen, C. C., and Zhang, L. 2004. "Rewards-allocation preferences of Chinese employees in the new millennium: the effects of ownership reform, collectivism, and goal priority", *Organization Science*, 15: 221–31.
Heuer, M., Cummings, J. L., and Hutabarat, W. 1999. "Cultural stability or change among managers in Indonesia", *Journal of International Business Studies*, 30, 599–610.
Hofstede, G. 1980. *Culture's Consequences: International Differences in Work-related Values*. Beverly Hills, CA: Sage Publications.
  1991. *Culture and Organizations: Software of the Mind*. London: McGraw Hill.
  2006. "What did GLOBE really measure? researchers' minds versus respondents' minds", *Journal of International Business Studies*, 37: 882–96.
Hong, Y. Y., Morris, M. W., Chiu, C. Y., and Benet-Martínez, V. 2000. "Multicultural minds: a dynamic constructivist approach to culture and cognition", *American Psychologist*, 55: 709–72.
House R. J, Hanges, P. J, Javidan, M., Dorfman, P., and Gupta V. 2004. *Cultures, Leadership, and Organizations: GLOBE Study of 62 Societies*. Newbury Park, CA: Sage.
Hung, K. H., Gu, F., and Yim, C. K. 2007. "A social institutional approach to identifying generation cohorts in China with a comparison with American consumers", *Journal of International Business Studies*, 38: 836–53.
Inglehart, R. 2006. "Mapping global values", *Comparative Sociology*, 5: 115–36.
Jaffe, G. 2007. "How courting sheiks slowed violence in Iraq", *Wall Street Journal*, 32, A1–A11.
Javidan, M., House, R. J., Dorfman, P. W., Hanges, P. J., and Sully de Luque, M. 2006. "Conceptualizing and measuring cultures and their consequences: a comparative review of GLOBE's and Hofstede's approaches", *Journal of International Business Studies*, 37: 897–914.

Kachelmeier, S. J., and Shehata, M. 1997. "Internal auditing and voluntary cooperation in firms: a cross-cultural experiment", *The Accounting Review*, 72, 407–31.
Kardiner, A., Linton, R., Du Bois, C., and West, J. 1945. *The psychological frontiers of society*. New York: Columbia University Press.
Kipnis, A. 1997. *Producing Guanxi: Sentiment, Self, and Subculture in a North China Village*. Durham, NC: Duke University Press.
Kirkman, B. L., Gibson, C. B., and Shapiro, D. L. 2001. "Exporting teams: enhancing the implementation and effectiveness of work teams in global affiliates", *Organizational Dynamics* 30: 12–29.
  Lowe, K. B., and Gibson, C. B. 2006. "A quarter century of Culture's Consequences: A review of empirical research incorporating Hofstede's cultural values framework", *Journal of International Business Studies*, 36: 285–320.
Kluckhohn, F., and Strodtbeck, F. 1961. *Variations in Value Orientations*. Evanston, IL: Row, Peterson.
Kogut, B. and Singh, H. 1988. "The effect of national culture on the choice of entry mode", *Journal of International Business Studies*, 41: 1–32.
Kostova, T. 1999. "Transnational transfer of strategic organizational practices: a contextual perspective", *Academy of Management Review*, 24, 308–24.
  2004. "Limitations of the culture perspective in teaching international management", in N. A. Boyacigiller, R. A. Goodman, and M. E. Phillips (eds.), *Crossing Cultures: Insights From Master Teachers*. New York: Routledge, pp. 185–200.
Kottak, C. P. 2006. *Cultural Anthropology* (11th edn). New York: McGraw Hill.
Lau, C. M. and Ngo, H. Y. 2001. "Organization development and firm performance: a comparison of multinational and local firms", *Journal of International Business Studies*, 32: 95–114.
Leung, K. 1997. "Negotiation and reward allocations across cultures", In. P. C. Earley and M. Erez (eds.), *New Perspectives on International Industrial Organizational Psychology*. San Francisco, CA: New Lexington Press/Jossey-Bass, pp. 640–75.
  Bhagat, R. S., Buchan, N. R., Erez, M., and Gibson, C. B. 2005. "Culture and international business: recent advances and their implications for future research", *Journal of International Business Studies*, 36, 357–78.

and Bond, M. H. 2004. "Social axioms: A model for social beliefs in multi-cultural perspective", *Advances in Experimental Social Psychology*, 36: 119–97.

Bond, M. H., Reimel de Carrasquel, S., Muñoz, C., Hernández, M., Murakami, F., Yamaguchi, S., Bierbrauer, G., and Singelis, T. M. 2002. "Social axioms: the search for universal dimensions of general beliefs about how the world functions", *Journal of Cross-Cultural Psychology*, 33: 286–302.

Su, S. K., and Morris, M. W. 2001. "Justice in the culturally diverse workplace: the problems of over and under emphasis of cultural differences", in S. Gilliland, D. Steiner, and D. Skarlicki (eds.), *Research in social issues in management: Vol. 1*. Greenwich, Connecticut: Information Age Publishing, pp. 161–85.

Lewis, G. J., and Harvey, B. 2001. "Perceived environmental uncertainty: the extension of Miller's scale to the natural environment", *Journal of Management Studies*, 38, 201–34.

Lim, K., Leung, K., Sia, C. L., and Lee, M. 2004. "Is e-commerce boundary-less? Effects of individualism-collectivism and uncertainty avoidance on internet shopping", *Journal of International Business Studies*, 35: 545–59.

Lin, N. 2001. *Social Capital: A Theory of Social Structure*. New York: Cambridge University Press.

Linton, R. 1936. *The Study of Man*. New York: Appleton-Century-Crofts.

Lip, E. 1988. *Chinese Beliefs and Superstitions*. Singapore: Graham Brash.

Lippman, T. W. 1995. *Understanding Islam*. New York: Meridian Books.

Liu, S. 2003. "Cultures within culture: unity and diversity of two generations of employees in stated-owned enterprise", *Human Relations*, 56: 387–417.

Luo, Y. 2000. *Guanxi and Business*. Singapore: World Scientific Press.

2007. "Continuous learning: the influence of national institutional logics on training attitudes", *Organization Science*, 18: 280–96.

Malinowski, B. 1944. *A Scientific Theory of Culture*. Chapel Hill, NC: University of North Carolina Press.

Marcus, A. 2003. "Fast forward: user-interface design and China: a great leap forward", *Interactions*, 10: 21–5.

Martinsons, M. G. 2004. "ERP in China – one package, two profiles: how and why the same software system implementation can produce fundamentally different results", *Communications of the ACM*, 47, 65–8.

Matten, D. and Geppert, M. 2004. "Work systems in heavy engineering: the role of national culture and national institutions in multinational corporations", *Journal of International Management*, 10: 177–98.

McClelland, D. C. 1961. *The Achieving Society*. Princeton, NJ: D. Van Nostrand.

Miller, K. D. 1992. "A framework for integrated risk management in international business", *Journal of International Business Studies*, 23: 311–31.

1993. "Industry and country effects on managers' perceptions of environmental uncertainties", *Journal of International Business Studies*, 24, 693–714.

Mol, S. T., Born, M. P. H., Willemsen, M. E., and Van Der Molen, H. T. 2005. "Predicting expatriate job performance for selection purposes: a quantitative review", *Journal of Cross-Cultural Psychology*, 36: 590–620.

Molinsky, A. 2007. "Cross-cultural code-switching: the psychological challenges of adapting behavior in foreign cultural interactions", *Academy of Management Review*, 32, 622–40.

Morris, M. W., Williams, K. Y., Leung, K., Bhatnagar, D., Li, J. F., Kondo, M., Luo, J. L., and Hu, J. C. 1998. "Culture, conflict management style, and underlying values: accounting for cross-national differences in styles of handling conflicts among US, Chinese, Indian and Filipina Managers", *Journal of International Business Studies*, 29: 729–48.

Mouly, V. S. and Sankaran, J. K. 2002. "The enactment of envy within organizations", *Journal of Applied Behavioral Science*, 38: 36–56.

Murdock, G. P. 1945. "The common denominator of cultures", in R. Linton (ed.), *Science of Man in the World Crisis*. New York: Columbia University Press, pp. 123–42.

Neo, B. S. and Chen, G. 2007. *Dynamic Governance: Embedding Culture, Capabilities and Change in Singapore*. Singapore: World Scientific Press.

Newman, K. L. 2000. "Organizational transformation during institutional upheaval", *Academy of Management Review*, 25: 602–19.

North, D.C. 1990. *Institutions, Institutional Change and Economic Performance*. New York: Cambridge University Press.

Oliver, C. 1991. "Strategic responses to institutional processes", *Academy of Management Review*, 16: 145–79.

Ong, A. 1987. *Spirits of Resistance and Capitalist Discipline: Factory Women in Malaysia*. Albany, NY: *State University of New York Press*.

1999. *Flexible Citizenship: The Cultural Logics of Transnationality*. Durham: Duke University Press.

Parboteeah, K.P. and Cullen, J.B. 2003. "Social institutions and work centrality: explorations beyond national culture", *Organization Science*, 14: 137–48.

Parkin, R. 1997. *Kinship: An Introduction to Basic Concepts*. Malden, MA: Blackwell.

Pelto, P. 1968. "The difference between 'tight' and 'loose' societies", *Transaction*, 5: 37–40.

Peng, M.W., Wang, D., and Jiang, Y. 2008. "An institution-based view of international business strategy: a focus on emerging economies", *Journal of International Business Studies* 39: 920–36.

Ralston, D.A., Egri, C.P., Stewart, S., Terpstra, R.H., and Yu, K.C. 1999. "Doing business in the 21st century with the new generation of Chinese managers: a study of generational shifts in work values in China", *Journal of International Business Studies*, 30: 415–27.

Redding, S.G. 1995. *The Spirit of Chinese Capitalism*. New York: Walter de Gruyter.

Rogers, E.M. 2003. *Diffusion of Innovations* (5th edn). New York: Simon and Schuster.

Rotter, J.B. 1966. "Generalized expectancies for internal versus external control of reinforcement", *Psychological Monographs*, 80, 1–28.

Schein, E. 2004. *Organizational Culture and Leadership* (3rd edn). New York: Wiley.

Schwartz, S.H. 1992. "Universals in the content and structure of values: theoretical advances and empirical tests in 20 countries", *Advances in Experimental Social Psychology*, 25: 1–65.

1994. "Beyond individualism/collectivism: New cultural dimensions of values", in U. Kim, H.C. Triandis, C. Kagitcibasi, S. Choi, and G. Yoon (eds.), *Individualism and Collectivism: Theory, Method, and Applications*. Thousand Oaks, CA: Sage, pp. 85–119.

Scott, R. 1995. *Institutions and Organizations*. Thousand Oaks, CA: Sage.

Shen, S.T., Woolley, M., and Prior, S. 2006. "Towards culture-centered design", *Interacting with Computers*, 18, 820–52.

Smith, P.B., and Bond, M.H. 1998. *Social Psychology Across Cultures* (2nd edn). Boston, MA: Allyn & Bacon.

Smith, P.B., Dugan, S., and Trompenaars, F. 1996. "National culture and managerial values: a dimensional analysis across 43 nations", *Journal of Cross-Cultural Psychology*, 27, 231–64.

Sia, S.K., and Soh, C. 2007. "An assessment of package-organisation misalignment: institutional and ontological structures", *European Journal of Information Systems* 16(5): 568–83.

Singh, K. 2007. "The limited relevance of culture to strategy", *Asia Pacific Journal of Management*, 24: 421–28.

Stahl, G.K. and Caligiuri, P.M. 2005. "The effectiveness of expatriate coping strategies: the moderating role of cultural distance, position level and the time on the international assignment", *Journal of Applied Psychology*, 90: 603–15.

Sternberg, R.J. 1986. "A framework for understanding conceptions of intelligence", in R.J. Sternberg and D.K. Detterman (eds.), *What is Intelligence? Contemporary Viewpoints on its Nature and Definition*. Norwood, NJ: Ablex, pp. 3–15.

Stewart, E.C., and Bennett, M.J. 1991. *American Cultural Patterns: A Cross-cultural Perspective*. Yarmouth, ME: Intercultural Press.

Stone, L. 2001. *New Directions in Anthropological Kinship*. Lanham, MD: Rowman and Littlefield.

Thomas, L.G. III and Waring, G. 1999. "Competing capitalisms: capital investment in American, German, and Japanese firms", *Strategic Management Journal*, 20, 729–48.

Tinsley, C.H., and Brodt, S.E. 2004. "Conflict management in Asia: A dynamic framework and future directions", in K. Leung and S. White (eds.), *Handbook of Asian Management*. New York: Kluwer, pp. 439–58.

Tong, C.K. and Yong, P.K. 1998. "Guanxi bases, xinjong, and Chinese business networks", *British Journal of Sociology*, 49: 75–96.

Trafimow, D., Triandis, H.C., and Goto, S.G. 1991. "Some tests of the distinction between the private self and the collective self", *Journal of Personality and Social Psychology*, 60: 649–55.

Triandis, H. C. 1972. *Analysis of Subjective Culture*. New York: Wiley.

Trompenaars, F. 1993. *Riding the Waves of Culture: Understanding Diversity in Global Business*. London: Nicholas Brealey.

Tsui, A. S. and Gutek, B. 1999. *Demographic Differences in Organizations: Current Research and Future Directions*. New York: Lexington Books/Macmillan.

Tsui-Auch, L. S. 2004. "The professionally managed family-ruled enterprise: ethnic Chinese business in Singapore", *Journal of Management Studies*, 41: 693–723.

Tung, R. L. 1998. "American expatriates abroad: from neophytes to cosmopolitans", *Journal of World Business* 33: 125–44.

van de Vliert, E. 2003. "Thermoclimate, culture, and poverty as country-level roots of workers' wages", *Journal of International Business Studies*, 34: 40–52.

2006. "Autocratic leadership around the globe: do climate and wealth drive leadership culture?", *Journal of Cross-Cultural Psychology*, 37: 42–59.

2007. "Climatoeconomic roots of survival versus self-expression cultures", *Journal of Cross-Cultural Psychology* 38, 156–72.

2008. Climate, wealth, and organization. In P. B. Smith, M. F. Peterson, and D. C. Thomas (eds.), *Handbook of Cross-cultural Management Research*. Thousand Oaks, CA: Sage, pp. 330–350.

and Smith, P. B. 2004. "Leader reliance on subordinates across nations that differ in development and climate", *Leadership Quarterly*, 15: 381–403.

and Van Yperen, N. W. 1996. "Why cross-national differences in role overload? Don't overlook ambient temperature!", *Academy of Management Journal* 39: 986–1004.

Van Yperen, N. W., and Thierry, H. (2008). "Are wages more important for employees in poorer countries with harsher climates?", *Journal of Organizational Behavior*, 29: 79–94.

Walder, A. G. 1995. "Local governments as industrial firms: an organizational analysis of China's transitional economy", *American Journal of Sociology* 101: 263–301.

Warner, M. 1996. "Human resources in the People's Republic of China: the 'three systems' reform", *Human Resources Management Journal*, 6: 32–43.

Weber, M. 1958. *The Protestant Ethic and the Spirit of Capitalism*. New York: Charles Scribner's Sons.

Wee, B. G. 1995. *Structure, Action and the Interpretive Flexibility of Quality Control Circles – An analysis of QCC Systems and Practice in Singapore*. PhD thesis, University of Hull, UK.

White, S. 2002. "Rigor and relevance in Asian management research: where are we and where can we go?", *Asia Pacific Journal of Management*, 19, 287–352.

Williams, K. and O'Reilly, C. 1998. The complexity of diversity: a review of forty years of research", in B. M. Staw and L. L. Cummings (eds.), *Research in Organizational Behavior*, vol. 20. Greenwich, CT: JAI Press, pp. 77–140.

Whiting, B. B. 1974. "Folk wisdom and child rearing", *Merrill-Palmer Quarterly* 20: 9–19.

Womack, J. P., Jones, D. T., and Roos, D. 1990. *That Machine that Changed the World*. New York: Rawson Associates.

Xu, D., and Shenkar, O. 2002. "Institutional distance and the multinational enterprise", *Academy of Management Review* 27: 608–18.

Yang. M. M. 1994. *Gifts, Favors and Banquets: The Art of Social Relationships in China*. Ithaca, NY: Cornell University Press.

2002. "The resilience of guanxi and its new deployments: a critique of some new guanxi scholarship", *China Quarterly* 170: 459–76.

Zellmer-Bruhn, M., Gibson, C. B., and Earley, P. C. 2002. *Some of These Things are Not Like the Others: An Exploration of Heterogeneity in Work*. Paper presented at the annual meeting of Academy of Management, Denver, CO.

When does culture matter?

CRISTINA B. GIBSON, MARTHA L. MAZNEVSKI, and BRADLEY L. KIRKMAN

Recent years of research in international management have been dominated by studies of culture's effect on dependent variables of interest to managers, including individual work behavior, effective organizational structures, and economic success. Reviews of research conclude that culture does have an impact, one that cannot be ignored (Adler and Bartholomew, 1992; Boyacigiller and Adler, 1991; Earley and Sing, 1995; Earley and Gibson, 2002; Kirkman, Lowe, and Gibson, 2004; Oyserman, Kemmelmeir, and Coon, 2002). For example, in their review of cultural values research published between 1980 and 2002, Kirkman, Lowe and Gibson (2004) describe sixty-one studies that provide empirical evidence for a relationship between cultural values and individual level outcomes, including change management behaviors (e.g., Eby, Adams, Russell et al., 2000); conflict management behaviors (e.g., Gabrielidis, Stephan, et al., 1997); behaviors in negotiations (e.g., Wade-Benzio, Okumura, Brett, et al., 2002); reward allocation (e.g., Gomez, Kirkman, and Shapiro, 2000); decision-making (e.g., Mitchell, Smith, Seawright, et al., 2000); human resource management (e.g., Earley, Gibson and Chen, 1999); leadership behaviors (e.g., Chan and Drasgow, 2001); individual behavior in groups (e.g., Gibson and Zellmer-Bruhn, 2001); personality (e.g., Tafarodi, Lang, and Smith, 1999); and work-related attitudes or emotions (e.g., Harpaz, Honig, and Coetsier, 2002).

However, at the same time, research and practice offer numerous examples of studies and observations in which culture had less effect than did unique personalities, strong leadership, or uniformity of practices (e.g., Earley and Gibson, 2002; Maznevski and Chudoba, 2000; Roth, Prasnikar, Okuno-Fujiwara, et al., 1991; Wetlaufer, 1999). Furthermore, in many scholarly studies culture's impact is statistically significant, but does not explain a large amount of variance indicating that other variables must be considered as important predictors alongside culture (e.g., Peterson, et al., 1995; Brett and Okumura, 1998; Gibson, 1999; Clugston, Howell, and Dorfman, 2000; Mitchell, Smith, Seawright, et al., 2000; Kirkman and Shapiro, 2001). While researchers are able to draw implications for managers, they cannot reach a high level of precision regarding the specific impacts and the circumstances in which culture should be a central focus, or when it might be less critical. For example, several studies have found relationships between collectivism and individual attitudes toward teamwork (e.g., Bochner, 1994; Casimir and Keats, 1996; Eby and Dobbins, 1997; Earley, Gibson, and Chen, 1999; Kirkman and Shapiro, 2000; Gibson and Zellmer-Bruhn, 2001). However, do these cultural proclivities come into play in every circumstance? Might there be situations, such as in times of crisis, when members of organizations have fairly universally positive attitudes toward teamwork?

Part of the problem is that such research often attempts to explain individual-level phenomena, such as attitudes and behaviors, with the group-level phenomenon of culture (Bond, 2002; Hofstede, 2001). Culture is a property of groups or societies, and its effect on individual outcomes is highly indirect and likely moderated by a variety of other variables. Some researchers suggest that culture should only be used to predict outcomes at the same level of analysis, such as aggregate rates of turnover, insurance use, or economic indicators (e.g., Franke, Hofstede, and Bond, 1991; Hofstede, 1997, 2001). However, managers have a strong need to predict patterns of behavior among employees, co-workers, and business partners in international settings; thus, management researchers should

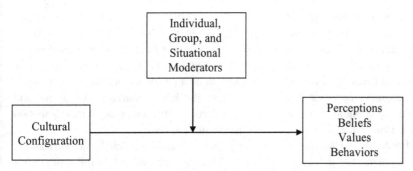

Figure 3.1 General model of causation: moderators of the impact of culture

not avoid these questions. In this sense, we agree wholeheartedly with Oyserman, Kemmelmeir, and Coon (2002, p. 110), who in their survey of the field of organizational psychology, suggested that:

> the essential goal of the field is to understand how culture influences how the mind works and to identify the cultural contingencies that moderate general processes of human cognition, affect and behavior. To take on this challenge, cultural psychologists must posit general principals that are likely to have different instantiations across cultures.

Individuals within a culture must think, evaluate, and behave in ways that are efficient, understandable to each other, and facilitate cooperation. This comprehensibility, in turn, is facilitated by similarity among the individual members themselves.

This presents a dilemma for the field of international management. On the one hand, researchers and managers need to understand the individual-level outcomes that are related to culture, so they can work closely with other people around the world and implement organizational innovations to enhance effectiveness across multinational locations. On the other hand, research examining the role of culture has not captured enough variance in the patterns of individual outcomes to make the specific recommendations managers need. In this chapter, we argue that the field's current limitations should not prevent us from articulating and researching questions of importance to international management theory and practice; rather, we as researchers should seek to re-conceptualize the relationship between culture and individual

outcomes in a way that explains the relationship with greater precision.

We take a superordinate position concerning the nature of culture's effect on individuals, shifting the focus of the field's discussion. In the past, much of the cross-cultural and international management research has been fueled by the desire to document that culture does matter (Oyserman, Coon, and Kemmelmeir, 2002). While this is an important endeavor, it lacks precision. Thus, instead of addressing whether or not culture makes a difference, we join others (Earley and Gibson, 2002; Leung, Bhagat, Buchan, *et al.*, 2005; Kirkman *et al.*, 2004; Leung, Su, and Morris, 2001) in addressing the issue of *when* it makes a difference (figure 3.1). We explore the nature of culture's effect on four categories of individual-level outcomes: perception, beliefs, values, and behavior. We identify how this relationship is moderated by a set of important contingent variables at three levels of analysis: individual, group, and contextual. Through this analysis, we develop a comprehensive model of the relationships between culture and individual outcomes. Before examining the relationships in depth, we will frame the discussion by defining culture, discussing the nature of cultural causation, and identifying the variables to be addressed.

Culture

In this research, we adopt the following definition of culture: culture is the configuration of basic assumptions about humans and their relationship to each other and to the world around them, shared by an identifiable group of people. Culture is manifested in individuals' values and beliefs, in expected norms for social behavior, and in artifacts such as social institutions and physical items. This definition is an extension of the cognitive approach that is embedded in many traditional definitions of culture (e.g., Brannen, Gomez, Peterson, *et al.*, 2004; Erez and Earley, 1993; Hofstede, 1980; Kluckhohn, 1954; Oyserman, Kemmelmeir, Coon, 2002; Shweder and LeVine, 1984). Several aspects of the definition require elaboration. First is the deliberate choice of the word "configuration," which is consistent with the approach set forth by Meyer, Tsui, and Hinings (1993). A configuration is a "multidimensional constellation of conceptually distinct characteristics that commonly occur together" (Meyer, Tsui, and Hinings 1993, p. 1175). As in any configuration, while specific elements of culture can be separated, analyzed, and compared with elements of other cultures in useful ways, the interaction of combined elements has effects different from those expected by a simple summation of the effects of the individual elements. Culture's effects cannot be well understood unless culture is seen as a gestalt created by combinations of elements.

Second, while we mostly "see" culture in its manifestations, it is the underlying assumptions that constitute the deep level of culture (Schein, 1984). These assumptions are held by individuals, often subconsciously, and are rarely questioned. They are learned in direct and indirect ways in childhood, and reinforced throughout life by pervasive social values and beliefs, expected norms, and artifacts in the culture's environment. They are foundational schemas – generalized abstracted ways of making meaning (Oyserman, Kemmelmeir, and Coon, 2002).

Third, culture does not concern all assumptions held by individuals – that set may be infinite or at least indefinable. Issues concerning the group's survival and social interaction bound the set of assumptions that define cultural configurations. Since prehistoric times humans have lived in groups, operating in social organizations to coordinate long-term survival and prosperity. For a wide variety of complex reasons, different groups developed different assumptions about how to interact to survive, and these are the substance of culture (Hofstede, 1980; Kluckhohn and Strodtbeck, 1961). As aptly put by Oyserman, Kemmelmeir, and Coon (2002, p. 114), cultures provide insight into how to be a person in the world, what makes for a good life, how to interact with others, and which aspects of situations require more attention and processing capacity.

This content is directly related to a fourth aspect of our definition: the notion that the assumptions are shared (Erez and Earley, 1993; Morgeson and Hofmann, 1999). In order for the assumptions to work – that is, for them to facilitate the survival and prosperity of the group – they must guide the culture's members to behave in a coordinated and consistent manner. Interestingly, this "sharedness" does not need to be absolutely complete. Cultures can be described on a continuum from strong to weak (Kilmann, Saxton, and Serpa 1986; Trompenaars, 1993), on which strong cultures are those with a high level of sharedness and weak cultures are those with less sharing of assumptions and beliefs. At some level, a weak culture ceases to be a culture at all, but the dividing line between what is and what is not a culture is sometimes difficult to discern.

Finally, the choice of the term "identifiable group of people" must be addressed. It is well accepted that many types of cultures exist, including cultures associated with national, ethnic, religious, professional, gender, age, class, and organizational dimensions. While international management researchers tend to focus on cultures associated with national and ethnic groups – as we will in this article – we acknowledge that other cultural affiliations exist and influence organizational phenomena. The identification of the cultural group is a recognition that the group operates in a coordinated way under a relatively cohesive set of assumptions about each other and the world around them.

The nature of culture as a causal variable

When we talk about culture causing individual-level outcomes, we are clearly crossing levels of analysis. While this is conceptually and methodologically difficult, it is not unreasonable (Klein, Tosi, and Cannella 1999; Klein and Koslowski, 2000). In fact, as argued by Morgeson and Hofmann (1999), collective constructs are generated by the interaction of individuals, and in return both influence and constrain individual outcomes. As a shared agreement about interpretation, evaluation and action, culture is one of many collective phenomena that affect individual outcomes.

We suggest that the collective configuration of culture affects individual outcomes through mechanisms defined by two dimensions: cognitive versus social, and passive versus active. First, culture provides a template for cognitive processes (Erez and Earley, 1993; Oyserman, Kemmelmeir, and Coon, 2002), and members use this template, or schema, to process information automatically. Cultural cognitions are brought into play passively, for example, in noticing information in advertising, interpreting the meaning of stories on the news, and evaluating performance indicators. Culture also plays a more active role in the cognitive process. Individuals notice things that do not fit their own schemas, and culture provides a means for resolving the resulting cognitive dissonance (Festinger, 1957). For example, an American working with a Chinese co-worker in a group may not even notice if the co-worker does not speak out loud as much as the American does, because his or her cultural template does not direct attention to silence or context (passive cognitive). However, if the American does notice the Chinese co-worker's relative quiet, a need for cognitive equilibrium will likely direct the American to conclude that the co-worker has nothing to contribute, consistent with the American cultural norms for interpreting silence (active cognitive).

In addition to cognitive processes, culture also affects individual outcomes through social mechanisms. Cultural scripts for social interaction implicitly guide everyday behavior, such as transactions in stores or at banks, greeting people, and holding meetings. While these scripts are a type of cognition (Lord and Foti, 1986), here we distinguish them from the notice–interpret–evaluate sequence of cognitive information processing. Without thinking, people follow cultural scripts passively in social settings. More actively, individuals are motivated to behave according to cultural norms to satisfy a need for social acceptance (Earley and Erez, 1993). This need is universal, although individuals differ in the relative strength of need for social acceptance (i.e., need for affiliation) compared to others (McClelland, 1961). Because culture is a shared agreement about effective social interaction, individuals who comply with the culture's norms are more socially accepted by others. Through this active social mechanism, individuals more or less consciously decide to think or act in accordance with the culture, even while recognizing that there may be alternative modes.

Cognition research has shown how pervasive the influence of schemas is, and how difficult they are to change (Flynn, Chatman, and Spataro, 2001; Rousseau, 1995). The need to reduce cognitive dissonance also has a powerful impact on thinking processes; and the need to be accepted socially, at least at a minimum level, is a very basic need. Social routines are incredibly resistant to change (Feldman, 2000). Because culture operates on individuals through both of these dimensions, it is hardly surprising that its influence is so strong. Culture's impact is certainly pervasive and important, yet we still have a need for greater precision in our understanding of cultural effects.

Having outlined the mechanisms through which culture affects individual outcomes, we can now state the research question more specifically. Rather than simply asking "when does culture matter?", we can ask: "What are the conditions that increase an individual's propensity to think, feel, value, or behave in accordance with culture?" "What are the conditions that increase an individual's propensity to think, feel, value or behave using alternate schemas or to satisfy alternate needs?" The more active and passive cognitive and social processes are moderated by other elements, the less predictive culture will be of individual outcomes.

Finally, although we will not focus on them in this chapter, two other points are important regarding the causal relationship between culture and individuals. First, in the long term the causal direction of the relationship is reciprocal. Individuals affect their environments, and culture is a dynamic, ever-changing result of individual interactions. In the short term, culture does not change radically. However, researchers should bear in mind the dynamic nature of culture, and the possibility that human interaction in organizations influences national culture (Gibson, 1994; Morgeson and Hofmann, 1999).

Second, our focus will be on culture as the main independent variable, and we explore other variables as moderators (e.g., personality or characteristics of the situation) of the impact of culture. One could equally examine other roles that culture can play in models (Kirkman, Lowe, and Gibson, 2006; Lytle *et al.*, 1995). For example, culture can function as a dependent variable of interest, with other factors, such as organizational structures producing changes in cultural values. The Kirkman, Lowe, and Gibson (2006) review mentioned earlier identified five such studies that involved cultural dimensions from Hofstede's (1980) research. For example, in one study, leaders described in interviews the process by which local cultures gradually changed to become more isomorphic with organizational cultures of multinational firms that entered the local markets (Gibson, 1994). Culture can also serve as a moderator that changes the nature of the relationship between two other variables. Kirkman, Lowe, and Gibson (2006) identified twenty-four such studies at the individual level. For example, Erez and Somech (1996) found that collectivism moderated the relationship between goal characteristics and group performance. We view such studies as particularly helpful in assessing the boundaries of organizational behavior research to test the robustness of a particular theory.

In selecting the focus for the role of culture in a given analysis, the issue is one of determining which phenomenon is more of interest in a particular research study. In international management research that is seeking to understand how certain individual level outcomes change across cultures, the approach outlined here, focusing on culture as the independent variable and individual level outcomes as the dependent variables, is appropriate.

Dependent variables: what culture affects

Culture has the potential to affect many phenomena important to international management, including those at the individual, group, and institutional levels of analysis. This chapter focuses on individual-level manifestations, which we discuss in terms of four categories: perceptions, beliefs, values, and behaviors. This section describes these categories and briefly reviews how each is influenced by culture.

Perception: do you see what I see?

Perception is the process by which individuals select, organize, and evaluate stimuli from the external environment (Singer, 1976). As demonstrated in numerous laboratory experiments (see Pryor and Ostrom, 1991 for a review) as well as in the field (Adler, 1997), perception is selective and involves schematic processing. Information is organized into cognitive frameworks or expectations, called schemas (Pryor and Ostrom, 1991). These cognitive structures guide the perceiver to attend to what is important, lend structure to otherwise ambiguous social experience, enable the perceiver to fill in gaps when information is missing, and allow the perceiver to anticipate what will come next (Abelson, 1981). As a result, we can "see" things that do not exist and not "see" things that do exist (Hall, 1976).

Culture has been shown to have a strong influence on the schemas we construct (see Triandis, 1994 for a research review). Many important schemas are developed through childhood socialization and pressures to conform, which are associated with cultural values and patterns (Gruenfeld and Maceachron, 1975; Witkin and Berry, 1975). Culture affects perception primarily through its influence on: (1) the content of the schemas; (2) the structure of the schemas; and (3) the propensity to process using schemas (Shaw, 1990). With regard to content, for example, research indicates that culture is related to the width of schema categories – how broad a category is – such that people from different cultures have systematically different category widths (Detweiler, 1978). With respect to structure, some cultures encourage high differentiation among dimensions of the environment, while other cultures encourage people to perceive the environment as a unidimensional, highly integrated whole (Gruenfeld and Maceachron, 1975; Witkin, 1967; Witkin and Berry, 1975). Finally, research also indicates that culture impacts the extent to which information is processed automatically. For example, culture determines whether we pay attention to the context in which an experience occurs (Markus and Kitayama, 1991), a phenomenon that has been referred to as high versus low context (Hall and Hall, 1988). In high context cultures, perception is likely to involve a comprehensive, controlled process (Shaw, 1990), while in low context cultures the perceptual process is quicker and more automatic.

Beliefs: what's related to what?

Beliefs are a person's subjective probability judgment concerning a relation between the object of the belief and some other object, value, concept or attribute (Fishbein and Ajzen, 1975, p. 131). Four characteristics of beliefs that are of special importance for the present analysis are: *confidence, centrality, interrelationship*, and *functionality* (Bar-Tal, 1990). Confidence differentiates beliefs on the basis of truth attributed to them. A person may have minimal confidence in some beliefs, and will express these using statements such as "maybe" or "possibly," while having absolute confidence in other beliefs and will state the latter ones in definite ways such as "definitely" and "absolutely" (Bandura, 1997). Centrality characterizes the extent of beliefs' accessibility in individuals' repertoire and their use in various considerations that individuals make. Some beliefs are very central, used often, and are relevant for a wide range of evaluations, decisions, judgments, or behaviors. Others are less central, peripheral beliefs that are only taken into consideration at specific times. Interrelationship describes the extent to which the belief is related to other beliefs in a network or system. For example, a person's belief about compensation systems may be related to a complex series of beliefs about economic and political systems. On the other hand, a person's two or three beliefs about the Arctic Sea might be relatively isolated. Finally, functionality differentiates beliefs on the

basis of the needs that they fulfill. Beliefs may be utilitarian in that they help people get rewards and avoid punishments; they may protect an individual's sense of self; they may express personal values; or they may serve a knowledge function, providing meaning, understanding, and organization to what we know (Bar-Tal, 1990; Gibson, 1999).

Evidence for the relationship between culture and beliefs has been gathered by researchers such as Miller (1984), who demonstrated that Americans are much more likely to use internal dispositions as beliefs about behavior (i.e., "He did it because he is dishonest") than external, context factors (i.e., "He did it because it was a hot day"). Conversely, Miller found that Indians tended to use context factors more often than dispositions.

Values: what is important?

A value is a belief that is prescriptive – an enduring belief that a specific mode of conduct or end-state of existence is socially preferable to an opposite mode of conduct or end-state of existence (Rokeach, 1973; Schwartz, 1992). Values guide the selection of the means and ends of specific actions, and serve as criteria by which objects, actions, or events are evaluated. Individuals differ with respect to the values they hold or consider important; however, groups can be described by shared value systems.

That culture influences values has been shown by many scholars and, indeed, the words "cultural values" abound in the literature (Erez and Earley, 1993; Hofstede, 1980; Rokeach, 1973; Schwartz, 1994; Triandis, 1994; Trompenaars, 1993). We typically adopt values during early socialization experiences as a function of childhood. As a child matures and is exposed to settings of increasing complexity, he or she is likely to reaffirm particular values congruent with the settings and weaken or change other values that are inconsistent with the settings. Major programs of research conducted by Hofstede (1980), Trompenaars (1993) and Schwartz (1992) provide some indirect evidence for the relationship between culture and values by demonstrating that values vary more between countries than within countries.

Behavior: what will I do?

In our framework, behavior encompasses the actions that people take on a daily basis in response to stimuli, choices, or situations. Anthropologists and social psychologists have researched the impact of culture on behaviors for decades (see Triandis, 1994, for an overview). We note that behavior is a distal outcome of culture. By this we mean that culture does not impact behavior directly, but rather that culture impacts behavior through its influence on other more proximal outcomes. In terms of very general categories of behavior, we have evidence that culture is related to aggressive behavior such as being dominant, competitive, or violent (Goldstein and Segall, 1983). In some societies aggression is commonplace, while in others it is virtually absent. Empirical research has also established that culture is related to helping behaviors such as providing direction, encouragement, or reassurance (Hinde and Groebel, 1991). Other research has demonstrated strong relationships between culture and conforming behavior and between culture and obedience (see Mann, 1980 for a review). Empirical work has also demonstrated links between culture and disclosure or intimacy (Gudykunst, 1983). Research based on Hofstede's (1980) framework has demonstrated links between culture and directive managerial behavior (Gallois, Barker, Jones, *et al.*, 1992), between culture and providing feedback (Cohen, 1991), and between culture and conflict reduction (Leung, 1988).

Relationships among dependent variables

Of course, separating perceptions, beliefs, values, and behaviors as we have done in this section is somewhat artificial, since the four categories are highly related to each other. What we believe and value influences what we notice and how we interpret it, all of which influences how we behave. Behavior and its effects on the environment in turn affect what we perceive and believe. The fact that culture affects each element in this continual process makes its influence both pervasive and complex. However, we are still left with the fact that sometimes its influence seems to be greater than others. Thinking about moderating effects in terms of different categories of individual outcomes (i.e., perceptions, beliefs, values, and behaviors) is therefore helpful in making sense of this complexity. We now turn to the proposed moderators of the relationship between culture and individual outcomes.

Moderator variables: when culture matters

To address the question of when culture influences these outcomes, we outline a framework to identify different types of moderators and their effects. In addition to the complexity created by "independent" and "dependent" variables at different levels of analysis, we propose that the relationship between culture and individual outcomes is moderated by variables at three levels of analysis: individual, group, and situational. In this section, we take each level of analysis and propose specific variables that moderate the relationship between culture and each of the four categories of outcomes. This discussion is not intended to identify all moderators of the relationship between culture and individual outcomes, but to illustrate this framework for understanding the role of categories of moderators. At the individual level, we explore personality dimensions, cognitive process variables, individual experiences, and self-identity. At the group level, we examine the role of small work group characteristics as well as larger social groups. At the situational level, we describe how elements of the environment and context can moderate the relationship. The discussion is summarized in table 3.1.

Individual-level moderators

Perhaps the most pervasive moderator at the individual level is that of personality, or characteristics which capture stable individual differences in personal traits. Research reported in the personality literature provides evidence for five major personality

Table 3.1 Moderators of the impact of culture

Level of Moderator	Outcome	Example Of Moderator Variable	Proposed Relationship: Culture Is A Stronger Predictor When
Individual	Perception	Personality trait: *Openness*	Openness is low (Digman, 1990).
		Experience: *Exposure to Other Cultures*	Exposure to other cultures is low (Pick, 1980; Toyne, 1976).
	Beliefs	Personality trait: *Conformity*	Conformity is high (Digman and Takemoto-Chock, 1981)
		Experience: *Lineal Descent*	Native or first generation emigrant status, rather than later generation emigrant status (Earley and Erez, 1997).
	Values	Personality trait: *Social Adaptability*	Social Adaptability is low (Digman, 1990; Lorr, 1986).
		Self-Identity: *Identification with Culture*	Identification with culture is high (Turner, 1987).
	Behavior	Personality trait: *Conscientiousness*	Conscientiousness is high (Tellegen, 1985; Hogan, 1986).
		Self-Identity: *Self-efficacy*	Self-efficacy is low (Bandura, 1997).
Group	Perception	Social Group: *Group Identification*	Group identification is high (Bettenhausen, 1991; Kernis, Grannemann, Richie, and Hart, 1988).
		Work Group: *Social Reality Construction*	Group's social reality construction is shared (Brown and Hosking, 1986; DiStefano and Maznevski, 2000).
	Beliefs	Social Group: *Group Homogeneity*	Group homogeneity is high (Bettenhausen and Murnighan, 1991).
		Work Group: *Group Polarization*	Group polarization is low (Isenberg, 1986; Ziller, 1957).
	Values	Social Group: *Strength of Organizational Culture*	Organizational culture is strong (Sackmann, 1992).
		Work Group: *Group Cohesion*	Group cohesion is high (Bettenhausen, 1991; Organ and Hammer, 1950).
Group	Behavior	Social Group: *Collectivism, Ingroup-Outgroup*	Culture is more collective (Kirkman and Shapiro, 1997). Within collective cultures, when dealing with members of ingroup (Triandis, 1994; Triandis *et al.*, 1988).
		Work Group: *Stage of Group Development*	In forming and storming stages than in norming and performing stages (Tuckman, 1965).
Situation	Perception	Dimension: *Economic Uncertainty*	Uncertainty is high immediately after currency crisis (Jordan, 1997; Pollack, 1997).
	Beliefs	Dimension: *Social Richness*	Social richness is lower in a rural than an urban environment (Triandis, 1994; Trompenaars, 1993).
	Values	Dimension: *Political Volatility*	Volatility is low and there are no changes in government structure (Earley and Erez, 1997).
	Behavior	Dimension: *Technological Environment is Strong vs. Weak*	Situation is weak, procedures and tools are ambiguous or highly complex (Mischel, 1973; Shoda, Mischel, and Wright, 1993).

factors that exist in all cultures (see Digman, 1990, for a review). These five factors have been given various labels; however, the general consensus seems to be that the following traits capture the essence of the five factors: social adaptability; conformity; conscientiousness; emotional stability; and openness (Benet and Waller, 1995; Digman, 1990; Yang and Bond, 1990). We argue that personality (i.e., the degree to which a person possesses these traits) will moderate the impact of culture on perceptions, beliefs, values, and behavior, as illustrated in the examples below.

Perception

An important personality characteristic that affects perception is openness, or the degree to which a person has an inquiring intellect and an independence of thinking (Digman, 1990). Persons characterized by openness will demonstrate openness to ways of perceiving other than those typical of their native culture. They are more likely to perceive in a manner that is independent of their culture. Thus, for those high on openness, there will be a lower relationship between culture and perception. For those low on openness, we would expect perception to be more dependent upon the cultural modes of thinking.

A number of other individual differences are likely to moderate the impact of culture on perceptions. For example, the extent of familiarity with other cultures influences how individuals process information. When a person has acquired extensive international experience, he or she may no longer perceive in a manner that is characteristic of his or her native culture; therefore, there may be little relationship between culture and perception. Several studies have shown that exposure to foreign cultures and business practices reduce cognitive differences between individuals from different cultures (Pick, 1980; Toyne, 1976). When a person has not been exposed to foreign cultures, the relationship between culture and perception will likely remain.

Beliefs

Personality characteristics such as conformity – a tendency to match one's self to others – will moderate the impact of culture on beliefs. People who are high on conformity tend to follow social norms (Fiske, 1949). They also tend to demonstrate "friendly compliance" with the status quo (Digman and Takemoto-Chock, 1981). Within a culture, then, those people who are characterized by the conformity personality characteristic are more likely to hold beliefs that are in line with their culture. Indeed, beliefs in alignment with the culture

will be central to the conformist's belief system. On the other hand, people low on conformity tend to demonstrate hostile noncompliance (Digman and Takemoto-Chock, 1981). These individuals are not likely to hold beliefs based on cultural characteristics, and any cultural beliefs they may hold are likely to be low on centrality (i.e., nonessential).

Another individual difference variable that will moderate the impact of culture on beliefs is lineal descent. People native to a given culture tend to demonstrate the strongest relationship between that culture and their belief system. They have high confidence in culturally aligned beliefs. As families immigrate from their native culture and spend more time in a new culture, they slowly take on the culture of their new home. This process has been referred to as acculturation (Earley and Erez, 1997). Over time as new persons are born into these families, successive generations demonstrate fewer and fewer of the characteristic beliefs of the original culture held by their ancestors; they may also have less and less confidence in culturally aligned beliefs. There will be little or no relationship between the family's original native culture and the beliefs held by these new generations.

Values

One personality characteristic that will moderate culture's affect on values is social adaptability, which has also been referred to as extraversion (Digman, 1990) and interpersonal involvement (Lorr, 1986). This trait captures whether or not a person is comfortable socially and the extent to which he or she is socially active. People who demonstrate social adaptability are more likely to change their values to fit the social setting they happen to be in at any given time. These persons tend to take to heart the old adage "When in Rome, do as the Romans do," thus demonstrating malleability in terms of what they deem important or desirable. Such individuals are not likely to be as driven by their own cultural assumptions in determining what will be valued. For them, culture will have little impact on their value system.

A second important individual difference moderator is the extent to which a person identifies with his or her culture. Not all individuals within a society identify with their national culture. According to social categorization theory, individuals view themselves as members of a number of groups and make personal self-categorizations regarding their membership within these groups (Turner, 1987). For example, one of the authors views herself as a member of the "female" gender group, the "academic" professional group, and the "North American" cultural group. She categorizes herself as a female above all else and identifies most strongly with this group. She does not identify with "North American" culture. Her values are characteristic of females in general, but not characteristic of North Americans as a cultural group. Thus, her level of identification with North American culture moderates the extent to which that culture impacts her values.

Behavior

A number of individual characteristics will moderate the impact of culture on behavior. For example, the personality trait conscientiousness, which has also been referred to as "constraint" (Tellegen, 1985) and "prudence" (Hogan, 1986) implies a degree of caution in one's actions. People described as conscientious or prudent are also characterized as having "good common sense" or a "practical wisdom." This suggests that people who are conscientious will comply with behaviors that are deemed acceptable in a given culture. For example, a particular society may incorporate a set of cultural assumptions concerning the importance of protecting the well-being of their in-group. In this society, a person with the conscientiousness personality trait is likely to demonstrate behaviors that promote the group's well-being. On the other hand, a person who does not have the conscientiousness trait may disregard these culturally prescribed behaviors and instead engage in behaviors that maximize self-interests.

An additional individual characteristic that moderates the relationship with behavior is self-efficacy, or a judgment of one's capability to accomplish a certain level of performance (Bandura, 1997). People who have a high sense of self-efficacy tend to pursue challenging goals that may be outside the reach of the average person. People with a strong sense of self-efficacy, therefore, may be more willing to step outside the culturally prescribed behaviors to attempt tasks or goals for which success is viewed as improbable by the majority of social actors in a setting. For these individuals, culture will have little or no impact on behavior. For example, Australians tend to endorse the "Tall Poppy Syndrome" (Gibson, 1994). This adage suggests that any "poppy" that outgrows the others in a field will get "cut down;" in other words, any over-achiever will eventually fail. Interviews and observations suggest that it is the high self-efficacy Australians who step outside this culturally prescribed behavior to actually achieve beyond average (Gibson, 1994; Jenner, 1982; Limerick, 1990).

Group-level moderators

Past research suggests that group-level moderators, such as characteristics of the group itself, can moderate the relationship between culture and individual outcomes. In fact, Meltzer (1963) reported that group averages of variables predicted individual attitudes and behavior better than the individual's own scores on the same variables, for dependent variables related to group-level phenomena, such as attitude towards an organization's program, and own activity on committee projects. Over the last decade, more and more organizations have adopted team-based approaches to carry out work both in the United States (Lawler, Mohrman, and Ledford 1995; Osterman, 1994) and in Asia, Europe, and Latin America (Gibson and Kirkman, 1999; Kirkman and Shapiro, 1997; Manz and Sims, 1993). As a result, more employees than ever before are working in formal groups to accomplish their tasks, and managers have an increased need to understand the interaction between cultural and group effects on individual outcomes. Relationships with two types of group-level moderators will be described here: moderators related to the larger social or cultural group to which the individual belongs, and moderators more characteristic of smaller work groups.

In general, the moderating effect of group-level variables is more complex in nature than that of individual-level variables, making culture's effects *seem* less systematic. If the group's characteristics are consistent with the culture's characteristics, they will reinforce the direct effect of culture, and the relationship between culture and individual-level outcomes will appear to be very strong. On the other hand, if the group's characteristics are inconsistent with the culture, they will counter the direct effect of culture, and the relationship between culture and individual-level outcomes will appear to be weak. Therefore, when culture matters depends not only on the group-level variables but on whether they reinforce or contradict the cultural configuration.

Perception

One social group level variable that will likely moderate the relationship between culture and perception is the extent of group identification. Some social groups are characterized by strong identification, such that a high proportion of group members know clearly and identify strongly with the group's defining features. In North America, for example, the Canadian media often characterize Canadians as having little sense of self-identity as compared to their US neighbors (e.g., Byfield, 1997). As demonstrated in laboratory and field studies, being part of an identifiable, interdependent social group lowers self-awareness and heightens group awareness (Bettenhausen, 1991; Kernis, Grannemann, Richie, *et al.*, 1988). Thus we would expect that members of a social group (or culture) characterized by strong group identification would notice more stimuli that are relevant to their group, and interpret them more in ways that are consistent with the group, than members of a social group with weaker group identification.

Another work-group level moderator is the extent to which groups develop a shared social reality, or a shared understanding of criteria for evaluating information and responses. Through social interaction in groups, members learn the labels with which they see and interpret their world (Bettenhausen, 1991). Group members, themselves, can influence the extent of the group's shared reality by explicitly de-centering to understand and take into account different individual perspectives, and integrating their perspectives with respect to

the task (Brown and Hosking, 1986; DiStefano and Maznevski, 2000). Members of groups which construct a strong, shared social reality are more likely to perceive and interpret stimuli based on that shared social reality, rather than based on schema related to culture.

Beliefs

Homogeneity is one social group-level moderator of the relationship between culture and beliefs. Social groups are more or less homogeneous on demographic characteristics such as age, gender, race, and education, or other factors such as ability or personality (Bettenhausen, 1991). Some national cultures are characterized by more homogeneity than others, such as Japan compared to Indonesia. The research conducted to date on homogeneity has focused on smaller groups, but the conclusions can be generalized cautiously to larger groups. Group members share more similar beliefs when their groups are homogeneous rather than heterogeneous (Bettenhausen, 1991; Levine and Moreland, 1990). In fact, in homogeneous groups, beliefs have a specific function: they serve to bind the group members together and help maintain homogeneity, reinforcing the cycle of cause and effect. Heterogeneous groups have many more of the characteristics that are associated with dissimilar beliefs, such as increased conflict (Jackson and Jackson, 1993; Pelled, Eisenhardt, and Xin 1999; Pfeffer, 1983), higher turnover (Jackson, Brett, Sessa, *et al.*, 1991; O'Reilly, Caldwell, Barnett 1989; Pfeffer and O'Reilly, 1987; Wagner, Pfeffer, and O'Reilley, 1984), and difficulty reaching consensus (Bettenhausen, 1991). We would expect that in a social group characterized by homogeneity, culture would be a better predictor of individuals' beliefs than in a more heterogeneous social group.

A work-group level moderator of the relationship between culture and beliefs is group polarization. Group polarization refers to the process by which group judgments tend to be more extreme than the judgments of individual members (Ziller, 1957). Group polarization tends to occur for two reasons: (1) group social comparison; and (2) persuasive arguments (Bettenhausen, 1991). In the first instance, group members alter their initial beliefs to be consistent with the group norm. In the second, group members modify their beliefs based on the arguments presented during group discussions. Regardless of the source of polarization (see Isenberg, 1986 for a meta-analysis demonstrating support for both social comparison and persuasive argument), in highly polarized groups the relationship between national culture and beliefs is likely to be weaker than in non-polarized groups. Again, centrality of beliefs is the issue: in highly polarized groups, group beliefs are more central than national cultural beliefs.

Values

One social group moderator of the relationship between culture and individual's values is the strength of the sub-culture (e.g., organizational culture) to which the individual belongs. Stronger sub-cultures are those in which more members strongly hold values that are consistent with each other (Sackmann, 1992). Individuals who belong to strong sub-cultures will likely have more values consistent with that sub-culture than with their national culture. For example, one of the authors has conducted research in a US company that has a very strong organizational culture, which differs from the national US culture on some important dimensions. In that organization, the company's sub-culture likely better predicts individuals' values than does the national culture.

A work-group moderator of culture's effect on individual values is group cohesion, or the degree to which members of a group are attracted to other members and are motivated to stay in the group (Organ and Hammer, 1950). When a group member is attracted to a group and motivated to stay, he or she is likely to have bought into the values of the group and accepted what the group believes (Bettenhausen, 1991). In these circumstances, the work group values may be stronger predictors than the national cultural values. Cohesiveness has been linked to a variety of positive outcomes such as group performance (George and Bettenhausen, 1990; Littlepage, Cowart, and Kerr, 1989; Wolfe and Box, 1988), lower turnover (George and Bettenhausen, 1990; O'Reilly, Caldwell, and Barnett, 1989), and group resistance to disruption

(Brawley, Carron, and Widmeyer, 1988). These outcomes, in turn, will also likely create more adherences to the values of the group.

Behavior

Specific dimensions of the culture itself can moderate the relationship between the cultural configuration and individuals' behavior. For example, in highly individualistic societies, a broader range of behaviors is sanctioned by societal norms than in highly collective societies. For example, in the US, individuality is encouraged, while in Japan "the nail that sticks out will be pounded down" (Kirkman and Shapiro, 1997). Therefore, in individualistic cultures an individual's behavior may not be as well predicted by other dimensions of the culture, or by the culture as a whole, than it is in collective cultures. Moreover, especially in collective cultures, people differentiate between: (1) "ingroup members," or groups of individuals with whom they share attributes that contribute to their positive social identity; and (2) "outgroup members," or groups with whom they do not share these attributes (Triandis, 1994; Triandis, Bontempo, Villareal, et al., 1988). Within collective cultures, then, behavior towards ingroup members may be more in line with cultural predictions than behavior towards outgroup members.

A work-group variable that will likely affect the relationship between culture and behavior is the group's stage of development. Tuckman (1965) argued that groups experience four stages: (1) forming, or the joining of members in a group; (2) storming, or the conflict that immediately results from struggles for power and leadership of the group; (3) norming, or the reaching of consensus on how the group will operate and what it will do; and (4) performing, or the actual accomplishment of tasks. Although other researchers have demonstrated that this lineal sequence has many variations (e.g., Gersick, 1989), there is little doubt that in the early life of a group, members have not yet negotiated consensus around how the group will operate or the types of things the group should do. During these stages, culture will have more of an impact on behavior since it will be used as the "default" set of assumptions from which to begin

(Bettenhausen and Murnighan, 1991). However, in later stages or after a period of punctuated change (Gersick, 1989), the group will have developed some idiosyncratic behavioral norms for carrying out work. Much of what happens in these latter stages will occur through shared behavior predicted by the group's characteristics rather than those of the national culture.

Situational moderators

In their recent essay on the state of the field of cultural psychology, Oyserman, Kemmelmeir, and Coon (2002, p. 113) highlight the importance of the situation in determining cognitive, affective, and behavioral consequences of culture. Specifically, they suggest that it is the "cultural-laden ways in which situations are construed – the subjective meaning they have for individuals" that ultimately determines culture's consequences. This approach integrates cultural psychology with social cognition by arguing that culture matters because it influences subjective construal of situations, and it is these subjective construals that should be the focus of our attention (Oyserman, Kemmelmeir, and Coon, 2002). Thus, culture influences the sense we make of social situations – what seems central versus peripheral, what is desirable or valuable, normative or accepted, ultimately influencing how information is perceived, encoded, processed and remembered. A related approach, "situated culture" focuses on everyday situations faced by individuals and argues that cultures differ in features of these situations and that these features carry with them certain ways of thinking about the self (Kitayama, 2002).

We argue that it is also useful to consider specific aspects of situations themselves, what we call "situational moderators" that can influence the relationship between cultural configurations and individual-level outcomes. Because of their familiarity to most management researchers, we will focus here on the set of environmental dimensions identified in the strategy and organizational design literature as having a contingent effect on the level of performance associated with a particular strategy or design. These dimensions include uncertainty, complexity, munificence, and volatility (Burns and Stalker, 1961; Downey, Hellriegel, and Slocum, 1975; Hickson, Hinings, Clegg, et al., 1988; Kotha and Nair, 1995; Lawrence and Lorsch, 1967). Recognizing that the degree of uncertainty or complexity (or any of these situational characteristics) is itself a matter of interpretation and perception that is open to cultural influences, we suggest that understanding the general (or average) perception of the characteristics in any given situation, and how that level of the situational moderator impacts culture's influence on outcomes, can provide important insights. We will illustrate the moderating capacity of situational characteristics here using different elements of the environment, including the political, economic, social, and technological arenas, to demonstrate the breadth of scope that must be considered in understanding situational impacts.

Perception

As described above, one of the main purposes for cognitive schemas is to filter stimuli: individuals tend to pay attention to stimuli that are identified as important by their schemas and to interpret the stimuli in ways consistent with the schemas (Lord and Foti, 1986). Schemas play a particularly influential role in the initial sorting out of highly uncertain situations – those in which many elements are simultaneously present and changing – since it is in these situations that the individual is exposed to a large amount of stimuli. After the uncertainty has been present for a while, however, the individual will refine his or her schema to incorporate the new stimuli and relationships (Feldman, 1986). Since culture provides an important basis for initial schema development, we would expect culture to be a better predictor of perception at the onset of high uncertainty than in relative certainty or long into a period of uncertainty.

For example, in the economic sphere immediately after the Korean currency crisis, Korean cultural leaders and the media identified the problem as individual consumers' overspending, and encouraged individual Koreans to do their part in turning the situation around. They implored people to stop spending money (especially on imports), to save electricity, to work for less pay, and, in sum, to "do your part in reducing the strain on the economy" (Jordan, 1997; Pollack, 1997). These perceptions and subsequent recommendations are consistent with a collective culture orientation, in which each person sacrifices his or her own interests for those of the whole group. This reaction contradicted economic experts who argued that the actions were more likely to lead to economic stagnation than to growth (Pollack, 1997). Culture was a much stronger predictor of perception during initial uncertainty than rational economic reasoning was.

Beliefs

People exposed to a richer, or more munificent, environment develop greater cognitive complexity – a more complex belief structure (Triandis, 1994; Trompenaars, 1993). When there are more stimuli and more relationships among stimuli in an environment that is not threatening, the individual develops more beliefs and more relationships among beliefs. Therefore, beliefs of individuals who have been exposed to a munificent and varied environment are less likely to be associated with culture than those of individuals who live in a more restricted environment.

This relationship can be seen perhaps most vividly with respect to the social environment. For example, many people who live in urban areas of multinational cities such as London, Toronto, and Hong Kong are exposed to cultural manifestations – including food, theatre, languages, and practices – originating from many parts of the world. These individuals often incorporate beliefs from other cultures into their own belief system in ways that differ from any of the original cultures. However, individuals from the same national cultures but more isolated areas of their countries do not have the opportunity to sample such exotic fare, and are more likely to maintain a belief structure more consistent with their national culture (Triandis, 1994).

Values

The relationship between an individual's culture and his or her values can also be moderated by

uncertainty in the environment, particularly by uncertainty related to volatility. Large changes in an individual's environment can affect values, especially if the changes threaten the stability of the individual's (or culture's) habitual way of life (Earley and Erez, 1997). In a society undergoing great changes, then, culture may be a weaker predictor of individual values than it is in societies undergoing less change.

This relationship can be seen in Russia, with respect to the political environment. Since the fall of Communism in 1991, individual Russians have embraced a wide variety of values. While some still value the hierarchy and traditions of Russia of the eighteenth century, others value a more western-style individualism and entrepreneurship (Ralston, Holt, Terpstra, et al., 1997). The same phenomenon has occurred in the Czech Republic, formerly part of Czechoslovakia, which was a member of the general alliance of communist countries. In 1989, Czechoslovakia underwent the "Velvet Revolution", after which the country split itself into two semi-autonomous republics, Czech and Slovakia, and created separate legislatures (Machann, 1991; McGregor, 1991). The Czech Republic is now an emerging capitalist system. As the new political and economic systems have unfolded, individuals' values appear to be evolving gradually as well (Earley, Gibson, and Chen, 1999; McGregor, 1991).

Behavior

The moderating relationship of situation on the role of culture in behavior can best be seen by classifying situations as "strong" or "weak" (Mischel, 1973; Shoda, Mischel, and Wright 1993). Strong situations are those in which environmental and social cues to behavior are clear, while weak situations do not present such unambiguous guides to behavior. An individual must interpret the events in weak situations with a more deliberate series of judgments to structure their own actions. Mischel (1973) and Shoda, Mischel, and Wright, (1993) suggest that individual differences (personality) influence action in weak situations, but that in strong situations individual differences are minimized. A parallel argument can be made for the influence of culture: in strong situations, cultural configuration will not predict behavior as much as it will in weak situations (Maznevski and Peterson, 1997).

This relationship can be illustrated with an example from the technological environment. In an organization, there may be very specific procedures and equipment for completing a task, such as tools for manufacturing and assembly, rules and computer programs for quality assessment and control, and software packages for components design. These are all strong situations. In other parts of the organization, a strategy design team may be given the ambiguous task to "develop a global go-to-market strategy for this new product line." This is a much weaker situation. In the strong situations, culture will influence behavior less than it will in the weak situations. Several researchers have obtained evidence that having standard scripts makes it much easier to transfer interorganizational knowledge because the process is standardized and does not have to be re-invented each time it occurs (Miner and Haunschild, 1995; Suchman, 1994; Zucker, 1987). Knowledge transfer is often ambiguous and uncertain, an inherently weak-situation process; by creating a strong situation with standard scripts, organizations decrease the ambiguity of the process and increase the likelihood that it will occur.

Discussion

We have presented a model which explicates numerous potential moderators of the relationship between the collective configuration of culture and the perceptions, beliefs, values, and behaviors of the people that belong to that culture. Using this approach, researchers can become much more specific about when culture matters, explaining more variance in individual outcomes across cultures and providing more insight for practicing managers. With so many moderators discussed, one begins to wonder whether culture ever matters at all. Our model does not imply that culture will have no influence on perceptions, beliefs, values, and behaviors. In fact, a large body of international management research has shown individual-level

differences associated with culture even without assessing the effect of these moderators, suggesting that the direct effect of culture is in fact quite pervasive (see Erez and Earley, 1993; Oyserman, Coon and Kemmelmeir, 2002 for reviews). To explain this, we return to the four mechanisms through which culture influences individual outcomes: passive cognitive, passive social, active cognitive, and active social. These mechanisms account for a large proportion of individuals' day-to-day information processing and social interaction, and it is only when the individual moves outside automatic mode – as influenced by the moderators identified here – that other elements will be more influential. Culture always matters, *but there are certain circumstances in which culture matters more, and others in which culture matters less.* We have attempted to present moderators that should help researchers and managers determine when culture matters more. We now turn to a discussion of implications for theory, research, and practice.

Implications for theory

This chapter highlights the importance of building and testing more complex relationships regarding the impact of culture on individual outcomes. One primary concern here is the challenge of crossing levels of analysis. As highlighted in the special forum in *Academy of Management Review* several years ago, this issue is just beginning to be incorporated into management research (Klein, Tosi, and Cannella, 1999). Given the centrality of culture (a collective construct) to international management involving the interaction of individuals (Bond, 2002; Oyserman, Coon, and Kemmelmeir, 2002; Morgeson and Hofmann, 1999), we suggest that international management research should be on the forefront of this type of inquiry. To expand this discussion, the relationships identified here could be elaborated upon in more detail, for example by linking different causal mechanisms with specific moderator variables.

In addition, much of the previous work on the impact of culture isolates one aspect of culture, usually individualism-collectivism, and examines its impact on people's behavior (e.g., Bochner, 1994; Cox, Lobel, and McLeod, 1991; Earley, 1989; Kim, Park, and Suzuki, 1990; Oyserman, Coon, and Kemmelmeir, 2002; Triandis, Bontempo, Villareal, *et al.*, 1988; Wagner, 1995). People's perceptions, beliefs, values, and behavior are likely to be influenced by more than one aspect of culture and more than one moderator of the relationship between culture and individual outcomes (Adler, 1997). Furthermore, aspects of culture are likely to work in concert (rather than singly) to form a more dynamic and complex explanation for individual outcomes (Kirkman and Shapiro, 1997). To be certain, the inclusion of multiple aspects of culture (i.e., one's cultural value "constellation") and multiple moderators must be balanced with pragmatic concerns such as survey lengths and the duration of interviews. However, to the extent that these limitations can be overcome, the inclusion of more variables will only ensure a more complete and relevant understanding of the complexity of culture.

Implications for research

Our literature review of cross-cultural studies revealed very few studies in which moderators of the relationship between culture and individual outcomes were measured (Earley, 1993 is an exception). We have pointed to a number of moderators that may affect the relationships between culture and individual outcomes. We believe that to advance the field of international management, future researchers must begin to include measures of moderators in their studies. To say that culture matters is not enough. International management research will advance to the extent that scholars can identify when culture is most likely to matter. We have provided direction for future research delineating which moderators may be most important depending upon whether investigators are examining perceptions, beliefs, values, or behavior.

We would also like to emphasize that our model necessitates changes in research design, particularly with regard to sampling and data analysis. Investigating the moderating effects we propose will require large, diverse samples. Statistical

analyses with moderated relationships require larger sample sizes to account sufficiently for additional variables and lower degrees of freedom (Nunnally and Bernstein, 1994). In addition, testing for moderation increases the probability of multicollinearity between main effects and interaction effects because the latter is basically a product of the former (Nunnally and Bernstein, 1994). The statistical "centering" of the interaction term will likely reduce the presence of multicollinearity, however (Aiken and West, 1991).

We also agree with Bond (2002) that is it particularly important for researchers to explore measurement techniques other than explicit, paper-and-pencil measures of declarative self-knowledge. For example, we view as promising differently focused measures such as ratings of others (Bond, Kwan, and Li, 2000), and different sources of ratings such as ratings by others (Leung and Bond, 2001), as well as interview-based content analysis of expressions of values, such as that pioneered by Gibson and Zellmer-Bruhn (2001). Fortunately, recent advances in statistical methods, including the increased accessibility of Hierarchical Linear Modeling for conducting regressions using data at multiple levels of analysis (Bryk and Raudenbush, 1992), should make this type of data analysis more feasible.

Implications for practice

As more and more managers become involved in the globalization of business, more fine-grained assistance is needed to help those managers take into account the important role of culture in affecting their employees' perceptions, beliefs, values, and behavior. This type of approach has been advocated at a general level by authors such as Adler (1997) and Earley and Erez (1997). However, managers have a need for more specific guidance. In an age of declining resources and increases in the rate of change, managers more than ever need help in focusing their time and energy more tightly. Once researchers have investigated the moderators we have discussed, we will be better able to make generalizations for managers about which of the moderators seem to be strongest, and subsequently make recommendations about the degree to which managers should include cultural considerations when designing organizations or policies.

Conclusion

Managers should always take culture into account when developing and implementing strategies or human resources practices in other cultures. Our experience in working with managers in these situations has suggested time and time again that there are very few instances, if any, that culture simply does not matter at all. Managerial responsibilities are often divided and focused on many different concerns simultaneously. With progress in these directions, we can begin to identify the particular times when an ignorance of culture will be highly detrimental to the success or failure of management initiatives in foreign cultures, and other times when the norms of culture will not be so salient. We hope that future research will provide an effective template for alerting managers to situations when they must focus their energy and take responsibility for the role of culture in their organizations' performance.

References

Abelson, R. P. 1981. "The psychological status of the script concept", *American Psychologist* 36: 715–29.

Adler, N. J. 1997. *International Dimensions of Organizational Behavior* (3rd edn). Cincinnati, OH: South-Western College Publishing.

and Bartholomew, S. 1992. "Academic and professional communities of discourse: generating knowledge on transnational human resource management", *Journal of International Business Studies* 23: 551–69.

Aiken, L. S. and West, S. G. 1991. *Multiple Regression: Testing and Interpreting Interactions*. Thousand Oaks, CA: Sage.

Bandura, A. 1997. *Self-efficacy: The Exercise of Control*. New York, NY: W. H. Freeman.

Bar-Tal, D. 1990. *Group Beliefs: A Conception for Analyzing Group, Structure, Processes and Behavior*. New York, NY: Springer-Verlag.

Benet, V. and Waller, N. G. 1995. "The big seven factors model of personality description: evidence for its cross-cultural generality in a Spanish sample", *Journal of Personality and Social Psychology* 69, 701–18.

Bettenhausen, K. L. 1991. "Five years of group research: what we have learned and what needs to be addressed", *Journal of Management* 17: 345–81.

and Murnighan, J. K. 1991. "The development and stability of norms in groups facing interpersonal and structural challenge", *Administrative Science Quarterly* 36, pp. 20–35.

Bochner, S. 1994. "Cross-cultural differences in the self-concept: a test of Hofstede's individualism/collectivism distinction", *Journal of Cross-Cultural Psychology* 25: 273–83.

Bond, M. H. 2002. "Reclaiming the individual from Hofstede's ecological analysis – A 20 year odyssey: comment on Oyserman et al. (2002)", *Psychological Bulletin* 128: 73–7.

Kwan, V. S. Y., and Li, C. 2000. "Decomposing a sense of superiority: the differential social impact of self-regard and regard for others", *Journal of Research in Personality* 34: 537–53.

Boyacigiller, N. A. and Adler, N. J. 1991. "The parochial dinosaur: organizational science in a global context", *Academy of Management Review* 16: 262–90.

Brannen, M. Y., Gomez, C., Peterson, M. F., Romani, L., Sagiv, L., and Wu, P. 2004. "People in organizations: culture, personality and social dynamics". in H. W. Lane, M. L. Maznevski, M. E. Mendenhall, and J. McNett (eds.), *The Blackwell Handbook of Global Management: A Guide to the Management of Complexity*. Malden, MA: Blackwell Publishing, pp. 26–54.

Brawley, L. R., Carron, A. V., and Widmeyer, W. N. 1988. "Exploring the relationship between cohesion and group resistance to disruption", *Journal of Sport and Exercise Psychology* 10: 199–213.

Brett, J. M. and Okumura, T. 1998. "Inter- and intracultural negotiation: U.S. and Japanese negotiators", *Academy of Management Journal* 41: 495–510.

Brown, M. H. and Hosking, D. M. 1986. "Distributed leadership and skilled performance as successful organization in social movements", *Human Relations* 39: 65–79.

Bryk, A. S. and Raudenbush, S.W. 1992. *Hierarchical Linear Models*. Newbury Park, CA: Sage.

Burns, T. and Stalker, G. M. 1961. *The Management of Innovation*. London: Tavistock Publications.

Byfield, T. 1997. "We erred when we stamped out our Canadian identity: name the four provinces that formed Canada", *The Financial Post*, p. 28.

Casimir, G. and Keats, D. 1996. "The effects of work environment and in-group membership on the leadership preferences of Anglo-Australians and Chinese Australians", *Journal of Cross-Cultural Psychology* 27: 436–57.

Chan, K.Y., and Drasgow, F. 2001. "Toward a theory of individual differences and leadership: Understanding the motivation to lead", *Journal of Applied Psychology* 86: 481–98.

Clugston, M., Howell, J.P. and Dorfman, P.W. 2000 "Does cultural socialization predict multiple bases and foci of commitment", *Journal of Management,* 26: 5–30.

Cohen, R. 1991. *Negotiating Across Cultures*. Washington, DC: United States Institute of Peace Press.

Cox, T.H., Lobel, S.A., and McLeod, P.L. 1991. "Effects of ethnic group cultural differences on cooperative and competitive behavior on a group task", *Academy of Management Journal* 34: 827–47.

Detweiler, R.A. 1978. "Culture, category width and attributions", *Journal of Cross-Cultural Psychology* 9: 259–84.

Digman, J.M. 1990. "Personality structure: Emergence of the rive-factor model", *Annual Review of Psychology* 41: pp. 417–40.

and Takemoto-Chock, N.K. 1981. "Factors in the natural language of personality: re-analysis, comparison, and interpretation of six major studies", *Multidisciplinary Behavior Review* 16: 149–70.

DiStefano, J.J. and Maznevski, M.L. 2000. "Creating value with diverse teams in global management", *Organizational Dynamics* 29: 45–63.

Downey, H.K., Hellriegel, D., and Slocum, J.W. Jr. 1975. "Environmental uncertainty: the construct and its application", *Administrative Science Quarterly* 20: 613–29.

Earley, P.C. 1989. "Social loafing and collectivism: a comparison of the United States and the People's Republic of China", *Administrative Science Quarterly* 34: 565–81.

1993. "East meets West meets Mideast: further explorations of collectivistic and individualistic work groups", *Academy of Management Journal* 36, 319–48.

and Erez, M. 1997. *The Transplanted Executive: Why You Need to Understand How Workers in Other Countries See the World Differently*. New York: Oxford University Press.

Gibson, C.B., and Chen, C.C. 1999. "'How did I do?' versus 'How did we do?' Cultural contrasts of performance feedback use and self-efficacy", *Journal of Cross-Cultural Psychology* 30: pp. 594–619.

and Gibson, C.B. 2002. *Multinational Teams: A New Perspective*. Lawrence Earlbaum and Associates: Mahwah, NJ.

and Sing, H. 1995. "International and intercultural management research: what's next?", *Academy of Management Journal* 28: pp. 327–40.

Eby, L.T., Adams, D.M., Russell, J.E.A., and Gaby, S.H. 2000. "Perceptions of organizational readiness for change: factors related to employees' reactions to the implementation of team-based selling", *Human Relations* 53: 419–42.

and Dobbins, G.H. 1997. "Collectivistic orientation in teams: an individual and group-level analysis", *Journal of Organizational Behavior* 18: 275–95.

Erez, M. and Earley, P.C. 1993. *Culture, Self-Identity, and Work*. Oxford: Oxford University Press.

and Somech, A. 1996. "Group productivity loss – the rule or the exception", *Academy of Management Journal* 39: 1513–37.

Feldman, J. 1986. "On the difficulty of learning from experience", in H.P. Jr. Sims and D.A. Gioia, *The Thinking Organization*. San Francisco, CA: Jossey-Bass Publishers, pp. 263–92.

2000. "Organizational routines as a source of continuous change", *Organization Science* 11: pp. 611–29.

Festinger, L. 1957. *A Theory of Cognitive Dissonance*. Palo Alto, CA: Stanford University Press.

Fishbein, M. and Ajzen, I. 1975. *Belief, Attitude, Intention and Behavior*. Reading, MA: Addison-Wesley.

Fiske, D. 1949. "Consistency of the factorial structures of personality ratings from different sources", *Journal of Abnormal Social Psychology* 44: 329–44.

Franke, R. H., Hofstede, G., and Bond, M. H. 1991. "Cultural roots of economic performance: A research note", *Strategic Management Journal* 12: 165–73.

Flynn, F. J., Chatman, J. A., and Spataro, S. E. 2001. "Getting to know you: the influence of personality on impressions and performance of demographically different people in organizations", *Administrative Science Quarterly* 46: 414–42.

Gabrielidis, C., Stephan, W. G., Ybarra, O., Dos Santos Pearson, V. M., and Villareal, L. 1997. "Preferred styles of conflict resolution: Mexico and the United States", *Journal of Cross-Cultural Psychology* 28: 661–77.

Gallois, C., Barker, M., Jones, E., and Callan, V. 1992. "Intercultural communication: evaluations of lecturers by Australian and Chinese students", in S. Iwawaki, Y. Kashima, and K. Leung (eds.), *Innovations in Cross-Cultural Psychology*. Amsterdam: Swets and Zeitlinger, pp. 86–102.

George, J. M. and Bettenhausen, K. L. 1990. "Understanding prosocial behavior, sales performance, and turnover: a group level analysis in a service context", *Journal of Applied Psychology* 75: 698–709.

Gersick, C. J. G. 1989. "Marking time: predictable transitions in task groups", *Academy of Management Journal* 32: 274–309.

Gibson, C. B. 1994. "The impact of national culture on organization structure: evidence from cross-cultural interviews", in S. B. Prasad (ed.), *Advances in International Comparative Management*, Vol. 9 Greenwich, CT: JAI Press, pp. 3–37.

1999. "Do they do what they believe they can? Group-efficacy beliefs and group performance across tasks and cultures", *Academy of Management Journal* 42: 138–52.

and Kirkman, B. L. 1999. "Our past, present, and future in teams: the role of human resource professionals in managing team performance", in A. I. Kraut and A. K. Korman (eds.), *Changing Concepts and Practices for Human Resource Management: Contributions from Industrial and Organizational Psychology*. San Francisco, CA: Jossey-Bass.

and Zellmer-Bruhn, M. 2001. "Metaphor and meaning: an intercultural analysis of the concept of teamwork", *Administrative Science Quarterly* 46: 274–303.

Goldstein, A. P., and Segall, M. H. 1983. *Aggression in Global Perspective*. New York: Pergamon.

Gomez, C. B., Kirkman, B. L., and Shapiro, D. L. 2000. "The impact of collectivism and ingroup/outgroup membership on the evaluation generosity of team members", *Academy of Management Journal* 43: 1097–106.

Gruenfeld, L. W. and Maceachron, A. E. 1975. "A cross-national study of cognitive style among managers and technicians", *International Journal of Psychology* 10: 27–56.

Gudykunst, W. B. 1983. *Intercultural Communication Theory*. Beverly Hills, CA: Sage.

Hall, E. T. 1976. *Beyond Culture*. New York, NY: Anchor Press/ Doubleday.

and Hall, M. 1988. *Hidden Differences: Doing Business with the Japanese*. New York, NY: Prentice Hall.

Harpaz, I., Honig, B., Coetsier, P. 2002. "A cross-cultural longitudinal analysis of the meaning of work and the socialization process of career starters", *Journal of World Business* 37: 230–44.

Hickson, D., Hinings, C. R., Clegg, S. R., Child, J., Aldrich, H., Karpik, L., and Donaldson, L. 1988. "Offense and defense: a symposium with Hinings, Clegg, Child, Aldrich, Karpik, and Donaldson", *Organization Studies* 9: 1–32.

Hinde, R. A. and Groebel, J. 1991. *Cooperation and Prosocial Behavior*. Cambridge, UK: Cambridge University Press.

Hofstede, G. 1980. *Culture's Consequences: International Differences in Work-Related Values*. Newbury Park: Sage.

1997. *Cultures and Organizations: Software of the Mind (Rev. ed.)*. New York, NY: McGraw-Hill.

2001. *Culture's Consequences: Comparing Values, Behaviors, Institutions and Organizations Across Nations*. Thousand Oaks, CA: Sage.

Hogan, R. 1986. *Hogan Personality Inventory*. Minneapolis, MN: National Computer Systems.

Isenberg, D. J. 1986. "Group polarization: a critical review and meta-analysis", *Journal of Personality and Social Psychology* 50: 1141– 51.

Jackson, S. E., Brett, J. F., Sessa, V. I., Cooper, D. M., Julin, J. A., and Peryronnin, K. 1991. "Some differences make a difference: individual dissimilarity and group heterogeneity as correlates of recruitment, promotions, and turnover", *Journal of Applied Psychology* 76: 675–89.

and Jackson, A. E. B. 1993. "Socialization amidst diversity: the impact of demographics on work team oldtimers and newcomers", in B. Staw and L. L. Cummings (eds.), *Research in Organizational Behavior*. Greenwich, CT: JAI Press, pp. 45–109.

Jenner, S. R. 1982. "Analyzing cultural stereotypes in multinational business: United States and Australia", *Journal of Management Studies* 19: 307–25.

Jordan, M. 1997. "South Koreans turn to thrift and patriotism to combat ills", *International Herald Tribune*, p. 1.

Kernis, M. H., Grannemann, B. D., Richie, T., and Hart, J. 1988. "The role of contextual factors in the relationship between physical activity and self-awareness", *British Journal of Social Psychology*, 27: 265–73.

Kilmann, R., Saxton, M. J., and Serpa, R. 1986. "Issues in understanding and changing culture", *California Management Review* 87–94.

Kim, K. I., Park, H., and Suzuki, N. 1990. "Reward allocations in the United States, Japan, and South Korea: a comparison of individualistic and collectivistic cultures", *Academy of Management Journal* 33: 188–98.

Kirkman, B. L. and Shapiro, D. L. 1997. "The impact of cultural values on employee resistance to teams: toward a model of globalized self-managing work team effectiveness", *Academy of Management Review*, 22: 730–57.

and Shapiro, D. L. 2000. "Understanding why team members won't share: An examination of factors related to employee receptivity to team-based rewards", *Small Group Research* 31: 175–209.

and Shapiro, D. L. 2001. "The impact of team members' cultural values on productivity, cooperation, and empowerment in self-managing work teams", *Journal of Cross-Cultural Psychology* 32: 597–617.

Lowe, K. B., and Gibson, C. B. 2006. "A quarter century of culture's consequences: a review of the empirical research incorporating Hofstede's Cultural Value Framework", *Journal of International Business Studies* 37: 285–320.

Rosen, B., Tesluk, P., and Gibson, C. B. 2004. "The impact of team empowerment on virtual team performance: the moderating role of face

to face interaction", *Academy of Management Journal* 47(2): 187–208.

Kitayama, S. 2002. "Culture and basic psychological theory – toward a system view of culture: commentary on Oyserman et al. (2002)", *Psychological Bulletin* 128: 89–96.

Klein, K. J. and Kozlowski, S. W. 2000. *Multilevel Theory, Research And Methods In Organizations*. Jossey-Bass: San Francisco.

Tosi, H., and Cannella, A. A. Jr. 1999. "Multilevel theory building: benefits, barriers, and new developments", *Academy of Management Review* 24: 243–8.

Kluckhohn, C. 1954. *Culture and Behavior*. New York, NY: Free Press.

Kluckhohn, F. and Strodtbeck, F. 1961. *Variations in Value Orientations*. Evanston, IL: Row, Peterson.

Kotha, S. and Nair, A. 1995. "Strategy and environment as determinants of performance: evidence from the Japanese machine tool industry", *Strategic Management Journal* 16: 497–518.

Lawler, I. E. E., Mohrman, S. A., and Ledford, Jr. G. E. 1995. *Creating High Performance Organizations: Practices and Results of Employee Involvement and Total Quality Management in Fortune 1000 Companies*. San Francisco, CA: Jossey Bass.

Lawrence, P. and Lorsch, J. 1967. *Organization and Environment*. Boston, MA: Harvard Business School Press.

Leung, K. 1988. "Some determinants of conflict avoidance", *Journal of Cross-Cultural Psychology* 19: 125–36.

Bhagat, R., Buchan, N. R., Erez, M., and Gibson, C. B. 2005. "Culture and international business: recent advances and future directions", *Journal of International Business Studies* 36: 357–78.

Su, S. K. and Morris, M. 2001. "Justice in the culturally diverse workplace: the problems of over and under emphasis of culture", in S. Gilliland, D. Steiner and D. Skarlicki (eds.), *Theoretical and Cultural Perspectives on Organizational Justice*. Greenwich, CT: Information Age Publishing, pp. 161–86.

and Bond, M. H. 2001. "Interpersonal communication and personality: self and other perspectives", *Asian Journal of Social Psychology* 4: 69–86.

Levine, J. M. and Moreland, R. L. 1990. "Progress in small group research", *Annual Review of Psychology* 41: 585–634.

Limerick, D. C. 1990. "Managers of meaning: From Bob Geldof's band aid to Astralian CEO's", *Organization Dynamics* 18: 22–33.

Littlepage, G. E., Cowart, L., and Kerr, B. 1989. "Relationships between group environment scales and group performance and cohesion", *Small Group Behavior* 20: 50–61.

Lord, R. G. and Foti, R. J. 1986. "Schema theories, information processing, and organizational behavior", in H. P. Jr. Sims and D. A. Gioia (eds.), *The Thinking Organization*. San Francisco, CA: Jossey-Bass Publishers, pp. 20–48.

Lorr, M. 1986. *Interpersonal Style Inventory: Manual*. Los Angeles, CA: Western Psychological Services.

Lytle, A. L., Brett, J. M., Barsness, Z., Tinsley, C. H., and Janssens, M. 1995. "A paradigm for quantitative cross-cultural research in organizational behavior", in B. M. Staw, and L. L. Cummings (eds.), *Research in Organizational Behavior* 17: 167–214.

Machann, C. 1991. "The 'ethnic situation' in Czechoslovakia after the revolution of November 1989", *Journal of Ethnic Studies* 18: 135–141.

Mann, L. 1980. "Cross-cultural studies of small groups", in H. C. Triandis and R. W. Brislin, (eds.), *Handbook of Cross-Cultural Psychology*, Vol. 5. Boston, MA: Allyn and Bacon, pp. 155–210.

Manz, C. C. and Sims, H. P. 1993. *Business Without Bosses: How Self-Managing Teams Are Building High Performance Companies*. New York, NY: Wiley.

Markus, H. and Kitayama, S. 1991. "Culture and self: implications for cognition, emotion, and motivation", *Psychological Review* 98: 224–53.

Maznevski, M. L. and Chudoba, K. 2000. "Bridging space over time: Global virtual team dynamics and effectiveness", *Organization Science* 11: 473–92.

and DiStefano, J. J. 1996. "The mortar in the mosaic: A new look at process and performance in diverse teams." Paper presented at Academy of Management Annual Meeting, Cincinnatti.

and Peterson, M. F. 1997. "Societal values, social interpretation, and multinational teams", in C. S. Granrose and S. Oskamp (eds.), *Cross-cultural Work Groups*, Thousand Oaks, CA: Sage, pp. 61–89.

McClelland, D. C. 1961. *The Achieving Society*. New York, NY: Van Nostrand Reinhold.

McGregor, J. P. 1991. "Value structures in a developed Socialist system: the case of Czechoslovakia", *Comparative Politics* 23: 181–200.

Meltzer, L. 1963. "Comparing relationships of individual and average variables to individual response", *American Sociological Review* 28: 117–23.

Meyer, A. D., Tsui, A. S., and Hinings, C. R. 1993. "Configurational approaches to organizational analysis", *Academy of Management Journal* 36, 1175–95.

Miller, J. G. 1984. "Culture and the development of everyday social explanation", *Journal of Personality and Social Psychology* 46: 961–78.

Miner, A. and Haunschild, P. 1995. "Population level learning", in B. Staw and L. Cummings (eds.), *Research in Organizational Behavior*. Greenwich, CT: JAI Press.

Mischel, W. 1973. "Toward a cognitive social learning reconceptualization of personality", *Psychological Review* 80: 252–83.

Mitchell, R. K., Smith, B., Seawright, K. W., and Morse, E. A. 2000. "Cross-cultural cognitions and the venture creation decision", *Academy of Management Journal* 43: 974–93.

Morgeson, F. P. and Hofmann, D. A. 1999. "The structure and function of collective constructs: implications for multilevel research and theory development", *Academy of Management Review* 24: 249–65.

Morris, M. H., Davis, D. L. and Allen, J. W. 1994. "Fostering corporate entrepreneurship: Cross-cultural comparisons of the importance of individualism versus collectivism", *Journal of International Business Studies*, 25, pp. 65–89.

Nunnally, J. C. and Bernstein, I. H. 1994. *Psychometric Theory* (3rd edn). New York, NY: McGraw-Hill.

O'Reilly, C. A., Caldwell, D. F., and Barnett, W. P. 1989. "Work group demography, social integration, and turnover", *Administrative Science Quarterly* 34: 21–37.

Organ, D. and Hammer, W. C. 1950. *Organizational Behavior*. Plano, TX: Business Publications.

Osterman, P. 1994. "How common is workplace transformation and who adopts it?", *Industrial and Labor Relations Review* 47: 751–782.

Oyserman, D., Coon, H. M., and Kemmelmeir, M., 2002. "Rethinking individualism and collectivism: evaluation of theoretical assumptions and meta-analysis", *Psychological Bulletin* 128: 3–72.

Kemmelmeir, M., and Coon, H. M. 2002. "Cultural psychology, a new look: reply to Bond (2002), Kitayama (2002), and Miller (2002)", *Psychological Bulletin* 128: 110–17.

Pelled, L. H., Eisenhardt, K. M., and Xin, K. R. 1999. "Exploring the black box: an analysis of work group diversity, conflict, and performance", *Administrative Science Quarterly* 44: 1–28.

Peterson, M. F., Smith, P. B., Akande, A., Ayestaran, S., Bochner, S., Callan, V., *et al.* 1995. "Role conflict, ambiguity, and overload: a 21-nation study", *Academy of Management Journal* 38: 429–52.

Pfeffer, J. 1983. "Organizational demography", in B. Staw and L. Cummings (eds.), *Research in Organizational Behavior*. Greenwich, CT: JAI Press, pp. 299–357.

and O'Reilly, C. 1987. "Hospital demography and turnover among nurses", *Industrial Relations* 36: 158–73.

Pick, A. D. 1980. "Psychological perspectives", in H. C. Triandis and W. Langer (eds.), *Handbook of Cross-Cultural Psychology: Basic Processes*. Boston, MA: Allyn and Bacon, pp. 117–153.

Pollack, A. 1997. "Will Korean frugality help or hurt?" *International Herald Tribune*, p. 7.

Pryor, J. B. and Ostrom, T. M. 1991. "Social cognition theory of group processes", in L. B. Resnick, J. M. Levine, and S. D. Teasley (eds.), *Perspectives in Socially Shared Cognition*. Washington, D.C.: American Psychological Association, pp. 147–183.

Ralston, D. A., Holt, D. H., Terpstra, R. H., and Kai-Cheng, Y. 1997. "The impact of national culture and economic ideology on managerial work values: a study of the United States, Russia, Japan, and China", *Journal of International Business Studies* 28: 177–207.

Rokeach, J. 1973. *The Nature of Human Values*. New York, NY: Free Press.

Roth, A. E., Prasnikar, V., Okuno-Fujiwara, M. and Zamir, S. 1991. "Bargaining and market behavior in Jerusalem, Ljubljana, Pittsburgh, and Tokyo: an experimental study", *The American Economic Review* 81: 1068–96.

Rousseau, D. M. 1995. *Psychological Cantracts in Organization*. London: Sage.

Sackmann, S. A. 1992. "Culture and subculture: an analysis of organizational knowledge", *Administrative Science Quarterly* 37: 140–61.

Schein, E. H. 1984. "Coming to a new awareness of organizational culture", *Sloan Management Review* 25: 3–16.

Schwartz, S. H. 1992. "Universals in the content and structure of values: theoretical advances and empirical tests in 20 countries", *Advances in Experimental Social Psychology* 25: 1–65.

Schwartz, S. H. 1994. "Beyond individualism/ collectivism: new cultural dimensions of values", in U. Kim, H. C. Triandis, C. Kagitcibasi, S.-C. Choi, and G. Yoon (eds.), *Individualism and Collectivism: Theory, Method, and Applications*. Thousand Oaks, CA: Sage Publications.

Shaw, J. B. 1990. "A cognitive categorization model for the study of intercultural management", *Academy of Management Review* 14: 626–45.

Shoda, Y., Mischel, W., and Wright, J. 1993. "The role of situational demands and cognitive competencies in behavior organization and personality coherence", *Journal of Personality and Social Psychology* 65: 1023–35.

Shweder, R. A. and LeVine, R. A. 1984. *Culture Theory: Essays on Mind, Self, and Emotion*. New York, NY: Cambridge University Press.

Singer, M. 1976. "Culture: a perceptual approach", in L. S. Samovar and R. E. Porter (eds.), *Intercultural Communication: A Reader* Belmont, CA: Wadsworth, pp. 110–119.

Suchman, M. C. 1994. "On advice of counsel: law firms and venture capital funds as information intermediaries in the structuration of Silicon Valley", Unpublished doctoral dissertation, Stanford University.

Tafarodi, R. W., Lang, J. M., and Smith, A. J. 1999. "Self-esteem and the cultural trade-off: evidence for the role of individualism-collectivism", *Journal of Cross-Cultural Psychology* 30: 620–40.

Tellegen, A. 1985. "Structures of mood and personality and their relevance to assessing anxiety with an emphasis on self-report", in A. Tuma and J. Maser (eds.), *Anxiety and the Anxiety Disorders*. Hillsdale, NJ: Erlbaum, pp. 681–706.

Toyne, B. 1976. "Host country managers of multinational firms: an evaluation of variables affecting their managerial thinking patterns", *Journal of International Business Studies* 7: 39–55.

Triandis, H. C. 1994. *Culture and Social Behavior.* New York, NY: McGraw-Hill.

Bontempo, R., Villareal, M. J., Asai, M., and Lucca, N. 1988. "Individualism and collectivism: cross-cultural perspectives on self-ingroup relationships", *Journal of Personality and Social Psychology* 54: 323–38.

Trompenaars, F. 1993. *Riding the Waves of Culture: Understanding Cultural Diversity in Business.* Avon: The Bath Press.

Tuckman, B. W. 1965. "Developmental sequences in small groups", *Psychology Bulletin* 63: 384–99.

Turner, J. C. 1987. *Rediscovering the Social Group.* Oxford, UK: Basil Blackwell.

Wade-Benzoni, K. A., Okumura, T., Brett, J., Moore, D. A., Tenbrunsel, A. E., and Bazerman, M. H. 2002. "Cognitions and behavior in asymmetric social dilemmas: a comparison of two cultures", *Journal of Applied Psychology* 87: 87–95.

Wagner, I. J. A. 1995. "Studies of individualism-collectivism: effects on cooperation in groups", *Academy of Management Journal* 38: 152–72.

Wagner, W. G., Pfeffer, J., and O'Reilley, C. C. 1984. "Organizational demography and turnover in top management groups", *Administrative Science Quarterly* 29: 74–92.

Wetlaufer, S. 1999. "Organizing for empowerment: an interview with AES's Roger Sant and Dennis Bakke", *Harvard Business Review* 77: 110–23.

Whitener, E. M., Maznevski, M. L., Saebo, S. R., and Ekelund, B. Z. 1999. "Testing the cultural boundaries of a model of trust: subordinate-manager relationships in Norway and the United States", paper presented at Academy of Management Annual Meeting, Chicago.

Witkin, H. A. 1967. "A cognitive-style approach to cross-cultural research", *International Journal of Psychology* 2: 233–50.

and Berry, I. W. 1975. "Psychological differentiation in cross-cultural perspective", *Journal of Cross-Cultural Psychology* 6: 4–87.

Wolfe, J. and Box, T. M. 1988. "Team cohesion effects on business game performance", *Simulations and Games* 19: 82–98.

Yang, K. and Bond, M. H. 1990. "Exploring implicit personality theories with indigenous or imported constructs: the Chinese case", *Journal of Personality and Social Psychology* 58: 1087–95.

Ziller, R. C. 1957. "Four techniques of group decision making under certainty", *Journal of Applied Psychology* 41: 384–8.

Zucker, L. 1987. "Institutional theories of organization", *Annual Review of Sociology* 13: 443–64.

PART II

Culture and Organization Theory

Culture and organization design: strategy, structure, and decision-making

RICHARD M. STEERS, LUCIARA NARDON, and CARLOS SANCHEZ-RUNDE

Cultural anthropologist Edward T. Hall relished using parables in his writings to make points about cultural differences that more serious scholarly treatments often obscure. One of his more popular parables continues to be salient today as organizations and their managers increasingly interact with their distant counterparts around the world. Hall (1960) recalled a time of a great flood that involved a monkey and a fish. When the flood came, the agile and experienced monkey quickly scrambled up a tree to escape the raging waters below. As she looked down from her safe perch, she noticed a poor fish struggling against the swift current. With the very best of intentions, she reached down and lifted the fish from the water, with predictable consequences for the fish. Unfortunately, as globalization takes hold around the world, more and more monkeys are increasingly trying to save more and more fish, frequently leading to confusion, misunderstandings, conflicts, and lost opportunities.

Most organizations today are increasingly going global, whether they wish to or not. In doing so, however, it would be incorrect to assume that these highly diverse organizations seek convergence in their strategies and structures for accomplishing their missions. Simply put, there is no such thing as a preferred global organization design. Many factors – including cultural differences – play important roles in determining how organizations are structured and work to achieve their goals. In this regard, organizational scholars risk losing their relevance to the extent that they lose sight of many of the key structural and managerial differences that proliferate around the world. This chapter is thus designed to encourage organizational scholars to pay increased attention to cultural and national differences as they work to develop the theories-in-use for tomorrow.

In this chapter, we provide a cross-cultural perspective on several interrelated issues relating to the design and structure of organizations. In particular, we begin with some observations that suggest a rethinking of management roles as they are influenced by, and in turn reinforce, cultural differences. Based on this, a comparative assessment of basic organization designs and their management implications in eight geographically dispersed countries is presented. Here we focus on general trends, not absolutes, realizing that all cultures manifest variations (both large and small) in the ways in which they influence national organizing frameworks. Next, general trends in employee participation and organizational decision-making across cultures are explored, again looking for general trends rather than doctrine. Finally, based on the materials discussed, suggestions for future research are suggested.

Rethinking the managerial role

A major conundrum in organizational studies is whether organizations are the products of managers or managers are the products of organizations. In point of fact, both are correct. Organizations and their managers exist in an often chaotic and interactive environment where causal relationships are not easily determined. Moreover, the cultural milieus in which these interactions transpire are themselves complex and highly interactive, and often lead to significant variations in the roles and responsibilities of senior and junior managers alike. As a result, in order to understand

71

both of these critical variables – management and organizations – it is necessary to view them under various cultural templates and examine the differences, nuances and all. We begin here with management and how views of management have (and in many cases, have not) evolved over time.

Traditional views of management

Definitions of *management* abound in the research literature on organizational studies. What is significant about these definitions, coming from all parts of the world, is their notable lack of much variance. Management is management, or so we are told. Dating from the early writings by Frederick Taylor, Henri Fayol, Max Weber, Mary Parker Follett, and others, in the late nineteenth and early twentieth centuries and continuing through to today, most writers have agreed that management involves the coordination and control of people, material, and processes to achieve specific organizational objectives as efficiently and effectively as possible. Indeed, business historian Claude George (1972) has discovered the roots of such a definition dating back to the ancient Samarians, Egyptians, Hebrews, and Chinese well over 3,000 years ago. Neither the concept nor the profession of management are new; indeed, they are a widely thought to be a central pillar of organized society.

Although this underlying definition remains the same, small variations around this theme can be found. Industrial engineers, dating from the time of scientific management proponent Frederick Taylor (1911), have long emphasized production or operations management and the necessity to structure jobs, people, and incentive systems in ways that maximized performance. Similarly, Henri Fayol (1916), also writing at the beginning of the twentieth century, emphasized the importance of standardized "principles" of management, including division of work, unity of command, unity of direction, and the subordination of personal interests to the general (i.e., organization's) interest. While Taylor focused on workers and Fayol focused on administrative structures, their mantra was the same: organizations must be managed through strength and logic.

Around this same time, social scientists and other academicians took a different perspective to the same phenomenon. Hugo Munsterberg (1913) launched investigations into the application of psychological principles to management and workers. In the process, he created the field of industrial psychology. In his book entitled *Psychology and Industrial Efficiency*, he asserted that the aim of this new discipline was "to sketch the outlines of a new science, which is to intermediate between the modern laboratory psychology and the problem of economics." Meanwhile, Max Weber (1927, English language edition) wrote extensively about how organizations organize and operate – or, more accurately, *should* organize and operate. Weber introduced the concept of "bureaucracy" as the most perfect form of organization. Obviously, this term has taken on very different and negative connotations in recent years, but this was its original meaning. As originally conceived, rules governed everything and little was left to chance. People were hired and promoted based on qualifications, not unlike the ancient Chinese civil service system at the time of Confucius. Power and authority were vested in offices, not individuals. However, even here, the conclusion was the same: rules and standard operating procedures, uniformly enforced by competent managers, would lead to efficient operations. The goal remained unchanged.

Now consider the advice of contemporary writers on management. While contemporary writers have added some depth to the ongoing dialog about the nature and role of management, they have not added much breadth. Consider two contemporary definitions of management (Robbins and Coulter, 2007; Hitt, Black, and Porter, 2007): "Management involves coordinating and overseeing the work activities of others so that their activities are completed efficiently and effectively," and management is "the process of assembling and using sets of resources in a goal-directed manner to accomplish tasks in an organizational setting." Once again, the desired end state remains unchanged.

This stability in our conception of management sees the managerial role as being one and the same across time and space. Indeed, in one of the most frequently cited studies of management, Henry Mintzberg (1973, 1993) concluded that "managers' jobs are remarkably alike," whether we are looking at foremen, company presidents, or government administrators. In the end, "the prime purpose of the manager is to ensure that his organization serves its basic purpose – the efficient production of specific goods and services." Mintzberg goes a step further and suggests that all managers serve ten basic managerial roles in varying degrees. These include; figurehead; leader; liaison; monitor; disseminator; spokesperson; entrepreneur; disturbance handler; resource allocator; and negotiator. These traits, in turn, can be organized into three clusters: (1) an *interpersonal* role, focusing on building and leading effective groups and organizations; (2) an *informational* role, focusing on collecting, organizing and disseminating relevant information in a timely fashion; and (3) a *decisional* role, focusing on making creative strategic and tactical decisions on behalf of the organization and securing broad-based support for such actions.

Culture and management practice

This line of reasoning seems to ignore, or at least downplay, the significant role that cultural differences can play in both the conceptualization and practice of management around the world. Consider, for example, how managers from around the globe describe the unique management styles found in their home countries: Malaysians expect their managers to behave in a manner that is humble, modest, and dignified.[1] Iranians seek power and strength in their managers. The French expect their managers to be cultivated – highly educated in the arts and mathematics. The most important mission for a Japanese manager is to develop a healthy relationship with his or her employees where employees and managers share the same fate; management is not seen as a dictatorship. Top managers in Japan must have an ability to manage people by leading them. Nigerians expect organizations to duplicate among managers and employees the social patterns also found at social and even tribal levels. Peruvian employees look for decisiveness and authority in their managers, even to the point of easily resisting attempts at introducing participation schemes. Americans are generally described as being schizophrenic in their choice of

managers; some people like leaders who empower and encourage their subordinates, while others prefer leaders who are bold, forceful, confidant, and risk-oriented. Finally, the Dutch tend to emphasize egalitarianism and are skeptical about the value of a manager. Terms like 'leader' and 'manager' sometimes carry a stigma. If a parent is employed as a manager, Dutch children will sometimes not admit it to their schoolmates.

One of the more interesting attempts to study culture as it relates to managerial roles was conducted by Andre Laurent (1983). He focused his attention on understanding the normative managerial roles (that is, what is expected of managers) and discovered significant differences across cultures. He asked managers from different cultures a series of questions dealing with effective management. His results demonstrate wide variations in responses across cultures, as shown in table 4.1. If managers from different countries differ so much in their descriptions of the correct managerial role, it is no wonder that significant differences can be found in actual management style across national boundaries.

A similar study conducted by Charles Hampden-Turner and Fons Trompenaars (1993) also found significant differences across managers based on culture, as shown in table 4.2. For example, managers in the US, Sweden, Japan, Finland, and Korea showed more overall drive and initiative than leaders in Portugal, Norway, Greece, and the UK. Likewise, managers in Sweden, Japan, Norway, and the US tended to be more willing to delegate authority than leaders in Greece, Portugal, Spain, and Italy. These findings, along with those of Laurent, suggest clearly that effective managerial behavior can easily vary across cultures.

Other studies support this conclusion. For example, one study found that British managers were more participative than their French or German counterparts (Hodgetts and Luthans, 2003). Two possible reasons were suggested for this. First, the UK is more egalitarian than France and the political environment supports this approach. And second, top British managers tend not to be involved in the day-to-day affairs of the business and delegate

---

[1] Personal communications to the authors by managers attending MBA and executive programs.

Table 4.1 Cultural differences in the ideal managerial role

Country	Percent of Managers Who Agree with Each Statement		
	"Managers must have the answers to most questions asked by subordinates."	*"The main reason for a chain of command is so people know who has authority."*	*"It is OK to bypass chain of command to get something done efficiently."*
China	74%	70%	59%
France	53%	43%	43%
Germany	46%	26%	45%
Indonesia	73%	83%	51%
Italy	66%	–	56%
Japan	78%	50%	–
Netherlands	17%	31%	44%
Spain	–	34%	74%
Sweden	10%	30%	26%
United States	18%	17%	32%
United Kingdom	27%	34%	35%

Source: Data from Andre Laurent reported in J. Saee. 2005. *Managing Organizations in a Global Economy*. Mason, OH: Thompson/Southwestern, pp. 39–42.

many key decisions to middle and lower-level managers. The French and Germans, by contrast, tend to prefer a more work-centered, authoritarian approach. While it is true that German codetermination leads to power sharing with employees throughout the organization, some have argued that this has resulted not from German culture but rather from German laws. By contrast, Scandinavian countries make wide use of participative leadership approaches, again following from their somewhat more egalitarian culture.

Meanwhile, Japanese managers tend to be somewhat authoritarian but at the same time listen to the opinions of their subordinates and involve them in key decisions. One study found that Japanese managers place greater confidence in the skills and capabilities of their subordinates than their counterparts in other cultures (Abbeglen and Stalk, 1985). Another feature of Japanese leadership is an inclination to give subordinates ambiguous, instead of highly specific goals. That is, many Japanese managers tell their workers what they want in a general way, but leave it to the workers to determine the details and the work plan. This contrasts sharply with typical US managers, who like to take a hands-on, management-by-objectives approach to project management.

To illustrate this point, let us return to Mintzberg's ten managerial roles. Although this model was initially designed around North American managers, it can also be useful in exploring on a conceptual level how culture and managerial roles can intersect. For the sake of example, table 4.3 illustrates how each of the ten managerial roles can be influenced by cultural differences. For example, considerable research has indicated that most people in individualistic cultures prefer managers who take charge, while most people in collectivistic cultures prefer managers who are more consultative. Similarly, managers in high context cultures frequently make extensive use of the context surrounding a message to get their point across, while managers in low context cultures tend to rely almost exclusively on specific and detailed messages and ignore much of the message context. In short, the managerial role keeps changing – not necessarily in major ways, but certainly in important ways – as we move across borders.

The strategic management cycle: a model

Based on this research, it is possible to develop a schematic representation highlighting the manner in which managers and managerial action interact

Table 4.2 Culture and desirable managerial characteristics

Country	Manager's Sense of Drive and Initiative	Country	Manager's Willingness to Delegate Authority
US	74	Sweden	76
Sweden	72	Japan	69
Japan	72	Norway	69
Finland	70	US	66
Korea	68	Singapore	65
Netherlands	67	Denmark	65
Singapore	66	Canada	64
Switzerland	66	Finland	63
Belgium	65	Switzerland	62
Ireland	65	Netherlands	61
France	65	Australia	61
Austria	63	Germany	61
Denmark	63	New Zealand	61
Italy	62	Ireland	60
Australia	62	United Kingdom	59
Canada	62	Belgium	55
Spain	62	Austria	54
New Zealand	59	France	54
Greece	59	Italy	47
United Kingdom	58	Spain	44
Norway	55	Portugal	43
Portugal	49	Greece	38

Source: Adapted from C. Hampden-Turner and F. Trompenaars. 1993. *The Seven Cultures of Capitalism*. New York, NY: Doubleday. Findings are expressed in percentages of agreement by managers.

with several of the more macro aspects of organizations, including their mission and values, strategy and goals, and structure. Historically, these relationships have been seen largely in terms of a one-way causal relationship. That is, mission determines strategy, which in turn determines structure, which governs management practice, which ultimately determines the extent to which the organization succeeded in achieving its mission. More recent evidence, as discussed below, suggests a far more complex and interactive relationship (see figure 4.1).

Specifically, while mission and values may help determine an organization's initial strategy and goals – at least in the early years of the venture – organization design and even management practices can also influence strategy in significant ways, especially as the organization matures and

is confronted by new challenges and economic realities. Likewise, strategy can influence structure, but so too can management practices. Finally, these interactive relationships are played out in a business environment that is itself multifaceted and interactive. This includes such external factors as geographic location; the cultural milieu(s) in which organizations work; legal conventions and local customs; variations in political and institutional support; a country or region's factor endowments; the specific sector of the economy where the organization does business (e.g., industry vs. services); available investments, technologies, and markets; and environmental challenges and goals. In other words, as will be discussed below, the simple strategy-structure-management paradigm in found to be sorely lacking in explanatory power as organization theory crosses borders.

Table 4.3 Cultural influences on managerial roles

Managerial Roles	Differences Across Cultures
Interpersonal Roles	
Figurehead	Figureheads have considerable symbolic value in some cultures; in others, being described as a figurehead is not seen as a compliment.
Leader	Individualistic cultures prefer highly visible "take charge" leaders; collectivistic cultures prefer more consultative leaders.
Liaison	Some cultures prefer informal contacts based on long-standing personal relationships; others prefer to use official representatives.
Informational Roles	
Monitor	Culture often influences both the extent of information monitoring and which specific information sources receive greatest attention.
Disseminator	In some cultures, the context surrounding a message is more important than the message itself; in others, the reverse is true.
Spokesperson	Culture often influences who is respected and seen as a legitimate spokesperson for an organization.
Decisional Roles	
Entrepreneur	Some cultures are highly supportive of innovation and change; others prefer the status quo and resist change.
Disturbance handler	Some cultures resolve conflict quietly; others accept and at times encourage a more public approach.
Resource allocator	Hierarchical cultures support differential resource allocations; egalitarian cultures prefer greater equality or equity in distributions.
Negotiator	Some cultures negotiate all items in a proposed contract simultaneously; others negotiate each item sequentially.

Source: Adapted from H. Mintzberg. 1973. *The Nature of Managerial Work*. New York, NY: Harper & Row and R. M. Steers and L. Nardon. 2006. *Managing in the Global Economy*. Armonk, NY: M. E. Sharpe.

Stakeholders and strategic choice

A key responsibility of management is to establish a coherent mission and a strategic plan to guide the firm in the efficient use of its financial, physical, technological, and human resources towards a clearly stated objective. In other words, strategy guides both structure and management, at least in theory. However, as was noted in the previous section, other factors, including local beliefs, values, and prevailing social norms, often play a role in the final determination of the outcomes. Just as these outside factors can influence organization design, so too can they influence strategy (see figure 4.1). In this section, we will examine how such differences can influence strategic considerations, including the role of stakeholders, the strategy-structure nexus, and various institutional factors.

Stakeholders and strategy formulation

Not surprisingly, a company's stakeholders (e.g., investors, customers, employees, etc.) can have a major influence on both the determination of the company's mission and its strategy. Various stakeholders place demands, expectations, and constraints on enterprise activity and, obviously, these demands frequently differ across the various stakeholders, some wanting better return on their investment and others that was a more socially or environmentally responsible organization. Most managers understand this. However, what is often overlooked is the fact that the nature and power of a stakeholder group can be influenced by the predominant culture in which the enterprise does business. We refer to this as the difference between a *centralized* and a *distributed* stakeholder model.

For example, as shown in figure 4.2, some companies routinely face a stakeholders group where power and influence is fairly centralized. In Korea, Mexico, the UK, and the US, for example, investors, customers, and governments often have considerable influence over enterprise mission and strategy, while employees and the public-at-large do not. At the same time, in Germany, Japan, and

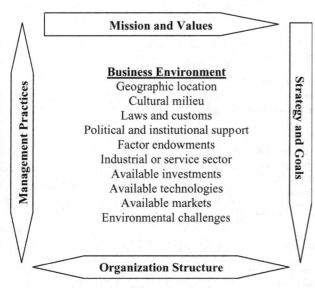

Figure 4.1 The strategic management cycle: a model

Sweden, the opposite situation often exists. That is, while investors, customers, and governments sometimes have a major influence over missions and strategies so, too, do employees and the public at large. Moreover, American or British firms doing business in Sweden or Germany, for example, often face this broader or more distributed stakeholder group and must accommodate these different constituencies.

To see how variations in the stakeholder's model can influence strategy, consider Volkswagen AG (Kothen, McKinley, and Scherer, 1999). This company has consistently pursued two seemingly contradictory goals: remaining a sales leader in the global auto industry while at the same time building and maintaining what some call a "worker's paradise" for its employees. On several occasions, however, these twin goals have come under attack as global auto sales plummeted. During one of these crises, sales dropped 20 per cent in one year, requiring a massive reduction in working hours by company employees. Indeed, the company determined that is had 30,000 more workers than it needed in Germany alone. Its supervisory board concluded that poor economic conditions would likely remain for several years and that in order to survive it had to find a way to quickly reduce its operating costs by 20 per cent to match the decline in sales.

However, as the company faced this challenge, the business and social environment in which key decisions would be made differed sharply from those the company would have faced in the US. Twenty per cent of company stock is owned by the state of Lower Saxony, where the company's principle manufacturing facilities are located. In addition, 90 per cent of all employees in Germany are unionized. Since the company's union contract required approval of over 80 per cent of the shareholders on all-important decisions, any cost-cutting plan that involved large lay-offs was highly problematic. Lower Saxony and the IG-Metall union also had strong representation on the company's supervisory board, where cost reduction strategies would be openly discussed. As a result, major lay-offs were not a viable option.

In addition to its governance structure, Volkswagen had spent decades developing a culture of cooperation and inclusion among all of its employees. Key features of this culture included the widespread dissemination of detailed information on the state of the company to employees, IG-Metall union, and works councils; a receptive climate for unions; informal codetermination in advance of formal decisions; an emphasis on consensus in decision-making; and a norm of implementing decisions once they are made.

Centralized stakeholder model

Distributed stakeholder model

Figure 4.2 Centralized vs. distributed stakeholder models

In creating and supporting this culture, VW was by no means abandoning its objectives of profitability and shareholder value. Instead, it believed (like many German companies) that all of the principal stakeholders of the company – including employees – should be protected in making major corporate decisions. In other words, capital and labor were seen as joint responsibilities of the company. From the standpoint of top management, VW had to find a solution that was acceptable to both sides. On the one hand, a reduction in labor costs was required to enhance operating efficiency and competitiveness, particularly in the face of reduced demand for its product. On the other hand, the method of achieving this cost reduction had to be acceptable to rank and file employees. Had managers in other countries (e.g., Australia, UK, US) faced this dilemma, the decision process would

probably have been much simpler due to the fewer powerful stakeholders at the table.

The strategy-structure nexus

Strategy experts offer very clear advice to global managers: first, create a specific, realistic, and clearly understood mission (or purpose) for a global enterprise. Next, articulate precisely what strategies will be employed in support of this mission. Then, managers should organize or reorganize the available human, physical, and financial resources and link them to appropriate management systems in order to maximize the collective (and hopefully integrated) efforts directed towards strategic goal attainment. Finally, once operations have begun, managers should apply a variety of control mechanisms to insure that the organization remains on track. Information on the effectiveness of the control systems then feeds back in a decreasing fashion to raise issues or questions at every stage along the path.

The problem here is that things are never as simple as they seem to be in theory. Organizations typically exist in highly complex and conflicting environments where managers must often act with an absence of crucial information. Moreover, as noted above, cultural differences are ever present to confuse things further. In the face of this uncertainly, there is seldom one best design for any organization. Rather, organizations and their managers must identify a design that best supports their overall global strategy.

Unfortunately, this basic paradigm raises a conundrum for many managers. Most strategy scholars suggest that there is a rational sequence between strategy and structure in which the former precedes the latter. Hence, a "rational" company first determines its overall goals and objectives and then designs (or redesigns) its organization structure to support the strategy. Unfortunately, while this practice may be common in the west, it is less common in other parts of the world, where local considerations often come into play. That is, the strategy-structure relationship is to a degree culture-bound. In many east Asian countries, for example, companies often first consider what resources they currently have – including human resources – and then, and only then, consider what strategies might best capitalize on these resources.

This "inverted" tendency can be explained by several factors. First, in many countries (not including the UK or US), it is sometimes very difficult to dismiss current employees, so managers are often more likely to consider how best to use their current employees. Labor laws and social legislation in the Netherlands, Germany, and the Scandinavian countries, for example, make it both difficult and costly to lay employees off, while in Japan, Malaysia, and Thailand, managers can lose face by demonstrating that they cannot make full use of the people they have. Secondly, in countries that use some form of reciprocal exchange relationships that are developed over time (e.g., *guanxi* in China), it is not always easy to make major changes in strategic partners or to find new ones. These two factors often create organizational inertia that is changed only with great difficulty or crisis.

As an example, much has been written about Nissan's first non-Japanese CEO, Carlos Ghosn (*The Economist*, 2007). For Ghosn and his top management team, deciding on an appropriate revised corporate strategy and organization design was not an easy task. In the end, Nissan adapted a number of "western" management methods to a Japanese company with considerable success. While some small structural changes were made to fit Nissan's new global strategy, many others were not. At the same time, however, Nissan competitors, Toyota and Honda, continue to make use of the more traditional Japanese structures and strategies – at least in their Japanese facilities. This seeming discrepancy raises several questions: Who decides what approach to structure and strategy is superior? How do organizations know when they have the best design? And who gets to define "best?"

Culture and institutional support

In addition to culture's influence on which stakeholder model (centralized or distributed) is implemented, culture can also influence the scope and nature of a country's institutional support for its industries (see table 4.4). Consider Germany's *Mittelstand* firms (SMEs in English), where an obsession with technology and quality has led to a loss of competitiveness in many global markets where price is a major determining factor in purchases. Instead of seeking major cost-cutting, many of these firms opted instead to sell exclusively in markets that preferred quality over price. In doing so, product quality (even at high costs) turned from a liability into an asset, and in this German institutions played an important role. German tax policies support SME firms and the German government provides financing for the country's expansive apprenticeship and training programs.

A company-specific example of institutional support can be seen in the case of Korea's Hyundai Motor Company. Hyundai's first entries into the global car markets were disappointing. Product quality was so poor that even low prices could

Table 4.4 Core cultural dimensions for select countries

Country Clusters	Hierarchy-Equality	Individualism-Collectivism	Mastery-Harmony	Monochronism-Polychronism	Universalism-Particularism
Anglo Cluster (e.g., Canada, UK, US)	Moderately egalitarian	Strongly individualistic	Strongly mastery-oriented	Strongly monochronic	Moderately universalistic
East/Southeast Asian Cluster (e.g., China, Japan, Malaysia)	Strongly hierarchical	Strongly collectivistic	Strongly-harmony-oriented	Moderately monochronic	Strongly particularistic
Germanic Cluster (e.g., Germany)	Moderately egalitarian	Moderately individualistic	Moderately mastery-oriented	Moderately monochronic	Strongly universalistic
Latin American Cluster (e.g., Mexico)	Moderately hierarchical	Moderately collectivistic	Moderately harmony-oriented	Strongly polychronic	Strongly particularistic
Latin European Cluster (e.g., France)	Moderately hierarchical	Moderately collectivistic	Moderately harmony-oriented	Moderately polychronic	Moderately particularistic
Sub-Sahara African Cluster (e.g., Nigeria)	Strongly hierarchical	Strongly collectivistic	Moderately harmony-oriented	Moderately polychronic	Strongly particularistic

Note: These core cultural dimension ratings represent central tendencies for selected country clusters (see Chapter 1 for details). Variations, sometimes substantial, around these central tendencies can be found in all clusters and countries.

not offset them. Over the years, Hyundai reengineered, not just its cars, but its whole company to the point where its cars are now ranked among the best in the world. Even so, the image of low, or at least mediocre, quality persisted, despite award after award for product quality from 2006 to 2008. The question was repeatedly raised how Korean-made cars could possibly be equivalent to up-scale German or Japanese cars. Ultimately, the company launched a new advertising campaign aimed at convincing consumers that a Hyundai may not be the high-status choice but it was certainly the intelligent choice (i.e., value for money), a strategy successfully used by Sweden's Volvo many years earlier. Hyundai's strategy was aided in no small way by a long history of government support for the country's heavy industries. This occurred largely through the industrial policy of the Korean government, which included government financial support, access to emerging technologies, and restricted markets for foreign imports.

On a more macro level, compare Japan and the US in terms of how their institutional environments may affect a company's strategic choice. If there is a principal difference in the business strategies of Japanese and US firms, it is Japan's preoccupation with gaining market share as opposed to a US preoccupation on short-term net profits or higher stock prices (Kono and Clegg, 2001).

This fundamental difference results from several differences in the two business environments that allow many Japanese firms to take a longer-term perspective than their US competitors. The institutional environment in which most US firms operate is characterized by a distant and oftentimes adversarial business-government relationship, where government is the principal regulator as opposed to being a partner. In addition, the principal purpose of a company in the US is to maximize stockholder wealth. Investors stress short-term transactions and returns on investment. A clear link exists between earnings per share and stock price. Managers are frequently offered stock options and large bonuses for superior (short-term) performance. Finally, undervalued companies are frequently subject to hostile takeovers.

Meanwhile, the Japanese institutional environment is significantly different. Strong and relatively permanent cooperative business-government relations permeate the business landscape, including government targeting of strategic industries and support of local industries. The principal purpose of a company is to build value over the long term to benefit investors, employees, and nation. Investors stress long-term stock appreciation instead of short-term earnings per share. Dividends are often paid at a constant rate as a percentage of par value of stock, not as a percentage of profits. Managers are seldom offered stock options or large bonuses for superior performance. Few outside board members are present to defend stockholder interests. Finally, undervalued companies are often protected by sister companies from outside takeovers (see below).

As a result of these differences, Japanese firms are often better positioned to focus their attention on attaining long-term strategic objectives (e.g., beating competitors) instead of immediate financial objectives. This competitive advantage occurs for three principal reasons: first, low profits and high retained earnings are more available to support growth. Second, close relationships with banks often allow the use of heavy debt to support growth. And, finally, Japanese stockholders routinely accept low dividends and management's absolute control over the firm.

Within this institutional framework, many Japanese firms are able to develop strategic plans to compete aggressively against western firms by using one or more of the following strategies. First, Japanese firms often compete with high-value products where the company can add value with knowledge instead of some other factor. For example, many Japanese firms tend to compete based on superior technology instead of cost (e.g., cameras, electronics, avionics). A highly educated and relatively highly paid workforce supports this strategy. Second, Japanese firms often stress continual improvements in quality and productivity to minimize costs and remain ahead of competitors. Japan's use of just-in-time production and TQM quality control systems are legendary in this regard. And, finally, many Japanese firms capitalize on the resources of their broad-based business networks, the *keiretsu* (see below). For example, Japanese companies routinely get financing from group banks and use group-based trading companies for product or services distribution.

Using these strategies, Japanese firms generally follow an incremental sequence of tactics to capture targeted markets. First, they enter a market at the low end with high quality products. Through continuous improvement, they then move to penetrate the market and build customer loyalty. Next, they move upscale in the market where profit margins are more substantial. Overseas manufacturing facilities are opened when a sufficient overseas market exists to ensure manufacturing economies of scale. Finally, profits from the venture are re-invested in improving existing products or developing new ones to remain one step ahead of competitors. The end result of this strategy is to force competitors to play a continual game of catch-up until their resources are depleted and they leave the market.

What we find, then, are instances where systematic differences can be found across cultures as they influence stakeholder composition and motivations and decisions relating to strategic choice. The theoretical and research implications of this will be discussed later in this chapter.

Organizing frameworks

If comparisons across cultures are done with sufficient precision, valuable lessons can be learned concerning why companies are often organized based on different principles in different parts of the world. Consider the example of Intel. As an Intel executive recently observed:

> Intel is not a very hierarchical company so a formalized organization structure is not a particularly good representation of how the company works. At the highest level, Intel is organized into largely autonomous divisions. It uses matrix management and cross-functional teams including IT, knowledge management, human resources, finance, legal, change control, data warehousing, common directory information management, and cost reduction teams (to name a few) to rapidly adapt to changing conditions. (www.Intel.com, 2006).

Yet Intel is not organized like many of its US competitors, including Hewlett-Packard, Apple, and IBM. Similarly, companies can also be structured very differently across national boundaries. That is, Intel is not organized like Hitachi, Matsushita, and Toshiba in Japan or BASF, Bosch, and SAP in Germany or Infosys, Tata, and Wipro in India.

These differences can prove useful when attempting to understand how global firms operate around the world. A company's unique organization design is like its own personal fingerprint. It can provide insights into a company's character, values, ambitions, management systems, and operating procedures. Comparing such designs can help us understand how cultural differences can influence how businesses operate and managers manage.

To this end, we focus here on comparing typical organization designs in eight geographically dispersed countries: China, Japan, France, Germany, Malaysia, Mexico, Nigeria, and the US. We highlight ways in which cultural differences can influence the methods by which companies structure and manage their organizations to do business in the global economy. This is done using the *core cultural dimensions* discussed in Chapter 1. In this overview, however, some caution is in order. First, space does not permit a detailed examination of companies in each culture; instead, we present overviews painting with broad strokes. Moreover, while this discussion is aimed at highlighting some organizational differences across the eight cultures, considerable variations often exist within each country. In other words, these comparisons are intended to highlight different trends; they are not meant as monolithic descriptions of culture and organization design. We begin with a look inside a typical US business organization.

The US corporation

Identifying a "typical" company in any culture is a challenge, but perhaps nowhere is this challenge more acute than in US firms. Like everywhere else, US companies reflect the culture(s) where they do business, and since the US is so strongly multicultural, it is not surprising to find major differences across companies – even in similar industries. Still, it is possible to develop a general portrait of what such a company looks like in terms of its basic organizing structure and management processes.

To accomplish this, it is useful to first consider how we might describe American culture. Based on the "Anglo" core cultural dimensions discussed

in Chapter 1 and summarized in table 4.4, we might begin by suggesting that the dominant central tendencies of American culture are moderately egalitarian, strongly individualistic, strongly mastery-oriented, strongly monochromic, and moderately universalistic (Nardon and Steers, 2009).[2] This description helps us build a platform – albeit an imprecise one – for further analysis.

Based on this overview, what happens when we add to this picture the observations of people who have spent considerable time with Americans? Journalists and social scientists from various countries have tried to do this for many years (Harris, Moran, and Moran, 2004). While acknowledging that the US probably has greater diversity than many other countries, these writers have nonetheless tried to characterize Americans using a small number of adjectives.

For starters, Americans tend to be highly individualistic. Perhaps no other country in the world stresses individual rights and responsibilities more than the US. Here, success is often seen as being determined by personal effort, and it is important to stay out of other people's business. At the same time, Americans tend to be materialistic. As a society that is focused on achievement, material possessions often represent symbols of success and conspicuous consumption can become a lifestyle. This belief often leads to a short-term focus that requires considerable energy to achieve immediate results. Americans also tend to be informal. They are often uncomfortable with formality and are quick to use first names and discuss personal details with new acquaintances. Many people also feel that the typical American is somewhat linear. They tend to be single-minded in the pursuit of their objectives and often rush headlong towards their goals with a determination that can border on obsession. They do things 24/7 and are never far from their cell phones, laptops, and BlackBerrys. Work frequently takes precedence over family and friends.

In addition, Americans can at times be a bit impatient. Time is seen as a measurable – and sometimes marketable – commodity that should be used wisely in the pursuit of one's objectives, whether business or pleasure. Compared to many other cultures, Americans are also more risk-oriented. They

---

[2] It should be remembered that the term "Anglo" came into widespread use by cultural anthropologies and social psychologists in the 1970s and 1980s to describe this cluster, and much has changed in the intervening years.

tend to be optimistic and opportunistic, and are often comfortable taking risks in order to achieve desired objectives. They are also seen by many as being superficial; they often ignore the details or conflicting positions underlying complex issues and prefer to focus on the proverbial big picture. They enjoy small talk, but have little patience with cultural niceties or ceremonial observances. They sometimes have difficulty building deep or lasting relationships. And they can be blunt. They often like to put their cards on the table from the start and are suspicious of anyone who does not reciprocate. Understanding nuances or subtleties in conversations is not their strong suit.

Americans are often described as being overly trusting and friendly towards people they hardly know. They come across to many foreigners as naïve and uninformed on matters of global importance. They are admired for their technical competence, but not their sophistication. However, they can also be very generous. On a per capita basis, Americans give more money to charities than anyone else on the planet. Some say this is because they have more money to give or because of US tax policies that reward charitable contributions, but there is more to it than this. There is a fundamental belief that people have a moral responsibility to support social causes, political causes, local causes, and even sometimes perfect strangers to an extent seldom seen elsewhere. Finally, many Americans tend to be a bit jingoistic and seem convinced that their country is the greatest in the world. There is no reason to discuss this; anyone who disagrees is simply wrong.

Obviously, all Americans do not fit this description? For starters, the US is a very heterogeneous society consisting of many strong cultures. Most of its citizens or their ancestors migrated to the US from various regions of the world in search of a better life and brought their cultures with them. It is therefore important to recognize that when people try to describe a "typical" American, they are often focusing on Anglo-Americans or, more accurately, European Americans. Other American cultures, including Asian Americans, African Americans, Native Americans, and so forth, can have very different cultural characteristics. And even among the European American community,

stark cultural differences can be found. Indeed, the individualistic nature of the US encourages and supports cultural diversity. Despite all of this, if so many observers from so many different backgrounds come to the same conclusions about the "typical" American, such observations are difficult to ignore.

Now, consider how the people characterized by this or similar description might build organizations. Such organizations would likely stress individual achievement and responsibility, control over the environment, a somewhat linear approach to decision-making, respect for rules and policies and a sense of order, and a belief that at least in theory anyone can rise to the top. As a result, a typical US organization is perhaps best described as a loosely coupled system with many key parts located outside of the company for purposes of efficiency and flexibility. American CEOs tend to have considerable power as decision-makers and leaders so long as they succeed. Indeed, we often hear about the "imperial CEO." If they do not succeed, however, they tend to disappear rather quickly. Partly as a result of this, many US firms tend to have a top-down decision-making style. When they need capital to expand the business, market research for a new product, or in-depth legal advice, they frequently go outside the company. Likewise, both manufacturing and service companies often rely on outside suppliers and distributors that have only a tenuous relationship to the company. And even inside the company, employees are often viewed as factors of production more than members. Indeed, in some American companies, "permanent" employees are routinely hired and fired based on variations in workloads. And the use of contingent workers is on the rise, partly to save money and partly to increase flexibility and operating efficiency. This organizing framework is illustrated in figure 4.3.

This exhibit illustrates a general paradigm for US firms. However, in view of the highly individualistic nature of the prevailing culture, it is not surprising to find a wide variation around this general model. US firms can be highly autocratic or highly participative, mastery-oriented or harmony-oriented, and so forth. Even so, a general model serves a useful purpose as a starting point for cross-cultural comparisons.

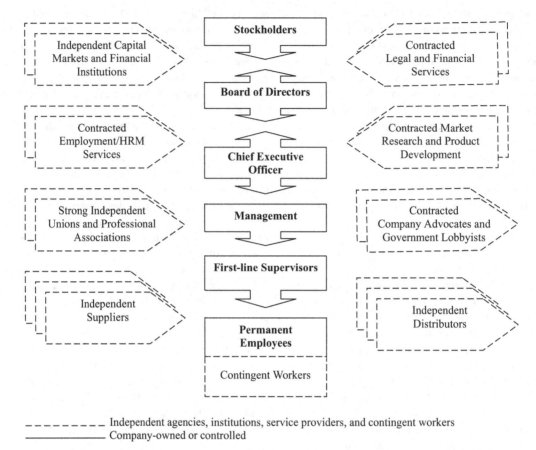

Independent agencies, institutions, service providers, and contingent workers
Company-owned or controlled

Figure 4.3 Organization design of a typical US corporation

Going beyond the US, it is clearly a mistake to assume that organization and management practices are identical – or even similar, in some cases – across the broad "Anglo" cluster. For example, when British managers are asked to compare North American and British managers and corporations, they typically offer one of two responses: either they are very similar or they are very different. Such is the heterogeneity of corporations on both sides of the Atlantic. Frames of references, as well as nuances, become both important and ambiguous. At the same time, when Canadians are asked to compare US and Canadian managers and organizations, they, too, can sometimes find sizable differences.

In order to delve a bit deeper here in this comparison, and commenting on British organizational trends, Nigel Nicholson (2008) has suggested that the major challenge is to understand how much of an organization's ethos or operating model comes from national cultures, sector cultures, or parent company cultures. At the national level, key inputs are obviously regulatory elements as well as governance norms and cultural factors, such as shared expectations of employees and other stakeholders. On these factors, only a few differences between the two cultures are noted. However, the typical governance rules in the UK are quite different. As a rule, British companies are far less tolerant of power aggregation than are their American counterparts. For example, they tend to oppose unitary boards of directors and strongly prefer the separation of Chairman and CEO and their councils (e.g., top team teams and boards).

They also dislike dual share voting systems, and have rules that prevent banks from owning major shares in companies.

In addition, British firms are also far less encumbered with layers of lawyers, spend far less money on government lobbying, and have generally weak trade associations. Management consultants do have influence on British firms, but less so than in the US. In general, then, Nicholson notes that British firms tend to be more liberal than those in the US and maintain more liquidity and fluidity in ownership. However, if British firms are more liberal in ownership and governance, they tend to be more conservative in management policies and practices. The ethos of British management is highly pragmatic, achievement oriented, and entrepreneurial, but often opposed to "out-of-the-box" thinking, weak on leadership, strong on financial management, and frequently poor on vision, community, and integration.

Adding to these observations, John Child (2008) cautions against placing too much emphasis on seeing ideal types and archetypes of British (or any other firms). For example, while many larger UK companies have been acquired by or merged into larger non-British firms, a strong entrepreneurial and SME sector remains. And, as in any country, there are large differences between traditional manufacturing and newer service firms.

Like Nicholson, Child points to differences in ethos as providing particularly significant contrasts between US and British firms. Indeed, he adds to Nicholson's list of features characterizing many larger British firms, including a short-term, cost-conscious orientation (hence a generally low emphasis on personal development and training), poor internal integration (both horizontal and vertical), and a continuing failure to dialogue adequately with employees. Finally, although some have suggested that the UK may be losing its individualistic culture to a degree, Child points out that in organizations that continue to use performance-based incentives, such as in many financial and consulting services, we still see high levels of initiative and a strong achievement orientation.

Speaking to differences between Canadians and their US counterparts, Nancy Adler (2008a) offers the following observations:

Compared to Americans, Canadians tend to understate their strengths and perhaps overstate their weaknesses. They do not usually claim to be the best at something. Canadians strongly believe in collegiality. For example, Canada is one of the leaders in creating Middle-country initiatives where a group of countries in the world tries to get something done (instead of trying to go it alone). Canadians tend to be more formal than Americans – titles and family names are important. Canadians are generally more polite and less confrontational than their American counterparts. Canadians are also less explicitly and publicly religious. Finally, Canadians believe in more collective responsibility across society in such areas as education and health care.

All of this is not to say that overlaps do not occur; obviously they do. However, assuming that Americans and Canadians live identical lifestyles or share identical values can only lead to lost opportunities for global managers.

In summary, some might argue that in making comparisons between American and UK firms – and, indeed, firms in Australian, Canada, and New Zealand – the key issue is whether within-group variance is larger or smaller than between-group variance. That is, commonalities can be found among all of the countries that comprise the so-called "Anglo" cluster. Part of the reason for these similarities can be found in the historic British influences in all of these cultures. Even so, in recognition of the strong individualism found in this cluster, it is not surprising to find it is difficult to make generalizations about organization design and management practice. At the same time, part of the differences here can be found in the increasing cultural heterogeneity of people inhabiting all of these countries. Diversity is increasing throughout. Indeed, as these countries become increasingly multicultural, perhaps the term "Anglo" will lose much of its meaning as a descriptor of this cluster of countries.

The Japanese keiretsu

Japan is often the country of choice when making comparisons with US, British, and other so-called "Anglo" countries. There are many reasons for this. Many westerners are somewhat familiar with Japan

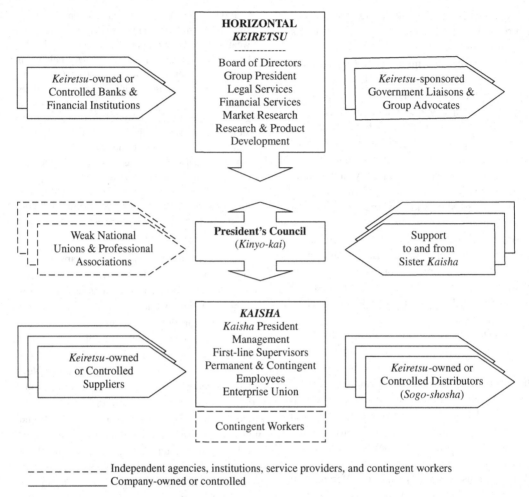

Figure 4.4 Organization design of a typical horizontal *keiretsu*

and its culture. Japan's economy remains strong in many business sectors and most geographical regions. Company names like Mitsubishi, Sony, Toshiba, Toyota, Nissan, Honda, etc., are household brands and countless people around the world own products manufactured by them. In view of this, we turn now to a look inside the typical Japanese organization.

Perhaps the best way to understand how Japanese firms work is to begin with some observations about the local culture. As shown in table 4.4 above, an overview of Japanese culture includes a strong belief in hierarchy, strong collectivism, a strong harmony orientation, moderate monochronism,

and strong particularism. Hierarchy beliefs in Japan can be seen in the deep respect shown to elders and people in positions of authority. In many circumstances, their directives are to be obeyed immediately and without question. This belief follows from early Confucian teachings (see below). Indeed, the concept of authority in Japan differs from that typically found in the west. Western views of authority see power generally flowing in one direction – down. The supervisor or manager gives directions; those below him or her follow them. Authority is a one-way concept. In Japan and many other Asian countries, by contrast, power still flows downwards but those exercising power must also look after the welfare and well-being of those they manage. In other words, a supervisor expects his or her directives to be followed without question, but will also spend considerable time guiding, coaching, and teaching subordinates so they can progress in their careers. Subordinates – and in many cases their families too – will be looked after. Thus, authority here is seen as a two-way street; both sides (superiors and subordinates) have a role to play. By deferring to those above you, you are in essence asking them to look after you.

Japan is also a highly collectivistic nation. Groups generally take precedence over individuals and people gain their personal identity through their group membership. An old saying, "The nail that sticks out will be hammered down," best exemplifies the importance of this belief. Contrast this to the old American and British saying, "God helps those who help themselves." As a result, employees naturally gravitate towards groups at work and group achievement often surpasses individual achievement on the job. Seniority-based (group) rewards are frequently preferred over performance-based (individual) rewards, particularly among older employees.

Harmony, both with other people and with nature, is also a strong characteristic. Japan's respect for its surrounding environment is legendary. This is not to say that Japanese refrain for changing or challenging nature; rather, they typically attempt this in ways that do as little harm as possible to the environment. Likewise, most Japanese will go to great lengths not to offend anyone or create open conflict or argumentation. As a result, communications in Japan tends to emphasize context at least as much as it does content. Non-verbal signs and signals are used to convey their thoughts in cases where their words might be constrained.

Japanese are frequently described as being moderately monochronic. That is, they tend to focus on one or only a few tasks at a time and clearly separate work and family as it relates to the workplace. And finally, many observes have noted that Japanese society tends to be highly particularistic. That is, while clear rules of law pervade society, exceptions are routinely made for friends and family or for powerful and influential people.

Japan's large vertically integrated *keiretsu* organizations (e.g., Sumitomo, Mitsui, Mitsubishi) represent a unique approach to organization that has served their companies and their country well over the years (Kono and Clegg, 2001). The design of these organizations is rooted in Japanese history and is successful largely because it is congruent with the national culture (Abbeglen and Stalk, 1985). In contrast to their Anglo-American and even to some extent some their European counterparts, Japanese firms tend to treat their employees as a fixed cost, not a variable cost, and relationships with suppliers tend to be closer and more stable over time. Executives have less power and decision-making is distributed throughout the firm (see below). Financing is more likely to come from inside the Japanese conglomerate's own financial institutions (e.g., company-owned banks or insurance companies), while marketing research and even legal advice frequently is typically done inside the firm. Finally, Japanese unions tend to be company unions and are more closely associated with company interests than is the case in the west.

To succeed in business, various individual Japanese companies (*kaisha*) join together to form a business group, or *keiretsu* network. The *keiretsu* provides financial, organizational, legal, and logistical support for its sister companies. For example, when Mitsubishi Motors (a *kaisha*) needs glass, sheet metal, electrical components, or fabric for its automobile assembly line, it is likely to secure most if not all of these materials from other companies within the Mitsubishi Business Group (a *keiretsu*). Obviously, not being a *keiretsu* member can lead to isolation and missed business opportunities. Indeed, it is this isolation from the open market – not being allowed membership in key business relationships – that many western companies object to in attempting to conduct business in Japan.

Japanese *keiretsu* can be divided into two basic types: horizontal (*yoko*) and vertical (*tate*). A *horizontal keiretsu* consists of a group of interlocking companies typically clustered around a main bank, a lead manufacturer, and a trading company, and overseen by a President's Council consisting of the presidents of the major group companies. Figure 4.4 illustrates how a horizontal *keiretsu* is organized. The "Big Six" horizontal *keiretsu* are Mitsui, Mitsubishi, Sumitomo, Fuyo, Sanwa, and Dai-Ichi Kangyo Bank Group. By contrast, a *vertical keiretsu* consists of a large manufacturing company surrounded by numerous small and subservient suppliers and distributors that keep the operations running smoothly, typically through a just-in-time (or *kanban*) production system. Toyota and Honda are good examples here.

A good example of a *horizontal keiretsu* can be seen in the Mitsubishi Business Group. Mitsubishi has a main bank (Mitsubishi Bank), a trading company (*Mitsubishi Shoji*), and a flagship manufacturer (Mitsubishi Heavy Industries). In addition, three financial firms are typically clustered around these three key companies: a life insurance company, a non-life insurance company, and a trust bank. Together, these financial firms, the trading company, and the group's key manufacturers give the *keiretsu* its unique identity. Beyond this are hundreds of large and small companies that are associated with the group. Senior managers from the principal companies are frequently assigned to serve in management positions in the smaller firms to assist with inter-company coordination support. Interlocking directorates are common to reinforce this family system.

Within each horizontal *keiretsu*, a *main bank* performs several functions. First, its most important role is providing funds for company operations, expansion, and research and development. These banks provide more than two-thirds of the financial needs of *keiretsu*-affiliated companies. Second, member companies frequently hold stock in sister companies (known as stable cross-shareholdings). Main banks are among the nation's largest shareholders for such firms, providing considerable stability for company management interested in long-term growth strategies. Third, main banks provide an important audit function for member companies in monitoring corporate performance and evaluating risk. Fourth, main banks provide the best source of venture capital for member companies interested in launching new but risky ventures. For instance, Sumitomo Bank provided massive start-up investments in member company NEC's initiative to capture the semiconductor market. Finally, main banks serve as the "company doctor" in rescuing sister companies that are facing bankruptcy. Since corporate bankruptcy can threaten public confidence in Japan's economic system, not just a specific business group, main banks often quietly provide financial support to keep ailing companies going until the firm can be re-organized or the problem resolved. This financial commitment to member companies can also create trouble for the *keiretsu*, however, when the main bank is required to bail out a noncompetitive company that should perhaps be sold off or dissolved.

The trading company, or *sogo shosha*, provides member companies with ready access to global markets and distribution networks. These companies (e.g., Mitsubishi Shoji or Sumitomo Busan) maintain offices throughout the world and are continually on the lookout for new or expanded markets. At the same time, their field offices collect and analyze market and economic intelligence that can be used by member companies to develop new products or otherwise get a jump on the competition. They frequently assist member companies with various marketing activities as well and facilitate imports into Japan for their business customers. In fact, historically, Japanese trading companies have been responsible for almost half of Japan's imports and three-fifths of its exports. Finally, the *sogo shosha* often provide significant credit (through the group's main bank) for small and medium-sized companies involved in business activities with member companies, again gaining advantage over foreign competitors that operate further from lines of credit.

Finally, although hundreds of companies may be affiliated with one *keiretsu*, only the principal companies are allowed to join the *Presidents' Council* (*shacho-kai*, or *kinyo-kai* in the case of Mitsubishi). This council (typically consisting of the CEOs of the top twenty to thirty group companies) meets monthly to discuss principal strategies for the group, as well as issues of coordination across the various sister companies. Since council meetings are private and no records are maintained, little is understood about how such councils actually work. At the very least, however, these meetings facilitate extensive cooperation across member companies on developing group strategy and group solidarity,

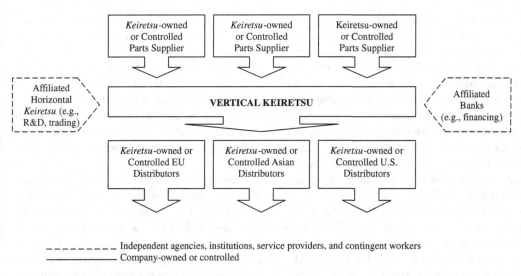

| Keiretsu-owned or Controlled Parts Supplier | Keiretsu-owned or Controlled Parts Supplier | Keiretsu-owned or Controlled Parts Supplier |

Affiliated Horizontal *Keiretsu* (e.g., R&D, trading)

VERTICAL KEIRETSU

Affiliated Banks (e.g., financing)

| Keiretsu-owned or Controlled EU Distributors | Keiretsu-owned or Controlled Asian Distributors | Keiretsu-owned or Controlled U.S. Distributors |

– – – – – – – – Independent agencies, institutions, service providers, and contingent workers
——————— Company-owned or controlled

Figure 4.5 Organization design of a typical vertical *keiretsu*

as well as mediating disagreements across member companies.

When most westerners think of a *keiretsu*, they have in mind the horizontal variety discussed above. However, the *vertical* (or pyramid) *keiretsu* can be just as powerful. Key vertical *keiretsu* include the major Japanese automobile firms such as Toyota, Nissan, and Honda, as well as some of the major electric giants like Sony, Toshiba, and Matsushita. An illustration of the organization structure of a vertical *keiretsu* is shown in figure 4.5. As noted above, a vertical *keiretsu* consists of a major company surrounded by a large number of smaller firms that act either as suppliers or distributors for the big firm.

In point of fact, there are two kinds of vertical *keiretsu*: a *production keiretsu*, in which a myriad of parts suppliers join together to create sub-assemblies for a single end-product manufacturer, and a *distribution keiretsu*, in which a single large firm, usually a manufacturer, moves products to market through a network of wholesalers and retailers that depend on the parent company for goods. Since most manufacturers have both *keiretsu* types (production and distribution), we can envision the two like an hourglass: an upside-down (production) pyramid on top in which individual parts suppliers provide various parts (e.g., fabric for car seats) to sub-component assembly

companies that ultimately provide subassemblies (e.g., completed seats) to the parent company in the center of the hourglass. Here, the parent company assembles the end products and prepares them for market. Next, these products are passed down into another (distribution) pyramid where they are distributed to wholesalers and ultimately to retail consumers.

In some cases, a leading company from a vertical *keiretsu* will form an alliance with a horizontal *keiretsu* to ensure solid financing and improved trading capabilities. Toyota is a member of the Mitsui Group, for example, in addition to running its own vertical *keiretsu*. Finally, numerous small supplier firms become quasi-members of the group and receive long-term purchasing contracts, as well as assistance with financing and sometimes research and development. These suppliers support the famous *kanban* (or just-in-time) inventory system that Japan is noted for and must remain loyal to one group. That is, when supplies on an assembly line get short, suppliers are automatically notified and replenish the factory in short order.

Japanese *kaisha* tend to view all regular employees (not including large numbers of continent workers or workers employed by company suppliers) as part of their permanent cost structure. As such, during difficult financial periods, most Japanese companies will go to great lengths to retain their workers (often called "salarymen"). This contrasts sharply with the situation in many Anglo-American firms, where lay-offs are frequently seen as an easy solution to financial exigency. If workers are seen as a fixed cost (instead of a variable cost), it makes sense to invest heavily in their training. Long-term employment will allow for sufficient payback of such training expenses. In this sense, western observers have suggested that Japanese companies treat their employees more like family members than employees.

Concern has frequently been expressed that employee commitment to their companies in Japan may be too strong. Many Japanese refuse to take all of the vacation time to which they are entitled – a practice seldom witnessed in the west. A commonly used Japanese word, *ganbatte*, typifies this overzealous commitment to work (Meek, 1999). Indeed, Japanese employees and even school children will often be heard to say to their friends or colleagues "*Ganbatte kudasai*" – never give up, try harder, do your best. On the positive side, *ganbatte* shows strong commitment to succeed on behalf of one's company or family. On the negative side, it often manifests itself in large numbers of work-related health problems. Health-care professionals routinely express concern about the large number of Japanese employees who overwork themselves to the point of becoming ill.

Finally, it is important to note that in view of Japan's long-running economic problems and increased global pressures for efficiency, several Japanese companies (e.g., Hitachi, Toshiba, NEC) have recently begun to back away from their former policies of ironclad job security and lifetime employment (Kono and Clegg, 2001). Other companies are beginning to place greater emphasis on individual performance and performance appraisals (Cullen and Parboteeah, 2005). Even so, the general characteristics of Japanese HRM systems remain relatively constant. Concern for the group, respect for age and seniority, and devotion to the company remain hallmarks of the typical Japanese firm. Indeed, when Fujitsu decided to initiate a western-style performance-based pay system, it proved to be a poor fit with Japanese culture and was toned down. Fujitsu's new system emphasizes worker enthusiasm and energy in tackling a job instead of actual goal accomplishment in annual performance evaluations (Tanikawa, 2001). Moreover, when Fujitsu announced that it was laying off 15,000 workers, or 9 per cent of its workforce, it made it clear that all involuntary lay-offs would take place in operations outside of Japan. Any Japanese workforce reductions would be accomplished through retirements and normal attrition.

There are over 70,000 labor unions in Japan, most of which are company-specific. These *enterprise unions* tend to include both workers and lower and middle-level managers. This differs from the situation in the US, for example, where most labor organizations are industrial unions that cross several companies in the same industry. Although many enterprise unions affiliate with national labor federations (which facilitate the annual spring wage negotiations, or *shunto*), these organizations are more decentralized than in the US. As a result, Japanese workers in enterprise unions typically do not experience the same degree of divided loyalties (union vs. company) that are often seen in the US among unionized workers. In addition, it is not uncommon for union members in Japanese companies to rise through the management ranks – even to the position of company president in some cases. This seldom occurs in the US, where the "white collar" managerial hierarchy is separate and distinct from "blue collar" workers and where junior managers are typically hired from among recent college graduates, not rank-and-file production workers. Even though enterprise unions are often linked to large nationwide industrial unions, industrial action is rare and most disputes are settled relatively amicably.

The lack of clear divisions between labor and management in Japanese firms often makes it possible to enlist workers at all levels in efforts to improve productivity and product quality. Quality and service are company-wide concerns from the top to the bottom of the organization, not just management concerns. Japan is noted for its widespread use of *quality circles*, small groups of workers who spend time (frequently their own) trying to improve operational procedures or product quality in their own area (Kono and Clegg, 2001).

These efforts help Japanese firms with their *kaizen*, a philosophy of continuous improvement that is also a hallmark of Japanese manufacturing firms (Lillrank and Kano, 1989).

In summary, the typical Japanese approach to organization and management is both different and effective, and represents a formidable threat to global competitors. Japanese firms have found a way to build their organizations in ways that draw support from the local environment and culture and mobilize their resources in ways that many western firms have difficulty understanding, let alone responding to. It is a model that prizes cooperation and mutual support among friends and all-out competition against all others.

The Chinese gong-si

When westerners attempt to describe Chinese culture, they invariably begin – correctly or incorrectly – with Confucianism. Contrary to popular western belief, Confucianism is a philosophy, not a religion. Kong Qui was a senior civil servant in China in the sixth century BCE. His western name, Confucius, is actually a Latin form of the title *Kongfuzi*, which means Great Master Kong. Kong Qui was a moral philosopher, best known for his thoughts on correct moral character and personal responsibility. Although he never published his thoughts or philosophy, his disciples collected them and subsequently published them in a classic book called the *Analects*. Known for his wisdom and insight, Kong Qui promulgated a code of ethical behavior that was meant to guide interpersonal relationships in everyday life. This code was summed up in the so-called *five cardinal virtues*, or principles, that suggest a way of living in the broader society that are still taken very seriously in many cultures today. These principles include filial piety, absolute loyalty to one's family and superiors, strict seniority in organization and personal relationships, subservience of women to men, and mutual trust and harmony between close friends and colleagues.

Kong Qui and his followers saw the universe – and hence society – as a hierarchical system ruled by an educated aristocratic elite. Concepts such as democracy and equality were disdained, while learning and education were highly prized. Confucian society stressed the virtues of self-discipline, hard work, diligence, and frugality (Wu and Grove, 1999). Hence, the fundamental nature of human relationships is not interactions among equals but rather interactions among unequals. That is, correct interpersonal behavior is determined by one's age, gender, and position in society, and a breach of this social etiquette carried with it severe penalties.

These five cardinal virtues are reinforced through rigid norms and sanctions that govern social relationships across the society. First, consider the concept of *guanxi*. *Guanxi* can be defined as a strong personal relationship between two people with implications of a continual exchange of favors. Others define it simply as good connections or tight social networks based on trust, common background, and experience. Two people have *guanxi* when they can assume that each is conscientiously committed to the other regardless of what happens. This bond is based on the exchange of favors (i.e., social capital), not necessarily friendship or sympathy, and it does not have to involve friends. It is more utilitarian than emotional. It also tends to favor the weaker of the two parties in ongoing exchanges, an outgrowth of the Confucian doctrine of looking after those less fortunate than oneself. Failing to meet one's obligations under this equity arrangement causes severe loss of face and creates the appearance of being untrustworthy.

The second factor in determining social relationships in China (and elsewhere in Asia) is *mientzu*, or face (i.e., dignity, self-respect, prestige). A central tenet of Confucianism is to maintain long-term social harmony (Earley, 1997). This is based both on the maintenance of correct relationships between individuals and on the protection of one's face. All social interactions must be conducted in a manner in which no party loses face. Face can be classified into two types: *lian* and *mianzi*. *Lian* is associated with personal behavior, while *mianzi* is something valuable that can be achieved. Under this system, a Chinese may be criticized for having no *lian* and will be seen as being unsuccessful if he has no *mianzi*. Normally, people of higher rank possess greater *mianzi*. Together they determine who has face, who gains it, and who loses it. As a result, face represents a key component in the exercise of *guanxi*. If a person has little *mianzi*, he or she has limited social capital with which to cultivate social connections.

Simply put, face represents the confidence society has in one's moral character. It represents one's self-image or reputation. The loss of face makes it impossible for an individual to function properly in the community. This occurs when an individual, either through his own actions or the actions of people close to him, fails to meet essential requirements placed upon him by virtue of his social position. Hence, if an individual cannot keep a commitment – however small – he loses face. Similarly, a person loses face when he or she is not treated in accordance with his or her station or position in society. Thus, a senior manager will lose face if it becomes known that a junior colleague is earning a higher salary or was promoted ahead of him.

The third important factor here is *renqing*, or personal obligations. These personal obligations accrue to individuals as a result of past *guanxi* relationships. That is, it involves unpaid debts or favors that are owed to others as a result of past favors in a continuing exchange relationship between friends and colleagues. In addition to various social expressions (such as offering congratulations or condolences and making gifts on appropriate occasions), *renqing* often includes a display of human empathy and personal sentiments. It focuses on social emotions – emotions played out in public – rather than personal emotions, which are frequently hidden from view. If one fails to follow the rule of equity in the exchange of *renqing*, one loses face, hurts the feelings of others, and looks inconsiderate. This applies even to one's closest friends. As such, some have translated *renqing* as "humanized obligations" instead of personal obligations, which implies that a continued exchange of favors with a sentimental touch is involved.

Fourth, consider the importance of *rank*. Confucian principles were designed to recognize hierarchy and differences between class members. As a result, the behavioral requirements of individuals differed according to who was involved in the relationship. Among equals, certain patterns of prescribed behavior existed. You can see this today when two strangers discover, upon meeting for the first time, that they both attended the same high school or college. An instant bond emerges and there is a sense of immediate camaraderie. On the other hand, for people from outside this common background or clan, there is frequent hostility or distrust. Foreign observers note that some people can be very blunt and impolite when talking with total strangers, yet very hospitable and generous when dealing with friends or acquaintances. It is a question of belonging.

Finally, within one's broad circle of acquaintances, there is a clear responsibility for maintaining *hé-xié*, or group harmony (*wa* in Japanese; *inwha* in Korean). Again, this principle stresses harmony between unequals. That is, it links persons of unequal rank in power, prestige, or position. Since strong personal relationships outside the family only tend to occur between persons of equal rank, age, or prestige, harmony is the means of defining all other necessarily more formal relationships. It is everyone's responsibility to continually maintain this harmony among one's acquaintances and family members, and considerable effort is invested in doing so, including gift giving.

In view of China's strong cultural traditions, it is not surprising that its companies, both large and small, reflect this heritage. Chinese companies are generally called *gong-si*. While the term *gong-si* originally referred to private family-owned enterprises, recent Chinese corporate law now uses this term to refer to all companies, regardless of whether they are large or small, family-owned or state-owned. To clarify this difference, smaller and medium-sized family-run enterprises are now often called *jia zu gong-si*. An illustration of a typical family-run firm is shown in figure 4.6.

Found throughout China, Taiwan, Singapore, and elsewhere around the world where overseas Chinese congregate, the Chinese family business tends to be a small entrepreneurial venture owned by family members and typically employing members of the extended family as well as others whom the family feels it can trust (Redding, 1990). These firms are particularly prevalent in Southern China and among overseas Chinese. As a rule, Chinese family firms are considerably smaller and exhibit greater independence than their Japanese or Korean counterparts.

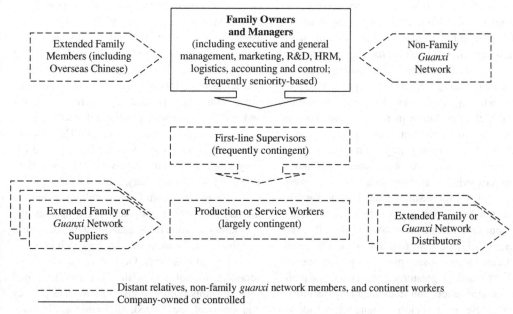

Figure 4.6 Organization design of a typical chinese family-owned *gong-si*

The dominant management style of the *gong-si* is patrimonialism, which includes paternalism, hierarchy, mutual obligation, responsibility, familism, personalism, and connections (Child, 1994; Chen, 2001). As a result, typical Chinese family business are often characterized by power and influence being closely related to ownership, autocratic leadership, and a personalistic style of management designed in part to pay honor to the founder or leader.

Following from Confucian thought, the family is the most fundamental revenue and expenditure unit. Within a family, each member contributes his or her income to a common family fund. Each member then has a right to a portion of these funds, while the remainder belongs to the family as a whole. The interests of the entire family take precedence over individual members and others outside the family. As a result, business owners tend to regard the business as the private property of the core family (not an individual), and are therefore reluctant to share ownership with outsiders or to borrow from individuals or organizations unrelated to the family in some way. Top management positions are often filled with family

members, sometimes despite a lack of managerial competence. Company size tends to be small. Over 90 per cent of these firms employ fewer than fifty people, including family members, and focus their energies on a small area of business – production, sales, or service (Redding, 1990).

Gong-si companies have little formal structure, few standard operating procedures, and little specialization (*Economist*, 2004). While they lack formal structure and procedures, personal relationships are likely to take precedence over more objectively defined concerns such as organizational efficiency. Who one knows is often more important than what one knows and employee loyalty is often preferred over actual performance. Decisions are frequently based either on intuition or on long-standing business relationships. According to Ming-Jer Chen, if these family firms have a competitive advantage, it lies in their small size, flexibility, network of connections, and negotiation skills (Chen, 2001).

As noted by many social scientists, cultures can sometimes evolve over time in response to external stimuli. China provides a good example of this. Perhaps one reason Chinese culture has endured for so many millennia is that it is at once both strong and flexible. Its roots are very deep, yet it is sufficiently flexible to adapt to shifting political sands (from empire to nationalism to communism to quasi-capitalism). As China has begun to prosper in response to its newfound economic freedoms, and as more young Chinese are exposed to western thought (e.g., capitalism, democracy, individualism), a clear evolution in management thought can be seen from older managers to younger ones (Ahmad, 2004). Many young Chinese managers, with greater educational opportunities and more overseas experience, are beginning to develop their own framework for business management that differs significantly from that of their parents. This new approach can perhaps best be described as a blend of old and new, east and west. The trend in Chinese management philosophy is changing rapidly towards a greater emphasis on competitiveness, innovation, and individual responsibility. Clearly, there are variations around this trend, so caution is in order about over-generalization. Even so, these changes are real and widespread. How they will influence future successes or failures of Chinese businessmen and women remains to be seen. What is clear, however, is that these changes pose a significant challenge for all partners doing business in the region, regardless of their home country.

The German Konzern

Germany is a country widely known and respected for its leading-edge technology and craftsmanship. It is also known as a high-cost producer. Combining these two attributes leads to its position in the global marketplace as a producer of innovative, high quality, and expensive goods and services. However, as globalization pressures continue and price points becomes an increasingly important factor for global consumers, the obvious question is how German companies can compete now and in the future. To explore this question, it is necessary to examine the unique approach to organization and management that is found in Germany and its Germanic neighbors.

A number of social scientists have attempted to describe German culture in general terms. Geert Hofstede, for example, has described the typical German as relatively individualistic (although not so extreme as Americans), high on uncertainty avoidance and masculinity, and relatively low on power distance (Hofestede 1980). Hall and Hall (1990) add that Germans tend to be very punctual about time, follow schedules closely, demand order, value their personal space, respect power and position, and seek detailed information prior to decision-making. Indeed, Hall and Hall quote a French executive as saying that "Germans are too busy managing to think creatively" (Hall and Hall, 1990). By way of summary, Table 4.4 (above) suggests that the dominant German culture includes a mastery orientation, moderate individualism and egalitarian, a strong rule-based orientation (i.e., universalistic), and a monochromic approach to time.

To foreign observers, Germans tend to be conservative, formal, and polite (Hill, 1997). Formal titles are important in conversations, and privacy and protocol are valued. In business, Germans tend to be assertive, but not aggressive. Although firms are often characterized by strict departmentalization, decisions tend to be made based on broad-based discussion and consensus building among key stakeholders. Negotiations are based on extensive assessments of data and plans and, since Germany is a low context culture (where message clarity counts), communication is explicit and easily understood by foreigners. Germans tend to be broadly educated, multilingual, and widely traveled. They are highly regarded for being trusted partners, as well as for their forward-looking human resource management policies. In recent years, perhaps because of this informed world view, Germany has witnessed an increased flexibility in cultural expressions. Still, differences remain.

As with companies in any country, it is difficult to generalize about the nature or structure of the typical German firm (*Konzern*). As in the US, German firms generally take one of two legal forms: a limited partnership designated by a *GmbH* (*Gesellschaft mit beschraenkter Haftung*) following the company name or a public stock company designated by an *AG* (*Aktiengesellschaft*) following the name. In German conglomerates, the parent company is often referred to as the *Muttergesellschaft* (mother company).

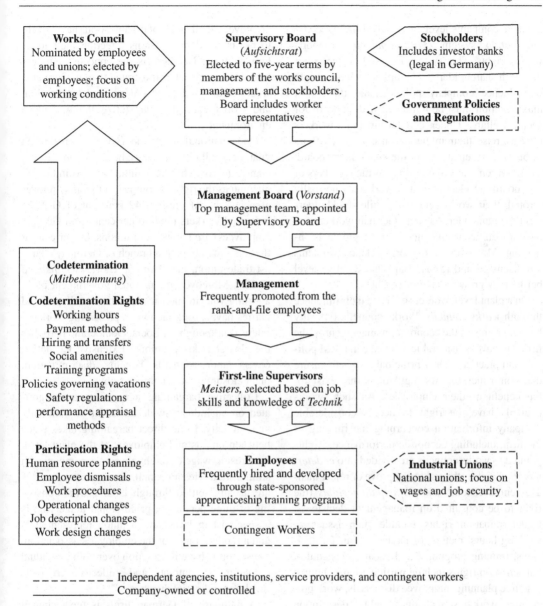

Works Council
Nominated by employees and unions; elected by employees; focus on working conditions

Supervisory Board
(*Aufsichtsrat*)
Elected to five-year terms by members of the works council, management, and stockholders. Board includes worker representatives

Stockholders
Includes investor banks (legal in Germany)

Government Policies and Regulations

Management Board (*Vorstand*)
Top management team, appointed by Supervisory Board

Codetermination
(*Mitbestimmung*)

Codetermination Rights
Working hours
Payment methods
Hiring and transfers
Social amenities
Training programs
Policies governing vacations
Safety regulations
performance appraisal methods

Participation Rights
Human resource planning
Employee dismissals
Work procedures
Operational changes
Job description changes
Work design changes

Management
Frequently promoted from the rank-and-file employees

First-line Supervisors
Meisters, selected based on job skills and knowledge of *Technik*

Employees
Frequently hired and developed through state-sponsored apprenticeship training programs

Industrial Unions
National unions; focus on wages and job security

Contingent Workers

– – – – – – – – Independent agencies, institutions, service providers, and contingent workers
———————— Company-owned or controlled

Figure 4.7 Organization design of a typical German *konzern*

From an organizational standpoint, German firms are typically led from the top by two boards. At the very top is the *supervisory board* (*Aufsichtsrat*), as shown below in figure 4.7. This board, much like a board of directors in US firms, is responsible for insuring that the principal corporate objectives are met over the long term. Its members are typically elected for five years and can only be changed by a vote of 75 per cent of the voting shares. A key function of the supervisory board is to oversee the activities of the *management board* (*Vorstand*), which consists of the top management team of the firm and is responsible for its actual strategic and operational management. These two boards are jointly responsible for the success or failure of German enterprise.

On a company level, a legally binding *codetermination* system (*Mitbestimmung*) supports worker rights. This system is based on the belief that both shareholders and employees have a right to influence company policies, and that profit maximization must be tempered with concern for social welfare. Under codetermination, workers may exercise their influence on corporate affairs through representatives on the supervisory board. Typically, one-half to one-third of the members of this board are elected by the workers – normally through their works council – while stockholders elect the remainder. As such, German workers can have a significant influence on strategic decision-making. Moreover, many serious labor problems are discussed and resolved at this executive level before they grow into major conflicts.

On a plant level, workers exercise their influence through *works councils*. Works councils typically have no rights in the economic management of the firm, but have considerable influence in HRM policies and practices. Their principal task is to ensure that companies follows regulations that exist for the benefit of their employees. As such, works councils have the right to access considerable company information concerning the running of the firm, including economic performance. Rights granted to works councils are divided into *codetermination rights* (the right to approve or reject management decisions) and *participation rights* (the right to be consulted on management decisions). Codetermination rights include such issues as working hours, method of payment, transfer decisions, training programs, and vacation schedules. Participation rights include participation in human resource planning, employee dismissals, work procedures, work design changes, and job description changes.

The German industrial relations system is highly standardized, extensively organized through state regulation, and characterized by formal recognition of employee rights at all levels of the firm (Schonfeld, 2004; *Economist*, 2004). This concept of fostering strong employee participation in corporate decision-making is generally referred to (especially in Europe) as *industrial democracy*. Industrial democracy refers to a consensus among national leaders and citizens in a country that employees at all levels of organizations have a right to be involved in decisions affecting their long-term welfare. Nowhere is the concept of industrial democracy better illustrated than in Germany, where strong industrial unions, codetermination, and works councils characterize the workplace environment.

On a national level, the German constitution guarantees all citizens the right to join unions and engage in collective bargaining. It also indirectly guarantees the right of companies to join employer associations. At present, 42 per cent of German industrial workers (and 30 per cent of all German employees) are members of unions; 80 per cent of these are members of a branch of Germany's largest trade union, the *Deutsche Gewerkschaftsbund* (DGB). Moreover, the national government plays a strong role in industrial relations. All political parties have strong factions representing workers' interests, although the Social Democratic Party has the closest links to unions. Extensive legislation covers labor standards, benefits, discrimination, plant closures, and employee rights.

Collective bargaining agreements are negotiated on an industry-wide basis, either nationally or regionally. Little direct bargaining takes place between unions and employers at the plant level. As a result, wage differentials across companies in similar industries are small. Employment disputes are usually settled through labor courts, consisting of three persons: a professional judge who is a specialist in labor law, a union representative, and a representative of the employer's association. These courts have jurisdiction over both individual employment contracts and collective contracts involving industrial disputes.

A hallmark of German firms is the technical competence they bring to the manufacture of so many diverse products. German engineering is world famous. A major reason for this lies in the training of managers and workers. Line managers in German firms are typically better trained technically than their European or American counterparts, with closer relations between them and technical experts in the firm. In contrast to American managers, most German managers are trained as engineers and have completed some form of craft apprenticeship training program. The typical

German organization is distinguished by its tightly knit technical staff superstructure, closely linked to supervisory and managerial tasks which, when combined, produce high levels of performance. Compared to French or British industry, German firms have a lower center of gravity; that is, they have less proliferation of administrative and support staff and more hands-on shop floor managers.

From the first-line supervisor (usually held by a *Meister*, or master technician) on up, managers are respected for what they know rather than who they are. They tend to be far less controlling than many of their US counterparts. Instead, it is assumed that workers and supervisors will meet deadlines, guarantee quality and service, and do not require close supervision. Independence within agreed upon parameters characterizes the working relationship between managers and the managed.

Behind the organizational facade of German firms is a particular notion of technical competence commonly referred to as *Technik*. This describes the knowledge and skills required for work (Brunstein, 1995). It is the science and art of manufacturing high-quality and technologically advanced products. The success of *Technik* in German manufacturing is evidenced by the fact that over 40 per cent of Germany's GDP is derived from manufacturing. Indeed, Germany is responsible for over half of all EU manufactured exports. It is for this reason that knowledge of *Technik* represents a principal determinant in the selection of supervisors and managers.

A principal method for developing this technical competence in workers begins with widespread and intensive *apprenticeship training* programs (Cullen and Parboteeah, 2005). It is estimated that over 65 per cent of 15- and 16-year-old Germans enter some form of vocational training program. Apprenticeship programs exist not only for manual occupations, but also for many technical, commercial, and managerial occupations. There are two principal forms of vocational training in Germany. The first consists of general and specialized training programs offered by vocational schools and technical colleges. The second, referred to as *dual system apprenticeship training*, combines in-house apprenticeship training with part-time vocational training leading to a skilled-worker

certificate. There are over 400 nationally recognized vocational certificates. Qualifications for each certificate are standardized throughout the country, leading to a well-trained workforce with skills that are not company-specific. This certificate training can be followed by attendance at one of the many *Fachschule*, or advanced vocational colleges. Graduation from a *Fachschule* facilitates the achievement of a *Meister*, or master technician, certification (see figure 4.8).

The dual system of apprenticeship training represents a partnership between employers, unions, and the government. Costs are typically shared between companies and the government on a two-thirds/one-third basis. Employers are legally required to release young workers for vocational training. German companies are also widely known for their strong support of company-sponsored training programs. Daimler, for example, regularly offers 180 vocational courses to its employees. Each year, the company has over 600 employees studying in vocational or modular management development courses, as well as over 4,000 employees who participate in some form of formal training at the company's training center. However, in recent years some have criticized the complexity of German apprenticeship programs, as well as the length of time required for certification (Miller, 2004). It has been argued that this lengthy certification procedure hinders entrepreneurship and Germany's competitive position in the world by limiting access to many professions, inhibiting change in those professions, and threatening creativity and innovation.

The French Société Anonyme

Next, consider organization and management in France. As in the US, it is difficult to pin down what it means to be French (Hill, 1997). Beginning with table 4.4 above, we note that the French are often seen as being moderately hierarchical, moderately collectivistic, moderately harmony-oriented, moderately polychromic, and moderately particularistic. Perhaps the key work here is "moderate." That is, French culture contains a dynamic that includes numerous opposing beliefs, values, attitudes, and behaviors. In such an environment, extremes tend

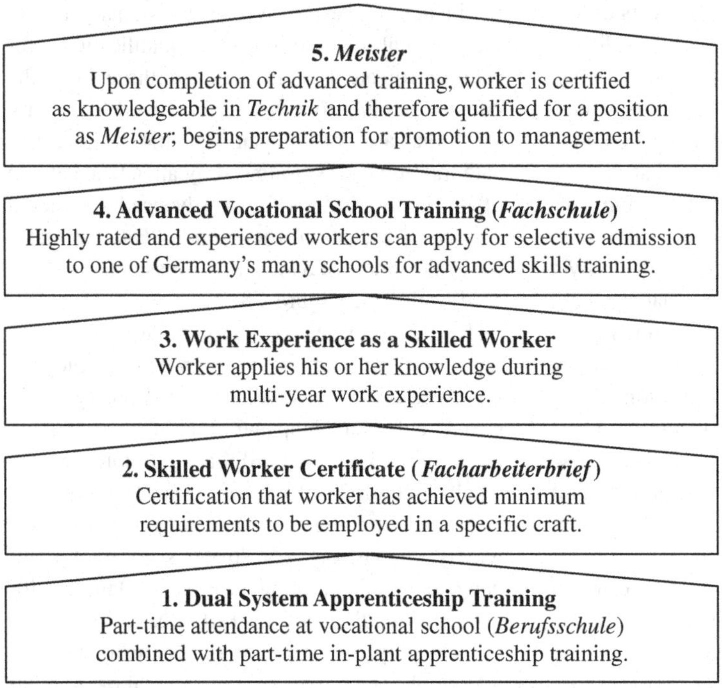

5. Meister
Upon completion of advanced training, worker is certified
as knowledgeable in *Technik* and therefore qualified for a position
as *Meister*; begins preparation for promotion to management.

4. Advanced Vocational School Training (*Fachschule*)
Highly rated and experienced workers can apply for selective admission
to one of Germany's many schools for advanced skills training.

3. Work Experience as a Skilled Worker
Worker applies his or her knowledge during
multi-year work experience.

2. Skilled Worker Certificate (*Facharbeiterbrief*)
Certification that worker has achieved minimum
requirements to be employed in a specific craft.

1. Dual System Apprenticeship Training
Part-time attendance at vocational school (*Berufsschule*)
combined with part-time in-plant apprenticeship training.

Figure 4.8. Germany's dual system of vocational training

to give way to a blend of tolerance, patience, and flexibility.

Going one step further, according to noted anthropologists Edward and Mildred Hall (1990), the French tend to be friendly, humorous, and frequently sarcastic. They admire people who have strong opinions and openly disagree with them, in contrast with many Americans who often prefer people that agree with them. As a result, the French are accustomed to conflict, and will frequently assume in negotiations that many issues simply cannot be reconciled. Many Anglo-Americans, by contrast, tend to believe that conflicts can frequently be resolved if both parties make the effort and are willing to compromise. Perhaps Americans are more optimistic, while French are more fatalistic.

In addition, personal relationships are very important to the French and can take considerable time to develop. The French tend to evaluate a person's trustworthiness based on first-hand experiences, while many Anglo-Americans tend to base such assessments on past achievements, reputation, or the evaluation by others.

In France, one's social class – aristocracy, upper bourgeoisie, upper-middle bourgeoisie, middle class, lower-middle class, and lower class – is important and social interactions are frequently influenced by stereotypes. Moreover, most French can expect little change in their social class, regardless of their accomplishments. It is very difficult to climb the social ladder. The French tend to be very status conscious, and sometimes enjoy displaying their status and culture to friends and strangers alike. As one French student replied when asked about the primary difference between the French and Americans, "The French have more culture" (Hooker, 2003, p. 234). While many Americans may reject this assertion, or even question what it means to have "more" culture, they too are sometimes seen bragging about their own cultural superiority.

A French company is typically referred to as a *société*, or association. Incorporated firms are referred to as *Société Anonyme*, or simply SA Compared to typical American and British firms, French organizations tend to be highly centralized, with rigid structures and reporting channels. As a result, decisions frequently take considerable time both to make and to implement. Foreigners frequently complain about encountering excessive bureaucratic red tape when dealing with French companies (Hickson, 1993). In addition, many French managers are seen as highly autocratic, and often more interested in protecting their personal turf than in working with others in the organization to achieve significant results. French managers seldom share information with subordinates in the belief that knowledge is power.

Reflecting a tradition of class-consciousness, there is often a large class distinction made at work between managers (or *cadre*) and workers (Barsoux and Lawrence, 1991). In the past, most senior executives of France's leading companies (as well as most of France's top political leaders) graduated from a small set of elite polytechnic universities called *grandes ecoles*. The program of study at these schools historically emphasized engineering and mathematics over business in the belief that anyone who can master mathematics can accomplish almost anything. However, this focus is now changing, and these institutions are globalizing at a rapid pace. More and more junior managers are now seeking MBA programs in Europe and elsewhere. School ties are routinely maintained and exploited throughout one's career.

On the job, French leaders are often formal, impersonal, and authoritarian. In interpersonal relations, they can be critical of individuals and institutions alike. A French schoolteacher observed that "the operating principle of French education is negative reinforcement" (Hall and Hall, 1990, p. 99). This tendency carries over to the workplace, where subordinates are routinely criticized. By contrast, Americans tend to believe a bit more in the value of positive reinforcement and incentives over punishment.

Rules and regulations proliferate in French organizations, much as they do in German firms. However, their use and implementation can be quite different. While many Germans use policies and procedures to improve the efficiency of operations, the French prefer *savoir faire* as a substitute for following structured procedures. Cultural expectations require German mangers to remain on schedule, maintain commitments, and deal with problems as they arise. By contrast, the more individualistic French are more likely to be concerned with following proper professional protocol. Even so, unlike the Germans, they will often ignore rules when they interfere with the attainment of a key goal (Brunstein, 1995).

In the workplace (and in contrast to the corporate cultures in many US and UK firms), many French employees are not motivated by competition or the desire to emulate their colleagues. Outsiders frequently claim that they do not have the same work ethic that many Americans and Asians have. French workers tend to avoid overtime work, work an average (and legally-mandated) 35-hour workweek, and receive one of the longest vacations in the world. While the French admire the industriousness of Americans and Asians, for example, they believe that quality of life is often more important than success at work, and attach great importance to their leisure time. However, few would argue that they work hard during regularly scheduled hours and have a reputation for high productivity. This reputation results in part from a French tradition of craftsmanship and in part from the fact that a high percentage of French workers are employed in small, independent businesses where quality is respected.

Many US managers believe that it is more difficult to get along with the French than with any other European nation. Not surprisingly, many French managers feel the same about Americans. Consider the following examples. According to Hall and Hall (1990), many US managers criticize their French managerial counterparts because for a number of reasons: they won't delegate; they won't keep their subordinates informed; they don't feel a sense of responsibility towards their subordinates; they refuse to accept responsibility of things; they are not team players; they are overly sensitive to hierarchy and status; they are highly authoritarian; they are not interested in improving their job skills or knowledge; they are primarily concerned with their own self-interest; and they are less mobile than Americans. Obviously, there are variations in such observations but, according to these noted anthropologies, this is the gist of American opinion.

At the same time, Hall and Hall (1990) quote several French managers who hold similarly negative opinions about their US counterparts: US managers in Europe are not creative; they are too tied to their checklists. Success is not achieved by logic and procedure alone. American executives are reliable and hardworking, and often charming and innocent. But they are too narrow in their focus; they are not well rounded. They have no time for cultural interests and lack appreciation for art, music, and philosophy. Too many American executives are preoccupied with financial reporting. This syndrome produces people who avoid decisions. Finally, Americans do not know how to present themselves; they sprawl and slouch and have no finesse.

It can be argued here that perhaps the perceptions on both sides are correct to some extent. Clearly, one factor that may help explain these differing perceptions is the fundamental difference between French and American cultures in terms of their time orientation. As noted above, most American are decidedly monochronic, meaning that they tend to stress a high degree of scheduling in their lives, concentration of effort on one activity at a time, and elaborate codes of behavior built around promptness in meeting obligations and appointments. Put more simply, many Americans tend to be a bit linear in their thinking and behavior, always focusing on the ultimate goal. By contrast, most French are polychronic, stressing human relationships and social interaction over arbitrary schedules and appointments and engaging in several activities simultaneously with frequent interruptions. To the French, one might suggest, the journey is probably more important than the ultimate destination.

The Malaysian Bumiputra firm

Malaysia is a nation of 21 million people. Fifty-nine per cent of the population is native Malay, often called *bumiputras* (or "sons of the soil"). Another 32 per cent of the population is ethnic Chinese and 9 per cent are of Indian origin. Islam is the official religion of Malaysia and nearly all Malays are Muslim. Non-Malays are free to choose other religions. The Chinese are largely Buddhist, with some Taoists, Christians, and Confucianists.

In fact, many Chinese practice multiple religions. Indians tend to be Hindu or Sikh, but some are Christian.

A person's ancestral background is often important in determining social status and future opportunities (Lewis, 1999; Gannon, 2001). Wealth is highly admired and many *bumiputra* Malaysians believe that success or failure is the result of fate or the will of God. Others, like the Chinese, have a somewhat greater tendency to believe that people control their own destiny. Malaysians from all three cultural backgrounds value the family above all else and often use family connections to gain employment and other advantages. Families, in turn, place a high value on personal loyalty and education as a means to get ahead. While all people identify with being Malaysians, they will often identify more strongly with their ethnic background than with their national citizenship.

Working with Malaysians can require a considerable degree of cultural sensitivity. Not only are one's status and position in the organizational hierarchy important, but also power distances tend to be very high. In business transactions, this means sending business representatives who are of at least an equivalent rank to one's prospective customers. Sending someone of lower rank can be deemed insulting. In the workplace, respecting older workers is important, even by managers who have greater authority. As in many Asian countries, age is highly respected and conveys a sense of both wisdom and authority over others.

Maintaining politeness and harmony are also important, and open conflict is avoided at any cost. Above all, visitors must not cause others to lose face in any of the three ethnic groups. Preserving respect and dignity, even in the face of disagreement, is fundamental to understanding all Malaysians.

Family relationships are important as families form the basis of this highly collectivistic society among all ethnic groups, Malays, Chinese, and Indians. Participative decision-making is commonplace, so long as group elders allow it. In negotiations, compromise and collaboration are preferred over confrontation, competition, or a winner-takes-all approach. This emphasis on moderation reflects both Chinese and Malay teachings.

As such, listening carefully to one's partners and watching for body language becomes critical in this high context culture.

Bumiputra firms tend to be run based on principles that are consistent with the Malaysian cultures. Organizations tend to be somewhat flat with power centered at the top. Many businesses are family owned and family run. Communication both within an organization and between organizations and their customers is often subtle and generally transmitted in an indirect style. Maintaining one's humility and modesty is crucial. Strong emotions are seldom exhibited, work activities tend to be polychronic, and work goals are modest. Managers are often hired based on family connections, although competence is also important. Status is important at all levels of the hierarchy.

While differences can obviously be found across Malaysia's *bumiputra* firms, common characteristics include the following: managers place a high value on protocol, rank, and status; self-confidence and ability to be sensitive to the needs of others are valued managerial qualities; managerial legitimacy is based on education and family background; social relationships are based on collectivist principles; business is largely based on long-term mutual trust; high context communication is important; employee selection is based on combination of family connections, cultural grouping, and skills and abilities; managers must show concern for subordinates' welfare; it is acceptable to terminate employment for poor performance; finally, Malaysian firms are reluctant to lay off employees during difficult economic times.

For many years, the government has supported an affirmative action program in hiring and promotion that favors the majority *bumiputras* over ethnic Chinese and Indians, arguing that such a program is necessary to overcome traditional Chinese dominance in business. *Bumiputra* employees are generally thought to be less aggressive and less experienced in business, and can be both humble and shy with strangers compared to the Chinese and Indians. *Bumiputra* firms often enjoy special access to government funding and government contracts.

Among ethnic Chinese, their cultural tendency towards collectivism often extends beyond the family into something called a *pok chow* (Gannon, 2001). *Pok chow* translates roughly as "gang contracting," and exists when groups of workers band together to seek and conduct work as a team. (Indeed, it represents an ancient Chinese version of the contemporary "western" self-managing team.) Members join together by mutual consent, determine their own work rules, division of labor, and procedures for dividing up their compensation. They frequently even elect their own leaders. They then sell their services to firms or other employers looking for work to be done. *Pok chow* crews are especially popular in the construction industry in Malaysia, where employers only have to deal with crew leaders and can dispense with other complicated organizational procedures or requirements.

The Mexican grupo

Cultural anthropologists and other social scientists tend to describe Mexican culture as being somewhat collectivistic, hierarchical, polychronic, paternalistic, group-centered, security-oriented, somewhat formal, and at times fatalistic (Kras, 1989; Engholm and Grimes, 1997). This certainly does not apply to all Mexicans; indeed, it does not even recognize that Mexico is a multicultural society with both European and native influences. Even so, foreign visitors frequently observe that Mexicans will at times go to great lengths to protect their dignity, uphold their honor, and maintain their good name. The uniqueness of the individual is honored in Mexico, and people are judged on their individual achievements, demeanor, trustworthiness, and character. Personal respect is a very important element in any relationship.

Mexican business culture operates under a strict status system. Most business is conducted between equals, and titles and social position are important. As a result, it is unlikely that a Mexican company president would meet with a mid-level representative of another firm, even an important foreign firm. Thus, smart international companies send presidents to meet presidents, vice presidents to meet vice presidents, and so forth. In addition, a personal introduction through a mutual friend is always helpful, as it is in many parts of the world.

Networking is also very important in Mexico. Cultivating personal relationships with those who may be in a position to help is crucial to successful business. These relationships are typically built on complex personal ties rather than legal contracts as is typical in much of the west. Being accepted as part of a network also entails reciprocity. This requires you to use your own contacts and connections (*palancas*) to help others when called upon for assistance. This is similar to the Chinese concept of *guanxi*. Success thus often depends in part on who you know.

Many Mexican companies take a paternalistic approach in their relations with their employees. This often means providing services that are not traditionally considered the responsibility of employers throughout much of the west. For example, many Mexican employees will expect the company to provide transportation to the work site. This is often accomplished by subcontracting privately owned buses to travel through the neighborhoods of the employees and gather the workers each morning. Many firms also provide cafeterias and feed their employees lunch each day.

In any culture, the use of time can tell us a great deal about how organizations (and societies) work. This is clearly true in Mexico. Time is frequently used intentionally to demonstrate who is more important. Making someone wait shows power, prestige, and status. At the same time, managers must be careful not to offend their counterparts and thereby risk losing business.

Another aspect of time is the sense of urgency with which business is done. Mexico is famous for the concept of *mañana*. The idea here is that there is always another day to complete today's work. While putting things off is commonplace, it would be incorrect to equate this phenomenon with laziness or an unprofessional work attitude. Rather, it represents a different approach to doing business – one that seeks to prioritize conflicting requirements. Mexicans tend to believe that there are other priorities in life than just work and that conditions often conspire to prevent the realization of plans as envisioned. Rather than get unduly stressed about multiple and often conflicting demands, they often take a more relaxed attitude, assuming that things will eventually get done. This is sometimes difficult for

many Anglo-Americans, Asians, and Europeans to comprehend. As such, foreigners must understand that when Mexicans promise something will be done by a certain time or date, they are often saying this to please the person they are dealing with rather that giving an straightforward appraisal of when the work will be done. In Mexico, unlike many other countries, such promises are not considered a contract or firm obligation. Time commitments are more likely to be made out of politeness and the need for having a ballpark idea of when the work will be completed.

When doing business in Mexico, proper contacts with various government departments can be vital for success. Most Mexican business people tend to be somewhat scornful of the effectiveness of political officials in general and often claim that they want little to do with them. However, in Mexico (as elsewhere) when a cabinet official, governor, or mayor launches a new program, those same business people often race to see who can be first on the scene to lend a hand and participate in the program. There is a reason for this. No political office in the US can compare in terms of raw power to that wielded by government officials in Mexico. Top government officials preside as if over a fiefdom and their decisions can have a significant impact on any business. Official contacts are of tremendous help to any business endeavor. Another benefit is that one's credibility within the business community increases proportionally to the depth and breadth of one's access to government officials.

In recent years, the Mexican government has taken significant steps to crack down on bribery and corruption at all levels. This is not to say that major bribery no longer exists, but it is much more subtle and is less likely to involve visitors from other countries. The tradition of bribery, or *mordida* (the bite), predates the Mexican Republic and one may still be asked for a "contribution" from time to time. Small-scale bribery often involves minor officials that regularly deal with foreign businesspersons or tourists who expect a small cash payment in return for their providing a service (e.g., extending a tourist card or visa).

A typical Mexican business group (*grupo*) consists of several highly diverse companies that operate in a climate of familial ties, mutual trust, and overall cooperation. *Grupos* are typically led by strong, powerful CEOs who are often also the principal stockholders. Member companies typically share operating philosophies, channels of distribution, marketing intelligence, and efficiencies of scale, even though they are legally separate entities.

Global executives observe that Anglo-American and Mexican managers frequently approach business matters in very different ways. Many of these differences are based on contrasting beliefs concerning what constitutes good management (Engholm and Grimes, 1997). For starters, consider the following: many Mexican managers see Anglo-American managers – particularly those from the US – as being too direct, too impatient, and too reluctant to accept blame. On the other hand, many Anglo-American managers see Mexican managers as being too polite, too indecisive, and too slow to act. In addition, many Anglo-Americans seek rational, linear decisions based on concrete and business-related evidence. By contrast, many Mexican managers use a more non-linear approach, considering other issues (e.g., personal relationships, traditions, and personal loyalties) and reaching decisions through extended discussions with various parties. Many Anglo-Americans see no problem in criticizing others in public or placing blame or responsibility for failure on specific individuals. By contrast, many Mexicans prefer to avoid placing blame and instead focus on the positive aspects of individual behavior or performance.

Many Mexicans value strong interpersonal relationships, human dignity, and the full enjoyment of life. There is a strong belief in the importance of achieving a suitable balance between home life and work life. By contrast, many Anglo-Americans seem to value aggressively attacking problems, egalitarian conduct, and accomplishing tasks at almost any price. Working long hours is assumed and, for many, a rich family life can be a detriment to career success. Finally, Mexican businesspeople typically negotiate contracts and deals in restaurants, hotels, conference rooms, or other neutral territory. Rarely will a Mexican company conduct extensive negotiations at its own place of business.

Foreign observers also suggest that management in Mexico tends to be somewhat more autocratic than is typically found in Anglo-American or European firms. However, while a manager in Mexico must be respected by his or her subordinates for being tough and decisive, he or she must also be seen as *simpatico*, or understanding. Managers in Mexico tend to exhibit a strong sense of paternalism, a caring for the personal side of their employees that is often absent and at times even resented north of the border. They must act like a *patron* and treat their subordinates like an extended family, like Japanese managers. Along with this, managers must also treat their employees with a strong sense of respect; personal slights frequently bring strong resentment. Mexican workers often require more communication, relationship building, and reassurance than employees in some "western" countries.

Finally, Mexican firms are characterized by strong centralized decision-making. While the necessity to decentralize many functions and responsibilities is recognized, it is clearly understood that the boss has the final say. Today, particularly in the larger firms, a new generation of younger and highly educated managers is beginning to gain prominence. This new generation is beginning to change corporate cultures to be more receptive to decentralization of decision-making.

The Nigerian firm

The sub-Saharan region of Africa is vast, and wide variations can be found across its various countries and cultures. Even so, as noted above in table 4.4, some notable general cultural trends can be identified. Perhaps the strongest cultural trends include a strong belief in hierarchy and collectivism, as well as a moderate belief in harmony and polychronic communication and time patterns. In addition, a strong particularistic orientation to rules, laws, and polices can also be found. Having said this, it is still useful to drill down a bit and focus on the cultural similarities and differences within a single country, like the West African nation of Nigeria.

Nigeria consists of three principal ethnic groups – the Hausa-Fulani, Yoruba, and Igbo – who collectively represent about 70 per cent of the population. Another 10 per cent of the population consists of groups numbering more than 1 million members each, including the Kanuri, Tiv, and Ibibio. More than 300 smaller ethnic groups account for the remaining 20 per cent of the population. As a nation, Nigeria's official language is English. This derives from the many years of British colonial rule, but is also used by the government to provide one unifying language. In addition, over 400 different dialects can be found across the country.

Nigeria is also a land of religious diversity, with Muslims living predominantly in the north and Christians predominantly in the south. Native religions, in which people believe in deities, spirits, and ancestor worship, are spread throughout the country. Many Muslims and Christians may also intertwine their beliefs with more unorthodox indigenous ones.

Along with South Africa, Nigeria is considered a super-power in the African continent and consequently Nigerians are generally proud of their country. It has the largest population in Africa and the land is endowed with vast quantities of natural resources. It is the sixth largest oil-producing nation and has a well-educated and industrious society.

At the same time, Nigeria consistently ranks very high on expert's lists of corrupt countries in which to do business. Bribery is endemic. Indeed, Transparency International, an organization dedicated to eliminating corruption in international business, ranked Nigeria as the world's most corrupt nation in its study of eighty-five countries (*Economist*, 1999).

Extended families are the norm in Nigeria and are in fact the backbone of the social system. Grandparents, cousins, aunts, uncles, sisters, brothers and in-laws all work as a unit through life. Hierarchy and seniority guide family relationships. Social standing and recognition is achieved through extended families. Similarly, a family's honor is influenced by the actions of its members. Individuals turn to members of the extended family for financial aid and guidance, and the family is expected to provide for the welfare of every member. Although the role of the extended family is diminishing somewhat in urban areas, there remains a strong tradition of mutual caring and responsibility among the members.

Nigeria is a hierarchical society. Age and position earns – even demands – respect. Age is believed to confer wisdom, so older people are granted respect. The oldest person in a group is revered and honored. In a social situation, they are greeted and served first. In return, the most senior person has the responsibility to make decisions that are in the best interest of the group.

Due to the diverse ethnic make-up of the country, communication styles vary. In the southwest, where the people are from the Yoruba tribe, people's communication employs proverbs, sayings, and even songs to enrich the meaning of what they say. This is especially true when speaking their native language, although many of the same characteristics have been carried into their English language usage. The Yoruba often use humor to prevent boredom during long meetings or serious discussions. They believe that embedding humor in their message guarantees that what they say is not readily forgotten. Meanwhile, Nigerians living in the south of the country tend to speak more directly. Nigerians also make extensive use of nonverbal behavior (e.g., facial expressions) to communicate their views.

In discussions, Nigerians frequently begin with a general idea and then slowly move to the specific, often using a somewhat circuitous route. Their logic is often contextual. That is, they tend to look for the rationale behind behavior and attempt to understand the context. Thus, behavior is viewed in terms of its surrounding context, and not simply in terms of what has been observed. As a result, what is not said is often more important than what is.

Organization and management in Nigeria – at least in medium- and large-scale firms – has been heavily influenced by British practices, although these practices have been modified to suit local cultures. Many observers have agreed with Choudhry (1986) that "the general tone of management is prescriptive, often authoritarian, inflexible, and insensitive." Bureaucracy and hierarchy seem to rule. Some have suggested that these characteristics can be traced to Nigeria's colonial past, where foreign administrators had little faith in the abilities of local employees and hence retained managerial authority at the top of the organization. The menial work that was assigned to subordinates was closely supervised, and no real authority was delegated. However, this is likely only part of the explanation, as Nigerian cultural trends also reinforce this approach to management style (Abudu, 1986). In any case, we frequently find situations in African firms where subordinates have little to do while their supervisors are overworked – a typical indication that managers are reluctant to delegate much autonomy. In this regard, Moses Kiggundu (1988) concludes that this form of organization often results in "a debilitating unwillingness to take independent action."

Another characteristic here is perhaps more directly influenced by local cultures. As Kiggundu (1988, p. 225) also observes in his study of African organizations:

> there would be an atmosphere of management by crisis as events would seem to take everybody by surprise. Conflicts would tend to be avoided, smoothed over rather than directly confronted, Although there would be a lot of activities in these organizations, very few people would be able to assess how well or badly they or the organization as a whole was performing.

In response to this negative portrait, Nzelibe (1986, p. 11) counters that we must remember that there may indeed be a fundamental conflict between western and African management thought. Specifically, he observes that "whereas Western management thought advocates eurocentrism, individualism, and modernity, African management thought emphasizes ethnocentrism, traditionalism, communialism, and cooperative teamwork."

In any case, most local and foreign researchers agree that the typical power structure and workflows lead to chronic inefficiencies. Top managers are authoritarian, paternalistic, autocratic, overworked, highly educated, articulate, and widely traveled. However, they seldom provide much in the way of visionary leadership. Organizations frequently do not have clearly stated or widely understood goals and objectives. They tend to be heavily politicized and have weak executive and management systems. Senior executives are often frequently seen as spending too much time outside

the organization working on political, religious, and family issues (Blunt and Jones, 1992).

On the other hand, middle managers often lack critical managerial skills and knowledge about the industry in which they are working. At the same time, according to Kiggundu (1988), many mid-level managers exhibit low levels of motivation, tend to be risk averse, are often unwilling to take independent action or show initiative, seem to prefer (or are at least used to) close supervision, and are unwilling to delegate. He goes on the point out that mid-level managers in a wide range of developing countries (i.e., not just in Africa) are frequently understaffed and are characterized by weak and/or inappropriate management systems and organizational controls.

Finally, lower level employees in Nigeria (and Africa more generally) are often described as being overstaffed and inefficient. Operators tend to be underutilized, underpaid, resistant to change, and rewarded based on factors unrelated to actual job performance. As a result, we often see low morale, lack of commitment, high turnover, and high absenteeism. Communication up and down the hierarchy tends to be poor.

Organizing frameworks: a comparative summary

So, what lessons can be drawn about organization design and management practices as they are potentially influenced by cultural variations across countries and cultures? Again, while numerous variations can be found within each culture, general trends can nonetheless be identified for purposes of making rough comparisons. As illustrated in table 4.5, a solid argument can be made that both of these critical components of organizational competitiveness have been found to have different central tendencies across countries based on their prevailing cultures.

In collectivistic cultures, for example, families – either extended families in China or corporate families in Japan – tend to overshadow how business enterprise is both organized and managed. By contrast, in more individualistic cultures like the UK or the US, relatively greater influence is placed on individual autonomy, personal accountability and achievement-based compensation. Likewise,

Table 4.5 Organizing frameworks: a comparative summary

Country	Organization Design Trends	Management Style Trends
Chinese *Gong-si*	Flat, fluid organizations with little structure; power centered in closely-knit family owners; large numbers of non-family contingent workers; hierarchical and autocratic; collectivistic.	Supervisory role focuses on direction and control; patriarchal; relationship-based management; family managers as generalists; emphasis on building trust and personal relationships (*guanxi*); somewhat monochronic; highly centralized and rapid decision-making with rapid implementation.
French *Société Anonyme*	Tall bureaucratic organizations; hierarchical and autocratic; status conscious; clear differentiation between management and workers.	Top-down autocratic management; supervisory role focuses on direction and control; somewhat relationship-based management; somewhat collectivistic and harmony-oriented; polychronic; slow and centralized decision-making with slow implementation.
German *Konzern*	Formal organizations with strict hierarchies; power dispersed across multiple stakeholders, including works councils and industrial unions.	Supervisory role focuses on technical expertise and consensus building; rule-based and somewhat linear management; formal; highly participative; slow consensual decision-making with moderate pace of implementation; strong apprenticeship training.
Japanese *Kaisha* and *Keiretsu*	Formal organizations consisting of closely-knit extended networks; hierarchical and autocratic; collectivistic; close affiliation with banks; strong trading companies; company unions.	Supervisory role focuses on paternalism and support, particularly at lower levels of the hierarchy; relationship-based management; strong group orientation; harmony-oriented; emphasis on trust and personal relationships; avoids overt conflict; emphasis on employee development and mutual commitments; employees as fixed cost; slow decision-making but rapid implementation.
Malaysian *Bumiputra* Company	Formal organizations consisting of multicultural and family-based networks; status and harmony-oriented; strongly hierarchical; collectivistic.	Supervisory role focuses on paternalism and support; patriarchal; relationship-based management; stresses harmony and respect; emphasis on trust and personal relationships; slow autocratic decision making with slow implementation.
Mexican *Grupo*	Formal organizations frequently organized like extended families; hierarchical; autocratic; somewhat collectivistic; respect for individuals important.	Supervisory role focuses on direction and control; patriarchal and autocratic; relationship-based and nonlinear management; use of connections (*palancas*); emphasis on trust and personal relationships; slow autocratic decision-making with slow implementation.
Nigerian Company	Autocratic and bureaucratic; hierarchical and patriarchal; somewhat collectivistic.	Supervisory role focuses on direction and control; relationship-based management; autocratic; centralized; resistant to change; close work-family integration; weak work ethic.
US Corporation	Often informal organizations comprising loosely-coupled systems; power based in stockholders and executive team; emphasis on efficiency and flexibility; moderately egalitarian; mastery-oriented.	Supervisory role focuses on direction and control; rule-based management; stresses individual achievement and responsibility; imperial CEO; highly-trained management cadre; flexible and innovative; respect for rules and policies and a sense of order; extensive use of contingent workers; linear, rapid, and somewhat autocratic decision-making but with slow implementation; employees as variable cost.

while formal organizations are stressed in both Malaysia and Germany, the former emphasizes centralized power and influence processes while the later emphasizes decentralization and collaboration. While organizations in both Mexico and Nigeria are often characterized as being hierarchical and autocratic, differences can often be found in the extent to which a general level of trust and a respect between superiors and subordinates exists. And while casual observers see both organization design and management practice in countries like Australia, Canada, the UK, and the US as being very similar, significant differences can also be found, as discussed above.

The theory development and research implications of these trends will be discussed below.

Participation and decision-making

A principal function of management is making timely, relevant – and hopefully wise – decisions concerning the future directions of the firm. Critical to this process is where, when, and how information is sourced for optimum results. In other words, who has useful and important information or viewpoints that can lead to better decisions and who can be ignored either for confidentiality or efficiency reasons? Clearly, there are considerable and often heated disagreements on this issue. At the heart of this disagreement is the issue of *employee participation*.

Not surprisingly, employee participation can take many different forms, both within and between cultures. In Japan, for example, culture and traditions dictate that managers consult with their workers on many aspects of individual and departmental performance. Individual employees are encouraged to step forward with ideas to improve operations or product development. As a result, employee suggestion systems abound in Japanese companies. However, organization-wide issues are typically left to senior managers. By contrast, Germany long ago enacted a series of federal laws that mandate employee participation in virtually all key decisions an organization makes. This form of participation normally takes place through elected representatives to management boards, rather than having individual employees step forward with ideas or suggestions. Finally, the situation in countries like Australia, Canada, Great Britain, and the US is somewhat difficult to describe, since it is characterized by wide variations in the amount of allowed participation. For example, some companies in these countries support broad-based employee participation, while others shy away from it. No cultural or legal mandates require participation, so prevailing organizational norms are set either by corporate culture or senior management. At the same time, Canada, which is often identified as being part of the Anglo cluster but is in fact strongly bi-cultural if not multicultural, is seen by many outside observers as being somewhat more participative than any of the other three.

As we consider these trends, however, two caveats must be kept in mind. First, most of the rigorous studies on the impact of employee participation and involvement were conducted among either English-speaking (typically British and North American) or Scandinavian (e.g., Norwegian, Swedish) employees. As a result, far less is known about the motivational potential of employee participation across other cultural groupings. The obvious unanswered question here is the extent to which theory actually translates into action around the world. Put another way, do employees in countries as diverse as Costa Rica, Egypt, India, Malaysia, and Nigeria, and all perform better if allowed high degrees of participation?

A second problem is a bit more esoteric. Specifically, throughout the employee participation movement, the actual concept itself remains only loosely defined. That is, what exactly does "participation" or employee involvement mean? How is the concept operationalized? And how far down the organizational hierarchy does actual participation actually exist? In point of fact, employee participation is operationalized in many different ways in different cultures around the world. Differences can also be found in the extent to which senior managers are actually committed to such participation or just give lip service to it or – worse still – use it as a form of exploitation by creating the impression that "your opinion counts" when in fact it does not.

The intersection of these two problems – the questionable universality of participation as a sound management principle and the variable implementation of participative principles – creates significant challenges for global managers. Simply put, can they trust what they have been taught about how much they should attempt to involve rank-and-file employees when sent to a new and unfamiliar work environment?

To address this challenge and delve further into the manner in which participation strategies are enacted around the world, we need an analytic framework to guide further study. While many such heuristics are available, we will make use of a long-standing framework initially developed by Victor Vroom and Phillip Yetton (1973; Yukl and Lepsinger, 2004). Their "normative decision model" has seen widespread use among scholars and managers, due in part to its strong empirical base and in part to its down-to-earth approach to

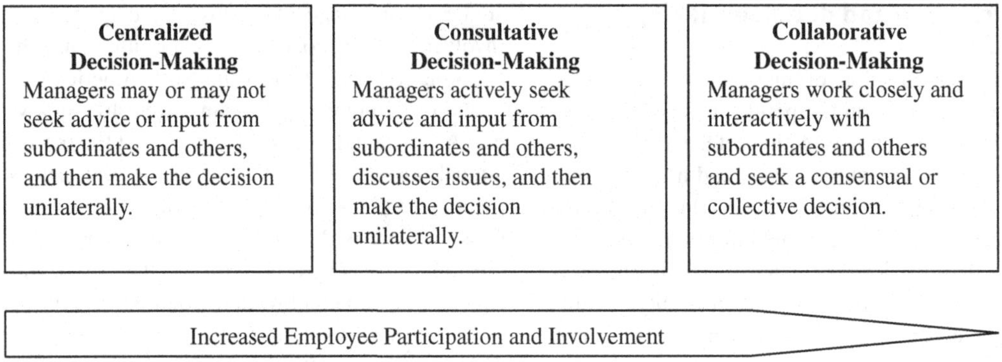

Centralized Decision-Making	**Consultative Decision-Making**	**Collaborative Decision-Making**
Managers may or may not seek advice or input from subordinates and others, and then make the decision unilaterally.	Managers actively seek advice and input from subordinates and others, discusses issues, and then make the decision unilaterally.	Managers work closely and interactively with subordinates and others and seek a consensual or collective decision.

Increased Employee Participation and Involvement

Figure 4.9 Approaches to organizational decision-making

understanding how decisions up and down the organizational hierarchy are actually made. The part of the model we use here is a classification scheme relating to the amount of participation allowed subordinates. As adapted from Vroom and Yetton, we identify three categories (see figure 4.9):

- *Centralized decisions*, where the manager-in-charge either makes a decision or solves a problem unilaterally or after brief discussions or input from subordinates or others. (Many researchers refer to this as "authoritarian" decision-making, but it is more accurate to characterize it as being unilateral in nature.)
- *Consultative decisions*, where the manager-in-charge actively seeks advice and input from subordinates and others – often working together as a team – but still makes a unilateral decision.
- *Collaborative decisions*, where the manager-in-charge works closely and interactively with subordinates and others and seeks a consensual or collective decision in which everyone had an opportunity to take part. (Vroom and Yetton (1973) refer to this as a "group decision.")

Centralized decision-making

If we look at a typical decision-making process in many of the so-called Anglo countries (e.g., Australia, Canada, UK, US), we often find a process much like that shown in figure 4.10 – but with obvious notable variations. We see, in essence,

centralized decision-making. Here problem identification is largely a managerial or supervisory responsibility; workers' opinions are often ignored or not offered in the first place. Once a problem or issue has been identified, it is management's responsibility to analyze and resolve it, often with the help of senior managers or outside specialists and consultants. Decisions are then passed down to lower-level employees in the form of changed work procedures. Not surprisingly, since the people at the bottom of the hierarchy often have little understanding of management's conclusions or intents, decision implementation tends to be slow, as management must convince workers to join the decision. Frequently, extrinsic rewards (i.e., externally administered rewards such a pay or bonuses) must be used instead of intrinsic rewards (i.e., internally administered rewards such as pride in accomplishment or job satisfaction) as a result of this process.

To see how this centralized decision-making process can work in the US, consider the example of executive selection at General Motors. For several years, and for a variety of reasons, GM's auto sales had declined precipitously. Despite continual pressure to resign and let someone else take the helm, CEO Rick Wagoner repeatedly sought the support of friendly members of the board of directors to continue in his leadership role. Finally, in 2008, when losses reached $40 billion a year, Wagoner was forced to admit that he was "somewhat stretched" in his job and needed

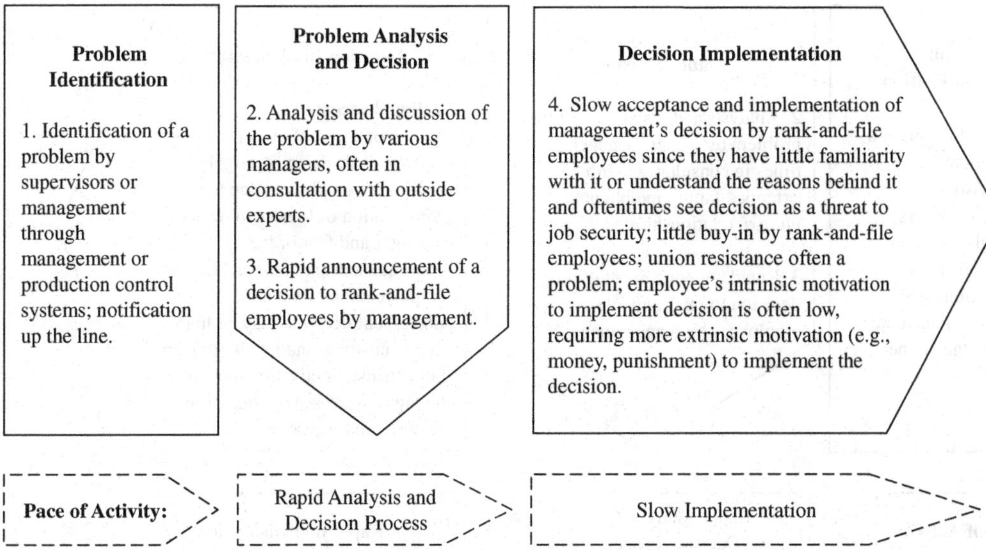

Problem Identification	Problem Analysis and Decision	Decision Implementation
1. Identification of a problem by supervisors or management through management or production control systems; notification up the line.	2. Analysis and discussion of the problem by various managers, often in consultation with outside experts. 3. Rapid announcement of a decision to rank-and-file employees by management.	4. Slow acceptance and implementation of management's decision by rank-and-file employees since they have little familiarity with it or understand the reasons behind it and oftentimes see decision as a threat to job security; little buy-in by rank-and-file employees; union resistance often a problem; employee's intrinsic motivation to implement decision is often low, requiring more extrinsic motivation (e.g., money, punishment) to implement the decision.

Pace of Activity:	Rapid Analysis and Decision Process	Slow Implementation

Figure 4.10. Centralized decision-making (e.g., US Corporation)

more help. His answer was to divide his current job into two, retaining the CEO and chairman's largely external role while promoting long-term GM executive Frederick Henderson to become the new Chief Operating Officer. Henderson had an established record as a turn-around artist within several of GM's divisions in both Asia and Europe, and Wagoner was convinced he could help with the company's transition into a more competitive organization. But Wagner's decision was taken largely unilaterally. It was "something I'd been thinking about for a while and talking to the board about" (Stoll and Spector, 2008). In view of the pivotal role played by a COO in any restructuring effort, it is interesting how few of the major stakeholders in GM's future (e.g., alliance partners, unions, division managers, suppliers, distributors, etc.) were actually involved in this decision. Wagoner proposed Henderson, the board agreed, and the decision was announced. At the same time, the board of directors voted to increase Wagoner's salary by 33 per cent (Stoll and Brulliard, 2008). It is interesting to note here that in other western countries, including Australia, the UK, the Netherlands, and Sweden, to name just a few, it is customary to allow company stockholders to vote on executive compensation; not so in the US (Lublin, 2008).

Meanwhile, the decision process described above in not dissimilar from that commonly found in Chinese *gong-si*, or family-based companies. Despite being a collectivistic country, China is still hierarchical, leading to centralized power in decision-making. As shown in figure 4.11, problem identification is typically done by either supervisors or owner-managers using fairly rigid management and production control systems; immediate knowledge up the line. The owner-managers then discuss and analyze the problem, often in consultation with extended family members or *guanxi* relationships. Because of the autocratic decision style, rapid announcement of a decision to rank-and-file employees by management is possible. Rapid acceptance and implementation of owner-manager's decision by largely contingent employees is also possible due to a combination of loyalty to owner-manager and fear of the consequences on non-compliance. Employees' intrinsic motivation to implement decision may be high due to customs and loyalty to firm, but extrinsic motivation may also be high due to importance of job security and income.

Problem Identification	Problem Analysis and Decision	Decision Implementation
1. Identification of a problem by supervisors or owner-managers through management or production control systems; immediate knowledge up the line.	2. Analysis and discussion of the problem by owner-managers, at times in consultation with extended family members or *guanxi* relationships. 3. Rapid announcement of a decision to rank-and-file employees by management.	4. Rapid acceptance and implementation of owner-manager's decision by largely contingent employees due to a combination of loyalty to owner-manager and fear of the consequences on non-compliance; employee's intrinsic motivation to implement decision may be high due to customs and loyalty to firm, but extrinsic motivation may also be high due to importance of job security and income.

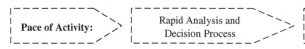

Pace of Activity:	Rapid Analysis and Decision Process	Rapid Implementation

Figure 4.11. Centralized decision-making (e.g., Chinese *gong-si*)

A good example of how Chinese family-based companies organize and make decisions can be seen in the case of the East Hope Group (Chen, 2001). This business conglomerate, now headquartered in Pudong, Shanghai, was originally founded by four brothers of the Liu family when they sold their watches and bicycles to raise the necessary $120 to start a very small agricultural business. Today, the East Hope Group was the largest animal feed producer – as well as the largest private enterprise – in China, with 10,000 employees working in 120 various business enterprises around the country. East Hope has recently expanded into real estate, heavy industries, financial investments and securities, and construction, and is a major shareholder in Minsheng Bank, the first privately owned bank in China. The four brothers and their families jointly own the East Hope Group Corporation, Ltd, while each brother heads of one of the firm's four separate and highly diverse divisions. Notably, the "dominant" family head is not the eldest, but the third brother, Liu Yonghao. In addition, Liu family members can be found throughout the key executive and managerial positions in all four divisions. When important decisions arise, family members meet to discuss strategies and tactics and make decisions about future courses of action. These decisions are then relayed to lower level non-family employees for implementation.

Consultative decision-making

Decision-making in a typical Japanese *kaisha* or *keiretsu* reflects Japanese culture and is seen by many observers as being quite distinct from the west. Not surprisingly, Japanese firms endorse the concept of decision-making based on consultations up and down the hierarchy (Kato and Kato, 1992). The system by which this is done is usually called *ringi-seido* (often shortened to simply *ringi-sei*), or circle of discussion as illustrated in figure 4.12. Outside of Japan, it is often called *consultative decision-making*.

When a particular problem or opportunity is identified, a group of workers or supervisors will discuss various parameters of the problem and try and identify possible solutions. At times, technical experts will be brought in for assistance. If the initial results are positive, employees will approach their supervisor for more advice and possible support. This entire process is generally referred to as *nemawashi*. The word *nemawashi* is derived from

Nemawashi
(informal discussions up and down hierarchy; nurturing ideas)

1. Problem identified by supervisors or workers.

2. Lower-level employees in a section or department work together to solve a problem and gain informal consensus around a possible solution.

3. Department heads, section chiefs, and supervisors meet informally to discuss and modify proposal. Technical experts consulted where needed to improve proposal.

4. Departmental consensus is reached on a specific proposal or plan of action. At this stage, considerable planning on the project has been completed.

Ringi-sho
(formal authorization process)

5. A formal written proposal (*ringi-sho*) is then drafted and passed up the chain of command for approval or rejection. Managers who approve of the plan stamp their name on it; managers who do not approve either refrain from stamping or stamp it on the reverse side.

Formal Decision

6. When *ringi-sho* document makes it to top management, it is likely to be approved since rank-and-file managers up the chain of command have already agreed to it.

Decision Implementation

7. Relatively rapid implementation of the decision (as opposed to questioning the decision) since widespread employees buy-in up and down the hierarchy has already been achieved; union resistance infrequent; employee's intrinsic motivation to implement the decision is typically very high since they participated in it.

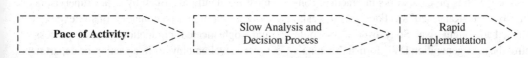

Pace of Activity: Slow Analysis and Decision Process   Rapid Implementation

Figure 4.12. Consultative decision-making (e.g., Japanese *keiretsu*)

a description of the process of preparing the roots of a tree for planting. The concept here is that if the roots are properly prepared, the tree will survive and prosper. Similarly, if a proposal is properly prepared, it too should survive and prosper.

When a group has achieved informal consensus, a formal proposal is then drafted for submission up the chain of command. This formal document, known as a *ringi-sho*, is then reviewed by successively higher levels of management. If a manager agrees with the proposal, he or she stamps his name on it; if not, he or she either refrains from stamping it or stamps it on the reverse side. By the time the document reaches upper management, it has become clear whether it has broad-based support or not. If it does enjoy support, in all likelihood top management will formally adopt the proposal. In this way, upper management frequently has little input into the decision-making process. If

a proposal has universal support up the chain of command, top managers will be hard pressed to oppose it.

While discussions concerning a particular decision or course of action are proceeding, two seemingly contradictory processes often occur that tend to confuse many westerners. In Japan, doing or saying the right thing according to prevailing norms or social custom is referred to as *tatemae*, while doing or saying what one actually prefers to do (which may be difficult) is referred to as *honne*. Thus, in a conversation or meeting, to some westerners a Japanese manager may speak in contradictions or, worse, speak insincerely. In reality, the manager may simply be saying what he believes he is obliged to say, while hoping that through subtle signals the recipient of the message will discover his true desire or intent. This can be confusing to many westerners and requires them to listen carefully and observe body language as well as formal speech (for example, reading someone's face). After all, Japan is a high context culture, while most western nations are not. As a result, when a mid-level manager signs off on a proposal, it can be difficult to determine whether this support is genuine or socially obligatory.

A key point to remember here: the *ringi-sei* process tends to result in slow decisions, often a disadvantage in a fast-paced competitive global business environment. However, this process yields considerable support for and commitment to the emergent solution when it is achieved. By contrast, many western decisions are typically made unilaterally much higher up in the management hierarchy but, once made, frequently face considerable opposition or apathy as managers and workers attempt to implement them. As a result, strategic planning is frequently accomplished more quickly in the west, while strategic implementation is frequently accomplished more quickly in Japan.

To see how this process works in practice, consider Toshiba (Kane, 2008). For several years, Toshiba had fought rival Sony over who would control the next-generation DVD format (Toshiba's HD DVD or Sony's Blu-ray). This was a battle of technology, movie studios, merchandisers, and customers. In 2008, when it finally became clear that Sony's Blu-ray format was going to win the battle, Toshiba's CEO Atsutoshi Nishida initially took no action. Instead, he spent considerable time thinking about both the DVD market in general and Toshiba's role in this changing market in particular. He discussed the matter with numerous colleagues up and down the corporate hierarchy. He talked with his alliance partners outside of Toshiba. Then he held more discussions and floated more proposals. Word came from throughout the organization that the company needed to remain in the DVD market, partly because of pride and partly because people reasoned that the company had the advanced technologies required to compete over the long term. In the end, instead of admitting defeat, Nishida built a consensus within Toshiba and among its partners to cease any further futile competition against Sony. At the same time, he began pushing his researchers to try and leapfrog Blu-ray technology with something even better for

the distant future. Consensus was also reached on a decision to push current marketing efforts harder to capture a larger market share for standard-format (or older) DVD players – a much larger market than the anticipated market for Blu-rays. He then announced quietly that Toshiba was yielding to Sony's Blu-ray. Within two months, Toshiba began shipping new models of standard-format DVD players at reduced costs to global markets.

Collaborative decision-making

Finally, the decision-making process found in many German, Dutch, and Scandinavian firms tend to be more participative than those countries in either the Anglo or the Asian cluster. This is due in large measure to the presence of codetermination laws and works councils. Collaborative decision-making can be highly complex due to the knowledge and power and of the various stakeholders (see figure 4.13). In this process, problems are most frequently identified by either supervisors or workers through a combination of job experience and sophisticated production control processes. Lower-level employees in a section or department begin by working with supervisors to help identify the underlying causes of the problem cause, as well as possible solutions. Next, department heads, section chiefs, and supervisors meet to discuss and develop a proposal to remedy the situation. Technical experts and works council members are frequently consulted as needed to achieve the best possible solution. The problem and possible solutions are then passed up management hierarchy. Management discusses the problem and possible solutions widely and then makes a formal decision, often in consultation and negotiation with works council members and the local industrial union leadership.

Resulting decisions are likely to be widely accepted by rank-and-file employees because of the representative process through which they were made; workers at all levels have had a voice throughout the process. As a result, decision implementation typically proceeds at a moderate pace since, although union resistance may still occur due to structural or contract issues. Employees' intrinsic motivation to implement the decision is

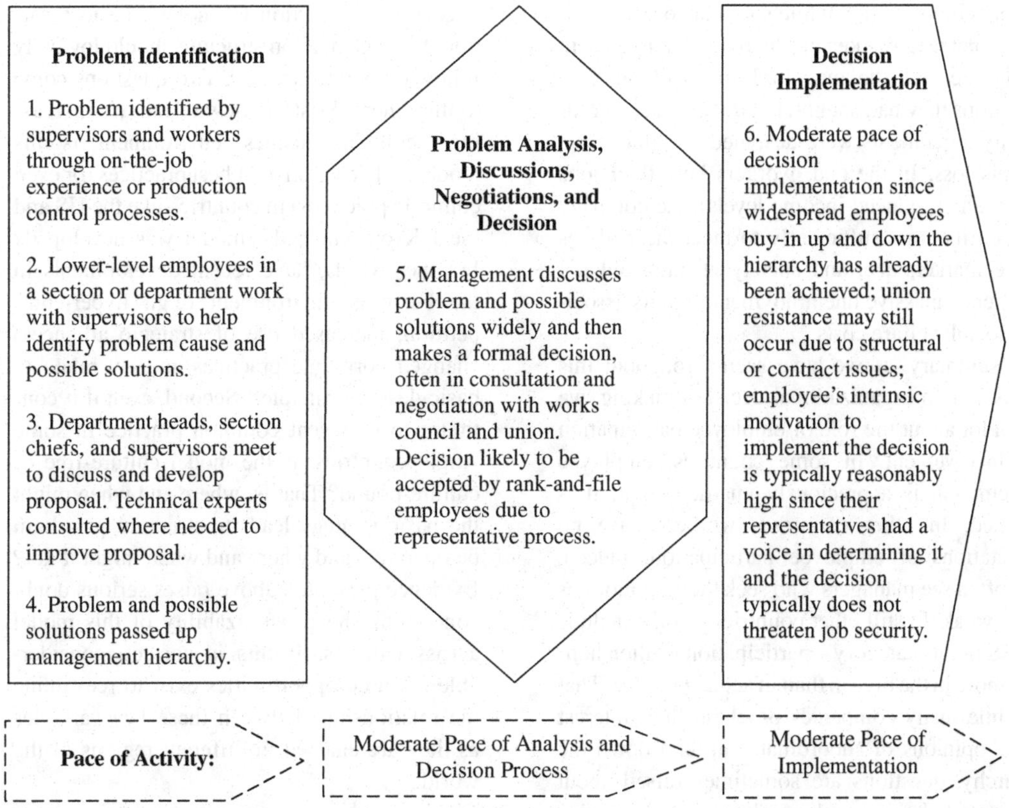

Problem Identification

1. Problem identified by supervisors and workers through on-the-job experience or production control processes.

2. Lower-level employees in a section or department work with supervisors to help identify problem cause and possible solutions.

3. Department heads, section chiefs, and supervisors meet to discuss and develop proposal. Technical experts consulted where needed to improve proposal.

4. Problem and possible solutions passed up management hierarchy.

Problem Analysis, Discussions, Negotiations, and Decision

5. Management discusses problem and possible solutions widely and then makes a formal decision, often in consultation and negotiation with works council and union. Decision likely to be accepted by rank-and-file employees due to representative process.

Decision Implementation

6. Moderate pace of decision implementation since widespread employees buy-in up and down the hierarchy has already been achieved; union resistance may still occur due to structural or contract issues; employee's intrinsic motivation to implement the decision is typically reasonably high since their representatives had a voice in determining it and the decision typically does not threaten job security.

Pace of Activity: → Moderate Pace of Analysis and Decision Process → Moderate Pace of Implementation

Figure 4.13. Collaborative decision-making (e.g., German *konzern*)

typically reasonably high, since their representatives had a voice in determining it and the decision typically does not threaten job security.

To see how collaborative decision-making works, consider again the example of Volkswagen AG (Kothen, McKinley, and Scherer, 1999). When threatened financially due to declining auto sales (discussed above), VW was required to follow a collaborative decision making process as part of Germany's legislated codetermination system. As the management and supervisory boards examined the problem, several traditional solutions – like early retirement, temporary reductions in working hours, and consensual termination agreements – were eliminated, due primarily to excessive costs associated with their implementation. The only viable solution from management's standpoint was

to reduce the working week of all employees without compensatory payments.

To accomplish this, VW needed agreement from its principal union, IG-Metall. At first, union representatives rejected even the basic idea of reducing the working week without compensation. Over time, however, they became convinced of the necessity of change. From then on, the question was how to achieve the company's goal with the minimum of pain for employees. Union leaders and works council members held focus groups with employees to discuss various options and seek suggestions and ideas. These proposals were summarized and fed back to management. After months of discussions and negotiations with works council members and union representatives, a compromise was finally reached that involved shortening working hours without compensation while simultaneously working to increase worker productivity. Management did not receive the magnitude of working hour reductions they had sought, but the increased productivity agreements were designed to compensate for this loss. In the end, workers kept their jobs (although at reduced income levels), the company reduced its costs sufficiently to meet the realities of the marketplace, and society at large did not experience massive unemployment with its associated social welfare costs.

In summary, as we have seen throughout this discussion on organizational decision-making, we hear a lot about the role of employee participation and involvement. In some countries, employee participation is a preciously guarded right; it is assumed. In other countries, workers have no expectations of employee participation; indeed, they often see managers who seek their opinions as being weak. In still other countries – some include the US in this category – participation is often honored more in the breach than in actual practice. That is, while many companies proclaim their interest in the opinions of subordinates up and down the hierarchy, questions are sometimes raised about the sincerity behind such proclamations. Is anyone really listening?

A future research agenda

In closing, it is important to note that there exists considerable research and thinking (as opposed to theory-building) focusing on the influence of cultural differences on the interrelationships between management, organizations, and decision-making. However, in our view, most of the more rigorous materials have become dated and precede the era of globalization, while most of the recent work is observational and anecdotal at best. In our judgment, it is time to our refocus serious research attention on this important topic. Several avenues exist for reasoned theory-building and solid empirical research, including the following:

1. *Strategy-structure relationships.* Most current writings concerning the strategy-structure relationship follow from the early work on General Motors by Alfred Chandler (1962). We believe it is time to question Chandler's basic assertion that organization structure should logically follow corporate strategy. Two questions come to mind here. First, in view of today's increasingly complex business environment, is this model still descriptive of best practices (or even common practices) in countries like the US and the UK on which the model was developed? In other words, have recent developments in the business environment (e.g., hyper-competition, increased use of strategic alliances) changed corporate practices as they relate to basic design principles. Second, even if it continues to represent common practice in some Anglo countries, is the model culture-free or culture-bound? That is, where and when might the basic strategy-leads-to-structure paradigm be operative and where and when might it not? Evidence presented above raises serious doubt concerning the generalizability of this model across cultures. If this is correct, considerable research opportunities exist to reexamine the relationships between these key variables as they are enacted in different regions of the world.

2. *Within- vs. between-group variance in organization design.* Considerable research has been done focusing on variances between organizing models in countries such as Canada, France, Germany, the UK, and the US. However, what is missing in our view is sustained research (on the scope of the GLOBE study) that examines the relative variance in organization design and management practices within specific countries and then compares these findings to variance across countries. The obvious question here is whether within-country variance is larger or smaller that between-country variance. Put another way, can we say that there remains a typical French organizing model compared to typical Mexican, German, or Chinese models? Moreover, as many management observers suggest, are management styles and organizing frameworks beginning to merge into one or more "global" models or is this assertion largely unfounded?

3. *Organization design and competitiveness.* An interesting line of research focuses on the

extent to which there exists a link between specific organization designs and organizational success. That is, are there universal design principles (e.g., flat vs. tall organizations, high vs. low participation, flexible vs. rigid, etc.) upon which organizations can build a foundation for competitive success in the global environment? Alternatively, are there country- or region-specific designs that are best suited to economic success in various parts of the globe?

4. *Patterns of organization change*. In many countries, change is the only constant, as managers continually attempt to refine organizational relationships to improve their competitiveness. This presents an interesting question for researchers who study organization change. Specifically, does culture play a role (significant or otherwise) in determining how far and how fast organizational change efforts go? That is, are some cultures more reluctant to initiate substantive (or even minor) changes to the organization's basic design or is change universal? Decades of research by cultural anthropologists and others suggest that propensity to change is often locally determined. If this is the case, what are the implications for more traditional cultures in the increasingly turbulent and uncertain global economy?

5. *Participation and decision-making*. Much has been written about decision-making styles and strategies. In this regard, our limited review above suggests is that decision-making strategies – particularly those involving relative degrees of employee participation – can vary systematically across cultures. Two research issues emerge here. First, to what extent is this conclusion correct? That is, can we conclude with reasonable certainty that German or Chinese or Japanese organizations use culturally distinct decision styles that systematically differentiate them from other cultures? And, second, can conclusions be drawn concerning the importance of encouraging employee participation for corporate performance and competitiveness or is the concept of participation largely value-based and embedded in certain cultural belief structures regardless of its actual utility for organizational success?

In summary, much has been learned in recent years about the nature and scope of management, organization design, and decision-making around the world. However, much more remains to be done, In this regard, we conclude with an observation made by Kurt Lewin (1951) almost sixty years ago: 'There is nothing so practical as a good theory.' We believe this adage continues to represent some of the best advice available for future organizational and management researchers. However, in closing, we should like to emphasize two words from this declaration. The first word is "theory." While the field of cross-cultural organizational research is rife with well-intentioned observations and vignettes, what is needed now is solid theory-based modeling efforts that attempt to introduce some explanatory power to what has been learned to date. We are seriously in need of well-reasoned theories upon which empiricists can build and managers can manage. In addition, however, a second word in Lewin's declaration also calls for attention: the word "practical." Kurt Lewin understood better than most that, while esoteric theories may be the playground of the intellectual elite, modeling without inherent logic, realism, clarity, and management application is of little use in the long run. What is needed, in our view, is the development of new theories and paradigms that marry managerial experience with scholastic wisdom. In short, we need theories that can work on the ground, not just at 10,000 meters up. In this way, we believe necessary progress can be made to the benefit of organizations and employees alike.

References

Abbeglen, J., and Stalk, G. 1985. *Kaisha: The Japanese Corporation*. New York: Harper & Row.

Abudu, F. 1986. "Work attitudes of Africans, with special reference to Nigeria," *International Studies of Management and Organization* 16(2): 17–36.

Adler, N. 2008a. Personal communication.

Adler, N. 2008b. *International Dimensions of Organizational Behavior*. Mason, OH: Thompson-Southwestern.

Ahmad, S. 2004. "Behind the mask: a survey of business in China", *The Economist*, March 20, pp. 3–19.

Barsoux, J. L., and Lawrence, P. 1991 "The making of a French manager", *Harvard Business Review*, July–August, pp. 1–8.

Blunt, P., and Jones, M. L. 1992. *Managing Organizations in Africa*. Berlin: Walter de Gruyter.

Brunstein, I. (ed.). 1995. *Human Resource Management in Western Europe*. Berlin: de Gruyter.

Chandler, A. 1962. *Strategy and Structure: Chapters in the History of the American Industrial Enterprise*. Cambridge, MA: MIT Press.

Chen, M. J. 2001. *Inside Chinese Business*. Boston: Harvard Business School Press.

Child, J. 1994. *Management in China During the Age of Reform*. Cambridge: Cambridge University Press.

2008. Personal communication.

Choudhry, A. M. 1986. "The community concept of business: a critique", *International Studies in Management and Organization* 16(2): 93.

Cullen, J. and Parboteeah, K. P. 2005. *Multinational Management: A Strategic Approach*. Cincinnati: Southwestern College Publishing.

Earley, C. 1997. *Face, Harmony, and Social Structure*. New York: Oxford University Press.

Economist. 1999. "Out of control", December 4, p. 44.

2004. "German industrial relations: slowly losing their chains", February 21, p. 49.

2007. "Face value: Tough Ghosn", September 15, p. 82.

Engholm, C. and Grimes, S. 1997. *Doing Business in Mexico*, Upper Saddle, NJ: Prentice Hall.

Fayol, H. 1916. *Administration Industrielle et Generale*. Paris: Dunod.

Gannon, M. 2001. *Understanding Global Cultures* (2nd edn). Thousand Oaks, CA: Sage Publications.

George, C. S. 1972. *The History of Management Thought*. Englewood Cliffs, NJ: Prentice-Hall.

Hall, E. T. 1960. "The silent language in overseas business", *Harvard Business Review*, May–June.

and Hall, M. 1990. *Understanding Cultural Differences: Germans, French, and Americans*. Yarmouth, ME: Intercultural Press.

Hampden-Turner, C. and Trompenaars, F. 1993. *The Seven Cultures of Capitalism*. New York: Doubleday.

Harris P. , Moran, R., and Moran, S. 2004. *Managing Cultural Differences*, (6th edn). Amsterdam: Elsevier.

Hickson, D. (ed.) 1993. *Management in Western Europe*. Berlin: de Gruyter.

Hill, R. 1997. *We Europeans*. Brussels: Europublications.

Hitt, M., Black, S., and Porter, L. 2005. *Management*. Upper Saddle River, NJ: Pearson-Prentice-Hall, p. 8.

Hodgetts, R. and Luthans, F. 2003. *International Management: Culture, Strategy, and Behavior*, (5th edn). New York: McGraw-Hill-Irwin.

Hofstede, G. 1980 (2001). *Culture's Consequence: International Differences in Work Related Values*. Thousand Oaks, CA: Sage.

Hooker, J. 2003. *Working Across Cultures*. Stanford, CA: Stanford Business Books.

Kane, Y. I. 2008. "Toshiba's plan for life after HD DVD", *Wall Street Journal*, March 3, p. B1.

Kato, H and Kato, J. 1992. *Understanding and Working with the Japanese Business World*. Englewood Cliffs, NJ: Prentice-Hall.

Kiggundu, M. 1988. "Africa", in R. Nath (ed.), *Comparative Management: A Regional View*. Cambridge, MA: Ballinger.

Kono, T. and Clegg, S. 2001. *Trends in Japanese Management: Continuing Strengths, Current Problems, and Changing Priorities*. London: Palgrave.

Kothen, C., McKinley, W., and Scherer, A. G. 1999. "Alternatives to organizational downsizing: a German case study", *Management* 2(3): 263–86.

Kras, E. 1989. *Management in Two Cultures: Bridging the Gap Between U.S. and Mexican Managers*. Yarmouth, Maine: Intercultural Press.

Laurent, A. "The cultural diversity of western conceptions of management", *International Studies of Management and Organization* XIII, (1–2): 75–96.

Lewin, K. 1951. *Field Theory in Social Science: Selected Theoretical Papers*. New York: Harper and Brothers.

Lewis, R. D. 1999. *When Cultures Collide*. London: Nicholas Brealey Publishing.

Lillrank, P. and Kano, N. 1989. *Continuous Improvement: Quality Control Circles in Japanese Industry*. Ann Arbor: Center for Japanese Studies, University of Michigan.

Lublin, J. 2008. "Say on the boss's pay", *Wall Street Journal*, March 7, p. B1.

Meek, C. 1999. "*Ganbatte*: understanding the Japanese Employee", *Business Horizons*, January–February, pp. 27–36.

Miller, J. 2004. "Employment rules hinder EU", *The Wall Street Journal*, August 16, p. A11.

Mintzberg, H. 1973. *The Nature of Managerial Work*. New York: Harper & Row.

1993. *Structure in Fives: Designing Effective Organizations*. Englewood Cliffs, NJ: Prentice-Hall.

Munsterberg, H. 1913. *Psychology and Industrial Efficiency*. Cambridge, MA: Riverside Press.

Nardon, L. and Steers, R. M. 2009. "The culture theory jungle: divergence and convergence in models of national culture", in R. Bhagat and R. M. Steers (eds.), *Handbook of Culture, Work, and Organizations*. Cambridge, UK: Cambridge University Press.

Nicholson, N. 2008. Personal communication.

Nzelibe, C. O. 1986. "The evolution of African management thought", *International Studies of Management and Organizations* 16(2): 11.

Redding, G. 1990. *The Spirit of Chinese Capitalism*. Berlin: de Gruyter.

Robbins, S. and Coulter, M. 2007. *Management*. Upper Saddle River, NJ: Pearson-Prentice-Hall, p. 7.

Schoenfeld, A. 2004. "Germany rethinks generous perks for civil servants", *Wall Street Journal*, April 5, p. A17.

Steers, R. M. and Nardon, L. 2006. *Managing in the Global Economy*. Armonk, NY: M. E. Sharpe.

Stoll, J. and Brulliard, N. 2008. "GM chief Wagoner gets 33% raise", *Wall Street Journal*, March 7, p. B6.

and Spector, M. 2008. "Wagoner outlines his role in GM's hierarchy", *Wall Street Journal*, March 5, p. B1.

Tanikawa, M. 2001. "Fujitsu decides to backtrack on performance-based pay", *New York Times*, March 22.

Taylor, F. 1911. *Scientific Management*. New York: Harper & Row.

Vroom, V. and Yetton, P. 1973. *Leadership and Decision-Making*. New York: Wiley.

Weber, M. 1927. *The Theory of Social and Economic Organization*. New York: Free Press.

Wu, W. and Grove, C. 1999. *Encountering the Chinese*. Yarmouth, ME: Intercultural Press.

www.Intel.com. 2006. August 19.

Yukl, G. and Lepsinger, R. 2004. *Flexible Leadership*. San Francisco, CA: Jossey-Bass.

Cross-cultural perspectives on international mergers and acquisitions

GÜNTER K. STAHL and MANSOUR JAVIDAN

Mergers and acquisitions (M&A) continue to be a highly popular strategy for achieving growth and diversification. The fastest growing type of M&A deal is the cross-border acquisition (Evans, Pucik, and Barsoux, 2002). Executives view cross-border acquisitions as an important strategy in extending their geographical reach and gaining rapid access to new markets and resources (Datta and Puia, 1995). The ultimate driver of cross-border M&A activity is the increase in global competition and the corresponding erosion of national boundaries. Companies have followed their customers as they respond to the pressures of obtaining scale in a rapidly consolidating global economy. In combination with other trends, such as increased corporate restructuring, reduced trade barriers, easier access to global pools of capital, and access to new markets and specialized resources, globalization has spurred an unprecedented surge in cross-border M&A (Evans et al., 2002; Finkelstein, 1999; Shimizu, Hitt, Vaidyanath, and Pisano, 2004).

However, despite their popularity and strategic importance, the track record of such transactions is not very encouraging. A meta-analysis by King, Dalton, Daily, and Covin (2004) of ninety-three published studies indicates that the post-acquisition performance of acquiring firms fails to surpass or tends to be slightly poorer than that of non-acquiring firms. This is consistent with previous research on M&A activity and financial performance that indicated that while the shareholders of target firms gain significantly from M&A, there is little evidence that value is created for the shareholders of acquiring firms (see Datta, Pinches, and Narayanan, 1992; Lubatkin, 1983 for reviews). The King et al. (2004) meta-analysis further revealed

that none of the antecedent variables most commonly used in empirical research to predict acquisition performance (degree of diversification of the acquirer, degree of relatedness, method of payment, and acquisition experience of the acquirer) explained variance in post-acquisition performance. Collectively, the findings of this meta-analysis imply that anticipated synergies are often not realized; and that unidentified variables explain significant variance in post-acquisition performance. King et al. (2004) conclude that: "despite decades of research, what impacts the financial performance of firms engaging in M&A activity remains largely unexplained" (p. 198).

While the King et al. (2004) meta-analysis did not compare the performance of international M&A with that of domestic transactions, M&A scholars and executives generally agree that cross-border M&A are difficult to implement. Due to their international nature, cross-border M&A involve unique challenges, as countries have different legal systems and regulatory requirements, accounting standards, employment systems, and so on (Aguilera and Dencker, 2004; Child, Faulkner and Pitkethly, 2001; Shimizu et al., 2004; Schuler, Jackson, and Luo, 2004). In addition to obstacles created by differences in the broader institutional environment, cultural differences in management styles and business norms, as well as the often unanticipated challenges inherent in communicating across long distances, dealing with problems arising from different communication styles, and, in some instances, cultural chauvinism and xenophobia (Goulet and Schweiger, 2006; Olie, 1990; Vaara, 2003), can undermine the success of M&A that otherwise have a sound strategic and financial fit. For example, the poor performance of

DaimlerChrysler, one of the most talked-about mergers of the past decade, is often attributed to a culture clash that resulted in major integration problems (Epstein, 2004; Vlasic and Stertz, 2000). In the DaimlerChrysler merger, differences in management philosophies, compensation systems, and decision-making processes caused friction between members of senior management, while lower level employees fought over issues such as dress code, working hours, and smoking on the job. Language also became an issue. While most managers on the Daimler side could speak some English, not all were able to do so with the ease and accuracy that is needed for effective working relationships. Among the Chrysler managers and employees, very few had any knowledge of German at all (Vlasic and Stertz, 2000).

Even mergers of companies with headquarters in the same country – while usually not classified as "international" – involve many of the same cultural challenges as those encountered in cross-border M&A. For instance, when Boeing acquired McDonnell Douglas, the two US companies had to integrate operations in dozens of countries around the globe (Finkelstein, 1999). The same is true for most other "single country" M&A, such as the merger of Sandoz and Ciba-Geigy to form the pharmaceutical giant Novartis. Although Sandoz and Ciba-Geigy had a common Swiss cultural heritage and shared the same vision and strategic goals, management had to overcome major obstacles to rebuilding trust and creating a new corporate culture (Chua, Engeli and Stahl, 2005).

Thus, there is a myriad of anecdotal and case study evidence to suggest that differences in culture between merging firms – at both national and corporate levels – represent a source of "cultural risk" (David and Singh, 1994) and a potential obstacle to achieving integration benefits. Despite this large body of anecdotal evidence, however, empirical research on the impact of cultural differences on M&A performance has yielded inconclusive – and often contradictory – results. While some studies (e.g., Datta and Puia, 1995) found national cultural differences to be negatively associated with M&A performance, others (e.g., Morosini, Shane and Singh, 1998) observed a positive relationship or found cultural differences

to be unrelated to the performance of firms engaging in M&A activity. Narrative reviews of this literature (Schoenberg, 2000; Schweiger and Goulet, 2000; Teerikangas and Very, 2006; Stahl and Voigt, 2005) have generally concluded that cultural differences present a 'double-edged sword' and a 'mixed blessing' in M&A. A recent meta-analysis of the existing body of research (Stahl and Voigt, 2008) suggests that differences in culture seem to affect post-merger integration outcomes in different, and sometimes opposing, ways depending on the type of outcome variables and various contextual factors. Overall, cultural differences accounted only for a small proportion of the variance in post-merger integration outcomes. Collectively, these findings suggest that the relationship between cultural differences and M&A outcomes is complex and that unidentified moderator variables might be obscuring the effect of cultural differences on M&A performance. For example, Waldman and Javidan (forthcoming) have recently suggested that the leadership styles of the executives in charge of the post merger integration can have a big impact on its success.

In this chapter, we provide an overview of extant theories and research findings on the role of culture in cross-border M&A. We suggest several possible explanations for the inconsistent findings that emerged from previous research into the performance implications of cultural differences in M&A, and discuss some of the conceptual and methodological ambiguities inherent in the "cultural distance" paradigm, which continues to dominate research in this field. We introduce an alternative cultural framework, based on the conceptual foundations and empirical findings of the GLOBE research program, and provide an in-depth look at how cultural differences at the national level can affect the integration process and, ultimately, the post-merger financial performance. We conclude with a discussion of open questions and future research directions.

Since the focus of interest is cross-border M&A, the main emphasis of this chapter is on national cultural differences and their impact on the post-merger integration process. While organizational cultural differences have important implications for partner selection and the management of the integration process (e.g., David and Singh, 1994; Larsson and Lubatkin, 2001; Weber, Shenkar and Raveh, 1996), our emphasis on national cultural differences seems justified in light of findings that suggest that even a powerful corporate culture will not render national influences insignificant; and that national culture may come through more forcefully in the face of a strong corporate culture (Schneider and Barsoux, 2003).

Our starting point is to focus on the concept of "integration," which is a central, but ill-defined, concept in M&A research.

The concept of integration

While some M&A (e.g., conglomerate mergers) may be motivated by purely financial considerations or undertaken as a means of diversifying risk, the *raison d'être* of related-business M&A is to improve the competitive position of one or both of the firms by generating synergies, whereby in combination the two firms create more value than each could achieve alone (Haspeslagh and Jemison, 1991; Hitt, Harrison, and Ireland 2001; Schweiger, 2002). In this type of M&A, some degree of interorganizational integration is necessary following the M&A transaction in order to achieve the strategic intent of the deal (Stahl, Mendenhall, Pablo, and Javidan, 2005). Pablo (1994) defines integration as "the making of changes in the functional activity arrangements, organizational structures and systems, and cultures of combining organizations to facilitate their consolidation into a functioning whole" (p. 806). As such, integration involves managerial actions taken to secure the efficient and effective direction of organizational activities and resources toward the accomplishment of common organizational goals.

There are different ways in which assets and people can be combined in a merger or an acquisition, largely depending on the strategic logic behind the deal, and each integration type has different organizational challenges associated with it (see Schweiger and Goulet, 2000, for an overview of integration frameworks). For example, companies that pursue a growth-through-acquisitions strategy, such as Cisco Systems or General Electric, tend to integrate acquired units by absorbing them into existing units or establishing autonomous units. Mega-mergers such as DaimlerChrysler, JPMorganChase or AstraZeneca, on the other hand, involve two entities of relatively equal size coming together and either taking the best of each company or forming a completely new organization that promises significant competitive advantage (Ashkenas, DeMonaco, and Francis, 1998; Bower, 2001; Epstein, 2004). These two scenarios require different approaches to cultural integration. Choosing an integration approach that does not match with the strategy or the desired cultural outcome can significantly reduce the value created by the merger (Evans, Pucik, and Barsoux, *et al.*, 2002; Schweiger, 2002; Stahl, 2006).

Marks and Mirvis (1994, 1998) provide an integration framework that focuses on the desired cultural 'end-state' for the new entity and the path to reach this. As illustrated by figure 5.1, they identify five integration approaches, depending on the degree of change required in either the acquirer, the target, or in both companies. When no cultural change in the acquired company is desired, it can be considered as a stand-alone or preservation acquisition. In this case, the acquired company will preserve its independence and cultural autonomy. This often occurs when the rationale behind the merger is to get hold of highly skilled individuals and retain them, or when adherence to the acquiring company's rules and systems could be detrimental to the target firm's competitive advantage. When a large amount of change in the acquired company is expected but with relatively little change for the acquirer, then *absorption* is the most likely path. The acquired company conforms to the acquirer's way of working, with a focus on full cultural assimilation. Such deals are particularly common when the acquired company is performing poorly, or when the market conditions force consolidation. An expectation of major cultural change in both entities results in a *transformation merger*, while the selective combination of the most appealing features of the two cultures is often described as a *"best of both merger"*. In contrast with best of both mergers, companies adopting a transformation strategy often use the

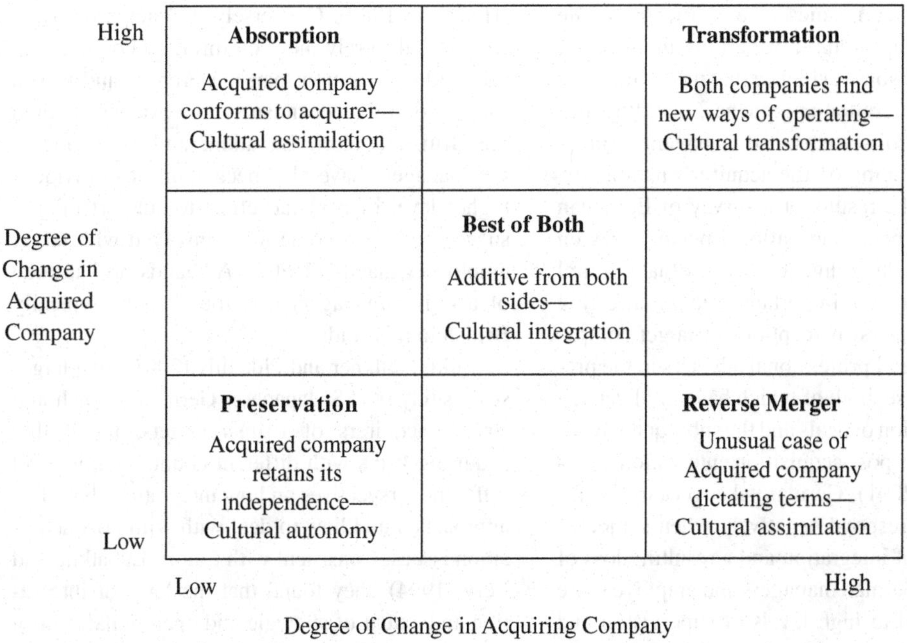

	High				
High	**Absorption** Acquired company conforms to acquirer— Cultural assimilation			**Transformation** Both companies find new ways of operating— Cultural transformation	
Degree of Change in Acquired Company			**Best of Both** Additive from both sides— Cultural integration		
Low	**Preservation** Acquired company retains its independence— Cultural autonomy			**Reverse Merger** Unusual case of Acquired company dictating terms— Cultural assimilation	
	Low				High

Degree of Change in Acquiring Company

Figure 5.1 Post-merger integration approaches and degree of cultural change envisioned
Source: Mirvis and Marks (1994). *Managing the Merger: Making it Work*. Upper Saddle River, NJ: Prentice Hall.

merger to break sharply with the past and to reinvent themselves. In rare cases, the culture of the acquirer is blended into that of the acquired firm in a *reverse merger*.

The five integration approaches depicted in figure 5.1 have different implications for the employees involved and for the management of the post-merger integration process (Haspeslagh and Jemison, 1991; Marks and Mirvis, 1998; Schweiger, 2002; Stahl, Pucik, Evans and Mendenhall, 2004). However, it is important to note that, within acquired or merged companies, different types of approaches may be used, based on functions, geographical areas and product lines. Therefore, it would be more precise to consider the impact of the integration approach at the level of business units or functions rather than at the firm level (David and Singh, 1994; Schweiger and Goulet, 2000). Moreover, there is evidence that the strategic choices discussed above cannot be considered in isolation from the cultural contexts within which the acquired and acquiring firms (or merger partners) operate.

Approaches to understanding the role of culture in mergers and acquisitions

In this section, we review two major streams of research within this field: cross-national comparison studies, which are concerned with the variation in approaches to M&A across nations or cultures; and intercultural interaction studies, which focus on the implications of cultural differences for the M&A process. These paradigms or foci differ in basic premises, frameworks, and methods (Boyacigiller, Kleinberg, Phillips, and Sackmann, 2003), and we will attempt to clarify some of the conceptual and methodological ambiguities inherent in these two research streams, particularly the "cultural distance" paradigm.

Cross-national comparison studies: cultural variations in mergers and acquisitions

Cross-national comparison studies are concerned with the question: Does national culture affect the approaches companies take to M&A? While research into the cultural variations in M&A is limited, there is some evidence that the preferences for types of integration approaches, due diligence processes, control systems, and management practices vary depending on the acquirer's nationality. For example, the results of a survey of European top executives regarding national perspectives on pre-acquisition due diligence suggest that cultural differences play an important role in affecting acquiring managers' perceptions of target companies and the use of professional advisors in the pre-acquisition phase, both of which have implications for the negotiation of deals and the subsequent management of the post-acquisition integration process (Angwin, 2001). German takeover targets, for example, may respond negatively when subjected to high levels of integration and a resulting loss of autonomy, as German managers and employees are not accustomed to high levels of supervision and control. Also, there is a longstanding tradition of industrial democracy through powerful workers' councils in Germany that is reinforced by a system of worker co-determination on supervisory boards, which supports shared decision making and flatter organizational structures. Angwin (2001) argues that such cultural and institutional factors must be considered in pre-acquisition due diligence as they are likely to cause problems during the integration period.

Research has also shown that managers from different countries are likely to implement different control systems and use different managerial practices in acquired firms. A study of US, British, and French acquirers of western European targets, for instance, found that French acquirers exercise higher formal control over targets than both British and US acquirers (Calori, Lubatkin, and Very, 1994). This is consistent with findings that indicate that French, more so than British, acquirers rely on managerial transfer and centralized headquarters-subsidiary controls over targets, so that power and influence resides at the hierarchical top (Lubatkin, Calori, Very, and Veiga, 1998). These patterns have been attributed to the French not only expressing a greater need for uncertainty avoidance, but also having a greater acceptance of power distance than both British and US acquirers

(Hofstede, 1980). Conversely, US acquirers have been found to rely more on informal communication and cooperation than the French, and to use formal control mechanisms more extensively than the British (Calori, Lubatkin, and Very, 1994). US managers have also been found to provide a higher level of personal effort to support merger success and to become more involved with target employees than the British. A "hands-off" attitude of acquirer managers was found to be typically British in this study.

Child, Faulkner and Pitkethly (2001), in a large-scale study of US, Japanese, German, French and British acquirers of British targets, found that acquiring firms with different country origins had different perspectives on how integration should be approached and how to deal with with post-acquisition issues. Consistent with Calori, Lubatkin, and Very (1994), they found that the level of integration and extent of strategic and operational control exercised varied by nationality. For example, US and French companies exercised greater strategic control over acquired firms than acquirers of other nationalities. In characterizing different integration approaches, Child, Faulkner and Pitkethly (2001) described US acquirers as "absorbers," French acquirers as "imperialists," and Japanese acquirers as "preservers." Although no consistent pattern emerged for the German sample, the results indicated that German acquirers, in a similar way to the Japanese, tend to avoid closely integrating their new acquisitions. Significant differences were also found in management philosophy, communication style and HR practices that acquirers of different nationalities applied to their acquisitions (Faulkner, Pitkethly, and Child 2002). For example, US firms were found to be very results orientated, quick to "hire and fire," and they tended to use HR practices as an integration tool (i.e., as a way of teaching the acquired company the "way to do things around here"). In contrast, Japanese acquirers adopted a more long-term approach, as manifested in lifetime employment, slow and steady career progression, and seniority-based promotion practices. At the same time, the available evidence suggests that cross-border M&A promote some degree of convergence in HR policies and practices toward accepted best practice. Practices such as result-oriented performance appraisal, individual performance-related pay, extensive training and development, and team-based work organization were common across nationalities, even if such practices were not widely used in the parent organization.

Child, Faulkner, and Pitkethly (2001) conclude from their study that acquiring companies of different nationality are able to achieve high levels of post-acquisition performance through introducing their own typical strategies, policies and practices. While this may be true, a substantial body of research on cross-border M&A suggests that post-merger integration practices to some extent need to be aligned with the cultural and institutional context within which the target firm or merger partner operates (e.g., Aguilera and Dencker, 2004; Calori, Lubatkin, and Very 1994; Goulet and Schweiger, 2006; Morosini and Singh, 1994; Schuler, Jackson, and Luo, 2004; Shimizu et al., 2004). For example, the findings of a study of cross-border acquisitions conducted by Morosini and Singh (1994) indicate that members of target firms in countries high on uncertainty avoidance tend to respond negatively when subjected to high levels of integration. Conversely, target firm members from national cultures low on uncertainty avoidance were found to respond more positively and perform more effectively when subjected to higher levels of integration. These findings suggest that a "culture-compatible" post-acquisition integration strategy implemented by the acquiring company can improve cross-border acquisition performance.

The results of a policy-capturing study conducted by Stahl, Chua and Pablo (2003) on a cross-national sample of German, Canadian and Singaporean managers and employees support the conclusion that the way target firm members react to an acquirer's integration approach is contingent on their cultural background. While the attractiveness of the acquirer's HR policies and compensation and benefits system was the most powerful predictor of the employee reactions to a takeover in all three groups, this study found significant differences in the way the German, Canadian and Singaporean employees reacted to an acquirer's integration approach and practices.

For instance, German employees responded more negatively to hostile takeover tactics, removal of autonomy, and acquisition by a foreign acquirer (as opposed to an acquirer from the home country) than Singaporeans. Conversely, for Singaporean employees, the history of collaboration between the two firms prior to the acquisition was a major factor in determining their reactions to the takeover, while for the German respondents the firms' interaction history was largely irrelevant. These findings suggest that the way target employees react to an acquirer's integration approach depends to some extent on their national origin. Therefore, companies engaged in cross-border acquisitions need to consider contingencies in the cultural and institutional contexts and adapt their approaches for integrating acquired firms accordingly.

Collectively, the results of the cross-national comparison studies reviewed in this section seem to support Goulet and Schweiger's (2006) observation that "acquirers may be culturally predisposed in the way they approach integration, and that targets may be culturally predisposed in the way they respond to integration" (p. 410). However, it is not clear from this research whether differing national tendencies in integration processes, management styles, and so on, are attributable to differences in culture or, more broadly, to differences in the institutional environment. Differences in government regulations, industry structure, access to financial resources through financial institutions, and a host of other factors embedded in the respective national contexts of merging companies may affect the M&A process (Aguilera and Dencker, 2004; Calori, Lubatkin and Very, 1994; Child, Faulkner, and Pitkethly, 2001; Shimizu et al., 2004). The hostile takeover bid of Mannesmann by Vodafone provides an instructive example. Vodafone not only had to deal with the German system of employee co-determination, but also with an entirely different ownership structure influenced by banks, opaque accounting and disclosure rules, a two-tiered board structure with a strong orientation towards consensus decision-making, different company laws, a German corporate culture with a strong orientation towards production and engineering, and a relatively weak 'equity culture' (Aguilera and Dencker, 2004). It also had to deal with a German government that was vehemently opposed to the takeover bid, as illustrated by Chancellor Gerhard Schröder's warning that a hostile takeover would undermine the principle of co-determination and "destroy the corporate culture" (Hoepner and Jackson, 2001: 36). Thus, in order to understand country-specific biases in the way companies approach, and employees react, to cross-border M&A, a thorough analysis of the wider institutional context is necessary.

Beyond cultural distance: intercultural interaction studies of cross-border mergers and acquisitions

While cross-national comparison studies are primarily concerned with the variation in M&A approaches across nations or cultures, intercultural interaction studies (Boyacigiller et al., 2003) focus on the implications of cultural differences for the M&A process. Key research questions addressed by this stream of research include: How do differences in culture between merging companies affect the attitudinal and behavioral responses of the employees involved, as well as the post-merger performance? When merging companies from different national cultures interact, what is the nature of the new culture that evolves or emerges? And how can the cultural frictions inherent in the integration process be avoided or managed?

Although research into these questions is theoretically and methodologically eclectic, the field of M&A integration research continues to be dominated by the "cultural distance" paradigm. In the international management literature, differences between national cultures are commonly conceptualized in terms of "cultural distance" (e.g., Drogendijk and Slangen, 2006; Harzing, 2004; Kogut and Singh, 1988; Morosini, Shane, and Singh, 1998). The central assumption underlying most of this research is an idea known as the "cultural distance hypothesis." In its most general form, it proposes that the difficulties, costs, and risks associated with cross-cultural contact increase with growing cultural differences between two individuals, groups, or organizations (Hofstede, 1980). Cultural distance has been shown to be significantly related to the choice of foreign entry

mode and the perceived ability to manage foreign operations (e.g., Kogut and Singh, 1988), organizational learning across cultural barriers (e.g., Barkema, Bell, and Pennings 1996; Javidan et al., 2005), the longevity of global strategic alliances (e.g., Parkhe, 1991), and cultural adjustment of expatriate managers (e.g., Black, Mendenhall, and Oddou, 1991).

Cultural distance is commonly measured in terms of differences in work-related values, using the Kogut and Singh (1988) index, a composite measure of Hofstede's (1980) dimensions of national cultures. Stahl and Voigt's (2008) meta-analysis revealed that the Kogut and Singh index is by far the most widely used cultural distance measure in research on cross-border M&A. It has been employed to examine the impact of national cultural differences on a wide range of M&A outcomes, including top management turnover (e.g., Krug and Nigh, 1998), acquiring firm managers' evalations of post-acquisition performance (e.g., Slangen, 2006), return on equity (e.g., Barkema, Bell, and Pennings, et al., 1996), sales growth (e.g., Morosini, Shane, and Singh, 1998), and cumulative abnormal returns (e.g., Markides and Oyon, 1998).

Despite its popularity, there are serious flaws inherent in the design of the Kogut and Singh index, and its conceptual foundations have been criticized for a number of reasons (Dow and Karunaratna, 2006; Harzing, 2004; Shenkar, 2001; Smith, 2002). For example, scholars have argued that the inconsistent results obtained in studies on the sequence of foreign direct investment, the choice of foreign entry mode, and foreign subsidiary performance might be due to false assumptions about the conceptual and methodological properties of the cultural distance concept (Harzing, 2004; Shenkar, 2001). In the context of M&A research, the use of the cultural distance construct in general and the Kogut and Singh (1988) index in particular is problematic because it may lead to several potentially erroneous understandings:

1. While the use of the Kogut and Singh (1988) index may be a convenient way to measure cultural distance, it masks important information regarding the specific nature of cultural

differences. In terms of impact on cross-border mergers, the effect is better understood by focusing on specific cultural dimensions rather than on overall cultural distance. Each cultural dimension may have a differential effect on each aspect of the organization, and some dimensions may have no effect at all. Barkema and Vermeulen (1998), for example, found that the relationship between a composite measure of Hofstede's cultural dimensions and international joint venture survival was caused entirely by only three of the five dimensions.

2. Dow and Karunaratna (2006) have argued that the importance of cultural dimensions cannot be determined in isolation from the dependent variables examined. The weighting of the dimensions needs to be determined empirically, in concert with the dependent variable(s) of interest. In the context of M&A research, for example, cultural differences on the power distance dimension may predict top management turnover following an acquisition, whereas differences on the uncertainty avoidance dimension may be associated with employee resistance. The Kogut and Singh (1988) index implicitly assumes that the differences in the scores on each of Hofstede's dimensions are equally important, irrespective of the outcome predicted by cultural distance.

3. Due to the differential impact of each cultural dimension, combining these dimensions into a composite measure of cultural difference provides a misleading picture (Harzing, 2004; Shenkar, 2001). Two pairs of cultures may have comparable overall cultural distance scores, although they differ on completely different aspects of culture. The impact of the cultural difference in one merger may be bigger because the companies diverge on the more important dimensions. The second pair may have a similar overall score, but since the score is due to the divergence in less important dimensions, they are not as affected by the difference. For example, Hofstede (1989) suggested that differences in uncertainty avoidance may be the most problematic for international joint ventures, an assumption supported by Barkema and Vermeulen (1998). Morosini and Singh's (1994)

research on cross-border acquisitions also suggests that uncertainty avoidance may be the most important cultural dimension in predicting performance. However, uncertainty avoidance was found to influence post-acquisition performance only when considered in conjunction with the acquirer's integration approach (i.e., a significant interaction effect emerged). Neither uncertainty avoidance nor any of the other Hofstede dimensions were directly related to performance. These findings suggest that the relationship between culture and M&A performance is complex and that cultural differences may interact with aspects of the integration design in influencing M&A outcomes.

4. Differences on cultural dimensions do not necessarily have a cumulative effect (Shenkar, 2001; Javidan et al., 2006). The consequence of the difference in one dimension may be compensatory to the difference in another dimension. In other words, the interaction effect between differences in cultural dimensions needs to be explored. For example, a company from a high power distance oriented culture may acquire a company from a lower power distance culture. This would lead the senior managers of the acquiring company to be more autocratic and hierarchically oriented. At the same time, the acquiring company may be from a more future oriented culture, which would lead the managers to plan over a longer horizon, focus on longer term issues and better anticipate future challenges. Thus, power distance can lead to higher performance due to greater emphasis on future orientation. An overall notion of cultural distance does not shed any light on such complex interactions and the dynamic interplay between different dimensions of cultural differences.

5. Cultural distance is almost universally measured by averaging the scores on Hofstede's (1980) cultural dimensions. While Hofstede's conceptual framework has been instrumental in furthering our understanding of cultures, it consists only of four dimensions. It is not clear that these dimensions provide an exhaustive picture of country cultures or that they are all relevant in terms of the impact on cross-border M&A (Javidan et al., 2006).

Other conceptual and methodological problems that arise in studies with a limited focus on cultural distance include a lack of attention to cultural elements other than work-related values (e.g., organizational practices); the largely unsubstantiated assumption that all members of an organization share the same cultural orientation and that this orientation is relatively stable over time; a lack of consideration of other dimensions or sources of cultural differences, such as differences in organizational, functional and industry cultures; and the fact that studies that examine the effects of pre-merger cultural differences on post-merger outcomes, almost by design, tend to treat the integration process as a "black box" (Stahl and Voigt, 2005; Teerikangas and Very, 2006). The latter concern is of particular importance in light of findings that suggest the impact of cultural differences on M&A performance may be mediated by integration process variables, and may further depend on moderator variables. For example, the results of a case survey by Larsson and Finkelstein (1999) suggest that differences in corporate culture can undermine the realization of synergies by causing employees to resist the changes more actively (a mediated effect). A study by Slangen (2006) found that differences in national culture had a negative effect on post-acquisition performance when the acquired unit was tightly integrated into the acquiring company, but had a positive effect on performance when the degree of integration was limited (a moderated effect). A more complex model of the effects of cultural differences in M&A would include both mediating processes and moderating variables.

We conclude that past research has been overly simplistic in assuming that post-merger outcomes can be predicted by a composite measure of cultural distance and in isolation from the wider integration process. The inconsistent – and often puzzling (Cartwright and Schoenberg, 2006) – results obtained in M&A performance research that uses cultural distance as the main explanatory construct may be due to problematic assumptions about the conceptual and methodological properties of the cultural distance construct, as discussed above. To advance our understanding of the cultural dynamics of cross-border M&A further, we

need both a more sophisticated conceptualization of culture, as well as a more accurate mapping of the mechanisms that link cultural differences to M&A processes and outcomes.

To address these issues and provide a better understanding of the effects of cultural differences in cross-border M&A, we draw next on the conceptual foundations and empirical results of the GLOBE research program (House *et al.*, 2004).

Impact of national culture on mergers and acquisitions: lessons from Project GLOBE

In this section, we use the findings of the GLOBE (Global Leadership and Organizational Behavior Effectiveness) research program to explore the impact of national culture on the dynamics of M&A integration. The GLOBE research program is a team of over 160 researchers who have been working together since 1992 and have collected data on cultural values and practices and leadership attributes from over 17,000 managers in sixty-two societies. For more information on this project, the reader can refer to House *et al.* (2004), and Javidan *et al.* (2006) or visit the GLOBE website (www. thunderbird.edu/wwwfiles/ms/globe/). The following is a brief explanation of each GLOBE cultural dimension:

1. *Assertiveness* is the extent a society encourages people to be tough, confrontational, assertive, and competitive versus modest and tender. Societies with highly assertive practices such as the US tend to have a 'can-do' attitude and tend to value competition.
2. *Future orientation* refers to the extent to which a society encourages and rewards future-oriented behaviors such as planning, investing in the future, and delaying gratification. Countries with strong future orientation practices, such as Singapore, are associated with higher propensity to save for the future and longer thinking and decision-making time frames.
3. *Gender differentiation* is the extent to which a society maximizes gender role differences. Countries such as Hungary are reported to have

the least gender-differentiated practices and tend to accord women a higher status and a stronger role in decision-making.

4. *Uncertainty avoidance* is defined as the society's reliance on social norms and procedures to alleviate the unpredictability of future events. Societies that are high on uncertainty avoidance practices, such as Germany, have a stronger tendency toward orderliness and consistency, structured lifestyles, clear specification of social expectations, and rules and laws to deal with situations.

5. *Power distance* is defined as the degree to which members of a society expect power to be unequally shared. Societies that are high on power distance practices, such as Russia, tend to expect obedience towards superiors and clearly distinguish between those with status and power and those without it.

6. *Institutional emphasis on collectivism vs. individualism* is defined as the degree to which individuals are encouraged by societal institutions to be integrated into groups within organizations and the society. Society institutional emphasis on collectivism consists of allocating resources and making opportunities available for members of the society to participate in societal legislative, economic, social, and political processes.

7. *Family collectivism* refers to the extent to which members of a society take pride in membership in small groups such as their family and circle of close friends. In countries like Iran, family members and close friends tend to have strong expectations of each other.

8. *Performance orientation* refers to the degree to which a society encourages and rewards members for performance improvement and excellence. In countries like Singapore and the US, training and development is highly valued. People have a "can-do" attitude and believe in taking initiative. They prefer a direct and explicit style of communication and tend to have a sense of urgency.

9. *Humane orientation* is defined as the degree to which a society encourages and rewards individuals for being fair, altruistic, generous, caring, and kind to others. In countries like Malaysia, human relations, sympathy, and support for others, especially the weak and the vulnerable are highly encouraged.

National culture and the dynamics of post-merger integration

Several authors have suggested that the post-acquisition integration process is a major determinant of the merger's eventual outcome (Datta, 1991; Haspeslagh and Jemison, 1991; Hitt *et al.*, 1991; Hitt, Hoskisson, and Ireland, 1990; Jemison and Sitkin, 1986; Larsson and Finkelstein, 1999; Morosini, 1999; Pablo, 1994; Schweiger and Lippert, 2005; Tetenbaum, 1999; Waldman and Javidan, forthcoming). While there seems to be a general agreement that the post-acquisition integration process is a critical link to merger success, the literature is rather fragmented as to why the integration process is so complex and in what way it is affected by cultural differences, especially in cross-border mergers. Several authors have discussed the issue of organizational or cultural fit in mergers (e.g., Buono and Bowditch, 1989; Sales and Mirvis, 1984). They argue that some form of compatibility or fit is required between the merging companies' cultures, styles, and procedures to enhance the chances of success. While this argument is intuitively appealing and has received some empirical support (Chatterjee, *et al.* 1992; Weber and Schweiger, 1989), it is rather static. By assuming that the mere existence of an organizational fit is sufficient, it does not provide an understanding of the dynamic nature of the post-acquisition process. We propose the notion of organizational alignment to emphasize the dynamics involved in the integration process. In other words, while the Marks and Mirvis framework in figure 5.1 represents either the starting point or the end point of the post merger process, in this section, we examine the dynamics of the post merger process from a cross cultural perspective.

Based on GLOBE findings, the extant literature, and logical extensions, we explore how the various national cultural dimensions can have an effect on the two merging companies' post-merger dynamics that influence the alignment process. The notion of organizational alignment refers to the extent the two large corporations attempt to combine and integrate their organizations to help achieve their strategic intent and enhance the post-merger firm's competitive position. Cultural differences directly and intensely affect the process of organizational alignment through their impact on three critical elements in the combining organizations: human capital, organizational capital, and social capital.

Culture and human capital

Human capital refers to the stock of intellectual and emotional energy in the firm (Barney, 1991; Barney and Wright, 1998; Huselid, 1995; Javidan, 1991; Lepak and Snell, 1999; Hitt, Bierman, Shimizu, and Kochhar, 2001; Polanyi, 1957, 1966). It reflects the state of employee competencies and their motivation to utilize these competencies towards the goals of the organization. Mergers have a direct impact on employees, as explained by Jack Welch, the former CEO of GE in *Fortune*, May 29, 1995:

> Having the company you work for acquired is probably the worst thing that can happen to somebody, other than the loss of a family member ... All the things you have learned – all the truths you have known – your boss, where you get your paycheck from, your security, change in one day.

Several authors have suggested that without employee support, the expected performance of a merger is rarely realized (Berry and Annis, 1974; Hambrick and Cannela, 1993; Sales and Mirvis, 1984; Weber, 1988). In a detailed study of sixty-one cases of mergers, Larsson and Finkelstein (1999) showed that employee resistance reduces the ability of the post-merger firm to realize the expected synergies. Most research evidence shows that employees tend to view mergers negatively (Larsson and Finkelstein, 1999) because of lay-offs, relocation, and generally negative impact on career plans and development, and career mobility (Gaertner, 1986; Walsh, 1989).

In a cross-border merger, two or more groups of employees come in contact. Each group has a stock of human capital consisting of the reservoir of skills and competencies along with the associated human resource policies and procedures that are designed to maintain and develop the required competencies. Cultural differences affect the stock of human capital because the competencies required and human resource policies existing in each firm have strong cultural underpinnings and evolve over time in harmony with national cultural values and practices (Schein, 1992; Tetenbaum, 1999). For example, after the acquisition of the Swiss company Pharmacia, the executives at the American company Upjohn faced resistance from Swiss employees against frequent progress reports and random drug tests and the headquarters' ban on alcohol consumption at lunch (Tetenbaum, 1999).

Based on GLOBE findings, the extant literature, and logical extensions, table 5.1 shows the impact of cultural differences on the stock of human capital in a cross-border merger.

The strong cultural underpinnings of human resource policies make it hard for the companies from different cultures to understand the historical evolution of each company's stock of human capital and to manage the integration of the two different approaches. Human capital evolves over time as a set of skills and competencies anchored in a set of human resource policies and actions. Altering any major element in a company's stock of human capital can cause major resistance and alienation because it could disentangle the web of interconnected elements and cause anxiety and uncertainty among employees (Hirsch and Andrews, 1983). There is some evidence that up to 47 percent of all senior managers in an acquired firm could leave within the first year of the acquisition and up to 72 percent within the first three years (Tetenbaum, 1999). Given that a major reason for mergers is learning and utilization of the acquired firm's intellectual capital, finding ways of keeping the experienced employees and executives is a major challenge.

Culture and organizational capital

Organizational capital refers to the variety of routines, processes, and procedures that a firm employs to achieve and maintain its competitive position (Day, 1992; Hamel and Heene, 1994; Heene and Sanchez, 1996; Hunt, 2000; Javidan,

Table 5.1 Impact of national culture on stock of human capital

Cultural Dimension	Organizations from countries with high practices scores tend to show the following attributes:
Performance Orientation	Skills and performance are key criteria for recruitment and selection; recruitment process is transparent; competition and cooperation are both encouraged and supported as long as they get results; strong emphasis on training, job rotation, and employee development; strong emphasis on goals and accountability; regular monitoring and feedback; reward system is based on performance and results; compensation differenttials can be quite large; jobs can be filled from within or from outside.
Future Orientation	Skills and capabilities are important for long-term success; strong emphasis on internal promotion and recruitment; strong emphasis on orienting, and training; strong emphasis on building a corporate culture; job rotation and employee development; bonuses are not a very critical part of the reward system; non-financial rewards are important.
Uncertainty Avoidance	Formal process of recruitment; emphasis on detailed job description; plethora of employee related manuals and HR policies; little flexibility; emphasis on quantitative job assessment and criteria; regular and frequent evaluations; rigid pay scales; more emphasis on base salary rather than bonuses.
Power Distance	Skills are not as critical in recruitment and hiring; hiring is done by the boss who makes a decision based on qualitative and vague criteria; job interview is the most critical piece; recruitment process is not transparent; competition and initiative are not valued highly; towing the line and not shaking the boat are important; little emphasis on employee development; socialization and building social networks are critical; little emphasis on goals; pleasing the boss is very important; assessment process is not transparent; politics play an important role in promotions and rewards.
Humane Orientation	Aggressiveness is not valued; feedback is not very direct; skills and performance are not very critical; recruitment criteria are rather vague; cooperation and teamwork is emphasized; internal competition is frowned upon; not much salary differential; emphasis on employee development and training; not very rigorous and frequent evaluation; emphasis on self-monitoring; employee focused goals; policies to support the employees' families may also be in place.
Assertiveness	Task-oriented HR policies; skills and performance are important criteria for selection; recruitment process is transparent; recruitment criteria are clear; emphasis on employment interview; internal competition is highly valued; employees are expected to manage their own development and career planning; accountability is taken seriously; compensation differentials can be large; regular evaluation and assessment.
Gender Egalitarianism	Egalitarian; diversity is a major criterion in recruitment; recruitment process is transparent; evaluation and compensation criteria are heavily weighted towards balancing various goals; emphasis on promotion from within; not very large salary differentials.
Institutional Collectivism	Group harmony is critical; employee participation in recruitment process; emphasis on team building; rewards tend to be group oriented rather than individualistic; rewards tend to be both financial and non financial; salary differentials are not large; emphasis on base salary; individual skills are not as critical; team-based skills are important.
Family Collectivism	Recruitment process is informal and unclear; criteria for selection are unclear and vague; skills and performance are not very important; evaluation process is infrequent and informal; feedback is indirect and not task oriented; HR policies and support mechanisms are limited; limited emphasis on employee training; salary differentials can be large; dominant coalitions tend to dominate decisions and policies.

1998; Nelson and Winter, 1982; Slater and Narver, 1995; Teece, Pisano, and Shuen, 1997). They are heterogeneous, intangible, path-dependent, and immobile (Hunt, 2000), enabling the firm to deploy its human and other resources to ensure competitive success. A firm's planning systems, control and accounting systems, information systems, and organizational structure are all embedded in its national and organizational culture. These systems and processes are designed to facilitate the firm's internal integration and external adaptation challenges. They are designed by individuals who, as fellow countrymen, share more or less similar experiences, acculturation processes, and developmental paths and share a generally similar mental programming (Hofstede, 1980, 2001). They bring these similar experiences into the design and operation of various organizational systems. Based on

Table 5.2 Impact of national culture on organizational capital

Cultural Dimension	Organizations from countries with high practices scores tend to show the following attributes:
Performance Orientation	Simple, competitive focused, analytical planning process, not very bureaucratic; comprehensive control, accounting, and information systems, organization structure typically simple and flat, project based, integrative. Divisional structure in large firms.
Future Orientation	Elaborate and analytical planning process, long-term oriented; elaborate information, accounting, and control systems. Large investment in R&D.
Uncertainty Avoidance	Elaborate and bureaucratic planning process, elaborate, very detailed and comprehensive information, control, and accounting systems. Hierarchical structure. Very little matrix or project-based organization. Detailed manuals and policies about every aspect of the organization. Detailed and clear reporting mechanisms; limited spans of control. Reliance on formal job descriptions for role definitions.
Power Distance	Limited planning process, information is power. Control, information, and accounting systems are designed to provide control to senior management. Not necessarily very reliable systems. Strict hierarchy. Detailed and clear reporting mechanisms. Arbitrary use of authority.
Humane Orientation	Structure is not hierarchical; tends to be relatively flat; information, accounting, and control systems are informal.
Assertiveness	Simple, competitive focused, analytical planning process, not very bureaucratic; comprehensive control, accounting, and information systems, organization structure typically simple and flat, project based.
Gender Egalitarianism	Structure is not very hierarchical. Matrix and project based structures are prevalent; coordinating mechanisms are popular; information, accounting, and control systems are simple. Relatively high percentage of women in key positions.
Institutional Collectivism	Flat, project based, integrative structure; information, accounting, and control systems are not very sophisticated. Authority is shared. Strong similarity of organizational structure and practices to institutional and industry norms.
Family Collectivism	Information, planning, accounting, and control systems are not very sophisticated. Very strong informal processes and structures.

GLOBE findings, the extant literature, and logical extensions, table 5.2 shows the potential ways that the different cultural dimensions can affect organizational capital.

In a cross-border merger, achieving synergy requires integration of many organizational systems. Cultural influences on organizational systems can make it very difficult to reconcile the differences and to achieve synergy. One of the authors was recently involved in a merger of two very large multinational corporations. Among many integration issues, a controversial problem was how to design a new employee expense reporting system. One company, representing a very strong humane orientated culture, was insisting that employees should have total freedom in using their credit cards and that the company should automatically pay the credit card company for the expenses incurred by the employee without requiring employees to get pre- or post-approval. The other company, representing a stronger power distance

culture was adamant that employees should receive pre-approval before incurring any expenses over a small limit, and should personally pay the credit company. They should then apply to their immediate supervisor for reimbursement. After a review of the expenses, the boss would approve reimbursement. The debate over the proper course of action for the post-merger company took over a year and caused substantial ill will among the executives from the two companies.

Culture and social capital

Several authors have discussed the concept of culture clash in mergers. It is generally argued that when two dissimilar cultures come into contact, they can produce feelings of anxiety and distrust (Ivancevich, Schweiger, and Power, 1987), hostility (Weber and Schweiger, 1989), and cultural collision (Buono and Bowditch, 1989). While the notion of culture clash is intuitively appealing, the literature does not provide a clear theoretical understanding of the dynamics of culture clash. It is not clear what culture clash is and how it comes about. To help fill this gap, particularly in relation to cross-border mergers, we examine the relationship between culture and the sociological concept of social capital.

The first systematic and comprehensive definition of the concept was provided by Bourdieu (1985), who defined it as "the aggregate of the actual or potential resources which are linked to possession of a durable network of more or less institutionalized relationships of mutual acquaintance or recognition" (p. 248). He further suggested that "the profits which accrue from membership in a group are the basis of the solidarity which makes them possible" (Bourdieu, 1985, p. 249). Bourdieu's concept of social capital has two key elements: the social relationships that allow access to resources, and the amount and quality of those resources (Portes, 1998). Burt, in further building on Bourdieu's work, defined social capital as "friends, colleagues, and more general contacts through whom you receive opportunities to use your human and financial capital" (Burt, 1992, p. 9). Putnam defined it as "features of social organizations, such as networks, norms, and trust, that facilitate action and cooperation for mutual benefit" (Putnam, 1993, p. 35).

While various other writers provide differing definitions, they all seem to agree on the basic notion of social capital as the "ability of actors to secure benefits by virtue of membership in social networks or other social structures" (Portes, 1998, p. 6). A distinguishing feature of social capital is its intangible nature. While organizational capital is in its bank accounts and its other assets, and human capital is in people's minds, social capital exists in the structure of relationships (Portes, 1998). The structure of relationships is represented by norms of trust and reciprocity, and by sufficiently strong ties that enforce these norms and make it possible for group members to make their resources available to their associates without having to go through a market exchange or having to build strong monitoring and reinforcement mechanisms (Coleman, 1988). In other words, social capital is the "glue that holds societies together" (Serageldin,

1998, p. I). But social capital does not come about naturally and overnight. It evolves and grows as a result of a group's common experiences and situations over time, which lead to "bounded solidarity" (Portes, 1998, p. 8) and result in building of trust and mutually enforceable norms. Trust is a critical element in development of social capital because it creates certainty and confidence among group members and thus reduces concerns about motives behind decisions and actions and enhances the motivation to contribute to the relationship. As a result, it reduces transaction costs and complexities in members' relationships.

The concept of social capital has direct relevance to cross-border mergers because while social capital can have valuable consequences for group members, it can have negative consequences in terms of how the groups interact with each other. Each of the firms entering into a cross-border merger can be conceptualized as possessing a particular level or stock of social capital. The particular stock of social capital is developed over time and as a result of common experiences and bounded solidarity both in the corporate setting and the national environment. Cross-border mergers bring two such structures of relationships into contact. There are several reasons for such an interaction leading to negative consequences.

First, in bringing two separate structures of trust together, mergers disrupt existing structures/networks, as illustrated by the following quote from Dan Vasella, CEO of Novartis: "Among all the corporate values, trust was the one that suffered most from the merger. A new organisation, a new boss, a new location – all of these destroyed existing networks and relationships" (Chua, Engeli, and Stahl, 2005, p. 386). The uncertainty caused by the disruption in the trust networks causes many side effects like stress, uncertainty, identity crisis, and resistance.

Secondly, the same strong ties that build trust, enhance the flow of information and communication, and provide benefits to group members, can act to constrain access to outsiders (Portes, 1998; Woolcock, 1997). The employees in the two merging firms may be reluctant to make their structures of relationships available to those in the other side because the relationships are based on bounded solidarity and enforceable trust developed over time. It is not easily feasible or desirable from the group members' perspective, to make the same level of relationship-based privilege and benefits available to others without the same common history or established trust. As Waldinger (1995) described it: "the same social relations that... enhance the ease and efficiency of economic exchanges among community members implicitly restrict outsiders" (p. 557).

In fact, it is plausible that the contact between the two sets of relations can lead to resistance, adversity, and opposition because exposure to another organization may cause feelings of uncertainty, ambiguity, and anxiety. To defend against these feelings, employees at each organization may cement their solidarity to their own structure of relationships because it gives them identity and feeling of self-worth. This is especially true in cases where the acquiring company, in its pursuit of synergy, attempts to make major changes in the target company's systems and operations to achieve integration. In such cases, the employees at the acquiring company may feel that since their firm has paid a premium to acquire the target firm, they are justified in imposing their ways on the other side. In other words, the purchase premium is seen as the justification for their solidarity. In contrast, those at the target firm may see this as an attack and use their own solidarity as the only defense left. These are some of the dynamics that can lead to culture clashes and dysfunctional consequences.

A third reason for possible clashes is the pressure for conformity in each firm. In return for membership and its privileges, members of each structure of relationships are expected to conform to its rules and norms. It is this level of social control that ensures enforceable trust and efficient transactions. The norms of conformity are critical for the group's survival but they can impede integration with another group in a cross-border merger because they constrain the members' freedom to accept the new group or new relationships. The fear of losing one's associates' trust or collegial attitudes can be a strong impediment to accepting the new processes, systems, or procedures in a cross-border merger.

In short, cross-border mergers expose two different sets of social capital to each other. Any intensive form of integration requires dismantling of the two old structures of relationships and creating a new stock of social capital. The extent to which the countries represented in the merger are different has a direct effect on the reaction from the members of the old sets of relationships. If the cultures are similar, for example, two companies in the Anglo cluster, the potential dysfunctional consequences could be limited. If the two cultures are significantly different, for example, one of an Asian culture and one from Nordic Europe, then the potential clashes can be more severe and the integration of the two companies will represent a bigger managerial challenge.

To summarize, most mergers and acquisitions take place to achieve some form of synergy. But achieving the desired synergy requires, in most cases, the ability to successfully integrate various aspects of the two companies. Successful post-merger integration, in turn, requires the ability to effectively manage the post-merger dynamics. Our approach to understanding these dynamics is through the notion of human, organizational, and social capital. Post-merger integration dynamics consists of the processes that resolve the issues regarding these three levels of capital while the two firms attempt to integrate their activities. National cultural differences of the two firms can have a big impact on their post-merger integration due to their potential impact on the issues relating to human, organizational, and social capital. In other words, it is not sufficient to identify cultural similarities and differences. We need to understand better how these similarities and differences influence the success of the merger by examining their impact on the post merger integration dynamics.

Linking cultural differences to post-merger integration outcomes: theoretical models and perspectives

In the previous section, we explored how cultural values and practices can affect a range of strategic, organizational, and integration process issues that are potentially relevant to the success of cross-border M&A. However, the cultural dynamics of M&A goes beyond the objective measures of the national cultures of the companies involved in the merger. Evidence suggests that M&A success and failure cannot be sufficiently accounted for by the pre-merger cultural differences, without taking the wider integration process and the context within which integration takes place into account (Stahl and Voigt, 2008). Next, we will review the major theoretical perspectives on the role of culture in M&A integration. These models and frameworks go beyond the "cultural distance paradigm," in that they specify the mechanisms by which cultural differences affect the post-merger integration process and, ultimately, the outcome of cross-border M&A.

The cultural fit or culture compatibility perspective

A central assumption underlying cultural fit models of M&A integration is that the degree of similarity or compatibility between the cultures of merging organizations is a critical determinant of the subsequent integration process (Cartwright and Cooper, 1996; David and Singh, 1994; Morosini and Singh, 1994). Perhaps the most widely cited model of this type is Cartwright and Cooper's (1993, 1996) model of culture compatibility. Its basic premise is that cultures vary in terms of the degree of constraint they impose on individuals, and that this has important implications for the integration process in M&A. Cartwright and Cooper propose that in mergers of equals ("collaborative marriages"), the cultures of the combining organizations must be similar or related types for the integration process to proceed smoothly, because the success of the merger depends on the ability to create a coherent "third culture," which combines elements of both pre-merger cultures. Since organizations generally strive to retain their own culture, mergers between companies with dissimilar cultures are likely to result in major integration problems. In cases where significant differences in power or size exist, and the acquirer or dominant merger partner imposes its culture on the target ("traditional marriages"), Cartwright and Cooper propose that the perceived attractiveness of the acquirer's culture relative to the target's is a more important factor in determining the integration success than cultural distance per se. According to the model, the perceived attractiveness of the acquirer's culture is dependent on the direction of the perceived culture change, that is, whether that culture is perceived as increasing or reducing the degree of autonomy. If the acquired employees expect the takeover to result in increased autonomy and other benefits, they are likely to accept the acquirer's culture and may even welcome the takeover. If, on the other hand, they perceive the changes as undesirable, they are likely to resist the takeover (Waldman and Javidan, forthcoming).

Although Cartwright and Cooper's (1993, 1996) model focuses primarily on differences in organizational culture and how they affect employee stress and attitudes toward the new organization, the logic can also be applied to the cultural issues inherent in cross-border M&A. Central to the GLOBE framework is the distinction between cultural practices and cultural values. On each of the nine GLOBE dimensions, a society is positioned in terms of both its cultural practices ("As Is" scores) and its cultural values ("Should Be" scores), the latter of which tell us something about the direction the members of a culture want their society and institutions to develop in the future. For the South Asian Cluster, for example, the GLOBE findings reveal a significant gap between cultural practices and cultural values on the power distance dimension, which implies that South Asians have a desire to work in organizations with less hierarchical structures, greater delegation of responsibility and less authoritarian leaders – desires that are in sharp contrast to current organizational practices. Cartwright and Cooper's (1993, 1996) model would suggest that, despite significant cultural differences, acquisition of a South Asian company by, say, a Europe-based firm would meet with little resistance on the part of the target firm employees, who may even welcome the takeover and see it as a liberation from autocratic and ineffective management, and a chance for increased autonomy, participation, and other benefits (e.g., better reputation, a more enlightened culture).

The acculturation perspective

Models of the post-merger acculturation process (Elsass and Veiga, 1994; Larsson and Lubatkin, 2001; Nahavandi and Malekzadeh, 1988; Sales and Mirvis, 1984) emphasize the dynamics of culture change, rather than stable cultural differences between the merging organizations. In anthropology, the term "acculturation" is defined as "changes induced in (two cultural) systems as a result of the diffusion of cultural elements in both directions" (Berry, 1980, p. 215). Consistent with this definition, Larsson and Lubatkin (2001) view acculturation in M&A as the outcome of a cooperative process whereby the beliefs, assumptions, and values of two previously independent work forces form a jointly determined culture. Acculturation is achieved through development of a common organizational language, mutual consideration, and values promoting shared interests. As such, acculturation is a prerequisite for M&A success, especially when high levels of integration are required (Waldman and Javidan, forthcoming).

While Larsson and Lubatkin (2001) view acculturation as an inherently cooperative process, others have suggested that acculturation outcomes can be positive and negative. For example, Nahavandi and Malekzadeh's (1988) model of acculturative stress proposes that the degree of congruence between the acquiring and acquired firms' preferred modes of acculturation will affect the amount of stress and conflict experienced during the integration period. They identified four acculturation modes, which define ways in which the two organizations involved in an acquisition adapt to each other and resolve emergent conflict: integration, assimilation, separation, and deculturation. From the acquired firm's point of view, the extent to which members want to preserve their own cultural identity and the degree to which they feel attracted to the acquirer's culture will determine their preferred mode of acculturation. The acquiring firm's preferred acculturation mode is largely determined by its diversification strategy and tolerance for diversity. The model suggests that incongruence, which occurs when the two firms do not agree on the mode of acculturation, will lead to high amounts of acculturative stress, interorganizational conflict, and disruption

for both individual and group functioning as the target firm members struggle to preserve their cultural identity. Congruence, on the other hand, will result in minimal acculturative stress and is likely to facilitate the implementation of the merger. The dynamic nature of the model suggests that, over time, the two companies may each move from one mode of acculturation to other modes and, therefore, the degree of congruence between the companies' preferred acculturation modes may change.

Models of the post-merger acculturation process such as the one proposed by Nahavandi and Malekzadeh (1988) highlight the dynamic processes by which the acquired and acquiring firms resolve the conflict that arises as a result of a takeover. Consistent with these models, a longitudinal case study of the acculturation process in a firm that had been acquired by a large US conglomerate (Sales and Mirvis, 1984) found that the acculturation outcome depended on the extent to which the acquired firm was allowed to determine its preferred mode of acculturation, to which the relationships between the members of the two companies were positive and involved reciprocity, and to which the acquired firm desired to retain its own cultural identity.

Social identity theory

Social identity theory has recently been applied to the study of conflicts in M&A (Bartels et al., 2006; Gaertner et al., 2001; Hogg and Terry, 2000; Marmenout, 2006; Terry, Carey, and Callan, 2001; Van Leeuwen and Van Knippenberg, 2003). At its centre is the observation that people define themselves according to their group membership (the in-group) and in relation to other groups (salient out-groups). Social identity theory is based on three principal ideas: categorization, identification, and comparison (Ashforth and Mael, 1989; Tajfel, 1982; Turner, 1982). First, individuals tend to classify people along stereotypical dimensions that accentuate differences between them. Perceptions of others thus become depersonalized and people are considered as group members rather than individuals. Second, individuals tend to identify with a group to which they think they belong. This is referred to as "social identity," which is part of an individual's self-concept. Finally, social comparison entails the evaluation of how the position of one's own group compares to that of other groups. Organizational members show a bias towards members of their own group and tend to hold a negative view about the members of the out-group in order to enhance the relative standing of their own group. If the out-group is perceived to be more attractive, and the individual cannot move to that group, a collective strategy will be adopted to favor the in-group and derogate the out-group (Marmenout, 2006).

Applied to cross-border M&A, social identity theory suggests that the mere existence of two different cultures is enough to lead to in-group out-group bias and conflict. It highlights the constructed nature of cultural perceptions in a merger situation: organizational members, while emphasizing their own positive distinctiveness, tend to exaggerate the differences between their own and the merger partner's culture. In an inter-group comparison situation:

> [group] members prefer and selectively recall information that suggests intergroup differences rather than similarities…This suggests that groups have a vested interest in perceiving or even provoking greater differentiation than exists and disparaging the reference group on this basis. (Ashforth and Mael, 1989, p. 31)

In-group bias and out-group derogation are likely to be greatest when there is a perceived external threat, such as a hostile takeover attempt, and when the out-group is perceived to be very different from the in-group (Elsass and Veiga, 1994). In such a situation, cohesiveness among the members of the target firm is likely to increase and the takeover attempt may be fiercely resisted (Krug and Nigh, 2001; Stahl and Sitkin, 2005). Importantly, social identity theory suggests that the process of cultural differentiation in M&A is influenced by the perceived relative status of the merger partners. In-group bias on the part of the lower-status group (i.e., the target firm) can be reduced if group members can join the higher-status group (i.e., the acquiring firm), thus achieving positive distinctiveness through social mobility (Marmenout, 2006). If, for example, the target firm members welcomed

the takeover, perhaps viewing the acquirer as being a savior, the intergroup structure might be one of cooperation rather than conflict or competition. In such a situation, forces of differentiation would be weak (Elsass and Veiga, 1994).

The trust-theoretical perspective

A trust-theoretical perspective on cross-border M&A suggests that cultural differences affect organizational members in ways largely similar to those proposed by social identity theory. There is extensive evidence in social psychology that perceived similarity tends to result in a higher degree of attraction towards the other party (Byrne 1971; Darr and Kurzberg, 2000). Research on organizational trust has shown that shared values, norms, and patterns of behavior facilitate the emergence of trust, while at the same time limiting the potential for conflict in a relationship (Kramer, 1999; Lewicki and Wiethoff, 2000; McAllister, 1995). In contrast, trust can erode and the potential for conflict increase when a party is perceived as not sharing key cultural values, because that party is perceived as operating under values and assumptions so different that the party's underlying world view becomes suspect (Sitkin and Roth, 1993). As a result of perceptual biases and basic cognitive processes such as social categorization (Kramer, 1999; Kramer, Brewer, and Hanna, 1996), the members of the out-group are often attributed negative characteristics and intentions, which may generate or reinforce feelings of suspicion, as the out-group members are being evaluated "as uniformly unethical or malevolent, incompetent, and ill-informed – and the in-group is viewed in the opposite terms" (Sitkin and Stickel, 1996, p. 212).

Similar processes can be observed in inter-organizational relationships (Stahl and Sitkin, 2005). For example, research on cooperative alliances between firms has shown that shared values facilitate the creation and maintenance of trust; conversely, value incongruence has been found to diminish trust (e.g., Anderson and Weitz, 1989; Sarkar, Cavusgil, and Evirgen, 1997). In M&A, fundamentally different values, goals, and beliefs concerning appropriate organizational practices may lead to feelings of suspicion and covert or overt political struggles between the two parties (Vaara, 2003). In a cross-border context, such politicization tends to be fueled by cultural stereotypes, nationalism, and even xenophobia. The resulting rift often unites people on the same side of national boundaries, further strengthening "us versus them" sentiments. The actions taken and the messages sent by the acquiring organization are particularly likely to be misinterpreted by employees in culturally distant countries, creating false impressions, which in turn trigger political behavior, feelings of mistrust, and conflicts (Olie, 1990; Risberg, Tienari, and Vaara 2003; Vaara, Tienari, and Säntti, 2003). Moreover, cultural differences at the national level are easy "attribution targets," implying that internal politics or power struggles may be seen or portrayed as being caused by cultural differences even in circumstances where this is not the case (Vaara, 2002). A trust-theoretical analysis thus suggests that the cultural differences inherent in cross-border M&A have a potentially adverse effect on a variety of processes and outcomes relevant to synergy realization, such as the emergence of a sense of shared identity among organizational members and the development of a new culture with common goals and values.

The capital market perspective

The capital market perspective on the role of culture in M&A holds that perceptions of cultural differences affect shareholder value by influencing expectations of investors about the future performance of the acquiring firm (Chatterjee et al., 1992). This prediction is based on the central tenet of financial economics that the stock market is efficient and incorporates all available information into its expectation of future firm earnings and into the current share price. While the validity of this premise has been challenged (e.g., Barney, 1988; Harrison et al., 1991), there is some evidence to suggest that the stock market may factor in the "human side" of a merger when estimating future consolidation costs and the financial impact of a merger (Chatterjee et al., 1992; Lubatkin, 1987). For example, Lubatkin (1987) argued that investors may evaluate M&A not only based on financial and strategic fit considerations, but also on

"softer," less tangible factors, such as the quality of human capital acquired. Consistent with this idea, Chatterjee et al. (1992) proposed that with the continual flow of anecdotal evidence from the popular press about the adverse effects of culture clashes in M&A, analysts may also factor in cultural fit considerations in the valuation of a merger. They found that differences in organizational culture, as manifested in incompatible management styles, were negatively associated with stock market gains. This supports the conclusion that "investors are generally skeptical about mergers where the cultures … are perceived to be incompatible, while they are supportive of mergers were the cultures appear to be compatible" (Chatterjee et al., 1992, p. 331).

Extending this argument to cross-border acquisitions, Datta and Puia (1995) showed that acquisitions involving countries with high cultural distance from the US had a stronger decline in shareholder wealth than those from countries with low cultural distance, reaching the conclusion that country culture plays a significant role in the perceived chances of success in cross-border mergers. The KPMG consulting firm has found similar results. They showed that mergers between US and UK companies were 45 percent more successful than the average, while those between American and other European firms were 11 percent less successful than the average return of all cross-border mergers. Datta and Puia (1995) suggested that the existence of significant cultural differences at the national level may be perceived by investors as a factor in increasing post-acquisition administrative and consolidation costs. Moreover, they argued that national cultural distance may result in an inadequate understanding of the foreign market and may cause an acquirer to overpay for the target firm. Perceived cultural differences may thus adversely affect the acquiring firm's market value.

The resource based view of the firm

While the bulk of the M&A literature emphasizes the "dark side" of culture, particularly the problems caused by cultural differences in the integration process, some scholars have argued for the opposite view that cultural differences can be a source of value creation and learning in M&A. This view is largely based on the assumption that differences rather than similarities between merging organizations create opportunities for synergies (Harrison et al., 1991; Shimizu et al., 2004). For example, Harrison et al. (1991) provided evidence that complementarities – but not similarities – are associated with superior acquisition performance. Combinations of complementary capabilities cannot easily be duplicated by other firms and may thus provide the acquirer with a possibility to earn abnormal returns from the acquisition. Research within the perspective of the resource-based view of the firm suggests that sustainable competitive advantage comes from valuable, rare, and inimitable resources that can be physical, financial, or human (Barney, 1991; Fiol, 1991). More specifically, in the context of M&A, Barney (1988) suggested that synergistic benefits would be reflected in the acquisition price unless they were either unanticipated or unique to the acquirer-target pair.

Drawing on the resource-based view of the firm, Morosini, Shane, and Singh (1998, p. 141) have argued that a cross-border acquisition can be interpreted as "a mechanism for the acquiring (or the target) firm to access different routines and repertoires that are missing in its own national culture, and which have the potential to enhance the combined firm's competitive advantage and performance over time." Under this perspective, acquisitions in culturally distant countries are potentially more valuable, because a greater cultural distance makes it more likely that the target firm will have capabilities that are significantly different from the acquirer's own set and which cannot be easily replicated. Thus, complementarities are more likely to exist. Consistent with this logic, it has been argued that acquisitions in unfamiliar cultures can enhance the development of technological skills, trigger new solutions, and foster innovation, as firms operating in different cultures and markets are exposed to a wider variety of ideas, practices and routines (Barkema and Vermeulen, 1998; Larsson and Finkelstein, 1999; Morosini, Shane, and Singh, 1998; Olie and Verwaal, 2004).

This is very much in line with suggestions that cultural diversity can be a positive force in cross-border mergers and alliances, in the sense that it can create an opportunity for the two sides to learn from each other and to create synergy (Stahl, 2006). For example, Carlos Ghosn, the CEO of Nissan and Renault, who is credited with the successful turnaround of Nissan, has repeatedly stressed that in the Renault-Nissan alliance, "cultural differences are seen more as an object of cross-fertilization and innovation ... Differences in culture are being used more and more as ways of listening to what different people can bring to the table to achieve our objectives for the future. So, it is a careful selection of best practices and best approaches" (cited in Emerson, 2001, p. 6).

Collectively, these arguments suggest that the cultural differences inherent in cross-border M&A can be a source of value creation. However, the benefits in terms of increased potential for capability transfer and resource sharing may be offset by the impediments in the integration process caused by cultural differences. In other words, the combined firm's ability to realize synergies from diversity depends on the top management's ability to overcome cultural differences and prevent them from causing dysfunctional relationships (Waldman and Javidan, forthcoming). GLOBE has shown that by leveraging similarities in goals and values, top management can appeal to common interests and channel diversity of views into productive outcomes (Javidan et al., 2005).

Organizational learning theories

Researchers adopting an organizational learning perspective have also emphasized the potential benefits of cultural differences in M&A. For example, research conducted by Barkema and Vermeulen (Barkema and Vermeulen, 1998; Vermeulen and Barkema, 2001) suggests that differences in cultures and systems may help acquiring firms to break rigidities and decrease inertia, develop richer knowledge structures, and foster innovation and learning. Even if acquired capabilities which had been embedded in a different cultural environment cannot be directly assimilated into the acquiring firm, the infusion of new knowledge and practices may boost the development of new knowledge. However, Björkman, Stahl and Vaara (2007) have argued that these benefits are likely to be realized only if the cultural differences between the merging firms are not so large that they disrupt the successful implementation of capabilities, resource sharing and interorganizational learning. As an example, if the styles of the top management teams are diametrically opposed to each other and organizational members do not share key values, it is unlikely that the target firm can add valuable strategic capabilities that can be leveraged by the acquirer. This is because cultural distance increases the likelihood that management styles and organizational practices, are incompatible and cause implementation problems (Slangen, 2006; Vermeulen and Barkema, 2001). Cultural differences are most likely to lead to complementary capabilities that fit with and enhance one another when they are moderately large. When taken together, these arguments suggest a curvilinear relationship between cultural distance and the success of the capability transfer and interorganizational learning.

In addition to focusing on capability transfer as it relates to synergy realization, reseachers have also examined the issue of learning through experience, with a focus on how organizations learn from past M&A activities in order to improve their management of and success with future M&A (Björkman, Tienari and Vaara, 2005; Finkelstein and Haleblian, 2002; Greenberg, Lane and Bahde, 2005; Hayward, 2002; Zollo and Singh, 2004). On the basis of empirical research, it is unclear whether more experienced companies have a higher probability of success when acquiring other companies (King *et al.*, 2004). Behavioral learning theory suggests there is a learning effect, and there is some evidence that previous experience influences subsequent acquisitions and their performance. However, experience does not always lead to improvements in performance. The evidence suggests that firms that make multiple acquisitions within the same industry seem to benefit most from past acquisition experience, but for dissimilar acquisitions experience often has a negative influence on acquisition performance (Finkelstein and Haleblian, 2002; Haleblian and Finkelstein, 1999). Also, the effect of experience is not linear. The best performing acquirers appear to be either those

without experience, who are unlikely to make inappropriate generalizations, or those who have engaged in a large number of acquisitions and have learned how to apply their knowledge (Haleblian and Finkelstein, 1999).

Research with a focus on learning through experience has important implications for management, as it suggests that learning does not develop simply from the accumulation of experience but rather it is through the investment of time and effort in activities that enable the firm to learn by institutionalizing the lessons learned from past experiences and building a core competency around M&A activity (Evans, Pucik, and Barsoux, 2002; Greenberg, Lane, and Bahde, 2005; Zollo and Singh, 2004). An essential part of this core competency is culture learning (Schweiger and Goulet, 2005; Stahl, 2006). GE Capital, the financial services arm of General Electric, for example, has developed a set of guidelines and process tools for integrating acquired companies, which has been applied successfully in scores of transactions (Ashkenas, DeMonaco and Francis, 1998). The GE integration framework provides guidance on what needs to be done at different stages of the acquisition process, and it highlights the key organizational issues and decision points, providing the appropriate methodology and required resources. As GE Capital accumulates more experience, it is continuously updated and fine-tuned. Key elements include: HR due diligence and cultural assessment; selection of the integration manager and assembling of the transition team; development of the communication strategy; formulation of the integration plan; assignment of accountability for specific integration tasks; and various process tools to accelerate the integration and deal with any resistance to change. GE Capital uses this integration framework worldwide, but they have realized that in many countries, especially those with hierarchical social systems, "cultural issues were getting in the way of fast and effective integration ... [because] newly acquired leaders didn't comfortably accept the autonomy that comes along with empowerment" (Ashkenas, DeMonaco and Francis, 1998, p. 176). To overcome cultural barriers, GE Capital developed a systematic process of cross-cultural analysis, which encompasses a structured three-day "cultural workout" session between GE Capital and the newly acquired management team. This process is now applied in most of GE's acquisitions, especially when the acquisition is made outside the US.

The social constructivist view

In a significant departure from the mainstream of ideas on the role of culture in M&A, social constructivists view culture as a system of shared or partly shared meanings or patterns of interpretation, which are produced, reproduced and continually changed by the people identifying with them (e.g., Gertsen, Søderberg, and Torp, 1998; Kleppestø, 1998; Vaara, 2002). This perspective emphasizes symbolization and sees culture as a dynamic and emergent phenomenon that comes into existence in relation to and in contrast with another culture, rather than as a relatively stable system of practices, norms and values. For example, Kleppestø (1993) views culture as a "constantly ongoing attempt of the collective to define itself and its situation" (cited by Gertsen, Søderberg, and Torp, 1998, p. 33). According to this view, each organization consists of numerous individuals with distinct self-identities that are socially produced and that help create meaning at both the individual and collective level. Organizational culture is seen as a complex process by which a distinct organizational identity is created and maintained by its members (Kleppestø, 1998; Vaara, Tienari, and Säntti, 2003). The exaggerated view of differences and lack of attention to similarities often observed in M&A can be interpreted as a collective sensemaking mechanism: "we" cannot establish an identity without stressing "our" uniqueness and "their" otherness (Kleppestø, 1998; 2005). Under this perspective, culture clash and many of the human resource problems surrounding the postmerger integration process can be best understood as a quest for identity, i.e., a result of organizational members' attempts to defend their individual, social and organizational identities, as they are being threatened by the takeover.

Proponents of a social constructivist perspective on M&A have argued that it is not cultural differences per se that create problems in the integration period, but rather the way cultural boundaries are drawn and a new organizational identity is developed (Gertsen, Søderberg, and Torp, 1998; Kleppestø, 1998; Vaara, Tienari, and Säntti, 2003). The view of cultural integration as an identity-building process and emergent phenomenon is consistent with other theoretical perspectives on the role of culture in M&A, most notably social identity theory (Tajfel, 1982; Turner, 1982). However, a fundamental difference between the social constructivist view of culture and other perspectives lies in their underlying assumptions about the ontological status of the concept of culture. While social constructivists view culture as a system of shared meanings and thus an essentially subjective representation, the bulk of the models presented in this chapter are rooted in a predominantly functionalist and objectivist understanding of culture as something "real" (Morgan and Smircich, 1980). The same is true for the underlying cultural concepts and frameworks, be it Schein's (1985) levels-of-culture model, the concept of culture adopted by the GLOBE research program (House et al., 2004), or Hofstede's (1980) definition of culture as "collective programming of the mind." Despite fundamental differences, however, the theoretical models and perspectives reviewed in this section seem to converge on two key assumptions: first, differences in culture influence post-merger integration outcomes; and, second, M&A success and failure cannot be sufficiently accounted for by pre-merger cultural differences alone, without taking the wider integration process into consideration.

Implications for future research and conclusions

In this chapter, we reviewed extant theory and research on the role of culture in M&A to explore how cultural differences can affect a range of strategic, organizational, and integration process issues that are potentially relevant to the success of cross-border M&A. By linking organizational and human resource perspectives on post-merger integration to notions drawn from the strategy and finance literatures on M&A, we hoped to gain a better understanding of the mechanisms through which cultural differences at the national level affect M&A performance. Collectively, the theoretical perspectives and empirical findings reviewed in this chapter indicate that the culture-performance relationship in M&A is considerably more complex than the "cultural distance" hypothesis suggests.

While the diverse theoretical perspectives and research streams discussed in this chapter have significantly advanced our understanding of the cultural dynamics of M&A, they have not been well integrated in the M&A literature. What we are still lacking is *the full story* or – less ambitious – a comprehensive framework that integrates concepts and ideas from various disciplines and acknowledges the deep complexity of the matter. Such a framework is unlikely to be complete without being able to account for the complex interaction between cultural differences and aspects of the integration design, and incorporating different levels of culture, intervening processes, moderating variables, and contextual factors. An integrative framework of the role of culture in M&A must also pay attention to the temporal dimension of the integration process, and be able to explain how and why cultural differences can be both an asset and a liability in M&A.

As mentioned at the outset, research into the performance implications of cultural differences in M&A continues to be dominated by the cultural distance paradigm, with the majority of studies relying on the ubiquitous Kogut and Singh (1988) index as a measure of cultural distance. The conceptual and methodological concerns surrounding the cultural distance construct, particularly research using the Kogut and Singh (1988) index, have been well documented in the international management literature (Dow and Karunaratna, 2006; Harzing, 2004; Shenkar, 2001; Smith, 2002). Harzing (2004) concluded from her discussion of the conceptual and methodological properties of the cultural distance concept in general, and the Kogut and Singh (1988) index in particular, that "this index should never have achieved the almost mythical and unassailable status it seems to have ... Of course, the continued use of, and overwhelming number of, references to this index has only reinforced its position" (p. 102). For future empirical studies, we recommend the use of alternative cultural distance measures (see Dow

and Karunaratna, 2006; Drogendijk and Slangen, 2006), which should be supplemented with a direct measurement of cultural differences.

Another concern that needs to be addressed in future research on the performance implications of cultural differences in M&A is the choice of outcome variable(s). Abnormal stock market returns, realization of operational synergies, accounting-based performance improvements, and behavioral and attitudinal measures represent very different dimensions of M&A success. How the investment community reacts to the announcement of an M&A may differ from the reactions of customers and employees – if for no other reason than that the interests of these constituencies are partially divergent and sometimes completely at odds. Also, different types of outcome measures vary in terms of the unit of analysis (individuals, groups, the organization, the capital market), objectivity and reliability (self-report measures, objective data), and time of measurement (shortly or some time after the announcement). Thus, they may share little common variance. It follows that M&A scholars are comparing apples and oranges when making conclusions about the effects of cultural differences in M&A without distinguishing between different types of outcome variables. Researchers would be well advised to follow King *et al.*'s (2004) recommendation to employ multiple outcome measures to facilitate cumulating research across disciplines and to improve the understanding of differences between different types of outcome measures.

Another limitation of existing research in this area is that most studies – particularly those focusing on cultural distance as the main explanatory variable – tend to promote a rather static view of the role of culture in M&A, in that they focus on pre-merger cultural differences and their relationship with some post-merger outcome. In so doing, M&A researchers have largely treated the integration process as a "black box." Based on this review, there are a number of integration issues that are dynamic in nature and deserve further exploration, including the question of how the sociocultural and task integration sub-processes (Birkinshaw, Bresman, and Håkanson, 2000) combine to facilitate the realization of synergies; how differences in culture may foster the transfer of capabilities, resource sharing and learning (Björkman, Stahl, and Vaara, 2007); and how merging companies can create a new identity and culture (Larsson and Lubatkin, 2001; Waldman and Javidan, forthcoming). These and other important aspects of the integration process cannot be easily uncovered through cross-sectional studies and survey designs. Longitudinal case studies (e.g., Sales and Mirvis, 1984; Yu, Engleman, and Van de Ven, 2005) and field experiments (e.g., Schweiger and Denisi, 1991; Schweiger and Goulet, 2005) can help establish causality and provide a richer understanding of the mechanisms by which cultural differences affect the success of M&A.

References

Aguilera, R. V. and Dencker, J. 2004. "The role of human resource management in cross-border mergers and acquisitions", *International Journal of Human Resource Management* 15: 1357–72.

Anderson, E. and Weitz, B. 1989. 'Determinants of continuity in conventional industrial channel dyads', *Marketing Science* 8 (4).

Angwin, D. 2001. "Mergers and acquisitions across European borders: National perspectives on preacquisition due diligence and the use of professional advisers", *Journal of World Business* 36: 32–57.

Ashforth, B. E. and Mael, F. 1989. "Social identity theory and the organization", *Academy of Management Review* 14: 20–39.

Ashkenas, R. N., DeMonaco, L. J., and Francis, S. C. 1998. "Making the deal real: how GE Capital integrates acquisitions", *Harvard Business Review* January–February, pp. 165–78.

Barkema, H. G., Bell, J. H., and Pennings, J. M. 1996. "Foreign entry, cultural barriers, and learning", *Strategic Management Journal* 17(2): 151–66.

and Vermeulen, F. 1998. "International expansion through start-up or acquisition: a learning perspective", *Academy of Management Journal* 41: 7–26.

Barney, J. 1988. "Returns to bidding firms in mergers and acquisitions: reconsidering the relatedness hypothesis", *Strategic Management Journal* 9(5): 71–8.

Barney, J. B. 1991. "Firm resources and sustained competitive advantage", *Journal of Management* 17(1): 99–120.

and Wright, P. M. 1998. "On becoming a strategic partner: the role of human resources in gaining competitive advantage", *Human Resource Management* 37: 31–46.

Bartels, J., Douwes, R., De Jong, M., and Pruyn, A. 2006. "Organizational identification during a merger: determinants of employees' expected identification with the new organization", *British Journal of Management* 17: S49–S67.

Berry, J. W. 1980. "Social and cultural change", in H. C. Triandis and R. W. Brislin (eds.), *Handbook of Cross-cultural Psychology*. Boston, MA: Allyn & Bacon.

Berry, J. W. and Annis R. C. 1974. "Acculturative stress: The role of ecology, culture and differentiation", *Journal of Cross Cultural Psychology* 5: 382–406.

Birkinshaw, J., Bresman, H., and Håkanson, L. 2000. "Managing the post-acquisition integration process: how the human integration and task integration processes interact to foster value creation", *Journal of Management Studies* 37(3): 395–425.

Björkman, I., Stahl, G. K., and Vaara, E. 2007. "Cultural differences and capability transfer in cross-border acquisitions: the mediating roles of capability complementarity, absorptive capacity, and social integration", *Journal of International Business Studies* 38: 658–72.

Tienari, J. and Vaara, E. 2005. "A learning perspective on sociocultural integration in cross-national mergers", in G. Stahl and M. Mendenhall (eds.), *Mergers and Acquisitions: Managing Culture and Human Resources*. Stanford, CA: Stanford University Press, pp. 155–75.

Black, J. S., Mendenhall, M., and Oddou, G. 1991. "Toward a comprehensive model of international adjustment: an integration of multiple theoretical perspectives", *Academy of Management Review* 16: 291–317.

Bourdieu, P. 1985. "The forms of capital", in J. G. Richardson, (ed.), *Handbook of Theory and Research for the Sociology of Education*. New York: Greenwood, pp. 241–58.

Bower, J. 2001. "Not all M&A's are alike – and that matters", *Harvard Business Review* 79(3): 92–101.

Boyacigiller, N., Kleinberg, J., Phillips, M. E., and Sackmann, S. 2003. "Conceptualizing culture: elucidating the streams of research in international cross-cultural management", in B. J. Punnett and O. Shenkar (eds.), *Handbook for International Management Research*. Ann Arbor: University of Michigan Press, pp. 99–167.

Buono, A. F. and Bowditch, J. L. 1989. *The Human Side of Mergers and Acquisitions: Managing Collisions between People, Cultures, and Organizations*. San Francisco: Jossey-Bass.

Burt, R. 1992. *Structural Holes: The Social Structure of Competition*. Cambridge, MA: Harvard University Press.

Byrne, D. 1971. *The Attraction Paradigm*. New York: Academic Press.

Calori, R., Lubatkin, M., and Very, P. 1994. "Control mechanisms in cross-border acquisitions: an international comparison", *Organization Studies* 15(3): 361–79.

Cartwright, S. and Cooper, C. L. 1993. "The role of culture compatibility in successful organizational marriage", *Academy of Management Executive* 7: 57–70.

1996. *Managing Mergers, Acquisitions, and Strategic Alliances: Integrating People and Cultures* (2nd edn). Oxford.: Butterworth and Heinemann.

and Schoenberg, R. 2006. "Thirty years of mergers and acquisitions research: recent advances and future opportunities", *British Journal of Management* 17: S1–S5.

Chatterjee, S., Lubatkin M. H., Schweiger D. M., and Weber Y. 1992. "Cultural differences and shareholder value in related mergers: linking equity and human capital", *Strategic Management Journal* 13(5): 319–34.

Child, J., Faulkner, D., and Pitkethly, R. 2001. *The Management of International Acquisitions*. Oxford: Oxford University Press.

Chua, C. H., Engeli, H. P., and Stahl, G. 2005. "Creating a new identity and high performance culture at Novartis", in G. K. Stahl and M. E. Mendenhall (eds.), *Mergers and Acquisitions: Managing Culture and Human Resource*. Stanford: Stanford Business, pp. 379–400.

Coleman, J. S. 1988. "Social capital in the creation of human capital", *American Journal of Sociology* 94: 95–121.

Darr, E. D. and Kurtzberg, T. R. 2000. "An investigation of partner similarity dimensions on knowledge transfer", *Organizational*

Behavior and Human Decision Processes 82: 28–44.

Datta, D. K. 1991. "Organizational fit and acquisition performance: effects of post-acquisition integration", *Strategic Management Journal* 12: 281–97.

Pinches, G. E., and Narayanan, V. K. 1992. "Factors influencing wealth creation from mergers and acquisitions: a meta-analysis". *Strategic Management Journal*, 13: 67–84.

and Puia, G. 1995. "Cross-border acquisitions: an examination of the influence of relatedness and cultural fit on shareholder value creation in US acquiring firms", *Management International Review* 35: 337–59.

David, K. and Singh, H. 1994. "Sources of acquisition cultural risk", in G. Krogh, A. Sinatra, and H. Singh (eds.), *The Management of Corporate Acquisitions*, Macmillan: Houndmills, pp. 251–92.

Day, G. S. 1992. "Marketing's contribution to the strategy dialogue", *Journal of the Academy of Marketing Science* 20: 323–30.

Dow, D. and Karunaratna, A. 2006. "Developing a multidimensional instrument to measure psychic distance stimuli", *Journal of International Business Studies* 37(5): 578–602.

Drogendijk, R. and Slangen, A. H. L. 2006. "Hofstede, Schwartz, or managerial perceptions? The effects of different cultural distance measures on establishment mode choices by multinational enterprises", *International Business Review* 15(4): 361–80.

Elsass, P. M. and Veiga, J. F. 1994. "Acculturation in acquired organizations: A force-field perspective", *Human Relations* 47(4): 431–53.

Emerson, V. 2001. "An interview with Carlos Ghosn, President of Nissan Motors, Ltd. and Industry Leader of the Year", *Journal of World Business* 36: 3–10.

Epstein, M. J. 2004. "The drivers of success in post-merger integration", *Organizational Dynamics* 33(2): 174–89.

Evans, P., Pucik, V., and Barsoux, J.-L. 2002. *The Global Challenge: Frameworks for International Human Resource Management*. New York: McGraw-Hill.

Faulkner, D., Pitkethly, R., and Child, J. 2002. "International mergers and acquisitions in the UK 1985–94: a comparison of national HRM practices", *International Journal of Human Resource Management* 13: 106–22.

Finkelstein, S. 1999. *Safe Ways to Cross the Merger Minefield. In: Mastering Global Business.* London: Financial Times Pitman Publishing, pp. 119–23.

and Halablian, J. 2002. "Understanding acquisition performance: The role of transfer effects", *Organization Science* 13: 36–47.

Fiol, M. 1991. "Managing culture as a competitive resource: An identity-based view of sustainable competitive advantage", *Journal of Management* 17(1): 191–211.

Gaertner, K. N. 1986. "Colliding cultures: the implications of a merger for managers' careers", paper presented at Academy of Management Annual Meeting, Chicago, IL.

Gaertner, S. L., Bachman, B. A., Dovidio, J., and Banker, B. S. 2001. "Corporate mergers and step family marriages: Identity, harmony, and commitment", in A. M. Hogg and P. J. Terry (eds.), *Social Identity Processes in Organizational Contexts*. Philadelphia: Taylor and Francis, pp. 265–82.

Gertsen, M. C., Søderberg, A.-M. and Torp, J. E. 1998. "Different approaches to the understanding of culture in mergers and acquisitions", in M. C. Gertsen, A.-M. Søderberg, and J. E. Torp (eds.), *Cultural Dimensions of International Mergers and Acquisitions*. Berlin: De Gruyter, pp. 17–38.

Goulet, P. K. and Schweiger, D. M.. 2006. "Managing culture and human resources in mergers and acquisitions", in G. K. Stahl, and I. Björkman (eds.), *Handbook of Research in International Human Resource management*. Edward Elgar, Cheltenham, pp. 405–29.

Greenberg, D. N., Lane, H. W., and Bahde, K. 2005. "Organizational learning in cross-border mergers and acquisitions", in G. Stahl and M. Mendenhall (eds.), *Mergers and Acquisitions: Managing culture and Human Resources*. Stanford, CA: Stanford University Press, pp. 53–76.

Halablian, J. and Finkelstein, S. 1999. "The influence of organizational acquisition performance on acquisition performance: a behavioral learning perspective', *Administrative Science Quarterly* 44(1): 29–56.

Hambrick, D. C. and Cannella, A. A. 1993. "Relative standing: a framework for understanding departures of acquired executives", *Academy of Management Journal* 36: 733–62.

Hamel, G. and Heene, A. 1994. *Competence-Based Competition*, New York: John Wiley.

Harrison, J. S., Hitt, M. A., Hoskisson, R. E. and Ireland, R. D. 1991. "Synergies and post-acquisition performance: Differences versus similarities in resource allocations", *Journal of Management* 17(1): 173–90.

Haspeslagh, P. and Jemison, D. B. 1991. *Managing Acquisitions: Creating Value Through Corporate Renewal*. New York: The Free Press.

Harzing, A.-W. 2004. 'The role of culture in entry-mode studies: from neglect to myopia?', *Advances in International Management* 15: 75–127.

Hayward, M. L. A. 2002. "When do firms learn from their acquisition experience? Evidence from 1990–1995", *Strategic Management Journal* 23(1): 21–39.

Heene, A., and Sanchez, R. 1996. *Competence-Based Strategic Management*. New York: John Wiley.

Hirsch, P., and Andrews J. A. 1983. "Ambushes, shootouts, and knights of the roundtable: the language of corporate takeovers", in Pondy, L., Frost, P., Morgan, G., and Dandridge, T. (eds.), *Monograph in Organizational Behavior and Industrial Relations, vol. 1: Organizational Symbolism*. Greenwich, CT: JAI Press, pp. 145–55.

Hitt, M. A., Bierman, L., Shimizu, K., and Kochhar, R. 2001. "Direct and moderating effects of human capital on strategy and performance in professional service firms: a resource-based perspective", *Academy of Management Journal*. 44: 13–28.

Harrison, J. J. and Ireland, R. D. 2001. *Mergers and Acquisitions: A Guide to Creating Value for Stakeholders*. Oxford: Oxford University Press.

Hoskisson, R. E., and Ireland, R. D. 1990. "Mergers and acquisitions and managerial commitment to innovation in M-form firms", *Strategic Management Journal*, 11 (special issue): 29–47.

Hoskisson, R. E., Ireland, R. D., and Harrison, J. S. 1991. "Effects of acquisitions on R&D inputs and outputs", *Academy of Management Journal* 34: 693–706.

Hoepner, M. and Jackson, G. 2001. *An Emerging Market for Corporate Control? The Case of Mannesmannn and German Corporate Governance*. MPIfG Discussion Paper

01/4. Koeln: Max-Planck-Institut fuer
Gesellschaftsforschung.

Hofstede, G. 1980. *Culture's Consequences:
International Differences in Work Related
Values*. Beverly Hills: Sage.

2001. *Culture's Consequences: Comparing Values,
Behaviors, Insitutions, and Organizations
Across Nations* (2nd edn.). Beverley Hills: Sage.

Hogg, M.A. and Terry, D.J. 2000. "Social
identity and self-categorization processes
in organizational contexts", *Acedemy of
Management Review* 25: 121–40.

House, R.J., Hanges P.W., Javidan M., Dorfman, P.,
and Gupta V. (eds.). 2004. *Culture, Leadership,
and Organizations: The GLOBE Study of 62
Societies*. Beverly Hills: Sage.

Hunt, S.D. 2000. *A General Theory of Competition*,
Thousand Oaks: SAGE.

Huselid, M.A. 1995. "The impact of human resource
practices on turnover, productivity, and
corporate financial performance", *Academy of
Management Journal* 38: 635–72.

Ivancevich, J.M., Schweiger, D.M., and Power,
F.R. 1987. "Strategies for managing human
resources during mergers and acquisitions",
Human Resources Planning 101: 19–35.

Javidan, M. 1991. "Leading a high commitment
organization", *Long Range Planning* 24(2):
28–36.

1998. "Core competence: What does it mean in
practice?", *Long Range Planning* 31(1).

House, R.J., Dorfman, P., Hanges P., and. Sully
de Luque, M. 2006. "Conceptualizing and
measuring cultures and their consequences: a
comparative review of GLOBE's and Hofstede's
approaches", *Journal of International Business
Studies*.

Stahl, G.K., Brodbeck, F., and Wilderom, C. 2005.
"Cross-border transfer of knowledge: Cultural
lessons from project GLOBE", *Academy of
Management Executive* 19(2): 59–76.

Jemison, D.B. and Sitkin, S.B. 1986. "Corporate
acquisitions: a process perspective", *Academy
of Management Review* 11(1): 145–63.

King, D.R., Dalton, D.R., Daily, C.M., and Covin,
J.G. 2004. "Meta-analyses of post-acquisition
performance: indications of unidentified
moderators", *Strategic Management Journal*
25(2): 187–200.

Kleppestø, S. 1993. *Kultur och identitet vid
företagsuppköp och fusioner*. Stockholm:
Nerenius och Santerus.

1998. "A quest for social identity: the pragmatics
of communication in mergers and acquisitions",
in M.C. Gertsen, A.-M. Søderberg, and
J.E. Torp (eds.), *Cultural Dimensions of
International Mergers and Acquisitions*. Berlin:
De Gruyter, pp. 147–166.

Kogut, B. and Singh, H. 1988. "The effect of
national culture on the choice of entry mode",
Journal of International Business Studies 19(3):
411–32.

Kramer, R.M. 1999. "Trust and distrust in
organizations: emerging perspectives, enduring
questions", *Annual Review of Psychology* 50:
569–98.

Brewer, M.B., and Hanna, B.A. 1996. "Collective
Trust and Collective Action", in R.M. Kramer
and T.R. Tyler (eds.), *Trust in Organizations:
Frontiers of Theory and Research*. Thousand
Oaks: Sage, pp. 357–389.

Krug, J.A. and Nigh, D. 1998. "Top management
departures in cross-border acquisitions",
Journal of International Management 4:
267–87.

and D. Nigh. 2001. "Executive perceptions in
foreign and domestic acquisitions", *Journal of
World Business* 36: 85–105.

Larsson, R. and Lubatkin, M. 2001. "Achieving
acculturation in mergers and acquisitions: an
international case survey", *Human Relations*
54(12): 1573–607.

and Finkelstein, S. 1999. "Integrating strategic,
organizational, and human resource
perspectives on mergers and acquisitions: a case
survey of synergy realization", *Organization
Science* 10(1): 1–26.

Lepak, D.P. and Snell, S.A. 1999. "The human
resource architecture: toward a theory of human
capital allocation and development", *Academy
of Management Review* 24: 31–48.

Lewicki, R.J. and Wiethoff C. 2000. "Trust, trust
development, and trust repair", in M. Deutsch
and P.T. Coleman, *The Handbook of Conflict
Resolution*. San Francisco: Jossey-Bass,
pp. 86–107.

Lubatkin, M. 1983. "Mergers and the performance of
the acquiring firm", *Academy of Management
Review* 8: 218–25.

1987. "Merger strategies and stockholder value",
Strategic Management Journal 8: 39–53.

Calori, R., Very, P., and Veiga, J.F. 1998.
"Managing mergers across borders: a two-
nation exploration of a nationally bound

administrative heritage". *Organization Science* 9: 670–84.

Markides, C. and Oyon, D. 1998. "International acquisitions: do they create value for shareholders?", *European Management Journal* 16: 125–35.

Marks, M.L. and Mirvis, P.H. 1998. *Joining Forces: Making One Plus One Equal Three in Mergers, Acquisitions, and Alliances*. San Francisco: Jossey-Bass.

Marmenout, K. 2006. "Antecedents of outgroup derogation in organizational mergers", paper presented at the Academy of Management Conference, Atlanta.

McAllister, D.J. 1995. "Affect and cognition-based trust as foundations for interpersonal cooperation in organizations", *Academy of Management Journal* 38: 24–59.

Mirvis, P.H. and Marks, M.L. 1994. *Managing the Merger: Making it Work*. Upper Saddle River: Prentice Hall.

Morgan, G. and Smircich, L. 1980. "The case for qualitative research", *Academy of Management Review* 5: 491–501.

Morosini, P. 1999. *Managing Cultural Differences*. Kidlington, Oxford: Elsevier Science.

 Shane, S., and Singh, H. 1998. "National cultural distance and cross-border acquisition performance", *Journal of International Business Studies* 29(1): 137–58.

 and Singh, H. 1994. "Post-cross-border acquisitions: implementing 'national culture-compatible' strategies to improve performance", *European Management Journal* 4: 390–400.

Nahavandi, A. and Malekzadeh, A.R. 1988. "Acculturation in mergers and acquisitions", *Academy of Management Review* 13(1): 79–90.

Nelson, R.R. and Winter, S.G. 1982. *An Evolutionary Theory of Economic Change*, Cambridge, MA: Belknap Press.

Olie, R. 1990. "Culture and integration problems in international mergers and acquisitions", *European Management Journal* 8: 206–15.

 and E. Verwaal. 2004. "The effects of cultural distance and host country experience on the performance of cross-border acquisitions". Paper presented at the Academy of Management Conference, New Orleans.

Pablo, A.L. 1994. "Determinants of acquisition integration level: A decision-making perspective", *Academy of Management Journal* 37(4): 803–37.

Parkhe, A. 1991. "Interfirm diversity, organizational learning, and longevity in global strategic alliances", *Journal of International Business Studies* 20: 579–601.

Polanyi, M. 1957. *Personal Knowledge: Towards a Post-Critical Philosophy*. London: Routledge and Kegan Paul.

 1966. *The Tacit Dimension*. Garden City, New York: Doubleday.

Portes, A. 1998. "Social capital: its origins and applications in modern sociology", *Annual Review of Sociology* 24: 1–24.

Putnam, R.D. 1993. "The prosperous community: social capital and public life", *American Prospective* 13: 35–42.

Risberg, A., Tienari, J. and Vaara, E. 2003. "Making sense of a transnational merger: media texts and the (re)construction of power relations", *Culture and Organization* 9(2): 121–37.

Sales, A.L. and Mirvis, P.H. 1984. "When cultures collide: Issues of acquisition", in J.R. Kimberly and R.E. Quinn (eds.), *Managing Organizational Transitions* (pp. 107–133). Homewood: Irwin.

Sarkar, M., Cavusgil, T., and Evirgen, C. 1997. "A commitment-trust mediated framework of international collaborative venture performance", in P.W. Beamish and J.P. Killing (eds.), *Cooperative Strategies: North American Perspectives*. San Francisco: New Lexington, pp. 255–85.

Schein, E.H. 1985. *Organizational Culture and Leadership* San Francisco: Jossey-Bass.

 1992. *Organizational Culture And Leadership* (2nd edn). San Francisco: Jossey-Bass.

Schneider, S. and Barsoux, J.L. 2003. *Managing Across Cultures*. London: Prentice Hall.

Schoenberg, R. 2000. "The influence of cultural compatibility within cross-border acquisitions: a review", *Advances in Mergers and Acquisitions* 1: 43–59.

Schuler, R.S., Jackson, S.E., and Luo, Y. 2004. *Managing Human Resources in Cross-border Alliances*. London: Routledge.

Schweiger, D.M. 2002. *M & A Integration: A Framework for Executives and Managers*. New York: McGraw Hill.

 and DeNisi, A.S. 1991. "Communication with employees following a merger: A longitudinal field experiment", *Academy Management Journal* 34: 110–35.

and Goulet, P. K. 2000. "Integrating mergers and acquisitions: an international research review", *Advances in Mergers and Acquisitions* 1: 61–91.

and Goulet, P. K. 2005. "Facilitating acquisition integration through deep-level cultural learning interventions: a longitudinal field experiment", *Organization Studies* 26: 1477–99.

and Lippert, R. L. 2005. "Integration: the critical link in M&A value creation", in M. Mendenhall and G. Stahl (eds.), *Mergers and Acquisitions: Managing Culture and Human Resources.* Stanford: Stanford University Press, pp. 17–45.

Serageldin, I. 1998. "Social capital and poverty", World Bank Working Paper No. 4: Social Capital Initiative.

Shenkar, O. 2001. "Cultural distance revisited: towards a more rigorous conceptualization and measurement of cultural differences", *Journal of International Business Studies* 32: 519–36.

Shimizu, K., Hitt, M. A., Vaidyanath, D. and Pisano, V. 2004. "Theoretical foundations of cross-border mergers and acquisitions: a review of current research and recommendations for the future", *Journal of International Management* 10(3): 307–53.

Sitkin, S. B. and Roth, N. L. 1993. "Explaining the limited effectiveness of legalistic 'remedies' for trust/distrust", *Organization Science* 4: 367–92.

and Stickel, D. 1996. "The road to hell: The dynamics of distrust in an era of 'quality' management", in R. Kramer and T. Tyler (eds.), *Trust in organizations.* Thousand Oaks: Sage, pp. 196–215.

Slangen, A. H. L. 2006. "National cultural distance and initial foreign acquisition performance: the moderating effect of integration", *Journal of World Business* 41(2): 161–70.

Slater, S. F. and Narver, J. C. 1995. "Market orientation and the learning organization", *Journal of Marketing* 59: 63–74.

Smith, P. B. 2002. "Culture's consequences: Something old and something new", *Human Relations* 55: 119–35.

Stahl, G. K. 2006. "Synergy springs from cultural revolution", *Financial Times*, October 6, 2006.

Chua, C. H., and Pablo, A. 2003. "Trust following acquisitions: a three-country comparative study of employee reactions to takeovers", Academy of Management Best Paper Proceedings, IM, N1–N6.

Mendenhall, M., Pablo, A., and Javidan, M. 2005. "Sociocultural integration in mergers and acquisitions", in G. K. Stahl and M. E. Mendenhall (eds.), *Mergers and Acquisitions: Managing Culture and Human Resources.* Stanford: Stanford University Press, pp. 3–16.

Pucik, V., Evans, P., and Mendenhall, M. 2004. "Human resource management in cross-border mergers and acquisitions", in A.-W. Harzing and J. van Ruysseveldt (eds.), *International Human Resource Management: An Integrated Approach* (2nd edn) London: Sage, pp. 89–113.

Stahl, G. K. and Sitkin, S. 2005. "Trust in mergers and acquisitions", in G. Stahl and M. Mendenhall (eds.), *Mergers and Acquisitions: Managing Culture and Human Resources.* Stanford, CA: Stanford University Press, pp. 82–102.

and Voigt, A. 2005. "The performance impact of cultural differences in mergers and acquisitions: a critical research review and an integrative model", in C. L. Cooper and S. Finkelstein (eds.), *Advances in Mergers and Acquisitions.* JAI Press: New York, pp. 51–83.

and Voigt, A. 2008. "Do cultural differences matter in mergers and acquisitions? A tentative model and meta-analytic examination", *Organization Science* 19: 160–76.

Tajfel, H. 1982. *Social Identity and Intergroup Relations.* New York: Cambridge University Press.

Teece, D., Pisano, G., and Shuen, A. 1997. "Dynamic capabilities and strategic management", *Strategic Management Journal* 18: 509–33.

Teerikangas, S. and Very, P. 2006. "The culture-performance relationship in M&A: from Yes/No to how", *British Journal of Management* 17(1): 31–48.

Terry, D. J., Carey, C. J., and Callan, V. J. 2001. "Employee adjustment to an organizational merger: an intergroup perspective", *Personality and Social Psychology Bulletin* 27: 267–80.

Tetenbaum, T. J. 1999. "Beating the odds of merger & acquisition failure: seven key practices that improve the chance for expected integration and synergies", *Organizational Dynamics*, Autumn, 1–12.

Turner, J. C. 1982. "Towards a cognitive redefinition of the social group", in H. Tajfel (ed.), *Social Identity and Intergroup Relations*, New York: Cambridge University Press, pp. 15–40.

Vaara, E. 2002. "On the discursive construction of success/failure in narratives of post-merger integration", *Organisation Studies* 23: 213–50.
2003. "Post-acquisition integration as sensemaking: glimpses of ambiguity, confusion, hypocrisy, and politicization", *Journal of Management Studies* 40(4): 859–94.

Tienari, J., and Säntti, R. 2003. "The international match: metaphors as vehicles of social identity-building in cross-border mergers", *Human Relations* 56(4): 419–51.

van Leeuwen, E. and Van Knippenberg, D. 2003. "Continuing and changing group identities: the effects of merging on social identification and ingroup bias", *Personality and Social Psychology Bulletin* 29: 679–90.

Vermeulen, F. and Barkema, H. G. 2001. "Learning through acquisitions", *Academy of Management Journal* 44(3): 457–76.

Vlasic, B. and Stertz, B. 2000. *How Daimler-Benz Drove off with Chrysler*. New York: Morrow.

Waldinger. 1995. "The other side of embeddedness: a case study of the interplay between economics and ethnicity", *Ethnic and Racial Studies* 18: 555–80.

Waldman, D. and Javidan, M. (forthcoming). "Alternative forms of charismatic leadership in the integration of mergers and acquisitions", *Leadership Quarterly*.

Walsh, J. P. 1989. "Doing a deal: mergers and acquisition negotiations and their impact upon target companies top management turnover", *Strategic Management Journal* 10: 307–22.

Weber, Y. 1988. *The Effects of Top Management Culture Clash on the Implementation of Mergers and Acquisitions*, unpublished doctoral dissertation, University of South Carolina.
and Schweiger, D. 1989. "Implementing mergers and acquisitions: the role of cultural differences and the level of integration", University of South Carolina Working Paper.

Shenkar, O., and Raveh, A. 1996. "National and corporate fit in mergers & acquisitions: an exploratory study", *Management Science* 4(8): 1215–27.

Woolcock, M. 1997. "Social capital and economic development: towards a theoretical synthesis and policy framework", *Theory and Society*, 1–57.

Yu, J., Engleman, R. M., and Van de Ven, A. H. 2005. "The integration journey: an attention-based view of the merger and acquisition integration process", *Organisation Studies* 26: 1501–28.

Zollo, M., and Singh, H. 2004. "Deliberate learning in corporate acquisitions: post-acquisition strategies and integration capability in US bank mergers", *Strategy Management Journal* 25: 1233–56.

Global culture and organizational processes

MIRIAM EREZ and GILI S. DRORI

At the end of the twentieth century, concern with globalization and its seemingly continuous intensification led to new stream of research in organizational studies focusing on the changes that globalization brings to organizations. Such studies on the impact of globalization on organizations came from a variety of disciplinary perspectives. To name a mere few directions of inquiry, psychologists introduced questions about identity formation and cultural intelligence in such new global environments (e.g., Erez and Gati 2004; Earley, Ang and Tan, 2006; Shokef and Erez, 2006), ethnographers observed rituals of global restructuring in organizations (e.g., Ailon-Suadi and Kunda, 2003; Soderberg and Vaara, 2003), sociologists analyzed added organizational components (Drori, Meyer and Hwang, 2006), and strategy researchers study new forms of organization and integration patterns (Ghoshal and Bartlett, 1990; Birkinshaw *et al.*, 2003).

This variety of disciplinary foci resulted in marked fragmentation of the field of globalization studies, between the micro- and macro-, or between the behavioral and institutional. With each discipline developing its respective research tradition, this fragmentation blinded us to the conceptual commonalities and the observed similarities across such disciplinary divides. Today, calls are made from across this divide to expand the respective perspectives and thus to broaden the scope of each research tradition: institutionalists (Djelic and Quack, 2008; Powell and Colyvas, forthcoming) and strategy researchers (Redding, 2005) alike call for the use of multidisciplinary approaches to study complex social changes. For structuralists, the call is to seek the microfoundations and to build a theory of action to explain structural change; for organizational behavior researchers the call is to acknowledge the impact of social institutions and

to integrate the structural context of behavior into their analyses.

In this work we take these calls as a challenge. Specifically, we proposed a model for how institutional and cultural characteristics of the global world influence the structure and culture of global work organizations and the mindset and self-identity of individuals situated in them. We differentiate our arguments from the following bodies of work: (a) from studies on the effects of globalization, which conceive of globalization as a process of economic interdependencies, by orienting our work towards world *cultural* effects; (b) from studies that focus on globalization-induced organizational change in general, by orienting our work towards change in *work-related* environment in particular; and, (c) from discipline-specific work that focuses on either micro- or macro- effects, by creating a bridge and a *multidisciplinary* viewpoint on such complex processes.

Overall, the goal of this chapter is to outline a multidisciplinary model for the study of global and cultural effects on work. Arguing that culture and work scholarship focused solely on national and organizational cultures and neglected to integrate the work on global culture, we start with a review of globalization and of global culture. We then organize the effects of global culture on organizations along three cultural processes – rationalization, professionalization, and actorhood – and direct our study towards work organizations. We then propose a multi-level model that describes the embeddedness of work organizations in varied and cross-cutting cultures. Based on this proposed model, we outline the specific institutional and behavioral outcomes: we describe how such world cultural influences are expressed in the workplace, with structural, normative, and behavioral manifestations. We conclude with commentary on global convergence, the relations between structure, culture and behavior, and paths for future study.

Rethinking globalization as an institutional process: from economics to culture, from exchange to transformation

Globalization is a new term (Guillén, 2001) but the process it describes has old roots in western and capitalist expansion worldwide. While the intensification of global exchange – in the flow of commodities, people, and money – has been gradually growing for several centuries now, certain historic events – particularly the structuration of the world polity after World War II and the subsequent end of the Cold War – brought globalization to its current peak. Common descriptions of globalization portray it as a process of intensifying interdependencies (Keohane and Nye, 2000; Govindarajan and Gupta, 2001; Foreign Policy, 2005, 2006, 2007), focusing on the obvious escalation of international exchanges of everything from capital and labor to commodities and diplomatic relations. This perspective, shared by neoliberal (Keohane and Nye, 1997; Bhagwati, 2004; Wolf, 2004) and critical (Chase-Dunn, 1998; Wallerstein, 2000; Sklair, 2001) thinkers alike, highlights a mechanistic image of the global system: global players are assumed to be rational and bounded social actors and their exchange relations are assumed to be based on purposive calculations of costs and benefits. Recent realist contributions (e.g., Slaughter, 2004) add an acknowledgement of the global or supranational sphere: this added layer of consolidated and intensifying exchange, often coordinated by intergovernmental networks (Diehl, 1997), reinforces the exchanges among units within this global system.

The descriptive power of such approaches, summarizing globalization as transference (exchange) and transformation (change through exchange; see Bartelson, 2000), highlights the economic and political dimensions of globalization but gives little consideration to its cultural features. Even when applied to the globalization of cultural items, such approaches highlight the role of media

and consumerism (e.g., Ritzer, 2004b), treat culture as yet another commodity, and regard culture as an instrumental feature of global influence. In this way, realist approaches to globalization give little attention to the abstract ontological and cosmological nature of global cultural institutions, seeing global culture as carrying themes and practices that interpret the meaning of being and offer an interpretive grid for events and actions. Such realist approaches neglect, therefore, to interpret the complexity of globalization as transcendence (dissolution of borders through such exchange; see Bartelson, 2000). First, by regarding culture as the residual factor (see, Thomas et al., 1987, p. 7) and by instrumentalizing any references to its influence, realist approaches fail to recognize fully the power of culture and norms in motivating social change. Second, realist expectations that competition, now global, will breed differentiation are challenged by the obvious isomorphic features of societies and organizations worldwide. This is clearly evident in regards to the globalization of culture, where there is little sense of competition per se and yet cultural spheres are rearranged as transnational social-scapes – from diasporic communities to media-scape (see Appadurai, 1996). Third, the realist definition of the social actor as rational and bounded is obviously challenged by the intense interconnectedness of entities and by the ceremonial nature of many common practices (see, Meyer et al., 1997). On all these three accounts, the realist instrumentalization and marginalization of the study of culture is challenged by obvious features of the globalization age (see Drori, 2008).

Culture, which is a complex notion with many permutations to its definition (see Mor-Barak, 2005 p. 169[1]), is commonly defined as the shared values and norms of a society. Still, "culture involves far more than *general values* and knowledge that influence tastes and decisions; it defines the *ontological value* of actors and action" (Meyer et al., 1987: 22; emphases in original text). Globalization, being a powerful cultural process, has ontological and cosmological dimensions (or values and meaning

---

[1] We return to this matter of the definition of culture later in our essay.

systems that interpret the world) that are added upon the "layers" of rapidly intensifying political and economic exchanges (Meyer *et al.*, 1997; Meyer and Jepperson, 2000; Drori *et al.*, 2003; Drori, 2008). Moreover, globalization is a dual-level process: it is (a) the process of diffusion of practices, ideas and objects worldwide, across and through social borders and (b) the process of consolidation of a world society, serving as a canopy for global processes (Drori, 2008). With this cultural and institutional perspective, the world has become the relevant "imagined community" (see Anderson, 1991), thus constituting a world society. The culture of this newly imagined global community serves as the "interpretive grid," the "software of the mind" (Hofstede and Hofstede, 2004), or the "mindset" (Govindarajan and Gupta, 2001) of globalization.

The cultures of globalization

Globalization has accelerated the opportunities for cross-cultural interfaces. International organizations – either multinational enterprises or global civil society organizations – provide an interaction site for people coming from a mosaic of cultures, working within the same organization structure and operating with a shared organization value system (Gelfand, Erez, and Aycan, 2007). For the last thirty years, researchers have struggled with the question of what is culture, what are the cultural coordinates mapping cultures, and how cultures differ from each other. This stream of research centered, however, on the national and sub-national levels of culture. Moreover, any cross-cultural comparisons, as in the work of Hofstede, Schwartz, or Trompenaar, reflected the then common image of the world as an international system, thus devoting no attention to the global per se. We propose that globalization, which transcends national and other cultural borders, formed a new layer of culture, namely global culture. After a short review of cross-cultural studies to date, we proceed to propose a multilevel approach to understand the complexity of culture in global contexts: from the emerging macro-level of global culture to the embedded levels

of national cultures, organizational cultures, and team cultures.

The study of cultural differences

Culture is commonly defined as a set of shared meaning systems (Shweder and LeVine, 1984), a set of mental programs (Hofstede, 1980), a shared knowledge structure that results in decreased variability in values and behavioral patterns (Erez and Earley, 1993) and as shared motives, values, beliefs, identities, and interpretations or meanings of significant events that result from common experiences of members of collectives and are transmitted across age generations (House *et al.*, 2004). Carried by organizations and manifested in their structures and procedures, culture shapes the core values and norms of society's members. These values are shared and transmitted from one generation to another through social learning processes of modeling and observation, as well as through the effects of individual actions (Bandura, 1986). Hence, from a behaviorist perspective, culture represents what a group learns over a period of time as that group solves its problems of survival in an external environment and its problems of internal integration (Schein, 2004), while, from a macro perspective, culture reflects the institutional normative guidelines and is anchored in institutional arrangements. The common denominator of all the above definitions is that culture is a social, or collective, feature, rather than an individual attribute. Still, this shared, or collective, feature of culture binds social groups at various levels of aggregation, from the smallest of work teams, through organizations and nation, to the grand level of the global.

Until recently, the national level has been considered to be the most macro level of culture. Numerous typologies were developed to assess cross-cultural differences in cultural values. First, in what came to be the defining study of the field, Hofstede (1980) differentiated among national cultures along the dimensions, or scales, of power distance, individualism (versus collectivism), masculinity (versus femininity), and uncertainty avoidance. Later, following an interest in Asian values in particular, he added a scale for long- (versus short-) time orientation (Hofstede and Bond, 1988). Second, House and his colleagues (2004), as a part of the GLOBE project, added to Hofstede's canonized axes also the dimensions of humane orientation, and performance orientation. They also further distinguished between societal level and group level norms in regards to the Hofstede axis of collectivism versus individualism and they altered the single dimension of masculinity-femininity into two distinct axes for gender egalitarianism and assertiveness. Third, Trompenaars and Hampden-Turner (1998), based on a study of managers in twenty-three countries, added the identification of national cultures along the dimensions of: universalism (versus particularism); individualism (versus collectivism); neutral (masking feelings, versus affective or emotional); specific (emphasis on shared and public space, versus diffuse or emphasis on private space); and achievement (versus ascription). Last, Schwartz (1992) assessed the cultural values at the individual level and aggregated them to the national level. In an attempt to offer a multidimensional map of how such axes of culture related to each other, Schwartz identified three polar value dimensions: autonomy versus embeddedness, egalitarianism versus hierarchy, and mastery versus harmony.

Inspired by this stream of empirical research on cross-cultural differences at the national level, several attempts were made to gauge culture at the organizational level. While organizational culture is defined as the normative system that is shared by members of the same organization, it is often conflated with work-related environments and thus captures specifically the notion of corporate culture. With that, several studies offer parameters for differentiating organizational or corporate culture. The first group of studies focuses on the cultural features of the work process. For example, Rousseau (1990) distinguished between three markers of organizational values: task-related values, interpersonal values, and personal, or self-growth values. Similarly, Deal and Kennedy (1982) categorize organizational culture by its feedback response, risk-taking, Mucho, and work hard/play hard tendencies. And, Hofstede et al. (1990) categorize organizational culture along the scales of process or results orientation, employee

or job orientation, closed or open system approach, tight or loose control, and normative or pragmatic orientation. The second group of studies focuses more specifically on the normative behavior of the employees in such cultural environments. For example, O'Reilly, Chatman, and Caldwell (1991) identified nine cultural values in organizations: innovation and risk-taking, attention to detail, outcome orientation, assertiveness, supportiveness, emphasis on rewards, team orientation, decisiveness, representing the three factor categories. And, a third group of studies defines organizational culture in reference to its environment. For example, Schein (2004) categorizes cultures by their relations with nature and time, thus capturing notions of truth, control, and human nature. And, in attempt to thwart the western nature of such classifications, Tsui, Wang, and Xin (2006) classify organizational cultures along the two dimensions of internal integration (marked by harmony, standardization, communication, employee development, employee contribution, leadership, and shared vision) and external adaptation (marked by results and quality, customer satisfaction, innovation, and outcome orientation).

Implied in these studies is the layering of such cultures. Hofstede and his colleagues, who in their study of organizational culture find that all value orientations are strongly associated with the nationality (Danish or Dutch) of the organization, comment that "having gone to study organizational value differences and having done so in two countries for reasons of convenience, we seem to have mainly caught national value differences" (Hofstede et al., 1990 p. 301). But even for Hofstede, this layering of cultures – organizational and national – was merely a problem of research design and not an outcome of the desire accurately to gauge the complexity of cross-cultural exchange during the era of globalization. Yet, with globalization only adding to this complex disarray of cultures, attention should be given to multiple levels of culture, beyond the organizational and national.

A multilevel approach to culture

As we entered the new millennium, a group of sociologists has begun studying institutional and cultural phenomena in the global context (Boli, 2001; Drori, 2005; Lechner and Boli, 2005; Boli 2006). Added to this set of cultures is also a mosaic of cultures reflecting ethnic, racial, religious, gender, and other group-specific norms and values[2] (Chao and Moon, 2005). Globalization, with its globe-spanning connections and thus with its transnational identities, has brought these cultures to engage each other, creating a complex picture of cross-cutting relations among the many cultures of globalization.

Erez and Gati (2004) proposed a dynamic multilevel model of culture in which they first explicated the relations among the many cultures of globalization. They also were the first to introduce the notion of global culture to discussions of culture and work. Their model includes both structural and dynamic dimensions: they described both: (a) the hierarchy of nested group-, organizational-, national-, and global cultures; and (b) the top-down (global-local) and bottom-up (local-global) processes through which one level of culture influences other levels. Through top-down (global-local) processes the macro level of the global work culture influences national, organizational, and team cultures, as well as influences the behavior of individuals according to these global norms. Reciprocally, through bottom-up processes, social groups and individuals labor to define and change their culture, and such changes build into aggregates that reinforce and constitute broader culture.

The Erez and Gati model allows for a classificatory description of any specific culture: together, these dimensions or markers provide a grid for identifying cultural variation. With its emphasis on the multiplicity of cultures, this model goes a long way in explaining the multiple, possibly contradictory, cultural demands on embedded organizations and individuals. It implies that, at any given historic moment and place, organizations and units are nested in multiple levels of cultures. And, the more cosmopolitan the unit is, the more levels of culture it is influenced by. In a similar vain, Arnett (2002) and Chao and Moon (2005) describe how the individual's identity is a mosaic of multiple

cultural influences and Gerhards and Haceknbroch (2000) show how even a person's name is subject to global and cultural modernization.

With its emphasis on the dynamic flow of cultural influences, this model also goes a long way in specifying the relations among nested cultures: seeing cultural influences as a series of effects. These nested cultural influences are interpreted in a variety of ways: they are understood as a form of capitalist imposition (Sklair, 2001), as a state of competition and contestation (Weiner, 2007), as a process of translation (Czarniawska and Sevon, 2005), as scale of embeddedness (Meyer et al., 1997), or as an instance of glocalization (Robertson, 1995). These understandings, each in its distinct way, explain dynamics of world society by addressing notions of change and variation. They also allow for explanations of action and behavior in globalization, addressing such common questions as "why are states complying with international laws?", "why are corporations adhering to global voluntary standards?", or "why do individuals conform to global fashions?"

But even the Erez and Gati model, with its recognition of the multiplicity of cultures and of the dynamic relations among them, leaves global culture underspecified. While global culture – which is presumably the broadest and most general of the cultures in globalization – is an entity of its own, and while it is recognized as changing through its interaction with other cultures, the specific norms, beliefs, traditions, and assumptions that bind world society remain unspecified. In the following sections, we outline the features of global culture, so at later sections we can describe the influences of global culture on organizations and work.

Global culture

Divisions and conflicts, rife worldwide, somewhat obscure the dramatic consolidation of a global culture, particularly since the end of World War II. Global culture encompasses the values and norms that are shared worldwide, across various political, economic, and other social divisions (see Featherstone, 1990; Lechner and Boli, 2005). It is "the cultural complex of foundational assumptions, forms of knowledge, and prescriptions for

---

[2] Which are commonly under-theorized in spite of their obvious stand as global "scapes."

action that underlie globalized flows, organizations, and institutions" (Boli, 2001, p. 6261). Like other cultures, global culture is a shared, or common, feature. As such, it marks the boundaries of the relevant social unit and implies that the "imagined community" has been extended to be a world society, whose existence became a presupposition in the age of globalization. Even the talk about global culture itself reifies the consolidation of a world society.

Global culture encodes the norms, models, and institutions that are made sacred and are treated as desiderata, presumably uniting a world society. As much as this global framework is general and as much as the concept of "culture" is illusive, there have been several attempts to specify the normative framework of the emerging world society. We describe here several studies, which while using different "sites" and different methods, all attempt at mapping global culture. We then draw global cultural principles from them.

Boli (2006) described the global moral order by categorizing the various celebrations (announcements and titles), certifications (licenses and professional ranking), and criticisms (public exposure and denunciations). In making such public displays as the Noble Prize, ISO audits, and organizational progress reports, world society praises virtue (moral standing) and virtuosity (instrumental competence) and admonishes transgression. These displays vary by degree of rationalization, between normative declarations where the criteria for compliance are explicitly codified and are made procedural (such as sainthood as a display of virtue and FDA approval as a display of virtuosity) and where the normative code is more ambiguous and subjective (such as corporate social responsibility as a display of virtue and UN World Heritage sites as a display of virtuosity; Boli, 2006, pp. 107–10). Lechner and Boli (2005), in a similarly sweeping review of the cultural role of international organizations (such as UN or the International Criminal Court) and their work (UN summits or ICC judgments), argued that these organizations serve as sites of global cultural practice and thus affirm, codify, and diffuse world norms.

Using one such "metric" for the scope of world norms, Drori (2005) analyzed the practice of UN dedications to describe what issues are declared most worthy by UN member states. She showed that among the 127 issues highlighted by UN dedications, 38 percent directly address issues of development and 40 percent address issues of rights, while matters relating to security, sovereignty, and culture are relatively marginalized (2005, pp. 182–3). The two central themes of UN dedication – development and rights – serve as prism for particular subjects, from health to food to colonialism. And, these two themes mark the scale for human achievement, highlighting "the core matters that UN collectively commits to uphold" and "the issues that are given special appreciation by world community" (2005, p. 183).

Mapping global culture by the scope of collective action on various issues was also at the basis of Boli and Thomas's (1997, 1999) investigation of international nongovernmental organizations. Seeing such organizations as the backbone of global civil society, Boli and Thomas categorized the growth in international nogovernmental organizations by field and that 44 percent of all global civic organizations in 1988 centered on issues of economic exchange, medicine and healthcare, and science. These issues are surely matters of social concern but they are also highly universalized: we accept that the principles or laws in these matters are true worldwide. Still, as Boli and Thomas described, many "softer" matters are increasingly matters of global social concern, reflecting the reorientation of world society since the late nineteenth century toward universalized and individualistic themes. As a result, there has also been a dramatic structuration of the field of human rights (Tsutsui and Wotipka, 2004) and the rights of specific groups (for example, women; Berkovitch, 1999) and a marked stagnation in organizing around collective themes, such as labor and religion (Boli and Thomas, 1997, p. 184).

This trend of individualization supported the emergence of a global identity as yet another scale of world cultural characteristics. Defined as the individual sense of belonging to and identification with universal matters, global identity builds upon a cosmopolitan ideology. This consciousness of a global community and this sense of humanity do not negate the identification with other groups, such as the nation or the ethnic group (see, Iriye, 2004, p. 9). Rather, global identity is unique in that it allows, with no conflict, for one to hold a multilayered sense of belonging and identification (Arnett, 2002; Norris, 2003; Erez and Gati, 2004; Erez and Shokef, 2008; Shokef and Erez, 2006). This global identity, which is conceptually separate from the globalizing tendencies towards individualism and actorhood, supports globalization. Another feature of the global citizens is the cultural intelligence (CQ) which is an individual's capability to deal effectively in situations characterized by cultural diversity, and "is needed to manage the stress of culture shock and the consequent frustration and confusion that typically result from clashes of cultural differences" (Earley, Ang, and Tan, 2006, p. 3).

Together, these investigations demonstrate the breadth and complexity of global culture and the multiple ways of gauging its scope. In spite of this variety, it is clear that there exists a core set of issues that is pronounced as global and is proclaimed as important and valued the world over. This core set of *issues* – extending from human rights, to environmentalism, to inequality, to development – surely goes much further than any trends of global consumer culture. Yet, in spite of this variety of issues, there are common themes or norms that outline a "sacred canopy" – to paraphrase Peter Berger – of global societal expectations. The primary cultural *themes* of this "canopy" are guided by progress (the aspiration for advancement of human life) and justice (the aspiration for moral and righteous life; Meyer *et al.*, 1987; 1997). These twin pillars of western, now global, culture serve as a prism for all other issues; subjects that are framed as related to either progress or justice become privileged over all others (Meyer *et al.*, 1987; 1997). Boli and Thomas (1999) add to this description by specifying five cultural tones that underlie the expansion of global civil society: (a) universalism; (b) individualism; (c) rational voluntaristic authority; (d) human purposefulness; and (e) world citizenship. These norms highlight the role of moral, purposeful,

and empowered agency, or actohood (Meyer and Jepperson, 2000) and its realization in rationalized ways of systematization and standardization (Jepperson, 2002, p. 257) and with scientization as the principal organizing logic (Drori and Meyer, 2006). Overall, progress, justice, and individualism emerge as the sanctified themes of the still evolving global normative consensus.

Global cultural processes

How are global cultural themes affecting organizations? The array of global norms, which reflects the complexity of human history and of current international arrangements, can be distilled into three global cultural processes: rationalization, professionalization, and actorhood.[3] These three cultural processes embody many of the global norms as well as capture their impact on, here, work environment. In the following section, we describe these three processes, as well as their structural and behavioral impacts on current world of work.

Rationalization

Rationalization pertains to systemization, standardization, routinization and thus formalization of social activity. It is defined as the "continuing efforts to systematize social life around standardized rules and around schemes that explicitly differentiate and then seek to link means and ends" (Jepperson, 2002, p. 257). Rationalization can be observed in the development of rationalized structures (articulated and formal role differentiation, evident in titles and organizational chart), rationalized procedures (articulated and formal description of processes, of such tasks as hiring or production), and rationalized accounts (articulated justifications for such behavior, displayed in advertising material or annual reports; see Drori, Meyer and Hwang, forthcoming). While systemization and formalization are sometimes explained by long-term competitive evolution and increasing socio-technical complexity, rationalization also involves cultural enactment based on perceptions of the relevant environment (Drori, Jang and Meyer, 2006). In this sense, rationalization is more than the mechanistic application of standard routines; rather, it involves

---

[3] This categorization is drawn from the conceptual framework developed in Drori, Meyer and Hwang, 2006.

an incorporation of a "spirit" of modernization, in Weberian terms.

Such rationalization draws from the culture of universalism: the articulated awareness that social issues are relevant worldwide, which is aided by scientized models for the universal applicability of natural and now social laws (see, Drori *et al.*, 2003; Drori and Meyer, 2006). Scientization is driving organizations to see themselves as comparable and compatible with other organizations. As a result, corporations of various sizes or various sectors, universities from various countries, and civil society organizations with various missions observe each other's routines, imitate each other's action, and refer to each other as models.

In constructing a sense of comparability, universalism also creates a sense of competition. This is most clearly evident in the emerging culture of ranking, where organizations are bluntly compared based on presumably universal criteria. For example, Hedmo, Sahlin-Andersson, and Wedin (2006) described the ranking of European educational programs and the related development of an accreditation system, and analyzing this as a process of modeling and enactment (with the benchmark being the American business education sector). And whereas this example of the ranking and accreditation of European MBA programs highlights regulatory regimes and thus the formal dimension of universal comparability, much of such universal comparability is informal. For example, rankings of such "qualities" as global integration, corruption, and good corporate citizenship are now common, imagining a shared and global scale for such comparisons. Similarly, work partners, even from across cultures and world regions, rely on common benchmarks of performance and quality, thus assuming comparability of their work processes across such social divides.

Rationalization also breeds standardization, or the emergence of consistent and uniform procedures for executing tasks. ISO initiatives – on quality control, environmental care and soon on social responsibility – are prime examples of global standardization: Mendel (2006) described them as abstract and highly normative rules, even if voluntary or "soft," that set common models for organizational tasks. Similarly, accounting puts order into

managerial chaos, standardizing risk management (Power, 2007) and creating categories for work and operations (Jang, 2006; Power, 2007). With voluntary rules (like ISO) and others more formal (like financial reporting), these rationalized steps create a regime of standardization (of everything from the design, quality, and delivery of both products and services), add pressure on organizations to comply with such standards, and thus fuel isomorphic tendencies among organizations. In short, rationalization, drawing from world norms of universality and related scientization, shapes organizations towards more formal and standardized forms. Universality drives comparability and thus bench-marking. Scientization drives models for how such comparability is to be executed, namely according to analytic schemes of both features and causality. In some sectors more than in others, such comparability takes the form of competition: this, we accept, is the basis for firms' behavior in the marketplace, but increasingly we see the implementation of bench-marking strategies in educational or philanthropic organizations. Competition, based on assumptions of universality, is the conceptual framework of the environment, which is thus defined as a market. Rationalization's impact on the workplace is in establishing an environment of comparability and competition and thus fueling standardization. While such competition also requires niche-carving, where organizations struggle to differentiate themselves from their competitors, they drive organizations to become innovative and mark innovation and change among the current desired features of organizations.

The obvious manifestation of these work-related features (comparability, competition, and standardization) is modeling: one mimics the form of the other with the assumption that they share common features, goals, or contexts. Such modeling is done on the basis of perceived success: one mimics the form that is associated with successful outcome. Such modeling is prevalent in both structural and behavioral ways. Structurally, modeling results in the adoption of universalized and scientized models and their diffusion from one context to another and thus takes the form of isomorphism. Either through strategic mimicry, or normative pressures, or through coercion (see

DiMaggio and Powell, 1983), organizations learn from each other and enact legitimate or seemingly successful scripts. Here, the influence of global scripts varies by the level of embeddedness in world society: more embedded organizations, which thus are more aware of the global scripts or under stronger influence of global model carriers, are more isomorphic. This is the case in regards to business schools (Hedmo, Sahlin-Andersson, and Wedin 2006), quality assurance practices in firms (Mendel, 2006), and national modes of governance (Drori, Jang, and Meyer, 2006). Overall, world norms of universality, which are translated to work-related culture of comparability, result in far-reaching modeling and subsequent similarity, with both structural and behavioral manifestations.

Professionalization

The global cultural emphasis on universalism also nourishes the work-related emphasis on professionalization. Only in a universalistic context can we imagine that professionals hold the principal knowledge and expertise. Professionalization refers to knowledge and expertise as drawn only from legitimate, or preferably certified, members of a profession. Not only are certification and accreditation themselves rationalizing procedures, but professionalization distinctly offers a legitimate basis for counseling organizations and their managers on how and what to execute their tasks. In a world described as chaotic and risky (Beck, 1992), where many of the social problems regarded as global (Ritzer, 2004a), professionals guide organizations in making what seems to be necessary adjustments: think tanks advise policy makers, consultancy agencies advise corporate heads, and psychologists advise team leaders. Professionalization is fueled by the massive expansion of education in general (Schofer and Meyer, 2005) and of professional education in particular (Moon and Wotipka, 2006). Therefore, professional advice, which draws from modern education system and its pedagogy and therefore draws authority from universal and certified knowledge, marginalizes former and alternative modes of competence and authority – such as seniority, royal title, or moral authority – which are assumed to draw from local and thus context-specific knowledge.

Lawyers, accountants, management consultants, medical doctors, scientists, and advertising agents alike base their authority in the universal principles of their profession. And, professional ties, among people and among organizations, serve as the medium for the transfer of scripts (forms and practices) across contexts.

Professionalization has obvious structural manifestations in the organization of work. First, professionalization changed the structure of modern economies by creating a sector of professional service firms (Greenwood and Suddaby, 2006). This rapidly growing sector is expanding to include more and more professions: while most studies center on law, accountancy, and business consultancy, the same principles apply also to the increasingly organized and universalized professions of human resources management ("head hunting"), banking and venture investment, and engineering and architecture. The normative guide for this sector is the authority to mold the practice of other organizations.

Second, professionalization contributed to formal role differentiation within organizations: it defined management as a profession, severing its ties with ownership, and created a sense of discrete organizational tasks associated with such roles. As a result, organizations of various sorts have similar formal posts: from general manager to financial officer to human resources manager, the work tasks for these managerial roles are distinct, as are the professional background, certification and professional ethos. The separation of profession and role from organizational context (goal or sector) contributes to mobility of people and of conceptual models alike across organizations and across contexts.

Third, the mix of rationalization and professionalization, which creates such notions as "best practice," delivers profound impact on organizations. By crystallizing "best practice" solutions to organizational crises, which are formulaic and standardized plans of action, professionals affirm the vision of organizations as comparable, of social rules as universal, and of professional expertise as the relevant authority. And, in so doing, they further encourage comparability and modeling, isomorphic tendencies across organizations, and global homogenization: see Ruef (2002) and McKenna, Djelic, and

Ainamo (2003) regarding management consultants; Djelic (1998) regarding economists; Dezalay and Garth (2002) regarding lawyers; and Power (1997) and Jang (2006) regarding accountants.

Professionalization also impacts behavioral patterns in work environments. It creates a professional ethos that affects the identification of professionals with their work: rather than identifying with their firm, professionals identify primarily with their profession (Stryker and Burke, 2000). As a result, the "distance" between an American doctor and a Chinese doctor, for example, is smaller than it is between an American doctor and an American farmer. It also contributes to mobility: because they identify themselves primarily as professionals, they easily transfer from one firm to another. Yet, professionalization also helps mitigate the cultural diversity that results from mobility and transnational exchange: it offers tools to manage diversity, coordinate activities, and streamline processes, assuming that cultural diversity itself is a universal phenomenon and thus remedied by standardized tools. Overall, professionalization further opens the organization in general and workplaces in particular to their environment, allowing for a whole host of "external" influences to permeate work situations. Professionalization thus transforms organizations and changes social relations within them.

Actorhood

Agentic tendencies in global culture constitute a culture of actorhood, where social entities are instilled with a strong sense of agency, authority, and "voice." Through education and personal development strategies, and with a basis in the scientized vision of the natural and social worlds as manageable and controllable, people and organizations are transformed into highly agentic and proactive social entities (Drori, Meyer, and Hwang, 2006; forthcoming). The social actor is conceived as having control over her or his environment and thus of their destiny. Thus, "actorhood" goes beyond individualism, even if it is related to it: "actorhood" constitutes an agent, or a proactive singular social actor. Globalization diffuses this profoundly western (or Judeo-Christian) concept of the person and its cosmological place, changing societies by

redefining the relations of authority between person and hegemon and between person and nature. The individual human person is the set as the basic unit of society (Meyer and Jepperson, 2000) and many social programs – from government services, to democracy, to social science methodologies – are constructed with this person as the organizing principle. Education has been a prime vehicle for this trend, instilling in individuals the capacity or motivation, as well as skills, for taking a proactive stand (Meyer and Jepperson, 2000; Schofer and Meyer, 2005). Over time, the individual human came to supersede other social units, organized around collectivist or traditional modes of authority, such as a clan or a nation. Still, while the individual human is the prime instance of actorhood, actorhood is still infused into a variety of social units: corporations, nations, charities, and other organizations are considered singular entities, speaking in one voice and bearing responsibilities as a collective, increasingly also in the legal and formal sense.

This global cultural emphasis on the role of personal agency, which is labeled "actorhood," profoundly impacted on work situations. It fueled a culture of entrepreneurship and innovation, especially in the past three decades. This has changed the relationship between of workers and their organization: structurally, it created channels for worker input into organizational processes; and, behaviorally, it engaged workers in modes of self-efficacy and self-motivation. It also altered the mode of authority and regulation, establishing modes of responsibility to replace other modes of control and compliance. Structurally, actorhood is manifested in agency-enhancing practices. Some such structural arrangements that constitute the worker as an agent – for example, programs of in-house training in firms, which are now operating in firms worldwide – build a culture of human resource management and train workers in skills that go further than the set required for their production role into a sphere enhancing their capacities in terms of vision, creativity, and entrepreneurship (Luo, 2006). Similarly, firms increasingly establish corporate social responsibility initiatives, thus creating a new worldwide norm for corporate good citizenship that reformulates the relationship between state, market, and society (Khagram and

Shanahan, 2006). With its new role, anchored in these new corporate procedures and units, the firm is asserting its role as a (responsible) social agent.

In summary, globalization reflects not only a remarkable intensification of global exchanges and flows and a dramatic thickening of international and transnational webs of relations, but also a major cultural change. Global culture, with its core themes of progress and justice, brings three profound changes to organizations: rationalization, professionalization, and actorhood. This change is also accompanied by a shift in the organizing logic from the particularistic (national, ethnic) to the universal (human, standardized, formal). With this extension of the social horizon to world society came a consolidation of a global culture, which combines the ideals of progress and justice and norms that enhance rationalization, professionalization, and actorhood. These norms are unquestionably anchored in the ideas and ideals of the western Age of Enlightenment. While some scholars thus interpret it as a mechanism of capitalist, or specifically American, political and economic domination, the more prevalent interpretation view global culture "in terms of the diversity, variety and richness of popular discourse, codes and practices which resist and play-back systemicity and order" (Featherston, 1990, p. 2). This image of a co-constitutive (not to say dialectic) social sphere, makes global culture particularly influential: it sets not only desiderata, at the ideational level, but also directly imprints organizations, behaviors and practices. In this sense, global culture is both dynamic and hyperactive, anchored in organizations that increasingly take a proactive role.

One may argue that the global culture is heavily embedded in western cultures and it may not reflect all the players in the global world. Global culture is in indeed western in essence. Also true is that western companies dominated 60 percent of the global activities, thus disseminating western values (Thurow, 2003). Yet, many of these global institutions and values penetrate non-western countries through multinational enterprises that operate both at the global and national levels. And so, while we recognize that globalization carries western ideals and thus it requires greater adjustment from developing nations, several Asian countries nevertheless rank highest on the scales of globalization (Foreign Policy, 2005, 2006, 2007). Also, while the growing economic gap between developed and developing countries sets a barrier for further globalization (Leung et al., 2005), many local organizations adopt the transnational features with the expectation, for a better fit with modern or global trends. Such hybrid or glocal forms are shown in corporate set-ups like malls and franchises (e.g., Helacioglu, 2000; Illouz and John, 2003), in local civic associations (e.g., Mato, 2000), and indeed in multinational organizations that are infused with global norms and the features of global culture. The following section examines how the global culture specifically impacts business organizations and the workplace.

World cultural impact on organizations and the workplace

Multi-cultural organizations at work

In spite of diverging views on what role organizations play in globalization[4], all social scientists recognize the obvious fact that globalization indeed shapes organizations. Globalization changes the map of financial resources for organizations: foreign direct investment and charitable donations, like trade and production, alike are now transnational, thus broadening the scope of economic exchange for organizations. Globalization also changed the regulatory and political map for organizations: international political alliances – on diverse issues such as trade and labor, governance and law, environmental conservation and rights – now set regulatory parameters for organizations, both local and global. Globalization changes the supply chain to be defined not only in terms of supply of the raw material, but also in terms of globally outsourcing portions of the work flow itself – from software development to call centers (Grossman and Helpman, 2005; Friedman, 2000, 2005). Finally,

---

[4] Variety of theoretical approaches: from conservatives (Abbott and Snidal, 1998) to neo-Marxists (Sklair, 2001; Chandler and Mazlich, 2005) to institutionalists (Boli and Thomas, 1997; 1999).

globalization facilitates the diffusion of knowledge and the mobilization of employees and managers across cultural and national borders. Overall, many factors – from technology to resources to scale – have shaped the impact of globalization on organizations. In this chapter we highlight the effects of global culture on organizations by applying a dynamic and multilevel model to describe the effects of global culture on organizations, and specifically on multinational organizations.

Multinational organizations are rapidly expanding: organizations as diverse in their goals as international governmental organizations, multinational corporations and transnational civil society associations are all creating an environment that is uniquely multinational. Added to this are organizations, even if national in operations, which are coming in exchange with global or other national organizations; for example, subcontractors in production.

Multinational organizations differ from all known local organizations by operating in the geographically dispersed and culturally diverse global environment. Furthermore, global organizations stand on local cultural subsidiaries that demand local responsiveness but, at the same time, they require global integration to maintain their unity as one organization (Bartlett and Ghoshal, 1989; Doz and Prahalad, 1991). Such organizations are, therefore, unique in the way they integrate global values together with the diverse values of their multiple subsidiaries. This integration of various cultural demands has been a particular challenge for multinational enterprises, where for example multiple cultures influence the work of multinational teams, where international regulation requires compliance worldwide, and where transnational mobilization calls for engagement of diverse stakeholders. Such organizations, in the age of globalization, are trapped between this "layering" of cultures, subject to the nested and cross-cutting relations among various "levels" of cultural environments.

The study of global cultural influences, in particular, on organizations has expanded, investigating the effects on governmental bureaucracies (Hwang, 2006; in regards to state planning agencies), educational institutions (Hedmo, Sahlin-Andersson, and Wedin 2006; Moon and Wotipka,

2006, with regard to universities), for-profit companies (Mendel, 2006; Luo, 2006, with regard to corporate practices). There is also a rich tradition, even if diverse theoretically, of studying globalization through organizations: from multinational corporations to intergovernmental organizations to transnational civil society organizations. While drawing from scholarly work on globalization and organizations, in this work we specifically focus on the impact of cultural globalization on work environments. We propose that the global work values carried by multinational organizations have unique characteristics that reflect the duality of the global world context and local national environment. In the following section, we explore, with specific examples, the structural and behavioral manifestations of the influence of global culture on workplace culture.

Global culture impact on global work values of multinational organizations

While there are numerous typologies of national and organizational cultures, there is no existing typology of the global work culture. Shokef and Erez (2006) define the *global work culture* as the shared understanding of the visible rules, regulations, and behaviors, and the deeper values and ethics of the global work context (Shokef and Erez, 2006). Their approach stems from ecological models which treat values as facilitating adaptation to the external environment by instructing what is right and what is wrong, good, or bad (Rokeach, 1973; Berry *et al.*, 1992; Erez and Gati, 2004). Accordingly, global work values facilitate adaptation to the global context in which business operations take place. In the next section we explicate the impact of global values on global work values.

In the following sections we describe several such impacts. We organize our descriptions along the three general global cultural processes described earlier: (1) rationalization; (2) professionalization; and (3) actorhood. We further articulate how each such global cultural process (in italics) carries or expresses particular global values (in bold) and how such values are then imprinting particular values, activities, and behaviors in work situations.

1. Rationalization

1A. Rationalized assumptions about *universalism*, which highly significant global values (Jepperson, 2002) drive organizations to see themselves as comparable to other organizations (Drori *et al.*, 2003; Drori and Meyer, 2006). Expressing such notions of comparability are global ranking machineries, which classify work organizations according to what is understood to be important criteria – from profitability to social responsibility. And, obviously, such ranking highlight the admired organizations, setting them as models for others to emulate. This ranking reifies the sense of competition, which is also carried by the ideas of the world as a market, and establishes that organizations are competing with each other on the top rank (Govindarajan and Gupta, 2001). This sense of competition guides organizations: for example, the corporate strategy of competitive performance orientation emphasizes the importance of bench-marking the company in reference to its competitors and verifying that its performance level is always above its competitors (Porter, 1985; Fiegenbaum, Hart, and Schendel, 1996). It is assumed that the rank, or relative position, affects the appeal to customers, employees and shareholders and thus influences the organization's long-term competitive advantage in the market. As a result, work values of *competitive performance* became an important global work value (Shokef and Erez, 2006).

1B. Rationalization and universalism inform ideas about the value of *standardization* (Loya and Boli, 1999; Drori, Jang, and Meyer 2006). It is assumed that standardization enhances comparability and thus competitive performance. With standardization translated into consistent and uniform procedures for executing tasks, work organizations came to focus on particular aspects of their practice that we set as standard (rather than on others that were assumed to be particularistic). For example, multinational organizations comply with the international standards of quality performance (e.g., ISO; Mendel, 2006) or with the international accounting standards of risk management (Jang, 2006; Power, 2007). This compliance reflects the global work value of *quality focus*, where organizational anxieties about comparability are translated into standard operations and procedures.

1C. The rationalization of the context, or environment, of organizations as a market, coupled with (a) the recognition of multicultural nature of such environment and (b) actorhood ideals about the place of the individual, have established recognition of the importance of customers. It is assumed that recognizing the layout of culturally diverse customers and identifying their diverse needs and unique preferences are crucial for the competitive advantage of companies (Yilmaz, Alpkan, and Ergun, 2005). In this way, the rationalization of the organization's environment has fueled the recognition of *customer orientation* as a core global work value (Kilduff and Dougherty, 2000). Also, customer orientation is defined as a practical strategy to enhance competitiveness.

1D. Consumed by concerns about competitiveness, organizations also turn to other strategies that are assumed to enhance their ranking and their performance. Among the novel strategies is innovation. Innovation is highlighted these days as the defining feature of successful organizations: new and unique products, services, and procedures – preferably of the kind that revolutionizes the field – win markets and gain success for the innovative organizations. And with the global environment described as highly dynamic, innovation and change are conceived as particularly crucial for adaptation to this highly uncertain context: innovation facilitates adaptation to such an environment as old strategies, goals, and work procedures may no longer be effective, or even functional (Friedman, 2000, 2005; Giddens, 2000; Kilduff and Dougherty, 2000). With that, *innovation* has evolved from a strategy (a response to a need or a crisis) to a core global work value that facilitates competitive performance.

2. Professionalization

2A. Professionalization reinforces universalistic global values. With science defining social laws as similar in relevance to the universalistic applications of natural laws (Drori *et al.*, 2003; Drori and Meyer, 2006) and with academic institutions becoming increasingly isomorphic in curriculum and output, professionalization homogenizes global work culture. Professional schools mimic each other's curriculum, using the same professional reading material and requiring similar accreditation exams that impose standard professional requirements. Today's students travel across national borders to join the best professional programs regardless of their geographical locations. Furthermore, professional schools, and in particular schools of management, open MBA programs outside their home country, bluntly disseminating knowledge across national borders. With the revolution of the internet, knowledge has become universal as well. Thus, professionals around the world share a common body of knowledge and professional values.

In regards to the global work context, professionalization helps create the synergy among professionals across geographically dispersed and culturally diverse subsidiaries. With that, *professionalization* enhances the sense of *interdependence*, explaining interdependence as a prerequisite for a united or integrated organization. High professionalism establishes shared professional goals and shared work procedures and thus interdependence, which is necessary for collaborative work among professionals and for knowledge sharing. Interdependencies strengthen organizational unity and homogeneity in the professional and managerial practices that are implemented across subsidiaries (Rosenweig and Nohria, 1994; Friedman, 2000, 2005; Govindarajan and Gupta, 2001; Kostova and Roth, 2002; Berson, Erez, and Adler, 2004). For example, managers working in multiple subsidiaries of one multinational company had a strong shared understanding of their task-related managerial roles of strategic planning and leading innovation and change (Berson, Erez, and Adler 2004). At the same time, interdependence is also associated with collectivistic values (Hofstede, 2001) and, consequently, it may have a negative consequences in both individualist and collectivist environments: in individualist cultures interdependence may be taken to mean a threat to the "space" of the individual and thus be less appreciated, whereas in collectivist cultures interdependence may strengthen the ingroup–outgroup division, thus inhibiting knowledge sharing across culturally diverse groups. Therefore, the meaning of interdependence may fracture through the lens of local cultural values.

2B. Rationalization and *professionalism* may also enhance trust across people in diverse cultures. *Trust* "concerns the willingness of one person or group to relate to another in the belief that the other's actions will be beneficial rather than detrimental, even though this cannot be guaranteed" (Child, 2001, p. 275). Implementing rationally based standard organizational rules and procedures, supported by universal professional rules and procedures, reduces ambiguity and increase predictability in organizations; predictability, stability, and reduced ambiguity enhance trust among members of the organization, between the organization and its partners (suppliers, customers, and shareholders), and among various units in the network of exchange (Giddens, 2000; Earley and Gibson, 2002). In this way, professionalization creates a platform for exchange that is then interpreted as stable enough to enhance trust. A culture of trust enhances shared knowledge, free communication and cooperation and its importance is amplified in a multicultural work environment.

3. Actorhood

3A. The global value of *actorhood* has direct implications to the importance of personal growth and respect for the individual in multinational organizations. In such complex organizations individuals may lose their sense of identification with the organization, and feel lost (Erez and Gati, 2004). Therefore, emphasizing individuals' personal development is important for enhancing the sense of self-worth and well-being of individual employees in multinational organizations (Erez and Gati, 2004) and is constructed as related to productivity and effectiveness. *Personal development* as an organizational value appears in existing typologies of organizational culture (Rousseau, 1990; O'Reilly, Chatman, and Caldwell 1991). Yet, while the interpretation of the same managerial practices as contributing or not to a person's sense of self-growth may vary across cultures (Erez and Earley, 1993) and while the meaning of personal growth may be shaped by the local national cultures of the subsidiaries, there is a clear expansion of human resources culture of this sort across the world (Luo, 2006). According to Luo's (2006) work, the agentic cultural tendencies of global culture, or actorhood, get embodied in corporate practices: for example, in-house training that goes beyond the skills for the work tasks and enhances ideals of self-growth and take-charge mentality.

3B. With the cultural focus changing towards the individual as an agent or a responsible and active social actor (which is the essence of actorhood) comes an a recognition of personal traits and attributes: personal characteristics (skills, motivation, temperament), rather than social attributes (race, ethnicity, gender), are ascribed greater importance, particularly in work environments. This results in greater *openness to cultural diversity* (Erez and Gati, 2004; Shokef and Erez, 2006). Openness to cultural diversity is defined as the degree of receptivity by individuals, groups, and organizations to perceived dissimilarity (Härtel, 2004). The cultural diversity of multinational organizations is a given: it is imprinted into their structure by the simple fact that they consist of various national subsidiaries. Cultural diversity is constructed as a possible functional problem, requiring managerial strategies to resolve tensions and inefficiencies resulting from such diversity. Such strategies call, for example, for effective communication and cooperation with each other (Maznevski, 1994; Govindarajan and Gupta, 2001). Yet, the openness to cultural diversity goes beyond this functional relation with efficiency of resources. It is also intertwined with the universalistic tendencies of global culture: universalistic approaches to people, which are expressed in discourses of rights and conceptualize members of diverse cultures as equal rather than as particular/peculiar, create a platform for cross-cultural cooperation. This is particularly strong within professional groups, such as accountants, management consultants, and academics, because their professional ethos is very universalistic, drawing from universalized laws of performance and conduct. In this sense, openness to cultural diversity draws from global culture but also directly impacts on the culture of work, by enabling work exchange to be situated within professional and universalistic discourses.

3C. Actorhood is also reflected in the *social responsibility* initiatives (Khagram and Shanahan, 2006), in organizations in general and in work organizations in particular. Such initiatives take the form of support for community education and health, protection of the environment, or enhancement of employee work conditions (Wood, 1991; Gardberg and Fombrun, 2006). They are understood as a requirement of social actors: to care for one's peers, individual or organizational, is in the nature of an actor and of a global citizen. Also, recognizing the diversity and fragility of one's communities and helping them to grow and develop reflects upon the sense of personal development of the individual employees who are members of these communities (Frederick, 1998; Gardberg and Fombrun, 2006). And, in the case of corporate responsibility, such initiatives reflect collective actorhood, seeing corporations as responsible collective citizens. While the concept of organizational social responsibility has different meanings in different countries (Gardberg and Fombrun, 2006), while it varies across sectors (Khagram and Shanahan, 2006), and therefore is influenced by local cultural values, the rapid expansion of such initiatives are a global wave.

Overall, we attribute work values to the influence of global values and see such direct link as particularly pronounced the more globally embedded the work organization is. However, are all these nine values adhered to a similar extent across all subsidiaries of the same multinational organization, or across different multinational corporations? Are these values homogeneous across locales? The answer to these questions depends on the level of global integration versus local responsiveness that characterizes the multicultural organization (Bartlett and Ghoshal, 1994). Organizations with a stronger structure of global integration are more likely to have a higher level of homogeneity in their global work values. The ones that are more concerned about local responsiveness may be less homogeneous in their global work values, allowing for more flexibility and a higher level of acceptance of cultural diversity with respect to some of the values. Overall, we propose that multinational organizations will maintain a higher level of homogeneity and global integration with respect to task-oriented values (Berson, Erez, and Alder, 2004) or externally adapted values (Tsui, 2006), such as global competitiveness, customer orientation, and quality focus. This homogeneity will be driven by the global world values of universalism, rationalization, and professionalization. On

Table 6.1. Observing global cultural effects on work organizations

Global Culture	Global Organization Work Culture		
	Structure and Institutions	Values	Global Actions Behaviors
1. Rationalization (Formalization standardization)	Adoption of universalized recipes, isomorphism; comparability	Competitive performance; quality assurance; innovation; customer orientation	Modeling; social learning
2. Professionalization (Authority drawn from certified knowledge)	Universal role and dask differentiation; universalized expert knowledge	Task interdependence; trust	Shared professional and managerial practices
3. Actorhood (Control, agency, and empowerment)	Empowerment strategies; democratization; rights procedures; skill	Acceptance of cultural diversity; social responsibility	Self-regulation, self-efficacy, self-growth; global identity

the other hand, the more interpersonal and personal oriented values (Berson, Erez, and Adler, 2004), or the internally integrated values (Tsui *et al.*, 2006) will be more influenced by the local national cultures, ascribing different meanings to the realization of the same values. For example, the values of personal development and the value of interdependence may have different meanings in different cultures. Yet, the value of acceptance of diversity should be homogenously interpreted as cultural diversity is a very salient characteristic of the global work context.

A proposed model of the interrelationships between global culture, global organizational values, and the individual's self-regulation and global identity

Our main claim is that global culture affects organizations in general and the workplace in particular, structural, cultural, and behavioral manifestations. We also argue that there are similar patterns between the structural and cultural dimensions and their behavioral manifestations. In this sense, structure, culture and behavior are not contradictory and their relations are not incongruous. Rather, we suggest, "action" (structure) and "acting" (behavior) are complementary dimensions of the profound change experienced in organizations, due to world cultural impact.

Here, "action" and "acting" serve as codes for disciplinary perspectives on organizations and

work environments. "Action" stands for sociological, structural perspective, highlighting consolidation of or change in organizational formats, institutional models, and overall marco-global and meso-organizational settings. "Acting," on the other hand, stands for an agentic view of the self, meaning to act as an agent and to influence intentionally one's functioning and life circumstances (Bandura, 2001). Through top-down processes, the macro-global institutions and culture shape the structural and cultural characteristics of the global work organizations. Members of multinational organizations share these global values that cross the boundaries of their local national cultures. These values shape their self and guide their cognitive, motivational and behavioral processes. Reciprocally, sharing the same value system strengthens the culture and tightens it (Erez and Gati, 2004). Employees who share similar cultural values develop a sense of belongingness to others in the global work organization which leads to the emergence of a global identity (Erez and Gati, 2004).

Table 6.1 and figure 6.1 portray the interplay between the cultural level of global world values, the organization culture of multinational organizations, and the individual global self-identity and behaviors. Global culture disseminates the values of rationalization, professionalism, and actorhood. Consistent with these values are the cultural values of multinational work organizations emphasizing competitive performance, quality, innovation, and customer orientation, reflecting the global value of rationalization; interdependence and trust, reflecting the value of professionalism; personal growth,

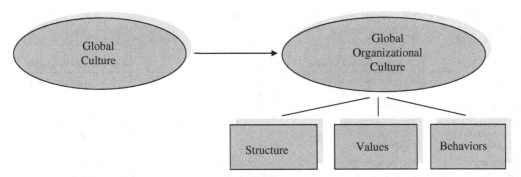

Figure 6.1. Modeling global cultural effects on work organizations

acceptance of cultural diversity, and social responsibility, reflecting the value of actorhood.

Given the complex structure of the multinational organizations, and the variations across subsidiaries with respect to local resources, politics, legal systems, and cultural values, multinational (hence multicultural) organizations cope with the tension between the forces towards universalism and isomorphism emphasizing global integration, and the forces towards local responsiveness to the particular characteristics of the local subsidiaries (Ghoshal and Nohria, 1993). Variations across multinational organizations reflect differences in the balance point between global integration and local responsiveness. Finally, at the individual level, the global world value of actorhood shapes the agentic self, or the acting self, who intentionally self-regulate behavior (Bandura, 2001). This acting self learns to adjust to the global work environment by modeling others, by using the cultural values as criteria for behaviors that result in a sense of self-worth and well-being, by strengthening one's self-efficacy through such positive experiences, and by developing a sense of belongingness to significant others in the global work environment, in the form of global identity.

The cause for such similarity of effects, across the "dimensions" of impact, is the shared global culture: global culture formulates the normative recipes for both action and acting, offering scripts for sense-making of an experience as well as guiding the course of action. As graphically outlined in figure 6.1 global world norms and values get imprinted into the workplace in ways that are both exhibited institutionally and culturally. These values are further manifested at the more micro level of the individual self and behavior.

The three global cultural tendencies have profoundly changed organizations in general and work environments in particular: (a) rationalization, by creating an environment of formal comparability, inducing the global work values of competitive performance, quality, innovation and customer orientation; (b) professionalization, by changing the basis for authoritative knowledge, and strengthening the interdependence among professionals beyond their cultural borders, and their mutual trust by sharing similar professional standards; (c) actorhood, by setting an expectation of proactive engagement of persons and organizations, initiating programs of social responsibility at the organizational level, empowering local subsidiaries to become profit centers, with local accountability and responsibility to the subsidiary's operations and success, and empowering individual employees to become active participant, to monitor and self-regulate their behaviors towards the accomplishment of the organizational goals. Together, these values contribute to reshaping of modern organizations. First, they support a flatter (rather than hierarchical) organizational structure: having employees act as agents, with better skills and greater sense of authority, and having authority drawn from professionalized and rationalized knowledge (rather than from superior position), employees are encouraged to get involved in the firm's decentralized decision-making. This is also true at the macro level: firms are encouraged to get involved in social policy-making, at the national and international level, and serve as partners to civil society and government in such policy forums. Second, these cultural tendencies together reformulate the mode of governance, replacing hierarchical forms of centralized planning (Hwang, 2006) with a novel combination of managerialism and participatory actorhood (Drori, 2006). In the workplace, these translate to the formation of voluntary standards (or "soft law" compliance procedures; Mörth, 2006), transparency and accountability measures, learning and feedback routines etc. (Ellis *et al.*, 1999) and, as described earlier, it also engages employees in new forms that extend beyond their production role. Third, the openness of the organization – to "external" professional advice as to out-sourcing of production tasks – combined with a heightened sense of responsibility and agency, result in a move towards embedded autonomy. "Connectivity to an interorganizational network and competence at managing collaborations have become drivers of the new logic of organizing" (Powell, 2001, p. 60). They result in the transformation of the "classic" multidivisional firm that transacts with its production-line partners into a "twenty-first-century firm" entangled in a heterogeneous network, internally and externally. This is also true at the micro level: the embedded autonomy of the employee serves as a strategy for encouraging both engagement and productivity in highly diverse work teams. Fourth, the openness and networked nature of relations encourage a learning culture, of dynamic change. Pressured by (perceived) competition and networked into a wide spectrum of partners, firms experiment with new methods and strategies. This responsive and adaptive organization continuously stays attuned to "best practice" ideas and maintains re-skilling of its workers. Building upon the descriptions set by Powell (2001), the new workplace is highly dynamic, less authoritarian, very open, and more networked than its historic predecessors and its less modern, or global, previous workplace or form.

Concluding comments

To conclude the discussion of our proposed model of the impact of global culture on work

environments, let us make several qualifications to these sweeping arguments.

First, in our focus on the effects of culture on organizations, and specifically on work environments, we are not oblivious to the obvious impact that other dimensions of globalization have had on such environments: for example, globalization transformed organizations through massive flows of foreign direct investments (Grossman and Helpman, 2005), by binding various organizations into new modes of governance (Ottaway, 2001), and by integrating technologies that mediate virtual work situations (Knorr-Cetina and Bruegger, 2002). Nevertheless, in this work we call particular attention to the effects of cultural means and to the more subtle, non-coercive, or "soft" means by which global cultural norms have transformed work environments.

Second, we provide here numerous examples from work in businesses or firms, but we think that such work features are similar in any complex organizations – be it for-profit or nonprofit, governmental or nongovernmental. In this way, work situations, and particularly transnational work situations, are similar in multinational firms (Nestle or Toyota), transnational civil society organizations (Global Exchange or Transparency International) and international governmental agencies (UN or the World Bank).

Third, while we argue that globalization exerts isomorphic pressures of work environments, we acknowledge that such general trends towards homogenization and convergence have not erased all variations. Rather, there are obvious variations in the impact of global culture on workplace environment: Moore (2005) demonstrates variations in routines and attitudes at work within a single global firm, while Morgan and Quack (2006) demonstrate variations in set-up and practices among firms bound by a single professional ethos. As said by Hedmo, Sahlin-Andersson, and Wedin, (2006, p. 326): "In this intertwined game, played between schools and regulators and between regional and global levels, it seems difficult to maintain regional distinctions." Here, there are obvious parallels with the literature on "glocalization," highlighting again the intersecting normative pressures of world, national, organizational, and professional cultures (e.g., Illouz and John, 2003; Helacioglu, 2000). All multinational companies cope with the need to balance global integration with local responsiveness, yet, they vary in the balance point, whether tilting towards the one pole or the other (Doz and Prahalad, 1991; Bartlett and Ghoshal, 1989).

Fourth, organizations are not only the targets of cultural influence, but rather they are also the carriers of global culture; they are not only subject to world cultural influence, but they are also involved, as institutional entrepreneurs, in the maintenance and change of global culture. In this sense, the relations between global culture and organizations are reciprocal and co-constitutive. With that, the distinctions made here about how globalization fuels organization, as a process of expansive scope, without considering the reciprocity in this relationship, is for analytic purposes only. In general, we suggest here that the social world is more complex than the analytic models that aim to describe it.

Fifth, while in this chapter we demonstrated how the global culture shapes the culture of global work organizations, we should also stress that the global work organization is also influenced by the national cultural values nested within its subsidiaries. These influences are more likely to shape relational values and values of personal growth that are less likely to be universal than the task-related values of performance competencies, and customer orientation.

The comparative study of culture and work has been a bifurcated field: attention has been given either to the structural features of culture and work or to the relational and behavioral aspects of culture and work. As reasoned by Powell and Colyvas, "We need both a richer understanding of individual motives and orientations, and deeper insight into how individuals interpret context" (forthcoming, p. 2 in draft). Following this call to enrich one perspective with another, we apply here a multidisciplinary approach to organizational change: we set out to describe how culture transforms institutions, their structure and their operations, while also impacting the behavior of individuals in such concrete organizational settings. Specifically, we proposed a model for how institutional and cultural characteristics of the global world influence the structure and culture of global work organizations and the mindset and self-identity of the individuals working in this global context. This bridging approach answers the call for a new analytic approach: to give attention to the interactions between the institutional, the cultural, and the cognitive–behavioral.

In our work here, we attempt to bridge the existing intellectual divide by showing how the structural–normative and the cognitive–behavioral are two facets of the same phenomenon. Normative values set the structure which supports their existence. These normative values are cognitively shared and similarly interpreted by people in the same cultural environment. The cognitively shared values filter down to become part of a person's self. Once internalized, these values serve as criteria for choosing the behavior that is most congruent with the internalized values and is most likely to enhance a person's sense of self-worth and well-being (Erez and Earley, 1993). Furthermore, recognizing that others share a similar value system strengthens a person's sense of social identity with these others (Tajfel and Turner, 1979), which takes the form of a global identity when these significant others are members of the global work organization, sharing the global work values (Erez and Gati, 2004).

As reviewed here, there are obvious connections between patterns of influence, or outcome of influence, at the three levels of the global world institutions and culture, at the organizational structure and culture of global work organizations, and at the cognitive, behavioral level of individuals working in global work organizations. For example, modeling, which draws from universalistic ideas and thus from assumptions of comparability across contexts, is exhibited at both the structural and the behavioral dimensions of workplace environments, as enactment and isomorphic tendencies and as mimicry of roles and behaviors, respectively. Overall, global normative codes influence the micro- and the macro-dimensions of work situations in parallel, suggesting that the micro- and the macro- are complementary facets of organizational change. This idea is somewhat captured in the seemingly contradictory term of "global microstructures" (Knorr-Cetina and Bruegger, 2002), where global conditions form virtual spheres of micro-integration that are anchored in work processes, routines, and structures. These global micro structures reflect the continuous tension between global integration and local responsiveness, where local cultural values introduce some variations into the universal and isomorphic forces that shape global organizations (Bartlett and Ghoshal, 1989; Doz and Prahalad, 1991).

Is there a sequence between micro and macro, in their relations with globalization or global culture? Does one mediate the effects of the other, in the context of globalization and in the study of culture? These questions are a variant of the chicken-and-egg conundrum. In our opinion, the relationships between the behavioral and the structural are not sequential relations, but rather reciprocal, co-constitutive relations. This reciprocity is highlighted in Erez and Gati's (2004) dynamic model of world cultural influence, where influences flow to and from the global to the individual through all mediating "levels" of cultures. In this way, influences surely work both ways: globalization enhances diffusion and isomorphism, whereas its similarity instills a sense of urgency for global convergence and existence of a global society. These influences shape the global work organizations and instill the global values and forms of organizing at the organizational level. Yet, such global work organizations are built upon diverse subsidiaries with diverse cultures, and social institutions. These influences shape the overall structure and culture of the multinational organizations and diffuse some divergence into the global work organizations. These organizations play the delicate game between global integration and local responsiveness, and converge to different equilibriums, depending on other factors such as national environmental factors within a host country, industrial structural factors, and organizational factors. High local responsiveness is necessary if a multinational organization attempts to maintain a strong and sustainable competitive position in a host country (Uadong, 2001). Competition intensity and demand heterogeneity in a host market affect the product differentiation and customer responsiveness needed to achieve a competitive position, which in turn influences local responsiveness. Reciprocally, multinational enterprises are carriers of values and behavioral norms that influence the global culture through bottom-up processes. Both levels of the global culture and the global work organization influence lower levels of value representation at the individual level. Sharing global work values strengthens employees' sense of global identity, which, in turn, through bottom-up processes, strengthens the global work values.

Several research paths follow from this call for multidisciplinary study of global culture and work. Currently, two complementary yet diverging strategies are common. One strategy, exemplified in Moore's (2005) study of the work environment in the London branch of a multinational German bank, focuses on a single location with multiple cross-cutting cultures, one of which is global culture. The second strategy, exemplified by Hofstede's (1980) canonized work, surveys multiple locations, exposing cross-national and cross-cultural variation. Both approaches analytically decompose complex work situations and are thus admirable. Their shortcoming, if any, is in the absence of a historical context: both approaches offer cross-sectional perspective, or a time-specific "snap shot," on the matter of culture and work. Yet, it is reasonable to expect that managerial ideas and world norms are period-specific: "scientific management" ideas dominated managerial thought after 1930s were subsequently replaced by a sequence of "in vogue" ideologies of TQM (1990s) or MBO (1950s–70s; see, Strang and Macy 2001). In this way, managerial ideologies, like other world cultural influences, are tied to a particular historic context, reflecting the economic, political and cultural nature of that era. We see urgency, therefore, in that future research should add a historical context for this process of influence of global culture by adding a longitudinal dimension to research strategy on issues of culture and work in the age of globalization.

References

Abbott, K. W. and Snidal, D. 1998. "Why states act through formal international organizations?", *Journal of Conflict Resolution* 42: 3–32.

Ailon-Souday, G. and Kunda, G. 2003. "The local selves of global workers: the social construction of national identity in the face of organizational globalization", *Organization Studies* 24 (7): 1073–96.

Anderson, B., 1991. *Imagined Communities: Reflections on the Origin and Spread of Nationalism* (2nd edn). London and New York: Verso.

Appadurai, A. 1996. *Modernity at Large: Cultural Dimensions of Globalization*. Minneapolis, MN: University of Minnesota Press.

Arnett, J.J. 2002. "The psychology of globalization", *American Psychologist* 57: 774–83.

Bandura, A. 1986. "Social cognitive theory of mass communication", in J. Bryant and D. Zillamn (eds.), *Media Effects: Advances in Theory and Research*. Hillsdale, NJ: Lawrence Erlbaum, pp. 121–50.

1997. *Self Efficacy: The Exercise of Control*. New York, NY: Freeman.

2001. "Social cognitive theory: an agentic perspective", *Annual Review of Psychology* 52: 1–26.

Bartelson, J. 2000. "Three concepts of globalization", *International Sociology*, 15 (2): 180–96.

Bartlett, C.A. and Ghoshal, S. 1989. *Managing Across Borders: The Transnational Solution*. Boston, MA: Harvard Business School Press.

and Ghoshal, S. 1994. "Changing the role of top management: beyond strategy and purpose", *Harvard Business Review* 72(6): 79–88.

Beck, U. 1992. *Risk Society*. London: Sage.

Berkovitch, N. 1999. *From Motherhood to Citizenship: Women's Rights and International Organizations*. Baltimore, MD: Johns Hopkins University Press.

Berry, J.W., Poortinga, Y.H., Segall, M.H., and Dasen, P.R. 1992. *Cross-cultural Psychology: Research and Applications*. New York, NY: Cambridge University Press.

Berson, Y., Erez, M., and Adler, S. 2004. "Reflections of organizational identity and national culture on managerial roles in a multinational corporation", *Academy of Management Best Paper Proceedings*, Q1–Q6.

Bhagwati, J. 2004. *In Defense of Globalization*. Oxford: Oxford University Press.

Birkinshaw, J., Ghoshal, S., Marcides, C.D., Stopford, J., and Yip, G. (eds.) 2004. *The Future of the Multinational Company*. London: John Wiley.

Boli, J. 2001. "Globalization and world culture", in *International Encyclopedia of the Social and Behavioral Sciences*. New York: Elsevier Science, pp. 6261–66.

2006. "The rationalization of virtue and virtuosity in world society", in M.L. Djelic and K. Sahlin-Andersson (eds.), *Transnational Governance: Institutional Dynamics of Regulation*. Cambridge: Cambridge University Press, pp. 95–118.

and Thomas, G.M. 1997. "World culture in the world polity", *American Sociological Review* 62: 171–90.

and Thomas, G.M. 1999. *Constructing World Culture: International Non-Governmental Organizations Since 1875*. Stanford, CA: Stanford University Press.

Chandler, A.D. Jr. and Mazlich, B. (eds.) 2005. *Leviathans: Multinational Corporations and the New Global Economy*. Cambridge: Cambridge University Press.

Chase-Dunn, C.K. 1998. *Global Formation: Structures of the World Economy*. Lanham, MD: Rowan and Littlefield.

Chao, G.T. and Moon, H. 2005. "The cultural mosaic: a metatheory for understanding the complexity of culture", *Journal of Applied Psychology* 90: 1128–40.

Child, J. 2001. "Trust – the fundamental bond in global collaboration", *Organizational Dynamics* 29 (4): 274–88.

Czarniawska, B., and Sevon, G. (eds.) 2005. *Global Ideas: How Ideas, Objects and Practices Travel in the Global Economy*. Copenhagen: Copenhagen Business School Press.

Deal, T.E. and Kennedy, A.A. 1982. *Corporate Cultures: The Rites and Rituals of Corporate Life*. Harmondsworth: Penguin Books.

Dezalay, Y. and Garth, B.G. (eds.) 2002. *Global Prescriptions: The Production, Exportation, and Importation of a New Legal Orthodoxy*. Ann Arbor, MI: University of Michigan Press.

Diehl, P.F. (ed.) 1997. *The Politics of Global Governance: International Organizations in an Interdependent World*. Boulder: Lynn Rienner Publications.

DiMaggio, P. and Powell, W.W. 1983. "The iron cage revisited: institutional somorphism and collective rationality in organizational fields", *American Sociological Review* 48: 147–60.

Djelic, M.-L. 1998. "Actors and institutional channels: emergence of a cross-national modernizing network", in M.-L. Djelic, *Exporting the American Model: The Postwar Transformation of European Business*. Oxford: Oxford University Press, pp. 95–127.

and Quack, S. Forthcoming. "Institutionalism and transnationalism", in R. Greenwood, C. Oliver, K. Sahlin, and R. Suddaby (eds.), *Handbook of Organizational Institutionalism*. London: Sage.

Doz, Y. and Prahalad, C. K. 1991. "Managing MNCs: a search for a new paradigm", *Strategic Management Journal* 12: 145–64.

Drori, G. S. 2005. "United Nations' dedications: a world culture in the making?", *International Sociology* 20: 177–201.

2006. "Governed by governance: the new prism for organizational change", in G. S. Drori, J. W. Meyer, and H. Hwang (eds.), *Globalization and Organization: World Society and Organizational Change*. Oxford: Oxford University Press, pp. 91–118.

2007. "Information society as a global policy agenda: what does it tell us about the age of globalization?", *International Journal of Comparative Sociology* 48: 297–316.

2008. "Institutionalism and globalization studies", in R. Greenwood, C. Oliver, K. Sahlin, and R. Suddaby (eds.), *Handbook of Organizational Institutionalism*. London: Sage, pp. 798–842.

Jang, Y. S. and Meyer, J. W. 2006. "Sources of rationalized governance: cross-national longitudinal analyses, 1985–2002", *Administrative Science Quarterly* 51: 205–29.

and Meyer, J. W. 2006. "Scientization: Making a world safe for organizing", in M.-L. Djelic and K. Sahlin-Andersson (eds.), *Transnational Governance: Institutional Dynamics of Regulation*. Cambridge: Cambridge University Press, pp. 32–52.

Meyer, J. W., and Hwang, H. (eds.) 2006. *Globalization and Organization: World Society and Organizational Change*. Oxford: Oxford University Press.

Meyer, J. W., and Hwang, H. Forthcoming. "Global organization: rationalization and actorhood as dominant scripts", in R. Meyer, K. Sahlin, M. Ventresca, and P. Walgenbach (eds.), *Ideology and Institutions*.

Meyer, J. W., Ramirez, F. O. and Schofer, E. 2003. *Science in the Modern World Polity*. Stanford, CA: Stanford University Press.

Earley, P. C., Ang, S., and Tan, J. S. 2006. "What is cultural intelligence and why does it matter?", in *CQ: Developing Cultural Intelligence at Work*. Stanford, CA: Stanford University Press, pp. 19–41.

and Gibson, C. B. 2002. *Multinational Work Teams: A New Perspective*. New Jersey: Lawrence Erlbaum.

Ellis, S., Caridi, O., Lipshitz, R., and Poper, M. 1999. "Error criticality and organizational learning: an empirical investigation," *Knowledge and Process Management* 6: 166–75.

Erez, M. and Earley, P. C. 1993. *Culture, Self-identity, and Work*. Oxford: Oxford University Press.

and Gati, E. 2004. "A dynamic, multi-level model of culture: from micro level of the individual to the macro level of a world culture", *Applied Psychology* 53: 583–98.

and Shokef, E. 2008. "The culture of global organizations", in P. Smith, M. Peterson, and D. Thomas (eds.), *Handbook of Cross-Cultural Management*. Thousand Oaks, CA: Sage, pp. 285–300.

Earley, P. C., Ang, S., and Tan, J. S. 2006. *CQ: Developing Cultural Intelligence at Work*. Stanford, CA: Stanford University Press.

Featherstone, M. 1990. "Global culture: An introduction," *Theory, Culture and Society* 7: 1–14.

Fiegenbaum, A., Hart, S., and Schendel, D. 1996. "Strategic reference point theory", *Strategic Management Journal* 17(13): 216–36.

Foreign Policy. 2005. "Measuring globalization", *Foreign Policy* 148: 652–66.

2006. "The globalization index", *Foreign Policy* 149: 74–81.

2007. "The globalization index 2007", *Foreign Policy* 163: 68–76.

Frederick, W. C. 1998. "Moving to CSR: What to pack for the trip", *Business to Society* 37(1): 40–59.

Friedman, T. L. 2000. *The Lexus and the Olive Tree: Understanding Globalziation*. New York, NY: Anchor.

2005. *The World is Flat: A Brief History of the Twenty-First Century*. New York, NY: Farrar, Straus and Giroux.

Gardberg, N. and Fombrun, G. 2006. "Corporate citizenship: creating intangible assets across institutional environments", *Academy of Management Review*, 31(2): 329–346.

Gelfand, M., Erez, M., and Aycan, Z. 2007. "Cross-cultural organizational behavior", *Annual Review of Psychology* 58: 479–514.

Gerhards, J. and Haceknbroch, R. 2000. "Trends and causes of cultural modernization: an empirical study of first names", *International Sociology* 15: 501–31.

Ghoshal, S. and Bartlett, C. A. 1990. "The multinational corporation as an interorganizational network", *The Academy of Management Review* 15: 603–25.

and Nohria, N. 1993. "Horses for courses: organizational forms for multinational corporations", *Sloan Management Review* 34: 23–35.

Giddens, A. 2000. *The Third Way and its Critics.* London: Polity Press.

Govindarajan, V. and Gupta, A. K. 2001. "Cultivating a global mindset", in V. Govindarajan and A. K. Gupta, *The Quest for Global Dominance: Transforming Global Presence into Global Competitive Advantage.* San Fransisco: Jossey-Bass, pp. 105–36.

Greenwood, R. and Suddaby, R. (eds.) 2006. *Professional Service Firms.* Elsevier Science.

Griswold, W. 1992. *Cultures and Societies in a Changing World.* Thousand Oaks, CA: Pine Forge Press.

Grossman, G. M. and Helpman, E. 2005. "Outsourcing and a global economy", *Review of Economic Studies* 72: 135–59.

Guillén, M. F. 2001. "Is globalization civilizing, destructive or feeble? A critique of five key debates in the social science literature", *Annual Review of Sociology* 27: 235–60.

Härtel, C. E. J. 2004. "Towards a multicultural world", *Australian Journal of Management* 29(2): 189–200.

Hedmo, T., Sahlin-Andersson, K., and Wedin, L. 2006. "The emergence of a European regulatory field of management education", in M.-L. Djelic and K. Sahlin-Andersson (eds.), *Transnational Governance: Institutional Dynamics of Regulation.* Cambridge: Cambridge University Press, pp. 308–27.

Helacioglu, B. 2000. "Globalization in the neighborhood: from the nation-state to bilkent center", *International Sociology* 15: 326–42.

Hofstede, G. 1980. *Culture's Consequences: International Differences in Work Related Values.* Thousand Oaks, CA: Sage.

2001. *Cultures Consequences: Comparing Values, Behaviors, Institutions, and Organizations Across Nations* (2nd edn). Thousand Oaks, CA: Sage.

and Bond, M. 1988. "The Confucius connection: from cultural roots to economic growth", *Organizational Dynamics* 16: 4–21.

and Hofstede, J. 2004. "Introduction: the rules of the social game", in G. Hofstede, *Cultures and Organizations: Software of the Mind.* New York, NY: McGraw-Hill, pp. 1–38.

Neuijen, N., Ohayv, D. D., and Sanders, G. 1990. "Measuring organizational cultures: a qualitative and quantitative study across twenty cases", *Administrative Science Quarterly* 35: 286–316.

House, R. J., Hanges, P. J., Javidan, M., Dorfman, P. W. and Gupta, V. (eds.) 2004. *Culture, Leadership and Organizations: The GLOBE Study of 62 Societies.* Thousand Oaks, CA: Sage.

Hwang, H. 2006. "Planning development: globalization and the shifting locus of planning", in G. S. Drori, J. W. Meyer, and H. Hwang (eds.), *Globalization and Organization: World Society and Organizational Change.* Oxford: Oxford University Press, pp. 69–90.

Illouz, E. and John, N. 2003. "Global habitus, local stratification, and symbolic struggles over identity: the case of McDonalds' Israel", *American Behavioral Scientist* 47: 201–29.

Iriye, A. 2004. *Global Community.* Berkeley, CA: University of California Press.

Jang, Y. S. 2006. "Transparent accounting as a world societal norm", in G. S. Drori, J. W. Meyer, and H. Hwang (eds.), *Globalization and Organization.* Oxford: Oxford University Press, pp. 167–95.

Jepperson, R. L. 2002. "The development and application of sociological neo-institutionalism", in J. Berger and M. Zelditch Jr. (eds.) *New Directions in Contemporary Sociological Theory.* Lanham, MD: Rowman and Littlefield, pp. 229–66.

Keohane, R. O. and Nye, J.S. Jr. 1997. *Power and Interdependence: World Politics in Transition* (2nd edn). Boston, MA: Little, Brown.

Keohane, R. O. and Nye, J. S. Jr. 2000. "Globalization: What's new? What's not? (And so what?)", *Foreign Policy* 118: 104–19.

Khagram, S. and Shanahan, S. 2006. "Dynamics of corporate responsibility," in G. S. Drori, J. W. Meyer, and H. Hwang (eds.), *Globalization and Organizations.* Oxford: Oxford University Press, pp. 196–224.

Kilduff, M. and Dougherty, D. 2000. "Editorial team essay – change and development in a pluralistic world: the view from the classics", *Academy of Management Review* 25: 777–82.

Knorr-Cetina, K. and Bruegger, U. 2002. "Global microstructures: the virtual societies of financial markets", *American Journal of Sociology* 107: 905–51.

Kostova, T. and Roth, K. 2002. "Adoption of an organizational practice by the subsidiaries of the MNC: institutional and relational effects", *Academy of Management Journal* 45: 215–33.

Lechner, F. J. and Boli, J. 2005. *World Culture: Origins and Consequences*. Oxford: Blackwell Publishing.

Loya, T. and Boli, J. 1999. "Standardization in the world polity: technical rationality over power", in J. Boli and G. M. Thomas (eds.), *Constructing World Culture: International Nongovernmental Organizations Since 1875*. Stanford, CA: Stanford University Press, pp. 169–97.

Leung, K., Bhagat, R., Buchan, N.R, Erez, M., and Gibson, C. B. 2005. "Culture and international business: recent advances and future directions", *Journal of International Business Studies* 36: 357–78.

Luo, X. 2006. "The spread of a 'human resources' culture: Institutional individualism and the rise of personal development training", in G. S. Drori, J. W. Meyer, and H. Hwang (eds.), *Globalization and Organization: World Society and Organizational Change*. Oxford: Oxford University Press, pp. 225–40.

Mato, D. 2000. "Transnational networking and the social production of representations of identities by indigenous peoples' organizations in Latin America", *International Sociology* 15: 343–60.

Maznevski, M. L. 1994. "Understanding our differences: Performance in decision-making groups with diverse members", *Human Relations* 47(5): 531–52.

McKenna, C. D., Djelic, M.-L., and Ainamo, A. 2003. "Message and medium: the role of consulting firms in globalization and its local interpretation", in M.-L. Djelic and S. Quack (eds.), *Globalization and Institutions: Redefining the Rules of the Economic Game*. Northampton, MA: Edward Elgar, pp. 83–107.

Mendel, P. 2006. "The making and expansion of international management standards", in G. S. Drori, J. W. Meyer, and H. Hwang (eds.), *Globalization and Organization*. Oxford: Oxford University Press, pp. 137–66.

Meyer, J. W., Boli, J. and Thomas, G. M. 1987. "Ontology and rationalization in the Western cultural account", in G. Thomas, J. W. Meyer, F. O. Ramirez, and J. Boli (eds.), *Institutional Structure: Constituting State, Society and the Individual*. Newbury Park: Sage.

Boli, J., Thomas, G. M. and Ramirez, F. O. 1997. "World society and the nation-state", *American Journal of Sociology* 103: 144–81.

and Jepperson, R. L. 2000. "The 'actors' of modern society: the cultural construction of social agency", *Sociological Theory* 18(1): 100–20.

Moon, H. and Wotipka, C. M. 2006. "The worldwide diffusion of business education, 1881–1999", in G. S. Drori, J. W. Meyer, and H. Hwang (eds.), *Globalization and Organization*. Oxford: Oxford University Press, pp. 121–36.

Moore, F. 2005. *Transnational Business Cultures: Life and Work in a Multinational Corporation*. Aldershot: Ashgate Publishing.

Mor-Barak, M. E. 2005. *Managing Diversity: Towards a Globally Inclusive Workplace*. Thousand Oaks, CA: Sage.

Morgan, G. and Quack, S. 2006. "The internationalization of professional service firms: global convergence, national path-dependence or cross-border hybridization?", in R. Greenwood and R. Suddaby (eds.), *Professional Service Firms*. Elsevier, pp. 403–31.

Mörth, U. 2006. "Soft regulation and global democracy", in M.-L. Djelic and K. Sahlin-Andersson (eds.), *Transnational Governance: Institutional Dynamics of Regulation*. Cambridge: Cambridge University Press, pp. 119–35.

Norris, P. 2003. "Global governance and cosmopolitan citizens", in D. Held and A. McGrew (eds.), *Global Transformations: An Introduction to the Globalization Debate*. Cambridge: Polity, pp. 287–93.

O'Reilly, C. A., Chatman, J., and Caldwell, D. F. 1991. "People and organizational culture: a profile comparison approach to assessing person-organization fit", *Academy of Management Journal* 34(3): 493.

Ottaway, M. 2001. "Corporatism goes global: International organizations, nongovernmental organization networks, and transnational business", *Global Governance*, 7: 265–292.

Porter, M. E. 1985. *Competitive Advantage*. New York, NY: The Free Press.

Powell, W. W. 2001. "The capitalist form of the twenty-first century: emerging patterns in western enterprise", in P. DiMaggio (ed.), *The Twenty-First Century Firm: Changing Economic Organization in International Perspective*. Princeton, NJ: Princeton University Press, pp. 33–68.

and Colyvas, J. A. Forthcoming. "The microfoundations of institutional theory", in R. Greenwood, C. Oliver, K. Sahlin, and R. Suddaby (eds.), *Handbook of Organizational Institutionalism*. London: Sage.

Power, M. 1997. *The Audit Society*. Oxford: Oxford University Press.

2007. *Organized Uncertainty: Designing a World of Risk Management*. Oxford: Oxford University Press.

Redding, G. 2005. "The thick description and comparison of societal systems of capitalism", *Journal of International Business Studies* 36: 123–55.

Ritzer, G. (ed.) 2004a. *The Handbook of Social Problems: A Comparative International Perspective*. Thousand Oaks, CA: Sage.

2004b. *The Globalization of Nothing*. Thousand Oaks, CA: Pine Forge Press.

Robertson, R. 1995. "Globalization, space, and modernity", *The European Legacy* 8(1): 37–60.

Rokeach, M. 1973. *The Nature of Human Values*. New York, NY: Free Press.

Rosenweig, P. M. and Nohria, N. 1994. "Influences on human resource management practices in multinational corporations", *Journal of International Business* 2.

Rousseau, D. M. 1990. "Assessing organizational culture: the case for multiple methods", in B. Schneider (ed.), *Organizational Climate and Culture*. San Fransisco: Jossey-Bass.

Ruef, M. 2002. "At the interstices of organizations: The explosion of the management consulting profession, 1933–1997", in K. Sahlin-Andersson and L. Engwall (eds.), *The Expansion of Management Knowledge: Carriers, Flows, and Sources*. Stanford: Stanford University Press, pp. 74–95.

Schein, E. H. 2004. *Organizational Culture and Leadership* (3rd edn). Somerset, NJ: John Wiley & Sons.

Schofer, E. and Meyer, J. W. 2005. "The world-wide expansion of higher education in the twentieth

century", *American Sociological Review* 70: 898–920.

Schwartz, S. H. 1992. "Universals in the content and structure of values: theoretical advances and empirical tests in 20 countries", *Advances in Experimental Social Psychology* 25: 1–65.

Shokef, E. and Erez, M. 2006. "Global work culture and global identity as a platform for a shared understanding in multicultural teams", in B. Mannix, Neale, M., and Chen, Ya-Ru (eds.), *National Culture and Groups: Research on Managing Groups and Teams*, vol 9. San Diego, CA: Elsevier JAI Press, pp. 325–52.

Shweder, R. A. and LeVine, R. A. (eds.) 1984. *Culture Theory: Essays on Mind, Self and Emotion*. New York, NY: Cambridge university Press.

Sklair, L. 2001. *The Transnational Capitalist Class*. Oxford: Blackwell.

Slaughter, A-M. 2004. "Sovereignty and power in a networked world order", *Stanford Journal of International Law* 40: 283–327.

Soderberg, A.-M. and Vaara, E. 2003. *Merging Across Borders: People, Cultures, and Politics*. Copenhagen: Copenhagen Business School Press.

Strang, D. and Macy, M. W. 2001. "In search of excellence: fads, success stories, and adaptive emulation", *American Journal of Sociology* 107: 147–82.

Stryker, S. and Burke, P. J. (2000). "The past, present, and future of an identity theory", *Social Psychology Quarterly* 63: 284–97.

Tajfel, H. and Turner, J. C. 1979. "An integrative theory of inter-group conflict", in W. G. Austin and S. Worchel (eds.), *The Social Psychology of Group Relations*. Monterey, CA: Brooks-Cole, pp. 33–47.

Thomas, G., Meyer, J. W., Ramirez, F. O., and Boli, J. 1987. *Institutional Structure: Constituting State, Society, and the Individual*. Newbury Park: Sage.

Thurow, L. (2003). *Fortune Favors the Bold*. New York, NY: Harper Collins.

Trompenaars, F. and Hampden-Turner, C. 1998. *Riding the Waves of Culture: Understanding Diversity in Global Business* (2nd edn). New York, NY: McGraw-Hill.

Tsui, A. S., Wang, H. and Xin, K. R. (2006). "Organizational culture in China: an analysis of culture dimensions and culture types", *Management and Organization Review* 2: 345–76.

Tsutsui, K. and Wotipka, C. M. 2004. "Global civil society and the international human rights movement: citizen participation in human rights international nongovernmental organizations", *Social Forces* 83: 587–620.

Wallerstein, E. 2000. "Globalization or age of transition? A long-term view of the trajectory of the World-System", *International Sociology* 15: 249–65.

Weiner, A. 2007. "Contested meanings of norms: Research framework", *Comparative European Politics* 5: 1–17.

Wolf, M. 2004. *Why Globalization Works?* New Haven, CT: Yale University Press.

Wood, D. J. 1991. "Corporate social performance revisited", *Academy of Management Review* 16: 693.

Yilmaz, C., Alpkan, L., and Ergun, E. 2005. "Cultural determinants of customer- and learning oriented value systems and the joint effects on firm performance", *Journal of Business Research* 58: 1340–52.

Cultural variations in the creation, diffusion and transfer of organizational knowledge[1]

RABI S. BHAGAT, ANNETTE S. McDEVITT,
and IAN McDEVITT

Since the early 1970s, scholars in the disciplines of economics and management have been predicting the onset of a post-industrial or information era, particularly in the G-8 countries. These predictions are largely derived from comprehensive analyses of these economies as well as those of other emerging economies such as South Korea, India, Brazil, and China. These analyses reflect that a series of significant shifts are under way from predominantly manufacturing-based economies to information, knowledge, and intellect-based economies (Leonard, 1995; Quinn, Anderson and Finklestein, 1996; Nonaka and Takauchi, 1995).

It is becoming clear that, as globalization increases interdependence of various economies of the world, the importance of creating, diffusing, and absorbing scientifically and strategically important knowledge also increases. In addition, the process of successfully managing joint ventures and cross-border strategic alliances demands that effective transfer of scientific (not necessarily organization-specific) and organizational knowledge (often specific to an organization) across nations and cultures take place effectively.

Reports on the economic structure of these societies are being driven by organizations that clearly possess the advantage of having access to knowledge that have clear competitive advantages (Ruggles and Holtshouse, 1999; Govindarajan and Gupta, 2001). In various academic journals, such as *The Journal of Information and Knowledge Management*, *Academy of Management Journal*, *Academy of Management Review*, *Management Science*, etc.,

there has been an outpouring of research and findings concerning the effects of organizational knowledge management on effectiveness.

Some authors have advanced the notion that knowledge is an "overwhelmingly productive resource" and a "primary competitive factor" in creating new theories and practices concerning organizational innovation and economic growth (Foray, 2004; Romer, 1989). Peter Drucker (1969, 1993) noted that traditional factors of production are easily available in the interdependent context of the various globalizing economies, but what is not easily accessible is scientific and organizational knowledge of high quality. These commodities are not found in all parts of the globalizing world, but are nevertheless more fundamental in both sustaining and accelerating competitiveness of most of the countries that are members of the World Trade Organization (WTO). *Business Week* (Engardio, 2007) discussed various ways in which the future of work is changing due to creation of new technologies in the era of global 24–7 workforce connected through internet in different parts of the world (Engardio, 2007). From the mid-1990s, there has been a series of systematic inquiries into the processes of creation, diffusion, absorption, and transfer of organizational knowledge (Nonaka and Takeuchi, 1995; Choo, 1998; Dierkes *et al.*, 2001; Govindarajan and Gupta, 1991, 2001; Teigland, Fey, and Birkinshaw, 2000; Bhagat *et al.*, 2002a; Bhagat, Ford, Jones, and Taylor, 2002b; Alvesson, M. and Karreman, D, 2001). Although the relevance of cultural variations on these processes is acknowledged (see Bhagat *et al.*, 2002a), there has not been an integrative review since the publication of Bhagat *et al.*,

[1] The authors thank H. C. Triandis, B. R. Baliga, Balaji Krishnan, and Karen Moustafa Leonard for their useful comments.

(2002a, 2002b). Two recent papers (Javidan *et al.*, 2005; Bhagat, Englis, and Kedia, 2007) attempt to fill that void, but there is still a distinct need for a systemic review of the role of cultural differences on these processes.

The objectives of this chapter are as follows:

1. Define the construct of *organizational knowledge* and discuss the utility of various modes of creation, absorption, and diffusion as proposed in Nonaka and Takeuchi (1995).
2. Examine the role of *cultural variations* on cross-border transfer of organizational knowledge with special attention to the role of individualism-collectivism, power distance, and a few other dimensions of cultural variations. Our goal is to discuss the role of the most important dimension of cultural variation, i.e., individualism-collectivism. While other dimensions of culture are clearly important, a detailed discussion of the role of these dimensions is beyond the scope of this chapter.
3. Discuss the significance of some of the factors (organizational, institutional, and cultural) which either facilitate or inhibit the creation, diffusion, absorption, and cross-border transfer of organizational knowledge.
4. Discuss future directions for research in this rapidly growing area which is vital for comparative as well as competitive advantage of multinational and global organizations.

Definitions

Before we discuss the issues of cultural variations into creation, diffusion, and transmission of organizational knowledge, it is important to provide a definition of organizational knowledge (see figure 7.1). *Knowledge* is defined as a multi-dimensional construct with multi-layered meanings. It reflects the notion of justified "true belief" (Nonaka, 1994, p. 15) and consists of a fluid mix of past experiences – both framed and not fully framed – contextual information, intuition, and insights that provides a valuable framework for assessing and possibly incorporating new experiences and information. Knowledge, according to

Davenport and Prusak (1998) essentially originates in the minds of the knowers (i.e., those individuals who are systematically pursuing search for knowledge) in the context of organizations. Knowledge gets systematically and sometimes not so systematically embedded in the archives of the organization, and at other times, in non-systematic forms reflected in organizational norms, practices, and routines. Organizational knowledge as a foundation for global competitiveness is of significant theoretical importance and spans many disciplines including economics, psychology, sociology, and information science. In the past decade, tremendous advances in communication technology have changed our understanding regarding how multinational and global organizations create, disseminate, and transfer knowledge across national and cultural boundaries.

Knowledge can be categorized into *explicit* (unambiguous, straightforward, and clear-cut) and *tacit* (implicit) categories (Polanyi 1966). Tacit knowledge is "… being understood without being openly expressed" (*Random House Dictionary of the English Language*, 1971), or knowledge for which we do not have words. Tacit knowledge is automatically evoked with little or almost no cognitive effort, i.e. it requires little effort to comprehend on the part of those who are accustomed to using tacit knowledge. Tacit knowledge has its foundation in the mental models, ingrained cultural beliefs, values, insights, and experiences. Tacit knowledge of a technical nature is demonstrated when people master a specific body of knowledge and develop habitual skills and abilities and can function as master craftsmen. People use metaphors, analogies, demonstrations and stories to convey their tacit knowledge to others (Stewart, 1997).

Polanyi (1958) notes that tacit knowledge is personal, difficult to communicate, highly specialized, and not easily traded in the external marketplace (Ghemawat, 1991). Explicit knowledge, on the other hand, can be codified, transmitted, and traded for its economic significance (Nonaka and Takeuchi, 1995). Reed and DeFillippi (1990) note that much tacit knowledge is embedded in the informal social networks and the organizational culture (Martin, 1992). Explicit knowledge

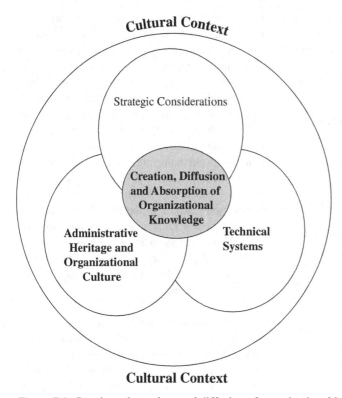

Cultural Context

Figure 7.1. Creation, absorption, and diffusion of organizational knowledge
Source: Bhagat, Englis, and Kedia (2007), p. 107.

is like a building block, whereas tacit knowledge provides the glue that holds these building blocks. At times, tacit knowledge may be a more valuable resource, but the difficulty associated in properly interpreting and articulating it makes its timely use problematic. Explicit knowledge, on the other hand, is easier to acquire and can be utilized more efficiently (Polyani, 1966). According to studies dealing with management knowledge transfer in international joint ventures (IJV) (Uzzi, 1997; Uzzi and Lancaster, 2003), Dhanaraj *et al.* (2004) find that relational embeddedness facilitates the transfer of tacit knowledge. Relational embeddedness is composed of emotional support, managerial expertise, investment of time, and level of trust to reflect the strength of social ties between parent companies and the newly formed IJV. In a related vein, Szulanski (1995, 1996) finds that the quality of relationships between the source and the recipient is the strongest predictor in studies dealing with transfer of best practices.

Cognitive aspects of tacit knowledge are concerned with an individual or group's images of social reality and expectations in the future, i.e., this knowledge is more focused on contextually grounded information (Nonaka, 1994). Tacit knowledge, to use another perspective, is the process of continuous knowing and is analog in character. Explicit knowledge, on the other hand, is discrete or digital. Much knowledge in international organizations that engage in transactions across nations and cultures is tacit and needs to be articulated to the extent that it can be in explicit form and codified. In general, quantifiable technologies and processes have their foundations in bodies of explicit knowledge and can be easily transferred (Teagarden *et al.*, 1995). In contrast, managerial, and marketing expertise tends to be more tacit (Shenkar and Li, 1999; Lane, Salk and Lyles, 2001). The point is that an individual or a team (face-to-face or virtual) may not able to communicate significant aspects of a body of knowledge because much of it may be tacit in character. However, such knowledge plays a crucial role in the enhancing the international competitiveness of organizations functioning across national borders and cultures. A significant amount of tacit knowledge may be articulated through continuous transactions between individuals and related inter-organizational mechanisms.

The importance of tacit knowledge is reflected in our work and personal lives. Incorporation of tacit knowledge enables us to drive a car, deal with children, and even settle a dispute among colleagues, etc. In other words, tacit knowledge can be viewed as "knowledge in action," in that there are special routines, actions, recognitions, and judgments that one may spontaneously engage in with little reflection (Schon, 1983).

Multinational and global organizations must engage in creating and transforming tacit as and explicit knowledge. Numerous studies have acknowledged the criticality of tacitness (Kogut and Zander, 1993; Zander and Kogut, 1995; Choi and Lee, 1997), but few have examined its exact importance in light of key theoretical concepts of knowledge transfer. Tacitness is often associated with Polanyi's (1966) observation that we can know more than we can tell. The dichotomy between tacit and explicit knowledge is based on whether knowledge can or cannot be codified and transmitted in a formal, systematic language or representation, and has been well documented (Kogut and Zander, 1993; Zander and Kogut, 1995; Choi and Lee, 1997).

Other dimensions that are important to consider deal with *simple versus complex* and *independent versus systemic* aspects of organizational knowledge. Simple knowledge can be captured and transmitted with relatively little information or effort. Complex knowledge involves more causal ambiguities and uncertainties and as a result, the amount of factual information that is required to create, diffuse, and absorb such knowledge is greater. Independent knowledge that can be generated without regard to the characteristics of the organization, whereas systemic knowledge reflects the characteristics of the organization or the system (i.e., the nature of the R & D laboratory or knowledge creating units). Consider statements such as: "IBM's way of doing things," the "Fed-Ex way of doing things," etc. (i.e., when the knowledge is systemic in character, it may not be easily transferred and applied in other contexts).

Creation, diffusion, absorption, and transfer of organizational knowledge constitute a continuous spiral of interactions through which some tacit knowledge may become explicit, and some explicit knowledge, tacit. Especially in the context of organizations that function across dissimilar cultures, a large amount of knowledge management involves effective handling of various forms of tacit knowledge. Certain types of tacit knowledge which are often foundations of the intellectual capital (Stewart, 1997) of the organization are either difficult or impossible to access. They lie in the accumulated experiences of key participants of the organization over the life cycle of the organization. It seems that tacit forms of knowledge are more commonly emphasized in the creation and diffusion process in East Asian and other collectivistic organizations (see Nonaka and Takeuchi, 1995 for case histories). In contrast, explicit knowledge is available in the form of files, library collections, databases, archives, and groupware, etc. Starting with the individual, the spiral of knowledge creation and diffusion moves and integrates relevant issues at the group and organizational levels. In the process, conversion from tacit to explicit knowledge and explicit to tacit knowledge begins to occur in routine as well as in a non-routine fashion. Furthermore, both of these types of knowledge get organizationally amplified, i.e., recognized for their validity and applicability for solving important problems. Four distinct modes of knowledge creation and diffusion occur as the process unfolds over time. They are: *combination, socialization, externalization,* and *internalization.*

Conceptualized as *combination,* the Mode 1 method of knowledge creation is concerned with the process of reconfiguring distinct bodies of existing explicit knowledge leading to the creation of new explicit knowledge. Creation and diffusion of knowledge in global and transnational organizations is a function of: (1) the extent of involvement of the organization in the global economy; (2) administrative heritage and organizational culture concerning the role of innovation, organizational learning; and (3) other institutional factors. These factors can serve as both facilitators and inhibitors of knowledge creation. Creation and diffusion of organizational knowledge is influenced by strategic considerations (i.e, strategic intent for knowledge creation with emphasis on innovation, and organizational climate supportive for innovation), technical systems (i.e., sophistication of research and development (R & D) laboratories, including centers for managing knowledge, and quality and accessibility of management information systems), and administrative heritage (i.e., top management commitment and other relevant historical practicing pertaining to creation, diffusion, and absorption of knowledge). Global information systems used to transfer explicit knowledge (e.g., design of artificial intelligence systems or specifics on robotics) between various subsidiaries in the form of continuous electronic data interchange (EDI) technology (Clarke *et al.*, 1991).

Mode 2 of knowledge creation and diffusion, which is called *internalization*, is concerned with transformation of explicit information and knowledge into tacit forms. Groups and individuals who create knowledge by engaging in this process do so by repeated performance of a task such that explicit knowledge of the various principles and procedures involved are converted and retained as tacit knowledge. The process of becoming an expert in the art of French cooking by practicing various recipes from the book by Julia Childs illustrates the process of creating knowledge with the mode of internalization. The trial and error that one needs to engage in makes one almost instinctively familiar and responsive to the various rhythms and practices that are necessary for cooking various types of French cuisine.

Mode 3 of knowledge creation and diffusion, which is called *externalization*, is concerned with converting tacit knowledge inherent in the distinctive context of the organization into explicit knowledge by articulating and sharing various metaphors, analogies, mental models, and heuristics. Perhaps the best example of externalization is found in the case of a team of software engineers who were sent to watch the hand movements of the head baker of Osaka International Hotel in Osaka, Japan. What this team tried to do is to develop a

series of computer programs which would imitate perfectly the hand movements of the baker so that the inside mechanisms of the bread machine would knead the dough of bread in the same fashion and using identical motions as the head baker. Firms like Asea Brown Boveri (ABB) have been very successful in the science of producing new knowledge by linking individuals with a special group-ware information technology such as Lotus Notes[tm] – mechanisms that had some capacity for encouraging the employees to attempt and succeed in turning much of their tacit knowledge into explicit knowledge by repeated trial and error (Sproull and Kiesler, 1991).

Mode 4 of knowledge creation and diffusion is called *socialization* and is concerned with the process of sharing experiences that creates a new type of tacit knowledge from existing sources of tacit knowledge. In this mode, the emphasis is on transforming tacit knowledge through the medium of shared experience and apprentices learn various skills and crafts, both physical and cognitive, by observing, assisting, and imitating the behaviors of experienced professionals. When young doctors learn to treat their new patients, they are often socialized by the senior doctors. Such socialization does not have explicit guidelines that one can read and think about in various books of medical practice. Much of the knowledge is conveyed by nonverbal means – the young apprentice learns the various techniques that the most seasoned professional uses in gaining the respect and confidence of the patients. Also, the art of learning to teach essentially relies on the process of socialization. Doctoral students do not become expert teachers by reading various books on how to teach, prepare exams, etc. They become experts by absorbing various forms of tacit information from the senior professors regarding how to design the syllabus, focus on the central themes of the subject, etc. Socialization as a mechanism for generating knowledge is likely to be more effective in the case of groups who are able to quickly interpret the nature of information that is present in various gestures, practices, non-verbal methods, and rituals. Groups which emphasize the combination mode do not make use of daily or even periodic forms of ritual for conveying valuable information in order to transform or create knowledge. Absorption of knowledge in the combination mode is quite different than the mode used for absorbing knowledge in the socialization mode.

The role of cultural variations

The cultural context(s) (contexts in the case of those subsidiaries or organizations located in dissimilar cultures yet highly interconnected by technical system of the organization) in which the organization functions is important in informing us as to which of the above modes is likely to be used more and when. Holden (2002) noted that one of the major problems in recent studies of knowledge management is that the diversity of countries in terms of language, culture, and ethnic background are not explicitly considered. A notable exception is a recent study by Haghirian (2003) involving transfer of knowledge from Japanese MNCs to their subsidiaries. If the country manager of the subsidiary of a Japanese MNC or global organization is not Japanese in origin, the transaction of organizational knowledge would be considerably slower. Also, proficiency in Japanese and perceptions of low levels of cultural differences between Japan and the country of the recipient organization positively influence transactions of knowledge. Kostova (1999) noted that while there has been recognition of strategic importance of organizational knowledge transfer, there is substantial evidence that some of these transfers are not smoothly implemented and successful. In addition to characteristics of the various barriers to the transfer process, there are others that are clearly rooted in the differences among administrative heritages, organizational culture, and societal culture-based differences. On many occasions, managers of subsidiaries expressed frustrations with the request for implementing another new program from the headquarters. In fact, subsidiary managers may choose not to implement a particular program by noting that "people here will not buy into these foreign practices." In some cases, the level of trust between the local managers from the parent company is low, leading to complete distortion of the knowledge management-based practice or implementing

something totally different. As interorganizational collaborations (e.g., joint ventures, strategic alliances, cross-border project teams) increase, the ability of knowledge workers in different industries expect interpersonal, intergroup, and interorganizational transactions based on trust and norms of reciprocity. However, interpersonal trust is often a function of perceived as well as real cultural differences and can be difficult to create in collaborative projects. We pay attention to the issue of trust in a later section.

Culture is to a society what memory is to an individual (Triandis, 1994, 1995, 1998). The definition of culture is broad, but in general it refers to differing patterns of customs, beliefs, roles, values, and attitudinal predispositions that members of a group who speak the same language has in a given geographical location. There are several important dimensions of cultural variations which are important in considering the issues of creation, diffusion, absorption, and transfer of knowledge. However, the literature in this area has tended to focus more heavily on the role of individualism-collectivism because this dimension reflects "deep structure of cultural differences among societies" (Triandis, 1995, 1998; Greenfield, 1999; Hofstede, 2001).

Individualism and collectivism are social patterns that define culture syndromes (Earley and Gibson, 1998; Hofstede, 1980, 1991; Triandis, 1994, 1995, 1998). *Individualism* may be defined as a social pattern that consists of relationships that exist among loosely linked individuals who view themselves as fairly independent of the various groups to which they may have belonged in the past or still belong. *Collectivism*, on the other hand, is a social pattern which consists of closely linked individuals who see themselves to belonging to one or more collectives (e.g. family, co-workers, ingroups, work organizations, etc.) and who are motivated by obligations to, duties towards, and prevailing norms in these groups. Collectivists are more inclined to give priority to the goals of the collectivists over their own personal goals and also prefer to sample information from the collective and ingroup to think about themselves and interpret available knowledge. Bhagat *et al.* (2002a) noted that this aspect of cultural variation influences how members of a society interpret, process, create, and transfer a body

Table 7.1 Relative emphasis of different types of human resource knowledge and mode of conversion in individualistic and collectivistic cultures

Dimensions of Knowledge	Individualistic Cultures	Collectivistic Cultures
Simple versus complex	No distinct preference for handling either type	
Tacit versus explicit	Explicit	Tacit
Independent versus systemic	Independent	Systemic
Mode of Conversion	Externalization Combination	Socialization Internalization

Adapted from Bhagat *et al.* 2002. *Academy of Management Review*, p. 209.

of information and knowledge. Research evidence discussed in Markus and Kityama (1991), Markus, Kityama, and Heiman (1996) indicate that people in individualistic cultures think of their "selves" as independent of the immediate social or work environment and tend to evaluate each piece of information as being independent from the context in which it is found. Collectivists, on the other hand, see their "selves" as functioning interdependently with significant others (e.g. ingroups, co-workers) in the social or work environment and search for contextually relevant cues in interpreting and using each piece of information (Kagitcibasi, 1997; Triandis, 1995, 1998).

When organizational knowledge management evokes episodes about organizational history, patterns of obligation, past practices, norms of doing things in a specific way as preferred by the ingroup, collectivists tend to perform better. In terms of paying attention to, comprehending, and putting knowledge into action, collectivists are more sensitive to context-specific information. What this means is that systemic and tacit knowledge are likely to be more valued by collectivists even though, as we have shown earlier, these forms of knowledge are more difficult to deal with. On the other hand, when organizational knowledge management processes emphasize personal attributes such as beliefs, feelings, and attitudes towards an object, person, or event, individualists tend to perform better. Simply put, individualists are more concerned with rational connections among various events in the causal chain of knowledge when they create, diffuse, absorb, and transfer knowledge.

Table 7.1 depicts the relative emphasis of individualistic versus collectivistic cultures in the creation, diffusion, and absorption of the three facets of knowledge: tacit versus explicit, simple versus complex, and independent versus systemic. It shows that individuals working in multinational or global organizations located in individualistic cultures do not differ from individuals working in collectivistic organizations in terms of their preference for simple versus complex types of knowledge. The number of causal uncertainties inherent in a body of knowledge does not necessarily make it difficult for a collectivistically inclined organization to be either more or less proficient in these three distinct phases of knowledge management. However, individualists prefer explicit forms of knowledge more than collectivists (Bhagat *et al.*, 2002b). Collectivists are prone to dealing with tacit forms of knowledge that are more contextually grounded than individualists. Therefore, it is logical to argue that collectivists are more comfortable in the creation, absorption, and diffusion of tacit forms of knowledge. Members of individualistic cultures are strongly predisposed to create knowledge that heavily relies on externalization as well as combination. Coding of information in a manner that can be understood by more individuals who might need the knowledge at one time or another is preferred in organizations that are largely individualistic in orientation. On the other hand, members of work organizations in collectivistic cultures are more inclined to favor socialization and internalization as modes of knowledge conversion. The level of comfort with information that is contextually embedded tends to be higher in collectivistic cultures. Now, we turn to the issue of cross-border transfer of organizational knowledge especially from individualistic context to collectivistic context and vice versa.

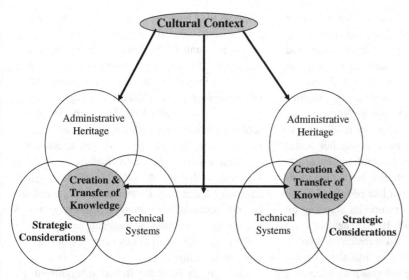

Figure 7.2. Societal culture and other organization-based variables influencing the cross-border transfer of organizational knowledge.
Source: Bhagat, Englis and Kedia (2007).

Individualism-collectivism and cross-border transfer of organizational knowledge

In figure 7.2, we depict the current state of thinking pertaining to the role of individualism-collectivism and the cross-border transfer of organizational knowledge (Bhagat *et al.*, 2002a). The authors advance the idea that the transfer of knowledge is more effective when it involves national contexts with identical cultural patterns of vertical individualism, vertical collectivism, horizontal individualism, and horizontal collectivism. By superimposing the dimension of horizontal versus verticality on the dimension of individualism-collectivism, four cultural grids are created (Triandis, 1995, 1998).

Transferring knowledge from individualistic cultures

In vertical individualistic cultures (found in nations like the US and UK), there is a clear preference for knowledge that is linear (i.e., cause-effect relationships are clearly specified), credible, and explicitly logical (Ji, Peng and Nisbett, 2000; Nisbett, Peng, Choi and Norenzayan, 2001; Triandis, 1994, 1998). Vertical individualists experience difficulty

in transferring knowledge to horizontal or vertical collectivists, since these groups are likely to be more sensitive to knowledge that are immediately relevant to ingroups and is relational in character (Kashima and Kashima, 1998). When collectivists (either horizontal or vertical types) communicate, they tend to put more emphasis on the nature of the *context versus content*. They also emphasize relational issues that were mutually agreed upon than what was precisely communicated. Relational orientation might at times overwhelm their search for rational elements in knowledge acquisition and transfer-related processes.

Tudjman (1991) suggests that individualists believe that knowledge can be articulated no matter how long it might take at times, can be organized and created from theoretical analyses and syntheses; whereas collectivists are inclined to emphasize the salience of context in understanding the significance of knowledge in addition to pure analysis. By noting this, we are not saying that collectivistic thinking is not conducive to advanced scientific analysis, rather it is different. One of the major strengths of collectivistic cultures that is not easily understood by members of individualistic cultures is that collectivists are better in their tendency to absorb, transmit, and transfer tacit information. On the other hand, in contrast, individualistic cultures (whether vertical or horizontal) are better equipped to process, absorb, and transfer information and knowledge that is linear, complex, and explicit such as scientific data, frameworks, and theories.

Horizontal individualists (members of countries like Australia, Sweden, Denmark, Norway, and other Scandinavian countries) are more effective in transferring knowledge to members of horizontal individualistic cultures. Horizontal individualists emphasize values of self-reliance, but unlike vertical individualists, they do not like people who like to stick out or display their superior standing on some issues (Triandis, 1995, 1998). They are more comfortable in absorbing and transferring knowledge that is clearly possible to articulate, organize, and logical, but ignore information concerning hierarchy, i.e., they are much less sensitive about distinctiveness of organizational status, position, or other similar attributes that might be of greater interest to vertical collectivists in the process of transferring and absorbing knowledge.

Transferring knowledge from collectivistic cultures

Bhagat *et al.* (2002b) suggests that members of collectivistic cultures are more effective in terms of transferring various types of organizational knowledge to other collectivistic cultures. Vertical collectivists are more sensitive to information and cues coming from individuals who have higher status or hold senior positions in organizational hierarchies. In transferring knowledge to organizations located in vertical collectivists cultures such as India, Brazil, China, Nigeria, and the Philippines, difficulties arise because, while the collectivistic contexts may facilitate transfer of knowledge, the subtleness of differences of horizontalness versus verticalness may cause difficulties in transferring some types of knowledge, especially those which contain unique information about hierarchies, more systemic, and sticky (Szulanski, 1996). In addition, particularly strict norms, a tendency to highlight information about relationships versus factual details, familiaism and other nepotism-based practices in some developing countries of the collectivistic world make it difficult to both transfer and absorb knowledge to other cultures.

Collectivists, regardless of whether they are of the horizontal or vertical variety, experience more difficulty in transferring knowledge to individualist regardless of whether these groups are vertical or horizontal in orientation. The point is that collectivists are more effective in transferring knowledge to as well as absorbing knowledge from other collectivists, whereas individualists are more effective in transferring knowledge to as well as absorbing knowledge from other individualists. A piece of information that has the potential to yield significant knowledge may be available in one culture, but not necessarily in another (Lillard, 1998). A knowledge item must be available and generally understood to be used in any setting. Consider the emotion term *lajya*.

Collectivists from the Indian subcontinent use this term to describe the emotion that combines the terms shyness, shame, and embarrassment. Women experiencing *lajya* may blush and have a false pulse. When people in a community where the term *lajya* is widely used, say that an individual is experiencing *lajya*, then he or she is definitely experiencing that emotion. However, to an outsider, the term does not have any direct meaning and he or she may not quite appreciate the subtle difference that one experiencing *lajya* feels from the feeling of shyness. Contextual activation of culture-specific knowledge deals with issues of *availability* and *chronic accessibility* (which refers to likelihood that a knowledge item will be accessed from one's long-term memory and a knowledge item gains chronic accessibility when it is repeatedly activated in a given context due to its importance). *Temporal accessibility* is also important and is concerned with the accessibility of a knowledge item without much delay, and it increases the probability that such knowledge can be immediately available for application. A knowledge item that is repeatedly accessed (i.e., recalled) by members of a cultural group is likely to be easily available for timely application (see Chiu and Hong, 2006 for further details).

The role of other cultural variations

There are other important dimensions of cultural variations (Lytle *et al.*, 1995) which also have implications for the creation, diffusion, absorption, and cross-border transfer of organizational knowledge. Dimensions such as *power distance* (Hofstede, 2001); *openness to change versus tendencies toward conservatism* (Smith and Schwartz, 1997; Ekstein and Gurr, 1975; Haire, Ghiselli and Porter, 1966), *past/present/future orientation* (Kluckholm and Strodtneck, 1961), *cosmopolitanism versus local orientation* (Merton, 1968; Rogers and Shoemaker, 1971; Kedia and Bhagat, 1988), *Confucian dynamism* (Chinese Culture Connection, 1987), *universalism versus particularism* (Glenn and Glenn, 1981), *holistic versus linear orientation* (Redding, 1980; Maruyama, 1994) have implications in the way knowledge gets generated, diffused, absorbed, and transferred in multinational and global corporations. For precise definitions of these dimensions, see Lytle *et al.* (1995). As we have emphasized earlier, individualism versus collectivism is, in our view, the most important dimension of cultural variation that is responsible for all of these three facets of organizational knowledge management. It reflects the central concerns of societies which differentiate as to how humans are socialized to think about various patterns of information and concepts into meaningful and sometimes not so meaningful clusters of ideas and constructs. More research needs to be conducted into the interaction of those dimensions that are particularly salient in a given situation. Based on the available evidence, it is clear that there has been an added emphasis on the role of the cultural individualism versus collectivism in the management of organizational knowledge as well as related intellectual processes. The terms *individualism* and *collectivism* are used to characterize cultures and societies (Triandis, 1988). The terms *idiocentric* and *allocentric* should be used to characterize individuals and their attitudinal and behavioral propensities (Triandis, 1989, 1994, 1995). It has been found that idiocentrics are more concerned with achievement-related activities and pay attention to information, signals, and knowledge that help them in accomplishing achievement-related tasks, but they do not like to work in groups; whereas allocentrics are more concerned with socially-relevant cues, information, and knowledge, and they are well connected with their social networks (Triandis *et al.*, 1988; Triandis, 1988).

We need to know more about informational processing propensities of idiocentrics (i.e., those who display stronger individualistic values in a context of collectivism) and allocentrics (those who display stronger collectivistic values in a context of individualism) and how they might pay differential attention to social cues in deciphering the centrality of messages. The distinction between the concepts of individualism and collectivism (conceptualized at the level of social group and cultures) from those of idiocentrics and allocentrics are important when we want to know more about how idiocentrics and allocentrics might interpret cues, information, and knowledge sent from cultures which are different from the cultures in which they were primarily socialized.

The social life of information (Brown and Deguid, 2000) is likely to be interpreted and valued differently across the individualism-collectivism divide and these interpretations take more selective forms when we consider the idiocentric-allocentric divide at the individual level. Brown and Deguid (2000) further note that while people learn conceptually complex tasks better alone, they are nonetheless enmeshed in various work groups which exercise strong influence in filtering. In other words, information, and knowledge that individuals receive in the work place have a strong social component, and there is going to be a significant difference in the way allocentrics and idiocentrics perceive and make use of information that is generated in the group context. Idiocentrics, regardless of the norms of the organizational and societal cultures in which they may work, are likely to be more vigilant about seeking information and knowledge that are particularly relevant for their performance in the work roles – they will tend to be field-independent as opposed to field-dependent in their propensity to search for and absorb information and knowledge. On the other hand, allocentrics are likely to rely more on information that is socially valued, validated and made available through social cues. The cultural variation of individualism-collectivism can inform us a great deal about phenomenon in the creation, diffusion, transmission, absorption, and transfer of organizational knowledge (Bhagat *et al.*, 2002a) Next, we turn our attention to the role of the cultural variation of power distance.

In order to understand the role of power distance in organizational knowledge management processes, it is important to understand the extent of the value of *paternalism* is a value of some importance in the MNCs or in the subsidiaries of the MNCs. Paternalism (Aycan, 2006) is a tendency on the part of senior managers to assume that they know what would benefit their subordinates – there is little consultation with the subordinates regarding the kinds of actions that they ought to initiate in situations that involve creation and absorption of knowledge. Managers who value paternalism and put emphasis on maintaining large power distances from subordinates are likely to view them as having little legitimate power (Lucas, 2006). They adopt the view that subordinates need to be instructed as to "how things are done around here." The process of adoption of new and innovative technologies, including better methods of data management and information processing systems, etc., become localized in the hands of those who are used to having it, using it, and benefiting from it. Innovative methods are difficult to implement in organizations that are characterized by large power distances (Almeida and Kogut, 1999). Implementation of such methods and techniques often have the unintended effects of lowering power distances between various levels of the organizations resulting in the experience of threat and dissonance. The willingness of the subsidiaries of multinational to reach compromising scenarios is based on:

1. The degree of technological endowments that each has.
2. The extent of strategic reciprocal interdependence that each has on the other.
3. The extent to which smooth transfer of knowledge is sustained by the existence of super-ordinate goals such as strong symbiotic values reflected in the charters of contracts, joint venture agreements, and various strategic alliances – the sincerity of the commitment of the senior managers in the transaction process also acts as a strong super ordinate goal which minimizes difficulties due to power distance-related differences.

When the supplying organization has relatively low levels of power and prestige compared to the recipient or acquirer organization, strong imbalances of perception relating to the role of such knowledge can also arise and become problematic, both in the short and the long term. A recent study by Wong, Ho, and Lee (2008) indicate that inter-unit transfer of knowledge is largely determined by the nature of criticality versus non-criticality of knowledge and the degree to which they are non-substitutable. Increasingly, there is evidence that differences in power between transacting units and organizations can affect the quality and flow of knowledge. The process becomes more complicated when an organization in the collectivistic context (e.g., Samsung Corporation of South Korea) supplies knowledge to an organization in an individualistic context (e.g., Microsoft or IBM in the US context).

In addition to the cultural variation of power distance, the role of *associative versus abstractive reasoning* (Glenn and Glenn, 1981; Bhagat et al., 2002a) is important. These authors note that individualistic cultures are likely to emphasize an abstractive mode of reasoning compared to collectivist cultures. In individualistic cultures, cause-effect relationships and the Judeo-Christian modes of thinking are valued, whereas in collectivistic cultures, emphasis on associative modes of thinking is more common. Associative thinking is not necessarily inferior to abstractive thinking (Bhagat et al., 2002b) – it is just different.

In associative mode of processing information and knowledge, relations among various events or processes are not necessarily sequentially and logically linked, cause-effect relationships are not necessarily of prime concern. Furthermore, the context of communication is of distinctive importance – societies emphasizing associative mode of processing information tend to be high-context (Hall, 1959; 1976). Scientific discoveries involving abstractive and systematic thinking are hallmarks of the majority of the countries in western Europe, the US, Canada, Australia, and New Zealand.

Abstractive mode of processing information is present in both work and non-work context in these societies. The associative mode of thinking is more common in east and south Asian, Latin America, and African societies (Glenn and Glenn, 1981). In the creation, diffusion, and transfer of tacit knowledge, an associative mode of reasoning is likely to be more helpful in some situations in these societies – especially in rural settings. It is our thesis that it is considerably difficult for an individual with an abstractive mode of reasoning to effectively transfer information and knowledge effectively with those who function primarily with an associative mode. Misinterpretation is often the result.

There is often a strong relationship between formal schooling and existence of syllogistic reasoning. Non-schooled central Asian peasants reflected these tendencies to the syllogisms that Luria (1976) posed to them. To take a famous example, when presented with the syllogism of the form: " ... in Siberia, all the bears are white: my friend, Ivan was in Siberia and saw a bear: what color was it?", children who had not been to school answered to the effect that "I have never been to Siberia, so I cannot say what color the bear was; Ivan is your friend, so ask him." This kind of response is typically recorded in many societies where cultures among non-schooled subjects. Interestingly, these kinds of response tendencies tend to diminish quickly with years of schooling in favor of a response pattern that one would likely make based on the logical requirements of the task (Cole et al., 1971; Scribner, 1975; Tulviste, 1979). Research reported in Cole (1990) clearly shows that formal schooling promotes a distinctive kind of theoretical thinking, a result consistent with expectations of the socio-historical context of the society. However, the nature of the theoretical thinking and the various underpinnings of knowledge management systems that are associated with it remains content-specific. For example, Tulviste (1979) demonstrated that where schooling is relatively recent phenomenon in the society, children learn to display theoretical thinking with respect to the content of the school and then slowly become proficient in applying it to everyday concepts that they need in their day-to-day functioning. These studies demonstrate the learning of important concepts is largely a function of culture-based socialization that is unique to each culture. Some of the dimensions of cultural variations that is likely to be useful in future theory development in this area are found

in Lytle et al., (1995). Future researchers should pay attention to these cultural dimensions.

Other factors affecting knowledge management

Some of the factors whose role needs to be carefully looked into along with the role of cultural variations are as follows:

1. Tendencies toward knowledge disavowal in organizations.
2. Lack of interpersonal and inter-organizational trust.
3. Incongruence between organizational cultures and administrative heritages of transacting organizations – especially when the organizations are located in dissimilar cultural contexts.
4. Absence of technical and signature skills (Leonard, 1995) on the part of key participants of transacting organizations.
5. Lack of adequate and sustained commitment on the part of senior managers.

Knowledge disavowal (Zaltman, 1979) is an issue of considerable importance in transferring organizational knowledge among organizations in the domestic context or across dissimilar national cultures. Of course, it becomes more complicated when dissimilar cultures are involved. Recipients of important knowledge pertaining to innovative practices (e.g., implementation of a new accounting system in lowering unnecessary costs) are unwilling to admit that this knowledge was somehow not generated by themselves, and therefore, may disown the knowledge or not implement it effectively, leading to disavowal. Kedia and Bhagat (1988) discussed the importance of this issue two decades ago, and there have been significant research on this topic in many forms.

Trust is a complex construct and has many definitions (Rousseau et al., 1998). The key characteristics of trust include that, without it, it is hard to transfer knowledge, since the risk and uncertainty is high for the exchange of intellectual capital (Boon and Holmes, 1991; Jones and George, 1998). The idea is that trust is a relevant factor only in risky situations, and without uncertainty in the outcome, trust has no role of any consequence. Trust is an essential concept in the process of knowledge creating and transfer. Once trust is established, reciprocity is a pattern of communication which allows individuals to share, and thus transfer knowledge within an organization. Lack of interpersonal and inter-organizational trust is even more critical and looms large in the context of knowledge creation, diffusion, absorption, and transfer in organizations. It plays a larger role when the issue of transfer involves dissimilar organizations across nations and cultures. The issue of trust is of vital importance and its presence often guarantees successful transfer and sharing of organizational knowledge. Trust functions as an ongoing mechanism of social control and reduces risks that the recipient organization will not use the knowledge in a detrimental fashion towards the transferring organization. The most important elements influencing building of trust is rooted in the degree of mutual confidence in the reliabilities of each other to come through and keep their commitments in times both good and bad.

Davenport and Prusak (1998) emphasize that, for processes of organizational trust to have their maximal positive impact, they must be initiated by the top management. In fact, there is significant evidence that tendencies towards engaging in trustworthy behaviors are not sustained at the lower levels unless the organizational culture and the administrative heritage of the organization provide key elements in the development and maintenance of trust on an ongoing basis, i.e., it must become an inviolate organizational norm. If key participants exploit various types of organizational knowledge for personal gain, they begin to adversely affect the spiral of knowledge creation.

Perceived levels of risks and uncertainty associated with sharing tacit (sometimes even personal but inherently useful) knowledge decreases when interpersonal trust and caring are important hallmarks in the organizational culture (Nonaka and Takeuchi, 1995; O'Dell and Grayson, 1998; von Krogh, 1998; Hansen, Nohria, and Tierny 1999; Lee and Ahn, 2005). Furthermore, trust also facilitates the process of knowledge transactions between members of internal and external project teams (Foos, Schum, and Rothenberg (2006). Uzzi (1997) found that interpersonal trust allows individuals

access to the sources of the other party and also engaging mutual problem-solving to resolve issues which might be tricky to begin with.

Values of trust and openness in organizational culture promote sharing of knowledge and tend to empower individuals (von Krogh, 1998). In a related vein, Nonaka (1990) noted that loyal and trusting relationships eliminate tendencies toward deception and other dysfunctional behaviors. The advantages of sharing knowledge, for example, lower transaction costs, are also accomplished in a climate of mutual trust regardless of whether the transacting parties are located in the same cultural context or across dissimilar cultures. Formal mechanisms of knowledge sharing work rather poorly in a culture of absence of trust, especially when such lack of trust is sustained at the higher levels (Andrews and Delahaye, 2000; Roberts, 2000; Zand, 1972). The distinction between interpersonal trust and organizational trust needs to be recognized. Interpersonal trust is a psychological state connoting the intention of one party to accept the vulnerability based on positive expectations of the intentions or behavior of the other party (Rousseau et al., 1998). The target of trust is the person, which is not based on their position, title, or because they represent an organization.

In most east Asian cultures, many business practices are conducted on mutual understanding and do not necessarily require elaborate rituals of building trust. However, in transacting organizational knowledge-related issues with western organizations, issues of trust become important. There is much less surveillance of behaviors which might be rooted in opportunism. Sincerity of intentions and a long history of cooperative transactions serve to improve trust as an organic foundation for smooth transfer of knowledge (Hauke, 2006).

Because most collectivistic cultures are based on the premise of relationship building, trust is important to the transfer of tactic knowledge, but less so for the transfer of explicit knowledge (Dhanaraj et al., 2004). However, one caveat should be made, in that high levels of trust may inhibit the transfer of external knowledge because of collective blindness (Van Wijk, 2005).

Subsidiaries of MNCs which are located in remote parts of the world do not show willingness to participate in knowledge management systems initiated by the headquarters unless they feel valued and trusted. Reciprocity in sharing knowledge is also sustained more effectively when there is a significant amount of trust in the past transaction processes. When conceptualized as a network of knowledge flows (Gupta and Govindarajan, 1991) among various units in dissimilar parts of the globe, we can clearly see as to why values of trustworthiness when enshrined in the entire context can significantly facilitate the global competitiveness of MNCs.

When the transacting organizations have incompatible organizational cultures and administrative heritages, it becomes problematic to transfer knowledge. When strategic processes initiated by either of the organizations do not match with those of the other, the flow of knowledge is inevitably affected. More research is needed on this issue. Other factors that can either facilitate or inhibit transfer of knowledge deal with the lack of *signature skills* on the part of key participants between the transacting organizations (Bhagat *et al.*, 2002b). Signature skills reflect composite clusters of insights and abilities that are uniquely available or created in an organizational context. The presence of similar types of signature skills in both the transferring and the recipient organization facilitates transfer of knowledge even when the organizations are located in dissimilar cultural contexts. The lack of technical skills and cosmopolitan orientation on the part of key participants cause further complications (Bhagat *et al.*, 2002b; Kedia and Bhagat, 1988).

Finally, the lack of sincere and ongoing commitment on the part of managers in the upper echelons of the transacting organizations exacerbates the difficulties surrounding cross-border transfer of organizational knowledge. If the senior managers involved in the transactions are not confident of the significance and the value of organizational knowledge that they are about to receive and therefore do not invest the necessary resources such as money, time, and personnel in with significant technical knowledge and signature skills in the acquisition process, then transfer of knowledge becomes an impossible. When these conditions are present, even cultural similarities (both organizational and societal level) do not necessarily facilitate smooth transfers.

General Electric (GE) has been a leader in managing knowledge among its worldwide operations and, in fact, a trend-setter since the early 1980s. It creates new practices such as work-out sessions and has been quite effective in diffusing these innovative practices throughout its divisions and subsidiaries throughout the world. The knowledge created in GE becomes institutionalized, and GE employees throughout its global system internalize GE practices. It has been noted that most people at GE believe that the organizational knowledge generated in the GE context tends to be superior in quality. Furthermore, they function with the belief that such knowledge is also a sustainable source of competitive advantage. Kostova *et al.*, (2004) note that there is a lot to be learned from GE's ongoing experience in knowledge management, particularly in terms of its creative ability to manage a holistic system and articulate a strong organizational culture and administrative heritage for fostering knowledge creation, diffusion, and transfer-related activities. In fact, it was former CEO Jack Welch who launched the concept of identifying best practices and the Crotonville Center. *Best practices* – a formal system for identifying, documenting, formalizing, disseminating, and implementing best practices in different divisions and subsidiaries of the organization helped GE to improve its performance in the stock market by a significant amount between 1981 and 2001. There is a strong emphasis on learning from other organizations that are known for competencies in various areas (e.g., Walmart in the area of customer satisfaction, Honda for new product development, etc.). The best practices initiative results in major overhaul of management thinking throughout the organization and helps develop important benchmarks. Furthermore, such practices channel the energy of the organization towards learning and implementing the best way to conduct important functions which were not effective in the past. In other words, a strong emphasis on knowledge management in the organizational culture of GE results in effective creation, diffusion, absorption, and also cross-border transfer of such knowledge. There are other examples of multinational and global organizations which are leaders in the management of organizational knowledge (Nonaka and Takeuchi, 1995; Ruggles and Holtshouse, 1999);

Tsui-Auch, 2001). A careful examination of these cases clearly reveals the important role of administrative heritages and organizational culture in initiating and sustaining the process of creation, diffusion, absorption, and cross-border transfer of organizational knowledge across dissimilar cultures when needed.

Where do we go from here?

In this chapter, we have argued that the creation, diffusion, absorption, and transfer of organizational knowledge both within the domestic as well as the international context, is of importance to multinational and global organizations. Organizational knowledge is a multidisciplinary construct, and effective understanding of its underpinnings from both a theoretical and an applied point of view requires that one adopts a multidisciplinary approach (see Dierkes *et al.*, 2001). The focus in our chapter has been on the role of cultural variations in the creation, diffusion, absorption, and transfer of organizational knowledge.

A multinational or global organization's ability to effectively monitor, absorb, and transfer newly acquired knowledge across its various subsidiaries and strategic alliance partners can enhance its competitive advantage (Almeida, Grant, and Song, 1998; De Long and Fahey, 2000; Bhagat *et al.*, 2002b). In order to create, sustain, diffuse, absorb, and transfer effective patterns of organizational knowledge both within the organization and across inter-organizational networks, it becomes necessary for these organizations continuously to assess the significance of strategic and technological developments in the industry. That is, not only do they need to generate innovative and competitive knowledge on their own, but they should carefully monitor the development of knowledge in other organizations that compete with theirs. These developments take place not only in the environmental and cultural contexts of the organization, but also in the inner circles, corridors, hallways, and centers of knowledge management of other multinational (MNCs) and global organizations.

Efforts to create knowledge successfully are not completed just by introducing an innovative idea that has significant potential for system-wide application and implementation. The process must be continuously evaluated and monitored. Senior managers, chief information officers, or vice presidents of knowledge management units should have genuine commitment to the processes of creation, diffusion, absorption, and transfer of knowledge throughout the entire organization. Research and development processes do not always guarantee the creation of important knowledge. Knowledge may be accidentally discovered as well. Experienced managers should be able to recognize the importance of such accidental knowledge in a timely fashion. Senior managers should institutionalize appropriate reward structure for recognizing the accidental discovery of knowledge.

Differences in abstractive versus associative modes of thinking (and other cultural variations) create significant difficulties in harnessing organizational knowledge that can often be systemic in character and have stickiness to it. These issues can be solved over time when organizational culture encourages sustained attention to creation and diffusion of knowledge. Kambayashi (2003), in an interesting monograph demonstrating the strong cultural influences on the use of information technology (IT) in the UK and Japan, shows that national cultural based variations play a strong role. Such variations shape the intricacies of interaction between various facets of information technology and the characteristics of organizations in both the UK and Japan. Future studies should be undertaken to validate, as well as extend the findings of Kamabayashi, and the generalizability of his findings should be examined in other cultural contexts such as Brazil, Russia, India, and China (members of the BRIC economies).

Phatak, Bhagat and Kashlak (2008) describe the spiral of knowledge creation (in exhibit 11.3, p. 337) and note that while the creation of new knowledge may start with an individual, it requires the conjoint operation of the three systems, i.e., technical, administrative, and strategic. Often knowledge may become stripped of its core scientific underpinnings in the process of being translated and transferred into the organizational culture of a dissimilar nation or culture. This may result in knowledge that is not only technically incorrect,

Table 7.2 Factors affecting the creation of knowledge in transnational and global organizations

	Facilitating Factors	Accompanying Processes
Strategic Considerations	• Strategic intent for knowledge creation	• Creating and leveraging knowledge in organizational network regardless of location and cultural context
	• Emphasis on innovation	• Promoting innovation at appropriate points in the value chain, not just at the headquarters
	• Tangible and administrative support for innovation	• Making resources available throughout network
Administrative Heritage	• Historical emphasis on knowledge creation	• Emphasizing incremental and continuous innovation
	• Values and practices of senior founders and managers	• Managerial values and practices infused throughout network for supporting knowledge creation
	• Nature of organizational communication and quality of professional interactions	• Processes, systems, and support infrastructure to facilitate creation of knowledge
Technical Systems	• Research and development (R&D) systems	• Ensuring compatibility and sophistication of R&D systems throughout the world (i.e., laboratories)
	• Sophistication of management information system	• Making continuous investments such as intranet, Internet, e-commerce, and ongoing innovation for accomplishing such sophistication
	• Quality and competence of technical and administrative staff	• Recruiting, developing, and retaining globally competent technical and administrative staff

Source: Bhagat, Englis, and Kedia (2007), p. 111.

but culturally inapplicable as well. It may also be the case that some abstractive types of knowledge get reduced to inaccurate forms of associative knowledge and do not result in meaningful implementation in some remote subsidiaries which are not in continuous contact with knowledge-creating units of the global organization or network.

In addition to acknowledging the role of cultural differences, one must recognize that effective knowledge transfer is facilitated when: (1) the organization has relatively porous boundaries for sensing important strategic and competitive knowledge; (2) the administrative heritage and organizational culture actively promotes receptiveness of "not invented here" type of knowledge as well as organizational knowledge that is created in the organization's own context; (3) the communication infrastructure and the level of technological sophistication are high. The various facilitating factors and their accompanying processes in the creation, diffusion, absorption, and transfer of organizational knowledge in transnational and global organizations are listed in table 7.2. Adequate consideration should also be given to the fact that information, especially in the organizational context, has a distinct social life span (Brown and

Deguid, 2000; Ruggles and Holtshouse, 1999). The significance of the social and cultural life of information becomes more salient in situations involving cross-border transfer (see table 7.3 and figure 7.3). These values enshrined in an organization have significant impacts on the process of learning of an organization (Argote and Todorova, 2007). The structural changes that are necessary and the levels of trust that can be generated are also greatly influenced by the joint action of cultural variations at the organizational, institutional, and societal levels. The values of the key participants of the transacting multinational and global organizations can either facilitate or hinder the effectiveness of transfer. If we gain better insights into the nature of those values and the extent to which they are determined by one's societal culture and/or the organizational culture, then we can begin to adopt appropriate measures to solve difficult issues (Goh, 2002; Huit, Ketchen and Slater, 2004).

The role of cultural variations is widely recognized in the comparative study of work organizations. Multinational and global organizations must find appropriate ways of creating, diffusing, and absorbing knowledge that they must employ

Table 7.3 Factors affecting the transfer of knowledge within and across transnational and global organizations

Similar	Within	Across
Strategic Considerations		
Strategic intent for knowledge creation	• Transferring knowledge in subsidiaries located in distinctive cultural contexts such as GM in US and Glaxco-Wellcome of UK. Strategic intent generally facilitates such processes.	• Transferring knowledge between two global organizations (i.e. IBM in the US with Fujitsu in Japan), differences in strategic intent generally prevents effective transfer in subsidiaries located in distinctive cultural contexts.
Emphasis on innovation	• Transfer of knowledge generally emphasizes creation of new knowledge at the point of absorption.	• Transfer of knowledge to fulfill licensing requirements and enhance functioning of recipient organization.
Tangible and administrative support for innovation	• Making resources available throughout network to facilitate knowledge transfer is easier to accomplish when there is significant top management support.	• Differs in available resources to facilitate knowledge transfer processes may lead to selective absorption, retention, and diffusion.
Administrative Heritage		
Historical emphasis on knowledge creation	• Knowledge transfer is more effective if emphasis is on continuous innovation throughout network.	• Differences in historical emphasis on knowledge management may lead to ineffective knowledge transfer.
Values and practices of founders and senior managers	• Likely consistency in managerial practices throughout network might aid knowledge transfers across subsidiaries.	• Differences in managerial values and practices infused throughout distinct organizations likely to inhibit successful knowledge transfer.
Nature of organizational communication and quality of professional interactions	• Processes, systems, and support infrastructure to facilitate creation of knowledge.	• Processes, systems, and support infrastructure to facilitate creation of knowledge.
Technical Systems		
Research and development (R&D) systems	• Likely compatibility of R&D systems throughout the world facilitates knowledge transfer.	• Differences in compatibility and sophistication of R&D systems throughout the world inhibits effective knowledge transfer.
Sophistication of management information system	• Continuous investments in MIS systems facilitate knowledge transfer.	• Differences in MIS systems inhibit effective transfer of knowledge.
Quality and competence of technical and administrative staff	• Competent technical and administrative staff facilitate knowledge transfer.	• Differences in skill levels of technical and administrative staff inhibit knowledge transfer.
Cultural Differences		
Individualism – Collectivism	Transferring implicit knowledge from a collectivistic context to an individualistic context, even though difficult, could still be accomplished with relative ease due to similarities in strategic considerations, administrative heritage, and technical systems.	Transferring implicit knowledge from a collectivistic context to an individualistic context will be more difficult due to differences similarities in strategic considerations, administrative heritage, and technical systems.
	Transferring explicit knowledge from a collectivistic context to an individualistic context, even though difficult, could still be accomplished with relative ease due to similarities in strategic considerations, administrative heritage, and technical systems.	Transferring explicit knowledge from a collectivistic context to an individualistic context will be more difficult due to differences similarities in strategic considerations, administrative heritage, and technical systems.

Table 7.3 (cont.)

Similar	Within	Across
Power Distance	Transferring implicit knowledge from a high power distance context to a low power distance context and vice versa, while difficult, could still be accomplished with relative ease due to above-mentioned similarities.	Transferring implicit knowledge from a high power distance context to a low power distance context and vice versa, will be more difficult due to differences similarities in strategic considerations, administrative heritage, and technical systems.
	Transferring explicit knowledge from a high power distance context to a low power distance context and vice versa, while difficult, could still be accomplished with relative ease due to above mentioned similarities.	Transferring explicit knowledge from a high power distance context to a low power distance context and vice versa, will be more difficult due to differences similarities in strategic considerations, administrative heritage, and technical systems.

Source: Bhagat, Englis and Kedia (2007), p. 111.

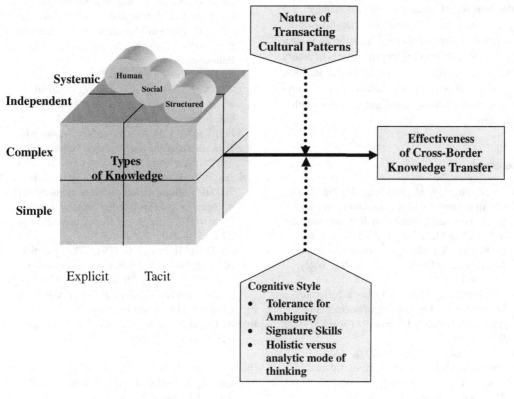

Note: ➡ Presumed Causal Influences

     •••➤ Presumed Moderating Influence

Figure 7.3 A model of knowledge transfer in a cross-border context
Source: Bhagat, Kedia, Harveston (2002), p. 206.

in building and sustaining competitiveness on an ongoing basis. In this chapter, we have provided a detailed appraisal of the role of cultural variation. The competitive advantage that multinational and global organizations (Ruggles and Holtshouse, 1999; Nonaka and Takeuchi, 1995; Kostova, Athanassiou, and Berdrow, 2004; Bhagat et al., 2007) will have depends on their intrinsic abilities to manage cultural variations in the process of knowledge creation and transfer.

It is our hope that ideas offered in this chapter will stimulate more creative theory development and empirical research in this area. In doing research for writing this chapter, we formed the distinct impression that effective research on the nature of creation, diffusion, absorption, and cross-border transfer of organizational knowledge is a long-term endeavor. Continuous triangulation of quantitative and qualitative methodologies is necessary, along with ongoing improvements in theory building. The journey may be long and arduous, but as it is well known in a famous Chinese saying, a journey of a thousand miles begins with a single step.

References

Almeida, P., Grant, R. M., and Song, J. 1998. "The role of the international corporations in cross-border knowledge transfer in the semiconductor industry", in M. A. Hitt, J. E. Ricart, and R. D. Nixon (eds.), *Managing Strategically in an Interconnected World*. New York, NY: Wiley, pp. 119–148.

Almeida, P. and Kogut, B. 1999. "Localization of knowledge and the mobility of engineers in regional networks", *Management Science* 45(7): 905.

Alvesson, M. and Karreman, D. 2001. "Odd couple: making sense of the curious concept of knowledge management", *Journal of Management Studies* 38: 995–1018.

Andrews, K. M., and Delahaye, B. L. 2000. "Influences on knowledge processes in organizational learning: the psychological filter", *Journal of Management Studies* 37: 797–810.

Argote, L. and Todorova, G. 2007. "Organizational Learning" in G. P. Hodgkinson and J. K. Ford (eds.), *International Review of Industrial and Organizational Psychology*, vol. 22. New York, NY: Wiley.

Ashkenas, R., Ulrich, D., Jick, T. and Kerr, S. 1998. *The Boundaryless Organization*. San Francisco: Jossey-Bass.

Aycan, Z. 1996. "Towards conceptual refinement and operationalization", in. U. Kim, K. Yang, and K. Hwang, (eds.), *Indigenous and Cultural Psychology: Understanding People in Context*. New York, NY: Springer Publishing.

Bartlett, C. and Ghoshal, S. 1986. "Tap your subsidiaries for global reach", *Harvard Business Review* Nov-Dec: 87–94.

Bhagat, R. S. Englis, P., and Kedia, B. L. 2007. "Creation, diffusion, and transfer of organizational knowledge in transnational and global organizations: where do we do from here?", in L. L. Neider and C. A. Schriescheim (eds.), *Research in Management: International Perspectives*. Charlotte, NC: Information Age Publishing.

Ford, D. L., Jones, C. A., and Taylor, R. R. 2002b. "Knowledge management in global organizations: implications for international human resource management", in G. R. Ferris and J. J. Martocchio (eds.), *Research in Personnel and Human Resource Management* vol. 21. New York, NY: Jai Press. pp. 243–274.

Kedia, B. L., Harveston, P. D., and Triandis, H., 2002a. "Cultural variations in the cross-border of organizational knowledge: an integrative framework", *Academy of Management Review* 27(2): 204–21.

Boon, S. D. and Holmes, J. G. 1991. "The dynamics of interpersonal trust: Resolving uncertainty in face of risk", in R. A. Hinde and J. Groebel (eds.), *Cooperation and Prosocial Behavior*. Cambridge: Cambridge University Press, pp. 190–211.

Brown, J. S. and Deguid, P. 2000. *The Social Life of Information*. Cambridge, MA: Harvard Business School Press.

Buchel, B. and Raub, S. 2002. "Building knowledge creating networks", *European Management Journal* 20: 587–96.

Chinese Culture Connection, 1987. "Chinese values and the search for culture-free dimensions of culture", *Journal of Cross-Cultural Psychology* 18: 143–64.

Chiu, C.-Y. and Hong, Y. 2006. *The Social Psychology of Culture*. New York, NY: Psychology Press.

Choi, C. J., and Lee, S. H. 1997. "A knowledge-based view of cooperative interorganizational relationships", in P. Beamish and J. Killing (eds.), *Cooperative Strategies: European Perspectives*. San Francisco, CA: New Lexington Press pp. 33–58.

Choo, C. W. 1998. *The Knowing Organization: How Organizations Use Information to Construct Meaning, Create Knowledge, and Make Decisions*. New York, NY: Oxford University Press.

Clarke, R. A., DeLuca, P., Gricar, J., Imai, T., McCubbrey, D., and Swatman, P. M. C. 1991. "The international significance of electronic data interchange", in S. Palvia, P. Palvia, and R. M. Zigli (eds.), *Global Issues of Information Technology Management*, pp. 276–307.

Cole, M. 1990. "Cultural psychology: a once and future discipline", in J. J. Berman (ed.), *Nebraska Symposium of Motivation: Cross-Cultural Perspectives*. Lincoln, NE: University of Nebraska Press.

Gay, G., Glick, J. A., and Sharpe, D. W. 1971. *The Cultural Context of Learning and Thinking: An Exploration in Experimental Anthropology*. New York, NY: Basic Books.

Davenport, T. H. and Prusak, L. 1998. *Working Knowledge: How Organizations Manage What They Know*. Boston, MA: Harvard Business School Press.

De Long, D. W. and Fahey, L. 2000. "Diagnosing cultural barriers to knowledge management", *Academy of Management Executive* 14: 113–27.

Dhanaraj, C, Lyles, M. A., Steensma, H. K., and Tihanyi, L. 2004. "Managing tacit and explicit knowledge transfer in IJVs: the role of relational embeddedness and the impact on performance", *Journal of International Business Studies* 35: 428.

Dierkes, M., Berthoin Antal, A., Child, J. and Nonaka, I. 2001. *Handbook of Organizational Learning and Knowledge*, Oxford: Oxford University Press.

Drucker, P. F. 1969. *The Age of Discontinuity*. New York, NY: Harper.
    1993. *Post capitalist society*. New York, NY: Harper.

Earley, P. C. and Gibson, C. B. 1998. "Taking stock in our progress on individualism-collectivism: 100 years of solidarity and community", *Journal of Management* 24: 265–304.

Eckstein, H., and Gurr, T. R. 1975. *Patterns of Authority*. New York, NY: John Wiley.

Engardio, P. 2007. *Business Week*, August 20–27, 2007.

Foos, T., Schum, G., and Rothenberg, S. 2006. "Tacit knowledge and the knowledge disconnect", *Journal of Knowledge Management* 10(1): 6–18.

Foray, D. 2004. *The Economics of Knowledge*. Cambridge, MA: MIT Press.

Ghemawat, P. 1991. *Commitment: The Dynamic of Strategy*. New York, NY: Free Press.

Glenn, E. and Glenn, P. 1981. *Man and Mankind: Conflicts and Communication between Cultures*. Norwood, NJ: Ablex Co.

Goh, S. C. 2002. "Managing effective knowledge transfer: an integrative framework and some practical implications", *Journal of Knowledge Management* 6: 23–30.

Govindarajan, V. and Gupta, A. 1991. "Knowledge flows and the structure of control within multinational firms", *Academy of Management Review* 16: 768–92.

Govindarajan, V. and Gupta, A. 2001. *The Quest for Global Dominance: Transforming Global Presence into Global Competitive Advantage*. San Francisco: Jossey-Bass.

Greenfield, P. 1999. "Three approaches to the psychology of culture: where do they come from?", paper presented at the Third Conference of the Asian Association of Social Psychology, Taiwan, August.

Gupta, A. and Govindarajan, V. 1991. "Knowledge flows and the structure of control within multinational corporations", *Academy of Management Review* 16: 768–92.

Haghirian, P. 2003. "Does culture really matter? Cultural influences on the knowledge transfer", Proceedings of the 11th European Conference on Information, Naples, Italy, pp. 1–21.

Haire, M., Ghiselli, E., and Porter, L. W. 1966. *Managerial Thinking: An International Study*. New York, NY: John Wiley.

Hall, E. T. 1959. *The Silent Language*. New York, NY: Doubleday.
    1976. *Beyond Culture*. New York, NY: Random House.

Hansen, M. T. Nohria, N., and Tierney, T. 1999. "What's your strategy for managing knowledge?", *Harvard Business Review* March-April: 106–16.

Hauke, A. 2006. "Impact of cultural differences in knowledge transfer in British, Hungarian and Polish enterprises." Foundazione Eni Enrico Mattel Note di Lafvaro Series Index (working paper). Milan.

Hofstede, G. 1980. *Culture's Consequences: International Differences in Work-Related Values*. Beverly Hills, CA: Sage.

1991. *Cultures and Organizations: Software of the Mind*. London: McGraw-Hill.

2001. *Culture's Consequences: Comparing Values, Behaviors Institutions, and Organizations Across Nations*. Thousand Oaks, CA: Sage.

Holden, H. 2002. *Cross-Cultural Management: A Knowledge Management Perspective*. Harlow: Financial Times/Prentice-Hall.

Huit, G., Ketchen, D., and Slater, S. 2004. "Information processing, knowledge development and strategic supply chain performance", *Academy of Management Journal* 47: 241–53.

Javidan, M., Stahl, G., Brodbeck, F, and Wilderom, C. P. M. 2005. "Cross-border transfer of knowledge: cultural lessons from Project GLOBE", *Academy of Management Executive* 19(2): 59–76.

Ji, L.-J., Peng, K, and Nisbitt, R. E. 2000. "Culture, control and perception of relationships in the environment", *Journal of Personality and Social Psychology* 78: 943–55.

Jones, G. R., and George, J. M. 1998. "The experience and evolution of trust: Implications for cooperation and teamwork", *Academy of Management Review* 23: 531–46.

Kagitcibasi, C. 1997. "Individualism and collectivism", in J. W. Berry, M. H. Segall, and C. Kagitcibasi (eds.), *Handbook of Cross-Cultural Psychology* vol. 3. Needham Heights, MA: Allyn and Bacon, pp. 1–50.

Kambayashi, N. 2003. *Cultural Influences on IT use: A UK-Japanese Comparison*. New York, NY: Palgrave McMillan.

Kashima, E. S. and Kashima, Y. 1998. "Culture and language: the case of cultural dimensions and personal pronouns use", *Journal of Cross-Cultural Psychology* 29: 461–86.

Kedia, B. and Bhagat, R. 1988. "Cultural Constraints on Transfer of Technology across Nations: Implications for Research in International and Comparative Management", *Academy of Management Review* 13(4): 559–71.

Kluckholm, F. and Strodtbeck, F. 1961. *Variations in Value Orientations*. Evanston: Row Peterson.

Kogut, B. and Zander, U. 1993. "Knowledge of the firm and the evolutionary theory of the multinational corporation", *Journal of International Business Studies* 24: 25–64.

Kostova, T. 1999. "Transnational transfer of strategic organizational practices: a contextual perspective", *Academy of Management Review* 24: 308–24.

Athanassion, N., and Berdrow, I. 2004. "Managing knowledge in global organizations", in H. Lane, M. Maznerski, M. E. Mendenhall, and J. McNett (eds.), *The Blackwell Handbook of Global Management: A Guide to Managing Complexity*. Oxford: Blackwell.

Lane, P. J., Salk, J. E., and Lyles, M. A. 2001. "Absorbtive capacity, learning, and performance in international joint ventures", *Strategic Management Journal* 22(12): 1139.

Lee, D. J. and Ahn, J. H. 2005. "Rewarding knowledge sharing under measurement inaccuracy", *Knowledge Management Research and Practice* 3: 229–43.

Leonard, D. 1995. *Wellsprings of Knowledge: Building and Sustaining the Sources of Innovation*. Boston, MA: Harvard Business School Press.

Lillard, A. S. 1998. Ethnopsychologies: cultural variations in theories of mind. *Pychological Bulletin* 123: 33–6.

Lucas, L. M. 2006. "The role of culture on knowledge transfer: the case of the multinational corporation", *The Learning Organization* 13(2/3): 257–75.

Luria, A. R. 1976. *Cognitive Development*. Cambridge, MA: Harvard University Press.

Lytle, A. L., Brett, J. M., Barnes, Z. I., Tinsley, C. H., and Janssens, M., 1995. "A paradigm for confirmatory cross-cultural research in organizational behavior", in L. L. Cummings and B. M. Stahl (eds.), *Research in Organizational Behavior* vol. 17 Greenwich, CT: JAI Press. pp 167–214.

Markus, H. R. and Kitayama, S. 1991. "Culture and the self: Implications for cognitions, emotions, and motivation", *Psychology Review* 98: 224–53.

Kitayama, S., and Heiman, R. J. 1996. "Culture and basic psychological principles", in E. T. Higgins and A. W. Kruglanski (eds.). *Social*

Psychology: Handbook of Basic Principles. New York, NY: Guildford Press, pp. 857–915.

Martin, J. 1992. *Cultures in Organizations: Three Perspectives*. New York, NY: Oxford University Press.

Merton, R. 1968. *Social Theory and Social Structure*. New York: The Free Press–Glencoe.

Maruyama, M., 1994. *Mindscapes in Management: Use of Individual Differences in Multicultural Management*. Aldershot: Dartmouth.

Peng, K., Choi, I., and Norenzayan, A., 2001. "Culture and systems of thought: holistic versus analytic cognitions", *Psychology Review* 108: 291–310.

Nonaka, I., 1990. *Knowledge Creation Management*. Tokyo: Touyoukeizai.

1994. "A dynamic theory of organizational knowledge creation", *Organization Science* 5: 14–37.

and Takeuchi, H. 1995. *The Knowledge Creating Company*. New York, NY: Oxford University Press.

O'Dell, C. and Grayson, C. J. 1998. *If Only We Knew What We Know: The Transfer of Internal Knowledge and Best Practice*. New York, NY: The Free Press.

Phatak, A. V., Bhagat, R. S., and Kashlak, R. J. 2008. *International Management in a Diverse and Dynamic Global Environment*. Boston, MA: McGraw-Irwin.

Polanyi, M. 1958. *Personal Knowledge*. Chicago, IL: University of Chicago Press.

1966. *The Tacit Dimension*. Garden City, NY: Doubleday.

Quinn, J. B., Anderson, P., and Finkelstein, S. 1996. "Leveraging intellect", *Academy of Management* 10: 7–27.

Random House Dictionary of the English Language, 1971. New York, NY: Random House.

Redding, S. G. 1980. "Cognition as an aspect of culture and its reaction to management processes: an exploratory view of the Chinese case", *Journal of Management Studies* 17: 127–48.

Reed, R. and DeFillippi. R. 1990. "Casual ambiguity, barriers to imitation and sustainable competitive advantage", *Academy of Management Review* 15: 88–102.

Roberts, J. 2000. "From know-how to show how? Questioning the role of information and telecommunication technologies in knowledge

transfer", *Technology Analysis and Strategic Management* 12: 429–43.

Rogers, E. M. and Shoemaker, F. F. 1971. *Communication of Innovations: A Cross-Cultural Approach*. New York, NY: Free Press.

Rousseau, D. M., Sitkin, S., Burt, R., and Camerer, C., 1998. "Not so different after all: a cross-discipline view of trust", *Academy of Management Review* 23: 393–404.

Rower, P. M. 1989. "Increasing returns and new developments in the theory of growth", National Bureau of Economic Research Working Paper No. 3098, Cambridge, MA: NBER.

Ruggles, R. and Holtshouse, D. 1999. *The Knowledge Advantage*. Dover, NH: Capstone.

Schon, D. V. 1983. *The Reflective Practitioner: How Professionals Think in Action*. New York, NY: Basic Books.

Scribner, S. 1975. "Recall of classical syllogisms: a cross-cultural investigation of error on logical problems", in R. Falmagne (ed.), *Reasoning: Representation and Process*. Hillsdale, NJ: Erlbaum.

Shenkar, O. and Li, J. 1999. "Knowledge search in international cooperative ventures", *Organizational Science* 10: 134–43.

Smith, P. and Schwartz, S. 1997. "Values", in J. W. Berry, M. H. Segall, and C. Kagitcibasi, *Handbook of Cross-Cultural Psychology: Social Behavior and Applications*, vol 3. Boston, MA: Allyn and Bacon, pp. 77–118.

Sproull, L. and Kiesler, S. 1991. "Computers, network, and work", *Scientific American* 265(3): 116–23.

Stewart, T. A. 1997. *Intellectual Capital: The New Wealth of Organizations*. New York, NY: Doubleday Currency.

1995. "Unpacking stickiness: an empirical investigation of the barriers to transfer best practice inside the firm", *Academy of Management Journal*, Best Paper Proceeding: 437–41.

1996. "Exploring internal stickiness: impediments to the transfer of best practice within the firm", *Strategic Management Journal* 17: 27–43.

Teagarden, M., Von Glinow, M., Bowen, D., Frayne, C. A., Nason, S. *et al.* 1995. "Toward building a theory of comparative research: an idiographic case study of the best international human resources management project", *Academy of Management Journal* 38(5): 1261–87.

Teigland, R, Fey, C. F., and Birkinshaw, J., 2000. "Knowledge dissemination in global R & D operations: an empirical study of multinationals in the high technology electronics industry", *Management International Review* 40(1): 49–78.

Triandis, H. C. 1994. *Culture and Social Behavior.* New York, NY: McGraw-Hill.

1995. *Individualism and Collectivism.* Boulder, CO: Westview Press.

1998. "Vertical and horizontal individualism and collectivism: theory and research implications for international comparative management", in J. L. Cheng and R. B. Peterson (eds.), *Advances in International Comparative Management*, vol. 12 Stamfort, CT: Jai Press, pp. 7–36.

Tsui-Auch, L. A. 2001. "Learning in global and local networks: Experience of Chinese firms in Hong Kong, Singapore, and Taiwan", in M. Dierkes, A. Berthoin Antal, J. Child, and I. Nonaka (eds.), *Handbook of Organizational Learning and Knowledge.* Oxford: Oxford University Press, pp. 716–32.

Tudjman, M. 1991. "Culture and information society: the Japanese way", *Information Process and Management* 27: 229–43.

Tulviste, P. 1979. "On the origins of theoretic syllogistic reasoning in culture and the child", *Quarterly Newsletter of the Laboratory of Comparative Human Cognition* 1(4): 73–80.

Uzzi, B. 1997. "Social structure and competition in interfirm networks: The paradox of embeddedness", *Administative Science Quarterly* 42: 35–67.

and Lancaster, R. 2003. "Relational embeddedness and learning: the case of bank loan managers and their clients", *Management Science* 49(4): 383.

Van Wijk, R., van den Bosch, F. A. J., Volberda, H. W., and Heinhuis, S. M.. 2005. "Reciprocity of Knowledge flows in internal network forms of organizing". Erasmus Research Institute of Management report series, *Research in Management.* Rotterdam: ERIM.

Von Krogh, G. 1998. "Care in knowledge creation", *California Management Review* 40: 133–53.

Wong, S. S., Ho, V. T., Lee, C. H. 2008. "A power perspective to interunit knowledge transfer: linking knowledge attributes to unit power and the transfer of knowledge", *Journal of Management* 34(1): 127–50.

Zand, D. 1972. "Trust and managerial problem solving", *Administrative Science Quarterly* 17: 229–39.

Zaltman, G., 1979. "Knowledge Disavowal in Organizations", in R. H. Kilmann *et al.* (eds.), *Producing Useful Knowledge for Organizations.* New York, NY: Jossey-Bass.

Zander, U., and Kogut, B. 1995. "Knowledge and the speed of the transfer and imitation of organizational capabilities: an empirical test", *Organization Science* 6: 76–92.

Cultural variations and the morphology of innovation

JOHN R. KIMBERLY and COLLEEN BEECKEN RYE[1]

The relationship between culture and innovation has intrigued researchers for generations. After much research and experimentation, what we know about the relationship is that innovation both shapes and is shaped by culture, and that both culture and innovation can be conceptualized as operating at multiple levels – national, regional, and organizational. We also know that in the management literature, culture has most commonly been conceptualized as an organizational variable – a constellation of norms and values, unique in some respects to every organization, that can, through its influence on the behavior of organizational members, either encourage and facilitate innovation or be an obstacle to it.

The focus in this handbook is on culture, organizations, and work. But what happens when we focus on the adoption and diffusion of innovation and seek to understand the role of culture in that process? We find that research on innovation has generally been concerned with one of two general classes of problems: the *production* of innovation or the *diffusion and adoption* of innovation. Culture is frequently invoked by researchers to explain either why one organization produces more innovations than another or why one organization adopts a given innovation whereas another either does not or adopts later than the other. And when managers wish to increase the "innovativeness" of their organizations in either of the senses noted above – production or adoption – they often introduce initiatives designed to change the culture in the belief that the sort of behavioral change they seek will follow. When conceptualized this way, culture is seen primarily as an organizational attribute that varies measurably from one organization to the next.

But what about the influence of national or regional culture on innovation? We see many

fewer studies of its relationship to innovation. Perhaps this is because it seems less tractable than organizational culture; or because, by focusing on only one country, most work on innovation effectively holds national and/or regional culture constant; or because of the research challenges that inevitably complicate cross national research. But, as the work of Guillen and others (Guillen, 2000; Guler, Guillen, and Macpherson, 2002; Polillo and Guillen, 2005) has shown, differences in national culture are related to differences in innovation. And in an era when the flow of people, ideas, and other resources across national borders is accelerating rapidly, we might expect that the level of interest in the relationship between national or regional culture and innovation would increase.

In this chapter, we are concerned with the adoption and diffusion of innovation across national borders, and we seek to clarify the influence of national and regional culture on this process. This effort has led us to see innovation differently from the way it is typically seen in the adoption and diffusion literature and to focus on what we call the *morphology of innovation*, or the way in which innovation may change as it spreads across national and regional borders. The most common research approach in the adoption and diffusion literature seeks to explain the propensity and timing of the adoption of an innovation. Typically, this research identifies those organizational characteristics that are thought to influence adoption, explores how these characteristics vary in the population of

[1] We are grateful to Jon Chilingerian for his comments on this chapter, and we thank Gérard de Pouvourville, Tom D'Aunno, and the authors of the chapters used in the preparation of this manuscript for their contributions. All errors and omissions are our own.

197

interest, and then examines how this variability is related to variability in adoption behavior. In this approach, organizations are the unit of analysis, and innovations are generally considered to be discrete objects or sets of practices. The influence of national or regional culture is rarely considered explicitly.

Research using this approach has two principal limitations, neither of which is obvious because both are implicit. First, one underlying assumption is that innovations are both discrete and static; perhaps this is because the organization is the unit of analysis and, as such, the dynamic characteristics of innovation have been overlooked, or perhaps it is because many of the innovations that have been researched, such as MRI machines or computers, are technologically embedded and at a superficial level appear to be fixed, concrete entities. Second, because the underlying assumption is that innovations do not change as they diffuse, research using this approach overlooks the possible influence of national or regional culture on the shape of innovation itself.

How might these limitations be addressed? We suggest that instead of looking at innovation and culture from an organizational perspective, where the organization is the unit of analysis, one might explore the way in which an innovation moves across national and regional borders and becomes incorporated in organizations as a function of varying institutional arrangements, historical circumstances, and power distributions. In other words, rather than assuming that innovations are discrete and static, one might explore whether and to what the extent innovations evolve and change as they diffuse and are implemented in different national and regional contexts, partly as a function of institutional, historical, and political differences in these contexts and partly as result of accumulation of experience with their use. In this approach, the innovation itself is the unit of analysis. Culture shapes the innovation, and this – along with the cultural values embedded in organizations – shapes implementation and, ultimately, diffusion.

We adopt this approach in the research we report in this chapter. We explore the relationship between national and regional culture and the ways in which innovation changes as it diffuses and is implemented. Specifically, we analyze cross-national data on the diffusion and implementation of an important innovation – patient classification systems (PCSs) – and examine how national culture shapes the way in which groups of stakeholders have modified this innovation to fit national and regional contexts. We then discuss the research implications of this view of the process.

Based on our analysis, we develop the concept of the *morphology of innovation*, or the way in which innovation changes as it spreads across national and regional borders. Our analysis leads us to conclude that *the implicit assumption that innovations are discrete, unchanging and culture-free, an assumption that is common in the adoption and diffusion literature, needs to be reevaluated.* Rather, many innovations are not discrete, change as they spread, and are culturally embedded. The case of patient classification systems suggests that rather than assuming that innovations are static, we need to consider the possibility that they are dynamic and, specifically, be aware of the fact that innovations are infused with cultural values that may evolve and change over time in accordance with the *logiques d'action* of influential stakeholders, those principles by virtue of which individuals and groups organize their behavior (Karpik, 1972). Although some innovations certainly evolve and change more than others as they diffuse, the exceptional case may in fact be the innovation that doesn't change at all.

A short history of patient classification systems

Patient classification systems (PCSs) are tools for comparing the outputs of health care providers. The first PCS was developed by a team of researchers at Yale University under the direction of Robert Fetter and John Thompson in the 1960s and 1970s. After a group of local physicians asked the team for help with utilization review in 1967, they experimented with industrial engineering techniques and assessed whether they were feasible in a hospital setting, where tens of thousands of unique hospital patient types existed (Chilingerian, 2008).[2] The team searched for an underlying structure to resource consumption that, at the same time, had clinical coherence. To this end, they applied the techniques of statistical process control to focus on similarities and used physician panels to understand clinical patterns (*ibid.*).

Based on this analysis, the Yale team eventually developed computer software, called grouper software, that would subdivide large datasets of patient records with cost data into meaningful categories from a resource and clinical perspective, an algorithm for so doing, and associated tools such as a cost modeling system. Specifically, they segmented 10,000 hospital diagnostic codes into twenty-three mutually exclusive, exhaustive categories called major diagnostic categories (MDCs), based on major organ systems inferred from diagnosis. They then segmented MDCs by three variables they found to be strongly associated with resource consumption – presence of a surgical procedure, presence of complications or co-morbidities, and patient age – in a decision tree structure (*ibid.*). The resulting categories, or diagnosis related groups (DRGs), were designed to segment clinically similar groups of patients by their resource requirements in hospital settings and provided a way – for the first time – to measure and compare the output of hospitals (*ibid.*).

On April 1, 1983, the US Congress adopted DRGs as a financing tool for Medicare hospital payments (Kimberly, D'Aunno, and Pouvourville, 2008). Under the US Prospective Payment System, DRGs are the underlying patient classification system, and Medicare prospectively pays hospitals a flat amount per patient diagnosis, which falls into one of over 500 DRG categories (CMS, 2007). DRGs were adopted in the hopes that prospective payment would promote cost control relative to the fee-for-service system that was previously in place. Significantly, the US was one of many countries struggling with increasing healthcare costs, and over time several other countries experimented with and adopted PCSs (Kimberly, D'Aunno, and Pouvourville, 2008). Implementation was earliest in a number of countries in western Europe, but followers have included developed countries around the globe. Countries implemented PCSs

for various purposes – financing (as in the US), but also as managerial, epidemiological, and planning tools.

Implementation within adopting countries has varied considerably, with much regional variation. For example, by 1991, twenty American states had adopted DRGs, and, by 1997, the US government reported eighteen different PCSs in use in the states for Medicaid and other payments (Chilingerian, 2008).[3] In Australia, the state of Victoria adopted a PCS first, and other states followed its lead, in both adoption and changes to the PCS (Duckett, 2008). And in Italy there has been substantial variation across regions in the adoption and implementation of disease classification schemes and DRG classification versions, although a law compelled them to adopt a uniform disease classification system in 2006, which also implied a shift to a new DRG classification system (Tedeschi, 2008).

Research methods

To examine the relationship between national and regional culture, innovation, and organization, we took the innovation – patient classification systems – as the unit of analysis and tracked how they evolved and changed over time, as well as why this happened. This way of framing the relationship differs from the more common research approach, that takes the organization as the unit of analysis and explores how variability at the organizational level influences adoption and implementation of a particular innovation and that implicitly assumes that the innovation is invariant across contexts.

Data collection began with a unique database of the histories of PCS adoption and implementation within sixteen countries. This database consisted of a series of book chapters, each describing the history of one country's experience with PCS, taken from a project designed to examine

---

[2] For example, Chilingerian (2008) reports that there were thirty-nine different ways to describe a cataract care process.

[3] DRGs are used in the same way across the US for Medicare payments, since Medicare is a federally sponsored program.

the crossnational diffusion of PCS (Kimberly, D'Aunno, and Pourvourville, 2008). Since process-oriented research questions require longitudinal research designs (Kimberly, 1976), it was imperative to have longitudinal data, which the histories provided. It was also desirable to have rich description to facilitate theory building, as well as accounts from individuals with first-hand experience of the events to increase validity of the data. The histories had these characteristics as well.

We selected a subset of these histories for inclusion in our study using theoretical sampling (Eisenhardt, 1989). Specifically, we selected countries so that they exhibited variation on a set of pre-specified characteristics, such as timing of initial adoption of PCS, timing of changes in PCS use, resulting use of PCS, and national context. The resulting subset of countries includes the US, France, Italy, Japan, and Germany. Table 8.1 delineates some salient characteristics of PCSs in these countries.

To analyze our data, we used grounded theory techniques (Glaser and Strauss, 1967; Strauss and Corbin, 1998; Strauss, 1987). Specifically, we coded country histories for categories of data related to: (i) important events in PCS adoption; (ii) factors shaping PCS adoption; (iii) characteristics of PCS; and (iv) what PCS means to the focal country. This code structure emerged from the data. We developed the code structure iteratively and, when a category was added for one country, we then revisited and coded all other countries for that category. We then iteratively developed codes within each of these categories across countries, as they emerged from the data (grouping, for example, PCS characteristics mentioned in the histories that were similar to each other on one or more dimensions). We completed these steps in NVIVO 7 (QSR International, Melbourne, Australia).

After these steps, we transferred and re-coded selected data into an Excel database to enable us to analyze the categories in the context of time, key to analysis of process (Kimberly, 1979). Specifically, we induced phases of innovation adoption and change based on the analysis of important events

and then re-coded categories three and four by phase.[4] For example, we tracked the components of innovation, as they existed in each country in each country's phases of innovation adoption and change. Additionally, we induced more detailed categories of factors shaping PCS development and coded them into an Excel database, enabling us to compare these factors across countries more easily.

A different view of innovation

Based on this analysis, we see innovation as a complex of components that may change as a function of the differential interests of influential stakeholders, platforms for action that are situated in institutional, historical, and political contexts. This view differs from most previous research, in which innovation is typically viewed as a more or less discrete entity as opposed to a changing complex of components, and institutional, historical, and political contexts as correlates of adoption of innovation as opposed to drivers of change in innovation configuration. Specifically, across the countries in our sample, we found that the basic components of PCS were similar. Further, innovation expanded over time in both breadth (number of components) and depth (number of elements of components) in predictable ways at this macro level of analysis. However, at a micro level of analysis, there was substantial variation, particularly in the ways in which components "looked" in each of the countries (or, types of elements in each component) and how components related to each other. This variation unfolded over time, reflecting the interests and agendas of influential stakeholders, often unique to each country and region.

In other words, as the innovation was adopted and implemented across countries and regions within countries, rather than being stable, the components of innovation changed. At a macro level of analysis, components expanded in breadth and depth in ways that were homogeneous across countries. At a micro level of analysis, components also changed in content and in their relationship to each other in ways that were heterogeneous across countries. We have come to call the process by

---

[4] Not enough information was provided in the histories to code category two reliably by phase.

Table 8.1. Variation in patient classification system adoption

Country	Year of Adoption	Origin of System	Goals and Purpose of the System	Difficulty/Duration of Adoption and Implementation	Extent of System Use
France	1982–1989 – US DRG research projects. 1986 – French DRG project-French grouper based on HCFA 1985 DRG system. 1994 PMSI implemented. 1996 – Full data, 1998 productivity report available. 1997–1998 – Discharge data recorded.	US Yale systems, with adaptation and refinements.	Financing hospitals (recent goal).	*Difficult* Conflicting policy, different payment rules for for-profit and non-profit providers.	Acute hospital care (medical, surgical, and obstetrics).
Germany	2005 – DRGs introduced in phases, beginning in 2002; much preparation work completed earlier.	Australian DRG system; Australian procedure code mapped to German code.	Increase hospital efficiency; contain health spending; reduce length of stay.	*Moderate* Change to DRGs was phased in; idea considered much earlier than 2002; stakeholders have varying views.	All hospital activity.
Italy	1994 – Capitation Act and related funding. 2002 – Italian version of ICD9-CM codes.	Based on US model.	Financial system to control growth of hospital costs, increase accountability for production.	*Difficult* 1994 to 2002 choppy uptake, differences among regions in diffusion and use/regional autonomy.	Inpatient hospital activity. Extends to nursing homes.
Japan	2001 – International scan and study for a case mix system. 2003 – Implemented for payment using ICD-10 codes.	Influenced by French and Australian systems for regional health planning and Belgium and Britain for incremental development.	Process oriented to reflect medical practice; hospital profiling and improved efficiency.	*Moderate* Incremental rollout. Strong IT system development; still opposition from physicians and hospitals.	Acute hospital care.
United States	1967 – Yale University research project based on ICD codes of 10,000 diagnoses then organized into 383 cases. 1980–1982 – 72 hospitals in New Jersey came under DRG payment. 1983 – Congressional law using DRGs as payment for Medicare beneficiaries.	Length of Stay as a standard measure; DRGs identified as the 'product of the hospital'.	Expected cost of hospital case mix. Government healthcare budget control tool.	*Moderate* 1980–1982 – New Jersey hospitals. 1983–1994 – diffused to every region in the US. 1991 – 20 states using DRG-based payment systems.	Inpatient care for Medicare beneficiaries (government sponsored health insurance for individuals over 65 years or disabled). 1992 – prospective payment system. 1997 – extended to outpatient, skilled nursing, long-term care, home care and rehabilitation. Current – APR-DRGs development of refined DRGs to capture severity and risk of mortality.

Source: Kimberly, D'Aunno, and Pourvourville (2008b).

which components and elements of an innovation change over time the *morphology of innovation*.

The components of PCS

We define *component* as a basic constituent of an innovation. In our taxonomy, components are composed of *elements*, or distinct parts of a component. In the case of PCS, components were similar across countries. Specifically, we found that the components are: (i) information; (ii) physical artifacts; (iii) knowledge; (iv) processes; and (v) organizational arrangements. Table 8.2 lists examples of elements of these components for each country in the sample. We explore each of these components in turn below.

Information

All countries in the sample began their adoption process with information, and information continued to drive the shape of the innovation over time. By information, we mean to include what some have called explicit knowledge, or "knowing about" how to do something (Grant, 2003). Specifically, information includes items such as research on the validity of other countries' PCSs in the focal country context or cost data collected from hospitals. For example, in Japan, the Ministry of Health, Labor, and Welfare (MHLW) conducted research on the validity of three different PCS alternatives early in the innovation's history within that country. They compared already existing PCSs and an early version of a new PCS, developed for Japan, to see if they were applicable to the Japanese hospital system and patterns of clinical practice found there. This research drove early discourse about PCS, which, when powerful physician stakeholders expressed concern that outside systems would curtail their medical practice, led to more MHLW research on PCS application in several European countries. The latter research eventually informed efforts to build an original PCS, based on Japanese clinical practice and process (Matsuda, 2008).

Physical artifacts

Countries in our sample developed the tools necessary for experimenting with and implementing a PCS. These include items such as databases, coding manuals, and software systems. While tools were developed, information about PCS continued to accumulate, sometimes within the physical artifacts (e.g. manuals) and sometimes through expanded efforts to compare other countries' experiences with the focal countries' circumstances. For example, between 1982 and 1985, France developed a pilot medical records database to test the creation of a French hospital database, a uniform hospital discharge dataset, and a computer system for assessing the technical feasibility of assigning DRG codes to uniform hospital abstracts (the Grenoble-based DOSTAM system). Some were part information, part physical artifact (e.g., the uniform hospital discharge dataset), but all contained tactile elements. All were necessary for the creation of a French PCS, which was adapted from the US system (Rodrigues and Michelot, 2008).

Knowledge

While agents in countries developed physical artifacts, and as artifacts came to be used in implementation of PCSs, knowledge began to accumulate. By knowledge, we mean what others have called tacit knowledge, or "knowing how" (Grant, 2003; Polanyi, 1962). Specifically, knowledge includes elements such as the coding know-how of hospital employees and the development know-how of government officials building physical artifacts. While knowledge builds, information and physical artifacts continue to accumulate as the country implements PCS, and, over time, some knowledge converts to information as it is codified. The French experience with PCS provides a good example of knowledge building. When France began experimenting with PCS, French hospitals did not have personnel trained to handle diagnosis and procedure coding, an essential component of PCS, and had never been legally compelled to register data on medical services provided, unlike hospitals in other countries. Both skills require a good bit of tacit knowledge. Once the tools required for experimentation with PCS were developed, people began to gain experience with coding and registration of services, and collectively built an infrastructure of knowledge on how to do those things. Eventually, most universities developed curricula in medical information (Rodrigues and Michelot, 2008).

Table 8.2 Innovation components and selected elements

Innovation Components and Selected Elements	United States	France	Italy	Japan	Germany
Information					
Research on validity of other alternatives	X	–	–	X	X
Research on validity of concept	X	X	X	X	–
Positive and negative lists	–	–	X	–	–
Patient data from hospitals	X	X	X	X	X
Cost data from hospitals	X	X	X	X	X
Physical Artifacts					
Grouper	X	X	X	X	X
Pilot medical records database	X	X	X	X	X
Uniform hospital discharge dataset	X	X	X	X	X
Information systems to help with coding	–	–	–	X	–
Information systems to enable payment	–	–	–	X	–
Costing manual	–	–	–	X	–
Software for costing studies	–	–	–	X	–
Knowledge					
Expertise in grouper software	X	X	X	X	X
Organizational expertise in coding	X	X	X	–	X
National education program in coding	–	X	–	–	–
Org expertise in managerial uses	–	–	–	X	–
Processes					
Classification system	X	X	X	X	X
Payment system	X	X	X	X	X
Cost accounting model	X	X	X	–	X
Budgeting model	–	X	–	–	–
Organizational Structure					
Governmental committees to evaluate PCS	X	X	X	X	–
Creation of departments within organizations	–	X	–	–	–
Creation of governmental agency	–	X	–	–	X
Committee of associations to evaluate PCSs	–	–	–	–	X
Creation of other PCS institutions	–	–	–	–	X

Processes

Usually at the same time as physical artifacts were developed, developers chose processes necessary for PCS. In particular, these processes included cost modeling systems, classification systems, and payment systems. For example, a committee in the Reagan administration was charged with developing the DRG approach and, eventually, recommended this approach to Congress. They developed a payment system, which Congress approved, whereby a hospital's DRG payment was calculated as follows: hospital's payment per discharge = DRG relative weight * standardized base payment. In its basic form, Medicare creates a standardized base payment rate (BP) that includes operating and capital costs which represents a national average unit price for medical care. Then, each DRG is assigned a relative weight (RW) that represents the expected resource consumption for a typical patient at an average hospital (Chilingerian, 2008).[5] Hospitals are paid the product of these two numbers for each diagnosis in each DRG, adjusted for geographic and organizational characteristics. By contrast, in Japan, there are two components of reimbursement – a per diem hospital fee (paid using the Japanese PCS) and a fee-for-service component (paid for surgical procedures and anesthesia, pharmaceuticals and expensive devices, and procedures that cost more than 10,000 yen / US $100). The per diem hospital fee is paid on a sliding scale depending on the amount of time that patients are in the hospital.[6] Further, a hospital coefficient is applied and calculated according to function and characteristics of the hospital facility (Matsuda, 2008).

Organizational arrangements

Finally, experimentation with and implementation of PCS required new organizational arrangements in all of the countries in our sample. This includes elements such as new committees, new governmental agencies, and new departments within hospitals. These are considered part of the innovation, because the innovation could not be developed or used without them. Importantly, as before, other components continued to change and expand as organizational arrangements developed. The French, for example, mandated that hospitals create medical records departments and created a national casemix agency (Rodrigues and Michelot, 2008). The Department of Planning at the Ministry of Health in Italy created a committee to study patient discharges from a sample of Italian hospitals to assess feasibility of PCS (Tedeschi, 2008).

---

[5] For example, a DRG with a relative weight of 1 is expected to consume half of resources as a DRG with a relative weight of 2 (Chilingerian, 2008).

[6] Up to a length of stay equaling the twenty-fifth percentile day in Japan for that diagnosis, the per diem rate is 15 percent more than a national standard per diem rate. However, from the day corresponding to the average length of stay in Japan for that diagnosis to that length of stay plus two standard deviations, the per diem rate is set for 15 percent less than the standard per diem rate (Matsuda, 2008).

Changes in components over time

One can see from table 8.2 that all countries in our sample possessed these basic components of PCS. However, it is clear that the elements of innovation within each component varied. For example, while research on the validity of other alternatives (including other existing PCSs, flat rate payment, etc.) shaped the resulting PCS in the US, Japan, and Germany, such research was less important in France and Italy. To take another example, while all countries developed knowledge, countries differed as to what types of knowledge were developed. Employees in French hospitals were not used to handling international coding systems and, as a result, lacked coding skills and needed to develop this expertise as part of PCS implementation. The US had a deep history of coding and registering diagnoses and procedures. However, developers had to gain tacit expertise in partitioning cost and procedure data.

It is less clear from table 8.2 that, while some elements appear to be similar, they may be used and/or adopted quite differently. For example, all countries in the sample adopted some form of a grouper, which is a basic tool required for the use of PCS. However, France transposed the American grouper, while Germany transposed the Australian grouper. All countries in the sample adopted some form of a classification system. However, the US, Japan, and France developed their own systems, while Germany adopted the Australian system (and Italian regions each adopted or developed different systems). While all countries in our sample eventually developed a payment process, the US adopted one in 1983, three years after the first demonstrated use of PCS as a payment mechanism (in the state of New Jersey), while France did not adopt one until 2004 – nineteen years after the release of the first French classification system and twenty-five years after the first demonstrated use in New Jersey.

Clearly, though it appears similar at a macro level of analysis, when viewed at a micro level of analysis PCS differs between adopting countries and, sometimes, between regions within adopting countries. The granularity of the micro level is not trivial, as adoption of elements such as a payment system, and choice in which payment system to adopt or develop, has significant consequences for how an innovation "looks" and functions – and diffuses.

So how exactly does PCS vary between countries, and how did this variation unfold over time? Table 8.3 shows how innovation elements changed over time in the first two adopters of PCS – the US and France (similar tables for other countries available from the authors upon request). Each line corresponds to one element of PCS and lists the year when it was adopted, developed, or changed; regional events and the type of component are denoted in each line, according to the table index.

In particular, it is clear that, as PCS diffused to countries and to regions within countries, the innovation expanded over time in breadth (number of components) and depth (number of elements of components). Concretely, in the US, a classification system and a grouper – two basic physical artifacts necessary for using a PCS – were developed early in the country's experience with PCS. However, once built, several committees (organizational arrangements) convened to build evidence on the validity of PCS (information), and hospital expertise with coding and governmental expertise with updating DRGs began to accumulate (knowledge). Over time, the innovation expanded to new settings based on accumulated information and knowledge (such as physician services in 1992) with new corresponding processes (here, the resource-based relative value scale, or RBRVS, for payment process for physician services) and new corresponding needs for information (here, collection of new cost data) (Chilingerian, 2008). In contrast, the French transposed the American classification system based on consulting assistance from the Yale team and information gathered from the US (information) and then, over time, developed proprietary versions (physical artifacts, processes) based on continued research (information). Employees in French hospitals gathered expertise in coding through pilot projects (knowledge) and, once a governmental decree mandated the establishment of medical records departments (organizational arrangements), this became part of routines in hospitals (additional knowledge). Over time, processes changed to accommodate the government's intended use of the innovation (process);

in particular, payment systems were developed only in the past several years when the government decided to use PCS as a financing tool for French hospitals (Rodrigues and Michelot, 2008).

As the components gradually expanded over time in breadth and depth, they also changed in meaning. This was visible in substantial variation over time in the types of elements in each component and how components related to each other. One can begin to see this in table 8.3. For example, the classification system first developed in France grew to become "more French" over time as developers moved from an American transposition in 1986 and created a proprietary classification system fitted to clinical practice patterns in France in 1996. The basic system of classification in the US, first used in hospitals from 1983, eventually expanded in 1992 and 1997 to include settings as diverse as physician services, outpatient services, skilled nursing care, long-term care, home health care, and rehabilitation services. Physical artifacts, organizational arrangements, processes, information, and knowledge expanded and changed to accommodate PCS in these new settings. For example, the grouper software was modified for new settings and operated on new kinds of cost data.

The data from these five countries lead us to speculate that changes in the meaning of innovation during diffusion were driven by the interests and agendas of influential stakeholders. The early US experience illustrates this process. Specifically, the original PCS developed by Fetter and Thompson at Yale was designed as a managerial tool for utilization review. Chilingerian (2008) notes that DRGs came to be adopted in the US not because the approach offered a perfect technical policy solution, but because the approach became closely aligned with the socio-cultural and political systems. In fact, there were several other alternative schemes designed as financing tools (for example, flat rates and price controls). However, New Jersey Health Commissioner Joanne Finley – former New Haven city public health officer, adjunct professor at Yale, and associate of Thompson – was faced with rising health-care costs and pressure from lawsuits to reform. In this midst of this, she remembered Thompson's innovation and encouragement to "try this new thing." In 1976, she requested a proposal

Table 8.3 Innovation elements over time in the United States and France

Year	United States	France
1967	Yale team begins work on PCS (OS)	
Early 1970s	Classification system (DRGs) (P)	
Early 1970s	Grouper and tools developed (PA)	
Early 1970s	System expertise builds at Yale team level (K)	
1976	*R:* Proposal for all-payer DRG system in NJ (I)	
1979	Pettengill and Vertrees committee conducts pilot (OS)	
	Pettengill and Vertrees report on DRGs (I)	
1980	Schweiker committee forms (OS)	
	R: 26 NJ hospitals receive DRG payments (P, PA)	
	R: System expertise builds at organizational level (K)	
1981	Schweiker report on DRGs and flat rates (I)	
	R: 40 more NJ hospitals receive DRG payments (P, PA)	
	R: System expertise builds at organizational level (K)	
1982	Report to Congress proposing DRGs (I)	Visit of French delegation to Yale (I)
	R: 30 more NJ hospitals receive DRG payments (P, PA)	Pilot medical records database (PA, P)
	R: System expertise builds at organizational level (K)	System expertise builds at governmental level (K)
1983	Payment system adopted for hospitals (P, PA, I)	*R:* DOSTAM system (Grenoble-based) (PA, P)
	HCFA expert committees form (OS)	System expertise builds at governmental level (K)
	System expertise builds at organizational level (K)	
	R: Processes begin to change as diffuse to states (P)	
1984	DRGs, RWs, BP reviewed and amended annually hereafter (P)	Pilot cost accounting and budgeting model (PA, P)
	System expertise builds at governmental level (K)	System expertise builds at governmental level (K)
1985		Uniform hospital discharge dataset (I, PA)
1986		Initial version of GHM classification released (P)
		(transposition and change of American classification system)
		Transposition of American grouper (PA)
		Adopt Fetter's cost modeling system (P)
		System expertise builds at organizational and governmental level (K)
1989		Private, for-profit hospitals required to be part of experiment (I, PA, P)
		Create Medical Information Departments (DIM) in hospitals (OS)
		System expertise builds at organizational level (K)

Table 8.3 (cont.)

Year	United States	France
1991	*R:* DRGs have diffused to 20 states (P, PA, I)	Recording of PMSI data mandatory (I)
		Setting up of DIM mandatory (OS)
		Hospital reform act (legalize DRG system) (P, PA, I)
		System expertise builds at organizational level (K)
1992	Use expands to physician services (P, PA, I)	Creation of a national per-case costs database (I)
	R: DRGs repealed in NJ (P)	System expertise builds at organizational level (K)
1994	*R:* DRGs have diffused to 25 states (P, PA, I)	Mandatory experimentation with all private and public hospitals (P, PA, I)
		PMSI adopted in all public and private not-for-profit hospitals (PA, P, I)
1995		System expertise builds at organizational level (K)
1996		PMSI adopted in all private for-profit hospitals (PA, P, I)
		System expertise builds at organizational level (K)
		R: Juppe reform introduces system of budget adj based on casemix (P)
1997	Use expands to outpt svcs, skilled nursing, long-term care, home health, and rehab svcs (P, PA, I)	Grouping with French GHM released (PA, P)
	R: 18 different PCS in place (P)	Transposition of another American grouper (PA)
1998		Law passed for experimentation of Tarification à la Pathologie (I)
2000		Taskforce created to implement Tarification à la Pathologie (OS)
		National casemix agency created (OS)
2002		Taskforce report (I)
2003		Law commands casemix financing by 2012 (I)
		Payment system adopted (P)
2004		Case mix based financing begins (P, PA, I)
		10th version of GHM classification released (P, PA)
Current	All Patient Refined DRGs in development (P, PA)	

Notes: R = Regional component
I = Information
PA = Physical artifact
P = Process
K = Knowledge
OS = Organizational structure

from the Yale team to design and implement an all-payer DRG system in New Jersey. Eventually, with private counsel and assistance of Jack Owen, the head of the New Jersey Hospital Association, Finley developed a proposal that accommodated the primary interests of key stakeholders, including urban hospitals, who wanted assistance for caring for poor patients; commercial insurers, who wanted relief from cost shifting; state legislators, who desired cost control to address Medicaid cost escalation; and the federal government, who encouraged states to experiment with different forms of reimbursement in order to develop a model for Medicare reform (Mayes, 2006; Chilingerian, 2008). This compromise resulted in the adoption of DRGs in New Jersey as a financial tool in a phased implementation from 1980–82.

In this example, institutional, historical, and political contexts shaped the way influential stakeholders perceived the innovation. Joanne Finley's historical institutional affiliations with Thompson led her to consider the innovation, and the institutional demands of a failing healthcare system encouraged her to look at the innovation as a solution for payment and controlling costs. Jack Owen and Joanne Finley were able to convince other influential stakeholders to accept the innovation as a payment mechanism given the backdrop of political upheaval (threatened lawsuits and escalating costs). Context combined with the *logiques d'action* of influential stakeholders to change the meaning of innovation from a managerial tool to a financial tool – first at the regional level, and then at the national level.

The morphology of innovation

We refer to the process by which components and elements of an innovation change over time as the *morphology of innovation*. It is clear to us that, as PCS diffused to countries and to regions, it changed in breadth, depth, and meaning, and that these changes were driven by the interests and agendas of influential stakeholders, situated in the demands of cultural contexts. While the presence of a set of basic components was similar across cultures, culture shaped the choice of elements within those components and the connections

between components. Culture drives the *shape* of innovation – the content and linkages implicit in the object of innovation. In short, *innovations are not culture-free*, as often assumed in the literature; instead, they are infused with cultural values that are embedded as they evolve and change over time in response to the interests and agendas of influential stakeholders. Organizations are the medium through which this process unfolds, and adoption and implementation should not be seen as the end point but rather as one part of the larger process of cultural adaptation.

Specifically, we believe that there are two separate levels at which innovations diffuse – a super-structural (macro) level and an operational (micro) level – and each level corresponds to a different process of adoption and implementation and contributes differently to morphology over time. At the super-structural level, influential stakeholders are concerned about finding solutions to specific problems as they arise over time. For example, in the US case, New Jersey state legislators were concerned about controlling increasing Medicaid costs, and urban hospitals desired relief in caring for poor patients. Over time, after the adoption of DRGs for hospitals, US legislators would be concerned with controlling costs in other settings, such as nursing homes and rehabilitation services. Views about the appropriateness of potential solutions emanate from their agendas and focus on the reproducibility of the innovation in the focal institutional, historical, and political contexts, as well as the comparability of the innovation with other alternatives. In the US, Secretary of Health and Human Services Richard Schweiker headed a committee that evaluated alternatives for financing tools; when they were about to recommend flat rates to Congress, however, he ordered them to develop the DRG approach, having been convinced of the viability of DRGs and assured of the political support of the American Hospital Association through Jack Owen (Chilingerian, 2008). At this level, certain components come to legitimate and define the innovation over time and, thus, we should expect these components to be reproduced more or less similarly among countries. In our case, all countries in our sample adopted some form of information, physical artifacts, processes, knowledge, and organizational arrangements. Within each of these components, certain elements were similar. For example, within physical artifacts, all countries adopted some form of a grouper, a tool that was perceived by stakeholders to be required for the use of PCS.

At the operational level, in contrast, influential stakeholders are concerned with the nuts and bolts of the innovation – functionality, usability, and "making it work" in the local context. This is where stakeholders tailor the innovation to meet local conditions. The Italian experience provides a good illustration of change at the operational level. In 1978, a national health-care system (Servizio Sanitario Nazionale, or SSN), replaced a system of health insurance funds. Before the 1990s, the central government administered payments to regions on the basis of actual expenditures. However, the SSN was reshaped in the 1990s through a process of increasing decentralization from the central government to regional governments, local health authorities (Aziende Sanitarie Locali, or ASLs), and public and private hospitals (Tedeschi, 2008). In this context, each Italian region has developed a distinctive version of organizational and funding models to meet local contextual demands (*ibid.*). PCS is incorporated in these funding models in a variety of different ways across the regions. Some regions use PCS alongside lump sum allocations for specific services (e.g., emergency rooms); other regions use PCS alongside different fee schedules for different types of organizations (e.g., lower fees for rural public hospitals); still others use PCS in conjunction with expenditure targets ceilings or targets or discretional allocations of extraordinary funds; and most use a combination of these (Jommi, Cantu, and Anessi-Pessina, 2001). Emilia-Romangna, Friuli V.G., and Tuscany historically negotiated, additionally, bilateral contracts between local health units (the predecessor to ASLs) alongside PCS (*ibid.*). Further, rates within each PCS vary between regions. Tedeschi (2008) reports that only five regions developed their own regional tariffs, though due to unique provisions in financing models, substantial differences among regional tariffs have appeared through time, ranging from +16 percent to −30 percent of national rates.

At the operational level, one might expect more variation in the elements of innovation as a result of variations in interests and cultural context. Matsuda (2008) notes that the Japanese government feels that it needs to provide objective data for future reforms; thus, one of the main purposes of the PCS project within that country is to collect these data through electronic claim systems that can be used to implement PCS. Therefore, one sees in table 8.2 that information systems to support PCS are relatively more important in Japan than other countries, where data collection is relatively less important to reform efforts. Further variation occurs because, while some elements appear to be similar, they may be used and/or adopted quite differently. For example, it is clear that the Italian payment process, described directly above, and the US and Japanese payment processes, described in the components of PCS section above, are very different; yet, they are all payment processes, an element within the process component of PCS innovation.

In short, culture drives the *shape* of innovation – the content and linkages implicit in the object of innovation. Innovations become infused with cultural values that are embedded in the innovation as it evolves and changes over time in response to the interests and agendas of influential stakeholders. *Culture conditions behavior, which drives demands of the innovation – which changes the innovation itself to conform to demands.* In this way, the innovation becomes "more French" or "more German" or "more Japanese" over time as elements are added, modified, subtracted, or re-linked to each other.

Our work on the diffusion of patient classification systems leads us further to posit that there are two dimensions of time in which innovations diffuse – *diffusion time* and *morphological time*. Figure 8.1 shows the diffusion curve for PCS in our sample and illustrates the difference between the two dimensions of time. In particular, Rogers (2003, p. 5) defines diffusion as "the process in which an innovation is communicated through certain channels over time among the members of a social system"; by implication, diffusion time connotes the amount of time it takes for an innovation to be communicated to members of the social system. Diffusion time occurs over the longer

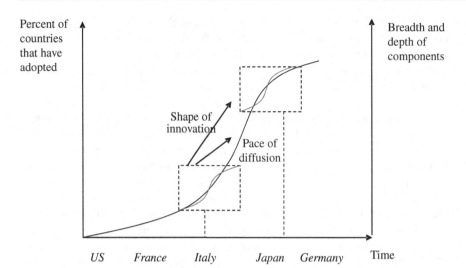

Figure 8.1 Diffusion time and morphological time

s-curve in figure 8.1 and is the dimension of time studied by most innovation researchers. However, we believe there is another dimension of time that is largely ignored in the literature – morphological time. We define morphological time as the amount of time it takes for groups within a social system, individually and in concert, to change an innovation to fit local context, where local can be defined at multiple levels of analysis, such as national, regional, and organizational levels. Morphological time occurs over the shorter s-curves (within boxes at each country's approximate "adoption") located along the aggregate diffusion curve.[7] The first y-axis represents the relevant dependent variable for diffusion time – percentage of countries (adopting units) that have adopted the innovation. The second y-axis represents the relevant dependent variable for morphological time – the breadth and depth of components of innovation present in the adopting unit. One might specify additional dimensions (not shown), such as the percentage of organizations within countries that have adopted the innovation or the breadth and depth of

components within particular organizations over time. Note that, while meaning of components is clearly important, meaning cannot be represented on the diffusion curve or on the morphology curve (as meaning is not reducible to one dimension; the traditional diffusion curve implicitly assumes that all innovations are the same); for this chapter, we leave it as implicit in the curve.

According to our data, morphology occurs semi-continuously along the diffusion curve and, importantly, the morphology of an innovation influences the pace of diffusion (i.e., shape of the diffusion curve) and the shape of the innovation as it diffuses (i.e., what is being adopted); both are shown by the arrows in figure 8.1. One can see semi-continuous morphology in table 8.3, where the US and France, two early adopters, are continuing to change their PCSs even today. Further, one can see in table 8.3 how certain events in precedent cases of adoption and implementation shape the design of future adoptions and can speed up the process or slow it down. For example, consultations with the Yale team, who designed the US system, significantly shaped the early adoption and development of PCS in France. The American DRG system and its elements became part of the choice set for France, who picked, chose, and re-worked elements to fit its local circumstances. Outside table 8.3, we know that the pace of German adoption, as well as

[7] We only proxy the shape of morphology curves as s-curves; the lack of previous research on morphology does not allow us to specify the shape with certainty. Data analysis on the shapes of morphology curves for PCS is on our current research agenda.

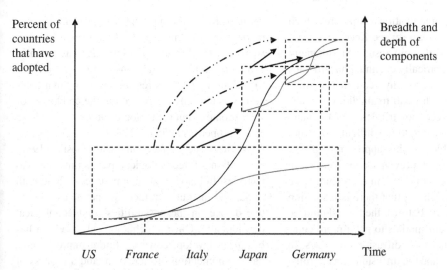

Figure 8.2 Effect of long and short morphological times on future diffusion and morphology

the shape of the innovation ultimately adopted and implemented, was influenced significantly by the existence of other alternatives, and the Germans eventually adopted the Australian system.

Length of morphological time for adopting units influences the pace of diffusion and the shape of the innovation as it diffuses. Specifically, contemporaneous circumstances influence the pace of diffusion and the shape of innovation at any time during diffusion, and sometimes previous adopters change innovation contemporaneously with other subsequent adopters' innovation adoption or morphology decisions. More concretely, figure 8.2 illustrates how long and sometimes short morphology curves can effectively transect processes occurring farther along in diffusion time and, in this way, influence those processes contemporaneously. Though France was an early adopter in the 1980s, its process of adoption of a financing process (an element of the process component) around 2000–2004 should have influenced all contemporaneous adopters, such as Germany, as well as the ongoing morphology of all previous adopters – to varying degrees depending on relationships between countries. This could occur, for example, as it provides another type of financing process to consider, which becomes an element in the choice set for financing processes, or it provides ongoing

impetus to potential adopters due to isomorphic pressures to conform (DiMaggio and Powell, 1983). Japan's ongoing morphology should have been a part of the German process, seen in figure 8.1 as an intersection of the Japanese and German morphology curves. Indeed, the data bear out these predictions, though relationships between countries and other factors are mediating variables. For example, the French PCS was among those considered by the German associations commissioned by the German Parliament to choose a PCS, but the Australian version was ultimately chosen, primarily due to the low fees charged by the Australian government (Neubauer, 2008).

Distinguishing between diffusion time and morphological time is conceptually appealing, but raises some thorny methodological problems. The distinction raises the question of whether the same innovation diffuses along the diffusion curve. If the innovation is not the same – if it evolves and changes – then a basic assumption of the diffusion research approach described earlier is called into question. Different versions of innovation may be adopted in different ways (Downs and Mohr, 1976). Also, culture is an unobserved variable in much multinational research. To the extent that culture drives both the shape of innovation (as found in this research) and the correlates of innovation (such as organizational structure, which is often infused with culture; see Kervasdoué and Kimberly, 1979), simultaneity results. Simultaneity tends to produce empirically declining hazard rates and, while problematic in any econometric strategy, it is particularly difficult to ameliorate in survival analysis, the econometric strategy of many diffusion researchers, due to the difficulty of using instrumental variables in this approach (Allison, 1995). Additionally, if previous adoptions drive the pace of current adoptions (in non-isomorphic ways, such as highlighting that there is a solution where there was none before), then we should be including these in our models to get a more complete picture of innovation diffusion processes. In summary, to understand the diffusion process fully, one must understand what is being diffused and why. Both change over time. This is the morphology of innovation.

Connections to other research approaches

The approach we are advocating here, although developed independently, is linked to others in the literature on innovation, particularly those in the tradition of the social construction of technology. The social constructionists argue that human action and economic, political, and other aspects of social context influence the shape of technology at a fundamental level (e.g., Bijker, Hughes, and Pinch, 1987; Bijker, 1995; Latour, 1987; Callon, 1986). Their view challenges technological determinism, or "the belief that technical forces determine social and cultural changes" (Bijker, Hughes, and Pinch, 1987). The technological determinists see the development of technology as proceeding along a predetermined path, largely devoid of cultural influence, and technologies' influence on society as for the most part unidirectional, whereas the social constructionists see social groups as having various interpretations of the meaning of technology, thereby influencing the shape of technological change (Bijker, 1995). Not surprisingly, research on the social construction of technology contrasts sharply with that in the classical diffusion of innovation tradition, with fixed and relatively stable technologies passing in linear fashion from engineer to user in the latter and all relevant social groups

participating in the ongoing development of technology in the former (Pollack and Stokes, 1996; Bijker, 1995). While our perspective has much in common with the social constructivists, we identify most closely with research positing that technology is not only interwoven in the conditions of social context, but technologies *in themselves* have social properties (Winner, 1980).

We also see connections with Dosi's (1982) conception of technological paradigms and trajectories. In his view, economic forces, along with social and institutional factors, operate as a selective device on the possibilities for technological development. Once a technological paradigm has begun to develop, however, future improvements have a momentum of their own, and a process of incremental change and problem solving activities follow along a technological trajectory bounded by the selected paradigm, in a fashion analogous to that described by Kuhn (1962) in science (Dosi, 1982). While our viewpoint embraces the concept of a technological paradigm selected by social factors and acknowledges the powerful exclusionary and inclusionary effects of paradigms on future innovation change, it emphasizes the progressive embodiment of social factors in the innovation itself, a process that unfolds both during selection and then as the innovation moves along a technological trajectory.

Finally, a small subset of the adoption and diffusion literature highlights the concept of reinvention. Rice and Rogers (1980, p. 500) define reinvention as "the degree to which an innovation is changed by the adopter in the process of adoption and implementation after its original development." Rogers (2003, p. 188) is on the right track when he contends that: "the general picture that emerges from studies of re-invention is that an innovation is not a fixed entity. Instead, people who use an innovation shape it by giving it meaning as they learn by using the new idea." This literature asserts that most reinvention occurs in the implementation stage of the innovation-decision process, after adoption of a discrete innovation that has already been developed (Rogers, 2003).

Our approach also highlights the importance of change over time in the components of an innovation. However, we emphasize the importance of users as well as history and other aspects of social context, and envisage a more fluid boundary between invention and innovation longitudinally.

Conclusions

By way of conclusion, we would like to reinforce four basic points.

First, the relationship between innovation and culture is more complex than the literature on adoption and diffusion would suggest. Innovations may change as they cross national and regional borders as a function of the interplay of the interests of various stakeholders – users, champions, sellers, and others – and on varying institutional arrangements, historical circumstances, and power distributions. Rather than assuming that innovations are static, researchers should at least allow for the possibility that they change and build this in to their theorizing and their empirics. They should, in other words, use the *morphology of innovation* as a point of departure for their work.

Second, as an area for future theorizing and empirical investigation, it would be useful to begin to develop morphological typologies of innovation. Some innovations, by their nature, may be more susceptible to change than others, and efforts to specify the qualities of innovation that make them more or less susceptible to change as they diffuse would be most welcome. Patient classification systems would, on the surface, appear to be more susceptible to change as they diffuse than, for example, intermittent positive pressure breathing machines, but it would not be wise simply to assume this to be true.

Third, the differences between diffusion time and morphological time should be explored further. Based on our analysis of the diffusion of PCSs, we posited that morphological time unfolds within diffusion time, but we did not address the question of how much an innovation can change and still be the same. We can make the case that PCS as an innovation was basically the same innovation in each of the five countries we examined, and that what we observed was local variation. However, it might well be that some change might be sufficiently frame-breaking to warrant thinking of the

result as an innovation in itself, with an entirely new diffusion trajectory. The development of an episode-based as opposed to an encounter-based system in the Netherlands, for example, could be viewed as an extension of PCS logic and hence as a case of morphology in the context of diffusion. However, it might also herald the advent of a radically different approach to resource allocation in health systems and therefore be viewed as a relatively radical departure from what was done previously and hence as an innovation in its own right.

Finally, we believe that a morphological model of innovation computes well with experience. The implicit assumptions of stability and concreteness found in much of the organizational research on adoption and diffusion of innovation may help simplify the job of the researcher, but, when examined carefully, they do not hold up well empirically. Our analysis of the diffusion of patient classification systems in five different countries suggests strongly that national and regional cultures play a significant role in shaping both the form and the pace of innovation and that to ignore this role is to seriously mis-specify the underlying process.

References

Allison, P. 1995. *Survival Analysis Using SAS: A Practical Guide*. Cary, NC: SAS Institute, Inc.

Bijker, W. E. 1995. *Of Bicycles, Bakelites, and Bulbs: Toward a Theory of Sociotechnical Change*. Cambridge, MA: The MIT Press.

Hughes, T. P., and Pinch, T. J. 1987. *The Social Construction of Technological Systems: New Directions in the Sociology and History of Technology*. Cambridge, MA: MIT Press.

Callon, M. 1986. *Mapping the Dynamics of Science and Technology*. London, Macmillan.

Centers for Medicare and Medicaid Services (CMS). 2007. "Overview to Acute Inpatient PPS". accessed on June 29, 2007 at www.cms.hhs. gov/AcuteInpatientPPS/.

Chilingerian. J. 2008. "Origins of DRGs in the United States: A technical, political, and cultural story", in J. R. Kimberly, G. Pouvourville, and T. A. D'Aunno (eds.), *The Globalization of Managerial Innovation: The Interplay of Politics, Policy and Functionality in*

Health Care, Cambridge: Cambridge University Press.

DiMaggio, P. J. and Powell, W. 1983. "The iron cage revisited: institutional isomorphism and collective rationality in organizational fields", *American Sociological Review* 48: 147–60.

Dosi, G. 1982. "Technological paradigms and technological trajectories", *Research Policy* 11: 147–62.

Downs, G. W. and Mohr, L. B. 1976. "Conceptual issues in the study of innovation", *Administrative Science Quarterly* 21(4): 700–14.

Duckett, S. J. 2008. "Casemix development and implementation in Australia", in J. R. Kimberly, G. Pouvourville, T. A. D'Aunno. (eds.), *The Globalization of Managerial Innovation: The Interplay of Politics, Policy and Functionality in Health Care*. Cambridge: Cambridge University Press.

Eisenhardt, K. M. 1989. "Building theories from case-study research", *Academy of Management Review* 14(4): 532–50.

Glaser, B. G. and Strauss, A. L. 1967. *The Discovery of Grounded Theory: Strategies for Qualitative Research*. Chicago, IL: Aldine Publishing. Co.

Grant, R. M. 2003. *Contemporary Strategy Analysis*. Malden, MA: Blackwell Publishing.

Guillen, M. F. 2000. "Corporate governance and globalization: is there a convergence across countries?", *Advances in Comparative International Management* 13: 175–204.

Guler, I, Guillen, M. F., and Macpherson, J. M. 2002. "Global competition, institutions, and the diffusion of organizational practices", *Administrative Science Quarterly* 47: 207–32.

Jommi, C., Cantu, E., and Anessi-Pessina, E. 2001. "New funding arrangements in the Italian National Service", *International Journal of Health Planning and Management* 16: 347–68.

Karpik, L. 1972. "Organisations et logiques d'action", *Sociologie du Travail* 4: 38–56.

Kervasdoué, J. and Kimberly, J. R. 1979. "Are organization structures culture-free? The case of hospital innovation in the US and France", in G. England, A. Negandhi, and B. Wilpert (eds.), *Organizational Functioning in a Cross-Cultural Perspective*. Kent, OH: Kent State University Press.

Kimberly, J. R. 1976. "Issues in design of longitudinal organizational research", *Sociological Methods & Research* 4(3): 321–47.

1979. "Issues in the creation of organizations – initiation, innovation, and institutionalization", *Academy of Management Journal* 22(3): 437–57.

D'Aunno, T. A., and Pouvourville, G. 2008a. Preface, in J. R. Kimberly, G. Pouvourville, T. A. D'Aunno (eds.), *The globalization of Managerial Innovation: The Interplay of Politics, Policy and Functionality in Health Care*, Cambridge: Cambridge University Press.

D'Aunno, T. A., and Pouvourville, G. 2008b. "The globalization of a management technology: the case of patient classification systems", in J. R. Kimberly, G. Pouvourville, T. A. D'Aunno (eds.), *The Globalization of Managerial Innovation: The Interplay of Politics, Policy and Functionality in Health Care*, Cambridge: Cambridge University Press.

Kuhn, T. 1962. *The Structure of Scientific Revolutions*. Chicago, IL: Chicago University Press.

Latour, B. 1987. *Science in Action*. Cambridge, MA: Harvard University Press.

Matsuda, S. 2008. "Diagnosis procedure combination – the Japanese original casemix system", in J. R. Kimberly, G. Pouvourville, T. A. D'Aunno (eds.), *The Globalization of Managerial Innovation: The Interplay of Politics, Policy and Functionality in Health Care*. Cambridge: Cambridge University Press.

Mayes, R. 2006. "The origins, development, and passage of medicare's revolutionary prospective payment system", *Journal of the History of Medicine and Allied Sciences* 62(1): 21–55.

Neubauer, G. 2008. "DRG-finals in Germany: Introduction of a comprehensive, prospective DRG-payment system until 2009". in J. R. Kimberly, G. Pouvourville, and T. A. D'Aunno (eds.), *The Globalization of Managerial Innovation: The Interplay of Politics, Policy and Functionality in Health Care*. Cambridge: Cambridge University Press.

Polanyi, M. 1962. *Personal knowledge: Towards a Post-critical Philosophy*. New York, NY: Harper Torchbooks.

Polillo, S, and Guillen, M. F. 2005. "Globalization pressures and the state: the global spread of central bank independence", *American Journal of Sociology* 110(6): 1764–802.

Pollack, N. and Stokes, C. 1996. "Designing technology at the conference table", *EASST Review* 15(1).

Rice, R. E. and Rogers, E. M. 1980. "Re-invention in the innovation process", *Knowledge* 1: 499–514.

Rodrigues, J. M. and Michelot, X. 2008. "France", in J. R. Kimberly, G. Pouvourville, and T. A. D'Aunno (eds.), *The Globalization of Managerial Innovation: The Interplay of Politics, Policy and Functionality in Health Care*. Cambridge: Cambridge University Press.

Rogers, E. M. 2003. *Diffusion of Innovations*. New York: Free Press.

Strauss, A. L. 1987. *Qualitative Analysis for Social Scientists*. Cambridge: Cambridge University Press.

and Corbin, J. M. 1998. *Basics of Qualitative Research: Techniques and Procedures for Developing Grounded Theory*. Thousand Oaks, CA: Sage Publications.

Tedeschi, P. 2008. "The first decade of case-mix systems in Italy", in J. R. Kimberly, G. Pouvourville, and T. A. D'Aunno (eds.), *The Globalization of Managerial Innovation: The Interplay of Politics, Policy and Functionality in Health Care*. Cambridge: Cambridge University Press.

Winner, L. 1980. "Do artifacts have politics?", *Daedalus* 109(1).

PART III

Culture and Organizational Behavior

Understanding leadership across cultures

MARCUS W. DICKSON, DEANNE N. DEN HARTOG, and NATHALIE CASTAÑO[1]

[c]ulture, in the sense of the inner values and attitudes that guide a population, frightens scholars
David Lander (2000, p. 2)

Recent polls suggested that Vladimir Putin, then President of Russia, maintained relatively high levels of popularity within Russia over several years. North Americans and western Europeans do not understand why (Pew Research Center, 2007). The 2008 Presidential election campaign in the US was heavily influenced by candidates' religious beliefs, and Europeans do not understand why (Wells, 2007). Terror attacks in Madrid in 2004 were quickly followed by the election of new national leadership that had campaigned on a promise to withdraw Spanish troops from Iraq – Spanish citizenry largely celebrated the withdrawal of troops as fulfillment of the new leadership's promise to bring troops home if the UN was not in control in Iraq, while American politicians and citizens described Spanish national leadership as capitulating to terrorists (Simons et al., 2004). In each of these cases, cultural differences in the ways in which people think about leadership led to misunderstanding and incorrect attributions about those in other cultures. Clearly, leadership and culture are a potent combination, and it is not surprising that scholars might be fearful of testing their well-established intra-culturally validated leadership theories across cultural boundaries.

Of course, when we look closely at the extant literature on leadership that has been conducted intra-culturally, there is quite a bit there that is none too clear. There is no consistently agreed-upon definition of "leadership," and consequently no clear understanding of the boundaries of the leadership construct space (e.g., Bass, 1997; Chemers, 1997). Thus, the study of leadership is already complex – adding a cultural component makes it infinitely more so. This is largely because, just as the construct

space of "leadership" is not well defined, the meaning and measurement of "culture" is also imprecise.

For many scholars, the favored approach has been to take a well-established framework of leadership (e.g., the transformational/charismatic model, or the Ohio State "structure/consideration" model), and to examine it cross-culturally. For many years, however, the lack of a well-established cultural framework to build upon in doing cross-cultural research (on leadership or other organizational topics) made it harder for researchers to reach theoretically sound conclusions and apply findings on leadership cross-culturally.

One of the pre-eminent researchers to develop such a framework is, of course, Geert Hofstede (1980; 2001). A central figure in the development of literature on culture variation and the dimension-based approach to assessing and classifying cultures, Hofstede has long argued that culture is often inappropriately applied in research settings. Often there is little theoretical justification for expecting cultural differences, and no model to identify what differences should be expected. Other researchers (e.g., Drenth and Den Hartog, 1998; Graen et al., 1997) have responded to Hofstede's critiques of the ways in which culture has been incorporated organizational research by posing fundamentally different questions about what cross-cultural research is, and what it is focused on. In essence, Hofstede's framework and the work of those following and building upon it have given some guidance on how to address the "cross-cultural" part of the "cross-cultural leadership" conundrum. The "leadership" part remains problematic.

One reason for this is the different meanings that "leadership" carries in different cultures. For example, in Anglo-Saxon countries, "leadership"

[1] We would like to thank Nathan Weidner and Heather Parr for their assistance in the preparation of this chapter.

generally has a positive connotation (i.e., a leader is typically seen as a heroic figure). However, direct translation of the word to other languages can invoke images of dictatorship (e.g., "leader" in German is "führer," and in Spanish is "jefe," both terms connoting directive or authoritarian styles of leadership; Bass and Stogdill, 1990; House *et al.*, 2004; Den Hartog and Dickson, 2004), or of other undesirable behaviors and characteristics. Similarly, in egalitarian societies the terms "followers" or "subordinates" are often seen as inappropriate; for example, in the Netherlands subordinates are more typically referred to as co-workers (*medewerkers*). This potential change or even loss of meaning in translation across languages represents an obvious issue in terms of measuring any construct. It is particularly the case, we find, in studying leadership.

A second reason that studying leadership across cultures is so difficult is that leadership is not the same thing across cultures. Daniel Etounga-Manguelle has said "Culture is the mother; institutions are the children" (Harrison, 2000, p. xxviii). As cultures vary, so too do the institutions within those cultures and leadership as a central component of institutional/organizational functioning varies as well. In individualistic societies, for example, leadership usually refers to a single person who guides and directs the actions of others, often in a very visible way. In more collectivistic societies, leadership is often less associated with individuals, and is more often seen as a group endeavor. In high power distance societies, leaders are seen as separate and apart from their followers, while in lower power distance societies, leaders are perceived as more approachable and less "different." The common North American celebration of leaders' accomplishments stands in stark contrast to Lao Tzu's still oft-quoted statement that: "A leader is best when people barely know he exists, when his work is done, his aim fulfilled, they will say: we did it ourselves."

---

[2] Bass and Stogdill (1990) contains an extensive review of the literature on leadership research conducted in multiple societies up to its publication date, and we commend it to the reader. We also look forward to the fourth edition of the *Handbook*, which Dr. Bass concluded shortly before his recent death, and we join leadership scholars worldwide in remembering Dr. Bass and his immense contributions to the study of leadership.

In this chapter, we will cover three main areas. First, we discuss the complex quest of researchers who have tried and are trying to further the understanding about leadership in different cultures. We then describe two opposing goals prevalent in cross-cultural leadership research – the quest to identify leadership universals, and the quest to identify cultural contingencies in leadership – and the outcomes of research from each perspective. Second, we briefly review some of the research related to cultural dimensions as well as alternative ways of looking at leadership in different cultures. We also discuss the impact this research has had on leadership behaviors and effectiveness. Finally, we draw some implications from the findings in this area that may help leaders make better decisions and be more effective when managing people.[2]

Cross-culturally defining leadership

One attempt at defining leadership cross-culturally comes from the Global Leadership and Organizational Behavior Effectiveness (GLOBE) Project. Robert J. House is the principal investigator of this long-term study and, along with several co-principal investigators and a multinational coordinating team, he led over 180 researchers from around the world in a study of the interacting effects of leadership, societal values, and organizational culture. The GLOBE Project was initially designed to assess both similarities and differences in the cultural semantic definition of leadership. Over 15,000 middle managers from more than 800 organizations in three industries in sixty-two countries were asked to describe leader attributes and behaviors that they perceived to enhance or impede outstanding leadership (House *et al.*, 2004). (Though we will review some of GLOBE's findings below, table 9.1 contains a brief summary of GLOBE results, as well as those of some other recent cross-cultural research on leadership.)

Before starting data collection, GLOBE researchers were faced with the difficult task of defining leadership in an encompassing way. One author of this chapter had the humbling experience of chairing the session at which the project's operational definition of "leadership" was to be established.

Table 9.1. Summary of findings from GLOBE and other recent cross-cultural research on leadership

Areas	Findings	Examples
Culture and leadership (Javidan, House, and Dorfman, 2004)	Culturally endorsed implicit theories of leadership (CLT): common observations and values concerning what constitutes effective and ineffective leadership by members of a culture.	
	• First order attributes: 21 primary factors.	Visionary, integrator, self-centered, participative, modesty, autonomous.
	• Second order attributes: consolidation of the 21 primary factors into six "second-order" global leadership dimensions:	
	(a) Charismatic/value-based leadership.	Visionary, inspirational, self-sacrifice, performance-oriented, integrity, decisive.
	(b) Team-oriented leadership.	Collaborative team orientation, integrator, malevolent, diplomatic, administratively competent.
	(c) Participative leadership.	Participative, autocratic.
	(d) Autonomous leadership.	Autonomous.
	(e) Humane-oriented leadership.	Humane-oriented, modesty.
	(f) Self-protective leadership.	Self-centered, status-conscious, conflict inducer, face-saver, procedural, bureaucratic.
	Universally endorsed outstanding leadership attributes.	Most attributes of the charismatic value-based and team-oriented leadership dimensions.
	Culturally contingent attributes.	Attributes in the participative, humane-oriented, and autonomous leadership dimension.
	Universally endorsed negative leadership.	Attributes in the autonomous self-protective leadership dimension.
Culture dimensions and leadership CLTs (Javidan *et al.*, 2004)	**Uncertainty avoidance:** positive predictor of self-protective, team-oriented, and humane-oriented leadership. Negative predictor of participative leadership.	
	Collectivism: positive predictor of charismatic/value-based and team-oriented leadership. Negative predictor of self-protective leadership.	
	Gender egalitarianism (masculinity-femininity): Positive predictor of participative and charismatic/valued-based leadership. Negative predictor of self-protective leadership.	
	Power distance: positive predictor of self-protective leadership. Negative predictor of charismatic/value-based and participative leadership.	
Leadership CLTs and cultural clusters (Javidan, *et al.*, 2004)	Charismatic/valued-based leadership valued the most in the Anglo cluster and the least in the Middle East cluster.	
	Team-oriented leadership valued the most in the Latin America cluster and the least in the Middle-East cluster.	
	Participative leadership valued the most in the Germanic Europe cluster and the least in the Middle-East cluster.	

Table 9.1. (cont.)

Areas	Findings	Examples
	Humane-oriented leadership valued the most in the Southern Asia cluster and the least in the Nordic Europe cluster.	
	Autonomous leadership valued the most in the Eastern Europe and the least in the Latin America.	
	Self-protective leadership valued the most in the Southern Asia cluster and the least in the Nordic Europe.	
Charismatic transformational leadership (Den Hartog, House, Hanges, Ruiz-Quintanilla, *et al.*, 1999)	Universally endorsed charismatic/transformational attributes.	Motive arouser, encouraging, communicative, trustworthy, dynamic, positive, confidence builder, and motivational.
	Culturally contingent charismatic transformational attributes.	Enthusiastic, risk taking, ambitious, self-effacing, unique, self-sacrificial, sincere, sensitive, compassionate, and willful.
	None of the universally endorsed negative leadership attributes described transformational/charismatic leadership.	
	Perceptual processes about leaders differ between upper versus lower hierarchical levels.	
	Equally endorsed attributes for both top and lower levels of leadership.	Being communicative, inspirational, and confidence builder.
	Attributes considered to be more important for top levels of leadership.	Being innovative, visionary, persuasive, long-term, oriented, diplomatic, and courageous.
	Attributes considered to be more important for lower levels of leadership.	Attention for subordinates, team building, and being participative.
Other	Cultural congruence proposition: leader behaviors are congruent with the cultural forces surrounding the leader.	Morris, Williams, Leung, Larrick, Mendoza, *et al.* (1998) showed that Chinese managers tend to rely on an avoiding conflict management style, possibly due to China's cultural values of conformity and tradition. US managers instead rely more on a competing conflict management style, which is more congruent with their culture of achievement values.
	Cultural difference proposition: deviation of leader behavior from dominant cultural values will encourage innovation and performance improvement.	
	Near universality of leader behavior proposition: some leader behaviors are universally accepted and considered effective regardless of the specific culture.	Apart from the GLOBE findings, Leslie and Van Velsor (1998) found that US and European managers perceive effective leaders as valuing personal influence, cooperation and acceptance of rules and procedures by external authority.

With what in retrospect we hope was simply the naïveté of youth (rather than a larger case of simple ignorance), he prepared a preliminary working definition, with the expectation that the assembled researchers would see its wisdom and quickly adopt it, thereby allowing everyone to get to an early dinner. Several hours later, when a definition was finally (and in some cases somewhat grudgingly) adopted, it bore little resemblance to the initial definition. Further, there were clear geographic "camps" advocating different conceptualizations of "leadership" – and these different conceptualizations were eventually replicated in the data collection phases of the project. Ultimately, social scientists and management scholars representing fifty-six countries from around the world defined "leadership" as "the ability of an individual to influence, motivate, and enable others to contribute towards the effectiveness and success of the organization of which they are members" (House *et al.*, 2004).

Although other attempts have been made to clarify what *leadership* means across cultures, several issues are omnipresent and problematic for all of these efforts (GLOBE included). Among these are the difficulties in measuring the differing cognitive prototypes that people of different cultures hold to characterize the construct of leadership, and the challenge of differentiating different conceptualizations of leadership from differing culture-specific behavioral enactments of similar cognitive conceptualizations of the construct of leadership (Den Hartog and Dickson, 2004).

Western – and particularly American – bias is still another issue that cross-cultural leadership faces (Den Hartog and Dickson, 2004; Graen *et al.*, 1997). Tsui, Nifadkar, and Ou (2007, p. 469) noted that:

> The intellectual leadership of cross-national research by U.S. scholars is a mixed blessing. Although they can provide expertise on theory, research design, and familiarity with the dominant research paradigm, they also may lead (unknowingly or unintentionally) the study down a path that is essentially an application or replication of (U.S.) domestic research rather than develop new theoretical insights on unique problems that are important in the comparison nations.

Of course, this bias is not unique to the study of cross-cultural aspects of leadership, but holds equally for the study of leadership in general. Although leadership researchers increasingly attempt to conduct studies in non-western/ non-westernized countries and some interesting comparative work has been done (e.g., Quang, Swierczek, and Chi, 1998; Xin and Tsui, 1996), researchers still tend to import American or other western leadership research as the basis of their models and measures. Far less work starts from more indigenous theories of leadership. Too often cross-cultural (leadership) researchers fail to consider the myriad ways in which cultural differences might systematically affect data collection, analysis, and interpretation, much less how such differences may affect the meaning, enactment, and effectiveness of leader behaviors (Den Hartog and Dickson, 2004; Dorfman, 1994; Matsumoto, 1994).

Universality vs. cultural contingency

An additional broad issue affecting the field of cross-cultural leadership research is the lack of clarity about what we are looking for in the first place. Cross-cultural leadership researchers are often torn between the quest to identify leadership "universals" that hold true across cultures, and the competing quest to apply theory to explain cultural contingencies in leadership (e.g., Hanges and Dickson, 2006). Far too often, the researchers themselves are not clear about their goals – again, we can point to the GLOBE Project for examples.

GLOBE's preliminary pilot studies to develop leadership scales yielded several items on which we found little variability across cultures. Of course, items on which there is no variability are not useful in the scale development effort, and the initial plan was to discard those items, as we would in any other project. It was only some time later that the principal GLOBE statistical experts paused and realized that it would be impossible to statistically identify leadership universals if the only items in the survey were those that showed cross-cultural variability. In short, we had not thought sufficiently clearly in advance about whether our goals were to identify universals or cultural contingencies. Unfortunately, we are not alone in this oversight.

Why does this matter? As Smith and Bond (1993, p. 58) point out:

> If we wish to make statements about universal or etic aspects of social behavior, they need to be phrased in highly abstract ways. Conversely, if we wish to highlight the meaning of these generalizations in specific or emic ways, then we need to refer to more precisely specified events or behaviors.

The implication for cross-cultural leadership research is that we must more clearly specify our research goals prior to blindly wandering down the research path. When our focus is on the identification of leadership universals, broader and more abstract conceptualizations of leadership constructs are necessary. When our goal is to understand or compare leadership practices common in a specific setting, then our constructs must be operationalized with much greater precision than is provided by common leadership assessment tools like the well-known Multifactor Leadership Questionnaire (MLQ; Bass and Avolio, 1990), the Leader Behavior Description Questionnaire (LBDQ; Fleishman, 1953 and others), or other similar questionnaire measures. For example, while a broad category such as *consideration* might be universally valued by subordinates, the specific behaviors that signal consideration to subordinates in different cultures very likely vary. We will provide more examples of this below, and turn now to consideration of leadership universals, and the research that has searched for them.

The quest for universality. Many researchers focused on identifying cross-culturally universal phenomena – including several leadership researchers (e.g., Bass, 1997) – have relied on Lonner's (1980) conceptualizations of cultural universality. As these different conceptualizations play out in several ways in the cross-cultural leadership arena, we briefly review these concepts now.

Lonner (1980) described the *simple universal* as a phenomenon that is constant throughout the world. Most of the phenomena that fit into this category are in the form of general statements or principles. Two examples are that humans are aggressive, and that humans communicate with each other. Both statements are true across all known human cultures, and so are considered simple universals. For most people, when they hear that something is "universal around the world," they expect the statement to refer to simple universals. If only that were so – the life of the cross-cultural researcher would be much easier. Lonner, of course, recognized that most phenomena that exist across cultures cannot be described as simple universals, and so he coined several other terms to reflect other conceptualizations of *universality*.

Variform universals are phenomena that, when investigated across cultures, go through subtle modifications. In other words, a variform universal refers to a case in which a general statement or principle holds across cultures, but the enactment of the principle differs across cultures. An example of variform universality is eye contact. In this case, responses would differ if people from different cultures were asked to interpret the meaning of a particular type, intensity, or duration of eye contact. In many Mediterranean cultures, eye contact during conversation is steady and from close quarters. Conversely, the Finnish conductor Esa-Pekka Salonen likes to cite the humorous adage from his homeland that, in a conversation, a Finnish introvert looks at his own shoes, while a Finnish extrovert looks at the other person's shoes (Ross, 2007). Thus, eye contact occurs during conversation and carries meaning around the world, but the precise meanings of eye contact vary systematically between cultures.

The *functional universal* focuses on the stability of relationships between variables. Functional universality occurs when the within-group relationship between two variables remains the same across cultures. That is, researchers interested in functional universals look for stable patterns and relationships that permit inferences without regard to situational factors. For example, Bass (1997) reports that research finds a consistent negative relationship between laissez-faire leadership and subordinate perceptions of the leader effectiveness across different cultures. Thus, it appears to be a functional universal that leaders who avoid their responsibilities are perceived to be ineffective.

Bass (1997) built on Lonner's (1980) framework to introduce another conceptualization of universality. He defined the *variform functional universal* as a case in which, even though the relationship between two variables is always found, both the relationship's magnitude and the behavioral enactment of the constructs change across cultures. An example given by Bass is that a relationship has been found between transformational leader behaviors and effectiveness; however, the magnitude of this behavior-effectiveness relationship varies across cultures, as does the nature of the behaviors seen as "transformational." Bass explicitly notes, for example (1997, p. 136), that:

> transformational leadership may be autocratic and directive or democratic and participative. Leaders can be intellectually stimulating to their followers when they authoritatively direct their followers' attention to a hidden assumption in their thinking. Leaders could also be intellectually stimulating when they ask whether their group would be ready to look together for hidden assumptions.

Our concern here is that the quest for universality in cross-cultural leadership research can lead researchers and theorists to ever broader and more abstract classifications of their constructs, or to ever broader definitions of universality. Clearly, a variform functional universal is a long way from a simple universal, and leadership that is participative and democratic is a long way from leadership that is autocratic and directive. When we expand our definitions to such an extent, we risk losing the ability to give guidance to actual leaders in actual leadership situations. As one student in a recent doctoral seminar asked: how useful is it to tell a soon-to-depart expatriate manager that he or she should exhibit transformational leadership because it is universal, but to follow that recommendation with the reminder that the behaviors that lead to subordinate perceptions of transformational leadership can vary across the full spectrum of leader behaviors? The reverse of course also holds true – assuming that the lack of simple universals means that it is impossible to make general statements about leadership, and thus that everything about leadership is determined by the context, will also yield ineffective advice to our soon-to-depart expatriate.

We see this difficulty – matching theoretical rigor with applicability – as one of the major challenges for cross-cultural leadership researchers as we attempt to move our field forward, and we see lack of clarity in research about whether the goal is to identify universals or cultural contingencies as one of the biggest barriers to overcoming that difficulty. Clearly, the search for leadership universals and leadership cultural contingencies are both important, and both can further the understanding of cross-cultural leadership and other cross-cultural phenomena. We see the most likely route forward in this regard to be continued development of theory that assists in understanding cultural variation. In short, we want to better identify cultural contingencies that make theoretical sense, and in so doing better understand the things that are, in fact, universal.

Identifying cultural contingencies

One useful approach to studying cross-cultural leadership is through the identification and measurement of cultural dimensions. This approach of classifying societies on the basis of either a dichotomous classification or on their location along a construct continuum is certainly not new. For example, Margaret Mead (1939) divided the societies she studied into two groups, with characteristics that today would label them as individualistic or collectivistic (see below). Many other subsequent researchers have done the same, on similar or on newly identified dichotomies and dimensions.

Though certainly not the first to propose dimensions upon which cultures vary, Geert Hofstede (1980, 2001) is well known for developing a framework for classifying countries based on prevalent work-related values. Hofstede's (1980) most well-known study was based on a survey among IBM managers and employees in more than forty-two countries. Following studies have included other countries and different samples (e.g., Hofstede, 2001), and the dimensions Hofstede developed and validated have been employed by a tremendous range of subsequent leadership researchers. We will briefly review some of the research related to the impact of these cultural dimensions on leadership behaviors and effectiveness.

Individualism-collectivism

A well-known culture dimension proposed by Hofstede (1980) is individualism versus collectivism. In brief, cultures characterized by individualism emphasize independence. In these societies, people are expected to take care of themselves and to look after their own interests and those of their close family members. Cultures characterized by collectivism, on the other hand, emphasize interdependence. In these societies, people distinguish between ingroups and outgroups, and these distinctions are generally ascriptive. Ingroups are cohesive and strong. People expect their ingroup to look after them, and they are loyal to it in return (Hofstede, 1980, 2001).

Schwartz (1999) described individualism and collectivism somewhat differently, as the extent to which people in societies are autonomous versus embedded in the group. High autonomy means that people are perceived as autonomous entities that find meaning in life through their uniqueness. Individuals in embedded cultures are perceived as part of the collective and are likely to find meaning and direction in life through participating in the group and identifying with its goals. Organizations tend to take responsibility for their members in all domains of life. In turn, individuals are expected to identify with and work toward organizational goals.

Individualism and collectivism are clearly linked to leadership and leader behavior. The results from GLOBE (House, et al., 2004) are relevant here. Though GLOBE researchers found some leader characteristics to be universally endorsed (a topic we address in detail later in this

chapter), the perceptions of most leader characteristics varied between cultures, and in many cases this variation reflected differences in individualism and collectivism. For example, being autonomous, unique, and independent were leader attributes that were found to be highly valued in individualist cultures, but not endorsed in collectivistic cultures (see Den Hartog et al., 1999; and Dorfman, Hanges, and Brodbeck, 2004 for a full list of attributes).

Research on transformational leadership suggests that some collectivist values fit well with certain transformational/charismatic leadership processes, such as the central role of the group and identification processes (Jung and Avolio, 1999). For instance, collectivists are more likely to identify with their leader's goals and the common purpose or shared vision of the group and organization, and typically exhibit high levels of loyalty (Jung, Bass, and Sosik, 1995). Members of collectivist cultures tend to have a stronger attachment to their organizations and tend to be more willing to put the group's goals before their own (e.g., Earley, 1989; Triandis, 1995). In contrast, people from individualist cultures tend to be more motivated to satisfy their own self-interest and personal goals. Individuals take care of themselves, and individual initiative, achievement, and rewards are central. As such, individualists may be more readily motivated by more short-term focused transactional leadership (Jung and Avolio, 1999).[3]

Masculinity-femininity

Another cultural dimension described by Hofstede (1998, 2001) is masculinity versus femininity. Masculinity implies dominant societal values stressing assertiveness and toughness, the acquisition of money and things, and not caring for others, the quality of life, or people. It is also characterized by aggressiveness, competition, and achievement orientation. On the other hand, feminine cultures value warm social relationships, quality of life, or people. People in these societies are expected to be modest and tender (Hofstede, 2001). Achievement motivation – on the part of both leaders and followers – and an acceptance of a "machismo style" of management should be higher in cultures high

---

[3] It is curious that several related leadership theories and models, all of which rely on characteristics more common in collectivistic societies (e.g., Bass and Avolio's full range theory of leadership; House's theory of charismatic leadership; Sashkin's theory of inspirational leadership, etc.) all emerged from scholars based in the US – one of the most, if not the most, individualistic societies.

on masculinity than in those low on masculinity (Triandis, 1994).

Hofstede (1998) has noted that the distinction between masculine and feminine aspects of the leadership role are well-established, and he points to the well-known "Managerial Grid" of Blake and Mouton (1964) and the earlier Ohio State studies on which the grid was based (e.g., Fleishman, Harris, and Burtt, 1955). These studies demonstrated the importance of "initiating structure" (a concern for task accomplishment, which Hofstede identifies as a masculine characteristic) and "consideration" (a concern for people and relationships, which Hofstede identifies as a feminine characteristic).[4]

Hofstede (1998) cites several provocative studies that highlight distinctions between societies classified as masculine or feminine. He goes on to assert that the nature of feminism that emerges in masculine and feminine cultures differs, with feminism in masculine cultures being a "competitive feminism," in which the opportunities available to men are made equally available to women (with obvious implications for leaders and leadership). In feminine cultures, however, a "complementary feminism" emerges, in which the roles of men and women are seen as interdependent, with respect urged for women because of the contributions that they can make to society precisely because they are different from men (with equally obvious, but different, implications for leaders and leadership).

Work by Williams and Best (1990) provides some support for these assertions, in that they showed that in countries classified as feminine, respondents showed greater differentiation in the characteristics they ascribed to men and women. Hofstede interprets this by saying: "In feminine countries, respondents do not feel inhibited in classifying an adjective as associated with men or with women, because this does not imply a positive or negative value judgment; women are as good or bad as men" (1998, p. 96). This could help to explain why the common assumption that women would advance to leadership roles more rapidly in feminine societies has not proven to be the case – research by V. Schein and others has shown that the "think manager-think male" (Schein, et al., 1996) mindset holds in many cultures (e.g., Schein and Mueller, 1992; Schein, et al., 1996; Sczesny, et al.,

2004), and it may be that women will advance more into leadership and executive roles in cultures of competitive feminism – where women and men are expected to compete on equal footing, with little acknowledgement of gender differences. Of course, to do so, these data suggest, women will need to behave in the typically masculine style seen as "managerial" or "leader-like" in those cultures.

Questions about masculinity/femininity as a dimension

This culture dimension is probably the one that has been critiqued the most. Criticisms regarding this dimension include issues of measurement and definition (e.g., this dimension includes various topics such as gender role division, assertiveness, dominance, and toughness in social relationships, being humane or focused on quality of life, and being performance or achievement oriented). Hofstede addressed these criticisms and expanded on the construct, including extensive discussion of its relationship with religious expression within a society (and to some extent, to leadership) in his 1998 book, *Masculinity and Femininity: The Taboo Dimension of National Cultures*. For many researchers, Hofstede's (1998) extended discussion of masculinity was still not fully persuasive. For example, two of the main elements of Hofstede's conception of masculinity were gender role division/gender egalitarianism, and assertiveness in interactions. Rather than approaching masculinity as an over-arching construct, House *et al.* (2004) measured these constructs separately, and demonstrated that they are not fully covariant.

Gender egalitarianism was defined by GLOBE as the degree to which each society seeks to minimize or maximize gender role differences (House *et al.*, 2004). GLOBE researchers assessed the extent

---

[4] Within the US-developed managerial grid framework, a "9,9 leader" (high on both initiating structure and consideration) was seen as the best type of leader for a great many work situations. However, the US is classed by Hofstede as relatively high on masculinity (1980; 2001), suggesting that the typical American manager would be more focused on initiating structure than on consideration – in other words, the commonly held cultural values and norms would yield leaders who were sub-optimal.

to which culturally endorsed implicit theories of leadership reflect gender egalitarianism. More gender egalitarian cultures endorsed charismatic leaders' attributes such as foresight, enthusiastic, and self-sacrificial as well as participative leader attributes such as egalitarian, delegator, and collectively oriented (Emrich, Denmark, and Den Hartog, 2004).

GLOBE defines assertiveness as the degree to which individuals in organizations or societies are assertive, tough, dominant, and aggressive in social relationships. Among other things, the GLOBE findings suggest a negative relationship between assertiveness and the endorsement of participative and team-oriented leadership attributes and a positive one with the endorsement of autonomous leader characteristics (Den Hartog, 2004). Assertiveness is linked to the preferred use of language in society. Being direct and unambiguous in expressing oneself is associated with this. GLOBE research supports the idea that in some cultures conversational directedness is valued, while in others it is rejected. Related research at the individual level found a negative correlation between assertiveness and indirect language use in the US, whereas North Koreans were significantly less direct in communication than Americans (Holtgraves, 1997). This difference is similar to that described initially by Hall in the 1950s, and more recently by Samovar and Porter (2004) and others in referring to high context and low context cultures. High context cultures (such as North Korea) assume a great deal of shared tacit knowledge and understanding among members, thus leading to much less direct communication. On the other hand, low context cultures (such as the US) assume very little tacit knowledge and understanding among members, thus leading to very explicit communications, including detailed contracts, explicit critique of performance in annual performance reviews by leaders, and more frequent required "updates" to a supervisor on how a task is progressing. These differences in assumptions about the appropriate way to behave towards a leader and as a leader are often deeply held, and are perceived by those holding them as simply reflecting common sense (e.g., Hanges, Lord, and Dickson, 2000). Consequently, leaders working across cultural boundaries from

masculine to feminine cultures or vice versa may find themselves feeling either "left out of the loop" or "too much in the loop," making them uncomfortable in either case.

Uncertainty avoidance

Uncertainty avoidance, as defined by Hofstede (1980), is the extent to which a society avoids ambiguity and uncertain situations. These societies try to avoid ambiguity by providing greater stability, establishing formal rules, and rejecting deviant behaviors. In short, these societies rely on social norms and procedures to avoid unpredictability of the future. As indicated, the GLOBE Project assessed the endorsement of leader attributes in different cultures and of the leader attributes that were found to vary across cultures several reflect uncertainty avoidance, including being habitual, procedural, risk-taking, formal, cautious, and orderly. These attributes were perceived as enhancing outstanding leadership in high uncertainty avoidance countries and not in those low on the dimension (Den Hartog et al., 1999; Dorfman, Hanges, and Brodbeck, 2004).

Uncertainty avoidance not only applies to leadership characteristics, but also to career advancement preferences. For instance, societies high on uncertainty avoidance tend to value such things as career stability, formal rules, and the development of expertise, all of which affect the perceptions and expectations that people hold (i.e., their leadership schemas; Hanges, Lord, and Dickson, 2000) about who should and will emerge as leaders. On the other hand, societies low on uncertainty avoidance are more flexible in roles and jobs, and have an emphasis on general rather than specialized skills. More job mobility is also typical in these societies. Again, these work characteristics affect the shared leadership schemas of organization and society members. One example comes from Stewart et al. (1994), who compared career management activities for young managers in Germany (a culture high on uncertainty avoidance) and the UK (a culture lower on uncertainty avoidance). The researchers found that the British leaders typically placed more emphasis on career mobility and generalization, while the German leaders spent more time in a single job or functional area and valued the development of specialized, task-related expertise.

Expectations that leaders have of subordinates, and that customers have of businesses, are also greatly influenced by uncertainty avoidance. For instance, in high uncertainty avoidance contexts, planning and detailed agreements are the norm, whereas in low uncertainty avoidance contexts flexibility in response to changing situations and innovation are more prominent (Dickson, Den Hartog, and Mitchelson, 2003).

Power distance

All over the world, the leadership role is associated with power and status; therefore, the ways in which power and status are divided in society is obviously relevant to the leadership role. Power distance refers to the extent to which members of a society believe that it is acceptable or desirable for those higher in the hierarchy to be treated with deference and respect, to be obeyed, and to have extra privileges (Hofstede, 1980, 2001). In short, it is the extent to which society accepts the fact that power in institutions and organizations is distributed unequally. Power distance is also related to the concentration of authority (Hofstede, 2001). For instance, in high power distance countries such as China, Mexico, and the Philippines, subordinates are less likely to directly challenge their supervisors. In contrast, subordinates in countries low in power distance (e.g., Finland, the Netherlands, Israel, and the US) are more likely to do so.

Similarly, Schwartz (1999) holds that any society is confronted by the question of how to guarantee the necessary responsible behavior of its members. To resolve this problem, hierarchical cultures emphasize the chain of authority and ascribed and hierarchically structured roles. An unequal distribution of power is legitimate and employees are expected to comply with management without questioning directives. In contrast, in egalitarian cultures people tend to view each other more as moral equals and a more participative way to motivate employees is found. Employees tend to have their say in things and share in goal-setting activities (Sagiv and Schwartz, 2000; Den Hartog and Dickson, 2004).

Leadership styles are clearly likely to vary between cultures based on power distance. That is, in high power distance societies, authoritarian leadership and more autocratic decision making are more likely to be accepted. In egalitarian cultures, employees expect to have a say in decisions affecting their work. For example, in studies comparing managers from France (a culture high in power distance) and Denmark (a culture low in power distance), French respondents consistently indicated that they were expected routinely to consult their supervisors, simply because he or she was the boss, whereas the Danish indicated they were only expected to consult their supervisors when he or she was likely to know the answer to their problem (Schramm-Nielsen, 1989; Sondergaard, 1988; both in Hofstede, 2001). In France, bosses were highly respected by virtue of their position, whereas in Denmark respect relationships were found to be independent of rank. A Danish boss could do the work of a subordinate without loss of prestige, but a French manager could not. Finally, the Danish firms were characterized by delegation of authority and flatter hierarchical structures (Schramm-Nielsen, 1989; Sondergaard, 1988; both in Hofstede, 2001). Related research shows that subordinates in high power distance countries are more reluctant to challenge their supervisors and more fearful in expressing disagreement with their managers than their counterparts in low power distance countries (Adsit et al., 1997).

The results from GLOBE (House, et al., 2004) are again relevant here. For example, the endorsement of attributes such as status-conscious, class-conscious, elitist, and domineering varied across high power distance cultures versus egalitarian cultures. Similarly, Dorfman et al. (1997) compared leader behavior in five western and Asian countries (the US, Mexico, Japan, Taiwan, and South Korea). They found that some leader behaviors were positively related to outcomes such as satisfaction with supervision and organizational commitment in all these nations, but other leader behaviors were not universally endorsed. They interpreted the differences they found as reflecting power distance. For instance, directive leadership only had positive outcomes in terms of satisfaction and commitment in Mexico and Taiwan (cultures relatively high on power distance). Participative leadership only had positive effects in the US and South Korea (cultures relatively low in power distance). In Mexico and the US, they were able to collect similar job performance data. They found that in Mexico only supportive and directive leadership were directly and positively related to performance, whereas in the US, only participative leadership had a direct and positive relationship with performance.

Employees' willingness to accept supervisory direction, and emphasis on gaining support from those in positions of authority, were also found to be affected by power distance. In a study by Bu, Craig, and Peng (2001) that compared the willingness to accept supervisory direction among Chinese, Taiwanese, and US employees, the researchers found that, overall, Chinese employees had the strongest tendency to accept direction and US employees the least. Consistency between the supervisory direction and company policies was most valued by Chinese. They also were less responsive to their own assessment of the merit of the directions they were given.

Recent research on power distance has also shown the effect it has specifically on transformational leadership in different cultures. Bass (1997) found that preferences for positive effects of transformational leadership have been found in many different cultures. However, the enactment of transformational leadership may take more as well as less participative forms. This seems likely to be linked to societal norms and values regarding power and status differentials. For example, in highly egalitarian/low power distance countries (e.g., The Netherlands and Australia), transformational leader behaviors are highly correlated with participation in decision making (Den Hartog, 1997; Feather, 1994). This suggests that transformational leaders may need to be more participative to be effective in highly egalitarian societies. On the other hand, in high power distance societies, transformational leadership may take a more directive form (Den Hartog *et al.*, 1999). Further research in this area is needed for a better understanding of the impact that societal values have on transformational leadership effectiveness.

In summary, research shows that power distance in society has an impact on aspects of leadership. Where power distance is low, people tend to prefer leadership that is more egalitarian and subordinates are more willing to criticize and speak up to their leaders. Where power distance is high, leaders tend to be less participative and more authoritarian and directive, with subordinates being less used to speaking up. Such directive leadership is also more effective in a high power distance context.

Conclusion to dimensions

Research done on cultural dimensions shows that there is still some ambiguity about the best way to implement the dimensional approach to culture. This, in turn, has an obvious impact in the way these dimensions can be applied to leadership.

Two main conclusions can be drawn from the information presented above. The first is that although cultural dimensions were treated one by one in this part of the chapter, it is likely the case that different cultural dimensions simultaneously affect leaders and followers – in other words, the dimensions are likely to interact. For instance, as Offerman and Hellman (1997) were validating Hofstede's (1980) initial culture study at IBM, they found that managers from low power distance countries tended to use more communication behaviors and were perceived as more approachable than managers from higher power distance countries. Simultaneously, managers with citizenship from high uncertainty avoidance countries tended to be more controlling, less delegating, and less approachable than those from low uncertainty avoidance countries. Considering these two dimensions together (say, in a 2 x 2 table of high/low power distance on one axis and high/low uncertainty avoidance on the other) leads to a clear understanding of the likely leadership behaviors of managers in those societies.

We also find that reviewing the literature on cultural dimensions and leadership reinforces our previously stated concern about the tension between research on how behaviors, styles, and traits vary in systematic ways across cultures, and research on how the magnitude of the relationship between leaders' activities and subsequent performance and follower perception of the leader is dependent on broader aspects of culture. Again, these two different trends (focusing on dimensions versus looking for universals) reflect fundamentally different implications for the study of leadership.

Finally, it is important to note that although Hofstede's cultural dimensions have been widely used, the dimensions – and the entire concept of scaling cultures based on a qualitative measurement scheme – have not been without criticism. Some of these critiques hold that Hofstede presents an overly simplistic dimensional conceptualization of culture; that the original sample came from a single multinational corporation (IBM), raising issues about the confound of corporate culture with societal culture; that his work ignores the existence of substantial within-country cultural heterogeneity; and that the measure itself is not valid.[5] We turn briefly to a summary of work by Jai Sinha as one example (of several possible examples) of a research program that does not rely on a dimension-based approach for the conceptualization of culture when examining culture's impact on leadership processes.

Cultural dimensions – too simplistic a model?

The tension between etic and emic approaches to research is present in the study of cross-cultural leadership, as it is in every domain of cross-cultural research. The work of Hofstede (1980, 2000) and others who provide dimensionalizations of cultural values lead to work focused on scaling societies based on the measurement of their cultural values, and to prediction of outcomes based on that measurement. However, others who take a more emic approach often focus not on the commonalities across cultures or the rank orderings of cultures on particular variables, but instead on the idiosyncrasies of cultures, and on explicating why the cultural dimensions are insufficient descriptors of the richness of life in a given culture. A particular example of this latter approach that is deserving of attention has been the work of Jai Sinha, with his extensive writings on India.

Sinha has specialized in exploring the various cultural aspects of the Indian people. In particular,

it seems to be his goal to differentiate Indian culture from its western influence in order to identify the aspects of Indian culture that are distinctly India's own. In particular, he has conducted research looking at the both collectivist and individualistic nature of Indians. He has argued that traditional Indian values argue for a collectivist nature, while a strong western influence – partially through education – is encouraging more individualistic intentions and behaviors amongst the Indian people (Sinha et al., 2001; 2002).

Sinha has also argued that researchers need to consider the perspective from which most cross-cultural research is being conducted. He points out that although the amount of research that was being done in India by Indian researchers soared in the 1960s and 1970s, these researchers were basing most of their models and arguments around previously established western perspectives instead of building theories and research that were truly their own, and truly descriptive of Indian culture. We and others (e.g., Tsui, et al., 2007) have similarly argued that the way for cross-cultural leadership research to move forward will be to look for commonalities among locally generated theory, rather than agreement in locally collected data using externally developed research models (e.g., Dickson, 2005). (We address this topic in more detail in our section on future directions for cross-cultural leadership research.)

Sinha further suggests that not only should more established countries like the US conduct research in Indian organizations and attempt to influence them and guide them towards better development, but researchers working out of third world countries need to be able to study more developed countries in order to assess from their own point of view the reasons for and descriptions of differences in organizational behaviors (Sinha, 2003). In this, Sinha mirrors the call by Leung (2007) for Asian researchers to enhance their efforts in investigating

---

[5] See Dickson, Den Hartog, and Mitchelson (2003) and Sivakumar and Nakata (2001) for lengthier discussions of the criticisms of Hofstede's work. For recent overviews and critiques see Kirkman, Lowe, and Gibson (2006) and McSweeney (2002).

indigenous constructs and developing indigenous theoretical explanations for phenomena.

It is from this perspective that he incorporates traditional Hindu words into many of his articles in order to offer a more Indian perspective on the research that he conducts. In this way he seems to advocate what he refers to as an exogenous process of indigenization, whereby western concepts and theories are considered through a more culturally relevant perspective (Sinha, 2003).

It is through this point of view that he has recently looked at the differences in managers' perceptions of their organizations and the society around them throughout India (Sinha., 2004). In this paper Sinha argues that India itself is so culturally diverse that it is not accurate or even possible to make generalizations about the country's culture as a whole. Instead, Sinha sought to identify both cultural aspects that would be pervasive throughout Indian culture and cultural aspects that would vary from region to region. Sinha further sought to identify what aspects of those regions may account for the variability in manager's perceptions of organizational culture in their region. These arguments by Sinha have significant implications for leadership and other researchers in highly heterogeneous nations or nations where there are distinct and overlapping sub-cultures.

Of course, Sinha's criticisms and those of other researchers who advocate non-dimension-based cultural conceptualizations do not negate the fact that Hofstede's work and work derived from it have had a major influence on cross-cultural organizational research, particularly in the leadership domain. Several researchers have used the dimensional framework to move beyond the single-culture level of analysis, to find groupings of cultures that share similar patterns of values and practices, and we turn now to the implications of these "culture clusters" for the understanding of leadership in a cultural context.

Culture clusters

Cross-cultural researchers have also used other approaches in their research. One such approach has been the creation of a set of culture clusters, or groupings of cultures that are similar to each other. The goal of these studies is to examine whether variability in values or behaviors or other cultural markers occurred at the level of the society/nation, or whether there was similarity across a larger grouping of nations. Ronen and Shenkar's (1985) oft-cited clustering of cultures (synthesizing the work of several prior scholars) gave rise to a variety of other similar efforts, the most recent of which are those by the GLOBE Project (House, et al., 2004), whose cluster analyses were based on the cultural values of the countries in their study.

While Ronen and Shenkar (1985) identified eight clusters (Arab, Near Eastern, Nordic, Germanic, Anglo, Latin European, Latin (Spanish) American, and Far Eastern), with forty-two cultures included, GLOBE identified ten country clusters (Anglo, Latin European, Nordic European, Germanic European, Eastern European, Latin American, Sub-Saharan Africa, Southern Asia, Arab and Middle Eastern, and Confucian Asian). The countries within each cluster share many similarities and differ significantly from countries in other clusters. Although the GLOBE Project included a wide variety of countries, there are still many societies that were not included. It could be possible that additional clusters emerge if more societies are added, but it seems quite likely that many societies not included in this data set would fit cleanly into one of the ten clusters identified. Additionally, while Ronen and Shenkar (1985) identified four cultures that they classified as independent, or not clustering meaningfully with any other culture (Brazil, Japan, India, and Israel), the GLOBE cluster analyses did not allow for cultures to stand alone. Consequently, as with any cluster analysis, the inclusion of entities that do not cleanly fit into a cluster could have led to other changes in cluster groupings (e.g., GLOBE placed the Netherlands in the Germanic cluster, rather than the Nordic European cluster). The issue of whether to allow independent cultures in such analyses remains a point for debate.

These clusters have several implications for leadership and other business issues. The direct implications will be discussed further in the chapter. (To see a complete list of the culture clusters refer to Gupta, Hanges, and Dorfman, 2002.) It is important to note, however, that the clusters are not impermeable boundaries, nor are they permanent descriptions of similarities of individual nations' cultures. Myers *et al.* (1995) point out, for example, that the process of Europeanization and the ever-increasing mobility and transience of the labor force (including managerial labor) will eventually lead to greater convergence in the preferred leadership styles of Europeans, even though at present the nations of Europe are generally divided by researchers into multiple culture clusters.

Leadership behaviors and attributes

It is an obvious advantage to know about certain personality characteristics that would help select effective leaders. A major question is whether these personal characteristics that are associated with effective leadership within a single country are also useful in other cultural settings. GLOBE is the largest project to date to attempt to address this question. In addition to measuring the values and practices of the different cultures, the GLOBE study also gathered information about the common leadership preferences in those cultures.

Universally endorsed leader characteristics. The GLOBE Project asked middle managers from over sixty countries to rate their perceptions of over 200 different leader attributes and behaviors. The main focus was directed towards whether these attributes and behaviors inhibited or facilitated a person's being an outstanding leader. The GLOBE Project reports approximately twenty leadership attributes that are universally endorsed as contributing to effective leadership, and others which are seen as universally undesirable (Den Hartog *et al.*, 1999). For instance, in all the countries that participated in the study, an outstanding leader is expected to be encouraging, motivational, dynamic, and to have foresight. On the other hand, outstanding leaders were expected not to be noncooperative, ruthless, and dictatorial. Many more leader characteristics were seen as culturally contingent, however (Den Hartog *et al.*, 1999).

Culturally contingent leader characteristics

Keating and Martin (2004) in their study of the Irish-German experience, include several examples of cultural contingencies across culture clusters that affect the perception of leadership effectiveness. For example, the German emphasis on planning and execution as key features of the leadership role (related to the higher than average uncertainty avoidance and future orientation scores for Germany) contrasts with the Irish tendency to see the leader role as one of responding to situations as they change (related to the lower than average uncertainty avoidance and future orientation scores for Ireland). While Irish-German multinationals and cross-national partnerships are growing in frequency, they are clearly not without their challenges arising from differing conceptualizations of leadership related to home country culture.

Den Hartog *et al.* (1999) also noted that in the vast majority of the cases, the degree to which a particular attribute was seen as inhibiting or facilitating outstanding leadership varied by culture. Most of the GLOBE findings for culturally contingent leader characteristics are related to how different cultures' responses to various leadership styles are in line with other work-related beliefs and values. The best way to describe these characteristics is relying on the cultural dimensions described earlier. For example, the dimension of power distance can be seen as the origin of several differences. "Elitist" and "domineering" are both leader attributes that differ widely in endorsement between cultures. In some cultures they are seen as contributing to outstanding leadership (i.e., high power distance cultures) and in some others they are seen as inhibiting outstanding leadership (i.e., low power distance cultures). More of the characteristics that vary across culture found by the GLOBE Project were already discussed in the section of "cultural dimensions related to leadership" in this chapter.

Leadership styles

The GLOBE Project also looked at major leadership styles by combining the behaviors and attributes into larger groupings of related items.

As was the case with some leadership behaviors and attributes, different leadership styles that were considered as most effective in some cultures were seen differently in others. GLOBE identified six major categories of leader behaviors and attributes (see also Dorfman *et al.*, 2004). The six dimensions with their respective leader characteristic are:

- Charismatic/value-based leadership: being visionary, inspirational, decisive, and having integrity.
- Team-oriented leadership: acting collaboratively, integrating, and being diplomatic.
- Participative leadership: being non-autocratic and allowing participation in decision making.
- Autonomous leadership: being individualistic, independent, and unique.
- Humane leadership: showing modesty, tolerance, and sensitivity.
- Self-protective leadership: being self-centered, status-conscious, and a face-saver.

Findings indicate that the universality and cultural-contingency positions hold for leadership styles as well (Den Hartog *et al.*, 1999; Dorfman *et al.*, 2004). Two of the leadership styles (charismatic leadership and team-oriented leadership) were strongly endorsed in all ten clusters. However, the extent to which they were valued changed across clusters. For instance, the endorsement of these two leadership styles was strongest in the Anglo, southern Asian, and Latin American clusters and was consistent but less strong in the rest.

The other leadership styles were found to be culturally contingent. Humane leadership was strongly endorsed in the southern Asia, Anglo, and sub-Saharan Africa clusters, and not so strongly endorsed in the Latin American and Nordic European cluster. Autonomous leadership was generally seen as neither facilitating nor inhibiting a leader from being effective. However, within the eastern and Germanic Europe clusters this leadership style was evaluated as slightly more positively related to being an outstanding leader than in other culture clusters. For self-protective leadership and participative leadership, there was substantial variability in the degree to which they were endorsed within the different country clusters (Den Hartog *et al.*, 1999; Dorfman *et al.*, 2004).

Implications for leaders

The research described thus far can be applied in several ways. By understanding the differences and similarities of societies in terms of work-related values, leaders are likely to make better decisions and be more effective when managing people. This section of the chapter will focus on practical applications of cross-cultural leadership research in two main areas. The first one is human resource practices; specifically reward systems, work teams, and personnel selection systems. The second area is mergers, acquisitions, and joint ventures.

Reward systems

Cross-cultural research in the area of performance appraisal and reward systems is particularly prone to portray American biases. For instance, the idea of individual achievement and pay for performance is so inherent in American thinking that managers believe that implanting this same system in other countries will yield the same typically positive results as found in the US. In reality, many cultures have other preferences and expect reward systems to follow their values. This, in turn, might result in resistance against pay for performance systems.

Reward systems are strongly linked to performance evaluation. For example, in more individualistic societies, evaluation systems tend to assess employee performance based on employee productivity, timeliness, quality of output, and job-specific knowledge and proficiency. The end result or output is emphasized more than the process, implying striving for performance criteria that are tangible, objective and observable (Aycan and Kanungo, 2001). In contrast, in highly collectivistic and high power distance cultures, employee loyalty tends to be valued at least as much as productivity. Measurable output and outcomes are important, yet more subjective social and relational criteria also play a strong role in evaluation systems (Aycan and Kanungo, 2001).

Who has a legitimate and accepted input in evaluation systems is also affected by culture. As mentioned above, subordinates in high power distance countries are typically more reluctant to challenge their supervisors and more fearful in expressing disagreement with their managers (Adsit *et al.*, 1997). Not only are people in such high power distance countries less likely to provide negative feedback to superiors spontaneously, the idea that subordinates would be allowed to provide feedback in more formal rating systems (e.g., 360 degree feedback) is also much more likely to be rejected in high power distance countries, because such upward feedback may be perceived as threatening status positions (Kirkman and Den Hartog, 2004).

Whether rewards are contingent upon performance also depends in part on the cultural context. For example, Aycan *et al.* (2000) found weak performance-reward contingencies in what she labels collectivist societies where contingencies other than performance affected rewards. Also, a preference for rewarding the group as a whole rather than the individual members is seen in these societies. In contrast, in individualistic societies the equity norm implies a stronger link between performance and reward (Aycan and Kanungo, 2001). In more individualistic societies like the US, UK, and Australia, rewards and recognition programs are thus commonly tied to individual performance. The notion of "sharing" rewards or credit for an accomplishment is probably as foreign a notion in individualistic countries as strongly individual focused recognition such as an "employee of the month" award might be in collectivistic countries like Japan, China, or Malaysia (Kirkman and Den Hartog, 2004).

Fairness is another aspect that is reflected in reward systems. People always want to be treated fairly; however, the things that constitute fairness will differ across cultures (Den Hartog and Dickson, 2004). In general, strongly collectivist societies prefer pay differences based on factors, such as age. On the other hand, individualist societies tend to prefer reward systems to be (at least in part) based on pay for performance. In both cases, people perceive the reward system they prefer as being fairer than other systems. A Chinese colleague made this particularly clear in her description of a Chinese garment factory staffed almost exclusively by women that was taken over by a new western owner. The new owners instituted a pay-for-performance plan similar to those implemented in all of their other factories. The male factory foreman explained the new plan and how it would benefit the employees, and pointed out how fair it was, because those who contributed the most to the company's performance would receive the most from the company. Several weeks later, the women of the factory overcame their cultural tendencies of high power distance and clear gender roles to approach the foreman and ask that the former pay system – in which those women who were older or who had more family members to care for were paid more – be restored, because it was "more fair."

Earley and Gibson (2002) provide a similar account in which an American expatriate manager applied a typical North American reward system – using public recognition as a form of reward, along with public presentation of bonuses for good performance – in an Asian context. In a cultural setting in which members prefer to recognize group contributions to a project's success, rather than having individuals singled out in front of their project team-mates, this reward system functioned as more of a system of punishments to those selected for individual recognition.

Clearly, fairness perceptions of reward systems can differ by culture, and managers and leaders need to be aware of these differences in order for their organizations to succeed.

Work teams

As globalization continues, diversity in teams becomes more and more common. Teams with members from different cultural backgrounds work together not only because there is a more culturally diverse workforce, but because task forces are also created with representatives from locations around the world. Early and Gibson (2002) point out that people from cultures high in masculinity may find it difficult to interact effectively with team members from cultures where gender is less of a consideration (i.e., low masculinity countries), especially in leadership situations. Long-established cognitive processes about something as basic as how to allocate tasks among group members are likely to be challenged (often by those least expected to challenge a leader's decision), and can lead to internal team dissension. Similarly, people from countries that are high in power distance may be uncomfortable in a leaderless group, which is a common work form for those in low power distance cultures. In high power distance cultures, management may also be less likely to allow teams a high level of autonomy (e.g. Kirkman, Lowe and Gibson, 2006). In these cultures, introducing team self-management activities such as setting their own goals or taking initiative without asking for permission from supervisors, thus requires careful attention.

Also, team members from high uncertainty avoidance cultures may prefer scheduled meeting times or firm deadlines, while those from low uncertainty avoidance cultures may find such practices constraining. For example, Germany and Ireland are similar on all of Hofstede's culture dimensions, except uncertainty avoidance (Germany ranks high and Ireland low). Rauch, Frese and Sonnentag (2000) compared the use of planning in German and Irish small enterprises. In Germany, customers will expect business owners to plan carefully and in more detail. In contrast, in Ireland planning is seen as less necessary and customers have less respect for plans, show unplanned behavior themselves and expect flexibility. Planning in too much detail will render small business owners inflexible. Thus, Rauch and colleagues expected and found that planning had a positive influence on small business success in Germany and a negative influence on small business success in Ireland. In other words, the cultural appropriateness of extensive planning (which relates to uncertainty avoidance) will influence its success.

Based on these findings, leaders of multinational teams need to recognize the needs of team members and develop norms that work for that particular team. Once potential points of disagreement are observed, the leader needs to act proactively and guide the group towards working outside their typical patterns to accommodate everyone's needs. This could be particularly difficult in that the team members from other cultures are often much more able to see other members' cultural values than their own. (In talking about cultural dimensions with executive education students in Taiwan recently, one of the authors found that the Taiwanese students readily understood the concept

of individualism and could point out the author's individualist assumptions and behaviors, but had a much more difficult time embracing the concept of collectivism, or of identifying their own behaviors and assumptions that reflected collectivism.)

Personnel selection systems

A primary task for leaders is to choose who will work for and with them. The processes by which this occurs vary widely across countries, as does the extent to which these processes are regulated by law. Also, the social validity of any given selection practice (i.e., the perceived fairness and acceptability of a practice) may differ across cultures, for example, testing is much less readily accepted in some cultures than in others (Aycan and Kanungo, 2001). The underlying value systems that guide personnel selection seem to be more similar within a culture cluster, thus making it easier to transfer personnel selection systems within clusters. For instance, in the Anglo cluster, laws and regulations mandating selection based on ability and potential, and barring the hiring of family members or in some cases friends on the basis of personal relationship, are quite common. On the other hand, in the South Asian cluster, the hiring of relatives and friends is viewed more positively – the referring family member is seen as being able to vouch for and ensure the reliability and performance of the family member to be hired, for example. Thus, a personnel selection system used in the US would potentially be more easily transferable to the UK than it would be to China. In sum, if a hiring system is seen as unfair (regardless of the "objective" fairness of the system from any given cultural perspective), there can be various negative consequences to the company (e.g., company's reputation can suffer, turnover might increase, and in some countries, greater chance for legal action), as well as the decreased likelihood of leader effectiveness.

Expatriates

Research in cross-cultural leadership can also have a useful application for organizations that send and receive expatriate managers and leaders. Expatriates are employees sent by their organization to a related unit in a foreign country to accomplish a job or organization related goal for a temporary period that is usually over six months and less than five years in one term (Aycan and Kanungo, 1997). Expatriates tend to be managers or professionals sent out for highly complex and responsible tasks that need to be performed in an intercultural environment (Sinangil and Ones, 2001). Recent research on expatriate managers has again confirmed the variability in preferred leadership styles across cultures, raising questions about who to select for expatriate assignments, and how to prepare them. For example, Stroh, Black, Mendenhall, and Gregersen (2005) summarize a range of research to conclude that high-involvement leadership – defined as focusing on both accomplishing tasks and on the needs of people, seemingly akin to "nine, nine leadership" in Blake and Mouton's (1964) "managerial grid" approach – is more effective outside the US than within the US, and is among the most effective leadership approaches. Leaders who are comfortable with this style may be more suited for expatriate assignments than those with less balanced emphases between task and people demands.

Some of the areas on expatriate research include expatriate training, adjustment, and job performance. We will address each of these topics in turn.

Many of the elements that make expatriates successful can be developed, and leaders can play an important role in developing these. For example, according to Black and Mendenhall (1990) cross-cultural training improves cultural awareness, interpersonal adjustment and managerial effectiveness. Several training methods can be used to develop the necessary skills that expatriates need to be successful in their overseas assignment. Some of the most commonly used training methods include the university model, the experiential model, behavior modification training, and the culture assimilator training (Herzfeldt, 2007). The university model relies on one-way communication methods to convey information to the trainees. Although widely used, this method is not the most suitable for intercultural training because training is mostly conducted in a classroom setting, does not address ambiguous situations, and the training is based on paper orientation instead of building

people-skills. The experiential model, on the other hand, exposes the trainees to situations similar to those that might be encountered in other cultures. Some of the techniques used in this model are role playing and simulations. The behavior modification training also focuses on learning, specifically on Bandura's (1977) social learning theory. This model has proven very useful because it focuses on behavioral dimensions of cultural competence (e.g., gestures and physical expression). Finally, the culture assimilator is one of the best-known and most frequent applied methods for intercultural training. It is based on critical incidents and aims to teach trainees to make the same attributions as members of the other cultures (Herzfeldt, 2007).

Adjustment is another area in which expatriate research has focused. Expatriate adaptation is composed of three different dimensions: work adjustment, social adjustment, and environmental adjustment. Work adjustment refers to the expatriate's comfort with the assigned tasks and responsibilities. Social adjustment refers to the degree of comfort the expatriate has when interacting with host country nationals at work and in other settings. Environmental adjustment refers to expatriate's comfort with the new culture (i.e., food, health care, and general living conditions; Herzfeldt, 2007).

Leaders can play a pivotal role in these three areas of expatriate adaptation. For instance, Toh and Denisi (2007) suggest that leaders can help expatriates to adapt to the new settings by making them feel more comfortable when dealing with peers, local supervisors and subordinates. Leaders can also help expatriates by familiarizing them to the national culture (e.g., values and expected behaviors) as well as the local language. Leaders can also help by training local workers on how to deal with expatriates and developing everyone's cultural sensitivity (Toh and Denisi, 2007).

Regarding environmental adjustment, research findings point that workers in collectivistic cultures are more likely to define expatriates in terms of social group identities (e.g., expatriate's nationality) (Toh and Denisi, 2007). Local workers in collectivistic societies tend to focus on the ingroup and outgroup distinctions. In this situation, expatriates tend to have more difficulties socializing and becoming a member of the ingroup (Toh and Denisi, 2007). Similarly, if the expatriate comes from a collectivistic culture, then their nationality tends to be more salient, making the process of socialization harder on them. In both cases it is likely that expatriates will be considered as an outgroup member causing a negative effect on the expatriate's adjustment (Toh and Denisi, 2007). By being aware of these cultural differences, leaders can address these issues to help expatriates and host country nationals be more sensitive to each other's needs and preferences.

Research on expatriate job performance has also yielded useful insights. For instance, in a meta-analysis conducted by Mol *et al*. (2005), cultural sensitivity and local language ability emerged as important predictors of expatriate job performance along with personality factors. More exploratory predictors (due to the small number of studies) found in the meta-analysis included tasks and interpersonal leadership, cultural flexibility and tolerance for ambiguity.

Conclusions

Cross-cultural research on leadership has been ongoing for many years now, and given the internationalization of both organizations and management research, this area is likely to continue to grow. The popularity of such research outlets as the *Advances in Global Leadership* series edited by Bill Mobley attest to the widespread recognition of the topic's importance. Indeed, significant advances in our understandings of leadership and how it plays out in different cultural contexts have been achieved, as have increases in our understandings of how leadership styles and behaviors interact to lead toward – or away from – leader effectiveness.

However, we are not as sanguine as some of our colleagues about the progress being made in cross-cultural organizational research (see Gelfand *et al*., 2006), particularly in regards to leadership. The quest for "leadership universals" has been an important aspect of cross-cultural leadership research in the past decade, though it is not clear that these research efforts have proven particularly

useful. For example, we have already mentioned Bass's (1997) argument that transformational leadership is universal across cultures. However, in order to make that argument, he was compelled to define the idea of "universality" quite broadly, noting that in some cultures transformational leadership will be participatory and democratic, while in others it will be authoritarian and directive. In other words, the behaviors of the leaders will vary greatly across cultures, but if they still exhibit the classic "Four I's" of transformational leadership (inspirational motivation, idealized influence, intellectual stimulation, and individualized consideration; Bass and Avolio, 1990), then, regardless of the drastically different behaviors, transformational leadership will still be declared to be a universal phenomenon. This variation is made greater when Bass's concept of *variform functional* universality is applied, meaning that the behaviors that make up a construct will vary across cultures, and the magnitude of the relationship between two constructs will vary across cultures, but nonetheless, it will still be considered to be universal.

For us, this seems to be a case when the quest to find universality leads to such a high level of abstraction that the professed universality may become less valuable for actual leaders. Telling an expatriate manager from Finland that transformational leadership is universal, and so he or she should rely on it during his or her assignment to Bolivia is unlikely to be useful advice if the behaviors that comprise transformational leadership differ drastically between the home culture and the host culture, especially if it is still unclear exactly what such behaviors would be. Similarly, an overly strong focus on situational specificity and subtle differences in every specific context may lead to radically rejecting the idea that leading in one culture might at least in some regards be similar to leading in another culture. This may also be less fruitful when thinking about how to generate optimally useful practical advice for leaders.

It is not surprising that the majority of the empirical research on leadership, and on cross-cultural issues in leadership, comes from western societies, and (to be redundant) more individualistic societies (Dickson, Den Hartog, and Mitchelson, 2003). This is clearly to the detriment for our understanding of cultural issues as they affect the leadership process, and we are hopeful that increasing numbers of researchers in other parts of the world will turn their attentions to this topic. We are also hopeful that as researchers take up this call, they do not simply import extant conceptualizations of leadership and test them in their own cultural context, but instead will generate their own indigenous theories of leadership and its antecedents, consequences, moderators, mediators, and covariates. Leung (2007) has called for Asian social psychologists to enhance their efforts at developing theory locally and at studying indigenous concepts: we would expand that call beyond Asia, and beyond social psychologists, and would (in an admittedly selfish move) emphasize the importance of a focus on organizational leadership in this new research.

Tsui and her colleagues (2007) echo this concern and this call, when they recommend that culture-oriented researchers "Go Native – Toward Country-Specific Research" (p. 467). They note the prevalence of US-based researchers and US-originated models in much cross-cultural research, including leadership research. However, as Ofori-Dankwa and Ricks (2000) pointed out, researchers using a "difference-oriented lens" may tend to pose questions and find results consistent with the lens used. The risk of this orientation is that the researchers might not be asking "the right questions" (Ofori-Dankwa and Ricks, 2000, p. 173), that is, studying issues that may be of low relevance to other cultures. Valid cross-cultural studies must start with substantive knowledge of relevant phenomena in all the contexts (Cavusgil and Das, 1997) before making meaningful comparisons between them" (Tsui et al., 2007, p. 467).

Such an approach requires a change in our understanding of our goals. We believe that the "local research" approach advocated by Tsui and colleagues (2007) will allow for more indigenous explanations of leadership to emerge, and it is at that point that more significant advances in understanding leadership across cultures will emerge. When we are able to compare explanations for leadership phenomena that make sense in a given cultural context, we can then find commonalities and discrepancies between these locally generated *theories*, rather than applying a priori theory

to locally generated *data*. In this way, we believe, will culture's impact on leadership be more readily and accurately assessed.

Finally, we take to heart Tsui et al.'s (2007) reminder that culture (in the sense of shared values and beliefs) is not the only cause of differences between cultures (in the sense of nations), and their recommendation to incorporate national differences other than cultural values into our research examining national differences in leadership or other organizational behavior topics. They advocate moving toward a "polycontextual approach" (p. 464) that incorporates various aspects of national contexts (e.g., physical, historical, political, social) as predictors of the ways of knowing that are common within nations, with these as predictors of the meanings of work that are commonly shared by a nation's residents, with these as predictors of employment outcomes (e.g., attitudes and behavior at work). Like many researchers from a more psychologically oriented tradition, we find ourselves perhaps overly focused on cultural values and beliefs. Tsui et al. (among others) remind us that leader behavior is not a simple linear function of cultural values, but is affected by a wide range of issues that lead to leaders' approaches to processing information, reaching decisions, attempting to influence peers and subordinates, and ultimately to leaders attempting to lead.

The late Bernard Bass and colleagues (Bass et al., 1979) concluded over twenty-five years ago that, more often than not, national boundaries matter in determining the goals, risk-taking propensities, interpersonal competence (what might now be called "emotional intelligence"), emotional stability, and style of leadership preferred and enacted by managers and leaders. The succeeding years have not changed those conclusions – the conclusions have simply expanded and broadened, as have our recognitions of the complexity of assessing and measuring these issues, and of the risks of being overly confident in our conclusions. Culture is perhaps less frightening to leadership scholars and researchers today but, like most frightening things, it still deserves to be treated with respect and caution. We join with Smith and Hitt (2005, p. 30) in saying that cross-cultural research – including cross-cultural research on leadership – is "not for the faint-hearted." It is, however, of critical importance, and we applaud the researchers who have taken on the challenge, and look forward to reading about (and contributing to!) the next steps in our understandings of this topic.

References

Adsit, D. J., London., M., Crom, S. and Jones, D. 1997. "Cross-cultural differences in upward ratings in a multinational company", *International Journal of Human Resource Management* 8(4): 385–401.

Aycan, Z. and Kanungo, R. N. 1997. "Current issues and future challenges in expatriate management", in Z. Aycan (ed.), *New Approaches to Employee Management*, vol. 4. Greenwich, CT: JAI Press, pp. 245–60.

and Kanungo, R. N. 2001. "Cross-cultural industrial and organizational psychology: a critical appraisal of the field and future directions", in N. Anderson, D. S. A. Ones, H. K. Sinangil, and C. Viswesvaran (eds.), *Handbook of Industrial, Work and Organizational Psychology*, vol. 1. London: Sage, pp. 385–408.

Kanungo, R. N., Mendoca, M., Yu, K., Deller, J., Stahl., J., and Kurshid, A. 2000. "Impact of culture on human resource practices: The model of culture fit", *Applied Psychology: An International Review* 49(1): 192–220.

Bandura, A. 1977. *Social Learning Theory*. New York, NY: general Learning Press.

Bass, B. M. 1997. "Does the transactional – transformational leadership paradigm transcend organizational and national boundaries?", *American Psychologist* 52(2): 130–9.

and Avolio, B. J. 1990. *Multifactor Leadership Questionnaire*. Palo Alto, CA: Consulting Psychologist.

Burger, P. C., Doktor, R., and Barrett, G. V. 1979. *Assessment of Managers: An International Comparison*. New York, NY: Free Press.

and Stogdill, R. M. 1990. *Handbook of Leadership: Theory, Research and Managerial Applications*. New York, NY: Free Press.

Black, J. S. and Mendenhall, M. 1990. "Cross-cultural training effectiveness: a review and theoretical framework for future research", *Academy of Management Review* 16(2): 291–317.

Blake, R. R. and Mouton, J. S. 1964. *The Managerial Grid*. Houston, TX: Gulf.

Bu, N., Craig, T. J., and Peng, T. K. 2001. "Acceptance of supervisory direction in typical workplace situations: a comparison of US, Taiwanese and PRC employees", *International Journal of Cross Cultural Management* 1(2): 131–52.

Cavusgil, S. T., and Das, A. 1997. "Methodological issues in empirical cross-cultural research: a survey of the management literature and a framework", *Management International Review* 37: 71–96.

Chemers, M. M. 1997. *An Integrative Theory of Leadership*. Mahwah, NJ: Lawrence Erlbaum Associates.

Chinese Culture Connection. 1987. Chinese values and the search for culture-free dimensions of culture. *Journal of Cross-Cultural Psychology* 18, 143–174.

Den Hartog, D. N. 1997. "Inspirational leadership". Amsterdam: Free University of Amsterdam (unpublished doctoral dissertation).

2004. "Assertiveness", in R. J. House, P. J. Hanges, M. Javidan, P. W. Dorfman, and V. Gupta (eds.), *Leadership, Culture, and Organizations: The GLOBE Study of 62 Societies*. Thousand Oaks, CA: Sage.

and Dickson, M. W. 2004. "Leadership and Culture", in J. Antonakis, A. T. Cianciolo, and R. J. Sternberg (eds.), *The Nature of Leadership*. Thousand Oaks, CA: Sage.

House, R. J., Hanges, P. J., Ruiz-Quintanilla, S. A., Dorfman, P. W., and GLOBE Associates. 1999. "Culture specific and cross-culturally generalizable implicit leadership theories: Are attributes of charismatic/transformational leadership universally endorsed?", *The Leadership Quarterly* 10: 219–56.

Dickson, M. W. 2005. "Is *anything* true on both sides of the Pyrenees? Questions and conundrums in cross-cultural research", invited presentation to the Institute for International Integration Studies, Trinity College, Dublin, Ireland.

Den Hartog, D. N., and Mitchelson, J. K. 2003. "Research on leadership in a cross-cultural context: Making progress, and raising new questions", *The Leadership Quarterly* 14: 729–68.

Dorfman, P. W., 1994. "Methodological problems in cross-cultural leadership research", Paper presented at Symposium on International Research, Society for Industrial & Organizational Psychology.

Hanges, P. J., and Brodbeck, F. C. 2004. "Leadership prototypes and cultural variation: the identification of culturally endorsed implicit theories of leadership", in R. J. House, P. J. Hanges, M. Javidan, P. W. Dorfman, and V. Gupta (eds.), *Leadership, Culture, and Organizations: The GLOBE Study of 62 Societies*. Thousand Oaks, CA: Sage.

Howell, J. P., Hibino, S., Lee, J. K., Tate, U., and Bautista, A. 1997. "Leadership in Western and Asian countries: Commonalities and differences in effective leadership processes across cultures", *The Leadership Quarterly*, 8(3): 233–74.

Drenth, P. J. D. and Den Hartog, D. N. 1998. "Culture and organizational differences", in W. J. Lonner and D. L. Dinnel (eds.), *Merging Past, Present, and Future in Cross-cultural Psychology: Selected Papers from the Fourteenth International Congress of the International Association for Cross-cultural Psychology*. Bristol, PA: Swets and Zeitlinger Publishers, pp. 489–502.

Earley, P. C. 1989. "Social loafing and collectivism: a comparison of the United States and the People's Republic of China", *Administrative Science Quarterly* 34(4): 565–81.

and Gibson, C. B. 2002. *Multinational Work Teams: A New Perspective*. Mahwah, NJ: Lawrence Erlbaum.

Emrich, C., Denmark, F., and Den Hartog, D. N. 2004. "Cross-cultural differences in gender egalitarianism: implications for societies, organizations, and leaders", in R. J. House, P. J. Hanges, M. Javidan, P. W. Dorfman, and V. Gupta (eds.), *Leadership, Culture, and Organizations: The GLOBE Study of 62 Societies*, vol. 1. Thousand Oaks, CA: Sage.

Feather, N. T. 1994. "Attitudes towards high achievers and reactions to their fall: theory and research concerning tall poppies", in M. P. Zanna (ed.), *Advances in Social Psychology*, vol. 26. New York: Academic Press, pp. 1–73.

Fleishman, E. A. 1953. "The description of supervisory behavior", *Personnel Psychology* 37: 1–6.

Harris, E. F., and Burtt, H. E. 1955. *Leadership and Supervision in Industry*. Columbus, OH: Ohio State University Press.

Gelfand, M. J., Leslie, L. M., and Shteynberg, G. 2006. "Cross-cultural theory/methods", in

S. Rogelberg (ed.), *Encyclopedia of Industrial and Organizational Psychology*. Thousand Oaks, CA: Sage.

Graen, G. B., Hui, C., Wakabayashi, M., and Wang, Z.-M. 1997. "Cross-cultural research alliances in organizational research", in P. C. Earley, and M. Erez (eds.), *New Perspectives on International Industrial/organizational Psychology*. San Francisco, CA: Jossey-Bass, pp. 160–189.

Gupta, V., Hanges, P. J., and Dorfman, P. W. 2002. "Cultural clusters: methodology and findings", *Journal of World Business* 37(1): 11–15.

Hanges, P. J. and Dickson, M. W. 2006. "Agitation over aggregation: clarifying the development of and the nature of the GLOBE scales", *Leadership Quarterly* 17: 522–36.

Lord, R. G., and Dickson, M. W. 2000. "An information processing perspective on leadership and culture: a case for connectionist architecture", *Applied Psychology: An International Review* 49: 133–61.

Harrison, L. E. 2000. "Why culture matters", in L. E. Harrison and S. P. Huntington (eds.), *Culture Matters: How Values Shape Human Progress*. New York: Basic Books, pp. xvii–xxxiv.

Herzfeldt, R. H. 2007. *Intercultural Training for International Placements*. Unpublished doctoral dissertation, Aston University, UK.

Hofstede, G. 1980. *Culture's Consequences: International Differences in Work-related Values* (abridged edn). Newbury Park, CA: Sage.

1998. *Masculinity and Femininity: The Taboo Dimension of National Cultures*. Newbury Park, CA: Sage.

2000. "Culture's recent consequences: using dimension scores in theory and research", *International Journal of Cross Cultural Management* 1(1): 11–30.

2001. *Culture's Consequences: Comparing Values, Behaviors, Institutions, and Organizations Across Nations* (2nd edn). Newbury Park, CA: Sage.

Holtgraves, T. 1997. "Styles of language use: individual and cultural variability in conversational indirectness", *Journal of Personality and Social Psychology* 73: 624–637.

House, R. J., Hanges, P. J., Javidan, M., Dorfman, P. W., and Gupta, V. (eds.) 2004. *Leadership, Culture, and Organizations: The GLOBE Study of 62 Societies*. Thousand Oaks, CA: Sage.

Javidan, M., House, R. J., and Dorfman, P. W. 2004. "A nontechnical summary of GLOBE findings", in R. J. House, P. J. Hanges, M. Javidan,

P. W. Dorfman, and V. Gupta (eds.), *Leadership, Culture, and Organizations: The GLOBE Study of 62 Societies*. Thousand Oaks, CA: Sage.

Jung, D. I. and Avolio, B. J. 1999. "Effects of leadership style and followers' cultural orientation on performance in group and individual task conditions", *Academy of Management Journal* 42(2): 208–18.

Bass, B. M., and Sosik, J. J. 1995. "Bridging leadership and culture: a theoretical consideration of transformational leadership and collectivistic cultures", *Journal of Leadership Studies* 2: 3–18.

Keating, M. A. and Martin, G. S. (eds.) 2004. *Managing Cross-Cultural Business Relatives: The Irish-German Experience*. Dublin: Blackwell.

Kirkman, B. L. and Den Hartog, D. N. 2004. "Team Performance Management", in H. Lane, M. Maznevski, M. Mendenhall, and J. McNett, (eds.), *Blackwell Handbook of Global Management*. Oxford: Blackwell, pp. 251–72.

Lowe, K. B., and Gibson, C. B. 2006. "A quarter century of Culture's Consequences: a review of empirical research incorporating Hofstede's cultural values framework", *Journal of International Business Studies* 37(3): 285–320.

Kluckhohn, F. R., and Strodtbeck, F. L. 1961. *Variations in Value orientations*. Evanston, IL: Row, Peterson.

Landes, D. 2000. "Culture makes almost all the difference", in L. E. Harrison and S. P. Huntington (eds.), *Culture Matters: How Values Shape Human Progress*. New York: Basic Books, pp. 2–13.

Lesley, J. B. and Van Velsor, E. 1998. *A Cross-national Comparison of Effective Leadership and Teamwork: Toward a Global Workforce*. Greensboro, NC: Center for Creative Leadership.

Leung, K. 2007. "Asian social psychology: achievements, threats, and opportunities", *Asian Journal of Social Psychology* 10(1): 8–15.

Lord, R. G. and Maher, K. J. 1991. *Leadership and Information Processing*. London: Routledge.

Lonner, W. J. 1980. "The search for psychological universals", in H. C. Triandis and W. W. Lambert (eds.), *Perspectives Handbook of Cross-cultural Psychology*, vol. 1. Boston: Allyn and Bacon, pp. 143–204.

Matsumoto, D. 1994. *Cultural Influences on Research Methods and Statistics*. Pacific Grove, CA: Books.

McClelland, D. C. 1985. *Human Motivation*. Glenview, IL: Scott, Foresman.

McSweeney, B. 2002. "Hofstede's model of national cultural differences and their consequences: a triumph of faith – a failure of analysis", *Human Relations* 55(1): 89–118

Mead, M. 1939. *From the South Seas – Coming of Age in Samoa*. New York, NY: Morrow.

Mol, S. T., Born, M. Ph., Willemsen, M. E. and Van der Molen, H. T.2005. "Predicting expatriate job performance for selection purposes: a quantitative review", *Journal of Cross-Cultural Psychology* 36(5): 590–620.

Morris, M. W., Williams, K. Y., Leung, K., Larrick, R., Mendoza, M. T., Bhatnagar, D., *et al*. 1998. "Conflict management style: Accounting for cross-national differences", *Journal of International Business Studies* 29(4): 729–47.

Myers, A., Kakabadse, A., McMahon, T., and Spony, G. 1995. "Top management styles in Europe: implications for business and cross-national teams", *European Business Journal* 7(1): 17–27.

Offermann, L. R. and Hellman, P. S. 1997. "Culture's consequences for leadership behavior: National values in action", *Journal of Cross-Cultural Psychology* 28(3): 342–51.

Ofori-Dankwa, J. and Ricks, D. A. 2000. "Research emphases on cultural differences and/or similarities: are we asking the right questions?" *Journal of International Management*, 6: 172–86.

Pew Research Center. 2007. "Rising environmental concern", in *47-Nation Survey: Global unease with Major World Powers*. Washingdon, DC: Pew Research Center.

Quang, T., Swierczek, F. W., and Chi, D. T. K. 1998. "Effective leadership in joint ventures in Vietnam: a cross-cultural perspective", *Journal of Organizational Change Management* 11: 357–72.

Rauch A., Frese, M., Sonnentag, S. 2000. "Cultural differences in planning/success relationships: a comparison of small enterprises in Ireland, West Germany, and East Germany", *Journal of Small Business Management* 38(4): 28–41.

Ronen, S. and Shenkar, O. 1985. "Clustering countries on attitudinal dimensions: a review and synthesis", *Academy of Management Review* 10: 435–54.

Ross, A. 2007. "The Anti-maestro", *The New Yorker*, April 30, pp. 60–3.

Sagiv, L. and Schwartz, S. H. (2002). "Values priorities and subjective well-being: direct relations and congruity effects", *European Journal of Social Psychology*, 30: 177–98.

Samovar, L. A., and Porter, R. E. 2004. *Communication Between Cultures* (5th edn). Florence, KY: Wadsworth.

Schein, V. E. and Mueller, R. 1992. "Sex role stereotyping and requisite management characteristics: a cross cultural look", *Journal of Organizational Behavior* 13: 439–47.

Mueller, R., Lituchy, T., and Liu, J. 1996. "Think manager – think male: a global phenomenon?", *Journal of Organizational Behavior* 17: 33–41.

Schramm-Nielfen, I. 1989. *Relations de Travail Entre Danois et Francais dans les Enterprises Privées*. Copenhagen: Integrated Modern Languages and Economics centre.

Schwartz, S. H. 1992. "Universals in the content and structure of values: theoretical advances and empirical tests in 20 countries", *Advances in Experimental Social Psychology* 25: 1–65.

1999. "Cultural value differences: some implications for work", *Applied Psychology: An International Review* 48: 23–48.

Sczesny, S., Bosak, J., Neff, D., and Schyns, B. 2004. "Gender stereotypes and the attribution of leadership traits: a cross-cultural comparison", *Sex Roles* 51: 631–45.

Simons, M., Fuchs, D., Burns, J. F., and Sanger, D. E. 2004. "Spanish premier orders soldiers home from Iraq", *New York Times*, April 19, 2004.

Sinangil, H. K. and Ones, D. S. 2001. "Expatriate management", in N. Anderson, D. S. A. Ones, H. K. Sinangil, and C. Viswesvaran (eds.), *Handbook of Industrial, Work and Organizational Psychology*, vol. 1. London: Sage, pp. 425–43.

Sinha, J. B. 1984. "Towards partnership for a relevant research in the third world", *International Journal of Psychology* 19: 169–77

2003. "Trends towards indigenization of psychology in India", in Yang, K. S., Hwang, K. K., Pedersen, P. B., and Daibo, I. (eds.), *Progress in Asian Social Psychology: Conceptual and Empirical Contributions*. Westport CT, Greenwood.

2004. "Facets of societal and organizational cultures and managers' work related thoughts and feelings", *Psychology and Developing Societies* 16: 1–25.

Sinha, T. N., Verma, J., and Sinha, R. B. N. 2001. "Collectivism coexisting with individualism: An Indian scenario", *Asian Journal of Social Psychology* 4: 133–45.

Vohra, N., Singhal, S., Sinha, R. B. N., and Ushashree, S. 2002. "Normative predictions of collectivist-individualist intentions and behavior of Indians", *International Journal of Psychology* 37: 309–19.

Smith, P. B. and Bond, M. H. (eds.) 1993. *Social Psychology Across Cultures: Analysis and Respectives*. Hertfordshire Harvester: Wheatsheaf.

Dugan, S., and Trompenaars, F. 1996. "National culture and the values of organizational employees: a dimensional analysis across 43 nations", *Journal of Cross-Cultural Psychology* 27(2): 231–64.

Smith, K. G. and Hitt, M. A. 2005. *Great Minds in Management: The Process of Theory Development*. Oxford: Oxford University Press

Sivakumar, K. and Nakata, C. 2001. "The stampede toward Hofstede's framework: avoiding the sample design pit in cross-cultural research", *Journal of International Business Studies* 32: 555–74.

Stewart, R., Barsoux, J. L., Kieser, A., Ganter, H. D., and Walgenbach, P. 1994. *Managing in Britain and Germany*. London: St Martin's Press/ MacMillan Press.

Stroh, L. K., Black, J. S., Mendenhall, M. E., and Gregersen, H. B. 2005. *International Assignments: Integration of Strategy, Research, and Practice*. Mahwah, NJ: Lawrence Erlbaum.

Toh, S. M. and DeNisi, A. S. 2007. "Host nationals as socializing agents: a social indentity approach", *Journal of Organizational Behaviour* 25: 281–301.

Triandis, H. C. 1994. "Theoretical and methodological approaches to the study of collectivism and individualism", in U. Kim, H. C. Triandis, C. Kagitcibasi, S. C. Choi, and G. Yoon (eds.), *Individualism and Collectivism: Theory, Method, and Applications*. Thousand Oaks, CA: Sage, pp. 41–51.

1995. *Individualism and Collectivism*. San Fransisco, CA: Westview Press.

Trompenaars, F. 1993. *Riding the Waves of Culture: Understanding Cultural Diversity in Business*. London: Economist Books.

Tsui, A. S., Nifadkar, S. S., and Ou, A. Y. 2007. "Cross-national cross-cultural organizational bahaviour research: advances, gaps, and recommendations", *Journal of Management* 33(3): 462–78.

Wells, M. 2007. "Could Christian vote desert Republicans?" Online article dated 27 July 2007, accessed December 12, 2007 from http://news.bbc.co.uk/2/hi/americas/6917947.stm.

Williams, J. E. and Best, D. L. 1990. *Measuring Sex Stereotypes: A Multination Study*. Newbury Park, CA: Sage.

Xin, K. R. and Tsui, A. S. 1996. "Different strokes for different folks? Influence tactics by Asian-American and Caucasian American managers," *The Leadership Quarterly* 7: 109–32.

CHAPTER 10

Global leadership: progress and challenges

JOYCE S. OSLAND, SULLY TAYLOR, and
MARK E. MENDENHALL

The extensive cultural variations described in this book make a strong argument for global leaders who possess cultural awareness, intercultural competence, and global knowledge relating to culture. Culture, however, is not the only contextual determinant that forms the Petri dish that creates global leadership (GL). The organizing principle for this chapter is the linkage among various components of the global context, the resulting GL sensemaking and competencies, and their development. Based on this framework, we review the limited empirical literature on global leadership and its development and identify the pathways for future research.

Global leadership has achieved a salient position in the international management literature during the past decade. The need to understand the nature of global leaders has emerged with the increasing internationalization and globalization of firms in which the dependence on vendors, employees, outsourced work, and customers from other countries is now seen as critical. Gunnar Hedlund (1986, p. 18) envisaged the current reality of global business in the mid-1980s:

> A radical view concerning globality is that we are witnessing the disappearance of the international dimension of business. For commercial and practical purposes, nations do not exist and the relevant business arena becomes something like a big unified "home market."

Similarly, global leaders deal with employees and stakeholders from a range of cultures and seldom have the luxury of understanding each culture in depth. Therefore, we suggest that they are forced to develop meta-level cultural skills, which we will discuss later, that go beyond those required of most domestic or expatriate leaders. Furthermore, the need for increased flexibility and responsiveness

has led to more "networked" firms, in which individuals far down from the top echelon are deeply immersed in global leadership activities such as leading global product or project teams or negotiating important agreements with foreign suppliers. Thus, the scope, importance, and extent of global leadership are growing in most multinational firms (MNCs), and developing global leaders is a high priority (Gregersen, Morrison and Black, 1998; Mendenhall et al., 2003; Suutari, 2002). Stroh and Caliguiri (1998) suggest that there seems to be a positive relationship between MNC financial success and their ability to successfully develop GL competencies.

Unfortunately, research indicates that businesses have an inadequate number of global leaders (Gregersen, Morrison and Black, 1998; Charan, Drotter, and Noel, 2001), and a future global leadership gap is predicted in for-profit, public, and non-profit sectors (Bikson et al., 2003). In a study by Mercer Delta (2006) that surveyed 223 senior executives from large firms in seventeen industries in forty-four countries, a majority of executives reported leadership shortages to deal with future global business risks that threaten corporate performance.

Management scholars have responded by producing both empirical and non-empirical work on the topic of global leadership. Most of this literature has taken a content approach ("what is it?"); to a lesser degree, scholars have focused on how to develop global leaders ("how do you get it?"). While these efforts have produced some solid lessons, as we will see in reviewing the literature, more foundational research is needed.

The chapter discusses the progress, challenges, and gaps in these areas: the global leadership construct, the global context, the sensemaking and competencies required of global leaders, development strategies and challenges, and implications for future research.

The global leadership construct

In spite of the increasing attention devoted to global leadership, one of its salient features is the lack of a clear construct definition. One reason for this ambiguity is the evolutionary nature of a nascent field. Early definitions of global leadership borrowed and extrapolated traditional, domestic leadership definitions (Yeung and Ready, 1995), but scholars quickly recognized that global leadership was far more complex than domestic leadership due to the pressures and dynamics of global competition (Weber et al., 1998) that broadened the scope of the leader's work. Adler clarified the issue when she wrote:

> Global leaders, unlike domestic leaders, address people worldwide. Global leadership theory, unlike its domestic counterpart, is concerned with the interaction of people and ideas among cultures, rather than with either the efficacy of particular leadership styles within the leader's home country or with the comparison of leadership approaches among leaders from various countries – each of whose domain is limited to issues and people within their own cultural environment. A fundamental distinction is that global leadership is neither domestic nor multidomestic (Adler, 2001, p. 77).

Thus, global leadership is also defined by what it is *not*; while their literatures contribute to our understanding of this phenomenon, GL is not the study of expatriate leaders, global managers, cross-cultural leadership, or comparative leadership. The most extensive, recent example of cross-cultural and comparative leadership is Project GLOBE (see Chapter 12), which identified indigenous leadership profiles for sixty-two countries. Global leaders deal with followers whose mental map of the "ideal leader" reflects these indigenous styles. Therefore, theirs is a meta-level form of leadership that has to understand and adapt to cultural expectations and practices and find a style that is more universally acceptable. When GLOBE researchers opined on global leadership, based on their findings about

cultural differences and diverse leadership styles, they hypothesized that global leaders require a global mindset, tolerance of ambiguity, and cultural adaptability and flexibility (Javidan et al., 2006).

Scholars quickly sought to explain the distinctive characteristics of GL. For the most part, they seem to agree that GL differs from domestic leadership in the complexity of their context and the issues they confront (Lane et al., 2004). Global leaders face a range of ever-changing environments that span geographies, cultures and socio-political systems (Rosen et al., 2000) and must successfully manage the intricate interdependencies among them so the firm can accomplish its goals. Based on the GL literature and the global context, Osland and Bird (2006, p. 123) concluded that global leadership: "differs from domestic leadership in degree in terms of issues related to connectedness, boundary spanning, complexity, ethical challenges, dealing with tensions and paradoxes, pattern recognition, and building learning environments, team, and community and leading large-scale change efforts – across diverse cultures." We will discuss the context of global leadership in more detail later on.

In brief, a global leader keeps people across a global organization on track and motivated toward achieving shared objectives. Drawing on Adler (2001) and Festing (2001), a succinct definition of global leadership is "a process of influencing the thinking, attitudes, and behaviors of a global community to work together synergistically toward a common vision and common goals" (Osland and Bird, 2006, p. 123). An expanded definition of global leaders, crafted by Allan Bird, captures Kotter's (1990) distinction between managers and leaders and provides more description:

> Global leaders are individuals who effect significant positive change in organizations by building communities through the development of trust and the arrangement of organizational structures and processes in a context involving multiple stakeholders, multiple sources of external authority, and multiple cultures under conditions of temporal, geographical and cultural complexity. (Osland et al., 2007, p. 2)

The second definition makes the assumption that not all global managers are global leaders. A third definition portrays global leadership as an organizational capacity to draw out the necessary GL expertise and influence when and where it is needed. This definition assumes that global leadership does not reside within just one individual but can be distributed and shared. In sum, global leadership is a process exerted by both individuals and organizations.

No treatise on the nature and definition of global leadership can escape without addressing this question: How does global leadership differ from leadership in general? Is it a different animal or simply a new subfield? We see GL as both a different animal and a subfield for these reasons.

1. In some ways, global leadership (GL) appears to be qualitatively different from "domestic" leadership. This position is supported by examples of research in related fields that documented differences between domestic and global/international work. A direct comparison of domestic and expatriate work found that expatriates reported significantly higher demands for social and perceptual skills, reasoning ability, and adjustment- and achievement-orientation personality requirements in their work (Shin, Morgeson and Campion, 2007). Critical incident interviews with fifty-five CEOs from various countries and industries yielded three universal competencies shared by global and domestic managers: sharpening the focus, building commitment, and driving for success (McBer, 1995). Competencies that varied by culture were: business relationships, the role of action, and the style of authority (McBer, 1995). Furthermore, Dalton and her colleagues found significant differences in the role performance of domestic and global managers (Dalton *et al.*, 2002). While extrapolation from research of this nature is sufficient to hypothesize a qualitative difference between domestic and global leaders, scholars have yet to directly compare and contrast the demands and competencies of domestic and global leadership.

2. Early GL findings indicate both shared similarities and differences of degree and kind with domestic leadership; the differences are due to contextual factors (Mendenhall, 2008). To name

just a few examples, vision, the ability to lead change, integrity, trust, and communication are essential leadership components, regardless of context. However, global leaders have to realize that trust takes different forms in different cultures and that intercultural communication entails expanded skills and more mindful attention. Thus, cultural variations require that leaders be more adaptive and expand their skill set.

3. The context in which global leaders work seem to demand additional skills that receive little or no mention in traditional leadership theory. Boundary spanning, for example, is not mentioned in Yukl's (2006) well-respected text on leadership. There are certainly numerous references to relations-oriented behaviors, but a list of these behaviors (Yukl, 2002, p. 66) does not capture the role boundary spanning plays in a global context, in particular with respect to joining and serving as a conduit for knowledge flows and social capital (Beechler, Søndergaard, Miller and Bird, 2004). Boundary spanning is an essential skill for global leaders given the multiplicities and interdependencies in their environment. In addition, interviews with expert global leaders revealed a pronounced reliance on social acuity (similar to the perceptual and social skills found in expatriates mentioned previously); in ambiguous situations where they do not completely understand multiple perspectives and cultural cues, global leaders learn to read people very closely and seek help from others when they themselves cannot decode what is occurring (Osland *et al.*, 2007). While effective domestic leaders no doubt also read people, they can assume greater accuracy when interpreting the cues they observe due to greater cultural homogeneity. Therefore, we argue that social acuity is a more conscious, salient skill for global leaders.

4. In addition to leadership theory, GL has multi-disciplinary intellectual roots in intercultural communication and competence, expatriation, global management, and comparative leadership (Osland, 2008a). Thus, the literature and theory GL draws upon is more extensive.

5. While the research on global leadership development (GLD) is limited, the development path

is not exactly the same for global and domestic leaders. While domestic and global executives learn the same way, the most important lessons for global leaders come from cultural experiences, which are more complex and do not always result in the same lessons (McCall and Hollenbeck, 2002). Furthermore, significant others play a greater role in GLD than with domestic executives (McCall and Hollenbeck, 2002). GLD relies on transformational experiences, such as expatriate assignments, extensive practice and challenging cross-cultural exposure. An expatriate experience is generally agreed to be the most effective way to develop global leadership (cf. Mendenhall, 2001), but not every assignment is equally challenging or leveraged for learning. In comparison with the development of domestic leaders, Mendenhall argues that GLD is less linear. This will be discussed in greater detail later on.

In sum, global leadership and development is both similar and different in degree and kind from domestic leadership and its development. The global context differentiates global leaders and irrevocably changes the way they think and behave. Assuming that global leadership is nothing more than "leadership plus culture" may prevent scholars and practitioners from fully understanding this phenomenon and developing new leadership theory. We hope that scholars will not follow the example of some corporate GL development programs that simply add a module on intercultural communication to their domestic leadership program and assume this is sufficient. Because scholars have seldom studied leaders in such an extreme context, there is a strong possibility that both our theory and developmental strategies will call for a new paradigm.

The global context

So far we have argued that the spread of globalization, and the resulting global context in which business takes place, has expanded the nature of leadership in global jobs. In this section we want to focus on the global context itself: "The term 'global' encompasses more than simple *geographic reach* in terms of business operations. It also includes the notion of *cultural reach* in terms of people and *intellectual reach* in the development of a global mindset" (Osland, Bird, Mendenhall and Osland, 2006, p. 197) and global skills. The crucible that shapes and challenges global leaders is the global context. Lane and his colleagues characterize the context of globalization in terms of flux and complexity, which is composed of three conditions: multiplicity, interdependence, and ambiguity (Lane, Maznevski, and Mendenhall, 2004):

- *Complexity* in terms of the number of factors, trends, challenges, and relationships to take into consideration and track.
- *Multiplicity* across a range of dimensions, such as more and different ways of doing business and organizing, more and different competitors, customers, governments, stakeholders, and contexts that add up to "many voices, viewpoints, and constraints" (Lane *et al.*, 2004, p. 9)
- *Interdependence* within and without the organization, along the value chain, in alliances, and among a host of stakeholders, sociocultural, political, economic and environmental systems.
- *Ambiguity* in terms of lack of information clarity, failure to understand cause and effect, equivocality, and difficulty in interpreting cues and signals, identifying appropriate actions and pursuing plausible goals.
- *Flux* in terms of quickly transitioning systems, shifting values and emergent patterns of organizational structure and behavior.

These characteristics appear in table 10.1, along with the addition of a fifth characteristic – cultural variations:

- *Cultural variations* in patterns of values, habits, expectations, language, and perspectives.

It could be useful to determine how to measure these contextual factors and test whether varying levels have a differential impact on characteristics of GL and GLD.

Table 10.1 The global context and global leadership sense-making and competencies

Global Context	Sensemaking	Global Leadership Competencies
Complexity	Meta-level sensemaking (higher-order) • Requisite variety in mental models • Understanding of paradox • Influencing and changing mental models (defragging) • Creating the correct shared vision	Global mindset • Cosmopolitanism • Cognitive complexity Inquisitiveness Influence stakeholders
• Multiplicity	Inclusive sensemaking • Determining whom to include • Perspective-taking • Determining which perspectives to heed • Collaborative decision-making	Span boundaries Cognitive complexity Influence stakeholders Multicultural teaming
• Interdependence	Systemic sensemaking • Engaging in stakeholder dialogue • Coordinating multiple sensemaking • Collaborative decision-making	Cognitive complexity Critical thinking Global knowledge Span boundaries Multicultural teaming Build trust Build community
• Ambiguity	Confident sensemaking • Seeking clarity from trusted network members • Narrowing the sensemaking "focus" • Gauging when enough is known to make decisions • Collaborative decision-making	Humility Inquisitiveness Integrity Resilience Build trust Make ethical decisions Influence stakeholders
Flux	Quick sensemaking • Refocusing the vision based on what's important • Innovative responses • Realignment • Rapid decision-making	Architecting Build trust Build community Lead change Resilience
Cultural Variations	Intercultural sensemaking • Decoding culture • Bridging cultural differences • Decisions that leverage culture	Mindful communication Build trust Multicultural teaming Intercultural competence Global mindset Humility Inquisitiveness Global knowledge Cosmopolitanism Cognitive complexity

Two process models of global leadership

To date, there are very few process models that describe how global leaders interact with the environment. Borrowing from the global management literature, Lane and his colleagues (Lane, Maznevski, and Mendenhall, 2004) contend that four interrelated processes are critical for managing global complexity:

• Collaborating – "the establishment of relationships characterized by community, flexibility, respect, trust, and mutual accountability" (Lane, Maznevski, and Mendenhall, 2004, p. 20).

- Discovering – "a set of transformation processes that lead to new ways of seeing and acting" (Lane, Maznevski, and Mendenhall, 2004, p. 20), dealing with learning and creating.
- Architecting – the "mindful design of processes that align, balance, and synchronize the different parts of the organization that provides a platform for coordinated response" (Lane, Maznevski, and Mendenhall, 2004, p. 20).
- Systems thinking – "the ability to see the interrelationships among components and levels in a complex system and to anticipate the consequences of changes in and to the system" (Lane, Maznevski, and Mendenhall, 2004, p. 21).

Two process models, the effectiveness cycle and sensemaking, are described below.

The effectiveness cycle

The effectiveness cycle (Bird and Osland, 2004, pp. 59–61), which describes what effective global managers do at the most basic level, consists of three stages:

Stage 1: *Perceive, analyze, and diagnose to decode the situation* – This involves matching characteristics of the current situation to past experiences, scanning for relevant cues or their absence, framing the situation in terms of experience and expectation, and setting plausible goals for the outcome.
Stage 2: *Accurately identify effective managerial action* – Given the situation and the desired outcome, which nuanced actions would be the most effective? This judgment relies on global knowledge, experience, contingency factors, and the ability to imagine and predict the results of various responses.
Stage 3: *Possess the behavioral repertoire and flexibility to act appropriately given the situation* – In this stage, the emphasis moves from cognition to behavior.

Thus, effectiveness is predicated on both cognitive and behavioral knowledge and skills developed over time.

Osland and Bird (2006) built on this model to concentrate on global leaders as experts who developed the specific form of expertise required by the global context. Grounding their work in the expert cognition literature, they wanted to develop an alternative to the countervailing competency approach to understanding GL. They were inspired by Klein's (1998; 2004) recognition-primed decision-making model, which describes how experts make decisions in extreme naturalistic settings. His simplified model begins with a "situation that generates cues that let you recognize patterns that activate action scripts which you assess by mental simulations using your mental models" (Klein, 2004, p. 26).

Osland and her colleagues' research on expert cognition in global leaders described their problem-solving and decision-making processes and methods for dealing with extreme uncertainty in challenging global leadership incidents (Osland *et al.*, 2007). Their findings indicate that the separation between the cognitive and behavioral aspects of the effectiveness cycle is not present in this sample. The global leaders use behavioral skills throughout the cycle as they bring together teams to help them diagnose situations and actively seek information from others in stage one. Similarly, they do not always know which actions are most effective in stage two, if they work with unfamiliar cultures or in novel situations in which no one has experience. Therefore, they sometimes request advice from others about appropriate actions. They seem much less needful of advice or help when it comes to executing their action scripts in stage three. Thus, throughout the cycle, global leaders are using cognitive and behavior skills and knowledge simultaneously or iteratively.

Beechler and Javidan (2007) also used the effectiveness cycle (Bird and Osland, 2004) to describe a global leader's response to the environment in their proposed model of global mindset and global leadership. Global mindset is the centerpiece of this model. Individuals who have a global mindset possess: (1) global intellectual capital (knowledge of the global industry, knowledge of global value networks, knowledge of the global organization, cognitive complexity, and cultural acumen); (2) psychological capital (positive psychological profile, cosmopolitanism, and passion for cross-cultural and cross-national encounters); and (3) social capital (structural, relational, and cognitive social capital). The outcome of global mindset and the behavioral repertoire reflected in the effectiveness cycle is the ability to influence people from different socio-cultural systems, which they link to successful global corporations. Their descriptions of the components of global mindset include many of the behavioral GL competencies identified in research. Questions regarding the breadth of the global mindset definition remain unanswered; this model also raises the cognitive-behavioral dichotomy.

Sensemaking

Yet another way to describe how global leaders interact with the environment is sensemaking (Osland et al., 2008). Sensemaking involves placing stimuli into a framework that enables people "to comprehend, understand, explain, attribute, extrapolate, and predict" (Starbuck and Milliken, 1988, p. 51). Within complex situations people "chop moments out of continuous flows and extract cues from those moments" (Weick, 1995, p. 43). When a cue is extracted from the general flow of stimuli, it is "embellished" and linked to a more general idea, most commonly to a similar cue from one's past (Weick, 1995). With respect to problem detection, Klein and his colleagues stated that "the knowledge and expectancies a person has will determine what counts as a cue and whether it will be noticed" (Klein et al., 2005: 17). In their data/frame model of sensemaking, they argue:

> that data are used to construct a frame (a story or script or schema) that accounts for the data and guides the search for additional data. At the same time, the frame a person is using to understand events will determine what counts as data. Both activities occur in parallel, the data generating the frame, and the frame defining what counts as data. (Klein et al., 2005, p. 20)

We agree with the Osland et al. (2008) working paper (which describes sensemaking in greater depth) that the various aspects of the global context lead to slightly different variations in sensemaking, as shown in table 10.1. Complexity leads to *meta-level sensemaking* and involves mental models that match the requisite variety in the environmental context, understanding paradox, giving up obsolete mental models and encouraging others to do the same, and creating an appropriate shared

vision. Multiplicity leads to *inclusive sensemaking* that incorporates the views and voices of the appropriate stakeholders. Perspective taking and figuring out which perspectives can be trusted or hold the most importance eventually lead to collaborative decision making. Interdependence leads to *systemic sensemaking*. This entails stakeholder dialogue to ensure that the interdependencies are well understood; it also involves understanding and coordinating the ways in which various entities make sense of their own context and engaging in collaborative decision-making. Ambiguity leads to *confident sensemaking* in the face of uncertainty. Global leaders seek clarity from people in their networks whom they trust. The sensemaking "focus" is gradually narrowed, and a determination has to be made regarding when enough information is known to serve as the basis for collaborative decisions. Flux requires *quick sensemaking*, which involves refocusing the vision based on what is important and coming up with innovative responses. It also means realigning the organization quickly and making rapid decisions.

Intercultural sensemaking is a result of cultural variations. It can be triggered when people are surprised by novel cultural variations, when they observe unexpected cultural behavior, or when they make a deliberate attempt to learn more about another culture (Osland, Bird, and Gundersen, 2007). Cultural trigger events, which are perceived differentially by individuals, can lead to intercultural sensemaking once they pass a certain threshold. Intercultural sensemaking is an ongoing process involving an iterative cycle of events: framing the situation, making attributions, and selecting scripts, which are undergirded by constellations of cultural values and cultural history (Osland and Bird, 2000). It is predicated on the assumption that culture is contextually based and paradoxical in nature (Kluckholm and Strodtbeck, 1961; Osland and Bird, 2002; Fang, 2006; Gannon, 2007). Intercultural sensemaking can lead to several outcomes: schema development, automaticity, cue identification, pattern recognition, increased mindfulness, emotional earmarks, and ascending restabilization at a higher level of cultural understanding (Osland, Bird and Gundersen, 2007).

None of the GL process models has been tested to date, and more research attention is needed in this area so the field is not limited to a competency approach.

Global leadership research – progress and challenges

This section presents what is known about global leadership to date and the gaps in our knowledge that should be addressed by future research. There are five published reviews of the GL literature (Hollenbeck, 2001; Suutari, 2002; Jokinen, 2005; Osland, Bird, Mendenhall and Osland, 2006; Osland, 2008b). A chronology of all the empirical research on global leadership and development we could locate is found in table 10.2.

Global mindset

A key component in any discussion of global leadership is the concept of global mindset, which is widely accepted as a foundational aspect of global leadership. No manager can become a global leader unless she develops a global mindset, but that is not the only requirement. As Kedia and Mukherji (1999) contend, global mindset is a necessary but not sufficient condition for global leadership. Over the past decade, definitions and descriptions of global mindset have proliferated; while the empirical testing of proffered models has grown, empirical research is still limited. We will briefly review the major characteristics of the literature in this area and identify the issues that still need to be addressed by theoretical and empirical research. For a recent and in-depth review of the global mindset literature, the reader is referred to Levy et al. (2007). We should note that Bouquet (2005) and others posited the amount of global mindset that is needed by a global leader may vary somewhat depending on its internationalization pressures. While "born global" firms are more likely to be led by leaders with global mindset (Harveston, Kedia, and Davis, 2000), Bouquet (2005) found that excessive attention to global issues by some leaders, which some might describe as too much global mindset, led to negative effects on firm performance. In general,

however, our stance is that a well-developed global mindset in fact enables global leaders to deploy it as appropriate and necessary, and that there is no such thing as "too much" global mindset.

The first major characteristic in this literature is the multilevel nature of global mindset, which has been discussed at the organizational, group and individual level. The writings of Perlmutter (1969), one of the earliest international management scholars to pinpoint this as an important element in global competitiveness, encompass both the organizational and individual level. His work focuses on the mindset of the top management of international organizations with regard to their operations abroad. Perlmutter (1969) and Perlmutter and Heenan (1979) distinguish between three main types of companies with international operations: those who are ethnocentric and see the rest of the world through the eyes of their home operations; those who are polycentric and viewed the world as a conglomeration of distinct, separate independent geographies with nothing in common; and those who are geocentric, who see the similarities as well as the differences among markets and peoples and strive to integrate and leverage where it makes sense. This last type has many of the elements of what has come to be seen as global mindset. Perlmutter's (1969) characterizations of the mindset of top management were later used to describe the international staffing patterns found in many global firms (c.f., Pucik, 1994). Others who have discussed global mindset from the organizational or group point of view include Bartlett and Ghoshal (1989; 1990), Jeannet (2000), Govindarajan and Gupta (2001), Levy (2005), Bouquet (2005) and Begley and Boyd (2003).

Because this chapter also emphasizes the development of individual global leaders, we will review more closely the literature that has discussed global mindset at this level. Two overarching foci can be distinguished in this research: a focus on the cognitive component of global mindset and another on the behavioral/attitudinal aspects. The cognitive component has received the lion's share of attention, both scholarly and empirical, in the last few years. Drawing on the original work by Perlmutter (1969) and Perlmutter and Heenan (1979), whose descriptions of the different ways top management

Table 10.2 A chronological list of empirical research on global leadership and global leadership development

Authors	Description	Method	Global Leadership Findings	Global Leadership Development Findings
Wills and Barham (1994)	Identifies success factors in international managers	Interviews with 60 senior international executives from companies in different countries and industries.	Relatively unchangeable intertwined core of cognitive complexity, emotional energy and psychological maturity might be more important than specific competencies or skills. Subthemes include: cultural empathy, active listening, humility, emotional self-awareness and resilience, risk acceptance, family emotional support, curiosity to learn, live in here and now, and personal morality.	Utilize holistic assessment procedures and systems. Consider the work/family balance.
Yeung and Ready (1995)	Identifies leadership capabilities in a cross-national study	Surveys of 1,200 managers from 10 major global corporations and 8 countries	Capabilities: articulate vision, values, and strategy; catalyst for strategic and cultural change; empower others; results and customer orientation.	
Adler (1997)	Describes women global leaders in politics and business	Archival data and interviews with women global leaders from 60 countries	Their number is increasing and they come from diverse backgrounds; are *not* selected by women-friendly countries or companies; use broad-based power rather than hierarchical power; are lateral transfers; symbolize change and unity; and leverage their increased visibility.	
Graen and Hui (1999)	Outlines challenges and success factors of global leaders and discusses their development.	Longitudinal study of Japanese global leaders	Career progress predicted by three behaviors occurring in first 3 years of career: (1) building effective working relationships characterized by trust, respect, and obligation with immediate supervisors; (2) networking derived from contacts at prestigious universities; (3) doing more than was expected in the face of difficult and ambiguous performance expectations.	Integrative approach to traditional global leadership development systems includes: cross-cultural leadership skills; transcultural competence development; third-culture-building capability; and cross-cultural creative problem-solving efficacy.
Black, Morrison, and Gregersen (1999)	Identifies capabilities of effective global leaders and how to develop them.	Interviews of 90 senior line and HR executives in 50 companies in Europe, North America and Asia and 40 nominated global leaders.	Capabilities: Inquisitive, character, duality, savvy.	Development occurs via training, transfer, travel, and multicultural teams.
Kets de Vries and Forent-Treacy (1999)	Describes excellent global leadership.	Case studies involving interviews with 3 global leaders (CEOs).	Described the background, development and characteristics of excellent global leaders. Identified best practices in leadership, structure, strategy, corporate culture.	

Table 10.2 (cont.)

Authors	Description	Method	Global Leadership Findings	Global Leadership Development Findings
Rosen, Digh, Singer, and Philips, (2000)	Identifies leadership universals.	Interviews with 75 CEOs from 28 countries; 1,058 surveys with CEOs, presidents, managing directors or chairmen; studies of national culture.	Leadership universals: personal, social, business, and cultural literacies, many of which are paradoxical in nature.	Leadership skills attributed to work experience, natural ability, role models, formal training, age and religion.
McCall and Hollenbeck (2002)	To identify how to select and develop global executives and understand how they derail.	Interviews with 101 executives nominated as successful global executives from 36 countries and 16 global firms.	Competencies: open-minded and flexible; culture interest and sensitivity; able to deal with complexity; resilient, resourceful, optimistic, energetic; honesty and integrity; stable personal life; value-added technical or business skills.	Strategy drives development. Learning about culture and adaptability is more difficult than business lessons. While they learn like domestic execs, cultural experiences are more complex and may have different lessons and significant. Others play a greater role. GLD is not an exact science. Global leaders and global jobs are not all alike. Global careers are hazardous. GLD is difficult but not impossible, and they take more responsibility for their own development.
Goldsmith, Greenberg, Robertson, and Hu-Chan (2003)	To identify global leadership dimensions needed in the future.	Thought leader panels; focus groups with 28 CEOs, focus/dialogue groups with at least 207 current or future leaders; interviews with 202 high potential next generation leaders; 73 surveys from forum group members.	Fifteen dimensions: integrity, personal mastery, constructive dialogue, shared vision, empowerment, developing people, building partnerships, sharing leadership, thinking globally, appreciating diversity, technologically savvy, customer satisfaction, anticipating opportunities, leading change, and maintaining competitive advantage.	
Bikson, Treverton, Moini, and Lindstrom (2003)	Examines impact of globalization on HR needs, global leadership competencies, and policies and practices needed to produce sufficient global leaders.	Structured interviews with 135 US HR and senior managers in public, for-profit, and non-profit sectors. Unstructured interviews with 24 experts on development policies and practices.	Insufficient number of future global leader who have the required integrated skill repertoire: substantive depth in organization's primary business; managerial ability (especially teamwork and interpersonal skills); strategic international understanding; and cross-cultural experience.	Recommendations include: encourage the development of portfolio careers and develop personnel policies to support them; internationalize university curricula; implement sector-specific near- and long-term programs to develop global leaders.

Kets de Vries, and Florent-Treacy (2002)	Describes how global leaders develop and succeed.	Field data from consultations and corporate action research projects in addition to over 500 interviews with senior executives who participated in INSEAD seminars.	Successful global leaders understand basic motivational need systems and stimulate the collective imagination of employees.	The basic foundation of GLD is: (1) family background including culturally diverse parents, early international experience, bilingualism; (2) early education in international schools, summer camps and international travel; (3) later education involving exchange programs, foreign language and international MBA programs; (4) spouses and children who are supportive, adventurous, adaptable and mobile.
Kets de Vries, Vrignaud, and Florent-Treacy (2004)	Describes the development of a 360-degree feedback instrument, GlobeInvent.	Based on semi-structured interviews with a number of senior executives.	Twelve dimensions – a psychodynamic properties: envisioning, empowering, energizing, designing, rewarding, team-building, outside orientation, global mindset, tenacity, emotional intelligence, life balance, resilience to stress.	
Caliguiri (2006)	Discusses developmental opportunities that should produce effective global leaders.	Job analysis of the global leadership task with focus groups and surveys of leaders from European and North American firms, complemented by a literature review of developmental methods for international jobs.	Offering the right people the right developmental opportunities will produce leaders who can effectly perform GL tasks and activities.	

Source: Adapted and updated from J. Osland, A. Bird, M. Mendenhall, and A. Osland (2006) "Developing Global leadership Capabilities and Global Mindset: A Review", in G. Stahl and I. Björkman (eds.). *Handbook of Research in International Human Resource Management.* Cheltenham: Edward Elgar, pp. 205–6; and J. Osland (2008) "An Overview of the Global Leadership Research", in M. Mendenhall, J. S. Osland, A., Bird, G., Oddou, and M. Maznevski, *Global Leadership: Theory and Practice.* London: Routledge, p. 41.

teams *think* about the global arena, scholars taking the cognitive approach to global mindset have searched for a theoretically sound and parsimonious way to define the construct. This approach is best represented by the works of Murtha, Lenway and Bagozzi (1998), Gupta and Govindajaran (2002), Harveston, Kedia and Davis (2000), Nummela, Saarenketo and Puumalainen (2004), Arora *et al.* (2004), Levy *et al.* (2007), Osland and Bird (2006), and Osland *et al.* (2007). All the approaches are based on the premise that the cognitive abilities of leaders of global firms are stretched further than domestic leaders by the heterogeneity and complexity of the international arena. Successfully responding to the demands of the local and the global environments, the need to both integrate and differentiate, and the requirement to pay attention to multiple constituencies and issues across the world is made possible by the greater cognitive complexity in the global leader. Murtha, Lenway, and Bagozzi (1998), Harveston, Kedia, and Davis (2000), and Nummela, Saarenketo, and Puumalainen (2004) focus on the strategic issues that confront global leaders and how these drive a requirement for managers to perceive and understand a cognitively complex array of information, issues, opportunities and threats. Murtha, Lenway, and Bagozzi (1998), for example, studied the cognitive shift that occurred in a group of 305 managers in a MNC as it evolved towards greater global engagement and a more global strategy over time. Harveston, Kedia , and Davis (2000) found a relationship between the global mindsets of managers in firms that are global at founding, thereby providing a link between the strategic requirements for complexity and cognitive capabilities. Pointing to the importance of the relationship between global mindset and global strategy to firm outcomes, Nummela, Saarenketo, and Puumalainen (2004) found a positive relationship between the global mindset of managers in a group of Finnish firms operating in globalized markets and the financial performance of the firm.

Other writers on global mindset, while recognizing the cognitive component of the construct, have placed greater attention on the behavioral dimensions. Both Adler and Bartholomew (1992) and Estienne (1997) emphasize that globally minded managers need both culturally specific knowledge and adaptation skills. Attitudes and skills as part of global mindset can also be found in the approaches of Kedia and Mukherji (1999), Rhinesmith (1992), Kobrin (1994) and Ashkenas *et al.* (1995). Many of these scholars explore the personal characteristics that leaders with a global mindset must have, such as a high tolerance for ambiguity, a high value for diversity and an openness to new experiences and peoples.

Drawing on the previous literature as well as work on cognitive complexity (Streufert and Streufert, 1978; Weick, 1979 and Bartunek, Gordon and Weathersby, 1983) and cosmopolitanism (Gouldner, 1957; Hannerz, 1996; Vertovec and Cohen, 2002a, 2002b) Levy *et al.* (2007) provide a definition of global mindset that encompasses two main dimensions: cognitive complexity and an openness to the others and the world. They define global mindset as: "a highly complex cognitive structure characterized by an openness to and articulation of multiple cultural and strategic realities on both global and local levels, and the cognitive ability to mediate and integrate across this multiplicity" (Levy *et al.*, 2007, p. 244). They marry this to the information processing requirements (Daft and Weick, 1984) to illustrate how global mindset aids global managers' attention, interpretation and action.

In something of a departure from both the cognitive and behavioral streams described above, Osland and Bird (2006) adopt the view that global leaders can be seen as "experts". A global mindset is thus seen as the expert mind that a global leader develops in order to be effective. Drawing on the literature on expert cognition (Sternberg and Davidson, 1994), Osland and Bird describe these global leaders as those who can make better global decisions because they have learned how to distinguish relevant information, see relevant patterns, build deep knowledge, perceive subtle cues, and select appropriate action scripts. The focus on the expert decision-making capability that a global leader must possess closely aligns this conceptualization to the *action* component of the information processing approach utilized by Levy *et al.* (2007) and, at the organizational level, Bouquet (2005). While this view of global mindset draws heavily on the idea of cognitive complexity that others have signaled as important dimensions (Levy *et al.*, 2007; Murtha, Lenway, and Bagozzi 1998; Nummela, Saarenketo, and Puumalainen 2004), their construct clearly acknowledges that a global leader can have different levels of global mindset ("novice," "advanced beginner," "proficient," "expert"), the experiential basis for the development of a global mindset.

As this review illustrates, the number of both theoretical and empirical writings on global mindset have increased exponentially over the last decade and produced identifiable streams. There seems to be a growing consensus based on this literature that global mindset requires greater cognitive complexity than a domestic mindset, as well as an openness to and interest in the variety and diversity of the world. Yet, in spite of the considerable progress that has been made, several important issues remain to be addressed by this literature. First, as indicated by the work of Osland and Bird (2006), there are few direct implications of much of this literature for global leadership development. Can the cognitive complexity and cosmopolitanism deemed important by various scholars actually be developed in individuals? While McCall and Hollenbeck's (2002) study of international managers indicates that experience is key, many questions still remain. What is the threshold level of experience a manager must have in order for a global mindset to develop? In what order, if any, should the dimensions of global mindset be developed? Because many of the studies to date have been largely cross-sectional and focused on the relationship to firm strategy, these questions have yet to be answered. In this regard, Osland and Bird's approach provides a useful framework that ties directly to established work on the development of experts, which may be helpful.

Other crucial questions remain concerning the global mindset construct. First, have all dimensions of a global mindset been identified or completely captured by current descriptions? While both a strategic and a behavioral/attitudinal (Levy *et al.*, 2007) dimension have been identified, other dimensions may emerge. Second, what is the relative importance of each dimension and the interdependence between them? Third, how should the identified dimensions by operationalized? Most measures of global mindset to date have been based on self-perceptions, and there has been little convergence around a single validated approach to measurement. Fourth, what level and kind of global mindset is required by a particular company or situation? Does a firm that is globalizing from the beginning need more cosmopolitanism than cognitive complexity in its global leaders, for example? All these issues are important considerations and barriers to the design of a sound global leadership development approach.

Global leadership competencies

Knowledge about how leaders influence the thinking, attitudes and behaviors of a global community is still somewhat elusive. Beyond global mindset, the ability to lead globally has often been defined in terms of competencies. Numerous studies have been conducted to determine what constitutes the right 'set' of competencies that defines a global leader (e.g., Black, Morrison and Gregersen, 1999; Kets de Vries and Florent-Treacy, 1999; Rosen *et al.*, 2000; Adler, 2001; McCall and Hollenbeck, 2002; Bikson *et al.*, 2003; Goldsmith *et al.*, 2003; Kets de Vries, Vrignaud, and Florent-Treacy, 2004). These studies differ greatly in sampled populations, definitions of GL success, and methodological approach; thus, comparability among them and definitive conclusions are difficult. The resultant lists of competencies overlap, separated at times only by semantic differences (Jokinen, 2005).

Conceptual frameworks

There are no original theories of global leadership. Most research has taken a content approach, similar to the trait research in the early days of domestic leadership. Three attempts, explained below, have been made to organize the approximately sixty competencies found in the GL literature. These conceptual frameworks have not been tested empirically as yet, but they are based on empirical research on GL competencies.

1. *Multidimensional construct of global leadership*. After reviewing the literature and listing the competencies, Mendenhall and Osland (2002) concluded that global leadership is a

multi-dimensional construct composed of six core dimensions: (1) cross-cultural relationship skills; (2) traits and values; (3) cognitive orientation; (4) global business expertise; (5) global organizing expertise; and (6) visioning.

2. *Integrated framework of global leadership.* Based on a review of the expatriate and global leader literature, Jokinen (2005) proposed an integrated theoretical framework of global leadership consisting of three types or layers of competencies: a fundamental core, mental characteristics and behavioral skills. The fundamental core is composed of self-awareness, engagement in personal transformation, and inquisitiveness. These characteristics are similar to prerequisites for developing other competencies; thus, they are not end-state competencies but indicators of global leadership potential. The second layer consists of mental characteristics that affect the way people approach issues and therefore guide their actions. It consists of optimism, self-regulation, motivation to work in an international environment, social judgment skills, empathy, cognitive skills, and the acceptance of complexity and its contradictions. The last layer is behavioral and refers to tangible skills and knowledge leading to concrete actions and results: social skills, networking skills, and knowledge. Jokinen notes that these competencies are continuums. She recommends, therefore, that "the emphasis shift from identifying specific lists of competencies to defining and measuring their ideal level in individuals" (Jokinen, 2005, p. 212).

3. *The pyramid model of global leadership.* The pyramid model, shown in figure 10.1, takes this form to reflect the assumption that global leaders have certain threshold knowledge and traits that serve as a base for higher-level competencies.[1] (For a thorough description of

the pyramid model, see Osland, 2008b). The five-level model suggests a progression that is cumulative, advancing from bottom to top. Level 1, the foundation, is comprised of *global knowledge*, which can be categorized as *know what, know who, know how, know when,* and *know why*. This taxonomy is borrowed from expatriate research (Berthoin Antal, 2000; Bird, 2001). Level 2 contains four specific *threshold traits*: integrity, humility, inquisitiveness and resilience. These are relatively stable personality traits; not everyone can develop them, which means they could be viewed as selection criteria.

Level 3 is composed of *attitudes and orientations*, the global mindset that influences the way global leaders perceive and interpret the world. This concept will be treated in greater depth in a following section, owing to its importance to global leadership. The first three levels, knowledge, personality traits and attitudes, become valuable only when translated into action. Therefore, Level 4 includes the *interpersonal skills* needed to cross cultures: mindful communication, creating and building trust, and the ability to work in multicultural teams.

Level 5 contains *system skills*, the meta-skills that encapsulate many other skills required for global work, such as cross-cultural expertise and the ability to both adapt to cultural differences and leverage them for competitive advantage. At this level, the central focus is the ability to influence people and the systems in which they work, both inside and outside the organization. It consists of boundary spanning, building community, leading change and creating a vision, architecting, influencing stakeholders, and making (ethical) decisions. The pyramid model does not capture the dynamic interactive aspect of the global leadership process; its contribution lies in the identification of different building blocks of global leadership and the simplification of a complex array of competencies. Figure 10.1 indicates, in the third column, the various competencies in the pyramid model that seem to relate to each aspect of the global context (the first column) and each type of sensemaking (the second column).

[1] The pyramid model was developed originally via a modified Delphi technique with a team of international management scholars, members of ION (International Organizations Network), who identified the key competencies of global managers (Bird and Osland, 2004). The model was subsequently expanded and adapted for global leaders based on a review of the recent global leadership literature (Osland, 2008).

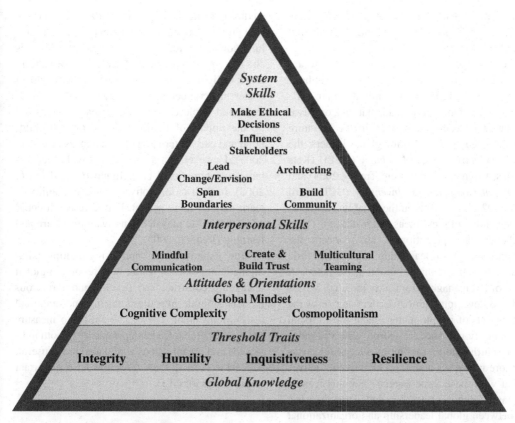

Figure 10.1. The pyramid model
Source: Adapted from A. Bird and J. Osland, "Global competencies: an introduction", in H. Lane, M. Maznevski, M. Mendenhall, and J. McNett (eds.), *Handbook of Global Management: A Guide to Managing Complexity*. Malden, MA: Blackwell, p. 67.

Global leadership antecedents and effectiveness outcomes

Little is known about the antecedents of global leadership. In the only known longitudinal study, the eventual career progress of Japanese global leaders (Graen and Hui, 1999, pp. 17–18) was predicted by three behaviors that occurred in the first three years of their career: (1) building effective working relationships characterized by trust, respect, and obligation with immediate supervisors; (2) networking derived from their contacts at prestigious universities; and (3) doing more than was expected in the face of difficult and ambiguous performance expectations. The last element, "difficult and ambiguous performance expectations," exemplifies the challenging experiences that constitute a common element in all models of global leadership development (Kets de Vries and Florent-Treacy, 2002; McCall and Hollenbeck, 2002; Osland *et al.*, 2006; Osland and Bird, 2008). A comparison of effective and ineffective global leaders found that the former group: had significantly higher conscientiousness scores and significantly lower neuroticism scores on the "Big Five" personality test; came from bicultural families; participated in more geographically distributed teams; had long-term international assignments; and were mentored by people from a different culture (Caligiuri, 2004). Other studies also found that global leaders had a diverse family background and international exposure and cultural contact during childhood (e.g., Kets de Vries and Florent-Treacy, 2002; McCall and Hollenbeck, 2002).

As one would expect in a new field, there are few assessment measures targeted at GL that have been validated (Bird, 2008). While there are various measures of intercultural adaptability, only two assessment measures mentioned in the literature were designed specifically for global leaders: the *Global Executive Leader Inventory* (GELI) (Kets de Vries, Vrignaud, and Florent-Treacy, 2004) and the *Global Competencies Inventory* (GCI) (Bird *et al.*, 2002). More work on the reliability and predictive validity of these measures is needed.

Scholars and practitioners alike accept the importance of global leadership, but there is little research to support this common-sense belief. A survey of HR managers from sixty large US MNCs identified developing global leaders as one of the three aspects of people management most crucial to organizational success (Stroh and Caliguiri, 1998). Furthermore, the more successful firms had more numerous and more effective initiatives to deal with these three aspects. For this reason, Stroh and Caliguiri (1998) concluded that there is a link between global leadership and organizational effectiveness. More research on this relationship would be helpful.

Implications for future global leadership research

Given the dearth of relevant longitudinal research, we have limited agreement and knowledge about both the antecedents and outcomes of global leadership. There is some agreement that global leadership consists of core characteristics, context-specific abilities, and universal leadership skills (Osland, 2008b). Yet there are still very important gaps in our understanding of what constitutes GL, including whether all competencies are equally important in every context. Research that directly measures GL behavior would be extremely helpful so that we could understand what global leaders actually do as they interact with their environment.

Researchers have indicated that there are most likely different profiles of global leaders (McCall and Hollenbeck, 2002; Osland *et al.*, 2007). Some

studies indicate the importance of a diverse family background and international exposure and cultural contact during childhood (e.g., Kets de Vries and Florent-Treacy, 2002; McCall and Hollenbeck, 2002; Caligiuri, 2004). If it is true that some global leadership competencies are developed in childhood and adolescence, more research is needed on the impact of family background and childhood and early international experiences (Jokinen, 2005). However, not all successful global leaders have an international background (Osland *et al.*, 2008). In their case, motivation and the ability to learn may be more salient. Future research could address the role played by motivation to learn and learning (Jokinen, 2005).

More exploratory research using multiple paradigmatic approaches would help refine the global leadership construct and develop more rigorous models to guide hypothesis testing and empirical tests (Mendenhall, 1999). The ability to measure the level of global leadership capacity in both individuals and organizations would also prove useful. The answers to all these questions have important implications for GLD.

Global leadership development research – progress and challenges

Due to its presumed importance to organizational performance, global leadership development (GLD) has captured the attention of many scholars and practitioners. From this mostly conceptual and non-empirical literature, several conclusions can be tentatively drawn about how global leaders are developed; these include: (1) the recognition that global leadership is transformative and takes time to develop; (2) that GLD is best done through experiential learning; (3) that GLD must be multi-method in its design; and (4) GLD should be a transparent process to all organizational members. A number of tools for GLD have also been identified, although the order in which they should be used, extent of use, and with whom have not been empirically established to date in the literature.

As can be seen from the findings in the right-hand column of table 10.2, the empirical literature on GLD is limited (Bikson *et al.*, 2004; Black,

Morrison, and Gregson 1999; Graen and Hui, 1999; Kets de Vries and Florent-Treacy, 2002; McCall and Hollenbeck, 2002; Stroh and Caligiuri, 1998; Caligiuri, 2006). Most asked subjects directly how GLD should or did occur. Caliguiri (2006) took a different tack, identifying ten global leader tasks, working backwards to determine the knowledge, skills, ability and other personal characteristics (KSAOs) that lead to their effective performance and making recommendations about training and development.

There are three extant process models of GLD: (1) a model derived from qualitative research that reflects the partnership between international executives and their organization (McCall and Hollenbeck, 2002); (2) the Chattanooga model, a conceptual model that has as its centerpiece the transformational aspect of GLD, accompanied by the moderators and antecedents (Osland et al., 2006); and (3) a variation of the Chattanooga model that focuses more specifically on developing GL expertise (Osland and Bird, 2008). For a description and comparison of these models, see Osland and Bird (2008). Personal transformation is a critical component of each model.

All models of GLD recognize that the competencies that a person needs in order to become a global leader require significant time to develop (Suutari, 2002; Mendenhall, 2006; Osland and Taylor, 2001; Tubbs and Schulz, 2006; Caliguiri, 2006). Most scholars argue that global leadership development does not involve adding discrete skills to some sort of "managerial skill portfolio." Instead, GLD involves adopting new skills and competencies while simultaneously expanding the scope and dimensionality of existing skills and competencies and shedding "comfortable" skills and skill routines that are less effective in global managerial contexts (Mendenhall, 2001).

According to Mendenhall (2006, p. 425), GLD occurs when people become self-aware of the degree to which they possess global leadership competencies and subsequently undergo a series of experiences, over time, which force them to utilize and practice these competencies. Because an individual must undergo such a deeply transformative experience in order to become a global leader, the current accepted train of thought by scholars is that

this process cannot be rushed nor accomplished through traditional, "classroom-type" training workshops and seminars.

With few exceptions, most of the scholars who have written about GLD fail to clearly establish the theoretical underpinnings of their proposed approaches to GLD, other than stating that GLD involves personal transformation processes. Scholars conceptualize how GLD might be achieved in two ways: (1) through the design of an effective human resource management system; or (2) through a managed process of personal transformation. While some scholars see these as intertwined (Oddou, Mendenhall and Ritchie, 2000), it is useful to distinguish one from the other to delineate implications for how organizations and individuals might/should go about developing global leaders.

The "HRM programmatic" approach

Representing the HRM approach, Suutari explicitly connects GLD to the resource-based view of the firm, stating that: "management development is part of creating the core competencies that lead to competitive advantage" (Suutari, 2002, p. 219). To create GL competencies, she argues that the firm must enact six strategic management design components, all of which involve a strong focus on the human resource management function. HR must become a "fully integrated global business partner" (Suutari, 2002, p. 221), and her arguments focus largely on what competencies can be developed through specific sets of HR tools. This emphasis on the tools and roles of the HR function puts the onus of GLD squarely on the shoulders of HR managers and the top management of firms, which is echoed in the work of Beechler and Javidan (2007) and Caliguri (2006). McCall and Hollenbeck (2002) also approach GLD somewhat from this viewpoint, arguing that the strategy and structure of a firm will determine its GLD requirements and process; firm-level characteristics will determine, for example, the number of executives and roles that need GLD, the kinds of assignments that are available to enhance GLD, and the locations and contexts in which these developmental processes will occur.

The "personal responsibility" focus

Other authors (Mendenhall, 2006; Osland, 2001) while not ignoring either the need to identify a set of competencies nor the role that HR can play in helping or hindering this personal transformation, emphasize that GLD is first and foremost a personal journey that involves a profound and irrevocable change in a person's worldview and behavior. While an HR system might be able to facilitate some of this development, they assume that in the end it is entirely up to the individual whether or not he/she develops global leadership skills.

Neither camp generally rejects the other's importance to GLD; they simply differ as to their primary focus. In Gestalt terms, for the "personal responsibility" camp of scholars, the personal responsibility for GLD growth is the figure while the efficacy of HR systems is the ground. For scholars who subscribe to the HR systems approach to GLD, the opposite view holds – HR practices and strategy constitute the figure while personal responsibility shifts to ground.

Oddou and Mendenhall (2008) draw on Black, Morrison, and Gregerson's (1999) concept of "remapping" to create a process model that encourages the individual to contrast, confront and replace his own values and behaviors with those outside his culture or country. This involves a high degree of personal knowledge (Mendenhall, 2006) and also a structuring of experiences that vary in intensity, importance and complexity (Osland and Bird, 2008) in order for a change in mental models to occur. All of these models are based on an individual model of learning and development, while the organization and its HR policies are seen as providing the context or support for the nurturance of transformative experiences inherent in GLD. Due to the deep personal transformation that must occur in GLD, organizations have less control over the process of developing global leadership than domestic leaders (McCall and Hollenbeck, 2002), and, indeed, organizations are seen as partners in this personal process rather than controllers or instigators. As we will see later in this chapter, this difference in perspective can have far-reaching implications for how GLD is approached in a dynamic organizational environment.

Lichtenstein and Mendenhall (2002) have contributed an additional theoretical lens through which GLD can be viewed. Drawing on the "new science" literature, they emphasize that the constructs of non-linearity, interdependence and emergence can be helpful in understanding the process of GLD. A key concept from these constructs that affects both the HRM and the personal transformation approaches to GLD is that the inputs to a process are often non-proportional to their subsequent outputs (Lichtenstein and Mendenhall, 2002, p. 7). That is, whether utilizing a theoretical approach that focuses on organizational systems such as HRM or on personal transformation, one cannot always predict the effect that a particular input (such as a training program, key job assignment, or overseas posting) is likely to create within an individual in terms of GLD. Given the inherent lack of surety and positivistic control in the GLD process by either the organization or the individual, caution is warranted in evaluating the claims, predictions, and recommendations by HR managers, consultants, scholars, and executives regarding the efficacy of any program designed to enhance GLD.

Figure 10.2 summarizes the relationship among the focus of accountability for GLD, training methods, and HR support. Oddou and Mendenhall (2008) cite Dodge (1993) in stating that in general, 20 percent of learning occurs in classroom situations, 30 percent of learning comes from information exchanges with others, and 50 percent of learning occurs during personal work/experiential experiences. Global competency development methods are linked in figure 10.2 according to their primary learning contexts: classroom, exchange, and experience. Also, figure 10.2 reflects the degree to which personal responsibility for transformative learning versus HRM programming is critical for given GLD methods. For *all* methods both play a role, but the primacy of focus shifts, depending on the nature of the method utilized. As illustrated in figure 10.2, the criticality of personal responsibility lessens at "classroom type" of GLD methods, while HRM programming is critical for that category of methods. Perhaps not surprisingly, the ambiguity over how to approach GLD from a theoretical perspective – as a strategic HRM problem intrinsically linked to firm competitiveness, or as a personal development process – is reflected in

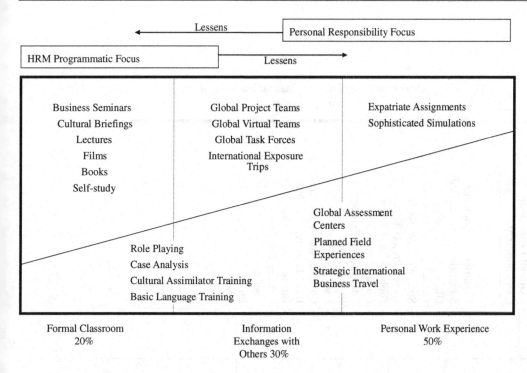

Figure 10.2. Integration of focus, training methods, and HR support

the ongoing debate over which competencies a global leader must develop.

Selection of GL candidates for development Programs

The lack of a single, cohesive model of GLD is reflected in the ongoing challenges with selecting candidates for development. In addition, there is no empirical evidence directly linking candidate selection criteria to superior GLD outcomes. Much of the empirical research in the GLD area has developed selection criteria post hoc, based on the qualities perceived to be associated with effective global leaders. An example of this can be found in McCall and Hollenbeck's (2002) study, where they derived the competencies that global leader candidates should be selected for based on their interviews with 101 global executives deemed successful by others. Thus, much of the writing in this area is related to the model of global leadership and GLD that particular authors have developed or used in their research or writings, thus making this

a particularly fruitful area for further exploration by researchers.

Some scholars recommend that candidates should already possess needed global leadership characteristics that are very difficult to develop in people "from scratch" (Osland, *et al.*, 2006). The threshold traits – inquisitiveness, integrity, resilience and humility – in the pyramid model reflect this belief, that is, the necessity of selecting individuals for GLD who already possess above average manifestations of these traits. There is also some consensus that there may be industry or firm strategy requirements that shape the type of global leader that is needed, which could also influence the selection of appropriate global leader candidates for development (Jokinen, 2005; McCall and Hollenbeck, 2002). More research is needed to answer the many selection challenges and questions that remain.

Another challenge is sorting out the level of competency required for a particular global leader role. Ignoring for the moment the question discussed above of how the requisite competencies were derived, the selection process must recognize

Ideal sequence of developmental learning of competencies

Global Context	Sensemaking	Global Leadership	Global Leadership Development
Complexity	**Meta-level sensemaking (higher-order)** • Requisite variety in mental models • Understanding of paradox • Influencing and changing mental models (defragging) • Creating the correct shared vision	Global mindset • Cosmopolitanism • Cognitive complexity Inquisitiveness Influence stakeholders	*Highest Potential for Competency Development* • Expatriate Assignments • Sophisticated Simulations • Global Assessment Centers • Planned Field Experiences • Strategic Business Travel • Global Project Teams • Global Virtual Teams • Global Task Forces • International Exposure Trips • Role Playing • Case Analysis • Cultural Assimilator Training • Basic Language Training • Business Seminars • Cultural Briefings • Lectures • Films • Books • Self-Study *Lowest Potential for Competency Development*
• **Multiplicity**	**Inclusive sensemaking** • Determining whom to include • Perspective-taking • Determining which perspectives to heed • Collaborative decision making	Span boundaries Cognitive complexity Influence stakeholders Multicultural teaming	
• **Interdependence**	**Systemic sensemaking** • Engaging in stakeholder dialogue • Coordinating multiple sensemaking • Collaborative decision making	Cognitive complexity Critical thinking Global knowledge Span boundaries Multicultural teaming Build trust Building community	
• **Ambiguity**	**Confident sensemaking** • Seeking clarity from trusted network members • Narrowing the sense-making "focus" • Gauging when enough is known to make decisions • Collaborative decision making	Humility Inquisitiveness Integrity Resilience Build trust Make ethical decisions Influence stakeholders	
Flux	**Quick sensemaking** • Refocusing the vision based on what's important • Innovative responses • Realignment • Rapid decision making	Architecting Building trust Build community Lead change Resilience	
Cultural Variations	**Intercultural sensemaking** • Decoding culture • Bridging cultural differences • Decisions that leverage culture	Mindful communication Multicultural teaming Intercultural competence Global mindset Humility Inquisitiveness Global knowledge Cosmopolitanism Cognitive complexity	

Figure 10.3. Relationship of global context, sensemaking, competencies, and development

that competencies are developed along a continuum rather than as absolutes (Jokinen, 2005). That is, a candidate may be in possession of some level of a particular competency that may be adequate for his/her next global leader assignment but insufficient for operating in higher global roles in the organization in the future. To what degree does the selection program accept this level of proficiency in a candidate, either for determining entry or successful completion of the program? How completely developed does a competency need to be at any particular point in a global leader's trajectory (Lichtenstein and Mendenhall, 2002)?

Equally challenging is determining the role of culture in selecting suitable GLD candidates. The determination of a particular candidate's level on a selection criterion or competency, such as inquisitiveness, may be culturally biased by the way in which it is measured. The home culture of the firm that devises the GLD selection process may deeply influence beliefs about what behavioral and other cues indicate mastery of a particular competency. Trying to determine the inquisitiveness of a Thai person via questions raised during an interview or his initiation of self-determined lines of inquiry in a project may lead to erroneous conclusions. Cultural blinders can also result in selecting people who later find themselves in awkward positions relative to their "ingroup" when they are expected to act in ways that contradict their norms about gender or age status. Conversely, people may not be viewed as potential candidates for reasons that have no credibility beyond their own cultural boundaries. This "similar-to-me" trap can affect all aspects of a GLD selection process.

The institutional context can influence GLD selection processes as well. The nature of the local labor market may determine the availability of not only the number of qualified candidates, but also the competencies that can be expected from candidates in a particular country. For example, "leading change" has not been encouraged in either educational institutions or companies in China, making the existence of such competencies in Chinese managers relatively rare. Should a company adjust its selection process to the institutional realities of the countries in which it operates?

Figure 10.3 simply juxtaposes the nature of the global context, the requisite sensemaking necessary to thrive in the global context, global competencies, and global leadership development methods. To be successful in a global environment, leaders have to be capable of engaging in the different types of sophisticated, complex global sensemaking shown in the second column. The categories of sensemaking rely upon various types of global competencies, as shown in the third column. In the vast majority of cases, global leaders do not come pre-fitted with high levels of expertise in all the global competencies required to engage in competent sensemaking. Thus, GLD methods are required to assist leaders in their competency development. The GLD methods that have the highest potential for the development of global leadership competencies are listed in descending order in the right-hand column in figure 10.3.

In an ideal world, managers would begin their global leadership competency development with basic, traditional learning methods and progressively move through the more sophisticated development processes as illustrated in figure 10.3. In practice, this ideal scenario rarely occurs. It requires a long-term, dedicated view to GLD within a firm. Such an approach requires a strong vision, adequate funding, and sophisticated HR maintenance procedures. More commonly, most companies opt for development methods at the extremes of the developmental learning continuum delineated in figure 10.3 – individuals are placed in expatriate assignments without adequate preparation or managers are given classroom-type training in the hope that such training will expand the attendees' skill portfolios. While cases can be found where such strategies have worked, they are the exceptions that prove the norm; namely, that there are no short-cuts to global leadership development.

Cases where leaders have thrived after being placed in "sink-or-swim" expatriate assignments and have emerged as competent global leaders have been attributed to the likelihood that these individuals already possessed high levels of expertise in global leadership competencies and were naturally high in "personal responsibility focus" in terms of their learning style. This, of course, supports the argument that firms spend more time in careful selection of people who already possess high levels of global competencies versus trying to develop global competencies in

Table 10.3 Eight major research directions needed in the global leadership field

Systematic analyses of the factors that promote or impede global leadership and mindset development (Osland, Bird, Mendenhall, and Osland, 2006, p. 219)
Consensus on the definition and parameters of global leadership and global mindset constructs (Osland, Bird, Mendenhall, and Osland, 2006, p. 219)
To avoid a Western bias, future research on global leadership, sensemaking, and mindset – and their development – should include globally diverse subjects and settings (Osland, Bird, Mendenhall, and Osland, 2006, p. 219)
As a necessity for advancing the field, existing global leadership models' propositions and hypotheses require empirical testing (Osland, Bird, Mendenhall, and Osland, 2006, pp. 218–19)
Alignment of HRM and organizational culture with firms' efforts to develop global leadership require investigation beyond single-sample case studies and anecdotal reports (Osland, Bird, Mendenhall, and Osland, 2006, p. 219)
Empirical research needs to be conducted on how the various global competencies influence each other, if they shift in their valences due to context or task or cultural distance or other variables, and under what conditions they develop or can or cannot be effectively deployed (Mendenhall, 2001)
There is a lack of sophisticated understanding regarding optimal sequencing of GLD methods, which methods and in what combinations are most effective during "in-country" vs. "pre-departure" training for expatriates, and whether it is possible to accelerate learning through the sequential process described in Figure 10.3 (Mendenhall, 2001)
There is a strong need for longitudinal research that investigates the global leadership development process in global leaders. The situation in this field is even worse than that of expatriate adjustment, where it has been note that: "Although [the] calling for longitudinal research is perhaps a shopworn recommendation in management scholarship, the situation in the expatriate area is especially grim, where fewer than 5 percent of the existing studies are longitudinal" (Bhaskar-Shrinivas, Harrison, Shaffer, and Luk, 2005, p. 273)

individuals who are at the norm or below the norm in their global competency expertise.

However, all the above considerations related to global leadership development are mostly conjecture as the paucity of empirical literature in the field does not allow at this time for clear prescriptive directions.

Conclusion

This chapter focuses on the progress, challenges and future research needs of the study of global leadership and its development. Despite shared commonalities with traditional leadership, we articulate how global leadership differs in degree and kind due to the global context in which it is practiced. Cultural variations, complexity (multiplicity, interdependence, ambiguity) and flux are the contextual determinants of global leadership. In an attempt to expand the competency approach found in most GL research, we present an integrated framework that takes a broader view of global leadership. This framework, the chapter's major contribution, illustrates how the above mentioned contextual determinants lead to global leadership, which is portrayed as different forms of sensemaking which

then entail particular competencies; the final component of the framework is the ideal sequence of the development training needed to learn these competencies. We have reviewed the limited empirical research on GL and GTD in relation to this framework.

The focus of this chapter has been the phenomenon of global leadership. Other than clarifying how it differs from traditional leadership, scholars have yet to look at the relationship between traditional leadership theories and GL. The study of global leadership could well have implications for indigenous leadership theories. For example, will the variables that determine effectiveness in global leadership expand the conceptualization of effectiveness in traditional leadership theory? Given the "extreme case" of global leadership, its ongoing development as a field of study could open up new avenues for research and theory-building for traditional leadership scholars.

The nascent field of global leadership has generated more questions than answers about the phenomenon. Be that as it may, global leadership is of paramount importance to corporations' ability to compete. Therefore, we end our chapter by summarizing in table 10.3 the eight most important questions, directions, and needs of the global leadership field that merit research attention and emphasis.

References

Adler, N. J. 2001. "Global leadership: Women leaders", in M. Mendenhall, T. Kuhlmann, and G. Stahl, *Developing Global Business Leaders: Policies, Processes and Innovations*. Westport, CT: Quorum Books, pp. 73–97.

and Bartholomew, S. 1992. "Globalization and Human Resource Management", in A. M. Rugman and A. Verbeke (eds.), *Research in Global Strategic Management: Corporate Response to Change*. Greenwich, CT: JAI Press, pp. 179–201.

Arora, A., Jaju, A., Kefalas, A. G., and Perenich, T. 2004. "An exploratory analysis of global managerial mindsets: a case of US textile and apparel industry", *Journal of International Management* 10(3): 393–411.

Ashkenas, R., Ulrich, D., Jick, T., and Kerr, S. 1995. *The Boundaryless Organization: Breaking the Chains of Organizational Structure*. San Francisco, CA: Jossey-Bass.

Bartlett, C.A. and Ghoshal, S. 1989. *Managing Across Borders: The Transnational Solution*. Boston, MA: Harvard Business School Press.

and Ghoshal, S. 1990. "Matrix management: not a structure, a frame of mind", *Harvard Business Review* 68(4): 138–45.

Bartunek, J. M., Gordon, J. R., and Weathersby, R. P. 1983. "Developing 'complicated' understanding in administrators", *Academy of Management Review* 8(2): 273–84.

Beechler, S. and Javidan, M. 2007. "Leading with a global mindset", in M. Javidan, R. Steers, and M. Hitt (eds.), *Advances in International Management: Special Issue on Global Mindset* 19: 131–69.

Søndergaard, M., Miller, E. L., and Bird, A. 2004. "Boundary Spanning", in H. W. Lane, M. L. Maznevski, M. E. Mendenhall, and J. McNett (eds.), *Handbook of Global Management: A Guide to Complexity*. Oxford: Blackwell, pp. 121–133.

Begley, T. M. and Boyd, D. P. 2003. "The need for a corporate global mind-set", *MIT Sloan Management Review* 44(2): 25–32.

Berthoin Antal, A. 2000. "Types of knowledge gained by expatriate managers", *Journal of General Management* 26(2): 32–51.

Bikson, T. K., Treverton, G. F., Moini, J. S., and Lindstrom, G. 2003. *New Challenges for International Leadership: Lessons from Organizations with Global Missions*. Sauta Monica, CA: Rand.

Bird, A. 2001. "International assignments and careers as repositories of knowledge", in M. Mendenhall, T. Kühlmann and G. K. Stahl (eds.), *Developing Global Business Leaders: Policies, Processes and Innovation*. Westport, CT: Quorum.

2008. "Assessing global leadership competencies", in M. Mendenhall, J. S. Osland, A. Bird, G. Oddou, and M. Maznevski, *Global Leadership: Research, Practice and Development*. London: Routledge, pp, 64–80.

and Osland, J. S. 2004. "Global competencies: an introduction", in H. Lane, M. Maznevski, M. Mendenhall, and J. Mcnett (eds.), *The Handbook of Global Management*. Oxford: Blackwell, pp. 57–80.

Stevens, M. J., Mendenhall, M. E., and Oddou, G. 2002. *The Global Competencies Inventory*. St Louis, MO: The Kozai Group, Inc.

Black, J. S., Morrison, A. J., and Gregersen, H. B. 1999. *Global Explorers: The Next Generations of Leaders*. New York, NY: Routledge.

Bouquet, C. A. 2005. *Building Global Mindsets: An Attention-Based Perspective*. New York: Palgrave Macmillan.

Caligiuri, P. M. 2004. "Global leadership development through expatriate assignments and other international experiences", Paper presented at the Academy of Management, New Orleans.

2006. "Developing global leaders", *Human Resource Management Review* 16(2): 219–28.

Charan, R., Drotter, S., and Noel, J. 2001. *The Leadership Pipeline*. San Francisco: Jossey Bass.

Daft, R. L. and Weick, K. E. 1984. "Toward a model of organizations as interpretation systems", *Academy of Management Review* 9(2): 284–95.

Dalton, M., Ernst, C., Deal, J., and Leslie, J. 2002. *Success for the New global Manager: What You Need to Know to Work Across Distances, Countries and Cultures*. San Francisco: Jossey-Bass and the Center for Creative Leadership.

Dodge, B. 1993. "Empowerment and the evolution of learning", *Education and Training* 35(5): 3–10.

Estienne, M. 1997. "The art of cross-cultural management: an alternative approach to training and development", *Journal of European Industrial Training* 21(1): 14–18.

Fang, T. 2006. "From 'onion' to 'ocean': paradox and change in national cultures", *International Studies of Management & Organization* 35(4): 71–90.

Festing, M. 2001. "The effects of international human resource management strategies on global leadership development", in M. Mendenhall, T. M. Kuhlmann and G. Stahl (eds.), *Developing Global Business Leaders: Policies, Processes, and Innovations*. Westport, CN: Quorum, pp. 37–56.

Gannon, M. J. 2007. *Paradoxes of Culture and Globalization*. Thousand Oaks, CA Sage Publications.

Goldsmith, M., Greenberg, C., Robertson, A., and Hu-Chan, M. 2003. *Global Leadership: The Next Generation*. Upper Saddle River, NJ: Prentice-Hall.

Gouldner, A.W. 1957. "Cosmopolitans and locals: toward an analysis of latent social roles – I", *Administrative Science Quarterly* 2(3): 281–306.

Govindarajan, V. and Gupta, A. K. 2001. *The Quest for Global Dominance: Transforming Global Presence into Global competitive Advantage*. San Francisco, CA: Jossey-Bass.

Graen, G. B. and Hui, C. 1999. "U.S. army leadership in the twenty-first century: challenges and implications for training", in J. G. Hunt, G. E. Dodge, and L. Wong (eds.), *Out-of-The-Box Leadership: Transforming the Twenty-First Century Army and Other Top Performing Organizations*. Stamford, Connecticut: Jai Press Inc, pp. 239–52.

Gregersen, H. B., Morrison, A. J., and Black, J. S. 1998. "Developing leaders for the global frontier", *Sloan Management Review* 40(1): 21–32.

Gupta, A. K. and Govindarajan, V. 2002. "Cultivating a global mindset", *Academy of Management Executive* 16(1): 116–26.

Hannerz, U. 1996. "Cosmopolitans and locals in world culture", in U. Hannerz (ed.), *Transnational Connections: Culture, People, Places*. London: Routledge, pp. 102–11.

Harveston, P.D., Kedia, B.L., and Davis, P.S. 2000. "Internationalization of born global and gradual globalizing firms: the impact of the manager", *Advances in Competitiveness Research* 8(1): 92–9.

Hedlund, G. 1986. "The hypermodern MNC: A heterarchy?" *Human Resource Management*, 25(1), pp. 9–35.

Heenan, D. and Perlmutter, H. 1979. *Multinational Organizational Development: A Social Architecture Perspective*. Reading, MA: Addison-Wesley.

Hollenbeck, G. P. 2001. "A serendipitous sojourn through the global leadership literature", in W. Mobley and M. W. McCall (eds.), *Advances in Global Leadership*. Stamford, CT: JAI Press.

Javidan, M., Dorfman, P., Sully de Luque, M., and House, R. 2006. "In the eye of the beholder: cross cultural lessons in leadership from Project GLOBE", *Academy of Management Perspectives* 20(1): 67–90.

Jeannet, J. P. 2000. *Managing with a Global Mindset*. London: Financial Times/Prentice Hall.

Jokinen, T. 2005. "Global leadership competencies: a review and discussion", *Journal of European Industrial Training* 29(2/3): 199–216.

Kedia, B. L. and Mukherji, A. 1999. "Global managers: developing a mindset for global competitiveness", *Journal of World Business* 34(3): 230–51.

Kets De Vries, M. F. R. and Florent-Treacy, E. 1999. *The New Global Leaders*. San Francisco, CA: Jossey-Bass.

and Florent-Treacy, E. 2002. "Global leadership from A to Z: creating high commitment organizations", *Organizational Dynamics* 30(4): 295–309.

Vrignaud, P., and Florent-Treacy, E. 2004. "The global leadership life inventory: development and psychometric properties of a 360-degree feedback instrument", *International Journal of Human Resource Management* 15(3): 475–92.

Klein, G. A. 1998. *Sources of Power*. Cambridge, MA: MIT Press.

2004. *The Power of Intuition: How to Use Your Gut Feelings to Make Better Decisions at Work*. New York, NY: Random House, Inc.

Pliske, R., Crandall, B., and Woods, D. 2005. "Problem Detection", *Cognition, Technology and Work* 7: 14–28.

Kluckhohn, F. and Strodtbeck, F. L. 1961. *Variations in Value Orientations*. Evanston, IL: Row, Peterson.

Kobrin, S. J. 1994. "Is there a relationship between a geocentric mind-set and multinational strategy?", *Journal of International Business Studies* 25(3): 493–511.

Kotter, J. P. 1990 "What Leaders Really Do", *Harvard Business Review* 68(3): 103–11.

Lane, H. W., Maznevski, M. L., and Mendenhall, M. E. (2004) "Hercules Meets Buddha", in H. W. Lane, M. Maznevski, M. E. Mendenhall, and J. McNett (eds.), *The Handbook of Global Management: A Guide to Managing Complexity*. Oxford: Blackwell, pp. 3–25.

Maznevski, M. L. Mendenhall, M. E., and McNett, J. (eds.) (2004). *The Handbook of global management: A guide & Managing Complexity*. Oxford: Blackwell.

Levy, O. 2005. "The influence of top management team attentional patterns on global strategic posture of firms", *Journal of Organizational Behavior* 26(7): 797–819.

Beechler, S., Taylor, S., and Boyacigiller, N. 2007 "What do we talk about when we talk about global mindset: managerial cognition in Multinational Corporations", *Journal of International Business Studies* 38: 231–58.

Lichtenstein, B. and Mendenhall, M. 2002 "Non-linearity and response-ability: emergent order in 21st century careers", *Human Relations* 55(1): 5–32.

McBer and Company 1995. "Mastering Global Leadership: Hay/McBer International CEO Leadership Study", Boston, MA: Hay/McBer Worldwide Resource Center.

McCall, M. R. and Hollenbeck, G. P. 2002. *Developing Global Executives: The Lessons of International Experience*. Boston, MA: Harvard Business School Press.

Mendenhall, M. 1999. "On the need for paradigmatic integration in international human resource management", *Management International Review* 39(3): 65–87.

2001. "New perspectives on expatriate adjustment and its relationship to global leadership development", in Mendenhall, M., Kuhlmann, T., and Stahl, G. (eds.), *Developing Global Business Leaders: Policies, Processes, and Innovations*. Westport, CT: Quorum Books, pp. 1–16.

2006. "The elusive, yet critical challenge of developing global leaders", *European Management Journal* 24(6): 422–29.

Mendenhall, M. 2008. "Leadership and the birth of global leadership", in M. Mendenhall, J. S. Osland, A. Bird, G. Oddou, and M. Maznevski, *Global Leadership: Research, Practice and Development*. London: Routledge, pp. 1–17.

Jensen, R., Gregersen, H., and Black, J. S. 2003. "Seeing the elephant: HRM challenges in the age of globalization", *Organizational Dynamics* 32(3): 261–74.

Kuhlmann, T., and Stahl, G. 2001. *Developing Global Business Leaders: Policies, Processes and Innovations*. Westport, CT: Quorum Books.

and Osland, J. S. 2002. "An overview of the extant global leadership research", Symposium presentation, Academy of International Business, Puerto Rico.

Mercer Delta 2006. "The global leadership imperative", presentation to the Human Resource Planning Society.

Murtha, T. P., Lenway, S. A., and Bagozzi, R. P. 1998. "Global mind-sets and cognitive shift in a complex multinational corporation", *Strategic Management Journal* 19(2): 97–114.

Nummela, N., Saarenketo, S., and Puumalainen, K. 2004. "A global mindset: a prerequisite for successful internationalization?", *Canadian Journal of Administrative Sciences* 21(1): 51–64.

Oddou, G. and Mendenhall, M. 2008. "Global leadership Development", in M. Mendenhall, J. S. Osland, A. Bird, G. Oddou, and M. Maznevski, *Global Leadership: Research, Practice and Development*. London: Routledge, pp. 160–174..

Mendenhall, M. E., and Ritchie, J. B. 2000. "Leveraging travel as a tool for global leadership development", *Human Resource Management* 39(2/3): 159–72.

Osland, J. 2001. "The quest for transformation: the process of global leadership development", in M. Mendenhall, T. Kuhlmann, and G. Stahl (eds.), *Developing Global Business Leaders: Policies, Processes and Innovations*. Westport, CN: Quorum Books, pp. 137–56.

Osland, J. 2008a. "The multidisciplinary roots of global leadership", in M. Mendenhall, J. S. Osland, A. Bird, G. Oddou, and M. Maznevski, *Global Leadership: Research, Practice and Development*. London: Routledge, pp. 18–33.

Osland, J. 2008b. "An overview of the global leadership literature", in M. Mendenhall,

J. S. Osland, A. Bird, G. Oddou, and M. Maznevski, *Global Leadership: Research, Practice and Development*. London: Routledge, pp. 34–63.

Osland, J. and Bird, A. 2000. "Beyond Sophisticated Stereotyping: Cultural Sensemaking in Context", *Academy of Management Executive* 14(1): 65–77.

Osland, J. and Bird, A. 2006. "Global leaders as experts", in W. Mobley, and E. Weldon (eds.), *Advances in Global Leadership*, vol 4. Stamford, CT: JAI Press, pp. 123–42.

Osland, J. and Bird, A. 2008. "Process models of global leadership development", in M. Mendenhall, J. S. Osland, A. Bird, G. Oddou, and M. Maznevski, *Global Leadership: Research, Practice and Development*. London: Routledge, pp. 81–93.

Osland, J., Bird, A., and Gundersen, A. 2007. "Trigger Events in Intercultural Sensemaking", Academy of Management Meeting, Philadelphia, PA.

Osland, J., Bird, A., Mendenhall, M. E., and Osland, A. 2006. "Developing global leadership capabilities and global mindset: a review", in G. K. Stahl and I. Björkman (eds.), *Handbook of Research in International Human Resource Management*. Cheltenham, UK: Edward Elgar Publishing, pp. 197–222.

Osland, J., Bird, A., Osland, A., and Oddou, G. 2007. "Expert Cognition in High Technology Global Leaders", *Proceedings of NDM8*, 8th Naturalistic Decision Making Conference, Monterey, CA.

Osland, J., Oddou, G., Bird, A., and Osland, A. 2008. "Global Leadership In Context", Working Paper, San José State University.

Osland, J. and Taylor, S. 2001. "Developing global leaders", www.HR.Com.

Perlmutter, H.V. 1969. "The tortuous evolution of the multinational corporation", *Columbia Journal of World Business* 4(1): 9–18.

and Heenan, D.A. 1979. *Multinational Organization Development*. Reading: Addison-Wesley.

Pucik, V. 1994. "The challenges of globalization: the strategic role of local managers in Japanese owned US subsidiaries", in N. Campbell, and F. Burtono (eds.), *Japanese Multinationals*. London: Routledge.

Rhinesmith, S. H. 1992. "Global mindsets for global managers", *Training & Development*. 46(10): 63–9.

Rosen, R., Digh, P., Singer, M., and Philips, C. 2000. *Global Literacies: Lessons on Business Leadership and National Cultures*. New York, NY: Simon and Schuster.

Shin, S. J., Morgeson, F. P., and Campion, M. A. 2007. "What you do depends on where you are: understanding how domestic and expatriate work requirements depend upon the cultural context", *Journal of International Business Studies* 38(1): 64–83.

Starbuck, W. H. and Milliken, F. J. 1988. "Executives' perceptual filters: what they notice and how they make sense", in D.C. Hambrick (ed.), *The Executive Effect: Concepts and Methods for Studying Top Managers* Greenwich, CT: JAI Press, pp. 35–65.

Sternberg, R. and Davidson, J. 1994. *The Nature of Insight*. Cambridge, MA: MIT Press.

Streufert, S. and Streufert, S. C. 1978. *Behavior in the Complex Environment*. Washington, DC: Winston.

Stroh, L. K. and Caligiuri, P. M. 1998. "Increasing global competitiveness through effective people management", *Journal of World Business* 33(1): 1–16.

Suutari, V. 2002. "Global leadership development: an emerging research agenda", *Career Development International* 7(4): 218–33.

Tubbs, S. L. and Schulz, E. 2006. "Exploring a taxonomy of global leadership competencies and meta-competencies", *Journal of American Academy of Business* 8(2): 29–34.

Vertovec, S. and Cohen, R. 2002a. *Conceiving Cosmopolitanism: Theory, Context, and Practice*. Oxford: Oxford University Press.

and Cohen, R. 2002b. "Introduction: Conceiving Cosmopolitanism", in S. Vertovec and R. Cohen (eds.), *Conceiving Cosmopolitanism: Theory, Context, and Practice*. Oxford: Oxford University Press, pp. 1–22.

Weber, W., Festing, M., Dowling, P. J., and Schuler, R. S. 1998. *Internationales Personalmanagement*. Wiesbaden: Gabler Verlag.

Weick, K. E. 1979. "Cognitive Processes in Organizations", in B. Staw (ed.), *Research in Organizational behavior*. Greenwich, CT: JAI Press, pp. 41–74.

1995. *Sensemaking in Organizations*. Thousand Oaks, CA: Sage.

Wills, S. and Barham, K. 1994. "Being an international manager", *European Management Journal* 12: 49–58.

Yeung A. K. and Ready D. A. 1995. "Developing leadership capabilities of global corporations: a comparative study in eight nations",

Human Resource Management 34(4): 529–47.

Yukl, G. 2002. *Leadership in Organizations* (5th edn). Upper Saddle River, NJ: Pearson Prentice-Hall.

2006. *Leadership in Organizations* (6th edn). Upper Saddle River, NJ: Pearson Prentice-Hall.

The role of cultural elements in virtual teams[1]

TARYN L. STANKO and CRISTINA B. GIBSON

The study of teams, which are formed when two or more individuals interact with one another as they work to reach a common goal, has generated a great deal of research over the last several decades. Classic studies of teams of workers, such as those conducted by Elton Mayo and his colleagues in the 1920s and 1930s (the "Hawthorne studies"), highlighted the idea that when people work in teams, rather than individually, significant team-level phenomena can occur. For example, in a series of experiments, Mayo and his colleagues found that when the employees they studied worked together and formed team loyalty, they experienced higher levels of motivation than when they had worked individually (Mayo, 1946; Roethlisberger and Dickson, 1939). Studies such as these thus triggered a surge of interest in the topic of teams.

In recent years increased attention has been paid to multinational teams, or teams where members come from different national or cultural backgrounds (Earley and Gibson, 2002). Over the last few decades the workforce has become increasingly diverse (Moghaddam, 1997) and some large organizations are now operating across greater geographic areas than in the past (McMichael, 2000). Thus, individuals cooperate in multinational teams that are increasingly diverse, and that sometimes span geographic boundaries. While there has been a steady increase in the number of studies that focus on how cultural differences may shape multinational team dynamics (Earley and Gibson, 2002), relatively less is known about the role that cultural differences play when teams

are also enabled by technology. In this chapter we review the most recent research that has been conducted examining these technology enabled teams, often referred to as virtual teams, and specifically explore how the issue of culture is dealt with in this body of research.

Virtual teams are variously defined as geographically dispersed (consisting of members spread across more than one location), electronically dependent (communicating using electronic tools such as e-mail or instant messaging), structurally dynamic (in which change occurs frequently among members, their roles, and relationships to each other), or nationally diverse (consisting of members with more than one national or cultural background) (Gibson and Gibbs, 2006; Kirkman and Mathieu, 2005; Martins, Gilson, and Maynard, 2004; Griffith, Sawyer and Neale, 2003). These dimensions are often related, such that when teams are geographically dispersed and electronic dependence is high, teams are often also culturally diverse, although this is not always the case. Teams with such characteristics are growing in number and importance – a study by the Gartner Group indicated that more than 60 percent of professional employees work in teams characterized by virtuality (Kanawattanachai and Yoo, 2002). Such teams potentially make it easier to acquire and apply knowledge to critical tasks in global firms (e.g., Sole and Edmondson, 2002). However, a review of the recent literature indicates ambiguous findings regarding the organizational performance implications of this relatively new form of teaming, and very little is understood about the role of culture in such teams. In fact, most researchers document challenges. Part of the problem is that the term "virtual" has been applied imprecisely in the literature (Gibson and Gibbs, 2006).

[1] This chapter is based upon work supported by the National Science Foundation under Grant #0422676. Any opinions, findings, and conclusions or recommendations expressed in this chapter are those of the authors and do not necessarily reflect the views of the National Science Foundation.

We attempt to bring more clarity to this growing domain of the literature through a conceptual review and synthesis of the research articles addressing virtuality published in the last six years. Specifically, we conducted a Web of Science search for articles published between 2000 and 2006 in the organizations, communication, psychology, international management, and information systems journals. Using variations of the search terms virtual, distributed, or dispersed we identified 418 articles. A total of 207 of these articles pertained to virtual, distributed or dispersed *work* (i.e., virtual gaming was also a common topic in the literature but was considered outside the scope of this chapter).

Our review focuses on four key areas: (1) conceptualizations and operationalizations of virtuality, in particular, exploring culture as a defining characteristic; (2) research designs utilized (i.e., experimental, field surveys, case studies); (3) the role of virtuality in the models investigated (i.e., whether it is considered an independent variable, moderator or dependent variable); and (4) outcomes of virtuality (dependent variables investigated). In each of these areas, we first summarize the state of the art and the limitations of the current research, and then we develop recommendations for future research, essentially laying out a plan for where we can go from here. In this regard, we emphasize the most promising directions for future research concerning cultural variations in virtual work.

Conceptualizations and operationalizations of virtuality

Early research on virtual work defined it as "work carried out in a location remote from the central offices or production facilities, where the worker has no personal contact with coworkers but is able to communicate with them electronically" (Cascio, 2000, p. 85), while virtual teams were initially defined as groups of geographically distributed coworkers that are assembled using a combination of telecommunications and information technologies to accomplish a variety of critical tasks (Townsend, DeMarie, and Hendrickson, 1998).

Definitions of this type assumed that teams could be viewed as either completely virtual or completely face-to-face, leading researchers to treat virtual teams as a single "ideal" type (Bell and Kozlowski, 2002, p. 16), and a common research design in the early experimental research was comparing manipulations of pure face-to-face versus pure computer-mediated interactions (e.g., Kiesler, Siegel, and McGuire, 1984; Spears and Lea, 1992; Straus and McGrath, 1994; Walther, 1995; Huang *et al.*, 2002).

Scholars have now shifted away from this dichotomy to focus on the extent of virtualness, recognizing that most teams can be described on a continuum of virtuality. Further, there is conceptual agreement that virtuality is multidimensional (Griffith, Sawyer, and Neale, 2003; Martins, Gilson, and Maynard, 2004; Kirkman and Mathieu, 2005), but the number and complexity of the dimensions varies from one conceptual framework to another. Of the 207 articles uncovered in the Web of Science search, 198 (96 percent) included more than one dimension and 108 (52 percent) included at least *three* dimensions.[2] For example, Nemiro (2002) defined virtual teams as geographically dispersed, relying heavily on information technology to accomplish work, with fluid membership. Majchrzak *et al.* (2000) defined virtual teams as those that are geographically distributed and reliant on technology, with a more malleable structure than traditional teams. Shin (2004) suggested that virtuality is the degree to which a group has temporal, cultural, spatial, and organizational dispersion, and communicates through electronic means. Paul *et al.* (2005) argued that virtual teams are those that cut across national, functional, and organizational boundaries and are connected by telecommunications and information technology. Kirkman and Mathieu (2005) included three dimensions: the extent to which team members use

---

[2] In many articles, authors offered a formal definition of what it means to be virtual. In these instances, identifying the number of dimensions in their conceptualization was straightforward. However, when no formal definition was offered, a feature was considered a defining dimension of virtuality when authors described it as "typical of" or "prevalent in" the teams under consideration.

virtual tools, the amount of informational value provided by such tools, and the synchronicity of team members' interaction. Finally, Harvey, Novicevic, and Garrison (2005) defined virtual teams as geographically and organizationally dispersed, with members who work in different time zones, in different nations around the world, with membership that is often temporary and structure that is transitory, and who communicate primarily via technology.

Summarizing across this growing literature, the most common characteristics conceptualized as comprising virtuality are geographic dispersion, electronic dependence, and national (or cultural) diversity. Specifically, in the Web of Science search, 201 (97 percent) of the articles included geographic dispersion, 176 (85 percent) included electronic dependence, and sixty-two (30 percent) included national/cultural diversity. However, a key limitation in this literature is that although virtuality is often conceptualized as multi-dimensional construct, *it is seldom empirically operationalized using multiple dimensions.* Amazingly, only fourteen articles (7 percent) operationalized virtuality using more than one dimension, and six of these included only two dimensions.

The appendix summarizes sixty-two articles which have included national/cultural diversity as a defining element of virtuality. It is important to note that even when national or cultural diversity is not formally included in the definition of virtuality, it is frequently mentioned in passing as an important feature that coincides with geographic dispersion (e.g., see Hinds and Mortenson, 2005). In addition, nearly one-third (sixty-four, representing or 31 percent) of the articles we reviewed included samples that consisted of team members in different countries. In most of these studies, national diversity is assumed to exist in these teams (even if it was not measured), and it is assumed that national diversity coincides with cultural diversity. As a result, authors often invoke cultural explanations for the causal mechanisms associated with the effects of national diversity as an element of virtuality.

For example, Gibson and Gibbs (2006) unpack four characteristics often associated with new "virtual" team designs – geographic dispersion, electronic dependence, structural dynamism, and national diversity – and in doing so, they examine a curious paradox. That is, although teams with these characteristics are often implemented by organizations to increase innovation, they often hinder it. They first tested the plausibility of their arguments using in-depth qualitative analysis of interviews with 177 members of fourteen teams in a variety of industries. A second study constituted a more formal test of hypotheses using survey data collected from 266 members of fifty-six aerospace design teams. They find that the four team design characteristics are not highly intercorrelated, that they have independent and differential effects on innovation, with negative effects documented in most teams.

In explaining the rationale for the negative relationship between national diversity and team innovation, Gibson and Gibbs (2006) argue that nationality is a superordinate determinant of cultural identity that is engrained from birth and is likely to be more salient than a particular organizational or functional culture (Hofstede, 1991; Earley and Mosakowski, 2000). Being a salient source of identity, national diversity can hinder internal team communication, conflict resolution and the development of a shared vision, because it creates different expectations for communication practices (Gibson and Vermeulen, 2003) and reduces identification with the team as a whole (Fiol, 1991; Hambrick et al., 1998). Thus, although collaborations that consist of members from different nations may have access to more information (Watson, Kumar, and Michaelson, 1993) as a result of different worldviews (Choi, Nisbett and Norenzayan, 1999), they have been found to be fraught with difficulties that can hinder innovation through misunderstanding, stereotyping, and the inability to reach agreement, make decisions, and take action (Adler, 1997). During multicultural collaboration, differences across cultural dimensions are likely to cause communication breakdowns (Kirkman and Shapiro, 1997; Gibson and Zellmer-Bruhn, 2001), making it difficult to aggregate and process information, particularly for knowledge that is uncodified (Nonaka and Takeuchi, 1995). In addition, high national diversity and identification with nationality likely result in social categorization, a process in which individuals from different groups (e.g., nations) make "ingroup/outgroup" distinctions purely on the basis of nationality, particularly when they have inadequate information about others involved (Whitener *et al.* 1998). These distinctions can result in stereotyping, distrust and suspicion of out-group members (Brewer, 1981), reducing team identification and integration as well as the team's ability to leverage information (Adler, 1997; Hambrick *et al.*, 1998).

Similarly, although they examined collocated teams, evidence in support of this across a large sample of a variety of team types was gathered by Gibson and Vermeulen (2003). These researchers found a strong negative relationship between team demographic heterogeneity (including nationality) and team learning behaviors, a set of actions teams are likely to engage in during innovation. In particular, developing a shared vision is precarious in nationally diverse teams, due to strong identification with subgroups (Fiol, 1991; Mathieu *et al.*, 2000), and this may hamper innovation.

Unfortunately, in the studies we reviewed, it is very rare that authors actually measure the cultural mechanisms directly. For example, Krebs, Hobman and Bordia (2006) compared the consequences of demographic dissimilarity for group trust in work teams in a virtual (computer-mediated) and a face-to-face (FTF) environment. They predicted that demographic dissimilarity (based on age, gender, country of birth, and major) would be negatively associated with group trust in the FTF environment but not in the computer-mediated environment. Partial support was found for the effectiveness of computer-mediated groups in reducing the negative consequences of dissimilarity. Age dissimilarity was negatively related to trust in FTF groups but not in computer-mediated groups. Birthplace dissimilarity (e.g., members were born in different countries from different regions such, such as Australia versus Asia) was positively related to trust in computer-mediated groups. The authors suggest that this may have been true because:

> more than half of participants high in birthplace dissimilarity were from collectivist cultures such as China and the Philippines ... in a work group situation, collectivists are more likely than individualists to sacrifice personal interests for the attainment of group goals ... and are more likely

to enjoy doing what the group expects of them ... thus individuals high in birthplace dissimilarity may have perceived higher levels of trust based on their collectivist values of a more cooperative attitude toward group work. (Krebs, Hobman, and Bordia, 2006, pp. 736–7)

However, the authors did not measure the underlying cultural values in their study, and so cannot discern evidence for this explanation.

As a second example, Hardin, Fuller, and Davison (2007) conceptualize global virtual teams as technology mediated, globally distributed, and culturally diverse. The authors surveyed 243 team members from universities in the US and Hong Kong during a series of virtual team projects. Although they propose differences based on cultural values, and even go to the extent of measuring individual-collectivism, they do not use these scores in their analysis. Rather, they compare Hong Kong and US team members. Results revealed that, regardless of national background, team members reported less confidence in their ability to work in virtual team environments than traditional face-to-face environments. Team members from the US reported higher self-efficacy beliefs (both group self-efficacy and virtual team self-efficacy) than team members from collectivist cultures. Furthermore, when the reference for efficacy beliefs changed from the individual to the group, the magnitude of change was greater for the Hong Kong versus US team members.

A few authors have actually modeled differences in cultural values. A noteworthy example is the investigation conducted by Swigger *et al.* (2004). The authors discuss the results of an ongoing project to investigate how cultural factors, as identified by the Cultural Perspectives Questionnaire (CPQ), affect the performance of distributed collaborative learning teams. Interestingly, the authors do not include national/cultural diversity as part of the formal definition of virtuality, rather they describe virtual teams as consisting of geographically dispersed members who use information and communication technology and have little, if any, face-to-face contact. However, the authors do measure fifteen cultural values among fifty-five two-person teams that consisted of one student from a US university and one from a Turkish university. Students were divided into culturally diverse work-teams and assigned programming projects to be completed using special collaborative software and none had face-to-face contact. The programming tasks ranged from simple design projects to more complicated programs that required extensive collaboration. Cultural distinctions between work-teams were based upon the students' responses to the CPQ. Project performance was evaluated with respect to programming accuracy, efficiency, completeness, and style.

The results of the Swigger et al. (2004) study indicate that a team's cultural composition is a significant predictor of its performance on programming projects. Findings suggest that the cultural attributes most strongly correlated to group performance were those related to attitudes about organizational hierarchy, organizational harmony, trade-offs between future and current needs, and beliefs about how much influence individuals have on their fate. For example, Swigger and her colleagues (2004) found that when team members had a high belief in hierarchy (in the importance of a rigid power structure for society), they performed more poorly than those teams with lower levels of such beliefs. In some cases, it was disparity in values within a team that triggered poor performance, such as when teams had members with both low and high levels of the "destiny predetermined" cultural value (the belief that outcomes of future events are predetermined). Moreover, the type of programming task affected the strength of the relationship between individual cultural attributes and performance, such that when the task was complicated, high scores in hierarchy values were even more strongly associated with lower project performance.

Extensions for future research

In summary, there is consensus that virtuality is multidimensional, but empirical research examining multidimensional conceptualizations is lagging far behind the theory. In a given paper, researchers often define virtuality as consisting of four or more dimensions, but then go on to select teams for inclusion based on only one or two dimensions, failing to measure the extent to which the dimensions vary among the teams (or perhaps even among the members). Hence, greater attention needs to be paid to the measurement of virtuality. Future research should develop and use measures that assess multiple dimensions of virtuality. Even if virtuality is not considered a variable in the relationships investigated (but rather is a selection criteria or boundary condition), we recommend that the teams be assessed on multiple dimensions to confirm assumptions about the sampling design, as well as to investigate potential variance within the sample.

That is, we argue that although we may be able to characterize teams or subunits based on the degree to which the team as a whole exhibits the multiple dimensions, at the same time, it is important to also assess each individual participant's perception, experience, or extent of each dimension, given individuals may vary within teams or subunits in the extent to which they perceive the element as a defining characteristic of the team. Current work suggests that individual perceptions of virtuality may have important implications for the psychological states of virtual workers, such as the extent to which employees experience work as meaningful (Gibson et al., 2007) and thus it is important to understand what factors shape these perceptions. Specifically, recent work by Gibson and her colleagues (Gibson et al., 2007) assessed perceptions of two dimensions of virtuality (electronic dependence and geographic dispersion) at the individual level among 177 virtual team members from fourteen teams and examined the relationship between these perceptions and the psychological states of team members. They found that geographic dispersion was negatively related to three psychological states, including experienced meaningfulness, experienced responsibility, and knowledge of results, while electronic dependence was negatively related to only experienced meaningfulness and experienced responsibility. Additionally, Gibson et al. (2007) found that, for at least one dimension of virtuality (geographic dispersion), these psychological states mediated the negative relationship between virtuality and team enabling conditions, such as trust and shared understanding. Given that psychological states are important in shaping team enabling conditions, these results point to the importance of understanding perceptions of virtuality at the individual level.

In addition, although national or cultural diversity is very frequently mentioned as characterizing virtual collaborations, very little research investigates this dimension empirically. We are in dire need of studies which measure and test the effects of the cultural element of virtuality, and the manner in which it potentially interacts with the other dimensions (or perhaps is independent of them). And we would like to emphasize the importance of measuring not just national background of participants, but also their cultural values, orientations, and perspectives. We agree with recent international management scholars in the call for inclusion of multiple dimensions of culture, beyond the Hofstede Cultural Orientation Framework, to enable extensions of current research which has relied so heavily on this framework (Kirkman, Lowe, and Gibson, 2006; Leung et al., 2005). For example, Gibson and Gibbs (2006) mention the potential importance of investigating teams which include some members with "high context" cultural orientation and others with "low context" cultural orientation, referring to the importance of nonverbal, contextual cues in communicating or interpreting messages (Hall and Hall, 1987; Gordon, 1991). Members of high context cultures tend to avoid negative or confrontational responses while communicating with members of their own work group in order to save face and preserve a sense of harmony within the group (Adler, Brahm, and Graham, 1992). Members of low context cultures, on the other hand, use explicit language to convey exactly what is meant in a much more direct manner, even if the message is negative or confrontational.

An equally promising cultural phenomenon to investigate in conjunction with the cultural element of virtuality is time perspective (Gibson, Waller, Carpenter and Conte, 2007; Waller, Conte, Gibson and Carpenter, 2001). Time perspective is a cognitive frame "used in encoding, storing, and recalling experienced events, as well as in forming expectations, goals, contingencies, and imaginative scenarios" (Zimbardo and Boyd, 1999: 1272–1273). It refers to the degree of emphasis placed on

the past, present, or future by an individual. Time perspective may play an especially critical role in teams that are highly virtual because it is considered to result largely from national culture, socialization, and life experiences (Hall, 1983; Jones, 1988; Kluckhohn and Strodtbeck, 1961; Zimbardo and Boyd, 1999), which often differ in such teams where collaboration of individuals from varied backgrounds, contexts, and cultures is needed. The cognitive temporal bias created by time perspectives leads to a habitual tendency to concentrate on the past, present, or future when collecting or evaluating information or making decisions (Gibson et al., 2007). Previous empirical work indicates a robust linkage between individuals' time perspectives and decision-making, goal commitment, and goal attainment (Zimbardo and Boyd, 1999); recent conceptual work suggests that differences in time perspective among team members may affect team outcomes under deadline conditions (Waller et al., 2001).

Another promising avenue which we encourage is examining awareness of cultural differences in virtual collaborations. This approach was used by Edwards and Sridhar (2005) in an examination of twenty-four virtual software development teams from Canada and India. The authors investigated how trust, task structure, and virtuality (operationalized as perceptions of cultural diversity among team members and perceptions of problems caused by time zone differences) affect multiple outcomes. Trust between the teams and well-defined task structure were found to positively influence the efficiency, effectiveness, and satisfaction level of the teams. Although no significant relationships were uncovered between awareness of cultural diversity and outcomes, the sample consisted of students rather than workers in organizational settings, and hence may underestimate the potential effects of individual perceptions. Therefore, we see this as a promising avenue for future research.

At the very least, researchers examining only one element of virtuality should explicitly state the rationale for doing so and should ensure that these research designs do not confound different elements. For example, studies which intend to examine geographic dispersion, divide subjects into two types of teams – (1) face-to-face; or

(2) geographically dispersed – and then require the geographically dispersed participants to use electronic communication, cannot tease out the potential differential effects of the geographic dispersion versus the electronic communication. Gibson and Gibbs (2006) found that these features have different effects, and proposed that they do so based on differential causal mechanisms (although they admit that a limitation of their design is that they could not examine these underlying processes in their study). Different causal mechanisms imply different managerial techniques in order to address unique challenges associated with the features. Future research should specifically investigate the unique causal mechanisms; designs that confound geographic dispersion and electronic communication do not enable such fine-grained analysis.

Research designs for investigating virtuality

Speaking more specifically to the issue of research designs, we found that the majority of articles addressing virtuality over the last six years have been theoretical, case studies, or experimental, with only a handful using field data to empirically assess virtuality along with the other variables of interest. Specifically, of the 207 articles extracted, three (1 percent) were meta-analyses, sixty-two (30 percent) were non-empirical (conceptual, review, and practitioner-oriented), forty-eight (23 percent) were case studies, fifty-nine (29 percent) were laboratory experiments (i.e., virtuality was manipulated or a selection criteria), and only thirty-five (17 percent) were field studies. Further, only nineteen (9 percent) of the studies actually measured one or more elements of virtuality in the field; the remaining field studies simply list virtuality criteria for team inclusion, but do not directly measure any given element of virtuality. We review each of these categories in turn in this section.

Meta-analyses

None of the three meta-analytic studies examined the role of culture as an element of virtuality. Dennis and Wixom (2001) conceptualized

virtuality as geographically and temporally dispersed work reliant on technology to communicate. They examined 119 relationships in sixty-one studies that included both virtual and collocated teams to make comparisons, with virtual teams defined as those that worked separated by distance or time. Across these studies, they found that decision quality is lower in virtual teams, but the number of ideas generated is the same as the number generated in face-to-face teams using group support software, and that decision time is shorter and satisfaction higher when teams are larger. In addition, process facilitation is associated with higher decision quality and satisfaction with the process.

Focusing on levels of analysis issues in investigating distributed teams that are reliant on communications technology, Gallivan and Benbunan-Fich (2005) reviewed all empirical studies of electronic collaboration from seven information systems journals for the period 1999–2003. Summarizing relationships across the thirty-six articles identified, they found that a majority of these studies contain one or more problems of levels incongruence that cast doubts on the validity of their results. They argue that these methodological problems are in part responsible for the inconsistent results reported in this literature, especially given researchers' frequent decision to analyze data at the individual level – even when the theory was formulated at the group level and when the research setting featured individuals working in groups – may very well have artificially inflated the authors' chances of finding statistically significant results.

Finally, most recently, DeRosa, Smith and Hantula (2007) compared electronic brainstorming groups, face-to-face groups, and nominal groups (individuals on their own) across seventy-six relationships reported in seventeen studies. Findings indicated that electronic brainstorming groups are more productive and more satisfied with the interaction process than face-to-face groups. Small nominal groups had more non-redundant ideas than small electronic brainstorming groups, but large electronic brainstorming groups had more non-redundant ideas than large nominal groups.

Conceptual, review, and case studies

The insightful article by Barczak, McDough and Athanassiou (2006) provides an example of a non-empirical piece which addresses the role of culture as an element of virtuality. The authors conceptualize global new product development teams as globally dispersed and culturally and functionally diverse. Summarizing ten years of research on leading and managing global, as well as traditional, new product development teams, they surface four key challenges facing global team leaders: team members who speak different native languages, have different cultural backgrounds, who reside in multiple countries, and who come from different organizations. For each challenge, the authors identify skills and attributes that global team leaders need to possess as well as actions they need to take to ensure the success of their global teams.

Kankanhalli, Tan and Wei (2006) offer an example of a case study which addresses culture. The authors conceptualize virtuality as: (1) technology mediation; (2) global distribution; (3) cultural diversity; and (4) rarely having face-to-face contact. They examined virtuality in three teams of graduate students from universities in the US, Europe, and Asia to develop propositions concerning the antecedents and effects of global virtual team conflict. They propose that cultural diversity, specifically in terms of individualism-collectivism, contributes to both task and relationship conflict while functional diversity results in task conflict. Further, they propose that the quantity of e-mail and lack of feedback inherent in technology mediated communication can contribute to task conflict. Finally, they suggest that the relationship between conflict and performance may be contingent upon task complexity, task interdependence, and conflict resolution approaches.

Experimental designs

In addition to the Swigger et al. (2004) study described above, which involved an experimental design, a second example of a laboratory experiment which included national/cultural diversity is a study by Paul, Samarah, Seeetharaman and Mykytyn (2005). Defining virtual teams as those that cut across national, functional, and organizational boundaries, and are connected by telecommunication and information technology, the authors investigated eighty-three subjects from the US and India, divided into twenty-two teams (nine culturally heterogeneous with US and Indian team member, four with all US members and nine with members from India) who worked on a decision task involving the adoption of a computer-use fee by an online university. Team members used a web-based group decision support system (GDSS) that allowed them the opportunity to discuss task options, critique suggestions, and vote on the result. Findings indicated that collaborative conflict management style positively impacted satisfaction with the decision-making process, perceived decision quality, and perceived participation of the virtual teams. Group diversity was found to have a moderating influence between collaborative style and group performance, and collaborative style was influenced by the individualistic-collectivistic orientations. Collectivistic orientations helped enhance the level of collaborative conflict management style prevailing in teams. Specifically, the authors found that the higher the individualistic orientation of a virtual team, the lower its collaborative conflict management style. When members of a virtual team were predominantly individualistic, there was very little tendency to pursue interests that were shared collectively by all in the group unless the collective interest matched the self interest (Paul et al. 2005, p. 209). As a result, the authors suggest that cooperation among individualists may be best induced by the "contingent receipt of personal incentives (for example, merit pay for effective team work)" while cooperation among collectivists "can be motivated by receipt of outcomes that benefit the entire membership (for example, safe work environment)." Thus, this research also indicates that the process to motivate team members may differ depending on their orientation.

Field studies

In addition to the Gibson and Gibbs (2006) study described above, a second example of a field study which included nationality/culture is the investigation conducted by Chudoba, Wynn, Lu, and Watson-Manhein (2005). Using the concept of discontinuities, or changes in expected conditions, the authors propose a virtuality index to assess how "virtual" a given setting is. The discontinuities included geography, time zone, organization, national culture, work practices, and technology. The index separately measures these aspects of virtuality and their effect on perceived team performance. An online survey administered to a stratified random sample of 1,269 members at Intel Corporation consisted of eighteen questionnaire items that asked individuals how frequently they experienced the discontinuities. Data clustered into three overarching discontinuities: team distribution, workplace mobility, and differences in work practices (people changing teams, working with those who use different types of technology, and cultural differences). Differences in work practices were negatively related to performance. Interestingly, being distributed, in and of itself, had no impact on team performance, and work practice predictability and sociability mitigated effects of working in discontinuous environments. As a result, the authors highlight the importance of developing a foundation for shared expectations in order to lessen the negative effects of discontinuities in virtual teams.

Longitudinal designs

We were very pleased to see that a total of twenty-eight studies included a longitudinal component. Of these, fourteen were case studies, thirteen were laboratory experiments, and one was a field study. Demonstrating the importance of change over time in virtual teams, Rutkowski, Vogel, Bemelmans, and van Genuchten (2002) conducted a study with a sample of 178 students from the Netherlands and China, to explore how individuals in virtual teams use technology and experience culture while working on projects over time. The authors describe virtual team members as being: (1) geographically dispersed; (2) culturally diverse; (3) temporary; (4) reliant on electronic communication; (5) and having a lack of face-to-face interaction. All teams of two to four students participated in an IT-focused project over a period of six weeks using the same

type of technology, an internet-based group support system, to communicate with one another, helping to reduce problems of technological discontinuities described above. A survey assessing cultural values and other variables was administered before the project commenced and again after the project was completed. Team members exhibited increased levels of shared meaning and shifts in beliefs over the course of the project. Specifically, before the project, the desire to have a set hierarchy, a leader for the group, and interdependence among group members were stronger for the Chinese participants than for the Dutch participants. Over the six-week period of virtual work on the project, the Chinese and Dutch members' beliefs converged, with both types of members reporting that hierarchy and having a leader for the group were less important than they had first believed. Interdependence became more important for the Dutch members. Consistent with several recommendations made by Chudoba *et al.* (2005) above, Rutkowski and colleagues (2002) argue that ensuring team members use similar types of technology and creating common ground through shared understanding of work requirements are critical steps in helping virtual team members overcome cultural differences. The results of this study suggest that because beliefs of virtual workers may shift over time, perhaps from experience working with people from diverse cultures, it is important to take a longitudinal approach to studying cultural phenomena in distributed teams.

Extensions for future research

Although non-empirical articles still represent approximately 30 percent of those published during the period we examined, we have reached a point in the development of the domain that empirical studies are keeping better pace with conceptual developments. This is a positive trend that we hope to see continue. We also appreciate the very rigorous work being done in the lab to isolate important features of virtuality and to tease out specific effects under controlled conditions. In particular, we know much more about communication processes and information sharing when work is more, rather than less virtual, as a result of these studies (e.g., Lowry *et al.*, 2006: Sarker, 2005; Sarker *et al.*, 2005; Whitman *et al.*, 2005). Although less work on the culture element of virtuality has been done in the lab, notable exceptions include (Sarker, 2005; Sarker *et al.*, 2005; Staples and Zhao, 2006), which have enriched our understanding of the effects of culture on conflict (Staples and Zhao, 2006) and how cultural values shape knowledge transfer in virtual settings (Sarker, 2005; Sarker *et al.*, 2005).

At the same time, we believe there are important dynamics associated with virtuality, such as the development of team cohesion, commitment, and the process of relationship building, that can only be truly understood in the field – that is, by examination of employees who work with some degree of virtuality on work tasks with important consequences to themselves and their organizations. Hence, we were dismayed at how few studies (less than 10 percent of those reviewed) measured dimensions of virtuality in the field among real workers. We need many more field studies using the careful measurement techniques we discussed in the previous section in order to increase our understanding of how virtuality operates in actual organizational settings. Including a longitudinal component to these studies is also critical, given early evidence that virtuality effects change over time, for example, trust (Kanawattanachai and Yoo, 2002; Krebs, Hobman, and Bordia. 2006; Wilson, Straus, and McEvily 2006) shared understanding (Baba *et al.*, 2004; Hasty, Massey, and Brown, 2006), and performance, such as perceived decision quality (Tan *et al.*, 2000). Other phenomena likely to operate very differently in longer term virtual work include identity dynamics, commitment to a team or task, and communication protocols.

The role of virtuality in organizational models

The role of virtuality in causal models has been somewhat limited. Across the 207 articles, the most common role of virtuality was as an independent variable (i.e., in a total of thirty-two (15 percent) of the studies reviewed). In these studies the effects, outcomes or consequences of one or more element

of virtuality were examined. Virtuality has also been conceptualized as a moderator. In this section, we review these two ways in which virtuality has been featured in prior studies, and discuss other possible roles that virtuality might play as an area ripe for future research.

Virtuality as independent variable

An example of a study in which virtuality is featured as an independent variable is that conducted by Cramton and Webber (2005). The authors conceptualize virtuality as having interdependence, a common purpose, working across locations and time, and using CMC much more than FTF, and indicate that virtual teams are likely to be culturally diverse (2005, p. 759). They examined the impact of virtuality on work processes and perceived performance in thirty-nine work teams from an international consulting firm. The teams were either entirely collocated (working together in the same office) or virtual (with at least 30 percent of team members working at other offices). Cramton and Webber (2005) surveyed the teams and found that the virtual teams had less effective work processes in terms of communication and coordination, than did the collocated teams. The authors reasoned that this is because the virtual teams are more likely to have different cultural and organizational backgrounds that generate contextual differences between members, yet members are not likely to identify and discuss these differences. Further analysis revealed that work processes partially moderated the negative relationship between virtuality and perceived performance.

These findings highlight the significance of effective work processes for virtual team performance, although the fact that work processes only partially mediated the relationship between virtuality and performance suggests that there may be other important factors at work. To push our understanding of these relationships further, Cramton and Webber (2005) argue that features such as the nature of the work being performed, how the work is structured, and the psychological consequences of virtual work, may be relevant. In particular, the authors also suggest that to better manage the challenges associated with geographic dispersion, such as divergent cultural values, it is important to facilitate connections between team members and between team members and the task.

Virtuality as moderator

A total of seven studies (3 percent) examined virtuality as a moderator. In these studies, the manner in which being virtual changes the nature of the relationship between some other feature of collaboration and outcomes are examined. For example, in addition to examining the direct impact of virtuality on task and affective conflict, Mortensen and Hinds (2001) also investigated whether virtuality moderated the relationship between shared identity and task and affective conflict. They conceptualized virtual teams as work groups that have (1) members who work in more than one geographic location, (2) are forced to rely heavily on communication technology, and (3) have national differences; and they argue that, with national differences, there are likely to be cultural differences represented on highly virtual teams (Mortensen and Hinds, 2001, p. 216). Among a sample of twenty-four product development teams from five companies, the authors compared teams that operated face-to-face to those that were nationally and internationally distributed (teams were considered nationally distributed if members were spread across more than one location in a single country; internationally distributed teams had members in more than one country). They found that team identity was associated with less task and affective conflict for distributed teams, but not for collocated teams. Further, task and affective conflict were negatively related to performance in the distributed teams, but not for the collocated teams. Because managers can cultivate a virtual team's shared identity by increasing interdependence among members and building common goals, these findings suggest that a team's shared identity may offer managers an important tool in helping distributed teams to manage conflict.

Virtuality as dependent variable

None of the studies uncovered in our search empirically examined virtuality as a dependent variable.

However, authors refer to a multitude of factors that precede (or result in) an organizations' use of virtual teams. Several features of work commonly cited as resulting in the use of virtual teams include: increased complexity and uncertainty of work (e.g. Barzcak, McDonough, and Athanassiou, 2006; Dani *et al.*, 2006), advances in information and communication technology (e.g. Dani *et al.*, 2006; Hinds and Mortenson, 2005; Ocker, 2005), the increasingly global nature of work and resources (e.g. Barczak, McDonough, and Athanassiou, 2006; Erik, 2005), and barriers to using traditional teams, such as time and expense (e.g. Fletcher and Major, 2006). For example, Barczak , McDonough, and Athanassiou, (2006, p. 28) state:

> As companies move into the global arena, they find the process of developing and launching new products becoming progressively more complex as they attempt to meet both global and local customer needs and integrate design and development expertise scattered around the world. To cope with these demands, many firms are turning to global new product development teams.

The authors conceptualize such teams as "complex, often composed of individuals who are culturally, ethnically and functionally diverse and who work and live in different countries where the firm has operations of varying sizes and capabilities" (2006, p. 28) and state that team members often speak different languages, have dissimilar cultural values, and have very little face-to-face interaction in the course of their work.

Likewise, Fuller, Hardin, and Davison, (2006, p. 210) state that:

> the use of virtual teams to accomplish work objectives is becoming increasingly prevalent in today's organizations (Griffith, Sawyer, and Neale, 2003; Jarvenpaa and Leidner, 1999; Jarvenpaa, Shaw, and Staples, 2004; Majchrzak *et al.*, 2004; Majchrzak *et al.*, 2000; Malhotra, *et al.*, 2001; Massey, Montoya-Weiss, and Hung, 2003; Montoya-Weiss, Massey, and Song, 2001). This trend is expected to continue (Lipnack and Stamps, 2000) for a variety of reasons, including reduced travel costs, increased organizational benefits from using the best talent regardless of location (Cairncross, 2001; Duarte and Snyder, 2001, Espinosa *et al.*, 2003), and the greater availability

of sophisticated technology to support such distributed work (Boudreau et al. 1998; Paul, 2006, Staples, Hulland, and Higgins, 1999).

Similarly, suggesting that "e-collaboration technology" (information and communication technologies that support communication, information sharing and coordination, and individuals and organizations) may be an important antecedent to virtuality, Erik (2005, p. 78) states:

> To meet the opportunities and challenges from increasing globalization of markets and industries, companies restructure their operations according to new business models (Boudreau et al. 1998). Virtual organizations (Mowshowitz, 1997), supply chain management (Robb, 2003), and collaborative commerce (c-commerce) (Bechek and Brea, 2001) are all examples of such business models, often implying tight collaboration among organizations in different parts of the world. The enabling infrastructure for these forms of distributed collaboration is e-collaboration technologies.

Extensions for future research

In summary, the virtuality literature is not yet characterized by creative use of the concept of virtuality in a variety of different conceptual roles. Rather, when it is measured, virtuality is typically viewed as an antecedent to other effects. Further, we would like to reiterate that in some studies, although elements of virtuality were measured, they were simply used as controls (e.g. Jarvenpaa, Shaw, and Staples, 2004; Kirkman, Lowe, and Gibson 2006), rather than as components of a causal model. In many other studies (e.g. Barut, Yildirim, and Kilic, 2006; Kotlarsky and Oshri, 2005; Panteli and Davison, 2005; Qureshi, Liu, and Voegl, 2006; Sarker et al., 2005; Sarker and Sahay, 2004; Tan et al., 2000) elements of virtuality were selection criteria or boundary conditions, rather than serving as measured variables for use in hypothesis testing.

We would like to encourage researchers to think about elements of virtuality as central components of causal models and as important variables to measure and include in hypothesis testing. While the line of research examining consequences of virtuality remains critical, we hope that researchers

will also consider virtuality as a moderator. We know from the handful of studies examining virtuality as a moderator that it can impact such relationships as those between conflict and performance (Mortensen and Hinds, 2001) and between teamwork and performance (Hoegl et al., 2007), but there are many other potential effects that virtuality may moderate, such as the positive relationship Qureshi, Liu, and Voegl (2006) found between positive communication and shared understanding. Given the importance of communication in virtual teams, this relationship may be even stronger in dispersed settings. Additionally, the positive relationship between communication and knowledge transfer found by Sarker (2005) may be weaker in virtual teams, suggesting it may be important to communicate more extensively in virtual teams than in collocated teams.

Further, we propose that more work is needed to examine the antecedents of virtuality. We know very little about whether virtuality is even a choice! We know even less about the factors that drive specific decisions regarding each element of virtuality. For example, are culturally diverse teams assembled primarily for the purposes of increasing creativity and innovation? For political or legal reasons? Based on strategic rationale, in order to increase local responsiveness of new products or to develop access to new markets? Coupled with such questions, it will be interesting to examine whether incorporating virtuality in organizational designs delivers on the motivations that underlie the establishment of such designs. This leads us to our final section regarding the outcomes of establishing virtuality.

Consequences of virtuality

Given that most research has examined virtuality as an independent variable, we thought it important to explore the range of consequences associated with virtuality in the research we reviewed. Consequences can be categorized into four major areas, including performance, attitudes and beliefs, team characteristics and processes, and technology use. We review each of these categories in this section.

Performance

A total of fourteen studies (7 percent) investigated the effects of virtuality on a variety of performance outcomes. Although most studies found significant relationships between virtuality and performance, in many cases the direction of the relationships were inconsistent across studies. For example, Dennis and Wixom (2001) found that virtuality was negatively related to decision quality, however, two earlier studies found a positive relationship between virtuality and decision quality (Huang *et al.*, 2002; Schmidt, Montoya-Weiss, and Massey, 2001). Similarly, while virtuality was found to be negatively related to innovation in one study (Gibson and Gibbs, 2006), a recent meta-analysis found that virtuality was positively related to brainstorming performance (DeRosa, Smith, and Hantula, 2007). Further, virtuality has been both positively (Staples and Zhao, 2006) and negatively (Cummings and Kiesler, 2005; Swigger *et al.*, 2004) related to performance on individual tasks and projects. The studies in our sample also demonstrate that virtuality may be significantly negatively related to team members' perceptions of performance (Chudoba *et al.* 2005; Cramton and Webber, 2005). One study by Fletcher and Major (2006) found that groups using audio communication only had lower perceived performance than FTF groups, although the two groups did not differ significantly in the number of errors they made. However, although it was not the focus of their study, Fletcher and Major (2006) found no significant differences in error rate or perceived performance between FTF groups and groups that communicated via audio and shared workspace, which perhaps is a more accurate reflection of a virtual team than groups using audio only.

As a noteworthy example, the study conducted by Staple and Zhao (2006) offers useful insight into how virtuality affects team performance. The authors define virtual teams as those that are geographically distributed, who rely on communication technology, who have members from different countries of origin, and whose members have different native languages and cultural values. Four types of teams were created that varied across two dimensions – (1) FTF vs. computer-mediated and (2) culturally homogenous vs. culturally heterogeneous – among a sample of 380 graduate and undergraduate students in Canada, resulting in seventy-two teams. Members were placed into teams based on their native language and individualism-collectivism values. The authors found that virtual culturally heterogeneous teams had significantly higher performance than FTF culturally heterogeneous teams. They suggest that computer-mediated communication may actually mask some of the cultural differences that are more obvious when working face to face, and thus reduce potential negative impacts of heterogeneity.

Attitudes and beliefs

A second category of consequences of virtuality, examined in a total of twelve (6 percent) of the studies reviewed, includes those pertaining to team member attitudes and beliefs, such as satisfaction (e.g. Golden, 2006b), commitment (e.g. Huang *et al.*, 2002), and trust (e.g. Polzer *et al.*, 2006). Among the articles examining the relationship between virtuality and different types of satisfaction, Golden (2006b) found that virtuality had a curvilinear relationship with job satisfaction, such that, up to a certain point, for increasing levels of virtuality there were increases in job satisfaction after which higher levels of virtuality then became negatively related to job satisfaction. Additionally, DeRosa *et al.* (2007) found a positive relationship between virtuality and satisfaction with the interaction process. However, a third study looking at satisfaction in virtual teams found that virtual teams had lower levels of group satisfaction with group experience than FTF teams (Whitman *et al.*, 2005). Additionally, Staples and Zhao (2006) found that virtuality, as measured by cultural diversity, was negatively related to satisfaction in virtual teams. Several studies also found that virtuality was positively related to commitment (Golden, 2006a), negatively related to turnover intentions and work exhaustion (Golden, 2006b), and that members of virtual teams react more negatively to unfair events (Tangirila and Alge, 2006). Finally, two studies found that virtuality was significantly related to trust, including Polzer *et al.*, (2006) and Wilson, Struas, and McEvily (2006). Polzer *et al.*

(2006) found that while virtuality in general has a negative impact on trust, groups with homogenous subgroups can have lower trust than completely diverse teams, suggesting that different dimensions of virtuality may have different effects on trust.

Interestingly, the study by Wilson, Straus, and McEvily (2006) demonstrated that trust evolves over time in virtual teams. Wilson, Straus, and McEvily (2006) describe virtual teams as "technology mediated-groups" that are separated by space and whose members use technology to communicate. The authors examined how trust in face-to-face teams differs from trust in computer-mediated teams among a sample of fifty-two four-person teams of undergraduate students in the US. The findings demonstrated that while trust started out lower in virtual teams, it rises over time so that eventually there are no significant differences in levels of trust between face-to-face groups and computer-mediated groups. These findings extend earlier work by Jarvenpaa and colleagues (1998, 1999) by explicitly comparing levels of trust in both FTF teams and virtual teams. Findings by Wilson, Straus, and McEvily. (2006) suggest that despite differences in early levels of trust compared to FTF teams, given enough time, virtual teams can build the trust they need to function successfully.

Team characteristics and processes

A third set of studies that examined consequences of virtuality (eighteen, or 8 percent of studies) focused on relationships with team characteristics and processes such as teamwork and team cohesion (e.g. Fletcher and Major, 2006; Huang et al., 2002; Hoegl and Proserpio, 2004; Staples and Zhao, 2006) coordination (Cummings and Kiesler, 2005), and conflict (Polzer et al., 2006). Recent research has found virtuality to be associated with higher levels of member contribution (Chidambaram and Tung, 2005), lower levels of perceived communication effectiveness (Whitman et al., 2005), and lower levels of collaborative conflict management style (Paul et al., 2004). A negative relationship was also found between virtuality and the availability of social information (Tangirala and Alge, 2006), work processes involving communication and coordination (Cramton and Webber, 2005;

Cummings and Kiesler, 2005; Hoegl and Proserpio, 2004) knowing what others expect, and having a sense of making progress on projects (Whitman et al., 2005). Whitman et al. (2005) also found that virtuality was positively related to perceptions that decision making was difficult. At the same time, positive effects of virtuality have been found on affective and task conflict in virtual teams (Hinds and Mortensen, 2005; Polzer et al., 2006, Staples and Zhao, 2006). Other studies examined the effect of virtuality on issues involving knowledge sharing among team members (e.g. Sarker, 2005; Akgun et al., 2005). For example, Sarker (2005) conceptualized virtual teams as those with members of different cultural backgrounds, different geographic locations, separated by space and time, whose communication is mediated by communication technology. Using survey data and e-mail messages among eighty-five students in eleven teams from the US and Thailand, Sarker's (2005) findings suggest that teams with higher levels of individualistic cultural values were more likely to transfer knowledge in virtual teams.

Technology use

Finally, the fourth set of virtuality consequences examined (in four, or 2 percent of studies) pertained to technology use. For example, using both survey and interview data from individuals across five organizations, Sapsed et al. (2005) examined the effects of virtuality (being co-located or dispersed) on team members use of multiple types of technology, including telephone, e-mail, videoconferencing, groupware, and websites, to complete several common information sharing tasks. They found that dispersed and co-located team members tend to use FTF interaction, e-mail, and project websites at about the same rate to deal with organizational tasks. However, Sapsed et al. (2005) did find important differences suggesting that dispersed team members used the telephone to a much greater extent than FTF teams, especially to verify and validate information. The authors also found that dispersed team members relied more heavily on videoconferencing for knowledge-intensive work than their co-located counterparts. In a second example, Timmerman and Scott (2006) demonstrated, among a sample of ninety-eight members of virtual teams in the US, that virtuality, as measured by number of time zones, number of locations, and importance of cultural diversity, was positively related to communication technology use.

Non-significant effects

Although the studies above demonstrate that potential virtuality has as a predictor of organizationally relevant outcomes, a number of studies also found non-significant relationships when virtuality was included as an independent variable. For example, Chidambaram and Tung (2005), Edwards and Sridhar (2005), and Whitman et al. (2005) found no relationship between virtuality and performance. Similar inconsistencies exist regarding virtuality and satisfaction; out of the seven articles assessing this relationship, three found no significant effects (Dennis and Wixom, 2002; Edwards and Sridhar, 2005; Timmerman and Scott, 2006). Likewise, while the three studies mentioned above found significant effects of virtuality on team cohesion, two found no relationship between the two variables (Timmerman and Scott, 2006; Chidambaram and Tung, 2005). Non-significant effects have also emerged in studies examining the effects of virtuality on use of technology (Mortensen and Hinds, 2001), internet self-efficacy (O'Malley and Kelleher, 2002), trust (Timmerman and Scott, 2006), commitment (Huang et al., 2002), communication quality and collaborative environment (Huang et al., 2002; Lowry et al., 2006), learning effectiveness (Edwards and Sridhar, 2005), and conflict (Mortensen and Hinds, 2001).

Extensions for future research

We view as particularly important research which helps to address the conflicting results regarding performance outcomes for virtuality. Given that six of the fourteen articles assessing the impact of virtuality on performance found a negative relationship (Chudoba et al., 2005; Cramton and Webber, 2005; Cummings and Kiesler, 2005; Dennis and Wixom, 2001; Gibson and Gibbs, 2006; Swigger

et al., 2004), another four found a positive relationship (DeRosa, Smith, and Hantula, 2007; Huang et al., 2002; Schmidt, Montoya-Weiss, and Massey 2001; Staples and Zhao, 2006), and four found no relationship or mixed results (Chidambaram and Tung, 2005; Edwards and Sridhar, 2005; Fletcher and Major, 2006; Whitman et al., 2005), it is clear that this is an issue of vital importance for researchers in this area to resolve. The two meta-analyses that examine the relationship between virtuality and performance do not provide much additional clarity, as Dennis and Wixom (2001) found that virtuality was negatively related to decision quality in virtual teams compared to face-to-face teams, while DeRosa et al. (2007) found that electronic brainstorming groups were more productive than face-to-face groups. Interestingly, five of the six studies where a negative relationship was found involved field research in which team members from corporate organizations. In contrast, nearly all of the studies that found a positive relationship between virtuality and performance, and the four studies that found no relationship or mixed results, involved student subjects.

Future research adopting a conceptualization of virtuality as a multi-dimensional continuum and examining performance effects over time may provide the insight needed to resolve this debate. Type and complexity of task is also likely to be a factor impacting whether virtuality has a positive or negative impact on performance (e.g. Straus and McGrath, 1994). For example, previous work has found that as task complexity increases, virtual teams perform less effectively than face-to-face teams (Straus and McGrath, 1994). It is very likely that tasks performed by teams in the field, such as software development projects (e.g. Cramton and Webber, 2005), will be far more complex than tasks completed in laboratory settings, such as the desert survival exercise (e.g. Potter and Balthazard, 2002; Staples and Zhao, 2006). This suggests that findings from laboratory studies may not generalize to teams in the field. Future research should either examine, or at least control for, task type and complexity to take these important factors into account.

We would also like to encourage research that examines the conditions under which effects of virtuality may turn from negative to positive. For example, in the Gibson and Gibbs (2006) study, each of the four elements of virtuality (geographic dispersion, electronic dependence, national diversity, structural dynamism) was negatively related to innovation. However, these authors found that the elements of virtuality were positively associated with innovation when a psychologically safe communication climate (PSCC) was in place. For example, such a climate helps to bridge national differences and reduce in-group/out-group bias (Gudykunst, 1991; Maznevski, 1994). Larkey (1996) has argued that the social categorization process that occurs in diverse teams often results in "divergence," defined as adherence to culturally based communication patterns. This can be contrasted with convergence, defined as adjustment of one's communication style to match one's partner. Convergence is more common when there is a PSCC, and it helps counterbalance in-group/out-group dynamics (Larkey, 1996), which can facilitate innovation.

Open and accommodating communication is an important antecedent of shared cognition (Gibson and Zellmer-Bruhn, 2001) in its absence team mental models have been found to diverge over time (Levesque, Wilson, and Wholey, 2001). Team members who communicate more supportively with one another are more likely to develop a common frame of reference and shared mental model (Klimoski and Mohammed, 1994). Further, the innovation process requires that the parties involved suspend judgment, remain open to others' ideas, and put forth the effort required to integrate new knowledge with existing knowledge to produce the innovation. When this occurs, exposure to new processes of working or a new approach to a problem may propel one to pursue previously unexplored directions or to integrate new ideas leading to novel and innovative solutions (Okhuysen and Eisenhardt, 2002; Perry-Smith and Shalley, 2003). In support of this, Gibson and Vermeulen (2003) found that the differences associated with national demographic heterogeneity in teams could be bridged if mild subgroups formed and created a psychologically safe environment. Through information exchange, members identified and developed more commonalities, reducing in-group/

out-group barriers and increasing information processing capacity (Gibson and Vermeulen, 2003).

Conclusions

In conclusion, although increasing attention has been paid to the issue of virtuality in the workplace in recent years, there are still important gaps in our knowledge that need to be addressed in future research. With regard to how virtuality is conceptualized and operationalized, our review demonstrates that while there is general agreement regarding the multi-dimensional nature of virtuality, few studies actually measured any dimension of virtuality, much less the multiple dimensions. Such assessment is integral to exploring the varied and potentially differential effects of different elements of virtuality. Additionally, as we have demonstrated, many researchers recognize the importance of culture as a key dimension of virtuality, and include teams with members from different countries in their studies. However, these same studies rarely empirically examine or include culture in their analytical models. Given the importance of cultural values in shaping a wide range of phenomena, future research should explore the cultural dimension of virtual teams in order for us to better understand virtual team characteristics and outcomes. Additionally, our review highlights the importance of expanding the scope of the research designs utilized (i.e., experimental, field surveys, case studies). While research using field studies is on the rise, there is still a great need for empirical examination of virtual work using teams facing real world challenges. Given the demonstrated importance of change over time (e.g. Kanawattanachai and Yoo, 2002; Krebs, Hobman, and Bordia, 2006; Wilson, Straus, and McEvily, 2006), future work examining such teams should also employ a longitudinal approach.

Our review also demonstrates that while there were a number of studies examining virtuality as an independent variable, very few studies included virtuality as a moderator, and none examined virtuality as a dependent variable. Many authors offered reasons for why virtual teams are being used so extensively by organizations (e.g., globalization, improved technology), yet these ideas have yet to be empirically tested to determine the antecedents of virtual team use. Finally, we document that virtuality is associated with a variety of consequences, ranging from virtual team member satisfaction to group cohesion and performance. While several studies found significant effects for virtuality among the outcomes studied, the findings were somewhat inconsistent, particularly with regard to performance. This underscores the importance of examining these phenomena among teams in the field over an extended period of time, to fully capture the complexity of virtual team experiences. Although virtuality research has come a long way in the past decade, we still have much to discover regarding this new form of collaboration.

References

Adler, N. J. 1997. *International Dimensions of Organizational behavior*. Cincinnati, OH: South-Western College Publishing.

Brahm, R., and Graham, J. L. 1992. "Strategy implementation: a comparison of face-to-face negotiations in the People's Republic of China and the U. S.", *Strategic Management Journal* 13: 449–66.

Akgun, A. E., Byrne, J., Keskin, H., Lynn, G. S., and Imamoglu, S. Z. 2005. "Knowledge networks in new product development projects: A transactive memory perspective", *Information and Management* 42: 1105–20.

Alavi, M. and Tiwana, A. 2002. "Knowledge integration in virtual teams: The potential role of KMS", *Journal of the American Society for Information and Technology* 53: 1029–37.

Baba, M., Gluesing, J., Ratner, H., and Wagner, K. 2004. "The contexts of knowing: natural history of a globally distributed team", *Journal of Organizational Behavior* 25: 547–87.

Barczak, G., McDonough, E. F., and Athanassiou, N. 2006. "So you want to be a global project leader?", *Research-Technology Management* 49: 28–35.

Barut, M., Yildirim, M. B., and Kilic, K. 2006. "Designing a global multi-disciplinary classroom: a learning experience in supply chain logistics management", *International Journal of Engineering Education* 22: 1105–14.

Bechek, B. and Brea, C. 2001. "Deciphering collaborative commerce", *Journal of Business Strategy* 22, pp. 36–8.

Bell, B. S. and Kozlowski, S. W. J. 2002. "A typology of virtual teams: implications for effective leadership", *Group and Organization Management* 27: 14–49.

Bing, J. W. and Bing, C. M. 2001. "Helping global teams compete", *Training and Development* 55: 70–1.

Boudreau, M., Loch, K., Robey, D., and Straub, D. 1998. "Going global: using information technology to advance the competitiveness of the virtual transnational organization", *Academy of Management Executive* 12: 120–8.

Brewer, M. B. 1981. "Ethnocentrism and its role in interpersonal trust", in M. B. Brewer and B. E. Collins (eds.), *Scientific Inquiry and the Social Sciences*. New York, NY: Jossey-Bass, pp. 345–60.

Cairncross, F. 2001. *Death of Distance: How the Communication Revolution is Changing Our Lives*. Boston, MA: Harvard Business School Press.

Cascio, W. F. 2000. "Managing a virtual workplace", *Academy of Management Executive* 14: 81–90.

Chidambaram, L. and Tung, L. L. 2005. "Is out of sight, out of mind? An empirical study of social loafing in technology-supported groups", *Information Systems Research* 16: 149–68.

Child, J. 2001. "Trust – The fundamental bond in global collaboration", *Organizational Dynamics* 29: 274–88.

Chinowsky, P. S. and Rojas, E. M. 2003. "Virtual teams: Guide to successful implementation", *Journal of Management in Engineering*, 19: 98–106.

Choi, I., Nisbett, R. E. and Norenzayan A. 1999. "Causal attributions across cultures: variation and universality", *Psychological Bulletin* 125: 47–63.

Chudoba, K. M., Wynn, E., Lu, M., and Watson-Manheim, M. B. 2005. "How virtual are we? Measuring virtuality and understanding its impact in a global organization", *Information Systems Journal* 15: 279–306.

Cramton, C. D. and Webber, S. S. 2005. "Relationships among geographic dispersion, team processes, and effectiveness in software development work teams", *Journal of Business Research* 58: 758–65.

Crossman, A. and Lee-Kelley, L. 2004. "Trust, commitment and team working: The paradox of virtual organizations", *Global Networks-A Journal of Transnational Affairs* 4: 375–90.

Cummings, J. N. and Kiesler, S. 2005. "Collaborative research across disciplinary and organizational boundaries", *Social Studies of Science* 35: 703–22.

Dani, S. S., Burns, N. D., Backhouse, C. J., and Kochhar, A. K. 2006. "The implications of organizational culture and trust in the working of virtual teams", *Proceedings of the Institution of Mechanical Engineers Part B – Journal of Engineering Manufacture* 220: 951–60.

De Leede, J. and Looise, J. C. 2001. "Demanding more than people can deliver: Exploring the issues of loyalty and commitment in enterprise collaborations", *Production Planning and Control* 12: 504–13.

Dennis, A. R. and Wixom, B. H. 2001. "Investigating the moderators of the group support systems use with meta-analysis", *Journal of Management Information Systems* 18: 235–57.

DeRosa, D., Hantula, D., Kock, N., and D'Arcy, J. 2004. "Trust and leadership in virtual teamwork: a media naturalness perspective", *Human Resource Management* 43: 219–32.

Smith, C. L., and Hantula, D. A. 2007. "The medium matters: mining the long-promised merit of group interaction in creative idea generation tasks in a meta-analysis of the electronic group brainstorming literature", *Computers in Human behavior* 23: 1549–81.

Dorsett, L. 2001. "A (fast) week in a digital collaboration space", *Training and Development* 55: 51.

Duarte, D. L. and Snyder, N.T. 2001. *Mastering Virtual Teams: Strategies, Tools, and Techniques That Succeed*. San Francisco, CA: Jossey-Bass.

Earley, P. C. and Gibson, C. B. 2002. *Multinational Work Teams: A New Perspective*. Mahwah, NJ: Lawrence Erlbaum.

Earley, P. C., and E. Mosakowski. 2000. "Creating hybrid team cultures: an empirical test of transnational team functioning", *Academy of Management Journal* 43: 26–49.

Edwards, H. K. and Sridhar, V. 2005. "Analysis of software requirements engineering exercises in a global virtual team setup", *Journal of Global Information Management* 13: 21–41.

Erik, B. 2005. "Experiences from global e-collaboration: Contextual influences on technology adoption and use", *IEEE Transactions on Professional Communication* 48: 78–86.

Espinosa, J. A., Cummings, J. N., Wilson, J., and Pearce, B. 2003. "Team boundary issues across multiple global firms", *Journal of Management Information Systems* 19: 157–90.

Fiol, C. M. 1991. "Managing culture as a competitive resource: an identity-based view of sustainable competitive advantage", *Journal of Management*, 17: 191–211.

Fletcher, T. D. and Major, D. A. 2006. "The effects of communication modality on performance and self-ratings of teamwork components", *Journal of Computer-Mediated Communication* 11: 557–76.

Fuller, M. A., Hardin, A. M., and Davison, R. M. 2006. "Efficacy in technology-mediated distributed teams", *Journal of Management Information Systems* 23: 209–35.

Gallivan, M. J. and Benbunan-Fich, R. 2005. "A framework for analyzing levels of analysis issues in studies of e-collaboration", *IEEE Transactions on Professional Communication* 48: 87–104.

Gibson, C. B., Cohen, S. G., Gibbs, J. L., Stanko, T. L., and Tesluk, P. 2007. "Investigating the "I" in virtuality: how do individual experiences of geographic dispersion and electronic dependence affect psychological states and workplace enabling conditions?", University of California, Irvine Working Paper.

and Gibbs, J. L. 2006. "Unpacking the concept of virtuality: the effects of geographic dispersion, electronic dependence, dynamic structure, and national diversity on team innovation", *Administrative Science Quarterly* 51: 451–95.

and Vermeulen, F. 2003. "A healthy divide: subgroups as a stimulus for team learning", *Administrative Science Quarterly* 48: 202–39.

Waller, M. J., Carpenter, M., and Conte, J. 2007. "Antecedents, consequences, and moderators of time perspective heterogeneity for knowledge management in MNO teams", *Journal of Organizational behavior*, 28: 1005–34.

and Zellmer-Bruhn, M. 2001. "Metaphor and meaning: an intercultural analysis of the concept of teamwork", *Administrative Science Quarterly* 46: 274–303.

Gillam, C. and Oppenheim, C. 2006. "Review article: Reviewing the impact of virtual teams in the information age", *Journal of Information Science* 32: 160–75.

Golden, T. D. 2006a. "Avoiding depletion in virtual work: telework and the intervening impact of work exhaustion on commitment and turnover intentions", *Journal of Vocational Behavior* 69: 176–87.

2006b. "The role of relationships in understanding telecommuter satisfaction", *Journal of Organizational Behavior* 27: 319–40.

Gordon, G. G. 1991. "Industry determinants of organizational culture", *Academy of Management Review* 16: 396–415.

Griffith, T. L., Sawyer, J. E. and Neale, M. A. 2003. "Virtualness and knowledge in teams: managing the love triangle of organizations, individuals, and information technology", *MIS Quarterly* 27: 265–87.

Gudykunst, W. B. 1991. *Bridging Differences: Effective Intergroup Communication*. Newbury Park, CA: Sage.

Hall, E.T. 1983. *The Dance of Life: The Other Dimension of Time*. Garden City, NY: Anchor Press.

and Hall, M. R. 1987. *Hidden Differences: Doing Business with the Japanese*. Garden City, NY: Doubleday.

Hambrick, D. C., Davison, S. C., Snell, C. and Snow, C. C. 1998. "When groups consist of multiple nationalities: towards a new understanding of the implications", *Organization Studies* 19: 181–205.

Hammond, J., Koubek, R. J., and Harvey, C. M. 2001. "Distributed collaboration for engineering design: a review and reappraisal", *Human Factors and Ergonimics in Manufacturing* 11: 35–52.

Hardin, A. M., Fuller, M. A., and Davison, R. M. 2007. "I know I can but can we? Culture and efficacy beliefs in global virtual teams", *Small Group Research* 38: 130–55.

Fuller, M. A., and Valacich, J. S. 2006. "Measuring group efficacy in virtual teams: new questions in an old debate", *Small Group Research* 37: 65–85.

Harvey, M., Novicevic, M. M., and Garrison, G. 2005. "Global virtual teams: a human resource capital architecture", *International Journal of Human Resource Management* 16: 1583–99.

Hasty, B. K., Massey, A. P., and Brown, S. A. 2006. "Experiences and Media perceptions of senders and receivers in knowledge transfer: an exploratory study", in *Proceedings of the 39th Annual Hawaii Conference in Systems Sciences*, vol. 7. Washington, DC: IEEE Computer Society.

Hertel, G., Konradt, U., and Voss, K. 2006. "Competencies for virtual teamwork: development and validation of a web-based selection tool for members of distributed teams", *European Journal of Work and Organizational Psychology* 15: 477–504.

Hinds, P. J. and Mortensen, M. 2005. "Understanding conflict in geographically distributed teams: the moderating effects of shared identity, shared context, and spontaneous communication", *Organization Science* 16: 290–307.

Hoegl, M., Ernst, H., and Proserpio, L. 2007. "How teamwork matters more as team member dispersion increases". *Journal of Product Innovation Management* 24(2): 156–65.

and Proserpio, L. 2004. "Team member proximity and teamwork in innovative projects", *Research Policy* 33: 1153–65.

Hofstede, G. 1991. *Cultures and Organizations: Software of the Mind*. New York, NY: McGraw Hill.

Huang, W. W., Wei, K. K., Watson, R. T., and Tan, B. C. 2002. "Supporting virtual team-building with a GSS: an empirical investigation", *Decision Support Systems* 34: 359–67.

Janssens, M. and Brett, J. M. 2006. "Cultural intelligence in global teams: a fusion model of collaboration", *Group and Organization Management* 31: 124–53.

Jarvenpaa, S. L., Knoll, K., and Leidner, D. E. 1998. "Is there anybody out there? Antecedents of trust in global virtual teams", *Journal of Management Information Systems* 14: 29–64.

Jarvenpaa, S. L. and Leidner, D. E. 1999. "Communication and trust in global virtual teams", *Organization Science* 10: 791–815.

Shaw, T. R., and Staples, D. 2004. "Toward contextualized theories of trust: the role of trust in global virtual teams", *Information Systems Research* 15: 250–67.

Jones, J. M. 1988. "Cultural differences in temporal perspectives: Instrumental and expressive behaviors in time", in J. E. McGrath (ed.), *The Social Psychology of Time: New Perspectives*. Beverly Hills, CA: Sage, 21–38.

Kanawattanachai, P. and Y. Yoo. 2002. "Dynamic nature of trust in virtual teams", *Journal of Strategic Information Systems* 11: 187–213.

Kankanhalli, A., Tan, B. C. Y. and Wei, K. K. 2006. "Conflict and performance in global virtual teams", *Journal of Management Information Systems* 23: 237–74.

Kiesler, S., Siegler, J. and McGuire, T. W. 1984. "Social psychological aspects of computer-mediated communication", *American Psychologist* 39: 1123–34.

Kirkman, B. L. and Mathieu, J. E. 2005. "The dimensions and antecedents of team virtuality", *Journal of Management* 31: 700–18.

Lowe, K. B., and Gibson, C. B. 2006. "A quarter century of Culture's Consequences: a review of empirical research incorporating Hofstede's cultural values framework", *Journal of International Business Studies* 37: 285–320.

Rosen, B., Gibson, C. B., Tesluk, P. E., and McPherson, S. O. 2002. "Five challenges to virtual team success: Lessons from Sabre, Inc", *Academy of Management Executive* 16: 67–79.

Rosen, B. and Shapiro. D. L. 1997. "The impact of cultural values on employee resistance to teams: toward a model of globalized self-managing work team effectiveness", *Academy of Management Review* 22: 730–57.

Klimoski, R. and Mohammed. S. 1994. "Team mental model: construct or metaphor?", *Journal of Management* 20: 403–437.

Kluckhohn, F. R. and Strodtbeck, F. L. 1961. *Variations in Value Orientations*. Evanston, IL: Row, Peterson.

Kotlarsky, J. and Oshri, I. 2005. "Social ties, knowledge sharing and successful collaboration in globally distributed system development projects", *European Journal of Information Systems* 14: 37–48.

Krebs, S. A., Hobman, E. V., and Bordia, P. 2006. "Virtual teams and group member dissimilarity: consequences for the development of trust", *Small Group Research* 37: 721–41.

Larkey, L. K. 1996. "Toward a theory of communicative interactions in culturally diverse workgroups", *Academy of Management Review* 21: 463–91.

Lee, O. 2002. "Cultural differences in e-mail use of virtual teams: A critical social theory perspective", *Cyberpsychology and Behavior* 5: 227–32.

Leung, K., Bhagat, R. S., Buchan, N. R., Erez, M., and Gibson, C. G. 2005. "Culture and international business: recent advances and their implications for future research", *Journal of International Business Studies* 36: 357–78.

Levesque, L. L., Wilson, J. M., and Wholey, D. R. 2001. "Cognitive divergence and shared mental models in software development project teams", *Journal of Organizational Behavior* 22: 135–44.

Lipnack, J. and Stamps, J. 2000. *Virtual Teams: People Working Across Boundaries with Technology*. New York, NY: John Wiley.

Lowry, P. B., Roberts, T. L., Romano, N. C., Cheney, P. D., and Hightower, R. T. 2006. "The impact of group size and social presence on small-group communication: does computer-mediated communication make a difference?" *Small Group Research* 37: 631–661.

Malhotra, A., Majchrzak, A., Carman, R., and Lott, V. 2001. "Radical innovation without collocation: a case study at Boeing-Rocketdyne", *MIS Quarterly* 25: 229–49.

Majchrzak, A., Malhotra, A., Stamps, J., and Lipnack, J. 2004. "Can absence make a team grow stronger", *Harvard Business Review* 82: 131–40.

Rice, R. E., Malhotra, A., and King, N. 2000. "Technology adaptation: the case of a computer-supported inter-organizational virtual team", *MIS Quarterly* 24: 569–600.

Martins, L. L., Gilson, L. L., and Maynard, M. T. 2004. "Virtual teams: what do we know and where do we go from here?", *Journal of Management* 30: 805–35.

Maruping, L. A. and Agarwal, R. 2004. "Managing team interpersonal processes through technology: A task-technology fit perspective", *Journal of Applied Psychology* 89: 975–90.

Massey, A., Montoya-Weiss, M. M., and Hung, Y. 2003. "Because time matters: temporal coordination in global virtual project teams", *Journal of Management Information Systems* 19: 129–59.

Mathieu, J. E., Heffner, T. S., Goodwin, G. F., Salas, E., and Cannon-Bowers, J. A. 2000. "The influence of shared mental models on team process and performance", *Journal of Applied Psychology* 85: 273–83.

May, A. and Carter, C. 2001. "A case study of virtual team working in the European automotive industry", *International Journal of Industrial Ergonomics* 27: 171–86.

Mayo, E. 1946. *The Human Problems of an Industrialized Civilization*. Boston, MA: Division of Research, Graduate School of Business Administration, Harvard University.

Maznevski, M. L. 1994. "Understanding our differences: performance in decision-making groups with diverse members", *Human Relations* 47: 531–52.

and Chudoba, K. M. 2000. "Bridging space over time: Global virtual team dynamics and effectiveness", *Organization Science* 11: 473–92.

and DiStefano, J. J. 2000. "Global leaders are team players: developing global leaders through membership on global teams", *Human Resource Management* 39: 195–208.

McDonough, E. F. and Cedrone, D. 2000. "Meeting the challenge of global team management", *Research-Technology Management* 43: 12–17.

Kahn, K. B., and Barczak, G. 2001. "An investigation of the use of global, virtual, and colocated new product development teams", *Journal of Product Innovation Management* 18: 110–20.

McMichael, P. 2000. *Development and Social Change. A Global Perspective*. Durham, NC: Duke University Press.

Moghaddam, F. M. 1997. "Change and continuity in organizations: Assessing intergroup relations", in C. S. Granose and K. Oskamp (eds.), *Cross-cultural Workgroups*. Thousand Oaks, CA: Sage, 36–60.

Montoya-Weiss, M. M., Massey, A. P., and Song, M., 2001. "Getting it together: temporal coordination and conflict management in global virtual teams", *Academy of Management Journal* 44: 1251–62.

Mortensen, M. and Hinds, P. J. 2001. "Conflict and shared identity in geographically distributed teams", *International Journal of Conflict Management* 12: 212–38.

Mowshowitz, A. 1997. "Virtual organization", *Communications of the ACM* 40: 30–37.

Nemiro, J. 2002. "The creative process in virtual teams", *Creativity Research Journal* 14: 69–83.

Nonaka, I. and Takeuchi H. 1995. *The Knowledge Creating Company*. New York, NY: Oxford University Press.

Ocker, R. J. 2005. "Influences on creativity in asynchronous virtual teams: a qualitative analysis of experimental teams", *IEEE Transactions on Professional Communication* 48: 22–39.

Okhuysen, G. and Eisenhardt, K. M. 2002. "Integrating knowledge in groups: how formal interventions enable flexibility", *Organization Science* 13: 370–87.

Olson, G. M. and Olson, J. S. 2000. "Distance matters", *Human-Computer Interaction* 15: 139–78.

O'Malley, M. and Kelleher, T. 2002. "Papayas and pedagogy: geographically dispersed teams and Internet self-efficacy", *Public Relations Review* 28: 175–84.

Panteli, N. and Davison, R. M. 2005. "The role of subgroups in the communication patterns of global virtual teams", *IEEE Transactions on Professional Communication* 48: 191–200.

and Fineman, S. 2005. "The sound of silence: the case of virtual team organising", *Behaviour and Information Technology* 24: 347–52.

Paul, D. 2006. "Collaborative activities in virtual settings: a knowledge management perspective of telemedicine", *Journal of Management Information Systems* 22: 143–76.

Paul, S., Samarah, I. M., Seetharaman, P., and Mykytyn, P. P. 2005. "An empirical investigation of collaborative conflict management style in group support system-based global virtual teams", *Journal of Management Information Systems* 21: 185–222.

Seetharaman, P., Samarah, I., and Mykytyn, P. P. 2004. "Impact of heterogeneity and collaborative conflict management style on the performance of synchronous global virtual teams", *Information and Management* 41: 303–21.

Pauleen, D. J. 2003. "An inductively derived model of leader-initiated relationship building with virtual team members", *Journal of Management Information Systems* 20: 227–56.

and Yoong, P. 2001a. "Facilitating virtual team relationship via Internet and conventional communication channels", *Internet Research-Electronic Networking Applications and Policy* 11: 190–202.

and Yoong, P. 2001b. "Relationship building and the use of ICT in boundary-crossing virtual teams: A facilitator's perspective", *Journal of Information Technology* 16: 205–20.

Perry-Smith, J. E. and Shalley, C. E. 2003. "The social side of creativity: a static and dynamic social network perspective", *Academy of Management Review* 28: 89–106.

Polzer, J. T., Crisp, C. B., Jarvenpaa, S. L., and Kim, J. W. 2006. "Extending the faultline model to geographically dispersed teams: How colocated subgroups can impair group functioning", *Academy of Management Journal* 49: 679–92.

Potter, R. E. and Balthazard, P. A. 2002. "Virtual team interaction styles: assessment and effects", *International Journal of Human-Computer Studies* 56: 423–43.

Qureshi, S., Liu, M., Vogel, D. 2006. "The effects of electronic collaboration in distributed project management", *Group Decision and Negotiation* 15: 55–75.

and Vogel, D. 2001. "Adaptiveness in virtual teams: Organisational challenges and research directions", *Group Decision and Negotiation* 10: 27–46.

Robb, D. 2003. "The virtual enterprise: how companies use technology to stay in control of a virtual supply chain", *Information Strategy: Executive Journal* 19: 6–11.

Robey, D., Khoo, H. M. and Powers, C. 2000. "Situated learning in cross-functional virtual teams", *Technical Communication* 47: 51–66.

Roethlisberger, F. J. and Dickson, W. J. 1939. *Management and the Worker: An Account of a Research Program Conducted by the Western Electric Company, Hawthorne Works, Chicago.* Cambridge MA: Harvard University Press.

Rosen, B., Furst, S., Blackburn, R. 2006. "Training for virtual teams: An investigation of current practices and future needs", *Human Resource Management* 45: 229–47.

Rutkowski, A. F., Vogel, D., Bemelmans, T. M. A., and van Genuchten, M. 2002. "Group support systems and virtual collaboration: the HKNet project", *Group Decision and Negotiation* 11: 101–25.

Vogel, D. R., Van Genuchten, M., Bemelmans, T. M. A., and Favier, M. 2002. "E-collaboration: The reality of virtuality", *IEEE Transactions on Professional Communication* 45: 219–30.

Sakthivel, S. 2005. "Virtual workgroups in offshore systems development", *Information and Software Technology* 47: 305–18.

Sapsed, J., Gann, D., Marshall, N., and Salter, A. 2005. "From here to eternity? The practice of knowledge transfer in dispersed and co-located project organizations", *European Planning Studies* 13: 831–51.

Sarker, S. 2005. "Knowledge transfer and collaboration in distributed US-Thai teams", *Journal of Computer-Mediated Communication* 10.

and Sahay, S. 2004. "Implications of space and time for distributed work: an interpretive study of US-Norwegian systems development teams", *European Journal of Information Systems* 13: 3–20.

Nicholson, D. B., and Joshi, K. D. 2005. "Knowledge transfer in virtual systems development teams: an exploratory study of four key enablers", *IEEE Transactions on Professional Communication* 48: 201–18.

Schiller, S. Z., and Mandviwalla, M. 2007. "Virtual team research: an analysis of theory use and a framework for theory appropriation", *Small Group Research* 38: 12–59.

Schmidt, J. B., Montoya-Weiss, M. M., and Massey, A. P. 2001. "New product development decision-making effectiveness: comparing individuals, face-to-face teams, and virtual teams", *Decision Sciences* 32: 575–600.

Shin, Y. Y. 2004. "A person-environment fit model for virtual organizations", *Journal of Management* 30: 725–43.

2005. "Conflict resolution in virtual teams", *Organizational Dynamics* 34: 331–45.

Sivunen, A. and Valo, M. 2006. "Team leaders' technology choice in virtual teams", *IEEE Transactions on Professional Communication* 49: 57–68.

Smith, P. G. and Blanck, E. L. 2002. "From experience: Leading dispersed teams", *Journal of Product Innovation Management* 19: 294–304.

Sole, D. and Edmondson, A. 2002. "Situated knowledge and learning in dispersed teams", *British Journal of Management* 13: 17–34.

Spears, R. and Lea, M. 1992. "Social influence and the influences of the 'social' in computer-mediated communication", in M. Lea (ed.), *Contexts of Computer-mediated Communication*. London: Harvester-Wheatsheaf, pp 30–65.

Staples, S., Hulland, J. S., and Higgins, C. A. 1999. "A self-efficacy theory explanation for the management of remote workers in virtual organizations", *Organization Science* 10: 758–76.

Staples, D. S. and Zhao, L. 2006. "The effects of cultural diversity in virtual teams versus face-to-face teams", *Group Decision and Negotiation* 15: 389–406.

Straus, S. and McGrath, J. E. 1994. "Does the medium matter? The interaction of task type and technology on group performance and member reactions", *Journal of Applied Psychology* 79: 87–97.

Swigger, K., Alpaslan, F., Brazile, R., and Monticino, M. 2004. "Effects of culture on computer-supported international collaborations", *International Journal of Human-Computer Studies* 60: 365–80.

Tan, B. C. Y., Wei, K. K., Huang, W. W., and Ng, G. N. 2000. "A dialogue technique to enhance electronic communication in virtual teams", *IEEE Transactions on Professional Communication* 43: 153–65.

Tangirala, S. and Alge, B. J. 2006. "Reactions to unfair events in computer-mediated groups: a test of uncertainty management theory", *Organizational Behavior and Human Decision Processes* 100: 1–20.

Timmerman, C. E. and Scott, C. R. 2006. "Virtually working: communicative and structural predictors of media use and key outcomes in virtual work teams", *Communication Monographs* 73: 108–36.

Townsend, A. M., DeMarie, S. M., and Hendrickson, A. R. 1998. "Virtual teams: technology and the workplace of the future", *Academy of Management Executive* 12: 17–29.

Vogel, D. R., van Genuchten, M., Lou, D., Verveen, S., van Eekout, M., and Adams, A. 2001. "Exploratory research on the role of national and professional cultures in a distributed learning project", *IEEE Transactions on Professional Communication* 44: 114–25.

Waller, M. J., Conte, J. M., Gibson, C. B., and Carpenter, M. A. 2001. "The effect of individual perceptions of deadlines on team performance", *Academy of Management Review* 26: 586–600.

Walther, J. B. 1995. "Relational aspects of computer-mediated communication: experimental observations over time", *Organization Science* 6: 186–203.

Watson, W. E., Kumar, K., and Michaelson, L. K. 1993. "Cultural diversity's impact on interaction process and performance comparing homogeneous and diverse task groups", *Academy of Management Journal* 36: 590–602.

Whitener, E. M., Brodt, S. E., Korsgaard, A. M., and Werner, J. M. 1998. "Managers as initiators of trust: an exchange relationship framework for understanding managerial trustworthy behavior", *Academy of Management Review* 23: 513–30.

Whitman, L. E., Malzahn, D. E., Chaparro, B. S., Russell, M., Langrall, R., and Mohler, B. A. 2005. "A comparison of group processes, performance, and satisfaction in face-to-face versus computer-mediated engineering student design teams", *Journal of Engineering Education* 94: 327–33.

Wilson, J. M., Straus, S. G., and McEvily, B. 2006. "All in due time: the development of trust in computer-mediated and face-to-face teams", *Organizational Behavior and Human Decision Processes* 99: 16–33.

Zhuge, H. 2003. "Workflow- and agent-based cognitive flow management for distributed team Cooperation", *Information and Management*. 40:419–429.

Zimbardo, P. G. and Boyd, J. N. 1999. "Putting time in perspective: a valid, reliable individual-differences metric", *Journal of Personality and Social Psychology* 77: 1271–88.

Appendix: Articles defining culture as an element of virtuality

Study Design[a]	Virtuality Conceptualization	Op.[b]	Measure[c]	Role	DV	Findings
Alavi and Tiwana (2002)	T	(1) geographically and (2) temporally dispersed, (3) little shared history, (4) diversity of expertise or (5) culture, (6) technology-mediated interactions	0	NA	NA	NA	Identified 4 key constraints to knowledge integration and application related to transactive memory (such as insufficient mutual understanding) and propose 4 solutions (such as creating searchable repositories of codified knowledge).
Baba et al. (2004)	CS	(1) globally distributed team – two or more nations: (2) culturally diverse, (3) physical distance, (4) temporal distance, interdependent, (5) reliant on technology	0	real team: 20 members across 7 global locations	NA	NA	Examines cognitive convergence in virtual teams. Authors find that, in addition to knowledge sharing, such things as similar learning experiences, bringing out knowledge using third parties were important in increasing cognitive convergence.
Barczak et al. (2006)	P	global new product development teams (1) globally dispersed (2) cultural diversity (3) functional diversity	0	NA	NA	NA	Identifies four key challenges to work in global virtual teams (1) Different languages (2) different cultural backgrounds (3) globally dispersed (4) members from different companies. The authors then identify steps required to meet these challenges.
Barut et al. (2006)	E	(1) global, members from different countries (2) multi-disciplinary (3) use communication technology (4) diverse cultures (5) geographically dispersed	0	groups had 4 students from 3 countries, used technology	NA	NA	This study found that perceptions of the importance of virtual work increased after participation in virtual teams as did experience with use of technology. The authors then offer practical feedback for administering global teams in the classroom.
Bell and Kozlowski (2002)	T	"ideal type" spans (1) organizational, (2) temporal, (3) functional, and (4) geographical boundaries, (5) cultural boundaries (6) short-lived, members are part of other virtual teams, (7) dependent on technology	0	NA	NA	NA	In this work, the authors identify differences between virtual and traditional teams, create a typology of the different kinds of virtual teams, and then identify key areas for future research.
Bing and Bing (2001)	P	(1) globally dispersed, (2) culturally diverse	0	NA	NA	NA	This article describes some of the challenges facing virtual teams (e.g. cultural differences) and some steps to overcome these challenges, such as periodic measurement of team progress.

Appendix (cont.)

Study Design[a]	Virtuality Conceptualization	Op.[b]	Measure[c]	Role	DV	Findings
Cascio (2000)	P	(1) geographically dispersed, (2) reliant on technology (3) often work across cultural boundaries (4) dynamic (5) multi-organizational	0	NA	NA	NA	This article explores some of the potential benefits (e.g. higher profits, environmental benefits) and downsides of using virtual teams (e.g. cultural issues, feelings of isolation). The author then describes different issues managers of virtual teams should consider to successfully implement virtual work arrangements.
Child (2001)	P	(1) crossing national, (2) organizational, (3) cultural, (4) functional boundaries	0	NA	NA	NA	This article explores the notion of trust and why it is so important for virtual work. Strategies for generating and sustaining trust in virtual teams are then discussed.
Chinowsky and Rojas (2003)	P	(1) electronic media, (2) without regard to geographic location (3) culturally and (4) functionally diverse	0	NA	NA	NA	The authors describe the challenges of successfully implementing virtual teams (e.g. cultural differences) and then outline strategies for managing these challenges, such as by increasing cultural understanding and emphasizing common goals.
Chudoba et al. (2005)	F	virtuality depends on discontinuities (factors associated with a decrease in cohesion) in (1) geography (2) time zone (3) organization (4) national culture (5) work practices and (6) technology	3	Survey asked individuals how frequently they experienced discontinuities	IV	Perceived perform.	Geographic dispersion had no impact on perceived performance, varieties of practice were negatively associated with performance, work practice predictability and sociability helped mitigate the negative impact of discontinuities. Employee mobility and variety of practices was negatively related to perceived performance.
Cramton and Webber (2005)	F	groups with common purpose, interdependent, (1) work across locations and (2) time, (3) use CMC much more than FTF, (4) likely to be culturally diverse	1	teams either (1) entirely collocated or (2) virtual (>30 percent dispersed)	IV	Work processes, perform.	Geographically dispersed teams have less effective work processes than collocated teams, and geographic dispersion is negatively related to perceived performance.
Crossman and Lee-Kelley (2004)	CS	(1) separated by time, (2) space, and (3) "may be" culturally diverse, (4) reliance on communication media	0	Members dispersed across several countries	NA	NA	Shifts occur in commitment over time in virtual teams. Thus, teams need to re-evaluate whether they will be long or short-term.

Study	Type	Definition	N	Operationalization	IV/DV	Variable	Summary
De Leede and Looise (2001)	T	(1) geographically dispersed, (2) potentially across countries, (3) diverse functions and (4) cultures, (5) hardly any constant membership, temporary, (6) technology-mediated	0	NA	NA	NA	This paper explores potential differences in the antecedents to commitment and loyalty in virtual teams compared to FTF teams. The authors argue that antecedents to commitment such as task variety and interdependence are likely to be higher in VTs and thus lead to higher commitment in VTs compared to FTF teams.
DeRosa et al. (2004)	T	teams that work across (1) space, (2) time, and (3) organizational boundaries using (4) technology to facilitiate communication and coordination (5) more likely to come from different cultures (p. 223)	0	NA	NA	NA	Using media naturalness theory, this article emphasizes the importance of human adaptation and evolutionary processes for trust and leadership in virtual work.
Dorsett (2001)	P	(1) geographically dispersed, (2) culturally diverse, (3) reliant on technology	0	NA	NA	NA	Managers need to focus on team processes, not just the technology, importance of everyone on team having access to the same technology.
Espinosa et al. (2003)	CS	(1) geographical, (2) temporal, (3) functional, (4) identity, (5) organizational boundaries, (6) mediated by CMC (7) distant collaborations are usually culturally diverse	0	Teams geographically dispersed and from different countries	NA	NA	The authors discuss five types of boundaries (e.g. geographical, functional) that impact distributed work and discuss measurement issues. They argue it is important to appropriately measure the boundaries studied, control for other important boundaries, and differentiate between the effects of each boundary.
Gibson and Gibbs (2006)	F	virtuality was conceived as having four dimensions (1) geographic dispersion (2) electronic dependence (3) national diversity (4) dynamic structure	4	(1) geographic dispersion (distance between locations), (2) electronic dependence (survey questions) (3) national diversity (4) dynamic structure	IV	innovation	The authors found that each of the four dimensions of virtuality studied were negatively related to innovation, although having a psychologically safe communication climate helps to reduce these negative relationships. Results also showed that the four dimensions of virtuality studied were not highly intercorrelated and explained unique variation in innovation.

Appendix (cont.)

Study/Design[a]	Virtuality Conceptualization	Op.[b]	Measure[c]	Role	DV	Findings
Gillam and Oppenheim (2006)	R	groups that work (1) across time (2) space (3) often across organizational boundaries (4) use technology to facilitate communication (5) often culturally diverse	0	NA	NA	NA	Argues that cultural issues are often ignored in the VT literature, reviews definition of virtual teams, common issues, common topics studied.
Hammond et al. (2001)	R	(1) linked through technology, (2) distributed across location, (3) discipline, (4) company loyalties, and (5) culture	0	NA	NA	NA	The authors develop a conceptual model of distributed engineering collaboration based on a sociotechnical theory framework in order to understand how technology changes both social interaction and the technical design process.
Hardin et al. (2007)	E	global virtual team: (1) technology mediated, (2) globally distributed, (3) cultural diversity	0	groups used technology and came from different countries, variables were not measured	NA	NA	Regardless of cultural background, team members reported less confidence in their ability to work in virtual team environments than FTF environments and that team members from individualistic cultures reported higher self-efficacy beliefs than team members from collectivist cultures.
Hardin, et al. (2006)	E	(1) often culturally diverse (2) mostly non-collocated (3) space (4) time and (5) organizational boundaries (6) using technology	0	not measured, groups used had no FTF	NA	NA	Group efficacy beliefs reached by consensus were higher than those of individual VT members. Results also showed that the aggregated method was a superior predictor. Group outcome perceptions were significantly related to team performance.
Hertel et al. (2006)	F	common task, (1) geographically dispersed,(2) reliance on electronic media (3) Teams often cross national and/or cultural boundaries (p. 482)	0	teams are geographically dispersed and use technology, but differences not measured	NA	NA	Developed and validated a measure of Virtual Team Competency using first students, and then organizational virtual teams.
Hinds and Mortensen (2005)	F	Distributed work groups that have (1) members who work in more than one geographic location. (2) technology enabled (3) cultural diversity stems from geographic distribution	3	(1) structural: e.g. # time zones, (2) psychological: (e.g. percentage of isolates) (3) cultural diversity	IV	Task, interper. conflict	VTs reported more conflict compared to the FTF teams. Shared identity moderated the relationship between distribution and interpersonal conflict while shared context moderated the relationship between distribution and task conflict. Spontaneous communication was associated with higher levels of shared identity and shared context, and moderated the relationship between distribution and conflict.

Study	Type	Definition	#	Sample	Analysis	Variables	Findings
Janssens and Brett (2006)	T	(1) culturally diverse (2) functionally diverse, (3) differing assumptions, (4) work on complex task that will have impact in more than one country	0	NA	NA	NA	Develops a "fusion" model of collaboration for virtual teams by focusing on the FTF interactions of team members.
Kankanhalli et al. (2006)	CS	global virtual team: (1) technology mediated, (2) globally distributed, (3) cultural diversity, (4) rarely have FTF,	0	globally dispersed, use technology, and are culturally diverse, but these are not measured	NA	NA	Cultural diversity proposed to contribute to task and relationship conflict while functional diversity argued to result in task conflict. Quantity of email and lack of feedback can lead to task conflict. Relationship between conflict and performance may depend on task complexity, interdependence, and conflict resolution approach.
Kirkman et al. (2002)	F	across (1) time (2) space (3) organizational boundaries with a common purpose. (4) May be culturally diverse, often (5) rely on technology (6) cross-functional	3	(1) proportion of FTF, 2) proportion at same location, 3) proportion spent on VT	NA	NA	Identifies 5 challenges related to building trust and cohesion, overcoming isolation, and selection and assessment of virtual team members and Sabre's coping strategies.
Kotlarsky and Oshri (2005)	CS	(1) globally dispersed, (2) reliant on technology, (3) facing time zone and (4) cultural challenges	0	teams explicitly chosen that were globally distributed across at least two locations	NA	NA	Argued that many past studies focus on technical issues for successful collaboration. This study found that "human-related" issues, such as social ties and knowledge sharing, were also key factors in successful teams.
Krebs et al. (2006)	E	(1) geographically distributed, (2) culturally diverse, (3) different experiences, (4) technology allows formation of these teams	1	FTF vs. CMC groups	MOD	Group diversity; trust	Use of CMC can reduce some of the negative impacts of group member dissimilarities on trust. Age dissimilarity was negatively related to trust in FTF groups but not in computer-mediated groups. Birthplace dissimilarity was positively related to trust in computer-mediated groups.
Lee (2002)	CS	(1) geographically dispersed, (2) use of communication technology (3) importance of cultural differences	0	selected a team that was globally dispersed and relied heavily on email	NA	NA	Cultural differences exist in preferences for using email and CMC with senior members of the team. Confucian cultural ideals suggest email is rude and therefore members use FTF with senior team members.

Appendix (cont.)

Study Design[a]	Virtuality Conceptualization	Op.[b]	Measure[c]	Role	DV	Findings
Maruping and Agarwal (2004)	T	work that spans (1) functional, (2) organizational, (3) temporal, (4) spatial, and geographic boundaries, interdependent tasks, common purpose, (5) linked by technology	0	NA	NA	NA	The authors link the different types of technology to key processes in virtual work (1) conflict management (2) motivation/confidence building and (3) affect management in order to highlight how virtual team members can use technology to become more effective. Additionally, the authors argue that time plays an important role.
May and Carter (2001)	CS	(1) geographically dispersed, (2) culturally diverse, (3) use of technology	0	examined effectiveness of technology use in group distributed globally	NA	NA	Results suggest that advanced information and telecommunication technology can help increase efficiency and flexibility of distributed work.
Maznevski and DiStefano (2000)	T	global teams are teams of managers (1) from many parts of a multi-national company, (2) usually conduct communication using technology, (3) different cultural and (4) functional backgrounds	0	NA	NA	NA	This study examines the idea that global teams are an ideal setting for training global leaders.
Maznevski and Chudoba (2000)	CS	Global virtual teams = (1) internationally distributed, (2) CMC use, (3) global in task, identify as team (4) culturally diverse	0	teams are globally dispersed	NA	NA	Apply AST and find that 1) GVT dynamics take on form of series of interaction incidents, 2) interaction incidents in effective GVTs take on repeating temporal pattern – rhythm of regular intensive FTF meetings punctuated by less intensive mediated incidents.
McDonough and Cedrone (2000)	P	(1) members are globally dispersed, (2) rarely meet FTF, (3) are from different cultures and (4) speak different languages, (5) use of technology to manage these teams	0	NA	NA	NA	This article focuses on issues involved with managing globally dispersed teams and offers advice for (1) motivating dispersed employees (2) creating a psychologically safe environment to stimulate creativity (3) and managing communication challenges.
McDonough et al. (2001)	F	global teams = (1) globally and (2) culturally diverse, VS virtual/ distributed = just geographically dispersed mostly in one country, but are culturally similar	0	asked if their companies used global or virtual teams (as defined to the left)	NA	NA	Results suggest that firms face different problems associated with managing each type of NPD team-global, virtual and colocated, suggesting that companies and their managers employ different solutions to these different problems.

Citation	Type	Definition		Sample	IV MOD	DV	Findings
Mortensen and Hinds (2001)	F	Distributed work groups that have (1) members who work in more than one geographic location, (2) forced to rely heavily on communication technology (3) national, so likely to be culturally diverse	3	FTF vs. geographically distributed; cultural heterogeneity; reliance on technology		Identity, conflict, tech relian.; use of tech.	Shared team identity was associated with less task conflict and less affective conflict for distributed teams. Task and affective conflict negatively associated with performance in distributed teams. May be more conflict in teams that rely heavily on technology.
Ocker (2005)	E	(1) geographically and /or (2) organizationally dispersed, (3) reliance on technology (4) diverse cultures prevalent	1	hybrid groups (combination of FTF and CMC) as well as pure virtual groups	NA	NA	Dominance, domain knowledge, and downward norm setting, lack of shared understanding, time pressure, and technical difficulties negatively affected creative performance. Stimulating colleagues, collaborative climate helped foster creativity.
Olson and Olson (2000)	R	(1) geographically dispersed, (2) reliant on technology, (3) culturally diverse	0	NA	NA	NA	Reviews literature comparing VT and FTF groups and shows how reality differs from high expectations for use of tech. Authors describe key factors regarding effective distributed work, such as creating common ground and coupling of work.
Panteli and Davison (2005)	E	(1) geographically dispersed, (2) communication technologies (3) likely cultural dispersion (4) ethnic dispersion (5) linguistic dispersion	0	teams had students from two universities in different countries, used CMC.	NA	NA	When subgroup salience was high, this created boundaries between the groups and prevented group cohesiveness.
Panteli and Fineman, (2005)	T	(1) geographically dispersed, common task, (2) most communication via technology, (3) culturally diverse	0	NA	NA	NA	This article explores the idea that silence in virtual teams has different meanings and implications than silence in traditional teams.
Pauleen and Yoong (2001)	CS	(1) temporary, (2) culturally diverse, (3) geographically dispersed, (4) reliant on technology	0	geographically dispersed and crossed boundaries (e.g. organizational, cultural, etc.)	NA	NA	Findings suggest that some electronic communication channels are more effective than others in building online relationships and that facilitators need to strategically use the channels available to them to effectively build online relationships.
Pauleen and Yoong (2001)	CS	(1) work across time and (2) distance (3) using information and communication technology, (4) often from different countries, (5) cultures, and (6) functions	0	geographically dispersed and crossed boundaries (organizational, cultural, etc.)	NA	NA	The authors offer four key recommendations for virtual team facilitators included emphasizing technology, training, organizational support, and experience to promote successful boundary crossing.

301

Appendix (cont.)

Study Design[a]	Virtuality Conceptualization	Op.[b]	Measure[c]	Role	DV	Findings
Pauleen (2003)	CS	(1) information and communication technology use (2) across time, (3) distance, (4) culture, (5) functions, (6) divisions, (7) organizations, FTF may also be an important factor in virtual teams	0	five teams are globally dispersed teams	NA	NA	Used grounded theory approach to explore leadership in VTs. VT leaders believe that building relationships with team members prior to beginning virtual work is critical to successful leadership. A theoretical framework is developed outlining the steps VT leaders take to build relationship with members.
Qureshi and Vogel (2001)	T	work across (1) time zones, (2) distance, geographically, and (3) organizational boundaries, (4) linked by communication technology, (5) often culturally diverse	0	NA	NA	NA	This work identifies future areas of research needed to better understand virtual work and how the organizational context in which it takes place plays a role.
Qureshi et al. (2006)	CS	(1) geographically (2) time dispersed (3) organizationally (4) using information technology to accomplish tasks (5) live in different countries and often culturally diverse	0	dispersed across countries, use technology to communicate, but not measured as a variable	NA	NA	Positive communication can bring about shared understanding, lack of mutual knowledge and shared language can make communication difficult, not establishing mutual knowledge can be detrimental to decision quality.
Robey et al. (2000)	CS	(1) geographically dispersed (2) functional, (3) cultural divides, (4) reliance on technology	0	cross-functional, distributed teams, culturally diverse	NA	NA	Findings suggest that virtual teamwork requires members to devise practices for coordinating work.
Rosen et al. (2006)	F	(1) geographically dispersed (2) use of technology (3) more likely to have cultural and (4) functional diversity	0	NA (members had experience in dispersed teams)	NA	NA	Perceptions of mgmt. support and more prioritizing led to more effective training. Culturally diverse teams reported higher levels of VT training effectiveness. Cultural sensitivity training was also related to higher perceptions of training effectiveness.
Rutkowski et al. (2002)	CS	(1) geographically dispersed, (2) culturally diverse, (3) temporary, (4) reliant on CMC (5) lack of FTF	0	Teams of students from different countries, used CMC	NA	NA	Videoconferencing key during episodes of conflict, should have synchronous work periodically, recommend a "sandwich structure" with FTF at beginning and end.
Rutkowski et al. (2002)	CS	(1) geographically dispersed, (2) culturally diverse, (3) temporary, (4) reliant on CMC (5) lack of FTF	0	teams of students from different countries, used CMC	NA	NA	The students in this study were successful in using group systems to solve problems, collaborate creatively, and overcome cultural barriers.

Citation	Type	Definition					Findings
Sakthivel (2005)	T	virtual work in offshore systems development necessarily involves (1) different cultures, (2) countries, where people are separated by (3) time and (4) distance	0	NA	NA	NA	The limitations of virtual work in the context of offshore systems development are discussed. The author then describes management processes that facilitate virtual work in offshore development projects.
Sarker and Sahay (2004)	CS	dispersed across (1) space and (2) time, (3) use of information and communication technologies (ICT) (4) "varying cultural assumptions" (p. 6)	0	formed teams that are cross-cultural and use technology	NA	NA	The authors identified some problems and potential strategies for dealing with the issues of time and space in virtual teams.
Sarker (2005)	E	(1) different backgrounds (2) different geographic locations (3) separated by space (4) and time (5) mediated by ICTs. Called them (6) "Cross-cultural, (7) ICT mediated,	1	cultural dimension used country as a proxy for IND-COL	IV	knowledge transfer	Results suggest that credibility and communication impact knowledge transfer in the cross-cultural distributed teams. Capability was not found to be related to knowledge transfer. Opposite to predictions, the individuals from the more individualistic culture that shared more knowledge than those residing in the collectivistic culture.
Sarker *et al.* (2005)	E	(1) temporary, (2) use of CMC (3) diverse backgrounds, (4) diverse expertise, (5) geographically dispersed, and responsible for a project with a limited timeframe	0	created teams students from two universities in different countries, had them use CMC	NA	NA	For an individual to be perceived as an effective knowledge transfer agent by dispersed team members they need to communicate extensively, be perceived as credible, have more collectivistic values.
Schiller and Mandviwalla (2007)	T	interdependent tasks, common purpose, (1) use CMC more than FTF; (2) geographically dispersed, (3) more likely to be involved in multi-cultural functions	0	NA	NA	NA	This article offers a toolkit for academics to understand current theories on virtual teams and the strengths and weaknesses of each.
Shin (2004)	T	the degree to which a group has (1) temporal, (2) cultural, (3) spatial, and (4) organizational dispersion, (5) communicating through electronic means	0	NA	NA	NA	Based on the degree of virtuality that a team has (e.g. temporal, spatial, cultural, and organizational), this work identifies what individual qualities may impact successful virtual work (e.g. willingness to trust, trustworthiness, valuing diversity).
Shin (2005)	P	(1) geographically dispersed, (2) reliant on technology, (3) work across time, space, (4) culture, and (5) organizational boundaries,(6) band and disband quickly	0	NA	NA	NA	This practitioner piece focuses on furthering understanding of conflict in virtual teams. The sources of conflict and methods for mitigating conflict are explored.

Appendix (cont.)

Study Design[a]	Virtuality Conceptualization	Op.[b]	Measure[c]	Role	DV	Findings
Sivunen and Valo (2006)	CS	(1) geographically dispersed, sometimes across time zones (2) communicate mainly through technology (3) functional and (4) cultural differences common	0	NA (groups were described as dispersed)	NA	NA	VT leader choice of technology was based on four factors, two person related: (1) accessibility (2) social distance, and two task related: (3) idea sharing (4) informing.
Smith and Blanck (2002)	P	(1) geographically dispersed, (2) culturally diverse (does mention virtuality, but only to say that it is "faddish" and hurts team performance)	0	NA	NA	NA	This practitioner piece offers advice on how to effectively manage virtual teams, in particular by building open communication and trust from the beginning through FTF meetings.
Staples and Zhao (2006)	E	(1) geographically distributed (2) reliance on communication technology (3) different countries of origin (4) differences in native language and (5) differences in cultural values	2	groups created: FTF vs CMC; culturally homogeneous vs. heterogeneous based on language and IND-COL values	IV	Team task effect.	Culturally heterogeneous teams were less satisfied and cohesive and had more conflict than the homogeneous teams, differences in team performance were not significant. Results suggest that among heterogeneous teams the performance of the virtual heterogeneous teams was superior to that of the FTF heterogeneous teams.
Tan et al. (2000)	E	Virtual teams = (1) geographically dispersed, (2) CMC, (3) temporary, (4) members typically consist of member from diverse cultural backgrounds	0	Teams 100 percent reliant on CMC; manipulation was use of dialogue technique	NA	NA	Dialogue helps VTs improve relational development and decision outcome, VTs working together over time outperform new teams in RD and DO.
Vogel et al. (2001)	CS	(1) geographically and (2) culturally dispersed, (3) reliant on technology	0	teams with students from two different cultures/countries	NA	NA	Several recommendations for managing virtual teams, some examples are; quick support, frequent monitoring, supportive mgmt style, create/find common ground.
Zhuge (2003)	E T	(1) geographically distributed teams who face (2) challenges in coordination (3) assumes cultural diversity	0	NA	NA	NA	This work outlines a model for thinking about cognition and work processes in distributed teams.

a. CS: Case Study, E: Experiment, F: Field, P: Practitioner, T: Theoretical
b. Represents the number of virtuality dimensions operationalized.
c. This column describes either the measures used to operationalized virtuality, or the context manipulated to represent a virtual environment for team members.

Cultural drivers of work behavior: personal values, motivation, and job attitudes

CARLOS SANCHEZ-RUNDE, SANG MYUNG LEE, and RICHARD M. STEERS

In his classic study of bureaucracy, French sociologist Michael Crozier observed long ago that while managers have long understood that organization structures, attitudes, and behaviors differ across cultures, "social scientists have seldom been concerned with such comparisons" (1964, p. 210). Unfortunately, many organizational researches continue to share this view today and all too frequently assume explicitly or implicitly – and in both cases, incorrectly – that relationships found between variables in one culture will likely transcend others.

This viewpoint is easily understood. Culture is a difficult variable to define or measure. Data collection is often difficult and expensive. Translation problems complicate both measurement and analysis. Personal biases, however unintentional, frequently cloud both the choice and location of a research topic and the interpretation of results. Causal relationships are problematic. Intercultural sensitivities often impose self-censorship on dialog and debate. And everything takes more time than originally planned. As a result, serious study of the relationship between culture and behavior presents researchers with a complex puzzle that is not easily understood. Even so, being difficult, expensive, complex, imprecise, sensitive, time-consuming, and risky does not excuse or justify ignoring what is clearly one of the most important variables in the study of human behavior in organizations: culture.

Fortunately, the omission of cultural perspectives in organizational research has been increasingly redressed in recent years such that there is now a reasonably solid body of research focusing on various aspects of organizations and management practice as they relate to employee motivation and

work behavior (Latham and Pinder, 2005; Porter, Bigley, and Steers, 2003; Erez, Kleinbeck, and Thierry, 2001; Leung *et al.*, 2005; Bhagat *et al.*, 2007). Many of our early theories of work motivation that were initially thought to be largely universalistic are now confirmed to be culture-bound to some degree or another. For example, recent empirical studies have demonstrated that cultural variations can have a significant influence on such phenomena as work values, equity perceptions, achievement motivation, causal attributions, social loafing, and job attitudes, to name a few. This is not to say that this research is anywhere near complete; it is not. However, it is fair to say that recent years have witnessed an increasing interest in the serious study of cross-cultural issues as they relate to organizational behavior (Hooker, 2003).

Even so, while many organizational scholars now recognize that cultural differences can have a significant influence on work behavior, a clear understanding of how or why this occurs remains elusive (Chao and Moon, 2005; Steers, Mowday, and Shapiro, 2004; Bhagat *et al.*, 2007). There is something about the concept of culture as it relates to organizational dynamics that makes it "difficult to identify," "fuzzy," "complex and multifaceted," and "amorphous" (Hall, 1992; Trice and Beyer, 1993; Baligh, 1994; Brislin, 1993). As anthropologist Edward T. Hall (1992, p. 210) observed:

> I have come to the conclusion that the analysis of culture could be likened to the task of identifying mushrooms. Because of the nature of the mushrooms, no two experts describe them in precisely the same way, which creates a problem for the rest of us when we are trying to decide whether the specimen in our hands is edible.

As a result, partial models with little empirical support have sometimes been offered as substitutes for science in the belief that a naïve theory is preferable to no theory at all. Thus, we are sometimes left with findings that certain actions may differ across national boundaries, but can only speculate concerning the underlying reasons behind such actions. For instance, recognizing that managers in different countries behave differently when confronting the same challenge is important for understanding management practices, but it is only the beginning of the journey for understanding social dynamics in the workplace.

Thus, the purpose of this chapter is to help redress this limitation by systematically reviewing our current knowledge base concerning the relationship between culture and work motivation, and then organizing these findings in such a way that improved modeling of this relationship becomes possible. This chapter is divided into several sections. First, cross-cultural influences on personal values are reviewed as they relate to work behavior. This is followed by a review of the research on culture and work motivation. Next, the role of culture in the formulation of job attitudes is examined. Following this three-part review, an attempt is made to integrate available empirical findings to explore the implications for managing and motivating employees around the world. Finally, by way of conclusion, several methodological considerations are discussed as they relate to future research on this topic.

Culture, beliefs, and work values

While interest in personal values dates from the early work of Lewin (1935) and Allport (1937), the systematic study of values in the workplace began in earnest only about forty years ago. Following from Triandis (1995, p. 15), a *value* can be defined as "a standard people can use to evaluate their own behavior and that of others." Values identify those aspects in life and work that people should focus on, as well as goals they should reach. Applied to work settings, *personal work values* represent a set of standards and goals to which people aspire and that have meaning to them on the job. For example, some employees place a high value on interesting or meaningful work, while others place a high value on rewards and incentives. In both cases, such findings help guide our understanding of present and future behaviors at work. Since personal work values are largely culturally derived, their importance in understanding organization and management around the world is clear.

Within the workplace, key questions emerge concerning how personal work values influence employee willingness and preparedness to contribute towards the attainment of organizational goals. However, adding a cross-cultural perspective to this analysis raises further questions concerning how variations across cultures may or may not affect employee attitudes and behavior in the workplace, as well as what managers might do to accommodate such variations where they are found to exist. For example, values concerning the relative importance of individualism vs. collectivism can influence the manner in which employees are willing to work together. If Americans are indeed more individualistic on average than their Japanese counterparts, the implications for both organization and management can be significant.

Personal work values have been studied systematically from a cross-cultural perspective since the mid-1960s (Guth and Tagiuri, 1965; England, 1975; Firestone and Garza, 2005). Subsequent researchers have built upon these initial efforts to the point that today we have a reasonably clear conception of how work-related values can influence behavior across cultures. While Guth and Tagiuri focused their attention on the relationship between managerial values in different cultures and corporate strategy formulation, England and his colleagues focused more directly on the impact of managerial values on employee behavior at work.

England developed the personal values questionnaire, which measures sixty-six personal values held by managers in different countries (England, 1975; Davis and Rasool, 1988). These values were then clustered into several dimensions for further analysis. England found significant differences in the personal values among managers in the five countries he studied: Australia, Japan, Korea, India, and the US. American managers tended to be high in pragmatism, achievement-orientation,

Table 12.1 Work priorities in selected countries

Work Goals	Belgium	Germany	Israel	Japan	UK	US
Convenient working hours	9	7	11	8	5	9
Interesting work	1	3	1	2	1	1
Interpersonal relations	5	4	2	6	4	7
Job autonomy	4	8	4	3	10	8
Job security	3	2	10	4	3	3
Job-person fit	8	5	6	1	6	4
Opportunities to learn	7	9	5	7	8	5
Pay	2	1	3	5	2	2
Promotion opportunities	10	10	8	11	11	10
Variety in job content	6	6	11	9	7	6
Working conditions	11	11	9	10	9	11

Source: Based on data reported in G. England, 1986 "National work meanings and patterns: constraints on management action, *European Management Journal* 4(3): 176–84; D. Thomas. 2002. *International Management: A Cross-Cultural Perspective*. Thousand Oaks, CA: Sage, pp. 210–12.

and a demand for competence. They placed a high value on profit maximization, organizational efficiency, and productivity. Japanese and Korean managers also valued pragmatism, competence, and achievement, but emphasized organizational growth instead of profit maximization. Indian managers stressed a moralistic orientation, a desire for stability instead of change, and the importance of status, dignity, prestige, and compliance with organizational directives. Finally, Australian managers emphasized a moralistic and humanistic orientation, an emphasis on both growth and profit maximization, a high value on loyalty and trust, and a low emphasis on individual achievement, success, competition, and risk.

As part of England's research, employees were asked to rank a list of common work goals in order of importance in their lives. The results for six countries are shown in table 12.1. These rankings illustrate that while differences can obviously be found across cultures, such differences may not be as significant as is commonly believed.

This initial work by England and his colleagues formed the basis for a subsequent international study of managerial values called the Meaning of Work Project (MOW International Research Team, 1987). This study sought to identify the underlying meanings that individuals and groups attach to work in the following industrialized nations: Belgium, Germany, Holland, Israel, Japan, the UK, the US, and Yugoslavia. Three dimensions were used in the study: (1) work centrality, defined in terms of the relative importance of work for employees; (2) work goals, defined as the relative importance of 11 work goals and values sought and preferred by employees; and (3) societal norms about working, which compared beliefs about work as an entitlement or an obligation. Differences were then compared across nations. For example, Japan was found to have a higher number of workers for whom work was their central life interest, compared to both Americans and Germans who placed a higher value on leisure and social interaction. A high proportion of Americans saw work as a duty, an obligation that must be met. Japanese workers showed less interest in individual economic outcomes from work than most Europeans and Americans (England and Quintanilla, 1989).

Another effort by an international research team to codify work values as they are influenced by national boundaries was initiated by Elizur et al. (1991). Their research led to the development of the Work Values Questionnaire, which identifies twenty-four values, including achievement, status, job interest, meaningful work, independence, recognition, supervisory support, pay and benefits. They surveyed eight countries (China, Germany, Holland, Hungary, Israel, Korea, Taiwan, and the US) and found interesting commonalties as well as differences across nationalities. Achievement was considered as the most important work value in China, Taiwan, Korea, and Israel, second most important in Holland, Hungary, and the US, and ninth in Germany. Job interest was ranked first in Germany, Holland, the US, second in Taiwan and Israel, third in Korea, seventh in Hungary, and eighth in China. Personal growth, recognition, esteem, advancement, and use of one's abilities ranked high for all nationalities except Germany and Hungary. By contrast, Germany and Hungary ranked having the support of both co-workers and supervisors as very high. Perhaps the major contribution of this study beyond the survey data is the creation of a well-designed research instrument for future use in the study of work-related values across cultures.

Additional country-specific studies, most notably comparing American and Japanese managers, have expanded our knowledge in this area. Hopkins et al. (1977) found Japanese managers to be significantly more fatalistic and more authoritarian than their American counterparts. Likewise, Hayashi, Harnett, and Cummings (1973) found Japanese managers to be more conciliatory and risk-oriented than Americans. Yamagishi and Yamagishi (1994) found that Americans are more trusting in other people in general, consider reputation more important, and consider themselves to be honest and fair, while Japanese see greater utility in dealing with others through personal relations. These findings are consistent with England's earlier findings (e.g., England and Koike, 1970). Other studies by Vogel (1963) and Lincoln and Kalleberg (1990) found Japanese managers to be consistently harder workers than their western counterparts.

Finally, personal work values among Korean employees were examined by Ungson, Steers, and Park (1997), who compared Korean work values with those found in other Asian cultures, as well as in western cultures. Several findings from these studies are relevant here. First, like the Vogel and Lincoln and Kalleberg studies among the Japanese, Ungson et al. found that Korean workers and managers exhibit a very strong work ethic. In interviews, Korean workers took pride in claiming that they worked even harder than the Japanese did. Supporting evidence for this can be seen in a 1994 study of average work hours in various countries, in which it was found that Korean workers on average worked longer hours and took fewer vacation days than workers in Thailand, Hong Kong, Taiwan, Singapore, India, Japan, and Indonesia (Steers, 1999). In this study, Indonesians worked the shortest number of hours per year, while Indians took the largest number of vacation days each year. Beyond long working hours, the Korean corporate culture was found to be typically characterized by a strong Confucian belief in absolute loyalty to the company, adherence to the will of superiors, a strong belief in paternalism, seniority as a prominent factor in promotion, group-oriented achievement instead of individual achievement, the importance of preserving group harmony even at the expense of individual fairness, and a heavy reliance on personal relationships in business relations instead of legal contracts.

In summary, the available research literature on culture and personal values consistently demonstrates a strong and significant relationship with work behavior (Erez, Kleinbeck, and Thierry, 2001; Bhagat et al., 2007). This is appears to be true regardless of whether western or non-western templates are used for either conceptualization or empirical research. As a result, it seems highly advisable to include the role of cultural differences in any future modeling efforts, as well as managerial actions, that involve one's self-concept, individual beliefs and values, and individual traits and aspiration levels. These individual factors, in turn, have been shown to be closely related to self-efficacy, work norms and values, and ultimately work motivation (Bandura, 1996; Locke, 2001).

Culture and work motivation

For our purposes here, *work motivation* can be defined as that which energizes, directs, and sustains employee behavior in the workplace (Porter, Bigley, and Steers, 2003). In other words, the concept of work motivation focuses on those aspects of both the individual and the situation that: (a) causes initial willingness to exert energy and effort; (b) directs this energy in one direction or another; and (c) sustains that effort over time. While personal beliefs and values (discussed above) are clearly one determinant of work motivation, other factors also contribute, including: (1) individual need strengths; (2) cognitions, goals, and perceived equity; (3) incentives, rewards, and reinforcement; and (4) social norms and belief structures governing levels of required effort. The role of culture on each of these four factors will be examined in turn.

Individual needs and work behavior

Need theories of motivation date from the seminal works of Murray (1938) and Maslow (1954). Both of these researchers argued that individuals are largely motivated by various needs that serve to guide behavior. When manifest, such needs focus individual drive towards endeavors aimed at satisfying these needs. Murray believed that people are motivated by perhaps two dozen needs (e.g., achievement, affiliation, autonomy, and power or dominance) that become manifest or latent depending upon circumstances. By contrast, Maslow suggested that needs are pursued by individuals in a sequential or hierarchical fashion from basic deficiency needs (physiological, safety, and belongingness) to growth needs (self-esteem, and self-actualization). The original works of Murray and Maslow were later adapted to the workplace by McClelland (1961) and Alderfer (1972), respectively. McClelland (1961) focused his efforts on the three needs of achievement, affiliation, and dominance (referred to as need for power), while Alderfer's (1972) ERG theory simplified Maslow's five needs into three somewhat broader ones: existence, relatedness, and growth.

Need hierarchies

An early cross-cultural application of Maslow's need hierarchy model to the workplace was completed by Haire, Ghiselli, and Porter (1961), who found systematic differences in managerial need strengths across cultures. Later studies found the need hierarchy structure proposed by Maslow to be similar, but clearly not identical, in such countries as Peru, India, Mexico, and the Middle East (Badawy, 1979; Buera and Glueck, 1979; Jaggi, 1979; Stephens, Kedia, and Ezell, 1979; Reitz, 1975). Subsequently, Hofstede (1980b) argued persuasively that Maslow's need hierarchy is not universally applicable across cultures due to variations in country values. Evidence from Blunt and Jones (1992) and, more recently, from Mitchell and Daniels (2003) support this conclusion.

Achievement motivation

While Maslow's model of motivation has received some attention in other cultures, greater efforts have been directed towards applying the Murray/McClelland model, especially as it pertains to the need for achievement. The basic thesis underlying much of McClelland's work is a hypothesized relationship between aggregate levels of achievement motivation and subsequent economic growth among nations. According to this reasoning, as achievement motivation levels rise within a nation, so too does the extent of entrepreneurial behavior and economic development (McClelland and Winter, 1969). As a result, McClelland argued for the development of large-scale national training efforts in achievement motivation for underdeveloped countries.

McClelland's basic thesis, while disarmingly simple, has generated considerable controversy in the research literature as it relates to the basis of work motivation across cultures. To begin with, the projective test typically used to measure achievement (thematic apperception test) is itself controversial, with a number of studies questioning its validity and reliability (e.g., Iwawaki and Lynn, 1972). Beyond this, several studies suggest that the relationship between achievement motivation and subsequent success on a national level is far more complex than first suggested. Iwawaki and Lynn (1972), for example, found national achievement motivation levels between Japan and the UK to be roughly identical, even though Japan's economic growth rate far exceeded the UK's. McCarthy, Puffer, and Shekshnia (1993) found similar results when comparing Russian and American entrepreneurs. However, Krus and Rysberg (1976) found that entrepreneurs from highly diverse cultures (in this case east Europeans compared to Americans) can also have significantly different levels of achievement motivation. And Salili's (1979) study of Iranian men and women suggests that gender may also influence achievement motivation. Here it was found that Iranian women had achievement motivation scores that more closely resembled their American female counterparts than their Iranian male counterparts.

Bhagat and McQuaid (1982: 669; see also Bhagat et al., 2007) concluded from their comprehensive review of this subject that achievement motivation patterns would likely "arise in different cultural contexts in different forms, stimulated by different situational cues and may be channeled toward accomplishing different types of goals." Thus, DeVos (1968) found that Indians and Chinese frequently achieve considerable economic success outside their native cultures, even though their native cultures have traditionally been seen as being low in achievement motivation. And Maehr (1977; Maehr and Nichols, 1980) suggested that achievement should not be conceptualized or evaluated exclusively in terms of economic success. While economic or academic success may be normative indicators of achievement in the west, other variables, such as family success or success in personal relationships, may be more salient indicators elsewhere in the world. Based on a series of cross-cultural studies, Heckhausen (1971) concluded that a major limitation of McClelland's theory was its lack of differentiation between the affective orientations of fear of success and fear of failure. Both of these sentiments tend to be more prevalent in non-western societies than western ones.

Several studies have also questioned whether the achievement motive could be seen as a collective or group motive, not just an individual one (Kleinbeck, Wegge, and Schmidt, 2001). DeVos and Mizushima (1973), for example, suggest that a major aspect of achievement motivation in Japan involves a need to belong and cooperate with others, thereby linking the need for affiliation to the need for achievement much more closely than is typically found in the west. Yu and Yang (1994) make the same argument for Korea. And, as noted elsewhere, the existence of a group achievement motive throughout much of East Asia is a preeminent driving force in many work environments, while individual achievement is neither valued nor rewarded; indeed, it is frequently punished (Abegglen and Stalk, 1985).

Support for this position comes from a study by Sagie, Elizur, and Yamauchi (1996). They studied managers in five countries (Holland, Hungary, Israel, Japan, and the US) to test the universality of achievement motivation theory. Their findings led them to conclude that achievement motivation is perhaps best conceptualized as consisting of three facets (behavioral modality, type of confrontation, and time perspective) and that different cultures will excel in each of the various facets. In general, achievement motivation was found to be highest for the more individualistic American sample and lowest for the more collectivist Hungarian and Japanese samples. However, the study also concluded that a clear distinction needs to be made between individual and collective achievement motivation to reflect cultural variations.

While considerable progress has been made concerning the role of need theories of motivation in different cultural settings, a major omission must also be noted. Specifically, the vast majority of the cross-cultural research on needs focused on higher-order needs (e.g., achievement or self-actualization) and frequently ignored lower-order needs. In this regard, it must be remembered that much of the world's working population, particularly in the less industrialized nations, remains of necessity focused on trying to meet the more basic lower-order needs like safety and security. Studies by Blunt (1976), and Jones (1988) found, for example, that Kenyan and Malawi managers both attached the greatest importance to security needs, not higher-order needs. And Elenkov (1998) found Russian managers stress security and belongingness needs as opposed to higher-order needs. Moreover, even within more industrialized nations, large working populations similarly remain focused on meeting lower-order needs. It may be only the fortunate few who have a realistic opportunity to pursue self-actualization or genuine achievement in the workplace.

Cognitions, goals, and perceived equity

Cognitive approaches to motivation remain a dominant force in the study of organizational behavior (Mitchell and Daniels, 2003; Van Eerde and Thierry, 2001; Porter, Bigley, and Steers, 2003). Included here are such theories as equity theory (Adams, 1965), goal-setting theory (Locke and Latham, 1990), and expectancy/valence theory (Vroom, 1964; Porter and Lawler, 1968). These theories are based largely on the assumption that people tend to make reasoned choices about their behaviors and that these choices influence, and are influenced by, job-related outcomes and work attitudes. While the majority of cognitive theories, as well as much of the empirical work relating to them, derive from American efforts, a number of studies have also been conducted to test the external validity of these models outside the US.

Equity theory

Equity theory focuses on the motivational consequences that result when individuals believe they are being treated either fairly or unfairly in terms of the rewards and outcomes they receive (Adams, 1965; Mowday, 1996). The determination of equity is based, not on objective reality, but on the individual's perception of how his or her ratio of inputs to outcomes compares to the same ratio for a valued colleague. Accordingly, when an individual thinks that he or she is receiving less money for the same work than the referent other, the person would likely seek some remedy to return to a state of perceived equity. Remedies could include a work slowdown, filing a grievance, seeking alternative employment, etc. It is also possible for the individual to find remedy by changing his or her referent other, perhaps by rationalizing why the other person actually deserved more pay. By the same token, the theory asserts somewhat more controversially that when individuals feel over-compensated, they will likely increase their work efforts, again to achieve a balanced state compared to their referent other.

Considerable research supports the fundamental equity principle in western work groups, particularly as it relates to conditions of underpayment. However, when the theory is applied elsewhere, results tend to be more problematic. Yuchtman (1972), for example, studied equity perceptions among managers and non-managers in an Israeli kibbutz production unit and found that, contrary to initial predictions, managers felt less satisfied than workers. He explained this finding by suggesting that in the egalitarian work environment managers may feel that they are being under-compensated vis-à-vis their value and effort on behalf of the organization. Results were interpreted as supporting the theory.

However, other international researchers have suggested that the equity principle may be somewhat culture bound (Hofstede, 2001; Fey, 2005). Notably in Asia and the Middle East, examples abound concerning individuals who apparently readily accept a clearly recognizable state of inequity in order to preserve their view of societal harmony. For example, men and women frequently receive different pay for doing precisely the same work in countries like Japan and Korea (Abegglen and Stalk, 1985; Chung, Lee, and Jung, 1997). One might think that equity theory would predict that a state of inequity would result for female employees, leading to inequity resolution strategies such as those mentioned above. Yet, in many instances, no such perceived inequitable state has been found, thereby calling the theory into question. A plausible explanation here may be that women workers view other women as their referent other, not men. As a result, so long as all women are treated the same, a state of perceived equity could exist. This is not to say that such women feel "equal"; rather, compared to their female reference group they are receiving what others receive. A state of equity – if not equality – exists. Kim, Park, and Suzuki (1990) lend credence to this explanation in their study of equity perceptions in Japan, Korea, and the US. Their results led them to conclude: "the most important general conclusion emerging from our study is that the equity norm is generalizable across countries. It appeared in all three countries" (1990, p. 195).

Goal-setting theory

A second prominent cognitive theory of motivation that has received considerable attention in the west is goal-setting theory. Goal-setting models focus on how individuals respond to the existence of specific goals, as well as the manner in which such goals are determined (e.g., level of participation in goal-setting, goal difficulty, goal specificity, etc.). Considerable evidence supports the conclusion that many employees perform at higher levels when given specific and challenging goals in which they had some part in setting (Locke and Latham, 1990; Locke, 2001). Despite the large number of US studies on this subject, few studies have been conducted in other cultures (Fey, 2005; Wegge, Kleinbeck, and Schmidt, 2001; Erez, Kleinbeck, and Thierry, 2001). Most of these focused on the influence of employee participation and were conducted either at a societal level, focusing on participative and collectivistic values (Ronen and Shenkar, 1985), or on organizational level practices and their impact on job attitudes (Haire, Ghiselli, and Porter, 1961; Heller and Wilpert, 1981). Locke and Schweiger (1979) also note that participation in the determination of work goals in Europe is institutionalized by law and anchored in political systems that stress egalitarian values, compared to countries like the US, where it is not.

However, a few studies have examined goal-setting effects at the individual level of analysis across cultures. French, Israel, and As (1960) were perhaps the first research team to compare participation in goal determination in the workplace. In contrast to previous findings among American workers, French *et al.* found that Norwegian workers shunned direct participation and preferred to have their union representatives work with management to determine work goals. It was argued that, in Norway, such individual participation would have been seen as being inconsistent with their prevailing philosophy of participation through union representatives.

More recently, Earley (1986) found that, again in contrast to the US, British workers placed more trust in their union stewards than their foremen, and therefore responded more favorably to a goal-setting program sponsored by the stewards than by management. Earley concluded that the transferability of management techniques such as participation in goal setting across cultural settings may be affected by prevailing work norms. To test this proposition, Erez and Earley (1987) studied American and Israeli subjects and found that participative strategies led to higher levels of goal acceptance and performance than the assigned strategy in both cultures. Culture did not moderate the effects of goal-setting strategies or goal acceptance, but it did appear to moderate the effects of strategy on performance for extremely difficult goals. For both samples, acceptance was significantly lower in the assigned than in the participative goal-setting conditions. However, only in the Israeli sample was acceptance highly related to performance under assigned goals.

Expectancy/valence theory

Both the equity and goal-setting principles can be found in the integrated expectancy/valence theory of work motivation (Vroom, 1964; Porter and Lawler, 1968). This theory postulates that motivation is largely influenced by a multiplicative combination of one's belief that effort will lead to performance, performance will lead to certain outcomes, and the value placed on these outcomes by the individual. Thus, if an employee believes that if she works hard she will succeed on a task, and that if she succeeds her boss will in fact reward her, and that if the rewards to be received are valuable to her, she will likely be motivated to perform. On the other hand, if any one of these three components is not present, her motivation level will fall precipitously. The second part of the theory uses the equity principle to examine the relationship between performance and satisfaction. This model predicts that subsequent job satisfaction is determined by employee perceptions concerning the equity or fairness of the rewards received as a result of performance. High performance followed by high rewards should lead to high satisfaction, while high performance followed by low rewards should lead to low satisfaction.

Unfortunately, while expectancy/valence theory lends itself conceptually to rich cross-cultural comparisons, it remains difficult to operationalize for purposes of empirical study. Eden (1975) applied it to a sample of workers in an Israeli kibbutz and found some support for the theory. Matsui and Terai (1979) also found expectancy/valence theory could be applied successfully in Japan. However, a key assumption of this model is that employees have considerable control over the means of performance, the outcomes they will work for, and their manager's ability to successfully identify and administer desired rewards. Unfortunately, all three of these variables can vary significantly by culture. While Americans tend to believe they have considerable control over their environment, people in many other countries do not. Workers in Muslim cultures, for example, tend to manifest a strong external locus of control and believe that much of what happens is beyond their control. One could argue, therefore, that expectancies work best in helping to explain worker behavior in those countries that tend to emphasize an internal locus of control.

Another caution concerning the applicability of western motivation theories in general to other cultures involves the role of attributions in the process of individual judgement. Attribution theory was largely developed in the US, based on laboratory experiments using predominantly white college undergraduates (Kelley, 1973; Weiner, 1980). This theory focuses on how individuals attempt to understand and interpret events that occur around them. One aspect of this theory which has been repeatedly demonstrated in American studies is the self-serving bias, which asserts that in a group situation a leader will tend to attribute group success to himself and group failure to others. Hence, a manager might conclude that his work team succeeded because of his leadership skills. Alternatively, this same manager may conclude that his team failed because of group negligence and despite his best efforts. Evidence by Nam (1995), however, suggests that this process may be influenced by cultural differences. In a comparison of Koreans and Americans, Nam found support for the self-serving bias among his American sample but not in his Korean sample. Following Confucian tradition, Korean leaders accepted responsibility for group failure and attributed group success to the abilities of the group members – just the opposite of the Americans. Clearly, work motivation theories, regardless of their theoretical foundations, must account for cultural variations before any assertions

can be made concerning their external validity across national boundaries.

Incentives, rewards, and reinforcement

A third category of work motivation research focuses on how incentives, rewards, and reinforcements influence performance and work behavior (Chiang, 2005; Erez, Kleinbeck, and Therry, 2001; Erez, 1996; Bhagat *et al.*, 2007). Here the critical issues involve self-efficacy; reward preferences; merit pay; uncertainty, risk, and control; and executive compensation.

Self-efficacy

Theoretical justification for this the impact of incentives and rewards can be found in both cognitive theories and reinforcement theories, including social learning theory, behavior modification, and behavioral management theory (Bandura, 1986, 1996; Luthans and Kreitner, 1985). Critical to much of this research is the role played by self-efficacy in helping determine behavior. Bandura (1986) has argued that incentives and reinforcements can be particularly meaningful if the employees have a high self-efficacy; that is, if they genuinely believe they have the capacity to succeed. Self-efficacy is important because it helps individuals focus their attention on task, commit to challenging goals, and seek greater feedback on task effort (Kanfer and Ackerman, 1996; Locke and Latham, 1990; Tsui and Ashford, 1994; Stajkovic and Luthans, 2003).

Reward preferences

Moreover, the specific rewards that employees seek from the job can vary across cultures. As Adler (1986; see also Huang and Van de Vliert, 2004) points out, some cultures emphasize security, while others emphasize harmony and congenial interpersonal relationships, and still others emphasize individual status and respect. For example, an early study by Sirota and Greenwood (1971) examined employees of a large multinational electrical equipment manufacturer operating in forty countries around the world and found important similarities as well as differences in what rewards employees wanted in exchange for good performance. Interestingly, in all countries, the most important rewards that were sought involved recognition and achievement. Second in importance were improvements in the immediate work environment and employment conditions such as pay and work hours.

Beyond this, however, a number of differences emerged in terms of preferred rewards. Some countries, like England and the US, placed a low value on job security compared to workers in many nations, while French and Italian workers placed a high value on security and good fringe benefits and a low value on challenging work. Scandinavian workers de-emphasized "getting ahead" and instead stressed greater concern for others on the job and for personal freedom and autonomy. Germans placed high on security, fringe benefits, and "getting ahead," while Japanese ranked low on personal advancement and high on having good working conditions and a congenial work environment.

Kanungo and Wright (1983) found similar results in their four-country study of outcome preferences among managers from Canada, France, Japan, and the UK. This study focused on the relative preferences expressed by the managers for three types of job outcomes: organizationally mediated (e.g., earnings, fringe benefits, promotion opportunities); interpersonally mediated (e.g., respect and recognition, technically competent supervision); and internally mediated (e.g., responsibility and independence, achievement). Results showed that the British managers strongly preferred internally mediated (or intrinsic) job outcomes, while their French counterparts preferred organizationally mediated (or extrinsic) outcomes. The British managers also placed a higher value on receiving respect and recognition, while the French placed more emphasis on the quality of technical supervision. Canadian managers of British heritage resembled their British counterparts in terms of outcome preferences, while Canadians of French heritage did not closely resemble their French counterparts. Finally, the Japanese were found to be more similar to the British and Canadians in their outcome preferences than to the French. Overall, the greatest cultural divergence in this study was found to be between the British and French.

Considerable research indicates that culture can also play a significant role in determining who gets rewarded and how. Huo and Steers (1993) observed that culture can influence the effectiveness of an inventive system in at least three ways: (1) what is considered important or valuable by workers; (2) how motivation and performance problems are analyzed; and (3) what possible solutions to motivational problems lie in the feasible set for managers to select from. Thus, while many independent-minded US firms prefer merit-based reward systems as the best way to motivate employees, companies in more collectivistic cultures like Japan, Korea, and Taiwan frequently reject this approach as being too disruptive of the corporate culture and traditional values (Milliman et al., 1995). Likewise, firms in environments characterized by long-standing political instability, like Venezuela or Ecuador, often stress group-based incentives to reinforce high team spirit and commitment to the organization.

Merit pay

Merit pay systems that are common in the US attempt to link compensation directly to corporate financial performance, thereby stressing equity. Other cultures believe compensation should be based on group membership or group effort, thereby stressing equality (Erez and Earley, 1993; Leung, 2001; Chiang, 2005). This issue requires an assessment of distributive justice across cultures, especially as it relates to individualism or collectivism. One example of this can be seen in an effort by an American multinational corporation to institute an individually based bonus system for its sales representatives in a Danish subsidiary (Schneider, Wittenberg-Cox, and Hansen, 1991). The sales force under study rejected the proposal because it favored one group over another. The Danish employees felt that all employees should receive the same amount of bonus instead of a given percent of one's salary, reflecting a strong sense of egalitarianism.

Similarly, a study of Indonesian oil workers found that individually-based incentive systems created more controversy than results (Vance, McClaine, Boje, and Stage, 1992). As one HR manager commented: "Indonesians manage their culture by a group process, and everybody is linked together as a team. Distributing money differently amongst the team did not go over that well; so, we've come to the conclusion that pay for performance is not suitable for Indonesia" (p. 323). Similar results were reported in studies comparing Americans with Chinese (Bond, Leung, and Wan, 1982; Leung and Bond, 1984; Miller, Giacobbe-Miller, and Zhang, 1998), with Russians (Elenkov, 1998), and with Indians (Berman, Murphy-Berman, and Singh, 1985). In all three cases, Americans expressed greater preference than their counterparts for rewards to be based on performance instead of equality or need.

In studies of individualism and collectivism as they relate to issues of reward equity and distributive justice, consideration must be given to the types of rewards available to the employees. As predicted in his study of American and Chinese managers, Chen (1995) found that Americans preferred reward systems that allocated material rewards based on equity but allocated socio-emotional rewards based on equality. In contrast, Chinese managers preferred both material and socio-emotional rewards to be allocated based on equity. Chen's finding with respect to material rewards supports the earlier finding by Kim, Park, and Suzuki (1990) in Japan and Korea. Chen explained his findings by differentiating between vertical and horizontal collectivism in organizations. Evidence was found in Chen, Meindl, and Hunt (1997) to support the hypothesis that the newfound support for performance-based rewards in China may be explained by the existence of vertical collectivism. Horizontal collectivism, on the other hand, works against the equity principle. It was suggested that "collectivists are capable of adopting differential distributive logic as long as such logic is believed to be beneficial to collective survival and prosperity" (1997, p. 64). Another factor that may help explain this seemingly counterintuitive finding regarding a Chinese preference for equity over equality may lie in the nature of the Chinese sample, which consisted mainly of younger workers, with an average age 34. (The subjects in the Kim et al. study were also young.) Thus, part of this change in views towards equity-based rewards may represent a shift in employee

values – especially among the young – as a result of the surge in China's new quasi-market economy. Evidence consistent with this argument can be found in Saywell (1999).

It is interesting to note in this regard that the bases for some incentive systems have evolved over time in response to political and economic changes. China is frequently cited as an example of a country that is attempting to blend quasi-capitalistic economic reforms with a reasonably static socialist political state. On the economic front, China's economy has demonstrated considerable growth as entrepreneurs are increasingly allowed to initiate their own enterprises largely free from government control. And within existing and former state-owned enterprises, some movement can be seen towards what is called a reform model of incentives and motivation. Child (1994; see also Tung, 1991) makes a distinction between the traditional Chinese incentive model in which egalitarianism is stressed and rewards tend to be based on age, loyalty, and gender, and the new reform model in which merit and achievement receive greater emphasis and rewards tend to be based on qualifications, training, level of responsibility, and performance. Child and Tung both point out, however, that rhetoric in support of the reform model frequently surpasses actual implementation on the factory floor.

Meanwhile, efforts to introduce western-style merit pay systems in Japan have frequently led to an increase in overall labor costs (Sanger, 1993). Since the companies that adopted the merit-based reward system could not simultaneously reduce the pay of less productive workers for fear of causing them to lose face and disturb group harmony (wa), everyone's salary tended to increase. Conceptual justification for these results is offered by Milliman et al. (1998). Similar results concerning the manner in which culture can influence reward systems, as well as other personnel practices, emerged from a study among banking employees in Korea (Nam, 1995). The two Korean banks were owned and operated as joint ventures with banks in other countries, one from Japan and one from the US. In the American joint venture, US personnel policies dominated management practice in the Korean bank, while in the Japanese joint venture, a blend of Japanese and Korean HRM policies prevailed. Employees in the joint venture with the Japanese bank were found to be significantly more committed to the organization than employees in the American joint venture. Moreover, the Japanese-affiliated bank also demonstrated significantly higher financial performance.

On the other hand, Welsh, Luthans, and Sommer (1993) argued that some western incentives might work in post-communist societies. They compared three common western incentive systems to determine their effectiveness among Russian textile factory workers: (1) tying valued extrinsic rewards to good performance; (2) administering praise and recognition for good performance; and (3) using participative techniques to involve workers in decisions affecting how their jobs were performed. Welsh *et al.* found that both extrinsic rewards and positive reinforcement – both considered behavioral management techniques – led to significantly enhanced job performance, while participative techniques had little impact on job behavior. The authors concluded that behavioral management techniques could represent a useful motivational tool in the post-communist culture under study. However, the researchers also suggested that the Russian employees might have been overly skeptical about the genuineness of the participatory techniques used in the study and may have been overly cautious about their genuine participation.

Uncertainty, risk, and control

Cultural differences concerning uncertainty, risk, and control can also affect employee preferences for fixed versus variable compensation. Pennings (1993) found, for example, that more risk-oriented American managers were frequently prepared to convert 100 percent of their pay to variable compensation, while more risk-averse European managers would seldom commit to more than 10 percent of their pay to variable compensation. Similarly, cultural variations can influence employee preferences for financial or non-financial incentives. Thus, Schneider and Barsoux (2003) note that Swedes will typically prefer additional time off for superior performance instead of additional income (due in part to their high tax rates), while if given a choice Japanese workers would prefer financial

incentives (with a distinct preference for group-based incentives). Japanese workers tend to take only about half of their sixteen-day holiday entitlement (compared to 35 days in France and Germany) because taking all the time available may show a lack of commitment to the group. Japanese workers who take their full vacations or refuse to work overtime are frequently labeled *wagamama* (selfish). As a result, *karoshi* (death by overwork) is a serious concern in Japan, while Swedes see taking time off as part of an inherent right to a healthy and balanced life.

Executive compensation

Much has been written about excessive executive compensation, particularly in the US. From a motivational standpoint, compensation is seen as the key to hiring and retaining the best executive leadership available. While it is true that incentive systems work, the question that many people are asking is how much money is necessary to hire and motivate the right CEO? In the US, we hear increasing concerns about the "imperial CEO," referring to what many consider to be excessive rewards that in many cases are not even tied to executive or corporate performance. In many cases, they are tied to the manipulation of stock prices, often by illegal or certainly unethical means. Issues of fairness abound.

What upset has many people is that while executives are making increasing amounts of money, rank-and-file workers are often making less, especially in the US. Consider the following fact: twenty years ago, the average American CEO made forty times the salary of the average factory worker in his or her company. Now this figure is well over four hundred times. Worse still, the US seems to be way out in front of other nations in terms of this imbalance between workers' and executives' pay. Another way to understand this is to look at average CEO compensation compared to the average factory worker on a country-by-country basis, as shown in table 12.2. While aggregate data always contain some systematic errors – for example, the data for Korea do not include owner-CEOs, who can become incredibly wealthy even if they are officially paid very little – it is difficult to believe that the magnitude of these results is far from accurate.

Table 12.2 Ratio of CEO compensation to average employee income

Country	Pay Ratio	Country	Pay Ratio	Country	Pay Ratio
US	475	UK	24	Netherlands	16
Venezuela	50	Thailand	24	France	14
Brazil	49	Australia	23	New Zealand	13
Mexico	47	South Africa	22	Sweden	12
Singapore	44	Canada	20	Germany	12
Argentina	44	Italy	20	Switzerland	11
Malaysia	42	Belgium	18	Japan	11
Hong Kong	41	Spain	16	South Korea	8

Source: R. M. Steers and L. Nardon. 2006. *Managing in the Global Economy*. Armonk, NY: M. E. Sharpe. Numbers express the ratios between the average CEO compensation and the average compensation received by the average factory worker in each country.

Hopefully, recent laws passed in the US and elsewhere, as well as stockholder suits and prosecutions for illegal activities, will begin to redress some of the more brazen inequities.

Social norms and belief structures

Finally, social or group norms can often play a significant role in determining motivational levels with organizations. Here we discuss two such examples of how social norms and prevailing belief structures can represent significant factors in job performance and productivity: social loafing and work and leisure.

Social loafing and free riders

A key concern of high performance work teams is maximizing the collective contribution of group members towards the attainment of challenging goals (Lawler, 1992). In a competitive global economy, such collective action becomes a strategic advantage that can differentiate winners from losers. As such, the tendency of select group members to restrict output in the belief that others will take up the slack represents a serious impediment to organizational effectiveness. Free riders and social loafing as social phenomena have been scrutinized in a small but important set of studies (Latane, Willaims, and Harkins, 1979). In this regard, Olson (1971) notes that individuals may loaf in a group setting because they assume that the actions of others will ensure the attainment of the

collective good, thereby freeing them up to redirect their individual efforts towards the attainment of additional personal gains. This perspective is consistent with agency theory of motivated behavior (Jensen and Meckling, 1976).

Social loafing can only be successful when individual behavior can be hidden behind group behavior. To accomplish this, group norms must support, or at least tolerate, a high level of individualism. It is therefore not surprising that such behavior tends to be more prevalent in organizations in America and western Europe than in East Asia (Earley 1989, 1993; George, 1992). Matsui, Kakuyama, and Onglatco (1987) found, for example, that Japanese workers performed better in groups than alone. Gabrenya, Latane, and Wang (1983, 1985) found similar results in a Taiwanese study.

Earley (1989) specifically tested this hypothesis among Chinese and American managers and found that individualistic-collectivist beliefs moderated the tendency towards social loafing. Specifically, he found that more social loafing occurred in the individualistic American group than in the more collectivist Chinese group.

Building on these results, Earley (1993, 1997) posited that while individualists would consistently perform better when working individually rather than in a group, collectivists would perform better either when working in an ingroup as opposed to in an outgroup condition or working individually. Since the basis of collectivism is rooted in allegiance to the group, such individuals would only exhibit this allegiance and subsequent effort when working with members with whom they have had a long and mutually supportive relationship. Working in groups where members were relative strangers would not engender the same cohesiveness or motivational pattern.

Earley (1993) tested this hypothesis using a sample of US, Chinese, and Israeli managers. Results supported the hypothesis. Collectivists anticipated receiving more rewards and felt more efficacious, both alone and as group members, and thus performed better, while working in an ingroup situation than while working in either an outgroup situation or working alone. Individualists, on the other hand, anticipated receiving more rewards and felt more efficacious, and thus performed better, when working alone than while working in either an ingroup or outgroup situation.

In conclusion, cultural differences have a strong influence on work motivation. Culture can influence individual need strengths, cognitive processes governing effort determination, interpretations of and responses to various forms of incentives, and output restriction mechanisms such as social loafing. What is perhaps surprising here is not so much the magnitude of this influence, but its breadth. Based on available findings, cultural differences seem to permeate many aspects of both the decision to participate and the decision to produce, the two fundamental decisions facing organizational members (March and Simon, 1958). In view of these findings, it is surprising how few studies of work motivation have intentionally incorporated cultural variables into either their models or their research designs.

Work and leisure

It is often said that people in some societies work to live, while others live to work. We hear that Americans work harder than Europeans, but that many Asians work harder than Americans. Several EU countries now have a standard thirty-five-hour workweek, while the norm in the US is closer to fifty. Many Europeans can retire at 55, while most Americans must work until 60 or 65. We see newspaper articles seeking to identify the "hardest working" people in the world, as well as the "laziest." We see wide variations in vacation

time taken across countries, ranging from one or two weeks in much of Asia to four or five weeks in much of Europe (see table 12.3 for examples). The unanswered question throughout this debate is whether working harder than anyone else is a badge of honor or a sign of necessity or, worse still, some deep psychological malfunction.

In the never-ending search for competitive advantage, a key variable is labor cost and productivity. Consider: not only does Europe have higher labor costs than the US, but the average European worker is significantly less productive than his or her American counterpart on an annual basis. One OECD study found that the average US worker produced $35,500 in goods and services annually, while the average European worker produced only $25,200, or 69 percent of their US counterparts (Viscusi, 2002). This suggests that European companies are at a significant competitive disadvantage in the global marketplace. Among other things, their goods and services will likely cost more. However, a second study found that the vacation-loving French and Belgians out-produce Americans on a per-hour basis (Brady, 2002). They work fewer hours but make each hour count more. At a certain point, the study concluded, there is a negative rate of return on productivity resulting from working too long. So, how do we calculate productivity: annually of hourly? Which is better for employees? Which is better for companies? And which is better for national economic development?

Now consider vacations. A *Business Week* survey found that Americans now take less vacation time than even the Japanese or Koreans (Brady, 2002). Specifically, the study found that on average employees took the following vacation times (including public holidays): forty-two days in Italy, thirty-seven days in France, thirty-five days in Germany, thirty-four days in Brazil, twenty-eight days in Britain, twenty-six days in Canada, twenty-five days in South Korea, twenty-five days in Japan, and thirteen days in the US Obviously these are averages, and considerable variations can be found across the workforce. Even so, consider the effects of such long hours on home life, personal relationships, and even health. In the US, the average employee gives back 1.8

Table 12.3 Vacation policies in selected countries

Country	Typical Annual Vacation Policy
France	2 1/2 days paid leave for each full month of service during the year.
Germany	18 working days paid leave following 6 months of service.
Hong Kong	7 days paid leave following 12 months of continuous service with same employer.
Indonesia	12 days paid leave after 12 months of full service.
Italy	Varies according to length of service, but usually between 4 and 6 weeks paid leave.
Japan	10 days paid leave following 12 months of continuous service, providing that employee has worked at least 80% of this time.
Malaysia	Varies according to length of service but usually between 8 and 16 days paid leave.
Mexico	6 days paid leave.
Philippines	5 days paid leave.
Saudi Arabia	15 days of paid leave upon completion of 12 months of continuous service with the same employer.
Singapore	7 days paid leave following 12 months of continuous employment.
United Kingdom	No statutory requirement. Most salaried staff receive about 5 weeks of paid leave; paid leave for workers based on individual labor contracts.
United States	No statutory requirement. Typically varies based on length of service and job function, usually between 5 and 15 days paid leave annually.

Source: Adapted from V. Frazee. 1997. "Vacation Policies Around the World", *Personnel Journal* 75: 9; and A. Phatak, R. Bhagat, and R. Kashlak. 2004. *International Management*. New York, NY: McGraw-Hill/Irwin, p. 125.

unused vacations days annually, worth $20 billion to employers.

Finally, consider health and job satisfaction. It might be suggested that while Europeans load up on vacation time, Americans load up on consumer products. As the work pace quickens, health-related problems are rising, most notably heart problems resulting from job-related stress. So is employee dissatisfaction. A recent poll among US workers found that, given a choice between two weeks of extra pay and two weeks of vacation, employees preferred the extra vacation by a 2:1 margin. However, the pressure to succeed and concern about the economy and job security frequently lead American workers in the opposite direction towards more work and less play.

While perhaps overly simplistic, the work vs. leisure conundrum provides an easy conceptual entry into cultural differences, especially as they relate to the world of work. It indicates how central work is in some people's lives. However, this debate is only part of a larger debate over the social and economic consequences of increasing globalization. Many people believe – correctly or incorrectly – that the quickening pace of globalization and the competitive intensity of the new global economy are changing how people live in ways not imagined earlier. The open question is whether these changes are for the better or for the worse.

Cultural drivers of work behavior: a managerial perspective

How can we make sense out of these various findings concerning the role of culture in work motivation? And what implications can be identified for global managers? To answer these questions, it may be useful to focus somewhat more generally on how *cultural drivers* create both the opportunities and constraints on efforts by managers and organizations to motivate their employees through incentive and reward systems (see figure 12.1).

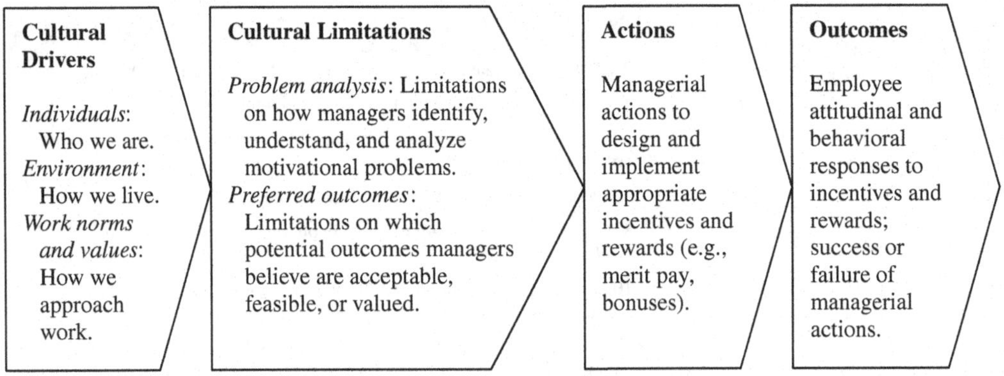

Cultural Drivers	Cultural Limitations	Actions	Outcomes
Individuals: Who we are. *Environment*: How we live. *Work norms and values*: How we approach work.	*Problem analysis*: Limitations on how managers identify, understand, and analyze motivational problems. *Preferred outcomes*: Limitations on which potential outcomes managers believe are acceptable, feasible, or valued.	Managerial actions to design and implement appropriate incentives and rewards (e.g., merit pay, bonuses).	Employee attitudinal and behavioral responses to incentives and rewards; success or failure of managerial actions.

Figure 12.1. Cultural drivers of work behavior: a managerial perspective

Cultural environment

Based on previous research, three factors emerging from one's *cultural environment* surroundings can be identified as a useful starting point for understanding work motivation decisions: 1) our concept of who we are as individuals; 2) how we live in our surrounding social and physical environment; and 3) how we approach work and society, particularly in terms of our work values and norms. In a very real sense, culture provides the stage upon which life events transpire.

Individual characteristics that can be influenced by cultural variations include the development of one's self-concept, personal values and beliefs, individual needs, traits, and aspirations (Locke, 2001; Eden, 2001; Bhagat *et al.*, 2007). Environmental characteristics that can be influenced by culture include family and community structures, values and norms, education and socialization experiences, occupational and organizational cultures, the status of economic development, and the political and legal system (Fey, 2005; Peterson and Ruiz-Quintanilla, 2003; Earley, 2001; Leung *et al.*, 2005).

For example, some cultures emphasize hard work and sacrifice, while others emphasize social relationships and enjoyment. Some stress individual achievement, while others stress group achievement. Some stress communal rewards, while others stress individual rewards. Culture also influences the beliefs and values of one's family and friends; younger members of a society learn what to believe in and what to strive for at least in part from older generations. Educational institutions are significantly influenced by culture, as are organizational and occupational values.

As a result of these individual and environmental characteristics, people enter the workplace already imbued with a set of culturally derived work norms and values about what constitutes acceptable or fair working conditions, what they wish to gain in exchange for their labor, how hard they intend to work, and how they view their career (Wood, George-Falvy, and Debrowski, 2001; Firestone and Garza, 2005). Included in this group of work norms and values are the general strength and quality of the employee work ethic, individual versus group achievement norms, proclivity towards egalitarianism, tolerance for ambiguity, social loafing or free rider, and norms concerning conformity and deviance from group wishes.

However, culturally based influences on work norms and values are not universal. Even in the most collectivistic societies, individual differences exist, although the magnitude of variation may differ by culture. Professionals tend to expect more from the workplace in terms of status, rewards, and freedom of action than most blue-collar workers in both Japan and the US, for example. Moreover, some cultures attempt to minimize status and reward differences between occupational groupings (e.g., Sweden), while others tend to enhance them (e.g., Korea). Individual and group assessments of equity, or what is deemed to be fair and just, seem to underlie this process across cultures.

In addition, culture influences self-efficacy beliefs through education and socialization experiences, as well as the level of incentives and disincentives that are offered to employees in exchange for their labor (Eden, 2001; Locke, 2001). As we might expect, incentives and disincentives are frequently influenced by such factors as education level, occupation, corporate personnel practices, level of economic prosperity, group norms, and the political and legal system in which people work.

Cultural drivers

The cultural environment, in turn, creates and reinforces normative beliefs and values that place at least two cultural limitaions on the acceptable actions, or *cultural drivers*, of both managers and employees. The first limitation focuses on *problem analysis*. That is, prevailing cultural environments can at times affect in no small way how problems are identified and understood by both managers and employees. Indeed, they can even sometimes help determine whether something is seen as a problem at all. For example, while managers in one culture (e.g., the USA) may focus very seriously on problems of employee absenteeism, managers elsewhere (e.g., Sweden) may see such behavior as more of a personal employee issue and acceptable within broader limits. The issue in these two cultures is not whether absenteeism is good or bad; rather, it is the magnitude or severity of the problem compared to other behaviors and actions.

In addition, cultural environments can influence the variety of possible solutions or *preferred outcomes* that are acceptable on the part of organizations, managers, and employees. Using the employee absenteeism example again, managers in some cultures (again, the US) may see strict punitive actions (e.g., financial penalties or termination) as either acceptable or even desirable when employees fail to come to work. In other cultures (again, Sweden), this may seem overly harsh and lacking in understanding of the underlying causes of the absences; such cultures may accept counseling but not termination. In still other cultures (e.g., Saudi Arabia), no action may be taken at all in the belief that absences are largely beyond the control

of individuals and, as such, should not be a legitimate issue for managers.

Another example can be seen in pay-for-performance or merit-based compensation systems. Considerable research (discussed above) indicates that in many western societies pay-for-performance compensation systems can significantly help to raise productivity, while in other cultures it frequently fail due to more egalitarian societal norms. In these examples and others, cultural drivers have the capacity to influence how problems are identified and diagnosed and how the array of possible solutions is considered by all parties.

Motivational strategies and outcomes

Finally, as illustrated in figure 12.1, in response to these cultural drivers, managers make constrained decisions focusing on acceptable *motivational* actions aimed at seeking remedies to the problem. These actions, in turn, are viewed and evaluated by employees as being either appropriate or inappropriate, acceptable or unacceptable, with corresponding *outcomes* in terms of attitudinal and behavioral consequences.

A good example of how this works can be seen in situations where organizations are experiencing financial exigency and wish to reduce their labor force to save costs. In the US, such a situation leads logically – and culturally consistently – to lay-offs. While widely recognized as causing hardships on people, lay-offs are often deemed to represent a prudent response to a financial crisis. In the Netherlands, by contrast, long-standing social legislation makes it much more difficult – and more costly – to downsize employees. As a result, Dutch organizations will often seek other remedies, such as highly lucrative employee buy-outs. Finally, in Japan, lay-offs are rare (although still possible), since the organization risks losing public reputation that can affect its business and future hiring opportunities. As a result, Japanese organizations frequently decide to transfer redundant employees to other parts of the organization or its subsidiaries. Thus, the same problem can lead to very different outcomes based on where the action occurs.

Culture and job attitudes

Following the classic work of Allport (1939), an *attitude* can be defined as a predisposition to respond in a favorable or unfavorable way to objects or persons in one's environment. In point of fact, attitudes represent a hypothetical construct since they are not observable and can only be inferred from self-reports and subsequent behaviors. They are generally thought to be unidimensional in nature, ranging from very favorable to very unfavorable. And attitudes are believed to be related to subsequent behavior. Attitudes are thought to consist of three interrelated components: (1) a cognitive component, focusing on the beliefs and thoughts a person has about another person or object; (2) an affective component, focusing on a person's feelings towards a person or object; and (3) an intentional component, focusing on the behavioral intentions a person has with respect to a person or object.

The importance of job attitudes in the workplace has been the subject of intensive examination since the early work of Brayfield and Crockett (1955). These studies have generally focused on one of three attitudes: job satisfaction (Locke, 1976; Porter and Lawler, 1968), job involvement (Lodahl and Kejner, 1965), and organizational commitment (Mowday, Porter, and Steers, 1982). However, while considerable research has focused on this subject within a single-country frame of reference (most notably the US), efforts to look at attitudes cross-culturally have been somewhat sparse. And, as noted by Bhagat and McQuaid (1882; Bhagat *et al.*, 2007), and in contrast to studies of work motivation, many of the early studies of cross-cultural influences on job attitudes were atheoretical in nature and somewhat simplistic in design. These studies examined bilateral relationships between job attitudes and specific outcome variables, such as performance or absenteeism in two different cultures. Hypotheses were frequently derived with little concern for extant theories underlying job attitudes and with little in-depth knowledge of the cultures under study.

In one early study, for example, Kraut and Ronen (1975) examined various facets of job satisfaction in a large multinational corporation with locations in five countries. Results indicated that country of origin was a better predictor of job performance than any of the facets of satisfaction. While an intriguing finding, little effort was made to consider the potential role of cultural variations in influencing such findings. In another study, Slocum (1971) found that the Mexican hourly workers exhibited greater job satisfaction than their American counterparts. Culture was identified as the reason for the significant differences, although little effort was made to examine why culture should make a difference. Moreover, the study did not explore economic or work environmental factors that could also help explain the findings.

Several studies examined the relationship between locus of control and job attitudes across cultures. Runyon (1973), for example, initially suggested that the relationship between locus of control and job involvement was culture bound. However, a subsequent investigation by Reitz and Jewell (1979) questioned this finding in a study of skilled and unskilled workers in Japan, Mexico, Thailand, Turkey, the former Yugoslavia, and the US. Results showed that, in all six highly divergent countries, workers with an internal locus of control were more involved with their jobs than those with an external locus of control. This finding, while significant for both genders, was stronger among men. Reitz and Jewell concluded that locus of control is, in fact, not culture-bound.

In a major study of job attitudes and management practices among over 8,000 workers in 106 factories in Japan and the US, Lincoln and Kalleberg (1990) concluded that Japanese workers were less satisfied but more committed than their American counterparts. The researchers explained this difference through an in-depth examination of both Japanese societal culture and corporate culture. For example, the age and seniority-grading system (*nenko*) prevalent in Japanese firms reinforces a family-like relationship between workers and companies; it shows concern for employee welfare. This, in turn, is reciprocated by workers in the form of stronger commitment to the organization, even if the jobs themselves are distasteful. By contrast, in the transitory culture that permeates many US firms, less mutual concern exists between employers and employees. Employees frequently

Table 12.4 Job satisfaction across cultures

Countries	% Employees Reporting High Job Satisfaction	Countries	% Employees Reporting High Job Satisfaction
Denmark	61	Argentina	38
India (middle class only)	55	Austria	36
Norway	54	Israel	33
United States	50	Brazil	28
Ireland	49	France	24
Canada	48	Japan	16
Germany	48	South Korea	14
Australia	46	China	11
Mexico	44	Czech Republic	11
Slovenia	40	Ukraine	10
United Kingdom	38	Hungary	9

Source: Adapted from M. Boyle. 2001. "Nothing is Rotten in Denmark", *Fortune*, February 19, pp. 242–3.

feel more like contract workers than members of the firm. As a result, lower commitment levels are reflected. (Whether this strong commitment exhibited by Japanese workers will continue in the face of an increasing emphasis on performance-based pay raises and promotions and more limited lifetime employment remains to be seen.) The prevalence of after-work socializing among Japanese workers (*tsukiai*) was also cited as another way for workers to reinforce their friendship ties and trust levels among themselves, thereby further solidifying their ties with the companies. Again, this contrasts sharply with the typical American practice of running for the parking lot or subway at the close of work.

In addition, Lincoln and Kalleberg argued that the differential job satisfaction levels between Japanese and American workers may occur because American culture stresses being upbeat and cheerful and putting the best possible face on events. By contrast, Japanese frequently bias their assessments in the opposite direction towards the self-critical and self-effacing. As such, using western questionnaires to ask questions about job satisfaction may prompt workers in the two cultures to respond in opposite ways, with one group overestimating their satisfaction levels and the other under-estimating them.

Aggregate work attitudes can change significantly over time as the result of structural changes in the political or economic environment. For example, Shin and Kim (1994) found that general job attitudes among Korean industrial workers declined sharply following the violent labor turmoil that erupted throughout that country in the late 1980s. Specifically, worker attitudes towards their supervisors and their companies declined (from 77 percent holding positive attitudes towards their supervisors and 91 percent holding positive attitudes towards their companies to 41 percent and 65 percent, respectively), as did their willingness to follow supervisory directions (from 94 percent to 59 percent). The rise of unionization and the ensuing labor disputes, largely sanctioned by the government, served to weaken the traditional psychological ties and obligations between workers and companies with a resulting decline in job satisfaction and commitment.

Moreover, findings by Huang and Van de Vliert (2004) suggest from their study of thirty-nine countries that job satisfaction was positively related to position in the organizational hierarchy in individualistic countries but not in collectivistic ones.

Finally, it is interesting to ask where employees report the greatest levels of satisfaction. As shown in table 12.4, the results are not unpredictable. The most satisfied employees are not necessarily found in richer countries or the countries of a particular continent. They are not found in countries that claim certain religious affiliations. Nor are they found exclusively in either large or small countries. Instead, the most satisfied employees tend to be found in those countries where the prevailing management systems and motivational programs are compatible with and supportive of local cultures. These findings caution against an unquestioning adoption of the "best practices" approach to management and motivation across diverse cultures.

In summary, cultural differences appear to have a significant influence on attitude formation, as well as on the consequences of attitudes once formed. This conclusion supports Triandis' (1971) signal work on this topic and has clear and important implications for both researchers and managers interested in how individuals and groups respond to events and actions in the workplace. Attitudes and accompanying trust levels influence the manner in which employees perceive and respond to reward systems. This, in turn, influences subsequent work motivation and performance. Thus, as suggested many years ago by Porter and Lawler (1968), ignoring the consequences of job-related attitudes on employee behavior and performance is done only at a manager's or organization's peril.

Implications for management

Based on this model, what lessons can be drawn concerning how to motivate employees in different cultures? To answer this question, we can combine the research on employee motivation discussed above with models of national culture (e.g., Hofstede, Hall, Trompenaars, GLOBE, etc.). For purposes of illustration, we will use five commonly used dimensions of culture: (1) the extent to which power and authority in a society are distributed hierarchically or in a more egalitarian and participative fashion, measured on a continuum from hierarchical to egalitarian; (2) the extent to which social relationships emphasize individual rights and responsibilities or group goals and collective action, measured on a continuum from individualistic to collectivistic; (3) the extent to which people seek to change and control or live in harmony with their natural and social surroundings, measured on a continuum from mastery to harmony; (4) the extent to which people organize

their time based on sequential attention to single tasks or simultaneous attention to multiple tasks, measured on a continuum from monochromic to polychromic; and (5) the extent to which rules, laws, and formal procedures are uniformly applied across societal members or tempered by personal relationships, in-group values, or unique circumstances, measured on a continuum from universalism to particularism (see Chapter 1 for details).

Using this approach, finding the most appropriate motivational strategies and techniques depends largely upon what culture managers are working in. Moreover, as noted in table 12.5, the differences across these culturally consistent motivational techniques can often be substantial (Latham and Pinder, 2005; Chao and Moon, 2005; Steers and Nardon, 2006). Consider just two examples: first, successful incentives programs in individualistic cultures would likely emphasize individual performance and emphasize financial rewards for outstanding performance, while such incentives in more collectivistic cultures would likely rely more heavily on group-based incentives and seniority-based rewards. As Akio Morita (1986:130), the late founder of Sony Corporation once observed: "To motivate employees, you must bring them into the family and treat them like respected members of it." While this assertion may make sense in Japan, it probably makes less sense in many other more individualistic cultures. Second, successful supervision in more hierarchical cultures would tend to be more directive, while supervision in more egalitarian cultures would tend to be more consultative. In both examples, it can be seen that the successful motivational strategy will likely vary based on prevailing cultural characteristics.

Conclusion and future research

Recent years have witnessed a significant increase in both the quantity and quality of research focusing on the role of cultural differences on work motivation and job attitudes. These newer studies are typically characterized by improved theoretical grounding, more rigorous research designs, improved measures, and more sophisticated data analytic techniques. As a result, we now have a

Table 12.5 Culture and trends in work motivation strategies

Core Cultural Dimensions	Motivational Strategies
Hierarchical cultures	Emphasize extrinsic rewards and large salary differentials. Provide clear directives to subordinates. Support decisive and powerful leaders. Reward subordinate compliance with management directives.
Egalitarian cultures	Emphasize intrinsic rewards and minimal salary differentials. Encourage participative or consultative decision-making. Support flexible and collaborative leaders. Reward constructive feedback and creativity.
Individualistic cultures	Emphasize extrinsic rewards (e.g., pay, promotion) tied to personal achievement. Emphasize individually based incentives. Stress personal responsibility for accomplishment. View employees as performers. Provide employees with autonomy and opportunities for advancement.
Collectivistic cultures	Emphasize intrinsic rewards (e.g., meaningful work) tied to commitment and loyalty. Emphasize group-based incentives. Stress group norms and moral persuasion. View employees as family members. Build teams and networks focused on task performance.
Mastery cultures	Create a competitive environment within the organization to stimulate best efforts. Emphasize performance-based incentives using monetary rewards. Showcase high performers. Encourage thinking big; conquering the environment. Provide assertiveness training programs.
Harmony cultures	Emphasize harmony and team effort for collective results. Emphasize seniority or membership-based incentives. Showcase team efforts and organization-wide accomplishments. Encourage respect for traditions and the environment. Encourage continued membership for entire work force.
Monochronic cultures	Provide simple and straightforward directions, one task at a time. Provide strict time limits for each project; require intermittent written progress reports. Focus on the job; keep personal relations to a minimum.
Polychronic cultures	Identify task requirements, but let employees choose how best to accomplish them. Provide flexible time limits for various tasks; check progress through personal discussions. Focus on personal relations as a means of succeeding on the job.
Universalistic cultures	State rules, regulations, and policies clearly and publicly. Enforce rules and regulations uniformly. Ties rewards to rule compliance. Where possible, provide employees with security and certainty. Where possible, make decisions based on objective criteria.
Particularistic cultures	Create opportunities for employees to develop social relationships at work. Invest time meeting with employees individually and in groups; build relationships and informal networks. Use influential people to help motivate. Account for extenuating circumstances in rule enforcement. Where possible, show patience with first-time rule-breakers. Keep your word; build trust with employees.

reasonable body of evidence from which to draw some initial conclusions.

Perhaps most importantly, research findings demonstrating the influence of cultural differences on work values, motivation, and job attitudes are now irrefutable. No longer can researchers ignore or trivialize the significance of culture in future studies on work behavior. This conclusion necessitates a reexamination of many of our current theories of both work attitudes and behavior, as well as management theories in general, to incorporate cultural factors as a more central conceptual variable.

An attempt has been made here to consider the role of culture as it specifically relates to work motivation and performance. However, more research and conceptualization along these lines would be of considerable benefit to the field in general. In view of the increasing globalization of markets, services, and manufacturing, ignoring cultural factors in corporate decision-making and action can have significant adverse economic repercussions for companies and countries alike. It is therefore hoped that this review will stimulate future endeavors by both researchers and managers to better understand the global realities of the workplace.

Research team composition

Despite this recent progress, however, the field can still do better. Several specific concerns relating to research on work motivation should be noted. Many of these criticisms of the organizational research literature in general also apply to the more specific research on work motivation and job performance. For example, while progress has been made in creating multinational research teams as one means of reducing national and cultural biases, the same cannot be said for creating multidisciplinary teams. In our view, much could be gained from incorporating the views of management scholars along with various social scientists, including psychologists, sociologists, economists, and anthropologists in serious studies of the motivational basis of employee behavior and performance. Seldom is such cooperation seen.

Conceptual rigor

The topic of work motivation across national boundaries requires a significant increase in rigorous, comprehensive, and theory-based studies that further our systematic understanding – and predictability – of behavioral phenomena in organizations around the world. Most of the studies in this domain focus on testing one small piece of one theory, ignoring a larger set of variables and relationships that in reality can frequently influence both attitudes and behavior. Seldom do we see the logic or preparation that can be found in

Lincoln and Kalleberg's (1990) study of Japanese and American employees or Earley's (1989; 1997) study of social loafing in China and the US These studies are theory-driven, technically accurate, and logical in their choice of samples.

In addition, comparative studies of the relative predictive powers of competing motivational models in and across cultures are seldom found in the literature, making progress in the important area highly problematic. In this regard, the study by Welsh, Luthans and Sommer (1993) comparing three western incentive systems among Russian workers may represent a model for others to emulate. Moreover, more intense efforts to model the various ways in which culture can influence individual behavior performance (like that recently published by Bhagat et al., 2007) are sorely needed. Finally, in addition to cross-national studies, more in-depth single-country studies focusing specifically on how culture actually influences attitudes and behavior would be helpful.

Sampling

In addition, the general failure to select samples that represent strategically different cultures for purposes of theory building has plagued cross-cultural research from its inception. All too frequently, we see samples of convenience that appear to be selected prior to any consideration of study variables or even theory. Indeed, some have referred to this problem as "vacation empiricism," and it hardly constitutes sound research. Instead, it represents a significant hurdle to further progress in the field. A good example of theory-driven strategic sampling combined with the use of a rigorous research instrument can be seen in the comparative work values study by Elizur et al. (1991). In short, what is needed is more theory-based sampling, not sampling-based theory.

It is also possible that some of the data we currently have on cultures are highly selective. Most of the field research reported here was conducted in work organizations, which routinely try to recruit and retain the best people available. As such, the people under study are generally likely to be more literate and better educated than the norm for a given society, and may not be representative of society as a whole. Conclusions based on such samples must be interpreted with caution.

Research instruments

Finally, more attention needs to be focused on the nature and quality of the research instruments under study. With the notable exception of Bond's (1987) Confucian dynamism scale, most variables under study in this field derive from western thought and consciousness. For example, why do we study job attitudes instead of face? Why do we study individual competitiveness instead of group harmony? Indeed, many research instruments employ western concepts that do not even have direct conceptual equivalents in some other cultures (e.g., job satisfaction). Other western concepts frequently used in questionnaires do not convey identical meanings across cultures (e.g., reward equity).

Translation problems in research instruments are also rampant, even when there is conceptual equivalency. Perhaps greater use of ethnographic methods would allow local employees to help identify those variables that are central areas of concern for purposes of study.

In summary, considerable progress has been made on this topic, and the role of cultural differences in work behavior is now better understood. However, despite this progress, we are left with the conclusion that serious efforts are still required to build on these current findings in an effort to extrapolate more of the essence of culture as a predictive variable in work motivation theory and research. We seem to remain largely mired in the realm of knowing *what* and, to some extent, knowing *how*. What would be particularly useful at this point would be expanding our understanding of *why*.

References

Abegglen, J. C., and Stalk, G. 1985. *Kaisha: The Japanese Corporation*. New York, NY: Basic Books.

Adams, S. 1965. "Inequity in social exchange", in L. Berkowitz (ed.), *Advances in Experimental Social Psychology*, vol. 2. New York, NY: Academic Press.

Adler, N. J. 1986. *International Dimensions of Organizational Behavior*. Boston: PWS-Kent, pp. 127–33.

Alderfer, C. P. 1972. *Existence, Relatedness, and Growth*. New York: Free Press.

Allport, G. W. 1937. *Personality: A Psychological Interpretation*. New York: Henry Holt.

Allport, G. W. 1939. "Attitudes". in C. Murchison (ed.), *Handbook of Social Psychology*. Worcester, MA: Clark University Press.

Badawy, M. K. 1979. "Managerial attitudes and need orientations of Middle Eastern executives: an empirical cross-cultural analysis", *Academy of Management Proceedings*, 39: 293–97.

Baligh, H. H. 1994. "Components of culture: Nature, interconnections, and relevance to the decisions on the organization structure", *Management Science*, 40: 14–27.

Bandura, A. 1986. *Social Foundation of Thought and Action: A Social Cognitive Theory*. Englewood Cliffs, N. J.: Prentice Hall.

Bandura, A. 1996. *Self-efficacy: The Exercise of Control*. New York, NY: Freeman.

Berman, J. J., Murphy-Berman, V., and Singh, P. 1985. "Cross-cultural similarities and differences in perceptions of fairness", *Journal of Cross-Cultural Psychology* 16(1): 55–67.

Bhagat, R. S. and McQuaid, S. J. 1982. "Role of subjective culture in organizations: a review and directions for future research", *Journal of Applied Psychology* 67(5): 653–85.

Van Scotter, J., Steverson, P., and Moustafa, K. 2007. "Cultural variations in individual job performance: implications for industrial and organizational psychology in the 21st century", *International Review of Industrial and Organizational Psychology*, 22: 235–64.

Blunt, P. 1976. "Management motivation in Kenya: Some initial impressions", *Eastern African Research and Development*, 6(1): 11–21.

and Jones, M. L. 1992. *Managing African Organizations*. Berlin: Walter de Gruyter.

Bond, M. H. 1987. "Chinese culture connection, Chinese values and the search for culture-free dimensions of culture", *Journal of Cross-Cultural Psychology* 18: 143–67.

Leung, K., and Wan, C. K. 1982. "How does cultural collectivism operate? The impact of task and maintenance contributions on reward distributions", *Journal of Cross-Cultural Psychology* 13(2): 186–200.

Boyle, M. 2001. "Nothing is rotten in Denmark", *Fortune*, February 19, pp. 242–243.

Brady, D. 2002. "Rethinking the rat race", *Business Week*, August 26, p. 143.

Brayfield, A. H. and Crockett, W. H. 1955. "Employee attitudes and employee performance", *Psychological Bulletin* 52: 396–424.

Brislin, R. 1993. *Understanding Culture's Influence on Behavior*. Fort Worth, TX: Harcourt Brace.

Buera, A. and Gluek, W. 1979. "Need satisfaction of Libyan managers", *Management International Review* 19(1): 113–23.

Chao, G. T. and Moon, H. 2005. "The cultural mosaic: A meta-theory for understanding the complexity of culture", *Journal of Applied Psychology* 90(6): 1128–40.

Chen, C. C. 1995. "New trends in reward allocation preferences: A Sino-U.S. Comparison", *Academy of Management Journal*, 38(2): 408–28.

Meindl, J. R., and Hunt, R. G. 1997. "Testing the effects of vertical and horizontal collectivism: a study of reward allocation preferences in China", *Journal of Cross-Cultural Psychology* 28(1): 44–70.

Chiang, F. 2005. "A critical examination of Hofstede's thesis and its application to international reward management", *International Journal of Human Resource Management* 16(9): 1545–63.

Child, J. 1994. *Management in China During the Age of Reform*. Cambridge: Cambridge University Press.

Chung, K. H., Lee, H. C., and Jung, K. H. 1997. *Korean Management: Global Strategy and Cultural Transformation*. Berlin: Walter de Gruyter.

Crozier, M. 1964. *The Bureaucratic Phenomenon*. Chicago: University of Chicago Press.

Davis, H. J. and Rasool, S. A. 1988. "A reconsideration of England's values research in cross-cultural management", in R. Farmer and E. McGoun (eds.), *Advances in International Comparative Management*. Greenwich, CT: JAI Press, pp. 109–25.

DeVos, G. A. 1968. "Achievement and innovation in culture and personality", in E. Norbeck, D. Price-Williams, and W. M. McCords (eds.), *The Study of Personality: An Interdisciplinary Approach*. New York, NY: Holt, Rinehart, & Winston.

and Mizushima, K. 1973. "Delinquency and social change in modern Japan," in G. A. DeVos (ed.), *Socialization for Achievement: Essays on the Cultural Psychology of the Japanese*. Berkeley, CA: University of California Press.

Earley, P. C. 1986. "Supervisors and shop stewards as sources of contextual information in goal-setting", *Journal of Applied Psychology* 71: 111–18.

1989. "Social loafing and collectivism", *Administrative Science Quarterly* 34: 565–81.

1993. "East meets west meets mideast: further explorations of collectivistic and individualistic work groups," *Academy of Management Journal*, 36(2): 319–48.

1997. *Face, Harmony, and Social Structure: An Analysis of Organizational Behavior Across Cultures*. New York: Oxford University Press.

2001. "Understanding social motivation from an interpersonal perspective: organizational face theory", in Erez, M., Kleinbeck, U., and Thierry, H. (eds.), *Work Motivation in the Context of a Globalizing Economy*. Mahwah, NJ: Lawrence Erlbaum Associates, pp. 369–79.

Economist The. 2000. September 30, p. 110.

Eden, D. 1975. "Intrinsic and extrinsic rewards and motives: replication and extension with kibbutz workers", *Journal of Applied Social Psychology* 5: 348–361.

2001. "Means efficacy: external sources of general and specific subjective efficacy", in Erez, M., Kleinbeck, U., and Thierry, H. (eds.), *Work Motivation in the Context of a Globalizing Economy*. Mahwah, NJ: Lawrence Erlbaum Associates, pp. 73–85.

Elenkov, D. S. 1998. "Can American management concepts work in Russia? A cross-cultural comparative study", *California Management Review* 40(4): 133–57.

Elizur, D., Borg, I., Hunt, R., and Beck, I. M. 1991. "The structure of work values: a cross-cultural comparison", *Journal of Organizational Behavior* 12: 21–38.

England, G. W. 1975. *The Manager and His Values: An International Perspective from the United States, Japan, Korea, India, and Australia*. Cambridge, MA: Ballanger.

1986. "National work meanings and patterns: Constraints on Management Action", *European Management Journal* 4(3): 176–84.

and Koike, R. 1970. "Personal values systems of Japanese managers", *Journal of Cross-Cultural Psychology* 1: 21–40.

and Quintanilla, A. R. 1989. "Major work meaning patterns in the national labor forces on Germany, Japan, and the United States", in S. B. Prasad (ed.), *Advances in International Comparative Management*. Greenwich, CT: JAI Press, pp. 77–94.

Erez, M. 1986. "The congruence of goal-setting strategies with socio-cultural values, and its effect on performance", *Journal of Management* 12: 585–92.

and Earley, P. C. 1987. "Comparative Analysis of Goal-Setting Strategies Across Cultures", *Journal of Applied Psychology* 72(4): 658–65.

and Earley, P. C. 1993. *Culture, Self-Identity, and Work*. New York: Oxford University Press.

Kleinbeck, U., and Thierry, H. (eds.). 2001. *Work Motivation in the Context of a Globalizing Economy*. Mahwah, NJ: Lawrence Erlbaum Associates.

Fey, C. F. 2005. "Opening the black box of motivation: A cross-cultural comparison of Sweden and Russia", *International Business Journal* 14(3): 345–367.

Firestone, J. M. and Garza, R. T. 2005. "Protestant work ethic and worker productivity in a Mexican brewery", *International Sociology* 20(1): 27–44.

Frazee, V. 1997. "Vacation politics around the world", *Personnel Journal*, 75:9.

French, J., P., Israel, J., and As, D. 1960. "An experiment in a Norwegian factory: interpersonal dimension in decision-making", *Human Relations* 13: 3–19.

Gabrenya, W. K., Latane, B., and Wang, Y. 1983. "Social loafing in cross-cultural perspective", *Journal of Cross-Cultural Psychology* 14: 368–84.

Latane, B., and Wang, Y. 1985. "Social loafing on an optimizing task: Cross-cultural differences among Chinese and Americans", *Journal of Cross-Cultural Psychology* 16: 223–42.

Gannon, M. J. and Newman, K. L. (eds.) 2001. *Handbook of Cross-Cultural Management*. London: Basil Blackwell, pp 190–216.

George, J. M. 1992. "Extrinsic and intrinsic origins of perceived social loafing in organizations", *Academy of Management Journal* 35: 191–202.

Guth, W. D. and Tagiuri, R. 1965. "Personal values and corporate strategy", *Harvard Business Review* 123–32.

Haire, M., Ghiselli, E. E., and Porter, L. L. 1961. *Managerial Thinking: An International Study*. New York, NY: Wiley.

Hall, E. T. 1992. *An Anthropology of Everyday Life: An Autobiography*. New York: Anchor.

Hayashi, K., Harnett, D. L., and Cummings, L. L. 1973. "Personality and behavior in negotiations: an American-Japanese empirical comparison", working paper. Fujinomiya, Japan: Institute for International Studies and Training.

Heckhausen, H. 1971. "Trainingskurse zur Erhoehung der Leistungsmotivation und der unternehmerischen Aktivitaet in einem Entwicklungsland: Eine nachtraegliche Analyse des erzielten Motivwandels", *Zeitschrift fuer Entwicklungspsychologie und Paedagogishe Psychologie* 3: 253–68.

Heller, F. A. and Wilpert, B. 1981. *Competence and Power in Managerial Decision Making*. Chichester: Wiley.

Hofstede, G. 1980a, 2001. *Culture's Consequence: International Differences in Work-Related Values*. Beverly Hills, CA: Sage Publications.

1980b. "Motivation, leadership, and organization: Do American theories apply abroad?", *Organizational Dynamics* 9(1), 42–63.

Hooker, J. 2003. *Working Across Cultures*. Stanford, CA: Stanford University Press.

Hopkins, M. E., Lo, L., Peterson, R. E., and Seo, K. K. 1977. "Japanese and American managers", *Journal of Applied Psychology* 96: 71.

House, R. J., Hanges, P. J., Javidan, M., Dorfman, P. W., and Gupta, V. 2004. *Culture, Leadership and Organizations: The GLOBE Study of 62 Societies*. Thousand Oaks, CA: Sage Publications.

Huang, X. and Van de Vliert, E. 2004. "Job level and national culture as joint roots of job satisfaction", *Applied Psychology: An International Review* 53(3): 329–48.

Huo, Y. P. and Steers, R. M. 1993. "Cultural influences on the design of incentive systems: the case of East Asia", *Asia Pacific Journal of Management* 10(1): 71–85.

Ilgen, D. R. and Sheppard, L. 2001. "Motivation in work teams," In Erez, M., Kleinbeck, U., and Thierry, H. (Eds.), *Work Motivation in the Context of a Globalizing Economy*. Mahwah, N.J.: Lawrence Erlbaum Associates, 169–180.

Iwawaki, S. and Lynn, R. 1972. "Measuring achievement motivation in Japan and Great Britain", *Journal of Cross-Cultural Psychology* 3: 219–20.

Jaggi, B. 1979. "Need importance of Indian managers", *Management International Review* 19(1): 107–113.

Javidan, M., Steers, R. M., and Hitt, H. 2008. *Advances in International Management: The Global Mindset*. Amsterdam: Elsevier.

Jensen, M. C. and Meckling, W. H. 1976. "Theory of the firm: Managerial behavior, agency costs, and ownership structure", *Journal of Financial Economics* 3: 305–60.

Jones, M. L. 1988. "Managerial thinking: an African perspective", *Journal of Management Studies* 25(5): 481–505.

Kanfer, R. and Ackerman, P. L. 1996. "A self-regulatory skills perspective to reducing cognitive interference", in I. G. Sarason and B. R. Sarason (eds.), *Cognitive Interference Theories: Methods and Findings*. New York, NY: Erlbaum.

Kanungo, R. N. and Wright, R. W. 1983. "A cross-cultural comparative study of managerial job attitudes", *Journal of International Business Studies* Fall: 115–28.

Kelley, H. H. 1973. "The process of causal attributions", *American Psychologist* 28: 107–29.

Kim, K. I., Park, H. J., and Suzuki, N. 1990. "Reward allocations in the U.S., Japan, and Korea: a comparison of individualistic and collectivistic cultures", *Academy of Management Journal* 33(1): 188–98.

Kleinbeck, U., Wegge, J., Schmidt, K. H. 2001. "Work motivation and performance in groups", in M. Erez, U. Kleinbeck and H. Thierry (eds.), *Work Motivation in the Context of a Globalizing Economy*. Mahwah, NJ: Lawrence Erlbaum Associates, pp. 181–210.

Kraut, A. I. and Ronen, S. 1975. "Validity of job facet importance: a multinational, multicriteria study", *Journal of Applied Psychology* 60: 671–77.

Krus, D. J. and Rysberg, J. A. 1976. "Industrial managers and n Ach: comparable and compatible?", *Journal of Cross-Cultural Psychology* 7: 491–496.

Latane, B., Williams, K. D., and Harkins, S. G. 1979. "Many hands make light the work: The causes and consequences of social loafing", *Journal of Personality and Social Psychology* 37: 822–832.

Latham, G. P. and Pinder, C. P. 2005. "Work motivation theory and research at the dawn of the twenty-first century", *Annual Review of Psychology* 56: 485–516.

Lawler, E. E. 1992. *The Ultimate Advantage: Creating the High Involvement Organization*. San Francisco, CA: Jossey-Bass.

Leung, K. 2001. "Different carrots for different rabbits: effects of individualism-collectivism and power distance on work motivation," in M. Erez, U. Kleinbeck and H. Thierry (eds.), *Work Motivation in the Context of a Globalizing Economy*. Mahwah, NJ: Lawrence Erlbaum Associates, pp. 329–39.

Bhagat, R., Buchan, N., Erez, M., and Gibson, C. 2005. "Culture and international business: recent advances and their implications for future research", *Journal of International Business Studies* 36: 357–78.

and Bond, M. H. 1984. "The impact of cultural collectivism on reward allocation", *Journal of Personality and Social Psychology* 47(4): 793–804.

Lewin, K. 1935. *A Dynamic Theory of Personality*. New York: McGraw-Hill.

Lincoln, J. R., and Kalleberg, A. L. 1990. *Culture, Control, and Commitment: A Study of Work Organization and Work Attitudes in the United States and Japan*. Cambridge: Cambridge University Press.

Locke, E. A. 1976. "The nature and causes of job satisfaction", in M. D. Dunnette (ed.), *Handbook of Industrial and Organizational Psychology*. Chicago, IL: Rand McNally.

2001. "Self-set goals and self-efficacy as mediators of incentives and personality", in M. Erez, U. Kleinbeck and H. Thierry (eds.), *Work Motivation in the Context of a Globalizing Economy*. Mahwah, NJ: Lawrence Erlbaum Associates, pp. 13–25.

and Latham, G. P. 1990. *A Theory of Goal-Setting and Task Performance*. Englewood Cliffs, NJ: Prentice Hall.

and Schweiger, D. M. 1979. "Participation in decision-making: one more look", in B. M. Staw (ed.), *Research in Organizational Behavior*, vol. 1. Greenwich, CT: JAI Press.

Lodahl, T. and Kejner, M. 1965. "The definition and measurement of job involvement", *Journal of Applied Psychology* 49: 24–33.

Luthans, F. and Kreitner, R. 1985. *Organizational Behavior Modification*. Glenview, IL: Scott, Foresman.

Maehr, M. L. 1977. "Socio-cultural origins of achievement motivation", *International Journal of Intercultural Relations* 1: 81–104.

and Nichols, J. G. 1980. "Culture and achievement motivation: a second look", in N. Warren (ed.), *Studies in Cross-Cultural Psychology*, vol 3. New York, NY: Academic Press, pp. 221–67.

March, J. G. and Simon, H. A. 1958. *Organizations*. New York, NY: John Wiley.

Maslow, A. H. 1954. *Motivation and Personality*. New York, NY: Harper.

Matsui, T., Kakuyama, T., and Onglatco, M. L. 1987. "Effects of goals and feedback on performance in groups", *Journal of Applied Psychology* 72: 407–15.

and Terai, I. 1979. "A cross-cultural study of the validity of expectancy theory of work motivation", *Journal of Applied Psychology* 60(2): 263–5.

McCarthy, D. J., Puffer, S. M., and Shekshnia, S. V. 1993. "The resurgence of an entrepreneurial class in Russia", *Journal of Management Inquiry* 2(2), 125–37.

McClelland, D. C. 1961. *The Achieving Society*. Princeton, NJ: Van Nostrand.

and Winter, D. G. 1969. *Motivating Economic Achievement*. New York, NY: Free Press.

Miller, D. J., Giacobbe-Miller, J. K., and Zhang, W. 1998. "A comparative study of Chinese and U.S. distributive justice values, goals, and allocative behaviors", in J. L. Cheng and R. B. Peterson (eds.), *Advances in International Comparative Management*. Greenwich, CT: JAI Press, pp. 185–206.

Milliman, J., Nason, S., Gallagher, E., Hou, P., von Glinor, M. A., and Lowe, K. B. 1998. "The impact of national culture on human resource management practices: the case of performance appraisal", in J. L. Cheng and R. B. Peterson (eds.), *Advances in International Comparative Management*. Greenwich, CT: JAI Press, pp. 157–83.

Nason, S., von Glinow, M. A., Hou, P., Lowe, K. B., and Kim, N. 1995. "In search of 'best' strategic pay practices: an exploratory study of Japan, Korea, Taiwan, and the United States", in S. B. Prasad (ed.), *Advances in International Comparative Management*. Greenwich, CT: JAI Press, pp. 227–52.

Mitchell, T. R. 1997. "Matching motivational strategies with organizational contexts", in L. Cummings and B. Staw (eds.). *Research in Organizational Behavior, Volume 19*. Greenwich, CT: JAI Press, pp. 57–149.

and Daniels, D. 2003. "Motivation", in W.C. Borman, D. R. Ilgen, and R. J. Klimoski (eds.), *Comprehensive Handbook of Psychology*, 5th edn, vol. 12, *Industrial and Organizational Psychology*. New York, NY: Wiley.

Morita, A. 1986. *Made in Japan: Akio Morita and Sony*. New York, NY: Dutton.

MOW International Research Team. 1987. *The Meaning of Working*. London: Academic Press.

Mowday, R. T. 1996. "Equity theory predictions of behavior in organizations", in R. M. Steers, L. W. Porter, and G. A. Bigley (eds.), *Motivation and Leadership at Work*. New York: McGraw-Hill, pp. 53–83.

Porter, L. W., and Steers, R. M. 1982. *Employee-Organization Linkages: The Psychology of Employee Commitment, Absenteeism, and Turnover*. New York, NY: Academic Press.

Murray, H. A. 1938. *Explorations in Personality*. New York, NY: Oxford University Press.

Nam S. H. 1995. "Culture, control, and commitment in international joint ventures", *International Journal of Human Resource Management*, 6: 553–67.

Nicholson, N. 2001. "An evolutionary perspective on change and stability in personality, culture, and organization, In In Erez, M., Kleinbeck, U., and Thierry, H. (Eds.), *Work Motivation in the Context of a Globalizing Economy*. Mahwah, N.J.: Lawrence Erlbaum Associates, pp. 381–394.

Olson, M. 1971. *The Logic of Collective Action*. Cambridge, MA: Harvard University Press.

Pennings, J. M. 1993. "Executive reward systems: A cross-national comparison", *Journal of Management Studies* 30(2): 261–80.

Peterson, M. F., and Ruiz-Quintanilla, S. A. 2003. "Cultural socialization as a source of intrinsic work motivation", *Group and Organization Management* 28(2), pp. 188–216.

Phatak, A., Bhagat, R., and Kashlak, R. 2004. *International Management*. New York, NY: McGraw-Hill/Irwin, p. 125.

Porter, L. W. and Lawler, E. E. 1968. *Managerial Attitudes and Performance*. Homewood, IL: Irwin.

Bigley, G., and Steers, R. M. 2003. *Motivation and Work Behavior*. New York, NY: McGraw-Hill.

Ralston, D. A., Gustafson, D. J., Cheung, F. M., and Terpstra, R. H. 1993. "Differences in managerial values: A study of U.S., Hong Kong, and PRC managers," *Journal of International Business Studies*: 249–275.

Reitz, H. J. 1975. "The relative importance of five categories of needs among industrial workers in eight countries", *Academy of Management Proceedings* 270–73.

and Jewell, L. N. 1979. "Sex, locus of control, and job involvement: a six-country investigation", *Academy of Management Journal* 22: 72–80.

Ronen, S. and Shenkar, O. 1985. "Clustering countries on attitudinal dimensions: a review and synthesis", *Academy of Management Review* 3: 435–54.

Runyon, K. E. 1973. "Some interactions between personality variables and management styles", *Journal of Applied Psychology* 57: 288–94.

Sagie, A., Elizur, D., and Yamauchi, H. 1996. "The structure and strength of achievement motivation: A cross-cultural comparison", *Journal of Organizational Behavior* 17: 431–44.

Salili, F. 1979. "Determinants of achievement motivation for women in developing countries", *Journal of Vocational Behavior*, 14(3): 297–305.

Sanger, D. E. 1993. "Performance related pay in Japan", *International Herald Tribune*, October 5, p. 20.

Saywell, T. 1999. "Motive power: China's state firms bank on incentives to keep bosses operating at their peak", *Far Eastern Economic Review*, July 8, pp. 67–68.

Schneider, S. C. and Barsoux, J. L. 2003. *Managing Across Cultures*. London: FT/Prentice-Hall.

Wittenberg-Cox, A., and Hansen, L. 1991. *Honeywell Europe*. Fontainebleau: INSEAD.

Shin, Y. K., and Kim, H. G. 1994. "Individualism and collectivism in Korean industry", in G. Yoon and S. C. Choi (eds.), *Psychology of the Korean People: Collectivism and Individualism*. Seoul: Dang-A, pp. 189–208.

Sirota, D. and Greenwood, M. J. 1971. "Understanding your overseas workforce", *Harvard Business Review* 14(1): 53–60.

Slocum, J. W. 1971. "A comparative study of the satisfaction of American and Mexican operatives", *Academy of Management Journal* 14: 89–97.

Stajkovic, A. D. and Luthans, F. 2003. "Social cognitive theory and self-efficacy: implications for motivation theory and practice", in

L. W. Porter, G. Bigley and R. M. Steers, *Motivation and Work Behavior*. New York, NY: McGraw-Hill, pp. 126–40.

Steers, R. M. 1999. *Made in Korea: Chung Ju Yung and the Rise of Hyundai*. New York, NY: Routledge.

Mowday, R. T., and Shapiro, D. 2004. "The future of work motivation theory", *Academy of Management Review* 29(3), 379–87.

and Nardon, L. 2006. *Managing in the Global Economy*. Armonk, NY: M. E. Sharpe.

and Sanchez-Runde, C. 2001. "Culture, motivation, and work behavior", in M. J. Gannon and K. L. Newman (eds.), *Handbook of Cross-Cultural Management*. Oxford: Blackwell, pp. 190–216.

Stephens, D., Kedia, B., and Ezell, D. 1979. "Managerial need structures in U.S. and Peruvian industries", *Management International Review* 19: 27–39.

Thomas, D. 2002. *International Management: A Cross-Cultural Perspective*. Thousand Oaks, CA: Sage, pp. 210–212.

Triandis, H. C. 1971. *Attitude and Attitude Change*. New York, NY: Wiley.

1995. "Motivation and achievement in collectivist and individualist cultures", in M. L. Maehr and P. R. Pintrich (eds.), *Advances in Motivation and Achievement: Culture, Motivation, and Achievement*, vol. 9. Greenwich, CT: JAI Press, pp. 1–30.

Trice, H. M. and Beyer, J. M. 1993. *The Cultures of Work Organizations*. Englewood Cliffs, NJ: Prentice-Hall.

Trompenaars, F. and Hampden-Turner, C. 1998. *Riding the Waves of Culture: Understanding Diversity in Global Business*. New York, NY: McGraw Hill.

Tsui, A. and Ashford, S. 1994. "Adaptive self-regulation: a process view of managerial effectiveness", *Journal of Management* 20: 93–121.

Tung, R. L. 1991. "Motivation in Chinese industrial enterprises", in R. M. Steers and L. W. Porter (eds.), *Motivation and Work Behavior*. New York: McGraw-Hill, pp. 342–51.

Ungson, G. R., Steers, R. M., and Park, S. H. 1997. *Korean Enterprise: The Quest for Globalization*. Cambridge, MA: Harvard Business School Press.

Van Eerde, W., and Thierry, H. 2001. "VIE functions, self-set goals and performance: an experiment", in M. Erez, U. Kleinbeck and H. Thierry (eds.), *Work Motivation in the Context of a Globalizing Economy*. Mahwah, NJ: Lawrence Erlbaum Associates, pp. 131–47.

Vance, C. M., McClaine, S. R., Boje, D. M., and Stage, H. D. 1992. "An examination of the transferability of traditional performance appraisal principles across cultural boundaries", *Management International Review*, 32(4): 313–26.

Viscusi, G. 2002. "U.S. Production Still Tops Europe's", *Register Guard*, August 27, p. B–1.

Vogel, E. F. 1963. *Japan's New Middle Class*. Berkeley, CA: University of California Press.

Vroom, V. 1964. *Work and Motivation*. New York: Wiley.

Wegge, J., Kleinbeck, U., and Schmidt, K. H. 2001. "Goal Setting and Performance in Working Memory and Short-term Memory Tasks", in M. Erez, U. Kleinbeck and H. Thierry (eds.), *Work Motivation in the Context of a Globalizing Economy*. Mahwah, NJ: Lawrence Erlbaum Associates, pp. 49–72.

Weiner, B. 1980. *Human Motivation*. New York: Holt, Rinehart & Winston.

Welsh, D. H. B., Luthans, F., and Sommer, S. M. 1993. "Managing Russian factory workers: the impact of U.S.-based behavioral and participative techniques", *Academy of Management Journal* 36(1): 58–79.

Wood, R. E., George-Falvy, J., and Debrowski, S. 2001. "Motivation and information search on complex tasks", in M. Erez, U. Kleinbeck, and H. Thierry (eds.), *Work Motivation in the Context of a Globalizing Economy*. Mahwah, NJ: Lawrence Erlbaum Associates, pp. 27–48.

Yamagishi, T. and Yamagishi, M. 1994. "Trust and commitment in the United States and Japan", *Motivation and Emotion* 18(2): 129–66.

Yu, A. B. and Yang, K. S. 1994. "The nature of achievement motivation in collectivist societies", in U. Kim, H. C. Triandis, C. Kagitcibasi, S. C. Choi, and G. Yoon (eds.), *Individualism and Collectivism: Theory, Method, and Application*. Thousand Oaks, CA: Sage, pp. 85–119.

Yuchtman, E. 1972. "Reward distribution and work-role attractiveness in the Kibbutz: Reflections on equity theory", *American Sociological Review* 37: 581–95.

Interdisciplinary perspectives on culture, conflict, and negotiation[1]

LYNN IMAI and MICHELE J. GELFAND

There is no doubt that many of the greatest scientific breakthroughs have been made possible through interdisciplinary research. From the mapping of the genome to understanding the global map of terrorism, it is clear that science benefits from multiple perspectives that require expertise from different disciplines. As noted in the recent report by the Committee on Facilitating Interdisciplinary Research (2004) of the National Academy of Sciences: "Interdisciplinary research (IDR) can be one of the most productive and inspiring of human pursuits – one that provides a format for conversations and connections that lead to new knowledge", (p. 16). Also aptly put by Karl Popper (1963), arguably one of the most influential philosophers of science in the twentieth century: "We are not students of some subject matter, but students of problems. And problems may cut right across the borders of any subject matter or discipline" (p. 88). Many of the problems that are studied in organizational behavior are of no exception, whether it is understanding the complex question of human motivation, group dynamics, or globalization. The value – if not the necessity – of interdisciplinary perspectives is indisputable. Organizational behavior, with its penchant for multiple perspectives, be it from sociology, psychology, economics, or related disciplines, is well positioned to continue to push its interdisciplinary envelope. Yet much is to be done to fully capitalize upon the differences that invariably bring the most creative research products. As noted in a recent editorial in *Science*: "In the years to come, innovators will need to jettison the security of familiar tools, ideas and specialties as they forge new partnerships" (Kafatos and Eisner, 2004, p. 1257).

It is with this interdisciplinary mandate that we ground our chapter on culture, conflict, and negotiation. Observations of cultural differences in negotiation go as far back as early as 400 BC, when the Greek historian Herodotus observed the "strangeness" of how ancient Egyptians traded with the Greeks (Herodotus, Marincola, and de Selincourt, 2003). Within the context of organizational behavior/psychology, which includes research from both management and psychology departments, the study of culture, conflict, and negotiation has grown considerably over the last three decades, examining cultural influences on negotiator cognition, behavioral processes, and negotiated outcomes across a wide range of cultures and settings (see Gelfand, Erez, and Aycan, 2007). Few areas have expanded in terms of their depth and breadth as quickly as negotiation, and by extension as negotiation and culture (Kramer and Messick, 1995).

Yet, looking beyond our disciplinary borders, it is clear that there are many disciplines examining cultural influences on conflict and negotiations, broadly defined as situations in which individuals and groups are managing their interdependence and have a perceived conflict of interest (Walton and McKersie, 1965). In this chapter, we turn to a wide array of disciplines, both closely related as well as distant, including legal anthropology, comparative law, communication science, experimental economics, cognitive anthropology, language and disputing, international relations, and primatology, in order to push the interdisciplinary envelope on culture and negotiation in organizational behavior. In each discipline discussed, we identify the predominant paradigmatic approach to the study of culture, conflict, and negotiation including the *major research questions asked*, the *unit of analysis* used, the way in which *culture is conceptualized*, the dominant *methodology* used, as well as the *cross-cultural* (i.e., comparative) versus *intercultural* (i.e., involving different cultures) nature of research. We then review

[1] This research is based upon work supported by the US Army Research Laboratory and the US Army Research Office under grant number W911NF-08-1-0144.

key representative work from each discipline. Our goal is not to provide an exhaustive review of the literature, but to provide several examples of proto-typical work conducted in each discipline. Finally, we discuss the implications of each discipline for the study of culture, conflict, and negotiation in organizational behavior/psychology by comparing and contrasting the discipline with our field, and identifying interesting questions for future research in culture, conflict, and negotiation. Table 13.1 summarizes our discussion below. Above all, we hope that, by looking *outward* to representative works on culture, conflict, and negotiation from a variety of disciplines, we will begin to understand better our *own* implicit assumptions in organizational behavior/psychology and, most importantly, will invite new perspectives and interdisciplinary collaborations. We begin with a review of cross-cultural conflict and negotiation research in organizational behavior/psychology as a starting point from which to compare paradigms in other disciplines. We then discuss culture, conflict, and negotiation research in legal anthropology, comparative law, language and disputing, cognitive anthropology, experimental economics, primatology, communication science, and international relations.

Organizational behavior/psychology

Cross-cultural research on conflict and negoti-ation within the field of organizational behavior/psychology generally takes a social-psychological approach to the study of culture, conflict, and negotiation, addressing the general question of *how do negotiators vary across nations in their perceptions, behaviors, and negotiation outcomes*, and a related question of *what are the challenges and opportunities faced in intercultural negoti-ations comprised of negotiators from different nations?* The *unit of analysis* tends to be the individual negotiator or the negotiation dyad. *Culture* is typically conceptualized using the framework of national differences in values (Hofstede, 1980; Schwartz, 1994; Triandis, 1995). The most common methodology used is experiments and surveys and there is a priority on examining psychological states (e.g., cognitions) of negotiators as well as economic value achieved. Research in this field

historically has focused on *intracultural compari-sons*, yet is increasingly examining *intercultural comparisons* as well.

Later, we also review in this section the closely related discipline of international business (IB), which unlike organizational behavior/psychology, tends to focus on actual business negotiations in the field. Research in IB examines questions pertain-ing to *intercultural* negotiations such as *what actual negotiators perceive to be critical for success and failure*, and *how third cultures develop during the negotiation process*, using methodologies such as surveys and interviews. Other studies in IB focus more at the *macro level of analysis*, examining nego-tiations that occur in international contexts such as *inter-firm negotiations, joint ventures, international alliances, and mergers and acquisitions.*

Key findings from organizational behavior/psychology

Research in organizational behavior/psychology (OB/psychology) has examined how culture, typic-ally conceptualized and/or operationalized through cultural value dimensions, affects negotiators' implicit theories about themselves, their counter-parts, and the negotiation task. Implicit in this work is the notion that the meaning of the negotiation context is not "objectively" defined, rather, nego-tiators cognitively construct the reality of the social context in which they are negotiating (Bazerman and Carroll, 1987). Consistent with this, Gelfand *et al.* (2001) found that Japanese and US students have different cognitive interpretations of *iden-tical* conflict episodes. For instance, US students perceived conflicts to be concerned with individual rights and autonomy, whereas Japanese students perceived conflicts to be concerned with viola-tions of duties and obligations. US students also perceived conflicts to be more about competition, whereas Japanese students perceived conflicts to be more about cooperation. These findings empirically illustrated that the same conflicts may be perceived quite differently across cultures, yet make "cultural sense" from both cultural vantage points. From a practical point of view, Gelfand *et al.* (2001) con-cluded that, in intercultural situations, meta-level

Table 13.1 Interdisciplinary perspectives on culture, conflict, and negotiation

Organizational Behavior/ Psychology

Major Questions and Processes Examined	Unit of Analysis	How Culture is Conceptualized	Typical Methodology	Cross-cultural or Intercultural	Key Assumptions	Example Studies
How do negotiations vary across nations?	Individual	Cultural value dimensions (e.g., Hofstede, 1980)	Experiments	Cross-cultural and intercultural	Cultural values are important explanatory variables in negotiation	Adair et al., (2001); Adler et al., (1987); Brett & Okumura (1998); Gelfand & Christakopoulou (1999); Gelfand et al., (2001);
What are the challenges faced in intercultural negotiators?	Dyad		Surveys		Negotiators construals and motives vary across cultures	Gelfand & Realo (1999); Graham (1984); Morris et al. (2004);
Major processes investigated: Negotiator cognitions, motivations, behavioral processes (verbal), and negotiated outcomes					Economic value is the most important outcome	Tinsley (1998); Wade-Benzoni et al. (2002)

Legal Anthropology

Major Questions and Processes Examined	Unit of Analysis	How Culture is Conceptualized	Typical Methodology	Cross-cultural or Intercultural	Key Assumptions	Example Studies	Implications for OB/ Psych
How do various societies resolve disputes?	Community level; Pre-industrial societies	Social structure	Ethnographies	Cross-cultural	Culture is inextricably tied to the social context	Felstiner (1974–1975); Gluckman (1955); Koch et al. (1976); Nader (1969); Nader & Todd (1978); Ross (1986, 1993)	Study interrelationship between social structural characteristics and cultural values such as collectivism
What factors within these societies explain their preferred method(s) of dispute resolution?		Nature of social networks: Multiplex vs. simplex ties	Case studies				
Major processes investigated: Societal preference for dispute resolution method (e.g., competitive win-lose procedures, i.e. adjudication, and less distributive procedures such as mediation and negotiation)		Nature of social organization: Technologically complex/rich vs. Technologically simple/poor. Economic and political integration					

Comparative Law

Major Questions and Processes Examined	Unit of Analysis	How Culture is Conceptualized	Typical Methodology	Cross-cultural or Intercultural	Key Assumptions	Example Studies	Implications for OB/Psych
How does culture influence the design of legal systems? Do legal systems in turn influence culture? How do individuals' attitudes of what are appropriate dispute resolution methods vary across cultures? Major processes investigated: Design of legal system (e.g., role of civil jury, lawyers, judge, role of experts) Individual perceptions of appropriate ways to resolve disputes (e.g., responsibility and punishment, purpose of apologies)	Individual Societal	Social structure Hierarchy vs. solidarity Shared psychological values, beliefs, norms (e.g., group harmony)	Legal materials Analyses of court cases Surveys	Cross-cultural	Culture influences disputing processes and disputing processes influence culture	Bierbrauer (1994); Chase (1997, 2005); Hamilton & Sanders (1992); Kawashima (1963); Lauchli (2000); Wagatsuma & Rosett (1986)	Test models that incorporate multiple levels of analysis, including societal culture, legal institutions, and individual attitudes Explore non-cultural explanations for country differences (e.g., institutional differences) in conflict behavior across cultures

LANGUAGE AND DISPUTING

Major Questions and Processes Examined	Unit of Analysis	How Culture is Conceptualized	Typical Methodology	Cross-cultural or Intercultural	Key Assumptions	Example Studies	Implications for OB/Psych
What does the language used during conflict reveal about the socio-cultural knowledge of speakers, as well as the rules of inference and interaction governing speakers' behaviors? Major processes investigated: Emic (culture-specific) assumptions about how conflict should be resolved	Groups in pre-industrial and industrial societies	Social Structure (e.g., Hierarchy)	Descriptive accounts of conflict discourse Transcripts Ethnographic records Audio and video records Dramatic scripts	Non-comparative ethnographies of particular groups	Culture is carried through language	Conley & O'Barr (1990); Corsaro & Rizzo (1990); Grimshaw (1990); Watson-Gegeo & White (1990)	Incorporate linguistic analysis in studying negotiation process across cultures Explore the role of culture-specific emotions in negotiation Study the impact of public displays of conflict on reinforcing cultural values in the broader community

Table 13.1 (cont.)

Cognitive Anthropology

Major Questions and Processes Examined	Unit of Analysis	How Culture is Conceptualized	Typical Methodology	Cross-cultural or Intercultural	Key Assumptions	Example Studies	Implications for OB/Psych
How do meaning systems vary across cultures? What are the implications of such cultural differences in meaning on intercultural perceptions during conflict? Major processes investigated: Knowledge structures, Stereotyping	Group (aggregated from individuals)	Culture is represented by how knowledge is structured and organized Culture is distributional	Cognitive sorting tasks Surveys Qualitative methods	Cross-cultural (knowledge organization) Intercultural (stereotyping)	Culture is cognition (knowledge structure and knowledge organization) Variation in knowledge structures within cultures is also an important aspect of culture along with its consensus	Medin et al., (2006)	Focus on knowledge structures and their organization in influencing conflict behavior Pay attention to the degree of consensus of values, attitudes, beliefs, and knowledge structures within a single culture instead of treating it as noise

Experimental Economics

Major Questions and Processes Examined	Unit of Analysis	How Culture is Conceptualized	Typical Methodology	Cross-cultural or Intercultural	Key Assumptions	Example Studies	Implications for OB/Psych
How do economic behaviors such as cooperation, fairness, and trust vary across cultures? Major processes investigated: Cooperation, competition, offer behavior, punishment, trust/ risk preferences	Individual Societal	Culture is generally equated with country Macro structural variables (e.g., benefits to cooperation, market integration)	Economic games with real incentives: Ultimatum games Trust games Prisoner's dilemma games	Cross-cultural	Significant findings for other-regarding behaviors across different countries provides universal evidence against pure self-interest Experiments need to have real incentives	Ashraf et al., (2006); Bohnet et al., (forthcoming, 2008); Buchan & Croson (2004); Buchan et al., (2006); Henrich (2000); Henrich et al., (2005); Oosterbeek et al., (2003); Roth et al. (1991)	Examine the role of real incentives in cross-cultural studies of conflict and negotiation Incorporate psychological constructs that are currently not studied (e.g., sanctions, fear of punishment) in addition to cultural values (e.g., collectivism) in explaining cultural differences in conflict behavior

Primatology

Major Questions and Processes Examined	Unit of Analysis	How Culture is Conceptualized	Typical Methodology	Cross-cultural or Intercultural	Key Assumptions	Example Studies	Implications for OB/Psych
How do various aspects of the social context influence various types of conflict behavior among primates? Major processes investigated: Aggression, reconciliation, third party alliance/ intervention	Captive groups	Social/ Ecological Context	Direct observations of naturally-occurring behaviors in captive groups in treatment vs. control conditions	Across different ecological contexts	Conflict behaviors found in primates have significant relevance to humans	Cords & Thurnheer (1993); de Waal (2000); Flack et al. (2005); Thierry (2000)	Examine differences in power distribution on effectiveness of certain conflict resolution procedures Examine reconciliation and relationship repair processes across cultures

Communication

Major Questions and Processes Examined	Unit of Analysis	How Culture is Conceptualized	Typical Methodology	Cross-cultural or Intercultural	Key Assumptions	Example Studies	Implications for OB/Psych
How does communication processes vary across cultures, and in particular, in conflict situations? What are the obstacles encountered when people form different cultures communicate? How can communication be improved in intercultural contexts? Major processes investigated: Face concerns and facework behaviors; conflict styles; verbal and non-verbal communication; anxiety and uncertainty	Individual Dyad	Shared psychological values (e.g., Collectivism vs. Individualism) Individual self-construals (e.g., Interdependent vs. Independent)	Experiments Surveys	Cross-cultural and intercultural	Face and facework are critical to conflict and negotiation Variables relevant to intercultural interactions (e.g., anxiety) can differ from those relevant to intracultural interactions	Andersen et al., (2002); Cai et al., (2000); Gudykunst (2005); Lim (2002); Oetzel & Ting-Toomey (2003)	Integrate intercultural communication theories into conflict and negotiation research (e.g., the role of motivation, anxiety and intergroup dynamics in intercultural negotiations) Study non-tangible resources (e.g., identity) which can be negotiated in addition to more tangible resources such as economic profit

Table 13.1 (cont.)

International Relations

Major Questions and Processes Examined	Unit of Analysis	How Culture is Conceptualized	Typical Methodology	Cross-cultural or Intercultural	Key Assumptions	Example Studies	Implications for OB/Psych
How does culture influence negotiators' perceptions and behaviors?	Individual Group	Shared values, beliefs, norms	Case studies Archives	Cross-cultural, although data is derived from intercultural settings	Cultural differences should be examined directly in intercultural contexts	Cohen (1991, 1997, 2000, 2001a, 2001b); Faure & Rubin (1993)	Study not only behaviors during the actual conflict, but also pre and post-conflict stages
When do cultural effects on negotiation become attenuated?		Critical perspective of what culture is not (see Zartman, 1993; Avruch, 1998)	Interviews Auto-biographies of Negotiators		Real-world negotiations are critical to study (real incentives, rich context)		Examine a wider range of contextual variables in intercultural negotiation settings (e.g., perception of power, language of negotiation, cultural distance, historical memory)
What kinds of metaphors are used to understand negotiation in various cultures?			Direct observations				
Major processes investigated: Negotiation perceptions and behaviors, pre-negotiation phases, behavioral styles/ strategies, post-negotiation procedures and relationships							Expand outcome variables to non-economic resources (e.g., quality of personal relationships, honor, face, status)

conflicts – those which arise from very different definitions of the conflict itself – may make it especially difficult to come to agreements.

Research in OB/psychology has shown that negotiators across cultures also are differentially susceptible to different judgment biases. Negotiators in the US are particularly susceptible to competitive judgment biases such as *fixed pie* biases and fail to adequately assess the priorities of their counterparts (Gelfand and Christakopolou, 1999). Negotiators in the US also tend to have *self-serving biases* of their own fairness, which tends to decrease joint value at the negotiation table (Gelfand *et al.,* 2002; Wade-Benzoni *et al.,* 2002). Finally, negotiators in the US are also more likely to make internal attributions of other negotiators' behavior (e.g., their personality) rather than the situation, causing more competition in negotiation (Morris, Leung, and Iyengar, 2004; Valenzuela, Sristava, and Lee, 2005).

Moving beyond the individual level, research has examined whether there are cross-national differences in the use of negotiation tactics and outcomes in negotiations, typically in laboratory simulations. Early research had compared tactics and outcomes of Americans with Japanese (Graham, 1984), Canadians (Adler, Graham, and Gehrke, 1987), Chinese (Adler, Brahm, and Graham, 1992), French (Campbell *et al.,* 1988), and Russians (Graham, Evenko, and Rajan, 1993), examining whether problem-solving tactics are *reciprocated* to the same extent in negotiations in different cultures (Adler, Graham, and Gehrke, 1987; Adler, Brahm, and Graham, 1992), and has explored whether outcomes vary across cultures (Adler, Graham, and Gehrke, 1987) among other questions. In general, numerous cross-cultural differences were observed in tactics and outcomes, yet without a clear definitive pattern. In some cases results were consistent with predictions, in some cases there were no differences, and in some cases, results were reversed from what was predicted (see Gelfand and Dyer, 2000 for a review).

More recent research has drawn upon and incorporated theories and measures of cultural value dimensions (e.g., Hofstede, Schwartz) into culture and negotiation research, lending more theoretical coherence to the field. Tinsley (1998), for example, examined how different dimensions of culture affect negotiators' preferences for different negotiation strategies. Cultural differences on hierarchical differentiation (acceptance of social inequality, such as in Japan), explicit contracting (using formal agreements, such as in Germany), and polychronicity (processing many tasks simultaneously, such as in the US) were related to preferences for using authorities, relying on external regulations, and integrating interests in conflicts, respectively. Others have found consistent patterns in cultural influences on preferences for information exchange strategies. A key finding is that US negotiators, who tend to be more individualistic and low context, are more likely to share information *directly* and they tend to achieve high joint gains through this strategy. By contrast, Japanese, Russian, and Hong Kong negotiators, who tend to be more collectivistic and high context, are more likely to share information *indirectly* through their patterns of offers and achieve high joint gains through this strategy (Adair and Brett, 2005, Adair *et al.,* 2004, Adair, Okumura, and Brett, 2001). Communication sequences are also affected by culture. Negotiators from collectivistic cultures use more flexible complementary sequences, and are better able to use direct and indirect forms of information exchange, as compared to negotiators from individualistic cultures (Adair and Brett, 2005; Adair, Okumura, and Brett, 2001).

Research in OB/psychology has increasingly examined situational factors that moderate cultural effects in negotiation. Several factors appear to *exacerbate* baseline cultural tendencies in negotiation, including accountability (Gelfand and Realo, 1999), high need for closure (Morris and Fu, 2001), and high ambiguity (Morris, Leung, and Iyengar, 2004). The nature of the relationship with one's counterpart also has a moderating impact in negotiations across cultures. For example, research has shown that negotiators from collectivistic cultures, far from always being cooperative, tend to be more competitive when they have strong egoistic motives and high aspirations (Chen, Mannix, and Okumura, 2003), are dealing with outgroup members or intergroup situations (Chen and Li, 2005; Probst,

Carnevale, and Triandis, 1999; Triandis *et al.*, 2001), and having little external monitoring (Gelfand and Realo, 1999).

Finally, research in OB/psychology has focused on the dynamics of *intercultural negotiations*. Micro OB/psychology research has tended to compare intracultural negotiations with intercultural negotiations using experimental role plays. For example, Brett and Okumura (1998) demonstrated that cultural differences in cognition have important consequences for intercultural negotiation outcomes. Specifically, they measured aspects of culture (individualism-collectivism and hierarchy-egalitarianism) and illustrated that they affected negotiators' schemas and scripts (i.e., related to self-interest, power, and information sharing). Their results strongly suggest that incompatible schemas and scripts made it more difficult to achieve integrative outcomes in intercultural, as compared to intracultural negotiations (see also Adair, 1999; Tinsley, 1998). Imai and Gelfand (2007) found that negotiators with high cultural intelligence (Earley and Ang, 2003) were better able to sustain integrative bargaining sequences and create higher joint gain.

By contrast, research coming from the international business tradition has focused on negotiators' *perceptions* of the factors that are critical for success and failure in *actual* business negotiations. For example, Tung (1982) found that Americans perceived that successful negotiations were attributable to the attitude of the US firm wanting to invest in a long-term relationship with China, product characteristics, and familiarity with Chinese culture in terms of business practices, social customs, politics, and language. Failed negotiations were perceived to be attributable to cultural differences in business practices, negotiating styles and communication breakdowns, product characteristics, and Chinese insincerity. In actuality, negotiation success was predicted by years of Americans' experience in trading with China, number of previous negotiations with the Chinese, reading books on Chinese practices, and hiring experts to train American negotiators (see also Lee and Lo, 1988; Tung, 1984; Stewart and Keown, 1989).

Some studies have examined how culture changes over time in intercultural negotiations. For example, Brannen and Salk (2000) examined how national cultural traits of two companies combined to create a *third negotiated culture* through continuous interactions among members from both sides. Following the merger of a German company and a Japanese company, the authors found that in the startup period where there is high stress among top team members due to the novelty of working together, cultural differences in management were highly salient. By the time adjustment period was reached, however, these cultural differences were negotiated to form a third culture (see also Faure, 2000).

Finally, research on negotiations that occur across international borders also exists at a more "macro-strategic" level which can be differentiated from the "micro-behavioral" paradigm discussed above (Weiss 2004, 2006). Within the macro-strategic paradigm, research examines interfirm negotiations (joint ventures, international alliances, and mergers and acquisitions) as well as the impact of foreign multinational enterprises (MNE) resources on the outcomes of market entry negotiations with host governments (i.e., percentage of subsidiary ownership obtained by MNEs). Although these negotiations occur in international contexts, culture does not play a prominent role in these studies (see Kobayashi, 1988; Nair and Stafford, 1998).

In sum, research on culture, conflict, and negotiation in OB/psychology has largely focused on cross-national differences in perceptions, behaviors, and outcomes in experiments, and to a lesser extent, in actual negotiations in the field. The primary focus is on *value differences* and related psychological constructs, and how they affect economic value achieved in negotiations in different countries. Increasingly, the field is advancing more dynamic approaches to culture and negotiation, illustrating that cultural differences can change depending on the proximal situation, as well as focusing on the development of third cultures. We next turn to the key questions, paradigms, and methodologies that characterize numerous other disciplines that are also examining culture, conflict, and negotiation, discussing how they can each complement and extend extant perspectives in OB/psychology in important ways.

Legal anthropology

Legal anthropology and its paradigm

Legal anthropology, a sub-discipline within social and cultural anthropology, refers to the study of legal systems in various societies around the world. We focus on a select number of representative works conducted prior to the 1980s within legal anthropology, as contemporary work in the field focuses primarily on law within the US. One of the *major questions* asked among the classic works in legal anthropology is: *how do various societies resolve disputes, and what factors within these societies explain their preferred method(s) of dispute resolution?* The paradigm used in this discipline to address this broader question appears to have a number of features different from cross-cultural organizational behavior/psychology. First, the *unit of analysis* is the social group, or community, of mostly pre-industrial societies. Second, *culture*, as conceptualized in OB/psychology and IB in terms of shared values is given a minimal role, and it is the *social structure* of the community that is of major emphasis in explaining dispute resolution. Third, the most common *methodologies* used are case studies and ethnography, which allow for rich, in-depth, contextual descriptions of how a particular group of people resolve real-life disputes. Finally, when generalizations are observed based on a collection of ethnographies, they are of *cross-cultural* rather than of intercultural nature (see Gluckman, 1955; Nader, 1969; Nader and Todd, 1978).

Key findings from legal anthropology

In examining how various traditional societies resolve disputes, legal anthropologists have identified a wide variety of dispute resolution procedures that are used across cultures, including avoidance, tolerance, coercion, negotiation, mediation, arbitration, and adjudication (Black, 1993; Koch, 1974, 1979; Nader and Todd, 1978). Given this spectrum of possible dispute resolution methods, one of the major foci in this discipline has been to understand how the *social structure* constrains or affords

certain predominant ways of managing disputes in a particular community. For example, pioneering figures in this field such as Gluckman (1955) and Nader and Todd (1978) argue that the *nature of social relationships* in a community determines the dominant mode of dispute resolution used. In communities with multiplex ties, where each individual relates to another by sharing several dimensions of activity such as work, kinship, and recreation, disputes tend to be resolved through more cooperative means (e.g., negotiation, mediation) resulting in compromise outcomes given that preservation of relationships is paramount. In contrast, in communities with simplex ties, where each individual relates to another through one dimension of activity such as only through work, disputes tend to be handled by more competitive procedures (e.g. arbitration, adjudication) win-lose outcomes resulting in given that the severing of relationships is not as consequential (Gluckman, 1955; Nader and Todd, 1978).

Even when adjudication is used, the more multiplex the social ties tend to be in a given society, the more emphasis there seems to be on compromise over win-lose outcomes. For example, Nader (1969) provides a rich description of court procedures among the Zapotec of Mexico. In this multiplex, Zapotec judges go to great lengths to "make balance" (*hacer el balance*) between the plaintiff and defendant to prevent direct confrontations that lead to win-lose outcomes that would disturb the broader community at large. Thus, unlike western court procedures, where the sole function is to settle the dispute assuming that the cause of the dispute is already known, the role of Zapotec court procedures is to find out what the trouble really is between the disputants from both perspectives. A Zapotec judge does not see the situation as if one party is clearly to blame, but sees both parties at fault to a certain extent. Thus, the judge's concern is not past-oriented in terms of establishing facts or guilt as it is in the West, but is future-oriented in terms of re-establishing disrupted personal relations. Nader (1969) observes that this style of dispute resolution can be found in ethnographic accounts of other societies including Korea (Hahm, 1969), India (Cohn, 1959), Norway (Aubert, 1967), and the Ndendeuli of southern Tanzania (Gulliver, 1969).

Other research in legal anthropology has focused on how contextual variables interact with the nature of social ties in influencing dispute resolution procedures and outcomes (Nader and Todd, 1978). For example, when the source of the dispute is a *scarce resource*, relationships can be sacrificed in favor of win-lose outcomes (Starr and Yngvesson, 1975). Starr's (1978) description of Turkish society supports this view where even within multiplex communities, disputes over inheritance among siblings, or male control over the behavior of unmarried sisters can lead to the severance of relationships. Another contextual variable is the *power difference* between disputants. Nader and Todd (1978) observed that in many small-scale societies, existing power relations are legitimized through law, as the judge favors the more powerful disputant (Nader and Todd, 1978). A related finding by Todd (1978) is that social status determines whether one has access to certain dispute resolution forums in the first place. For example, Bavarians distinguish village members who have "*charakter*" (i.e., a personal characteristic describing how tightly one follows social norms) versus those who do not and only by having *charakter* can one gain social status and have access to preferred dispute resolution procedures.

Legal anthropologists also examine the relationship between the broader social organization and dispute resolution in different societies. Felstiner (1974–1975), for example, argued that non-government adjudication and mediation are more likely to be prevalent in technologically simple poor societies (TSPS), wherein social organization consists of extended family units, stable marriages that are often arranged and serve as liaisons between families, extra-nuclear family relationships that provide political and economic support, financial assistance in old age from family, low mobility of residence and vocation, and a lack of large-scale bureaucratic organizations. By contrast, avoidance is more likely to be prevalent in technologically complex rich societies (TCRS), wherein social organization is characterized by nuclear family units, relatively unstable marriages, extra-nuclear

family relationships that do not provide economic and political support, financial assistance in old age from the state, high mobility of residence and vocation, and the presence of large-scale bureaucratic organizations. Felstiner (1974–1975) reasoned that adjudication and mediation is more prevalent in TSPS than TCRS because it requires the presence of a social group that can apply normative rules to evaluate and sanction disputants, as well as the backing of coercive power that can enforce win-lose outcomes. Such factors are more characteristic of TSPS than TCRS, as face-to-face groups such as kin, factions, and villages can rule win-lose outcomes and disputants have no other choice than to adhere to such outcomes in order to maintain the overall functioning of the larger community. By contrast, avoidance is theorized to be more characteristic of TCRS than TSPS, as it is more likely to occur when the costs of severing the relationship between disputants are relatively low (see Danzig, 1973; Lowy, 1973; for criticisms, see also Newman, 1983) for economic perspective on the relationship between social complexity and legal institutions).

Koch, Sodergren, and Campbell (1976) also studied the extent to which the political integration of a society is related to dispute resolution practices. For example, in his own ethnographic work on the Jale of New Guinea, Koch (1974) describes how Jale communities are divided by several residential compounds consisting of a common men's house and family huts of its married members. Residents of the common men's house usually belong to several patrilineal lineages where each holds land as corporate estate. Since no political office exists for either the residential compounds or for the village as a whole, disputing parties resort to coercion which frequently escalates into warfare (for other examples, see Brogger, 1968; Fortes and Evans-Pritchard, 1940; Gluckman, 1959; Hoebel, 1954; Nader, 1965; Shapera, 1956). Indeed, among fifty pre-industrial societies, Koch *et al.* (1976) found that political integration (i.e., political authority above level of local community, strong centralized government, and relatively fixed mode of succession to political office) was associated with more use of triadic (i.e., adjudication, arbitration, mediation) than dyadic procedures (i.e., coercion, avoidance, negotiation) of dispute resolution (for criticisms on Koch, Sodergren, and Campbell, 1976, see Ross, 1993).

More recently, Ross (1986, 1993) examined how social structure relates to varying levels of conflict across societies. Coding ninety ethnographies of pre-industrial societies on economic and political complexity, patterns of marriage, strength of social linkages across communities within a society, inter-community trade, and the existence of fraternal interest groups, Ross (1986, 1993) found that societies with greater degrees of cross-cutting ties (i.e., people from one social group such as ethnicity, religion, gender, etc. have connections with people in other types of that social group) had lower levels of internal conflict. He reasons that, in societies with many cross-cutting ties across different communities, it is harder for individuals to rally support from others for purely their own interests, given others are likely to have loyalties to numerous social groups. Interestingly, this same process that characterized societies with low internal conflict also seemed to be related to high external conflict. Furthermore, Ross (1986, 1993) found that the psycho-cultural environment, that is, the cultural level disposition of these low-conflict societies were characterized by greater affection and warmth, as well as less overt aggression and male gender-identity conflicts.

Legal anthropology: summary and implications for organizational behavior/ psychology

Research in legal anthropology places major emphasis on social structure in explaining preferred methods of dispute resolution as well as overall levels of conflict across societies. Unlike cross-cultural organizational behavior/psychology, conflict is studied at the societal level, and psychological values at the individual level are not examined. Synergies across legal anthropology and OB/ psychology abound. One fruitful partnership would be to examine the interrelationship between social structural characteristics and culture-based psychological values such as collectivism. For example, does the shared value of collectivism develop as

social ties become more multiplex in a given society? How do cultural differences in cognitions and preferred conflict strategies vary depending on the nature of network ties? Are cultural differences in attitudes toward dispute resolution procedures such as mediation and negotiation in part explained in part by differences in social structural variables? More generally, the psychological tradition in OB would benefit from integrations with more macro social-structural and political context which has fruitfully been examined in legal anthropology.

Comparative law

Comparative law and its paradigm

At the broadest level, comparative law is concerned with the similarities and differences of *modern* legal systems across countries. Major questions that are asked in this discipline can vary from very macro questions such as, *how does culture influence the design of legal systems and do legal systems in turn influence culture?* to very micro questions such as, *how do individuals' perceptions vary across cultures in terms of the appropriate ways of resolving disputes?* Given such questions, the *unit of analysis* in comparative law can vary widely from country-level to individual-level. In terms of the treatment of *culture*, theory typically focuses on shared values as in organizational behavior/ psychology, yet these values are rarely measured and cross-country comparisons are common. *Methodologically*, comparative law currently does not have a single predominant approach, and relies on a diverse set of methods such as analyses of legal materials (e.g. publications from institutes for law), court cases, as well as surveys. Finally, as the name of this discipline indicates, the relationship between culture and disputing is examined through focusing on *cross-cultural* comparisons.

Key findings from comparative law

At a more macro, institutional level of analysis, Chase (1997, 2005) proposes that culture leads to differences in the design of legal systems among modern states. For example, he contrasts the American common law (i.e., adversarial) system and the European civil law (i.e., inquisitorial) system and how cultural values underlie the different roles played by the civil jury, the lawyers, the judge, and experts in each legal system. In the American common law system, the *civil jury* plays an extremely important role in civil litigation compared to the European civil law system. Chase (2005) argues that the prominent role of the civil jury in America is consistent with *egalitarianism* because laypeople with no expertise, regardless of education or social status are given power superior to that of the judge (Damaska, 1997). It is also consistent with *individualism* because of the significant power given to each individual, where a single hold-out verdict can lead to the end of the trial. Furthermore, in the American common law system, parties are given control of *pre-trial discovery*; that is, the power to investigate facts prior to trial. For example, each party can require from their opponent to submit oral questions and answers under oath (i.e., depositions and interrogatories) and produce files for inspection by the adversary (i.e., document discovery). This process reflects American egalitarianism because it "levels the playing field" for the economically weaker party, and it also reflects individualism because it allows attorneys to pursue their own course of action. In continental Europe, where it is less egalitarian and less individualistic, pre-trial discovery is considered unnecessary and intrusive (Schlesinger *et al.*, 1998). The *role of the judge* also varies significantly across cultures due to egalitarianism. Whereas the judge in the American common law system plays a largely passive role except when making a ruling, the judge in the European civil law system plays a more active role, for example, in questioning witnesses for examination and cross-examination (Cappelletti and Garth, 1987) as well as gathering and presenting the facts (Langbein, 1985). Finally, in addition to proposing that culture leads to differences in the design of legal systems, Chase (2005) also argues that there is a *reflexive relationship* in that legal systems also reinforce the broader culture in the society. He argues, "a set of social practices predominant in one area of human life, such as disputing, can

importantly influence practices, beliefs, and norms in other areas of society" (p. 127), and that this process occurs because disputing is dramatic, public, and engages attention; disputing is endorsed by cultural leaders; and because the court procedures become ritualized through repetition.

Hamilton and Sanders (1992) similarly argue that there is a mutually causal relationship between culture and legal institutions in the US and Japan. For example, they discuss how the American social structure and values characterized by low hierarchy and low solidarity are consistent with legal procedures that tend to be less inquisitorial and more adjudicative, whereas the Japanese social structure and values characterized by high hierarchy and high solidarity are more in line with legal procedures that tend to be more inquisitorial and less adjudicative. Hamilton and Sanders (1992) also propose that such differences in legal institutions in turn influence individual-level attitudes regarding the law such as on responsibility and punishment. They showed, for example, that Americans form attributions of responsibility based on the behavior of the actor, whereas the Japanese form attributions of responsibility based on the obligations the actor has towards others. Similarly, when making suggestions for punishment for the actor, Americans tend to give sanctions that isolate the actor, whereas the Japanese tend to give sanctions that focus more on restoring the relationship between the actor and the victim, similar to the findings on multiplex ties discussed in legal anthropology previously.

Kawashima (1963) also compares cross-cultural differences in the *usage* of law in the US and Japan. He argues that the Japanese hesitation to go to court (evidenced in lower litigation rates, smaller number of lawyers, and smaller number of claims brought to court) can be explained by the Japanese cultural value of group harmony. He specifically argues that because judicial decisions threaten the harmony of social groups as they regulate conduct by universalistic standards instead of mutual understanding, using litigation in Japan has been condemned as morally wrong and rebellious. For this reason, the prevailing form of dispute resolution in Japan has been through extrajudicial means of reconciliation such as the government institutionalized system of mediation, or *chotei*. Since Kawashima's (1963) work, similar arguments have been made for the role of culture in explaining Japan's low litigation rates (e.g., Kim and Lawson, 1979; Sato, 2001; Smith, 1987). However, other critics point out that there are alternative non-cultural explanations for low litigation rates in Japan. For example, Haley (1978) argued that institutional factors such as the low number of judges and lawyers available in Japan, shaped by the country's governing elites, explains lower litigation rates in Japan, not the cultural values of disputants per se. Ramseyer (1988) takes an economic perspective and argues that the lower litigation rates in Japan can be explained by rational decision-making processes concerning dispute resolution that would allow individuals to maximize their wealth and litigated outcomes. Yet, recently, Feldman (2007) argued that both institutional and economic/rational explanations are not contradictory with cultural explanations. Culture is what makes the governing elites shape the legal institution in the first place, and culture is what gives meaning to what is the most rational course of action.

The Japanese theme of valuing group solidarity and reconciliation is also reflected in Wagatsuma and Rosett's (1986) research on the functions of apologies in the US and Japan within legal contexts. They argue that, in Japan, the act of apologizing is not so much about acceptance of liability and responsibility as it is in the West, but is an act that signals the repairing of difficult relationships. Thus, sincerity of apologies in the US depends on genuine thoughts and whole-heartedness, whereas sincerity of apologies in Japan depend on performing the correct acts that restore relationships. Therefore, the Japanese can feel that they are not at fault, yet still think it is necessary to apologize to the other party. In the legal context, apologies are given higher priority in Japan than in the US. For example, in criminal law, letters of apology are used as an alternative to filing criminal charges, or in some cases may lead the judge to impose a milder sentence in a given trial. In contrast, apologies are generally avoided in the US for the fear of being accused of admitting responsibility.

Focusing at the more micro individual-level, Bierbrauer (1994) studied cultural differences

in attitudes towards the law, focusing on Kurds, Arabs, and Germans. Theorizing that collectivists (Kurds, Arabs) should place higher value on tradition and religion than individualists, Bierbrauer (1994) hypothesized and found that, compared to Germans, Kurds, and Arabs indicated less willingness to allow state law to intervene in family related matters (as it damages relationships), gave higher legitimacy for tradition and religion to handle disputes, preferred informal settlements, wanted apologies from the perpetrator to a greater degree, wanted family involved in third-party dispute resolution, valued harmony and compliance over formal rules in resolving disputes, and expected the judge to make greater allowance for gender and social status (see also Lauchli, 2000, who discusses similar notions regarding the influence of Confucian values on dispute resolution in China).

Comparative law: summary and implications for organizational behavior psychology

In summary, the major focus of comparative law is to determine how culture influences legal systems in various modern states. Disputing processes within the field are theorized at multiple levels of analysis, from the legal institution to the individual. Many creative synergies exist across comparative law and cross-cultural conflict and negotiation research in OB, most notably developing multi-level models that incorporate societal culture, legal institutions, and individual-level disputing behaviors. For example, research combining these disciplines might examine if normative disputing procedures at the institution level mediate the influence of societal culture on schemas and scripts for negotiation. Do individuals socialized in cultures with adjudicative legal institutions have schemas for negotiation that emphasizes win-lose outcomes while individuals from cultures with inquisitorial legal institutions have schemas for negotiation that emphasizes compromise outcomes? Debates regarding the relative importance of cultural values as an explanation for country differences in legal systems as compared to economic and institutional factors are common in comparative law. Cross-cultural OB/psychology would benefit from integrating such comparative explanations. Finally, it would also be interesting to examine the *reflexive* nature of culture and disputing in organizational behavior/psychology, for example, how changes in culture can evolve from changes in conflict and negotiation processes.

Language and disputing

Paradigm of study in language and disputing

The study of discourse or talk during conflict in various societies is not a single discipline but an approach taken by scholars that cuts across anthropology, linguistics, sociology, and psychology. The *major question* asked when using this approach is: *what does language used during conflict reveal about the socio-cultural knowledge presumed by speakers, as well as the rules of inference and interaction governing speakers' behaviors?* (Watson-Gegeo and White, 1990). In studying language during conflict, the *level of analysis* varies, depending on the particular context in which the conflict takes place. For example, conflict talk can occur within a dyad, or can occur within a group of individuals. *Culture* is treated as the particular social group to which the speakers' belong, including both pre-industrial and industrial societies. In terms of *methodology*, descriptive accounts of conflict discourse are examined employing sources such as transcripts, ethnographic records, audio and video records, as well as dramatic scripts. Finally, the vast majority of studies are non-comparative ethnographies of discourse during conflict, although several *cross-cultural comparisons* do exist (see Brenneis, 1988 for extensive review on language and disputing).

Key findings from language and disputing

Through ethnographic analyses of transcripts of conflict discourse across a wide range of pacific pre-industrial societies, Watson-Gegeo and White (1990) illustrate that cultural concepts such as those of person and emotion, as well as the nature of the social structure, are systematically related to the way in which conflict is conceptualized and resolved. For example, in most of the pacific societies studied, the concept of shame was the outcome of conflict and institutionalized practices such as reconciliation meetings existed for alleviating such shame. Furthermore, as discussed in Watson-Gegeo and White (1990), conflict discourse revealed that the social structure of the society influences various aspects of the conflict resolution process, including who controlled the process, the goals and outcomes of the process, and who participated in the process. For example, the political organization of the society was related to the extent to which the conflict resolution processes were controlled by officials and leaders. In the hierarchically organized Samoa, reconciliation meetings (*fono*) are called either when a social norm has been breached or when there is threat to the harmony of village life. These meetings are characterized by tight organization and control by chiefs, as well as orators who speak on behalf of the chiefs (Duranti, 1990). By contrast, in egalitarian Melanesia, discussion of conflict and decision-making meetings do not involve hierarchy (Watson-Gegeo and White, 1990). In hierarchical societies, the expected goals and outcomes of disputes were also explicit. For example, in the Hawaiian *ho'oponopono* ("to set things right"), or the family gathering for the discussion of interpersonal problems led by the household leader, the expected goal is always to clarify each individual's responsibility for actions and the expected outcome is always apology and forgiveness (Boggs and Chun, 1990). Social structure also influences the directness versus the indirectness of conflict discourse. For example, in hierarchical societies, the status of the powerful is signaled in direct speech. In contrast, in egalitarian societies, indirect discourse is used between disputants to avoid direct confrontations. For example, the Managalase of New Guinea manage contentious issues by presenting their own interpretations of affairs indirectly through the use of metaphors and allegories (McKellin, 1990). Finally, social structure also influences the *participation structure* or the constraints on who can say what to whom, how and when (Philips, 1972). In problem-solving contexts, multiple voices are allowed in an interactive dialogue through the assistance of mediators (e.g., Hawaiian ho'oponopono, the Samoan fono), whereas in contexts that create prescriptive, normative accounts of disputes to the public, lengthy interpretive accounts are given by pre-selected individual speakers. In such cases, because conflict resolution reflects socio-moral statements, who participates and how participation is managed is politically charged, and is reflected in the degree to which the event is planned in advance in terms of mutually agreed upon issues to be discussed. For example, in the Fiji pancayat, witnesses are already interviewed by committee members before the session is held, thus, committee members carefully control what witnesses say as well as what the general public observes. As Brenneis (1990) notes, in a society where the restoration of social ties is critical and individual emotions are de-emphasized, disputants are left satisfied despite such constraints on participation because the pancayat allows disputants and the public to share in the social experience of highly valued, non-individualized, collective moods.

Conflict discourse has also been studied among children in industrial societies. For example, Corsaro and Rizzo (1990) video-taped and studied cross-cultural similarities as well as differences in conflict talk among American and Italian nursery school children. In terms of similarities, children from both cultures mostly disputed about the nature of play, or how an act should be carried out in playing, as well as displaying oppositional exchanges. In both cultures, disputes over the nature of play involved children's attempts to come to shared understanding of play events. Despite these similarities, however, there were important cultural differences. Overall persuasiveness and verbal routines were much more important among Italian children than American children. That is, Italian children enjoyed engaging in disputes (*discussione*) as an end in itself using artful, creative dialogue. For example, Italian children emphasized style in their arguments, engaging in complex conflict talk by using interruption devices in turn-taking ("*ma scuza*" "but excuse me"), prefacing disagreements, using emphasis markers with "*ma*" (but), and format

tying, or repeating elements of an opponent's prior turn when talking.

Conflict discourse has also been studied in industrial societies in legal contexts. For example, although not focusing on cultural differences, Conley and O'Barr (1990) found that the style of accounts given by litigants varied depending on the social background of American litigants. For example, litigants of lower socioeconomic background tend to give relational accounts that emphasize status and relationships, filled with background details that are considered relevant to the litigant but irrelevant and inappropriate to the court. Such relational accounts were perceived by the court to be imprecise and tangential, whereas litigants of higher socioeconomic background tended to give rule-oriented accounts that emphasize rules and laws, leaving out information that pertains to motivation and feelings. The rule-oriented approach is correlated with the exposure to social power in the literature and rule-based cultures of business and law. When two sides of a dispute are given with different styles of accounts, Conley and O'Barr (1990) argue that the court is inherently biased in favor of the rule-oriented litigant.

Finally, in addition to the influence of culture/ community on conflict discourse, Grimshaw (1990) discusses how sociological variables such as power, affect, and stakes act as constraints on the occurrence and intensity of conflict discourse. For example, in Corsaro and Rizzo's (1990) study previously discussed, the children disputed with each other but did not challenge teachers of higher authority. It seems that the greater the discrepancies in power between disputants, the less likely that the less powerful will challenge the more powerful. Furthermore, the greater the discrepancies in power, the more likely for the conflict talk to be indirect, overtly neutral, and of lower intensity. However, if the stakes are high, subordinates may challenge superiors with greater power.

Language and disputing: implications for organizational behavior/psychology

In summary, the field of language and disputing relies on rich descriptive accounts of conflict discourse in various societies to examine culture-specific characteristics of conflict resolution. Like legal anthropology and comparative law, the role of the social structure of societies is theorized to have an important role in the dynamics of conflict. The analysis of discourse or talk and how it constrains and affords the definition and resolution of disputes is an approach that can be integrated with research in OB/psychology. For example, as discussed in Watson-Gegeo and White's (1990) collection of ethnographies, shame plays a central role in the nature of conflict resolution processes in many societies, yet research on culture and negotiation in OB/psychology rarely examines emotions. Research on language and disputing also calls attention to collective outcomes of disputing. For example, the work by Brenneis (1990) highlights that bystanders are at least as important as disputants themselves in some societies, as they come to experience collective mood which helps further to strengthen socio-moral norms. Finally, with some exceptions (see Leung, 1987; Tinsley and Brett, 1997), there is little attention to culture and mediation in the organizational behavior literature, yet third-party involvement in conflict resolution is widespread in many societies worldwide.

Cognitive anthropology

Paradigm of cognitive anthropology

Broadly put, cognitive anthropology is the study of the relationship between culture and human thought (Robertson and Beasley, 2007). More specifically, this field examines how people in various cultures understand and organize the material objects, events, and experiences that make up their world according to their indigenous cognitive categories (Robertson and Beasley, 2007). One of the *major questions* asked is: *how do meaning systems vary across cultures and what are the implications of such cultural differences for intercultural conflict?* The most relevant work in this tradition is that of Medin, Ross, and Cox (2006) on culture, meanings, and resource conflict. In their research, the authors focus on cultural differences in meanings of nature, or more specifically, the knowledge organization of the concept of nature as a source for intercultural misperceptions and conflict over natural resources between Native American Indians

and European Americans. In this tradition, *culture* is typically not defined in terms of shared values but as "the causally distributed patterns of ideas, their public expressions, and the resultant practices and behaviors in given ecological contexts" (Medin, Ross, and Cox, 2006, p. 28). Thus, culture is viewed as distributional, and the variation in values and norms *within* cultures is also considered an important aspect of culture along with its consensus. Thus, in terms of *levels of analysis*, Medin and colleagues' work focuses at the group level. The *methodology* used includes both qualitative and quantitative approaches. For example, cognitive sorting tasks, open-ended explanations of sorting, as well as surveys on values and beliefs are all used, and associated methods have been developed to assess levels of agreement in the structure and distribution of knowledge in cultural groups (e.g., the Cultural Consensus Model (CCM); Romney, Weller, and Batchelder, 1986). Finally, the authors focus on *cross-cultural* differences in knowledge organization, as well as *intercultural* misperceptions and stereotyping that result from such cultural differences in knowledge organization.

Key findings from cognitive anthropology

Medin, Ross, and Cox (2006) found that conflict over natural resources over (i.e., fish) between the Menominee Native American and European American fishermen are due to cultural differences in knowledge organization of nature (i.e., fishing), and that these differences are associated with negative intercultural stereotyping. The authors found that European Americans conceptualize nature in terms of sports, where the emphasis in fishing is placed on fair chase and competition to obtain "trophy game." In contrast, the Menominee conceptualize nature in terms of ecology, where the emphasis in fishing is placed on simply catching food. Cultural differences in the knowledge organization of nature were reflected in a number of cognitive tasks that examined expert fishermen's knowledge of fish among the two cultural groups. For example, when asked to freely sort species of fish into categories and provide a justification for why they did so, European Americans were more likely than the Menominees to use categories with evaluative dimensions such as prestigious sport fish versus garbage fish and give taxonomic and morphological justifications. On the other hand, the Menominee, more than European Americans, were likely to categorize based on ecological relations. The authors found this differential salience of ecological information despite the same level of knowledge base across the two groups. In a separate study, participants were asked to look at pairs of fish and describe how they influenced each other in nature. While European Americans tended to report only relations of adult fish, consistent with an interest in only catching the biggest fish for sports, the Menominee took into account the whole cycle of each species, consistent with an interest in overall ecology. Again, both groups had similar levels of knowledge base about interactions among fish.

In addition to knowledge organization of fish, European Americans and the Menominee had different goals for the practice of fishing. For example, the European Americans highly prioritized fishing as a challenge to outsmart fish, whereas the Menominee highly prioritized fishing for food. However, broad commonalities were also observed across the two groups. For example, both groups rank-ordered the desirability of fish species similarly, and both groups condemned selling fish, keeping undersized fish, and fishing on spawning beds. Despite such similarities in values, however, there were many intercultural misperceptions. For example, the Menominee overestimated European Americans' focus on catching trophy-size fish, and underestimated the importance of fishing as an activity to pass down to future generations as well as being close to nature. European Americans, on the other hand, showed the largest discrepancy where they underestimated the Menominee's focus on fishing as a way to relax, and overestimated the approval of selling fish, keeping under-sized fish, and fishing on spawning beds, when in fact both groups condemned these practices. Finally, it was found that cultural differences in knowledge organization as discussed above were correlated with individual-level stereotyping. For example, the more European American individuals had stronger conceptualization of nature as sports, the more likely they were to have intercultural misperceptions.

Cognitive anthropology: summary and implications for organizational behavior/psychology

In summary, cognitive anthropology focuses on cultural differences in knowledge structure and knowledge organization instead of cultural values. An interesting finding of Medin, Ross, and Cox's (2006) work is that knowledge organization can be a source of intercultural misperceptions, despite the two cultures sharing similar broader values which is a promising focus for organizational behavior/psychology. The notion in cognitive anthropology that the variability of beliefs, values, and norms (as opposed to its consensus) within one culture should not be treated as noise is also a meta-theoretical and empirical focus that should capture more attention in OB/psychology. For example, as they note, ignoring within-group differences can lead to the over-interpretation of cultural differences, as a consequence of researchers ignoring within-group differences (Medin, Ross, and Cox 2006).

Experimental economics

Experimental economics and its paradigm

Traditionally, economics was regarded as a non-experimental science that solely relied on findings from real-world markets and economies. However, in the last two decades, controlled laboratory experimentation, with its advantage of allowing researchers to make causal conclusions, emerged as a vital methodology forming the branch of experimental economics. To date, this sub-discipline has allowed the testing of theoretical predictions on various aspects of economic behavior, as well as the major assumption of economics itself, that behavior is determined purely through self-interest and rational decision-making. Studies that specifically focus on culture in this field investigate *major questions* such as, *how do economic behaviors such as cooperation, fairness, and trust vary across cultures?* examined at the individual and societal *levels of analysis*. Furthermore, most studies treat *cultural differences* synonymously with country differences except for more recent field experiments that are being conducted across small-scale pre-industrial societies by economic anthropologists. In either case however, cultural values or associated constructs are rarely measured. The methodologies used involve experiments that utilize various types of economic games where participants are always given real incentives (i.e., money). Finally, *cross-cultural comparisons* rather than intercultural comparisons are most common in experimental economics.

Key findings from experimental economics

Numerous experiments provide evidence against the previously held major assumption of economics, the selfishness axiom, which states that individuals seek to maximize their own material gains. In fact, it has been observed that people often forgo material gains in order to act pro-socially. Such evidence comes from experiments conducted with university students in numerous countries, although culture was not the explicit focus (see Camerer, 2003 for extensive review). That people often behave pro-socially can also be found using various types of economic games discussed below.

Ultimatum games

For example, the ultimatum game (UG) involves two people, where the first player called the "proposer" is allotted a sum of money and can offer a proportion of the sum to the second player, the "responder." The responder who knows the amount of the initial sum can either accept or reject the proposer's offer. If the responder accepts, he or she receives the offer and the proposer gets the remainder of the money (initial sum minus the offer). If the responder rejects the offer, neither party gets anything. If individuals were acting selfishly to maximize their own gains, it would be predicted that responders should accept any positive offer, and proposers would not send any money in the first place. However across many studies, what is consistently observed is that proposers offer around 40–50 percent of the initial sum, with responders rejecting approximately 20 percent of the time (Henrich *et al.*, 2005). Thus, it seems that proposers are sensitive to fairness norms, where they would rather give up money than to treat others unfairly and risk being punished.

Early cross-cultural studies found little variability in offer and rejection rates in different countries (Henrich *et al.*, 2005). For example, Roth, Prasnikar, Okuno-Fujiwara, and Zamir (1991) found similar offer and rejection rates in the US, Japan, Yugoslavia, and Israel, and any differences found between these countries were small. Cameron (1999) also found similar rates in Indonesia. More recently, however, Henrich (2000) observed a more peculiar finding when comparing UG behavior through field experiments between the Machiguenga men of the Peruvian Amazon and UCLA students. He found that offer rates among the Machiguenga were much smaller (mean of 26 percent) than previous findings (mean of 40–50 percent). Thus, unlike what has been previously observed among university students in hundreds of experiments, the Machiguenga had no intention of sharing equally nor had any expectation of receiving equal shares from others.

In a more extensive cross-cultural project, Henrich *et al.* (2005) conducted field experiments in fifteen small-scale pre-industrial societies, exhibiting a wide range of economic and cultural conditions (i.e., horticulturalists, nomadic herders, small-scale agriculturalists). Comparing UG behavior across these societies, they found that the selfishness axiom was violated in some way in all societies. However, a significant degree of variability was observed across the groups, with offer rates ranging from 26–58 percent, which is far greater than the 40–50 percent typically seen among university students in industrialized societies. Interestingly, offer rates were positively associated with the degree of *market integration* in the society, or the degree to which people engage in market exchange, sociopolitical complexity, and settlement size. Offer rates were also positively associated with the degree of *payoffs to cooperation*, or the extent to which non-immediate kin are involved in economic life. Replicating previous findings, the Machiguenga who are almost entirely economically dependent on their own families exhibited one of the lowest offer rates among the societies studied. Henrich *et al.* (2005) discuss how experimental play in UG behavior in these societies mirror patterns of interactions in everyday life. For example, the Au and Gnau of Papua Guinea offered more than half of the initially allotted money but many of these offers were rejected. Such a pattern can be explained within a societal context in which people seek status through gift giving. Gift-giving creates a strong obligation for the receiver to reciprocate in the future and places the receiver in a subordinate status; thus, excessively large gifts are frequently refused. By contrast, the Hadza exhibited low offers and high rejection rates. In everyday life, the Hadza avoid sharing meat and look for opportunities not to share (Marlowe, 2004), and cooperation is only enforced by fear of punishment by means such as informal social sanctions, gossip, and ostracism (Blurton Jones, 1984).

In another study, arguing that it is problematic not to measure cultural traits when comparing UG behaviors across cultures, Oosterbeek, Sloof, and van Kuilen (2004) coded thirty-seven papers conducted between 1982 and 2003 on various cultural dimensions based on where each study was conducted, and examined whether there were any relationships between cultural traits and UG offers/ rejection rates. They found that neither individualism nor power distance had any significant effects. However, they found that respect for authority had a negative association with offer rates.

Buchan, Croson, and Johnson (2004) also used the ultimatum game in their cross-cultural study, but focused on fairness beliefs in the US and Japan in various situational contexts. For example, the authors compared American and Japanese fairness beliefs when the proposer had greater power than the responder (i.e., had an alternative in case the deal did not go through with the responder) versus when the proposer had equal power with the responder (i.e., had no alterative). Buchan, Croson, and Johnson (2004) found that for Americans, what was considered fair offers (by the proposer) and demands (by the responder) were lower when the proposer had power than when the proposer did not have power. In contrast, for the Japanese, what was considered fair offers and demands were higher when the proposer had power than when the proposer did not have power. In other words, Americans believed that it is fair for the proposer with greater power to take the larger share of the money, whereas the Japanese believed that it is fair for the proposer with the greater power to earn smaller portions of the money and share more of the surplus with the weaker partner. Buchan, Croson, and Johnson (2004) explains that this is consistent with American and Japanese differences on the meaning of power. In the US, power is coercive, while in Japan, there is an interdependent relationship between the powerful and the powerless, where the powerful takes care of its subordinate in exchange for loyalty.

Trust games

Trust is another aspect of economic behavior that is studied cross-culturally in experimental economics. In studying trust, researchers often use the investment game (Berg, Dickhaut, and McCabe, 1995), which is played by a sender and a receiver. The sender is allotted an initial sum of money, and is told that he or she is free to keep the entire money or can split it with the receiver. Whatever amount of money sent to the receiver is tripled by the experimenter and given to the receiver. The receiver then decides whether to keep the entire tripled amount or to send some back to the sender. If both parties trusted each other, each would end up better off than if acting out of pure self-interest. For example, if the sender trusts the receiver and sends all of the ten dollars, the receiver gets thirty dollars, some of which he or she can send back. If the receiver reciprocates the sender's trust and sends back half of thirty dollars, each player ends up with fifteen dollars. By contrast, if the individuals purely acted out of self-interest, the sender would keep all of the ten dollars, and the receiver gets nothing.

Using this paradigm, recent work has examined whether culture influences levels of trust, and whether culture interacts with various social contexts in influencing levels of trust. For example, Buchan, Johnson, and Croson (2006) examined other-regarding preferences (ORP), which is a general term for constructs such as trust, reciprocity, and altruism, under ingroup versus outgroup contexts in the US, China, Japan, and Korea. Overall, the authors found few differences in ORPs across countries, although they did find that the Chinese sent slightly more money to receivers than the Americans. Furthermore, in terms of social context, the authors found that Americans send and return more money when players are ingroup members, whereas the Chinese send and return more money when players are outgroup members. Buchan, Johnson, and Croson (2006) explain this pattern of results by speculating that ingroup biases among the Chinese may be more common in naturally occuring social groups. In another study, Buchan and Croson (2004) found similar results where Americans were less likely to expect proposers to act in trusting ways as the social distance between proposers and receivers increased, whereas this pattern was weaker for the Chinese. Finally, Buchan, Croson and Dawes (2002) found that culture and social identity interact to influence the propensity to trust and reciprocate. Individualists were found to trust and reciprocate more when interacting with ingroup members than strangers, whereas collectivists behaved the same way across these two conditions. The authors also found that the Americans and Chinese sent and returned higher amounts than Koreans and the Japanese, providing some evidence for varying norms of trust and reciprocity across countries.

More recently, Ashraf, Bohnet, and Piankov (2006) focused on the question of what motivates people to trust and be trustworthy across the US, Russia, and South America using dictator and investment games. More specifically, they examined whether people trust others purely through "calculative" expectations of the other's trustworthiness (i.e., a belief) or through unconditional kindness (i.e., the enjoyment of trusting others). The authors also examined whether people who have been shown trust become trustworthy because of reciprocity or unconditional kindness. They found that trust (i.e., amount of money sent) is predicted more by the expectation of trustworthiness than unconditional kindness, and that trustworthiness (i.e., proportion of money received that is returned) is predicted more by unconditional kindness than reciprocity. Similar trust behaviors were observed among the US, Russia, and South America.

While the previous studies focus more on individual-level trust, other research has theorized on why there are country-level differences in trust, which is believed to lead to differences in economic performance. Buchan et al. (2002, 2006) discuss multiple perspectives on why societies differ in trust. For example, some emphasize culture (Ouchi, 1981; Fukuyama, 1995; Strong and Weber, 1998; Doney, Cannon, and Mullen, 1998), religion (La Porta et al., 1997), ease of communication (Fishman and Khanna 1999), presence of sanctioning mechanisms for non-cooperation (Yamagishi, 1988a, 1988b, Yamagishi and Yamagishi, 1994; Yamagishi, Cook, and Watabe, 1998), differing social/economic systems (Henrich et al., 2001, 2005), as well as degree and type of associative networks (Putnam, 1993). Zak and Knack (2001) also discuss sanctioning systems in terms of formal institutions (e.g., legal systems, the securities and exchange commission, investigative agencies) and informal systems (e.g., reputation and ostracism), as well as societal-level homogeneity, unequal distribution of income and discrimination. Furthermore, Zak and Fakhar (2006) provide evidence that societal-level trust across forty-one countries is correlated with consumption of plant-based estrogens and the presence of estrogen-like molecules in the environment. In their empirical study, Bohnet, Herrmann, and Zeckhauser (forthcoming) discuss some of these sources of country-level differences in trust in explaining why people in the Gulf (Emirates, Kuwaitis, Omanis) require a higher probability of trustworthiness from others in order to trust, compared to people in the West (Swiss, Americans). They theorize that in the Gulf, people are not inclined to trust strangers given the lack of formal institutions like contracts and the law. Instead, people in the Gulf trust familiar people where trust is promoted through social networks and informal social sanctions (See also Bohnet, Greig, Herrmann, and Zeckhauser, 2008 for other work on betrayal aversion in six countries).

Experimental economics: summary and implications for organizational behavior/ psychology

In summary, both experimental economics and organizational behavior/psychology examine how individual behavior such as cooperation, fairness, and trust vary across cultures, utilizing tightly controlled experiments in order to test theoretical predictions. Although both disciplines rely on similar methodologies, one major difference is that experimental economics consistently provide real incentives (i.e., money) for participants in studying their behavior, whereas organizational behavior/psychology is less consistent, sometimes using real incentives and at other times relying on other methods such as course credit. Experimental economics examines additional societal-level factors such as market integration, payoffs to cooperation, and sanctioning systems as sources of cultural differences. As with other potential "mergers" across disciplines, the simultaneous examination of both the rich psychological and contextual approach to culture, conflict, and negotiation in OB/psychology can be fruitfully integrated with the incentives and societal-level factors found in economics. For example, it would be fruitful to examine the condition under which values explain differences in conflict and negotiation across cultures as compared to incentives and sanctions.

Primatology

Paradigm of primatology

Conflict resolution is one major area of research in the discipline of primatology, or the study of primate behavior. Given the focus on non-human primates, culture as is conceptualized in this field is not examined; however, the influence of the social/ecological context on primate conflict resolution behaviors is commonly examined. We focus specifically on these studies in identifying lessons that can be learned from primatology for the study of culture and conflict in organizational behavior/psychology. In the most general sense, the *major question* asked in these studies is: *how do various aspects of the social context/structure influence various types of conflict behavior among primates?* The *level of analysis* in these studies is the group, where primates are usually studied in captive groups. While *culture* is not studied explicitly, there is a focus on the the social/ecological context. The *methodologies* used in studying primates vary depending on the nature of the research question; however, at a general level, the frequency of naturally occurring behaviors of interest in a treatment condition

is compared to the frequency of the same behavior in a controlled condition. Finally, the cross-cultural–intercultural distinction is not relevant in this discipline; however, comparisons of conflict behavior can be made across different social/ecological contexts.

Key findings from primatology

In examining the relationship between social/ecological context and conflict behaviors, one area of research in primatology has focused on how the various ways in which the *distribution of power* in primate societies affects the manifestation of aggression and post-conflict reconciliation behaviors among primates. For example, among different species of macaques, the extent of rigidity in the social hierarchy has been found to covary with conflict management patterns (Thierry, 2000). Rhesus and Japanese macaques that live with strong power asymmetries engage in highly uni-directional conflict, where the target of aggression flees or submits to the aggressor. Furthermore, post-conflict reconciliation behaviors between previous opponents are rare. By contrast, among Sulawesi Island macaques that live with weak power asymmetry, aggressive acts often elicit protests and counterattacks from the target (Thierry, 2000). Furthermore, post-conflict reconciliation behaviors between previous opponents are frequent. In explaining the origins of such power asymmetries, van Schaik (1989) argues that all animals live in groups for protection from predators, but such group living creates intragroup and inter-group competition for resources. In macaques, females create kin-bonded coalitions (i.e., the dominants) to face overt competition, both between individuals within a group and between groups. In cases where predation risks are high, the costs of leaving the group among subordinates are higher, thus, the subordinates remain in the group and dominants end up taking most of the resource share, creating despotic relationships among unrelated members within the group. By contrast, when predation risks are low, subordinates are not forced to remain within the group, and because dominants benefit from subordinates remaining within the group to cooperate against external threats, a

relatively equal division of resources results producing egalitarian relationships among non-kin.

The distribution of power in primate societies
has also been examined in relation to *third-party
policing*; that is, the physical intervention by a
third party of a conflict between two primates. For
example, among pigtailed macaques, Flack, de
Waal, and Krakauer (2005) found that policing is
only effective when exercised by a small number of
powerful individuals within the society where the
risk of physically intervening is of negligible cost
to them. Furthermore, Flack, Krakauer, and de Wall
(2005) found that, in pigtail macaques, knocking
out the high power intervenors caused the social
system to destabilize, leading to more conflict, less
socio-positive interaction, and less reconciliation
among other macaques. Flack Girvan, de Waal,
and Krakauer (2006) further found that policing
has a direct function of preventing injuries and
damaged relationships as well as indirect functions
of altering the social resource network in a way in
which group living is made more advantageous.
For example, with policing, individual macaques
had significantly more play and grooming partners, more beneficial affiliative contagion (i.e., A
grooms B, B grooms C, etc.), more cooperation
among individuals with unequal access to social
resources, and more interaction-partner diversity
(i.e., the prevention of formation of cliques of
similar macaques).

In addition to the distribution of power within
primate societies, the *value of relationships*
is another type of social contextual variable
conceptualized to influence reconciliation behaviors among primates. Reconciliation refers to
the friendly reunion between former opponents
soon after an aggressive confrontation (de Waal,
2000). Research generally supports that reconciliation is more likely to occur after conflict between
parties that have a relationship of high social or
reproductive value. For example, in a study by
Cords and Thurnheer (1993), pairs of long-tailed
macaques were trained so that popcorn was only
obtainable by acting in a coordinated fashion with
their partner by sitting side by side with each other.
Macaques that were trained to cooperate were
three times more likely to reconcile after an

induced conflict than those who were not trained
to cooperate.

Another social contextual variable, *crowding*,
also seems to affect conflict management patterns
among primates. For example, van Wolkenten *et al.*
(2006) found that crowding decreased aggression,
play, and social grooming in capuchin monkeys
(related to chimpanzees), suggesting that primates
may avoid social encounters and adopt a conflict
avoidance strategy. Indeed, many studies have supported the coping model, that animals respond to
crowded conditions by modifying their behavior
to reduce the severity of aggressive encounters
(Aureli and de Waal, 1997; de Waal, 1989; de
Waal, Aureli, and Judge, 2000; Judge, 2000; Judge
and de Waal, 1997). Chimpanzees have also been
found to increase friendly and appeasing interactions, although aggression increased slightly (de
Waal, 1982). However, in a different study of
chimpanzees, Aureli and de Waal (1997) found
that all forms of social behavior were decreased,
along with decreases in both intense and mild
aggression. Furthermore, Rhesus macaques have
been found to increase grooming while aggression
remained constant. In shorter-term crowding studies, rhesus monkeys have been shown to engage in
mild aggression and increase submissive signals,
but also decrease grooming (Judge, 2000).

Primatology: summary and implications
for organizational behavior/psychology

In summary, primatology is another discipline in
which conflict resolution is a major area of study.
Although culture is not examined per se, it does
study a number of social/ecological contextual variables, including distribution of power, policing,
value of relationships, and crowding and their
impact on various conflict management behaviors.
One implication of this discipline for the study of
culture, conflict, and negotiation in OB/psychology,
is examining the role of differences in power distribution at a societal level on conflict resolution. For
example, future research can examine questions
such as, what role does power distance between
negotiators have for conflict resolution across cultures? What are the effects of cultural differences

in power distance on effectiveness of third-party interventions? Furthermore, while conflict resolution has been studied, the act of reconciliation or relationship repair has received scant attention in organizational behavior/psychology, especially in cross-cultural contexts. Finally, borrowing from the primatology literature, we can expand our current individual-level understanding of culture such as cultural values (e.g., individualism-collectivism) and move towards a more ecological understanding of culture. In other words, focusing on higher level social/ecological differences may illuminate where cultural values come from. For example, it is possible that population density (e.g., crowding) may influence micro-level cultural values and behavior in conflict and negotiation situations.

Communication

Communication and its paradigm

Communication is a highly diverse discipline, and at the most general level examines how people exchange messages in order to create meaning across various contexts, cultures, channels, and media. Here, we focus on the cross-cultural and intercultural sub-disciplines within communication science which examine major questions such as: *How does communication vary across cultures, in conflict situations and more generally across situations? What are the obstacles encountered when people from different cultures communicate? How can communication be improved in intercultural contexts?* as well as, *how do cultural values influence negotiation behavior and outcomes?* The *units of analysis* in these areas, similar to cross-cultural organizational behavior are most typically at the individual level or the dyad level. *Culture* is often conceptualized as shared values and/or assessed through individuals' self-construals at the individual level. The research *method* used includes a variety of experimental paradigms such as questionnaire surveys and behavioral simulations. Finally, unlike organizational behavior that has predominantly focused on cross-cultural comparisons, the communication field has had a long history of distinguishing such *cross-cultural*

comparative research from *intercultural* research (Gudykunst and Mody, 2002).

Key findings from communication

Comparative research on communication

One major contribution of the communication sciences to the study of culture and conflict is derived from Ting-Toomey's *Face-Negotiation Theory* (see Ting-Toomey, 2005, for a review). This theory examines cross-cultural differences in *face*, or "the claimed sense of favorable social self-worth that a person wants others to have of him or her" (Ting-Toomey and Kurogi, 1998, p. 187), which can be threatened, maintained, or enhanced, especially in emotionally vulnerable situations such as conflict. Face can be focused on the concern for one's own image (self-face), another's image (other-face), or both (mutual-face). Face-negotiation theory also examines cultural differences in *facework*, or the behavioral tendencies individuals have in maintaining or restoring face loss (Ting-Toomey, 2005). For example, while face and facework are universal communication phenomena, the meaning of face and how individuals enact facework differ across cultures. Individualists tend to have higher self-face concerns and use more self-oriented facework strategies whereas collectivists have higher other-face concerns and use more other-oriented facework strategies (Ting-Toomey et al., 1991; Oetzel et al. (2001). In addition, individualists tend to use direct, face-threatening conflict styles such as dominating, whereas collectivists tend to use more indirect, mutual face-saving conflict styles such as avoiding and obliging (Elsayed-Ekhouly and Buda, 1996; Gabrielidis et al., 1997; Ohbuchi, Fukushima, and Tedeschi, 1999; Oetzel and Ting-Toomey, 2003; Ting-Toomey and Kurogi, 1998; Ting-Toomey et al., 1991). Face and facework strategies also vary across high and low power distance societies. Ting-Toomey and Kurogi (1998) argue that in small power distance cultures, high status members tend to use verbally direct facework strategies such as disapproval and threatening strategies, while low status members tend to use defensive strategies to restore face loss. In contrast, in large power distance cultures, high status members tend to use verbally indirect facework strategies such as indirect questioning and relational pressuring, while low status members use self-effacing and self-criticizing strategies to accept face loss. As well, individuals in small power distance cultures use horizontal facework which minimizes status differences, whereas individuals in large power distance cultures use vertical facework which maximizes status differences (Oetzel et al., 2001).

Contextual factors also interact with culture in influencing face concerns. For example, Ting-Toomey (2005) argued that individualists are less likely to distinguish between ingroup and outgroup members during conflict, and consequently have self-face concerns when dealing with members from either group. By contrast, collectivists make a greater distinction between ingroups versus outgroups, and only have other-face concerns when dealing with ingroup members while having self-face concerns for outgroup members. In the experimental work on negotiation, Cai, Wilson, and Drake (2000) also illustrate the importance of another contextual factor – negotiators' roles (e.g., buyer or seller) – and how they differentially influence dyads high and low on collectivism (see also Drake, 2001).

Other work in the communication sciences have focused on cross-cultural variability in verbal and non-verbal communication styles that may have relevance for culture and conflict and negotiation research and problems experienced in intercultural contexts (see Gudykunst and Mody, 2002 for detailed review on cross-cultural verbal and non-verbal communication). For example, cultures vary in the value placed on speech (Lim, 2002). In the West, there is a rich tradition of placing great value on speech where words are assumed to carry universal meaning, whereas in the East, words are considered to be only part of the total communication context (see also Hall, 1976 on high and low context communication). Language style also varies considerably across cultures. For example, unlike English, Asian languages are characterized by various status-markers (e.g., honorific prefixes and suffixes, different sets of inflectional endings) and mechanisms to maintain group-orientedness (e.g., dropping of pronouns; see Kashima and Kashima, 1998). Cultures vary in their speech acts, or the task that is perceived to be important in communicating. For example, while factual answers are valued in the West, courtesy is valued in the East (Hall and Whyte, 1960). Related work shows that individualism is associated with the importance of clarity in conversation, whereas collectivism is associated with the importance of social-relational constraints such as minimizing impositions (Kim, 1994, 2005; Miyahara and Kim, 1993; Miyahara et al., 1998). Finally, culture also affects non-verbal aspects of communication that has relevance for conflict and negotiation (Andersen et al., 2002). Immediacy refers to actions that communicate interpersonal closeness through behaviors such as smiling, touching, eye contact, open body positions, and vocal animation. High contact cultures include South America, southern and eastern Europe, and the Middle East, whereas low contact cultures include Asia and northern Europe (Hall, 1966). Furthermore, it is argued that situations in which it is appropriate to show positive versus negative emotions differ across cultures. In high power distance cultures, people only show positive emotions toward high status members, and negative emotions to those with lower status (Andersen and Bowman, 1999; Matsumoto, 1991; Porter and Samovar, 1998).

Intercultural communication

Research in communication has long distinguished cross-cultural comparative research from intercultural research. One representative theory of effective intercultural communication is Gudykunst's (2005) anxiety/uncertainty management (AUM) theory, which was designed to explain interpersonal and intergroup communication effectiveness between ingroup members and strangers. The theory posits that interacting with strangers elicits uncertainty, a cognitive phenomenon of not being able to predict the stranger's attitudes, feelings, and behaviors, as well as anxiety, the affective equivalent of uncertainty. Gudykunst (2005) argues that communication effectiveness is a function of uncertainty and anxiety levels being above the minimum threshold and below the maximum threshold. Put simply, when uncertainty and anxiety are below the minimum threshold, one does not make an effort to communicate effectively because of over-confidence in the predictability of the stranger's behavior, as well as the lack of adrenaline. Communication is also not effective when anxiety and uncertainty are above the maximum threshold because one then lacks the confidence to be able to predict others while feeling overwhelmed.

AUM theory identifies a number of factors that influence the likelihood that uncertainty and anxiety are effectively managed. Ways in which people react to strangers, such as having tolerance for ambiguity, reduces uncertainty and anxiety, and prevents people from relying on their first impressions in interpreting others. How people socially categorize strangers also matter; for example, having positive stereotypes of strangers help decrease uncertainty and anxiety. Situational factors also influence uncertainty management processes. For example, the greater the power the ingroup has over strangers, the less the anxiety (Goodwin, Operario, and Fiske, 1998). Also, the connectedness and inclusion one feels towards strangers reduces uncertainty (Berger and Calabrese, 1975; Gudykunst, Chua, and Gray, 1987) and anxiety (Stephan and Stephan, 1985). Gudykunst (2005) also argues that the extent to which uncertainty and anxiety management leads to effective communication largely depends on a person's level of mindfulness, which includes skills such as learning about strangers' perspectives by being open to novelty, being alert to distinctions, having an implicit awareness of multiple perspectives, and having an orientation in the present (Langer, 1997). Research thus far generally supports AUM theory (see Gudykunst and Nishida, 2001; Gudykunst, Nishida, and Chua, 1986; Gudykunst and Shapiro, 1996; Hubbert, Gudykunst, and Guerrero, 1999).

Communication: summary and implications for organizational behavior/ psychology

In summary, research on culture and conflict/ negotiation in communication shares a number of similarities with the foci in OB/psychology. Both tend to focus on the individual/dyad level of analysis, and use similar methodologies such as questionnaire surveys and negotiation simulations. Numerous research traditions in communication could be fruitfully integrated with research in OB/ psychology to enrich our understanding of culture, conflict, and negotiation. For example, it would be worthwhile to move beyond just examining cognitive sources of intercultural misunderstanding in negotiation (i.e., interpretation issues), and incorporate the role of motivation, uncertainty and anxiety, and intergroup dynamics, borrowing from AUM theory. Examining the dynamics of non-verbal aspects of communication such as immediacy behaviors and emotional displays in comparative and intercultural conflict and negotiation research will be an important complement to extant work on verbal communication styles in culture and conflict/negotiation research. Integrating this further with other disciplines that focus on social structure is also an exciting frontier. Finally, the communication literature is also rich in its focus on nontangible resources that can be negotiated across cultures (e.g., identity, relationships, face) which can expand the economic focus in cross-cultural OB/psychology research.

International relations

Paradigm of international relations

International relations, a branch of political science that is concerned with foreign affairs among nation states is another discipline that examines culture and conflict, specifically in the context of international diplomatic negotiations. This field investigates *major questions* such as: *how does culture influence negotiators' perceptions and behaviors? When do cultural effects on negotiation become attenuated? What kinds of metaphors are used to understand negotiation in various cultures?* Research in IR is generally conducted at the individual and group levels of analysis. Although these topics of inquiry are similar to those asked in organizational behavior/psychology, international relations differs significantly in that there is generally a lack of consensus among scholars in international relations regarding the *relevance of culture* in negotiation. Consequently, there is a lot of discussion in the literature on *how culture should be treated* as a construct (see Zartman, 1993). Unlike organizational behavior/psychology, the *methodology* employed in international relations are more qualitative, including case studies, archives, interviews, autobiographies of negotiators, as well as direct observations conducted in the field. Finally, while *cross-cultural comparisons* are made in international relations, they are always derived comparing negotiators from different cultures as they directly engage in intercultural negotiations.

Key findings from international relations

In his book on negotiations across cultures, Cohen (1991, 1997) relies on detailed historical examples of bilateral diplomatic negotiations (during the post-war period) between the US and other non-western states, as well as supplementary evidence from autobiographies and interviews of diplomats in order to study how culture influences negotiation behavior. Integrating across case studies, Cohen (1991, 1997) observes that such abstract cultural differences are indeed reflected in specific behaviors at various stages of negotiation. In the *pre-negotiation stage*, individuals from high context cultures (Cohen, 1991, 1997) prefer to establish personal relationships with their counterparts prior to negotiating, to a much larger extent than individuals from low context cultures. For example, in the 1984 negotiations over reforms in Japan's financial markets, the abrupt manner of Treasury Secretary Donald Reagan who was seen as if he was cutting a deal on Wall Street offended many Japanese who considered diplomatic negotiations to be a more interpersonally delicate issue (*Economist*, October 27, 1984). In addition to establishing personal relationships prior to negotiating, in high context cultures, negotiators go to great lengths in order to prevent uncertain processes and outcomes that can lead to loss of face and shame. For example, the Japanese have evolved a number of strategies to prevent surprises such as gathering as much information as possible about their counterparts prior

to negotiating and relying on informal contacts for pre-negotiation assurances, commitments, and guarantees.

Cohen (1991, 1997) identifies a number of cultural differences in behaviors *during the actual negotiation* as well. For example, during opening moves, negotiators from high versus low context cultures seem to differ in their expectations of when it is appropriate to reveal information. Americans, who assume an equal playing field, expect negotiators to start revealing information immediately, but with expectation of reciprocity from their counterparts, resembling the procedures of adversarial law. The Japanese, however, who feel that initial disagreement is overly aggressive and impolite, expect negotiators to reveal information later on in the negotiation. Consequently, it seems that in intercultural contexts, such differences in the timing of information-sharing leads Americans to be at a disadvantage compared to the Japanese (Cohen, 1991, 1997).

The way in which negotiators present their arguments to their counterparts is another type of behavior with significant cultural variability during negotiations. Edmund Glenn, a former state department interpreter argued from practical experience that negotiators from various cultures generally use one of three styles of persuasion (Cohen, 1991, 1997): (1) the factual-inductive style, where persuasion is based on concrete factual details (instead of grand philosophical debates) which serve as basis for conclusions; (used by the State Department, Congress, and in American legal training); (2) the axiomatic-deductive style, where persuasion focuses on broader principles first which serve as the basis for more practical applications; and (3) the affective-intuitive style, where persuasion is based on emotion rather than logic. Differences in the American factual-inductive style and the Egyptian axiomatic-deductive style have caused miscommunications in diplomatic negotiations during the Middle East conflict in the 1960s. For example, President Johnson was confused when the only message sent from Egyptian President Nasser was the desire to be understood. In using an axiomatic-deductive style, President Nasser was trying to establish the broader principles of their relationship (i.e., whether their relationship was one of mutual respect, whether Egyptian concerns and Israeli concerns were to be given equal considerations etc.), rather than going straight to the practical, concrete details. In addition to the factual-inductive and axiomatic-deductive styles, cultures seem to differ on whether emotion or logic is predominantly used by negotiators in making arguments. For example, in hierarchical cultures such as Japan, negotiators often take on a supplicant posture and employ emotional appeals instead of logic when interacting with opponents of stronger power such as the US. For example, in the 1971 Japanese monetary crisis, the Japanese depended on the mercy of the US, arguing that Japan "is a small nation, poor in natural resources, and therefore dependent on foreign trade" (Angel, 1988).

Cohen argues that culture also influences the immediate context in which negotiation behaviors take place, for example, whether negotiators can exercise discretion as representatives of a group. For example, Mike Smith (interviewed by Cohen, March 11, 1996), a former deputy US trade representative notes that compared to Americans, the Japanese have smaller discretion during negotiation. Similar observations have been made of other hierarchical cultures, including Mexico (Bowers, interviewed by Frederick Williams, March 11, 1996), Egypt, China, and India (Cohen, 1997).

Finally, Cohen (1991, 1997) observes that not only does culture influence behaviors before and during negotiation, but *at the end of negotiation* as well. For example, negotiators from different cultures prefer varying degrees of formality or explicitness of agreements. Americans for instance, prefer explicit formal contracts that are to be implemented, whereas negotiators from high-context cultures prefer more informal agreements (e.g., unwritten arrangements) that have room to conceal embarrassing outcomes to save face, and are more flexible in terms of changes to be made in the future. In addition to the form of agreements, another cultural difference as it relates to the final stages of negotiation is the effect deadlines have on the subjective experience and behaviors of negotiators. For Americans, time is perceived to be a commodity that can be wasted, and negotiators are

particularly sensitive to the pressure to settle as deadlines approach, compared to negotiators from high context cultures. Especially given their shorter-term conception of negotiations coupled with impatience, Americans are often left at a disadvantage in diplomatic negotiations (Cohen, 1991, 1997).

While Cohen (1991, 1997) focused primarily on historical case studies, Faure (1999) conducted direct observations of intercultural negotiations in the field for six years, with a specific focus on China-US negotiations in order to study cross-cultural differences in negotiation. More specifically, he identifies how culture influences various aspects of negotiation, in terms of actors, structure, strategies, process, and outcome. First, in terms of *actors*, or general characteristics of negotiators, Faure (1999) observes that the Chinese are significantly influenced by historical memories of past international relations, often in the scale of hundreds to thousands of years, and use moral debt owed to China as a tactic in weakening the position of negotiators from different countries. Second, culture also seems to influence the *structure* of negotiations. He observes that it is typical for the number of individuals for a single negotiation party in China to consist of fifteen to thirty people, far greater than the American norm. Furthermore, it is more common in China than in the US for the real decision-maker to not be present in the negotiation in order to save face. Finally, in business contexts, the Chinese often view that they have more *power* than Americans, as they perceive themselves to be buyers and foreigners to be sellers. Third, culture influences negotiation *strategy*, where the Chinese adopt different metaphors when interacting with foreign versus domestic negotiators. For example, he argues that the metaphor used when interacting with foreigners is "mobile warfare," where counterparts are perceived to be barbarians, and strategies include competitive tactics such as frightening the other, making false concessions, inducing guilt, and wearing down their opponents physically and psychologically. In contrast, in domestic negotiations or in intercultural negotiations where the foreigner is perceived to understand some aspects of Chinese culture, the relevant metaphor becomes a "joint quest," where foreigners are perceived as civilized people and tactics involve more cooperative behaviors such as highly ritualized activity, indirect communication, and politeness. Finally, in terms of negotiation *process* and *outcomes*, Faure (1999) identifies similar patterns to Cohen (1991, 1997). For example, the Chinese spend more time on relationship-building prior to negotiation, use more emotional appeals, and prefer loose agreements and implementation over formal contracts, under the joint quest metaphor.

In other work in international relations, researchers have identified contextual factors that most likely *attenuate* or *bolster* the main effects of culture on negotiation. For example, Faure and Rubin (1993) studied a collection of case studies on intercultural river disputes and the negotiation of allocation of resources in geographically neighboring countries. Integrating across case studies, they identified several limiting or exacerbating conditions of cultural influences on negotiation. First, they argue that greater the cultural distance between the parties in an intercultural negotiation, the more complications arise. Second, they also argue that the more power asymmetry there is between the parties, the party with the least power is less likely to be influenced by culture, as behavior will be determined by compliance to high status parties. Finally, the greater the number of parties involved in the negotiation – that is – the more multilateral the negotiation is, the more likely that the main effects of culture are dampened.

While the discussion so far has focused on cultural comparisons of actual negotiation behaviors, in another stream of research, Cohen (2000, 2001a, 2001b) makes cultural comparisons of *language* used in the domain of negotiation as a window into how particular societies conceive of and frame negotiation. In other words, through language, culture-specific metaphors for negotiation are identified. In English-speaking cultures such as the US and the UK, the analysis of words reveal that a number of metaphors are used to construe negotiation as an activity. First, many negotiation-related terms are linked to the settlement of labor-management disputes which implies that negotiation as an activity is one in which rules

and procedures for conciliation are established. Thus, negotiations in the US and the UK involve non-violent tactics, disputes are resolved fairly and effectively, the party with lower power will not be ignored, and outcomes result from compromise and mutual concessions. Second, Americans conceptualize negotiation as similar to engineering, where they have a very "can do" attitude in believing that every conflict, akin to a scientific "problem" can be resolved through dispassionate, rational analysis. Third, Christian theology is another theme of negotiation, where words such as "good faith" implies that negotiators have a sincere commitment to resolve conflict with an honest intention of implementing agreements. Finally, words such as "equal playing field," "play by the rules," and "fair play" suggest that negotiation is conceptualized similarly to sports, where the contest of negotiation is ruled by fairness (Cohen, 2001a).

In Arabic cultures by contrast, negotiation is conceptualized very differently. For example, the theme of honor is pervasive as evident in the words relevant to negotiation such as "sharaf" (standing, honor), "ird" (dignitiy, honor), and "wajh" (face, reputation). In Arabic culture, clan rivalry is endemic and conflict arises over many issues, including women, land, property, and family name, each with the risk of igniting blood revenge or retribution, "tha'r." The word for conflict, "niza", does not distinguish between "dispute" and "conflict" as in the West, and is consistent with the tendency for disputes over trivial matters to quickly turn into issues of honor. Furthermore, the word for "compromise" ("hal wasat") does not have the positive connotation as it does in the west, as compromise over principles such as honor is viewed negatively. In addition to the theme of honor, Islamic ethics is another predominant theme in negotiation in Arabic cultures. For example, in "tahkim," or formal arbitration, the goal of the arbitrator is not just to make a judicial ruling, but to reconcile the antagonists as judicial rulings that reflect moral lessons for the society at large (Cohen, 2001a).

In Hebrew, negotiation involves religious themes, including the Bible, Judaism, and Jewish law which give negotiations a moralistic tone, as well as Zionism and war which give negotiations a combative tone (Cohen, 2000). In Jewish culture, political negotiations are grounded in "shakla vetarya," or the studying and debate of the Talmud 'and Mishna. Thus, negotiation is conceptualized as an intellectual duel and problems are never definitively resolved, as the presence of a solution would imply closure (Cohen, 2000).

International relations: summary and implications for organizational behavior/psychology

In summary, international relations and organizational behavior/psychology focus on the question of how culture influences negotiation perceptions and behavior. However, unlike organizational behavior/psychology, which relies on laboratory experiments, international relations relies on qualitative methods that allow for rich contextual descriptions of how culture impacts real-life political negotiations. Given the qualitative nature of the data, however, these observations may not be statistically representative. Furthermore, with no variables held constant, the observations are suggestive tendencies at best, or hypotheses for future research (Cohen, 1991, 1997). The review illustrates numerous interesting avenues for future synergies across disciplines. For example, research in OB/psychology tends to examine how culture impacts actual, one-shot negotiations, and the case studies reviewed in this section suggest that it is critical to examine how culture influences negotiators before and after the actual negotiation. For example, it would be interesting to examine whether culture influences the ways in which outcomes of previous negotiations influence the dynamics of current negotiations, and whether culture influences how and when negotiation agreements are implemented. It would also be worthwhile to examine cultural differences in negotiators' perception of time and deadlines. The international relations literature helps to identify a number of contextual variables, such as power asymmetries, that may interact with culture in influencing intercultural negotiation behavior. In addition, the work on metaphors shows that language is not a neutral entity, but one that carries

culture (see also Gelfand and McCusker, 2002). Thus, it is important to study not only intercultural negotiations that are conducted in English, but those that are conducted in other languages as well. Other contextual variables for future intercultural negotiation research include cultural distance between the two cultures, multilateral negotiations, and negative historical memory (e.g., Faure, 1999). As with the communication literature, IR research on culture, conflict, and negotiation suggests that non-economic outcomes, including the quality of personal relationships, status, face, and honor, are critical to examine in future research.

Conclusion

We began this chapter with a call for interdisciplinary research on culture, conflict, and negotiation, arguing that the complexity of this topic invites and even demands knowledge from multiple disciplines. In order to start the interdisciplinary conversation, we reviewed prototypical work from a wide range of disciplines, including organizational behavior/psychology, legal anthropology, comparative law, language and disputing, cognitive anthropology, experimental economics, primatology, communication, and international relations, highlighting their commonalities and their differences. Not surprisingly, while all are concerned with how culture influences conflict and negotiation, different disciplines have a penchant for different research questions, different units of analysis, different ways in which culture is conceptualized, and different methodologies. By highlighting key insights and approaches from many disciplines to culture, conflict, and negotiation, we are beginning to map the scientific terrain that collectively address relevant factors in the broad topic of culture, conflict, and negotiation.

We have much optimism that the most important new insights in the area of culture, conflict, and negotiation will come from creative interdisciplinary mergers in theory and methods. Throughout the chapter, we gave examples of natural "cultural mergers" between OB/psychology and other disciplines studying culture, conflict, and negotiation. For example, the psychological perspective offered in OB/psychology can be fruitfully integrated with notions of social structure (legal anthropology), ecology (primatology), linguistic analyses (language and disputing), incentives (experimental economics), power and history (international relations), institutional factors (comparative law), variance in cultural meanings (cognitive anthropology), among others. OB/psychology research on culture and negotiation will likewise benefit from methodological approaches that have proved useful in its sister disciplines.

At the same time, it is worth noting that interdisciplinary research on culture, conflict, and negotiation will likely itself be subject to the very same difficulties that have been identified in managing interdependence across cultures. Scientific disciplines have their own cultures, and interdisciplinary teams will invariably find that they are managing culture conflict as they study this very phenomenon. Differences in worldviews, scientific language, and priorities that are entrenched in different disciplinary paradigms will make the research process both more rewarding but more difficult (and time-consuming). As well, new structures and scientific outlets will need to be created to counter the discipline-focused tradition that characterizes academe. Yet like other topics covered in the *Handbook*, culture, conflict, and negotiation is complex, multi-level, and dynamic topic that requires deep and diverse cultural perspectives from many disciplines. We hope this chapter will help to start to build such necessary interdisciplinary bridges.

References

Adair, W. L. 1999. "U.S. and Japanese mental models for negotiation", paper presented at the Conference of the International Association of Conflict Management, San Sebastian, Spain, June.

and Brett, J. M. 2005. "The negotiation dance: time, culture, and behavioral sequences in negotiation", *Organizational Science* 16: 33–51.

Brett, J. M., Lempereur, A., Okumura, T., Shikhirev, P., Tinsley, C. H., and Lytle, A. 2004. "Culture and negotiation strategy", *Negotiation Journal* 20: 87–111.

Okumura, T., and Brett, J. M. 2001. "Negotiation behavior when cultures collide: the United States and Japan", *Journal of Applied Psychology* 86: 371–85.

Adler, N. J., Brahm, R., and Graham, J. L. 1992. "Strategy implementation: a comparison of face-to-face negotiations in the People's Republic of China and the United States", *Strategic Management Journal* 13: 449–66.

Graham, J. L, and Gehrke, T. S. 1987. "Business negotiations in Canada, Mexico, and the U.S.", *Journal of Business Research* 15: 411–29.

Andersen, P. A., and Bowman, L. 1999. "Positions of power: Nonverbal influence in organizational communication", in L. K. Guerrero, J. A. DeVito, and M. L. Hecht (eds.), *The Nonverbal Communication Reader: Classic and Contemporary Readings* Prospect Heights, IL: Waveland, pp. 317–34.

Hecht, M. L., Hoobler, G. D., and Smallwood, M. 2002. "Nonverbal communication across cultures", in W. B. Gudykunst and B. Mody (eds.), *Handbook of International and Intercultural Communication* (2nd edn). Thousand Oaks, CA: Sage, pp. 89–106.

Angel, R. 1988. "Meeting the Japanese challenge, 1969-1971: balance-of-payments problems force the Nixon administration to act", *Pew Program in Case Teaching and Writing in International Affairs*. Case 135, pp. 13–14.

Ashraf, N., Bohnet, I., and Piankov, N. 2006. "Decomposing trust and trustworthiness", *Experimental Economics* 9: 193–208

Aubert, V. 1967. *Rettssosiologi (translation: sociology of law*. Oslo, Universitets-forlaget.

Aureli, F., and de Waal, F. B. M. 1997. "Inhibition of social behavior in chimpanzee under high-density conditions", *American Journal of Primatology* 41: 213–28.

Avruch, K. 1998. *Culture and Conflict Resolution*. Washington: US Institute of Peace Press.

Bazerman, M. H. and Carroll, J. S. 1987. "Negotiator cognition", *Research in Organizational Behavior* 9: 247–88.

Berg, J., Dickhaut, J., and McCabe, K. 1995. "Trust, reciprocity and social history", *Games and Economic Behavior* 10: 122–42.

Berger, C. R., and Calabrese, R. J. 1975. "Some explorations in initial interaction and beyond: toward a theory of interpersonal communication", *Human Communication Research* 1: 99–112.

Bierbrauer, G. 1994. "Toward an understanding of legal culture: variations in individualism and collectivism between Kurds, Lebanese, and Germans", *Law and Society Review* 28: 243–64.

Black, D. 1993. *The Social Structure of Right and Wrong.* San Diego, CA: Academic Press.

Blurton Jones, N. 1984. "Selfish origin of human food sharing: tolerated theft", *Ethology and Sociobiology* 5: 1–3.

Boggs, S. T., and Chun, M. N. 1990. "Ho'oponopono: a Hawaiian method of solving interpersonal problems", in K. Gegeo-White and G. M. White (eds.), *Disentangling: Conflict Discourse in Pacific Societies.* Stanford, CA: Stanford University Press, pp. 122–60.

Bohnet, I., Grieg, F., Hermann, B., and Zeckhauser, R. 2008."Betrayal aversion: Evidence from Brazil, China, Oman, Switzerland, Turkey, and the United States", *American Economic Review* 98: 294–310.

Herrmann, B., and Zeckhauser, R. "The requirements for trust in Gulf and Western countries", (forthcoming) *Quarterly Journal of Economics.*

Brannen, M. Y., and Salk, J. E. 2000. "Partnering across borders: negotiating organizational culture in a German-Japanese joint venture", *Human Relations* 53: 451–87.

Brenneis, D. 1988. "Language and disputing", in D. Siegel, A. Beals, and S. Tyler (eds.), *Annual Review of Anthropology.* Palo Alto: Annual Reviews, pp. 221–37.

Brenneis, D. 1990. "Dramatic gestures: the Fiji Indian pancayat as therapeutic event", in K. Gegeo-White and G. M. White (eds.), *Disentangling: Conflict Discourse in Pacific Societies.* Stanford, CA: Stanford University Press, pp. 214–38.

Brett, J. M. and Okumura, T. 1998. "Inter- and intra-cultural negotiation: U.S. and Japanese negotiators", *Academy of Management Journal* 41: 495–510.

Brogger, J. 1968. "Conflict resolution and the role of the bandit in peasant society", *Anthropological Quarterly* 41: 228–40.

Brunner, J. A., and Taoka, G. M. 1977. "Marketing and negotiating in the People's Republic of China: Perceptions of American businessmen who attended the 1975 Canton Fair", *Journal of International Business Studies* 8: 69–82.

Buchan, N. R., and Croson, R. T. 2004. "The boundaries of trust: own and other's actions in the U.S. and China", *Journal of Economic Behavior and Organization* 55: 485–504.

Croson, R. T., and Dawes, R. M. 2002. "Swift neighbors and persistent strangers: a cross-cultural investigation of trust and reciprocity in social exchange", *American Journal of Sociology* 108: 168–206.

Croson, R. T., and Johnson, E. J. 2004. "When do fair beliefs influence bargaining behavior: experimental bargaining in Japan and the United States", *Journal of Consumer Research* 31: 181–90.

Johnson, E. J., and Croson, R. T. 2006. "Let's get personal: an international examination of the influence of communication, culture, and social distance on other regarding preferences", *Journal of Economic Behavior and Organization* 60: 373–98.

Cai, D. A., Wilson, S. R., and Drake, L. E. 2000. "Culture in the context of intercultural negotiation", *Human Communication Research* 26: 591–617.

Camerer, C. F. 2003. *Behavioral Game Theory: Experiments in Strategic Interaction.* Princeton, NJ: Prince University Press.

Cameron, L. 1999. "Raising the stakes in the Ultimatum game: experimental evidence from Indonesia", *Economic Inquiry* 37: 47–59.

Campbell, C. G., Graham, J. L., Jolibert, A., Meissner, H. G. 1988. "Marketing Negotiations in France, Germany, U.K. and the U.S", *Journal of Marketing* 52: 49–62.

Cappelletti, M. and Garth, B. G. 1987. "Chapter 1: Introduction – Policies, trends, and ideas in civil procedure", *International Encyclopedia of Comparative Law* 16: 25–6.

Chase, O. G. 1997. "Legal processes and national culture", *Cardozo Journal of International and Comparative Law* 7: 81–90.

2005. *Law, Culture, and Ritual.* New York, NY: New York University Press.

Chen X. and Li, S. 2005. "Cross-national differences in cooperative decision-making in mixed-motive business contexts: the mediating effect of vertical and horizontal individualism", *Journal of International Business Studies* 36: 622–36.

Chen, Y. R., Mannix, E. A., and Okumura, T. 2003. "The importance of who you meet: effects of self- versus other-concerns among negotiators in the United States, the People's Republic of China, and Japan", *Journal of Experimental Social Psychology* 39: 1–15.

Cohen, R. 1991. *Negotiating Across Cultures*. Washington: US Institute of Peace Press.

1997. *Negotiating Across Cultures* (2nd edn.). Washington: US Institute of Peace Press.

2000. "Meaning, interpretation, and international negotiation", *Global Society* 14: 317–35.

2001a. "Language and conflict resolution: the limits of English", *International Studies Review* 3: 25–51.

2001b. "Language and negotiation: a Middle East lexicon", Retrieved November 1, 2007, from Language and Diplomacy website: http://diplo. diplomacy.edu/books/language_and_diplomacy/ bookasp.asp?url=texts/excerpts/cohen.htm.

Cohn, B. S. 1959. "Some notes on law and change in North India", *Economic Development and Cultural Change* 8: 79–93.

Committee on Facilitating Interdisciplinary Research, National Academy of Sciences, National Academy of Engineering, and Institute of Medicine. 2004. *Facilitating Interdisciplinary Research*. Washington, DC: The National Academies Press.

Conley, J. M. and O'Barr, W. M. 1990. *Rules Versus Relationships: The Ethnography of Legal Discourse*. Chicago, IL: Chicago University Press.

Cords, M. and Thurnheer, S. 1993. "Reconciling with valuable partners by long-tailed macaques", *Ethology* 93: 315–25.

Corsaro, W. and Rizzo, T. 1990. "Disputes in the peer culture of American and Italian nursery-school children", in A. Grimshaw (ed.), *Conflict Talk: Sociolinguistic Investigations in Arguments in Conversations* Cambridge, MA: Cambridge University Press, pp. 21–66.

Damaska, M. R. 1997. *Evidence Law Adrift*. New Haven, CT: Yale University Press.

Danzig, R. 1973. "Toward the creation of a complementary decentralized system of criminal justice", *Stanford Law Review* 26: 1–54.

De Waal, F. B. M. 1982. *Chimpanzee Politics: Power and Sex Among Apes*. Baltimore, MD: Johns Hopkins University Press.

1989. "The myth of a simple relation between space and aggression in captive primates", *Zoo Biology Supplement* 1: 141–8.

2000. "Primates: A natural heritage of conflict resolution", *Science* 289: 586–90.

Aureli, F., and Judge, P. G. 2000. "Coping with crowding", *Scientific American* 282: 76–81.

Doney, P. M., Cannon, J. P., and Mullen, M. R. 1998. "Understanding the influence of national culture on the development of trust", *Academy of Management Review* 23: 601–20.

Drake, L. E. 2001. "The culture-negotiation link: integrative and distributive bargaining through an intercultural communication lens", *Human Communication Research* 27: 317–49.

Duranti, A. 1990. "Doing things with words: conflict, understanding, and change in the Samoan 'fono'", in K. Gegeo-White and G. M. White (eds.), *Disentangling: Conflict Discourse in Pacific Societies*. Stanford, CA: Stanford University Press, pp. 459–89.

Earley, P. C. and Ang, S. 2003. *Cultural Intelligence: Individual Interactions Across Cultures*. Stanford, CA: Stanford University Press.

Economist 1984. October 27.

Elsayed-Ekhouly, S. M. and Buda, R. 1996. "Organizational conflict: A comparative analysis of conflict style across cultures", *International Journal of Conflict Management* 7: 71–81.

Faure, G. O. 1999. "The cultural dimension of negotiation: the Chinese case", *Group Decision and Negotiation* 8: 187–215.

2000. "Negotiations to set up joint ventures in China", *International Negotiation* 5: 157–89.

and Rubin, J. Z. 1993. *Culture and Negotiation*. Newbury Park, CA: Sage.

Feldman, E. A. 2007. "Law, culture, and conflict: dispute resolution in postwar Japan", *Public Law and Legal Theory Research Paper Series, Research Paper No. 07–16*.

Felstiner, W. 1974–1975. "Influences of social organization on dispute processing", *Law and Society Review*, 9: 63–94.

Fishman, R. and Khanna, T. 1999. "Is trust a historical residue? Information flows and trust level", *Journal of Economic Behavior and Organization* 38: 79–92.

Flack, J. C., de Waal, F. B. M, and Krakauer, D. C. 2005. "Social structure, robustness, and policing cost in a cognitively sophisticated species", *American Naturalist* 165: E126–E139.

Girvan, M., de Waal, F. B. M. and Krakauer, D. C. 2006. "Policing stabilizes construction of social niches in primates", *Nature* 439: 426–29.

Krakauer, D. C., and de Waal, F. B. M. 2005. "Robustness mechanisms in primate societies: a perturbation study", *Proceedings of the Royal Society London* B 272: 1091–9.

Fortes, M. and Evans-Pritchard, E. E. 1940. *African Political Systems*. Oxford: Oxford University Press.

Fukuyama, F. 1995. *Trust: The Social Virtues and the Creation of Prosperity*. New York, NY: Free Press.

Gabrielidis, C., Stephan, W. G., Ybarra, O., Dos Santos Pearson, V.M., and Villareal, L. 1997. "Preferred styles of conflict resolution: Mexico and the United States", *Journal of Cross-Cultural Psychology* 28: 661–77.

Gelfand, M. J., and Christakopoulou, S. 1999. "Culture and negotiator cognition: Judgement accuracy and negotiation processes in individualistic and collectivistic cultures", *Organizational Behavior and Human Decision Proceeses* 79: 248–69.

and Dyer, N. 2000. "A cultural perspective on negotiation: Progress, pitfalls, and prospects", *Applied Psychology: An International Review* 49: 62–99.

Erez, M., and Aycan, Z. 2007. "Cross-Cultural Organizational Behavior", *Annual Review of Psychology* 58: 479–514.

Higgins, M., Nishii, L. H., Raver, J. L., Dominguez, A., Murakami, F., Yamaguchi, S., and Toyama, M. 2002. "Culture and egocentric perceptions of fairness in conflict and negotiation", *Journal of Applied Psychology* 87: 833–45.

and McCusker, C. 2002. "Metaphor and the cultural construction of negotiation: a paradigm for theory and research", in M. Gannon and K. L. Newman (eds.), *Handbook of Cross-Cultural Management*. New York, NY: Blackwell, pp. 292–314.

Nishii, L. H., Holcombe, K. M, Dyer, N., Ohbuchi, K., and Fukuno, M. 2001. "Cultural influences on cognitive representations of conflict: interpretations of conflict episodes in the United States and Japan", *Journal of Applied Psychology* 86: pp. 1059–74.

and Realo, A. 1999. "Individualism-collectivism and accountability in intergroup negotiations", *Journal of Applied Psychology* 84: 721–36.

Gluckman, M. 1955. *The Judicial Process Among the Barotse of Northern Rhodesia*. Manchester: University Press for the Rhodes-Livingstone Institute.

1959. *Custom and Conflict in Africa*. Glencoe, IL: The Free Press.

Goodwin, S. A., Operario, D., and Fiske, S. T. 1998. "Situational power and interpersonal dominance facilitate bias and inequality", *Journal of Social Issues* 54: 677–98.

Graham, J. L. 1984. "Comparison of Japan and U.S. business negotiation", *International Journal of Research in Marketing* 1: 51–68.

Evenko, L. I. and Rajan, M. N. 1993. "An empirical comparison of Soviet and American business negotiations", *International Journal of Business Studies* 23: 387–418.

Grimshaw, A. 1990. *Conflict Talk: Sociolinguistic Investigations in Arguments in Conversations*. Cambridge: Cambridge University Press.

Gudykunst, W. B. 2005. "An anxiety/uncertainty management (AUM) theory of strangers' intercultural adjustment", in W. B. Gudykunst (ed.), *Theorizing About Intercultural Communication*. Thousand Oaks, CA: Sage, pp. 419–58.

Chua, E. G., and Gray, A. J. 1987. "Cultural dissimilarities and uncertainty reduction processes", *Communication Yearbook* 10: 456–69.

and Mody, B. 2002. *Handbook of International and Intercultural Communication* (2nd edn). Thousand Oaks, CA: Sage.

and Nishida, T. 2001. "Anxiety, uncertainty, and perceived effectiveness of communication across relationships and cultures", *International Journal of Intercultural Relations* 25: 55–73.

Nishida, T., and Chua, E. 1986. "Uncertainty reduction in Japanese-North American dyads", *Communication Research Reports* 3: 39–46.

and Shapiro, R. 1996. "Communication in everyday interpersonal and intergroup encounters", *International Journal of Intercultural Relations* 20: 19–45.

Gulliver, P. H. 1969. "Dispute settlement without courts: the Ndendeuli of Southern Tanzania", in L. Nader (ed.), *Law in Culture and Society*. Chicago, IL: Aldine, pp. 24–68.

Hahm, P. C. 1969. *Religion and Law in Korea*. Berkeley, CA: Kroeber Anthropological Society Press.

Haley, J. O. 1978. "The myth of the reluctant litigant", *Journal of Japanese Studies* 4: 359–89.

Hall, E. T. 1976. *Beyond Culture*. Garden City, NY: Doubleday/Anchor.

and Whyte, W. F. 1960. "Intercultural communication", *Human Organization* 19: 5–12.

Hamilton, V. L. and Sanders, J. 1992. *Everyday Justice: Responsibility and the Individual in Japan and the United States*. New Haven, CT: Yale University Press.

Henrich, J. 2000. "Does culture matter in economic behavior: ultimatum game bargaining among the Machiguenga", *American Economic Review* 90: 973–80.

Boyd, R., Bowles, S., Camerer, C., Fehr, E., Gintis, H., and McClreath, R. 2001. "In search of homo economicus: behavioral experiments in 15 small-scale societies", *American Economic Review* 91: 73–84.

Boyd, R., Bowles, S., Camerer, C., Fehr, E., Gintis, H., McElreath, R., Alvard, M., Barr, Al., Eensminger, J., Henrich, N. S., Hill, K., Gil-White, F., Gurvan, M., Marlowe, F. W., Patton, J. Q., and Tracer, D. 2005. "'Economic man' in cross-cultural perspective: Behavioral experiments in 15 small-scale societies", *Behavioral and Brain Sciences* 28: 795–855.

Herodotus, Marincola, J. M. and de Selincourt, A. 2003. *The Histories*. London, UK: Penguin Classics.

Hoebel, E. A. 1954. *The Law of Primitive Man: A Study in Comparative Legal Dynamics*. Cambridge, MA: Harvard University Press.

Hofstede, G. 1980. *Culture's Consequences: International Differences in Work-Related Values*. Newbury Park, CA: Sage.

Hubbert, K. N., Gudykunst, W. B., and Guerrero, S. L. 1999. "Intergroup communication over time", *International Journal of Intercultural Relations* 32: 13–46.

Imai, L. and Gelfand, M. J. 2007. "Culturally intelligent negotiators: the impact of CQ on intercultural negotiation effectiveness",

Academy of Management Best Paper Proceedings.

Judge, P. G. 2000. "Coping with crowded conditions", in Aureli, F., and de Waal, F. B. M. (eds.), *Natural Conflict Resolution*. Berkeley, CA: University of California Press, pp. 129–54.

and de Waal, F. B. M. 1997. "Rhesus monkey behavior under diverse population densities: coping with long-term crowding", *Animal Behavior* 54: 643–62.

Kafatos, F. and Eisner, T. 2004. "Unification in the century of biology", *Science* 303: 1257.

Kashima, E. S. and Kashima, Y. 1998. "Culture and language: the case of cultural dimensions and personal pronoun use", *Journal of Cross-Cultural Psychology* 29: 461–86.

Kawashima, T. 1963. "Dispute resolution in contemporary Japan", in von Mehren (ed.), *Law in Japan: Legal Order in a Changing Society*. Cambridge, MA: Harvard University Press, pp. 41–8.

Kim, C. and Lawson, C. M. 1979. "The law of the subtle mind: The traditional Japanese conception of law", *International and Comparative Law Quarterly* 28: 491–513.

Kim, M. 1994. "Cross-cultural comparisons of the perceived importance of conversational constraints", *Human Communication Research* 21: 128–51.

2005. "Culture-based conversational constraints theory: individual- and culture-level analyses", in W. B. Gudykunst, (ed.), *Theorizing About Intercultural Communication*. Thousand Oaks, CA: Sage, pp. 93–118.

Kobayashi, N. 1988. "Strategic alliances with Japanese firms", *Long Range Planning* 21: 29–34.

Koch, K. F. 1974. *War and Peace in Jalemo: The Management of Conflict in Highland New Guinea*. Cambridge, MA: Harvard University Press.

1979. "Introduction: Access to justice: an anthropological perspective", in K. F. Koch (ed.), *Access to Justice Vol. 4: The Anthropological Perspective: Patterns of Conflict Management: Essays in the Ethnography of Law*. Alphen aan den Rijn: Sijthoff and Noordhoff, pp. 1–16.

Sodergren, J. A. and Campbell, S. 1976. "Political and psychological correlates of conflict management: a cross-cultural study", *Law and Society Review* 10: 443–66.

Kramer, R. M., and Messick, D. M. 1995. *Negotiation as a Social Process: New Trends in Theory and Research*. Thousand Oaks, CA: Sage.

Langbein, J. H. 1985. "The German advantage in civil procedure", *University of Chicago Law Review* 52: 823–66.

Langer, Ellen J. 1997. *The Power of Mindful Learning*. Reading, MA: Addison-Wesley.

La Porta, R., Lopez-de-Salannes, F., Shleifer, A., and Vishny, R. 1997. "Trust in large organizations", *American Economic Review Papers and Proceedings* 87: 333–8.

Lauchli, U. M. 2000. "Cross-cultural negotiations, with a special focus on ADR with the Chinese", *William Mitchell Law Review* 26: 1045–73.

Lee, K. H., and Lo, W. C. 1988. "American business-people's perceptions of marketing and negotiations in the People's Republic of China", *International Marketing Review* 5: 41–51.

Leung, K. 1987. "Some determinants of reactions to procedural models for conflict resolution: a cross – national study", *Journal of Personality and Social Psychology* 53: 898–908.

Lim, T. 2002. "Language and verbal communication across cultures", in W. B. Gudykunst and B. Mody (eds.), *Handbook of International and Intercultural Communication* (2nd edn). Thousand Oaks, CA: Sage, pp. 69–88.

Lowy, M. J. 1973. "Modernizing the American legal system: an example of the peaceful use of anthropology", *Human Organization* 32: 205–9.

Marlowe, F. W. 2004. "What explains Hadza food sharing?", in M. Alvard (ed.), *Research in Economic Anthropology: Socioeconomic Aspects of Human Behavioral Ecology* (vol. 23). Greenwich, CT: JAI Press, pp. 67–86.

Matsumoto, D. 1991. "Cultural influences on facial expressions of emotion." *Southern Communication Journal* 56: 128–37.

McKellin, W. H. 1990. "Allegory and inference: Intentional ambiguity in Managalase negotiations", in K. Gegeo-White and G. M. White (eds.), *Disentangling: Conflict Discourse in Pacific Societies*. Stanford, CA: Stanford University Press, pp. 335–70.

Medin, D. L., Ross, N. O., and Cox, D. G. 2006. *Culture and Resource conflict: Why Meanings Matter*. New York, NY: Russell Sage Foundation.

Miyahara, A., and Kim, M. S. 1993. "Requesting styles among 'collectivists' cultures: a comparison between Japanese and Koreans", *Intercultural Communication Studies* 6: 104–28.

Kim, M. S., Shin, H. C., and Yoon, K. 1998. "Conflict resolution styles among 'Collectivist' cultures: a comparison between Japanese and Koreans", *International Journal of Intercultural Relations* 22: 505–25.

Morris, M. W., and Fu, H. 2001. "How does culture influence conflict resolution? A dynamic constructivist analysis", *Social Cognition* 19: 324–49.

Leung, K., and Iyengar, S. S. 2004. "Person perception in the heat of conflict: negative trait attributions affect procedural preferences and account for situational and cultural differences", *Asian Journal of Social Psychology* 7: 127–47.

Moser, L. J. 1986. "Cross-cultural dimensions: U.S.-Japan", in D. B. Bendahmane and L. Moser (eds.), *Toward a better understanding: U.S.-Japan Relations*, Washington DC: Foreign Services Institute, pp. 21–36.

Nader, L. 1965. "Choices of legal procedure: Shia Moslem and Mexican Zapotec", *American Anthropologist*, 67: 394–99.

1969. "Styles of court procedure: to make the balance", in L. Nader (ed.), *Law in Culture and Society*. Chicago, IL: Aldine pp. 69–91.

and Todd, H. F. 1978. *The Disputing Process: Law in Ten Societies*. New York, NY: Columbia University Press.

Nair, A. S. and Stafford, E. R. 1998. "Strategic alliances in China: Negotiating the barriers", *Long Range Planning* 31(1): 39–46.

Newman, K. 1983. *Law and economic organization: a comparative study of pre-industrial societies*. New York, NY: Cambridge University Press.

Oetzel, J. G. and Ting-Toomey, S. 2003. "Face concerns in interpersonal conflict. a cross-cultural empirical test of the face negotiation theory", *Communication Research* 30: 599–624.

Ting-Toomey, S., Matsumoto, T., Yokochi, Y., Pan, X., Takai, J., and Wilcox, R. 2001. "Face and facework in conflict: a cross-cultural comparison of China, Germany, Japan, and the United States", *Communication Monographs* 68: 235–58.

Ohbuchi, K., Fukushima, O., and Tedeschi, J. T. 1999. "Cultural values in conflict management: goal orientation, goal attainment, and tactical decision", *Journal of Cross-Cultural Psychology* 30: 51–71.

Oosterbeek, H., Sloof, R., and van Kuilen, G. 2003. "Cultural differences in ultimatum game experiments: evidence from a meta-analysis", *Experimental Economics* 7: 171–88.

Ouchi, W. 1981. *Theory 2*. Reading, MA: Addison-Wesley.

Philips, S. U. 1972. "Participant structures and communicative competence: Warm Springs children in community and classroom", in C. B. Cazden, V. P. John, and D. Hymes (eds.), *Functions of Language in the Classroom*, New York, NY: Teachers College Press, pp. 370–94.

Popper, K. R. 1963. *Conjectures and Refutations: The Growth of Scientific Knowledge*. New York, NY: Routledge and Kegan Paul.

Porter, R. E. and Samovar, L. A. 1998. "Cultural influences on emotional expression: implications for intercultural communication", in P. A. Andersen and L. K. Guerrero. (eds.), *Handbook of Communication and Emotion: Research, Theory, Applications, and Context*. San Diego, CA: Academic Press, pp. 449–62.

Probst, T. M., Carnevale, P. J., and Triandis, H. C. 1999. "Cultural values in intergroup and single-group social dilemmas", *Organizational Behavior and Human Decision Processes* 77: 171–91.

Putnam, R. D. 1993. *Making Democracy Work: Civic Traditions in Modern Italy*. Princeton, NJ: Princeton University Press.

Rahim, M. A. 1983. "A measure of the styles of handling interpersonal conflict." *Academy of Management Journal*, 26: 368–76.

Ramseyer, J. M. 1988. "Reluctant litigant revisited: rationality and disputes in Japan", *Journal of Japanese Studies* 14: 111–12.

Robertson, T., and Beasley, D. 2007. *Anthropological theories: A guide prepared by students for students*. Retrieved November 1, 2007, from Department of Anthropology College of Arts and Sciences The University of Alabama. Available at www.as.ua.edu/ant?Faculty/murphy/436/coganth.htm.

Romney, A. K., Weller, S. C., and Batchelder, W. H. 1986. "Culture as consensus: a theory of culture and informant accuracy", *American Anthropologist* 88: 318–38.

Ross, M. H. 1986. "A cross-cultural theory of political conflict and violence", *Political Psychology* 7: 427–69.

1993. *The Management of Conflict: Interpretations and Interests in Comparative Perspective*. New Haven, CT: Yale University Press.

Roth, A. E., Prasnikar, V., Okuno-Fujiwara, M., and Zamir, S. 1991. "Bargaining and market behavior in Jerusalem, Ljublijana, Pittsburgh and Tokyo: an experimental study", *American Economic Review* 81: 1068–95.

Sampson, E. E. 1993. "Identity politics: challenges to psychology's understanding", *American Psychologist* 48: 1219–30.

Sato, Y. 2001. *Commercial Dispute Processing and Japan*. New York, NY: Kluwer Law International.

Schlesinger, R. B., Baade, H. B., Herzog, P. E., and Wise, E. M. 1998. *Comparative Law* (6th edn). New York, NY: Foundation Press.

Schwartz, S. H. 1994. "Beyond individualism/collectivism: New cultural dimensions of values", in U. T. H. C. Kim (ed.), *Individualism and Collectivism: Theory, Method, and Applications. Cross-cultural Research and Methodology Series*, vol 18. Thousand Oaks, CA: Sage, pp. 85–119.

Shapera, I. 1956. *Government and Politics in Tribal Societies*. London: C. A. Watts.

Smith, J. C. 1987. "Ajase and Oedipus: ideas of the self in Japanese and Western legal consciousness", *Osaka University Law Review* 34: 1.

Starr, J. O. 1978. *Dispute and Settlement in Rural Turkey: An Ethnography of Law*. Leiden: E.J. Brill.

and Yngvesson, B. 1975. "Scarcity and disputing: Zeroing-in on compromise decisions", *American Ethnologist* 2: 553–66.

Stephan, W. G., and Stephan, C. W. 1985. "Intergroup anxiety", *Journal of Social Issues* 41: 157–75.

Stewart, S. and Keown, C. 1989. "Talking with the dragon: negotiating in the People's Republic of China", *Columbia Journal of World Business* 24: 68–72.

Strong, K. and Weber, J. 1998. "The myth of the trusting culture: a global, empirical assessment", *Business and Society* 37: 157–83.

Thierry, B. 2000. "Covariation of conflict management patterns across macaque species", in F. Aureli and F. B. M. de Waal (eds.), *Natural Conflict Resolution* Berkeley, CA: University of California Press, pp. 106–28.

Ting-Toomey, S. 2005. "The matrix of face: an updated face-negotiation theory", in W. B. Gudykunst (ed.), *Theorizing About Intercultural Communication* Thousand Oaks, CA: Sage, pp. 71–92.

Gao, G., Trubisky, P., Yang, Z., Kim, H. S., Lin, S. L., and Nishida, T. 1991. "Culture, face maintenance, and styles of handling interpersonal conflict: a study in five cultures", *International Journal of Conflict Management* 2: 275–96.

and Kurogi, A. 1998. "Facework competence in intercultural conflict: an updated face-negotiation theory", *International Journal of Intercultural Relations* 22: 187–225.

Tinsley, C. H. 1998. "Models of conflict resolution in Japanese, German, and American cultures", *Journal of Applied Psychology* 83: 316–23.

and Brett, J. M. 1997. "Managing work place conflict: a comparison of conflict frames and resolution in the US and Hong Kong". Best paper proceedings of fifty-seventh annual meeting of Academy of Management, Boston, MA.

Todd, H. F. 1978. "Litigious marginals: character and disputing in a Bavarian village", in L. Nader and H. F. Todd (eds.), *The Disputing Process: Law in Ten Societies*. New York, NY: Columbia University Press, pp. 86–121.

Triandis, H. C. 1995. *Individualism and Collectivism*. Boulder, CO: Westview.

Carnevale, P., Gelfand, M. J., Robert, C., Wasti, S. A., Probst, T., Kashima, E. S., Dragonas, T., Chan, D., Chen, X. P., Kim, U., De Dreu, C., Van de Vliert, E., Iwao, S., Ohbuchi, K., and Schmitz, P. 2001. "Culture and deception in business negotiations: a multilevel analysis", *International Journal of Cross-cultural Management* 1: 73–90.

Tung, R. L. 1982. "U.S.-China trade negotiations: practices, procedures, and outcomes", *Journal of International Business Studies* 13: 25–37.

1984. "How to negotiate with the Japanese", *California Management Review* 26: 62–77.

Valenzuela, A., Srivastava, J., and Lee, S. 2005. "The role of cultural orientation in bargaining under incomplete information: differences in causaul attributions", *Organizational Behavior and Human Decision Processes* 96: 72–88.

Van Schaik, C. P. 1989. "The ecology of social relationships amongst female primates", in V. Standen and R. A. Foley (eds.), *Comparative Socioecology*. Oxford: Blackwell, pp. 195–218.

Van Wolkenten, M. L., Davis, J. M., Gong, M. L. and de Waal, F. B. M. 2006. "Coping with acute crowding by capuchin monkeys (Cebus paella)", *International Journal of Primatology* 27: 1241–56.

Wade-Beonzoni, K. A., Brett, J. M., Tenbrunsel, A. E., Okumura, T., Moore, D. A., and Bazerman, M. H. 2002. "Cognitions and behavior in asymmetric social dilemmas: A comparison of two cutlures", *Journal of Applied Psychology* 87: 87–95.

Wagatsuma, H., and Rosett, A. R. 1986. "The implications of apology: law and culture in Japan and the United States", *Law and Society Review* 20: 461–98.

Walton, R. E., and McKersie, R. B. 1965. *Behavioral Theory of Labor Negotiations: An Analysis of a Social Interaction System*. New York, NY: McGraw-Hill.

Watson-Gegeo, K. and White, G. M. 1990. *Disentangling: Conflict Discourse in Pacific Societies*. Stanford, CA: Stanford University Press.

Weiss, S. E. 2004. "International business negotiations research: revisiting 'bricks, mortar, and Prospects'" in B. J. Punnett and O. Shenkar, (eds.), *Handbook for International Management Research*. Ann Arbor, MI: University of Michigan Press, pp. 415–74.

2006. "International business negotiation in a globalizing world: reflections on the contributions and future of a (sub) field", *International Negotiation* 11: 87–316.

Yamagishi, T. 1988a. "Exit from the group as an individualistic solution to the public good problem in the United States and Japan", *Journal of Experimental Social Psychology* 24: 530–42.

1988b. "The provision of a sanctioning system in the United States and Japan", *Social Psychology Quarterly* 51: 265–71.

Cook, K. S., and Watabe, M. 1998. "Uncertainty, trust, and commitment formation in the United

States and Japan", *American Journal of Sociology* 104: 165–94.

and Yamagishi, M. 1994. "Trust and commitment in the United States and Japan", *Motivation and Emotion* 18: 9–66.

Zak, P. J. and Fakhar, A. 2006. "Neuroactive hormones and interpersonal trust: international evidence", *Economics and Human Biology* 4: 412–29.

and Knack, S. 2001. "Trust and growth", *The Economic Journal* 111: 295–321.

Zartman, I. W. 1993. "A skeptic's view", in G. O. Faure and J. Z. Rubin (eds.), *Culture and Negotiation* Newbury Park, CA: Sage, pp. 17–21.

14 The complexity of trust: cultural environments, trust, and trust development

NANCY R. BUCHAN

The topic of trust has spawned a vast literature across multiple academic fields of inquiry and has produced some of the most cited papers within the field of management alone (e.g. Mayer, Davis, and Schoorman, 1995). Yet in many ways, the state of our understanding of trust development is similar to the story of the group of blind men touching different parts of an elephant. First, while we know many things about trust, there is little understanding of how the pieces of knowledge fit together. Second, significant stages within the trust development process remain virtually unexplored. Third, there is little recognition that the whole is likely much more complex than the sum of the parts. That is, trust development is dynamic and fluid, changing in nature from context to context, and is influenced by a multiplicity of economic, sociological, psychological and political factors in the cultural environment of the trust relationship.

An example of failure in the trust literature to integrate knowledge is that we seldom simultaneously examine the internal psychology of the trustor (McAllister, 1995; Jeffries and Reid, 2000) in conjunction with the external social context of trust relationships (Cook, Hardin, and Levi, 2005)). For example, the internal psychology of the trustor (whether relatively more rationally or intuitvely based) and the external social context of the relationship (whether perhaps a legal contract versus a relational one exists between partners) must be studied in conjunction because they are likely to interact with and influence the nature of trust extended, the attributions made regarding the trustworthiness of the partner, and ultimately, the potential for future growth trust or decline. Highlighting this point, when discussing relationships in which there exists a monitoring system, Mayer, Davis and

Schoorman (1995, p. 730) ask: "To what extent does cooperation that can be attributed to external motivations develop trust?".

There are also significant stages in the trust process which are almost wholly unexplored. For example, the work of Shapiro, Shepard and Cheraskin (1992), Lewicki and colleagues (Lewicki and Bunker, 1995; Lewicki, McAllister, and Bies, 1998; Lewicki and Wiethoff, 2000) and Mayer, Davis, and Schoorman (1995) has been instructive in suggesting that trust changes in character over time, and that there is likely a feedback loop whereby the forms of trust are "linked and build on each other as a relationship develops" (Lewicki and Bunker, 1995, p. 167). What remains ambiguous, however, is what is the trigger for the feedback loop? In their model of trust, Mayer, Davis, and Schoorman (1995), suggest that outcomes serve as a catalyst for further trust growth or decline. I propose that this explanation is overly simplistic. First, it is not always the case that information about a partner's trustworthiness is fully available or unambiguous. Second, regardless of whether such outcomes are clear or ambiguous, their impact on the future development or decline of trust is likely far from direct. Rather, it is suggested that outcomes are first filtered through a "relationship accounting" mechanism employed by the trustor. Psychological and sociological factors in relationship context determine whether the mechanism operates restrictively or leniently, whether positive or negative outcomes are acknowledged or ignored, and whether such outcomes prompt future trust development.

Finally, and perhaps most importantly, the complexity of trust development is not fully appreciated. Although trust is studied in numerous disciplines, we have relatively little understanding of the influence of sociological, psychological, economic, legal, or political factors in the cultural environment on the nature of trust or trust development. Furthermore, that knowledge which we do have is largely based on research in the US. Schoorman, Mayer, and Davis (2007) suggest that the greatest potential for cross-cultural research lies in understanding how propensities to trust vary across cultures and in understanding to what degree the nature of trust (e.g. whether it is relatively more benevolence or ability based) differs across cultures. National and cultural differences in the propensity toward generalized trust has certainly been the most studied topic within cross-cultural trust research (e.g., La Porta *et al.*, 1997; Putnam, 1993; Yamagishi, 1988b), yet it is proposed that to understand cultural differences in trust fully, we need to examine the influence of culture at every stage in the trust development process. As with the trust process itself, the nature of culture's influence on trust is much more complex than that which meets the eye. It is not enough to demonstrate that country X is more generally trusting than country Y. What we need to understand is, given the relationship context and the influence of a multiplicity of factors in the cultural environment, what is the nature of trust and how is it likely to develop over time?

The conceptualization of trust proposed in this chapter brings together and builds upon literature from economics, sociology, social psychology, law, political science, and business in an effort to address these weaknesses in the trust literature and to bring the whole elephant into view. In Section I, a dynamic model of trust is presented that meticulously breaks down the trust process and demonstrates the influence of contextual factors at various junctures within the process. Furthermore, as called for by Jeffries and Reed (2000), this model clarifies the interplay of the trustor's rationality and intuition at specific stages of the trust process, and details its influence in each. Because most of the research which informs the model was conducted in the west, the section ends by proposing a trajectory for trust development for western-based cultures. Having first established an understanding of the detailed and complex nature of the trust process, Section

II presents a full examination of the influence of factors in the cultural environment on each step of the process. Drawing on research that has occurred in less developed and/or non-western contexts, this examination reveals that culture is intrinsically intertwined in trust relationships, that the nature of trust is likely culturally determined, and that different trajectories for trust development may exist depending on the cultural environment studied.

Section 1: A multidimensional model of trust

In this section the model of the trust development process is presented. At the heart of the model is the definition of trust. This model draws from the general definition of trust proposed by Orbell, Dawes, and Schwarz-Shea (1994); trust is the expectation of another's behavior in a situation involving vulnerability where one may prefer the partner to do "a," but he/she has incentive or potential to do "b." This definition concurs with a broad interdisciplinary body of research conceptualizing trust as an expectation of another's behavior in a situation in which the trustor's outcomes are vulnerably dependent on the other's behavior (e.g., Deutsch, 1958; Pruitt and Kimmel, 1977; Gambetta, 1988; Coleman, 1988; Williamson, 1993; Hardin, 2002), however it adds clarity to the most commonly cited definitions of trust because of its specificity in identifying what the trustor is trusting the trustee to do. Trust as an expectation of behavior is exemplified by the statements of Volvo's manager of CRM when discussing the turnover of a data warehouse to a partner: "We state publicly that Harte-Hanks is our agent of record for customer analytics, and we expect that Harte-Hanks will give us additional support on site. We expect that they will supply us with a steady stream of good ideas and that they won't rip us off" (Leon, 2003, p. 40).

The key question is, on what is that expectation based? As Mayer, Davis and Schoorman (1995) summarize, a consensus in prior literature suggests that trust is based on assessments of a trustee's competence and benevolence.[1] Trust in a partner's competence is the expectation that the party has the skills, abilities and knowledge necessary for task performance (Gabarro, 1978); in the language of the definition, the partner is able to do "a." For example, a firm expects its new subcontractor to fill its second order satisfactorily (rather than fill it with lemons), because the order was competently filled the first time (Lorenz, 1992).

Trust in a partner's benevolence is the extent to which an individual is perceived to be genuinely interested in a partner's welfare and is motivated to seek joint – as opposed to individual – gain (Larzelere and Huston, 1980); thus the partner wants to do "a" because it would add to the joint outcomes of the relationship. For example, a member of a deeply trusting alliance allows their partner to act on their behalf because they believe that the partner will act to the benefit of the alliance rather than personal gain (Lewicki and Bunker, 1995).

The proposed model of trust deviates from standard convention however, because of its consideration of the social context of the trusting relationship, i.e. in its consideration of the incentives for the trustee to be trustworthy. In doing so, the model captures what Hardin refers to as encapsulated trust: "I trust you because your interest encapsulates mine, which is to say that you have an interest in fulfilling my trust" (Hardin, 2002, p. 3). For example, it is in your partner's interest to continue a relationship, to maintain a reputation, or to avoid network sanction.

Trust in the partner's incentives is the expectation based on knowledge of the incentive structure surrounding the relationship that your partner will not harm your interests but promote them; thus the partner's incentives motivate them to do "a" and not "b." Wal-Mart trusts P&G to work cooperatively rather than uncooperatively and produce and provide the goods it needs because of the hostages it has staked in the relationship (Kumar, 2000).

The inclusion of the trustee's incentives in this conceptualization is controversial; clearly the existence of incentives for the trustee to be trustworthy decrease the level of vulnerability for the trustee. Taken to the extreme, if no vulnerability exists there is not trust, only cooperation (Mayer,

Davis, and Schoorman, 1995; Cook, Hardin, and Levi, 2005). Yet, consideration of such incentives is crucial if we are to understand the role of the social context, as well as individual psychology, in trust building and dynamics. In research investigating the process of trust building and decline in professional relationships, the "self-interested" or "egotistic" incentives of the parties are necessarily considered, whether they relate to reputation, social sanction, idiosyncratic investments, or contracts (Lorenz, 1992; Rousseau et al., 1998; Zucker, 1986; Doney and Cannon, 1997; Lewicki and Bunker, 1995). Sometimes these relationships are seen as launching pads for initiating deeper levels of trust, such as when one enters into a relationship with a new firm because of its reputation but subsequently trusts the firm because it is perceived to have dealt in a trustworthy manner. Sometimes they are seen to lead to trust's stagnation, such as when a firm attributes its partner's cooperation only to the presence of a contract and the threat of sanction, rather that to trustworthy behavior (Rousseau et al., 1998; Malhotra and Murnighan, 2002). It is essential that we study these forms of incentive-based trust in order better to understand what consequences will occur.

In summary, trust is the expectation of behavior (where the expectation is based on the partner's competence, their benevolence, and on knowledge of the incentive structure surrounding the relationship) in a situation involving vulnerability where one may prefer the partner to do "a" but they have the incentive or potential to do "b."

With this definition of trust in hand, a model of the trust development process is now outlined (figure 14.1) and will be discussed in detail in the following sections. At the foundation of the trust

---

[1] Mayer, Davis and Schoorman add a third factor, integrity, to their model of trust. They define integrity as the "trustor's perception that the trustee adheres to a set of principles that the trustee finds acceptable," and support integrity's inclusion in their model by likening it to "value congruence," as discussed by Sitkin and Roth (1993). As discussed in the next section, such adherence to acceptable principles or value congruence is more accurately described as a part of social identity which influences the nature of trust in a relationship, rather than serving as one of the expectations on which it is based.

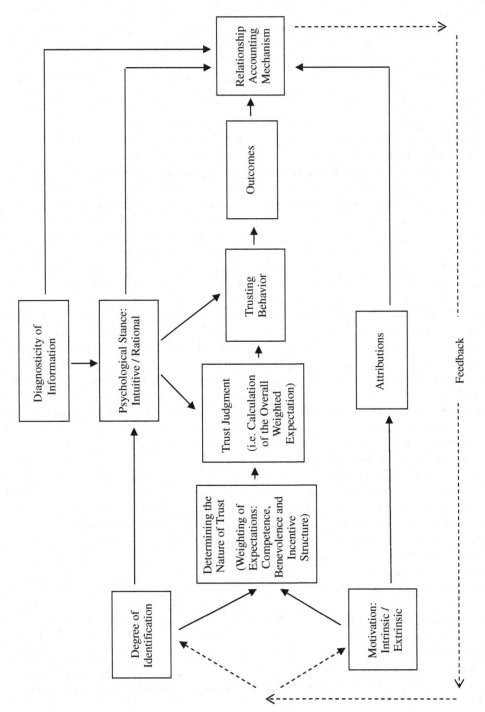

Figure 14.1 The trust development process

process are two factors; the degree of identification between the parties in the relationship, and the degree to which the trustor's motivations are internally or externally driven. The interaction of these factors determines the weighting of the three expectations and thus the nature of trust in the relationship. Based upon the weighted calculation of the three trust expectations, the trustor then makes a trust judgement and may extend trusting behavior. At this point, the proposed model permits the likelihood that trust may not be purely rational. Specifically, the trustor's psychological stance – whether intuitive or rational – will influence the type of trust judgements made, the biases in those judgements, and whether or not the trust judgement leads to trusting behavior. Furthermore, the psychological stance itself is influenced by the degree of identification between the parties and the degree of diagnostic information regarding the trustee. Trusting behavior, if extended, then leads to outcomes. Unlike prior models of the trust process, these outcomes do not feed back to the start of the trust process directly but instead are filtered through a relationship accounting mechanism. The accounting mechanism operates strictly or loosely as a function of factors in the sociological and psychological relationship context; the diagnosticity of information regarding the trustor's behavior and the relationship outcomes, the psychological stance of the trustor, and the attributions they are making about their own and the trustee's behavior. Once filtered through the accounting mechanism, the outcome information feeds back to influence the identification between the parties and the trustor's motivation, prompting trust growth or decline.

Determining the nature of trust

As discussed, trust is proposed to be based on three expectations; expectations of competence, expectations of benevolence, and expectations based on the incentive structure surrounding the relationship. The weighting of the three trust expectations will be determined by the degree of identification in the relationship and by the nature of the trustor's motivation.

Degree of identification

Kramer, Brewer, and Hanna state: "the willingness of individuals to engage in trust behavior in situations requiring collective action is tied to the salience and strength of their identification with an organization and its members" (1996, p. 359). Identification has the following three bases. (1) The *cognitive* base is derived from the effects of categorization on social perception and judgement which lead to the presence of ingroup biases and an increase in perceived similarity with other members. Additionally, within the partnership there is a tacit understanding regarding the norms and values that govern their relationship, and with it comes a bias in causal attributions made (i.e., the tendency to give ingroup members the benefit of doubt or to attribute infractions to external factors). (2) The *motivational* base proposes that because of the heightened perception of similarity with other group members, members shift from thinking of individual outcomes to a shared common fate. (3) The *affective* base of identification suggests that people derive emotional satisfaction from being part of a cooperative group (Kramer, Brewer, and Hanna, 1996).

Ring (1996) applied social identity theory to the development of cooperative interorganizational exchanges and described the process of identity-building as "sensemaking." Sensemaking occurs in two ways, through "separate knowing," which is directed at the transaction itself and at factors such as the predictability and functional competence of the parties, and through "connected knowing," which is focused on the actors in the transaction, allowing them to become connected to the others' ideas, values and objectives.

The present conceptualization of trust proposes that levels of identification in a relationship can change over time. The most typical path of development begins with lower levels of identity (where trust is based mainly on a partner's competence), and moves to higher levels of identity (where trust is based on a partner's benevolent motives). A positive feedback relationship is generated whereby the more frequently parties interact positively, the more frequently will they share information, the more intense will be their familiarity, mutual understanding, and concern for one another, and the greater will be their common resources, shared norms and values and their belief in a common fate (Rousseau *et al.*, 1998; Doney and Cannon, 1997; Lewicki and Bunker, 1995).

Proposition 1: The level of identity between parties will most influence the weighting of the expectations of competence and of benevolence in a relationship. As the level of identity between parties increases, the weighting of the expectation of a partner's competence decreases, and the weighting of the expectation of benevolence increases.

Motivation for exchange behavior

Social psychologists, Tyler and Huo, assume two core types of human motivation: "the forces exerted on an individual by external contingencies in his or her environment, and the motivational forces of his or her own attitudes and values" (2002, p. 26). The locus of motivation has been demonstrated to have significant effects on trust and cooperation.

Tyler and Huo's research concerning trust, cooperation and the law, suggests that behavior based on intrinsic motivations has an advantage over behavior motivated by external contingencies (i.e., factors in the social context). Intrinsically motivated behavior is driven by an internal desire to cooperate and to take responsibility for cooperative action because it is perceived as the correct behavior. Because of these intrinsic motivations, business partners can put fewer resources into supporting costly relationship governance or control mechanisms. "Organizations cannot recognize and reward every cooperative act, nor can they detect and punish every failure to cooperate ... successful cooperation depends, at least in part, on the willingness of individuals to engage voluntarily in behaviors that further collective aims" (Kramer, Brewer, and Hanna, 1996, p. 358).

Examples of extrinsically motivated business trust relationships may include relationships in the presence of legal contracts, relationship specific investments or "hostages," economic sanctions, or network governance (e.g., Ring and Van de Ven, 1992; Shapiro, Sheppard, and Cheraskin, 1992; Jones, Hesterly, and Borgatti, 1997). Conversely, intrinsically motivated trust relationships are exemplified by the relational contracts often found in interfirm relationships. These "incomplete contracts" rely on a shared understanding of relational norms to voluntarily govern behavior (Wathne and Heide, 2000).

In this model, extrinsically motivated trust applies to relationships where the trustor's motivation is based primarily on assessments of the social, legal or economic constraints in the social context that influence the exchange (e.g., I trust my JV partner because they have staked their reputation on this relationship). In contrast, intrinsically motivated trust applies to relationships where the trustor's motivation is based primarily on their own values and attitudes regarding what is appropriate in a given situation (I trust my JV partner because we have all got to give a bit to make this work). To the degree that the trustor's motivation to trust is primarily internal or external, expectations based upon the incentives surrounding the trust relationship will receive relatively greater weighting than will expectations of competence or benevolence.

Proposition 2: To the degree that the trustor's motivation to trust is based primarily on assessments of the social, legal, or economic constraints in the social context that influence the exchange or on their own values and attitudes regarding what is appropriate in a given situation, expectations based upon the incentives surrounding the trust relationship will receive relatively greater weighting relative to expectations of competence or benevolence.

The weighted trust expectations

Many researchers have acknowledged that identification is crucial to the formation of trust in business relationships (e.g. Shapiro, Sheppard, and Cheraskin, 1992; Lewicki and Bunker, 1995; Ring, 1996); very few researchers have recognized the importance of the trustor's motivation in such relationships (Weber, Malhotra and Murnighan, 2005 is an exception). The model proposed here is the first to suggest that it is the interplay of these two factors – identity and motivation – that leads to the differential weighting of the three trust expectations and to different trust relationships.

Figure 14.2 depicts the interaction of motivation and identity and its influence on the nature of the trust relationship. When identification is

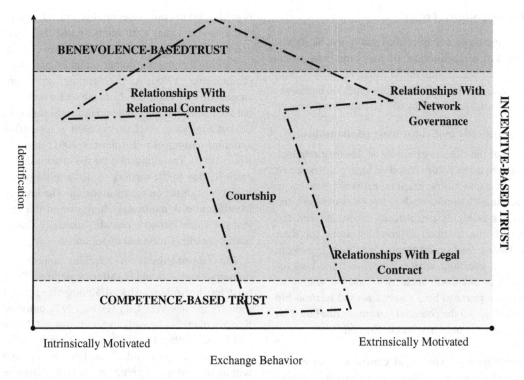

Figure 14.2. Taxonomy of trust: a western Trust Trajectory

low and the trustor's behavior is relatively more intrinsically motivated, expectations of competence will likely be most heavily weighted in the relationship. When identification is high and the trustor's behavior is highly intrinsically motivated, the trust relationship is most likely to be based on expectations of benevolence. It is when the level of identification is in the middle ranges that incentive-based trust relationships are most likely to arise. Some of the incentive-based relationships will be extrinsically motivated, such as relationships with legal contracts (when identity is relatively low) or relationships with network governance (when identity is relatively high). Some of the relationships will be relatively more intrinsically motivated, such as courtship (when identity begins relatively low but increases over time), and relationships with relational contracts (where identity is relatively high). The characteristics of competence-based, incentive-based,

and benevolence-based trust relationships are discussed in this section.

Competence-based trust

Competence-based trust relationships are typically of short duration or scope such that little is known about the partner on which to build identification and the exchange is conducted in the absence of contextual constraints. The key question is: can the partner deliver?

Pfizer president, Henry A. McKinnel, alludes to expectations of competence in the beginning stages of a Pfizer alliance: "You really need to focus on what brings each party to the relationship ... There has to be recognition of each other's capability ... As always we started out a bit suspicious of each other. Now we have expanded the relationships and it's gotten to be a win-win" (Arino, de la Torre, and Ring, 2001, p. 120).

Incentive-based trust

Because they are so numerous and varied, incentive-based trust relationships are likely the most prevalent trust relationship found within business (Cook, Hardin, and Levi, 2005). Four types of incentive-based trust relationships will be considered here.

Extrinsically motivated trust relationships

Two of the clearest examples of this trust relationship are relationships based on legal governance or contracts, and those based on network governance. Because these relationships are ones in which the trustor is highly extrinsically motivated and the trustee has a strong external incentive for their behavior, trust would seem to be almost irrelevant. Yet, in situations where competence and benevolence is unknown, such trust (and the testing of it) may prove to be a catalyst for the relationship and allow for the potential growth of trust based on competence or benevolence (Zucker, 1986).

Relationships with legal contract The motivation for this relationship is highly extrinsic due to the trustor's consideration of the legal constraints on the relationship (Ring and Van de Ven, 1992). The level of identification is low initially: some knowledge of the partner's competence or reputation may be known but identification in the relationship is not developed.

Contract-based governance underlies a number of interfirm relationships including partnerships, coalitions, franchises, and research consortia (Ring and Van de Ven, 1992). The potential for growth from a contract-based relationship is exemplified in the relationship between Nike and Amdahl, the new vendor of its mainframe processor:

> The vendor detected the problem remotely and had the repairman on site, the failed part off-line, and the replacement component picked and shipped almost before we knew anything had happened. Amdahl proved as good as they said they were, and that went a long way toward building trust (Cassel, 1996, p. 29)

Relationships with network governance In relationships involving network governance, trust

is predicated not only on economic considerations but also on social constraints, particularly the extent to which the current relationship is embedded within a network of other social relationships (Granovetter, 1985). At the extreme, such constraints involve exclusion from the social network, but the constraints also function through more subtle, but damaging, mechanisms such as reputation and third-party gossip (Ensminger, 2001; Burt and Knez, 1995). The motivation for the relationship is extrinsic due to the trustors' consideration of the social constraints on the relationship. The level of identification is moderately high due to the fact that the social network contains mutually shared norms regarding trust and opportunism.

The embeddedness of relations appears in numerous contexts and in differing degrees. Such trust has been demonstrated among the apparel industry in New York City (Uzzi, 1997), automobile distribution channels in South Korea (Hagen and Choe, 1998), the formal credit card market in Russia (Guseva and Rona-Tas, 2001), and within the informal credit markets in Vietnam (McMillian and Woodruff, 1999). Landa suggests that socially based trust has the highest propensity to develop in underdeveloped economies where there exists little perceived government efficacy and thus a high degree of uncertainty regarding formal contracts:

> Questionnaire surveys of and interviews with Chinese middlemen engaged in the marketing of smallholders' rubber in Singapore and West Malaysia in 1969 revealed that (a) the marketing of smallholders' rubber was dominated by a middleman group with a tightly knit kinship structure from the Hokkien-Chinese ethnic group; (b) that mutual trust and mutual aid formed the basis for the particularization of exchange relations among Chinese middlemen; and (c) that within the Chinese economy transactions among middlemen were based on credit; while Chinese middlemen used cash transactions with indigenous smallholders to reduce contract uncertainty ... The real significance of the visible, surface structure of the (ethnically homogeneous middleman group) EHMG lies in its underlying deep structure; the invisible codes of ethics, embedded in the personalized exchange

relations among the members of the EHMG, which function as constraints against breach of contract and hence facilitate exchange among Chinese middlemen. (1994, p. 351)

Intrinsically motivated trust relationships

In intrinsically motivated trust relationships both parties are interacting according to their own values or attitudes with the goal of developing a deeper trusting relationship. Two clear examples of intrinsically motivated relationships are courtship (Doney and Cannon, 1997) and interactions with relational contracts (Macneil, 1978).

Courtship   In courtship, trust is predicated on the predictability of the trustee's actions, which relies on information rather than deterrence, and which develops over time (Doney and Cannon, 1997). The motivation for the relationship is moderately intrinsic; although no formal or informal contract is in place, consideration is given to the trustee's potential loss of reputation or of the relationship in cases of opportunism. The key motivation is to build the relationship. The level of identification is moderately low initially; although there is little knowledge regarding the partner some information regarding the partner's competence or reputation will likely be known. This information is continually being accumulated with each exchange; as it does so, there is potential for the development of shared resources, norms, and a common fate, and therefore, a growth in identification. A representative from Xerox discusses the courtship process:

> Mutual dependency and common goals are meaningless if a supplier lacks capability to meet customer requirements. An incompetent but well-intentioned supplier is still incompetent. In order to trust a supplier, the customer has to be confident that the supplier is competent...Thanks to Xerox's pioneering work, most leading companies now use benchmarking techniques to test supplier competency in a broad range of areas such as new technology, delivery lead times, and price competitiveness. The most capable suppliers welcome such comparisons as opportunities to prove their prowess. (Laseter, 1997, p. 24).

Through repeated opportunities to prove their competence, there is potential for the development of trust which is increasingly benevolence based, one in which the question shifts from "are you the right one for me?" (Fournier, 1998) to "what can we achieve together?' (Mayer, Davis, and Schoorman, 1995). This development path suggests, for example, that a firm beginning a new partnership should be conscientious in repeatedly demonstrating its competence; in doing so, parties will deepen their understanding of each other and, based on a belief in each other's intentions, their relationship will have the potential to move into a more collaborative effort in the future.

Relationships with relational contracts   Here trust is predicated not on legal contracts but on the social constraints implicit in the relational contract, that is, a variety of norms and informal agreements governing the relationship (Macneil, 1978; Zaheer and Venkatraman, 1995). Consistent with relational exchanges, such relationships assume a history of interaction; past experiences serve as important factors in how the parties will conduct themselves in present and future exchanges (Dwyer, Schurr, and Oh, 1987; Ring and Van de Ven, 1994). Foremost "is the possibility of significant gains in joint – and consequently individual – payoffs as a result of effective communication and collaboration to achieve goals" (Dwyer, Schurr, and Oh, 1987, p. 14).

The motivation for the relationship is moderately intrinsic; the trustor's behavior is motivated by consideration of shared norms which specify the sharing of benefits and burdens and also the permissible limits on behavior (Heide and John, 1992; Macneil, 1978; Wathne and Heide, 2000). The level of identification is moderately high because of these shared norms and the development and maintenance of them reflects a shift toward collective goals and a "we-ness" in the relationship (Jap and Ganesan, 2000).

In a study of governance structures in network dyads, Larson (1992) examined seven entrepreneurial alliances which were stable and cooperative, and were evaluated by the participants as having contributed significantly to the firm's success and rapid growth. An account from one of these alliance participants is as follows:

> Over time you build a history of situations, compromises, and solutions. You learn the unwritten roles and how they want to play the game, which makes it incredibly easier to do business ... Its like a balance, a scale – in return for commitment on their part we say we are committed to you and we prove it. So it's a quid pro quo. It's a balanced relationship that says you make investments, we make investments; you take risks, we take risks; you perform, we perform. That's the basis on which you build trust ... (1992, p. 89)

Benevolence-based trust

Benevolence-based trust is predicated not on a conscious calculation of consequences, but rather emerges from identification with the other party's desires and intentions in the relationship (Lewicki and Bunker, 1995). It is based on the belief that whatever actions the partner takes, such actions will be a good-faith effort to help the trustor (Tyler and Huo, 2002).

The motivation for the relationship is highly intrinsic; the trustor's motivation is based on the perception that the two parties are in cooperation and both desire to increase joint welfare. The level of identification in the relationship is high; as Doney and Cannon suggest, inferences of benevolent intentions are likely to result when "the two parties have developed shared values or norms that enable one party to understand the other partner's objectives and goals better" (1997, p. 37).

Though one may suspect that benevolence-based relationships occur only among intimate interpersonal dyads, empirical evidence demonstrates that such relationships occur between individuals and legal authorities (Tyler and Huo, 2002), between consumers and a beloved brand (Fournier, 1998), and even between firms. Such a relationship is exemplified by the relationship between Motoman, a leading supplier of industrial robotic systems, and Stillwater Technologies, a contract tooling and machining company and a key supplier to Motoman:

> The two companies are so tightly integrated that not only do they occupy office and manufacturing space in the same 165,000 sq. ft. facility, but their telephone and computer systems are linked, and they share a common lobby, a conference room, training rooms, and an employee cafeteria ... The relationship is based on trust and handshake, not a written contract. "No one piece of paper defines this arrangement," says Phillip V. Monnin, chairman and CEO of Motoman. "This is a virtual partnership. Its like a joint venture without all the paperwork. We are two independent companies cooperating as close to the line of intimacy as you can get. We almost live in each other's shorts ... The symbiotic relationship does make the two of us together bigger than we are individually ... If we see a better way to do something we share it with each other because we're all working for the same thing." (Sheridan 1997, pp. 69–70)

In summary, through an understanding of the degree of identification in a relationship and of the nature of the trustor's motivations, one is able to discern which of the trust expectations is most heavily weighted in the relationship. Analysis of interaction of these two factors (identity and motivation) provides a structure that is sufficiently comprehensive to understand the nature of trust in virtually every business context.

The psychological stance of trust

Thus far, this conceptualization of trust sits firmly in the rational choice paradigm (Coleman, 1988; Williamson, 1993; Hardin, 2002), which, as Kramer suggests in his review of trust, "remains arguably the most influential image of trust within organizational science" (Kramer, 1999, p. 572). Based upon the weighted calculation of the three trust expectations described above, a trustor makes a trust judgement. The trust judgement involves multiplying each expectation times the trustor's value for that expectation (e.g., the weight of the competence expectation times how competent you believe the trustee to be), and then summing across expectations. At this point, however, as shown in the middle of figure 14.1, the model deviates from strict rational choice by admitting the influence of intuitive factors such as social and emotional influences on trust judgements and behavior.

The trust process will mostly likely not be strictly rational because as Kahneman suggests, each of us has two systems – a system of intuition and a system of reasoning – and the two systems run concurrently; utility cannot be divorced from emotion:

> The operations of System 1 (intuition) are fast, automatic, effortless, associative, and often emotionally charged; they are governed by habit and are therefore difficult to control or modify. The operations of System 2 (reasoning) are slower, serial, effortful, and deliberately controlled; they are also relatively flexible and potentially rule-governed. (Kahneman, 2003, p. 1451)

Thus, although the calculation of trust is proposed to be a rational process, it is virtually certain that intuition will play a role in influencing the trust judgement and in prompting or inhibiting trust behavior, as will be discussed in this section. Intuition and emotion will also influence the attributions made about the partner's behavior once outcomes are obtained, as will be addressed when the relationship accounting mechanism accounts is introduced.

The influence of rationality and intuition on trust judgements

The role of intuition and emotion in trust relationships is likely to be greatest both when there is a dearth of information regarding the trustee and when there is an abundance. In the first circumstance, there is a lack of diagnostic information available regarding the trustee's competence, benevolence or incentives in the relationship. In this sense, intuition-based trust is much closer to generalized, rather than to specific trust. Generalized trust is the belief in the benevolence of human nature in general; specific trust concerns trust in specific contexts and in established relationships (Yuki et al., 2005). In cases of generalized trust, characteristics of both the trustor and the trustee influence expectations of trustee behavior. The most influential characteristic of the trustor is their general propensity to trust other people (Mayer, Davis and Schoorman, 1995, Rotter, 1967); propensities have been shown to vary by race, religion, nationality and gender (e.g., Yuki et al., 2005; Glaeser et al., 2000, Croson and Buchan, 1999). Characteristics of the trustee reflect: (a) category based trust, which is predicated on the trustee's membership in a social or organizational category (Buchan, Croson, and Dawes, 2002; Williams, 2001; Orbell, Dawes, and Schwartz-Shea, 1994); and (b) perception based trust (Doney, Cannon, and Mullen, 1998), which is predicated on perceived attributes of the trustee (e.g., capability, competence, expertise, likeability).

To the degree that specific knowledge about the trustee's characteristics is absent, the intuitive system of calculation is likely to play a greater role and one's own propensity to trust becomes influential in the trust judgement. Gill et al. (2005) suggest the reason for this is based on Kahneman and Tversky's (1973) finding that people tend to interpret ambiguous information in a way that is congruent with preexisting beliefs, for example in a way congruent with their propensity to trust. Thus, for example, although I know little about the person who placed the classified advertisement, the fact that she is a woman and comes from the Midwest (like me), combined with the fact that I tend to believe that most people are generally trustworthy, may induce me to trust that the car she is selling me really does have 88,000 miles on the odometer, not 188,000.

A second situation is in relationships in which much is known about the partner and there is a high level of identity between the parties. In this case, the trust judgement is likely to be heavily influenced by intuition and biased toward expectations of benevolence. McAllister (1995) contrasts cognition based trust with affect based trust and suggests that affect based trust is grounded in the idea of benevolence, the expectation of reciprocal care and concern. Furthermore, in the course of trust development in managerial relationships, cognitive trust is likely to come first and affective trust will follow only after a greater investment of time and commitment to the relationship, and to learning about one another. Indeed, Lawler, Thye and Yoon (2002) suggest that the emotional effects of an exchange result from a social bonding process through which the group or partnership becomes an object of intrinsic or expressive value. Thus, it is likely that a high degree of identity between the parties will bias one's psychological stance toward intuition, and such intuition will bias the trust judgement in favor of expectations of benevolence (that is, expectations of benevolence will receive extra weighting, and the other two expectations will receive less, relative to the weightings determined in the trust determination step in the trust process).

Proposition 3: The psychological stance of an individual in a given relationship – whether intuitive or rational – will play a role in influencing trust judgements. In situations in which there is scarce or ambiguous information as to the trustworthiness of the partner, intuition will heavily influence judgements biasing them toward one's propensity toward generalized trust. In situations in which there exist high levels of identity between the partners, intuition will bias judgements toward overweighted expectations of benevolence, in contrast to competence and incentive structures.

The influence of rationality and intuition on trusting behavior

The intuitive system influences the trust process not only through its effect on trust judgements, but also in prompting or inhibiting trusting behavior. To understand this process fully, it is first necessary to understand the relationship of trust to risk.

Trust is conceptualized as distinct from risk. Researchers agree that trust entails the perception that one "will be worse off if he trusts and his trust is not fulfilled than if he does not trust" (Deutsch, 1958, p. 266). Without risk, trust becomes mere prediction, or simply the "ability to forecast another party's behavior" (Doney and Cannon, 1997, p. 37). The question is, how does trust relate to risk? Some propose that trust is a risk reduction mechanism (e.g., Nooteboom, Berger and Noorderhaven, 1997). The perspective proposed here is that trust is instead a stimulus to support activities in situations of risk (e.g., Luhmann, 1988; Mayer, Davis, and Schoorman, 1995). It is the "booster rocket" that lets you jump from a secure situation into one where the outcomes are unknown and potentially damaging (Yamagishi and Yamagishi, 1994).

As discussed by Wieselquist *et al.*: "Strong trust frees individuals from anxiety regarding their relationships, allowing them to risk increased dependence on a partner" (1999, p. 961).

Yet, how is it possible that even though people have access to the same information in an exchange relationship and may have formed the same trust expectation, some people will then go on to act on that trust expectation and exhibit trusting behavior, and others will not? The reason for this is that people vary in their risk preferences, i.e. their tendency toward risk aversion or risk seeking (Kahneman and Tversky, 1979). Although formal theories of "risk preferences" had not yet been articulated, Deutsch (1958) recognized the concept and the influence it would have in risky situations, explaining that people have "security levels" required for action which differ from person to person and situation to situation. Therefore, System 1 is likely to promote or inhibit trusting behavior through an individual's risk preferences. It is important to note that it is precisely because of individual differences in risk preferences that the distinction between trust as an expectation as proposed here, versus trust as a willingness or intention (e.g., Mayer, Davis, and Schoorman, 1995; Wicks, Berman, and Jones, 1999) is necessary. Trust expectations do not always lead to the willingness to trust, and neither to trusting behavior.

Proposition 4: The psychological stance of an individual in a given relationship – whether intuitive or rational – will play a role in prompting or inhibiting trust behavior. Intuition is likely to influence – through risk preferences – the degree to which a trustor acts on the trust expectations, that is, when a trust judgement leads to trusting behavior.

The work of Weber, Malhotra and Murnighan (2005) raises an important point about trust and risk. They suggest there are times that "irrational trust" (that is, an extreme level of trust) is necessary to jumpstart relationships and prompt a partner's trustworthiness. Although the rational trust paradigm suggests that trust is best developed incrementally, experimental work suggests that trustors are better off trusting completely or not at all, rather than trusting just a little (Pillutla, Malhotra, and Murnighan, 2003). "Large acts of trust are inherently less ambiguous; they provide clearer signals of trust, making it difficult to downplay the significance of the trustor's act or to justify non-reciprocity" (Weber, Malhotra, and Murnighan, 2005, p. 11).

Proposition 5: In some situations, the extension of "irrational trust" – and the existence of risk seeking preferences to prompt it – may be necessary to begin a trusting relationship.

Outcomes and the relationship accounting mechanism

Depending on their trust judgement and risk preferences, the trustor may then engage in trusting behavior which then leads to outcomes. It is at this point that Mayer, Davis and Schoorman (1995) suggest that the feedback loop begins; the outcomes of a trusting relationship, whether positive or negative, serve as a catalyst for future trust growth or decline. The model proposed here suggests that this description of trust dynamics is overly simplistic. It is proposed that the true catalyst for the reinitiation of the trust process (and trust growth or decline), is the relationship accounting mechanism employed by the trustor (refer to the far right of figure 14.1). The relationship accounting mechanism serves as a filter for outcomes; factors in the social and psychological context determine the extent to which the accounting mechanism operates restrictively and whether positive or negative outcomes are acknowledged and/or acted upon.

The relationship accounting mechanism

Relationship accounting systems refer to how two actors keep track of their ongoing exchanges. A *restrictive* accounting system is one that "must be continually balanced – debts are repaid quickly (often in kind- and careful track is kept of each person's contributions)." A *relaxed* accounting system is one which "books are allowed to remain unbalanced for long periods, and exact tabs are not kept on each party's contributions" (Kollock, 1993, p. 770).

To illustrate the concept of relaxed accounting systems, sociologist Peter Kollock relates two anecdotes. One concerns firms who have long-term ongoing exchange relationships as portrayed in the study of non- and incomplete-contractual business relationships by Macaulay (1963). These firms, Kollock suggests, are careful to avoid legal recourse for breach of contract except for the most severe situations in order to preserve the personal relationship between the two firms. This avoidance is done even when the aggrieved firm knows it could achieve a better settlement by filing suit over a specific violation. A second anecdote reads as follows:

> When Hurricane Gilbert devastated the Blue Mountain coffee growing region in Jamaica in 1988, Japanese importers quickly offered to help rebuild the area. The grateful coffee growers allowed the Japanese importers to buy up the vast majority of their coveted crop, despite higher offers from American and European importers. As one Jamaican coffee manager put it: "We have Americans and Europeans who call up all the time and say, look, we'll pay you $11 a pound (the price at the time was $7.50). Well, that's fine for one shot, but what do you do four years hence, when the next hurricane hits? That's when you remember the Japanese, and the lesson for us has been taking care of clients like that first. (Kollock, 1993, p. 770).

The work of social psychologists helps to clarify in what types of relationships restrictive or relaxed accounting systems might be employed. Tyler and Huo (2002) describe an outcome assessment process which proceeds along an outcome-based versus process-based trust continuum. They argue that greater identification leads one to evaluate trust experiences based on process or procedural terms rather than on outcome terms. Thus, restrictive accounting may apply to those trust relationships where strict record is kept of outcomes and instances of opportunism are closely tracked and immediately responded to. Relaxed accounting applies to those relationships higher in identity, where the outcome is secondary to whether one was treated fairly and whether one perceives the motives of the partner to have been benevolent. In fact, Tyler and Huo argue that trust in the motives of the other party provides a cushion against possible resistance in accepting negative outcomes.

Clark's research (1984; Clark, Powell, and Mills, 1986) also suggests that there are two types of relationships based upon the way in which interactions are accounted for. In exchange relationships members give benefits with the expectation of receiving comparable benefits soon after. In communal relationships members feel responsibility and demonstrate concern for the needs of the other, and receipt of a benefit or obligation does not create a specific debt to return a comparable benefit. Because of their characterization as relationships in which partners demonstrate concern for the needs of the other, communal relationships indicate ones in which there exist higher levels of identity. Importantly, similar to the work of Tyler and Huo (2002), Clark's research demonstrates the tendency to under-account in the interest of preserving the high identity relationship. Her experiments have shown that when establishing communal relationships, people will not only follow communal norms, but will actively avoid following exchange relationship norms (including strict record keeping) to avoid any perception on the other's part that they may prefer an exchange relationship.

Therefore, in this model, the relationship accounting system refers to the propensity of the trustor to record or keep track of individual transactions, and to act on the outcomes whether through rewarding or sanctioning the trustee. In a restrictive accounting system, every outcome is tracked and acted upon, when possible. In a relaxed system, each outcome may not be recorded, or, even if it is, the trustor may not immediately take action to redress that outcome. The method of accounting used is influenced by the level of identity in the relationship.

Proposition 6: Restrictive accounting systems will most likely be employed in relationships in which there exist low levels of identity; relaxed accounting systems will most likely be employed in relationships with relatively high levels of identity.

The diagnosticity of information and attributions

The diagnosticity of information refers to the extent to which there exists perfect information on which to assess the trustworthiness of a partner. There are two junctures in the trust process where the diagnosticity of information is key. The first, as discussed earlier, is at the point of the trust judgement; the less diagnostic is the information regarding the trustee, the more likely will the intuitive system influence the trust judgement. The second juncture comes at the interpretation of outcomes.

Outcome interpretation is problematic. A first problem is that of performance evaluation; performance evaluation is especially difficult when the performance being evaluated – such as that of a recently formed joint venture – occurs in an uncertain and risky environment (Anderson, 1985) and the construction of the measures itself is difficult. Anderson (1990) suggests that in such situations parties will, by default, rely on easily accessible measures such as profitably. Yet, she notes, in risky and uncertain environments (such as that for a newly formed joint ventures), the use of such measures is likely to negatively misstate the venture's performance.

A second problem, that of "noise," has been studied experimentally by psychologists, sociologists and economists (e.g. Bendor, Kramer, and Stout, 1991; Wu and Axelrod, 1995; Van Lange, Ouwerkerk, and Tazelaar, 2002). Specifically, noise is defined as "discrepancies between intended and actual outcomes for an interaction partner due to unintended errors" (Van Lange, Ouwerkerk, and Tazelaar, 2002, p. 768). These errors are quite common and may be due to exogenous shocks such as the economy, the behavior of customers, suppliers, or the workforce which affect the payoffs a trustor obtains as a result of a trustee's behavior but which are not perfect knowledge to both parties in the relationship (Bendor, Kramer, and Stout, 1991, p. 692).

Not all forms of noise, however, are likely to have the same influence on relationships. According to Van Lange, Ouwerkerk and Tazelaar (2002), negative noise (i.e., when the actual outcome is more negative for the trustor than intended by the trustee) is likely to have a stronger and more salient effect on a trustor's attributions about the partner's motives than is positive noise. Two key reasons for this are: (a) people are more motivated to form personality impressions and make attributions when their outcomes are affected negatively rather than positively); and (b) because of the fundamental attribution error, people are more likely to explain behaviors and their effects in terms of the partner's underlying traits and intentions, rather than by situational variables which actually may have produced the effects.

The diagnosticity of information is important because it influences how the trustor accounts for outcomes. The research presented here suggests outcomes may be interpreted as overly negative in risky and uncertain environments, and furthermore, negative noise will have a greater effect on the trustor's attributions than will positive noise.

Proposition 7: Outcomes are likely to be interpreted as overly negative in risky and uncertain environments, and negative attributions about the partner will be more salient than positive ones to the degree that the trustor's outcomes are negatively affected.

Other influences on the formation of attributions

Based upon their research, Miller and Remple state: "Trust grows in situations that allow for an unambiguous attribution of positive motives to the partner's behavior" (1994, p. 696). Yet, as just discussed, such situations – in which information regarding the trustworthiness of the partner is fully diagnostic – are relatively rare. Additionally, the diagnosticity of information is only one element influencing the development of the trustor's attributions. Within this process it is also necessary to account for the influence of the nature of trust in the relationship and for the psychological stance of the trustor on attributions.

Formation of negative attributions

The nature of the trustor's motivation has a powerful influence on trust because of the attributions the trustor makes for his own behavior, and the implications those attributions have for future trust. Bem's self-perception theory (1972) and specifically, the overjustification effect suggests that people try to understand their own behavior by making attributions depending on whether the behavior was motivated intrinsically or extrinsically, and importantly,

that extrinsic motivation will undermine intrinsic motivation. That is, if I attribute my trusting behavior to the fact that a contract was present (an extrinsic motivation), in the future my trusting behavior is less likely to be motivated by my intrinsic desire to do so, and instead a contract may be necessary to prompt trusting action.

Compounding the trustor's own behavioral attributions are the attributions he makes about *the trustee's* behaviors. Attribution theory (Heider, 1958; Kelley, 1967) suggests that I may attribute my partner's compliance to the existence of the contract (a situational attribution) rather than to their desire to be trustworthy (a dispositional attribution) when the situational constraint is salient (as a contract would be) and when variance of the behavior is low (i.e., most people comply with contracts). Thus, in the future, I may not believe that the trustee will be trustworthy if no contract is in force.

Furthermore, both partners are making such attributions about each other, reinforcing the negative effect. These attributions provide the rationale for the argument that contracts and other external mechanisms of exchange governance are more likely to inhibit future trust than to prompt it (e.g., Malhotra and Murnighan, 2002; Sitkin and Roth, 1993). Therefore, the trust extended in extrinsically motivated encapsulated trust relationships bears relatively little potential for the development of deeper intrinsically motivated, benevolence-based trust. The existence of extrinsic trustor motivations and situational constraints on the trustee may set a negative path dependency from which it is extremely difficult to deviate.

Proposition 8: Negative attributions regarding the partner's behavior are most likely to develop in extrinsically motivated, incentive-based trust relationships. Because of the cycle of these negative attributions, it will be difficult for the partners in such relationships to develop a trust relationship which is intrinsically motivated and based upon the motives of the partner.

Formation of positive attributions

There do exist situations in the trust process when positive attributions about the trustee are likely. As identity builds within a relationship, and the trustor is increasingly intrinsically motivated, the relationship moves closer to benevolent based trust. In such cases the psychological stance of the trustor begins to switch gears. The intuitive process becomes more prominent than the purely rational, and the affective and emotional bases of identity begin to complement and then may even to begin to dominate the cognitive base. Becasue the trustor is now interested more in the emotional rewards of the relationship, when they perceive the partner to have been trustworthy, they will derive satisfaction knowing that they voluntarily took a chance on the partner and it paid off (Kramer, Brewer, and Hanna, 1996). It follows naturally, then, that with the heavier reliance on the intuitive process comes a tendency to resist negative motivational attributions about the partner, and to give them the benefit of the doubt, that is, one has a "reservoir of goodwill" for the partner (Kumar 2000).

Miller and Rempel (2004) show that changes in trust over time could indeed be predicted by the tendency of trustors to make motivational attributions that "went beyond their evaluation of how their partner had behaved," and furthermore that it was the "willingness or unwillingness of people to attribute positive motives to their partner even when they felt their partner had behaved badly that predicted whether trust increased or decreased two years later" (2004, p. 703).

Therefore, it is likely that as trust relationships grow in identity and become increasingly intrinsically motivated (that is, as they become benevolence-based trust relationships), there will be a tendency for the trustor to make positive attributions regarding the partner's motives, even in the face of outcomes that are potentially negative for the trustor. Although the psychological processes within trust relationships of this nature are not purely rational, the research cited here suggests that they may be adaptive in the sense that the (potentially biased) positive attributions are associated with the growth of further trust.

Proposition 9: As trust increasingly becomes benevolence-based, there is likely to be an increased tendency for the trustor to make positive attributions regarding the partner's motives, *regardless of the actual outcomes in the relationship. Such intuitively based attributions are likely to lead to further initiation of trust.*

The effectiveness of the accounting mechanism

The relationship accounting mechanism could easily be influenced to function in an overly restrictive or overly relaxed manner because of the number of influences on the accounting mechanism and because each of the influences may be heavily intuition-based and possibly biased. Yet, both over and under accounting can have negative consequences for relationships, and thus, achieving a balance between the two is crucial to prompting trust growth or decline.

The danger of underaccounting

Although many times the tendency to "give the benefit of the doubt" in benevolence-based trust relationships may prove beneficial to further trust growth, there is also a distinct danger inherent in the under accounting of trust violations in such relationships. The dynamics of cognitive disconfirmation, and the levels of emotion based identification in the relationship inhibit acknowledgement of a partner's opportunism; such opportunities when left unchecked will be damaging to the trustor's outcomes and ultimately will undermine the further growth of trust in the relationship (Jeffries and Reed, 2000). For example, it is likely that precisely these dynamics were at play among the self-managing teams in Langfred's study (2004) which demonstrated that high levels of team trust are associated with reduced team performance. The high levels of trust among team members – the effects of cognitive disconfirmation and high levels of emotion involved – rendered monitoring of each team member by the others less likely, in the end hampered team performance.

To guard against such danger, individuals and firms in benevolence-based trust relationships should at least occasionally remember Ronald Reagan's adage to "trust but verify." The above recommendation entails incorporating elements of incentive-based trust into benevolence-based relationships. Although this may be a bit of a "cold shower" for the intuitive trustor, Joni (2004) suggests that an occasional accounting may not only be useful for the relationship, but should be welcomed. Joni (2004) discussed the use of an independent auditor for the relationship, this auditor could be an objective third party, or possibly even another supplier; if both parties are honest brokers in the relationship, they may appreciate having their trust verified, and this verification will serve to reaffirm the partners' trust and may lead them to deeper levels of it.

The danger of over accounting

There is also danger to the development of future trust presented by overaccounting of violations; the danger seems to be most prevalent in situations of low information diagnosticity. According to Anderson (1990), a disproportionate number of joint ventures – those entering new product classes or markets, R&D ventures, and experimental manufacturing ventures – can be classified as "ignorant" in Ouchi's taxonomy of performance assessment (1979). In these situations, "formal and frequent performance evaluation is of little use in reducing the parent's risk and uncertainty. Indeed, carrying out a formal evaluation may be counterproductive" (Anderson, 1990, p. 27). Anderson's analysis indicates that overly restrictive accounting in these situations may serve to steer the management of the joint ventures in the wrong direction (by emphasizing the wrong inputs), or may simply shut down the venture prematurely (based on readily available, but not necessary relevant, profitability measures).

Additionally, the economic model of Dutta, Bergen, and John (1994) suggests that there may be situations where the costs associated with instituting a self-governance device – which is often relied upon by firms in situations presenting performance evaluation problems (Rindfleisch and Heide, 1997) – that is strict enough to eliminate opportunism may actually outweigh the benefits. They investigated a manufacturer's policy toward exclusive territory dealers who sell across their assigned territories (i.e., bootleg). The results of their research demonstrate that optimal enforcement policies will generally tolerate some level of bootlegging. Thus, there may be times when

underaccounting may be an economically rational strategy even if that means tolerating less than diagnostic information.

Psychologists, sociologists, and economists who have studied noise also suggest that underaccounting – and specifically, a strategy of generosity – proves to be the best performing and most adaptive in noisy environments. Bendor, Kramer, and Stout (1991), Kollock (1993), Wu and Axelrod (1995) and Van Lange, Ouwerkert, and Tazelaar (2002) have all demonstrated – through computer simulations or experiments – that in noisy social dilemmas a generous strategy (e.g., tit-for-tat plus 1) outperforms a strategy of strict reciprocity (tit-for-tat). Van Lange, Ouwerkerk, and Tazelaar (2002) suggest that the "beliefs of trust and benign intent that are challenged by negative noise … are overcome by adding a bit of generosity to TFT" (2002, p. 777).

The implications of this discussion are paradoxical. In relationships with a strong degree of benevolent based trust, it may be prudent to be more vigilant and less relaxed in tallying and reacting to the partner's opportunism. However, in situations which are noisy, but in which one hopes to further develop a trusting relationship, a less stringent accounting of the partner's violations may be more efficient and effective in limiting potential negative attributions regarding the partner.

Proposition 10: Underaccounting is most likely to occur in benevolence-based trust relationships; in such relationships a relatively more restrictive accounting system is called for and may actually prove to strengthen trust. Overaccounting is most likely to occur in relationships in noisy contexts. In these cases strict accounting is often not the most efficient strategy to improve performance nor the most effective strategy in increasing trust.

The trigger for feedback in the trust process

To sum up the trust development process, one might think in terms of a trust trajectory as depicted in figure 14.2. Even if a relationship begins at the most basic level of outcome-based trust, the path of least resistance to building benevolence-based trust is one on which the partners continually seek to develop higher levels of identification through repeated positive interactions and on which they are consistently intrinsically motivated. The further away the trust relationship deviates from this trajectory (and becomes more extrinsically motivated by relying on the imposition of hostages, for example), the more likely will there be friction inhibiting further trust growth from negative extrinsic and situational attributions, especially in noisy relationship contexts. The closer the trust relationship is to this trajectory, the more likely is intuition to influence the trustor's relationship accounting mechanism, and the more likely are they to make positive attributions regarding the trustee. The positive accounting of outcomes then triggers a feedback loop that then increases the level of identity in the relationship, and prompts an even more intrinsic motivation for trust. A key to the trust trajectory is its bandwidth between intrinsic and extrinsic motivation. To guard against under- or overaccounting a trustor needs latitude to be able to rely on, or back off of, external incentives in the environment. In this way, trustee behavior that is legitimately trustworthy will have the best chance of being accurately accounted for.

Finally, it is important to note that the research and evidence in support of this trajectory, with the exception of the discussion of network-based trust relationships, is largely based in western countries and particularly in the US. Therefore, the trajectory shown in figure 14.2 applies mainly to western countries. As will be discussed in the next section of this chapter, culture is likely to influence each step of the trust process in significant ways. The consequence of these cultural differences is that alternative trust trajectories will be proposed. Thus, trust development is considered to be culturally determined.

Proposition 11: Within western countries the path of least resistance to building benevolence-based trust is one on which the partners continually seek to develop higher levels of identification through repeated positive interactions and on which they are consistently intrinsically motivated. However, to guard against under or over accounting a trustor needs latitude to be able to rely on *or back off of external incentives in the environment in order that legitimately trustworthy behavior will have the best chance of being accurately accounted for.*

Section II: Cultural influences on the trust development process

An advantage of a clearly delineated model of trust development is that it permits us to more easily examine where in the trust development process, why, and in what way, culture is likely to exert the greatest influence. In the following section the influence of culture on each step of the trust development process is discussed. Table 14.1 presents a list of macro-level and micro-level cultural influences on each step of the trust process. This list is not a comprehensive summary of all cross-cultural trust research; rather, it is an overview of arguments from a wide variety of disciplines that are relevant to understanding the influence of culture on trust.

The definition of "cultural dimension" used here is deliberately expansive, such that it provides for discussion of a wide variety of macro- and micro-level influences on trust; for example, the micro-level dimensions include collectivism and individualism at the individual level as well as the degree of an individuals' civic involvement, the macro-level dimensions encompass nation-based analyses as well as factors such as the rule of law, the percentage of people in a country belonging to a particular religion, or the number of phones per capita. This broad perspective is in line with the comprehensive definition of culture prescribed by Triandis:

A broad definition of culture is that it is the human-made part of the environment. It can be split into material and subjective culture. Material culture consists of such elements as dress, food, houses, highways, tools, and machines. Subjective culture is a society's "characteristic way of perceiving its social environment" (Triandis, 1972, p. viii, 3). It consists of ideas about what has worked in the past and thus is worth transmitting to future generations. Language and economic, educational, political, legal, philosophical, and religious systems are important elements of culture. Ideas about aesthetics, and how should people live with others, are also important elements. Most important are unstated assumptions, standard operating procedures, and habits of sampling information from the environment (Triandis, 2002).

Degree of identification

As demonstrated in the model of trust, one's degree of identification with an individual or group fundamentally influences the nature of trust between them. At the core of theories of identification is the notion of one's increased perception of similarity and belongingness to a group and the development of ingroup biases. A strong body of research, grounded in cross-cultural psychology, suggests that both the nature of group formation (of the sense of similarity and belongingness in a partnership or group) and of ingroup biases are likely to differ culturally, and specifically, across individuals who are collectively versus individually oriented.

Within collectivist cultures, ingroups are few, more permanent, and are formed on the basis of shared personal characteristics such as family, village, or clan. Among individualist cultures, by contrast, ingroups are plentiful, temporary and flexible, and are based on the common interests of members (Triandis, 1988; Han and Choe, 1994). Given the relative rigidity of ingroup boundaries in collectivist societies, it is not surprising that ingroup biases are more strongly held and more significantly demonstrated among naturally occurring groups in collectivist societies compared with such groups in individualist societies (Triandis, 1988).

Research by Buchan and colleagues (Buchan, Croson, and Dawes, 2002; Buchan, Johnson, and Croson, 2006) confirms that even in experimental settings using minimal group manipulations, individualist participants form group identities easily and demonstrate significant ingroup biases. In that same research, however, collectivist participants formed no such group distinctions or biases. In fact, Chinese participants, who tended to have the strongest collectivist orientations of any participants in the research, demonstrated

outgroup biases, seemingly in resistance to the artificial boundary that had been erected between them and their natural group members (i.e., participants were from the same university within each culture).

The implications of this research for trust development are that the foundation of the trust development process, the development of identity between parties, is likely to take much longer to build when the relationship involves collectively oriented parties than when the relationship occurs only among individually oriented parties. Indeed, as discussed by Farh *et al.* (1998), even though institutional rules may replace family connections in some Chinese or Taiwanese contexts, kinship remains a key element of guanxi and thus, individuals to whom one is related will simply be trusted more than non-related individuals. Pushing this connection even farther, the research by Yuki *et al.* (2005) suggests that the very basis of identification differs across cultures; while common identity may be more important in the individually oriented US, a common bond may be more important in collectively oriented societies.

How, then, does one develop trust when working with a collectively oriented partner? Perhaps the best example is set by collectivists themselves; when collectivists develop relationships with outsiders they "take great time and care to evaluate a partner and nurture the relationship so that the outsider can eventually be brought into the ingroup" (Farh *et al.*, 1988, p. 87). Such time and care was obviously on display in the relationship between Jamaican coffee exporters and their Japanese importers discussed earlier; on both sides concerns for the immediate transaction were secondary to concerns for relationship – and identity – building.

Proposition 12: Both the nature of group formation and of ingroup biases are likely to differ culturally, and specifically, across individuals who are collectively versus individually oriented. The development of identity between parties, is likely to take much longer to build when the relationship involves collectively oriented parties than when the relationship occurs only among individually oriented parties.

Table 14.1. Macro-level and Micro-level Cultural Influences on Trust

Element of Trust Process	Role within Process	Author	Cultural Dimension	Macro-Level*	Micro-Level**	Summary of Relevant Arguments / Findings
Degree of Identification	**Nature of ingroup formation**	Triandis *et al.* 1988; Han and Choe, 1994	Collectivism and individualism		X	In collectivist cultures ingroups are few, more permanent, formed on the basis of shared personal characteristics. In individualist cultures, ingroups are plentiful, temporary and flexible, based on common interests of members.
	Nature of ingroup formation; ingroup / outgroup bias	Farh, *et al.*, 1998	Nation based (Taiwan and mainland China)	X		Although family connections may be replaced by institutional rules in some contexts, kinship is a key element of guanxi and individuals to whom one is related are trusted more than non-related individuals.
	Nature of ingroup formation; ingroup/ outgroup bias	Huff and Kelley, 2003	Collectivism and individualism (within Japan, Korea, Hong Kong, Taiwan, China, Malaysia, US)		X	Collectivists display stronger ingroup biases than individualists; when collectivists develop relationships with outsiders they take "great time and care to evaluate a partner and nurture the relationship so that the outsider can eventually be brought into the ingroup" (p. 87).
	Nature of ingroup / outgroup bias	Triandis, 1995	Collectivism and individualism		X	Ingroup biases among natural ingroups in collectivist societies are likely to be much stronger than ingroup biases among natural individualist ingroups.
	Nature of ingroup formation; ingroup/ outgroup bias	Buchan, Croson and Dawes, 2002	Collectivism and individualism (within China, Japan Korea, US)		X	Individualists perceived greater similarity between themselves and experimentally manipulated ingroup members than among themselves and manipulated strangers; collectivists showed no significant differences. Individualists demonstrated an ingroup bias; collectivists did not.
	Nature of ingroup / outgroup bias	Buchan, Johnson and Croson 2005	Collectivism and individualism (within China, Japan Korea, US)		X	Among experimentally manipulated ingroups and outgroups; individualist participants demonstrated a strong ingroup bias; collectivist participants did not demonstrate a bias or sent more to the outgroup (to compensate for the construction of the artificial group boundary).
	Nature of ingroup / outgroup bias	Yuki, *et al.* 2005	Nation based (Japan and US)	X		Japanese and Americans demonstrate ingroup biases in trust. Japanese also extend trust to outgroup members with whom they have indirect personal connections. Suggests that common identity may be of more importance in US; common bond may be more important in Japan.

Motivation: intrinsic / extrinsic	Environmental (Extrinsic) Constraints to Influence the Relationship	Yamagishi et al. 1988a 1988b, 1994, 1998	Nation based (Japan and US)	X		Japanese display more trust toward ingroup members in the presence of mechanisms to reduce the uncertainty of trustee's actions (systems of sanctioning and monitoring); Americans display trust even in absence of such mechanisms.
	Environmental (Extrinsic) Constraints to Influence the Relationship	Hayashi et al., 1999	Sense of control (within Japan and the US)	X		Japanese expect partner to cooperate only when they feel a sense of control over partner's behavior (whether the control was real or illusory); Americans cooperated because of beliefs about benign intent. Reveals differing emphases on beliefs about nature of social relations versus beliefs in human nature.
	Environmental (Extrinsic) Constraints to Influence the Relationship	Malhotra, Kim and Buchan, 2007	Nation-based (South Korea and US); Independent / Interdependent self-construal	X	X	Although South Koreans / Collectivists are less generally trusting than Americans / Individualists, they are more willing to provide personal information to online marketing firms than are Americans when mutual monitoring and sanctioning mechanisms are present.
Determining the nature of trust	Influences on Expectations Based on Incentives	Hagen and Choe, 1998	Japan	X		Identifies several institutional mechanisms (such as subcontractor grading and a dual-vendor policy) and societal sanctioning mechanism (such as ostracism) that promote trust and cooperation in distribution channels
	Influences on expectations based on incentives	Landa 1994	Underdeveloped economies with little perceived governmental efficiency (China)	X		In response to underdeveloped economic environment and little perceived governmental efficiency, the solution to the difficulty of locating trustworthy partners lies in creation of embedded network that provides both information and sanctions, often by reliance on middlemen.
	Influences on expectations based on incentives	Cook, Rice, and Gerbasi 2004 citing Guseva and Rona –Tas (2001) and Radaev (2002), etc.	Transition economies with weak rule of law (Russia and Eastern Europe)	X		The lack of institutional support and backing of contracts along with an environment of corruption and exploitation gives rise to the creation of personal networks, organizations and institutions to facilitate interactions, enable the assessment of trustworthiness, and provide monitoring and enforcement
	Influences on expectations based on incentives	Rao, Pearce and Xin 2005; Pearce 2001	Nonfacilitative governments (China, Hong Kong, Thailand, US)	X		In response to nonfacilitative governments, mangers will develop networks of mutually committed personal relationships based on reciprocal exchange. These networks provide protection, information and dependence management.
	Influences on Expectations Based on Incentives	McMillan and Woodruff (1999a, 1999b)	Lack of contract law and enforcement (Vietnam)	X		The absence of legal enforcement combined with the risk of finding trading partners gives rise to relational mechanisms – networks which are used to determine credit worthiness or partner and to sanction defaulting customers.

Table 14.1. (cont.)

Element of Trust Process	Role within Process	Author	Cultural Dimension	Macro-Level*	Micro-Level**	Summary of Relevant Arguments / Findings
Psychological stance; intuitive / rational	An intuitive stance often leads to reliance on one's / General propensity to trust	La Porta et al., 1997	% of population belonging to a hierarchical religion (40 country analysis)	X		The correlation between general trust and membership in hierarchical religions is −0.61.
	General propensity to trust	Fishman and Khanna, 1999	Number of phones per capita (40 country analysis)	X		The number of phones per capita exerts a strong positive influence on the level of general trust in a society (40 country analysis).
	General propensity to trust	Putnam, 1993	Degree of civic involvement		X	A high degree of civic involvement (in voluntary associations) in society increases general levels of trust.
	General propensity to trust	Ingelhart, 1997	Stable democracy	X		WVS data from 43 countries show correlation of .72 between stable democracy and interpersonal trust.
	General propensity to trust	Mackie, 2001	Post-marital residence, Female age of marriage, Forms of service (work outside/inside the home)	X		Suggests that the interplay of social factors (post-marital residence (in/out of parents' home), female age of marriage and forms of service (whether inside/outside of home) may contribute to differences in levels of general trust across 12 western European countries.
	General propensity to trust	Yamagishi et al., 1988a, 1988b, 1994, 1998	Nation based (Japan and US)	X		Americans display more generalized trust (toward everyone including strangers). Japanese reliance on assurance mechanisms potentially limits their ability to develop greater generalized trust.
	General propensity to trust	Huff and Kelley, 2003	Collectivism and Individualism		X	Collectivists have stronger ingroup bias resulting in lower general propensities to trust and lower organization trust for external partners.
	General propensity to trust	Cook, Rice, and Gerbasi, 2004	Transition economies with weak rule of law	X		Personal networks (which developed to compensate for the lack of legitimate government control) often impede further transformation to system of trusting and trustworthy police, judges, governments and citizens.
	General propensity to trust	Rao, Pearce and Xin, 2005 (in line with Inglehart, 1999 and Ingelhart and Baker, 2000).	Rule of Law, Corruption, Political and Economic Risk (4 countries studied)	X		Populations in countries with weak rule of law, high levels of corruption, and greater political and economic risk were less trusting of others than populations in countries with the opposite conditions; the establishment of reciprocal exchange relationships (which led to specific trust) among managers is insufficient to overcome the negative effect of non-facilitative government on general trust
	Propensity toward intuitive vs. (calculative) rationality	Buchan and Croson, 2004	Nation based (China, US)	X		A "rational" trust decision is one in which trust is correlated with what one expects to receive back (trustworthiness). Americans fit the rational framework, Chinese do not.

Construct	Reference	Dimension			Description
Propensity toward intuitive vs. (calculative) rationality	Den Hartog, 2004	Assertiveness		X	Individuals from high assertiveness societies are more likely to use (more rational) calculative processes and more likely to emphasize capability in trust judgements than are individuals from low assertiveness societies.
Propensity toward intuitive vs. (calculative) rationality	Tan and Chee, 2005	Chinese Singaporeans	X		Affective influences such as personal relationships take priority over cognitive influences such as professional credentials (competence) in trust judgements; demonstrated influence on trust of factors unique to context such as filial piety, respect for authority, shared collective effort, harmonious relationships, magnanimous behavior.
Propensity toward intuitive vs. (calculative) rationality	Doney, Cannon and Mullen, 1998	Uncertainty avoidance		X	Individuals in high uncertainty avoidance cultures are more likely to use prediction, intentionality, capability and transference processes to establish trust. Individuals in low uncertainty avoidance cultures are more likely to use calculative processes.
Propensity toward intuitive vs. (calculative) rationality	Suuly de Luque and Javidan, 2004	Uncertainty avoidance		X	Individuals in high uncertainty avoidance cultures are more likely to establish rules to promote predictability of behavior and prefer long term, established relationships than individuals in low uncertainty avoidance cultures.
Propensity toward intuitive vs. (calculative) rationality	Malhotra, Kim and Buchan, 2007	Independent / interdependent		X	Independently oriented people tend to make the trust decisions based on a rational weighing of costs and benefits; Interdependently oriented people tend to make trust decisions based upon the beliefs and actions of those in their group.
Risk preferences (link psychological stance and trusting behavior)	Douglas and Wildavsky, 1982; (as cited by Weber and Hsee, 2000)	5 distinct culture worldviews or patterns of interpersonal relationships (hierarchical, individualist, egalitarian, fatalist, hermetic)	X		The perception of risk is a collective, socially constructed phenomenon; each culture selects which risks to attend to and which to ignore. Cultural differences are explained in terms of contribution to maintaining way of life; e.g. hierarchical groups perceive industrial and technical risks as opportunities whereas egalitarian groups perceive them as threats to their social structure.
Risk preferences (link psychological stance and trusting behavior)	Palmer, 1996	Douglas and Wildavsky categories (reduced): Hierarchical, individualist, egalitarian		X	When making risk judgements, hierarchists considered all variables in the rational judgement (gains and losses, outcome levels and probabilities); egalitarian judgements only reflected consideration of loss or harm; individualists provided lowest risk judgements for an array of risky investments and opportunities.
Risk preferences (link psychological stance and trusting behavior)	Bontempo, et al., 1997	Nation based (Hong Kong, Taiwan, Netherlands, US)	X	X	Differences in risk preferences followed a Chinese-western division. Probability of loss had a larger effect on perceived risk for Netherlands and US samples. Magnitude of loss had a larger effect on perceived risk for Hong Kong and Taiwan samples.

Table 14.1. (cont.)

Element of Trust Process	Role within Process	Author	Cultural Dimension	Macro-Level*	Micro-Level**	Summary of Relevant Arguments / Findings
	Risk preferences (link psychological stance and trusting behavior)	Weber and Hsee, 1998; Hsee and Weber, 1999; Weber and Hsee, 2000	Nation based (US, Poland, Germany, China)	X		Participants in China are systematically less risk averse in risky financial decisions than are participants in the US; however, differences across cultures are mainly due to differences in the way respondents perceived the risk of the decisions. Proposed "cushion" hypothesis: member of collectivist cultures can afford to take greater financial risks because their social networks will "cushion" them against catastrophic outcomes.
	Risk preferences (link psychological stance and trusting behavior)	Hsee and Weber, 1999	Differences in social networks		X	Test of cushion hypothesis: (a) Results demonstrate that size and quality of social networks mediate the relationship between culture and risk preference. (b) Chinese participants are more risk-seeking relative to Americans only in the domain of financial risks not in social domains
	Risk preferences (link psychological stance and trusting behavior)	Weber, Hsee and Sokolowska, 1999	Risk-taking content of American and Chinese proverbs	X		Chinese proverbs endorse risk-taking more than American proverbs, but Chinese only perceived the risk-taking advice in the financial domain; Within the proverbs, social concerns rate equal to financial or material concerns in (collectivist) China, but are of smaller importance in (individualist) US.
	Risk preferences (link psychological stance and trusting behavior)	Cook, et al., 2005	Risk-taking (within Japan and the US)	X		Risk taking is a crucial element in trust building for Americans, but not for Japanese. Americans were more willing than Japanese to take risks to build trust; when risk taking opportunities were not present, Americans were less cooperative than Japanese counterparts.
Diagnosticity of Information	**Influence on the psychological stance and relationship accounting mechanism**	Farh, et al., 1998; Tsui and Farh, 1997	Nation based (Taiwan and mainland China)	X		Guanxi is most pervasive within inner circle of power in large companies when task complexity is high and performance outcomes are ill defined.
	Influence on the psychological stance and relationship accounting mechanism	McMillan and Woodruff, 2000; Landa, 1994; Grief, 1995; Cook, Rice, Gerbasi, 2004, etc.	Ineffective contract enforcement and rule of law by government	X		In response to ineffective contract enforcement and rule of law by government organized private orders will arise between traders and among firms, their suppliers and customers. Key functions are to expand economic activity, provide information about who has broken a contract, and coordinate a response to such breaches.
	Influence on the psychological stance and relationship accounting mechanism	Rao, Pearce and Xin, 2005	Economies with non-facilitative governments	X		In response to non-facilitative governments, personal relationships serve as a key source of information regarding who is powerful and who is reliable.

				Macro-level*	Micro-level**	
Attributions	**Focus and content of attributions**	Maddox and Yuki, 2006	East Asians and westerners (Asian Americans – European Americans; Japanese – Americans)	X		East Asians focus more on distal, indirect causes (situational factors, groups are responsible, many possible causes) and take much more information into account. Westerners focus on proximate causes (personal factors, single persons are responsible, few possible causes) and take relatively much less information into account.
	Focus and content of attributions	Griffith, Zhang and Cavusgil, 2006	Collectivly / Individually oriented nations; Risk-taking / Risk avoiding nations; hierarchical / egalitarian nations	X		People from individually-oriented nations, risk-avoiding nations, and hierarchical nations attribute noncooperative incidents (NCI) to intentional actions; people from collectively oriented nations, risk-taking nations and egalitarian nations attribute NCI to unintentional actions.
	Focus and content of attributions	McGill, 1995	Nation based (Thailand / US)	X		To explain a successful strategy, Thai managers made external attributions (due to external circumstances or group), US managers made internal (personal) attributions. To explain an unsuccessful strategy, Thai managers made internal attributions, US managers made external attributions.
Relationship accounting mechanism	**Use of restrictive vs. relaxed accounting system**	Rao, Pearce and Xin, 2005	Economies with non-facilitative governments	X		Managers cope with the lack of government facilitation by building reciprocal exchange relationships in which exchanges of help, advice and approval occur over time. The greater the exchange in such relationships, the greater their trust in one another. In such relationships, the nature of the return is unspecified and future obligations are diffuse.
	Use of restrictive vs. relaxed accounting system	Lee, Pillutla and Law, 2000	Power distance		X	Procedural justice matters more in the trust in supervisor relationship for individuals with low power distance orientations than for individuals with high power distance orientations. The former may be less likely to extend the benefit of the doubt.
	Use of restrictive vs. relaxed accounting system	Farh, et al., 1998	Nation based (Taiwan and mainland China)	X		Different principles of interaction and social treatment apply between individuals who are connected by different guanxi bases. Kinship ties imply role obligation without expectation of reciprocity. Familiar ties imply favors and generosity with expectation of reciprocation. Strangers will be treated with caution and discretion.
	Use of restrictive vs. relaxed accounting system	McMillan and Woodruff, 1999	Lack of contract law and enforcement (Vietnam)	X		In absence of "shadow of law" firm suffering breach of contract maintain relationship with partner, "patiently" trying to get paid. Will investigate reason for breach and will negotiate if reason was outside of partner's control. Are hesitant to retaliate for fear for damaging partner's relationships with other trading partners.

* Macro-level: Environmental or cultural variable occurs and is discussed at the aggregate or country level
** Micro-level: Environmental or cultural variable occurs and is discussed at the individual level

Motivation: intrinsic/extrinsic

The combination of the degree of identification between the parties and the locus of motivation for the trustor influence the nature of trust in a given relationship. Motivations to trust vary across contexts and even within the same person depending on the relationship context; increasingly we understand that important differences exist in motivational tendencies cross-culturally as well. Specifically, a vast literature produced by experimental sociologist Toshio Yamagishi and colleagues (e.g., 1988a; 1988b; Yamagishi and Yamagishi, 1994; Yamagishi, Cook, and Watabe, 1998) demonstrates that when initiating new trust relationships Japanese are motivated by factors in the relationship environment, particularly the presence of an informal system of monitoring and sanctions to reduce the uncertainty of the partner's actions. Americans, on the other hand, are more likely to rely on their intrinsic beliefs regarding the benign intent of human nature.

Yamagishi supports his findings by pointing to the work of cultural anthropologist Ruth Benedict (1946), who proposed that in Japan informal mutual monitoring and sanctioning constitute the foundation of social order. Thus, Yamagishi, Cook, and Watabe (1998) argue, differences in trust and cooperation among Japanese and Americans are not due to the "individualistic view of culture," that is, the proposition that relative to Americans, Japanese place greater priority on group welfare over individual interests (1998, p. 168). But, rather, they are due to an "institutional view of culture," in which the closed nature of Japanese society breeds a sense of mutual dependence and control such that in the absence of such group constraints, Japanese feel insecure entering into trust relationships (1998, p. 168; Hayashi et al., 1999).

Malhotra, Kim, and Buchan (2007) extended this research to a South Korea-US comparison to study the decision to trust in the context of online privacy. Their results demonstrate that like the Japanese, South Koreans are more influenced than Americans in their trust decisions by the presence of monitoring and control mechanisms to insure that the information would not be misused. Additionally, they show that those participants who have interdependent self-construals are more likely to be influenced by societal control mechanisms than are participants who have independent self-construals.

This research suggests that in Japan and Korea, a trustor's decisions are most strongly motivated by extrinsic consideration of the social structure of their environment whereas in the US trust decisions are motivated more by the trustor's intrinsic beliefs regarding human nature, and furthermore these differences may be due to differences associated with collectivism and individualism at the individual level. It must be noted, however, that the meta-analysis of collectivism and individualism by Oyserman, Coon, and Kemmelmeier (2002) demonstrates that, unlike South Korea, Japan is not significantly more collectively oriented than is the US; furthermore, the extent to which collectivist or individualist tendencies are demonstrated is a function of the measurement items used. Clearly, more work is needed to fully understand the factors that contribute to the cultural orientation underlying this emphasis on extrinsic social structure versus intrinsic beliefs.

Proposition 13: In Japan and Korea, a trustor's decisions are most strongly motivated by extrinsic consideration of the social structure of their environment whereas in the US trust decisions are motivated more by the trustor's intrinsic beliefs regarding human nature. This difference may be due to differences associated with collectivism and individualism at the individual level.

Weighting of the three trust expectations

When the trustor's motivation is relatively extrinsic and levels of identity between the parties are low, expectations of competence are likely to be most heavily weighted in the trust calculation. When motivation is intrinsic and high levels of identity have developed, expectations of benevolence are likely to be most heavily weighted. Expectations based on the trustee's incentives to be trustworthy are likely to be most heavily weighted when the trustor's motivation is extrinsic and there exists a significant incentive for the trustee to be trustworthy, be it reputational concerns, network constraints, or a contract, for example. Although later in the trust development process we will see cultural influences biasing the weighting of the expectations of competence and benevolence, a solid body of research indicates that a priori there are particular environments that have a high propensity for the growth of specific incentives for the trustee.

As discussed, strong network-based incentives exist for the trustee in Japan and South Korea. Indeed, Hagen, and Choe's (1998) research demonstrates the power of informal institutional and societal mechanisms in prompting trusting and trustworthy behavior within Japanese distribution networks. It is interesting to note in Japan and South Korea the pervasiveness of network-based trust incentives, which are largely social in nature, in contrast to the rarity of legal contracts in those countries. This tendency is explained by Gesteland who, drawing on Hall's theory of high and low context cultures (Hall, 1959), discusses the meaning of what he calls "transaction-oriented" (or low context) versus "relationship-focused" (or high context) cultures (Gesteland, 1999). In transaction-oriented cultures such as the US, a legal contract strictly delineates the parameters of the exchange between the parties; in relationship-focused cultures, the exchange is adaptable as per nature of the relationship. That is, in transaction-oriented cultures, the contract defines the content of the exchange, the responsibility of the parties, and the deadline for its completion. In relationship-focused cultures such as Japan and South Korea, the exchange is grounded in a fluid (personal) relationship which carries with it the implicit understanding that renegotiation may need to occur in the face of unforeseen circumstances.[2] Salacuse (2001) highlights these different emphases and perspectives on relationships versus contracts across cultures and suggests they represent one of the most complex aspects of cross-cultural negotiations.

In light of the differing emphasis and perspective on contracts across cultures, it is significant that a solid body of research indicates that network-based incentives for the trustee are most likely to arise in emerging market environments where there is weak rule of law and little enforcement of contracts. For example, experimental research as well as empirical field research has demonstrated

the strength of such network relationships among privately owned firms in Vietnam (McMillan and Woodruff, 1999b), the non-profit sector in eastern Europe (Rose-Ackerman, 2001), entrepreneurial markets (Radaev, 2004) and credit card markets in Russia (Guseva and Rona-tas, 2001). Yet, interestingly, once stronger and more legitimate institutional enforcement mechanisms take hold, typically the emphasis on network-based incentives diminishes relative to growth in use of contracts to foster trust relationships (McMillan and Woodruff, 1999a; Johnson, McMillan and Woodruff, 2002).

The theoretical impetus for network commitments lies in the desire to reduce social uncertainty. In transitional market environments with weak rule of law and little contract enforcement, two types of uncertainty exist. First is the uncertainty of finding a reliable partner with whom to trade (Cook, Rice and Gerbasi, 2004); second is the uncertainty created by the risk of opportunism by the exchange partner, such as might be incurred when the quality of the product exchanged is not easily determined (Kollock, 1994). Oftentimes, securing commitments with specific partners is the most viable solution in such situations, and extended commitment is likely to provide information about the relative trustworthiness of the counterpart (Kollock 1994; Cook, Rice, and Gerbasi, 2004). In essence, the relationship evolves into a safe haven, protecting one from opportunistic partners, and traders will remain in this haven even to the exclusion of more potentially profitable exchanges (Yamagishi and Yamagishi, 1994). Thus, committed networks of exchange are most likely to become networks of trust under situations of risk.

---

[2] This difference in emphasis on contracts versus relationships is starkly portrayed in Trompenaars and Hampen-Turner's (1998) example of a trading relationship involving bauxite between individuals from a particularist versus universalist culture (correlated with high context and low context cultures, respectively). In that situation the bottom had fallen out of the bauxite market and the buyer from the particularist culture believes that they and the partner need to work out new terms for the exchange in the interest of the overall welfare of both parties in the relationship. By contrast, the seller from the universalist culture believes there is no such need for renegotiation since a contract is binding and final.

There is evidence that trust networks may not necessarily be permanent features of an economy but rather only a stage in market transition. Evidence from research in eastern Europe and Russia suggests that as institutional legitimacy and rule of law increases, people begin to place more reliance on the courts as arbiters in the case of contract failure rather than on network governance (Rose-Ackerman, 2001). Furthermore, McMillan and Woodruff find that courts have a perceptible effect on the level of trust in traders relationships with their consumers: "people who say the courts are effective grant 5% more trade credit on average"(1999a, p. 223).

When one compares the reliance on network relationships versus contracts in Japan and South Korea relative to what is seen in transition economies, an obvious question arises. If, as research seems to indicate, the typical path of trust development in transition economies moves from one based on network relationships to one invested more in contracts and the law, why do trust relationships in the developed markets of Japan and South Korea remain closely tied to network structures? I would suggest that the difference lies in the relationship-focused versus transaction-oriented nature of the cultures involved. In cultures that are most strongly relationship focused, the idea of using a legal contract – a piece of paper – to jumpstart trust in a new partnership is anathema to what a relationship really means. Reduction of social uncertainty is tied to the potential strength of the new relationship and its place within the network structure of the trustee's other relationships. In cultures that are relatively more transaction-oriented, the reduction in social uncertainty needed to enter into new trust relationships may be provided by the incentive of legitimate institutions and an enforceable legal contract.

If this is true, it will be interesting to witness what happens in the case of Vietnam, a country which is relatively relationship-focused, like Japan and South Korea, but which is likely to experience the same type of transition to more legitimate legal institutions seen in eastern Europe. In their examination of private sector relationships in Vietnam during the 1990s, McMillan and Woodruff (1999b) first point to the research by Barton (1983) in Vietnam in the 1960s to understand the market's evolution. At that time, business was based on and limited to personal relationships among ethnic Chinese and network reputational and enforcement mechanisms were in force. In the 1990s, however, there was no significant influence of an ethnic Chinese network on the propensity to form relationships and, in general, strict kin or clan social connections were used to initiate just one-quarter of new relationships in Vietnam, even in the absence of legal contract enforcement. Rather, relationships were bolstered by a hybrid structure of incentives, often relying on a broader network:

> To compensate for the inadequacy of the courts, the firms use repeated-game incentives. Contracting is supported by the threat of loss of future business. Of interest however, the managers told us they are reluctant to sanction trading partner ... To ensure compliance the firms rely on other devices to supplement the shadow of the future ... Community sanctions sometimes support transactions with reneging risks. Firms often scrutinize prospective trading partners before beginning to transact, checking the firms' reliability via other firms in the same line of business or familial connections (McMillan and Woodruff, 1999a, p. 638).

This research suggests that even in the presence of contract enforcement, the relationship-focused Vietnamese will likely continue relying on network relationship and socially based incentives to counter social uncertainty when starting trust relationships.

Proposition 14a: Expectations of trustworthiness based on the incentive structure surrounding the relationship (specifically, network-based trust) are likely to be most heavily weighted in relationship-focused countries such as Japan and South Korea and in transition economies.

Proposition 14b: As facilitative institutions and legitimate contract enforcement develop in transition economies, there is likely to be a shift in reliance to legal contracts in new trust relationships. Cultures, such as Vietnam, that are relatively more relationship-focused however are likely to continue to emphasize network-based trust.

Psychological stance: Intuitive or rational

One's psychological stance – whether intuitive or rational – influences and often biases trust judgment and trusting behavior in predictable ways and each of these ways has been shown to vary across cultures.

General propensities to trust

In situations in which little is known about the partner's benevolence or the incentives that prompt them to be trustworthy, trust resembles not specific but generalized trust, i.e. the belief in the trustworthiness of others in general. Generalized trust is strongly influenced by one's propensity to trust, and propensity to trust varies across cultures.

In the mid to late 1990s an upsurge of interest in the topic of generalized trust resulted from the publication of research linking generalized trust to a nation's economic prosperity (Fukuyama, 1995), to the degree of economic growth in a country (Knack and Keefer, 1997) and to the degree of governmental and economic stability in a country or region (Putnam, 1993). The implications of this research are that levels of generalized trust vary across societies. Since then, a host of publications have demonstrated that generalized trust levels are correlated with such things as the percentage of population belonging to a hierarchical religion in a country (La Porta *et al.*, 1997), the number of phones per capita in a country (Fishman and Khana, 1999), the typical post-marriage residence in a country, the average female age of marriage, the typical form of employment (Mackie, 2001) and the degree to which the country's population is civically involved (Putnam, 1993).

Other research has related generalized trust to the cultural dimensions already discussed. First, Huff and Kelley (2003) demonstrate in six countries differences in general trust across people with collectivist or individualist orientations. Because of the strength of their ingroup biases, Huff and Kelley argue, collectivists find it difficult to trust anyone outside their immediate group and thus have lower organizational trust for external partners and lower propensities for general trust. Second, there is solid body of evidence to demonstrate that populations who engage in the incentives provided by social network governance are likely to have lower levels of general trust. Yamagishi and colleagues have shown that Japanese have lower levels of general trust than Americans (Yamagishi, 1988a, 1988b; Yamagishi and Yamagishi, 1994, Yamagishi, Cook, and Watabe 1998). Others have demonstrated that populations in countries with weak rule of law are likely to form social networks to facilitate trust, but paradoxically, in promoting trust within the network, they are also decreasing their own propensities toward general trust (Cook, Rice, and Gerbasi, 2004; Rao, Pearce, and Xin, 2005).

This paradox is supported by Cook and Hardin (2001). They cite Stolle's (1998) finding that members of groups with weak within-group trust have higher levels of generalized trust than do members of groups with strong within-group trust. Cook and Hardin explain that the very tactics that foster strong within-group trust also "commonly foster distrust of outsiders. Namely they can lower the possibility for intergroup trust within society" (2001, p. 335). The implications of this are that strong network-based trust relationships, by lowering generalized propensities to trust, may actually serve to inhibit the development of non-network based trust relationships.

As discussed, one mechanism that may counter low generalized trust propensities is the development of confidence in institutions and legal contract enforcement. These incentives have proven in the Czech Republic or Poland, for example, to reduce social uncertainty to the degree that trustor's formally bound in network relationships would feel comfortable trusting a non-network member (Rose-Ackerman, 2001; Johnson, McMillan, and Woodruff, 2002). Yet, in line with the earlier discussion, legal mechanisms are not likely to significantly counter low generalized trust in collectivist, relationship-oriented societies.

Proposition 15a: Propensities toward generalized trust are likely to be relatively lower among people with collectivist orientations and among populations who engage in the incentives provided by social network governance.

Proposition 15b: Strong network-based trust relationships, by lowering generalized propensities to trust, may serve to inhibit the development of non-network based trust relationships.

Propensity toward intuitive versus calculative rationality

When someone relies on intuition in making a trust judegment, they are using what Kahneman describes as System 1 (Kahneman, 2003). Their judgement is likely to be automatic, associative, emotionally charged, and typically governed by habit. When one relies on calculative rationality in the trust judgement, they are using System 2; the judgement is likely to be slower, more effortful and deliberate, and potentially rule-governed. There is robust evidence to suggest that the propensity toward intuitive versus calculative rationality may vary across collectivist and individualist orientations and across individuals with differing degrees of uncertainty avoidance.

Tan and Chee (2005) examined the trust judgements of Chinese Singaporean managers and demonstrated that affective influences such as personal relationships, shared collective effort and harmonious relations take priority over cognitive influences such as professional credentials that would signal competence. Buchan and Croson's (2004) experimental study of trust between Chinese and American students and trust "targets," ranging from foreign strangers to one's own parents, revealed that there was a strong correlation between the trust American students would extend and the trustworthiness they expected in return, demonstrating that their trust judgement was in line with economic rationality. Yet there was no such correlation between trust extended and trustworthiness expected for Chinese students; rather, norms regarding different bases of guanxi (depending on type of relationship) seemed to be at play (Farh et al., 1998). Malhotra, Kim, and Buchan (2007) studied decisions to trust among on-line survey respondents in South Korea and the US and tested and classified the respondents based on their independent versus interdependent orientations (which are correlated with individualist and collectivist orientations, respectively). Independently oriented participants tended to make trust decisions based on a rational weighing of costs and benefits; interdependently oriented participants tended to trust based upon the beliefs and actions of those in their group.

The theoretical propositions of Doney, Cannon, and Mullen (1998) and the empirical work of Suuly de Luque and Javidan (2004) suggest that individuals in high uncertainty avoidance cultures are more likely to use processes such as predictability and transference when making trust judgements. That is, people in high uncertainty avoidance cultures prefer to establish rules to promote predictability of behavior and prefer to trust in long-term relationships, or to trust those who are known to them or at least known by someone in their network. Individuals in low uncertainty avoidance cultures are more likely to use a calculative process.

The implication of these cross-cultural differences in propensities toward intuitive (System 1-based) versus rational (System 2-based) trust judgements are that: (a) trust judgements are likely to be intuitively based and biased toward expectations of benevolence among people with interdependent (collectivist) orientations and within societies that display high uncertainty avoidance (that is, expectations of benevolence will be overweighted, and the other two expectations will be underweighted, relative to the weightings determined in the trust determination step on the trust process); and (b) there will likely be less bias in the weighting of expectations within the trust judgements of independently oriented individuals (individualists) and within societies that display low uncertainty avoidance.

Proposition 16: Trust judgements are likely to be intuitively based and biased toward expectations of benevolence, in contrast to competence and incentive structure, among people with interdependent (collectivist) orientations and within societies that display high uncertainty avoidance.

Risk preferences

Risk preferences influence the trust process by regulating the propensity of people – when given the same information regarding trust expectations – to act on their trust judgement and extend trusting behavior. Research examining risk attitudes and preferences across cultures demonstrates that people differ most in the extent to which they view a given situation as involving risk.

In 1982 political scientist Aaron Wildavsky and anthropolgist Mary Douglas developed the "cultural theory of risk" (Douglas and Wildavsky, 1982). According to this theory, the perception of risk is a collective, socially-constructed phenomenon and each culture selects which risks to attend to and which to ignore. Cultural differences in risk perception are explained in terms of the contribution to maintaining a way of life made by this decision to attend or ignore (Weber and Hsee, 2000). Douglas classifies social structures along two axes; the "grid" axis refers to the degree to which an individual's choices are delimited by society, the "group" axis refers to the degree of solidarity among members of society. Various combinations of "grid" and "group" yield five main classifications of world views; hierarchical, individualist, egalitarian, fatalist, plus a fifth, asocial.[3] Individualists, for example, value personal initiative in the marketplace and fear any threats that might hamper free exchange. Egalitarians tend to cling to traditional ways of life and view technology as a threat to their social structure. Hierarchists rely on experts who can establish rules to keep society within proper bounds and view technology as something that can be exploited within those bounds. It should be noted that Sjoberg (1997) found difficulty in classifying individuals according to the grid by group framework and suggested that more empirical research was needed to determine the extent to which the cultural theory of risk explains cultural differences in risk perceptions.

Research concerning cross-cultural risk perception by psychologists Elke Weber and Chris Hsee provides clearer evidence that risk preferences tend to be contextually based (Weber and Hsee, 1998; Hsee and Weber, 1999; Weber and Hsee, 2000). Specifically, experiment participants in China have systematically proven to be less risk averse in financial decisions than participants from the US, but have shown little difference in decisions involving social or medical domains. This difference is not due to risk attitudes (i.e., how much risk an individual will tolerate) but instead to systematic differences in risk perception; Chinese participants percieved the financial decision as being less risky than did Americans. To explain these findings, Hsee and Weber tested and

provided solid support for the "cushion hypothesis"; members of collectivist cultures believe they can afford to take greater financial risks because their social networks will "cushion" them against catastrophic loss.

This research suggests that cultures systematically vary in risk perceptions and that the risks they attend to or ignore seemed to be based on the degree to which such risk threatens social structure. For example, contrary to their risk-seeking tendency in financial decisions, Chinese participants were much more risk averse in the social domain; because of its importance to – and insurance of – their well-being, they could not risk losing the social cushion. The implication of these findings for the trust process is that the context of the trust decision may be a key to understanding whether and when the trust judgement leads to trusting behavior.

A final observation regarding risk and culture comes from the experimental research of Cook et al. (2005), which suggests that risk taking is a crucial element in initiating trust relationships for Americans, but not for Japanese. Americans were more willing than Japanese to take risks to build trust but when risk-taking opportunities were not present Americans were less cooperative than their Japanese counterparts. Furthermore, despite the greater propensity for risk-taking, Americans were no better than Japanese at improving levels of cooperation. This research suggests that the trust-building process differs across cultures, and that such trust building efforts may have different starting points.

In light of this research it would be informative to test the propositions of Weber, Malhotra, and Murnighan (2005) cross-culturally. As discussed, those authors proposed that sometimes "irrational trust" is necessary to initiate trust relationships. Cook et al.'s (2005) research suggests that these findings may differ across countries; it seems likely that the "irrational trust" approach to trust building may be more effective in western countries.

Proposition 17a: Cultures systematically vary in risk perceptions and the risks they attend to or

---

[3] Typically, only the first three classifications are included in analyses of risk preferences due to the low number of people classified as fatalists or asocials.

ignore seemed to be based on the degree to which such risk threatens social structure.

Proposition 17b: Evidence from Japan and the US suggests the trust-building process differs across cultures, and that such trust building efforts may have different starting points.

Diagnosticity of information

The diagnosticity of information influences the trust process at two junctures; at the point of the trust judgement and in the interpretation of outcomes. When information diagnosticity is poor: (a) the psychological stance is more likely to operate intuitively than by calculative rationality; and (b) the interpretation of outcomes may be biased in a negative manner.

The most predictable influence of culture on the diagnosticity of information is that in cultures in which network-based governance is a primary basis for trust relationships, personal relationships will serve as a key source of information regarding the reliability of the trustee, their behavior, and outcomes (e.g. Rao, Pearce, and Xin, 2005; McMillan and Woodruff, 1999b). This is because the health of such networks is based upon the accurate monitoring of behavior and is tied to the perceived strength of the network's ability to enforce group norms and punish group defectors. Furthermore, guanxi – and the information such relationship ties provide – is likely to be most influential in situations when performance

---

[4] Griffith, Zhang and Cavusgil (2006) put forward a number of propositions to delineate the influence of national character on attribution making; people from individually oriented nations, risk-avoiding nations, and hierarchical nations attribute noncooperative incidents (NCI) to intentional actions; people from collectively oriented nations, risk-taking nations and egalitarian nations attribute NCI to unintentional actions. Yet this framework presents contrasting hypotheses within a particular cultural type. For example, the individualist nature of the US would suggest the there is, in the US, a tendency to make intentional attributions for NCIs. However, the risk-taking propensity and the relatively egalitarian nature of the US would suggest a tendency toward unintentional attributions. Unfortunately, the authors do not provide propositions regarding how these contradictions within national culture types might be resolved.

evaluation is most difficult (Farh *et al.*, 1998; Tsui and Farh, 1997). This is because, in the absence of clearly diagnostic information, greater weight will be given to the information close relationships can provide.

The implications of these findings are that networks are a source of highly diagnostic information. This degree of diagnosticity will prompt less intuition in the trust judgement and will provide for less bias in attributions.

Proposition 18: Personal relationships in networks are a source of highly diagnostic information regarding the trustee and their behavior. This degree of diagnosticity will prompt less intuition in the trust judgment and will provide for less bias in attributions.

Attributions

According to the trust development process, negative attributions regarding a trustee's behavior are most likely to develop in relationships in which the trustee's motivation to trust is extrinsically based; positive attributions are likely to develop in relationships in which the trustee's motivation is intrinsic and social identity between the parties is high. Evidence from cross-cultural research suggests that due to differences in the method of attribution creation across cultures, the content of attributions and its influence on the relationship accounting mechanism is likely to be more complex.

Maddux and Yuki (2006) summarize a large body of research from cross-cultural psychology that suggests that East Asians focus more on distal, indirect causes of outcomes (situational factors, groups are responsible, many possible causes) and take much more information into account. Westerners focus on proximate causes to explain outcomes (personal factors, single persons are responsible, few possible causes) and take relatively much less information into account.[4] This research suggests that when accounting for outcomes and the trustee's behavior, East Asians are more likely to attribute positive outcomes (and thus trustworthiness) to the situation and existence of the network, and to attribute perceived negative outcomes to a confluence of causes, thus ultimately providing the trustee greater benefit of the doubt. Westerners, on the other hand, are more likely to attribute both positive and negative outcomes to the trustee themselves, thus more definitively ascribing trustworthiness or untrustworthiness.

Interestingly, McGill's experimental results in Thailand and the US (1995) suggests there may be a culture by context interaction when managers are making attributions about their own behavior. When explaining the success of a strategy they developed, Thai managers made external attributions – the success was due to the group or to external circumstances; American managers made internal, or personal, attributions. When explaining reasons for the strategy's failure, the attributions were reversed. Thai managers made internal attributions and American managers made external ones. This research suggests that, in the case of positively perceived outcomes, Thai trustors are more likely to attribute the outcome to the partner's trustworthiness or to the strength of the network and American trustors are more likely to attribute the outcome to their own well-made trust decision. In the case of negatively perceived outcomes, American trustees are more likely to attribute the outcomes to the trustee's lack of trustworthiness, while Thai managers are more likely to make internal attributions regarding their (lack of) ability to make trust judgements.

The implications of this research for the trust development process across cultures are that in the case of positive outcomes, Americans (and possibly westerners) are likely to believe they made the correct decision to trust and to conclude that the trustee acted in a trustworthy manner. Thais (and possibly East Asians) are likely to put even more emphasis on the relationships within their network and its influence in prompting trustworthy behavior from the trustee. In the case of negative outcomes, Americans (westerners) are likely to see the trustee as having been untrustworthy. Thais (East Asians) are likely to question their trust judgements but yet give the trustee the benefit of the doubt.

Proposition 19: Attributions for the trustor's and trustee's behavior are likely to differ across cultures and by context. Westerners are more likely to focus on proximate causes and make personal attributions. East Asians are likely to focus on distal causes and attribute events to a confluence of causes including the group and situation.

Relationship accounting mechanism

The relationship accounting mechanism operates strictly or loosely, depending on the psychological stance of the trustor, the degree of identification between the parties, the diagnosticity of information and the attributions made by the trustor about his own, and the trustee's behavior. Differences across culture also influence the rigidity of the accounting mechanism.

The network-based trust relationships that arise in countries with non-facilitative governments and a lack of contract enforcement typically operate in the relaxed manner appropriate to communal relationships (Rao, Pearce, and Xin, 2005; McMillan and Woodruff, 1999a). As discussed by Rao, Pearce, and Xin (2005), managers in those economies tend to build reciprocal exchange relationships (Molm, Takahashi, and Peterson, 2000); in such relationships the nature of the return is unspecified and future obligations are diffuse. Farh *et al.* (1998) suggest that, within China, the accounting mechanism may operate differently in relationships with different guanxi bases. Kinship ties imply that the mechanism will operate very loosely without specific expectations of reciprocity. Familiar ties imply a slightly stricter mechanism; extension of favors but with expectation of reciprocity. Lastly, the mechanism is likely to operate very strictly in relationships with strangers where caution and discretion are applied. A final study demonstrates the influence of power distance on the accounting mechanism. Specifically, Lee, Pillutla, and Law (2000) show procedural justice matters more in the trust-in-supervisor relationship for individuals with low power distance orientations than for individuals with high power distance orientations. The former may be less likely to extend the benefit of the doubt.

The implications of this research for trust development are that the accounting mechanism is most likely to operate in a relaxed manner in the network-based trust relationships of transition economies, and among individuals with high power distance orientations. Interestingly, the pattern of relationships that has evolved in Taiwan and China seems to be a bit more finely grained such that the operation of the accounting mechanism varies across networks and relationships, with kin-based relationships accorded the most relaxed accounting.

Proposition 20: The accounting mechanism is most likely to operate in a relaxed manner in the network-based trust relationships of transition economies, and among individuals with high power distance orientations. Due to the existence of different bases of guanxi, in China and Taiwan operation of the mechanism will vary according to relationships; it will be most relaxed in kin-based relationships.

Summary of cultural influences on the trust development process

This research suggests that culture influences each stage of the trust development process. Yet, a key shortcoming of existing research on trust and culture is that it has largely been confined to western countries and mainly to the US, as stated earlier, as well as to a handful of other countries such as Japan, China, Taiwan, and South Korea, along with Vietnam, Russia, and those eastern European countries typically classified as transitional economies. Therefore, the conclusions that can be drawn are limited in scope and remain untested in large areas of the world with differing cultural contexts; South America, the Middle East, South Asia, and Africa. Despite this limitation, the body of knowledge accumulated thus far regarding the influence of culture on trust suggests that there are likely culturally determined trust trajectories which differ from that proposed for typical western countries.

Trust trajectory in East Asia

In East Asia, the path of trust development seems to be determined by the foundations of social structure in society. These societies display collectivist tendencies regarding ingroup/outgroup

relations: among collectivist societies ingroups are few, permanent, and intensely loyal, with members displaying prominent biases toward anyone in the outgroup (e.g., Triandis, 1988; Han and Choe, 1994; Huff and Kelley, 2003). One key difference among East Asian nations is the basis for ingroup relations. In Japan the focus of ingroups is the work group;[5] in Chinese-based societies, the focus of the ingroup is the family (Redding, 2003). As Benedict (1946) proposed, in Japan mutual monitoring and sanctioning constitute the foundation of social order, and this seems to hold true in varying degrees throughout the East Asia.

This cultural context has given rise to relationships with network governance to reduce social uncertainty and facilitate network-based trust and exchange. The networks are founded on shared norms and values governing the relationships and thus the level of identity in these relationships is high. The trustor's motivation is based on the assurances of trustworthiness that the network provides and, thus, is extrinsic in nature. There is no need to look beyond the network to independently discern the trustee's competence or benevolence, essentially that is a function performed by network mechanisms, and as such expectations of the incentive structure surrounding the relationship are the most heavily weighted expectations in the trust judgement. The trustee is likely to rely on their intuition rather than calculative rationality in trust judgements. Therefore, their decision-making is biased toward benevolence and their risk-taking trusting behaviors are biased towards ones which will not harm the social structure of their society. When making attributions, East Asians are likely to focus on distal, indirect causes of outcomes and, when combined with their bias toward benevolence and the high levels of identity in the relationship, East Asian trustors are much more likely to give the trustee the benefit of the doubt. Acting as a counterweight to reduce the intuitive and benevolence bias, highly diagnostic information regarding the trustworthiness of the trustee is provided through network relationships. Since preservation of the network is of primary concern, behavior that endangers it will almost

---

[5] A dramatic illustration of this was by appointment by Sony of Howard Stringer, an American citizen, as its CEO in 2005.

Taxonomy of trust: culturally influenced trust trajectories

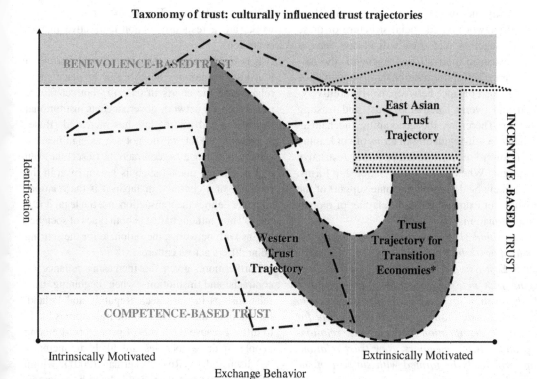

*Applies to transition economies with a relatively more transaction-focused orientation

Figure 14.3. Taxonomy of trust: culturally influenced trust trajectories

certainly be detected. The relationship accounting mechanism operates in a communal fashion. As in reciprocal exchanges, not every outcome is tracked nor acted upon, and neither is immediate reciprocation expected. The normal ebb and flow of relationships is recognized and respected within these relationship-focused cultures.

The strength of trust within the networks therefore develops over time yet, due to their low propensity for generalized trust, the scope of trust relationships within China, Japan, South Korea, or Vietnam, expands very slowly. As the example in Vietnam illustrated, this expansion is likely to be supported by a network, albeit not solely a kin-based one. Indeed, for members of the outgroup in China, which Francis Fukuyama famously described as a "low-trust" country due to its tight kin-based networks (1995), development of trust within a network would seem to be an almost impossible task. Yet Redding suggests

(perhaps overly optimistically) that the potential exists:

> They negotiate very hard, they demand high returns, they need the assurance of interpersonal trust, and their organizations are highly dependent on individuals. Defection by self-seeking subordinates, often taking product knowledge or customers with them, is hard to guard against in a culture boiling with entrepreneurship. This risk is in part counterbalanced by a powerful set of unspoken ethics surrounding trust. For those in the network, the bonds are unbreakable through good times and bad. The successful Westerner will take time, and the very successful will become an honorary Chinese. (Redding, 1995, p. 69).

It is proposed that the trust trajectory for East Asians begins with trust that is based in relationships with network governance and then develops in identification (see Figure 14.3). The trajectory is straight up, rather than moving toward intrinsically motivated trust; the relationship-focused, network-based social structure of these cultures suggests that trust will always have a strong extrinsic motivation. In general, the natural character of these relationships is one which provides for a balance between overly intuitively-based and overly calculative trust and trusting behavior. Therefore, the accounting mechanism seems to be self-regulating in terms of not leaning too far toward overly-relaxed or overly-restrictive accounting. When a new trust relationship forms, it will likely be done so with some support of the network, for example through relaying of reputation information.

Proposition 21: Because of the relationship-focused, network-based social structure of society, within East Asian countries the trust trajectory begins with network-based trust relationships. The motivation for the relationships is likely to remain extrinsic, however, there is potential for increased identification between the relationship and network members. New trust relationships will likely be formed with support of the network.

Trust trajectory in transitional economies (Russia and eastern Europe)

The trust trajectory in transitional economies such as those in Russia and eastern Europe is very similar to that seen in East Asia; however, there are significant differences both in the inception of the trajectory and in its direction. In Russia and eastern Europe, the lack of facilitative institutions and credible mechanisms for contract enforcement has given rise to relationships with network governance to reduce social uncertainty and facilitate network-based trust and exchange. The proposition forwarded here is that the difference between the networks seen in Russia and eastern Europe and those in East Asia is that the networks in East Asia are a natural result of values regarding the role of social relationships within those societies.

[6] Rose-Ackerman discussed the support of Levi and Stoker (2000) and Rothstein (2000) for this view, but acknowledges the argument of Putnam that high levels of interpersonal trust improve the responsiveness and trustworthiness of institutions. Clearly, it is an empirical question yet to be resolved.

In Russia and eastern Europe by contrast, the networks are a response to non-facilitative market conditions.

It is for this reason that, even though people in transition economies have begun to place more reliance on the courts in case of contract failure rather than on network governance as institutional legitimacy and rule of law has increased (Rose-Ackerman, 2001), we do not see as significant a switch to reliance on contracts in East Asia even in a developed market such as Japan. Even in the presence of a contract, in Japan it is the relationship that defines the transaction, not the legal document. Thus, although trust in both types of societies begins with networks, the rationale for the starting point differs across cultures.

Furthermore, given the increasing reliance on contracts and institutions when beginning trust relationships in the Czech Republic and Poland, for example, the direction of the trajectory is likely to differ because the levels of general trust among people in these societies are likely to increase. As discussed by Rose-Ackerman (2001), within transition societies there is likely to be a contest between existing trust networks that emerged as coping mechanisms versus confidence in new institutions. It is proposed that, as institutions within a society are increasingly seen as more trustworthy, there will be a growth of generalized trust in those societies as well.[6] As generalized trust, increases among the population, there will be a greater tendency to enter into relationships with non-network members. Furthermore, with the growth of institutional legitimacy, the less relationship-oriented is a culture, the less likely will trustors be to avoid relationships that risk harming the network-based social structure, and the less strongly will the network monitoring and enforcement mechanisms be enforced or relied upon.

Therefore, the trust trajectory for transition economies that are relatively more transaction-focused than relationship-oriented is one that begins at network-based governance but then moves back toward contract-based trust relationships as institutions become more facilitative and trustworthy and the population gains in generalized trust. The potential to develop competence-based trust relationships with non-network members increases, leading to potential increases in identification and to courtship-based relationships and to more instrinsically motivated trust.

Proposition 22: As a means to cope with non-facilitative institutions and lack of contract enforcement, the trust trajectory in societies within transition economies will begin with network-based trust relationships. As institutions gain in legitimacy and the rule of law strengthens, generalized trust among the population increases. People will begin to rely more on legal contracts to start relationships. The potential to develop competence-based trust relationships with non-network members increases, leading to potential increases in identification and to increasingly more intrinsically motivated trust.

Conclusion

The goal of this chapter is to provide a more comprehensive and complex understanding of the nature of trust and the trust process, and importantly to offer a detailed understanding of how and why the nature of trust and the trust process are likely to differ across cultures. The implications of this conceptualization are relevant for management theorists and practitioners alike.

First, by walking through the trust process step by step and gaining an understanding of the potential influence of culture at each juncture, both the richness and the weaknesses in our knowledge of the interplay of culture and trust are exposed. Based on cultural research in psychology, sociology, political science, economics, and business, three different culturally based trust trajectories were proposed. The existence of three distinct trajectories demonstrates that trust is a product of a multiplicity of influences and that the effect of each will differ according to factors in the local cultural environment; market conditions, social structure or cultural orientations, for example. Given that examinations of trust have not been conducted in large portions of the world – Africa, South America, the Middle East, etc. – it is glaringly apparent that we do not understand the nature or process of trust in areas of the world that are not only of economic but also of strategic importance. A contribution of this

chapter is to demonstrate that simply mapping a western trust trajectory to the trust patterns exhibited in other cultures is a dire mistake. It would seem equally erroneous simply to map the trust trajectories provided here to the cultures not yet studied, even if, on the surface, cultural similarities are apparent. For example, although Vietnam shared many of the same characteristics in its cultural environment as did other transition economies in eastern Europe, the trust trajectories are proposed are quite different. Therefore, it is crucial that we gain a more comprehensive understanding of all the social, psychological, political and economic factors that influence trust relationships in other cultural environments in order to be able to predict the nature and process of trust development in those cultures.

This conceptualization highlights another issue; because of its dynamic nature, trust is continually in flux; it is built, deepened, possibly weakened, and built again. Furthermore, this process may start with a single individual in each firm, and there must exist the allowance for this process to play out over and over again as trust spreads throughout both firms in the relationship. As demonstrated in the description of an aircraft engine venture between GE and SNECMA: "trust starts with the two people immediately involved … There were only two people who trusted each other, but they gradually buried this deeper and deeper in the organization" (Wolff, 1994, p. 12). This chapter highlights the need to deal with this dynamism differently depending on the cultural context.

Jeffries and Reed (2000) studied cognitive and affect-based trust at the individual and organizational levels and indeed suggest that there is circularity in the relationship between the micro and macro levels. Furthermore, they, as well as Anderson and Jap (2005), argue that too much trust at the interpersonal level can be harmful to a company's interest and propose that to prevent such harm, personnel be put on a rotation system – moving key relationship personnel every two years – to inhibit the growth of these "too close" relationships with individuals from the partner firm. In this conceptualization, the psychological, sociological, political, and economic influences on trusting relationships were presented in detail, and from this understanding a different remedy for this harmful trust problem is suggested. Given that close trusting relationships are not easily forged and may take years to grow (Larson, 1992), pulling the point person from that trusting relationship may do more harm than good to a company's overall interests and might better be seen as a last resort. This is particularly true, and the harm of such a remedy is likely to be exacerbated, in business cultures which are relationship oriented, rather than transaction focused, and where a personal relationship between parties must precede any exchange (Hall, 1959; Gesteland, 1999).

Thus, it is first suggested that the companies transfer focus from the individual benevolence-based (and emotion laden) trust elements in the relationship to the institutionalized incentive-based ones, in order to put in place mechanisms to guard against such trust. For example, for companies within western cultures, the company can institutionalize an accounting system for its relationships (based on principles similar to the model of Dutta, Bergen and John, 1994) which would signal when underaccounting is being undertaken by a given individual who may be swayed by their strong benevolence-based trust with the partner, and when action is both warranted and cost effective. As mentioned earlier, such verification of the basis of trust for each company may actually prove to strengthen the trust relationship between them (Joni, 2004). For companies in cultures where the dominant form of trust-relationship is network based, greater reliance should be put on the monitoring and enforcement functions of social networks.

As Schoorman, Mayer and Davis (2007) suggested in their recent analysis of trust literature, some of the greatest opportunity within trust research lies in deepening understanding of the role international and cross-cultural dimensions play in the trust process. This conceptualization has demonstrated that their sentiment could not be more true. In fact, it is proposed here that influence of culture is a great deal more complex than Schoorman, Mayer and Davis (2007) or other trust researchers to date have suggested. The goal of this chapter was to illustrate how a multiplicity of factors within the cultural and relationship environment influence the nature of trust and the trust process. In doing so, the complexity of culture's influence is revealed and the immense potential for future research into the interplay of culture and trust is introduced.

References

Anderson E. 1985. "The salesperson as outside agent or employee: a transaction cost analysis", *Marketing Science* 4: 234–54.

1990. "Two firms, one frontier: on assessing joint venture performance", *Sloan Mangement Review* 31(2): 19–30.

and Jap, S. D. 2005. "The dark side of close relationships", *Sloan Mangement Review* 46(3): 75–82.

Arino A., de la Torre J., and Ring, P. S. 2001. "Relational quality: Managing trust in corporate alliances", *California Management Review* 44: 109–31.

Barney, J. B. and Hansen, M. H. 1994. "Trustworthiness as a source of competitive advantage", *Strategic Management Journal* 15: 175–90.

Barton, C. A. 1983. "Trust and credit: some observations regarding business strategies of overseas Chinese traders in south Vietnam", in L. Y. C. Lim and P. L. A. Gosling (eds.), *The Chinese in Southeast Asia:* Singapore: Maruzen.

Bendor J., Kramer R. M., and Stout S. 1991. "When in doubt: cooperation in a noisy prisoner's dilemma", *Journal of Conflict Resolution* 35: 691–719.

Benedict R. 1946. *The Chrysanthemum and the Sword; Patterns of Japanese Culture*. Boston, MA: Houghton Mifflin.

Bem, D. J. 1972. "Self-perception theory", *Advances in Experimental Social Psychology* 6: 1–62.

Blois K. 2003. "Is it commercially irresponsible to trust?", *Journal of Business Ethics* 45: 183–93.

Bowles S. and Gintis H. 2004. "Persistent parochialism: trust and exclusion in ethnic networks", *Journal of Economic Behavior and Orgainzation* 55: 1–23.

Brockner J., Siegel, P. A., Daly, J. P., Tyler T., and Martin C. 1997. "When trust matters: the moderating effect of outcome favorability", *Administrative Science Quarterly* 42: 558–83.

Buchan N. and Croson R. 2004. "The boundaries of trust: own and others' actions in the U. S. and China", *Journal of Economic Behavior & Organization* 55(4): 485–504.

Croson, R. T. A., and Dawes, R. M. 2002. "Swift neighbors and persistent strangers: a cross-cultural investigation of trust and reciprocity in social exchange", *American Journal of Sociology* 108(1): 168–206.

Johnson, E. J., and Croson, R. T. A. 2006. "Let's get personal: an international examination of the influence of communication, culture and social distance on others regarding preferences", *Journal of Economic Behavior and Organization* 60(3): 373–98.

Burt, R. S. and Knez M. 1995. "Kinds of third-party effects on trust", *Rationality and Society* 7: 255–92.

Cassel, H. E. 1996. "Building the dream team: how data centers and vendors become partners", *Journal of Systems Management* 47(2): 28–31.

Chiang, F. F. T. and Birtch, T. A. 2007. "Examining the perceived causes of successful employee performance: an east-west comparison", *International Journal of Human Resource Management* 18(2): 232–48.

Clark, M. S. 1984. "Record keeping in two types of relationships", *Journal of Personality and Social Psychology* 47: 549–57.

Powell, M. C., and Mills J. 1986. "Keeping track of needs in communal and exchange relationships", *Journal of Personality and Social Psychology* 51: 333–8.

Coleman, J. S. 1988. "Social capital in the creation of human capital", *American Journal of Sociology* 94 (Supplement): S95–S120.

Cook, K. S. and Hardin R. 2001. "Norms of cooperativeness and networks of trust", in M. Hecter and K. Dieter-Opp (eds.), *Social Norms*. New York, NY: Russell Sage Foundation, pp. 327–47.

Hardin R., and Levi M. 2005. *Cooperation without Trust?* New York, NY: Russell Sage Foundation.

Rice, E. R. W., and Gerbasi A. 2004. "The emergence of trust networks under uncertainty: the case of transitional economies – insights from social psychological research", in J. Kornai B. Rothstein and S. Rose-Ackerman (eds.), *Creating Social Trust in Post-Socialist Transition*. New York, NY: Palgrave Macmillan, pp. 193–212.

Yamagishi T., Cheshire C., Cooper R., Matsuda M., and Mashima R. 2005. "Trust building via risk taking: a cross-societal experiment", *Social Psychology Quarterly* 68(2): 121–42.

Croson, R. T. A. and Buchan, N. R. 1999. "Gender and culture: international experimental evidence from trust games", *American Economic Review* 89: 386–91.

Dake K. 1991. "Orienting dispositions in the perception of risk – an analysis of contemporary worldviews and cultural biases", *Journal of Cross-Cultural Psychology* 22(1): 61–82.

1992. "Myths of nature – culture and the social construction of risk", *Journal of Social Issues* 48(4): 21–37.

Dasgupta P. 1988. "Trust as a commodity", in D. Gambetta (ed.), *Trust: Making and Breaking Cooperative Relations*. Oxford: Blackwell, pp. 108–37.

Davies, G. H. 2001. "ASPs: the crucial questions", *Sunday Times*, April 22, New Solutions.

Den Hartog, D. N. 2004. "Assertiveness", in R. J. House, P. J. Hanges M. Javidan, P. W. Dorfman, and V. Gupta (eds.), *Culture, Leadership, and Organizations: The Globe Study of 62 Societies*. Thousand Oaks, CA: Sage, pp. 395–436.

Deutsch M. 1958. "Trust and suspicion", *Conflict Resolution* 11: 205–79.

Doney, P. M. and Cannon, J. P. 1997. "An examination of the nature of trust in buyer-seller relationships", *Journal of Marketing* 61 (April): 35–51.

Cannon, J. P., and Mullen, M. R. 1998. "Understanding the influence of national culture on the development of trust", *Academy of Management Review* 23: 601–20.

Douglas M. and Wildavsky A. 1982. *Risk and Culture: An Essay on the Selection of Technical and Environmental Dangers*. Berkeley, CA: University of California Press.

Dunn, J. R. and Schweitzer, M. E. 2005. "Feeling and believing: the influence of emotion on trust", *Journal of Personality and Social Psychology* 88: 736–48.

Dutta S., Bergen M., and John G. 1994. "The governance of exclusive territories when dealers can bootleg", *Marketing Science* 13: 83–99.

Dwyer, R. F., Schurr, P. H., and Oh S. 1987. "Developing buyer-seller relationships", *Journal of Marketing* 51: 11–27.

Eisler, A. D., Eisler H., and Yoshida M. 2003. "Perception of human ecology: cross-cultural and gender comparisons", *Journal of Environmental Psychology* 23(1): 89–101.

Elangovan, A. R. and Shapiro D. 1998. "Betrayal of trust in organizations", *Academy of Management Review* 23: 547–66.

Ensminger J. 2001. "Reputations, trust, and the principal agent problem", in K. S. Cook (ed.), *Trust and Society*. New York, NY: Russell Sage Foundation, pp. 185–201.

Farh, J. L., Tsui, A. S., Xin K., and Cheng, B. S. 1998. "The influence of relational demography and guanxi: the Chinese case", *Organization Science* 9(4): 471–88.

Fishman R. and Khanna T. 1999. "Is trust a historical residue? Information flows and trust levels", *Journal of Economic Behavior and Organization* 38(1): 79–92.

Flynn, F. J. 2003. "How much should I give and how often? The effects of generosity and frequence on favor exchange on social status and productivity", *Academy of Management Journal* 48: 539–53.

Folger R. and Konovsky, M. A. 1989. "Effects of procedural and distributive justice on reactions to pay raise decisions", *Academy of Management Journal* 32: 115–30.

Fournier S. 1998. "Consumers and their brands: developing relationship theory in consumer research", *Journal of Consumer Research* 24: 343–73.

Fukuyama F. 1995. "Social capital and the global economy", *Foreign Affairs* 74(5): 89–103.

Gabarro, J. J. 1978. "The development of trust, influence, and expectations", in T. Athos and J. J. Gabarro (eds.), *Interpersonal Behavior: Communication and Understanding in Relationships*. Englewood Cliffs, NJ: Prentice Hall, pp. 290–303.

Gambetta D. 1988. "Can we trust trust?", in D. Gambetta (ed.), *Trust: Making and Breaking Cooperative Relations*. Oxford: Blackwell, pp. 213–37.

2005. *Streetwise: How Taxi Drivers Establish Customers' Trustworthiness*. New York, NY: Russell Sage Foundation.

Gesteland, R. R. 1999. *Cross-Cultural Business Behavior: Marketing, Nnegotiating and Managing Across Cultures*. Copenhagen: Copenhagen Business School Press.

Gill H., Boies K., Finegan, J. E., and McNally J. 2005. "Antecedents of trust: establishing a boundary condition for the relation between propensity to trust and intention to trust", *Journal of Business and Psychology* 19: 287–301.

Glaeser, E. L., Laibson, D. I., Scheinkman, J. A., and Soutter, C. L. 2000. "Measuring trust", *Quarterly Journal of Economics* 115: 811–46.

Granovetter M. 1985. "Economic action and social structure: the problem of embeddedness", *American Journal of Sociology* 91: 481–510.

Grayson K. and Ambler T. 1999. "The dark side of long-term relationships in marketing services", *Journal of Marketing Research* XXXVI: 132–41.

Griffith, D. A., Zhang C., and Cavusgil, S. T. 2006. "Attributions of noncooperative incidents and response strategies: the role of national character", *Journal of World Business* 41(4): 356–67.

Gupta V., Sully de Luque M., and House, R. J. 2004. "Multisource construct validity of globe scales", in R. J. House, P. J. Hanges M. Javidan P. W. Dorfman, and V. Gupta (eds.), *Culture, Leadership, and Organizations: The Globe Study of 62 Societies*. Thousand Oaks, CA: Sage, pp. 152–77.

Guseva A. and Rona-Tas A. 2001. "Uncertainty, risk, and trust: Russian and American credit card markets compared", *American Sociological Review* 66: 623–46.

Hagen, J. M. and Choe S. 1998. "Trust in Japanese interfirm relations: Institutional sanctions matter", *Academy of Management Review* 23: 589–600.

Hall E. 1959. *The Silent Language*. New York, NY: Anchor Press.

Han G. and Choe S. 1994. "Effects of family, region, and school network ties on interpersonal intentions and the analysis of network activities in Korea", in U. Kim, H. C. Triandis, C. Kagitcibai, S. C. Choi and G. Yoon (ed.), *Individualism and Collectivism: Theory, Method, and Applications*. Thousand Oaks, CA: Sage, pp.189–99.

Hardin. R. 2002. *Trust and Trustworthiness*. New York, NY: Russell Sage Foundation.

Hayashi N., Ostrom E., Walker J., and Yamagishi T. 1999. "Reciprocity, trust, and the sense of control", *Rationality and Society* 11(1): 27–46.

Heide, J. B. and John B. 1992. "Do norms matter in marketing relationship?" *Journal of Marketing* 56: 34–44.

Heider F. 1958. *The Psychology of Interpersonal Relations*. New York, NY: Wiley.

Henrich J., Boyd R., Bowles S., Camerer C., Fehr E., Gintis H., McElreath R., Alvard M., Barr A., Ensminger J., Henrich, N. S., Hill K., Gil-White F., Gurven M., Marlowe, F. W., Patton, J. Q. and Tracer D. 2005. "Economic Man", in "Cross-Cultural Perspective: Behavioral Experiments in 15 Small-Scale Societies", *Behavioral & Brain Sciences* 28(6): 795–855.

Henslin, J. M. 1968. "Trust and the cab drive", in Truzzi (ed.), *Sociology and Everyday Life*. Englewood Cliffs, NJ: Prentice Hall, pp. 138–58.

Hsee, C. K. and Weber, E. U. 1999. "Cross-national differences in risk preference and lay predictions", *Journal of Behavioral Decision Making* 12(2): 165–79.

Huff L. and Kelley L. 2003. "Levels of organizational trust in individualist versus collectivist societies: a seven-nation study", *Organization Science* 14(1): 81–90.

Jap, S. D. and Ganesan S. 2000. "Control mechanics and the relationship life cycle: implications for safe guarding investments and developing commitment", *Journal of Marketing Research* 37: 227–46.

Jeffries, F. L., and Reed R. 2000. "Trust and adoption in relational contracting", *Academy of Management Review* 4: 873–82.

Johnson, M. D. and Selnes F. 2004. "Customer portfolio management: toward a dynamic theory of exchange relationships", *Journal of Marketing* 68(2): 1–17.

Johnson S., McMillan J., and Woodruff C. 2002. "Courts and relational contracts", *Journal of Law Economics and Organization* 18(1): 221–77.

Jones C., Hersterly, W. S., and Borgatti, S. P. 1997. "A general theory of network governance: exchange conditions and social mechanisms", *Academy of Management Review* 22: 911–45.

Jones, G. R. and George, J. M. 1998. "The experience and evolution of trust: implications for cooperation and teamwork", *Academy of Management Review* 23: 531–46.

Joni S. 2004. "The geography of trust", *Harvard Business Review* March: 83–8.

Kahneman D. 2003. "Maps of bounded rationality: psychology for behavioral economics", *American Economic Review* December: 1449–75.

and Tversky A. 1973. "On the psychology of prediction", *Psychological Review* 80: 237–51.

and Tversky A. 1979. "Prospect theory: an analysis of decision under risk", *Econometrica* 47: 263–91.

Kelley, H. H. 1967. "Attribution theory in social psychology", in D. Levine (ed.), *Nebraska Symposium on Motivation*. Lincoln, NE: University of Nebraska Press, pp. 192–240.

and Thibaut, J. W. 1959. *The Social Psychology of Groups*. New York, NY: Wiley.

Kim, P. H., Dirks, K. T., Cooper, C. D., and Ferrin, D. L. 2006. "When more blame is better than less: the implications of internal vs. external attributions for the repair of trust after a competence vs. integrity-based trust violation", *Organizational Behavior and Human Decision Processes* 99(1): 49–65.

Knack S. and Keefer P. 1997. "Does social capital have an economic payoff? A cross-country investigation", *Quarterly Journal of Economics* 112(4): 1251–88.

Kolbasuk M., McGee J., and Wilder C. 2001. "Mantra of collaboration: trust but verify", *Information Week* 848: 40.

Kollock P. 1993. "An eye for and eye leaves everyone blind: Cooperation and accounting systems", *American Sociological Review* 58: 768–86.

1994. "The emergence of exchange structures – an experimental study of uncertainty, commitment, and trust", *American Journal of Sociology* 100(2): 313–45.

Korsgaard, M. A., Schweiger, D. M., and Sapienza, H. J. 1995. "Building commitment, attachment, and trust in strategic decision-making teams: the role of procedural justice", *Academy of Management Journal* 38: 60–84.

Kramer, R. M. 1999. "Trust and distrust in organizations: emerging perspectives, enduring questions", *Annual Review of Psychology* 50: 569–98.

Brewer, M. B., and Hanna, B. A. 1996. "Collective trust and collective action: the decision to trust as a social decision", in R. M. Kramer and T. R. Tyler (eds.), *Trust in Organizations*. Thousand Oaks, CA: Sage, pp. 357–89.

Kumar N. 2000. "The power of trust in manufacturer-retailer relationships", *Harvard*

Business Review November–December: 92–106.

La Porta R., Lopez DeSilanes F., Shleifer A., and Vishny, R. W. 1997. "Trust in large organizations", *American Economic Review* 87(2): 333–8.

Landa, J. T. 1994. *Trust, Ethnicity, and Identity.* Lansing, MI: University of Michigan Press.

Langfred, C. W. 2004. "Too much of a good thing? Negative effects of high trust and individual autonomy in self-managing teams", *Academy of Management Journal* 47: 385–99.

Larson N. 1992. "Network dyads in entrepreneurial settings: a study of the governance of exchange relationships", *Administrative Science Quarterly* 37: 76–104.

Larzelere, R. F. and Huston, T. L. 1980. "The dyadic trust scale: toward understanding interpersonal trust in close relationships", *Journal of the Marriage and Family* (August): 595–604.

Laseter, T. M. 1997. "You need more than trust", *Purchasing* 123(4): 23–6.

Lawler, E. J., Thye, S. R., and Yoon J. 2002. "Emotion and group cohesion in productive exchange", *American Journal of Sociology* 106: 616–57.

Lee C., Pillutla M., and Law, K. S. 2000. "Power-distance, gender and organizational justice", *Journal of Management* 26(4): 685–704.

Leon M. 2003. "Building trust", *Computerworld* 37(40): 40.

Levi M. and Stoker L. 2000. "Political trust and trustworthiness", *Annual Review of Political Science* 3(1): 475–507.

Levin, D. Z. and Cross R. 2004. "The strength of weak ties you can trust: the mediating role of trust in effective knowledge transfer", *Management Science* 50: 1477–90.

Lewicki, R. J. and Bunker, B. B. 1995. "Trust in relationship: a model of development and decline", in B. B. Bunker and J. Z. Rublin (eds.), *Conflict, Cooperation and Justice.* San Francisco, CA: Jossey-Bass, pp. 133–172.

McAllister, D. J., and Bies, R. J. 1998. "Trust and distrust: new relationships and realities", *Academy of Management Review* 23: 438–58.

and Wiethoff C. 2000. "Trust, trust development, and trust repair", in M. Deutsch and P. T. Coleman (eds.), *The Handbook of Conflict Resolution.* San Francisco: Jossey-Bass, pp. 86–107.

Lewis J. and Weigert A. 1985. "Trust as a social reality", *Social Forces* 63: 967–85.

Lorenz, E. H. 1992. "Trust and the flexible firm: international comparisons", *Industrial Relations* 31(Fall): 455–72.

Luhmann N. 1988. "Familiarity, confidence, trust: problems and alternatives", in D. Gambetta (ed.), *Trust: Making and Breaking Cooperative Relations.* Oxford: Blackwell, pp. 94–107.

Macaulay S. 1963. "Non-contractual relations in business: A preliminary study", *American Sociological Review* 28: 55–69.

Mackie G. 2001. "Patterns of social trust in western Europe and their genesis", in K. S. Cook (ed.), *Trust in Society:* New York, NY: Russell Sage Foundation.

Macneil, I. R. 1978. "Contracts: adjustment of long-term economic relationship under classical, neoclassical, and relational contract law", *Northwestern University Law Review* 72: 854–906.

Maddux, W. W. and Yuki M. 2006. "The 'ripple effect': cultural differences in perceptions of the consequences of events", *Personality and Social Psychology Bulletin* 32(5): 669–83.

Malhotra D. and Murnighan, J. K. 2002. "The effects of contracts on interpersonal trust", *Administrative Science Quarterly* 47: 534–59.

Malhotra, N. K., Kim, S. S., and Buchan, N. R. 2007. "A cross-cultural study of individuals' reactions to information privacy threats", CIBER Working Papers Series; http://mooreschool. sc.edu/moore/ciber/ciber-workingpapers.htm.

Mansbridge J. 1999. "Altruistic trust", in M. E. Warren (ed.) *Democracy and Trust.* Cambridge: Cambridge University Press.

Mayer, R. C., Davis, J. H., and Schoorman F. D. 1995. "An integrative model of organizational trust", *Academy of Management Review* 20(3): 709–34.

McAllister, D. L. 1995. "Affect – and cognition – based trust as foundations for interpersonal cooperation in organizations", *Academy of Management Journal* 38: 24–59.

McGill A. L. 1995. "American and Thai managers explanations for poor company performance – role of perspective and culture in causal selection", *Organizational Behavior and Human Decision Processes* 61(1): 16–27.

McMillan J. and Woodruff C. 1999a. "Dispute prevention without courts in Vietnam", *Journal of Law Economics amd Organization* 15(3): 637–58.

and Woodruff C. 1999b. "Interfirm relationships and informal credit in Vietnam", *Quarterly Journal of Economics* 114(4): 1285–320.

Miller, P. J. E. and Rempel J. K. 2004. "Trust and partner-enhancing attributions in close relationships", *Personality and Social Psychology Bulletin* 30: 695–705.

Mishra, A. K. and Spreitzer, G. M. 1998. "Explaining how survivors respond to downsizing: the roles of trust, empowerment, justice and work redesign", *Academy of Management Review* 23: 367–588.

Molm L., Takahashi N. and Peterson G. 2000. "Risk and trust is social exchange: an experimental test of a classical proposition", *American Journal of Sociology* 105: 1396–427.

Moorman C., Zaltman G., and Deshpande R. 1992. "Relationships between providers and users of market research: the dynamic of trust within and between organizations", *Journal of Marketing Research* 29: 314–28.

Nooteboom B., Berger H., and Noorderhaven, N. G. 1997. "Effects of trust and governance on relational risk", *Academy of Management Journal* 40: 308–38.

Orbell, J. M., Dawes R., and Schwartz-Shea P. 1994. "Trust, social categories, and individuals: the case of gender", *Motivation and Emotion* 18: 109–28.

Ouchi, W. G. 1979. "A conceptual framework for the design of organization control mechanisms", *Management Science* 25: 833–48.

Oyserman D., Coon H. M., and Kemmelmeier M. 2002. "Rethinking individualism and collectivism: Evaluation of theoretical assumptions and meta-analyses", *Psychological Bulletin* 128(1): 3–72.

Palmer, C. G. S. 1996. "Risk perception: an empirical study of the relationship between worldview and the risk construct", *Risk Analysis* 16(5): 717–23.

Parkhe A. 1993. "Strategic alliance structuring: a game theoretic and transaction cost examination of interfirm cooperation", *Academy of Management Journal* 36: 794–829.

Pillutla M. M., Malhotra D., and Murnighan J. K. 2003. "Attributions of trust and the calculus of reciprocity", *Journal of Experimental Social Psychology* 39(5): 448–55.

Pruitt, D. G. and Kimmel, M. J. 1977. "Twenty years of experimental gaming: critique, synthesis, and suggestions for the future", *Annual Review of Psychology* 28: 363–92.

Putnam R. D. 1993. *Making Democracy Word: Civic Traditions in Modern Italy*. Princeton, NY: Princeton University Press.

Radaev V. 2004. "How trust is established in economic relationships when institutions and individuals are not trustworthy: the case of Russia", in J. Kornai, B. Rothstein, and S. Rose-Ackerman (eds.), *Creating Social Trust in Post-Socialist Transition*. New York, NY: Palgrave Macmillan, pp. 91–110.

Rao A. N., Pearce J. L., and Xin K. 2005. "Governments, reciprocal exchange and trust among business associates", *Journal of International Business Studies* 36(1): 104–18.

Redding G. 1995. "Overseas Chinese networks: understanding the enigma", *Long Range Planning* 28(1): 61–9.

2003. "The evolution of business systems", *Research Series*. Euro-Asia Center, INSEAD.

Rempel, J. K., Holmes, J. G., and Zanna M. P. 1985. "Trust in close relationships", *Journal of Personality and Social Psychology* 49: 95–112.

Rindfleisch A., and Heide, J. B. 1997. "Transaction cost analysis: past, present, and future applications", *Journal of Marketing* 61: 30–54.

Ring, P. S. 1996. "Fragile and resilient trust and their roles in economic exchange", *Business and Society* 35: 148–75.

and Van De Ven, A. H. 1992. "Structuring cooperative relationships between organizations", *Strategic Management Journal* 13: 483–98.

and Van De Ven, A. H. 1994. "Developmental processes of cooperative interorganizational relationships", *Academy of Management Review* 19: 90–118.

Rose-Ackerman S. 2001. "Trust and honesty in post-socialist societies", *Kyklos* 54(2/3): 415–43.

Rothstein B. 2000. "Social capital and institutional legitimacy", *The 2000 Annual Meeting of the American Political Science Association*, August 31 – September 3.

Rotter, J. B. 1967. "A new scale for the measurement of interpersonal trust", *Journal of Personality* 35: 651–65.

Rousseau, D. M., Sitkin, S. M., Burt, R. S., and Camerer C. 1998. "Not so different after all: a cross-discipline view of trust", *Academy of Management Review* 23: 393–404.

Salacuse J. W. 2001. "Renegotiating existing agreements: how to deal with 'life struggling against form' ", *Negotiation Journal* 17: 311–31.

Schoorman F. D., Mayer R. C., and Davis J. H. 2007. "An integrative model of organizational trust: past, present, and future", *Academy of Management Review* 32(2): 344–54.

Shapiro, D. L., Sheppard, B. H., and Cheraskin L. 1992. "In theory: Business on a handshake", *Negotiation Journal* 8: 365–77.

Sheppard, B. H., and Sherman, D. M. 1998. "The grammars of trust: a model and general implications", *Academy of Management Review* 23: 422–37.

Sheridan, J. H. 1997. "An alliance built on trust", *Industry Week* 246(6): 67–71.

Sitkin, S. B., and Roth, N. L. 1993. "Explaining the limited effectiveness of legalistic 'remedies' for trust/distrust", *Organization Science* 4: 367–92.

Sjoberg L. 1997. "Risk decision and policy", *Explaining Risk Perception: An Empirical Evaluation of Cultural Theory* 2(2): 113–30.

Stolle D. 1998. "Bowling together, bowling alone: the development of generalized trust in voluntary associations", *Political Psychology* 19(3): 497–525.

Sully de Luque M. and Javidan M. 2004. "Uncertainty avoidance", in R. J. House, P. J. Hanges, M. Javidan, P. W. Dorfman, and V. Gupta (eds.), *Culture, Leadership, and Organizations: The Globe Study of 62 Societies.* Thousand Oaks, CA: Sage, pp. 602–53.

Tan, H. H. and Chee D. 2005. "Understanding interpersonal trust in a Confucian-influenced society", *International Journal of Cross Cultural Management* 5(2): 197–212.

Tax, S. S., Brown, S. W., and Chandrashekaran M. 1998. "Customer evaluations of service complaint experiences: implications for relationship marketing", *Journal of Marketing* 62: 60–77.

Triandis H. C. 1972. *The Analysis of Subjective Culture.* New York, NY: Wiley.

Triandis H. C. 1988. *Individualism and Collectivism.* Boulder, CO: Westview Press.

2002. "Subjective culture", in W. J. Lonner, D. L. Dinnel, S. A. Hayes, and D. N. Sattler (eds.), *Online Readings in Psychology and Culture.* Bellingham, DC: Center for Cross-Cultural Research, Western Washington University.

Trompenaars F. and Hampden-Turner C. 1998. *Riding the Waves of Culture: Understanding Diversity in Global Business.* New York, NY: McGraw-Hill.

Tsui A. S. and Farh, J. L. L. 1997. "Where guanxi matters – relational demography and guanxi in the Chinese context", *Work and Occupations* 24(1): 56–79.

Tyler, T. R., and Huo, Y. J. 2002. *Trust in the Law: Encouraging Public Cooperation with the Police and Courts.* New York, NY: Russell Sage Foundation.

Uzzi B. 1997. "Social structure and competition in interfirm networks: the paradox of embeddedness", *Administrative Science Quarterly* 42: 35–67.

Van Lange, P. A. M., Ouwerkerk, J. W., and Tazelaar, M. J. A. 2002. "How to overcome the detrimental effects of noise in social interaction: the benefits of generosity", *Journal of Personality and Social Psychology* 82: 768–80.

Walter R. and Delin J. 2003. "Cooperative brands: the importance of customer information for service brands", *Design Management Journal* 14: 63.

Wathne, K. H. and Heide, J. B. 2000. "Opportunism in interfirm relationships: forms, outcomes, and solutions", *Journal of Marketing* 64: 36–51.

Weber, J. M., Malhotra D., and Murnighan, J. K. 2005. "Normal acts of irrational trust: motivated attributions and the trust development process", in B. M. Staw and R. M. Kramer (eds.), *Research in Organizational Behavior* 27: 1–22.

Weber E. U. and Hsee C. 1998. "Cross-cultural differences in risk perception but cross-cultural similarities in attitudes towards perceived risk", *Management Science* 44(9): 1205–17.

and Hsee C. K. 2000. "Culture and individual judgment and decision making", *Applied Psychology – An International Review – Psychologie Appliquee – Revue Internationale* 49(1): 32–61.

Weber J., Malhotra D., and Murnighan J. K. 2005. "Normal acts of irrational trust: motivated attributions and the trust development process", *Research in Organizational Behavior* 27.

Wicks, A. C., Berman, S. L., and Jones, T. M. 1999. "The structure of optimal trust: moral and strategic implications", *Academy of Management Review* 24: 98–116.

Wieselquist J., Rusbult, C. E., Foster, C. A., and Agnew C. R. 1999. "Commitment, pro-relationship behavior, and trust in close relationships", *Journal of Personality and Social Psychology* 77: 942–66.

Wildavsky A. and Dake K. 1990. "Theories of risk perception – who fears what and why", *Daedalus* 119(4): 41–60.

Williams M. 2001. "In whom we trust: group membership as an affective context for trust development", *Academy of Management Review* 26: 377–96.

Williamson, O. E. 1985. *The Economic Institutions of Capitalism: Firms, Markets, Relational Contracting*. New York, NY: The Free Press.

1993. "Calculativeness, trust, and economic organization", *Journal of Law and Economics* XXXVI: 453–86.

Wolff, M. G. 1994. "Building trust in alliances", *Research Technology Management* 37(3): 12–16.

Wu J. and Axelrod R. 1995. "How to cope with noise in the iterated prisoner's dilemma", *Journal of Conflict Resolution* 39: 183–9.

Yamagishi T. 1988a. "Exit from the group as an individualistic solution to the free rider problem in the United States and Japan", *Journal of Experimental Social Psychology* 24(6): 530–42.

1988b. "The provision of a sanctioning system in the United-States and Japan", *Social Psychology Quarterly* 51(3): 265–71.

2001. "Trust as a form of social intelligence", in K. S. Cook (ed.), *Trust and Society*. New York: Russell Sage Foundation, pp. 121–47.

Cook K. S., and Watabe M. 1998. "Uncertainty, trust, and commitment formation in the United States and Japan", *American Journal of Sociology* 104(1): 165–94.

and Yamagishi M. 1994. "Trust and commitment in the United-States and Japan", *Motivation and Emotion* 18(2): 129–66.

Yuki M., Maddux W. W., Brewer M. B., and Takemura K. 2005. "Cross-cultural differences in relationship- and group-based trust", *Personality and Social Psychology Bulletin* 31(1): 48–62.

Zaheer A., McEvily B., and Perrone V. 1998. "Does trust matter? Exploring the effects of interorgainzational and interpersonal trust on performance", *Organizational Science* 9: 141–59.

and Venkatraman N. 1995. "Relational governance as an interorganizational strategy: an empirical test of the role of trust in economic exchange", *Strategic Management Journal* 16: 373–92.

Zucker, L. G. 1986. "Production of trust: institutional sources of economic structure, 1840–1920", *Research in Organizational Behavior* 8: 53–111.

Cultural variations in work stress and coping in an era of globalization

RABI S. BHAGAT, PAMELA K. STEVERSON, and
BEN C. H. KUO[1]

Globalization of businesses is a reality that is defining how people from different nations and cultures work together. Over 63,000 multinational and global corporations and 821,000 foreign subsidiaries employ over 90 million people worldwide. The United Nations estimates that about 175 million people live outside the country of their birth. In addition, there has been a great deal of inter-connectedness of work activities in the form of development of 24/7 call centers and outsourcing of various business processes, etc. The expansion of international trade has grown faster than the growth of even the most rapidly growing economies of Asia and South America (i.e., China, Vietnam, India, Brazil, and Argentina). The internet and various forms of computer-mediated communication are redefining the scope of work in multinational and global organizations that function across across disimilar cultures and national borders.

While this increased level of interconnectedness in the global economy has been expanding the global GDP, it has also ushered in a new era of major restructuring of both work and work organizations. This new era has created stressful experiences for workers including increased pressures to perform as well as *how* to perform in order to meet the demands of the global marketplace. Quick, Cooper, Nelson, Quick and Gavin (2003) noted that new technologies, coupled with rapid expansion of multinational and global organizations, have created highly competitive and stressful environments leading to transformations in managerial roles, working hours, work-life balance,

employee attitudes, organizational commitment, and the psychological contract (Cooper, 1998) and the organization. Many commentators in reflecting on the quality of work life in this new era have observed that such major restructuring of work and the attendant stressful experiences have not been known since the Industrial Revolution (see *Business Week*, August 21–27, 2007). In many ways, this has led to development of smaller organizations competing for their share of the global market and fewer workers doing more hours of work in environments where they feel less secure. In terms of pay and related compensation, the real wages and salaries of workers in the US, which is the largest economy in the world, are barely higher than they were in 2000 (Mandel, 2007). While such wage stagnation is not noted in the emergent economies, there are interesting and disturbing reports regarding the increase of work load, office politics, and competition. In a study of Indian call centers, Skeers (2005) reported a high level of exploitation of workers – the employees were under constant stress because of their workload, competitive pressures, and surveillance. When these call center employees were monitored for the number of calls that they received, the average call time and time between calls, they felt that they were being dehumanized. Close circuit cameras and electronic monitors kept track of the time that workers spent at their desk, the time spent for short breaks, and even the time in the bathroom. Such a situation is not necessarily confined to employees in call centers, professionals and managers of many global organizations are spending longer times on their jobs, face chances of occupational obsolescence, and are continuously watching for opportunities in other organizations located not only in their home countries but in other countries as well. These

[1] The authors would like to thank James C. Quick, James R. Van Scotter, James C. Segovis, and Dianna Stone for their helpful comments on an earlier draft of this chapter.

individuals also report a great deal of conflict with the demands of their non-work lives. New centers for research focusing on the antecedents and consequences of work family conflicts have emerged in the US, Spain, Canada, and other countries in the European Union (EU).

Stress is a stimulus or a series of stimuli that originate in the physical, social, or psychological environment requiring the person to respond and/or adapt. Typically, an individual is able to maintain a healthy and balanced state and function normally in response to stressful encounters in daily lives. However, negative effects of stress emerge when the experienced level of stress exceeds the capacity of the individual and his or her personal and social resources to cope with the stress (McGrath, 1976; Beehr and Bhagat, 1985; Cooper, Dewe, and O'Driscoll, 2003). The level of stress experienced by an individual depends on one's cognitive appraisal of the degree of threat to one's physical or psychosocial well-being and one's beliefs about the likelihood of effectively dealing with the negative consequences of environmental threats (Lazarus and Folkman, 1984). The interaction of the perception of threat and the perception of control determine the actual experience of stress. The most intense experience of stress occurs when one encounters stimuli perceived as a threat to well-being, particularly when one believes the consequences of the threat cannot be counteracted. The presence of threats, along with perceptions of an inability to control or counteract the threats, elicits high levels of stress in the individual which, in turn, are likely to be associated with psychological strain and resulting influences on valued work outcomes (i.e., job performance, job satisfaction, organizational commitment, turnover, etc.).

Work absorbs the energy and attention of a majority of adults in all industrialized societies. Occupational problems often take their toll in terms of decreased life satisfaction (Campbell, Converse, and Rodgers, 1976), psychological strain (Jex and Beehr, 1991; Kahn and Byosiere, 1992; Bhagat et al., 1994; Beehr, 1995; Sears, Urizar, and Evans, 2000), lowered mastery and self-esteem (Pearlin, Lieberman, Menaghan, and Mullan, 1981; Bhagat and Allie, 1989), burnout (Maslach, 1998) and physical outcomes such as ulcers, hypertension, and angina (Gaines and Jermier, 1983; Quick et al., 2003; Macik-Frey, Quick and Nelson, 2007).

Individuals experience stress not only in modern complex and globalized societies, but also in agricultural, pre-industrial and developing societies as well. Hooker (2003) noted that cultural patterns as well as various religions evolve in dissimilar ways in order to deal with different kinds of environmental and ecological stressors around the world. Far from being countries which have a monopoly on the ongoing experience of stressful encounters, the US and other industrialized countries in the G-8 network have enjoyed one of the least stressful environments in the world. The kinds of stressors that Americans and other members of the industrialized world experience tend to differ from those of the developing world (Hooker, 2003). The environment is basically stable and predictable in these national and cultural contexts (Triandis, 1994). In contrast to the stability of the western world with its day-in day-out hassles of daily life (e.g., a traffic jam on the way to work), there are areas of the world where there are frequent power outages, the transportation system is highly unreliable, and medical services are inadequate or even lacking. The food and water supplies may also be inadequate or contaminated, and the economy is often paralyzed by hyperinflation and bouts of massive unemployment. The national government may be in a constant state of crisis, corruption rules the bureaucratic processes, and terrorist acts are frequent. Hooker (2003) explained that these experiences are inherently stressful to the members of these countries.

Workers in developing countries may have problems adapting to new stressors or face exploitation. Chadhoury (2004) discussed the Oxfam report, based on the experiences of workers in twelve countries – Bangladesh, Chile, China, Colombia, Honduras, Kenya, Morocco, Sri Lanka, South Africa, Thailand, the UK, and the US – which found that large western retail companies have benefited from the globalization of production in developing countries to the detriment of workers, especially women. For example, in China, there are reports of forced labor, violations of shop floor standards, corporal punishment and physical assaults, violations of the right to work, and violations of occupational safety and health (Chan, 2001).

As we examine the stress phenomenon in the era of globalization, we believe that research on work stress has to go beyond the issues addressed by Kahn and Byosiere (1992) in the *Handbook of Industrial and Organizational Psychology*. They recommended that organizational stress researchers should focus on the nature of context in which stress responses occur along with the consequences for the individual. The nature of the context we need to consider concerns country and culture-specific variations in work stress, coping and well-being. Compared to the large and systematic body of research that evolved since the classic work of Kahn and his colleagues (Kahn, Wolfe, Quinn, and Snoek, 1964; Kahn, 1973; Kahn, 1981), investigations that incorporate the role of international and cultural variations on work stress and coping have yet to reach a state of maturity. At the time of writing this chapter, it remains unclear how relevant the existing western conceptual frameworks, theories, and findings research are in non-western contexts. The purpose of this chapter is to provide:

1. a historical perspective on international and cultural variations on organizational stress with special attention to the role of coping strategies;
2. a theoretical framework on stress and coping with a cultural perspective;
3. an examination of the role of employee assistance programs (EAPs) and other organizational interventions for managing the deleterious effects of the new kinds of stresses in the era of a global economy; and
4. future research implications.

Historical perspective on international and cross-cultural stress research

Work stress has been an important domain of sustained research over the past four decades. There have been a number of theoretical frameworks concerning the antecedents and consequences of experienced stress (Beehr, 1995). With the exception of the work reviewed in Wong and Wong (2006),

all of the dominant theories have been created by researchers from individualistic nations of the world (see McGrath, 1976; Beehr and Bhagat, 1985; Beehr, 1995; Cooper, 1998; Cooper *et al.*, 2001, Quick and Tetrick, 2003). For example, three prominent models that have driven stress research include: the person-environment fit theory (stress arises from a misfit between the person and environment) (French, Rogers, and Cobb, 1974), Karasek's (1979) demand-control-support model (stress is a response to the demands of work and one's control over those demands), and House's (1981) framework of occupational stress (experienced stress reflects the total process including environmental sources of stress, perceptions of stress, and responses to stress). Additional prominent frameworks include Beehr and Bhagat's (1985) uncertainty theory of occupational stress (stress is multiplicative function of perceived uncertainty of obtaining outcomes, perceived importance of these outcomes, and duration of the perceived uncertainties), and Edwards, Caplan, and Van Harrison's (1998) more rigorous approach to person-environment fit theory (French, Rodgers, and Cobb, 1974). While these frameworks have been useful in explaining the phenomenon of organizational stress in the western Europe, the US, and Canada, they do not take into account the role of cultural variations. Research conducted in the US, UK, Germany, Sweden, France, and Australia – i.e., countries with a strong individualistic orientation (with high emphasis on independent self-construal) do not easily generalize to work organizations in countries with a collectivistic orientation (with high interdependent self-construal) despite the fact 80 percent of the world's population live in countries predominated by collective values (Triandis, 1994). Although there is growing recognition that organizational and occupational stresses affect valued work outcomes in developing nations and emergent economies of the world (Bhagat, Steverson, and Segovis 2007a, 2007b, Quick *et al.*, 2003, Macik-Frey *et al.*, 2007), there have seldom been any comprehensive attempts to provide a theoretical framework that explicitly considers the role of cultural variations (Folkman and Moskowitz, 2004). The work of Bhagat, Steverson, and Segovis (2007a, 2007b) incorporating the role of culture in relation to employee assistance programs is a notable exception to this trend. Until recently, theories of work stress underestimated the importance of groups and cultures which limit the usefulness of the findings.

In a twenty-one nation study of middle managers, the extent of role conflict, role ambiguity, and role (work) overload was related to national scores on power distance (i.e., the extent inequity is accepted), individualism, uncertainty avoidance, and masculinity (Peterson *et al.*, 1995). Interestingly, country characteristics were related more to variations in role stresses than to differences in personal and organizational characteristics. Power distance and collectivism were positively related to role overload and negatively related to role ambiguity (Peterson *et al.*, 1995).

Spector *et al.* (2002) collected data on role conflict, role ambiguity, and role overload from middle managers in work organizations in twenty-four nations. The cultural dimensions of individualism-collectivism and power distance were closely related to these role stressors. Also, they found that these three role stressors varied more as a function of national and cultural variations, compared to personal, demographic, and organizational characteristics.

Perrewé *et al.* (2002) examined the relationship among role stressors (i.e., role ambiguity, role conflict), general self-efficacy (GSE), and burnout in nine countries. Findings supported that GSE had a universally negative association with burnout. Furthermore, in eight of the nine countries, self-efficacy mediated the relationships between role ambiguity and role conflict with burnout (Perrewé *et al.*, 2002).

Spector *et al.* (2004) investigated differences in job stressors among working college students and university support personnel from mainland China, Hong Kong, and the US. Significant differences were found for role ambiguity, role conflict, job autonomy, and interpersonal conflict. Role ambiguity was significantly higher for workers in Hong Kong than those in the China and the US. However, role ambiguity was also significantly higher in the US sample than in the mainland Chinese sample. Both Hong Kong and mainland China were significantly higher than the US for role conflict,

but there was no significant difference between the two Asian countries. Mainland China and the US were significantly higher than Hong Kong for perceived job autonomy. Finally, workers in Hong Kong were found to have the highest level of interpersonal conflict while workers in the US had the lowest level.

Narayanan, Menon, and Spector (1999) explored work stress for female clerical workers in India and the US in a qualitative study. Participants were asked to describe a concrete stressful event that occurred at work. The job stressors Indian workers cited most were lack of structure/clarity, lack of reward and recognition, equipment problems and situational constraints, and interpersonal conflict. In contrast, US workers most commonly reported work overload, lack of control/autonomy, and the perception of time/effort wasting.

In the next section, we discuss cultural perspectives on coping with stress. Because culture functions for a society in the same way as memory functions for an individual (Triandis, 1994, 1995, 1998, 2002), each culture provides culture-specific mechanisms (i.e., buffers and filters). These mechanisms evolve over time; typically they are directed towards coping with stress regardless of whether its origin is rooted in the domain of work or nonwork. *Coping* refers to the way individuals try to directly or indirectly manage, change or adapt to the experience of stress through cognitive efforts or action oriented strategies.

Cultural perspectives on coping with stress

While coping with stress is a universal experience shared by individuals from all cultures, the mechanism and process through which stressors are appraised and evaluated, and coping responses are selected vary significantly from culture to culture (Chun, Moos, and Cronkite, 2006; Lam and Zane, 2004; Lazarus and Folkman, 1984). Conceptually, Lazarus and Folkman (1984) posited that: (1) an individual's internalized values, beliefs, and norms are critical in defining his or her appraisal of stresses and delimiting options of coping responses evoked by the person; and (2) the appropriateness of an individual's coping response is bounded by his or her cultural norms. However, the extant stress and coping research, generated over the last three decades, has received criticism for being overly "acontextual" and lacking realism (Folkman and Moskowitz, 2004; Somerfield and McCrae, 2000). This includes the fact that empirical efforts to articulate the relationship between culture and coping have been very scarce (Dunahoo et al., 1998; Wong, Wong, and Scott, 2006).

Western-based, individualistic assumptions of stress-coping in the extant literature

To address the specific cultural dimensions associated with the stress and coping process, the broad theoretical context and conceptual assumptions of the stress-coping literature, in which culture-based coping research is embedded, needs to be carefully considered first. Folkman and Moskowitz (2004) observed that the emphasis on personal control, personal agency, and direct action within major stress and coping theories reflects an individualistic value orientation in the extant literature. Despite the fact that culture is implicated as a pivotal factor in the stress-coping process based on Lazarus and Folkman's (1984) original person-environment fit paradigm, subsequent empirical works established in this tradition have not investigated cultural factors adequately (Aldwin, 1994; Wester, Kuo, and Vogel, 2006). Hence, the extant stress-coping research and theories have been criticized for being overly western, European American in perspective (Utsey, Adams, and Borden, 2000; Wong, Wong, and Scott, 2006), with a partisan view toward "rugged individualism" (Hobfoll, 1998; Dunahoo et al., 1998), and action-oriented coping (Phillips and Pearson, 1996).

From this popular perspective, coping is typically subcategorized into problem-focused coping (cognitive efforts to redefine the problem and to select among alternative options and actions, etc.) versus emotion-focused coping (cognitive efforts to lessen emotional distress) (Parker and Endler, 1996; Pearlin and Schooler, 1978), both of which have been said to organize around the "self" and treat "I" as the central point of reference in stress and coping process (Hobfoll, 1998). For example, Bhagat et al. (1994) explored organizational

stress in seven national contexts (US, India, West Germany, Spain, New Zealand, Australia, and South Africa). They found that: (1) organizational stress was significantly correlated with experienced strain in all seven countries; (2) decision latitude had an independent effect in all of the seven countries studied; (3) problem-focused coping had significant independent effects in five countries; and (4) emotion-focused coping did not have a moderating effect or an independent effect in any of the seven countries (Bhagat et al., 1994). Later work by Bhagat and his colleagues found that South African managers were more likely to use emotion-focused coping to manage stress and that they differed from managers in the US, who were more likely to use a problem-focused coping style, even when controlling for organizational type and technology (Bhagat et al., 2001).

Findings such as the above have led scholars to question the generalizability of this intrapersonal, and agentic view of coping to fully account for the coping repertoires of persons from relational and collective cultures, such as individuals of Asian (Kuo, Roysircar, and Newby-Clark, 2006; Phillips and Pearson, 1996) and African backgrounds (Utsey et al., 2000; Utsey, Brown, and Borden, 2004).

However, there has been a limited, but increasing amount of empirical work within the cross-cultural and the multicultural psychological research that have attempted to identify between-group variability in cultural coping preferences, and to link these differences to meaningful cultural variables (Kuo et al., 2006). Many of these studies are established outside of industrial and organizational psychology, and stem from research contributions made in social, community, health, clinical and counseling psychology. Thus, the focus of this section is twofold: (1) comprehensively to survey empirical studies and systematically present findings that evidence cultural variations in stress and coping; and (2) subsequently to discuss and consider significant cross-cultural, theoretical constructs that underpin divergence in coping across cultures.

Cultural differences in coping

Cultural differences in coping preferences have been explored cross-culturally as a function of nationality.

Typically, this line of research involves comparing samples from diverse countries on the basis of a coping measure. Taking an etic (culturally-universal) assumption, this approach presumes that while cultural divergence in coping may exist, the underlying dimensions constituting coping can be measured in a similar manner across cultures (see Tweed and Delongis, 2006; Tweed, White, and Lehman, 2004 for more detail discussions). Operating from this vantage point, a number of international studies have identified significant group differences in coping behaviors among samples of different national groups.

In one study involving adolescents from five countries, Oláh (1995) found youth from European countries, including Hungary, Italy, and Sweden, adopted assimilative, operative, confrontative behaviors when facing stressful circumstances. These coping methods characterize attempts, on the part of European youth, to cope by forcing or modifying the stressor to be in line with what one wishes (e.g., assimilative coping). By contrast, Asian youth from India and Yemen reported a greater use of accommodative, emotion-focused coping when faced with stress. Oláh noted that the use of emotion-focused responses reflect Asians' inclination to adjust oneself to stay in line with the demands of the environmental stressors. Similarly, O'Connor and Shimizu (2002) found that Japanese university students in Japan were significantly more likely to use emotion-focused coping, in terms of escape-avoidance and positive reappraisal, than British students in the UK.

When confronted with social issues (e.g., pollution, discrimination, fear of global war, and community violence), Frydenberg et al., (2001) found that adolescents from Northern Ireland engaged more frequently in non-productive strategies, such as self-blame, tension reduction, and not coping, as well as, socially oriented strategies, such as seeking friends and social support for help more frequently than did adolescents in Colombia and Australia. Colombian adolescents, on the other hand, engaged in problem solving, spiritual support, social action, professional help-seeking, and worrying in response to the stressors more often than did the other two groups.

National differences in coping can also reflect the sociopolitical environment in which an individual is immersed and the kind of stressors faced. For example, Frydenberg et al. (2003) found clear distinction in the coping patterns of war-torn Palestinian youth that differentiated them from adolescents from Australia, Colombia, and Germany. More specifically, Palestinian youth reported the use more of seeking to belong, investing in close friends, ignoring the problem, not coping at all, seeking professional help, social action, social support, solving the problem, spiritual support, and working hard as ways of dealing with their stress. This group was also least likely to engage in physical recreations to help offset their stress. Australian adolescents, on the other hand, reported coping more often by seeking relaxing diversion and tension reduction, which included physical recreation. In the case of Palestinian youth, it was apparent that the constant ethno-political conflicts experienced by these young people directly limited the kind of coping options available to them.

Ethnic differences in coping

Even within the same national context, ethnic differences in coping are also evident. A number of multicultural studies have investigated coping's relationship to the psychological well-being and help-seeking behaviors of ethnic minorities. In a study examining coping and help-seeking for personal, interpersonal, and academic stressors among African American and Latino American college students, both groups were found to be similar in considering family and religion to be highly important coping resources to them (Chiang, Hunter, and Yeh, 2004). However, on closer inspection, Latino students were significantly more likely to turn to their parents for help than were African students, whereas African American students considered their involvement in religious activities to be more important in coping with stress than did Latino students. This latter finding was explained by the African-centered worldview which places spirituality and religion in high regard. In a study of first-year college students' responses to personal problems and their help-seeking attitude, African Americans reported less likely than Asian Americans and White Americans to engage in wishful thinking as a coping strategy (Sheu and Sedlacek, 2004).

However, Asian Americans reported a greater use of avoidant coping as compared to their white American and African American counterparts. The authors attributed this avoidance tendency to Asian preference for secondary control – a coping strategy that involves accepting rather than changing one's life circumstances.

Some consistent ethnic differences in coping were also identified across studies with samples representing diverse developmental stages. For instance, in a study of adolescents in Australia conducted by Neill and Proeve (2000), Southeast Asian secondary students were found to endorse "reference to others" as a coping resource more so than did their European counterparts. This other-centered coping preference was observed in Wong and Reker's (1985) study of older adults in Canada. When older adults were asked about the ways they respond to stress arising from aging, Chinese older adults reported to access more external help from others (i.e., families, friends, experts and God) and to use more "palliative strategies" (i.e., modifying their reaction towards the stressor) than their Caucasian counterparts. A similar preference was indicated in Yeh and Wang's (2000) study of Asian American college and graduate students. The investigators found that, instead of seeking professional help, Asian participants coped with psychological problems by keeping the issues within the family, seeking help from families, friends, and social groups, and engaging in social and familial activities. Overall, these studies point to common, shared predispositions among Asians for non-directive coping (e.g., avoidance) and collective or relational coping.

Research on similarities as well as differences in coping among ethnic subgroups has also revealed distinctive cultural coping patterns across groups. In a study by Yeh and Inose (2002), Chinese, Korean, and Japanese immigrant youth in the US were interviewed to explore their coping with cultural adjustment difficulties. The results indicated that Korean youth utilized religious coping more than Chinese and Japanese. On the other hand, Japanese youth utilized more social support than did the other two groups. Finally, both Korean and Japanese youth endorsed creative activities as a way of coping more often than did Chinese

youth. In yet another study on Asian Americans, Yeh and Wang (2000) compared the ways in which undergraduate and graduate students in the US of Chinese, Korean, Indian, and Filipino descents coped with mental health problems. Collectively as Asians, the participants generally reported similar coping resources and methods, but the relative importance assigned to the various coping strategies differed significantly across the four groups. Koreans were particularly distinct from the other Asian groups; they relied more heavily on coping through accessing religious sources and they also engaged in more negative coping through substance use.

Cultural variations on stress and the coping process indicate the existence of an intricate relationship between culture and stress responses. The findings in this area call for meaningful conceptualizations and robust interpretations of how and why individuals of dissimilar cultural backgrounds select and employ different coping styles (Lam and Zane, 2004; Kuo et al., 2006). Research suggests the presence of deep-level and ingrained dimensions of cultural variations that selectively predispose individuals towards preferring one style of coping over another. The search for culture-based explanations of stress and coping closely reflects recent developments in cross-cultural psychology research. Smith, Bond and Kagitcisbasi (2006), for example, emphasize the need to "unpack culture" by discerning and applying valid cultural constructs (i.e., individualism-collectivism, one's view of the world to include global mindset, associative versus abstractive modes of thinking, etc.) in order to gain better insights. Several recent empirical studies (e.g., Kuo et al., 2006; Tweed et al., 2004; Yeh, Arora, and Wu, 2006) and comprehensive summaries in Wong and Wong (2006) echo the same concerns. It is important for us to ask the question: "What are the cultural dimensions along which individuals and groups vary in their coping strategies and preferences?" To address this issue adequately, we present empirical evidence and interpretation related to the role of coping in situations involving self-construal, acculturation, and collectivism-individualism. Subsequently, we consider their implications for future research on stress and coping in work organizations.

Coping and interdependent versus independent self-construal

Individuals' self definition, in terms of independence and interdependence, has been shown to vary across cultural groups and to influence a person's cognitions, emotions, and motivations (Markus and Kitayama, 1991; Singelis, 1994). The independent selfhood is characterized by qualities of individualism, autonomy, self sufficiency, and self containment, and the reference point is one's internal thoughts, feelings, and actions (Markus and Kitayama, 1991). The interdependent selfhood, on the other hand, is represented by qualities of collectivism, relatedness, and social connection, and the point of reference is others' reactions and responses. Some attempts have been made to extend the theory of self construal to cross-cultural and cultural coping research. The outcomes of these studies appear to support the independent-interdependent self construal as a valuable and promising cultural framework to conceptualize cultural variations in coping (e.g., Cross, 1995; Lam and Zane, 2004).

Earlier work by Cross (1995) found that more independent East Asian students in the US were more likely to cope with direct attempts and plans to deal with their adjustment stress than less independent East Asian students. These direct coping approaches, in turn, helped East Asian students in reducing their perception of stress levels. In contrast, East Asian students who were more interdependent were found to report more adjustment stress, and their interdependence was not related to the use of direct coping. However, adopting a culture-based measure that distinguished and assessed coping in terms of collective, avoidance, and engagement coping, Kuo and Gingrich (2004) revealed differential relationships between self-construals and the three types of coping in a sample of Asian and Caucasian Canadian undergraduate students. Regardless of ethnicity, more independent students were more likely to adopt engagement coping only (conceptually aligned with the problem-focused coping) for stress that arose from interpersonal conflict. More interdependent students were found to use all three types of coping, including collective and avoidant strategies for the same interpersonal

stress scenario. The study further demonstrated that an interdependent tendency also affects individuals' stress appraisal process. More interdependent participants regarded the interpersonal conflict scenario presented in the study to be more stressful than did less interdependent participants.

Adopting a control-based model of coping, Lam and Zane (2004) tested the mediating effect of self-construals between ethnicity and preference for primary versus secondary control coping strategies among Asian American and White American college students. The result showed that interdependent self-construal partially mediated the ethnic effect on secondary control among Asian Americans. In other words, in responding to scenarios of interpersonal stress Asian Americans appeared to use more secondary control, that involves modifying one's thoughts and feelings to accommodate the external stressor. The authors linked this effect to Asian Americans' cultural values on social dependence and connectedness. By contrast, independent self-construal fully mediated the ethnic effect on primary control among White Americans. That is, White Americans showed a clear preference for primary control, which entails modifying the environment to fit the person's needs. Lam and Zane attributed this finding to western cultural values on autonomy and mastery of the environment.

Similar coping patterns were identified in Tweed et al., (2004) study of Japanese, Asian Canadians and European Canadians. The study utilized a combined etic-emic approach that integrated items from the ways of coping checklist (etic) and a number of Japanese-specific coping items (emic) to assess coping in terms of "externally targeted control" (altering or modifying the environment) versus. "internally targeted control" (modifying oneself to meet the environmental demand). The study hypothesized that each of these controls would correspond to collectivism-oriented individuals (i.e., East Asians) versus individualism-oriented individuals (i.e., European Canadians), respectively. The results supported the predictions that Japanese and other Asian respondents used more internally targeted coping strategies (e.g., accepting responsibilities, waiting things out, using self-control), whereas Euro-Canadians used more externally targeted coping strategies (e.g., confrontation). The authors contended that changes within oneself as a method of coping is more prevalent among Japanese and Asian Canadians because of interdependent self orientation, and the Buddhist and the Taoist beliefs.

Collectively, these studies extend previous understanding of the effect of self-construal on various aspects of psychological phenomena (Markus and Kitayama, 1991) to include cross-cultural stress and coping experiences. As such, cultural typology of self serves as a meaningful cultural construct in better understanding the process through which stress appraisal and coping strategy selection occur among individuals of diverse ethnic and cultural backgrounds.

Coping and acculturation

By definition, acculturation occurs when two autonomous cultures come into first-hand contact with each other and result in changes with either or both of the groups (Redfield, Linton, and Herskovits, 1936). According to the theory of acculturation, during cultural transition individuals undergo significant changes in language, behaviors, cognitions, personality, identity, attitudes, psychological well-being, and even in their stress and coping experiences (Berry, 1997; Zheng and Berry, 1991). A limited number of studies on cross-cultural adaptation among immigrants have suggested that cultural variability in coping approaches may be a function of acculturation levels.

Mena, Padilla, and Maldonado's (1987) study of coping mechanisms among four generation groups of immigrant college students in the US showed that the participants' generation status had an effect on the use of coping strategies and the experiences of acculturative stress. For instance, the late immigrant group reported a greater use of active coping methods than individuals from early immigrant and later-generation backgrounds. The second- and third-generation respondents, on the other hand, relied more on social networks as a coping mechanism than the first- and the mixed-generation group. It was assumed that second- and third-generation immigrants, being more acculturated in the US, were afforded with more interpersonal resources

and social networks as their sources of coping. In a Canadian study of cultural adjustment among individuals of varying immigration statuses, Zheng and Berry (1991) found that Chinese sojourners, being the most recent and the least acculturated newcomers to Canada, reported more areas of stresses and problems (e.g., homesickness, loneliness, etc.) than Chinese Canadian students and European Canadian students. The same group also tended to use more positive coping (e.g., more tension reduction and information-seeking), and less passive coping (e.g., wishful thinking and self-blame) than European Canadian students.

Inferring from these findings, it appears that coping patterns can vary along the dimension of one's acculturation level. In view of these findings, Kuo et al., (2006) postulated that the relationship between generational/immigrant status and preferred coping approaches might actually be mediated by degrees of acculturation. To examine this relationship, three cohorts of Chinese adolescents in Canada, including Chinese Canadians, late-entry Chinese immigrants, and Chinese sojourners, were assessed and compared based on measures of culture-based coping and acculturation (Kuo et al., 2006). Consistent with the authors' predictions, there were significant group differences in acculturation and coping patterns across the three cohort groups. In particular, Chinese adolescents in the less acculturated cohorts (e.g., Chinese sojourners) preferred more collective coping and avoidance coping methods in managing their acculturative stresses than those belonging to more acculturated cohorts (e.g., Chinese Canadians). The authors suggested that less acculturated immigrant adolescents might also adhere more strongly to traditional Asian values of collectivism and interpersonal harmony. As such, collective and avoidance (e.g., not rocking the boat) coping behaviors were favored by these adolescents.

These preliminary findings suggest that acculturation might be a critical factor in discerning cultural variations in coping, particularly among ethnic minorities and immigrants. Nonetheless, the conclusion on the interaction between acculturation and coping is quite tentative. It awaits further substantiation by additional conceptual development and empirical investigation.

Coping and individualism versus collectivism

One's tendency to construe one's "self" either in the independent or interdependent mode is essentially shaped by the predominance of individualism vs. collectivism in one's culture (Markus and Kitayama, 1991; Triandis, 2001). As we have seen earlier, Western, individualistic values and assumptions have guided research in this area for a long time. Recently, however, the cultural variation of collectivism has been receiving increased research attention focused on the intricate interplay between culture and coping strategies in a number of Asian samples (see Kuo et al., 2006; Yeh and Wang, 2000; Wong and Wong, 2006). Research involving African and African American samples are also on the rise (Utsey, Adams, and Borden, 2000; Utsey, Brown and Borden, 2004). These studies are concerned with articulating the role of "collective coping" in these predominately collectivistic samples.

The importance of coping by relying on relational and collectivistic values has been found in a study involving Chinese working parents in Hong Kong (Shek and Cheung, 1990). The results supported a clear distinction between two types of coping among the Hong Kong Chinese: "reliance on the self" versus "seeking help from others." Soliciting assistance from others (i.e., one's spouse, friends, parents, in-laws, relatives, supervisors, professionals, and even fortune-tellers) reflect different facets of coping. In a similar vein, later research on various subgroups of Asians lend further credence for the thesis that Asians have strong preferences for an ingroup-based coping style (Neill and Proeve, 2000; Yeh et al., 2001 and Chang, 2001). Termed as "collective coping" (Kuo et al., 2006; Yeh and Wang, 2002), it highlights that collectivists tend to cope by engaging others who are strongly connected in their social network.

Such emphasis on collective-coping has also been observed in Africo-centric frameworks. For example, Utsey and his associates found that community-based as well as spiritually-oriented approaches in dealing with stress are more frequently used by individuals of African descent (Utsey et al., 2000; Utsey et al., 2004). It is known that Africo-centric worldview places a strong emphasis on spirituality, affect sensitivity, expressive communication, and harmony with nature and temporal rhythms, and time as a social phenomenon. In addition, interpersonal orientation, multifaceted perception, and the tendency towards optimistic versus pessimistic orientations are also emphasized (Belgrave et al., 1997).

In a related vein, Utsey, Adams, and Bolden (2000) identified four types of coping behaviors (that are essentially culture-specific or emic in character) in people of African descent. These coping behaviors were carefully derived from data collected by using a culturally sensitive scale, called the Africultural coping systems inventory (ACSI). The first factor, termed *cognitive/emotional debriefing* style, represents adaptive reactions to environmental stressors by *detaching* oneself from the stressors and focusing on the positive aspects of the situation or event. The authors asserted that this type of coping has probably evolved out of centuries of racial oppression. The second coping style, termed the *spiritual-centered* factor, represents strategies being utilized to maintain an individual's sense of harmony with the universe. The third coping style, the *collective* factor, entails efforts to seek resolution and comfort through the social support of members of one's own in-group and others in the community. The fourth coping style, the *ritual-centered* factor, highlights the importance of engaging in spiritual rituals (e.g., lighting candles or burning incense) that are rooted in African societies. A later study involving the ACSI further supported the existence of these four coping styles for African Americans (Utsey, Brown, and Borden, 2004). These studies were conducted without an individualistic bias and it clearly informs us that in-group norms and other collectivistic values, spiritual rituals and practices are of profound significance in these cultural groups.

Kuo et al.'s (2006) study probed into the structure of coping among Asian samples by utilizing the cross-cultural coping scale (CCCS). The study found that collective coping, which is rooted in "ingroup" focused strategies, interpersonal and social resources located in one's immediate context, is quite different from the problem-focused and emotion-focused coping strategies that have guided research since the work of Lazarus and his associates in the early 1980s. Validated across three samples of Asians and Caucasians in the US and Canada, the CCCS supported the importance of collective coping along with avoidance and engagement modes of coping. It was also found that collective coping was preferred more by participants who were high in interdependent mode of self-construal, who were lower in acculturation level in the host country, and who engaged in more conservative religious beliefs and practices.

Yeh and her colleagues have also constructed a collectivism-based model of coping (Yeh, Arora, and Wu, 2006). Corresponding to the model is the collectivistic coping scale (the CCS) – a scale that was designed to capture the collective aspects of stress and coping among American ethnic minorities (Yeh et al., 2003). The scale was tested across six studies with diverse samples. The result of factor analysis of the CCS supported a seven-factor model of collectivistic coping which consists of: family support, respect for authority figures, intra-cultural coping, relational universality, forbearance, social activity, and fatalism. The scale was shown to be correlated with measures of collectivism, social support, collective self-esteem, and fusion with others.

Zhang and Long (2006) have examined collective coping within the context of work-related stress among overseas Chinese professionals in Canada. The authors developed and tested an occupational collective coping scale (i.e., the collective coping scale). The authors defined collective coping as coping activities that "function to orient attention to relationship with in-group members and maintenance of interpersonal relationships" (Zhang and Long, 2006, p. 571). More specifically, collective coping encompasses seeking support from one's in-group, conforming to one's ingroup norm, and using group action to cope. Across three studies on the development of the scale, the factor results pointed to three coping factors: collective, engagement, and disengagement coping. Incidentally, these coping factors were conceptually closely to those identified by Kuo et al. (2006) pertaining to non-work related stressors. Zhang and Long further revealed that those participants who identified strongly with Chinese traditional values and beliefs preferred collective coping.

The centrality of collectivism in the coping process among culturally diverse individuals finds additional support from a study focusing on the differential effects of personal, collective, and social identity on coping with mental health problems among native Japanese (Yeh et al., 2001). The authors defined the collective identity as the aspect of the self that is prescribed by the importance of family, ethnic group, community, religion, and language. The salience of collectivistic values was highlighted by Japanese students' preference for coping with the assistance from their friendship networks, and families and siblings, as opposed to mental health services providers. Moreover, collective identity was found to be a significant positive predictor in determining Japanese students' tendency to assess help from family as their ways of coping.

Additionally, collective coping was also found to play a critical role in facing serious trauma, grief, and loss among Asian Americans. In a rare qualitative study, Yeh, Inman, Kim, and Okubo (2006) interviewed eleven Asian Americans who had lost family members to the World Trade Center terrorist attack on September 11 2001. Based on open-ended, structured interviews, the study showed that the coping strategies adopted by these Asian participants in dealing with their tragedies were overrepresented by collective strategies. In fact, six of the eight key coping mechanisms reported by the participants mapped onto the characteristic of collective coping in terms of familial coping, intra-cultural coping, relational universality, forbearance, fatalism, and indigenous healing. The above studies together highlight the significance of collectivism as reflected in the stress and coping process among Asians.

Following on from the broad cultural perspectives on coping with stress described above, a specific conceptual model to guide future research in this area is presented in the next section. This model is adapted from earlier conceptualizations advanced in Bhagat, Steverson, and Segovis (2007a, 2007b).

Cross-cultural variations of the stress process: a conceptual model

Figure 15.1 demonstrates that both work (i.e., organizational) and non-work (i.e., personal

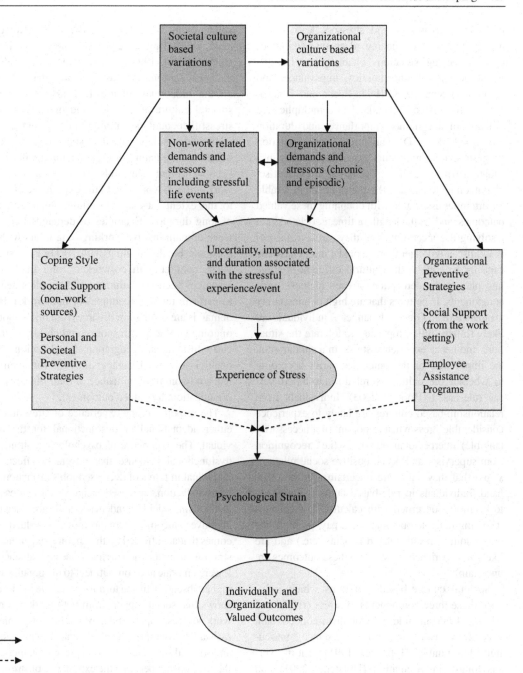

Figure 15.1. A conceptual model of cross-cultural and cross-national variations of the stress and coping process (adapted from Bhagat *et al.*, 2007a).

life related) demands and stressors lead to the possibility of experiencing decision-making or problem-solving situations characterized by different degrees of uncertainties, importance, and duration (Beehr, 1998, 1995, Beehr and Bhagat, 1985). Stress is conceptualized as a multiplicative function of uncertainty, importance, and duration (i.e., $S = U_c \times I \times D$). This multiplicative function suggests that an individual experiences stress in a situation where: (a) he or she has an important set of outcomes to obtain; (b) there are considerable uncertainties associated with obtaining these valued outcomes; and (c) the length of time associated with resolving the uncertainties (if they can be resolved) is significantly longer than he or she might have the capacity to cope with. Cultural differences come into play in the perception of each of these three components. In cultures that are high in uncertainty avoidance (e.g., Greece, Japan, etc.) individuals are likely to have little propensity to tolerate the situations and hence experience stress. In a similar vein, the importance of the outcomes varies according to whether the culture is relationship-based versus rule-based (Hooker, 2003). Individuals from relationship-based cultures are likely to experience considerable stress when important (not necessarily tangible) interpersonal outcomes (i.e., recognition from supervisor and peers, positive social relationships) that they value are uncertain. On the other hand, individuals in rule-based cultures are likely to be more concerned with calculative exchanges involving tangible outcomes (i.e., pay, promotional opportunities, health related benefits, etc.) and are likely to experience stress when these outcomes are uncertain.

Societal culture-based variations which influence these three components of stress (Beehr and Bhagat, 1985) include individualism-collectivism, uncertainty avoidance, power distance, masculinity-femininity (Hofstede, 1991), short- versus long-term orientation (Hofstede, 2001) and other variations such as those found in the World Values Survey, Triandis (1994, 1995, 1998, 2002), Trompenaars (1993), Bond (1996) and Chinese Culture Connection (1987). Organizational culture-based variations such as process versus results orientation, employee versus job orientation, parochial versus professional orientation, loose

versus tight control (Hofstede, 2001, Hofstede et al., 1990), fragmented versus integrative dimensions (Martin, 1993), etc. influence the kinds of demands (chronic versus episodic) that impinge on the individual. Figure 15.1 also shows that societal culture affects the kind of stressors and stressful encounters that might emerge in the lives of individuals. Not only that, societal culture also influences the nature of organizational values that become salient. Demands from the domains of work and non-work lead to the experience of stress to the extent they are uncertain, important, and of long duration. Examples of demands from the work domain involve working long hours without adequate breaks, dealing with an abrasive supervisor, conflict with co-workers, and inadequate resources such as equipment and supplies needed to perform the job. Examples of non-work related demands are death of or divorce from one's spouse, ongoing conflicts with spouse and children, financial difficulties, geographical relocation, and health issues (see Bhagat et al., 1985 for an empirical study on the significance of total life stress for organizationally valued outcomes).

The response to the experience of stress may be either adaptational or dysfunctional for the individual. The experience of psychological strain is a dysfunctional response that adversely affects the individual in terms of decreased job satisfaction and life satisfaction, increased incidence of depression, alcoholism, suicidal tendencies, and other negative affective outcomes. Organizationally valued outcomes that are affected by the ongoing experience of strain are decreased job performance and satisfaction, lowered morale and commitment to the organization, higher absenteeism and turnover, etc. The model also shows that social support from both work and non-work sources, coping style, availability of employee assistance programs as well personal, organizational, and societal strategies for stress prevention moderate the relationship between the experience of stress and psychological strain (see figure 15.1).

The role of social support is crucial. Individuals experiencing higher levels of social support, whether from supervisors, co-workers or family, experience lower of levels of psychogical strain including decreased incidences of burnout (Maslach, 1976; Dignam, Barrera, and West, 1986; Leiter, 1990).

Furthermore, effective individual coping skills as well as the availability of well-designed employee assistance programs are helpful in managing the stress (Bhagat, Steverson, and Segovis, 2007a, 2007b).

We have discussed the role of coping in ameliorating the effects of stress on psychological strain in an earlier section. It is sufficient to note that cultural variations play a stronger role in determining the type of coping strategy many instinctively prefer as a result of socialization in a given national or cultural context. Next, we discuss the role of employee assistance and other organization-based intervention strategies designed to lower the effects of stressful experiences on pyschological strain and individually and organizationally valued outcomes.

Role of EAPs and other organizational interventions

Workplace stress is a global concern. Understanding how culture and nationality may affect employee stress and coping is important for a global society. Interventions to prevent and cope with the effects of stress need to be sensitive to cultural differences. What works with one ethnic group or in one country might not work in another.

Work stress interventions consist of three categories based on western research; different approaches may be needed in different countries (Liu and Spector, 2005). First, primary intervention requires intervention at the level of stressors (Cooper, Dewe, and O'Driscoll, 2003). Efforts to reduce the stressors themselves necessitate understanding context-specific work stressors. Work redesign efforts such as job enrichment (adding tasks or responsibility or authority) and job rotation have the potential to reduce stress but need to take into account the individual's needs, values, and abilities.

Secondary interventions such as stress management training (i.e., relaxation exercises, biofeedback) help employees cope with stressors (Cooper, Dewe, and O'Driscoll, 2003). However, some specific techniques might be effective in one type of culture (i.e. individualistic) but not in others (i.e., collectivistic). For example, Liu and Spector (2005)

discussed that assertiveness training to learn to speak up to management might be effective in the low power distance US, while not effective in a high power distance country such as India, where assertiveness with managers might be viewed as inappropriate and as a challenge to managerial authority that would eventually result in increased stress.

Tertiary interventions involve treatment for individuals who are experiencing physical and psychological disorders (Cooper, Dewe, and O'Driscoll, 2003). Medical treatment of physical disorders and psychotherapy are examples of tertiary intervention. Medical treatment involves activities such as employee examinations, disability reviews, and urgent medical care. Most organizations are not well equipped to provide extensive or long-term care related to stress and must rely on outside health care referrals. Psychotherapy involves activities such as insight-oriented psychotherapy and supportive counseling. In particular, psychotherapy requires competence on the part of the therapist to successfully work with people of different cultural backgrounds (Kuo, and Gingrich, 2004; Kuo, Kwantes, Towson, and Nanson, 2006). In this context, it should be mentioned that psychotherapy as a technique is not necessarily universally accepted. In fact, there are stigmas associated with the use of psychotherapy and other person-directed techniques in East and South Asian cultures (Chiu and Hong, 2006) as well as in other cultures.

Many western companies offer limited counseling at the workplace or outside referrals through employee assistance programs (EAPs). Managers or the employee themselves can refer or be referred to the EAP. The primary goal of the EAP is to maintain or restore the health and productivity of valuable employees. EAPs are primarily rooted and evolve out of the cultural context of western and vertical individualistic societies (Bhagat *et al.*, 2007a, 2007b). Although they do exist in one form or another in other parts of the world (non-Western and collectivistic societies), the state of globalization in the locale, economic realities, and societal and organizational culture-based variations strongly affect their evolution, maintenance, and effectiveness. There are also cultural variations in the propensity to seek mental health related counseling

Table 15.1 An organizational culture-based matrix of the prevalence of styles of coping, social support mechanisms, and differential emphasis of EAPs (adapted from Bhagat et al., 2007b)

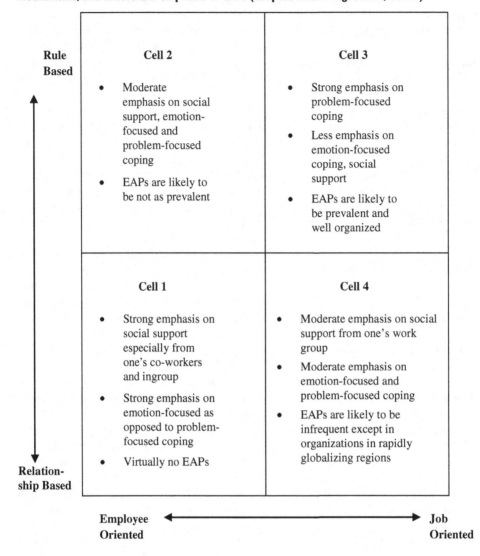

	Rule Based	**Cell 2**	**Cell 3**

Rule Based

Cell 2
- Moderate emphasis on social support, emotion-focused and problem-focused coping
- EAPs are likely to be not as prevalent

Cell 3
- Strong emphasis on problem-focused coping
- Less emphasis on emotion-focused coping, social support
- EAPs are likely to be prevalent and well organized

Cell 1
- Strong emphasis on social support especially from one's co-workers and ingroup
- Strong emphasis on emotion-focused as opposed to problem-focused coping
- Virtually no EAPs

Cell 4
- Moderate emphasis on social support from one's work group
- Moderate emphasis on emotion-focused and problem-focused coping
- EAPs are likely to be infrequent except in organizations in rapidly globalizing regions

Relationship Based

Employee Oriented ⟷ Job Oriented

(Kuo *et al.*, 2006) and to use EAPs (Bhagat *et al.*, 2007b). In table 15.1 we provide an organizational culture-based matrix of the prevalence of the styles of coping, social support mechanisms, and differential emphases of employee assistance programs based on the work of Bhagat *et al.*, (2007a).

As table 15.1 shows, cell 1 consists of work organizations that are largely employee oriented and also concerned with maintaining harmonious relationships in the workplace. Such organizations are found in rural areas of countries that are largely untouched by globalization. Small family owned organizations in horizontal or vertical collectivistic cultures (such as rural China, India, Brazil, Mexico, most rural parts of Latin America, the Middle East, and Africa, as well as the Israeli kibbutz) are likely to exhibit the tendencies of strong social support and strong emotion-focused as opposed to problem-focused coping. In Mexico, for example, work relationships, like other relationships in the non-work context, are strongly guided by the cultural tradition of simpatía (Diaz-Guerrero, 1967; Triandis, Marin, Lisansky, and Betancourt, 1984; Marin and Marin, 1994; Triandis, 1994). People value relationships and seek ways to maintain high degrees of social harmony in work as well as in their personal life. A strong concern for others in the immediate network is also characteristic of many East Asian cultures (Bond, 1996). EAPs are virtually unknown in these work cultures. Workplaces which are characterized by the cultural prototype as depicted in cell 2 are likely to moderately emphasize social support mechanisms, culture-specific (i.e., emic) coping strategies. EAPs in these contexts are likely to be somewhat uncommon. However, work organizations in urban sectors of the emergent economies and rapidly globalizing countries (e.g., South Korea, China, Taiwan, and India) are likely to exhibit these tendencies. Workplaces in cell 3 are found in highly industrialized and information intensive societies like those in the G-8 countries perhaps with the exception of Japan (which is the second largest economy but is highly collectivistic in orientation). The US, Australia, Canada, and a large part of western Europe have organizations whose cultural prototype fit this pattern (i.e. strongly job oriented and rule-based). There are both explicit and subtle messages in the work context that one must deal with stressful situations by adopting a problem-focused coping. Emotion-focused coping is to be avoided at all costs, especially in the workplace. Sanchez-Burks (2002, 2004) suggests that organizations located in countries such as the US will have a strong preference for putting aside affective and relational concerns away from work. EAPs are likely to be highly institutionalized and often available on a regular basis in this work context. Our research reveals that even in the collectivistic context of Japan (which is one of the G-8 countries) heavy emphasis placed on job and role orientation is also fostering the need for institutionalized EAPs in recent times. When Japan embarked on the path of rapid industrialization and reconstruction after World War II, workplaces

at that time did not have any organized and institutionalized EAPs to assist employees in times of distress. Social support was the primary method of coping with stress in this highly collectivistic East Asian country. Work places in cell 4 are job oriented and relationship-based. In these workplaces, there is likely to be a moderate emphasis on social support from one's ingroup as well as a moderate emphasis on problem-focused and emotion-focused styles of coping. There is likely to be an emphasis on the principle of gunaxi, that is a sense of interconnectedness with and caring for one's ingroup members (Leung and White, 2004; Hooker, 2003, p. 183). EAPs are likely to be infrequent except in rapidly globalizing regions. Examples of organizations in cell 4 are likely to be found in South Korea, Singapore, Taiwan, Thailand, and globalized urban regions of China (i.e., Shanghai, Canton, Beijing, etc.) and India (i.e., Bangalore, Bombay, Chennai, etc.).

Implications for future research

Although embedded in the research traditions of Europe and North America, the seminal coping model of Lazarus and Folkman (1984) has remained uncontested for more than four decades (Wong, Wong and Scott, 2006). The limited scope of western research models necessitate that future researchers utilize multicultural perspectives for the benefit of science and practice. Learning how people in dissimilar cultures experience and cope with stress can enhance our understanding and provide guidance for workplace interventions.

Although some studies have employed measures of coping, most have not dealt with the effectiveness of coping strategies in reducing stress. Pearlin and Schooler (1978) found little effectiveness of coping strategies aimed at reducing stress at work although they were effective in reducing stress in interpersonal relationships – in other words, mechanisms for dealing with stress that are idiosyncratically appropriate in one context may be relatively ineffective in another. We identify the following issues that need to be adequately addressed in future theory development and research concerning the role of cultural variations in work stress and coping.

Issue 1

A theory like transactional theory of stress and coping developed by Lazarus and his associates in the 1960s and then tested in numerous settings in the 1980s and 1990s (Lazarus and Folkman, 1984; Lazarus, 1991; Lazarus, 1999; Lazarus, 2000; Lazarus, 2003) eschews the notion that the nature of work stresses is not identical across different situations and/or different cultural contexts, nor do such stresses impact individuals with uniform effects. The transactional theory of stress clearly emphasizes the notion that the etiology of work stress as well as strategies directed for coping with work stress must be viewed within a longitudinal and process-oriented perspective. That is, neither the individual nor the work organization, nor the culture in which the work organization is embedded, is solely responsible for the transaction between stress and coping response. To place the emphasis of stress and coping squarely on the individual or on the context (organizational or societal culture-based) alone, fails to adequately account for the intricacies of human stress and cognition in the workplace. The conceptual model presented in this chapter is advanced to focus on the longitudinal process of work stress and coping. To appreciate the process fully, one must examine the unfolding bi-directional transaction interactions between the experienced stress from the environmentally imposed conditions and the individual's response within his or her societal and/or work culture. Such coping can be personal in etiology, i.e., problem-focused coping and other action-oriented strategies that one can creatively and sometimes not so creatively engage in. Also, cultural contexts may provide appropriate social support related mechanisms in the form of informational, affective, structural and instrumental supports. Future research should be directed towards understanding the complex processes that underlie the role of cultural variation in stress and coping.

Issue 2

Researchers should also focus on developing research instruments that consider the temporal nature and importance of stress. Stress can be acute or chronic, a one-time event, episodic, or an ongoing phenomenon. Current research instruments do not articulate this temporal differentiation. It is important to capture day-in and day-out stress experiences (e.g., daily hassles) as well as acute stress experiences (e.g., downsizing of company or job loss). Also, the importance of the stressor may vary among individuals and among individuals in different work organizations. Future research instruments should be designed to capture the degree of importance of the stress phenomenon.

Issue 3

Another area for researchers to focus on is the subjectivity inherent in research instruments. Self-report measures are heavily utilized (e.g., Spector et al., 2002; Bhagat et al., 1994; Bhagat, Vansotter et al., 2007) and will continue to be an important method for collecting information on stressful experiences, coping strategies, as well as perceptions of culture specific values inherent in the work and organizational contexts. However, it should be noted that while self-report based data collection generally yields psychometrically valid and reliable data in western contexts, such methods are not valid in countries and cultures where individuals have tendencies toward responding with *acquiescence bias*, i.e., a tendency to respond to questionnaire items either passively or by using one end of the attitudinal stem. Arab cultures in the Middle East are particularly known for this bias (Triandis, 1994; Van de Vijver and Leung, 1997) and while item response theories can be employed to correct for some of psychometric errors that creep in, the fact is that we need to move towards more unobtrusive, objective, archival, and creative methods for collecting stress and coping related information from individuals of dissimilar cultures. More emphasis needs to be placed on ethnographic and qualitative modes of data collection in cultures where such methods are likely to yield better insights into the the experience of stress and coping.

Issue 4

Research in this area should also be concerned with the key themes that lie at the intersection of theoretical concerns dealing with: (1) technological advances in the work place; (2) virtual work across nations and borders; (3) ageing of the work force in many but not all countries; and (4) the advancement of globalization. Macik-Frey *et al.* (2007) discussed the significance of these issues in their review of research on occupational health and psychology. They made important observations which are applicable in improving theoretical rigor and methodological robustness in the area of cultural variations of work stress and coping. Technological advances in the workplace result in improved individual and group productivity, higher levels of organizational effectiveness and better economic growth rates for nations. However, rapid technological changes result in unexpected and potentially problematic outcomes that make it difficult to discern the exact etiology of the stressful experiences of the employees and also the nature of interventions that need to be adopted to adequately address the distressing outcomes of the experiences. The impact of a virtual world where rapid advances in computer-mediated technologies eliminate space and time boundaries and challenge individuals continuously to monitor the pace of their work to keep up with the demands of clients located in different parts of the world both Western and non-Western. The issues are multi-faceted. Not only are individuals affected but also their spouses and immediate family members might be confronted with stressful health-related problems not previously seen by work stress researchers. Research centers, such as the one dealing with work-family issues located in IESE Business School in Barcelona, Spain, are beginning to provide useful insights but the search for knowledge that can be helpful for understanding the basic issues as well as for managing adverse outcomes continues to be outpaced by newer problems rapidly emerging in this era of virtual world and rapidly globalizing economies. The aging of the population in the US, as well as in much of the world, challenges work organizations today and in the future. Not only are people living longer, but they are living healthier lives with the expectation that the average age of workers will continue to increase as older workers strive to remain actively engaged. However, there is some evidence (Spiezia, 2002) that older workers are exiting the workforce earlier either by choice or force and that this is not always in their best interest economically. There are financial implications for organizations and nations in countries where the percentage of older workers is increasing rapidly. These implications exacerbate stressful thoughts on the part of older workers in pre-retirement years. Important insights need to be gained in this area. While significant in-roads have been made in Scandinavian countries and in the US (research largely sponsored by the National Institute of Occupational Safety and Health), there is little knowledge in this area from rapidly developing BRIC (Brazil, Russia, India, China) economies and other emergent economic zones where there is an uneven growth of older workers employed in different sectors of these economies. We urge future researchers to pay attention to this important area of research and generate comparative bodies of research and findings so that better interventions can be designed for individuals and their families in dissimilar cultures.

Along with the ageing issue, the increasing globalization of the workplace has obvious implications for health and well-being of the workers. Macik-Frey *et al.*, (2007) note that this is not simply a US issue and that globalization of occupational health and stress related issues is a major initiative of the World Health Organization started in 2000. The issue of national and cultural differences in the perception of physical and mental health, distress, and impact of work-related stressors on a growing percentage of working women and children demand urgent attention. Work-specific locus of control, which is generally higher in western countries and relates positively with physical well-being in the workplace, is found to be uncorrelated with physical well-being in a majority of the twenty-four cultures studied by Spector *et al.* (2002). Additional research of this kind, linking personality and specific individual-difference variables with cultural variations in the prediction of emotional and physical well-being, will be useful as globalization expands.

Since the review of occupational stress literature in Quick *et al.* (2003), Ganster and Schaubroeck (1991), Danna and Griffin (1999) and Quick and Tetrick (2003), we have seen a modest increase of research concerning the role of national and cultural differences in work stress and coping. We have argued in this chapter that such research has a unique role to play in examining the interaction of cultures, organizations, and work which is the primary focus of this handbook. Research in this area is not going to be for the faint-hearted because of complications involving theory and measurement, as we have discussed. However, it is our sincere hope that when research is conducted in the context of a robust theoretical framework as presented herein, important findings will emerge and the journey of a thousand miles will begin successfully with a few successful but bold steps.

References

Aldwin, C. M. 1994. *Stress, Coping, and Development*. New York, NY: Guilford Press.

Beehr, T. A. 1995. *Psychological Stress in the Workplace*. London: Routledge.
   1998. "Research on occupational stress an unfinished enterprise", *Personnel Psychology* 51: 835–44.
   and Bhagat, R. S. 1985. *Human Stress and Cognition in Organizations: An Integrative Perspective*. New York, NY: John Wiley Interscience Series on Organizational Assessment and Change.

Belgrave, F. Z., Townsend, T. G., Cherry, V. R., and Cunningham, D. M. 1997. "The influence of an Africentric worldview and demographic variables on drug knowledge, attitudes, and use among African American youth", *Journal of Community Psychology* 25(5): 421–33.

Berry, J. W. 1997. "Immigration, acculturation, and adaptation", *Applied Psychology: An International Review* 46: 5–34.

Bhagat, R. S. and Allie S. M. 1989. "Organizational stress, personal life stress and symptoms of life strains: an examination of the moderating role of sense of competence", *Journal of Vocational Behavior* 35: 231–53.

   Ford, D., O'Driscoll, M., Frey, L., Babakus, E., and Mahanyele, M. 2001. "Do South African managers cope differently from American managers? A cross-cultural investigation", *International Journal of Intercultural Relations* 25: 301–13.

   McQuaid, S. J., Lindholm, H., and Segovis, J. 1985. "Total life stress: a multimethod validation of the construct and its effects on organizationally valued outcomes and withdrawal behaviors", *Journal of Applied Psychology* 70(1).

O'Driscoll, M. P., Babakus, E., Frey, L. T., Chokkar, J., Ninokumar, B. H., Pate, L. E., Ryder, P. A., Fernandez, M. J.G., Ford, D. L., Jr., and Mahanyele, M. 1994. "Organizational stress and coping in seven national contexts: a cross-cultural investigation". in G. P. Keita and J. J. Hurrell, Jr. (eds.), *Job Stress in a Changing Workforce*. Washington, DC: American Psychological Association, pp. 93–105.

Steverson, P. K., and Segovis, J. C. 2007a. "Cultural variations in employee assistance programs in an era of globalization", in D. L. Stone and E. F. Stone-Romero (eds.), *The Influence of Culture on Human Resource Management Processes and Practices*. New York, NY: Taylor and Francis, pp. 207–33.

Steverson, P. K., and Segovis, J. C. 2007b. "International and cultural variations in employee assistance programmes: implications for managerial health and effectiveness", *Journal of Management Studies* 44(2): 222–42.

Vanscotter, J. S., Steverson, P. K., and Moustafa, K. S. 2007. "Cultural variations in job performance: implications for industrial and organizational Psychology in the 21st century". in G. P. Hodgkinson and J. K. Ford (eds.), *International Review of Industrial and Organizational Psychology*, vol. 22. New York, NY: Wiley, pp. 235–63.

Bond, M. H. (ed.). 1996. *The Handbook of Chinese Psychology*. Hong Kong: Oxford University Press.

Campbell, A., Converse, P. E., and Rodgers, W. L. 1976. *The Quality of American Life*. New York, NY: Sage.

Chadhoury, R. R. 2004. "Corporate exploitation of women", *Businessline, 1*. Retrieved March 3, 2008 from ABI/INFORM Trade and Industry Database.

Chan, A. 2001. *China's Workers Under Assault: The Exploitation of Labor in a Globalizing Economy*. Armonk, NY: Sharpe.

Chang, E. C. 1996. "Cultural differences in optimism, pessimism, and coping: predictors of subsequent adjustment in Asian American and Caucasian American college students", *Journal of Counseling Psychology* 43: 113–23.

Chiang, L., Hunter, C. D., and Yeh, C. J. 2004. "Coping attitudes, sources, and practices among Black and Latino college students", *Adolescence* 39: 793–815.

Chinese Culture Connection, 1987. "Chinese values and the search for culture-free dimensions of culture", *Journal of Cross-Cultural Psychology* 18: 143–64.

Chiu, C. and Hong, Y. 2006. *Social Psychology of Culture*. New York, NY: Psychology Press.

Chun, C. A., Moos, R. H., and Cronkite, R. C. 2006. "Culture: a fundamental context for the stress and coping paradigm", in P. T. P. Wong and L. C. J. Wong (eds.), *Handbook of Multicultural Perspectives on Stress and Coping*. New York NY: Springer, pp. 29–53.

Cooper, C. L. 1998. *Theories of Organizational Stress*. New York, NY: Oxford University Press.

Dewe, P., and O'Driscoll, M. 2003. "Employee assistance programmes", in J. C. Quick and L. E. Tetrick (eds.), *Handbook of Occupational Health and Psychology*. Washington, DC: American Psychological Association, pp. 289–304.

Cross, S. E. 1995. "Self-construals, coping, and stress in cross-cultural adaptation", *Journal of Cross-Cultural Psychology* 26: 673–97.

Danna, K. and Griffin, R. W. 1999. "Health and well-being in the workplace: a review and synthesis of the literature", *Journal of Management* 25: 357–84.

Diaz-Guerrero, R. 1967. *Psychology of the Mexican: Culture and Personality*. Austin, TX: University of Texas Press.

Dignam, J. T., Barrera, M., Jr., and West, S. G. 1986. "Occupational stress, social support and burnout among correctional officers", *American Journal of Community Psychology* 14: 177–93.

Dunahoo, C., Hobfoll, S. E., Monnier, J., Hulsizer, M. R., and Johnson, R. 1998. "There's more than rugged individualism in coping: Part 1: Even the Lone Ranger had Tonto", *Anxiety, Stress, and Coping* 11: 137–65.

Edwards, J. R., Caplan, R. D., and Van Harrison, R. 1998). "Person-environment fit theory: conceptual foundations, empirical evidence, and directions for future research", in Cooper, C. L. (eds), *Theories of Organizational Stress*. New York, NY: Oxford University Press, pp. 28–67.

Folkman, S. and Moskowitz, J. T. 2004. "Coping: pitfalls and promise", *Annual Review of Psychology* 55: 745–74.

French, J. R. P., Rodgers, W. L., and Cobb, S. 1974. "Adjustment as a person-environment fit". in G. Coelho, D. Hamburg, and J. Adams (eds.), *Coping and Adaptation*. New York, NY: Basic Books, pp. 316–33.

Frydenberg, E., Lewis, R., Ardila, R., Cairns, E., and Kennedy, G. 2001. "Adolescent concern with social issues: an exploratory comparison between Australian, Colombian and Northern Irish students", *Peace Conflict. Journal of Peace Psychology* 7: 59–76.

Lewis, R., Kennedy, G., Ardila, R., Frindte, W., and Hannoun, R. 2003. "Coping with concerns: an exploratory comparison of Australian, Colombian, German, and Palestinian adolescents", *Journal of Youth and Adolescence* 32: 59–66.

Gaines, J. and Jermier, J. M. 1983. "Emotional exhaustion in a high stress organization", *Academy of Management* 26(4): 567–86.

Ganster, D. C. and Schaubroeck, J. 1991. "Work stress and employee health", *Journal of Management* 17: 235–71.

Hobfoll, S. E. 1998. *Stress, Culture, and Community: The Psychology and Philosophy of Stress*. New York, NY: Plenum Press.

Hofstede, G. 1991. *Cultures and Organizations: Software of the Mind*. London: McGraw-Hill.

2001. *Culture's Consequences: Comparing Values, Behaviors, Institutions and Organizations across Nations* (2nd edn). Thousand Oaks, CA: Sage.

Neuijen, B., Ohayv, D. D., and Sanders, G. 1990. "Measuring organizational cultures: a qualitative and quantitative study across twenty cases", *Administrative Science Quarterly* 35(2): 286–316.

Hooker, J. (2003). *Working Across Cultures*. Stanford, CA: Stanford University Press.

House, J. S. 1981. *Work Stress and Social Support*. Boston, MA: Addison-Wesley.

Jex, S. M. and Beehr, T. A. 1991. "Emerging theoretical and methodological issues in the study of work-related stress." in K. Rowland and G. Ferris (eds.), *Research in Personnel and Human Resources Management* (vol. 9). Greenwich, CT: JAI Press, pp. 311–365.

Kahn, R. L. 1973. "Conflict, ambiguity and overload: three elements in job related stress", *Occupational Mental Health* 3: 2–9.

1981. *Work and Health*. New York, NY: Wiley.

Kahn, R. L. and Byosiere, P. 1992. "Stress in organizations", in M. D. Dunnette and L. M. Hough (eds.), *Handbook of Industrial and Organizational Psychology* (2nd edn). Palo Alto, CA: Consulting Psychologists Press, Inc, vol. 3, pp. 571–650.

Wolfe, D. M., Quinn, R., Snoek, J. D., and Rosenthal, R. A. 1964. *Organizational Stress*. New York, NY: Wiley.

Karasek, R. A. 1979. "Job demands, job decision latitude, and mental strain: implications for job design", *Administrative Science Quarterly* 24: 285–311.

Kuo, B. C. H. and Gingrich, L. 2004. "Correlates of self-construals among Asian and Caucasian undergraduates in Canada: cultural patterns and implications for counseling", *Guidance and Counseling* 20: 78–88.

Kuo, B. C. H., Kwantes, C. T., Towson, S., and Nanson, K. M. 2006. "Social beliefs as determinants of attitudes toward seeking professional psychological help among ethnically diverse university students", *Canadian Journal of Counseling* 40: 224–41.

Roysircar, G., and Newby-Clark, I. R. 2006. "Development of the Cross-Cultural Coping Scale: Collective, Avoidance, and Engagement strategies", *Measurement and Evaluation in Counseling and Development* 39: 161–81.

Lam, A. G. and Zane, N. W. 2004. "Ethnic differences in coping with interpersonal stressors: a test of self-construals as cultural mediators", *Journal of Cross-Cultural Psychology* 35: 446–59.

Lazarus, R. S. 1991. *Emotion and Adaptation*. New York, NY: Oxford University Press.

1999. *Stress and Emotion*. New York, NY: Springer.

2000. "Toward better research on stress and coping", *American Psychologist* 55: 665–73.

2003. "Does the positive psychology movement have legs? *Psychological Inquiry* 14(2): 93–103.

and Folkman, S. 1984. *Stress, Appraisal, and Coping*. New York, NY: Springer Publishing.

Leiter, M. P. 1990. "The impact of family resources, control coping, and skill utilization on the development of burnout: a longitudinal study", *Human Relations* 43: 1076–83.

Leung, K. and White, S. 2004. "Taking stock and charting a path for Asian management." in

K. Leung and S. White (eds.), *Handbook of Asian management*. Norwell, MA: Kluwer Academic Publishers.

Liu, C. and Spector, P. E. 2005. "International and Cross-cultural issues", in J. Barling, E. K. Kelloway, and M. R. Frone (eds.), *Handbook of Work Stress* Thousand Oaks, CA: Sage, pp. 487–515.

Macik-Frey, M., Quick, J. C., and Nelson, D. L. 2007. "Advances in occupational health: from a stressful beginning to a positive future", *Journal of Management* 33(6): 809–40.

Mandel, M. 2007. "Which way to the future?", *Business Week*, August 21 and 27 pp. 45–46.

Marin, G. and Marin, B. V. 1991. *Research with Hispanic Populations*. Newbury Park, CA: Sage.

Markus, H. R. and Kitayama, S. 1991. "Culture and the self: implications for cognition, emotion, and motivation", *Psychological Review* 98: 224–53.

Martin, J. 1993. *Cultures in Organizations*. New York, NY: Oxford University Press.

Maslach, C. 1976. "Burned out", *Human Behavior* 5: pp. 16–22.

1998. "A multidimensional theory of burnout", in C. L. Cooper (ed.), *Theories of Organizational Stress*. Oxford: Oxford University Press, pp. 68–85.

McGrath, J. E. 1976. "Stress and behavior in organizations". in M. D. Dunnette (ed.), *Handbook of Industrial and Organizational Psychology*. Chicago, IL: Rand McNally.

Mena, R., Padilla, A. M., and Maldonado, M. 1987. "Acculturative stress and specific coping strategies among immigrant and later generation college students", *Hispanic Journal of Behavioral Sciences* 9: 207–25.

Narayanan, L., Menon, S., and Spector, P. E. 1999. "A cross-cultural comparison of job stressors and reactions among employees holding comparable jobs in two countries", *International Journal of Stress Management* 6: 197–212.

Neill, L. M. and Proeve, M. J. 2000. "Ethnicity, gender, self-esteem, and coping styles: a comparison of Australian and South-East Asian secondary school students", *Australian Psychology* 35: 216–20.

Noh, S., Beiser, M., Kaspar, V., Hou, F., and Rummens, J. 1999. "Perceived racial discrimination, depression, and coping: A study of Southeast Asian refugees in Canada", *Journal of Health and Social Behavior* 40: pp. 193–207.

O'Connor, D. and Shimizu, M. 2002. "Sense of personal control, stress and coping style: a cross-cultural study", *Stress and Health* 18: 173–83.

Oláh, A. 1995. "Coping strategies among adolescents: a cross-cultural study", *Journal of Adolescence* 18: 491–512.

Parker, J. D. A. and Endler, N. S. 1996. "Coping and defense: an historical overview", in M. Zeidner and N. S. Endler (eds.), *Handbook of Coping: Theory, Research, Applications*. New York, NY: Wiley, pp. 3–23.

Pearlin, L. I., Lieberman, M. A., Menaghan, E. G., and Mullan, J. T. 1981. "The stress process", *Journal of Health and Social Behavior* 22: 337–56.

and Schooler, C. 1978. "The structure of coping", *Journal of Health and Social Behavior* 19: 2–21.

Perrewé, P. L., Hochwarter, W. A., Rossi, A. M., Wallace, A., Maignan, I., Castro, S. *et al.* 2002. "Are work stress relationships universal? A nine region examination of role stressors, general self-efficacy, and burnout", *Journal of International Management* 8(2): 163–87.

Peterson, M. F., Smith, P. B., Akande, A., Ayestaran, S., Bochner, S., Callan, V., *et al.* 1995. "Role conflict, ambiguity, and overload: a 21-nation study", *Academy of Management Journal* 38: 429–52.

Phillips, M. R. and Pearson, V. 1996. "Coping in Chinese communities: the need for a new research agenda", in M. H. Bond (ed.), *The Handbook of Chinese Psychology*. New York, NY: Oxford, pp. 429–440.

Quick, J. C., Cooper, C. L., Nelson, D. L., Quick, J. D., and Gavin, J. H. 2003. "Stress, health, and well-being at work", in J. Greenberg (ed.), *Organizational Behavior: The State of the Science* (2nd edn). Mahwah, NJ: Lawrence Erlbaum Associates.

and Tetrick, L. E. (eds.). 2003. *Handbook of Occupational Health Psychology*. Washington, DC: American Psychological Association.

Redfield, R., Linton, R., and Herskovits, M. 1936. "Memorandum for the study of acculturation", *American Anthropologist* 38: 149–52.

Sanchez-Burks, J. 2002. "Protestant relational ideology and (in)attention to relational cues in work settings", *Journal of Personality and Social Psychology* 79(2): 919–29.

2004. "Protestant relational ideology: the cognitive underpinnings and organizational implications of an American anomaly", in R. Kramer and B. Staw (eds.), *Research in Organizational Behavior*, vol. 26. Stanford, CT: Jai Press.

Sears, S. F., Urizar, G. G., Jr., and Evans, G. D. 2000. "Examining a stress-coping model of burnout and depression in extension agents", *Journal of Occupational Health Psychology* 5(1): 56–62.

Shek, D. T. L. and Cheung, C. K., 1990. "Locus of coping in a sample of Chinese working parents: reliance on self or seeking help from others", *Social Behavior and Personality* 18: 327–46.

Sheu, H. B., and Sedlacek, W. E. 2004. "An exploratory study of help-seeking attitudes and coping strategies among college students by race and gender", *Measurement and Evaluation in Counseling and Development* 37: 130–43.

Skeers, J. 2005. "Study documents exploitation in Indian call centres", retrieved July 24, 2007 from the World Socialist website of the the International Committee of the Fourth International at: www.wsws.org/articles/2005nov2005/indi-23n.shtml.

Singelis, T. M. 1994. "The measurement of independent and interdependent self-construals", *Personality and Social Psychology Bulletin* 20: 580–91.

Smith, P. B., Bond, M. H., and Kagitcibasi, C. 2006. *Understanding Social Psychology Across Cultures: Living and Working in a Changing World*. London: Sage.

Somerfield, M. R. and McCrae, R. R. 2000. "Stress and coping research: methodological challenges, theoretical advances, and clinical applications", *American Psychologist* 55: 620–5.

Spector, P. E., Cooper, C. L., Sanchez, J. I., Siu, O. L., Salgado, J., and Ma, J. 2004. "Eastern versus Western control beliefs at work: An investigation of secondary control, socioinstrumental control, and work locus of control in China and the US.", *Applied Psychology: An International Review* 55: 38–60.

Cooper, C. L., Sanchez, J. I., Sparks, K., Bernin, P., Büssing, A., et al. 2002. "A twenty-four nation/province study of work locus of control, well-being, and individualism: how generalizable are western work findings", Academy of Management Journal 45(2): 453–66.

Spiezia, V. 2002. "The graying population: a wasted human capital or just a social liability?" International Labour Review 141(1–2): 70–113.

Triandis, H. C. 1994. Culture and Social Behavior. New York, NY: McGraw-Hill.

1995. Individualism and Collectivism. Boulder, CO: Westview.

1998. "Vertical and horizontal individualism and collectivism: theory and research implications for international comparative management", Advances in International Comparative Management 12: 7–35.

2001. "Individualism-collectivism and personality", Journal of Personality 69: 907–24.

2002. "Generic individualism and collectivism", in M. Gannon and K. Newman (eds.), The Blackwell Handbook of Cross-Cultural Management. Oxford: Blackwell Business Publishing, pp. 16–45.

Marin, G., Lisansky, J., and Betancourt, H. 1984. "Simpatía as a cultural script of Hispanics", Journal of Personality and Social Psychology 47: 1363–75.

Trompenaars, F. 1993. Riding the Waves of Culture: Understanding Cultural Diversity in Business. London: Nicholas Brealey Publishing.

Tweed, R. G. and DeLongis, A. 2006. "Problems and strategies when using rating scales in cross-cultural coping research", in P. T. P. Wong and L. C. J. Wong (eds.), Handbook of Multicultural Perspectives on Stress and Coping. New York, NY: Springer, pp. 203–221.

White, K., and Lehman, D. R. 2004. "Culture, stress, and coping: internally- and externally-targeted control strategies of European Canadians, East Asian Canadians, and Japanese", Journal of Cross-Cultural Psychology 35: 652–68.

Utsey, S. O., Adams, E. P., and Bolden, M. 2000. "Development and initial validation of the Africultural Coping Systems Inventory", Journal of Black Psychology 26(2): 194–215.

Brown, C., and Bolden, M. A. 2004. "Testing the structural invariance of the Africultural Coping Systems Inventory across three

samples of African descent populations", Educational and Psychological Measurement 64(1): 185–95.

Van de Vijver, F. J. R. and Leung, K. 1997. Methods and Data Analysis for Cross-Cultural Research. Newbury Park, CA: Sage.

Wester, S. R., Kuo, B. C. H., and Vogel, D. L. 2006. "Multicultural coping: Chinese-Canadian adolescents, male gender role conflict, and psychological distress", Psychology of Men and Masculinity 7: 87–104.

Wong, P. T. P. and Reker, G. T. 1985. "Stress, coping, and well-being in Anglo and Chinese Elderly", Canadian Journal on Aging 4: 29–37.

and Wong, L. C. J. 2006. Handbook of Multicultural Perspectives on Stress and Coping. New York, NY: Springer.

Wong, L. C. J., and Scott, C. 2006. "Beyond stress and coping: the positive psychology of transformation", in P. T. P. Wong and L. C. J. Wong (eds.), Handbook of Multicultural Perspectives on Stress and Coping. New York, NY: Springer, pp. 1–26.

Yeh, C. J., Arora, A. K., and Wu, K. A. 2006. "A new theoretical model of collectivistic coping", in P. T. P. Wong and L. C. J. Wong (eds.), Handbook of Multicultural Perspectives on Stress and Coping. New York, NY: Springer, pp. 55–72.

Chang, T., Arora, A., Kim, A. B., and Xin, T., 2003. "Development of the collectivist coping scale: report from six studies", Paper presented at the 2003 Annual Convention of the American Psychological Association, Toronto, Canada.

Inman, A., Kim, A. B., and Okubo, Y. 2006. "Asian American collectivistic coping, response to 9/11", Cultural Diversity and Ethnic Minority Psychology 12: 134–48.

and Inose, M. 2002. "Difficulties and coping strategies of Chinese, Japanese, and Korean immigrant students", Adolescence 37(145): 69–82.

Inose, M., Kobori, A., and Change, T. 2001. "Self and coping among college students in Japan", Journal of College Student Development 42: 242–56.

and Wang, Y. W. 2000. "Asian American coping attitudes, sources, and practices implications for indigenous counseling strategies", Journal of College Student Development 41: 94–103.

Zhang, D. and Long, B. C. 2006. "A multicultural perspective on work-related stress development of a collective coping scale", in P. T. P. Wong and L. C. J. Wong (eds.), *Handbook of Multicultural Perspectives on Stress and Coping* New York, NY: Springer, pp. 555–576.

Zheng, X. and Berry, J. W. 1991. "Psychological adaptation of Chinese sojourners in Canada", *International Journal of Psychology* 26: 451–70.

Cultural values and women's work and career experiences[1]

RONALD J. BURKE

Women have entered the workplace in increasing numbers during the past two decades in all developed and developing countries. This trend has paralleled women's pursuit of education, particularly education in the professions such as business management, engineering, computer science and technology. Women have made great strides in entering professional and entry-level managerial jobs (Adler and Izraeli, 1988, 1994).

The International Labour Organization (ILO) (2004b) reported recent information in 2004. They concluded the following. The proportion of women in the labor force continues to increase. These participation rates, however, are uneven (e.g., East Asia, eighty-three women in the workforce for every 100 men, Middle East, forty women in the workforce for every 100 men). Female unemployment rates worldwide were slightly higher than those of males, but again there was considerable regional variability. Females were less likely to be in regular wage and salaried employment than men. Women who worked were more likely to work in agriculture and services. Women earned less income than men, a gap that has decreased only marginally and slowly. Countries having higher rates of female participation in the workforce also had lower birth rates

Women in management research is now increasingly being conducted in a greater number of countries reflecting both the globalization of business and the international competition for talent and the increasing numbers of women pursuing professional and managerial careers (Davidson and Burke, 2000; Burke and Nelson, 2001). Cross-cultural research on women in management issues, however, still

remains an under-researched and under-developed area of study (Cahoon and Rowney, 2000).

What do the numbers show?

Although some had predicted that women would achieve the ranks of senior executive leadership by now, the reality is that few women had reached senior management. It has been suggested that women in management worldwide encounter a glass ceiling, an invisible yet impenetrable barrier that limits women's career advancement. The absence of women at executive levels is universal. Less than 10 percent of corporate board directorships are held by women; only two women had CEO positions in the US Fortune 500 companies. We have a fairly reasonable understanding of the progress women have made so far and the obstacles that have prevented qualified women from reaching executive levels (Powell, 1999).

Statistics compiled by the ILO show that progress is being made in many countries. Wirth (2001) reported that in about half of forty-one countries having comparable data for 1998–99, women held between 29 and 30 percent of legislative, senior official and managerial jobs. Those countries included Austria, Germany, Greece, Israel, Peru, and Singapore. In sixteen of the forty-one countries, women held between 31 and 39 percent of these jobs. These countries included New Zealand, Poland, Portugal, and the UK. In other countries (Korea, Sri Lanka), women held less than 10 percent of these jobs. Wirth had no data from Africa but the United Nations (2000) estimated that women held about 15 percent of these jobs across twenty-five African countries.

In a 2004 update based on forty-eight countries, using the same classifications as Wirth (2001), women

[1] Preparation of this chapter was supported in part by York University. This review builds on the work of my colleague, Marilyn Davidson, University of Manchester.

increased their share of these jobs between 1 and 5 percent in twenty-six countries between 1996–99 and 2000–2002. Some countries showed large increases (e.g., Costa Rica, 24 percent) others showed decreases (e.g., Canada, 4 percent, Ireland, 6 percent).

The numbers of women in senior executive positions in various countries is difficult to obtain. In the US, women held 15 percent of board directorships (Catalyst, 2006). Women held 8 percent of "clout titles" and 5 percent of the most highly paid executive jobs (Catalyst, 2002a, 2002b). In the UK, women held 10 percent of all board directorships (Singh and Vinnicombe, 2005). In France, women held 5 percent of the top positions in the top 200 companies (ILO, 2004a). In Greece, women held 6 percent of the board seats of the top fifty firms on their stock exchange and state-owned corporations.

When it comes to female corporate officers, Canada has been shown to lag behind the US, but the gap is closing. In 2006, almost 66 percent of Canada's 500 largest companies had at least one female corporate officer, compared to 87.2 percent of US Fortune 500 companies (Catalyst, 2007). The largest disparity involved the proportion of companies with multiple women officers – 39.2 percent in Canada compared to 67.7 percent in the US.

Catalyst (2007) reported that in 2006, women held 5.4 percent of the top jobs in Canada's 500 largest companies, up from 4.5 percent two years earlier and 3.9 percent four years ago. CEOs/Presidents 4.2 percent, 2 percent gain from 2004; top earners 5.4 percent, 0.9 percent gain; clout titles 7.3 percent, 0.2 percent gain; corporate officers 15.1 percent, 0.7 percent gain; 16.2 percent of women in the "executive pipeline" headed for higher jobs, up from 14.8 percent two years earlier and 12.5 percent four years ago.

Some things seem to be difficult to change. Women continue to be paid less than men (Blau and Kahn, 2007). Women continue to face discrimination (Roth, 2007). Women continue to face barriers to career progress because they are women (Helfat, Harris, and Wolfson, 2006). It is safe to conclude that women in management face barriers to advancement in all countries, and the barriers appear to be greater at higher organizational levels. Perhaps the main barriers these women face lies in the attitudes and stereotypes that men have of women (Catalyst, 1996; 1997; 2004).

In almost all countries management is seen as a career suitable only for men. Therefore, it is dominated by men. Even in countries where women are better educated than men (e.g., Indonesia), relatively few women are in management especially at the senior levels. Women in most countries report barriers to career progress and tend to be concentrated in traditionally female jobs (education, human resources communication). Women are scarce in engineering, technology, natural resources, and manufacturing.

Countries also vary in how much organizational support is provided to women in the workplace. North American organizations began implementing a range of initiatives in the 1990s, with organizations in the UK and Australia joining this movement soon after. Organizations in Europe (e.g., France, Germany, and the Netherlands) became active in the late 1990s and early 2000s.

Culture obviously plays a key role. Both Italy and Japan have long valued traditional roles of women staying home to look after children. In Japan, women between the age of 30 and 45 exit the workforce to have children. In Japan, this is typically one child, resulting in a decreasing population. The absence of suitable child care also contributes to women staying at home after giving birth, figures in Japan being higher than in the US and Europe. Some countries (e.g., Norway, Spain, Portugal) are more likely to legislate equality in the form of a specified percentage of individuals at a particular level (e.g., on boards of directors) must be women. Other countries (US, UK, Canada) are less likely to adopt this approach.

We had several objectives in mind for this chapter which included:

• Understanding more about the status of women at work and women in management in a number of countries throughout the world.
• Shed light on the role of country culture on women's career advancement and international career assignments.
• Encourage the exchange of research findings as well as company "best practice" efforts.
• Encourage more research in the area, and more collaborative research across countries.

- Raise the issues in utilizing the best talents available.

The central question here is whether there is a relationship between cultural or societal values and the work experiences of women, particularly those working in managerial and professional jobs. Do women have different work and career experiences in countries having different cultural values? Are societal level values reflected in the organizational and/or occupational cultures of these countries? Unfortunately, there is relatively little research data that address these questions. It requires large-scale studies involving considerable resources; thus we will consider only two represented by the work of Geert Hofstede (1980, 1998, 2005) and of Robert House and his colleagues (House *et al.*, 2004). We will also make reference to studies that compare a small number of countries and to studies that examine the relationship of an organization's cultural values and the experiences of women.

The current body of research falls into the following themes:

Cross-cultural research on women in management

Country comparisons

- Careers of women in France and Canada (Symons, 1984).
- Male and female earnings differences in two Caribbean countries (Coppin, 1998).
- Sex role stereotyping and requisite management characteristics in three countries (Schein and Mueller, 1992).
- Portrayal of women in television commercials in two countries (Wiles and Tjerniund, 1991).
- Gender and power: sex segregation in higher education in two countries (Cole, 1998).
- Gender empowerment (equality) in 102 countries (Drew, 1999).
- Cultural origin, sex and work values in three countries (Akhtar, 2000).

- Portrayal of men and women in magazine advertising in two countries (Cheng, 1997).
- Managerial styles among female executives in two countries (Osland, Synder and Hunter, 1998).
- Sources of work family conflict among women and men in two countries (Yang *et al.*, 2000).
- Career priority patterns among managerial women in four countries (Burke, 2000).
- Occupational sex segregation in three Nordic countries (Melkas and Anker, 1997).
- Intergenerational correlations in labour market status in two countries (Couch and Dunn, 1997).
- Experiences of female entrepreneurs in three countries (Kolvereid, Shane, and Westhead, 1993).
- Career prospects patterns among managerial women in Turkey (Burke, Koyuncu and Fiksenbaum, 2007).
- Experiences of female international managers from four countries (Stone, 1991).
- Women's employment patterns in two occupations in two countries (Kidd and Shannon, 1996).
- Female education and adjustment programs in 59 countries (Rose, 1995).
- Masculinity/femininity and women's experiences in a large number of countries (Hofstede, 1980).

Women in non-North American countries

- Career strategies of Filipino women (Burke, Divinagracia, and Mamo, 1998).
- Career experiences of Indian women managers (Nath, 2000).
- Work experience and satisfaction among women managers (Richardsen, Mikkelsen and Burke, 1997).
- Career priority patterns in Bulgaria (Burke, Todorova, Kotzeva & McKeen 1994).
- Employment women in China (Granrose, 2006; Korabik, 1992).
- Career priority patterns in Singapore (Burke, *et al.*, 1997).
- Female labour market in Italy over time (Maione, 2000).
- Women management in Israel (Izraeli, 1987).

Broad conceptual pieces

- Women expatriates (Linehan and Walsh, 1999).
- Social economic changes, life stress and career success (Yang, 1998).

Edited collections

- Women on corporate boards of directors (Burke and Mattis, 2000).
- Women in management in Europe (Davidson and Cooper, 1993).
- Women in management in twenty-one countries (Adler and Izraeli, 1994).
- Dozens of research monographs by the ILO and other government agencies (United Nations).
- Successful women of the Americas (Punnett *et al.*, 2006).

Omar and Davidson (2001) review some key differences across cultures and national boundaries that affect women in management. These include having a noble and aristocracy heritage (Indonesia); the influence of Confucianism (Taiwan, Singapore); the influence of Islamic beliefs (Malaysia, UAE); the centrality of family, marriage and motherhood (Israel, Singapore), the promise of affirmative action and Equal opportunity legislation (US, Canada); population policies (Singapore); family policies (Japan); having a military connection (Israel, Indonesia); requirement to be geographically mobile (Japan); and marriage or pregnancy (Japan). There were large country difference in marital and parental status of women managers and professionals but not male managers (most married with children). There was also more work-home conflict in some countries (US, UK) than in others (Asia, Turkey).

Networking requires that women socialize and interact with men both at and outside of work. This can be difficult for many women in some countries (e.g., Muslim countries particularly). Muslim women wearing the hijab may encounter unique challenges. Thus, considering potential differences across cultures at both the local and societal context is important. This includes a patriarchical social system, the existence of strong gender stereotypes, the presence of ethnic stereotypes, and the effects of cultural and religious beliefs (family gender roles, marriage pressure, motherhood pressure).

Country comparisons

Davidson and Burke (2004), in an edited collection, reviewed information from twenty-one countries, relevant to the studies of women in the workforce in each. These included countries in the European Union, Europe, North and Central America, Australia, Asia, South America and Africa. They drew the following conclusions.

Women have entered the workplace in increasing numbers over the past two decades in all developed countries. But the pace of change in relation to women managers and professionals was typically slow and uneven in different countries and cultures (Wirth, 2001). Although women in many countries comprised half the growth in professional schools (law, business), and are gaining the necessary experience (Catalyst, 2000a), they still encounter a "glass ceiling" (Davidson and Burke, 2000; Powell and Graves, 2003).

Similarities and differences between country labor force characteristics

A common trend was an increase of women in paid employment over the past twenty years, particularly married women with children and part-time workers. But the percentage of women in the workforce ranged from a high of 52 percent (Netherlands) to a low of 30 percent (Turkey). The demographic work profiles among working women in these two countries were also very different. In addition, ethnic, and religious differences were present in some countries. For example, in Israel, 53 percent of Jewish women worked compared to only 18 percent of Muslim women.

Childcare issues

Provision of childcare facilities was a concern in most countries and considered a key requirement for encouraging women to enter business and management. Women in China tended to receive adequate childcare (the "one child" policy) and work without interruptions, but few Chinese women occupied managerial or professional positions compared to their British or North American counterparts.

Occupational gender segregation

Occupational segregation by gender (both horizontally and vertically, hierarchically) has persisted in all countries. The occupations women hold and areas of work they manage have remained fairly constant over the past few decades. China and Russia have the least occupational gender segregation, but women are still concentrated in clerical or lower level manual work. In Russia (unlike many countries), women dominated certain occupations (doctors, engineers, economists) but those occupations were assigned lower status than in countries where they were categorized as "male occupations."

Even in countries that have introduced legislation supporting equality (US, Australia) most employed women were in two occupations – clerical and services, human services such as education and health care.

Pay

In every single country, the pay gap between women's and men's earnings persists. Despite slow gains in closing this gap, it ranges from women earning 80 percent of men's pay in Canada and Poland to 65 percent in Russia and Norway, despite Norway's having the strongest legislation in the EU.

Women pursuing education

With the exception of China (35 percent) and Mexico (49 percent), over 50 percent of higher education students in all countries were female. But women students in the majority of countries were still concentrated in the social sciences and liberal arts with men dominating in the physical sciences, engineering and information technology. The least gender segregated courses of study were found in China, Poland, and Russia. In some countries (Belgium, Canada, the Netherlands) some courses of study have become feminized, in that over 50 percent of the students were female. Russia has shown a decrease in women engineering students over the past decade from almost 60 percent to 30 percent.

Women in management

Women occupy about one-third of the managerial jobs in the twenty-one countries examined. This figure has increased slowly; women, however, tend to occupy lower rather than higher level managerial jobs. China, for example, has one of the highest percentages of full-time female workers, but very few women managers. Women in North America occupy only 5 percent of senior-level executive positions.

Socio-economic, class ethnic, and religious composition

In the US, black women are the largest group of minority women; there are significant differences in black and white women's career progress. In Canada, Asian women (Chinese) are the largest female management group of minority women. The women in management literature has generally ignored the experiences of minority women in various countries and cultures (Omar and Davidson, 2001).

Women entrepreneurs

Between 6 percent and 50 percent of entrepreneurs/self-employed were women and these figures were increasing worldwide. The dominant type of self-employment continues to be unincorporated businesses without paid help. The majority of female-owned businesses were small and often stereotypically female (mainly in the service sector). But the latter is slowly changing, particularly among more highly educated women in North America, the UK and Europe. But women entrepreneurs earn less than their male counterparts and experience difficulties in obtaining financial support and with discrimination.

Legislation

Affirmative action/equal employment legislation in North America has increased the proportion of women in management, but not increased numbers of women at senior ranks. Equal pay legislation has not yet closed the gap in pay differentials observed in every country.

Davidson and Burke (2004) suggest we need a large-scale study that examines societal and cultural values and perceptions by large numbers of women (preferably managerial and professional) of their work environment/work experiences and their satisfaction with work, extra-work and their psychological well-being. It would also be useful to collect descriptive data on their employing organizations and their work situation characteristics (organizational level, organizational size, job tenure). Until such time, we can only speculate on the role of social and cultural values and women at work, or draw limited conclusions from the available country studies and country comparisons.

Conclusions and the future

In twenty-one countries – positive aspects include:

- More women in management.
- More supportive government policies.
- More supportive organizational practices.
- Changing family roles and responsibilities.
- Availability of more widespread support systems.
- Improved economic and labour market conditions.
- Changes in demographic characteristics offering more opportunities to women.

In twenty-one countries – negative aspects include:

- Pace of change often slow.
- Men still dominate senior executive positions, CEO and board directorships.
- Women still face discrimination and gender, ethnic, cultural and religious stereotyping.
- In some countries (e.g., Australia, UK, Canada, and Norway) the proportion of women as managers seems to have plateaued; e.g., in Norway, there is a prediction that at current rate of overall

increases, will take sixty-two years to achieve gender equality in senior management and 115 years before equality reached on corporate boards.

Factors which continue to limit women's advancement in management careers:

- Discrimination and prejudices.
- Organizational culture/policies and practices.
- Ineffectual discriminatory legislation.
- Societal norms regarding women's roles and women's educational attainment.
- Labour demands, economics etc can all have both positive and negative effects.
- Continued legislative initiatives.
- Enforcement of EO/Affirmative action.
- Changes related to organizational attitudes toward equality and diversity.
- Changes related to organizational work/family initiatives.
- Acknowledging the business sense re the management of diversity initiatives.
- Changes in societal attitudes (including the media) and individual's behavior.
- Educators and organizations to understand the barriers encountered by women.
- Managerial women need to understand why they are experiencing particular work situations.

Women managers in Hong Kong and Britain

Venter (2002) conducted a study of 401 male and female managers (164 in Hong Kong, 237 in Britain) using first a survey followed by interviews with twenty-three women in Hong Kong and twenty-four in Britain. She considered three areas of contextual difference: the impact of industrialization and economic growth in each country, their socio-political environments, and contrasting cultural values. Although all female respondents were managers, British women were depressed and defeated by their experiences of discrimination. The Chinese women managers described their experiences differently; they expected discrimination from their male colleagues but viewed this as a minor irritant that would not stop their career progress. Hong Kong women worked extra hard to overcome these barriers. Hong Kong women tended to value risk; British women tended to value security. British women blamed men's attitudes for their limited progress; Hong Kong women believed a lack of hard work accounted for their slow progress – external versus internal causes respectively.

In Britain, industrialization had been slower and carried out over a long period of time; in Hong Kong, the pace was rapid and women were needed as resources, given the growth in jobs. Britain has a welfare safety net; in Hong Kong, the family serves as a source of support and help – individualistic versus collectivistic values. British women managers wanted to be treated the same as their male colleagues. Hong Kong women managers wanted to have their feminine qualities – though different from masculine ones – to be valued similarly. They did not want to be the same as men. Thus, though the lives and work experiences of these two groups of women managers were similar in may respects, their interpretations of their experiences differed somewhat.

Using the sixty-one nation GLOBE database, Gupta, Hanges and Dorfman (2002) identified ten cultural clusters: South Asia, Anglo, Arab, Germanic Europe, Latin Europe, Eastern Europe, Confucian Asia, Latin America, Sub-Saharan Africa, and Nordic Europe. Cultural clusters allow one to understand intercultural similarities and intercultural differences. This information has practical usefulness for organizations in identifying cultures to expand into that are more similar and thus less risky.

Think manager – think male

Schein (2007) reviews how the "think manager – think male" attitude has changed in the thirty-five years since she first introduced this notion. This research has carried out over thirty years in the US and internationally. Over this period, corporate males in the US continued to see woman as less qualified than men for management positions. Women were less likely than men to be seen as having requisite management characteristics among male management students in the US, UK, Germany, China, and Japan.

Schein's early work (1973, 1975) showed that women were perceived by both male and female managers as less likely than men to possess the characteristics, attitudes, and temperaments required of successful managers. Later studies in the 1980s and 1990s showed that men's attitudes remained unchanged. Women's attitudes changed modestly, in that women now rated women's characteristics more similar to those required for success in a managerial job (Sczesny, 2003).

Studies conducted in other countries were consistent with the 1970s findings. That is, both women and men in Germany, the UK, China and Japan believed that men had requisite characteristics for success in the managerial job (Schein, Mueller, and Jacobson, 1989). There was some variations across the four countries in the degree to which women had the requisite skill (none in Japan, moderate in the UK).

Schein et al. (1996), in a study of male and female business students in five countries (China, Germany, the UK, Japan, the US), found that the correlations between descriptions of "men in general" and "successful managers" were strong in all countries for both male and female students. Perception of these targets were made on a list of ninety-two adjectives for describing people. The correlations between descriptions of "women in general" and "successful managers" were zero among males and positive but low among female students. In all five countries, the degree to which female students' descriptions of the "successful manager" and of "women in general" was correlated, was significantly correlated with masculinity; the less masculine a country, the more some characteristics of women were present in assessments of "successful managers."

Countries differ in the extent to which males and females "should" be managers – typically high among males in all countries; sometimes high and sometimes low among females, depending on the culture. In addition, levels of career ambition among men and women likewise vary according to national culture. Men in masculine societies value ambition and competitiveness; women in such societies can aspire to advancement, but on male terms. In feminine societies career advancement is optional for both men and women (Hofstede and Hofstede, 2005).

Think managers – think male has remained strong in males in spite of the gains that women in management have made and legislative and political efforts that support women in the workplace.

Men, however, seen to be unaware of the impact of their attitudes and stereotypes on women's careers. Men attribute the absence of women on senior levels to their absence of experience, not having enough experience, and an unwillingness to work the long hours required to succeed in a senior level position. The stability of "think manager – think male" continues to be a major impediment to women's career progress.

Tackling "think manager – think male"

It is important to continue the legal pressure to reduce barriers to women's advancement. These address the overt discriminatory practices. It is also useful to address corporate values and policies that limit women's progress. These include the long work hours culture, performance evaluations too closely tied to "face time," supporting work-family initiatives and ensuring that women are considered for key training and development activities as well as international assignments (Schein and Davidson, 1993).

Working time of couples

Medalia and Jacobs (2008) examined working time of married couples in twenty-eight countries. Work time predicts work-family conflict, unequal amounts of working time for men and women predicts gender inequality and, and some countries have suggested reducing work hours. Earlier work based on ten countries indicated that US couples worked more than any other country in this sample; 12 percent of US dual earner couples worked 100 or more hours per week. In the twenty-eight country sample, countries with long work week hours for men also had long work week hours for women. Men had longer work week hours than women. There were also large country differences in the percentage of dual career couples by country. Parents also worked fewer hours per week than did non-parents; this effect being larger for women than men. The US sample, while still working long

hours, no longer the longest hours. About one third of couples in Poland, Hungary and Taiwan worked 100 hours a week or more compared to 19 percent of couples in the US. The impact of these findings on family functioning and children cries out for attention.

There also was a relationship between Hofstede's masculinity scores for these countries and hours worked per week by couples. Not surprisingly, more couples tended to work more hours per week in the more masculine countries.

Work experiences, work outcomes, and psychological health

Burke (2001) surveyed work and career experiences as well as emotional well-being in samples of managerial and professional women in five countries: Bulgaria, Canada, Norway, the Philippines and Singapore. The survey was first conducted in Canada then used in the other countries translated as required using the back-translation method. The samples were different on various demographics and work situation characteristics.

In short, the pattern of findings was fairly consistent across all five countries. First, almost all multiple-time measures had acceptable levels of internal consistency, reliability in all countries. Second, respondents, reporting more positive work experiences (e.g., greater acceptance, training, and development) reported more favorable work outcomes (greater job satisfaction, lower intention to quit). Third, favorable work experiences were related to more positive psychological well-being in all countries. Fourth, more favorable work outcomes were also positively correlated with levels of psychological well-being.

The samples of managerial and professional women in these five countries showed significant country differences on several measures of demographic and work situation factors. These differences reflected their countries, educational, business and economic circumstances and the nature of women's movement into managerial and professional roles. Although culture was not measured, the five countries represent different cultural values and economic conditions. These differences were reflected in the mean values on the measures of work experience and satisfactions. Perhaps not surprisingly, there were marked country differences on measures of work experience, work satisfactions and emotional well-being, perhaps reflecting the country differences mentioned above. In spite of these differences, the work experiences examined were related to the success and satisfaction measures in very similar ways.

There were also some similarities in the findings across the five countries. First, almost identical measures revealed generally acceptable levels of internal consistency reliabilities in each of the five samples. Second, relationships among the variables of central interest (work experiences, work satisfactions, emotional well-being) were very similar in each of the five samples, despite significant sample differences on work situation and personal demographics, absolute levels on the variables of central interest and potentially great cultural and social values and histories.

Thus, the variables of central interest in this study were related to each other in ways that seemed to transcend large differences between the five samples. In all cases, particular work experiences were associated with work satisfactions and emotional well-being, and the work satisfactions were associated with emotional well-being measures in similar ways.

Career priority patterns across cultures

In a similar vein, Burke (2000) examined career priority patterns among samples of managerial and professional women in Bulgaria, Canada, Norway, and Singapore. Schwartz (1989) had earlier made the distinction between career-primary women and career-family women. Data were collected using questionnaires. Career priority patterns were assessed by a one-time scale anchored by career-primary and career-family archetypes. Women in all four countries shared similar career priority patterns, endorsing patterns that tended to both career and family.

These five countries are also likely to be similar in other ways related to the experiences and advancement of women in management. First,

relatively few women would have achieved executive leadership positions in large private sector organizations in them. Second, many of the barriers women in these countries face in their efforts to advance their careers (e.g., prejudice, negative stereotypes, greater responsibility for home and family duties, a less supportive and accepting workplace) would be very similar, though perhaps differing subtly in degree.

One possible explanation for these findings is that career development experiences of women are those that address common needs across countries and cultures. That is, needs for respect, recognition, support training and development opportunities, and the absence of additional barriers because of one's gender (overload, conflict) – if satisfied – are likely to be associated with work satisfaction and career benefits for women in all cultures. These results are likely to be evident in samples of men from those five countries as well.

Gender differences

If women and men in the same profession report similar work experiences, job and career satisfaction, and levels of psychological well-being, would that represent signs of progress? My colleagues and I have been involved in several studies of men and women in different occupations in various countries. These include psychologists in Australia, professors and physicians in Turkey, police officers in Norway, and MBA graduates in Canada.

These studies showed a similar pattern of findings, though some of the outcome measures varied. First, women and men in these studies differed significantly on personal demographic characteristics, findings commonly found in studies of gender differences. Males were at higher organizational levels, earned more income, were more likely to be married and, if married, to have children, to be older and with more work experience and longer organizational tenure. Second, men and women reported similar levels of workaholic behaviors, job and career satisfaction, future career prospects, intent to quit, extra-work satisfactions, and psychological well-being.

Women international managers

Linehan (2001) notes the low number of female international managers, citing 14 percent of global assignees being women in the US and 6.5 percent of global assignees in Australia. She interviewed fifty senior women managers who had at least one international career move. These women worked in England, Belgium, France, Ireland, and Germany and were employed in a wide variety of industries. While all were based in Europe, the sample did not reflect women's presence in the five countries included.

The career experiences of these fifty women contained experiences noted more generally in the women in management field (hitting the glass ceiling early). All believed they needed senior management experience before being considered for an overseas assignment. Many encountered a glass border as well, stereotyped attitudes of country senior managers about women's availability and sustainability and preferences for international assignments.

The women believed that generally similar skills were essential for both female and male managers working internationally, but that female managers need "additional qualities." Most believed that the stereotype of the white male manager persisted in all countries they had worked in, with some modest country differences and age differences in attitudes of their male colleagues (younger, more favorable). The career experiences and choices that had to be made by these women were common across all the countries in which they were based.

Supporting women's career advancement

Some light has been shed on the types of work experiences likely to be associated with women's career development. Morrison, White, and Van Velsor (1987), in a three-year study of top female executives, identified six factors which contributed to the women's career success. These were: help from above, a track record of achievements; a desire to succeed; an ability to manage subordinates; a willingness to take career risks; and an ability to be tough, decisive and demanding. Three derailment factors were common in explaining the failure of some female managers to achieve expected levels. These were: inability to adapt; wanting too much (for oneself or other women); and performance problems.

Furthermore, to be successful, women, more than men, needed help from above, needed to be easy to be with, and to be able to adapt. These factors related to developing good relationships with men in a male-dominated environment (also see Ragins, Townsend, and Mattis, 1998). Women, more than men, were also required to take career risks, be tough, have strong desires to succeed and have an impressive presence. These factors could be argued to be necessary to overcome the traditional stereotype of women such as being: risk averse, weak and afraid of success. Unfortunately, the narrow band of acceptable behavior for women contained some contradictions. The most obvious being: take risks but be consistently successful; be tough but easy to get along with; be ambitious but do not expect equal treatment; and take responsibility but be open to the advice of others, i.e., more senior men. These findings suggest that additional criteria for success were applied to women so that women had to have more assets and fewer liabilities than men.

As part of the same study, Morrison and her colleagues (1987) also examined the experiences of women who had advanced to levels of general management. They identified four critical work experiences: being accepted by their organizations; receiving support and encouragement; being given training and developmental opportunities; and being offered challenging work and visible assignments (Morrison, 1992). In speculating about their future success, these career-successful women perceived that there were even more constraints and less support now than in lower-level positions. Many reported exhaustion and talked about their futures involving doing something very different from what they were currently doing. In a series of follow-up interviews, Morrison, White, and Van Velsor (1992) obtained information from approximately one-third of their original sample and found that although some women had made progress, many were still stuck (see White, Cox, and Cooper, 1992, for similar findings based on a UK sample).

Aycan (2004) undertook two studies in Turkey exploring factors influencing women's career development. The first considered gender-role stereotypes and attitudes towards women's advancement 318 males and females completed the "Women As Managers Scale" (WAMS). While general attitudes toward women in management were slightly positive, females had significantly more positive attitudes than did males. Both women and men had moderate beliefs about women's competencies to carry out work and family responsibilities successfully. Other surveys in Turkey showed overwhelming belief that Turkish women's real place was in the home. But both women and men believed that women's status in work like should be improved.

In her second study, she interviewed fifty-two women in top and or middle management to better understand individual, organizational, and family-related factors influencing women's career advancement. These women attributed their career success primarily to personal characteristics (decisiveness, love for the job, integrity, self-confidence). Work was always important to these women. Most indicated few organizational supports as well as few systemic barriers. Surprisingly, few reported encountering a glass ceiling.

The socio-cultural context seemed to impact women's career advancement in two ways. First, gender role stereotypes emphasized women's family-related responsibilities – a potential barrier. Second, attitudes toward women's career advancement held by both women and men created another barrier. The latter likely affects the support women get from their spouses/partners and organizations.

Vinnicombe and Bank (2003) extensively interviewed nineteen women who had won the Veuve Clicquot Business Women of the Year Award, an award given to outstanding women executives and entrepreneurs. Their book distills how these women made it to the top, their views and definition of success and how their work fits into their lives. They identified ten key factors for success among the executive women. These were: confidence; self-promotion; risk-taking; visibility; career acceleration; mentoring; portfolio careers;

international experience; positive role models; and a management style compatible with that of male colleagues.

These factors overlap considerably with findings obtained from successful women in the US (Morrison, White, and VanVelsor, 1987) and Turkey (Aycan, 2004).

Canadian women business school graduates

Data were collected from 792 women graduates of the same Canadian business school, a 55 percent response rate. The sample tended to be in early career (one to ten years' work experience), fairly young (average age about 30), married (about 66 percent), and childless (66 percent). Three versions of the questionnaires were developed, each having about 270 respondents.

Three work and career experiences were included: support and encouragement; training and development; and feeling accepted. In addition, use of career strategies and levels of supervisor support were considered. Dependent variables included work outcomes (job satisfaction, career satisfaction, future career prospects, intent to quit) and psychological well-being (psychosomatic symptoms).

The following results were observed. First, women participating in more training and development activities, and women rating these activities more useful were more job and career satisfied and less likely to quit. Second, women reporting more positive work and career experiences also reported higher levels of job and career satisfaction, future career prospects and less intention to quit. Third, women making greater use of career strategies indicated higher levels of job and career satisfaction. In addition, women reporting higher levels of supervisor support also indicated greater job and career satisfaction.

Women in banking in Turkey

Data were collected from 286 females in managerial and professional jobs in a large Turkish bank, a 72 percent response rate. The majority were 40 years of age or younger (69 percent), married (79 percent), had children (76 percent), had one or two children (87 percent), held bachelor's university degrees (79 percent), were in lower or middle management jobs (82 percent), had worked continuously since graduation (68 percent), had only worked full-time (77 percent), worked for the bank ten years or more (53 percent), had ten years or less of job tenure (75 percent) and worked between forty-one and fifty hours per week (56 percent).

Five supportive work and career experiences were included: negative attitudes towards women; equal treatment; support; career barriers; and use of male standards. Work attitudes included measures of engagement, job and career satisfaction, and intent to quit. Measures of psychological well-being, included psychosomatic symptoms, emotional exhaustion, physical well-being, and emotional well-being.

Hierarchical regression analyses were undertaken, controlling both personal and work satisfaction characteristics, before considering the relationship of the work and career experience on the various dependent variables. Supportive work and career experiences had significant relationships with all three engagement measures. Negative attitudes towards women had significant negative relationships with all three; equal treatment and support had positive relationships with two of the three. Work and career experiences had significant relationships with two of the three work outcomes (job and career satisfaction); women indicating fewer negative attitudes toward women, and women indicating higher levels of support, indicated higher levels both job and career satisfaction. Finally, work and career experiences had a significant relationship with all measures of psychological well-being; women indicating more negative attitudes towards women and women indicating less support reported higher levels of distress on each measure.

Early career women managers in Australia

Data were collected from ninety-eight women graduates of the same business school in early career, a 10 percent response rate. Most were 30 years of age or younger (77 percent), had undergraduate degrees (80 percent), were single or divorced (60 percent), childless (78 percent), worked full-time (87 percent), had graduated within the past five years (55 percent), were in non-management or lower management jobs (65 percent), had worked continuously since graduation (69 percent), had short organizational and job tenure (77 percent and 93 percent having five or fewer years) and worked between forty-one and fifty hours per week (46 percent).

Five areas of supportive practice were considered: management support; policies and resources; administration; training and development; and recruiting and external rotations. Dependent variables included work outcomes (job and career satisfaction, intent to quit), psychological well-being (psychosomatic symptoms, emotional exhaustion, physical and emotional well-being) and three areas of extra-work satisfaction (family, friends, community).

Again, hierarchical regression analyses were undertaken controlling for both personal and work situation characteristics before examining the relationship of the work and career experiences with the various dependent variables. The five organizational practices were combined into a total score.

Organizational practices had significant relationships with both job and career satisfaction (but not intent to quit). In addition, organizational practices had a significant relationship with both psychosomatic symptoms and exhaustion (but not with physical or emotional well-being). Women indicating more supportive practices also reported fewer psychosomatic symptoms and less emotional exhaustion. Finally, supportive practices were found to have no relationship with measures of extra-work satisfaction.

In a separate analysis, women indicating more mentor functions also indicated greater job and career satisfaction, more optimistic future career prospects and fewer psychosomatic symptoms.

Implications

Turning now to the benefits of undertaking these supportive organizational practices, the data shows wide-ranging positive outcomes. That is, women describing more supportive organizational practices also indicated more job and career satisfaction and higher levels of psychological well-being. Others (Mattis, 2005; Giscombe, 2005; Hammond, 2002) have reported favorable job and career consequences of supporting women's career advancement but few have studied psychological well being. Extending the benefits of organizational practices supporting women to a consideration of their psychological health seems to be a logical extension given the association of job and career experiences with psychological well-being more generally (Nelson and Burke, 2002).

Finally, these findings have a direct bearing on practice. We have come to considerable understanding of the qualities that are part of work environments that are supportive of the career aspirations of women (and men). These include: top management support and commitment to the exercise; the explicit use of gender in decision-making in recruitment; career planning and employee development; the development of policies and procedures consistent with the goal of supporting women; the provision of rewards for providing the required support and achieving agreed upon goals for women's advancement; and becoming a model (in the wider community) of what can be accomplished through commitment, resources and effort.

In addition to these context efforts, other initiatives follow logically from them. These include providing support and encouragement to women, offering women challenging and visible work assignments, providing training and development opportunities and supporting cultural values accepting of women (Morrison, 1992). In addition, considerable progress has been made in integrating work-family concerns (Nelson and Burke, 2002).

National culture and women's work experiences

Interest in cultural differences, both between nations and between organizations, has increased. Hofstede's book (1980) was one of the first to raise objections about the universal validity of recently established management and organizational theories. Culture is a collective phenomenon shared with others from the same social environment in which it is learned. Culture is learned. Cultures are therefore relative; a culture is neither good nor bad. It is therefore inappropriate to apply one's norms and values to assess other (and different) cultures. Cultural values are also less likely to change over time but practices within cultures are more amenable to change. Hofstede and Hofstede (2005) use the term "software of the mind" to capture the notion of cultures as mental programming. It refers to patterns of thinking, feeling and habitual behaving or acting learned throughout one's lifetime. These "messages" are learned mostly in one's early childhood.

In one forty-five nation study (Barry, Bacon, and Child, 1959), males were higher on self-reliance, achievement, and independence whereas females were higher on nurturing, responsibility, and obedience. Sex differences in socialization emphases are associated with sex difference in behavior (Segal et al., 1990).

Hofstede (1980, 1983, 1991, 1993) has written about the ways in which country culture constrains or limits managerial practice or theories. Hofstede (1980) collected data from 88,000 women and men working for IBM in sixty-five countries using questionnaires. He considered values (an individual attribute) and culture (a collective attribute). Values are acquired early in one's life and reflect the culture in which one lives (software of the mind).

Hofstede identified four cultural values in this work: power distance (PD); uncertainty avoidance (UA); collectivism – individualism (CI); and masculinity-femininity (MF). We will review a sample of findings based on the MF dimension here, the dimension most likely to have an influence on the work and career experience of women. Countries received a score on the MF index reflecting the tendency of both men and women to endorse work goals more popular among men than among women (e.g., advancement and earnings versus friendly atmospheres and physical work conditions). Countries where both women and men endorsed work goals of men were high on masculinity, more masculine countries had greater value differences between men and women in the same jobs, had higher levels of work centrality, and, together, with low UA, had high levels of need for achievement. Masculinity was also negatively correlated with the percentage of women in professional and technical jobs (at least in the wealthier countries), and positively with the segregation of the sexes in higher education. Every society embraces many behaviors as more suitable for males, and others for females (sex roles); men are more concerned with work and economic roles, women with family and taking care of others. Males are assertive; females are nurturing. Males and females accept these behaviors as a function of sex-role socialization. This typically leads to a bias against women in organizations.

Organizations in masculine societies provide more opportunities for men in management ranks and emphasize work over family life, independence over dependence, results over process, equity over equality, facts over intuition, assertiveness over consideration, and dealing with conflict through fighting rather than cooperation or negotiation (Erez, 1994). Masculinity scores at the country level were also correlated with higher levels of stress, the belief that individual decisions were better than group decisions, the belief that employees dislike work, and knowing important people is more important than ability. People in more masculine countries live to work; people in more feminine countries work to live. Higher masculine countries stress the importance of leading, independence, and self-motivation and devalue the importance of helpfulness to others. In high masculine countries, fewer men are positive about having women in leadership positions.

High masculine countries include Japan, Austria, Switzerland, Germany, Italy, Venezuela, Mexico, and Columbia; low masculine countries include Finland, Denmark, Norway, Sweden, the Netherlands, Spain, Portugal, and France.

Management itself is a masculine concept developed in masculine countries (e.g., UK, US). Hofstede and Hofstede (2005) highlight some of the following differences related to masculinity-femininity likely to affect women's work and career experiences (see table 16.1).

Hofstede and McCrae (2004) report relationships between Hofstede's national culture dimensions and the Big 5 personality factors in thirty-three countries. They found masculinity to be significantly positively correlated with

openness to experience and neuroticism and significantly negatively correlated with agreeableness. Masculinity scores at the country level were uncorrelated with country scores on extraversion or conscientiousness. Regression analyses indicated positive relationships of masculinity with neuroticism and openness to experience and a negative relationship with extraversion. Masculinity had no relationship with either conscientiousness or agreeableness in these more complex analyses. The causes of these relationships are open to speculation however. These findings suggest that more feminine societies are likely to be more productive (e.g., more emotionally stable, more agreeable). In fact, over time, the wealthy countries have become more feminine.

Children's well-being

UNICEF (in 2007) measured six aspects of the well-being of 10–15-year-old children in twenty-one rich countries. These included: material conditions, health and safety; educational opportunities; family and peer relations; engaging in high-risk behaviors; and assessments of subjective well-being. The top countries included the Netherlands, the Scandinavian countries, Spain, and Switzerland. The bottom two countries were the USA and the UK. Hofstede found that 42 percent of country differences in child well-being could be explained by the masculinity-femininity dimension (r = .65, p < .01). Children in feminine countries were found to be happier. Neither national wealth nor any of the other cultural dimensions played a role here.

Robert House and his colleagues examined the role of societal culture and organizational culture in understanding leadership in sixty-two societies (Gupta, Hanges, and Dorfman, 2002; House et al., 2004; Javidan. and House, 2001, 2002). House and his colleagues (2004) divided Hofstede's masculinity-femininity into two dimensions – assertiveness and gender egalitarianism. Their research also considered both cultural practices (as they saw it now) and cultural values (how they hoped/believed things should be). They also distinguished between organizational cultures and societal

Table 16.1 Masculinity-femininity and women's work and career experiences

Feminine Societies	Masculine Societies
Job choice based on intrinsic interest	Job choice based on career opportunities
Men and women study the same subjects	Men and women study different subjects
Conflicts dealt with by compromise and negotiations	Conflicts dealt with by fighting
Rewards equality	Stress results, reward equity
Want to work less	Want to work more
Work to live	Live to work
More leisure time over money	More money over leisure time
Careers are optimal for both women and men	Career compulsory for men, optimal for women
More women in high level management jobs	Few women in top level management jobs

cultures. They found that societal culture dimensions were generally highly correlated with their measures of organizational culture dimensions.

GLOBE is a multi-phase, multi-method project examining the relationship between societal culture, organizational culture, and leadership. About 150 researchers from sixty-one cultures/countries representing all regions of the world took part. Data were collected in three industrial sectors in all societies: telecommunications, food and finance. Phase 1 involved the development and testing of the research instruments. Phases 1 and 2 focused on data collection and preliminary analyses. Data were collected from almost 17,000 middle managers from approximately 825 organizations in sixty-one countries. Some countries, however, included no women middle managers (a revealing fact by itself) and the gender of respondents was not obtained in still other countries.

Gender egalitarianism refers to the degree to which an organization and a society minimizes gender role differences while promoting gender equality. They found that societies scoring higher on gender egalitarianism had a higher proportion of women earning an income. Gender egalitarianism was also positively correlated with longevity. Respondents in societies scoring low on gender egalitarianism wanted to have more gender egalitarianism. In addition, countries with higher GNP also wanted to have more gender egalitarianism (Emerich, Denmark and Den Hartog, 2004).

Gender egalitarianism cultural values were positively associated with participative leadership, and to a lesser degree with charismatic leadership and negatively correlated with self-protective leadership.

In the GLOBE study, the mean for gender egalitarian practices was the lowest of all the means of the cultural dimensions examined. And respondents preferred their societies to be less male dominated. High gender egalitarian countries were: Hungary, Russia, Poland, Slovenia, and Denmark. Low gender egalitarian countries were South Korea, Kuwait, Egypt, Morocco, Zambia, and Turkey. Countries that wanted to be more gender egalitarian were: England, Sweden, Ireland, and Canada. Countries that believed they should be low on gender egalitarianism were Egypt, Qatar, Kuwait, China, Georgia, and Morocco.

Societies scoring higher on gender egalitarianism had more women in higher education and in the workforce, had higher levels of both human development and psychological health, and scored lower on a mastery orientation. Gender egalitarianism was also positively and significantly correlated with GNP per capita. Societies scoring higher on gender egalitarianism had higher levels of male-female social equality, women's economic activity, women's purchasing power, and women in government.

Kabasakal and Bodur (2002), again using the GLOBE data, examined the Arabic Cluster (Egypt, Morocco, Turkey, Kuwait, Qatar). These countries are highly masculine. They score low on gender egalitarianism, but aspire to score higher (the should be dimension). Islam defines males in ways that create a masculine society. Turkey has a high percentage of women as physicians and professors, these coming from higher socio-economic families, but women are relatively few in top management ranks or parliament.

Future research

The Hofstede and GLOBE projects are the most comprehensive studies of cultural values and behavior in organizations. Although these projects did not focus on women, they are the largest studies to date that shed light on cultural values and women's work and career experiences. In fact, Hofstede went on to specifically address gender (Hofstede, 1998). It is unfortunate that both projects have created conflict between the two research teams (Leung, 2006; Hofstede, 2006; Javidan et al., 2006; Smith, 2006; Earley, 2006; Graen, 2006; and House et al., 2006), as well as with external reviewers. These events are likely to make it more difficult for studies that more directly consider cultural values and women's work experiences. Such studies require vast resources, cooperation between researchers in several countries, and a long time frame; these elements are hard to marshal at the best of times.

While shedding some light on women at work, the large-scale studies of Hofstede and the GLOBE team were not explicitly designed to examine women's work and career experiences. Key questions become: Do we need a large-scale international study of national, cultural values, organized initiatives supporting women's advancement and women's work career and family experiences? And if we do what would it entail? These two ground-breaking studies have been criticized and some cross-cultural scholars have downplayed the usefulness of additional large-scale studies, calling instead for more intermediate level investigations, employing more qualitative approaches (Earley, 2006).

What would a large-scale study need to include?

- Multiple sectors.
- Large samples of women (and men).
- Measures of cultural values.
- Indicators of individual experiences at work, in their careers, in their families and communities, psychological and physical well-being, personal demographic, and work situation characteristics, characteristics of their employing organizations,

organizational initiatives supporting women's advancement, and their use of these.
- Country-level data on the percentages of a woman in the workforce, percentage of women in management and professional jobs, percentage of women on boards of directors, percentage of women enrolled in various college and university programs (e.g., business law, engineering), percentage of women graduates from these programs, national policies, and programs, national policies and programs supporting maternity, paternity and childcare, legislation relevant to women at work (equality, pay equality, harassment) among others.

References

Adler, N.J. and Izraeli, D. N. 1988. *Women in management worldwide.* Armonk, NY: M.E. Sharpe.

and Izraeli, D. N. 1994. *Competitive Frontiers: Women Managers in a Global Economy.* London: Blackwell.

Akhtar, S. 2000. "Influence of cultural origin and sex on work values", *Psychological Reports* 86: 1037–49.

Aycan, Z. 2004. "Key success factors for women in management in Turkey", *Applied Psychology: An International Review*, 53: 453–77.

Barry, H., Bacon, M. K., and Child, I. L 1957. "A cross-cultural survey of some sex differences in socialization", *Journal of Abnormal and Social Psychology* 55: 327–32.

Blau, F. D. and Kahn, L. M. 2007. "The gender pay gap: have women gone as far as they can?", *Academy of Management Perspectives* 21: 7–23.

Burke, R. J. 2000. "Career priority patterns among managerial women: a study of four countries", *Psychological Reports* 86: 1264–66.

2001. "Managerial women's career experiences, satisfaction and well-being: a five country study", *Cross Cultural Management* 8: 117–33.

Divinagracia, L. A. and Mamo, E. 1998. "Use of career strategies by Filipino managerial women", *Women in Management Review* 13: 217–20.

Kong, Y. P. and McKeen, C. A. 1997. "Managerial and professional women in Canada and Singapore", *The Asian Manager* 10: 78–82.

Koyuncu, M., and Fiksenbaum, L. 2007. "Career priority patterns among managerial and professional women in Turkey", *Women in Management Review* 22(5): 405–17.

and Mattis, M. C. 2000. *Women on Corporate Boards of Directors: International Challenges Opportunities*. Dordrecht: Kluwer.

and Nelson, D. L. 2001. *Advancing Women's Careers: Research and Practice*. London: Blackwell.

Todorova, I., Kotzeva, T., and McKeen, C. A. 1994. "Patterns of priority in careers among managerial and professional women in Bulgaria: costs of the mommy track?", *Psychological Reports* 75: 1019–26.

Cahoon, A. R. and Rowney, J. 2000. "Valuing diversity in a global economy: the sad state of organization and gender", in R. T. Golembiewski (ed.), *Handbook of Organizational Behavior*. New York, NY: Marcel Dekker Inc, pp. 457–90.

Catalyst. 1996. *Women in Corporate Leadership: Progress and Prospects*. New York, NY: Catalyst.

1997. *Closing the Gap: Women's Advancement in Corporate and Professional Canada*. New York, NY: Catalyst.

2002a. *Women in Leadership: A European Business Imperative*. New York, NY: Catalyst.

2002b. *2002 Catalyst Census of Women Corporate Officers and Top Wage Earners in the Fortune 500*. New York, NY: Catalyst.

2004. *Women and Men in US Corporate Leadership: Same Workplace, Different Realities?* New York, NY: Catalyst.

2006. *2005 Catalyst Census of Women Board Directors of the Fortune 500*. New York, NY: Catalyst.

2007. *2006 Census of Women Corporate Officers and Top Earners in the Financial Post 500*. Toronto: Catalyst.

Catalyst/Opportunity Now. 2000. *Breaking the Barriers: Women in Senior Management in the UK*. New York, NY: Catalyst and Opportunity Now.

Cheng, H. 1997. "'Holding up half the sky?' A sociocultural comparison of gender-role portrayals in Chinese and US advertising", *International Journal of Advertising* 16: 293–19.

Cole, M. 1998. Gender and power: a comparative analysis of sex segregation in Polish and American higher education, 1965–1985", *Sociology* 32: 277–98.

Coppin, A. 1998. "A comparison of male-female earnings differences across two Caribbean economies", *Journal of Developing Areas* 32: 375–94.

Couch, K. A. and Dunn, T. A. 1997. "Intergenerational correlations in labour market status: a comparison of the Baltic states and Germany", *Journal of Human Resources* 32: 210–32.

Davidson, M. J. and Burke, R. J. 2000). *Women in Management: Current Research Issues*. Thousand Oaks, CA: Sage.

and Burke, R. J. 2004. *Women in Management Worldwide: Facts, Figures and Analysis*. London: Ashgate.

and Cooper, C. L. 1993. *European Women in Business and Management*. London: Paul Chapman.

Drew, R. 1999. "Best countries for women to work in", *Management Review* 88: 10–16.

Earley, P. C. 2006. "Leading cultural research in the future: a matter of paradigms and taste", *Journal of International Business Studies* 37: 922.

Emerich, C. G., Denmark, F. L., and Den Hartog, D. N. 2004. "Cross-cultural differences in gender egalitarianism", in R. J. House, P. Hanges, M. Javidan, P. Dorfman and V. Gupta (eds.), *Culture, Leadership, and Organizations: The GLOBE study of 62 Societies*. Thousand Oaks, CA: Sage, pp. 343–93.

Erez, M. 1994. "Toward a model of cross-cultural industrial and organizational psychology", in H. C. Triandis, M. D. Dunnette and L. Hough (eds.), *Handbook of Industrial and Organizational Psychology* (2nd. edn), vol. 4. Palo Alto, CA: Consulting Psychologists Press.

Giscombe, K. 2005. "Best practices for women of colour in corporate America", *Supporting Women's Career Advancement* 266–94.

Graen, G. 2006. "In the eye of the beholder: cross-cultural lesson in leadership from Project GLOBE: a response viewed from the Third Culture Bonding (TCB) Model of cross cultural leadership", *Academy of Management Perspectives* 20: 95–101.

Granrose, C. S. 2006. *Employment of Women in Chinese Cultures*. Cheltenham: Edward Elgar.

Gupta, V., Hanges, P. J., and Dorfman, P. 2002. "Cultural clusters: methodology and findings", *Journal of World Business* 37: 11–15.

Hammond, V. 2002. Advancing women's executive leadership, in R. J. Burke and D. L. Nelson (eds.), *Advancing Women's Careers*. Oxford: Blackwelll Publishers, pp. 333–46.

Helfat, C. E., Harris, D., and Wolfson, P. J. 2006. "The pipeline to the top: women and men in the top executive ranks of US corporations", *Academy of Management Perspectives* 20: 42–64.

Hofstede, G. 1980. *Culture's Consequences: International Differences in Work-related Values*. Newbury Park, CA: Sage.

1983. "The cultural relativity of organizational practices and theories", *Journal of International Business Studies* 14: 75–89.

1991. *Cultures and Organizations: Software of the Mind*. London: McGraw-Hill.

1993. "Cultural constraints in management theories", *Academy of Management Executive* 7: 81–94.

1998. *Masculinity and Femininity: The Taboo Dimension of National Cultures*. Thousand Oaks, CA: Sage.

2001. *Culture's Consequences: Comparing Values, Behaviors and Organizations Across Nations*. Thousand Oaks, CA: Sage.

2006. "What did GLOBE really measure? Researchers' minds versus respondents' minds", *Journal of International Business Studies* 37: 882.

and Hofstede, G. J. 2005. *Cultures and Organizations: Software of the Mind*. New York, NY: McGraw-Hill.

and McCrae, R. R. 2004. "Personality and culture revisited: linking traits and dimensions of culture", *Cross-Cultural Research* 38: 52–88.

House, R. J., Hanges, P. J., Javidan, M., Dorfman, P. W., and Gupta, V. 2004. *Culture, Leadership and Organizations: The GLOBE Study of 62 Societies*. Thousand Oaks, CA: Sage.

Javidan, M., Dorfman, P. W., and Sully de Luque, M. 2006. "A failure of scholarship: response to George Graen's critique of GLOBE", *Academy of Management Perspectives* 20: 102–14.

House, R., Javidan, M., Hangers, P., and Dorfman, P. 2002. "Understanding cultures and implicit leadership theories across the globe: an introduction to Project GLOBE", *Journal of World Business* 37: 3–10.

ILO. 2004a. *Breaking the Glass Ceiling: Women in Management Update*. Geneva: International Labour Organization.

2004b. *Global Employment Trends for Women 2004*. Geneva: Switzerland.

Izraeli, D. N. 1987. "Women's movement into management in Israel", *International Studies of Management and Organization* 16: 76–90.

Javidan, M. and House, R. J. 2001. "Cultural acumen for the global manager: lessons from Project GLOBE", *Organizational Dynamics* 29: 289–305.

and House, R. J. 2002. "Leadership and cultures around the world: findings from GLOBE: an introduction to the special issue", *Journal of World Business* 37: 1–2.

House, R. J., Dorfman, P. W., Hanges, P. J., and Sully de Luque, M. 2006. "Conceptualizing and measuring cultures and their consequences: a comparative review of GLOBE's and Hofstede's approaches", *Journal of International Business Studies* 37: 897–915.

Kabasakal, H. and Bodur, M. 2002. "Arabic cluster: a bridge between East and West", *Journal of World Business* 37: 40–59.

Kidd, M. P. and Shannon, M. 1996. "The gender wage gap: a comparison of Australia and Canada", *Industrial and Labour Relations Review* 40: 729–46.

Kiscombe, K. 2005. "Best practices for women of color in corporate America", in R. J. Burke and M. C. Mattis (eds.), *Supporting Women's Career Advancement*. Cheltenham: Edward Elgar, pp. 266–94.

Kolvereid, L., Shane, S., and Westhead, P. 1993. "Is it equally difficult for female entrepreneurs to start businesses in all countries?", *Journal of Small Business Management*, 31: 42–58.

Korabik, K. 1992. "Women hold up half the sky: the status of managerial women in China", *Advances in Chinese Industrial Studies* 3: 197–211.

Leung, K. 2006. "Editor's introduction to the exchange between Hofstede and GLOBE", *Journal of International Business Studies* 37: 881.

Linehan, M. 2001. "Women international managers: the European Experience", *Cross Cultural Management* 8: 68–80.

and Walsh, J. S. 1999. "Senior female international managers: breaking the glass border", *Women in Management Review* 14: 219–30.

Maione, V. 2000. "The female labour market in Italy from an historical perspective", *Women in Management Review* 15: 90–104.

Mattis, M. C. 2005. "Best practices for supporting women engineers' career development in US corporations", in R. J. Burke and M. C. Mattis (eds.), *Supporting Women's Career Advancement*. Cheltenham: Edward Elgar, pp. 247–65.

Medalia, C. and Jacobs, J. A. 2008. "Working time for married couples in 28 countries", in R. J. Burke and C. L. Cooper (eds.), *The Long Work Hours Culture: Passion and Addiction*. London: Elsevier.

Melkas, H. and Anker, R. 1997. "Occupational segregation by sex in Nordic countries", *International Labour Review* 136: 341–63.

Morrison, A. M 1992. *The New Leaders*. San Francisco, CA: Jossey-Bass.

White, R. P., and Van Velsor, E. 1987. *Breaking the Glass Ceiling*. Reading, MA: Addison-Wesley.

White, R. P., and Van Velsor, E. 1992. *Breaking the Glass Ceiling*: Reading, MA: Addison-Wesley.

Nath, D. 2000. "Gently shattering the glass ceiling: experiences of Indian managers", *Women in Management Review* 15: 44–55.

Nelson, D. L., and Burke, R. J. 2002. *Gender, Work Stress, and Health*. Washington, DC: American Psychological Association.

Omar, A. and Davidson, M. J. 2001. "Women in management: a comparative cross-cultural overview", *Cross Cultural Management* 8: 35–67.

Osland, J. S., Synder, M. M. and Hunter, L. 1998. "A comparative study of managerial styles among female executives in Nicaragua and Costa Rica", *International Studies of Management and Organization*. 28: 54–73.

Powell, G. N. 1999. "Reflections on the glass ceiling: recent trends and future prospects", in G. N. Powell (ed.), *Handbook of Gender and Work*. Thousand Oaks, CA: Sage, pp. 325–45.

and Graves, L. 2003. *Women and Men in Management*. Newbury Park, CA: Sage.

Punnett, B. J., Duffy, J. A., Fox, S. Gregory, A., Litucky, T. R., Monserrat, S. I., Olivas-Lujan, M. R., and Santos, N. M. B. F. 2006. *Successful Professional Women of the Americas*. Cheltenham: Edward Elgar.

Ragins, B. R., Townsend, B., and Mattis, M. C. 1998. "Gender gap in the executive suite: CEOs and female executives report on breaking the glass ceiling", *Academy of Management Executive* 12: 28–42.

Richardsen, A. M., Mikkelsen, A., and Burke, R. J. 1997. "Work experiences and career and job satisfaction among professional and managerial women in Norway", *Scandinavian Journal of Management*. 13: 209–18.

Rose, P. 1995. "Female education and adjustment programs: a cross-country statistical analysis", *World Development* 23: 1931–49.

Roth, L. M. 2007. "Women on Wall Street: despite diversity measures, Wall Street remains vulnerable to sex discrimination changes", *Academy of Management Perspectives* 21: 24–35.

Schein, V. E. 1973. "The relationship between sex role stereotypes and requisite management characteristics", *Journal of Applied Psychology* 57: 95–100.

1975. "Relationships between sex role stereotypes and requisite management characteristics among female managers", *Journal of Applied Psychology* 60: 340–4.

2007. "Women in management: reflections and projections", *Women in Management Review* 22: 6–18.

and Davidson, M. J. 1993. "Think manager, think male", *Management Development Review* 6: 24–8.

and Mueller, R. 1992. "Sex role stereotyping and requisite management characteristics: a cross-cultural look", *Journal of Organizational Behavior* 13: 439–47.

Mueller, R., and Jacobson, C. 1989. "The relationship between sex role stereotypes and requisite management characteristics among college students", *Sex Roles* 20: 103–10.

Mueller, R., Lituchy, T., and Liu, J. 1996. "Think manager-think male: a global phenomenon?", *Journal of Organizational Behavior* 17: 33–41.

Schwartz, F. N. 1989. Management women and the new facts of life, *Harvard Business Review*. January-February: 65–76.

Sczesny, S. 2003. "A closer look beneath the surface: various facets of the think manager/think male stereotype", *Sex Roles* 49: 353–63.

Segall, M. H., Dasen, P. R., Berry, J. W., and Poortinga, H. 1990. *Human Behavior in Global Perspective: An Introduction to Cross-Cultural Psychology*. New York, NY: Pergamon.

Singh, V. and Vinnicombe, S. 2005. *The Female FTSE Report 2005? New Look Women Directors Add Value to Corporate Boards*. Cranfield: Cranfield University.

Smith, P. B. 2006. "When elephants fight, the grass gets trampled: the GLOBE and Hofstede projects", *Journal of International Business Studies* 37: 915.

Stone, R. J. 1991. "Expatriate selection and failure", *Human Resource Planning* 14: 9–22.

Symons, G. L. 1984. "Career lives of women in France and Canada: the case of managerial women", *Work and Occupations* 11: 331–346.

Venter, K. 2002. *Common Careers, Different Experiences: Women Managers in Hong Kong and Britain.* Hong Kong: Hong Kong University Press.

Vinnicombe, S. and Bank, J. 2003. *Women with Attitude: Lessons for Career Management.* London: Routledge.

White, B., Cox, C., and Cooper, C. L. 1992. *Women's Career Development.* Oxford: Blackwell Publishers.

Wiles, C. R. and Tjernlund, A. 1991. "A comparison of role portrayal of men and women in magazine advertising in the USA and Sweden", *International Journal of Advertising* 10: 259–67.

Wirth, L. 1998. "Women in management: closer to breaking through the glass ceiling", *International Labour Review* 137: 93–102.

2001. *Breaking the Glass Ceiling: Women in Management.* Geneva: International Labour Office.

Yang, N. 1998. "An international perspective on socio-economic changes and their effects on life stress and career success of working women", *SAM Advanced Management Journal* 63: 15–27.

Chen, C. C., Choi, J., and Zhou, Y. 2000. "Sources of workplace conflict: a Sino-US comparison of the effects of work and family demands", *Academy of Management Journal* 43: 113–123.

Intercultural training for the global workplace: review, synthesis, and theoretical explorations

DHARM P. S. BHAWUK[1]

Globalization has led to increased interconnectedness among nations and we are much more interdependent than we were in the past. This interdependence requires us to work with people from different cultures, and it also requires many of us to live in cultures far away and quite different from our own. Despite the similarities offered by technology and urban centres, differences persist, and the vision of a homogeneous world is quite unlikely and perhaps flawed. The variety of religions and languages present in the world today offers ample evidence that, if anything, humankind loves diversity. So we need to prepare ourselves to have a meaningful dialogue with people from different cultures to help each other solve our problems and also to learn from each other. Intercultural training as a field of research has become all the more relevant in today's shrinking world.

Just like we are all lay social psychologists, all of us interculturalists, those who have spent some time away from home in a foreign culture, are also lay intercultural trainers – we can teach what we

have learned just like any other knowledge or skill. However, since intercultural training has developed a rich literature as an academic discipline, which is grounded in theory, it offers opportunity to researchers and professionals to provide a systematic approach to developing, implementing, and evaluating intercultural training programs. This chapter intends to contribute to the extant literature by providing a theoretical framework for the systematic development of intercultural training programs, which can be used both in professional training and academic courses.

Three major reviews of the field of intercultural training (Bhawuk and Brislin, 2000; Landis and Bhawuk, 2004; Bhawuk, Landis, and Lo, 2006) have helped synthesize and extend the field of intercultural training in the new millennium. Bhawuk and Brislin (2000) provided a historical perspective tracing the evolution of the field, and concluded that the field has always been theory driven (Hall, 1959, 1966; Fiedler, Triandis, and Mitchell, 1971; Triandis, 1975). They noted that in recent times it had become more so with the integration of culture theories (Triandis, Brislin, and Hui, 1988; Cushner and Brislin, 1997; Brislin and Yoshida, 1994a; Bhawuk, 1998, 2001; Bhawuk and Brislin, 1992). Landis and Bhawuk (2004) presented a number of nested models leading to a comprehensive theoretical framework, such that through a program of research the framework could be evaluated by testing each of these models. Bhawuk, Landis, and Lo (2006) synthesized the fields of acculturation and intercultural training breaking new theoretical grounds for the development of various intercultural training strategies, and also presented its applicability for training military personnel (Landis and Bhawuk, 2005). This paper notes the

[1] This paper is dedicated to Professors Harry Triandis, Richard Brislin, and Dan Landis, from whom I have learned everything about culture and intercultural training. I would like to thank Harry Triandis, Dan Landis, Vijayan P. Munusamy, Keith Sakuda, Julia Smith, Rabi Bhagat, and Richard Steers, for their critical comments that helped me improve the paper significantly. I am grateful to Mr Ray S. Leki of the US State Department, who is a veteran of the Peace Corps and a very dear friend, for sharing his forthcoming book *Travel Wise: How to be Safe, Savvy, and Secure Abroad*. An earlier draft of this paper was presented at the 17th Annual Conference of Psychology, National Academy of Psychology (NAOP), Kanpur, India, December 17–19, 2007.

major contributions of these reviews, and further builds on them by synthesizing various theoretical ideas to propose an approach to intercultural training that is grounded in theory and can be utilized by business and government or non-government organizations.

Theory building in intercultural training

A review of the field of intercultural training shows that it has been led by stalwarts like Edward Hall, Harry Triandis, Richard Brislin, Dan Landis, and Bill Gudykunst, who helped the field grow with an emphasis on theory building from its earliest days. It is notable that Hall (1959, 1966) presented both a theory of culture and how it could be applied to train people to be effective while working abroad. Triandis, along with his colleagues, not only invented the culture assimilator (sometimes called the intercultural sensitizer), but presented many theoretical frameworks to provide the foundation of intercultural training as well as to develop and evaluate culture assimilators and other training programs (Triandis, 1972, 1975, 1977, 1994, 1995a, 1995b; Triandis, Brislin, and Hui, 1988; Fiedler, Mitchell and Triandis, 1971). Brislin not only presented the seminal books on intercultural training (Brislin and Pedersen, 1976; Brislin, 1981) helping the crystallization of the field, but also presented the first handbook (Landis and Brislin, 1983), the first cultural general assimilator (Brislin *et al.*, 1986; Cushner and Brislin, 1996), and two volumes of exercises in which each exercise was grounded in a theory (Brislin and Yoshida, 1994a, 1994b; Cushner and Brislin, 1997).

Landis founded the *International Journal of Intercultural Relations* in 1977 and continues to edit it. This journal is dedicated to building international understanding through intercultural training, which meets high standards of scientific rigor. Landis also developed many specialized culture assimilators including ones for use in the US military (see Landis and Bhagat, 1996), edited three editions of the *Handbook of Intercultural Training* (Landis and Brislin, 1983; Landis and Bhagat, 1996; Landis, Bennet, and Bennet, 2004),

led to the creation of the *International Academy of Intercultural Research* in 1999, and served as its Founding President. Gudykunst contributed by developing theories of intercultural communication and applying them to the field of intercultural training (Gudykunst, 2005). Of course, other researchers and practitioners have also contributed to the field significantly in many other ways, but the contribution of these researchers especially deserves to be noted for their theoretical contribution.

Bhawuk and Brislin (2000) reviewed the literature and traced the historical evolution of the field over the past fifty years. They noted that the culture assimilators were still being used and researched (Albert, 1983), whereas though simulation programs continue to be developed and used for intercultural training, they are not subjected as much to evaluation, and that there were many more tools like the intercultural sensitivity inventory and category width available for the evaluation of intercultural training programs. They noted two measure evaluation reviews, one by Black and Mendenhall (1990) and the other by Deshpande and Viswesvaran (1992), which showed that intercultural training programs do have positive outcomes for the trainees. Black and Mendenhall (1990) reviewed twenty-nine studies that had evaluated the effectiveness of various training programs, and concluded that because of cross-cultural training provided to participants, there were positive feelings about the training they received, improvement in their interpersonal relationships, changes in their perception of host nationals, reduction in culture shock (Oberg, 1960) experienced by them, and improvement in their performance on the job, establishing the general effectiveness of intercultural training programs. These findings were further supported in a meta-analysis of twenty-one studies in which the effect of cross-cultural training was examined on five variables of interest: self development of trainees, perception of trainees, relationship with host nationals, adjustment during sojourn, and performance on the job (Deshpande and Viswesvaran, 1992). Thus, the effectiveness of intercultural programs has stood various independent evaluations (see also meta-analysis by Morris and Robie, 2001). However, Mendenhall, *et al.* (2004) presented evidence that tempered the positive findings of the earlier studies.

Triandis (1995a) noted that, in general, field studies, but not the laboratory studies, have showed positive effect of cross-cultural assimilator training on most of the above mentioned variables. However, in a recent laboratory study comparing three types of culture assimilators with a control group, Bhawuk (1998) found that a theory-based "Individualism and Collectivism Assimilator" (ICA) had significant effects on a number of criterion measures such as intercultural sensitivity inventory, category width measure (Detweiler, 1978, 1980), attribution making, and satisfaction with training compared to a culture-specific assimilator for Japan, a culture-general assimilator (Brislin et al., 1986), and a control group. It must be noted that few studies have used behavioral measures over and above paper and pencil type dependent variables (Weldon, et al., 1975 and Landis, Brislin, and Hulgus, 1985, are the exceptions), thus raising questions about the impact of culture assimilators on the behaviors of trainees.

Bhawuk and Brislin (2000) noted that behavior modification training was one of the new developments in the field. Behavior modification training is necessary for habitual behaviors that people are not usually aware of, especially behaviors that are acceptable, even desirable, in one's own culture but which may be offensive in another culture. For example, in Latin American cultures, people give an *abrazo* or an embrace to friends which is not an acceptable behavior in the US; or in Greece when people show an open palm, called *moutza*, they are showing utmost contempt, and not simply waving or saying hello (Triandis, 1994). A *moutza* needs to be avoided, whereas an *abrazo* needs to be acquired. There are many examples of such behaviors, and the only way to learn them is through behavior modeling, by observing a model do the behavior and then practicing the behavior many times. Despite its theoretical rigor and practical significance, this method has not been used much in cross-cultural training programs because it is expensive, requiring a trainer who constantly works on one behavior at a time.

Harrison (1992) examined the effectiveness of different types of training programs by comparing groups that received culture assimilator training (i.e., Japanese Culture Assimilator), behavioral modeling training, a combined training (i.e., behavioral modeling and culture assimilator), and no training (i.e., control group). He found that people who received the combined training scored significantly higher on a measure of learning than those who were given other types of training or no training. This group performed better on the role-play task compared to the control group only, but not to the other two groups. This study provides further evidence for the impact of assimilators on behavioral tasks.

Bhawuk and Brislin (2000) noted another development that deals with the role of culture theory in cross-cultural training (Bhawuk, 1998; Bhawuk and Triandis, 1996), and the development of a theory-based culture assimilator, which is based on the four defining attributes and the vertical and horizontal typology of individualism and collectivism (Triandis, 1995b; Bhawuk, 1995, 1996, 2001). Bhawuk and Triandis (1996) proposed that culture theory could be effectively used in cross-cultural training. Bhawuk (1998) further refined this model by integrating the literature on cognition and stages of learning, and presented a model of stages of intercultural expertise development and suggested that a theory-based assimilator using fewer categories is likely to be more effective because it does not add to the cognitive load experienced during a cross-cultural interaction. He carried out a multimethod evaluation of cross-cultural training tools to test the model (Bhawuk, 1998), and found that, trainees who received the theory-based individualism and collectivism assimilator (ICA), compared to a culture-specific assimilator for Japan, a culture-general assimilator (Brislin et al., 1986), and a control group, were found to be significantly more interculturally sensitive, had larger category width, made better attribution on given difficult critical incidents, and were more satisfied with the training package. The findings of this study show promise for using overarching theories like individualism and collectivism in cross-cultural training. They concluded that the development of the field of cross-cultural training over the past fifty years showed an encouraging sign of evolution of more theoretically meaningful training methods and tools. It could be expected that more theory-based training methods and material are likely to be developed in the future. In this chapter, a framework is presented for the development of intercultural training programs that includes not only culture theories but also other theoretical ideas thus extending the field.

Landis and Bhawuk (2004) proposed a nested framework of testable models of intercultural training and learning. The first building block of their framework included such variables as intention to learn new cultural behavior, social support, host reinforcement, and spouse and family support to the sojourner. They posited that behavioral rehearsal would often be needed in the intercultural context, because people are learning new behaviors while living in another culture, and acquisition of such behaviors would necessarily follow the social learning theory (Bandura, 1977). The acquisition of these new cultural behaviors would be moderated by social support as well as host reinforcement. If spouse and other family members as well as the expatriate community support the target person to acquire these new behaviors, the person is likely to do a better job of learning these behaviors. Similarly, if the host nationals the sojourner is working with support the acquisition of the new behaviors, and encourage the sojourner, then the learning process is likely to be more effective. And building on the psychological literature, they posited that behavioral intention would be the best predictor of intercultural behaviors. This model could be tested for a number of intercultural behaviors like learning foreign languages, learning gestures and body language, and so forth.

Landis and Bhawuk (2004) presented other models as the antecedents to the above model. For example, intercultural effectiveness is often evaluated based on how well the tasks get done, and so they argued that in most intercultural interactions tasks take central stage, and centrality of goal is likely to have direct impact on behavioral intentions and ultimately intercultural behaviors. Interestingly, the role of task completion in the intercultural context has not been tested in the literature, and thus does provide an opportunity to build and test theory. Another antecedent of intercultural behavioral intention would be affect (Landis

and Bhawuk, 2004). Affect could vary along two dimensions. First, people could be different on their predisposition to change emotionally; some are ready to change versus others needing much more convincing or cajoling. Second, some people are more apt to express their emotions than others. Both of these affect related aspects have implications for overseas adjustment, and people need to become self-aware, and then learn to adapt their style to be effective in another culture. For example, in some cultures emotion is not to be expressed publicly, whereas in others it is not honest to hide one's emotion.

Of the two other models that Landis and Bhawuk (2004) presented in their framework, one linked intercultural sensitivity, social categorization, behavioral disposition, and intercultural behaviors, whereas the other posited that intercultural behavior would be a function of perceived differences in subjective culture (Triandis, 1972), the greater the cultural distance, the stronger the affective reaction. They suggested that individuals would seek information only up to a point where more stress becomes a deterrent for information seeking. They proposed that testing each of the models would require many experiments, and each of the studies could be viewed as a crucial experiment (Platt, 1964) needed to build a theory of intercultural behavior. Integrating these five models, a general model of intercultural behavior process with its many antecedents is derived. Thus, they presented models testable through smaller studies, and also in its totality through a program of research. By testing these five models, and linking them together, the larger framework could be tested.

Landis and Bhawuk (2004) noted that intercultural training researchers have been concerned with the development of the best training approach for most of the past fifty years, as much as they have been concerned about the evaluation of the effectiveness of intercultural training programs. They recommended that the discipline needed to start boldly building bridges between associated research disciplines. Following their recommendation, Bhawuk, Landis, and Lo (2006) took the first step toward such a theoretical bridge building, and attempted to synthesize the literature on intercultural training and acculturation. They attempted to integrate Berry's (1990) four-part typology into a theoretical framework developed by Landis and Bhawuk (2004), which seemed to open new avenues toward synthesizing these two disciplines. They also explored how different training tools could be effectively used to train people who are employing different acculturating strategies. For example, they noted that it is reasonable to treat those who are using the integration strategy differently from those who are using the marginalization, separation, or assimilation strategies. This approach should also serve to bridge intercultural training and other research disciplines like sojourner adaptation, stress management techniques, and learning theories.

Bhawuk, Landis, and Lo (2006) also noted various applications of individualism and collectivism in intercultural training, and suggested that perhaps acculturation literature should also take advantage of this theory more rigorously, which would further help bridge the two disciplines through a common theoretical foundation. They also attempted to synthesize intercultural sensitivity and acculturation literature by showing commonality between Bhawuk and Brislin's (1992) approach to intercultural sensitivity, and Bennett's (1986) "Developmental Model of Intercultural Sensitivity" (see also Hammer, Bennett, and Wiseman, 2003). In this chapter, some of these ideas are further developed in the context of developing the content of intercultural training programs. To do this a theoretical framework is developed, which is discussed in detail below.

A theoretical framework for the development of intercultural training programs

The theoretical framework presented in figure 17.1 helps synthesize various elements of the intercultural training literature, and also proposes future directions for research in intercultural training. At the core of the framework lie the fundamental issues and ways to prepare expatriates for their sojourn. The four elements at the core include: (a) basic processes of intercultural learning; (b) self-preservation (or survival issues); (c) cultural-theoretic framework;

and (d) socio, political, and economic framework. They represent areas of research, theory, and practice from which the content of intercultural training can be derived. These four elements constitute the foundational knowledge necessary to be effective in international assignments, and being grounded in theory could be viewed as associative rather than declarative knowledge (Anderson, 2000).

We can evaluate the importance of these four elements from two perspectives: from the perspective of the sojourner who is planning to travel abroad and from the perspective of pedagogy or how we can prepare the person best to be effective abroad. Self-preservation is the most important element because one cannot be effective if one's safety and survival is threatened, and the sojourners need to be prepared about how to be safe before any other information and concepts are presented to them. From the perspective of pedagogy, one could argue that the trainees may neglect learning the survival skills if they do not understand the basic processes involved in intercultural learning. After all, even the concepts of safety and survival are culturally defined. Motivated by pedagogy, the learning models are discussed first.

The second circle represents general intercultural skills that the expatriates must acquire and use in the behavioral settings pertinent to their industry and organization. The airlines industry works differently from the oil and gas industry not only because the external environment presents differently to each industry but also because each industry develops its own symbols and rituals since they serve different clientele and their products and services are different. These skills are less related to a particular culture, and in that sense could be viewed as culture-general skills (as opposed to cultural-specific). Organizational cultures are nested in the industrial culture but are also shaped by their national cultures, especially in human processes and the management of human resources. It is often assumed that sojourners understand the culture of the organization, and if they are going from headquarter of the organization they may even be viewed as experts on organizational routines and procedures.

The third circle in figure 17.1 represents the mission and goals of the organization. This circle

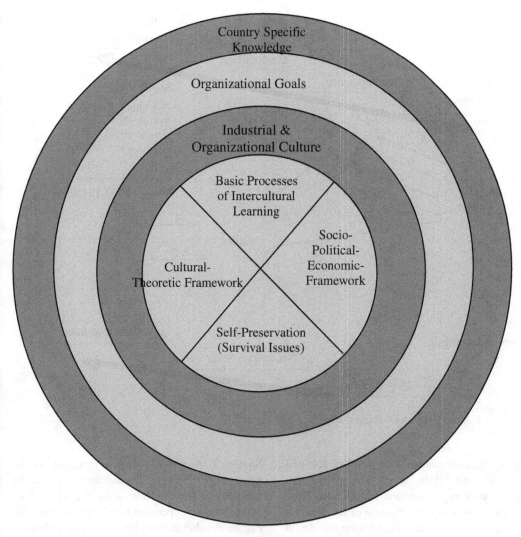

Figure 17.1. Developing intercultural training programs: a theoretical framework

represents outcomes at the higher level that the organization desires to achieve in its operations abroad, which put intercultural demands on the expatriates. Clearly, effective accomplishment of organizational objectives will require more complex and adept intercultural skill. The outermost circle represents culture-specific information expatriates need to operate effectively in a particular culture. Once expatriates have obtained the foundational knowledge and awareness (innermost circle) and the culture-general skills (second circle) that support the overall objectives of the organizations (third circle), then the final step is to learn specific information about the culture in which they will work (outermost circle). By first learning the foundational knowledge and culture-general skills, expatriates will be better able to assimilate cultural-specific training when it occurs, and much of it is likely to occur on the site while living in another culture. It should be noted that traditionally intercultural training programs have been more focused on the outer circle with the objective of orienting people to the target culture. It is plausible that for this reason many intercultural

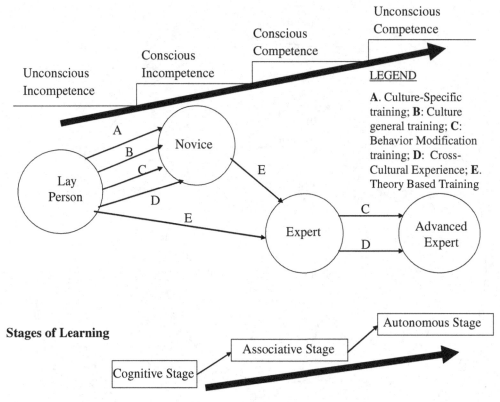

Figure 17.2. A model of cross-cultural expertise development

training programs remain at the level of do's and don'ts (Bhawuk, 1990), which neither facilitates acquisition of meta-cognition nor learning-how-to-learn. In what follows, the core of the model is discussed in detail, since this forms the foundation of intercultural training.

I Basic processes of intercultural learning

A model of cross-cultural expertise development

Building on the notion that theories have a role in the development of expertise, Bhawuk (1998) proposed a model of intercultural expertise development (see figure 17.2). A "lay person" is defined as one who has no knowledge of another culture, an ideal-type for all practical purposes, considering that even the

Sherpas in the remote Nepalese mountains or the pygmies in Africa have been exposed to people from other cultures. There is some evidence that people who have spent two or more years in another culture develop cross-cultural sensitivity through their intercultural interactions, even in the absence of any formal training (Bhawuk and Brislin, 1992). It is proposed that people with extended intercultural experience, or those who have gone through a formal intercultural training program (e.g., a culture-specific orientation) that discusses differences between two cultures, will develop some degree of intercultural expertise and are labeled "novices." In other words, "novices" are people with some intercultural skills or expertise, usually for a culture other than their own. These are people who are still in the first stage of learning (e.g., the cognitive or declarative stage, Anderson, 2000). These people are likely to explain a cultural difference in terms of behavioral observations such as "One does not say 'No' directly in Japan," "Nepalese men do not do household chores," and so forth, which often leads to a do's and don'ts list.

"Experts" are novices who have acquired the knowledge of culture theories which are relevant to a large number of behaviors so that they can organize cognitions about cultural differences more meaningfully around a theory (e.g., the way experts use Newton's second law of motion to classify physics problems). These are the people who are at the second stage of learning (e.g., the associative or proceduralization stage; Anderson, 2000). It is proposed that people can arrive at this stage by going through a theory-based intercultural training program.

"Advanced experts" are experts who have not only the knowledge of the theory, but also have had the amount of practice needed to perform the relevant tasks automatically. These are the people who are at the third stage of learning (i.e., the autonomous stage; Anderson, 2000). Since behavior modification training allows people to learn new behaviors by observing models and then practicing the target behaviors, a behavior modeling training following a theory-based training, will enable "experts" to become "advanced experts." Thus, the model of intercultural expertise development posits that intercultural training using culture theory will make a person an expert, whereas training that does not use theory will only result in novices; and to be an advanced expert one needs to go through behavioral training to practice different behaviors so that the behaviors become habitual. Figure 17.2 is a diagrammatic representation of this model. Also shown in the figure are the linkages between stages of learning and stages of intercultural expertise development.

Levels of competence

Extending the work of Howell (1982) to cross-cultural communication and training, Bhawuk (1995, 1998) suggested that there are four levels of cross-cultural competence: *unconscious incompetence*; *conscious incompetence*; *conscious competence*; and *unconscious competence*. Unconscious incompetence refers to the situation when one misinterprets others' behavior but is not even aware of

it; this is the situation when a sojourner is making incorrect attributions, usually based on his or her own cultural framework. When a person is at this level of competence, things do not work out the way one expects and one is not sure why things are not working. This characterizes the situation when a sojourner is experiencing culture shock or culture fatigue (Oberg, 1960). A person at this level of competence is a "lay person" in the model presented earlier (see figure 17.2).

Conscious incompetence refers to the situation when the sojourner has become aware of his or her failure to behave correctly, but is unable to make correct attributions since he or she lacks the right knowledge. The sojourner is learning by trial and error. This level of competence is exemplified by a tennis player who tries to improve his game without coaching or study, by simply playing more. The sojourner who is trying to figure out cultural differences through direct experience, or non-theory based training programs, fits the description of this level of competence and is called a "novice" in the model.

Conscious competence is the third level and the crucial difference between this and the previous level is that the person at this level communicates with *understanding*. The person understands why something works or does not work (i.e., he understands the covert principles and theories behind overt behaviors). A person at this level of competence is called an "expert" in the model.

It is suggested that level two in the competency hierarchy is *mechanical-analytical*, in that a behavior that is less effective than another is dropped, whereas level three is *thoughtful-analytical*, in that not only is an effective behavior selected but also an explanation of why a behavior is effective or ineffective becomes available (Howell, 1982). In the cross-cultural setting, at this level a sojourner is still not naturally proficient in his or her interactions with the hosts and has to make an effort to behave in the culturally appropriate way. For example, people who do not use "please" or "thank you" in their own culture and are at the third level of competence, have to remind themselves and make a conscious effort to use these words in social interactions in a culture where they are expected to use them.

When a person receives enough practice then a behavior becomes part of one's habit structure and one does not need to make an effort to behave in a culturally appropriate way; one has become so acculturated that one can almost pass as a native. This is the fourth and the highest stage of competence, unconscious competence, and corresponds to the "advanced expert" in the model. At this level, although the person fully understands the reasons for behaving in a certain way in another culture, neither mechanical nor thoughtful analysis is required and a person responds "correctly" automatically (i.e., the response is habitual).

Cognitive stages of expertise development

Anderson (2000) described how people develop expertise. According to him, skill learning occurs in three steps. The first step is a cognitive stage, in which a description of the procedure is learned. In this stage, the names and definitions of concepts and key entities are committed to memory. Therefore, knowledge is "declarative," and people have to make an effort to recall and apply what they have learned. Typically, learners rehearse the facts in first performing the task. For example, an individualist (e.g., an American manager) who is new in a collectivist culture (e.g., Japan) and faces an interpersonal situation in which he or she wants to disagree or reject an offer, idea, or solution, would recall the fact that people in Japan prefer not to be direct and forthright and use many euphemisms for saying "No." The knowledge of this information is declarative and in this situation the manager would rehearse this fact as he or she interacts with the Japanese. A natural feeling at the end of the interaction may be "Boy, that was difficult," "That was not bad," "I hope it is easier the next time," and so forth, depending on one's feeling of success or failure with the interaction. In this stage of learning, the person is aware of the entire process of recalling knowledge and applying it to the situation.

The second stage is called the associative stage, in which people convert their declarative knowledge of a domain into a more efficient procedural representation. Starting with the cognitive stage, learners begin to detect many of their mistakes in performing a task or skill, and eliminate some of these mistakes. Further, with practice they remember the elements of the procedure and their sequence. As learners get in the associative stage, they no longer have to rehearse the knowledge before they can apply it, and they follow a procedure that they know leads to a successful result. In the cross-cultural context described above, the American manager would interact with the Japanese worker without a need to recall or rehearse the fact that the Japanese do not say "No" directly. The manager will be able to smoothly get into the discussion, find a suitable excuse to disagree, and use a proper expression of negation so that the worker does not lose his or her face. Thus, in this stage people learn the steps of performing a task, and while performing it follow each step in the proper sequence. This is referred to as "proceduralization."

It is suggested that sometimes the two forms of knowledge, declarative and procedural, can coexist; for example, a person speaking a foreign language fluently can also remember many rules of grammar. In the context of intercultural interaction, it is likely that both declarative and procedural knowledge will coexist since the sojourner needs to constantly keep the rules of the host culture in mind to contrast it with proper behavior in his or her own culture. Only in the extreme case of a person going "native" (i.e., a person assimilating completely in the host culture) is it likely that there will be a singular presence of procedural knowledge. Complete assimilation is reflected in the sojourner's inability to explain why the hosts (or the person himself or herself) behave in a certain way; and the person is likely to say "That is the way to do it."

The third stage, in which the skill becomes more and more habitual and automatic, develops through practice and is called the "autonomous stage." People know the task so well that they can perform it very quickly without following each and every step. Speed and accuracy are the two characteristics of this stage; people perform the skills quickly and with few or no errors. In the scenario discussed earlier, the American manager in Japan would be able to convey an equivalent of saying "No" very quickly and without making an error to upset the host, when he or she is in this stage of expertise development. A Japanese worker is likely to think of this person as "so much like us," "extremely polite," and so forth. People who are in this stage are sophisticated users of knowledge in a particular domain (a particular culture in the case of intercultural interactions) and use broad principles to categorize and solve the problems of the domain.

It is suggested that there is no major difference between the associative and the autonomous stages, and that the autonomous stage can be considered an extension of the associative stage. In this stage, usually skills improve gradually, and since verbal mediation does not exist learners may be unable to verbalize knowledge completely. In effect, the autonomous stage refers to behaviors that have become habitual through extended practice. This stage is especially relevant to intercultural interactions, since sojourners are driven by habits acquired in their own culture, and acquire behaviors suitable for the host culture slowly, stage by stage, from the cognitive to the associative to the autonomous stage. Often these new behaviors are opposite of the behaviors learned in one's own culture. For example, the American manager in the example above has to stop being direct and forthright, something valued in the US, and start being indirect and vague, something valued in Japan. As mentioned earlier, if the sojourners do not want to go "native" (i.e., become just like the host culture nationals), they would need to be proficient in interactions with the hosts, but at the same time also be able to verbalize knowledge about behaviors in the host culture so that they retain their home culture's identity.

The development of expertise is reflected in how people (experts versus novices) solve problems. When experts and novices are asked to solve physics problems, specifically to find out the velocity of the freely sliding block at the end of an inclined plane, it is found that novices worked backward, step by step, starting by writing the formula to compute the unknown (the velocity), then writing the formula for another unknown in the first formula (acceleration), and so on; and then moving forward, computing each of the unknowns, until the solution is found (Anderson, 2000). On the other hand, experts solved the same problem in the opposite order, by using theories (e.g., Newton's second law of motion) and computing directly

what could be computed, and then moving on to finally solve the problem. The backward reasoning method followed by the novices loads the working memory and can result in errors, whereas the forward reasoning method followed by experts is superior in that it is more accurate as it does not load the working memory. To be able to use the forward reasoning method, the user must be conversant with all the possible forward solutions and then be able to decide which one will be relevant to the problem at hand, and this requires a good deal of expertise.

In cross-cultural interactions, the forward reasoning method is likely to be followed by experts, since it is possible to predict human behavior given the setting and other characteristics of the situation. In fact, a central premise of social learning theory (Bandura, 1977) is that people anticipate actions and their consequences (i.e., people can decide how they would behave in a situation based on their past observation and experience). In a cross-cultural situation, for example, knowing that collectivists are sensitive to the needs of their ingroups, to motivate the employees an expert may use the strategy of creating incentives that are useful to their ingroups. More research is needed to understand the differences in the strategies adopted by experts and novices. It makes intuitive sense to think that experts would use theories to guide their interactions in intercultural situation.

Disconfirmed expectation and the processes of learning-how-to-learn

Disconfirmed expectation refers to situations where sojourners expect a certain behavior from the host nationals, but experience a different one. Simply stated, one's expectations are not met or confirmed. Intercultural communication effectiveness can be enhanced if we prepare ourselves not to come to a hurried conclusion about the cause of hosts' behavior when the hosts do not meet our expectations, since such a conclusion can lead to a negative stereotype. A negative stereotype may prejudice future interactions with hosts resulting in interpersonal problems. Disconfirmed expectancies underlie many situations where differences in work ethics, roles, learning styles, use of time and space, and so forth occur.

Frustrations associated with disconfirmed expectation are a part of a basic psychological process that is also found in primates. For example, in an experiment a monkey is shown spinach in a box a number of times, and is thus socialized to expect spinach in the box. Later, when spinach is replaced by another item unknown to the monkey, the monkey is found to show frustration and anger when it opens the box and does not find the spinach, which it expected to see (Overmier, 2006). Thus, it is not surprising that we humans, too, are frustrated by disconfirmed expectations. Often service quality is compared to what we expect, and thus often a poor quality is nothing but an expression of a disconfirmed expectation. Of course, intercultural interactions are likely to be full of disconfirmed expectations, and if we are not to be shocked out of our wits, which is what culture shock (Ward, Bochner, and Furnham, 2001) is, we have to learn to deal with disconfirmed expectations.

It is posited here that disconfirmed expectations offer an opportunity for us to learn. In fact, when our expectations are met, we are practicing behaviors that we already know, and such situations lead to mastery of such behaviors to the level of automaticity, leading such behaviors to become habitual. But when we face a disconfirmed expectation, we have a choice of ignoring it as an aberration, similar to a poor service situation, or we can reflect on the situation and see if there is something to be learned. In intercultural settings, often there is a cultural behavior to be learned when we face a disconfirmed expectation. But unlike the motivated self-learner, others find this opportunity frustrating. Thus, to the motivated sojourner or expatriate disconfirmed expectations offer what Vygotsky (1978) called zone of proximal development where meaningful new learning takes place beyond the previous ability level of the learner. Below, disconfirmed expectation is synthesized in the learning how to learn model (Kolb, 1976; Hughes-Weiner, 1986).

Building on Kolb's (1976) learning styles model, Hughes-Weiner (1986) presented a learning-how-to-learn model applicable to the field of intercultural communication and training. The basic idea presented by Hughes-Weiner is that, starting with concrete experience, a learner can move to reflective observation, abstract conceptualization, and active experimentation. Here Kolb and Hugh-Weiner's ideas are further developed synthesizing the concepts of disconfirmed expectation, emic (culture specific knowledge), and etic (culture general or universal knowledge) (See figure 17.3). In an intercultural setting, we can stop at a concrete experience in which we do not understand the behavior of the host, and we can make an attribution that the actor is not a nice person (or even worse that he is a jerk or she is mean) or that the host culture is not a good culture (or even worse that this is a backward culture), and continue to act in the future the same way that we acted in such situations in the past. In other words, we happily move on, even if the hosts are not feeling good. Our behavior would support the notion that we are all ethnocentric (Triandis, 1990), and we would continue to be ethnocentric. This state fits with the intercultural development model (Bennett, 1986), and the person is clearly not only ethnocentric but also uninterested in self-growth.

If we do reflective observation, we learn about cultural differences, and often some emic aspect of the host culture emerges. We also learn about our own culture, especially if the other cultural practices are drastically different from our own, which is mediated by cultural distance. Therefore, stopping at reflective observation leads to some personal intercultural growth. However, stopping here may end up into one learning many do's and don'ts about a particular culture. If we go beyond reflective observation, and develop abstract conceptualization, we acquire theoretical insights, which help us organize many experiences coherently into one category, and we can learn many such theoretical ideas. This leads to culture general understanding, and is a clear advancement from the earlier stage. We develop an understanding of etics or universals and understand emics as cultural representations of those etics. This helps us understand our own culture better in that we know why we do what we do. Also, it helps us internalize that our own cultural practices are not universals but emic reflections of some etics.

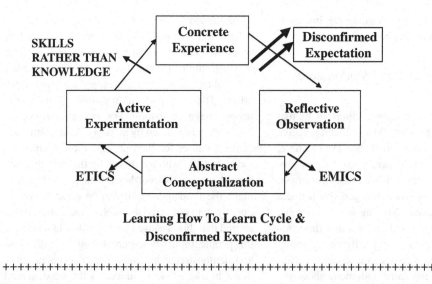

Learning How To Learn Cycle &
Disconfirmed Expectation

+++

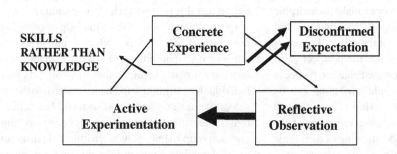

Path 2: Becoming an Expert Bi-Culturalist

Figure 17.3. Disconfirmed expectation and learning how to learn

Such internalization would weaken our natural ethnocentric cocoon and help us progress toward cultural relativism. In this phase, learning is supplemented by understanding. However, if we stop at this phase, we may have insights but our behavior may not show our understanding.

Active experimentation completes the cycle in that the learner is now testing theories and ideas learned. One is not only a "nice-talk- interculturalist" but an interculturalist who goes in the field, and tries out his or her learning. It is also plausible that people living in another culture for a long time move from reflective observation to active experimentation, simply bypassing the abstract conceptualization phase (See figure 17.3). This is similar

to behavioral modification training, except that the person is learning the behavior on the job and does not have much choice but to learn the behavior to be effective while he or she is living abroad. The pressures of adapting to a new environment and culture combined with the desire to be effective can lead one to master various behaviors in a new culture as a sojourner, without much abstract conceptualization. Thus, it is plausible that one can become an effective biculturalist (see figure 17.2). However, due to the lack of abstract conceptualization, one may continue to cultivate some bitterness resulting from the frustration from the external pressure requiring one to adapt. Thus, we see that disconfirmed expectation and learning how to learn are meta-skills that intercultural training can impart to be effective in intercultural communication.

Isomorphic attribution and fundamental attribution error

A major source of misunderstandings in human relationships is that two individuals do not perceive similar causes for a specific behavior. For example, if an employee is late for work, he or she may perceive that missing the bus was the cause of lateness, whereas his or her supervisor may perceive laziness as the cause of lateness. Making non-isomorphic attributions (Triandis, 1975) means that the same behavior is seen as having very different meaning. Isomorphic attribution refers to a sojourner making approximately the same judgment about the cause of a behavior as do people in the host culture (Triandis, 1975). When people make isomorphic attributions, they do not impose their own cultural perspective in deciding about the cause of a particular behavior. Instead, they use the perspective of the host culture in analyzing the behavior. It should be noted here that isomorphic attribution can be made at the emic level following a disconfirmed expectation using reflective observation, or at the etic level with a deeper understanding of their emic representations by developing abstract conceptualization as discussed earlier. In other words, isomorphic attribution made by novices and experts are not the same. Researchers and practitioners should both find this new insight useful, as theory clearly has a role in intercultural expertise development.

There is some evidence that we all suffer from the fundamental error of attribution. In the attribution process, often we make trait attribution for others behavior if they perform poorly (i.e., the other person is incapable of doing the task, is not smart, etc.), whereas we make contextual attribution for ourselves (i.e., the reason for poor performance is lack of resource, lack or support from the supervisor, poor team building, etc.). This process is reversed in that when others are successful we attribute it to external factors (i.e., they got lucky, they were spoon fed, we supported them all along, etc.) but when we are ourselves successful we attribute it to our trait (i.e., we are smart, we work hard, etc.) (Ross, 1977).

Fundamental error of attribution is further enhanced across cultures, and since we are all ethnocentric (Triandis, 1990), it makes sense to make trait attributions for our successes and blame other external factors for our failures, and to reverse it for others. There are also cultural differences in how people make attribution. For example, collectivists, as they are driven by modesty, tend to attribute external causes for their success more so than do individualists, who are driven by the idea that one should toot one's own horn. Thus, individualists make the fundamental attribution error more frequently than collectivists. Morris and Peng (1994) argued that this is caused by the cultural worldview that people implicitly acquire through socialization, and demonstrated in a multiple experiment study that Chinese are less subject to the fundamental attribution error than Americans, supporting the notion that this process varies across cultures.

Often, collectivists attribute the help of others as the cause of their success, whereas individualists attribute it to their ability. On the other hand, collectivists attribute failure to lack of effort; whereas individualists attribute it to factors external to themselves like task difficulty and so forth. For collectivists, the attribution process varies across ingroup and outgroup members, whereas individualists do not differentiate between ingroups and outgroups in making attributions (Triandis, 1995b). This will be discussed further in the later section on individualism and collectivism.

II Self-preservation (keeping security and survival issues in mind)

When we live in our own culture, we know how to go about doing various activities, and also know where not to go and when. This is not obvious when we live in another culture. For example, taking a taxi from the airport to the city may be a simple task in one culture, but not so safe in another culture. Most big airports in India provide the service of prepaid taxi to ensure safety of the passengers. I know of a returning young Indian who got robbed by the taxi driver simply because he had ignored the safety procedure and taken a non-registered taxi. Often local people know what activities are to be avoided or what part of the city should be avoided at what time of the day or night. Sojourners need to acquire this information and pay special attention to avoid difficult situations.

Sometimes sojourners get carried away when they have lived in a new culture and feel comfortable. This may sound like being over cautious, but it is better to be over cautious while living abroad. For example, having traveled to the US many times, and having lived there for two years, early in my sojourn I found myself in a precarious situation waiting for a bus in downtown Los Angeles at 1.00 a.m. while returning from the Disney Land with my wife and two little children. It was a scary situation with a police patrol car going around every few minutes and many shady looking people sauntering on the street. I called my cultural informant who was alarmed to learn my situation but was not able to come and fetch us because he lived too far away from there. He calmly gave me directions about how I could go to a safer street where a five star hotel was located. I had unwittingly put myself and my family in a difficult situation, which could have been easily avoided.

To begin with when we are living abroad, we are often so different that we do not quite fit into the social settings. People recognize us as a foreigner, and we become self conscious. Also, when we are in a completely new setting we have to learn about the place and people, and it is normal to experience cognitive load in such situations as we experience much ambiguity. This is enough to trigger a sense of insecurity, and people often complain about experiencing moderate level of anxiety. It is not unusual to feel that people of the host culture are staring at us. One does gets over it slowly over time, if things go right. But if the assignment is only for a short duration, and one has to be in social settings, then it is important to become aware of one's own discomfort, and to learn to perform one's tasks despite the nagging feeling of insecurity. It should be noted that it is harder for military personnel not to stick out when they are abroad because they are not only a foreigner, but also a person in military uniform, distinct from the locals. And if they are in hostile environment, say US soldiers and civilians in Iraq

or Afghanistan, then safety must not be taken for granted, and all precautions must be observed.

When we live in our own culture we also have our emotional support group that is often take for granted because the members of this group are there for us when we need them. When we are in another culture we have no access to this support group, and thus need to develop one. It is difficult to talk about life circumstances that are personal in nature and cause stress. For example, an illness or death in the family, own or family members' marital problems, and so forth take a lot of energy, and when we are away from home thinking about these matters, it can be quite debilitating.

Most often we are not prepared to deal with our own death or the death of close ones in the family. Talking about these matters is hard, yet accidents do happen, and people die unexpectedly. When we are in our own culture, we deal with them as they arise, and that is what most of us do. However, when we are abroad, we have distance and expenses between us and family, and we may regret not knowing what a dear one had wished for us to do. Before going abroad for a long assignment, it is necessary to talk about these matters with one's family and close friends and relatives, and prepare them to some degree for the unforeseen circumstances. Living instructions about how one should be cremated or dealt with if incapacitated is necessary. Having a will and leaving a power of attorney for somebody to take care of our financial and other personal matters is also helpful. Preparing for these emotional issues provides extra energy because one has fewer things to worry about when living abroad.

It is also important to think about the future, and the implications for oneself and other family members should one decide to marry someone from another culture while living abroad. It is not unusual for people to fall in love and develop a serious relationship with someone while living abroad, and it is good to think about such matters before they arise. Doing so helps with preparedness by reducing the stress arising from personal, emotional, and existential self-preservation. Leki (2007) has discussed the personal safety issues at length in his book, and provides an inventory that people can use to learn about their own safety needs while planning to travel abroad. He also provides practical tips to prepare for personal safety when living abroad.

The safety and survival issues have not received much attention in intercultural research beyond examining the nature of culture shock (Oberg, 1960; Ward, Bochner, and Furnham, 2001) and its consequences. Expatriates are expected to learn about safety matters and not much time is spent in counseling them to prepare for the target culture. For example, I personally know of people who took international assignments thinking that their troubled marriage would heal in an exotic place. Unfortunately, the new place adds more stress and invariably makes things worse, leading to breakup of a marriage. We cannot make progress unless organizations start providing training on this topic. Leki (2007) presents a way to start such training but much research is needed before we can evaluate what works or does not work and why.

III Socio-political-economic framework

Economic circumstances have profound effects on the work and social life of people, and personal income constrains an individual's choice of activities. Personal wealth also affects a person's perspectives on many social issues. Individuals from economically advanced countries generally enjoy greater levels of cosmopolitanism and participation in the global economy, whereas those from economically developing countries tend to have a life concerned with more immediate issues of survival. Thus, globalization has different meaning for economically developed and developing countries. Bhawuk (2005) presented a framework to capture the asymmetric economic conditions between nations. By categorizing countries as either developed or developing nations, it is possible to identify the distinct approaches people use to make decisions in these societies. This framework is useful in understanding differences resulting from variations in economic systems between developed and developing countries over and above their cultural dissimilarities. A discussion of such economic differences allows for building synergy across cultural differences, since differences

emerging from economic factors are presumed to be workable, and less likely to be the source of value-based conflicts.

Governments base their business policies on the overall economic condition of the country. National policies for stimulating economic development are grounded in the tenets of development economics. As nations progress through the various stages of economic development (Porter, 1990), national strategies, priorities, and values shift to meet the demands of a more affluent population. Policies and beliefs surrounding macroeconomic issues such as *Comparative Advantages, Role of Government*, and *Role of Business in Society* change with growing national wealth. Expectations of businesses also evolve as an economy develops, and change often occurs across both business and social categories.

Businesses within a market compete against each other through competitive advantages, but countries compete against each other through comparative advantages. Production capabilities compare differently across borders, as each country has a different mix of talents and costs associated with its production factors of labor, raw materials, and infrastructure. Developing countries tend to specialize in low cost labor, while developed countries tend to specialize in capital-intensive production. International managers must recognize the specific strengths and weaknesses of each country and adjust their decisions appropriately.

Businesses in different countries also share different relationships with their governments. Developing economies often follow more centralized planning, allowing a greater role for governments in shaping business policies. During the initial stages of economic development, guidance from the government has historically led to greater economic growth as seen in the success of Japan and the Asian Dragons (Korea, Singapore, Taiwan, and Hong Kong). Organizations operating in foreign countries must recognize the political imperatives of each nation, and adequately address them in their business strategies. Many times political imperatives may encourage governments to actively intervene to protect local firms against foreign competition. Rigidly adhering to an inappropriate strategy under such conditions would invariably lead a multinational to failure.

As businesses commit more resources to a specific country, they inevitably establish stronger ties to the community. Gaining acceptance from the local community can be considered a benchmark for business success, but the nature of the relationship must constantly be evaluated against the expectations for businesses' role in society. Social and cultural expectations strongly guide expected corporate responsibilities, but economic factors also play a considerable role. Literature on cultural complexity shows that developed countries tend to be more complex than the developing countries and exhibit more individualistic tendencies. Some may argue that developed countries are more democratic and open to progressive social change, but a better statement is that economic development leads to inevitable conflicts between a society's traditional values and introduced beliefs of the international community.

Economic forces also shape the *intrinsic motivation* of people. In a comparative study of Chinese and US workers, Chen (1995) found that financial incentives were more important for the Chinese than the US workers. These differences between developed and developing countries are supported in two large cross-cultural studies. Diener and colleagues found that happiness or subjective well-being is a function of income in the developing countries but not in the developed (Diener, 2000). Similarly, Inglehart (1997) found that developed countries are post materialist in that people expect their national governments to focus on providing more opportunity for individual participation in government decisions and defending freedom of speech. On the other hand, the developing countries were found to be materialist in that people in these countries expected their national government to focus on keeping order within the country and keeping prices at minimum.

Individuals' awareness and acceptance of the global community is also influenced by economic circumstances. Workers from nations with minimal exposure to globalization are likely to view convergence of business practices with contempt or suspicion. Expatriates imposing their foreign approaches on local communities may be viewed against the historical backdrop of colonization. The recent activism against globalization is a symptom of this mistrust. Support for the World Trade Organization can often be divided between developing and developed countries. Few governments from developed countries take active stances against globalization, but the majority of governments that openly dissent with globalization initiatives are from developing countries.

The economic framework discussed above captures some aspects that are important for sojourners in their adaptation to the host culture, which are not covered by culture theories like individualism and collectivism, and thus offers to be valuable for intercultural training. This framework can be further enriched by adding political and social dimensions so that differences resulting from religion, form of government, and other sociopolitical institutions and practices can also be captured. Some critical incidents are already available (Bhawuk, Munusamy, and Sakuda, 2007). As discovered in the Contrast American Method (Stewart, 1966), a cross-cultural training method where Americans are asked to compare host cultures to their home culture, training is most effective in situations where cultural differences can be contrasted. Similarly, by using developing and developed countries as prototypes, we can discuss socio-political-economic differences effectively in cross-cultural training programs.

IV Cultural-theoretical framework: four defining attributes of individualism and collectivism

Etymologically, individualism and collectivism allude to individual- and collective-centric worldviews and ways of life. When people act to maximize their personal gains, they are referred to as individualists, whereas when people behave to help the community or society, they are referred to as collectivists. These terms have been used by social scientists in much the same way. However, following the work of Hofstede (1980), Triandis and his collaborators developed a program of research in the 1980s and 1990s that led the terms to become popular psychological constructs used at the individual as well as cultural levels (Triandis, 1995b). At the cultural level, the terms *individualism* and *collectivism* are used, and cultures are referred to as being individualistic or collectivist. At the individual level the terms *idiocentrism* and *allocentrism* are used to denote individualism and collectivism respectively and are thought of as personality types (Triandis *et al.*, 1985). However, idiocentric people are found in collectivist cultures, and allocentric people are found in individualist cultures. The literature on these constructs has developed further in the last twenty years, and many people have started to refer to these ideas as the theory of individualism and collectivism (Bhawuk, 2001).

The supporters of the theory of individualism and collectivism find clear antecedents and consequences of these constructs, and they also find this culture theory useful in explaining and predicting human behavior in many social contexts (Triandis, McCusker, and Hui, 1990; Wheeler, Reis, and Bond, 1989). Measurement instruments for these constructs have been demonstrated to be reliable and valid in many areas of social research. Hundreds of journal articles have been published using these constructs, and much practical application for cross-cultural psychology, communication, marketing, and international management have also been found, making these constructs extremely popular (Triandis, 1995b). However, some critics find the empirical evidence wanting (Oyserman, Coon, and Kemmelmeier, 2002). Others have complained about their catchall nature and how researchers use them as residual concepts to explain cultural differences in many social behaviors (Schwartz, *et al.* 1994). Criticism aside, the reason this theory is chosen over others is because of its explanatory compatibility with other theories (see Triandis, 1995b; Triandis and Bhawuk, 1997), as well as its applicability to intercultural training (Bhawuk, 2001; Triandis, Brislin, and Hui, 1988) and its usefulness in the measurement of intercultural sensitivity (Bhawuk and Brislin, 1992).

The core of individualism and collectivism lies in the concept of self (Markus and Kitayama, 1991; Triandis, 1989). It is generally accepted that in individualist cultures people view themselves as having an independent concept of self, whereas in collectivist cultures people view themselves as having an interdependent concept of self. An individualist's concept of self does not include other people, roles, situations, or elements of nature (Beattie, 1980). On the other hand, a collectivist's concept of self includes other members of family, friends, people from the workplace, and even elements of nature. People in western countries like the US, the UK, Australia, and Germany, have an independent concept of self, and they feel a more pronounced social distance between themselves and others, including the immediate family. People in Asia, Africa, Latin America, and elsewhere have an interdependent concept of self, and social distance between an individual and his or her parents, spouse, siblings, children, friends, neighbors, supervisors, subordinates, and so forth is small.

Concept of self can be viewed as *digital* or *analogue*: digital for individualists and analogue for collectivists (Bhawuk, 2001). When individualists think of themselves and others, they are clear that their self only includes themselves. "This is me, but that is not me. My mother is not a part of me. My child is not a part of me. They are separate from me." There is no overlap between their selves and others. In other words, their view of themselves is digital. On the other hand, when collectivists think of people in their family (e.g., parents, spouse, children, siblings, and so forth), they feel these people are a part of their selves. For example, one's thinking may proceed like this: "My father is a part of me, not completely me, but somewhat a part of me. My child is a bigger part of me compared to my father, not completely me, but, yes, a good part of me." The same feeling holds in case of other relatives, friends, and even neighbors (Hsu, 1981). Thus, they have an analogue self. Of course, the biological self is digital for individualists as well as collectivists. It is the socially constructed self that is digital or analogue.

Differences in concepts of self lead to much difference in communication style (Kim and Sharkey, 1995; Kim *et al.* 1996). For example, people with independent concept of self are likely to be more direct in their communication than people of interdependent concept of self (Hara and Kim, 2004). People with interdependent concept of self are likely to be more sensitive to the idea of face saving (Ting-Toomey, 1988) than people with independent concept of self. People with independent concept of self are likely to communicate organizational schedules and deadlines more firmly, with a stipulation of punishment if schedule is not followed. People with interdependent concept of self are likely to have more tacit communication about resource sharing than those with independent concept of self. People with interdependent concept of self are likely to prefer face-to-face communication more than those with independent concept of self.

Concept of self also impacts the leadership styles found in different cultures. In collectivist cultures leaders are expected not only to be task focused but also to be nurturing in their relationship with their subordinates. This finds support in indigenous leadership research in countries like India, Japan, Philippines, and Mexico. It is also reflected in such cultural concepts like *simpatia* or being *simpatico* (Triandis *et al.* 1984), which means being pleasant and interpersonally sensitive in Latin America and among Hispanics and Latinos in the US. Similarly, in the Philippines the word *pakikisama* (Enriquez, 1979, 1986), which includes managerial characteristics like understanding, concern for employee welfare, kindness and helpfulness, and a pleasant and courteous disposition toward subordinates, indicates a people focus in leadership. In Japan, *amae* is a characteristic of intimate relationships where people presume that those with whom they have an intimate relationship will indulge them (Doi, 1981; Johnson, 1993). Yamaguchi (2004) calls it indulgent dependence where a child, spouse, junior student, or a subordinate seeks help from a parent, spouse, senior student, or supervisor even if he or she actually does not need help. This means that subordinates could expect to be supported by superiors even if their behavior is not perfect. This is not the situation in individualistic cultures, where leaders are not expected to nurture the subordinates beyond maintaining a professional relationship. In fact, in these cultures, both superiors and subordinates prefer to keep each other at arm's length (Bhawuk, 2004).

Task focus and people focus have been researched in leadership literature, starting with the early work at Ohio State University and the University of Michigan. The theory of individualism and collectivism helps explain why in collectivist cultures there is a more pronounced focus on people and relationships because of the collectivists' sense of interdependence and their need to keep harmony among people with whom they interact closely. On the other hand, in the individualist cultures there is a clear emphasis on task, even at the expense of relationships (Bhawuk, 2004). Further support for cultural difference in interdependence is found in the acceptance of paternalism in various cultures. For example, 80 percent of the Japanese and about 65 percent of the samples from middle European countries accepted paternalism, whereas only 51 percent of representative American samples did so (Dorfman *et al.* 1997).

Bhawuk (2001) argued that, depending on how people view themselves, they develop different types of affinity to groups. For example, those with the independent concept of self develop ties with other people to satisfy their self needs, and may not give importance to the need of other people, i.e., everybody takes care of his or her own needs first before thinking about the need of other people. However, those with interdependent concept of self develop ties with other people to satisfy the needs of the self as well as the members of the collective included in the self. This is the second defining attribute of individualism and collectivism, and focuses on the relationship between self and groups of people (Triandis, 1995b).

There are many aspects of interaction with groups that deserve our attention. First, as mentioned above, individualists give priority to their self-goals, whereas collectivists give priority to their ingroup goals (Triandis, 1995b; Triandis *et al.*, 1985; Triandis, 1989; Earley 1994, 1993). Second, individualists tend to take advantage of groups, and may indulge in social loafing (Earley, 1989), more so than collectivists. However, collectivists are likely to social loaf as much when interacting with outgroup members in a group setting. Third, collectivists make significantly large concessions to ingroup members in a negotiation task than they would to outgroup members, whereas individualists tend not to differentiate between ingroup and outgroup members (Carnevale, 1995; Triandis, 1989; Triandis *et al.*, 1988; Earley, 1993). Fourth, individualists tend to allocate rewards based on the equity principle, where as collectivists use equality for ingroup members, and equity for outgroup members (Leung and Bond, 1982; Bond, Leung, and Wan, 1982; Kim, Park, and Suzuki, 1990).

Early socialization leads people to interact with groups differently. For example, both collectivists (e.g., Japanese) and individualists (e.g., American) students are found to be motivated to learn when they are rewarded for learning (Haruki *et al.* 1984). However, contrary to expectations, the Japanese students, unlike the American students, showed motivation to learn even when the teacher was rewarded. The authors explained this phenomenon by suggesting that the socialization practices for children were different in the US and Japan, and that the Japanese children were socialized to observe and respond to others' feelings early on. A Japanese mother may say "I am happy" or "I am sad" to provide positive or negative reinforcement rather than directly saying "You are right" or "You are wrong," which is usually the case in the US.

Another reason for making this distinction is the collectivists' perception of a common fate with their family, kin, friends, and coworkers (Triandis, 1989; Triandis, McCusker, and Hui, 1990; Hui and Triandis, 1986). For example, divorce results many times for individualists because people are unwilling to compromise their careers, whereas collectivists often sacrifice career opportunities to take care of their family needs (ingroup goals) and derive satisfaction in doing so (Bhawuk, 2001). The reason for giving priority to the ingroup goals could be the narrowness of the perceived boundary between the individual and the others or smaller social distance between the self and others.

Individualists are likely to be monochronic in their use of time when interacting with other people, whereas collectivists are likely to be polychronic in their use of time when dealing with ingroup members, but monochronic in their use of time with outgroup members. Collectivists are likely be informal while communicating with ingroup members but formal while dealing with outgroup members, whereas individualists are likely to be informal (US) or formal (British and German) when dealing with ingroup or outgroup. Individualists are likely to emphasize the value for the person in trying to inspire people toward organizational goals,

whereas collectivists are likely to emphasize the value for the group. Telling people, "You should do this task because it is good for you," is likely to be a motivation strategy for individualists, whereas "You should do it because it is good for the collective" (e.g., family, unit, organization, etc.) is likely to be inspirational to collectivists. Shame is a likely tool for collectivists to discourage people from social loafing, whereas guilt is the likely tool for individualists (Bhawuk, 2004).

The third defining attribute focuses on how the self is viewed vis- à-vis the larger society, or how the self interacts with the society (Bhawuk, 2001). Those with independent concept of self do what they like to do, or what they think is good for them, i.e., they pursue their individual desires, attitudes, values, and beliefs (Triandis, 1995b). Since this meets the need of most of the people in a culture where most people have an independent concept of self, the individualistic society values people doing their own things. However, people with interdependent concept of self inherit many relationships and learn to live with these interdependencies. Part of managing the interdependencies is to develop goals that meet the need of more than one's own self. In the process of taking care of the needs of one's ingroup members, a social mechanism evolves in collectivist cultures, which is driven by norms. Thus, for those with interdependent concept of self it is much easier cognitively to resort to methods that have been tried in the past for interacting with people at large. Hence, the difference in following own attitude versus norms of the society becomes a salient difference between individualist and collectivist cultures (Triandis, 1995b).

One reason for the collectivists' desire to conform results from their need to pay attention to what their extended family, friends, colleagues, and neighbors have to say about what they do and how they do Hsu (1981). A sense of duty guides them towards social norms both in the workplace and interpersonal relationships. Individualists, on the other hand, are more concerned about their personal attitudes and values. They care much less than collectivists about what their family members have to say, let alone the extended family, friends, or neighbors. Often, in individualist cultures there are fewer norms about social and workplace behaviors, whereas in collectivist cultures there are many clear norms (Triandis, 1995b). It should be noted that it is not true that individualist cultures do not have norms, or that collectivist cultures do not have people doing what they like to do. Granted that there are exceptions, in individualistic cultures there are fewer norms and those that exist are not severely imposed, whereas in collectivist cultures not only norms are tightly monitored and imposed but also anti-normative behaviors are often hidden from public eyes (Triandis and Bhawuk, 1997).

In collectivist cultures there are likely to be more norms for interpersonal communication than in individualist cultures. Thus, in collectivist cultures effective communication is likely to include that which follows social prescription, i.e., how is something said is critical, whereas in individualist cultures effective communication is likely to be communication that produces a desired outcome, i.e., what is said is critical. In collectivist cultures the non-verbal behaviors are likely to be critical because such behaviors contextualize communication, whereas in individualist cultures non-verbal behaviors are less significant since context is, by comparison, less important. In collectivist cultures, e.g., in Japan, phenomena like *tatemae* (expected public behaviors, which could be opposite of how a person feels or would like to act) and *honne* (true or private feelings that is often kept to oneself) are likely to exist because knowing and maintaining norm is important (See Doi, 1986, pp. 35–48, for a discussion of these concepts), whereas in individualistic cultures such differences are unnecessary because people are attitude, value, and belief driven.

Lastly, there are critical difference between individualism and collectivism in how interpersonal relationships are maintained, as well as the nature of social exchange between self and others. In individualist cultures, social exchange is based on the principle of equal exchange, and people form new relationships to meet their changing needs based on cost benefit analysis. Thus, individualists are rational in their social exchange. In collectivist cultures people have an interdependent concept of self and they inherit many relationships. Therefore, people in collectivist cultures view their relationships as long term in nature and are unlikely

to break even a poor (i.e., not cost-effective) relationship. Thus, collectivists value relationships for their own sake and nurture them with unequal social exchanges over a long period of time.

Individualists tend to use exchange relationships, while collectivists tend to use communal relationships. In an exchange relationship, people give something (a gift or a service) to another person with the expectation that the other person will return a gift or service of equal value in the near future (Clark and Mills, 1979). The characteristics of this type of relationship are "equal value" and "short time frame." People keep a mental record of exchange of benefits and try to maintain a balanced account, in an accounting sense. In a communal relationship people do not keep an account of the exchanges taking place between them (Clark and Mills, 1979); one person may give a gift of much higher value than the other person, and the two people may still maintain their relationship. In other words, it is the relationship that is valued and not the exchanges that go on between people when they are in a communal relationship.

In collectivist cultures usually there are a series of exchanges between two people in which what is given never quite matches what is received. Thus, the exchange goes on for a long time unless the series is broken by some unavoidable situation. In this type of relationship people feel an equality of affect (i.e., when one feels up, the other also feels up; and when one feels down, the other also feels down). In contrast, in individualist cultures people exchange goods and services when they have common interests, and only if the benefits justify the costs. Individualists move on to new relationships when a relationship does not meet their needs.

We are likely to find variation across cultures in what is exchanged, and also across rural and urban settings. For example, in rural settings the exchange is likely to involve goods (vegetables, fruits, food items, etc.) and services (helping in field or yard, helping with children, etc.). It was found that in a Mexican peasant village usually there was a series of exchanges between two people in which what was given never quite matched what was received (Foster, 1967). Thus, the exchange went on for a long time unless the series was broken by some unavoidable situation. It also seems that there may be class difference in the exchange between people. For example, in many collectivist cultures, unlike the lower classes, among the middle class and the affluent people there are not many financial transactions (borrowing money or sharing financial resources) among the extended family members, but they provide emotional support to each other through social gatherings.

Again, this defining attribute of individualism and collectivism explains many differences in communication patterns across cultures. For example, interpersonal communication is marked by exchange of resources for collectivists, but not for individualists. Collectivists do not need to constantly communicate to maintain relationships, whereas individualists do. Individualists need to communicate, and stoppage of communication marks the end of a relationship, whereas collectivists can stop communication without breaking a relationship, and can actually pick up a relationship even after a gap of many years. Communication is peripheral to the relationship for collectivists, whereas for individualists it is central to the relationship.

The rational versus relational differentiation in social exchange also has important implications for leadership. According to leader-member exchange (LMX) theory (Graen and Scandura, 1987; Graen and Uhl-Bien, 1991; Graen and Wakabayashi, 1994), managers are able to influence their subordinates to produce beyond formal organizational expectations by developing "mature leader relationships," which are characterized by extracontractual behavior, mutual trust, respect, liking, superordinate goals, in-kind type of reciprocity, indefinite time span of reciprocity, and high leader-member exchange. However, those managers who do not develop mature leader relationships focus on cash and carry type of reciprocity, immediate time span of reciprocity, and low leader-member exchange. They often indulge in formal, contractual, mostly unidirectional downward influence processes. The exchange relationship obtains the desired behaviors from subordinates by exacting behavioral compliance through external control, while the communal relationship promotes an internalization of values and goals by the subordinate, and desired behaviors from subordinates are obtained through the

subordinates' self-control. It is evident that mature leader relationships are developed over a long term and resemble the communal relationship, whereas "immature" leader relationships reflect a short-term perspective of managers and focus on exchange relationships. Since people are socialized to value long-term relationships in collectivist cultures, the high LMX style of leadership is preferred in these cultures. In individualist cultures, though many managers do develop high LMX styles, in the long run people prefer to maximize their individual gains, and so a low LMX style of leadership is more prevalent (Bhawuk, 2004).

Many cultural differences in leadership styles have been found in studies on Japanese and American managers in multinational organizations in the US and Japan. For example, the American managers were found to have an underdeveloped sense of obligation to their co-workers and company. Therefore, the absenteeism rate among American managers was comparable to that of the workers (Graen and Wakabayashi, 1994). This lack of commitment is attributed to the individualists' exchange relationship perspective of the job, and the preference for a low LMX style of leadership. According to the Japanese philosophy, the managers and workers invest in their mutual relationships and build mutual obligations over a number of years, usually a lifetime, of work contact. This mutual obligation completely rules out the possibility of insubordination. In effect, if workers are resisting a manager's decision, the manager may have committed a mistake and is better off discussing the problem with the workers rather than imposing disciplinary sanctions (Graen and Wakabayashi, 1994). Again, the difference results from the preference for a high LMX leadership style in Japan.

Thus, we can see that the theoretical framework of individualism and collectivism offers a parsimonious framework to discuss many basic cultural differences that can be found across many pairs of cultures that are individualistic or collectivist. Triandis, Brislin, and Hui (1988) presented a list of advice for individualists going to collectivist cultures, and vice versa, which has been proven to be useful. Bhawuk (2001) presented four sets of behaviors capturing the four defining attributes of individualism and collectivism, which have been shown to be effective for intercultural training (Bhawuk, 1998). Therefore, there is much value in using this framework in intercultural training programs.

Discussion

The field of intercultural training has evolved significantly in the last fifty years, and, despite its theoretically rigorous foundations, there has not been a clear direction about how intercultural training programs should be developed. This could be attributed to the natural course of development of the field in which various individuals have contributed from narrow theoretical perspectives. This was reflected in the early discussion of whether intercultural training should follow the university model of classroom lectures or use the experiential training method (Harrison and Hopkins, 1967). Another discussion in the literature has been about the culture specific versus culture general approaches to training (Bhawuk, 1990). Clearly, there is much need for a theoretical framework for the development of intercultural training programs that synthesizes various theoretical perspectives and addresses many of the issues raised in the literature. This chapter is a small step in that direction.

This chapter synthesizes many of the theoretical concepts discussed in the intercultural training literature to present a framework that can be used to develop intercultural training programs. It is argued here that, for people to develop intercultural competence, they need to understand the process of skill acquisition, and learn how to learn so that they can continue to learn beyond a formal training program while living abroad. The concepts of disconfirmed expectation and isomorphic attribution are two basic concepts that are important to understand and can help in the process of skill acquisition. A clear understanding of the cognitive process of skill acquisition similarly provides the much needed cognitive framework for skill acquisition. The theoretical framework of individualism and collectivism helps organize the intercultural expertise at the abstract level much like what cognitive psychologists refer to as a theoretical organizing package or TOP.

The economic framework presented in the chapter at the core helps to go beyond cultural theories that are psychological or sociological in nature. This is presented as a first step, and clearly there is a need for developing frameworks that would capture other socio-political perspectives. Such additions in the future would make the framework more comprehensive, and aid people in their intercultural skill acquisition. An idea implicit in the framework is that intercultural skill is multidimensional, and thus there is a need to approach its acquisition by following a multimethod approach. This has been an idea hitherto neglected in the literature.

The addition of the need for self-preservation at the core of intercultural training programs is another contribution of the chapter, which has been hitherto neglected in intercultural training literature. Researchers and practitioners alike in their zeal of preparing people to be effective in their sojourn often neglect the basic issues of survival, or assume that the sojourners would take care of such issues themselves. This is a mistake, and all training programs must stress the need for self-preservation, which is not only unique to us individually, but also has some cultural underpinnings depending on who the sojourners are and where they are going to live. For example, there are likely gender differences that need to be addressed, as women have to deal with many more issues when moving from one culture to another than men have to do, and this issue needs to be further researched. Clearly, there are many aspects of survival that we all need to worry about and without taking care of these issues we simply cannot be effective in our work or social interactions. This has become a particularly important issue in view of the increased terrorist activities that the world has seen in the last few years, but I would like to note that this has always been a critical factor, and one that has not been given much attention in the literature.

The outer circles of the model deal with organizational, industry, and culture specific level issues, and were noted to make the model complete. Unfortunately, they could not be developed fully, and are important future research topics.

Intercultural training literature has been theoretically grounded in the individual differences perspective, and there is a need to develop multilevel models including organizational and industrial levels of analyses. It could be argued that people working in the information technology industry are going to need to adapt to different circumstances than people working in the oil exploration industry, the environment protection area, the financial industry, or the healthcare industry. Similarly, people working for a large multinational like IBM or Bank of America or NGOs like the UNICEF or The World Bank would need to adapt to different contexts and histories. Thus, preparing people associated with different industries and organizations going to different cultures necessarily would require a multilevel training program that would build on the core that was developed in some detail in this chapter. This model can also be used to organize college courses in intercultural training or communication, so that students are able to organize their personal intercultural skill development in a systematic way.

References

Albert, R. D. 1983. "The intercultural sensitizer or culture assimilator: a cognitive approach", in D. Landis and R. W. Brislin (eds.), *Handbook of Intercultural Training: Issues in Training Methodology* (vol. 2). New York, NY: Pergamon, pp. 186–217

Anderson, J. R. 2000. *Cognitive Psychology and Its Implications* (5th edn). New York, NY: Worth Publishing.

Bandura, A. 1977. *Social Learning Theory*. Englewood Cliffs, NJ: Prentice-Hall.

Beattie, J. 1980. Review article: "Representations of the self in traditional Africa", *Africa* 50(3): 313–20.

Bennett, M. J. 1986. "A developmental approach to training for intercultural sensitivity", *International Journal of Intercultural Relations* 10: 179–95.

Berry, J. W. 1990. "Psychology of acculturation: understanding individuals moving between cultures", in R. W. Brislin (ed.), *Applied Cross-Cultural Psychology*. Newbury Park, CA: Sage, pp. 232–253.

Bhawuk, D. P. S. 1990. "Cross-cultural orientation programs". in R. W. Brislin (ed.), *Applied Cross-cultural Psychology*. Newbury Park, CA: Sage, pp. 325–46.

1995. *The Role of Culture Theory in Cross-cultural Training: A Comparative Evaluation of Culture-specific, Culture General, and Theory-based Assimilators*. Unpublished doctoral dissertation, University of Illinois at Urbana-Champaign.

1996. "Development of a culture theory-based assimilator: applications of individualism and collectivism in cross-cultural training", *Best Paper Proceedings*, Academy of Management Annual Meeting, Cincinnati, pp. 147–50.

1998. "The role of culture theory in cross-cultural training: a multimethod study of culture-specific, culture-general, and culture theory-based assimilators", *Journal of Cross-Cultural Psychology*, 29(5): 630–55.

2001. "Evolution of culture assimilators: toward theory-based assimilators", *International Journal of Intercultural Relations*, 25(2): 141–63.

2004. "Individualism and collectivism", in *Encyclopedia of Leadership*, Vol. 2. Thousand Oaks, CA: Sage, 706–10.

2005. "Communication between of managers of two worlds: discovering cultural standards". Workshop presented at IMI 6th Annual Conference on Enhancing Cross-Cultural Effectiveness: Strategies and Skills for Business, Education, Training and Development Professionals, March 10–11, American University, Washington DC.

and Brislin, R. W. 1992. "The measurement of intercultural sensitivity using the concepts of individualism and collectivism", *International Journal of Intercultural Relations* 16: 413–36.

and Brislin, R. W. 2000. "Cross-cultural training: a review", *Applied Psychology: An International Review*, 49(1): 162–91.

Landis, D. and Lo, K. 2006. "Intercultural training", in. D. L. Sam and J. W. Berry (eds.), *The Cambridge Handbook of Acculturation Psychology*, Cambridge: Combridge University Press, pp. 504–24.

Munusamy, V. P., and Sakuda, K. 2007. "Preparing global business leaders: application of an economy-based theoretical framework to intercultural training", paper presented at the Academy of Management Conference, Philadelphia, August 3–8.

and Triandis, H. C. (1996). "The role of culture theory in the study of culture and intercultural training". in D. Landis and R. Bhagat (eds.), *Handbook of Intercultural Training*, Newbury Park, CA: Sage, pp. 17–34.

Black, J. S., and Mendenhall, M. 1990. "Cross-cultural training effectiveness: a review and theoretical framework for future research", *American Management Review* 15:113–36.

Bond, M. H., Leung, K., and Wan, K. C. 1982. "The social impact of self-effacing attributions: the Chinese case", *Journal of social Pychology* 118: 157–66.

Brislin, R. W. 1981. *Cross-cultural Encounters: Face to Face Interaction*. New York, NY: Pergamon.

Cushner, K., Cherrie, C., and Yong, M. 1986. *Intercultural Interactions: A Practical Guide*. Beverly Hills, CA: Sage.

and Pedersen, P. 1976. *Cross-cultural Orientation Programs*. New York, NY: Gardner.

and Yoshida, T. 1994a. *Intercultural Communication Training: An Introduction*. Thousand Oaks, CA: Sage.

and Yoshida, T. (eds.) (1994b). *Improving Intercultural Interactions: Models for Cross-cultural Training Programs*. Thousand Oaks, CA: Sage.

Carnevale, P. J. 1995. "Property, culture, and negotiation", in R. Kramer and D. M. Messick eds. *Negotiation as a Social Process*. Newbury Park, CA: Sage, pp. 309–23.

Chen, C. C. 1995. "New Trends in Rewards Allocation Preferences: A Sino-U.S. Comparison", *Academy of Management Journal* 38(2): 408–28.

Clark, M. S. and Mills, J. 1979. "Interpersonal attraction in exchange and communal relationships", *Journal of Personality and Social Psychology* 37: 12–24.

Cushner, K. and Brislin, R. W. 1996. *Intercultural Interactions: A Practical Guide* (2nd edn). Thousand Oaks, CA: Sage.

and Brislin, R. W. (eds.) 1997. *Improving Intercultural Interactions: Models for Cross-Cultural Training Programs*, Vol. 2. Thousand Oaks, CA: Sage.

and Landis, D. 1996. "The intercultural sensitizer", in D. Landis and R. Bhagat (eds.). *Handbook of Intercultural Training, (2nd edn)*. Thousand Oaks: Sage, pp. 185–202.

Deshpande, S. P. and Viswesvaran, C. 1992. "Is cross-cultural training of expatriate managers effective: a meta analysis", *International Journal of Intercultural Relations*, 16: 295–310.

Detweiler, R. 1978. "Culture, category width, and attributions: a model building approach to the reasons for cultural effects", *Journal of Cross-Cultural Psychology* 9: 259–84.

1980. "Intercultural interaction and the categorization process: a conceptual analysis and behavioral outcome", *International Journal of Intercultural Relations*, 4: 275–95.

Diener, E. 2000. "Subjective well-being: the science of happiness and a proposal for a national index" *American Psychologist* 55(1): 34–43.

Doi, T. 1981. *The Anatomy of Dependence: The Key Analysis of Japanese Behavior* (2nd edn) trans. John Bester. Tokyo: Kodansha International.

1986. *The Anatomy of Self: The Individual Versus Society*, trans. M. A. Harbison. Tokyo: Kodansha International.

Dorfman, P. W., Howell, J. P., Hibino, S., Lee, J. K., Tate, U., and Bautista, A. 1997. "Leadership in western and Asian countries; commonalities and differences in effective leadership processes", *Leadership Quarterly*, 8(3): 233–74.

Earley, P. C. 1989. "Social loafing and collectivism: a comparison of the United States and the People's Republic of China", *Administrative Science Quarterly*, 34: 565–81.

1993. "East meets west meets mideast: further explorations of collectivistic and individualistic work groups", *Academy of Management Journal* 36: 319–48.

1994. "Self or group? Cultural effects of training on self-efficacy and performance". *Administrative Science Quarterly* 39: 89–107.

Enriquez, V. G. 1979. "Towards cross-cultural knowledge through cross-indigenous methods and perspectives", *Philippine Journal of Psychology* 12: 9–15.

1986. "Kapwa: a core concept in Filipino social psychology", in V. G. Enriquez (ed.), *Philippine World View*. Pasir Panjang, Singapore: Institute of Southeast Asian Studies.

Fiedler, F. E., Mitchell, T. R., and Triandis, H. C. 1971. "The culture assimilator: an approach to cross-cultural training", *Journal of Applied Psychology*, 55: 95–102.

Foster, G. *Tzintzuntzan: Mexican Peasants in a Changing World*. Boston, MA: Little, Brown.

Graen, G. B., and Scandura, T. 1987. "Toward a psychology of dyadic organizing", *Research in Organizational Behavior* 9: 175–208.

and Uhl-Bien, M. 1991. "The transformation of professionals into self-managing and partially self-designing contributors: toward a theory of leadership making", *Journal of Management Systems*, 3(3): 33–48.

and Wakabayashi, M. 1994. "Cross-cultural leadership making: bridging American and Japanese diversity for team advantage", in H. C. Triandis, M. D. Dunnette, and L. M. Hough (eds.), *Handbook of Industrial and Organizational Psychology* (2nd edn). Palo Alto, CA: Consulting Psychologists Press, pp. 769–827.

Gudykunst, W. B. (ed.) 2005. *Theorizing about Intercultural Communication*. Thousand Oaks, CA: Sage.

Hall, E. T. 1959. *The Silent Language*. New York, NY: Doubleday.

1966. *The Hidden Dimension*. New York, NY: Doubleday.

Hammer, M., Bennett, M., and Wiseman, R. 2003. "Measuring intercultural sensitivity: the intercultural development inventory", *International Journal of Intercultural Relations*, 27: 421–44.

Hara, K., and Kim, M. S. 2004. "The effect of self-construals on conversational indirectness", *International Journal of Intercultural Relations*, 28: 1–18.

Harrison, J. K. 1992. "Individual and combined effects of behavior modeling and the culture assimilator in cross-cultural management training", *Journal of Applied Psychology*, 77: 952–62.

Harrison, R., and Hopkins, R. L. 1967. "The design of cross-cultural training: an alternative to the university model", *Journal of Applied Behavioral Science*, 3: 431–60.

Haruki, Y., Shigehisa, T., Nedate, K., Wajima, M., and Ogawa, R. 1984. "Effects of alien-reinforcement and its combined type on learning behavior and efficacy in relation to personality", *International Journal of Psychology*, 19: 527–45.

Hofstede, G. 1980. *Culture's Consequence*. Beverly Hills, CA: Sage.

Howell, W. S. 1982. *The Empathic Communicator*. Bellmont, CA: Wadsworth Publishing Company.

Hsu, F. L. K. 1981. *Americans and Chinese: Passage to Difference* (3rd edn). Honolulu, HI: University of Hawaii.

Hughes-Weiner, G. 1986. "The 'learning how to learn' approach to cross-cultural orientation", *International Journal of Intercultural Relations* 10: 485–505.

Hui, C. H. and Triandis, H. C. 1986. "Individualism-collectivism: a study of cross cultural researchers", *Journal of Cross-Cultural Psychology*, 17: 225–48.

Inglehart, R. 1997. *Modernization and Postmodernization: Cultural, Economic, and Political Change in 43 Societies*. Princeton, NJ: Princeton University Press.

Johnson, F. A. 1993. *Dependency and Japanese socialization: Psychoanalytic and Anthropological Investigations into Amae*. New York, NY: New York University Press.

Kim, K. L., Park, H., and Suzuki, N. 1990. "Reward allocations in the United States, Japan, and Korea: a comparison of individualistic and collectivistic cultures", *Academy of Management Journal* 33(1): 188–98.

Kim, M. S., Hunter, J. E., Miyahara, A., Horvath, A., Bresnahan, M., and Yoon, H. J. 1996. "Individual- vs. culture-level dimensions of individualism and collectivism: effects on preferred conversational styles", *Communication Monographs* 63: 29–49.

and Sharkey, W. F. 1995. "Independent and interdependent construals of self: explaining cultural patterns of interpersonal communication in multi-cultural organizational settings", *Communication Quarterly*, 43: 20–38.

Kolb, D. A. 1976. "Management and the learning process", *California Management Review*, 18(3): 21–31.

Landis, D., Bennett, M., and Bennett, J. 2004. *Handbook of Intercultural Training*, (3rd edn.) Thousand Oaks, CA: Sage.

and Bhagat, R. 1996. *Handbook of Intercultural Training*, 2nd Edn. Thousand Oaks, CA: Sage.

and Bhawuk, D. P. S. 2004. "Synthesizing theory building and practice in intercultural training", in D. Landis, M. Bennett, and J. Bennett (eds.), *Handbook of Intercultural Training* (3rd edn) Thousand Oaks, CA: Sage, pp. 451–66.

and Bhawuk, D. P. S. 2005. "Equal opportunity training in the military: toward a synthesis of theory and practice", *Proceedings of the 5th Biennial EO/EEO Research Symposium* organized by the Defense Equal Opportunity Management Institute (DEOMI), February 17–18, Cocoa Beach, Florida.

and Brislin, R. 1983. *Handbook of Intercultural Training*. Elmsford, NY: Pergamon Press.

Brislin, R. W., and Hulgus, J. 1985. "Attribution training versus contact in acculturative training: a laboratory study", *Journal of Applied Social Psychology*, 15: 466–82.

Leki, R. S. 2007. *Travel Wise: How to be Safe, Savvy, and Secure Abroad*. Boston, MA: Intercultural Press.

Leung, K. and Bond, M. H. 1982. "How Chinese and Americans reward task-related contributions: a preliminary study", *Psychologia* 25: 32–9.

Markus, H. R., and Kitayama, S. 1991. "Culture and the self: implications for cognition, emotion, and motivation", *Psychological Review*, 98: 224–53.

Mendenhall, M. E., Ehnert, I., Kühlmann, T. M., Oddou, G., Osland, J. S., and Stahl G. K. 2004. "Evaluation studies of cross-cultural training programs: a review of literature from 1988–2000", in D. Landis and J. Bennett (eds.), *The Handbook of Intercultural Training*. Thousand Oaks, CA: Sage, pp. 129–44.

Morris, M. A. and Robie, C. 2001. "A meta-analysis of the effects of cross-cultural training on expatriate performance and adjustment", *International Journal of Training and Development* 5: 112–25.

Morris, M. W., and Peng, K. 1994. "Culture and cause: American and Chinese attributions for social and physical events", *Journal of Personality and Social Psychology* 67: 949–71.

Oberg, K. 1960. "Culture shock: adjustment to new cultural environments", *Practical Anthropology* 7: 177–82.

Overmier, J. B. 2006. Keynote address given to the 16th Annual Conference of Psychology, National Academy of Psychology, Mumbai, India, December 14–16.

Oyserman, D., Coon, H. M., and Kemmelmeier, M. 2002. "Rethinking individualism and collectivism: evaluation of theoretical assumptions and meta-analyses", *Psychological Bulletin* 128: 3–72.

Platt, J. R. 1964. "Strong inference: certain systematic methods of scientific thinking may produce much more rapid progress than others", *Science* 146:(3642), 347–53.

Porter, M. 1990. *The Competitive Advantage of Nations*. New York, NY: Macmillan.

Ross, L. 1977. "The intuitive psychologist and his shortcomings: distortions in the attribution process", in L. Berkowitz (ed.), *Advances in Experimental Social Psychology* (vol. 10). New York: Academic Press, pp. 173–220.

Schwartz, S. H. 1994. "Beyond individualism and collectivism: new cultural dimensions of values", in U. Kim, H. C. Triandis, C. Kagitcibasi, S. Choi, G. Yoon (eds.), *Individualism and Collectivism: Theory, Method, and Applications*. Thousand Oaks, CA: Sage.

Stewart, E. 1966. "The simulation of cultural differences", *Journal of Communication* 16: 291–304.

Ting-Toomey, S. 1988. "A face-negotiation theory", in Y. Kim and W. Gudykunst (eds.), *Theories of Intercultural Communication*. Newbury Park, CA: Sage.

Triandis, H. 1972. *The Analysis of Subjective Culture*. New York, NY: Wiley.

1975. "Culture training, cognitive complexity, and interpersonal attitudes", in R. W. Brislin, S. Bochner, and W. Lonner (eds.), *Cross-cultural Perspectives on Learning*. Beverly Hills, CA: Sage, pp. 39–77.

1977. "Theoretical framework for evaluation of cross-cultural training effectiveness", *International Journal of Intercultural Relations*, 1: 19–45.

1989. "The self and social behavior in differing cultural contexts", *Psychological Review* 96: 506–20.

1990. "Theoretical concepts of use to practitioners", in R. W. Brislin (ed.) *Applied Cross-cultural Psychology*. Thousand Oaks, CA: Sage, pp. 34–55.

1994. *Culture and Social Behavior*. New York, NY: McGraw-Hill.

1995a. "Culture specific assimilators", in S. Fowler, and M. Mumford (eds.), *Intercultural Sourcebook*, vol. 1. Yarmouth, ME: Intercultural Press.

1995b. *Individualism and Collectivism*. Boulder, CO: Westview Press.

and Bhawuk, D. P. S. 1997. "Culture theory and the meaning of relatedness", in P. C. Early and M. Erez (eds.), *New Perspectives on International Industrial/Organizational Psychology*. New York, NY: New Lexington Free Press.

Bontempo, R., Villareal, M. J., Asai, M., and Lucca, N. 1988. "Individualism and collectivism: cross-cultural perspectives on self-in-group relationships", *Journal of Personality and Social Psychology* 54: 328–38.

Brislin, H. and Hui, C. 1988. "Cross-cultural training across the individualism-collectivism divide", *International Journal of Intercultural Relations* 12: 269–89.

Leung, K., Villareal, M., and Clark, F. L. 1985. "Allocentric vs. idiocentric tendencies: convergent and discriminant validation", *Journal of Research in Personality* 19: 395–415.

Marin, G., Lisansky, J., and Betancourt, H., 1984. "*Simpatia* as a cultural script of Hispanics", *Journal of Personality and Social Psychology* 47: 1363–75.

McCusker, C., and Hui, C. H. 1990. "Multimethod probes of individualism and collectivism", *Journal of Personality and Social Psychology* 59: 1006–20.

Vygotsky, L. 1978 *Mind in Society: The Development of Higher Psychological Processes*, Cambridge, MA, Harvard University Press.

Ward, C., Bochner, S., and Furnham, A. 2001. *The Psychology of Culture Shock.* London: Routledge.

Weldon, D. E., Carlston, D. E., Rissman, A. K., Slobodin, L., and Triandis, H. C. 1975. "A laboratory test of effects of culture assimilator training", *Journal of Personality and Social Psychology* 32: 300–10.

Wheeler, L., Reis, H. T., and Bond, M. H. 1989. "Collectivism-individualism in everyday social life: the middle kingdom and the melting pot", *Journal of Personality and Social Psychology* 57: 79–86.

Yamaguchi, S. 2004. "Further clarifications of the concept of amae in relation to dependence and attachment", *Human Development* 47: 28–33.

PART IV

Future Directions in Theory and Research

Improving methodological robustness in cross-cultural organizational research

FONS J. R. VAN DE VIJVER and RONALD FISCHER

Some of the largest and best known cross-cultural psychological projects come from the domain of organizational research; good examples are Hofstede's (1980, 2001) study on attitudes of IBM employees and the GLOBE study which involved sixty-two countries (House *et al.* 2003). However, these large projects are somewhat atypical in that most cross-cultural organizational studies involve two or three cultures. The current chapter provides an overview of basic issues in cross-cultural organizational research. The combination of a large interest in cross-cultural organizational research and the lack of a formal training of many researchers in cross-cultural methods create the need to reflect on these basic issues. The central question is how we can improve the methodological robustness of our research which, as we expect, will contribute to the validity and replicability of the conclusions derived from our research. We do not discuss the theories that are used in this field but focus on the methodological issues that are common to cross-cultural research (a good overview of current theories can be found in Smith, Bond, and Kagitcibasi, 2006).

The chapter deals with two kinds of methodological issues. The first involves the basic question of the comparability of constructs and scores across cultures (Poortinga, 1989). Comparability of scores across individuals obtained in a mono-cultural setting is typically taken for granted. We readily compare scores from participants in different organizations once we have established an adequate reliability and factorial composition of the instrument. Managers routinely use survey instruments and tests developed in different cultural contexts to make decisions about selecting or promoting employees, to judge morale and

satisfaction of staff or to evaluate effectiveness of training programmes, interventions or organizational effectiveness. However, the implicit assumption of comparability cannot be taken for granted in cross-cultural research. Comparability can be challenged in various ways. For example, cross-cultural differences in views on controversial topics such as abortion and soft-drug use may be influenced by differences in national laws, the societal climate of (in)tolerance surrounding these topics, and ensuing differences in social desirability. Our chapter primarily focuses on these factors in the context of cross-cultural applications of standard instruments or tests.

The second issue discussed in this chapter involves the multilevel design of cross-cultural organizational studies. Models have been developed in the last decades to account for the complex data structure of such studies which involve participants nested in organizations nested in cultures (Dansereau, Alutto and Yammarimo, 1984; Raudenbush and Bryk, 2001; Muthén, 1991, 1994). Cross-cultural psychological studies often draw inferences on cultures on the basis of individual-level scores. Multilevel analyses therefore need to address the following questions:

(a) What is the most appropriate level of analysis (individual, group, organization, industry, national culture, etc.)?
(b) Do concepts that exist at more than one level have the same meaning at all levels (isomorphism across levels)?
(c) What is the linkage of constructs across levels (e.g., influence of higher-level constructs on lower-level constructs)?

The first question needs to be addressed theoretically as well as methodologically. Researchers need to specify their appropriate level of theory and then measure the variables at this level. Much cross-cultural research uses aggregated scores. Any statistical test of differences in means, such as a *t* test or analysis of variance, assumes that the meaning of scores does not change after aggregation. We assume that the mean score is a good reflection of the standing of the culture on the underlying construct. Techniques are available to address what level is empirically justified. We also know that scored aggregation can lead to a change of meaning. Additional constructs can influence country-level differences. The statistical models that have been developed can address the question to what extent scores that are aggregated still have the same meaning after aggregation. For example, do scores on leadership preference still reflect this construct after scores have been aggregated at country level or are country-level differences influenced by additional constructs such as social desirability? Finally, we can investigate the relationships across levels. The most common question that can be statistically addressed refers to the prediction of a psychological variable (e.g., leadership preferences) by means of individual-level variables (e.g., education), organizational-level variables (e.g., size), and country-level variables (e.g., power distance and Gross National Product).

The first section of the chapter deals with scoring comparability; a taxonomy of bias and equivalence is presented that allows us to systematically describe levels of comparability. The second section deals with multilevel issues. Conclusions are drawn in the final section.

Bias and equivalence

An important question to consider in the initial stages of a project involves the choice of instrument. There are essentially three options: use an existing instrument; adapt an existing instrument; or develop a new instrument (Van de Vijver, 2003). Even in a project in which an existing (usually western) instrument has to be used, it is still important to consider the appropriateness of the existing instrument in the target culture. Appropriateness depends on linguistic, cultural, and psychometric criteria. Linguistic criteria involve the denotative and connotative meaning of stimuli and their comprehensibility. Cultural criteria involve the compliance with local norms and habits. Psychometric criteria characteristics involve the common criteria of validity and reliability.

The first option, called adoption, amounts to a close translation of an instrument in a target language. This option is the most frequently chosen in empirical research because it is simple to implement, cheap, has a high face validity, and retains the opportunity to compare scores obtained with the instrument across all translations. The aim of these translations often is the comparison of averages obtained in different cultures (does culture A score higher on construct X than does culture B?). Close translations have an important limitation: they can only be used when the items in the source and target language versions have an adequate coverage of the construct measured and no items show bias. Standard statistical techniques for assessing equivalence (e.g., Van de Vijver and Leung, 1997) should be applied to assess the similarity of constructs measured by the various language versions. However, even when the structures are identical, there is no guarantee that the translations are all culturally viable and that a locally developed instrument would cover the same aspects.

The second (and increasingly popular) option is labeled adaptation. It usually amounts to the close translation of some stimuli that are assumed to be adequate in the target culture, and to a change of other stimuli when a close translation would lead to linguistically, culturally or psychometrically inappropriate measurement (e.g., a questionnaire has the item "invite your boss over for a birthday party at your house") to express the idea of emotional closeness in organizations. However, the implicit assumption that birthday parties are a culturally important institution is not universally valid. A behavior could then be identified that comes close to the original in terms of psychological meaning (e.g., a meeting with a superior in an informal family setting).

The third option is called assembly. It involves the compilation of an entirely new instrument. It is the preferable choice if a translation or adaptation process is unlikely to yield an instrument with satisfactory linguistic, cultural, and psychometric accuracy. An assembly will lead to an emic, culture-specific instrument. An assembly maximizes the cultural suitability of an instrument, but it will preclude any numerical comparisons of scores across cultures.

There is no single best option. The choice for either option should be based on various factors. If the aim is to compare scores obtained with an instrument in different cultures, a close translation is the easiest procedure. However, the cultural adequacy of the instrument in the target culture has to be demonstrated. The "quick and dirty" practice of preparing a close translation, administering it in a target culture, and comparing the scores in a *t* test without any concern for the cultural and psychometric adequacy of the measure is hard to defend. If the aim is to maximize the ecological validity of the instrument (i.e., to measure the construct in a target culture as adequate way), an adaptation or assembly is preferable. Culture-specific items can increase the validity of research findings in specific cultural contexts and give us a better contextual understanding of the psychological processes (Bhagat and McQuaid, 1982), but they also decrease the comparability of the findings across cultural groups. Statistical tools, such as item response theory and structural equation modeling, can deal with an incomplete overlap in indicators across cultures (Van de Vijver and Leung, 1997). However, if the number of culture-specific items is large, the comparability of the construct or of the remaining items may be problematic. The maximization of cross-cultural comparability and of local validity may be incompatible in such cases. In the remainder of the chapter, we will deal with issues which are especially important for adopted and adapted instruments.

Bias

Bias refers to the presence of nuisance factors that challenge the comparability of scores across cultural groups. If scores are biased, their psychological meaning is culture dependent and cultural differences in assessment outcome are to be accounted for, partly or completely, by auxiliary psychological constructs or measurement artifacts.

The occurrence of bias has a bearing on the comparability of scores across cultures. The measurement implications of bias for comparability are addressed in the concept of *equivalence* (see Johnson, 1998, for a review). Equivalence refers to the comparability of test scores obtained in different cultural groups. Obviously, bias and equivalence are related; it is sometimes argued that they are mirror concepts. Bias, in this view, is synonymous to nonequivalence; conversely, equivalence refers to the absence of bias. This is not the view adopted here because, in the presentation of cross-cultural research methodology, it is instructive to disentangle sources of bias and their implications for score comparability.

Bias and equivalence are not inherent characteristics of an instrument, but arise in the application of an instrument in at least two cultural groups and the comparison of scores, patterns or item values. Decisions on the presence or absence of equivalence should be empirically based. The need for such validation and verification should not be interpreted as blind empiricism and the impossibility of implementing preventive measures in a study to minimize bias and maximize equivalence. On the contrary, not all instruments are equally susceptible to bias. For example, more structured test administrations are less prone to bias influences than are less structured sessions (assuming that the test administrations are adequately tailored to the cultural context and the test administration is not based on western manuals that neglect local communication conventions). Analogously, comparisons of closely related groups will be less susceptible to bias than comparisons of groups with a widely different cultural background.

Identification of bias and verification of equivalence are core theoretical as well as methodological problems of cross-cultural survey research (Smith, Bond, and Kagitcibasi, 2006). The validity of any comparison critically depends on the solution of these two issues. Malpass (1977) pointed out that methodological problems in cross-cultural research are often theoretical problems in disguise. If we measure some construct in two or more samples, we need to understand any potential variable

Table 18.1 Sources of bias in cross-cultural assessment

Type of Bias	Source of Bias
Construct bias	• Only partial overlap in the definitions of the construct across cultures (e.g., filial piety, as described in the main text).
	• Differential appropriateness of the behaviors associated with the construct (e.g., items do not belong to the repertoire of one of the cultural groups).
	• Poor sampling of all relevant behaviors (e.g., short instruments are used to cover broad constructs).
	• Incomplete coverage of all relevant aspects/facets of the construct (e.g., not all relevant domains are sampled).
Method bias	Sample bias
	• Incomparability of samples (e.g., caused by differences in kinds of organizations, education, or motivation across cultures).
	• Differences in environmental administration conditions, physical (e.g., recording devices) or social (e.g., class size).
	• Ambiguous instructions for respondents and/or guidelines for administrators.
	Administration bias
	• Differential expertise of administrators/interviewers.
	• Tester/interviewer/observer effects (e.g., halo effects).
	• Communication problems between participant and interviewer (e.g., participant is not sufficiently proficient in language of testing).
	Instrument bias
	• Differential response styles (e.g., social desirability, extremity scoring, acquiescence).
	• Differential familiarity with stimulus material and/or response procedures (particularly relevant in cognitive testing).
Item bias	• Poor translation (e.g., linguistically equivalent translation of a word does not exist in source and target language).
	• Ambiguous items (e.g., double barreled items).
	• Nuisance factors (e.g., item may invoke additional traits or abilities).
	• Cultural specifics (e.g., incidental differences in connotative meaning and/or appropriateness of the item content).

that can have an impact on the scores in one of the samples. The central issue is that respondents may be responding to the researcher or administrator, the social context in which the research takes place and the specific task in other ways than we believe they are. It is important to understand the "mind of the other" (Malpass, 1977), the meaning that is created by participants in different groups. The purpose of establishing equivalence is to examine this similarity in meaning. When we address the equivalence, we operationalize this similarity in meaning. For example, if the items of an instrument show similar associations with each other in different cultures, we argue that these items measure the same underlying constructs in these groups.

Sources of bias: construct, method, and item. In order to detect and/or prevent bias, we need to recognize what can lead to bias. Table 18.1 provides an overview of sources of bias, based on a classification by Van de Vijver and Tanzer (2004; cf. Van de Vijver and Poortinga 1997). Sources of bias are numerous, thus the overview is necessarily tentative.

Construct bias occurs when the construct measured is not identical across groups. Construct bias precludes the cross-cultural measurement of a construct with the same measure. Detection of construct bias requires some intimate familiarity with the culture being studied, which can be achieved by conducting local pilot studies in the initial stages of a project or using local insiders (see below). Embretson (1983) coined the term *construct underrepresentation* to describe the situation where an instrument insufficiently represents all the domains and dimensions relevant for a given construct in a given culture. There is an important difference between our term *construct bias* and Embretson's term. Whereas construct underrepresentation is a problem of instruments measuring broad concepts with too few indicators which can usually be overcome by adding items relating to these domains/dimensions, construct bias can only be overcome by adding items relating to new domains/dimensions. Clearly, identification of construct bias calls for detailed culture-specific knowledge.

Cross-cultural differences in the concept of depression are one example. Another empirical example can be found in Ho's (1996) work on filial piety (defined as a psychological characteristic associated with being "a good son or daughter"). The Chinese conception, according to which children are expected to assume the role of caretaker of elderly parents, is broader than the western. An inventory of filial piety based on the Chinese conceptualization covers aspects unrelated to the concept among western subjects, whereas a western-based inventory will leave important Chinese aspects uncovered. In western-based organizational settings, commitment has been conceptualized as a three-componential model (Cohen, 2003; Meyer and Allen, 1991; Meyer *et al.* 2002), differentiating affective, continuance and normative forms of commitment. Affective commitment is the emotional attachment to organizations and characterized by a genuine want or desire to belong to the organization as well as congruence and identification with the norms, values and goals of the organization. Continuance commitment focuses on the alleged costs associated with leaving or altering one's involvement with the organization, implying a perceived need to stay. Normative commitment is considered as a feeling of obligation to remain with the organization, capturing normative pressures and perceived obligations by important others.

The extent to which such definitions capture the understanding of commitment in different cultural contexts is yet unclear (Fischer and Mansell, 2008; Wasti and Oender, 2008). A meta-analysis by Fischer and Mansell (2008) showed that the three components showed considerable, but incomplete overlap in lower income contexts indicating that the components might not be functionally equivalent across economic contexts. Wasti (2002) argued that continuance commitment in a Turkish context is too narrowly defined. In more collectivistic contexts, loyalty and trust are important and strongly associated with paternalistic management practices. Therefore, employers are more likely to give trusted jobs to family members or friends, involving these individuals into relationships of dependency and obligation. This practice, in turn, leads to efforts to maintain "face" and one's credibility and attempts to return the favor. These normative pressures therefore become part of continuance commitment, involving both financial and rational considerations (investments, benefits as found in western contexts) as well as social costs (loss of face and credibility).

Yang and Bond (1990) presented indigenous Chinese personality descriptors and a set of American descriptors to a group of Taiwanese subjects. Factor analyses showed differences in the Chinese and American factor structures. Similarly, Cheung *et al.* (1996) found that the western-based five-factor model of personality (McCrae and Costa 1997) does not cover all the aspects deemed relevant by the Chinese to describe personality. In addition to the western factors of *extraversion, agreeableness, conscientiousness, neuroticism* (emotional stability), and *openness*, two further factors were found relevant for the Chinese context: *face* and *harmony*.

Construct bias can also be caused by differential appropriateness of the behaviors associated with the construct in the different cultures. An example of this comes from research on intelligence. Western intelligence tests tend to focus on reasoning and logical thinking (e.g., Raven's Progressive Matrices), while omnibus tests also contain subtests that tap into acquired knowledge (e.g., vocabulary scales for the Wechsler scales). When western respondents are asked which characteristics they associate with an intelligent person, skilled reasoning and extensive knowledge are frequently mentioned, as well as social aspects of intelligence. These social aspects are even more prominent in everyday conceptions of intelligence in non-western groups. Kokwet mothers (Kenya) expect that intelligent children know their place in the family and the fitting behaviors for children, such as proper forms of address. An intelligent child is obedient and does not create problems (Segall *et al.* 1990).

Construct bias is also apparent in commitment research. Since Cole's (1979) initial comparison of behavioral commitment levels in Japan and the US, there has been a great interest in differences and similarities in commitment across cultural groups. However, researchers soon found out that high levels of behavioral commitment among Japanese workers (indicated by low turnover) were not strongly correlated with attitudinal commitment, as was found in the US. Therefore, the behavior of (or thoughts about) leaving one's organization was a good indicator of attitudinal commitment in the US, but not in Japan (for reviews, see Besser, 1993; Lincoln and Kalleberg, 1990; Smith, Fischer and Sale, 2001).

An important type of bias, called *method bias*, can result from such factors as sample incomparability, instrument differences, tester and interviewer effects, and the mode of administration. Method bias is used here as a label for all sources of bias emanating from factors often described in the methods section of empirical papers or study documentations. They range from differential stimulus familiarity in mental testing to differential social desirability in personality and survey research. Identification of methods bias requires detailed and explicit documentation of all the procedural steps in a study.

Among the various types of method bias, sample bias is more likely to increase with cultural distance. Recurrent rival explanations (which become more salient with a larger cultural distance) are cross-cultural differences in social desirability and stimulus familiarity (testwiseness). The main problem with both social desirability and testwiseness is their relationship with country affluence; more affluent countries tend to show lower scores on social desirability (see Chapter 13). Subject recruitment procedures are another source of sample bias in cognitive tests. For instance, the motivation to display one's attitudes or abilities may depend on

the amount of previous exposure to psychological tests, the freedom to participate or not, and other sources that may show cross-cultural variation.

Administration bias can be caused by differences in the procedures or mode used to administer an instrument. For example, when interviews are held in respondents' homes, physical conditions (e.g., ambient noise, presence of others) are difficult to control. Respondents are more prepared to answer sensitive questions in self-completion contexts than in the shared discourse of an interview. Examples of social environmental conditions are individual (versus group) administration, the physical space between respondents (in group testing), or class size (in educational settings). Other sources of administration that can lead to method bias are ambiguity in the questionnaire instructions and/or guidelines or a differential application of these instructions (e.g., which answers to open questions are considered to be ambiguous and require follow-up questions). The effect of test administrator or interviewer presence on measurement outcomes has been empirically studied; regrettably, various studies apply inadequate designs and do not cross the cultures of testers and testees. In cognitive testing, the presence of the tester is usually not very obtrusive (Jensen, 1980). In survey research there is more evidence for interviewer effects (Singer and Presser, 1989). Deference to the interviewer has been reported; subjects were more likely to display positive attitudes to a particular cultural group when they are interviewed by someone from that group (e.g., Aquilino, 1994). A final source of administration bias is constituted by communication problems between the respondent and the tester/interviewer. For example, interventions by interpreters may influence the measurement outcome. Communication problems are not restricted to working with translators. Language problems may be a potent source of bias when, as is not uncommon in cross-cultural studies, an interview or test is administered in the second or third language of interviewers or respondents. Illustrations for such miscommunications between native and nonnative speakers can be found in Gass and Varonis (1991).

Instrument bias is a common problem in cognitive tests. An interesting example comes from

Piswanger's (1975) application of the Viennese Matrices Test (Formann and Piswanger, 1979). A Raven-like figural inductive reasoning test was administered to high-school students in Austria, Nigeria, and Togo (where the medium of instruction is Arabic). The most striking findings were cross-cultural differences in item difficulties related to identifying and applying rules in a horizontal direction (i.e., left to right). These differences were interpreted as bias due to the different directions in writing Latin and Arabic.

The third type of bias distinguished here refers to anomalies at item level and is called *item bias* or *differential item functioning*. According to a definition that is widely used in education and psychology, an item is biased if respondents with the same standing on the underlying construct (e.g., they are equally intelligent), but who come from different cultures, do not have the same mean score on the item. The score on the construct is usually derived from the total test score. Of all bias types, item bias has been the most extensively studied; various psychometric techniques are available to identify item bias (e.g., Camilli and Shepard, 1994; Van de Vijver and Leung, 1997). In a globalized working environment, the standardized application of uniform managerial and human resource practices requires that we test the applicability of test items for different populations. Item bias primarily applies to instruments where the same items are used to measure the construct in different samples. Including emic items that are non-comparable across groups can be informative for cultural purposes, but such items mostly preclude direct comparison.

Although item bias can arise in various ways, poor item translation, ambiguities in the original item, low familiarity/appropriateness of the item content in certain cultures, and the influence of cultural specifics such as nuisance factors or connotations associated with the item wording are the most common sources. For instance, if a geography test administered to pupils in Poland and Japan contains the item "What is the capital of Poland?," Polish pupils can be expected to show higher scores on the item than Japanese students, even if pupils with the same total test score were compared. The item is biased because it favors one cultural group

across all test score levels. Even translations which are seemingly correct can produce problems. A good example is the test item "Where is a bird with webbed feet most likely to live?" which was part of a large international study of educational achievement (cf. Hambleton, 1994). Compared to the overall pattern, the item turned out to be unexpectedly easy in Sweden. An inspection of the translation revealed why: the Swedish translation of the English was "bird with swimming feet," which gives a strong clue to the solution not present in the English original.

How to deal with bias

The previous section contains real and fictitious examples of bias. It is important to note that bias can affect all stages of a project. Minimizing bias is thus not an exclusive concern of developers, administrators, or data analysts. Since bias can challenge all stages of a project, ensuring quality is a matter of combining good theory, questionnaire design, administration, and analysis. The present section presents various ways in which the types of bias discussed above can be dealt with.

A taxonomy of the main approaches to deal with bias is presented in table 18.2 (cf. Van de Vijver and Tanzer, 2004). Rather than attempting to provide an exhaustive taxonomy (which goes beyond the scope of the present chapter), an attempt is made to provide an overview of solutions that have been presented in the past and to suggest directions in which a possible solution may be found in the event that the table does not provide a ready-made answer.

It should be emphasized that the focus of this chapter is on comparative studies. Within this context, culture-specifics constitute a potential challenge to be overcome. This focus on similarity is sometimes seen as a focus on universal aspects and the denial of culture-specifics. We do not concur with this view as some of the most interesting cross-cultural differences may reside in the cultural specifics. Emic research which tries to understand the culture from within is very important and informative for organizational research (Bhagat and McQuaid, 1982). Knowledge of emic concepts is critical for conducting studies of that culture,

Table 18.2 Strategies for identifying and dealing with bias

Type of Bias	Strategies
Construct bias	• Decentering (i.e., simultaneously developing the same instrument in several cultures).
	• Convergence approach (i.e., independent within-culture development of instruments and subsequent cross-cultural administration of all instruments).
Construct bias and/or method bias	• Use of informants with expertise in local culture and language.
	• Use samples of bilingual subjects.
	• Use of local pilots (e.g., content analyses of free-response questions).
	• Nonstandard instrument administration (e.g., "thinking aloud").
	• Cross-cultural comparison of nomological networks (e.g., convergent/discriminant validity studies, monotrait-multimethod studies.
	• Connotation of key phrases (e.g., examination of similarity of meaning of frequently employed terms such as "somewhat agree").
Method bias	• Extensive training of interviewers.
	• Detailed manual/protocol for administration, scoring, and interpretation.
	• Detailed instructions (e.g., with sufficient number of examples and/or exercises).
	• Use of subject and context variables (e.g., educational background).
	• Use of collateral information (e.g., test-taking behavior or test attitudes).
	• Assessment of response styles.
	• Use of test-retest, training and/or intervention studies.
Item bias	• Judgmental methods of item bias detection (e.g., linguistic and psychological analysis).
	• Psychometric methods of item bias detection (e.g., Differential Item Functioning analysis).

even if the study would be culture-comparative. However, from a methodological vantage point, cultural specifics need to be handled with care as, by definition, they are difficult or even impossible to compare across cultures. So, the focus on bias in comparative research is not meant to eliminate culture-specifics but to tell these apart from more universal aspects and to ascertain which aspects are universal and which are culture specific.

The first example of dealing with *construct bias* is cultural decentering (Werner and Campbell, 1970). A modified example can be found in the study of Tanzer, Gittler, and Ellis (1995). Starting with a set of German intelligence/aptitude tests, they developed an English version of the test battery. Based on the results of pilot tests in Austria and the US, both the German and English instructions and stimuli were modified before the main study was carried out. In the so-called convergence approach estimates are independently developed in different cultures and all instruments are then administered to subjects in all these cultures (Campbell, 1986).

A second set of remedies aims at a combination of construct and method bias. Another example is a large acculturation project, called ICSEY (International Comparative Study of Ethnic Youth). The project studies both migrant and host adolescents and their parents in thirteen countries, including migrants from about fifty different ethnic groups. Prior to the data collection, researchers met to decide on which instruments would be used. Issues like adequacy of the instrument vis-à-vis construct coverage and translatability (e.g., absence of colloquialisms and metaphorical expressions) were already factored into the instrument design, thereby presumably avoiding various possible problems in later stages. Other measures taken include using informants with expertise in local culture and language, samples of bilingual individuals, local pilots (e.g., content analyses of free-response questions), nonstandard instrument administration (e.g., thinking aloud), and a pretest study of the connotation of key phrases.

The cross-cultural comparison of nomological networks constitutes an interesting possibility to examine construct and/or method bias. An advantage of this infrequently employed method is its broad applicability. The method is based on a comparison of the correlations of an instrument that may have indicators that vary considerably across countries with various other instruments. The adequacy of the instrument in each country is supported if it shows a pattern of positive, zero, and negative correlations that are expected on theoretical grounds. For example, views towards waste management, when measured with different items across countries, may have positive correlations with concern for the environment and air pollution and a zero correlation with religiosity. Nomological networks may also be different across cultures; Tanzer and Sim (1991) found, for example, that good students in Singapore worry more about their performance during tests than do weak students, whereas the contrary is commonly reported in many other countries. For the other components of test anxiety (i.e., tension, low confidence, and cognitive interference), no cross-cultural differences were found. The authors attributed the inverted worry-achievement relationship to characteristics of the Singaporean educational system, especially the "kiasu" (fear of losing out) syndrome, which is deeply entrenched in the Singaporean society, rather then to construct bias in the internal structure of test anxiety.

Various procedures have been developed that mainly address method bias. A first proposal involves the extensive training of administrators/interviewers. Such training and instructions are required in order to ensure that interviews are administered in the same way across cultural groups. If the cultures of the interviewer and the interviewee differ, as is common in studies involving multicultural groups, it is important to make the interviewers aware of the relevant cultural specifics such as taboo topics.

A related approach amounts to the development of a detailed manual and administration protocol. The manual should ideally specify the test or interview administration and describe contingency plans on how to intervene in common interview problems (e.g., specifying when and how follow-up questions should be asked in open questions).

The measures discussed attempt to reduce or eliminate unwanted cross-cultural differences in administration conditions so as to maximize the comparability of scores obtained. Additional measures are needed to deal with cross-cultural differences that cannot be controlled by careful selection and wording of questions or response alternatives. Education is a good example. Studies involving widely different groups cannot avoid that the samples studied differ substantially in educational background, which in turn may give rise to cross-cultural differences in scores obtained. In some studies it may be possible to match groups from different groups on education by sampling subjects from specified educational backgrounds. However, this approach can have serious limitations; the samples obtained may not be representative for their countries. This problem is particularly salient in comparisons of countries with a population with large differences in average educational level. For example, if samples of Canadian and South African adults are chosen that are matched on education, it is likely that at least one of the samples is not representative for its population. Clearly, if one is interested in a country comparison after controlling for education, this poor representativeness does not create a problem. If the two samples are obtained using some random sampling scheme, educational differences are likely to emerge. The question may then arise to what extent the educational differences can be held responsible for observed test score differences. For example, to what extent could differences in attitudes toward euthanasia be explained by educational differences? If individual-level data on education is available, various statistical techniques, such as covariance and regression analysis, can be used as to determine to what extent the observed country differences can be explained by educational differences (Poortinga and Van de Vijver, 1987). The use of such explanatory variables provides a valuable tool to examine the nature of cross-cultural score differences.

A perennial issue in survey research is the prevalence of response effects and styles, especially social desirability and acquiescence. Their role in cross-cultural research as a source of unwanted cross-cultural score differences should not be underestimated. For some of the response styles, questionnaires are available; for example, the Eysenck Personality Questionnaire (Eysenck and Eysenck, 1975) has a social desirability subscale that has been applied in many countries. When response styles are suspected of differentially influencing responses as obtained in different cultural groups, the administration of a questionnaire to assess the response style can provide a valuable tool to interpret cross-cultural score differences.

There is empirical evidence indicating that countries differ in their usage of response scales. Hui and Triandis (1989) found that Hispanics tended to choose extremes on a five-point rating scale more often than white Americans, but that this difference disappeared when a ten-point scale was used. Similarly, Oakland, Gulek, and Glutting (1996) assessed test-taking behaviors among Turkish children, and their results, similar to those obtained with American children, showed that these behaviors are significantly correlated with the WISC-R IQ.

There are two kinds of procedures to assess item bias: judgmental procedures, either linguistic or psychological, and psychometric procedures. An example of a linguistic procedure can be found in Grill and Bartel (1977). They examined the Grammatic Closure subtest of the Illinois Test of Psycholinguistic Abilities for bias against speakers of nonstandard forms of English. In the first stage, potentially biased items were identified. Error responses of American black and white children indicated that more than half the errors on these items were accounted for by responses that are appropriate in nonstandard forms of English.

Equivalence

Four different types of equivalence are proposed here (cf. Van de Vijver and Leung, 1997; for a discussion of many concepts of equivalence, see Johnson, 1998). *Construct inequivalence* amounts to comparing *apples and oranges* without raising the level of comparison to that of *fruit* (e.g., the comparison of Chinese and western *filial piety*, discussed above). If constructs are inequivalent, comparisons lack a shared attribute, which precludes any comparison.

Structural or functional equivalence is found if an instrument administered in different cultural groups shows structural equivalence measures the same construct in all these groups. Structural equivalence has been addressed for various cognitive tests (Jensen 1980), Eysenck's personality questionnaire (Barrett *et al.* 1998), and the so-called five-factor model of personality (McCrae and Costa, 1997). Structural equivalence does not presuppose the use of identical instruments across cultures. A depression measure may be based on different indicators in different cultural groups and still show structural equivalence.

The third type of equivalence is called *measurement unit equivalence.* Instruments show this if their measurement scales have the same units of measurement, but a different origin (such as the Celsius and Kelvin scales in temperature measurement). This type of equivalence assumes interval- or ratio-level scores (with the same measurement units in each culture). Measurement unit equivalence applies when the same instrument has been administered in different cultures and a source of bias with a fairly uniform influence on the items of an instrument affects test scores in the different cultural groups in a differential way; for example, social desirability and stimulus familiarity influence scores more in some cultures than in others. When the relative contribution of both bias sources cannot be estimated, the interpretation of group comparisons of mean scores remains ambiguous.

At first sight, it may seem unnecessary or even counterproductive to define a level of equivalence with the same measurement units, but different origins. After all, if we apply the same interval-level scale in different groups, scores may be either fully comparable or, as in the case of nonequivalence, fully incomparable. The need for the concept of measurement unit equivalence may become clear by looking at the impact of differential social desirability or stimulus familiarity on cross-cultural score differences in more detail. Differential social desirability will create an offset in the scale in one of the cross-cultural groups: a score of, say, five in group A may be comparable to a score of nine in group B because of a higher social desirability in group B. Observed group differences in mean scores are then a mixture of valid cross-cultural differences and measurement artifacts. A correction would be required to make the scores comparable (Fischer, 2004). It may be noted that the basic idea of score corrections needed to make scores fully comparable is also applied in covariance analysis, in which score comparisons are made after the disturbing role of concomitant factors (bias in the context of the present chapter) has been statistically controlled for.

Only in the case of *scalar (or full score) equivalence* can direct comparisons be made; this is the only type of equivalence that allows for the conclusion that average scores obtained in two cultures are different or equal. Scalar equivalence assumes the identical interval or ratio scales across cultural groups. It is often difficult to decide whether equivalence in a given case is scalar equivalence or measurement equivalence. For example, ethnic differences in intelligence test scores have been interpreted as due to valid differences (scalar equivalence) as well as reflecting measurement artifacts (measurement unit equivalence). Scalar equivalence assumes that the role of bias can be safely neglected. However, verification of scalar equivalence relies on inductive evidence. Thus it is easier to disprove scalar equivalence than to prove it (cf. Popper's falsification principle). Measuring presumably relevant sources of bias (such as stimulus familiarity or social desirability) and showing that they cannot statistically explain observed cross-cultural differences in a multiple regression or covariance analysis is an example of falsifying a rival hypothesis.

Structural, measurement unit, and scalar equivalence are hierarchically ordered. The third presupposes the second, which presupposes the first. As a consequence, higher levels of equivalence are more difficult to establish. It is easier to verify that an instrument measures the same construct in different cultural groups (structural equivalence) than to identify numerical comparability across cultures (scalar equivalence). But one should bear in mind that higher levels of equivalence allow for more detailed comparisons of scores across cultures. Whereas only factor structures and nomological networks can be compared in the case of structural equivalence, measurement unit and full score or scalar equivalence allow for more fine grained analyses of cross-cultural similarities and differences, such as comparisons of mean scores across cultures in *t* tests and analyses of (co)variance.

The use of exploratory and confirmatory factor analysis in establishing equivalence. The most common technique for establishing structural equivalence is factor analysis. Both exploratory and confirmatory factor analysis can be used to address structural equivalence. The former amounts to a comparison of factor loadings (computational details can be found in Van de Vijver and Leung, 1997). Suppose that an instrument to measure organizational commitment is administered to employees in two countries. The same number of factors is extracted in both countries. The solution of one country is then rotated to the solution of the other country. This step is necessary to correct for the rotational freedom in exploratory factor analysis. In the last step of the procedure the agreement is computed for each factor extracted. A common statistic to compute the factorial agreement is known as Tucker's (1951) phi, originally proposed by Burt. This statistic computes the identity of two factors up to a positive multiplying constant. Factors in different countries with identical eigenvalues should have identical factor loadings, whereas factors with different eigenvalues are first corrected by multiplying the loadings with a positive constant so as to equate their eigenvalues. Allowing eigenvalues to differ across cultures before comparing the loadings is based on the reasoning that factors with different reliabilities across cultures can still measure the same underlying construct.

There are two different ways in which factor structures can be compared across cultures. The first procedure involves a pairwise comparison of factor structures across all countries. This strategy can quickly become cumbersome is the number of countries involved is large. A comparison of n countries involves $n \times (n - 1)/2$ comparisons. Comparing ten cultures already amounts to forty-five comparisons. The second procedure involves a comparison of all cultures to a single target culture (in which an instrument measuring the instrument was developed and validated) or to a pooled solution (to which all countries contribute either equally or weighted by their sample size). If the number of countries is relatively small, a researcher may decide to compare each country to the pooled solution of the other countries to avoid that a country contributes to the overall solution to which it is compared. The number of comparisons to be made is equal to the number of countries involved; a ten-country study would involve ten comparisons. The procedure in which a single solution for all countries is used as reference has become standard both in exploratory and confirmatory factor analysis. The reasons for this choice are computational simplicity and scientific parsimony (a single model accounts for the data in all countries). However, the procedure is problematic if there are homogeneous clusters of countries with different solutions. Suppose that we administer an instrument to measure depression in various countries and that the items cover both somatic and psychological symptoms of depression. It is known from the literature that various (non-western) cultures are less likely to endorse the psychological symptoms than the somatic symptoms (Van de Vijver and Tanaka-Matsumi, 2008). It may well be that the instrument is unidimensional in western cultures and bidimensional in non-western cultures. Pairwise solutions are better equipped to identify such homogeneous clusters. A cluster analysis of factorial agreement indices would show the different clusters which is more difficult to find in the analysis of a pooled solution.

Confirmatory factor analysis follows a different procedure. Compared with the exploratory factor analytic procedure, the testing of structural equivalence using confirmatory factor analysis is based on more rigorous statistical procedures and includes more parameters than factor loadings. Suppose that our scale of organizational commitment measures two correlated factors in both countries. The evaluation of equivalence in a confirmatory factor analysis consists of a number of hierarchically ordered tests. The first step tests whether the factor analytic solutions in the two countries have the same configuration which means that the same indicators should load on the same factors. This constellation is called "configural invariance." Assuming that an acceptable fit is found for this model, we can proceed to the next step by selecting parameters of the model that should be identical across cultures. It is

customary to test the identity of factor loadings in the next step ("measurement weights"), followed by a test of the identity of regression intercepts of the observed variables on their latent factors, identity of factor covariances, the identity of the structural residuals (i.e., identity of error components of the latent factors), and finally the identity of measurement residuals (i.e., identity of the error components of items). Examples from the organizational literature can be found in Ployhart et al. (2003) and Vandenberg and Lance (2000).

In our view, there are two kinds of problems with the use of structural equation modeling in cross-cultural organizational research. The first issue involves the assumption (often implicitly made in empirical applications of invariance tests) that a positive outcome of a test of invariance demonstrates that there is no bias in the instrument. The assumption is also used in the context of differential item functioning. An instrument from which all bias items have been removed is assumed to show valid cross-cultural score differences. The assumption is not correct. It is correct to argue that a failure to find invariance points to the presence of bias; however, it is quite possible that there is bias even if a test of invariance produces favorable results. The problem is a consequence of the absence of a rigorous test of construct bias in standard tests of invariance. An instrument that measures filial piety according to its western conceptualization leaves out important aspects of the concept in a non-western context, even if the instrument would show the highest level of cross-cultural invariance. There is a second and related assumption in invariance testing that also requires scrutiny; we refer here to the assumption, again often implicit, that a comparison of means based on instruments that have shown invariance shows cross-cultural differences that are only related to the target construct. The assumption is problematic because the influence of sources of method variance with a pervasive influence on items, such as acquiescence or social desirability, may not have been ruled out. It should be pointed out that the problematic nature of these assumptions is not a consequence of the statistical properties of structural equation models but of their current usage. There are indeed examples of cross-cultural studies in which structural equation modeling is used to examine the influence of acquiescence on cross-cultural score differences (Welkenhuysen-Gybels, Billiet, and Cambré, 2003).

A second problem in the use of structural equation modeling in cross-cultural studies involves the use and interpretation of fit statistics. There is a rich literature on fit statistics. Cheung and Rensvold (2002) conducted a simulation study to evaluate various fit statistics to test invariance in two-country comparisons. They suggest the use of increases in Bentler's comparative fit index, Steiger's gamma hat, and McDonald's noncentrality index in invariance testing. Their results, though very useful, should be complemented by more empirical studies in which the suitability of these guidelines are tested and by more Monte Carlo studies in which extensions to commonly applied fit indices such as the AGFI and to larger numbers of countries are studied. We do not yet know how we can adequately evaluate model fit in cross-cultural projects that involve dozens of countries. It has been proposed that an alternative way of overcoming fit problems could be the use of so-called item parcels (e.g., Little et al., 2002). Items are combined in parcels so as to reduce the impact of item particulars on model fit such as differential skewness and kurtosis of items across countries. Cross-cultural differences in these distributional properties can lead to a poor fit, although they may be minor and psychologically trivial. The use of item parcels could hold an important promise for cross-cultural research. However, their current usage is hampered by two factors. The first is the absence of generally accepted ways as to how items should be clustered. The second is related to the first; it has been demonstrated that bias in items may remain unnoticed if biased items are included in parcels with unbiased items (Meade and Kroustalis, 2006).

Explaining cross-cultural differences

Experienced cross-cultural researchers know that it is often easier to find significant cross-cultural differences in mean scores than to provide a conclusive interpretation of these differences. An important methodological aspect of cross-cultural research is to rule out alternative interpretations (Campbell, 1986). For example, suppose that a study shows that turnover intention is higher among employees in a US company than in a Japanese company. A first interpretation could be that the observed difference reflects a real cross-cultural difference which is in line with the lower labor market mobility of Japanese workers (as compared to American workers). However, various alternative interpretations could be offered. The first one would be that the construct or particular items are biased (e.g., the factor structure of the instrument is not the same in the two countries or some items are inadequate for the American employees). It could also be that the nature of the companies was different (e.g., the Japanese company is known to be a good, well paying employer), that the educational level of the employees was different (e.g., the Japanese employees were less schooled which makes them less mobile), or that the Japanese workers were less inclined to admit that they consider to quit their job. A common way to examine the validity of these interpretations is to include relevant operationalizations in the research so that its impact can be investigated. For example, a social desirability questionnaire is administered and a covariance analysis is carried out to examine whether cross-cultural differences are significant after social desirability differences in the two countries have been taken into account. The validity of our original interpretation of the cross-cultural differences (in terms individualism – collectivism) increases when we can rule out more alternative interpretations.

The search for validations of cross-cultural differences has an interesting and possibly unexpected corollary. Suppose that the differences in the above example are no longer significant if country differences in social desirability have been taken into account. Such a finding has an important psychological implication: the cross-cultural differences in turnover intention have to be seen as differences in social desirability. Japanese and American employees with the same level of social desirability are expected to have the same turnover intention. We may think that we observe cross-cultural differences in turnover intention, but what we actually observe are correlates of cross-cultural differences in social desirability. The cross-cultural literature contains various examples of how cross-cultural differences in target variables are shown to be reflections of other variables. For example, many differences between immigrant groups and mainstreamers in the acculturation literature are a function of the differences in socioeconomic status or education of the groups. Arends-Tóth and Van de Vijver (2008) found that the more traditional family values of non-western immigrant groups in the Netherlands (as compared to the Dutch mainstream group) can be largely explained by differences in education. Immigrants and mainstreamers with the same educational background do not show substantial differences in family values.

The methodological approach to validate interpretations of observed score differences in cross-cultural studies is known as "unpackaging" (Bond and Van de Vijver, 2008; Whiting, 1976). The idea is that observed score differences in target variables should be the starting point of further inquiry and that an examination of the antecedents of these differences is required; the differences should be "unpackaged." This process of unpackaging may involve the confirmation of intended interpretations (e.g., a measure of individualism – collectivism is administered and can statistically account for the observed cross-cultural differences in turnover intention); the process may also involve the disconfirmation of non-target explanations (e.g., the educational level of employees is measured so that we can statistically examine whether cross-cultural differences in education can explain away the differences in turnover intention). If researchers have a larger number of cultural groups, multilevel analyses can provide a powerful and elegant alternative for addressing bias issues. Conceptually similar to the "unpackaging," culture level variables can be used to examine whether they explain the observed cultural differences at the individual level. Although equivalence and multilevel approaches are often treated as separate topics, both approaches can be used to address questions of bias and equivalence (if large samples are available; see Fontaine, 2008).

Multilevel issues in organizational research

The literature on multilevel issues in organizational research has a comparatively long tradition. This is not surprising, given that managers have to deal with issues at the level of individuals, dyads, work groups, departments, and whole organizations. If organizational theories do only apply at one level (let us say the individual) and are misspecified at another level (work group or department), then organizational survival might be threatened and the manager could potentially lose his/her job if such theories were applied at the wrong level. Interest in multi-level research has increased exponentially over the last few decades with an associated sophistication and diversification of approaches (Kozlowski and Klein, 2000). Special issues on level issues in prestigious journals such as *Academy of Management Review*, *Leadership Quarterly*, and *Journal of International Business Studies* have been published, and there have been dedicated books and book series on the topic from organizational perspectives (e.g., Dansereau Alutto, and Yammarino, 1984; Klein and Kozlowski, 2000a; Yammarino and Dansereau, 2002–2007). The conceptual and statistical models that have been developed allow for an integrated treatment of the three basic issues of multilevel modeling mentioned before (What is the appropriate level of a theory (and data)? Is there a change in meaning of the same construct after (dis)aggregation?) Nevertheless, the research practice shows a more fragmented picture.

Identifying the appropriate level of theory and data

The first step for any research project should be the identification of the appropriate level to which generalizations should be made (Klein, Dansereau, and Hall, 1994). Are we proposing a theory that explains the motivation of individuals, interaction patterns between individuals in teams or the behavior of larger organizations? Although this may seem rather straightforward, the definition of the appropriate level can often be quite ambiguous. For example, many constructs such as justice perceptions, self-efficacy, or affect were thought to capture individual-level constructs, but, more recently, researchers have demonstrated these processes can also be described at higher levels; see work on justice climate (Colquitt, Noe, and Jackson 2002), group efficacy (Bandura, 1997), and group affect (George and James, 1993).

To help with the development of theory and research, Klein, Dansereau, and Hall (1994) outlined three alternative assumptions underlying any theoretical model: *homogeneity, independence,* and *heterogeneity.*

Homogeneity (or wholes in Dansereau, Alutto, and Yammarino's (1984) terminology) refers to the homogeneity of subunits within higher level units. Variability within units is seen as error. Using individuals within groups as an example, "group members are sufficiently similar with respect to the construct in question that they may be characterized as a whole" (Klein, Dansereau, and Hall 1994, p. 199). A single value or characteristic is then seen as sufficient to describe the group as a whole. Aggregation of responses by individuals within groups is justified if individuals within a specific unit agree with each other about the psychological meaning of the construct. In the theoretically ideal case, true variation only occurs between groups or units, but not within (James, 1982) and true effects exists only between units, phenomena are shared and identical within units and within-unit variability is error. In cross-cultural psychology, the common definition of culture as a shared meaning system (e.g., Hofstede, 1980, 2001; Rohner, 1984) would follow a homogeneity assumption.

The second assumption is *independence.* Subunits are independent from higher-level units. For example, individuals would be free of group influence. This assumption is made by many statistical tests (e.g., individual scores are independent from each other). This assumption treats group membership as irrelevant and the only true variation is between individuals (e.g., individual differences). Psychological approaches to human behavior have often been criticized for strongly adhering to this assumption (Sampson, 1981).

The final assumption is called *heterogeneity,* *"frog-pond", within-group* or *parts effect* (e.g., Dansereau et al., 1984). Comparative or relative effects are theorized and absolute effects are not important. A frog may be comparatively small in a big pond, but the same frog would appear large if the pond was smaller. The main assumption is therefore that effects are context-dependent, with any score depending on the respective level of scores in the unit of interest. The classical example is social comparison processes (Festinger, 1954). Individuals compare themselves with others and the standing relative to the standard or referent is important. Therefore, individuals vary within groups, the group itself is a meaningful entity and necessary as a contextual anchor, but variations between groups are not the key focus.

These theoretical issues have implications for both operationalization of constructs and sampling. Having theoretically defined an intended level of analysis, researchers need to decide how to best operationalize their theoretical constructs. Composition models (Chan, 1998) address how constructs can be measured at various levels. They "specify the functional relationship among phenomena or constructs at different levels of analysis ... that reference essentially the same content but that are qualitatively different at different levels" (Chan, 1998, p. 234). These models are helpful for conceptual precision in construct development and measurement since they deal with the content of dimensions and item wording.

Most constructs can be defined and investigated at various levels. Values as an example have been measured at the level of the individual, organization, and nation. At the level of the individual we would deal with an individual construct, whereas at the organization or nation level it reflects a collective construct. This distinction between individual and collective constructs is important (Morgeson and Hofmann, 1999). Individual-level constructs pertain to individuals and may reflect neuro-physiological or genetic processes, individual learning or specific and idiosyncratic life experiences. It may also be possible to describe the average level of any individual-level construct within a particular group. Aggregations of individual level constructs are possible, but the nature and function of such aggregates remains purely at the individual level.

In contrast, collective constructs clearly operate at the higher collective level and can not be broken down to the individual level. Morgeson and Hofmann (1999, p. 253) highlight that: "Collective structures emerge, are transmitted and persist through the actions of members of the collective (or the collective as a whole)." Speaking of the

Table 18.3 A classification of aggregate and collective constructs

Name of model	Level of observation	Agreement within group	Referent
Selected score model	Collection of individuals	Not necessary	Individual
Summary index model	Collection of individuals	Not necessary	Individual
Dispersion model	Collection of individuals	Not necessary	Individual
Referent shift model	Collective	Necessary	Aggregate
Aggregate model	Collective	NA	Aggregate
Consensus model	Fuzzy	Necessary	Individual

"collective climate" of an individual, for example, would be inappropriate and most people would agree that this does not make sense. Collective climate needs a group context to become meaningful. As Morgenson and Hofmann (1999, p. 252) put it:

> Mutual dependence (or interdependence) between individuals creates a context for their interaction. This interaction, in turn, occasions a jointly produced behavior pattern, which lies between the individuals involved. Collective action, thus, has a structure that inheres in the double interact rather than within either of the individuals involved. As interaction occurs within larger groups of individuals, a structure of collective action emerges that transcends the individuals who constitute the collective.

We briefly describe six different composition models. The statistical properties and origins of the model are more fully described in Chen, Mathieu, and Bliese (2004), Fischer (2008) and Hofmann and Jones (2004). We will describe these models in relation to individuals, organizations and nations, although these models are applicable to any other theoretical level (dyads, teams, departments, industries, regions, etc.).

The first three models in table 18.3 describe collections of individuals. The *selected score model* refers to an aggregate defined through a specific score at the individual level. This model most often applies to boundary conditions. For example, in the team productivity literature, team performance might be constrained by the lowest performing individual (Steiner, 1972). Therefore, one selected score would identify the higher level score, but the score is still at the level of the individual.

The *summary index model* describes groups through the aggregate of a variable of interest at the

individual level. We could, for example, measure the personality of all group members and then assign the average personality profile to each group. Therefore, the mean of an individual level variable is assigned to a whole work group. According to Hofmann and Jones (2004), the summary index model reflects the mean or sum of a construct for a collection of *individuals*, but it does not provide any meaningful information about the collective (work group in our example). These mean scores are therefore best interpreted as the central tendency of individuals.

The final individual level model is the *dispersion model*. Here, the variability or distribution of characteristics or properties rather than their central indices are of interest. It is similar to the previous summary index model in that it represents descriptive statistics of individuals within a unit or group. This variability is most commonly assessed using indicators of within-group variance (e.g., Naumann and Bennett, 2001). Value diversity within groups can be assessed with dispersion models (Williams and O'Reilly, 1998).

Collective constructs can be measured using the next three models in table 18.3. According to Hofmann and Jones (2004), both the referent-shift models and aggregate properties models provide clear and non-ambiguous assessment of true collective constructs. *Referent-shift models* were developed in climate research (Chan, 1998; Glick, 1985) to avoid conceptual confusions between individual (psychological) and organizational (collective) climate. Referent-shift models ask individuals to answer items focusing on the higher-level unit of investigation (work group or organization). Therefore, the referent is changed from "I" to "we" or "this group." Hence, a value item would look like "In this workgroup, people value power."

An essential step for referent-shift models is the assessment of agreement prior to aggregation. Data should only be aggregated if there is sufficient agreement (see below). Hence, the marked characteristics of this model are (a) focusing responses of individuals on the higher unit (instead of self-reports) and (b) an evaluation of agreement to justify aggregation (since agreement would indicate a collective construct). Referent-shift models are similar to summary-index models in that both require reports of individuals. However, summary-index models measure self-reports of individuals about their own characteristics, attitudes, abilities or values and these reports are aggregated without assessing agreement.

The second model of collective constructs is the *aggregate properties model*. This is the simplest model in that the construct directly reflects the higher unit. For example, the number of individuals working in an organization, the number of hierarchical levels or distributions of experts throughout departments are clear indicators of organizational-level characteristics. Expert ratings are also valid (e.g., ratings on organizational performance or innovation characteristics by the CEO).

The final model in this typology is the *consensus model*. Compared to the other two models, it is conceptually more complex, ambiguous or fuzzy (Hofmann and Jones, 2004). It may indicate a collective construct, since it is essentially an individual-level construct, but for which agreement exists. For example, if ratings of an item such as "I am happy" were found to be homogeneous within work groups or organizations, it would be justified to aggregate the scores to a higher level (this dependency at the individual level would also lead to biases and wrong statistical estimates at the individual level if not aggregated; Barcikowski, 1981; Bliese and Hanges, 2004; Kenny and Judd, 1986). Therefore, this model is similar to both the summary index model (by using individual-referenced items) and referent-shift consensus model (by showing sufficient agreement).

Hofmann and Jones (2004) prefer referent-shift models over direct-consensus models because direct-consensus models are ambiguous by providing an index of the shared level of individual-level characteristics within the culture, whereas the referent-shift consensus model represents the collective construct directly. Hofmann and Jones (2004) treat direct-consensus models as (indirect) markers for true collective constructs with referent-shift models being preferred for measuring collective constructs (Klein, Dansereau, and Hall, 1994; Kozlowski and Klein, 2000; Morgeson and Hofmann, 1999).

Assessment of agreement

Agreement is essential for developing true collective construct measures. A number of indicators are available and there has been a healthy debate in the literature about the appropriateness and empirical cut-off criteria for sufficient agreement that justify aggregation. One of the older and widely used indices is r_{wg}, developed by James, Demaree and Wolf (1984, 1993). This index focuses on consensus or agreement within a single unit; for example, a work group. This index compares the variability of a variable within a work group to some expected variability. If the observed variability is substantially smaller than the expected variance, the resulting value of r_{wg} is closer to 1, suggesting high agreement and that aggregation is possible. The index ranges from 0 to 1, although negative or values larger than 1 are possible (James, Demaree, and Wolf 1984; Klein and Kozlowski, 2000b). In contrast to reliability estimates that are based on the inter-item correlation, this index uses information about the variability (variance) within units.

Over the years, this index has been used widely but also has been strongly criticized. Brown and Hauenstein (2005) discussed a number of shortcomings of this indicator, among others the dependence on the number of scale options (the more scale options, the higher the agreement with everything else being equal), the dependence on the sample size (the greater the sample size, the higher the agreement, everything else being equal) and problems with the assumption of the null distribution (which is typically a rectangular distribution). They proposed an alternative measure a_{wg}. The maximum possible variance at the mean is being used as the null distribution. Agreement is then calculated as the 1 minus twice the observed variance divided by the maximum possible variance. The range of the index varies between -1 and 1.

A value of 1 means perfect agreement, a value of -1 indicates perfect disagreement and a value of 0 indicates that the variability is fifty percent of the possible variance at the mean. There are no statistical significance tests associated with a_{wg}. A .70 cut-off value has been proposed as a heuristic for moderate agreement, with values of less than .59 being seen as unacceptable if the construct is supposed to reflect group-level constructs (Brown and Hauenstein, 2005). Previous research has focused on agreement around specific and well-defined aspects in small groups within organizations. The critical values calculated by Brown and Hauenstein (2005) are based only on groups smaller than twenty; consequently those guidelines might be overly conservative with larger groups (such as organizations or nations). However, the index is a significant improvement since it overcomes several shortcomings of the widely used r_{wg}.

A second class of statistics to evaluate the extent to which perceptions are shared are intra-class correlations (ICC) (James, 1982; Shrout and Fleiss, 1979). Two types are commonly in use, ICC(1) and ICC(2). The first is essentially based on a random one-way analysis of variance and provides an estimate of the proportion of the total variance of a measure that is explained by unit membership (Bliese, 2000). A second interpretation of ICC(1) is as an estimate of the extent to which any one rater may represent all the raters within a group, the question of whether raters are interchangeable (James, 1982). The advantage of ICC(1) over other estimates such as eta-squared is that it is independent of group size (Bliese, 2000; Klein and Kozlowski, 2000b).

ICC(2) is used to answer the question about reliability of group means within a sample. ICC(2) values like any measure of reliability should exceed .70 to be judged as acceptable. This index is a variant of ICC(1), basically ICC(1) adjusted for group size (Bliese, 2000). Similar to other measures of reliability (e.g., Cronbach's alpha), the larger the group size, the larger ICC(2). This is based on the logic that group means based on many people per group are more stable and reliable than group means derived from only a few members. One important difference between r_{wg} and ICC is that r_{wg} focuses on agreement within each group separately (yielding one estimate for each group separately), whereas

ICC compares the variability within groups to the variability between groups (yielding one estimate across all groups). One problem that may emerge is that the interrater agreement varies substantially between groups. This can be incorporated in theoretical models as the concept of climate strength (Schneider, Salvaggio, and Subirats, 2002) and its effects can be tested (Colquitt, Noe, and Jackson 2002; Lindell and Brandt, 2000).

The identification of the appropriate level of data and analysis also has implications for sampling. Theoretical concerns are important again. Many nations have long histories of immigration and cultural heterogeneity (US, Canada, India, Switzerland, Malaysia, etc.), whereas other nations have been traditionally been more homogeneous in their cultural make-up (Japan, France, Portugal, etc.). Economic migrants also increase cultural diversity in many nations around the world. Rohner (1984) argued that cultural systems consist of equivalent and complimentary meaning systems. Researchers therefore need to identify those elements that are equivalent (shared by all cultural insiders) and those that are complimentary (where cultural knowledge is specific to roles and groups). Researchers should sample their research participants in line with the focus of their study. In the case of multicultural samples due to presence of minorities, migrants or the organizational context (multinationals, subsidiaries), indices of dispersion can be included in the theoretical model (e.g., Fischer et al., 2005). In these situations it can be tested whether cultural effects are stronger if they are widely shared within a nation. The above-mentioned indicators of agreement can be used and implemented in research design and analysis. It is also possible to develop models of cultural dispersion to explain cultural phenomena. Gelfand, Nishii, and Raver (2006) developed a multilevel theory of tightness-looseness to account for variability in individual and organizational variables. These theoretical innovations are exciting avenues to explain cultural phenomena as well as addressing issues of increasing cultural change.

A variance approach to levels research

Dansereau, Alutto, and Yammerino, (1984) developed a variance-based approach to test the appropriate level of a theory. Their "within and between analysis" (WABA) is a complex set of statistical techniques based on ANOVA logic to represent relationships. WABA can be used to test (a) the extent to which a construct varies within- or between-units (WABA I) and (b) to which extent two or more variables covary primarily within-units, between-units or both within- and between-units (WABA II). Therefore, WABA I can be used to assess to what extent variables measured at a lower level can be aggregated to a higher level. WABA II then offers a set of techniques to analyse the appropriate level of the relationships among variables. Data for each variable are divided into within-entities (deviation from the unit average) and between-entity (between unit averages). There are three basic steps. First, each variable is examined to what extent it varies mainly between groups (suggesting homogeneity within groups), within groups (suggesting heterogeneity within groups) or both between and within groups (suggesting individual differences rather than homogeneity or heterogeneity). Second, the relationships between variables are examined to see whether correlations are mainly a function of between-group covariances, within-group covariances and within- and between covariances. These two steps are then assessed for consistency and integrated to draw some overall conclusions about the most appropriate level of analysis (see Dansereau, Alutto, and Yammarino, 1984; Yammarino and Markham, 1992).

The unique aspect of WABA is the availability of tests of practical significance (E, A, and R tests) in addition to statistical significance (t, F and Z tests). These tests of practical significance are geometrically based and do not rely on sample size (degrees of freedom). WABA can also be used to study moderator effects (termed multiple relationship analysis MRA) (Schriesheim, Castro, and Yammarino, 2000).

WABA is a fairly flexible technique that has relatively few assumptions (essentially all the assumptions of ANOVA and regression analyses; see Castro, 2002). The technique does not make any assumptions about the appropriate level of relationships and researchers can test alternative levels of analysis. Therefore, dependent and independent variables are not constrained to any particular level of analysis and researchers can explore the most appropriate level. This is also a limitation since the analyses are completely data driven and testing all possible relationships may not make much theoretical sense (George and James, 1993). However, for the final test of bivariate relationships (WABA II), the relationships need to be at the same level. MRA also requires that the moderator is at a higher level (see Castro, 2002). The practical tests (the E-test in WABA I) has been criticized for being too conservative when group sizes increase (Bliese and Halverson, 1998). With large groups (e.g., using organizations or nations), achieving practical significance becomes difficult. George and James (1993) also noted that restrictions of between-group variance (e.g., when sampling multiple teams from one organizations) may lead to misspecifications of the WABA I equations. A final limitation that might be of particular interest for cross-cultural researchers is that WABA is not applicable in cases in which the relationship between variables x and y differs depending on the group (a person x situation/group interaction). If the relationships differ significantly across groups, the fundamental WABA equation will be meaningless since it follows the logic of ANCOVA that assumes equality of regressions lines (George and James, 1993). This is a concern for cross-cultural researchers, since it is a well-known phenomenon that relationships can be culture-specific (see, for example, the discussion of functional and structural equivalence above). Nevertheless, WABA has much to be recommended for cross-cultural research, since the technique can integrate various seemingly divergent multi-level perspectives (Dansereau and Yammarino, 2006).

Assessing changes of meaning of the same construct after aggregation

The previous section was concerned with the determination of the appropriate level of analysis. The implicit assumption was that the meaning of constructs remains the same. Organizational researchers using the methods described above have been less concerned with meaning changes during aggregation. In contrast, this has been a central concern for the approaches that are discussed next.

It is important to note that the methods described in these two sections have been independently developed and an integration is needed (see Peterson and Castro, 2006). Methods that were discussed in the bias and equivalence section can be used to address changes in meaning since it is a different form of equivalence (equivalence of meaning across levels).

Establishing factor structures at more than one level

Hofstede (1980) using a large cross-cultural dataset showed that the factor structures at the individual and national level can be different. This finding has led to a substantive interest among cross-cultural researchers in the structure of constructs at various levels. As discussed previously, WABA shows that within- and between structures are independent and can lead to completely different relationships. There are three statistical techniques that have been used for establishing equivalence across levels: multidimensional scaling, exploratory factor analysis and confirmatory factor analysis (for a more detailed description see Fontaine, 2008; Fischer, 2008; van de Vijver and Leung, 1997).

First, it would be important to analyze the structure at the individual level. As discussed before, within and between-group covariances are mathematically independent. Therefore, it is best to compare factor structures pairwise between nations or better, compare each nation with a pooled factor structure that gives equal weight to each group (and removes the between-group covariance component). Using the total covariance matrix across all participants irrespective of groups will lead to a mixing of within and between-effects. This should be avoided since it blurs the relative structures. Once an acceptable factorial structure (using acceptable agreement across individual solutions, see above) is found across cultural groups, it can be tested to what extent this individual-level structure has a comparable structure at the aggregate level. The aggregated between group correlation or covariance structure is factor analyzed or analyzed using multi-dimensional scaling. This between-group structure is then compared to the average individual-level solution (Muthén, 1994; van de Vijver and Poortinga, 2002). As we have discussed

previously, it would be important to test within-group agreement and between-group variability prior to aggregation. Sufficient between-group variability is obviously necessary, otherwise there would be nothing to model at the higher level. Therefore, this step of assessing between-group variability (the use of ICC(1)) is included in most recommendations of multi-level factor analysis (e.g., Muthén, 1991, 1994; van de Vijver and Poortinga, 2002).

The comparison of individual solutions at the individual level followed by a comparison with the aggregated matrix is a necessary step for all three techniques (although programmes like MPlus now allow simultaneous estimation of within- and between-group structures, see Fontaine, 2008). For MDS and EFA, an additional step is necessary. As discussed above, the structures need to be rotated to maximal similarity to allow comparisons across levels. Factorial agreement indices are available (see van de Vijver and Leung, 1997) and allow estimation of the similarity at the factor-level. CFA does not require this rotational sub-step. CFA is also more sophisticated, in that it allows for theory-driven constraints of parameters across levels and provides statistical tests for differences of individual parameters across levels. However, a drawback of CFA is that this technique has more assumptions (e.g., multivariate normality), fit indices are sample size dependent and there is a continuing debate about appropriate indicators of fit (see the discussion above).

In summary, the question of changes in meaning of constructs across levels due to aggregation is contentious, but can readily be addressed through multidimensional scaling or factor analysis at both levels. The structures can then be compared and inferences about the similarity or differences can be made. The previous section on the appropriate level of analysis has also demonstrated that it is theoretically possible that structures will be different since the within- and between-group covariance matrices are mathematically independent. These MDS and factor analytical techniques can be implemented without examining agreement or variance components. However, the two questions are complementary and ideally should be integrated.

Relationship between different constructs across levels

The final question addresses how different constructs are related across levels. We can distinguish three broad types of models: single-level models, cross-level models and homologous multi-level models (Klein and Kozlowski, 2000b). Single-level models are the most common models in that they are dealing with relationships between construct at one level of theory only. This level may be the individual, group, organization or nation-level. Psychologists and management researchers are most familiar with individual-level models, management researchers often deal with models at the team or organizational level and cross-cultural psychologists and sociologists are also familiar with models at the nation-level. Since single level models do not deal with constructs at a higher or level of analysis, they are straightforward analyzable using traditional analytical techniques such as correlation, multiple regression or structural equation modeling. If single-level models are conceptualized at a higher level and based on aggregation of lower-level data, all the steps addressed in relation to the first two questions need to be followed.

Cross-level models are the most complex models since they conceptualize relationships between variables across different levels. Organizational researchers are most familiar with top-down approaches that model effects of higher level variables on lower level variables (e.g., organizational climate influencing employee job satisfaction or performance). The alternative process of emergent or bottom-up processes is equally plausible, but empirical research on such processes is as yet sparse (Kozlowski and Klein, 2000). This is an area which has much potential for further theoretical development, particularly since it addresses essential questions such as how collectives develop and can be changed. Such research needs to be time-sensitive since emergent processes are slower and show delayed effects compared to top-down models (Klein and Kozlowski, 2000b). The statistical technique most suited to address emergent processes at this stage is WABA.

However, in the following we will focus on the three broad types of top-down models (Klein and Kozlowski, 2000b, Klein, Dansereau, and Hall 1994): direct effects, moderator and frog-pond cross-level models. The first model conceptualizes and examines direct or main effects of a higher level variable on one variable at a lower level. For example, we could estimate whether macro-economic development or thermal climate at the nation-level affects the willingness of individuals to volunteer within nations (van de Vliert, Huang, and Levine, 2004). In this case, both macro-economic and thermal climate are clear nation-level variables and their effect on the means within nations are estimated. Cross-level direct effects models can be used for unpackaging cultural effects and to investigate bias issues. When a large number of cultural samples is available (ideally twenty or more samples), researchers can first estimate the cross-cultural differences (e.g., using ICC(1)). As discussed above, these differences are often ambiguous to interpret and can arise due to substantive processes as well as a number of biases. If this variability can be explained using variables at a higher level (e.g., individualism-collectivism, national wealth), biases can be eliminated as alternative explanations or the relative effect of potential bias can be estimated (by examining how much variance is unexplained after accounting for the explanatory variables of interest).

Cross-level moderator models are complementary to direct effect models since they additionally examine whether a higher level variable changes the relationship between two lower level variables. More complex models are also possible. For example, Huang, van de Vliert, and van der Vegt (2006) studied whether power distance at the nation-level changed the relationship between employment involvement and participative climate on employee voice (a proactive tendency to make suggestions about improvements) at the organizational level. Therefore, the dependent variable at the organizational level was employee voice, the two independent variables at the organizational level were participative climate and formalized employee involvement, the independent variable at the nation-level was power distance. They found a three-way interaction across levels. Power distance changed the relationship between employee involvement and employee voice, but only if participative climate is high. In high power distant nations, formalized employee involvement is associated with increased employee voice, but only if there is a strong participative climate. Cross-level moderator models can also be used to address bias issues. For example, acquiescence and extreme responding are forms of method bias that threatens measurement unit and full-score equivalence. Smith and Fischer (2008) tested whether individual differences and culture-level variables together explain variability in these response styles. They found significant interactions, highlighting that individual dispositions and cultural variables have interactive effects on the willingness of respondents to acquiesce or express extreme opinions in survey research. For example, interdependent individuals in contexts in which it is acceptable to express affect freely (high affective autonomy) were more likely to agree to items irrespective of content. In contexts that were low on affective autonomy, the level of agreement was low irrespective of the interdependence of individuals.

The final set of cross-level models is cross-level frog-pond models. These models are related to the heterogeneity assumption described above since it models the effects of individual group members standing within a group on individual-level outcomes. An example is the relationship between performance of individuals and their self-efficacy, depending on the average level of performance within the team. In a high performing team, an individual with less than average work performance is likely to experience lower esteem. However, if the same individual was placed in a low performing team, his/her previously mediocre performance would be above average and the level of self-esteem might improve. In essence, the relative standing within the team is of importance rather than absolute levels. WABA II is best suited to test such frog-pond models (Klein and Kozlowski, 2000b).

The last group of multilevel models discussed here are homologous multilevel models. These models are somewhat similar to single-level models since they do not specify relationships across levels, but only relationships within levels. However, these models also specify that relationships between variables hold at multiple levels of analysis. The great appeal and value of such models for researchers is that generalizations across level can be made, substantially enhancing the generality and applicability of theory. A drawback of these models is that the demand for similar structures and functions across levels leads to abstract and simplified theoretical models that are no longer of any practical value (Klein, Cannella, and Tosi, 1999; Klein and Kozlowski, 2000b). To date, no such model has been proposed and empirically tested. Consequently, these models have much theoretical appeal, but their practical utility and usefulness is yet unproven. Chen, Bliese, and Mathieu (2005) have recently proposed conceptual frameworks and statistical procedures for such models and this may help to generate more theory and empirical tests (for a critique of these approaches see Dansereau and Yammarino, 2006).

Conclusion

A sound methodology can enhance the validity of findings. This truism is also true in cross-cultural organizational research. The appropriate uses of methodological tools can help to improve the interpretability of cross-cultural studies. Thus, various sophisticated tools are available to address the question of whether in instrument measures the same in different cultures. Examples are exploratory and confirmatory factor analyses and the numerous techniques that can be employed to identify differential item functioning. We have seen tremendous developments in cross-cultural research methods in the last decades. However, these techniques are not always fully exploited. We still come across too many studies in which cross-cultural differences in means scores are taken at face value without any concern for the comparability of scores across cultures. Progress in cross-cultural organizational research will depend on a combination and integration of sophisticated theorizing and adequate use of the tools that are available. It is remarkable that some methodological considerations have been widely accepted, such as problems with low internal consistencies and interrater reliabilities, while other recommendations regarding the testing of equivalence are often more preached than practiced.

We have paid much attention in the chapter to current developments in multilevel models. We consider these models to be possible spearheads of new developments in cross-cultural organizational behavior research. Multilevel models combine innovations in theory and development. We consider these models to be particularly important because they enable the study of individuals, organizations, and cultures in a joint model. As a consequence, we can now model the interaction of variables at different levels.

We expect that a further integration of theory and methods and a more refined use of methodological tools in cross-cultural research will help to increase the replicability of cross-cultural research findings, to bolster our conclusions against alternative interpretations, and to generate theories that better stand testing in a cross-cultural framework.

References

Aquilino, W. S. 1994. "Interviewer mode effects in surveys of drug and alcohol use", *Public Opinion Quarterly* 58: 210–40.

Arends-Tóth, J. V. and Van de Vijver, F. J. R. 2008. "Cultural differences in family, marital, and gender-role values among immigrants and majority members in the Netherlands", *International Journal of Psychology* (in press).

Au, K. Y. 2000. "Intra-cultural variation as another construct of international management: a study based on secondary data of 42 countries", *Journal of International Management* 6: 217–38.

Barcikowski, R. S. 1981. "Statistical power with group mean as the unit of analysis", *Journal of Educational Statistics* 6: 267–85.

Bandura, A. 1997. *Self-Efficacy: The Exercise of Control*. New York, NY: Freeman.

Barrett, P. T., Petrides, K. V., Eysenck, S. B. G., and Eysenck, H. J. 1998. "The Eysenck Personality Questionnaire: an examination of the factorial similarity of P, E, N, and L across 34 countries", *Personality and Individual Differences* 25: 805–19.

Besser, T. L. 1993. "The commitment of Japanese workers and U.S. workers: a reassessment of the literature", *American Sociological Review* 58: 873–81.

Bhagat, R. S. and McQuaid, S. J. 1982. "Role of subjective culture in organizations: a review and directions for future research", *Journal of Applied Psychology* 67: 653–85.

Bliese, P. D. 2000. "Within-group agreement, non-independence and reliability: implications for data aggregation and analyses", in J. K. Klein and S. W. J. Kozlowski (eds.), *Multilevel Theory, Research and Methods in Organizations. Foundations, Extensions, and New Directions*. San Francisco, CA: Jossey-Bass. pp. 349–381

and Halverson, R. H. 1998. "Group size and measures of group-level properties: an examination of eta-squared and ICC values", *Journal of Management* 24: 157–72.

and Hanges, P. J. 2004. "Being both too liberal and too conservative: the perils of treating grouped data as though they were independent", *Organizational Research Methods* 7: 400–17.

Bond, M. H. and van de Vijver, F. J. R. 2008. "Making scientific sense of cultural differences in psychological outcomes: unpacking the magnum mysterium", in F. J. R. van de Vijver and D. Matsumoto (eds.), *Research Methods in Cross-Cultural Psychology*. New York: Oxford University Press.

Brown, R. D. and Hauenstein, N. A. 2005. "Interrater agreement reconsidered: An alternative to the r_{wg} indices", *Organizational Research Methods* 8: 165–84.

Camilli, G. and Shepard, L. A. 1994. *Methods for Identifying Biased Test Items*. Thousand Oaks, CA: Sage.

Campbell, D. T. 1986. "Science's social system of validity-enhancing collective believe change and the problems of the social sciences", in D. W. Fiske and R. A. Shweder (eds.), *Metatheory in Social Science*. Chicago, IL: University of Chicago Press, pp. 108–135.

Castro, S. L. 2002. "Data analytical methods for the analysis of multilevel questions: a comparison of intraclass correlation coefficients, $r_{wg(j)}$, hierarchical linear modelling, within and between-analysis and random group resampling", *Leadership Quarterly* 13: 69–93.

Chan, D. 1998. "Functional relations among constructs in the same content domain at different levels of analysis: a typology of compositional models", *Journal of Applied Psychology* 83: 234–46.

Chen, G., Bliese, P. D., and Mathieu, J. E. 2005. "Conceptual framework and statistical procedures for delineating and testing multilevel theories of homology", *Organizational Research Methods* 8: 375–409.

Mathieu, J. E., and Bliese, P. D. 2004. "A framework for conducting multilevel construct validation", in F. J. Yammarino and F. Dansereau (eds.), *Research in Multilevel Issues: Multilevel Issues in Organizational Behavior and Processes* 3: 273–303. Oxford: Elsevier.

Cheung, F. M., Leung, K., Fan, R. M., Song, W. Z., Zhang, J. X., and Zhang, J. P. 1996. "Development of the Chinese Personality Assessment Inventory", *Journal of Cross-Cultural Psychology* 27: 118–99.

Cheung, G. W. and Rensvold, R. B. 2002. "Evaluating goodness-of-fit indexes for testing measurement invariance", *Structural Equation Modeling* 9: 233–55.

Cohen, A. 2003. *Multiple Commitments in the Workplace: An Integrative Approach.* Mahwah, NJ: Lawrence Erlbaum.

Cole, E. R. 1979. *Work, Mobility and Participation: A Comparative Study of American and Japanese Industry*, Los Angeles, CA: University of California Press.

Colquitt, J. A., Noe, R. A., and Jackson, C. L. 2002. "Justice in teams: antecedents and consequences of procedural justice climate", *Personnel Psychology* 55: 83–109.

Dansereau, F., Alutto, J. A., and Yammarino, F. J. 1984. *Theory-Testing in Organizational Behavior: The 'Variant' Approach.* Englewood Cliffs, NJ: Prentice Hall.

and Yammarino, F. J. (eds.) 1998. *Leadership: The Multiple-Level Approaches.* Stamford, CT: JAI Press.

and Yammarino, F. J. 2006. "Is more discussion about levels of analysis really necessary? When is such discussion sufficient?" *Leadership Quarterly* 17: 537–52.

Embretson, S. E. 1983. "Construct validity: construct representation versus nomothetic span", *Psychological Bulletin* 93: 179–97.

Eysenck, H. J. and Eysenck, S. B. G. 1975. *Manual of the Eysenck Personality Questionnaire.* London: Hodder and Stoughton.

Festinger, L. 1954. "A theory of social comparison processes", *Human Relations* 7: 117–40.

Fischer, R. 2004. "Standardization to account for cross-cultural response bias: a classification of score adjustment procedures and review of research in JCCP", *Journal of Cross-Cultural Psychology* 35: 263–82.

2008. "Multilevel approaches in organizational settings: opportunities, challenges and implications for cross-cultural research". in F. J. R. Van de Vijver, D. A. van Hemert, and Y. H. Poortinga (eds.), *Individuals and Cultures in Multilevel Analysis.* Mahwah, NJ: Erlbaum pp. 173–196.

Ferreira, M. C., Assmar, E. M. L., Redford, P., and Harb, C. 2005. "Organizational behaviour across cultures: theoretical and methodological issues for developing multi-level frameworks involving culture", *International Journal for Cross-Cultural Management* 5: 27–48.

and Mansell, A. 2009. A meta-analytic approach. *Journal of International Business Studies*, in press.

Fontaine, J. R. 2008. "Traditional and multilevel approaches in cross-cultural research: an integration of methodological frameworks" in F. J. R. Van de Vijver, D. A. Van Hemert, and Y. H. Poortinga (eds.), *Individuals and Cultures in Multilevel Analysis.* Mawhaw, NJ: Erlbaum pp. 65–92.

Formann, A. K. and Piswanger, K. 1979. *Wiener Matrizen-Test. Ein Rasch-skalierter sprachfreier Intelligenztest* [The Viennese Matrices Test. A Rasch-calibrated non-verbal intelligence test]. Weinheim, Germany: Beltz Test.

Gass, S. M. and Varonis, E. M. 1991. "Miscommunication in nonnative speaker discourse", in N. Coupland, H. Giles, and J. M. Wiemann (eds.), *Miscommunication and Problematic Talk.* Newbury Park, CA: Sage, pp. 121–45.

Gelfand, M. J., Nishii, L. H., and Raver, J. L. 2006. "On the nature and importance of cultural tightness-looseness", *Journal of Applied Psychology* 91: 1225–44.

George, J. M. and James, L. R. 1993. "Personality, affect and behavior in groups revisited: comment on aggregation, levels of analysis and a recent application of within and between analysis", *Journal of Applied Psychology* 78: 798–804.

Glick, W. H. 1985. "Conceptualising and measuring organizational and psychological climate: pitfalls in multilevel research", *Academy of Management Review* 10: 601–16.

Grill, J. J. and Bartel, N. R. 1977. "Language bias in tests: ITPA grammatic closure", *Journal of Learning Disabilities* 10: 229–35.

Hambleton, R. K. 1994. "Guidelines for adapting educational and psychological tests: a progress report", *European Journal of Psychological Assessment* 10: 229–44.

Ho, D. Y. F. 1996. "Filial piety and its psychological consequences", in M. H. Bond (ed.), *Handbook of Chinese Psychology*. Hong Kong: Oxford University Press, pp. 155–65.

Hofmann, D. A. and Jones, L. M. 2004. "Some foundational and guiding questions for multi-level construct validation" In F. J. Yammarino and F. Dansereau (eds.), *Multilevel Issues in Organizational Behaviour and Processes*, vol. 3 Amsterdam: Elsevier, pp. 305–16.

Hofstede, G. 1980. *Culture's Consequences: International Differences in Work-Related Values*. Beverly Hills, CA: Sage.

2001. *Culture's Consequences: Comparing Values, Behaviors, Institutions and Organizations Across Nations*, 2nd edn. Thousand Oaks, CA: Sage.

House, R. J., Hanges, P. J., Javidan, M., Dorfman, P., and Gupta, V. 2003. *GLOBE, Cultures, Leadership, and Organizations: GLOBE Study of 62 Societies*. Newbury Park, CA: Sage.

Huang, X., van de Vliert, E., and Van der Vegt, G. 2006. "Breaking the silence culture: stimulation of participation and employee opinion withholding cross-nationally", *Group and Organization Review* 1: 459–82.

Hui, C. H. and Triandis, H. C. 1989. "Effects of culture and response format on extreme response style", *Journal of Cross-Cultural Psychology* 20: 296–309.

James, L. R. 1982. "Aggregation bias in estimates of perceptual agreement", *Journal of Applied Psychology* 67: 219–29.

Demaree, R. G., and Wolf, G. 1984. "Estimating within-group interrater reliability with and without response bias", *Journal of Applied Psychology* 69: 85–98.

Demaree, R. G., and Wolf, G. 1993. "r_{wg}: An assessment of within-group interrater agreement", *Journal of Applied Psychology* 78: 306–9.

Jensen, A. R. 1980. *Bias in Mental Testing*. New York, NY: Free Press.

Johnson, T. P. 1998. "Approaches to equivalence in cross-cultural and cross-national survey research", *ZUMA Nachrichten Spezial* 3: 1–40.

Kenny, D. A. and Judd, C. M. 1986. "Consequences of violating the independence assumption in analysis of variance", *Psychological Bulletin* 99: 422–31.

Klein, K. J., Cannella, A., and Tosi, H. 1999. "Multilevel theory building: Benefits, barriers and new developments", *Academy of Management Review* 24: 243–8.

Dansereau, F., and Hall, R. J. 1994. "Level issues in theory development, data collection and analysis", *Academy of Management Review* 19: 195–229.

and Kozlowski, S. W. J. (eds.). 2000a *Multilevel Theory, Research and Methods in Organizations. Foundations, Extensions, and New Directions*. San Francisco, CA: Jossey-Bass.

and Kozlowski, S. W. J. 2000b. "From micro to macro: critical steps in conceptualizing and conducting multilevel research", *Organizational Research Methods* 3: 211–36.

Kozlowski, S. W. J. and Klein, J. K. 2000. "A multilevel approach to theory and research in organizations: contextual, temporal and emergent processes", in J. K. Klein and S. W. J. Kozlowski (eds.), *Multilevel Theory, Research and Methods in Organizations. Foundations, Extensions, and New Directions*. San Francisco, CA: Jossey-Bass, pp. 3–90.

Lincoln, J. R. and Kalleberg, A. L. 1990. *Culture, Control and Commitment: A Study of Work Organization and Work Attitudes in the United States and Japan*. New York, NY: Cambridge University Press.

Lindell, M. K. and Brandt, C. J. 2000. "Climate quality and climate consensus as mediators of the relationship between organizational antecedents and outcomes", *Journal of Applied Psychology* 85: 331–48.

Little, T. D., Cunningham, W. A., Shahar, G., and Widaman, K. F. 2002. "To parcel or not to parcel: exploring the question, weighing the merits", *Structural Equation Modeling: A Multidisciplinary Journal* 9: 151–73.

Malpass, R. S. 1977. "Theory and method in cross-cultural psychology", *American Psychologist* 32: 1069–79.

McCrae, R. R. and Costa, P. T. Jr. 1997. "Personality trait structure as a human universal", *American Psychologist* 52: 509–16.

Meade, A. W. and Kroustalis, C. M. 2006. "Problems with item parceling for confirmatory factor analytic tests of measurement invariance", *Organizational Research Methods*, 9: 369–403.

Meyer, J. P. and Allen, N. J. 1991. "A three-component conceptualization of organizational commitment", *Human Resource Management Review* 1: 61–89.

Stanley, D. J., Herscovitch, L. and Topolytsky, L. 2002. "Affective, continuance, normative commitment to the organization: a meta-analysis of antecedents, correlates and consequences", *Journal of Vocational Behavior* 61: 20–52.

Morgeson, F. P. and Hofmann, D. A. 1999. "The structure and function of collective constructs: implications for multilevel research and theory development", *Academy of Management Review* 24: 249–65.

Muthén, B. O. 1991. "Multilevel factor analysis of class and student achievement components", *Journal of Educational Measurement* 28: 338–54.

1994. "Multilevel covariance structure analysis", *Sociological Methods and Research* 22: 376–98.

Naumann, S. E. and Bennett, N. 2001. "A case for procedural justice climate: development and test of a multilevel model", *Academy of Management Journal* 43: 861–89.

Oakland, T., Gulek, C., and Glutting, J. 1996. "Children's test-taking behaviors: a review of literature, case study, and research of children", *European Journal of Psychological Assessment* 12: 240–46.

Peterson, M. F. and Castro, S. L. 2006. "Measurement metrics of aggregate levels of analysis: implications for organization culture research and the GLOBE project", *Leadership Quarterly* 17: 506–21.

Piswanger, K. 1975. *Interkulturelle Vergleiche mit dem Matrizentest von Formann* [Cross-cultural comparisons with Formann's Matrices Test]. Unpublished doctoral dissertation, University of Vienna, Vienna.

Ployhart, R. E., Wiechmann, D., Schmitt, N., Sacco, J. M., and Rogg, K. 2003. "The cross-cultural equivalence of job performance ratings", *Human Performance* 16: 46–79.

Poortinga, Y. H. 1989. "Equivalence in cross-cultural data: an overview of basic issues", *International Journal of Psychology* 24: 737–56.

and Van de Vijver, F. J. R. 1987. "Explaining cross-cultural differences: bias analysis and beyond", *Journal of Cross-Cultural Psychology* 18: 259–82.

Raudenbush, S. W. and Bryk, A. S. 2002. *Hierarchical Linear Models*, 2nd edn. London: Sage.

Rohner, R. P. 1984. "Toward a conception of culture for cross-cultural psychology", *Journal of Cross-Cultural Psychology* 15: 111–38.

Sampson, E. E. 1981. "Cognitive psychology as ideology", *American Psychologist* 7: 730–43.

Schneider, B., Salvaggio, A. N., and Subirats, M. 2002. "Climate strength: a new direction for climate research", *Journal of Applied Psychology* 87: 220–9.

Schriesheim, C. A., Castro, S. L., and Yammarino, F. J. 2000. "Investigating contingencies: an examination of the impact of span of supervision and upward controllingness on Leader-Member Exchange using traditional multivariate within and between entities analysis", *Journal of Applied Psychology* 85: 659–77.

Segall, M. H., Dasen, P. R., Berry, J. W., and Poortinga, Y. H. 1990. *Human Behavior in Global Perspective. An Introduction to Cross-Cultural Psychology.* New York, NY: Pergamon Press.

Shrout, P. E. and Fleiss, J. L. 1979. "Intraclass correlations: uses in assessing rater reliability", *Psychological Bulletin* 86: 420–28.

Singer, E. and Presser, S. 1989. "The interviewer", in E. Singer and S. Presser (eds.), *Survey Research Methods*. Chicago: University of Chicago Press, pp. 245–246.

Smith, P. B., Bond, M. H., and Kagitcibasi, C. 2006. *Understanding Social Psychology Across Cultures: Living and Working in a Changing World*. Thousand Oaks, CA: Sage.

and Fischer, R. 2008. "Acquiescence, extreme response bias and levels of cross-cultural analysis", in F. J. R. van de Vijver, D. A. Van Hemert, and Y. H. Poortinga (eds.), *Individuals and Cultures in Multilevel Analysis*. Mahwah, NJ: Erlbaum, pp. 283–311.

Fischer, R., and Sale, N. 2001. "Cross-cultural industrial/organizational psychology", in C. L. Cooper and I. T. Robertson (eds.), *International Review of Industrial and Organizational Psychology* vol. 16. New York, NY: Wiley, pp. 283–311.

Steiner, I. 1972. *Group Processes and Productivity*. New York: Academic Press.

Tanzer, N. K., Gittler, G., and Ellis, B. B. 1995. "Cross-cultural validation of item complexity in a LLTM-calibrated spatial ability test", *European Journal of Psychological Assessment* 11: 170–83.

and Sim, C. Q. E. 1991. *Test Anxiety in Primary School Students: An Empirical Study in Singapore*. Research Report 1991/6. Graz, Austria: Department of Psychology, University of Graz.

Tucker, L. R. 1951. *A Method for Synthesis of Factor Analysis Studies*. Personnel Research Section Report No. 984. Washington, DC: Department of the Army.

van de Vijver, F. J. R. 2003. "Test adaptation/ translation methods", in R. Fernández-Ballesteros (ed.), *Encyclopedia of Psychological Assessment*. Thousand Oaks, CA: Sage, pp. 960–64.

and Leung, K. 1997. *Methods and Data Analysis for Cross-Cultural Research*. Newbury Park, CA: Sage.

and Poortinga, Y. H. 1997. "Towards an integrated analysis of bias in cross-cultural assessment", *European Journal of Psychological Assessment* 13: 29–37.

and Poortinga, Y. H. 2002. "Structural equivalence in multilevel research", *Journal of Cross-Cultural Psychology* 33: 141–156.

and Tanaka-Matsumi, J. 2008. "Cross-cultural research methods". in D. McKay (ed.), *Handbook of Research Methods in Abnormal and Clinical Psychology*. Thousand Oaks, CA: Sage.

and Tanzer, N. K. 2004. "Bias and equivalence in cross-cultural assessment: an overview", *European Review of Applied Psychology* 54: 119–35.

van de Vliert, E., Huang, X., and Levine, R. V. 2004. "National wealth and thermal climate as predictors of motives for volunteer work", *Journal of Cross-Cultural Psychology* 35: 62–73.

Vandenberg, R. J. and Lance, C. A. 2000. "A review and synthesis of the measurement invariance literature: Suggestions, practices and recommendations", *Organizational Research Methods* 3: 4–70.

Wasti, S. A. 2002. "Affective and continuance commitment to the organization: test of an integrated model in the Turkish context", *International Journal of Intercultural Relations* 26: 525–50.

and Ondev, C. 2008. "Commitment across cultures: progress, pitfalls, and prepositions." in H. Klein, Becker, T., and J. P Meyer (eds.), *Commitment in Organizations: Accumulated Wisdom and New Directions*. Philadelphia, PA: Lawrence Erlbaum.

Welkenhuysen-Gybels, J., Billiet, J., and Cambré, B. 2003. "Adjustment for acquiescence in the assessment of the construct equivalence of Likert-type score items", *Journal of Cross-Cultural Psychology* 34: 702–22.

Werner, O. and Campbell, D. T. 1970. "Translating, working through interpreters, and the problem of decentering", in R. Naroll and R. Cohen (eds.), *A Handbook of Cultural Anthropology*. New York, NY: American Museum of Natural History, pp. 398–419.

Whiting, B. 1976. "The problem of the packaged variable", in K. Riegel and J. Meacham (eds.), *The Developing Individual in a Changing World*, vol. 1. The Hague: Mouton, 303–309.

Williams, K. Y. and O'Reilly, C. A. 1998. "Demography and diversity in organizations: a review of 40 years of research", in B. Staw and L. L. Cummings (eds.), *Research in Organisational Behaviour* 20: 77–140. Greenwich, CT: JAI Press.

Yammarimo, F. J. and Dansereau, F. 2002–2007. *Multilevel Issues in Organizational Behaviour and Processes*, vols. 1–7. Amsterdam: Elsevier.

and Markham, S. E. 1992. "On the application of within and between analysis: are absence and affect really group-based phenomena?" *Journal of Applied Psychology* 77: 168–76.

Yang, K. S. and Bond M. H. 1990. "Exploring implicit personality theories with indigenous or imported constructs: the Chinese case", *Journal of Personality and Social Psychology* 58: 1087–95.

CHAPTER 19 Culture, work, and organizations: a future research agenda

RABI S. BHAGAT

With increasing globalization and tremendous increases in foreign direct investments in various parts of the world since the 1990s, there has been a significant increase in understanding the functioning of organizations in distinctive cultural contexts of the world. The cross-cultural study of organizations is concerned with systematic investigations of work attitudes and organizational behavior of participants in different cultures. Today, it is almost impossible to find a major multinational and global organization that does not employ a significant percentage of foreign-born individuals. In some of these organizations, they occupy important managerial jobs in the upper echelons. These individuals often come from culturally dissimilar countries. In order to facilitate their functioning as well as assimilation into the mainstream organizational culture, global and multinational organizations will need to be concerned with the nature of cultural variations and the degree of cultural fit between these workers and the employing work organization may be increased.

Research on cultural variations on both macro and micro aspects of organizational behavior has existed since the publication of classic books such as *Industrialism and Industrial Man: The Problems of Labor and Management in Economic Growth* (Kerr *et al.*, 1964) and *Managerial Thinking: An International Study* (Haire, Ghiselli, and Porter, 1966). In these pioneering books, a primary interest was to understand the nature of convergence and divergence of managerial practices and cultures in dissimilar countries of the world. Since then, there have been a significant number of empirical studies dealing with comparisons of values, attitudes, cognitive styles, work ethics, etc. of individuals working in different parts of the globe.

Research involving cultural variations accelerated, especially after the publications of Geert Hofstede's 1980 *Cultural Consequences: International Differences in Work-Related Values*, which provided a much firmer grasp of cultural differences in forty countries with respect to four theoretically robust cultural dimensions. The second publication dealing with unique features of Japanese management styles published as *Theory Z* (Ouchi, 1981) provided substantial evidence linking organizational culture-related variations to organizational performance. The rate of publications linking important facets of national culture-based variations with organizational processes and the nature of work as perceived and experienced in different nations has increased significantly. We seem to have come closer toward a better understanding of how cultural processes in different parts of the world affect various important organizational processes including organizational effectiveness.

Cross-cultural studies in historical perspective

In her extensive review of the literature, Roberts (1970) noted the field of cross-cultural organizational behavior was fragmented, no systematic paradigms had emerged, and the findings were rarely integrated with the mainstream literature on organizational functioning. She expressed disappointment in her review, even though she entitled her paper "On looking at an elephant: an evaluation of cross-cultural research related to organizations" given the growing volume of research from the mid-1960s. Child (1981), in his assessment of cross-national study of organizations, made the interesting observation that there was a tendency on the part of researchers to use the construct of culture and cultural differences as an excuse for intellectual laziness. National differences found in various organizational processes where interpreted as cultural difference and no careful conceptual reasoning was advanced as to why cultural differences would be synonymous with national differences.

Bhagat and McQuaid (1982), in their review, expressed similar sentiments and advocated the construct of subjective culture (a more precise construct advanced by Triandis and his colleagues in 1972, which referred to a group's characteristic way of perceiving and interpreting its social environment) in studies linking cultural influences on behavior in and of organizations. Later reviews (Bhagat *et al.*, 1990; Arvey, Bhagat, and Salas, 1991) noted a pervasive lack of theoretical rigor and a similar lack of methodological robustness.

Much cross-cultural research conducted before 1982 was concerned with mean group differences without attempting to explain or understand why cultures should differ on the variables that were being investigated. If Mexican workers had lower levels of job satisfaction compared to US workers and experienced higher levels of work-family conflict compared to Canadian workers, is it necessarily due to differences in cultural orientations among these countries? Is it also possible that economic factors, company policies relating to the nature of tasks they perform, as well as concerns of the company in matters pertaining to work-family issues could be responsible as well? No systemic attempt was made to explain differences in the phenomenon in terms of precise theoretically robust issues. In addition, there was hardly any attempt made to integrate cross-cultural findings with mainstream theory and research or organizational function. Often, cultures were selected as "targets of opportunity" and in accordance with the travel plans of the principal investigator. Furthermore, the flow of knowledge seemed to proceed from a uni-cultural (often western) view of organizational functioning to a multi-cultural view without adequate theoretical explanations or conceptual grounding.

However, research reviewed in Bhagat *et al.* (1990) echoed a positive note. They noted that research on all of the topical areas reviewed had reasonable foundations on specific theoretical frameworks. However, there was a general trend

of debate concerning the applicability of western theories to other dissimilar cultures (often East Asian and South Asian countries). They also noted that studies were not concerned with mean group differences as much as in the past. Observed differences were being carefully interpreted in terms of more rigorous theoretical constructs which had their roots in cross-cultural psychology. Findings were also beginning to be accumulative and important practical issues could be addressed with the findings that were beginning to emerge and get established.

There were distinct signs of improvement in the adaptation of back translation procedures for collection of cross-cultural data. There were recognitions that the researcher had to educate himself or herself about various contextual influences as well as socio-cultural and emic (i.e., culture-specific) antecedents of behavior. However, differences between people across cultures were not being interpreted against a background of similarities as recommended strongly by Malpass (1977). Lack of emic content was responsible for some of the difficulties associated with the findings. This was exacerbated by imposing western- (often US) based theoretical perspectives on local phenomena in cultures that were not only non-western in nature, but had significantly different histories and evolutionary patterns.

Future research directions

Much has been accomplished, but much more remains to be done. Fifteen years ago, Triandis assessed the accomplishments of cross-cultural research in organizational behavior and concluded that many of the ideas guiding research were somewhat "vague" (Triandis, Dunette, and Hough 1994, p. 156). There was not a widely accepted definition of culture and that we did not have a good way of sorting out differences which had their roots in psychological as opposed to culture-based functioning of humans in different parts of the world. The point is that there is a psychic unity of mankind and many observable human phenomena such as deep affection of mothers toward their children, deep interpersonal affect and exchanges between spouses that are trans-cultural and have evolved through centuries of ecological functionalism. While cultural differences have their roots in different ecological contexts as well, they evolve primarily due to selective needs of certain psychological and social practices to have more importance in those contexts. So, there is a growing need to distinguish between psychological versus cultural roots of both observable and implicit organizational behavioral processes.

There is also a need to be clear about generalizability of results. What is true in the cultures of Japan or China or Vietnam may be less true in the sub-continent of India, Sri Lanka, and other countries in South Asia. The tendency quickly to generalize results over large regions is problematic and should be avoided in the future. He emphasized the need for researchers to be more involved in the rigorous theoretical issues. For example, what is the impact of culture and cultural variations on work attitudes, job-specific self esteem, and work stress? In a similar vein, how are negotiations between managers from two distinct cultures (i.e., US and Japan) affected by differences in subjective culture as well as in organizational culture of their companies? Triandis (1994) also advocated use of multi-method strategies since any single method is likely to be confounded with cultural differences. Advanced statistical techniques should be employed to correct for response biases and culture-specific methods of responding to questionnaires.

In our review of the literature, we find a distinct positive trend towards more rigorous studies linking cultures, organizations, and work. There have been new avenues of research and theoretically more interesting questions are being asked every year. The findings of this research are being used in organizational practices and there is hope that cross-cultural aspects of organizational behavior and international business will benefit from rigorous findings that are beginning to emerge in the past decade. However, it is necessary for us to identify some areas of research that are particularly of relevance as the world continues to globalize even more. They are noted as follows:

1. The changing workplace of tomorrow

With new technologies transforming work places at a rapid rate, there is a need to understand the impact of these new technologies on organizational structure, global strategies, creation of organizational knowledge, as well as the kind of adaptational behaviors that they require. New types of leadership, especially of the transformational kind, are going to be more important, not only in western countries, but also in the emerging economies of the world such as the BRIC countries (Brazil, Russia, India, and China).

Patterns of work motivation, work ethic, and attachment to traditional forms of organizational roles are going to change as new technologies begin to erode sharp boundaries between work and non-work roles. Gone are the days when one's work concerns essentially stayed confined in the domain of work. In the global cities of the world such as New York, London, Tokyo, Frankfurt, Paris, Chicago, Bombay, Beijing, Shanghai, San Paulo, etc., the distinction between what kind of work should be performed at work and what needs to be performed in the domain of non-work are beginning to blur.

While this is creating significant stressful experiences in the global economy, it is also creating important opportunities for working women in both individualistic and collectivistic parts of the world. It is no longer the case that various types of technologies induced changes in the western world only. We encounter significant changes in parts of the world that were relatively unaffected by technological changes occurring in the domain of work. In a recent visit to India, the first editor of this volume encountered some managers who had permanently returned from their well-paying jobs in the US to the global city of Bangalore. While they were being paid less compared to what they made in the US, they reported significant satisfaction from the fact that their jobs were relatively stable and that they were able to maintain satisfactory relationships with their spouses, children, and other important family members that are particularly valuable in the collectivistic context of Indian society. This was not expected; I expected the Indian managers to report happiness with their pay and ethnic communities in the US cities, where they had comfortable homes and better amenities of life.

The point is that members of different cultures react differently to changing patterns of work due to rapid innovations in technologies that have impacted work as well as work organizations in recent times. We need to know how cultural values interact with changing patterns of work and how organizational structures and managerial leadership might facilitate smooth transitions of workers from work roles of yesterday to the work roles of tomorrow. We have not seen a great deal of research in this area, and it is necessary for future researchers to focus on this phenomenon on the changing nature of work in dissimilar cultural contexts around the globe. We believe that important insights that will be generated in this area will be of considerable value, not only for advancing theory, but for also improving quality of life both in the domains of work and non-work – an area of research that is of significance in the majority of the globalizing nations.

2. Globalization and culture change

An evolving area of research that should occupy the interest of organizational researchers is concerned with the relationship between globalization and culture change. Does globalization, especially increasing economic interdependence among the members of the countries who belong to the World Trade Organization (WTO), produce selective cultural changes? The demographic changes and interaction of different cultures in various global cities of the world that necessarily accompany the process of globalization have important implications for coordination of knowledge on various ethnic communities and cultural identities that evolve in these enclaves.

One line of argument states that developing countries that are rapidly globalizing and which aspire to become like globalized countries of the west may begin to regard western economic policies as a reference point, not only in matters of economic development, but also in the realm of cultural restructuring and changes. Essentially,

this reflects the central thesis of the convergence hypothesis – a theoretical notion that occupied the interests of US social scientists as well as organizational scholars in the 1960s. While this is indeed taking place in some parts of the world, the point is that globalization is not necessarily leading to homogenization of cultures. If this is the case, then organizations in dissimilar cultures will emphasize distinctive cultural values in various practices – deeply reflecting the central concerns of the people of those contexts.

Hofstede (2001) and Triandis (2002) argued that cultural differences in organizational behavior-related processes will persist because some of the dominant cultural orientations are quite fundamental to the way humans sample and organize information from their social environment. People who are used to sampling more social information from their environment are not likely to become more effective in sampling task-related information just because the work environment is changing rapidly. It can happen, but the process of change will indeed be slow. In other words, globalization will produce dissimilar outcomes in the way people in different cultures converge towards some central tendencies that reflect largely western (primarily US) values. The essence of the divergence hypothesis that individuals would retain the predominant values of their ethnic and national cultures and are not likely to gravitate toward the western pattern. To put it another way, a non-westerner from the Middle East may be happy to bite into a Big Mac, but not necessarily accept the Magna Carta, the core of western civilization.

Smith, Bond, and Kagiticibasi (2006) distinguish between the concepts of modernity and convergence. While early studies of modernity and the evolution of modern man (Inkeles and Smith, 1974) focused on industrialization, it is important to note that industrialization is not the only stimulus for inducing cultural changes in different parts of the world. Rapid rates of urbanization and proliferation of communication media on an international scale provide great impetus for inducing cultural changes. As organizational researchers, we would expect these changes to create different types of values, work ethics, and organizational cultures in different geographical locales of the world.

Currently, over 85 percent of the movie audiences throughout the world watch films made in the US (United Nations Development Program, 2004). The number of television sets in the world is over 24 percent of the world's population (United Nations Development Program, 2004). The popular TV channels, such as CNN, BBC, and Sky Network, expose a very large percentage of the world's population to the significance of values, not only of the western world, but of the non-western nations as well. The question arises as to what kinds of values are likely to emerge as significant guides in different parts of the world.

These issues can be explored by cross-cultural organizational researchers to the extent we are willing to abandon our western-based ethnocentric perspectives and adopt a multi-cultural view of the world. While materialism and values championing the triumph of materialism over spiritualism and religious concerns are some of the guiding principles of the western societies – this is not necessarily true for many countries in Asia, Latin America, and Africa. There will be selective adoption of western practices, and we need to know the extent of their impact on organizational behavior and processes. Simply put: the relationship between economic and other aspects of globalization with culture changes taking place in various parts of the world is not necessarily a simple one. The impacts of such changes on work organizations of tomorrow are also rather complex, and it is important that we turn our attention to such issues which have not captured the imagination of the majority of cross-cultural organizational researchers today.

3. Changing nature of collaboration across national borders and cultures

A new kind of phenomenon occurring in the global economy is the process of cross-border collaboration among organizations located in dissimilar cultures. Strategic alliances among companies are used to describe a variety of inter-firm cooperation agreements ranging from launching shared research programs to formal joint ventures and minority equity participation. The key challenges surrounding the management of the various types of alliances are based on the nature of trust among the transacting organizations. Even in the best of circumstances, trust between individuals is difficult to maintain and sustain over long periods of time. It becomes even more difficult when trust involves significant cross-cultural differences. Research on this topic of cultural issues in the creation and maintenance of trust was non-existent in the 1980s and 1990s. It is indeed heartening to note that research on trust and also on cross-cultural differences in creating joint ventures and alliances is getting its due attention from organizational scholars in various parts of the world.

4. Cultural issues in conflict management and negotiation

As organizations begin to engage in strategic alliances and joint ventures with organizations located in dissimilar cultures, issues of managing conflicts and negotiation begin to emerge as important themes. Research in this area was non-existent in the 1980s and 1990s, but in the past decade, there have been significant insights generated into the cultural variations that are responsible for creating as well as solving conflicting situations in cross-border contexts. Well-known business schools are offering training programs for senior executives of multinational and global corporations as well as political leaders and sports entrepreneurs of many countries on the topic of negotiation. While it is not clear to what extent the art of cross-cultural negotiation can be taught effectively, we are still much better off in having some interesting insights into how members of different cultures approach the process of negotiation and conflict management. Often, these issues can be difficult to manage, and global organizations can encounter significant losses unless senior executives learn the cultural underpinnings of negotiation and conflict management across national borders.

5. Cultural differences in knowledge management, organizational innovation, and learning

Karl Weick (1995) noted in his endorsement of the book *The Knowledge Creating Company* by Nonaka and Takeuchi (1995) that knowledge creation is to the 1990s what pursuit of excellence was in the 1980s. Organizational knowledge is no longer being viewed as a necessary element in maintaining the international competitiveness of multinational and global organizations. It is critical that global organizations must learn the process of managing knowledge effectively on an ongoing basis. They need to innovate, and to understand the cycles of managing knowledge and various phases of innovation.

These processes, as we have shown in various chapters in the section dealing with macro organizational behavior, are heavily dependent on various types of cultural processes, both in the context of organizations and in societies. Work on virtual work teams is very important in learning about how organizations create and implement knowledge. Work in this area is progressing rapidly; however, more research needs to be conducted in order to provide better insight regarding how multinational and global organizations create, diffuse, absorb, and transfer knowledge. In the area of cross-cultural issues on knowledge management, much of it has been based on sound theoretical work. However, more empirical work involving the process of creating and managing knowledge cycles in various globalizing countries of the world is needed at this point in time.

In fact, knowledge on organizational learning will not only improve effectiveness of modern, complex organizations in the western context, but also will enhance functioning of organizations in parts of the world where corruption, nepotism, paper fetish, and other inefficient practices exist (Kiggundu, Jorgensen, and Hafsi, 1983). The utilization of organizational research (whether created in the West or in other globalizing countries of the world) will be more effective when one knows more about how organizations learn to adopt new techniques and methods.

6. Issues of leadership across cultures

Progress in this area of cross-cultural organizational behavior research has been substantial. Pioneered by Robert J. House of the Wharton Business School and his sixty-one collaborators from different parts of the world, the GLOBE project on how leadership is perceived in different parts of the world has made lasting contributions in enhancing our understanding of cross-cultural variations in the functioning of leaders. We know that leaders are perceived differently in various cultural contexts and that we need to sensitize leaders of multinational and global corporations to these issues.

Closely related to this topic of cross-cultural research on leadership concerns regarding how leaders develop global mindsets in order effectively to assimilate conflicting patterns of information from various operations of the firm are also gaining attention. While empirical work on the antecedents and consequences of global leadership is yet to develop, we get a clear picture regarding the utility of this construct in cross-cultural organizational research.

7. When and how culture and cultural variations matter

This issue is of significant importance in future studies. Cultural variations do not matter in all types of cross-national transactions. They matter in some situations more than others: they matter more in situations where fundamental cultural values are either challenged or questioned in the process of expanding global operations of multinational firms. As long as individuals and groups do not feel threatened that their cultural orientations will be lost, they are likely to be less resistant to minor changes in organizational practices and cultures. Cultures matter more in some contexts than in others and at some times more than others (Leung et al., 2005). Proper identification of this context and times will aid future research in significant ways.

There is no doubt that we have come a long way since Karlene Robert's review of the cross-cultural literature (Roberts, 1970). There is considerable excitement in the field. A large number of researchers from various countries of the world are beginning to collaborate on important research projects that are yielding important insights into how culture and cultural differences affect organizational behavior at both macro and micro levels. Research methodologies are considerably more sophisticated than was the case in the 1970s and 1980s, and sophisticated statistical techniques can also detect unique kinds of moderating and mediating influences of types of cultural variations (see Lytle *et al.*, 1995 for a comprehensive list of cultural differences). Advances in theory development as reflected in the January, 2002 issue of *Psychological Bulletin*, also provide interesting insights as well as caution regarding when cultural interpretations are appropriate and when they are not. We believe that cross-cultural research teams composed of investigators from different countries of the world will be able to identify theoretically rigorous hypotheses that need validation. This is already taking place, and we need to see more vigorous attempts in integrating research findings from other emerging areas in the field. We hope and believe that this handbook represents one useful step in this direction.

References

Arvey, R. D., Bhagat, R. S., and Salas, R. 1991. "Cross-cultural and cross-national issues in personnel and human resources management: where do we go from here?", in K. M. Rowland and G. Ferris (eds.), *Research in Personnel and Human Resources Management*, 9: 367–407. Greenwich, CT: JAI Press.

Bhagat, R. S. and McQuaid, S. J. 1982. "Role of subjective culture in organizations: a review and direction for future research", *Journal of Applied Psychology* 67(5): 653–85.

Bhagat, R. S., Kedia, B. L., Crawford, S. E., and Kaplan, M. R. 1990. "Cross-cultural issues in organizational psychology: emergent trends and discussion for research in the 1990s", in C. L. Cooper and I. T. Robertson (eds.), *International Review of Industrial and Organizational Psychology*. New York, NY: Wiley.

Child, J. 1981. "Culture, contingency, and capitalism in the cross-national study of organizations", in L. L. Cummings and R. M. Straw (eds.), *Research in Organizational Behavior*, vol. 3. Greenwich, CT: JAI Press, pp. 303–56.

Haire, M., Ghiselli, E., and Porter, L. W. 1966. *Managerial Thinking: An International Study*. New York, NY: Wiley.

Hofstede, G. 1980. *Cultural Consequence: International Differences in Work-related Values*. Beverly Hills, CA: Sage.

Hofstede, G. 1991. *Cultures and Organizations: Software of the Mind*. New York, NY: McGraw-Hill.

Hofstede, G. 2001. *Culture's consequences: Comparing values, behaviors, institutions, and organizations across nations* (2nd edn). Thousand Oaks, CA: Sage.

Inkeles, A. and Smith, D. H. 1974. *Becoming Modern: Individual Change in Six Developing Countries*. Cambridge, MA: Harvard University Press.

Kerr, C., Dunlop, S. T., Harbison, F. H., and Myers, C. A. 1964. *Industrialism and Industrial Man: The Problems of Labor and Management in Economic Growth*. Cambridge, MA: Harvard University Press.

Kiggundu, M. N., Jorgensen, J. J., and Hafsi, T. 1983. "Administrative theory and practice in developing countries: a synthesis". *Administrative Science Quarterly* 28:65–84.

Leung, K, Bhagat, R. S., Buchan, N., Erez, M., and Gibson, C. 2005. "Culture and international business: recent advances and future directions", *Journal of International Business Studies* 36(4): 357–78.

Lytle, A. L., Brett, J. M., Barsness, Z. I., Tinsley, C. H. and Janssens, M. 1995. "A paradigm for confirmatory cross-cultural research in organizational behavior", in L. L. Cummings and B. M. Staw (eds.), *Research in Organizational Behavior*, vol. 17. Greenwich, CT: JAI Press, pp. 167–214.

Malpass, R. S. 1977. "Theory and method in cross-cultural psychology" *American Psychologist* 32: 1069–79.

Nonaka, I. and Takeuchi, H. 1995. *The Knowledge Creating Company: How Japanese Companies Create the Dynamics of Innovation*. New York, NY: Oxford University Press.

Ouchi, W. G. 1981. *Theory Z: How American Business Can Meet the Japanese Challenge*. New York, NY: Perseus.

Roberts, K. H. 1970. "On looking at an elephant: an evaluation of cross-cultural research related to organizations", *Psychological Bulletin* 74: 327–50.

Smith, P. S., Bond, M. H., and Kigiticabasi, C. 2006. *Understanding Social Psychology Across Cultures: Living and Working in a Changing World*. London: Sage.

Triandis, H. C. 1994. "Cross-cultural industrial and organizational psychology", in H. C. Triandis,

M. D. Dunette and L. Hough (eds.), *Handbook of Industrial and Organizational Psychology*, (2nd edn), vol. 4. Palo Alto, CA: Consulting Psychologists Press.

Triandis, H. C. 2002. "Generic individualism and collectivism", in M. Gannon and K. Newman (eds.), *The Blackwell Handbook of Cross-cultural Management*. Oxford: Blackwell Business Publishing, pp. 16–45.

Triandis, H. C., Dunette, M. D., and Hough, L. (eds.) 1994. *Handbook of Industrial and Organizational Psychology* (2nd edn), vol. 4. Palo Alto, CA: Consulting Psychologists Press.

United Nations Development Program 2004. Human Development Report. New York: Oxford University Press.

Weick, K. E. 1995. *Sensemaking in Organizations*. London: Sage.

Index

acculturation process in M&As 134
achievement motivation 309–11
active mechanisms of cultural influence 49, 60
actorhood, global cultural process 157–8, 161–3
affinal kinship 32
AG (German public stock company) 94
aggregate constructs 505–7
allocentric characteristics 183
Anglo cluster 18–19, 82, 84–5
Arabic cluster 18–19, 456–7
assertiveness cultural dimension 126, 129, 130
associative versus abstractive reasoning 184–5
attribution
    fundamental attribution error 474
    in trust relationships 385–90, 397, 404–5
    isomorphic 474

behavior
    cultural influences 52, 53, 55, 57–8, 59–60
    regulation by social norms 25
behavior modification training 464
behavioral CQ (cultural intelligence) 27
beliefs
    characteristics of 51
    context-free 24–5
    cultural influences 51, 53, 54, 56–7, 59
bias
    cross-cultural research methodology 493–500
    Western/US bias in leadership research 223, 231
Boeing, acquisition of McDonnell Douglas 119
Britain see UK
bureaucracy, origin of the concept 72
business groups in Japan and Korea 27

Canadian firms, organization design and culture 84, 85
capital market perspective on cultural differences in M&As 136
centralized decision-making 108–10
centralized stakeholder models 76–8
China
    Confucian principles 91–3
    cultural conflict in a transition economy 38–9
    guanxi 27, 33, 91–2
    kinship systems 32–3
    preferred managerial style 74
Chinese family firms 92–3 see also Chinese gong-si

Chinese gong-si
    centralized decision-making 109–10
    organization design and culture 91–4
Chinese guanxi capitalism 33
cognitive anthropology research, cross-cultural conflict and
    negotiation 339, 350–2
cognitive CQ (cultural intelligence) 27
cognitive dissonance 49
cognitive mechanisms of cultural influence 49, 60
cognitive styles, relationship with economic activities
    35–6
collaborative decision-making 108, 112–14
collective constructs 505–7
collectivism, and group behavior 53, 57 see also
    individualism-collectivism cultural dimension
combination mode of knowledge creation and diffusion
    177–8, 179, 180
communication science research, cross-cultural conflict and
    negotiation 337–8, 357–60
comparative law research, cross-cultural conflict and
    negotiation 337, 346–8
complex versus simple knowledge 177, 180
confirmatory factor analysis 501–3
conflict and negotiation cross-cultural research
    cognitive anthropology perspective 339, 350–2
    communication science perspective 337–8, 357–60
    comparative law perspective 337, 346–8
    experimental economics perspective 339, 352–5
    international relations perspective 340–1, 360–4
    language and disputing perspective 340, 348–50
    legal anthropology perspective 336, 343–6
    organizational behavior perspective 335, 342–3
    primatology perspective 341, 355–7
    value of interdisciplinary perspectives 334–5, 364
conformity, moderator of cultural influence 53, 54
Confucian principles 91–3
consanguineal kinship 32
conscientiousness, moderator of cultural influence 53, 55
consultative decision-making 108, 110–12
coping, definition 421 see also stress at work
core cultural dimensions
    hierarchy-equality 10–11
    individualism-collectivism 10, 11–13
    mastery-harmony 10, 13–14
    monochronism-polychronism 10, 14–16
    universalism-particularism 10, 16–17

Printed in the United States
by Baker & Taylor Publisher Services